Understanding Human Behavior

An Introduction to Psychology
4th Edition

James V. McConnell
The University of Michigan

Understanding Human Behavior

An Introduction to Psychology

4th Edition

Holt, Rinehart and Winston
New York   Chicago   San Francisco   Philadelphia
Montreal   Toronto   London   Sydney   Tokyo
Mexico City   Rio de Janeiro   Madrid

Publisher John Michel
Editor Daniel M. Loch
Senior Developmental Editor Rosalind Sackoff
Senior Project Manager Arlene Katz
Production Manager Pat Sarcuni
Art Director Lou Scardino
Administrative Editor Jeanette Ninas Johnson
Cover Design Albert D'Agostino
Interior Design Caliber Design Planning
Photo Researcher Inge King

Library of Congress Cataloging in Publication Data

McConnell, James V.
   Understanding human behavior.

   Bibliographies
   Includes index.
   1. Psychology. I. Title

BF121.M42   1982   150   82-15689
ISBN 0-03-062329-4

Address correspondence to:
383 Madison Avenue
New York, N.Y. 10017
All rights reserved
Printed in the United States of America
Published simultaneously in Canada
3 4 5 6   039   9 8 7 6 5 4 3 2 1

CBS COLLEGE PUBLISHING
Holt, Rinehart and Winston
The Dryden Press
Saunders College Publishing

Dedication

For Roz, Johnna, and Louise,
For Art and Gerry, Ted and Mary,
For Don,
For Brian and Chris, Grant and Micki
And most of all, with great thanks to all the students. . . .

Preface

When the third edition of this text appeared late in 1979, I was quite pleased by how well it had turned out. At that time, what I noticed most were the improvements over the second edition. But when I reread the book in 1982, all I could see were things that needed changing. If you compare this edition with the previous ones, you'll see at once what I mean. Why did I change my viewpoint so drastically in just three years? For several reasons.

To begin with, psychology is a rapidly-changing discipline. A great deal has happened in our field in the past few years, and a textbook such as this one must be constantly updated if it is to remain abreast of current developments. Second, the success of UHB is built on feedback from instructors and students. And since the publication of the third edition, we've gotten comments and suggestions for improvement from hundreds of people who have used the book in the classroom. So there were things that simply had to be added—or altered—to keep the book current and useful.

More than this, I sensed in 1981 that it was time for a thorough overhaul of the book's *perspective.* Psychology is such a complex field that no one person can hope to master all its different areas. So I asked ten of the best-known scholars and educators in psychology to read those parts of UHB that matched their areas of expertise. They became the "Senior Editorial Consultants" for this edition, and their criticisms led me to make extensive revisions both in what is covered in this edition and in the manner in which the material is offered. I cannot emphasize too strongly how much these people have contributed to making the fourth edition pedagogically and scientifically more sound than was any earlier edition.

Thus UHB-4 is significantly better than the earlier version in at least two important ways. First, there are a great many new things in the fourth edition that didn't appear in the first three editions, mostly because the data simply weren't available by 1979. Second, thanks to the suggestions and comments made by the Senior Editorial Consultants (and by other people), we have found more effective ways to present much of the old material. In fact, for reasons I will shortly make clear, I rewrote every page of the book this time round. However, at the strong urging of most of the "users" of UHB-3, we have deliberately kept intact those elements of the first three editions that students and teachers found particularly valuable and useful.

In discussing UHB-4, then, I would like to describe three things: (1) What's new; (2) what's similar to the previous editions (but greatly improved); and (3) what things appeared to satisfy readers the most about UHB-3 and hence are relatively unchanged in this edition.

What's New

1. The "stories" that begin and end each major chapter in the book help set UHB apart from most other introductory textbooks. They serve many functions: They introduce the student to the topics to be covered within the chapter, they are rewarding experiences for many readers, and they "humanize" psychology in ways that tables of data and descriptions of experiments never can hope to. Indeed, most students list the stories as *one of the main reasons they like UHB so much.* I have written four new stories for this edition, mostly to replace ones that either seemed out of date or that pleased only a limited sample of readers.

2. One of the most exciting and rapidly-developing areas of psychology has to do with the discovery that the two hemispheres of the human brain appear to have rather different functions. Since UHB-3 appeared, Roger Sperry has won a much-deserved Nobel Prize for his pioneering studies on how the two hemispheres function. I have revised much of the material on the brain to take into account the most recent findings available to me by publication date. (One point I missed, however, because the data were published after the fourth edition went to press. In the 25 June, 1982 issue of *Science* C. de Lacoste-Utamsing and R. L. Holloway present data suggesting that there are actual *physical differences* between male and female corpus callosums in humans. These authors believe that these physical differences may help explain gender and sex-role differences in men and women.)

    But I have added other new material on the nervous system as well. Thanks to suggestions by William Uttal (and others), there is now much more detail on how the neuron functions. In addition, I have covered Paul MacLean's Triune Theory of the Brain as well (see Chapter 4), because it helps put into perspective some of the data on violence and aggression.

3. Because so many students liked Chapter 1 so much, I have kept the story of "Joe" more or less intact. Joe's story is an important one, and many students report that learning about his problems helps them see the "human side" to the behavioral sciences. But I have added material on the various fields of psychology, and information on what the profession of psychology is all about. I have also clarified the description of the scientific method and added to the coverage of experimental design. The general thrust of the chapter remains the same, however, for experience suggests that it is helpful in getting students to see that what goes on inside their brains influences their social responses—and vice versa.

4. Ten years ago, most people assumed that there were but one or two neurotransmitters. Recent evidence suggests there are, in fact, hundreds of quite different transmitter molecules. Five years ago, most people believed that a given neuron secreted but one (and only one) transmitter substance. Now it seems likely that each neuron secretes a wide range of different transmitters. These new data give us insights into the effects of drugs on behavior (mentioned in Chapter 3) that we never had before.

    More than this, we are just beginning to appreciate the effects that the endorphins have on human behavior. These natural pain killers not only induce such psychological experiences as "runner's high," but also seem to be involved in drug dependency, opiate addiction, and the placebo effect. And, as I note in Chapter 17, there are fascinating hints that "externalizers" may produce more endorphins than do "internalizers." If so, the amount of endorphins a given individual secretes may also be related to how "suggestible" the person is, and to the amount of time the person spends in fantasizing.

5. While we have known for some time that violence on TV can induce aggressive responses in viewers, it is only recently that we have learned what types of viewers are most affected. I report these data in Chapter 4, along with the good

news that some scientists have recently discovered ways of "desensitizing" violence-prone children to the bad effects of television.

6. The important role that olfaction plays in influencing both perceptions and behaviors—particularly those involving sexual stimuli—becomes clearer year by year. Some of the latest research findings are covered in Chapter 6.

7. Twenty years ago I suggested that sensory deprivation might be used as a therapeutic tool. Ten years ago scientists in Oklahoma showed that sensory deprivation might help autistic children who suffer from "input overload." A few years ago, John Lilly suggested that normal people could benefit from a type of sensory isolation called "tanking," but many psychologists disagree with Lilly's conclusions. I discuss all this in Chapter 8, and have included some preliminary results of research on autistic children that Donald E. P. Smith and I have been conducting for the past three years. We believe that the basic problem these children have is that they cannot voluntarily control their sensory inputs as most normal children do. Our research suggests that, when you give them new ways of filtering out inputs *electronically,* many previously "mute" autistic children show an increase in verbalization and the beginnings of true self-control.

8. Following suggestions from Robert Bolles and David Edwards, I have completely reworked the chapters on motivation (particularly Chapter 11). I have not only added new material on drive theory, but have greatly increased the material on emotions and moved it to Chapter 13. The latest findings on gender differences and sex roles are covered in Chapter 12.

9. I've added much more material on cognitive behavior modification to Chapter 15, and have reworked the material on memory (Chapter 16), including new data on the aphasias and on item storage and retrieval. This chapter also includes new research by Elizabeth Loftus on the effects of present inputs on past memories.

10. Pain is a difficult topic to discuss in simple terms, because subjective pain is influenced not only by sensory inputs, but also by personality type, past experience, perception, memory, motivation, and (you guessed it!) the amount of Substance P and the endorphins present in the body. This material—plus the latest research on hypnosis—is covered in Chapter 17.

11. Chapters 18–24, which cover developmental psychology and personality, are probably the most thoroughly revised of all. Thanks to comments by Nancy Cantor and Neil Salkind, I have tried to bring the major issues in developmental psychology into clearer focus. In the past two or three years, several research projects have yielded exciting new data on what newborn infants can and cannot do, and how infants are "pre-wired" to respond to their parents in various ways (and vice versa). These data appear in Chapters 18 and 19. You will find much more detailed descriptions of Piaget's theory in Chapter 20. His concept of cognitive "schemata" appears not only in this chapter, but also in Chapter 9 (perception) and Chapter 16 (memory).

Chapter 21, which covers dynamic personality theories, now includes an extensive discussion of social learning theory and draws heavily on recent work by Nancy Cantor and her colleagues. The discussions of Freudian theory have benefitted considerably from suggestions by Brian Bate. Thanks to him, too, there is more material in Chapter 23 on Gestalt therapy and TA.

12. At Leona Tyler's suggestion, I have rewritten and updated the material on psychological testing (Chapter 22). The material on intelligence now includes several theoretical positions not covered in earlier editions, and a much more balanced discussion of the pros and cons of psychometrics.

13. Despite Freud's belief that personality development more or less ends during adolescence, we now know that people are capable of psychological growth throughout their lives. Many of the myths we have about the capabilities and attributes of older individuals have recently been exploded. The chapters on

human development (18–20) and on personality (21–24) cover this new material on "life-long development and aging."

14. The discussion of abnormal psychology in UHB-3 was based on a preliminary draft of the American Psychiatric Association's *Diagnostic and Statistical Manual-III*. Chapter 23 in the present edition is based on the final version of DSM-III, which appeared in 1980.

No other recent development in the field of clinical psychology has caused as much turmoil as has DSM-III. However, like it or not (and most psychologists seem not to care much for it), DSM-III is here to stay and will have a tremendous effect on both clinical theory and practice for many years to come. I have tried to cover the strengths and weaknesses of DSM-III as objectively as I could. But ignoring it—as some readers have suggested—was out of the question. Any textbook that does not present and evaluate DSM-III simply does not do justice to this rapidly-changing field.

15. Since DSM-III appears to lean more toward "curing symptoms" than "curing underlying causes," I have also updated the long-standing conflict between traditional therapists and the practitioners of behavior modification and social learning theory. (In truth, since the social learning theorists have leaned so far in Piaget's direction in recent years—and since Piaget is not all that distant from Freud—one suspects that a rapprochement of sorts between the opposing views might occur in the near future.)

16. In the past two or three years, it has become apparent that Attribution Theory has gained dominance in the field of social psychology. Person perception (which also has its roots in Piaget's theories) has become more prominent, as well. At Jeffrey Z. Rubin's suggestion, Chapters 25 and 26 reflect this bias and present the latest applications of Heider's and Kelley's insights into social processes.

17. In the 1950's, no part of social psychology seemed to hold more promise than the Yale group's research on persuasion and attitude change. But by the 1980's, much of this work had been called into question. I tell why—and try to give an evaluation of this aspect of the social process—in Chapter 27. This chapter also includes new material which seems to support Ted Newcomb's original (and classic) study of attitude stability among women who attended Bennington College many years ago.

18. In the final chapter ("A Conclusion"), I have added new information on what the field of psychology might be like in the year 2000 A. D. The emphasis here is on application of knowledge for, about the time that UHB-3 was published, the number of psychologists working in applied areas surpassed the number working in university and research settings. From here on out, then, our students are more likely to find jobs in clinical and organizational settings than in the classroom or the laboratory. The final chapter includes a discussion of what this fact means to all psychologists.

19. Last, but surely not least, we have included one or more cartoons by Sidney Harris in each chapter. I have long admired Harris's work—which appears in *American Scientist, Omni, Discover,* and many other magazines. He is one of the very few humorists who really "understands" science, and his gentle spoofs add a marvelous new dimension to UHB-4.

What's Revised or Improved

There are many physical improvements in UHB-4. The most important thing to note is that, while we've increased the coverage of most of the important areas of psychology, we also did a judicious amount of "pruning." Thus the book actually is almost 100 pages *shorter* than was the third edition. I've condensed most of the "stories," eliminated some theoretical discussions, and chopped out material that seemed outdated.

We've also gone to a smaller page size, which makes the book easier for students to handle. In the process, we re-evaluated all the art work and graphic material. I think you will find many improvements in this aspect of the book.

But the most significant change of all is a very subtle one. In the spring of 1978 I purchased a Lanier word processor that is really a miniature computer. When writing UHB-3, I "put the book on the computer." Thus when it came time to prepare this edition, I was able to do an extensive amount of "fine tuning" of the material that I probably wouldn't have bothered with had the revision been made using the usual "cut and paste" method. Although the previous editions of UHB have scored high on "readability" and "human interest" tests, this version is surely the best. The sentences are shorter, as are the paragraphs. However, the summaries are longer and much more complete. These points are important, since recent studies suggest (a) that most textbooks show a *decrease* in readability and understandability from one edition to the next, and (b) that students learn as much from summaries as from the text itself. Thus, as a pedagogical tool, UHB-4 is vastly improved.

More than this, the future is finally here. My machine stores material on floppy disks, and the computer experts figured out a way to set type for UHB-4 straight from those disks. Thus as I prepared the final draft, I was actually setting type for the book itself. UHB-4 is one of the first major textbooks to be produced in this manner. Letting the author "set type" not only saves time—and thus makes the book more current when it first appears—but also dramatically reduces the number of typographical errors and other mistakes which always seem to creep into texts during the composition stage.

UHB has always had the reputation of being one of the most comprehensive and yet most integrated texts on the market. The fourth edition continues this tradition. However, I have placed less emphasis on General Systems Theory than in previous editions. There is a bit more of the history of psychology in Chapter 5—and considerably less about the holistic approach—than was the case in UHB-3. Rather than leaning so heavily on the systems approach for integration, I have tried to show the interconnections *between* other theories (such as Piaget's and Social Learning Theory) and *across* research findings (such as the influence of the endorphins on so many aspects of the human experience). My guess is that most readers will find this change an important and desirable one.

But in making all these changes, I have tried to keep both the teacher and the student in mind. For, even at its best, a text is no more than an adjunct to what goes on in the classroom. The instructor remains of paramount importance. However, teachers often need more help than authors have time or space to offer in the text itself. This time round, therefore, we have moved the references to the *Instructor's Manual*. Our studies show that teachers rely on this material much more than students, and that students who do consult the list of references usually need an instructor's guidance. The *Instructor's Manual* has also been organized in a chapter-by-chapter order rather than topically. At the end of the IM you will find a set of approximately 100 transparency masters, which are keyed to the text. The IM also contains a great many helpful hints and suggestions that both beginning and experienced teachers will find of value.

More than a million students have read one of the first three editions of this text, and we have kept their needs in mind while preparing UHB-4. Al Siebert and Tim Walter have greatly revised their outstanding *Student Manual,* while Ray Schrader and Reid Jones have reorganized and rewritten their *Unit Mastery/PSI Workbook.* Eugenia Scharf and Brian Bate have prepared a bank of test questions that is far better than any we've had before. The Test Bank will be available in printed form as well as a computer disk for either the Apple II or TRS 80.

We have doubled the number of slides to a total of 300. We have also worked to better integrate the slides with the text chapters.

There is a new addition to the package for this edition. As a discipline, psychology is so dynamic that it is almost impossible to read all the new literature and research. To help keep you in the forefront of the research, we are providing a set of abstracts for a select group of topics. We plan to provide 20–30 abstracts for each text chapter and to publish a new set of abstracts for each year of the fourth edition of UHB.

What's Much the Same:

So much has been changed or revised in this new edition that I feel compelled to assure both teachers and students of one important thing: We have managed to retain all those good things that have made UHB so popular in the past. As I mentioned earlier, the "stories" that begin and end each major chapter are still there, as are the glossary terms in the right-hand margin of each double-page spread, as was the case in UHB-1. The stories, the "running glossary," the simple language, and the integrated approach to psychology are the four features of the previous editions that students found particularly useful to them in their attempts to master the field of psychology.

There is no doubt that UHB-4 is as different from other introductory psychology textbooks as were the first three editions. If you read *Teaching of Psychology*—the journal put out by Division Two of the American Psychological Association—you know that research performed both in the US and in Canada shows that students rate UHB *higher than any other text.* I take great pride in this fact, for I have tried to write the book so that it will both *please and teach* the introductory student. To me, these are two of the most important goals of any psychology text—that readers enjoy what they read, and understand and remember the material *for a long time thereafter.* As best we can tell, UHB both "pleases and teaches" better than any other book that we have been able to test.

I have tried, as well, to present psychology in such a way that most readers will give at least passing consideration to making it their undergraduate major. As I have noted elsewhere, it doesn't help any of us if our classes (and texts) are so boring that most of our students can't wait to finish the introductory class so that they can take something more interesting.

The question remains, "What should a student get out of the introductory psychology course? Facts? An understanding of what psychology is all about?" Many of the so-called encyclopaedic texts contain a lot of facts, true. But how many students who read them can appreciate or recall those facts a month after the final exam? It seems to me that these texts miss the real point of what a college course should be about—that of encouraging *long-term changes* in human thoughts, feelings, and actions. According to a recent survey published in *Teaching of Psychology,* UHB cites at least as many facts and research studies as does the average psychology text, but explains the data and theories in such a way that the facts "come to life" and thus are important and real enough to be memorable and useful to the reader.

Finally, UHB-4 is as personal a book as the previous editions were. Our research shows that most students are put off by a very formal, academic approach to their first psychology course. The students are interested in *people*—themselves and others—and not in esoteric data, statistical equations, and the fine points of experimental design. Many of us who teach the first course forget that 95 percent of our students are *not* psychology majors. And probably 90 percent of them will *never* perform a real psychological experiment. Why then should we rub their noses in scientific esoterica when that's the last thing that will "turn them on" to psychology? UHB-4 is a practical, people-oriented textbook that deals in real-life issues and gives students material that they can put to practical use immediately. Is there any better way to make science understandable to students than by exciting their interest and giving them practical rewards for learning?

And perhaps that's the most important thing I learned from working with my Lanier word processor. This mini-brain will do what I tell it to do—if I give it the right inputs. I don't need to "motivate" it to respond, other than punching keys. The human brain must be programmed in much the same way, but humans have hearts that "pump emotions" as well as blood. Ordering a student to learn usually doesn't work very well, and no one has yet found a set of simple "brain buttons" to press that will ensure that undergraduates memorize a textbook as readily and as rapidly as my word processor memorizes data on floppy disks. Thus teaching and writing remain as much a psychological art as they are a psychological science.

If you are judging textbooks, don't just look at the pretty pictures, or at the number of literature citations, or at the names and concepts listed in the index. Instead, always judge a text *by the results that it gets.* That is, judge a book by how much the *typical reader* actually understands and remembers. If you do, you probably will learn as much about people, and how they differ from computers, as I have learned by working with my word processor.

In brief, I'm all for using computers if and when they will help me achieve my personal goals. But my chief aim remains that of helping *people*—helping teachers teach, and helping students learn to love and appreciate psychology as much as I do.

My sincere hope is that UHB-4 will help us all achieve those goals better than did any of the previous editions. And what better reason could one have for revising any textbook?

James V. McConnell

Acknowledgments

According to the title page, this is "my" book. Nothing could be farther from the truth. It takes the combined efforts of hundreds of people to produce a decent introductory psychology text. The author gets most of the credit, but the others do much of the real work. Yet without their contributions, no book would ever see final publication. In this brief note, let me acknowledge my great indebtedness to many individuals.

To begin with, there is Louise Waller, the editor of the first edition, who helped UHB through its considerable birth pangs. It was she who fought so hard to help me realize the dream we both had of what a textbook could be like.

Then there is Johnna Barto, who guided me through the editorial anxieties and uncertainties of the second and third editions. I owe Johnna great gratitude. Francoise D. Bartlett and Jeanette Ninas Johnson took over the editorial reins at the last moment on the third edition, when Johnna moved on to greener pastures. To both Fran and Jeanette, a warm and hearty vote of thanks for their help with both the third and fourth editions.

Rosalind Sackoff is the editor of the current edition, and much of the credit for making this version "the best ever" goes to her. She was a joy to work with, a very talented colleague and contributor, and someone I am happy to call "friend."

My special blessings too to Ray Ashton, Editor-in-Chief, for his considerable efforts to make UHB so successful. My thanks also to John Michel and Dan Loch for their bright ideas, their concern, and their continued support. They helped plan the fourth edition, and always put pride and educational accomplishment before mere profit—rare traits in the publishing world.

I would also like to thank Stan Frank, Harry McQuillen, John Wood, and Jean Smith for their many kindnesses.

Louis Scardino and Caliber Design Planning designed the book and supervised the illustration program. Inge King researched all the new photographs. Albert d'Agostino designed the marvelous cover. Pat Sarcuni guided matters wisely and well through the production process. My special thanks to Vic Calderon for his continued assistance in matters large and small.

Arlene Katz efficiently shepherded the book through the editorial process, coordinating all of the day-to-day activities that take the manuscript to bound book.

In final analysis, a good share of the success of the previous editions was due to the enthusiastic reception given UHB by many HRW marketing and salespeople. I cannot begin to name them all, but would like to extend thanks particularly to Lisa Bayard, George Bergquist, Lucienne Allard, Barbara Anson, Russ Boersma, Tim Baughman, Neil Cronin, Dave Cummins, Paul Davidson, Paul Dunn, Donna Fletcher, Dora Guzman, David Hall, Cecile Higgins, Tom Hogan, Sue Juhre, Tim Kent, Bobby Knight, John Lannefeld, Carl Leonard, Toni Linstedt, Jim Lizotte, Cathie MacIver,

Roger MacQuarrie, Charles McKissick, Earl McPeek, Ann Meyer, Chuck Pensinger, Tom Pohlman, Paula Rosenblatt, Marcia Staley, Randy Terry, Dennis Thetford, Karen Torre, Vern Tupper, and Don Welch.

Many of my professional colleagues gave generously of their time in reading all or parts of the manuscript and offering their thoughtful comments. In particular, there are the "senior Consultants" who gave so willingly of their collective wisdom: William Uttal, University of Michigan; Robert Bolles, University of Washington; David Edwards, Iowa State University; Neil Salkind, University of Kansas; Sandra Scarr, Yale University; Nancy Cantor, Princeton University; Brian Bate, Cayuhoga Community College; Leona Tyler; Theodore Newcomb, University of Michigan; Jeffrey Rubin, Tufts University.

There are also my colleagues, Tim Walter, Al Siebert, Jon Gosser, Reid Jones, and Raymond Shrader, whom I must acknowledge. They read the manuscript and offered many helpful suggestions. Siebert and Walter are also the authors of the excellent *Student Manual* that accompanies the book, while Shrader and Jones are the authors of the *Personalized Instruction* materials that many students use. Jon Gosser prepared the subject index.

I would also like to thank the following people for their letters, reviews, criticisms, and useful comments: Robert Burke, South Dakota State University; Michael Bergmire, Jefferson College; Patricia Tuntland, Pima College; Joan Rosen, Miami Dade Junior College; Dave Schroeder, University of Arkansas; Clinton Anderson, Providence College; James Wheeler, Meremac Community College; Rita Heberer, Belleville Area College; Paul Watson, University of Tennessee, Chattanooga; Margaret Condon, Northeastern Illinois University; Barton Meyers, Brooklyn College; Garvin Chastain, Boise State University.

Then there are my many friends in Ann Arbor and elsewhere, comrades all, who gave me most of my ideas and whose names I have taken in vain in some of the short stories. To my poker-playing cronies—Brian Healy, W. Robert Dixon, John Holland, Peter Steiner, Dan Rubinfeld, Chuck Phillips, and Ralph Heine—my thanks for keeping me amused (and broke) during the book's gestation period.

Last, but most assuredly not least, it is my students—past and present—who deserve my thanks. They taught me how to write; they shaped me into learning more about psychology and about people than I had any intention of learning. Whatever is best in this book is their doing, not mine.

Bless 'em all.

J. V. McC.

October 1982
Ann Arbor, Michigan

Senior Editorial Consultants

Part 1 *Biological Bases*
William Uttal, University of Michigan

Part 2 *Sensation and Perception*
William Uttal, University of Michigan

Part 3 *Motivation*
Robert Bolles, University of Washington
David Edwards, Iowa State University

Part 4 *Learning and Memory*
Robert Bolles, University of Washington

Part 5 *Maturation and Development*
Neil Salkind, University of Kansas
Sandra Scarr, Yale University

Part 6 *Personality*
Nancy Cantor, Princeton University
Brian Bate, Cayuhoga Community College
Leona Tyler

Part 7 *Social Psychology*
Theodore Newcomb, University of Michigan
Jeffrey Rubin, Tufts University

Contents

Part 2   Sensation and Perception   135

The beginning entries:

Part 7 Social Psychology   589

Statistical Appendix   670

Name Index   684

Subject Index   688

Introduction 1

"Getting It All Together"

It was a cold and rainy spring afternoon when Joe first showed up in my life. I had come back to my office after class somewhat drenched from the rain that poured out of a gray and angry sky. And there was Joe, sitting anxiously in the chair in front of my desk. We shook hands, then I asked him to wait a moment while I returned an urgent phone call that had come in while I had been in class.

As I was talking on the phone, I inspected Joe carefully out of the corner of my eye. He was a relatively plain-looking, dark-haired young man who seemed to be in his mid-twenties. His clothes were inexpensive but fairly well cared for. I got the impression that he was quite nervous, for his dark brown eyes darted constantly about the room and his hands trembled a bit as he lit a cigarette. I wondered what his problem was, and why he had brought it to me since I couldn't recall ever having seen him before. As soon as I finished talking on the telephone, Joe answered both questions.

"Dr. McConnell, I need help," he said rather loudly the moment I put down the receiver. "I'm sorry to bother you with it, because you're not my teacher or anything. But, well, several of my friends have taken your courses and . . ." Joe shrugged his shoulders and leaned forward a bit in his chair. "And I've read your introductory psych book, you know, and I liked it a lot. It helped me a lot because, well, one of my friends brought it to me while I was incarcerated in the mental hospital. Uh, yes, the book. You see, it was the only thing I had to read while I was incarcerated."

At this point Joe broke out in nervous laughter. "Can you believe that I read a book about crazy people when I was in a mental hospital? Oh, my. I had to do something to keep from going crazy, uh, so I read your book from cover to cover. I need, yes, I really do need your help because, uh, it wasn't fair what they did to me, and now they want to put me back in the hospital."

The Puzzle of Human Behavior

When you meet someone like Joe who's just gotten out of a mental hospital, how do you *see* that person? Do you view the person as being "sick," or "insane," or as a "fugitive from the funny farm"? Or do you see the individual as "a human being in distress who needs your help"? These questions are important because, generally speaking, the way you *perceive* people pretty much determines the way you will feel about them and the way you will treat them.

For my part, I tend to view someone like Joe as a mystery begging to be solved—a human "jigsaw puzzle" the person and I must jointly put together so that we both get a better picture of what the individual is really like. We usually begin with small details—fitting this little piece together with the next. At first, we usually focus on what's happening to the person in her or his present situation. Then we look at what experiences the person has had in the past. Next, we try to discover what future goals the individual has. Eventually, when we get enough of the small details in place, we can often begin to make plans about how this particular human being would like to grow, change, or solve her or his immediate problems.

So, at this point in my conversation with Joe, I sat back to think things over. What clues did I have so far about this puzzling young man named Joe?

To begin with, he was a middle-class male who either was in college now or had been a student in the recent past. He was neatly dressed, but in old clothes. I presumed, therefore, that he had little money but that he was still interested in "looking good" when he appeared in public. He had a good vocabulary, but his speech was a bit disjointed and broken up—a most important clue to his problems, as you will soon learn. He was nervous and frightened because "they" had put him in a mental hospital and now wanted him to go back.

Most important of all, *he wanted to make some changes in his life.* Otherwise, he never would have come to me asking for help.

As we talked further, Joe gave me many more clues as to what he was really like. Some of these "pieces of the jigsaw puzzle" fit into place right away. Other clues I simply missed, or I failed to recognize how important they were to understanding Joe when they first surfaced.

If you would like to learn some of the skills involved in understanding human behavior, why don't you follow along as Joe and I continue our conversation? Try to see Joe as I saw him, that blustery spring day when he first walked into my life. And as Joe and I fit the parts of his own unique "jigsaw puzzle" together, perhaps you will discover some things about yourself that you never really knew before.

Dead as a Brass Doorknob

It takes guts to admit that you've been "put away" in a mental hospital, and I respect people who are not ashamed to talk about what's happened to them. So I smiled at Joe and said, "I'm sorry to hear that you've had problems, and I don't blame you for wanting to make sure that 'they' don't send you back. But who are 'they'? And come to think of it, who are you?"

Joe's laugh was high and tightly pitched, almost a giggle. "I'm Joe X," he said, telling me his whole name. As it happened, although he lived some 60 miles from the University, I had heard of his family because his father was a prominent person. (I have changed Joe's name and some other details in order to protect his privacy, but the rest of the story is true.)

"So you're Joe," I said, reaching over the desk to shake his hand. "I'm glad to meet you. And I'm delighted that you liked my textbook *Understanding Human Behavior*, even if you did read it in rather unusual circumstances. But you still haven't said who 'they' are."

Joe hung his head in apparent embarrassment. "They're my parents. What can you do when your own mother and father have you locked away in a mental hospital because they think you're crazy?" He shook his head in dismay. "Oh, uh, I still love them. I guess. But, uh, it's hard to live with." He looked up at me quickly, waving his hands in a circle in front of his chest. "It's like this, you know," he said, waving his hands some more, almost as if he were trying to show me the *shape* of his own despair.

"Why do you think your parents had you committed, Joe?"

"Because I died," he said in a flat tone of voice.

I'm sure I frowned noticeably. "You died?"

Joe nodded. "I lay there on the ground for maybe ten minutes, dead as a brass doorknob. Uh, brass, you know, it conducts electricity. Uh, like I did, I guess."

Curiouser and curiouser. "*You* conducted electricity?"

"Like a brass doorknob. Um, the psychiatrist my parents sent me to said the 'death trauma' drove me crazy. Not everybody who dies comes back, you know. Uh, well, he said I haven't resolved my fears and anxieties about being dead, and coming back, and all that sort of thing."

Joe paused and lit another cigarette. His hands were shaking even more violently now than when I had first come back to my office. And no wonder.

"Joe, how did it happen? When did you die, and how did you manage to come back?"

He shrugged his shoulders. "Oh, it was years ago. Uh, maybe eight years ago this month. I was, you know, out there flying a kite, that was the crazy part of it. Uh, you shouldn't fly a kite on a rainy day, not near the power lines anyhow. Er, at least that's what they told me after I died and came back."

Joe stopped for a moment, frowning. "The psychiatrist always wanted me to talk about my feelings when I died. He said I had to relive the experience until all the feelings I had when I was dead came out into the open. Um, but that's ridiculous. I didn't *have* any feelings when I died, only when I came back. Uh, I mean, do you want me to talk about my feelings too?"

I smiled. "Joe, you can talk about anything you want to talk about. But frankly, I'd rather hear the facts first, and the feelings second. I gather you were flying a kite on a rainy day, and the kite struck some power lines. I would imagine that the electricity came down the kite string and knocked you out."

Joe nodded vigorously. "Killed me dead. Fifteen thousand volts, they said. I mean, I wasn't even breathing for five or ten minutes. Uh, I guess I would have stayed dead, lying there on the

"DELUSIONS OF GRANDEUR?
I AM GRAND!"

ground, but my brother saw it happen and he called for help. Uh, there was this doctor living next door, you see, and my brother yelled for him, and the doctor came and, oh, you know, he did that thing . . ." Again Joe's hands fluttered in front of his chest. "He breathed air back into my lungs, and resuscitated me. But, but my brain was killed, you know what I mean?"

Some "Shocking Facts" about Brain Damage

I knew what Joe meant. The jolt of electricity had stopped his heart from beating, and Joe's brain had been without blood and oxygen for several minutes. Some of the nerve cells in Joe's brain had surely died. Pumping air into Joe's lungs might have brought his heart and the rest of his body back to life, but brain cells are among the most sensitive bits of tissue in the body. Once Joe's nerve cells had been damaged, no medicine known to modern science could repair or replace them.

The fact that Joe had "died" and returned to life was, of course, the single most important clue to understanding his present predicament. As Joe's psychiatrist had known full well, such an experience leaves many scars on an individual's personality. But Joe's *psychological problems* were complicated by the *physical damage* that had occurred to his brain cells—as well as by the *social reactions* of his family and friends. In order to put the pieces of Joe's jigsaw puzzle together, I first had to learn something about how his body, mind, and social environment *interacted* with each other.

As you probably know, certain parts of your brain influence rather specific aspects of your thoughts, feelings, and behaviors. As we will see in Chapter 4, nerve cells in the front part of your brain have control over the muscles in your arms and legs. If these brain cells were damaged, you might spend the rest of your life in a wheelchair. Your *mind* might still be capable of "willing" your arms and legs to move. But if your brain cells were so damaged that they couldn't carry out your mental orders, your *body* would remain permanently paralyzed.

Other parts of your brain control your ability to speak. If you had an accident and injured these cells, you probably would experience rather severe problems trying to say things out loud. Your mind might still be able to "think" words, but your lips and vocal cords might not be able to respond by saying precisely what you were thinking (see Chapter 16).

Judging from Joe's behavior—most of which seemed entirely normal—he had recovered

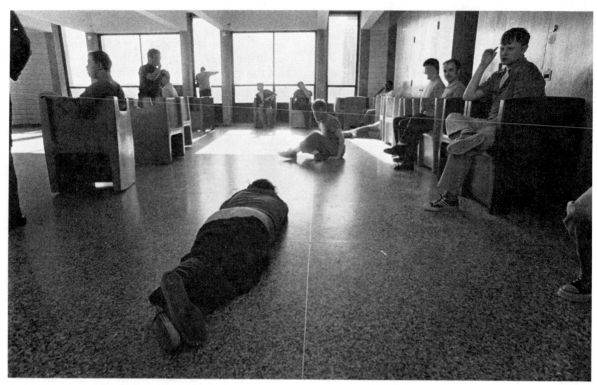
A ward in a mental hospital.

rather well from his terrifying experience. So his present problems couldn't entirely be due to the fact that he had suffered minor brain damage as a teenager. Therefore, to find out more about him, I asked him what it was like to die and then come back to life.

Joe giggled loudly. "I can't remember. I just can't remember! Isn't that crazy? The most important thing in my life, and I can't remember anything at all about what it was like to be dead. Uh, the doctor said that the damage to my brain probably caused me to forget. *Amnesia*, he called it. Um, but you know, the funny thing is that I can recall everything that happened afterward, and what happened earlier that day up to a few minutes before I got electrocuted, but I can't remember anything, oh, you know, any special feeling at all about being dead."

He rubbed his hands together, and then held them to his chest. "It was, I mean, like when you're asleep and you don't dream and you don't recall being asleep but the time is gone when you wake up. Uh, I guess I was scared about the whole thing, and my parents were awfully upset, and yes, yes, they took me to the hospital in the ambulance. I remember that. And, well, of course my mother kept crying about how God had given me back from the realm of the dead, and um, it was a

sign I had work to do yet. I told it all to the psychiatrist a hundred times, and um, he said someday I might remember if I can relive the experience enough times and release the blocked up fears and anxieties. But, why can't I remember it? Do you know?"

I thought I might. "Joe, as I point out in my book, there are a lot of studies showing that if something shocks or damages your brain, you lose your memory for everything that happened for 30 minutes or so *before* the accident. Oddly enough, you usually can remember what happened immediately *afterward*—but not what had happened to you just prior to the shock. That's what the phrase 'retrograde amnesia' really means—a memory loss that extends back in time from the moment of the accident."

"Yeah, but what puzzles me is that I died immediately *after* the shock, not before it. So, er, why don't I remember what came afterward?"

"Joe, the electricity was just the first shock you got. When you died, your brain stopped operating for a period of a few minutes. And then just as suddenly, it came back to life and started working again. Don't you think all that stopping and starting up was something of a shock to your brain too?"

Joe nodded. "Oh, yes. Nobody ever explained it to me that way. Uh, but if I can't remember it, why did it drive me crazy?"

What Is Insanity?

I looked at Joe very, very carefully. He seemed determined to convince me that he was "off his rocker." Yet his behavior so far had been fairly normal. True, his speech seemed a little disturbed, and from time to time his hands "fluttered" in an odd way—but I didn't really understand the significance of those facts until much later on. Despite his relatively normal behavior, however, Joe had worked with a psychiatrist for many years, he had spent time in a mental hospital, and he was very worried about being hospitalized again. Little wonder he was convinced he was "crazy." My problem now was to find out who and what had done the convincing. "Who decided you were insane, Joe?"

The young man gave me a puzzled look. "Uh, my parents, I guess. Like, you see, they sent me to see the psychiatrist in the first place."

"What made them do that?"

"I guess I screwed up, or something. I, well, maybe I did. You see, after I died, things didn't go so good for a while."

"What do you mean?"

Joe's hands flew about wildly for a moment. "It's like that, you know. It just didn't go very well. Oh, uh, I did okay in school. I finished high school, and came here to the University. Uh, I never did take one of your courses, because I was majoring in sociology. And then I got a job for a while, too—in Chicago. But they didn't like me there, so I, uh, came back home. And then the problems with my parents got worse, um, so they made me go see the psychiatrist, you know?"

"No, Joe, I don't know about the problems with your parents, because you haven't told me about them. Why don't you do that now?"

He shook his head forlornly. He sighed. He lit another cigarette. It seemed to me that we were, at last, getting down to the real facts about his present situation.

"Well," he said, puffing nervously on the cigarette, "I can't figure my mother out. Oh, you know. She says she loves me, and when I was in the hospital, she used to hold me in her arms and sing hymns to me. Er, she wanted me to be a preacher. But my daddy wanted me to go to college and become a lawyer. Um, they both were pretty angry when I went into sociology instead. And I used to have these spells, you know, when I just couldn't get it together. I ran off a couple of times, and uh, I used to get headaches and couldn't go to school all the time. So they sent me to the doctor."

"The psychiatrist?" I asked.

"No, the brain doctor, the neurologist. Oh man, he measured my brain waves and things like that. Er, he said I had irreversible brain damage from dying and I'd never be normal."

"So?"

Joe gave an eloquent shrug. "So he gave me some pills to take, to calm down my brain. They helped some, I guess, but mostly they just made me sleepy. Uh, I still had headaches and couldn't always get it together. Uh, so mother insisted that I go see this psychiatrist, um, and he kept asking me about how it felt to be dead and come back. And, uh, he wanted me to tell him about all my impulses and angers and bad feelings. Er, I told him all that, but I just felt worse, and some days I just stayed in bed, and my parents kept picking on me to get up and get things done." Joe shook his head sadly.

After a moment I said, "Why do you think your parents responded that way, Joe?"

"I guess they wanted me to be a success, and here I was a big disappointment to them. They just couldn't see inside me, you know, see what I was thinking and feeling, and how hard it was to act the way they wanted me to. And, uh, they just kept telling me my brain was damaged and I had to strive to overcome it and be like everybody else. Nothing I did seemed to be what they wanted. Uh, and one day I got very upset and we had a big argument about it all, and, and, mother called the psychiatrist and they decided I was crazy. And, oh, God, they said I needed complete rest and I felt so bad and my head hurt so much that I agreed. Uh, so they sent me to the mental hospital."

Joe paused for a very long time. Tears came to his eyes, and he opened his hands in resignation. Then he said, "I hated the hospital, and I didn't know why I was there, really. Except it was what my parents wanted, and, er, I figured they knew what they were doing. My social worker at the hospital said it was mostly my parents' fault, uh, that they didn't know how to give me the right environmental support. Oh, my. I don't know if I believe that, uh, but I know I don't want to go back to that hospital, Dr. McConnell. That place is hell on wheels. But if you can't work and support yourself, and you can't stand living with your parents, and you feel bad lots of the time, and you have brain damage, uh, doesn't that mean you're insane?"

Insanity versus Mental Illness

Insanity is a legal term, and as such, it's a "label" that psychologists don't use very much. If a judge decides that you cannot tell the difference between right and wrong, or that you are not able to resist criminal impulses, you may be certified as being "insane" by that judge. You then will lose some of your legal rights, and you may be sent to an institution. Thus, technically speaking, you are legally *sane* unless and until a judge signs papers saying that you are legally *insane*.

Psychologists and psychiatrists prefer to use the terms "mental illness" and "unable to cope" rather than "insane," mostly because we are more concerned about helping unhappy people get well than we are about pinning legal labels on them. Judges usually are more concerned about protecting the public and determining legal rights and wrongs.

So, to me, Joe wasn't "insane," although it did seem that he was very unhappy and very disturbed about a lot of things. But it was just as obvious that he had many strengths and many good points. And I was as interested in what Joe could do, and *do well*, as I was in what things in life troubled him.

Calling someone "mentally ill" doesn't usually tell you much about how to help the person get well. As we will see in later chapters, there is no universally agreed-upon treatment for most types of mental disorders—mainly because there is no real agreement as to what causes people to become mentally disturbed.

But we do know of several things that can give you difficulties. (1) Some psychological problems are primarily caused by physical or chemical damage to the nervous system. (2) Other problems seem mostly to be a result of how your mind reacts to (and copes with) various sorts of highly emotional and stressful experiences. And (3), still other so-called "mental difficulties" are actually due to the person's having learned inappropriate behavior patterns, or due to the social situation the person presently is in.

What we call "mental illness," then, can be the result of biological problems. Or psychological problems. Or problems having to do with the person's behavior or social environment. More likely, what we call "mental illness" occurs *because an individual has all three types of problems at once.*

For the most part, psychologists can best help you recover from "mental illness" if we view you from a biological perspective, *and* from a psychological perspective, *and* from a social or behavioral perspective *all at the same time*. That is, we need to perceive you as being an incredibly complex person who has a body, a mind, and who lives among and reacts to other people. If we were to look at *just* your physical reactions, or *just* your mental processes, or *just* your social behaviors, we probably would come up with a very limited set of solutions to your present problems.

My problem as I spoke to Joe was that I couldn't see what *his* problems really were. Although he said he was "brain damaged," his actions seemed pretty normal. He had finished college, and he used complex language rather well. Nor did his thought processes seem disturbed or unusual to me. He behaved politely, he responded to what I said in a logical way, he maintained good eye contact as he spoke to me, and he seemed to have his emotions under control.

And yet there *was* something unusual about Joe that I couldn't quite put my finger on.

Science as a "Detective Story"

Science is, to a great extent, the fine art of solving mysteries. Nature gives us a puzzle—human or otherwise. For some reason—perhaps due to our own peculiar nature as human beings—we are motivated to solve the puzzle. We can either use our "hunches" and make wild guesses about the answer—which is what people did for most of the history of civilization. Or we can adopt a logical process of some kind in trying to find the solution to the puzzle.

Even today, most people prefer using their guesses and their *subjective* feelings when trying to unravel any mystery that they encounter. And that's fine—as a starting point. But ever since the Middle Ages—when the scientific method was first developed—a growing number of individuals have tried to apply a logical, *objective* approach to the solution of human problems.

This objective approach is called the *scientific method*, and it is based on the belief that most mysteries have *natural* or *measurable causes*. To use the scientific method properly, you must follow several steps:

1. First, you have to recognize that a mystery of some kind exists that needs solving, and that the mystery probably has a natural cause. We might call this step *perceiving the problem*.
2. Then you make as many *initial observations* about the mysterious circumstances as you can. And you try to make your observations as exact and complete as possible.
3. You use the results of your initial observations to come up with a *tentative solution* or "first guess" as to what the answer is. Scientists often call this step "making an hypothesis." The solution you pick, however, will be determined by how you view the problem—and the world. If you think events that take place in the world around you are affected primarily by *supernatural powers*, then the scientific method won't help you much. But if you believe that a mysterious event might have a

natural cause, then perhaps you can state your "tentative solution" or hypothesis in a way that will help you determine what that cause is.

4. Next, you draw up a plan for *testing objectively* whether or not your first hunch about the solution was correct. This test may merely involve making further observations about the puzzling affair. Or it may involve performing an experiment in which you "do something" to the puzzle in order to get a reaction of some kind.

5. Whether you merely observe things, or whether you undertake an experiment of some kind, you then look over the data and try to decide as unemotionally as possible whether your tentative solution to the problem was right or wrong. If your initial hypothesis was wrong, you will revise it and make some more observations. But if your first hunch was correct, you probably will refine your solution to the mystery by *testing it again and again*. And to do so, you will again need to make predictions about future events.

6. If these further predictions turn out to be accurate, then most likely your solution to the puzzle was correct. But if your predictions were incorrect, you should realize that you goofed up somewhere along the way. And you will have to start the problem-solving process all over again.

The Importance of Objectivity

The key concept in any definition of the scientific method is *objectivity*. And "being objective" means standing back and looking at the puzzle as unemotionally and impersonally as you can.

True, your subjective, personal feelings are very useful in *motivating* you to want to solve problems, but your emotions can cloud your judgment if you don't know how to control them when necessary.

For example, Joe's parents loved him and hence were motivated to help him. But they became so upset that they simply couldn't view their family situation as a problem to be understood and perhaps solved. Had they done so, they might have guessed somewhere along the line that part of Joe's difficulties lay in *the way that they treated him*. As it was, their emotions got in the way. Because they couldn't shoulder part of the blame themselves, they preferred to see Joe's "craziness" as being entirely *inside Joe*. Thus, when the social worker at the mental hospital suggested that Joe's parents might be partially responsible for the way Joe acted, they rejected her hypothesis—without ever testing it scientifically.

Psychology became something of a science when we first learned to see ourselves as others see us—that is, when we learned to view people as *highly complex systems* whose feelings, thoughts, and actions are influenced by their biological inheritance, their past experiences, and the world around them.

Psychology is thus that junction point at which biology and the social environment interact to influence the development of our minds and bodies.

We will have more to say about what psychology is—and how it developed—in the next few chapters. For the moment, let's see how we might apply the scientific method to Joe's problem.

The "Mystery" of Joe

I could see Joe's body, and I could measure it objectively. His *mind* was hidden to me, however. The word "mind" comes from an Old English term meaning "memory." *Webster's New Collegiate Dictionary* defines mind as, "that element or complex of elements in an individual that feels, perceives, thinks, wills, and especially reasons." The same book also calls mind, "The conscious mental events and capabilities in an organism." Mind, then, has to do with your *inner* experiences. But if there is one fact that almost all psychologists are agreed upon, it's this one: What goes on inside your mind is a *private set of events* we can never inspect directly. However, by being objective—by talking with you and observing your reactions, by giving you "mental tests," by watching how you interact with other people, and by drawing on the results of thousands of scientific studies—we can often gain a pretty good notion of what you are like "inside."

So, I couldn't see *directly* if Joe was "mentally ill" or "legally insane," because I couldn't observe his mind. But I had watched his actions and reactions as objectively as I could and, frankly, I was still rather puzzled. Which is to say that I didn't yet have enough data about Joe to guess at a tentative solution to the mystery of his present existence.

And just as frankly, I don't know that I ever would have gained much insight into Joe's problems had fate not happily intervened.

There came a knock at my office door, and a student stuck her head in to remind me that I had promised to discuss her research with her.

Joe seemed to panic. He wrung his hands almost violently. "Uh, oh my, I don't mean to intrude. You've got to see this student, okay, but, listen, I really need your help, you know? I mean, I don't want to go back to that, that *place*, and I

A "typical family." Psychologists study both normal and abnormal behavior patterns.

know you can help me, uh, if you really want to." He stopped momentarily, and tears clouded his eyes. "But maybe you don't want to . . ."

"Yes, Joe, I really want to help you if I can." I smiled. "Anybody who read my book in a mental hospital obviously needs help, right?"

Joe smiled too. "Uh, could I buy you a beer after you see this person? I mean, that way we could converse in private for a while."

Mind Talk, Body Talk

An hour or so later, I met Joe at a nearby campus hangout. As I sat down, I noticed he had a large pitcher of beer in front of him. The pitcher was about two-thirds empty. When the waitress came up, I ordered a Coke. (If you're going to engage in scientific problem-solving, it helps to remain sober.)

"Gee, Dr. McConnell, I'm glad I came to see you today. Gee. I mean, I feel better already," Joe said, finishing his glass of beer and pouring himself another one.

"I'm glad you came to the office today, too. Been waiting long?"

Joe laughed. "I drank a couple of bottles, you know, and then, and then I ordered up this, this . . ." He pointed at the pitcher. "Oh, you know, the beer. The beer, uh, pitcher." He took a big swallow from his glass and refilled it.

"You seem to be enjoying yourself."

"I guess I am, really. Uh, I feel more *together* now, you know what I mean? Like this!" He swirled his hands around in a circle.

As I realized later, Joe had just given me several important clues to his problems:

First, he was apparently under considerable tension and, as I soon discovered, often used alcohol to relieve his feelings of stress.

Second, he probably suffered from some slight damage to the speech centers in his brain. All of us resort to using our hands to describe things now and again. But Joe had been doing it a bit too often. I didn't know precisely what his speech problem was, but I was reasonably sure that he had one and that it was related to what had happened to his brain when Joe temporarily "died."

Third, "getting it together" was easier for Joe when he was intoxicated. Why that was so will take a bit of explaining.

As we will see in the next chapter, your brain is divided into two halves, the left hemisphere and the right. If you are right-handed, the left half (or hemisphere) of your brain tends to dominate much of what you do. If you are left-handed, the situation is much more difficult to describe. So we will postpone talking about left-handed people until Chapter 2.

If you are right-handed, your left hemisphere is the seat of your self-awareness and of your logical decision-making processes. This half of your brain also controls speech and most other body movements. All of your conscious thoughts, then, are "mind talk" that originate in the left half of your brain.

The right half of your brain, on the other hand, is the seat of such creative abilities as spatial (three-dimensional) perception and pattern recognition. Under most circumstances, your right hemisphere is "silent," which is to say that it does not directly control what you say and consciously think. However, the right half of your brain does seem to take the lead in emotional responses and so it affects your speech, thoughts, and actions *indirectly*.

The conscious (left) half of your brain is not directly aware of what goes on in the silent (right) half of your brain. But most evidence suggests that your "silent hemisphere" monitors, perceives, and responds emotionally to whatever your "talking hemisphere" does. What we often call "body talk" or "body language," then, is actually a set of responses that appears to be controlled by the "silent half" of your brain.

As we will see in Chapter 3, drugs such as alcohol can disrupt the dominance of the "talking half" and thus let the "emotional half" of your brain express itself more freely. What Joe had just said and done gave me the hunch that—when Joe was a trifle intoxicated—the logical, conscious half of his brain didn't cooperate very well with the emotional, perceptual half of his brain.

Of course, I didn't line up all of these hunches in logical order the very instant Joe had said, "Uh, I feel more *together* now, you know what I mean?" But I did realize that Joe was decidedly more "different" in the bar than he had been in my office—and that helping Joe to "get it all together" might end up being more difficult than I had previously imagined.

I took a swig of my Coke. "Now that you're more 'together,' Joe, why don't you tell me something about yourself?"

Joe's Story

Joe finished off his glass of beer and poured himself yet another. "Uh, oh, I guess I'm really just like everybody else, you know. Uh, um, well, what else did you care to have me talk about?"

"Tell me where you live. Tell me about your parents. Tell me anything you think is important."

Joe nodded seriously. "You don't know my parents, do you? Uh, my mother, oh, did I tell you sometimes I hate her? Um, did you know that hate is dark green? Dark green hatred. I always thought it was red, uh, like red roses, you know?" Joe giggled. "Or like cheap red wine."

"You were talking about your mother, Joe."

"Oh, yes. Er, she cried a lot after I died, uh, but I told you that, didn't I? Yes, well, what didn't I tell you about my parents? Uh, my parents, well, I guess I really love them, mostly, anyway, but, uh, I wish my parents hadn't put me away in that mental hospital." Joe reached over and grabbed my arm, as if to emphasize his sincerity. "Don't let them put me back in that hospital, please!"

I tried to reassure Joe that I would do the best I could. His talk was becoming more and more disjointed, and his emotions weren't under the firm control he had shown while sitting in my office. However, it seemed to me that we were getting much closer to the "real Joe," and I wanted to give him a chance to show me anything about himself that he thought was important. So I prompted him again.

"About your mother, Joe. Is she a very religious person?"

Joe nodded his head vigorously. "Oh, yes, very religious, my mother. Uh, mother, yes, she has a lot of free time, uh, and she spends most of it down at the church. Uh, oh yes, that church is something else, big and beautiful, and it's located just off Woodward Avenue. Uh, er, varoom, you know?"

"Varoom?"

"Sure, varoom, varoom, VAROOM! The cars racing down Woodward Avenue."

Woodward Avenue runs right through the heart of Detroit. For decades, hot-rodders have raced their souped-up cars down the Avenue trying both to out-accelerate everyone else and to avoid getting a speeding ticket.

"You raced your car down Woodward when you were young?"

"Uh, yes, particularly right after I died. Um, er, dying is pretty scary, you know. Well, I get scared by lots of things, mostly spiders and snakes. Uh, oh, I almost got bitten by a snake, once, in Florida. A funny little coral snake, you know, with big long fangs." Joe made a funny face as he stuck his teeth out like fangs. "Uh, I didn't tell you about that, did I? You want me to talk about the snake?"

I suppose I stared at Joe silently for several seconds. He simply wasn't making much sense. He was jumping from one subject to another like a jack rabbit skipping across hot concrete. This is the sort of jumbled up, "word salad" pattern of speech you might sometimes observe in mental patients diagnosed as being *schizophrenic*. And yet he surely hadn't seemed schizophrenic when he sat in my office.

"Joe, you were talking about your mother, and I do wish . . ."

"RIGHT!" Joe said very, very loudly.

I frowned. I don't like being interrupted.

". . . and I do wish you'd continue on the subject."

Joe smiled. "What subject?"

"Your mother, Joe. Your mother. You said she spent a lot of her time in church."

Joe nodded his head. "Um, yes, she goes to church a lot, particularly on Sundays. Uh, oh, last Sunday I went over to visit a friend of mine, the one who gave me your book to read in the mental hospital. Oh, yes, that hospital was terrible, with all those crazy people in it."

Joe paused for a moment, wringing his hands again. "Do you think that dying, uh, like I did was what made me crazy?"

"I don't think you're 'crazy,' Joe, although . . ."

"GOOD!" he shouted.

I "Lose My Cool"

Another interruption. I was trying to be objective and "cool" about Joe's unusual verbal behavior, but for the moment I reacted very subjectively. That is, I *attributed* Joe's behavior to a character trait called "rudeness" (see Chapter 25 for a discussion of the "attribution process"). Had I maintained an objective viewpoint of Joe, I would have accepted *whatever he did* and then—standing back at arm's length—tried to figure out what caused his unusual behavior and how we might help him gain better control over his own actions.

But instead of looking at him objectively as "Joe-whose-mystery-needs-solving," I looked at him subjectively and emotionally as "Joe-who-ought-to-know-better." So I got a bit angry at his impoliteness—and momentarily missed the most telling clue of all as to what was wrong with him.

"Look, Joe, you want me to help you stay out of the mental hospital, right? Well, you can't go around interrupting people without annoying them. They think you ought to know better. And if you don't know better, then maybe there's something wrong with you, if you know what I mean."

Joe nodded that he understood.

"I'd guess that part of your problem is that you bother people because you don't do the things they expect you to do. Or say the things they expect you to say. Joe, most of us don't like things that are highly unpredictable, because we fear they may be out of control. When people don't do what we would do under the same circumstances, we often figure they're 'mentally ill,' and lock them up in mental hospitals because we're afraid of what they might do next. Just as you were afraid of that coral snake down in, in, . . ."

"In Florida. I told you that."

"Well, yes, Florida," I stammered, and then regained a bit of my own self-control. Joe might be 'crazy,' but he certainly wasn't dumb. He didn't seem to know where he might be going verbally, but he certainly remembered where he had been. Whatever else was wrong with him, his Long-term Memory seemed to be functioning well.

Joe giggled again. "There was a guy in the hospital who saw snakes all the time," he said, moving his left arm across the checkered tablecloth as if it were a snake about to strike at me. "Snakes, crawling all over his hospital bed. Uh, er, my hospital social worker said I came from a disturbed family milieu and needed 'family therapy' so my folks and I could get along better." Joe looked around wildly, as if trying to find something he had lost. "Uh, um, it is a far, far better thing I do than I have ever done before."

I pulled him gently back on target. "What did your psychiatrist say was wrong with you, Joe?"

"He said I lacked impulse control, and I suffered from anxiety and confused thought patterns. Um, yes, oh, oh! Patterns. Look at the patterns on this tablecloth, they're, you know . . ." Joe crossed and uncrossed his arms rapidly.

"What did your psychiatrist say ought to be done about your impulse control and your anxiety?"

"He said I needed to work through my death fears so I could get my psychosexual development back on track. Uh, my, do you think you can track down what's wrong with me?"

"Perhaps. With your help. Why did your psychiatrist send you to the mental hospital, Joe?"

"He said I wasn't responding to treatment because I was brain-damaged, hopelessly so. Uh, oh, really, I cross my heart and hope to die. Uh, er . . ."

Again I reached out verbally and pulled Joe down to reality. "Who told your psychiatrist your brain damage was hopeless?"

"The neurologist who examined me after the accident read my brain waves, I told you that, uh, and he said I suffered extensive brain damage when I died. Oh, uh, oh, I only died that one time, you know."

"I know, Joe. And you came back. But what did the neurologist suggest should be done to help you?"

Joe giggled. "He prescribed a whole bunch of pills, but then he said it was hopeless because the pills didn't help. Uh, yes, help, beer certainly helps me get it all together." He lifted his glass, took a swig, and saluted me. "Do you think I can get it all together so I don't have to go back to the hospital, or am I hopelessly crazy like the doctors said?"

Three Explanatory Views of Human Behavior

What would you have thought had you been in my place? Was Joe crazy, or mentally ill, or hopelessly brain-damaged, or schizophrenic, or merely the product of a disturbed family environment? Or was he all of these things, and perhaps a lot more?

What did the experts say? As Joe talked, I realized that in his quest for understanding himself, he had encountered three different people with three quite different views of what his problem really was.

The Biological Viewpoint

First, immediately after his accident, Joe had seen a neurologist who had made a thorough examination of his brain. By recording Joe's brain waves and by testing Joe in many other ways, this physician had been able to spot various areas of nerve cells that were behaving abnormally. The neurologist then made a *biological* diagnosis of Joe's problems.

Like most physicians, the neurologist *perceived* Joe as being primarily a complex biological machine. Thus the neurologist saw Joe's problem as being in his body, not in his mind or his social environment. Joe's brain-wave record was abnormal; therefore he had lost some neural tissue when he died. Some of the nerve cells that remained intact were now behaving abnormally. From a purely *biological* point of view, it is the actions of your nerve cells that control the thoughts and reactions of your mind. Joe's nerve cells were acting up, hence (to the neurologist) Joe was acting up.

Unfortunately, the neurologist could not bring those lost nerve cells back to life. All he could do was to prescribe pills that might reduce the abnormal responses Joe's nerve cells were making. For the neurologist apparently thought that if he could *force* Joe's nerve cells to act in a normal fashion, that would in turn *force* Joe's mind to react in a normal fashion as well.

Well, what do you think? Obviously there is a connection between what goes on inside your brain and what goes on inside your mind. But does that fact mean that we explain everything about your consciousness, your personality, your feelings and emotions *solely* in terms of the flow of electricity through your nervous system? Or should we take a broader view of what makes you tick?

The Intra-Psychic Viewpoint

When Joe's parents were disturbed by his actions, they sent him to see a psychiatrist. Psychiatrists are physicians who have been trained in psychology as well as in medicine. Like most psychiatrists—and like most psychologists, for that matter—Joe's psychiatrist took an *intra-psychic* view of him.

Most psychologists and psychiatrists believe that everything that goes wrong (or right) about a person's psyche or mind or behavior cannot be explained in simple, biological terms. Instead of just looking at how a person's brain functions in order to understand her or him, therefore, they must try to look (as best they can) at what goes on *inside the individual's mind*. The term *intra-psychic* actually means "inside the mind."

So those scientists with an intra-psychic viewpoint primarily study your *mental processes*. They do so in many ways: (1) by observing what you do; (2) by giving you standardized tests of various kinds, and then comparing your responses with those that other people make (see Chapter 22); and (3) by listening very closely to what you say about your own thoughts and feelings. The intra-psychic psychologists then try to explain your actions in terms of your perceptions, motives, values, and past experiences.

Someone with a biological viewpoint will usually perceive your thoughts and feelings as being *caused by* and hence *reducible to* physical processes in your brain. An intra-psychic psychologist will admit that what goes on inside your body is important, but believes that your mental processes are too complicated to be reducible to mere patterns of electrical activity inside your brain.

When I looked at Joe physiologically, I saw him as a "biological machine" with abnormal brain activity that no surgeon could ever hope to repair. But when I looked at Joe from the intra-psychic viewpoint, I saw him as a self-directed, conscious human being with his own unique set of goals and values. True, he had to "make do" with a damaged brain, but the human mind and body are incredibly flexible. Surely, if Joe got the proper help, he should be able to compensate (at least somewhat) for those lost nerve cells by finding new ways to achieve his personal goals.

From the biological viewpoint, your body exercises almost complete control over your mind. From the intra-psychic standpoint, however, your mind dominates most of your bodily activities.

Both viewpoints are necessary and can be very useful in helping you understand yourself (and others). But both viewpoints are—in and of themselves—incomplete.

The Social/Behavioral Viewpoint

Joe was neither a biological machine whose behavior was as predictable as a robot's, nor was he just a disembodied mind floating freely in space like a lonely star. Joe was a *social being*, whose thoughts and behaviors were strongly influenced

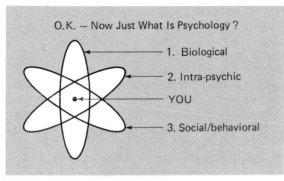

Fig. 1.1. Three views of human nature make up the holistic approach to psychology.

by the people and things around him, and whose thoughts and behaviors strongly influenced the people he was around.

Joe had a mother and father, and he had friends and lovers. In the past he had had classmates, playmates, teachers, supervisors, bosses, doctors, social workers, and psychiatrists. At the moment, he was talking with a psychologist, smiling frequently at the waitress who served him beer, and looking occasionally at all the other people in the bar. In his brief lifetime he had met and interacted with thousands of other individuals, all of whom had played their parts in helping make Joe what he was today.

Joe had learned to talk (and think) in English because that's the language his parents and friends taught him. He picked his own clothes, but his choices were obviously affected by the people around him. His values were, for the most part, identical to the values held by almost everyone he knew. Indeed, from the *social/behavioral viewpoint*, there was little about Joe's actions and emotions that couldn't be explained in terms of what he had learned from his social environment.

Joe's social worker at the mental hospital had diagnosed Joe's difficulties as stemming chiefly from "a disturbed family atmosphere." Which is to say she believed that most of Joe's abnormal thoughts and actions were the result of how his parents (and perhaps other people) had treated Joe both before and after his accident. And surely there was some truth to the social worker's diagnosis of what caused Joe's problems. As I discovered later on, Joe's mother was too protective of him immediately after he "died." Instead of encouraging him to learn how to cope with his physical disability, she rewarded him for "staying sick." She paid close attention to his every mistake—blaming his failures on his "poor, damaged brain." And with an excess of maternal

affection, she overwhelmed his attempts to stand on his own two feet.

But, after a while, when Joe became too dependent on her, she tired of the game and started demanding that he "shape up." A young man with a healthy brain might well have done so. Joe didn't—because he hadn't gotten the special training he needed in order to bring his damaged nerve cells and his thoughts under his voluntary control.

Both his parents probably would have been happy to help him—had they known what to do. But because they perceived the problem as being "inside his head," they didn't realize that *they* had to change their behaviors toward Joe in order to help *him* learn how to change his behaviors toward them. So they sent him first to a neurologist, second to a psychiatrist, and third to a mental hospital.

By the time the social worker suggested "family therapy," Joe's parents were convinced his case was hopeless. And since he couldn't take care of himself, and because his "crazy talk" and "strange actions" were unpredictable and frightening to them, Joe's parents decided the safest place for him was in a mental institution.

The Holistic Approach

Which of the three viewpoints—the biological, the intra-psychic, or the social/behavioral—gives you the greatest understanding of Joe and his problems?

The answer is, *all three of them taken together.* Like Joe, you are an incredibly complex living system. There is a biological side to your nature, a mental side, and a social side. You cannot hope to understand yourself—or Joe, or anyone else—unless you are willing to view human beings from these three different perspectives (see Fig. 1.1).

Psychology stands at that scientific crossroad where genetics, biochemistry, biology, sociology, and anthropology meet to form that unique organism we call the individual human being. Although some people tend to emphasize one or two of the three major viewpoints, the trend in psychology today is to take a *holistic approach* toward understanding and solving human problems.

And if you are to learn to understand yourself better—or to understand Joe, your parents, your friends, and your loved ones—you too must learn to see people as being complex *systems* made up of interacting parts. For example, consider Joe. Several specialists had looked at parts of him from their own restricted viewpoints. They had sincerely done their best—but they had failed to help him very much. What Joe needed most, it seemed to me, was someone who could help him put *all his parts together* to form an integrated whole. Since I believe in a holistic approach to solving human problems, I tried to do just that. As it happened, I was lucky, for Joe soon gave me the final clue I needed in order to put a number of pieces of his jigsaw puzzle together.

(For a more complete description of the holistic approach, please see Chapter 5.)

Joe and the Three Viewpoints

What had I learned about Joe so far?

From a biological viewpoint, I knew that he had suffered brain damage when he had "died" and come back to life.

From an intra-psychic view I knew that he still had strong emotions connected with that death episode, that he had even stronger fears he would be sent back to the mental hospital, and that he seemed highly motivated "to get well."

From a social/behavioral point of view I knew that he couldn't support himself, that he had problems getting along with his parents, and that many of his behaviors were so unusual that he disturbed the people around him.

Joe also had a "memory problem," but I wasn't sure what it was. He could remember what he had said five minutes ago, but not what he had said 15 seconds ago. When I asked him a question, his first sentence would be "on target," but then he lost his sense of direction and would wander aimlessly from one topic to another. Yet, if I gave him a *cue* as to what he was supposed to be talking about, he would pick up right where he had left off. He would complete one or two sentences, and then off he would drift again.

Odd, to say the least. Why couldn't Joe "talk in a straight line"? Was this the sort of behavior that had led his psychiatrist to say that Joe lacked "impulse control"?

I looked him carefully in the eyes and said, "Joe, I'm going to ask you a question, and I want you to try very hard to give me a complete answer. Please keep your mind on the answer and don't go drifting off. Okay?"

Joe nodded his head vigorously.

"Okay, Joe, tell me about the time you died, just like you told me this afternoon in my office."

Joe nodded again. "Well, I was out flying this kite of mine one windy spring day . . ."

I nodded to show I was listening.

". . . and it had rained, you know?" Joe looked directly at me, but I didn't respond. "Uh, yes, er, the rain in Spain falls mainly on the plain, uh."

"Kite, Joe."

"Oh, yes. I was running along trying to get the kite to catch the wind and go up in the air. Um, well, I caught an airplane once and flew all the way to the coast. Yes, uh, I just coast along when I have something to drink, don't you like to do that too?"

I was beginning to get angry. "Listen, Joe, you just aren't concentrating. You were talking about the day your kite string hit the power line and . . ."

"RIGHT!" Joe screamed.

And then the lightning bolt hit.

The Miracle of Normal Speech

For just an instant after Joe interrupted me again, my anger almost got out of control. Indeed, I really wanted to smack him one because his impoliteness and his inability to concentrate frustrated me so much.

And then, suddenly, some part of my mind took hold, throttled my angry response, and gave me what I can only call an objective flash of insight.

Joe was basically a very polite person, and yet here he was interrupting me. Polite people don't interrupt you unless they have a reason for doing so. What was Joe's reason? What was he trying to tell me?

Looking at Joe subjectively—seeing him as *Joe*—I had projected my own values and expectations on him. He had been quite sincere when he asked for my help, and he obviously appreciated my talking with him. But when he cut me off in mid-sentence, I forgot his sincerity and immediately *attributed* his response to "rudeness." Standing back and looking at the situation from a psychological distance, I realized that Joe must have some other reason for continually interrupting me. The bolt of mental lightning hit when I realized what it was.

Joe was giving me the kind of verbal reassurance and feedback he needed in order to concentrate.

We take it for granted that if you are "normal" you can answer a question that requires you to string several thoughts or sentences together in logical A-B-C sequence. But in order to get sentence "B" in its right place—after "A," and in front of "C"—you have to remember both "A" and "C" while you are saying "B." And it seems very unlikely that one single part of your mind/brain can "talk" and "remember" at the same time.

As I pointed out earlier, the left hemisphere of your brain is the "talking half." The left hemisphere therefore must execute the complex muscle movements involved in your saying the A-B-C sequence of sentences. But recent research suggests that while your left hemisphere is talking, your right hemisphere (1) *remembers* what the A-B-C "pattern" is supposed to be; (2) *monitors* or keeps track of what you're actually saying; and (3) then *provides feedback* to your left hemisphere to keep it "on target" in completing the A-B-C sequence.

We will have much more to say in the next chapter about how the two hemispheres of your brain cooperate to produce logical speech. The point to remember now is this one: You can't carry on a "normal conversation" with someone unless one part of your mind listens to (monitors) what another part of your mind is saying out loud.

Since each sentence Joe said was complete in and of itself, I presumed that the talking part of his mind (or brain) was working quite well. But the monitoring part seemed easily distracted. Joe could get out the first sentence in a sequence, but by the time he reached the final words in the sentence, he had forgotten what it was he had just said or where he was trying to go.

Joe covered up his forgetfulness very cleverly—he simply began a second sentence using the last word or two he had just said. The fact that this second sentence had no relationship to the first didn't appear to bother him, perhaps because the "monitoring" part of his brain wasn't all that interested in being logical anyhow.

But Joe *could* concentrate if I helped him listen to himself. That's what some part of his mind/brain was trying to tell me by shouting "GOOD," and "RIGHT" at me. I *had a hunch* that if I would just do the same thing for him, perhaps he could speak and think as logically as I could.

A "Tentative Solution" to Joe's Problem

A hunch, no matter how good, is little more than an unproved explanation of something. Once I had my flash of insight about what was wrong with Joe, I could have told him what I thought, and then left the proving up to him. But psychologists simply are not built that way. Once we perceive a "tentative solution" to a problem, we have an urge to put the solution to the test—either in the real world, or in a scientific laboratory.

My hunch led me to predict that if I nodded my head continuously and shouted encouraging feedback to Joe—as he had done when he interrupted me—he would be able to string several sentences together in logical order. And so I tried it.

Looking squarely at Joe to catch his gaze, I said, "Joe, you were talking about the kite, remember. Tell me about the kite, Joe."

"I was running along . . ."

"YES," I said loudly, nodding my head.

". . . trying to get the kite to catch the wind . . ."

"YES!"

". . . when the kite got caught on a power line . . ."

"GOOD!"

". . . and fifteen thousand volts came down the kite string . . ."

"RIGHT!"

". . . and killed me deader than a doorknob . . ."

"YES!"

". . . but my brother called the doctor who lived next door . . ."

"RIGHT!"

". . . and he resuscitated me . . ."

"GOOD!"

". . . and the ambulance came and took me to the hospital . . ."

"YES! YES!"

". . . and I lived happily ever after." Joe giggled, and poured himself some more beer.

I sat back in amazement. It had worked all right, but frankly I felt like a fool. Here I was, sitting in a public place, shouting and nodding my head violently at Joe. The people around us probably thought I was the one with "mental problems."

And, in a sense, I was. Other people Joe knew—seeing Joe either from a very subjective or a very narrow point of view—behaved "sanely" toward him by giving him little or no feedback when he tried to talk. I suspected that Joe's damaged brain couldn't produce the feedback he needed to hold a logical conversation, so he continually strayed from the subject. I gave him "crazy" feedback, and that seemed to help Joe think and talk relatively sanely. I didn't *know* this was the case, and there are many other possible explanations of why Joe spoke as he did. But this was the "tentative solution" that had occurred to me, and my "test" seemed to show I might have been right.

Independent, Dependent, and Intervening Variables

When psychologists perform experiments to test their hypotheses, they typically "do something new or unusual" to some organism or group. Then they sit back to see how the thoughts or actions of the person or group change.

When you "do something new or unusual" to an individual, you decide on the ways you are going to *vary* that person's environment. Since you make the choice, this *variable* in the experiment is "independent" of the subject's wishes. Psychologists call "what you do to a subject" in a scientific study the *independent variable* because it is under the experimenter's control.

When you act, people react. The subject's reaction is called the *dependent variable* because the response the person makes obviously depends on what you've done to the individual.

Why do subjects react as they do? Psychologists aren't always sure. But when we find that a certain act of ours almost always evokes the same response in someone else, we can often "make hunches." These hunches or hypotheses are our ways of explaining what goes on inside the person's mind or brain that *connects* the act with the reaction. Put another way, we guess at what processes inside the person "intervene" between the independent and dependent variable. Psychologists call these internal processes *intervening variables.*

Suppose you show a young girl a kitten because you want to see how she will react to it. She smiles and pets the animal. "Ah, ha!" you say. "She petted the kitten because she loves cats." Showing the girl the kitten is the *independent variable* because you could have shown her a snake. Smiling and petting are *dependent variables* because her response depended on what you showed her. If you'd shown her a snake, she might have run away. "Love" is an *intervening variable* because it's your explanation of why she responded as she did.

You can *see* kittens and petting behaviors. So independent and dependent variables are things that you can measure objectively. But you *can't see* "love" or "fear" or "mental illness." Thus intervening variables are usually *internal processes* that you can't measure directly. Indeed, you can't even be sure they actually exist. You merely presume that they do, because intervening variables give you a way of explaining the relationship you have observed between the independent and the dependent variables.

In Joe's case, the "independent variable" was the type of feedback that I gave him. The "dependent variable" was his speech—did he stay "on target," or not? The "intervening variable" was my hypothesis about what caused Joe's speech problems. Joe could talk, but he couldn't remember what he had just said. I suspected that, because of his accident, the part of his brain that should have been "monitoring" his speech wasn't functioning properly. And so it couldn't give him the feedback he needed to talk in A-B-C fashion. I reasoned that, if I gave Joe strong external feedback, I could substitute for the damaged part of his brain and he would speak logically. And he

did. I also suspected that if I varied my tactics and gave Joe no feedback at all, he wouldn't be able to tie his sentences together in A-B-C fashion. And that's what happened. Thus my hypothesis about what was taking place inside Joe's head—the intervening variable that explained his reactions—had stood the first test.

The "Between-Subjects" Design

But is one such test ever enough? Certainly not! You and I both know that Joe's behavior could have changed for many reasons, none of which had anything to do with giving him better feedback.

This point is so important, it may help to repeat it. Any time you try to explain an experiment in terms of an intervening variable, *there always will be other explanations for your results.* So, in science, you keep testing your hunches again and again. If the intervening variable you've dreamed up is a good one, it will accurately predict the outcome of your subsequent experiments. If it fails to do so, you should abandon your hypothesis and hunt for a new and better one.

Now, suppose you and I had been working together as a team, and we wanted to run some additional tests to see if my hunch about Joe was correct. What could we do next? If we had been studying the general subject of "the importance of feedback in maintaining mental concentration," would you be satisfied that we had used just one subject—a young man named Joe? After all, Joe might not be "representative" of other people at all. So, just to make sure of the *generality* of our hypothesis about feedback, we'd want to take a *random sample* of 100 other Joes and try the same thing on them. The sample would have to be "randomly selected" so we could be sure our results would apply to all Joes everywhere. We would call these 100 Joes our *experimental group,* because we were experimenting (trying something new) on them.

Suppose again that all 100 of our experimental subjects changed the same way that Joe did. Could we now be sure that our hunch was correct?

No, we'd need to find another 100 Joes and study how they reacted when we *didn't* give them appropriate feedback. These subjects would be called our *control group,* or *comparison group,* because we would want to compare their results with those of our experimental group.

To put the matter another way, we would want to give *different* independent variables to two groups. Or we would give *different amounts* of

Clinical psychologists often perform experimental studies based on just one person.

the same independent variable to two groups. In either case, we'd hope that the responses the groups made would vary in predictable and dependable ways. We call this type of experiment a *between-subjects design*.

Our initial hunch had led us to hypothesize that the "experimental Joes" would almost all be able to concentrate, while the "control Joes" would not. If the behaviors of the two groups differed as we had predicted, then we could place some faith in the *validity* or "realness" of our hunch. (As we will see in many later chapters, the use of control groups is one of the most important features of the experimental method.)

Whenever possible, psychologists like to test their hunches on large numbers of experimental and control subjects—simply because the more subjects we use, the more faith we can have in the "generality" of our results.

Unfortunately, in this case we have but one Joe to work with.

The "Within-Subjects" Design

When we test our theories on just one subject whose problem may be unique, we often employ a "within-subjects" rather than a "between-subjects" design. That is, we let each subject serve as her or his own control group. Making use of the "within-subjects" design, we first observe the subject without trying to change the person's behavior (Condition A). Then we do something to the subject (such as giving the person more appropriate feedback) to see how the subject's behavior alters. We call this Condition B.

Since Condition A differs markedly from Condition B, we have the same two independent variables as when we used an experimental group and a control group. But with the "within-subjects" design, one person acts as both groups *at different times*.

Next, to make sure that it was the variation in conditions that *caused* the change in the subject's response, we repeat the A-B sequence at least once more. If it turns out that the subject's response shifts in a predictable fashion each time we alternate Conditions A and B, then we can be reasonably sure that it was *what we did* that *caused the change*.

Using Joe as His Own Control

Giving Joe little or no feedback was Condition A in this case. Condition B was giving him strong feedback, and his response was so different that I could hardly believe my eyes and ears. So I asked him another question and sat passively (Condition A again) while he tried to answer. Joe got the first sentence out beautifully. Then he said, "Uh, er, well . . ." for about 15 seconds, his hands pumping away as he desperately tried to remember what he had just said. Then his mind "jackrabbited." He picked up on the last word in his first sentence, and his second sentence darted off in an entirely different direction from the one I had pointed him toward.

When Joe came to the end of this second sentence, he stammered for a few seconds, his hands chopped the air, and once more he flew off on a tangent.

So I switched back to Condition B by nodding and shouting "RIGHT" at him loudly every 3 or 4 seconds. Again he responded by speaking as normally and as sensibly as you and I might speak.

So far, so good. However, there was one more hunch I wanted to test, so I asked Joe yet another question. But this time, instead of nodding my head and shouting encouragement, I leaned across the table and tapped Joe rhythmically on his right arm. Each time he said a word or two, I struck his arm lightly with my finger. He spoke quite logically and coherently—as long as I tapped. When I stopped tapping, he drifted off almost immediately.

By now I was reasonably convinced that—particularly when he was a little intoxicated—Joe's mind simply wasn't generating the kind of *internal* feedback it needed in order to talk logically. The *external* feedback I gave Joe as he talked helped a lot, but I knew I wouldn't be satisfied until I had helped Joe "get it all together" so that he could produce the internal feedback he needed to speak in A-B-C fashion.

Most of us take it for granted that we can think and speak logically. Because we are so accustomed to this behavior, we seldom stop to see it for the miracle it is. Thus we miss the fact that *all of us* surely need some kind of internal or external feedback in order to make sure that we are saying what we ought to say (or behaving the way people think we ought to behave). It is only when someone as unusual as Joe comes along that we are forced to see ourselves in a new light.

What You Can Learn from Joe—And from This Book

Learning about psychology doesn't consist of finding a set of magic keys that will unlock the "great secrets of your mind." Rather, understanding human behavior is chiefly a matter of discovering thousands of things that you've been doing and thinking and feeling all your life—but were never really aware of.

Many fields of knowledge can offer you a *subjective* understanding of human behavior. Art,

literature, and religion are good examples of how valuable a subjective approach to the study of human nature can be. But psychology offers you two things that no other field can offer: (1) a set of *objective* facts about how you think, feel, and behave; and (2) theories and insights that attempt to explain in *objective* terms why you think, feel, and act as you do.

What Psychologists Do

There are many types of psychologists. Some psychologists *generate* facts and theories; others *apply* this information in real-life settings. Many psychologists do both.

Experimental psychologists mostly work in scientific laboratories. They perform experiments to help develop a basic understanding of human nature. There are many different types of experimentalists. Some study such processes as perception, learning, or motivation in human and animals subjects. Others, such as the biological psychologists, investigate such things as the effects of drugs and surgery on performance. Developmental psychologists look at how people grow and mature from infancy to old age. Social psychologists study the behavior of people in groups and organizations. Educational psychologists are primarily interested in how humans learn in schools and other educational settings. Most experimentalists teach at colleges and universities. Others work in government and industrial laboratories.

More than half of the psychologists in the US work in what are called "applied settings." *Clinical psychologists*, for example, try to help people like Joe solve their problems. Most clinical psychologists work in clinics or hospitals, or treat patients in their own offices. *Counseling psychologists* usually offer expert advice on personal or educational problems. Some counseling psychologists are in private practice; others work in schools or clinics. *Industrial psychologists* tend to work for business or government organizations. For the most part, they deal with personnel problems and management decision making.

Experimental psychologists may observe behavior either in the laboratory or in real-life settings. They also develop tests and take surveys. Applied psychologists may also develop knowledge in a variety of ways. But chiefly they conduct interviews, give tests, and apply information gathered from experiments and surveys. Clinical and counseling psychologists usually deal with one person at a time, although occasionally they work with groups. Industrial psychologists tend to focus on work groups and organizations.

Your author, James V. McConnell.

The Author's Biases

Some psychologists are primarily teachers. Although they may do some research, and may occasionally work with people like Joe, their main goal is passing information along to the students who take their classes or read their textbooks.

As you will see in Chapter 16, I spent many years studying the biochemistry of memory in a scientific laboratory. In recent years, though, I have devoted most of my time to writing and teaching. And, like all other teachers, I have my own set of biases or subjective viewpoints about people and psychology. I've mentioned some of these prejudices already. But there are others you should be aware of too, if you are to be able to read this book with both subjective enjoyment and objective understanding.

1. To begin with, I believe the study of human behavior is the most fascinating, most awe-inspiring, most important occupation imaginable. I hope that some of my enthusiasm for psychology rubs off on you by the time you finish the book, for it is the greatest gift I can give you.
2. I believe that learning should be made as rewarding as possible; indeed, that learning should be both challenging *and* fun. My way of

doing that is to focus on the experiences of real people (such as Joe), and to use these real people as examples. I teach by analogy, by telling stories. Sigmund Freud once said that, "Analogies prove nothing, but they do make us feel at home." Freud might have added that analogies also make a marvelous instructional technique.

3. There is a fair amount of scientific evidence suggesting that students remember best that part of a course which is most dramatic, most stimulating. So I have begun and ended each chapter with a story or a case history built around the lives of real or imagined human beings. Some of the stories actually happened; a few are pure fiction; most of them are mixtures of fact and imagination. You may find that you can *understand* the people in the stories much better after you have read the scientific material that comes between the opening and closing fiction.

But understanding is of little value if you don't remember what you've learned. So one of my purposes in printing the stories is to reward you for trying to remember the factual material. However, as you will see in Chapter 11, what is motivating and rewarding to one person may be punishing to another. If you are not fond of fiction, you might ask your teacher if you can skip the stories.

4. At various points, I have included "thought questions" that often are not answered directly in the text. The purpose of these questions is to push your mind beyond the facts on the printed page. However, if you find these questions a bore, or if the answers don't come easily, pass the questions by or ask your instructor to help you.
5. I place a great deal more faith in facts than I do in theories and opinions. Most arguments in science revolve around speculations and interpretations of data—not around the data themselves.

In science, you usually gather data first, then try to understand the meaning of those data. If you try to understand before you have enough facts, you run the danger of seeing what you want to see—instead of seeing what is objectively *there*.

6. There are two ways of gathering facts—in controlled settings such as the laboratory, and in less formal settings such as a clinician's office. Both clinical and experimental studies are necessary, because they give us different types of data. Clinical studies tell us a lot about a single person or subject, but don't necessarily give us

data that are true of people in general. Experimental studies typically tell us something about people in general, but we cannot always apply these data meaningfully to one particular individual whom we happen to be working with.

7. To my way of thinking, the scientific method is one of humanity's most glorious achievements. It is surely the most powerful way we have of determining objective facts and of testing our theoretical notions about why people act and think and feel as they do.

You have theories about human behavior, just as I do. But unless you have studied psychology before, the chances are very good that your present theories are based more on your subjective impressions than on objective data. Thus you may find that many of your feelings or theories about yourself and others are challenged or contradicted by the facts presented in this textbook. I do not ask that you give up your present views, merely that you try to examine afresh your notions about people in the light of what new information this book gives you.

When I met Joe, his behaviors forced me to re-examine many of my own notions about what controls "logical thought patterns" and "mental concentration" in normal people. I would hope that, when you meet people like Joe in this book, you too will be willing to look at them with as little bias and prejudice as possible.

8. I am an incurable optimist. I believe that, through the wise and humane application of the *holistic approach*, we can all come closer to achieving our personal goals in life (see Chapter 5). And with luck we can also help make the world a more rewarding and less desperate place in which to live. This moral viewpoint, like most others, rests on faith as well as on science; but it is a faith that is shared by most psychologists or they wouldn't *be* psychologists.

I also believe that you must pay for what you get in life—that we all suffer the consequences of our actions. A psychologist can tell you how to get good grades in school, how to get along better with your parents and friends, how to achieve a greater degree of self-actualization and personal happiness, and perhaps even help you be more successful in business if you're interested. But advice is the smallest coin in circulation. You won't get A's, or happiness, or money, or maturity unless you are willing to put forth the effort to do so on your own, to make the most of what you have and what you know.

All of which brings us back to Joe again.

Getting It All Together

Joe wanted desperately to get better, so he wouldn't have to return to the mental hospital. Once we learned about the problems he had in paying attention to his own behavior, I could give him some suggestions about what he had to do to solve his problems. I could help him plan his goals, plot his progress, and I could give him encouragement. But Joe—and only Joe—was the one who had to put it all together. That is, it was his personal responsibility to make the necessary changes in his thoughts and actions.

We started simply. I told Joe what I had been doing while we talked. That is, I showed him how I had been giving him external feedback to help him keep his thoughts on target. I suggested that, when he had "died," he might have lost the neural circuits that let him generate his own internal feedback. But I was confident that, if he tried hard enough, he could learn how to use other (undamaged) parts of his brain to do this on his own. And after he "got it all together" inside his own head, he could then go on to the even more challenging task of finding out how to get along better with other people.

Teaching Joe to listen to himself while talking turned out to be fairly easy. The next time we met, I recorded our conversation on tape. After he tried to answer a question, or tell a story, I played back what he had said so he could hear his own voice. I suggested that he use his left hand to tap on his right arm while he talked (you'll understand why I did this after you read Chapter 2).

Although he found it a tiring experience at first, Joe soon acquired some of the self-monitoring skills he needed. At the start, he had to pound on his right arm rather vigorously to keep himself on track. Later, he began to "fade out" the arm-tapping. Eventually just nodding his head or gently clenching one of his fists was enough to get him through a long sequence of sentences—even when he was a trifle intoxicated.

Then, without any help from me, Joe began to make some significant changes in the way he lived. He started getting up early every day so that he could look for work. When he did find temporary employment, he set goals for himself every day and tried to keep to them by drawing a graph showing his progress.

Finally, without telling me, he simply packed up his bags and headed for the Coast. He called me a few days after he got there.

"I wanted to do it on my own," he said over the phone. "And my parents just wouldn't let me. So I came out here. Uh, I think it's bound to work, because out here, they don't know me as 'crazy Joey,' I'm just plain Joe."

"You're not plain at all, Joe. You're pretty special."

"Yeah, but I want to be special-good, not special-crazy, if you know what I mean."

I did. And he is. You can spend your whole professional life as a psychologist without finding anyone who teaches you as much about human behavior as Joe taught me. Surely I owe him a great deal more than he ever owed me.

Joe told me that he had called his parents when he arrived on the Coast. They were relieved to find that he was all right, and promised to help him financially if he got a job. So he did that too. The last time I heard from him, he was doing fairly well. He told me that he hoped to come back home some day—but not until he was sure he could prove to his parents that he really had "gotten it all together."

Just before we finished our last conversation, I asked him what he liked most about life now.

"Being in control," he responded. "Even if I have to clench my fist now and then to keep things going straight, I'm doing what I want to do because I know what I'm doing. I know what my body is doing, I know what my head is doing, and I pay attention to what other people are doing to me and what I'm doing to them. Um, knowing about yourself, it's a great feeling. I really enjoy it a lot."

And, at a very practical and personal level, that's what "understanding human behavior" is all about—learning more about yourself and others.

I hope you enjoy it too.

Recommended Readings

At the end of each chapter, I will list several books or articles that you might read if you want to go into the content of that chapter more deeply. Should you wish a more detailed list of readings (chapter by chapter), ask your instructor for help.

You might also look over the references that are mentioned in the *Student Manual to Understanding Human Behavior*, by Al Siebert and Tim Walter, that accompanies this textbook. In addition to its list of reference materials, the *Student Manual* contains many helpful hints on how to study for examinations, how to organize your time, and how to get involved in psychology by doing studies and experiments on your own. If you are having difficulties with any of the courses you are taking, or if you aren't getting as good grades as you think you ought to be getting, you may find the *Student Manual* of practical value. (There is a separate manual for those of you taking the course on television or as a personalized course of instruction.)

There are also several general source materials that you can investigate. One of the most useful I know of is *The Encyclopedia of Human Behavior* by Robert M. Goldenson (Garden City, N.Y.: Doubleday & Company, 1970). General references, such as the *Encyclopedia Britannica*, contain a surprisingly large number of articles on psychological topics, most of which are written by experts.

Psychology Today is far and away the best popular magazine dealing with behavioral topics, but articles on the behavioral sciences also appear in *Discover*, *OMNI*, and *Science 83* (which becomes *Science 84* in 1984, *Science 85* in 1985, and so forth). There are also dozens of scientific journals, most of which focus on one particular aspect of human or animal behavior. Any psychology teacher or librarian will surely be happy to help you find the journal most interesting to you.

Biological
Bases
of Behavior

1

The Brain 2

Did You Know That . . .

Your brain looks something like a wrinkled mushroom?

Your brain contains at least 15 billion nerve cells (neurons)?

The cortex, or outer layer of your brain, contains most of the "decision-making centers" that influence what you do, feel, and think?

The major function of your brain is to process information?

Some four million people in the United States suffer from epilepsy?

Brain waves are the result of electrical excitation occurring in thousands or even millions of your brain cells?

The left half of your brain looks like a mirror image of the right half?

If you are right-handed, the left hemisphere of your brain is dominant and controls the right half of your body?

If you are right-handed, your left hemisphere contains your "speech center," and seems responsible for most language?

If you are right-handed, your right hemisphere seems primarily responsible for pattern perception and for some aspects of your emotional reactions?

If a surgeon separated the two hemispheres of your brain, you might end up with two quite separate and distinct "minds" inside your skull?

"On the Other Hand"

"Young man, you are an epileptic?"

Patrick looked the woman over carefully. Her closely cropped white hair was peppered with black, rather like ashes sprinkled on fresh snow. She was wearing a colonel's uniform with a lot of gold braid on it. The other soldiers seemed to be afraid of this woman, so Pat guessed she was a pretty important person. But Dr. Tavela had told him not to fear people just because they wore fancy uniforms. So Pat looked straight at the woman and said, "I used to be."

Colonel Garcia picked up a yellow pencil and began tapping it slowly on her desk. She looked squarely at the youth sitting in front of her for a moment, then said, "Before Dr. Tavela operated on you, then, you were subject to epileptic attacks?"

"Yes."

"These attacks occurred frequently?"

Pat shivered a bit, then ran his fingers nervously over the plaster cast on his left hand. It had been six weeks now since he had last felt the "aura," that strange feeling which hit him each time just before he had an epileptic seizure. He had gone six weeks now without the headaches—without once losing consciousness, falling to the floor, and embarrassing himself by "having a fit." Despite the bandages on his head and all the terrible things that had happened since his operation, Pat felt so different now that he tried not to think of what the seizures had been like. But since she asked, Pat answered truthfully. "The attacks came several times a day, sometimes."

Colonel Garcia turned to the officer sitting beside Patrick in front of her desk. "Captain Hartman, this has been confirmed?"

The blond-haired man nodded quickly. "Yes, Colonel. When Patrick was three, a severe fever caused considerable damage to his cortex. We have tested him on the EEG machine. Abnormal, spike-shaped brain waves show up in the motor areas of his right hemisphere. Epileptic seizures are almost always associated with 'spikes' in the motor cortex."

"Yes, of course," the woman responded, gazing back at Patrick. "And after the operation, you have been free of these attacks?"

Pat tried to smile politely. "Yes, ma'am."

"Then how did you hurt your left hand?"

Pat rubbed his right hand over the plaster cast covering his entire left hand and forearm. Only the tips of his fingers were free of the plaster. "After the operation, I couldn't walk very well at first. I fell and broke my hand."

Colonel Garcia looked back at Captain Hartman. "This too is confirmed?"

"Yes, Colonel. The X-rays show a compound fracture of the metacarpal bone. The wound is about three weeks old. Patrick will not be able to use his left hand freely for another month or so—except to scratch his nose."

Patrick gently rubbed a finger along the side of his nose.

"Was Dr. Tavela angry with you for breaking your hand?" the woman asked.

Patrick frowned. "He was angry because he said I might have hurt my head. But then, just before he left, he smiled and said it was a good sign."

"A sign of your recovery?"

Pat thought about it a moment. "He didn't say."

"I wish he had," Colonel Garcia said, then breathed a deep sigh. "Patrick, although Dr. Tavela lived in a foreign country, he was our friend."

Pat interrupted. "You mean he was your spy. Anyhow, that's what the secret police said when they questioned me."

Colonel Garcia glanced uneasily at Captain Hartman, then back at the boy. "You know Dr. Tavela was a good man, and he would want you to cooperate with us. I know you have told your story many times, Patrick. But I would like to hear it again. Tell me everything that happened, if you don't mind."

The young man shrugged his shoulders. "I don't mind."

"First, why were you sent to see a surgeon in a foreign country? Are there no good physicians here?"

"Because they said that Dr. Tavela was the only doctor in the world who did the sort of operation I needed."

"Dr. Tavela was a brilliant neurosurgeon," Colonel Garcia said quietly. "We will miss him. But tell me what happened to you at his clinic."

"He gave me a lot of tests for a week or so, and then my seizures got real bad. He said it was the stress that made them worse. Then they shaved my head and put me to sleep and he cut out the part of my brain that was making me sick."

"How soon afterward could you get up out of bed?"

"After a few days. Just to go to the bathroom. I guess it was a week or so before I could really walk much."

Colonel Garcia nodded sympathetically. "You said Dr. Tavela gave you some tests before the operation. Did he test you afterward?"

"Yeah. He had this sort of mask that I looked into. It blocked off part of what I could see. Then he showed me things and asked what they were."

The woman smiled with growing excitement. "What sort of things did he show you?"

"Oh, pictures of cows and horses. Circles and squares. Sometimes he showed me printed words and asked me to read them. Sometimes he made me wear earphones and then he asked me to do things or say things."

"What kind of things?"

"Oh, point at a circle, or say words like 'cat' and 'dog.'"

Colonel Garcia leaned forward eagerly. "And perhaps he showed you some letters and numbers, perhaps he talked about a chemical formula?"

Pat laughed. "That's what the secret police asked, too. Did I know anything about chemistry? And did Dr. Tavela read me the name of a formula, or anything like that?"

"And you said . . ."

"I said that he never read anything to me except the Bible. Mostly Proverbs."

"Why Proverbs?"

Patrick had never thought to question the actions of the adults around him. "I don't know. He seemed to like them. He said they contained all the wisdom of Solomon."

A startled look appeared on Captain Hartman's face. "Colonel . . ."

The woman interrupted. "Yes, Captain, I know. Tavela's first name was Solomon. You will please get a copy of the Bible from the library."

Captain Hartman rose and left the room.

Putting the pencil carefully down on her desk, Colonel Garcia continued. "Patrick, just before Dr. Tavela was killed by the secret police, someone brought him a copy of a very important secret formula."

"That would be the funny little man in the dark overcoat, I suppose," Patrick said, trying to be helpful.

"Perhaps so, Patrick. Tell me about him."

Pat picked at one of the bandages on his head with his right hand. "It was that last day, you know, the day the secret police came and . . . and . . ."

"I know. Go on, please."

"Well, I had the earphones on and was looking into the mask. Dr. Tavela was showing me some pictures and asking me questions over the earphones. Sometimes it hurt a little."

"Hurt?"

"Yeah. My ears. Sometimes he would whisper in one ear while he was making a very loud noise in the other. The noise hurt sometimes."

"What did he whisper to you, Patrick?"

Pat sighed. "I couldn't hear most of the time because of the noise. I guess he asked me to point to something, sometimes with my left hand, sometimes with my right. "

"But your left hand is in a cast."

"I can point with my fingers," Pat said, poking his left index finger at the pencil on the woman's desk to demonstrate his abilities. "That wasn't the problem."

"What was the problem, Patrick?"

"You're going to think this is pretty funny. I could *do* what he told me to do over the earphones. I pointed my left fingers at the thing he wanted me to touch. But I never was sure what it was he had asked me to do, even when I did it just like he said to do it." The young man stopped, a puzzled look on his face. "I mean, how can you *do* something when you don't know what it is you're supposed to be doing?"

Colonel Garcia frowned. Then she said, "Tell me about the man in the overcoat, please."

"Well, Dr. Tavela was testing me when this man came into the lab. He looked nervous and excited, I guess. He pulled on Dr. Tavela's arm, and they went out of the room for a while. Then, when Dr. Tavela came back, he was awful excited too. He said that something good had happened, something he had been waiting for a long time." Patrick's left hand reached out and touched the pencil again, almost unconsciously.

"And then . . ."

"And then he said we had work to do. So he whispered at me for a long time, maybe half an hour or so, and had me point to things again and again."

Colonel Garcia leaned forward. "What sort of things, Patrick? Numbers and letters?"

"That's what the secret police asked, but I don't know. I really don't!" Patrick's voice cracked with emotion. "I couldn't see the things, I just pointed at them with my left hand. The usual cat and dog pictures, I guess. That's what we usually worked on."

"You told the secret police about this?"

"Of course, but they didn't believe me at first. So they hooked me up to a polly . . . a polly . . ."

"A polygraph, Patrick. That's what you would call a 'lie detector.'"

"Yeah, well, they stuck this wet, metal thing on the palm of my right hand. It was connected with wires to a machine that made squiggles on a sheet of paper. And they asked me questions and looked at the squiggles." Patrick sighed deeply. "They did it for hours and hours and hours. One man kept insisting that I was lying and said they ought to give me a whipping for lying so much."

"Did they punish you?"

Patrick shook his head. "No, the other man kept saying that the squiggles showed I was telling the truth. And I was!"

Colonel Garcia nodded sympathetically. "I believe you, Patrick. You see, the secret police thought that Dr. Tavela had given you the formula. We put a lot of pressure on them, but they wouldn't release you until they made sure that you didn't know what it was."

The woman picked up the pencil again and tapped it nervously. "He must have known they would arrest him shortly, and I'll bet a million dollars he told you something. He must have hidden some clue deep within your brain, where the secret police couldn't find it, but we could."

"He didn't tell me anything, ma'am." Patrick started to cry a little. "Except, when the police came to the door to get him, he told me to be brave, and tell the truth. He said he was glad I had broken my hand, and that whenever I was troubled, I should read the Bible and seek out understanding."

Captain Hartman entered the Colonel's office bearing a tattered book. "You'd be surprised how difficult it was to find a copy of the Bible around this place," he said, handing the book to the woman.

Colonel Garcia gave the man a bemused look, then turned to Patrick. "What part of Proverbs did Dr. Tavela read to you the most?"

"The third chapter, I think it was."

The woman leafed through the book, found a place, then began to read.

"'Understanding is more precious than rubies: and all the things thou canst desire are not to be compared unto her. Length of days is in her right hand; and in her left hand riches and honor.'"

Patrick became excited. "Yes, that's it. He read that verse to me several times."

Colonel Garcia put the Bible face down on the desk, and picked up the pencil in her right hand. She tapped it gently on the desk, again and again. After a moment she stared at Patrick's left hand, encased as it was in the plaster cast. She gazed intently at the bandages on his shaven head. Next she looked at the innocent smile on the young man's face.

Then she laughed warmly, jubilantly. "Of course!" she said loudly.

Captain Hartman was startled. "Have you found the secret, Colonel?"

"Of course I have, Captain. Where the secret police failed, I have succeeded. Thanks to Dr. Tavela's clue from the Bible, and my knowledge of Patrick's problems, I know the truth." She got up and walked around the desk, pulling up a chair to sit by Patrick. She hugged him in her arms momentarily, then gently touched his head.

"What an appropriate place to hide a secret," she said.

(Continued on page 49.)

Your Brain

Your brain is the master organ of your body. During open heart surgery, a machine can take over for your heart, just as a machine can take over some of the functions of your kidneys. But even with mechanical methods of cleaning and pumping your blood, you remain YOU—which is to say that your thoughts, dreams, hopes, and general behavior patterns aren't much affected by mechanical substitutes for most of your bodily functions.

However, even a small amount of damage to certain *critical parts of your brain* may—under certain circumstances—cause you to lose consciousness for the rest of your life. More extensive damage might even cause rather dramatic changes in your personality. Why? Because your brain is the seat of your self-awareness, the locus of your intelligence, your compassion, and your creativity. All of your mental activities—your thoughts, emotions, and feelings—and all of your bodily processes are affected by the functioning of your brain.

On the other hand, sometimes people can sustain massive damage to major portions of their brains and still recover all the mental and physical abilities they had before the damage occurred. So, while your brain is very much the master organ of your body, YOU are a great deal more than the mere sum of all the complex physical activities that occur inside your skull.

A Note on the Glossary Items

Most texts have word lists or glossaries at the end of the book that give definitions of technical terms. These glossaries are often difficult to find and to use, and few of them tell you how to say the word aloud. In this book, we have reserved the top of the right-hand column of each odd-numbered page for definitions and explanations of the sometimes complicated words or phrases you may encounter in each chapter. We call this the "running glossary." Every time you see a **boldfaced** word on a page, you will know that the word is defined (and often a pronunciation given) in the "running glossary" at the top of the right-hand column of the next odd-numbered page.

If you already understand the boldfaced word, don't bother checking it out immediately. However, if you have any doubts about the meaning of the word—or if you are interested in the Latin or Greek derivation of the term—you may wish to check the item at once, without having to lose your place by turning to the back of the book (where the glossary is located in most other texts).

Also, when you study for an examination, you may find it helpful to check all the terms in the "running glossary" since many of the key words or thoughts will appear there. Most of these same important terms will also be **boldfaced** in the summary that appears at the end of most chapters.

If you run across a word you don't understand that does *not* appear in the "running glossary," please check the index at the end of the book to see if the word is defined elsewhere in the text. There is both an index of people's names and an index of subjects at the end of the book.

The pronunciations given in the definitions are in the "Midwestern dialect" that is used by many radio and TV announcers and newscasters. Pronunciations of many words vary from one part of the country to another. If you have doubts about how to say a word, please ask your teacher about it.

And finally, one very important point: Any dictionary contains thousands of words that you know, as well as thousands that you don't know. I hope you will use the "running glossary" in this text as you would a dictionary. Don't be upset if I define terms you think every student ought to be familiar with. I selected all the terms in the glossary by asking several hundred students to circle every word they didn't understand. The items that appear are those that *at least 10 percent* of these students weren't sure of—including some words that have no direct connection with the science of psychology.

This book is for *everybody*—for people with large vocabularies, and for people with limited knowledge but a large desire to learn. If you know most of the words defined in the "running glossary," congratulations! However, you should remember that other students may need all the help any of us can give.

Still and all, your brain is the single most important part of your body. Thus if you are to understand why you think and feel and act as you do, you *must* first have some notion of how this master organ operates. Therefore, we will begin our survey of the field of psychology by looking closely at your brain and nervous system.

Inputs, Internal Processes, Outputs

First, let us see what your brain actually looks like. If you enjoy analogies, consider this one for a moment. In a very limited sense, your brain is like

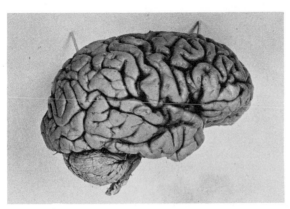

Fig. 2.1. The human brain, viewed from the right. The *cerebellum* (a Latin word meaning "little brain") at the bottom of the photograph is not a part of the cerebrum, but rather is one of the "lower centers." The cerebellum is involved in coordinating such complex movements as walking, playing the piano, driving a car, and so on. **(left)**

Fig. 2.2. Your brain in an imaginary mirror. **(right)**

a wrinkled mushroom packed tightly inside a bony shell we call the skull (see Fig. 2.1). Not counting the skull, your brain weighs about 1.3 kilograms (3 pounds). It is made up of more than 15 billion (15,000,000,000) nerve cells. The physiological activities of these nerve cells help determine what you think and feel and learn and do. But these nerve cells—or **neurons**, as they are called—do not all have the same tasks to perform. Sometimes groups of your neurons function rather independently. More often, they cooperate to achieve some common goal.

As we will see in Chapter 5, psychologists often consider business organizations to be "complex social systems," much as your body is a "complex living system." To make this point clearer, let's compare your body to a corporation. This analogy is pertinent, since the word "corporation" actually comes from the Latin word meaning *body*.

All living systems have three main types of functions—**inputs**, **internal activities**, and **outputs**. A large manufacturing company such as Ford takes in orders from customers and purchases raw materials. These are its *inputs*. The cars that Ford produces are its *outputs*. But producing cars also takes "information processing" and "decision making," which are *internal processes*. The management at Ford serves as the brain of that corporation and thus makes the decisions that keep the company functioning smoothly.

In similar fashion, you must decide what food to eat, what information to study for your next exam, and how you should act in most situations. Food and information are *inputs* to your body; decision making and digestion are *internal activities*; and what you say and do are your *outputs*. Your brain is your own "top management" that helps run your body in an efficient manner.

Corporate Organization

Ford could not survive unless its management team was organized into various levels or types of decision making. At the top are the executive officers, who send orders *down* the organizational ladder to "middle-level management." The men and women in middle-level management supervise the various internal functions that keep the organization alive and carry out the orders they receive from top management. Middle-level managers also send messages *up* to the executive officers letting them know how things in the factories are going.

At the bottom of the organizational chart are the front-line supervisors and workers. Some of these lower-level employees receive messages from the outside world, process them, and send them up the chain of command. Other employees produce most of the actual "outputs" of the car company. But what these people do, for the most part, is to follow instructions they receive from higher management.

Organization of Your Brain

Your brain is organized in "levels" much as is Ford. For instance, a large collection of neurons (nerve cells) gathered together at the very top of your brain serves as your own "top management." These neurons make up what is called the **cortex** of your brain.

Cortex is a Latin word meaning the "bark" of a tree or the "skin" of a mushroom. The thin outer skin of a mushroom is often darker and tougher than the tissue inside, and the cortex or thin outer layer of your brain is likewise different from the neurons inside. Your cortex contains millions of very special neurons that seem to be intimately related to your "stream of consciousness," or your moment-to-moment thoughts. It is mostly in your cortex that conscious decisions are made about what your own "corporation" or body is going to do. But your cortex must have informational inputs to process if it is to function properly, and it must have ways of sending messages to the muscles in your body if you are to produce the proper outputs.

Sensory and Motor Pathways

Information about the outside world flows into your cortex along a number of routes called **sensory pathways**. Your eyes, ears, nose, tongue, and skin all send messages to your brain about what is happening around you—and inside you. These inputs go first to the lower parts of your brain, and then to your cortex. Your cortex pays attention to this incoming sensory information, checks its memory files, and then decides what you should do or think or feel in a given situation. Paying attention, checking memory files, and making decisions are some of the ways in which your cortex *processes* sensory inputs.

Once your cortical "top management" has processed an input and decided on a response, it sends command messages along **motor pathways** to your body's muscles and glands telling them how to react. But before these messages reach your muscles, they must first pass through the lower parts of your brain.

Lying beneath your cortex are a large number of "middle management" **neural sub-centers**. For the most part these sub-centers merely screen out trivial inputs before sending the urgent ones up to your cortex, or they execute commands they receive from the top levels of your brain. But these lower centers are most important to your very existence for they control such *automatic* responses as breathing and digestion. They also execute the complex muscle movements involved in walking and running. For example, when you decide to walk to class, the *decision* to do so is made in your cortex. But are you conscious of each tiny movement the muscles in your legs and feet must make to get you there? Surely not, for you would be hard-pressed to keep up with the millions of different neural commands that the lower centers in your brain must issue to your muscles each time you take a simple stroll. Your neural sub-centers handle these movements automatically, without conscious effort on your part. However, in emergency

situations, your cortex may assume direct and voluntary control over many of your automatic responses.

But, for the most part, your cortical "top management" is free to dream and scheme as it wishes, leaving most of your physical behavior to be directly controlled by the lower parts of your brain.

Question: *If you had to consciously think about keeping your heart pumping and your lungs breathing, what would happen when you went to sleep at night?*

The Cerebrum

If you would like to get a better feel for the physical structure of your brain, you might try this little **demonstration**. Pause for a moment and go look at yourself in a mirror (see Fig. 2.2). If by some magic the flesh and bone of your head could be made invisible, you would see the front part of your brain as you stared into the mirror. Viewed this way, your brain would look much like the mountain ranges along the California coast as seen from an airplane. That is, your brain would appear to be a series of rounded hills with deep valleys in between.

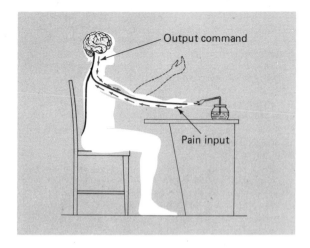

Output command

Pain input

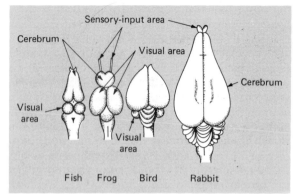

Sensory-input area

Cerebrum

Visual area

Cerebrum

Visual area

Visual area

Fish   Frog   Bird   Rabbit

Fig. 2.3. When a child's finger touches a hot object, a "pain input" is flashed up the nerves in the child's arm, to the spinal cord, and thence to the brain. The brain "processes" this input immediately, and sends an "output message" down the spinal cord ordering the muscles in the child's arm to move away from the object. **(left)**

Fig. 2.4. The brains of lower animals are made up chiefly of sensory-input areas and motor-output areas (such as the cerebellum). The larger the cerebrum is in relation to the rest of the brain, the more complex the behavior the organism is typically capable of. Your cerebrum makes up the major part of your brain and is more than 100 times larger than the cerebrum of the rabbit. **(right)**

The outer crust of this brainy landscape is, as we said, the *cortex*. It is about 0.65 centimeters (1/4 inch) thick. This cortical "peel" covers the biggest part of your brain, which is called the **cerebrum** (from the Latin word for "brain").

Your cerebrum sits on top of the rest of your brain much as the huge cap of a mushroom sits on top of its skinny stem. Sensory inputs flow up the narrow stem of your brain to your cerebrum. Your lower brain centers do the "preliminary processing" of this incoming information, acting on some inputs and screening out others. Mostly, though, these lower centers send inputs on to your cortex for final decision making. Output commands from your cortex flow down through the lower centers and on to your muscles and glands (see Fig. 2.3).

If you could look at your brain from the top, all you would see would be the cortical covering, or the cap of the cerebral mushroom. The lower centers, or sub-units, are all buried deep in your cerebrum or in the stem itself.

Evolution of the Cerebrum

In evolutionary terms, the cerebrum has been one of the last parts of the brain to develop. If you inspected the brains of lower animals, you would find that a human has a better-developed cerebrum than a monkey, that a monkey has more cerebral tissue than a dog, a dog more than a rat, a rat more than a pigeon, and a pigeon more than a goldfish (see Fig. 2.4). Most psychologists believe that, in general terms, the better developed an animal's cerebrum is, the more complex its behavior patterns are likely to be.

Very simple animals, such as worms and insects, have brains made up of just "the stem of the mushroom." Lacking cerebrums, they must make do with what in humans are called "the lower cen-

ters." The simplest forms of life, such as single-celled organisms, don't even have brains at all.

Complex intellectual functions—such as writing song lyrics and performing scientific experiments—are controlled by your cerebrum and its cortex. Perhaps this fact explains why biology students are able to study the earthworm, but no one has ever noticed a worm taking notes on human behavior. It takes a very large corporate structure indeed to produce such complex outputs as songs or automobiles.

The Brain and Behavior

Most companies manufacture a specific product or a series of products that keeps them in business. From a biological point of view, your brain *manufactures thoughts and behaviors*.

The primary purpose of your brain is to create neural, muscular, and glandular reactions, just as Ford's primary purpose is to produce cars and profits. The "employees" that make up your corporate brain and produce your thoughts, feelings, and behaviors are your individual nerve cells, or neurons. When your neurons are functioning well, they take in messages properly and make the right "corporate decisions." In consequence, your reactions flow off this neural assembly line in satisfactory fashion. When your neurons become sick or disturbed, various parts of this input-output process are badly upset.

If your *input* neurons were damaged or drugged, you might suffer from various kinds of **hallucinations**. That is, you could (1) see things that weren't there; (2) hear voices when no one is speaking; or (3) fail to detect important changes in your sensory environment. We will discuss these problems in the next chapter, when we investigate the effects that various drugs can have on your brain.

If your *processing* neurons are disturbed, several things may happen to you: (1) you could suffer a memory loss; (2) you might under-react or over-react to emotional situations; (3) your judgment might become clouded; (4) you could faint or fall into an abnormal sleep called a **coma**; or (5) your cortex might become so confused that it issued orders which led other people to think that you were "mentally ill." We will have a great deal more to say about some of these problems in later chapters.

If for any reason your *output* neurons start functioning abnormally, their behavioral product can sometimes be as clumsily put together as would be an automobile assembled by drunks. Damage to the output systems of your brain can lead to any of the following: (1) a loss of muscular coordination; (2) paralysis of the muscles in your arms, legs, or any other part of your body; or (3) a condition known as **motor epilepsy** or a **grand mal seizure**. We will have more to say about the abnormal condition called epilepsy later in the chapter. For the moment, let's see how your neurons function under normal conditions.

Question: Suppose a young man was hit over the head in a fight, and his doctor suspected brain damage even though the man's skull wasn't broken. How could the doctor get a rough idea of the location of any injury to the man's brain without having to open up his skull and look inside?

The Neuron

The major purpose of the individual nerve cells in your brain is to *pass information from one part of the body to another*. Although neurons vary considerably among themselves in size and shape, they all have three main parts—the **dendrites**, the **soma** (cell body), and the **axon**. As you will see, all three parts of the neuron are involved in transmitting "neural messages" through your body—and hence help produce thoughts and behaviors.

Cerebrum (sair-REE-brum). The big, thick "cap" on the top of your brain. Humans have bigger cerebrums than any other animal. The word "cerebral" (meaning "mental") comes from "cerebrum." Most of your important mental functions take place in your cerebrum.

Hallucinations (hal-LOO-see-NAY-shuns). Seeing or hearing things that aren't really there. If you attend a horror movie, and see a "ghost" on the way home, the ghost is probably an hallucination manufactured by your fear, rather than being a true sensory input.

Coma (KO-mah). An unusual form of deep sleep from which the person usually cannot be easily awakened. Often caused by drugs, fever, or brain injury.

Motor epilepsy (EP-ee-LEP-see). A type of muscular seizure or attack usually caused by damage to the brain.

Grand mal seizure (grahn mahl). Perhaps the most dramatic, terrifying type of motor epilepsy. The French words *grand mal* mean "big sickness" (the final "d" in "grand" is not pronounced).

Dendrite (DEN-dright). Tiny fibers at the front or "input" end of a neuron that are chemically excited by neuro-transmitters released into the synapse.

Soma (SO-mah). The cell body of a neuron. Contains the cell nucleus (NEW-klee-us). The center or main part of a neuron that "processes" some types of inputs to the cell.

Axon (AX-on). The "tail" or "output" end of a neuron. Axonic end-fibers release neural transmitters into the synapse which stimulate the next neuron in line.

Metabolism (mett-TAB-boh-lism). From a Greek word meaning "change." The sum total of biological processes inside the cell that (a) build up energy to be released, and (b) repair the cell and keep it functioning in a normal fashion.

The Dendrites

The front end, or *input* side, of a cortical neuron is a network of tiny fibers called *dendrites*. The dendrites project out from the cell body to make contact with surrounding nerve cells. The major activity of the dendrites is to receive information from other nerve cells. We will see how the dendrites accomplish this miracle in a moment. Dendrites also generate electrical activity that causes the *brain waves* we will discuss later on.

The Soma

The main part, or body, of the cell is called the *soma*. The soma seems to have two major functions. First, like the dendrites, it can receive inputs from other neurons. But second and just as important, the soma is the neuron's "housekeeper." Most of the complex chemical reactions called cellular **metabolism** which keep the cell functioning in a healthy fashion take place inside the soma.

In a manner of speaking, the soma is the *processing* part of the nerve cell. Many of the drugs that affect human behavior do so because they speed up or slow down the chemical reactions which occur naturally and continuously in the cell body of the neuron.

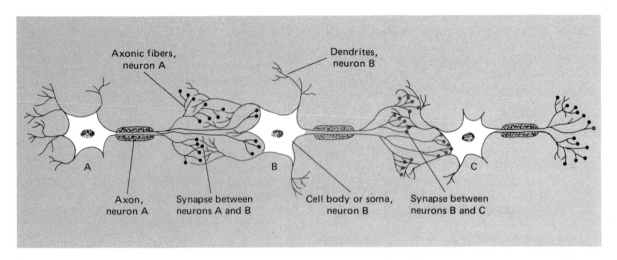

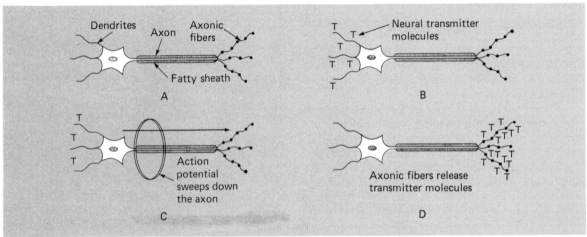

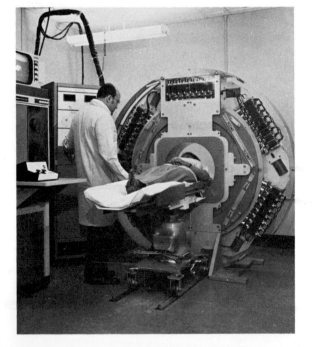

Fig. 2.5. Three neurons in a row. The axonic fibers of A make synapse with the dendrites and cell body of B, and the axonic fibers of B make synapse with the dendrites and cell body of C. **(top)**

Fig. 2.6. Transmitter molecules (T's) excite the dendrites of a neuron, causing the neuron to fire. During "firing," a wave of electro-chemical activity sweeps down the axon causing the axonic fibers to release more T's (transmitters) which stimulate the next neuron in line. **(middle)**

New techniques allow scientists to take three-dimensional x-ray photographs of the brain. **(left)**

The Axon

The action end, or *output* area, of the neuron is called the *axon*. The axon stretches back from the soma like a telephone cable. At the end of the axon are tiny fibers which make contact with the dendrites and cell bodies of nearby neurons, or with the muscles and glands in the rest of the body. The axon is the *output area* of the neuron because the axonic fibers actually pass messages along to other nerve cells, and to the muscles and glands. Many axons are covered with a fatty sheath that apparently serves to speed up neural transmission (see Chapter 17).

As we will see in a moment, the axonic fibers come close to, but *do not touch*, the dendrites and cell bodies of the neurons and muscles they make contact with.

Action Potentials

One of the major functions of the neuron is to send information from one part of your body to another. Each nerve cell contains a certain amount of stored-up electrical energy—the **resting potential**—that it can discharge in short bursts. The battery in your car releases a similar burst of stored-up electrical energy when you turn the ignition key. These bursts of energy are called **action potentials**.

The action potential is one of the key parts of the complex electro-chemical process by which your neurons pass messages from one part of your body to another. For example, consider three nerve cells in your brain that are connected together in sequence, in *A-B-C* fashion. As Fig. 2.5 shows, the axon of *A* makes contact with the dendrites and soma of *B*, and the axon of *B* makes contact with the dendrites and soma of *C*.

A, *B*, and *C* all have a certain (and very similar) resting potential to call upon when necessary. When a message is to be passed from *A* to *C*, a chemical change occurs in the axon of *A* that affects both the dendrites and the cell body of *B*. Neuron *B* responds by releasing its stored-up electrical energy. That is, when *A* stimulates *B*, an action potential sweeps down the length of *B*'s axon in much the same fashion as fire sweeps down a fuse. When the action potential reaches the tips of *B*'s axonic fibers, it causes a chemical change to occur that sets off a similar burst of electrical energy in neuron *C* (see Fig. 2.6).

Thus, the message passes from *A* to *B* to *C* as each cell produces an action potential which stimulates the next neuron in line.

Neural Firing

Whenever an action potential passes along a neuron's axon, we say that the nerve cell has **fired**, because the action involved is much like the firing of a gun. For example, consider how a gun actually "fires." There is a great deal of potential energy stored in the chemical gunpowder in a bullet. When you pull the trigger on a gun, you translate this *potential* chemical energy into the *active* energy of an explosion, and the bullet is propelled down the barrel of the gun. And when a neuron fires, it translates its resting potential into an action potential.

Resting potential. The amount of electrical energy stored up by a nerve cell that can be discharged in a short burst. The amount of money you have to spend at any one time is, in a sense, your "financial potential."

Action potential. The wave of electro-chemical energy that sweeps down the axon of a neuron when the nerve cell releases its resting potential and hence "fires."

Fired. When a neuron converts its resting potential into an action potential, we say that the nerve cell has "fired."

Synapse (SIN-aps). The extremely narrow, fluid-filled space between two nerve cells. Transmitter chemicals released by the axonic end fibers of one neuron cross the synapse and stimulate the dendrites and cell body of the next neuron in line, causing that neuron to fire. If the axon of nerve cell *A* can stimulate the dendrites and cell body of *B*, we say the two neurons "make synapse."

Let's carry the bullet analogy a step further. The neuron behaves in some ways as if it were a machine gun loaded with electro-chemical bullets. To begin with, a machine gun either fires, or it doesn't. The bullets travel at the same speed whether you fire one or a hundred in a row. In similar fashion, a neuron either fires, or doesn't fire. All its action potentials are of the same strength whether the neuron produces one of them a second, or a hundred.

Second, if you press and release the trigger on a machine gun very quickly, you can fire the shells slowly, one by one. But if you hold the trigger down, you can fire off whole bursts of bullets in a second or two. In like manner, if you tap lightly on your arm, the receptor (input) nerve cells in your skin will fire at a very slow rate—a few times a second. If you press very hard on your arm, these same input neurons can fire hundreds or even thousands of times per second.

Every time you move a muscle—or think a thought, or experience an emotion—you do so in part because one group of nerve cells in your brain *fires off messages* like a machine gun to your muscles, glands, or other groups of neurons.

The Synapse

Now, let us go back to neurons *A*, *B*, and *C*. As we noted, the axonic end-fibers of *A* come close to, *but do not actually touch*, the dendrites of cell *B*. The space between *A*'s axonic fibers and *B*'s dendrites is called the **synapse**. This synapse (or gap) is so tiny that you would have trouble seeing it even using the most powerful microscope.

The synaptic space between two nerve cells is really a *small canal*—a canal filled with fluid that contains many different types of chemical substances. These chemicals all have a definite effect on your behavior.

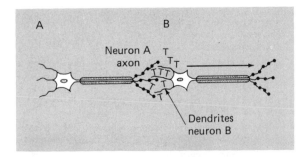

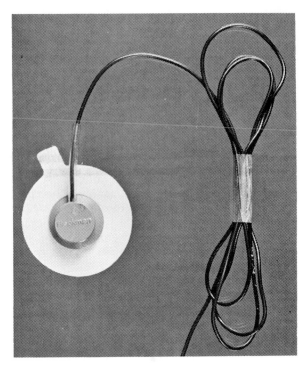

Fig. 2.7. When neuron A fires, its axonic fibers release transmitter (T) molecules into the synapse with neuron B. These molecules bind to receptor sites on the dendrites and cell body of B, causing B to fire. **(top left)**

Fig. 2.8. An electrode. **(right)**

Fig. 2.9. A patient hooked up to an EEG machine. **(bottom left)**

When a neuron fires, the action potential causes the axonic fibers to release tiny drops of chemicals into the synaptic gap or canal. These chemicals move across the synaptic canal and stimulate the dendrites and soma of the next cell. These stimulating chemicals are called **neural transmitters**, because they *transmit* information from one cell to another. The more neural transmitters that *A*'s axonic end-fibers release into the synaptic fluid between *A* and *B*, the more often cell *B* will be triggered into firing (see Fig. 2.7).

Nerve Cell Functions

Nerve cells have many functions. There are neurons in your eyes and ears—called **receptor cells** or input neurons—that detect changes in the world around you and relay information about those changes to your brain. Specialized **processing cells** react to this incoming sensory information by checking your memories to determine the input's importance and emotional value, and then decide how your body should react.

Motor neurons relay the output decision to your muscles and glands, thus causing your body to go into action. When a motor neuron fires, it releases *neural transmitters* into the synaptic canal between its own axon and the muscle it connects to. These transmitter chemicals cross the synaptic gap and cause the muscle to twitch or contract. Even the most complex muscular reactions—a rock musician playing a crashing chord on a guitar, or a secretary typing 100 words a minute on a typewriter—are made up of *orderly patterns of individual muscle contractions*. And all these reactions are brought about by the *orderly firing of motor neurons* and the release of transmitter chemicals at the **neuro-muscular synapse** (nerve-muscle connection).

If all your neurons were connected in simple *A-B-C* fashion, your behaviors would be no more complex than those of an earthworm. In fact, in the decision-making centers of your brain, the dendrites of any nerve cell *B* are likely to receive messages from axonic fibers from a thousand or more different *A*s. And *B*'s own axonic end-fibers are likely to pass messages along to the dendrites of a thousand or more *C*s. Thus any given neuron in your brain is likely to make contact with *thousands* of its neighboring neurons.

The EEG

Under normal conditions, the nerve cells in your brain act together in small units. But each unit (and each individual neuron) works toward the common goal of keeping you alive and functioning well. If a scientist wanted to get an idea of how your brain was performing, she or he might place one or more small pieces of metal—called **electrodes**—on the outside of your head (see Fig. 2.8). These electrodes would be connected by wires to an **electro-encephalo-graph**, or EEG machine (see Fig. 2.9).

This EEG machine translates electrical energy from your brain into *visual patterns on a screen*—much as a television set translates electrical energy into patterns you can see on the picture tube. Each time a nerve cell close to the electrode becomes excited (or "fires"), the electrode sends an electrical impulse to the EEG machine. This impulse is displayed visually on the EEG's picture tube (or perhaps printed out on a sheet of paper).

If, by some chance, all the cells in your brain near the electrode were silent for a second or two, the picture tube would show a flat, horizontal line. If one or two cells fired at exactly the same time, the line would have a tiny pip or bump in it. If 1,000 cells fired at exactly the same time, the peak would be very high indeed. And if, half a second later, 500 of these cells fired again, the screen would show a second peak about half the size of the previous one (see Fig. 2.10).

In a sense, the EEG gives you the same sort of fuzzy, imprecise picture of what is going on inside the skull that you would get if you stood outside a huge football stadium and tried to guess what was happening inside by listening to the roar of the crowd. Standing outside the stadium, you could tell whether the football game was exciting, and when an important play had been made. But you couldn't always tell which team had the ball, or what the score was—much less what individual members of the crowd were doing or experiencing.

The EEG electrode "listens" outside the skull to the electrical noise made inside by thousands of individual neurons, but all it can tell you is how active the *bulk* of the nerve cells are, not the precise behavior patterns of each *single* neuron.

Brain Waves

When you are actively engaged in thought—as when you are mentally trying to work through a difficult problem—your EEG record will show a rapid but rather irregular pattern of electrical activity. We call this sort of electrical output **beta waves**, or the **activity pattern** (see Fig. 2.11). The appearance of this irregular brain wave pattern on the EEG usually means that your mind is engaged in some kind of "deliberate mental processing."

Neural transmitters (NEWR-al TRANS-mitt-ers). Chemicals released into the synapse by the axonic fibers of one neuron that cause the second neuron to fire. Chemicals that thus "transmit a message" from one neuron to the next.

Receptor cells. Nerve cells in your eyes, ears, skin, and the rest of your body that receive information about your own body and the world around you. Input neurons.

Processing cells. Nerve cells in your brain that respond to information coming from the receptor cells.

Motor neurons. Output neurons. Nerve cells with very long axons. The dendrites and cell body of your motor neurons are usually in a motor center in your brain. The axon stretches out like a telephone cable from the brain to make synapse with other neurons and from thence to individual muscles somewhere in your body.

Neuro-muscular synapse (NEWR-roh). The synapse or connection point between a motor neuron and a muscle.

Electrode (ee-LEK-trode). A device used to detect electrical activity in the brain. Disk-electrodes are coin-shaped pieces of metal that can be placed against the head to read brain waves. Needle-electrodes are thin wires inserted through holes in the skull directly into the brain.

Electro-encelphalo-graph (ee-LEK-tro en-SEF-uh-low graf). An electronic machine that makes a graphic record of brain waves. **Cephalo** is the Greek word for "head."

Beta waves (BAIT-tah). Low voltage, rapid brain waves with rather a random pattern that signal alertness or awake attention.

Activity pattern. Another name for beta waves.

Alpha waves (AL-fa). When you are resting peacefully with your eyes closed, the visual regions of your brain at the back of your head will show a brain wave that repeats itself about 9–12 times per second. These are alpha waves. If you are listening to music with your eyes closed, the visual regions of your brain will show alpha waves, but the hearing regions will typically show the activity pattern. When you are reading a good book, the situation is often reversed–the visual brain will show the activity pattern and the hearing regions of your brain will show alpha waves.

Delta waves (DELL-tah). Much of the time when you are deeply asleep, your brain will produce big waves that repeat themselves 0.1–4 times per second.

The visual areas of your cortex are located primarily on the rear surface of your brain. When you relax and close your eyes, these visual parts of your brain will show regular but rather fast waves called **alpha waves** (see Fig. 2.11).

When you go to sleep, your brain wave activity generally slows down. The large, slow *sleep waves* that occur when you are deeply asleep are called **delta waves**. (We will have more to say about sleep and delta waves in the next chapter.)

The Cerebral Hemispheres

Now that you've learned something about how your neurons work, let's go back to your brain's basic structure. As we noted earlier, your cerebrum has "mountains" and "valleys" to it. The biggest "valley of the brain" is a deep groove that runs down the center from front to back, dividing

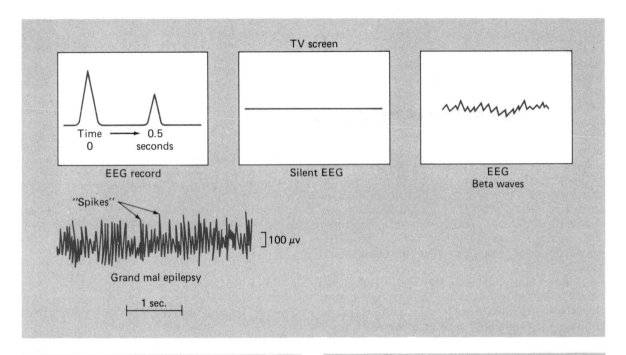

TV screen

EEG record

Silent EEG

EEG
Beta waves

"Spikes"

]100 μv

Grand mal epilepsy

1 sec.

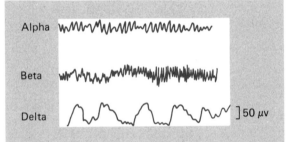

Alpha

Beta

Delta

]50 μv

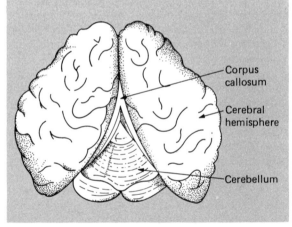

Corpus callosum

Cerebral hemisphere

Cerebellum

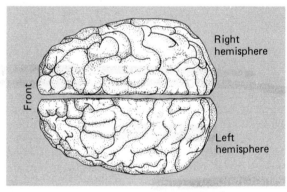

Front

Right hemisphere

Left hemisphere

Fig. 2.10. Examples of EEG records. **(top)**

Fig. 2.11. Alpha waves in the brain made up of electrical waves that have a frequency of 9–12 or so cycles per second. The delta waves register on an EEG machine as large, slow waves with a frequency of about 0.1–4 cycles per second. **(middle left)**

Fig. 2.12. A top view of the human brain showing the left and right hemispheres. **(bottom left)**

Fig. 2.13. The two cerebral hemispheres of the brain connected by the corpus callosum. **(right)**

your brain in two sphere-shaped parts called the **cerebral hemispheres** (see Fig. 2.12). These hemispheres are physical *mirror images* of each other, just as the left half of your face is (more-or-less) a mirror image of your right half, and your left hand is a mirror image of your right hand.

Despite the fact that your two cerebral hemispheres are reversed images of each other, however, there are major differences between them—just as there are functional differences between your right and left hands. Many things that you can do easily with one hand are very difficult for you to perform with the other. For example, if you are right-handed—as about 90 percent of the people in the world are—you write with your right hand but probably have trouble doing so with your left. If you are left-handed, you will typically write better with your left hand than you do with your right.

Now, ask yourself this question: If you are right-handed, why can't you write with your left hand since it is a mirror image of your right? The answer seems to lie in your *brain*, not in your *hands*.

As confusing as it may seem to you at first, your *right* cerebral hemisphere mainly controls the *left* side of your body, and your *left* cerebral hemisphere mainly controls the *right* side of your body. Thus the left half of your brain controls your right hand (and foot), and the right half of your brain controls your left hand (and foot).

If you are right-handed, your *left* hemisphere is your **dominant hemisphere**. A better name for the left half of your brain, however, might be "executive hemisphere," since this is the side of your brain that *executes* most of your body movements. When you write, your "executive left hemisphere" issues the orders that your right hand and fingers follow. And when you speak, it is this same "dominant" left side of your brain that makes your tongue, lips, and vocal cords move. Even when you think or scheme about something by "talking to yourself," you probably do so with this same "executive" or dominant left hemisphere.

Your *right* hemisphere is called by many names—**minor hemisphere**, "perceptual" hemisphere, "emotional" hemisphere, or "monitoring" hemisphere. It understands language, but neither talks nor writes except under rather unusual circumstances.

If certain "language areas" in your executive (left) hemisphere were damaged, you might lose the ability to say what you want to say in logical terms. You might even be unable to understand the meaning of spoken words. This inability to communicate is called **aphasia**, and its primary cause is damage to the speech centers in the dominant or "talking" hemisphere of the cerebrum.

If you are left-handed, it may be that the right half of your cerebrum is the "talking hemisphere" and produces most of your spoken and written language. Or it may be that your left hemisphere is dominant despite the fact that you are left-handed. However, in some left-handers, both hemispheres share the ability to speak and write, and neither of them is really "dominant." We don't really know why the pattern of hemispheric dominance is so confused in left-handed people.

The Corpus Callosum

As we said, the two cerebral hemispheres of your brain are separate and distinct from each other. But they are joined together by a bridge of very

---

Cerebral hemispheres (ser-REE-bral HEM-ee-spheres). The two halves of the globe-shaped or spherical cerebrum.

Dominant hemisphere. The half of the cerebrum that dominates or controls such activities as speech. Also called the "talking," "executive," and "major" hemisphere.

Minor hemisphere. The non-dominant half of the cerebrum which is a "silent partner" to the dominant or major hemisphere. Also called the the "perceptual" hemisphere, and the "emotional" hemisphere.

Aphasia (a-FAZE-ya). The inability to recognize the meaning of words, or to speak or write in meaningful terms. Some experts limit aphasia to an inability to process spoken language, and use the term agraphia (a-GRAF-ya) to refer to the inability to process written language. Either disorder is usually a symptom of some kind of brain damage.

Corpus callosum (KOR-pus kah-LOW-sum). The bridge of nervous tissue that connects the major and the minor hemispheres.

---

special tissue—much as the Northern Hemisphere is joined to the Southern Hemisphere by a narrow bridge of land we call Central America.

The tissue connecting the two hemispheres of your brain is called the **corpus callosum**, two Latin words meaning "thick or hardened body" (see Fig. 2.13). The corpus callosum contains a large number of axonic fibers that act like telephone cables running from one side of your brain to the other. Your "talking" hemisphere and your "perceiving" hemisphere keep in touch with each other *primarily* through your corpus callosum.

Sensory inputs that reach one of your hemispheres are almost automatically flashed to the other. Thus, if one of your hemispheres learns something, it usually shares the information with the other hemisphere almost immediately.

The situation is similar with your behavioral *outputs*. Suppose, for instance, your left hemisphere sends a message to the muscles in your right hand telling them to write the word "dog" with a pencil. Your dominant hemisphere would immediately let your right hemisphere know what it had commanded your hand to do.

Your left hemisphere is dominant as far as the execution of most muscle movements is concerned, but emotional reactions are controlled to a great extent by your right hemisphere. If you experienced something that upset or aroused you, your right hemisphere would send out the neural commands that caused you to blush, smile, laugh, or even "feel sick to your stomach." But your "emotional" hemisphere would also send a message across the corpus callosum to let your left "executive" hemisphere know what was happening—in case you might need to respond to the situation with more than a blush or a smile.

Your left hemisphere, then, *directly controls* the right half of your body. Your right hemisphere

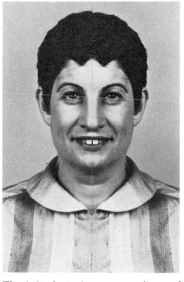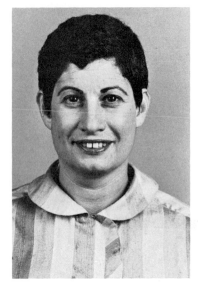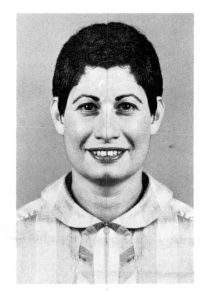

The left photo is a composite made up of the left half of a woman's face joined to its mirror image. The right photo shows the right half of the woman's face joined to its mirror image. The "normal" view of the woman is in the middle. The left half of the face is controlled by the right (emotional) hemisphere. When photos such as these were shown to subjects, most of them selected the "left" composite photos as displaying the most emotional expression. Notice too that the right half of the face (controlled by the dominant left hemisphere) is larger, as is customary in most right-handed individuals.

directly controls the left half of your body but, for the most part, rather passively yields control of most coordinated body movements to the left hemisphere. However, your right hemisphere does take the lead when it comes to such simple emotional reactions as laughing or crying.

Question: Because our society is built primarily for "right-handed" people, some parents attempt to impose right-handedness on children who are naturally left-handed. What might happen to speech development in a left-handed child who was forced to learn to write and speak with the "wrong" hemisphere of its brain?

Why a Dominant Hemisphere?
At birth (or shortly thereafter), one hemisphere starts to gain the lead over the other and eventually takes over major control of the whole body. Why the left hemisphere usually "wins out" is a matter for **conjecture**, but psychiatrist George F. Michel reported in the May 8, 1981 issue of *Science* that 65 percent of the newborn infants he studied preferred to lie with their heads turned to the

right. Only 15 percent of the infants showed a distinct preference for lying with their heads turned to the left. At 5 months of age, almost all of the children who had shown a "head right" orientation at birth reached for things with their right hands, while almost all of the infants with a "head left" orientation reached for objects with their left hands.

Michel believes that almost all infants are born with a tendency to orient their heads one way or another. This inborn "head orientation" then *determines* which hand—and which half of the brain—becomes dominant in later life.

Once the right hemisphere has become dominant, how does it exercise control over the left hemisphere? R.W. Doty and his colleagues reported in 1979 that the left half of the brain actively *inhibits* the right half. Thus, if you are right-handed, your right hemisphere is "passive" because your left hemisphere *suppresses* any attempts the right might make to speak or "take control" of your body movements. These "suppression orders," of course, are sent from the left hemisphere to the right across the corpus callosum.

Now, with all these facts in mind, can you guess what would happen to you if your corpus callosum were cut, and the two hemispheres of your brain were suddenly disconnected?

This is precisely the question that psychologists R.W. Sperry and R.E. Myers were trying to answer when, in 1953, they performed their first split-brain operations on cats. They ended up making one of the most exciting discoveries in modern psychology. Sperry has continued in this field of research for the past 30 years. In 1981 he was awarded the Nobel Prize in medicine and physiology for his split-brain studies.

Two Minds in the Same Body

The surgical technique used by Sperry and Myers involved opening up the cat's skull, then slicing the animal's corpus callosum. They also split the optic nerve that runs from the cat's eyes to its brain.

Normally, sensory input from *each* eye goes to *both* cerebral hemispheres along the **optic nerve**. When Sperry and Myers cut the corpus callosum—and also split the optic nerve—they left the cat's *eyes* as isolated from each other as were the *two halves of its cerebrum*. Now, whatever the animal's left eye saw was recorded only in the left hemisphere. And whatever the animal's right eye saw was recorded only in the cat's right hemisphere.

Immediately after the operation the cats had difficulty coordinating their movements. But, after a while, their behavior became fairly normal again. Either the two hemispheres had learned to cooperate with each other, or both sides of the brain took turns in controlling the entire body.

Once a cat seemed recovered from the surgery, Sperry and Myers gave the animal a variety of behavioral tests. First they blindfolded its left eye and taught the cat to solve a visual problem using *just* its right eye (and, of course, just the right hemisphere of its brain). The cat learned this lesson very well.

Next, they covered the trained right eye with the blindfold and tested the cat on the same problem with its untrained left eye (and left hemisphere). The question was, would any information about the problem have "leaked" from the right half of the cat's brain to the left?

The answer was a resounding *no*. Using just its untrained left eye, the cat appeared to be entirely ignorant of what it had learned with its right eye. When Sperry and Myers trained the left eye in similar fashion, the right eye (and hemisphere) seemed unaware of what the left part of the brain had learned.

Sperry and Myers concluded that the cat now had two "minds," either of which was capable of learning *on its own*—and of responding intelligently to changes in the world around it *on its own*.

Subsequent experiments with rats and monkeys gave similar results. However, the animals recovered so nicely that if you hadn't known about their operation, you probably wouldn't have guessed that there were two more-or-less independent "entities" inside each animal's body.

Conjecture (kon-JEKT-sure). From a Latin word meaning "to throw together." A conjecture is a guess or hypothesis (high-POTH-ee-sis).

Optic nerve (OP-tick). The visual input pathway that runs from each eye to the brain. Half of the optic nerve from each eye runs to the left brain, half to the right brain. In order to make sure that input from the cat's left eye went only to its left hemisphere, and that input from the right eye went only to the right hemisphere, Sperry and Myers had to cut half of the optic nerve from each eye.

The split-brain surgery was seemingly safe and relatively easy to perform in animals. But what would the operation do to a human, and why would anyone want to find out? To answer that question, we must look once more at that odd and unfortunate condition known as epilepsy.

Epilepsy

Although 4,000,000 people in the US suffer from epilepsy, most of us have little understanding of what causes the condition. Nor do most of us appreciate the the problems that epileptic individuals must face. Just for a moment, then, try to imagine what it might be like if you were unfortunate enough to sustain brain damage and have an epileptic attack.

If the site of the damaged nerve cells was in the *input* or *processing* areas of your brain, you might never recognize that you suffered from epilepsy. In fact, it was not until very recently that we realized that epilepsy could affect these parts of your nervous system. For seizures in the input and processing areas of the brain typically lead to little more than momentary lapses in consciousness.

If the injured neurons were in your *output* system, however, you would suffer from *motor epilepsy*—a condition that is very hard to overlook. During a full-blown motor seizure, most of the muscles in your body would suddenly contract. As your lungs squeezed shut, the air forced out might cause you to moan or scream. You would lose consciousness and fall to the ground, stiff as a board. For a moment or two, you would stop breathing. Then your arms and legs would begin twitching or jerking rhythmically, and you might lose control of your bladder and bowels.

Your motor seizure would be over and done with in five minutes or less, but you would be confused and sleepy—or have a headache—for some time thereafter. Typically, you would have little or no memory either of what led up to the seizure itself, or for the period of confusion that followed. Within an hour or so, you might be completely back to normal—until the next attack hit.

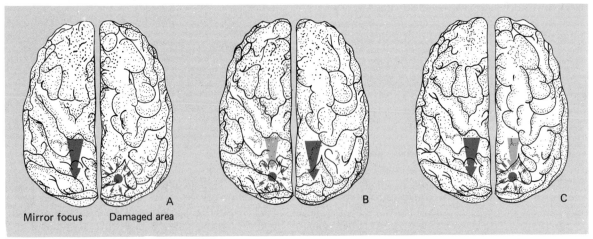

Mirror focus   Damaged area

A   B   C

Fig. 2.14. A. Damaged cells in the left hemisphere cause abnormal electrical activity in nearby cells—and send an "excited" message to their "mirror image" cells in the right hemisphere. B. The "mirror image" cells are stimulated to fire by this abnormal input, and feed an "excited" message back to the right hemisphere. C. Soon the whole brain is "on fire" with neural excitation, and an epileptic seizure results. Cutting the corpus callosum "cuts the feedback loop" and reduces the likelihood of a seizure.

If your epilepsy resulted from mild brain damage—or if the attack was caused by an overdose of some drug such as alcohol—your seizures would occur infrequently. But if your brain damage were severe, your attacks might happen several times a day—so frequently that you did not regain consciousness between seizures. This rare condition must be treated promptly, for it can lead to death.

Hypersynchrony

As we noted earlier, the neurons in your brain tend to function in small but relatively independent units. In brain-damaged people, however, *all* the nerve cells in a given part of the brain occasionally begin to fire in unison. We call this type of neural activity **hypersynchrony**, and it typically shows up on an EEG record as **spikes** (see Fig. 2.10).

When hypersynchrony occurs, huge and jagged waves of electrical activity sweep across the surface of the brain like a thunderstorm sweeping across the Atlantic Ocean. And just as you can tell something about the intensity of an Atlantic storm by measuring the size and shape of the ocean waves it stirs up, so you can tell something about that "stormy condition" called epilepsy by reading EEG records taken when a seizure occurs.

Epilepsy and the Corpus Callosum

The brain damage that causes most epileptic seizures usually has a specific **locus** or location on *one side of the brain*. If you took an EEG record from this damaged area, you would see continual "spike" responses.

But remember that the two hemispheres are more-or-less "mirror images." What would happen if you took an EEG record at the same point in the undamaged hemisphere? In fact, the EEG record from the unscarred hemisphere would usually look pretty normal. However, at the onset of an epileptic attack, you would detect spikes on *both sides of the brain*.

How could there be spike responses coming from apparently healthy tissue?

Almost every neuron in your *left* hemisphere has a nerve cell in your *right* hemisphere that is its "identical twin," or mirror image. Many of these nerve cells are tied together by axonic fibers that pass through the corpus callosum. Whenever a neuron in your dominant hemisphere fires, it may send a "command message" telling its mirror-image cell in the minor hemisphere to fire too. And whenever the mirror-image neuron fires, it sends a message back to the dominant hemisphere saying that it *has* fired.

These command messages are the primary way in which your dominant hemisphere coordinates muscular activities on both sides of your body.

Whenever an epileptic seizure begins at a point in one hemisphere, the mirror-image neurons in the other hemisphere receive a "seizure message" via the corpus callosum. This "seizure message" causes the mirror-image neurons to fire very, very rapidly themselves. The cells may even start showing spike activity on their own as they "catch fire" from all the stimulation they are receiving from the other hemisphere. So the spike activity begins to build up simultaneously at the *same spot in both hemispheres.*

In addition, the mirror-image neurons may send seizure messages back to the original site of the trouble. This return message from the undamaged hemisphere sets off even more spiking in the damaged area, which then sends even wilder messages back to the mirror-image cells, which causes them to fire even more rapidly.

Each time the seizure message flashes back and forth across the corpus callosum, a few more cells in each hemisphere get caught up in the spiking. Within a few seconds, the whole brain can become involved, and a *grand mal* attack occurs.

An epileptic seizure, therefore, is a good example of what is called a **positive feedback loop** (see Fig. 2.14).

"Cutting the Feedback Loop"

When medical doctors learned of the Sperry-Myers split-brain operation, they reasoned that if they cut the corpus callosum and separated the two hemispheres of the brain, they could *cut the positive feedback loop* that typically causes an epileptic attack. And, by "cutting the loop," they might prevent full-blown seizures from occurring in patients whose seizures couldn't be controlled by drugs or other medical treatment.

And the doctors were right. They tried the operation on a middle-aged man whom we shall call John Doe. During the Korean War, John Doe had served in the armed forces. After parachuting behind the enemy lines, he had been captured and put in a concentration camp. While in the prison camp, he had been struck on the head several times with a rifle butt.

Shortly thereafter, John Doe's epileptic seizures began. By the time he was released from the concentration camp, his brain was in such bad physical shape that drugs couldn't help very much. His seizures increased in frequency and intensity until they were occurring a dozen or more times a day. Without the split-brain operation, John Doe would probably have died—or committed suicide, as had many other epileptic patients with similar problems.

After the surgeons cut John Doe's corpus callosum, his seizures stopped almost completely—just as the surgeons had expected. Obviously, "cutting the positive feedback loop" had prevented the *grand mal* attacks from occurring. But, when the doctors split John Doe's brain, they apparently cut his "mind" into two separate but similar personalities as well. Each of these

Hypersynchrony (HIGH-purr-SINK-kron-ee). "Hyper" means high or above. "Synchrony" means coordinated activities. Neurons show hypersynchrony when too many of them fire in unison.

Spikes. Unusual, very large bursts of electrical activity that usually are symptoms of brain damage when they appear on an EEG record.

Locus (LOW-cuss). From the Latin word meaning "place" or "site."

Positive feedback loop. The term "feedback" means "getting information *back* from some outside source that lets you know what you are doing." When you curse someone, and the person hits you in response, you have just gotten feedback about your cursing. A feedback loop is a circle of responses. If each response in the feedback loop gets larger and larger, the feedback loop is positive, and an explosion often takes place. The "squeal" that sometimes comes from a public address system is another example of a positive feedback loop.

"minds" seemed to exist more-or-less independently of the other, and each of them had its own unique claim on his body.

As far has his mind was concerned, John Doe had suddenly become Siamese twins!

John-Doe-Left and John-Doe-Right

Immediately after the operation, John Doe was able to communicate in almost normal fashion. Some of his speech was slurred, as if he didn't have complete control over the muscles in his tongue. But his thinking seemed clear and logical, and he suffered no noticeable loss in intelligence.

But John Doe did have moments of confusion, and he was often unable to coordinate his body movements and his emotional reactions. Every now and then, he reported, the left half of his body "did odd things," *as if it had a will of its own.*

John Doe was right-handed, so his "talking hemisphere" controlled his right hand and leg. Occasionally, when John was dressing, his right hand would zip up his pants (as it normally did) and John would start to go about his business. Moments later, however, his left hand (controlled by the right hemisphere), would casually reach down and unzip his pants. His left hand did other odd things too, mostly in fairly emotional situations. These behaviors almost always embarrassed John Doe's dominant hemisphere, because he could offer no logical (verbal) explanation for why his left hand was behaving so peculiarly.

The doctors soon began to suspect that when John Doe answered their questions and reported his thoughts, it was *only* his left hemisphere that was doing the talking. Indeed, the left side of his brain seemed blissfully unaware of the perceptions and emotions that were occurring in his right hemisphere. And since his right hemi-

An unusually large number of painters and musicians are left handed. What does this fact tell you about the brain?

sphere couldn't communicate via the corpus callosum, it offered its comments behaviorally—by occasionally doing odd things that would *disrupt* the ongoing flow of behavior controlled by John Doe's left hemisphere.

The psychologists working with John Doe soon devised ways of communicating with either side of his brain without the other side's knowing what was going on. John-Doe-Left responded *verbally* to most questions the psychologists asked, since this hemisphere possessed full language control. John-Doe-Right could not talk, but he could *point to things* (with the left hand) in response to questions that John-Doe-Left couldn't hear.

Question: As soon as John-Doe-Left responded out loud to a question that only it could hear, why would John-Doe-Right usually know what the question had been?

Similar Personalities

Psychological tests showed that both John Does had remarkably similar personalities—except for language ability, they were about as much alike as identical twins. Their attitudes and opinions seemed to be the same; their perceptions of the world were the same; and they woke up and went to sleep at almost the same times.

There were differences, however. John-Doe-Left could express himself in language and was somewhat more logical and better at orderly planning than was John-Doe-Right. John-Doe-Right tended to be somewhat more aggressive, impulsive, emotional—and frequently expressed frustration with what was going on. This frustration apparently was caused by the fact that John-Doe-Right often knew what he wanted to say or do, but was unable to express himself verbally.

The split-brain operation was so successful in reducing epileptic attacks that it was tried with more than a dozen patients who might otherwise have died from uncontrollable seizures. In some of these patients, one hemisphere (usually the dominant one) was able to gain control of both sides of the body. In most cases, however, the two halves learned to cooperate and share control, but the dominant hemisphere was in the driver's seat most of the time. In one or two patients, though, neither half of the brain ever gained the ability to coordinate all bodily movements.

How the Hemispheres Differ

The split-brain studies have given us fascinating insights into the ways that the two hemispheres may function in individuals with intact brains. The research to date suggests that if you are right handed, your left hemisphere is much better at handling written and spoken language, and at executing sequences of coordinated movements. However, the right half of your brain seems superior at perceiving and remembering visual patterns, at processing emotional responses, and at "monitoring" your actions than is your left hemisphere.

Let us now examine in some detail the experiments which led to these conclusions.

Visual Perception, "Monitoring," and the Right Hemisphere

Research performed by Roger Sperry (and many others) suggests that the right hemisphere is much better at *perceiving visual patterns* than is the left. In one experiment, Sperry showed a male patient a complex design and then asked the man to reproduce the pattern by putting colored blocks together. When the patient used his left hand (right hemisphere), he completed the task rapidly. But when the man tried to match the design using his right hand (left hemisphere), he proceeded slowly, clumsily, and made many mistakes. And much to the annoyance of both Sperry and the patient, the man's left hand often tried to "correct" the mistakes the right hand made.

The right hemisphere not only seems to *perceive* complex visual patterns better than the left, it also seems to *remember* them more readily. In research reported in 1978 by Michael Gazzaniga and Joseph LeDoux, a split-brain patient was asked to reproduce patterns with either the left or right hand. The superiority of the left hand was much greater when the patient had to create the pattern from memory than when the pattern was physically present.

Oddly enough, there are no reports of cases in which the left hemisphere tries to correct any responses made by the right half of the brain. Indeed, as we will soon see, the left hemisphere usually tends to *deny responsibility* for any of the right hemisphere's actions. It would appear, then, that the right hemisphere is better at "monitoring" the activities of the left than the left hemisphere is at observing and recording the activities of the right.

Emotions and the Right Hemisphere

There is a fair amount of data connecting the right hemisphere with emotionality. For instance, sev-

Strokes. Brain damage usually caused by ruptured blood vessels. When deprived of blood, the neurons in a given area of the brain die. The stroke victim then loses the psychological and biological functions controlled by that part of the brain.

eral studies suggest that most smiles, grins, and frowns begin on the *left* side of the face in right-handed individuals—as surely would be the case if the *right* hemisphere took the lead in expressing joy or sorrow. Research on brain-damaged patients tends to confirm the role of the right hemisphere in emotional reactions. For example, in 1979 Elliott Ross and Marek-Marsel Mesulam reported the case histories of two people who suffered from **strokes** that affected the right half of the brain.

One of these patients—a 39-year-old woman—had to give up teaching school for a time after her stroke because she no longer could "put emotion into her speech and actions." All of her words came out in a flat tone of voice, and neither her pupils at school nor her own children at home could tell when she "meant business" when she talked. To compensate, she learned to say things like "I am angry and mean it" when she wanted to express dissatisfaction. She found it impossible to laugh, and was unable to cry even at her father's funeral. Some six months after the stroke, she started to regain the ability to express her feelings, and two months later she was once more able to express emotions normally. Apparently, undamaged parts of her brain had been able to "take over" the right-brain functions that were lost when the stroke occurred.

The other patient described by Ross and Mesulam was a 62-year-old surgeon whose right-hemisphere stroke left him with what his wife called "a nasty disposition." This man too was unable to make the tone of his voice match the mood that he wanted to express. He spoke in the same emotionless way no matter what he felt, a fact that distressed him as much as it did his wife. Unlike the schoolteacher, however, the surgeon did not recover the ability to "emote" even five years after the stroke.

Similar evidence about the importance of the right hemisphere in processing emotional responses comes from a split-brain patient studied by Roger Sperry and his associates. They showed pictures of various people and things to the woman's right hemisphere and asked her to evaluate the visual stimuli by giving a "thumbs up" or "thumbs down" response with her left hand. Her left hemisphere then tried to guess (and describe verbally) what the right was looking at.

Throughout the testing, the left hemisphere seemed to be playing a game like "20 questions" with the right. The right hemisphere would view a photo—of Adoph Hitler, for instance—and would give a vigorous "thumbs down" response. The left hemisphere would then attempt to figure out what the right had seen. When the left hemisphere guessed wrong, the right would respond with a "thumbs down." When the left was "on target," it got a "thumbs up" response and other positive emotional clues from the right. Indeed, as Sperry reports, he often had to restrain the woman's left hand from "tracing the initials" of the name of the object to help the left hemisphere with its guesses.

At one point in the testing, Sperry and his colleagues showed the woman's right hemisphere a photograph of herself. She responded, "Oh, No! Where'd you g— . . . what *are* they?" Then she laughed loudly and said, "Oh, God!" After a moment—in quite a different tone of voice—the woman asked hesitantly if there were people in the photograph. Sperry believes that the first (and rather emotional) reaction came from the right hemisphere before the left had time to exercise its usual dominance. Once the left hemisphere had gained control, though, it hesitantly asked about the picture in very unemotional tones.

Language and the Left Hemisphere

The split-brain research—and many other studies with both normal and brain-damaged individuals—suggests strongly that language is *primarily* processed on the left side of the brain. For instance, in 1978, Ruben Gur and his colleagues at the University of Pennsylvania gave 13 right-handed males various tasks to solve. Half of these tasks involved the use of complex language, while the other half of the problems involved the visual perception of incomplete patterns. When the subjects were working on the verbal problems, the blood flow through their *left* hemispheres increased markedly, but the blood flow through their *right* hemispheres did not increase at all. And those subjects who did best at solving the visual problems showed an increased blood flow through their *right* hemispheres, but not through the *left* half of their brains.

In a similar set of experiments, David Galin and his associates at the Langley Porter Institute in San Francisco found that normal subjects show increased electrical activity in their left hemispheres when attempting to solve verbal tasks, but increased activity in their right hemispheres when solving tasks of **spatial ability**.

Galin believes that "each hemisphere is specialized for a different cognitive style—the left for

an analytical, logical mode for which words are an excellent tool, and the right for a holistic **Gestalt** mode, which happens to be particularly suitable for spatial relations."

Cooperation across the Corpus Callosum

If it seems highly unlikely to you that you have two minds locked away inside your skull, the reason is not hard to find. Although the split-brain research suggests that each of your hemispheres *specializes* in certain types of tasks, for the most part the two halves of your brain *cooperate* so quickly and efficiently that they operate as a "functional unit" rather than as two separate entities. It is only when the two hemispheres are isolated that their differing abilities can readily be measured. And even these "differences" are not always obvious to the split-brain patient.

Roger Sperry reports that, following the operation, none of his split-brain patients was aware that "anything was missing." Although their left (verbal) hemispheres had lost most of what we call **depth perception**, and could no longer hear music in "full stereophonic sound," the patients did not become aware of this loss until it was demonstrated to them in the laboratory.

The patients often verbally rejected those few responses that clearly came from their right hemispheres. When Sperry would show a picture of some kind to the right hemisphere, the left hand would identify the picture correctly—but the patient would frequently deny having seen anything. And, just as often, when the patient's left hand would "correct" the right hand as it tried to reproduce a pattern, the patient would say something like, "Now, I know it wasn't *me* who did that!"

Case of J.W.

Studies in which only part of the corpus callosum is cut tell us even more about how the hemispheres communicate with each other. For example, in 1981 Michael Gazzaniga and his colleagues reported the case history of J.W., a bright young man whose epileptic seizures became so severe that he underwent split-brain surgery when he was 26. The operation took place in two stages, however. During the first stage, the surgeon cut *just the rear half* of the callosum. Then, 10 weeks later, the surgeon cut the *front half* as well. Gazzaniga and his co-workers gave J.W. psychological tests several times—before any surgery at all, after the first stage of the operation, and again after the entire corpus callosum had been cut.

Prior to the operation, when the word "knight" was shown just to J.W.'s right hemisphere, he immediately said the word aloud. After the rear half of the callosum was cut, however, J.W. gave the following response when his right hemisphere was again shown the word "knight": "I have a picture in my mind but can't say it . . . Two fighters in a ring . . . Ancient . . . wearing uniforms and helmets . . . on horses . . . trying to knock each other off . . . Knights?"

Two important points about the first part of the study:

1. When part of his callosum was still intact, J.W.'s left hemisphere did not deny having experienced stimuli presented to the right half of his brain. Instead, he claimed that he could "see" the stimulus in his mind, but just couldn't name or describe it very well.
2. When the rear half of his callosum was cut, J.W.'s right hemisphere could no longer send *specific stimuli* (such as words) to the left hemisphere. But it could transmit a *general impression* of the stimulus across the callosal tissue that still remained. His left hemisphere could then make educated guesses about what his right hemisphere was viewing.

After his entire corpus callosum was cut, though, J.W. was unable to report anything at all about the stimuli presented to his right hemisphere. Indeed, he now denied having "seen" anything at all, and his guesses at what the right hemisphere had been shown were no better than chance.

Gazzaniga believes that words and other *specific* sensory information pass back and forth between the two hemispheres in the rear half of the corpus callosum. However, the front half of the callosum apparently is the highway across which the two hemisphere exchange cognitive and emotional information (thoughts, feelings, and "meanings").

Question: When J.W.'s right hemisphere was shown the word "knight" after the first operation, his left hemisphere responded by talking about "two fighters in a ring wearing ancient armor." But the printed word "knight" sounds just the same as "night" when the two words are spoken aloud. What does the fact that J.W.'s left hemisphere didn't confuse "knight" with "night" tell you about what kind of sensory information the right hemisphere was sending to the left?

The Whole Brain versus the Split Brain

The chances are very good that no surgeon will ever cut your corpus callosum, and that you will not suffer the type of stroke which destroys your

Spatial ability (SPAY-shull). The ability to perceive or deal with objects in three-dimensional space. Also the ability to perceive three-dimensional patterns.

Gestalt (guess-SHTALT). A mental or perceptual pattern. From the German word meaning "figure," "pattern," or "good form." The ability to see something "as a whole"—rather than just see its parts—is the ability to "form a Gestalt."

Depth perception. The ability to see the world in three dimensions. The ability to judge how far away objects are.

Linear (LINN-ee-ur). Having to do with straight lines. When you connect your sentences together in A-B-C fashion, you are using "linear logic" to convey a thought pattern.

ability to express emotions. What then can all this study of brain-damaged individuals tell you about the normal functioning of the whole, intact brain? Although the split brain research does give a partial answer to this question, you should realize four things:

1. Almost all of the theories we have today are "subject to being recalled," which is to say that they may be drastically changed as new data come from the laboratory. For example, in 1783 the noted British poet William Cowper wrote, "If man had been intended to fly, God would have provided him with wings." What would Cowper have thought of today's jet airplanes? (And do you *really* believe that, if your corpus callosum were cut, you would end up with two separate and distinct minds inside your skull?)
2. Long before Sperry and Myers performed the first work on split-brain patients, Sigmund Freud stated that different parts of the mind seemed to perform quite different tasks. Freud thought that logic and rational thought took place in what he called "the conscious regions of the mind," while creativity and artistic perceptions were products of what he called "the unconscious portions of the mind." Not everyone agreed with Freud. But there is a striking parallel between his descriptions of "conscious" and "unconscious" mental processes and the functions shown by the left and right hemispheres in the split-brain studies.
3. Until recently, many experimental psychologists assumed that the "mind" was a highly complex biological machine that "processed information" much as a giant IBM computer might "process data." Other psychologists preferred to view the mind as a mental (or even spiritual) thing. But almost everybody thought of the mind as being a *single* system. The incredible conclusion some scientists draw from the split-brain research, however, is that you have *at least two different types of brains*, and thus two different types of "mind."

One half of your brain apparently takes in information from the outside world and processes it in a **linear** or logical fashion, rather as most modern computers do. This half of your brain is concious, verbal, and takes care of your daily behavior patterns in an orderly manner.

The other half of your brain—your right hemisphere, if you are right handed—seems to operate in quite a different manner. It deals with "patterns," "meanings," and "emotions" rather than with "bits of information." Although this half of your brain can talk under certain circumstances, it normally is non-verbal. It perceives the world in what seems to be a *holistic* fashion. It apparently monitors the actions of the other hemisphere, and gives emotional feedback to the left side of your brain to keep its thoughts and behaviors "on target" (see Chapter 5). Your right hemisphere also has its own type of consciousness, which seems to resemble *a waking dream* more than the sort of "ordinary awareness of the world" that occurs in the left hemisphere (see Chapter 3).

There are many computers that "process data" much as your left hemisphere does. To date, however, there are no computers that can deal with the world in the creative, holistic manner that your right hemisphere does. It is the *combination* of the two types of mental processes—the logical plus the creative—that makes the human mind infinitely more complex and interesting to study than is the ordinary computer.

4. We have known for centuries that certain drugs seem to have a strong influence on the way most people think and act. Some of the effects caused by these drugs—such as a dream-like state of consciousness and enhanced creativity—may well be caused by a disruption of the orderly flow of thoughts and emotions back and forth across the corpus callosum.

To understand better how your *whole brain* works when it is functioning normally, then, we must once more turn to the abnormal—to the influence of drugs on human behavior.

Summary

1. The **brain** is the master organ of your body that coordinates or controls many of the functions of the other organs.
2. The largest parts of your brain are the two **cerebral hemispheres** that sit atop the stem of your brain like the cap on a mushroom.
3. The thin outer covering of the cerebral hemispheres is called the **cortex**. Most of the functions of the brain that relate to conscious decision making are located in the cortex.
4. Your brain contains at least 15 billion nerve cells or **neurons**.
5. Most cortical neurons have three main parts—the **dendrites**, the cell body or **soma**, and the **axon**.
6. The main purpose of most neurons is to pass messages from one part of the body to another. These messages are really waves of electro-chemical energy called **action potentials**.
7. When the dendrites are stimulated by **neural transmitters**, the action potential sweeps down the axon like a bullet speeding down the barrel of a gun.
8. When the action potential reaches the end of the axon, it causes the axon to release **neural transmitters** into the **synapse**—the fluid-filled space between the axon of one neuron and the dendrites and cell body of a second neuron.
9. Neural transmitters released into the synapse excite the dendrites of the second neuron. It responds by **firing**, or generating an action potential of its own. The first neuron thus transmits a message to the second chemically.
10. **Sensory input neurons** receive information from the outside world and transmit this information to **neural sub-centers**, which then pass the information along to your cortex which decides how to respond.
11. **Command messages** telling your muscles to respond go out from the brain via **motor neurons**.
12. Your brain generates many types of electrical waves that show up on an **EEG** machine. When you are actively thinking, your brain produces **beta waves**. When you are resting peacefully with closed eyes, the visual areas in your brain generate **alpha waves**. When you are deeply asleep, your EEG record will show **delta waves**.
13. The two hemispheres of your brain are connected by a bridge of tissue called the **corpus callosum**.
14. Damage to various parts of the brain can

cause a condition known as **epilepsy**. Epileptic seizures show up on an EEG machine as **spike-shaped brain waves**.

15. If epileptic seizures become too frequent or severe, a surgeon may cut the corpus callosum. This **split-brain operation** may leave the patient with "two minds in the same body."

16. In right-handed people, the left hemisphere is **dominant**, has the power of speech, and controls coordinated movements of the body.

17. The minor or **perceptual/emotional hemisphere** can understand most language, but usually does not speak. It seems more specialized to handle perceptual patterns and emotional expression than is the dominant hemisphere.

18. In split-brain patients, the minor hemisphere can communicate with the outside world by moving the left hand.

19. What we call **conscious awareness** seems a function of the talking hemisphere, while **unconscious** creativity and artistic ability seem more a function of the perceptual/emotional half of the brain.

(Continued from page 28.)

"What an appropriate place to hide a secret," Colonel Garcia said, caressing Patrick's head again.

"I don't understand," said Captain Hartman. "How can the boy have a secret in his brain that the police over *there* could not discover?"

Colonel Garcia beamed. "Because Tavela knew more than they did, for one thing. Because they are atheists and God-haters, for another."

"Are you trying to tell me that Tavela hid the secret in Patrick's *soul*?" Captain Hartman said, a touch of sarcasm in his voice.

"Not quite, Captain, but perhaps you are closer than you know." The woman turned to the young man sitting beside her. "Tell me, Patrick, did you mention the Bible to the secret police when they questioned you?"

"Yes."

"And I'll bet they laughed, didn't they? And spoke of fairy stories and capitalist fancies, didn't they?"

Patrick nodded his agreement.

"But 'understanding is more precious than rubies,' Patrick. Don't ever forget that. Tavela knew we would understand. And we do."

"I don't understand at all," said Captain Hartman.

Colonel Garcia grew serious. "It is simple, when you know how the brain actually works. Patrick, when Dr. Tavela operated on you, he cut your corpus callosum, didn't he?"

"Yes, I think that was it. He said it would stop the seizures."

Nodding, Colonel Garcia continued. "And then he tested the two hemispheres of your brain to determine what each could see and hear and respond to."

"What has that got to do with the formula?" asked the Captain.

"*Everything*, if you understand the third chapter of Proverbs. You see, the 'mask' that Patrick looked into was a device which presented stimuli to just one half of his brain. If Dr. Tavela showed something to the left hemisphere, Patrick would be conscious of it and could answer questions about it verbally." She looked at the young man. "Is that not so? Didn't he ask you what you could see?"

"All the time," replied Patrick. "Sometimes I could tell him, and sometimes I couldn't."

"But even if you couldn't tell him what you saw, you could point to it with your left hand, couldn't you? Not with your right hand, of course, but with your left hand?"

Patrick considered the matter. "Yeah, you're right."

"Ah," said Captain Hartman. "I think I see what you mean. 'And in her left hand is riches and honor.' When Tavela knew the police were coming for him, he had half an hour to hide the secret formula where we could find it later. Not in the cast or in the bandages, because the police would check them."

Patrick nodded excitedly. "Yes, they took off my cast and changed my bandages. And they took lots of X-rays."

"And they didn't find anything, because they rejected the clue to the Bible," continued the Colonel.

Hartman smiled. "Because Dr. Tavela had hidden the formula in the right half of Patrick's brain. But how did he do that?" he asked.

"He must have whispered it in Patrick's left ear," replied Colonel Garcia. "Sounds from the left ear are recorded strongly in the right hemisphere, and but very weakly in the left half of the brain."

Hartman seemed confused. "But his left hemisphere doesn't *know* what the formula is at all!"

"That's what the loud noise was for, Captain. To block out the very weak whispering. Patrick's left hemisphere heard loud noises and missed the whispering. Patrick's right hemisphere heard very weak noises and loud whispering. So it knows, but Patrick doesn't, eh?" She smiled at the young man. "You really aren't conscious of what the formula is, are you?"

"No," he said, a puzzled look on his face.

Hartman's confusion continued. "But the secret police gave Patrick extensive polygraph tests, Colonel Garcia."

The woman laughed. "You missed another clue, Captain. Tell me, why do you think Dr. Tavela said it was lucky that Patrick broke a bone in his *left* hand?"

"Oh, of course," replied Hartman. "Because of the cast on Patrick's left hand, the police had to put the polygraph electrodes on the palm of his right hand."

"Which is controlled by the left half of Patrick's brain . . ." said the Colonel.

"Which *wasn't* conscious of the secret and hence couldn't give it away."

"Exactly." The woman picked up the pencil from her desk and wrote "Yes" and "No" on a sheet of paper. Then she put the paper close to Patrick's left hand. "Now, Patrick, I'm going to ask you some questions, but I don't want you to answer out loud. Instead, I want you to point to 'Yes' or 'No' on the paper with your *left* hand. All right?"

"All right," he responded, his left hand moving toward the paper.

"Patrick," the Colonel continued, "I want to talk to your right hemisphere. If you hear what I am saying, please point to 'Yes.'"

Patrick's fingers touched "Yes."

"Patrick, did Dr. Tavela tell you the secret formula?"

"No," said Patrick out loud. But his left hand pointed to "Yes."

"Weird," muttered Captain Hartman.

Patrick stared at his left hand in amazement. "I don't understand what I'm doing."

Colonel Garcia gave the young man a hug. "In the world of espionage we tell our agents, 'Never let your right hand know what your left is doing.' You are the only person I know of who can actually follow that advice. Because of your special brain, you have helped us, and Dr. Tavela, and even yourself. Be proud of that." Then she sighed and stood up. "Come, Patrick. It is time that your left hand had a long talk with one of our chemists."

Patrick's left hand pointed to "Yes."

Recommended Readings

Brown, T.S., and Patricia M. Wallace. *Physiological Psychology* (New York: Academic Press, 1980).

Galin, David. "Implications for psychiatry of left and right cerebral specialization," *Archives of General Psychiatry*, 31 (1974), pp. 572–583.

Gazzaniga, Michael S., and J.E. LeDoux. *The Integrated Mind* (New York: Plenum Press, 1978).

Sperry, R. W. "Hemisphere deconnection and unity in conscious awareness," *American Psychologist*, 23 (1968), pp. 723–733.

Springer, S.P., and G. Deutsch. *Left Brain, Right Brain* (San Francisco: Freeman, 1981).

Sterman, M.B. "Biofeedback and epilepsy," *Human Nature*, vol. 1, no. 5 (1978), pp. 50–57.

Sleep, Drugs, and Altered States of Consciousness

3

Did You Know That . . .

"Consciousness" is a "primitive term" that is almost impossible to define?

One way to alter consciousness is by speeding up or slowing down your brain's activity level?

Your body has regular physiological rhythms that vary according to the time of day?

No one really understands why people sleep and dream?

You go through several 90-minute sleep cycles nightly?

You dream more just before you awaken?

When you dream, your muscles are paralyzed so you won't act out your dreams?

Some people are able to control what they dream about?

Nightmares frequently occur after you've stopped taking sleeping pills?

Your brain produces natural pain-killers called endorphins that are similar to morphine?

Pregnant women secrete extra amounts of endorphins just before labor?

"Runner's high" may be due to endorphins?

Under controlled conditions, alcoholics cannot tell the difference between tonic water and vodka?

Most of the psychological effects of alcohol may be due to the drinker's expectations rather than to the drug itself?

People in the US spend 30 billion dollars a year on cocaine?

LSD was once used in the treatment of alcoholism?

There is no evidence that marijuana causes long-term health problems, but the drug can cause rather severe short-term disturbances?

"Perchance to Dream"

The Washington Bureaucrat leaned back in his overstuffed chair, puffed on his pipe, and meditated quietly as he looked at the man and woman sitting in front of his desk. They were nice people, really—bright, eager academics—and he did want to help them. They needed research funds to study some savages living in a jungle in South America, and were obviously good at their jobs. But it was a pity they knew so little about the savages who lived in that "jungle by the Potomac" called Washington, D.C.

"Look," the Bureaucrat said, putting down his pipe. "It's a simple trade-off, really. You, Dr. Ogdon, and your husband are both psychologists. You want to go study language development in some very primitive people who live near the Amazon. Right?"

Susan Ogdon looked at her husband and then nodded assent.

"Well," continued the Bureaucrat, "Our department wants someone to study marijuana use, and in just the same sort of backwoods people. We don't care what language these people speak or how they learn to speak it. But we do want to find out how pot-smoking affects their lives, their health, and their ability to get along in the world. You make our study for us, and we'll pay for the research." The Bureaucrat picked up his pipe again and leaned back in his chair. "What you choose to do on your spare time is your own affair, naturally. If you want to study language development on the side, we couldn't care less."

The woman cleared her throat. "What do you wish us to prove for you?"

The Bureaucrat sat bolt upright. "Nothing! Nothing at all! We have no preconceived notions of what your findings will be." The man paused, remembering how upset the Deputy Assistant Secretary got at the mere mention of marijuana. "Well, no *official* preconceived notions, you understand. But truthfully, we'll accept and let you publish whatever results you get."

"Why us?" asked Roger Ogdon.

"Because you've been there, and you know the people. Otherwise you wouldn't want to do your own research there." The Bureaucrat's voice softened and he put on his warmest smile. "Speaking personally, I do happen to be quite interested in language development. But the department simply is not able to fund such projects these days. So, when I read the proposal you sent us on language development in primitives, I thought . . ." He let his words drift slowly toward the ceiling like verbal pipe smoke.

The woman's face brightened. "Roger," she said, turning to her husband. "I do believe we ought to consider it. But we'd surely have to think some about how to measure the effects of long-term marijuana smoking on *anybody*, much less on the natives."

"You're right, Sue," Roger Ogdon said. He turned in his chair and looked straight at the Bureaucrat. "Why do you want us to study Amazon primitives? If you want to know the effects of pot-smoking on American citizens—and I suspect you do—why not do your research right here in Washington? Surely there are enough people in government who . . ."

"You're thinking of the Previous Administration," said the Bureaucrat quickly. "But really, you two, you know we can't get a really random sample of long-term pot smokers here, because the people who would volunteer wouldn't be representative. Besides, I suspect those natives have been smoking pot for many generations. You can look for long-term genetic effects as well as measuring the problems it gives them today."

Sue Ogdon frowned. "I thought you said you had no preconceived notions of what we'd find. What if there aren't any long-term genetic effects, or any real problems today?"

Now it was the Bureaucrat's turn to frown. These people were giving him a mild headache. Surely they saw that he was trying to help them. Why didn't they just take the money, and do what they were told? He reached in a desk drawer and took out an aspirin. Taking a sip of water, he swallowed the tablet quickly.

"Look, Dr. Ogdon," he said. "I will be frank with you. It would greatly please certain people upstairs if you found that marijuana had bad effects on the natives. Maybe that's what you'll find, and maybe not. But let's get things straight. I don't care what you find. Just plan the best study possible, use as many controls as you can, and get the facts. We'll pay the bills no matter what."

"Haven't you supported similar studies before?" asked the woman.

The Bureaucrat's face went slightly white. "Er, yes, I believe so. A couple, perhaps. But the more research is repeated, the more firmly we can believe in the data. As my senior professor in graduate school said, 'Replication is good for the soul.'"

Susan Ogdon persisted. "What did the other investigators find?"

"Now, now," said the Bureaucrat in a soothing tone of voice. "I'd rather you approached this problem with fresh minds. Just make sure that you measure the biological, psychological, and social effects of marijuana use, and do so as objectively as you can. That's the important thing."

Roger Ogdon was puzzled. "I don't think I've read the results of those 'couple of studies' you've already funded."

"Well," said the Bureaucrat, reaching for another aspirin. "I don't believe we've published the results yet. Later this year, perhaps . . ." He let his words drift off again.

Susan Ogdon frowned in surprise. "You mean, you didn't publish the results because the data didn't come out the way you expected them to? Then why do you want to pay for still another study whose results you may have to suppress?"

The Bureaucrat put down his pipe in an angry gesture. "Listen to me. You both are psychologists, and you're supposed to be able to understand why people and organizations act like they do. You know perfectly well that it takes a long time for an organization to change its mind on a subject. It takes a lot of data to accomplish that miracle, and a lot of gentle pushing from inside. You go do the study, and report *anything* you find. Do your own work on the side, if you wish. And leave it up to me to see that your data have the maximum impact. Okay?"

The man and woman exchanged glances. Then the man said, "Well, I think we understand each other. We'll go plan a study, and submit a proposal to you. If we agree on the details, you'll get us the funding. And, as you said, any other research we do 'on the side' is our business."

The Bureaucrat beamed. "Marvelous! I hoped you'd see it that way. Now, let's go find a drink somewhere and celebrate!"

(Continued on page 77.)

Consciousness

This chapter is about the biological basis of altered states of **consciousness**. It touches as well on drugs—how they affect your body and brain, how they influence the workings of your mind, how they alter your behavior, and how they affect your relationships with other people. This chapter also discusses that blissful state called sleep, and those sometimes unblissful experiences we call dreams and nightmares. Sleep and dreaming are good examples of altered states of awareness.

However, if you wish to find out some new things about drugs, sleep, and dreams, you will have to pay a small price for that pleasure. That is, you will have to learn a bit more about the *systematic interactions* among your brain, your mind, and your social environment. For unless you know something about what goes on inside your brain, and how the **synapse** really works, the new information about your states of mind may not make much sense to you.

So let us begin with what may seem a dumb question. What do we mean by the term *consciousness*? After all, if the main theme of this chapter is *altered* states of consciousness, perhaps we had better first make sure that we know what it is we're altering.

Primitive Terms

Every science has what are called **primitive terms**. That is, every science has ideas or concepts which are so elemental that they are exceptionally difficult to define.

For example, "energy" and "matter" are two primitive terms in the field of physics. You must have a rough notion of what these words mean, but you should also realize that great philosophical battles have been fought over their exact definitions.

In biology, there is probably no term more difficult to define than "life." Biologists have spent many centuries trying to pin down just what "life" is—and isn't. But, in truth, there is no one definition for "energy" or "matter" or "life" that all scientists will agree is completely accurate.

Psychology has its primitive terms too. One of these is *consciousness*. (Another, in case you're wondering, is *mind*.) The dictionary gives many definitions of "consciousness," most of which have to do with awareness, awakeness, understanding, being alert, or even being alive. Some of the dictionary meanings have to do with *self-awareness*, or the experience of knowing that you are having the experience of knowing. But no two psychologists will agree completely on the precise meaning of "consciousness" (nor of "mind," for that matter).

One reason that primitive terms give us fits is that these "elementary concepts" often refer to processes or conditions, rather than to things or objects. For instance, it is much easier to define a track shoe than it is to define the act of running. *Objects*, such as track shoes, usually have a location in space, and can be measured accurately. *Processes* such as running often have no clear-cut beginning or end, and there are very few processes that you can hold a ruler to or weigh on a scale.

Conscious awareness is an *internal mental process* which is even more difficult to talk about than is that behavioral process we call running. For self-awareness is something that occurs inside your head and can't be seen or observed directly. Anyone with eyes can tell whether you are running or standing still, but not even a psychologist can read your mind. All a psychologist can do, really, is to look at your actions and listen to what you say, and then make educated guesses about the mental processes that go on inside your head.

What can we do, therefore, to discover what consciousness is all about? Well, if we begin with the notion that consciousness refers to a process— *a sequence of events*—rather than to a "thing" we can touch or smell or see, then we're off to a good start in defining this primitive term.

And define it we must, for *consciousness* is one of the most controversial yet important concepts in all of psychology.

The Process of Consciousness

The following five points are perhaps as close as we can come (at the moment) to defining the process of consciousness scientifically:

1. You take in information from the world around you (and from your own body).
2. You recognize that you have (or haven't) experienced these inputs before.
3. You make decisions about what these sensory inputs mean, and what their emotional value might be to you.

4. You respond to the inputs.
5. You notice what the consequences of your actions and feelings are.

If we include "self-consciousness" in our definition, we must add a sixth point—namely, that you are aware of what you have done and can describe your inner processes verbally if asked to do so.

This definition surely gives us a better "handle" to study and discuss consciousness than we had before, since we know that inputs, internal processes, outputs, and feedback are necessary to the experience of self-awareness. And even if we cannot inspect your consciousness directly, we can at least measure the inputs, outputs, and feedback that so strongly influence what you think and feel. And we can deal objectively with your verbal report of your own "self-consciousness."

There is one more point that we should make about consciousness. If it is a process, then it *exists in time*. Indeed, it is hard to imagine any definition of consciousness that doesn't include an awareness of *duration*, or the passage of time. For example, when you are awake, you are surely aware of the hours ticking away, one by one.

On the other hand, it's quite unlikely that you consciously mark off the hours when you are deeply asleep. Perhaps that's one reason why we assume that you're *not conscious* when you're fast asleep. But what happens when you dream? Aren't you aware of temporal relationships when you're dreaming of winning a race (or when you're running away from some monster in a nightmare)? Is dreaming then a form of consciousness, or of non-consciousness?

In truth, both sleep and dreaming are two everyday examples of what we call "altered states of consciousness." Let's look at them more closely, both to learn about these fascinating if ordinary events, and to learn more about normal or "unaltered" states of consciousness.

Sleep and Dreams

Although you may not be consciously aware of it, your body goes through rather regular **physiological cycles** every day. Your temperature, for instance, is usually lowest in the middle of the night (if that is when you normally go to sleep), begins to rise a few hours before you get up in the morning, reaches the "normal" 37° **Celsius** (98.6° **Fahrenheit**) a few hours after you wake up, and then begins to fall again a few hours before the time you typically go to bed.

This **diurnal** temperature change is very slight—usually no more than a degree or so—but it does seem to occur in just about everybody. *Why* this diurnal rhythm occurs, no one is really sure. But we do know that it takes place even in people who are totally inactive throughout the day.

Temperature and Sleep

The relationship between your body temperature and how long you sleep is an interesting but complex one. In your normal environment, long-standing habits and social demands usually exert a strong influence on when you fall asleep and when you wake up. However, suppose we put you in a sound-proof room with no windows, gave you all the necessities of life, and told you to sleep whenever you wished. What would happen then? This is precisely the question that Charles Czeisler and his colleagues asked, and the answer they gave late in 1980 was a surprising one.

Czeisler and his co-workers isolated 12 male volunteers for periods ranging from 16 to 189 days and let them sleep on any schedule they wished. Although the subjects had no cues as to what time of day it was, their bodies still maintained the normal **daily temperature cycle**. And the men still tended to fall asleep when their body temperatures were lowest and to awaken when their temperatures were rising toward the 37° C.

Consciousness (KON-shuss-nuss). The act or process of being aware, particularly of one's surroundings and bodily condition. Also, being alert, understanding what is happening.

Synapse (SINN-aps). The fluid-filled space between two neurons. See Chapter 2.

Primitive terms. Concepts or ideas that are basic to a particular science—so basic that the science cannot exist without these concepts. Because the terms are so fundamental, they cannot be readily defined except in their own terms.

Physiological cycles (FIZZ-see-oh-lodge-uh-kal). Changes in bodily activities that occur regularly and dependably, and that usually are strongly influenced by the outside world, or that are inherited, or both. The menstrual period in women is an example of a human physiological cycle that repeats itself about every 28 days.

Celsius (SELL-see-us). The European temperature scale in which water freezes at 0°. Named for the Swedish scientist Anders Celsius who developed the scale in the early 1700's.

Fahrenheit (FAIR-en-height). The US temperature scale in which water freezes at 32°. Named for G.D. Fahrenheit, a German scientist who developed the scale about 30 years before Celsius.

Diurnal (dye-YOURN-all). Anything that occurs every day. A physiological cycle with a "period" of 24 hours.

Daily temperature cycle. When isolated from sunlight and normal "time" cues, humans show a diurnal cycle of about 25.5 hours rather than 24 hours. The subjects in Czeisler's experiment thus followed the lunar 25.5-hour cycle rather than the solar 24-hour cycle.

"I'LL HAVE TO GET DR. CURTIS TO REDUCE HIS DOSAGE OF THE MOOD-ELEVATOR."

"peak." Under these circumstances, the men slept an average of 7.8 hours.

Occasionally, however, the subjects would fall asleep when their temperatures were close to the daily "peak." Under these conditions, the men slept an average of more than 14 hours—and some of them slept for 20 hours or more. In almost all cases, however, the subjects *awakened* during that part of their daily cycle when their temperatures were *rising*.

Oddly enough, there seemed to be little connection between how deprived of sleep the men were and how long they actually slept, nor was there any relationship between sleep-deprivation and how sleepy the subjects felt. Rather, they almost always reported being sleepy at the lowest point in their temperature cycle, and feeling alert when their temperature was highest.

We will have more to say about this experiment in a moment, when we discuss dreaming. But first we have to ask a most important question: Why do you bother to go to sleep at all?

The Function of Sleep

Sleep is obviously an interruption in your normal stream of consciousness—that much is clear. But scientists are still uncertain as to what sleep actually is or what functions it serves. True, we all need to rest now and again to recover from the day's activities. But does unconscious sleep help

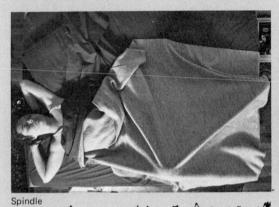

Spindle

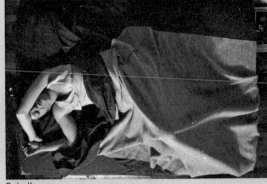

Spindle

Fig. 3.1A. In first of normal sleep's four stages, small, fast brain waves appear on EEG record **(below sleeper).**

Fig. 3.1B. In second stage, brain shows short bursts of activity (resembling spindles) as light sleep begins to deepen.

Spindle

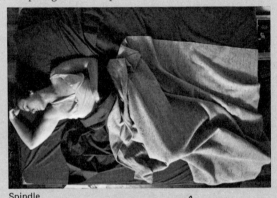

Spindle

Fig. 3.1C. In the third stage, larger, slower brain waves appear as the half-hour descent to deep sleep continues.

Fig. 3.1D. Fourth stage, with large delta waves, is followed by ascent to lighter sleep, then to dreaming (REM sleep).

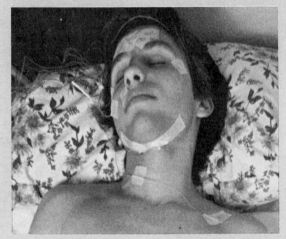

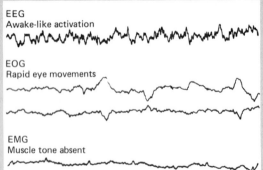

EEG
Awake-like activation

EOG
Rapid eye movements

EMG
Muscle tone absent

Fig. 3.1E. In REM sleep, when dreams take place, a volunteer's polygraph shows brain waves similar to waking state **(top row),** intense rapid eye movement **(middle),** and virtually no activity of chin muscles **(bottom).**

your body recover more than would "deep rest" in which you stayed peacefully awake? According to J.A. Horne, of Loughborough University in England, the answer is "no." In a 1979 review paper, Horne states that the major function of sleep is to *restore the brain*. The rest of your body, Horne says, can repair itself just as nicely during "deep rest" as it does when you are unconscious.

But the question still remains, if the main function of sleep is to let your brain restore itself *physiologically*, why do you have to be unconscious for the restoration to occur? We don't know the answer to that one. But there is growing evidence that sleep is important *psychologically* because it allows you to dream. And if sleep refreshes your body, dreams may be necessary for you to store the day's memories away and "freshen up your mind."

Sleep Cycles

Sleep is part of your daily activity cycle, but there are several different types or stages of sleep, and they too occur in cycles.

If you are an average sleeper, your sleep cycle will go something like this:

1. When you first drift off into slumber, your eyes will roll about a bit, your muscles will relax, and your breathing will slow and become quite regular. Your brain waves slow down a bit too, with alpha waves predominating for the first few minutes. This period is called *Stage 1 sleep*, and it is little more than a transition from being awake to being asleep. According to Wilse Webb, you spend from 1 to 10 percent of a night's sleep in Stage 1.
2. For the next half hour or so, as you relax more deeply, you will be in *Stage 2* of the sleep cycle. It is during this stage that your brain shows **sleep spindles** (see Fig. 3.1), which are bursts of waves that occur about 12–14 times per second. According to Webb, you spend from 40 to 60 percent of a night's sleep in Stage 2.
3. *Stage 3* sleep is a brief transition period, during which your brain waves slow down even more and sleep spindles tend to disappear. From 3 to 12 percent of sleep generally occurs at the Stage 3 level.
4. Then, about 40–60 minutes after you lose consciousness, you will have reached the deepest sleep of all. Your brain will show **delta waves**, and it will be very difficult for anyone to awaken you. This is *Stage 4* sleep, and it is during this stage that sleep-talking, sleep-walking, nightmares, and (in young children) bedwetting occur. Webb states that from 5 to 25 percent of your night's sleep is at Stage 4.

Sleep spindles (SPIN-dills). Bursts of brain waves with a frequency of 12–14 cycles per second that occur during Stage 2 sleep.

Delta waves. Large, slow brain waves with frequencies of less than 4 cycles per second. See Chapter 2.

Beta waves. The "activity pattern." Small, rapid brain waves that signal the person is alert or conscious.

REM. Rapid eye movement sleep that occurs toward the end of each 90-minute sleep cycle. It is during this period that most dreaming seems to occur.

5. You may think that you stay at this deep fourth stage all the rest of the night, but that turns out not to be the case. Instead, about 80 minutes after you fall into slumber, your brain activity will increase slightly. The delta waves will disappear, to be replaced by the **beta waves** that signal an active or "awake" brain. Your eyes will begin to dart around under your closed eyelids as if you were looking at something occurring in front of you. This period of *R*apid *E*ye *M*ovements is called **REM** sleep, and you spend from 15 to 35 percent of the night in REM sleep.
6. You are most likely to awaken during REM sleep (which is, in its way, somewhat similar to Stage 1 of the sleep cycle). But if you don't awaken, after 8 to 15 minutes of REM sleep, your brain waves will slow again. If this was your first cycle of the night, you probably will slip down all the way to Stage 4 sleep once more. Later in the evening, you may go only as deep as Stage 2 or 3. Whatever the case, some 80 minutes later your brain waves will speed up and you will go through another REM period.

If you are like most people, you will experience four to five complete sleep cycles per night, but both the quality and the intensity of the experience changes the longer you stay asleep (see Fig. 3.2). Your first cycle usually yields the deepest sleep, and your first REM period is typically the shortest. But no matter how many sleep cycles you experience during the night, you are more likely to awaken during an REM period than at any other time.

The length of the sleep cycle varies considerably from one species to another, and within a species it varies according to the age of the individual organism. Rats typically go through a full cycle in 10–13 minutes; children do so in 50–60 minutes; adult humans take 85–110 minutes; and adult elephants require about 120 minutes. (As we will see, however, there is considerable variation even among adult humans as to the number of cycles per night an individual needs or wants.)

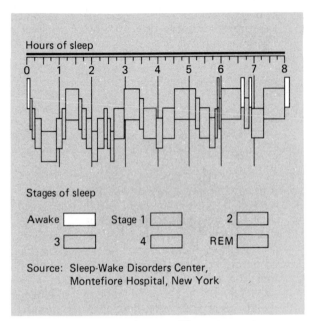

Fig. 3.2. A good night's sleep. Wakefulness gives way to deep sleep, then to the REM stage where most dreams occur. As the night wears on, dreams tend to lengthen.

In the figure:

Hours of sleep

Stages of sleep

Awake | Stage 1 | 2
3 | 4 | REM

Source: Sleep-Wake Disorders Center, Montefiore Hospital, New York

REM Sleep

It is during REM sleep that most dreams seem to occur. It is also during this period that most males experience an erection of the penis, and most females experience vaginal swelling and sometimes a hardening of their nipples. This sexual arousal typically occurs during each REM sleep period.

Dreaming seems to be primarily a function of the right hemisphere. Scientists from several laboratories have found that the right half of the brain is much more active electrically during dreaming than is the left. And Roger Sperry notes that while many of his split-brain patients reported having vivid dreams prior to the surgery, they reported no dreams at all after the operation. However, patients in other laboratories have given different reports, so the question is still in some doubt. It does seem clear, though, that the right hemisphere takes the lead during dreaming.

Dream "Paralysis"

During REM sleep and dreaming, you are almost incapable of moving. The muscles in your body are relaxed and capable of movement during both light and deep sleep. However, as you slip into REM sleep, most of the **voluntary muscles** in your body become *paralyzed*. Although your brain often sends orders to your muscles telling them to move, they simply don't respond. In more

technical terms—as we will see later in this chapter—we can say that REM sleep is accompanied by extensive *muscular inhibition*.

No one knows why this muscular inhibition takes place during REM sleep, but many scientists speculate that it serves to keep you from acting out your dreams. At least that is what Adrian Morrison at the University of Pennsylvania reported in 1981 to be true of cats. Morrison destroyed a very small amount of tissue in one of the lower brain centers of his animals. While awake, the cats behaved normally. When an REM period occurred during their sleep, though, the animals raised their heads, moved about, and struck out at imaginary objects. Morrison believes that the lower brain center he destroyed *actively inhibits* the acting out of dream behavior in normal animals.

Question: Why might you have trouble consciously remembering your dreams unless you say the dream out loud as soon as you awaken? And when you first awaken in the morning, why might you have difficulty "talking sensibly and getting your act together" for a short period of time?

Effects of Sleep Deprivation

If you are like the average person, you can tolerate up to 40 hours or so of sleeplessness without suffering too many ill effects. According to Wilse Webb, however, if you stay awake for more than 40 hours, you will probably begin to show an increased irritability and impulsiveness. Your decision-making processes will be affected, and you will react more slowly and make poorer intellectual judgments than you would when rested.

If you are deprived of sleep for 100 hours or more, you will very likely show considerable stress and even signs of mental disturbance. Which is to say that you will become almost as hostile and suspicious as are people who suffer from a "mental illness" called **paranoid schizophrenia**.

Whenever you are allowed to sleep after being severely deprived, your cycles may change to include much *more* Stage 4 (deep) sleep than usual—and a good deal *less* REM sleep than usual. However, as C.A. Czeisler and his associates note, you are unlikely to sleep for more than 11–16 hours even after you've been kept awake for 10 days straight.

If you are like most people, according to researchers Frederick Baekeland and Ernest Hartmann, you get from 7.5 to 8.0 hours of sleep per night. About 5 percent of the population regularly choose to sleep less than 6 hours a night, while another 5 percent will sleep more than 9 hours if given the chance. Baekeland and Hartmann call these people "short sleepers" and "long sleepers," and they differ from each other in a great many ways.

"Long" and "Short Sleepers"
The subjects of Baekeland and Hartmann's research were 20 young men who were identified as "short sleepers" and another 20 men who were "long sleepers." Each subject was given two nights to adapt to bedding down in a laboratory situation. Then Baekeland and Hartman attached an EEG machine to the men in order to study the sorts of brain waves the subjects showed while they were asleep.

Baekeland and Hartmann report that there were differences both in the type of sleep patterns the two types of sleepers showed and in their basic personalities. The "short sleepers" dozed off almost immediately and got but 5.5 hours of sleep. The "long sleepers" took much longer to get to sleep, but once **in the arms of Morpheus**, slept for about 8.8 hours.

Oddly enough, both groups averaged some 75 minutes of Stage 4 (deep) sleep per night. This fact led Baekeland and Hartmann to conclude that you get most of your really profound sleep during the first few hours you are in bed. However, the "long sleepers" averaged *almost twice as much REM sleep* per night as did the "short sleepers." And this need for lengthier sleep seems to stem at least in part from the personality characteristics of the men themselves.

"Short Sleepers"
Baekeland and Hartmann report that the "short sleepers" had been more-or-less average in their sleep needs until the men were in their teens. But, at about age 15 or so, the men voluntarily began cutting down their nightly sleep time because of pressures from school, work, and other activities. These men tended to view their nightly periods of unconsciousness as bothersome interruptions in their daily routines.

In general, these "short sleepers" appeared ambitious, active, energetic, cheerful, conformist in their opinions, and very sure about their career choices. They often held several jobs at once, or worked full- or part-time while going to school. And many of them had a strong urge to appear "normal" or "acceptable" to their friends and associates. When asked to recall their dreams, the "short sleepers" often claimed they hadn't dreamt at all. In similar fashion, their usual way of dealing with psychological problems apparently was to deny that the problem existed.

Voluntary muscles. Any muscles over which you have conscious control, such as the ones involved in talking, walking, or writing.

Involuntary muscles are those over which you have little or no conscious control, such as the ones involved in keeping your heart beating, your lungs breathing, or that help your stomach digest food.

Paranoid schizophrenia (PAIR-uh-noid skits-zoh-FREE-knee-uh). The major symptoms of this type of "mental illness" are illogical thought patterns, changeable delusions, and sometimes vivid hallucinations. Delusions of persecution ("they're controlling my mind by radio waves") are most common.

In the arms of Morpheus (MORE-fee-us). Morpheus was the Greek god of dreams. To go to sleep is to fall into the arms of Morpheus. The drug morphine gets its name from this same Greek god.

Introverted (INN-trow-ver-ted). A term made famous by the Swiss psychiatrist, Carl Jung. Introverted people spend much of their time looking inward, inspecting their own thoughts, feelings, and values.

"Long Sleepers"
The "long sleepers" had been lengthy sleepers since childhood. They seemed to enjoy their sleep, protected it, and were quite concerned when they were occasionally deprived of their desired 9 hours of sleep. They tended to recall their dreams much better than did the "short sleepers." Baekeland and Hartmann describe the "long sleepers" as being shy, anxious, **introverted**, inhibited, passive, mildly depressed, and unsure of themselves (particularly in social situations). A number of them, for instance, were still virgins at age 25–30. Several openly stated that sleep was an escape from their daily problems.

The Two Groups Compared
Baekeland and Hartmann suggest that "short sleepers" might be afraid of the subjective experiences that accompany dreaming. Indeed, the men seemed to curtail their sleep deliberately in order to escape any fantasies that might force them to inspect their own thoughts and feelings more carefully. By contrast, "long sleepers" seemed to need lengthy REM times in order to work out their personal uncertainties, fears, and conflicts during that altered state of consciousness we call dreaming.

Since Baekeland and Hartmann published their research, several other scientists have reported similar results. In 1979 Robert Hicks and his colleagues at San Jose State University reported a study of 500 college students. Hicks and his group found that the less students said they slept, the more likely the students were to be "hard-driving" types who experienced considerable stress in life. Hicks fears that "short sleepers" may be particularly prone to heart attacks later in life.

Dr. William Dement

In fact, people who sleep either too much or too little may be at risk as far as their health is concerned. In 1979, D.F. Kripke and his associates found that men and women who reported they usually slept either less than 4 hours or at least 10 hours were more likely to die within the next 6 years than were people who got normal sleep. The cause of death was typically a heart attack, stroke, cancer, or suicide—all related to stress. The risk factor was present in people of all ages, but was highest in individuals over 70.

A normal sleep pattern thus seems related both to good psychological and physical health.

Dreams

People have studied dreams and dreaming since the dawn of time, but it has only been in the last century that we have had the tools to investigate the subject scientifically.

The presence of "brain waves" in animals was discovered by Richard Caton in 1875. But it wasn't until 1930 that a German scientist named Hans Berger developed the first practical EEG machine. Thus it was Berger who first noted the changes in brain waves that occur during waking and sleep periods. (Alpha waves are still sometimes called the *Berger rhythm* in his honor.) Before Berger's pioneering studies, all we could do was to ask people to give us their *subjective* impressions about their sleep experiences. Thanks to the *objective* data we have gotten from EEG records, we have learned more about sleep in the past 50 years than we did in the previous 50,000.

The Dream Cycle

We've always known that sleeping people dream, but we didn't know much about the frequency of dreaming until the early 1950's. Prior to that time, scientists could do little more than record what people remembered about their dreams. Some people insisted they never dreamt at all; other individuals were confident that they dreamed the

whole night long. We now know, however, that everyone dreams *several times a night*, during each sleep cycle. For in 1953 Nathaniel Kleitman and Eugene Aserinski discovered the connection between REM sleep and dreaming by waking up their subjects at various times during the sleep cycle.

Kleitman and Aserinski noted that, if they woke up their subjects during deep sleep (Stages 3 and 4), the subjects seldom reported they were dreaming. However, if the subjects were awakened during initial light sleep (Stage 1), or particularly during REM sleep, the subjects frequently stated they had been dreaming. Furthermore, the subjects could almost always give rather vivid descriptions of what they had just dreamed. (If they were asked about their dreams later on, however, the subjects seldom could remember.)

It now seems fairly clear that, when you are in Stage 4 sleep, your sensory inputs are almost entirely cut off. In deep sleep, your cortex does little or no "processing" of incoming information, and only the lower centers of your brain are really functional. As each of your sleep cycles ends, however, a new one usually begins with REM sleep. Your cortex becomes active again, your eyes frequently begin to dart about under your eyelids, beta waves appear on your EEG record, and you rise gently but quickly from unconsciousness into the twilight zone of dreaming.

Question: During which part of the sleep cycle would it be most difficult to awaken you? Why?

Dream Frequency

According to Kleitman (and most other authorities), you probably have several dreams a night. In fact, you usually have several dreams within each REM period. Each dream probably runs from a few seconds to several minutes in length. And since REM periods at the beginning of your sleep tend to be the shortest, you probably dream less in the early evening than later on.

Dream Deprivation

Since all humans seem to dream nightly, we may assume that dreaming serves some necessary function. Although we are still not entirely sure what that function is, we now know that depriving people (or animals) of REM sleep can have fairly unpleasant effects. In 1960, Stanford University scientist William C. Dement reported data suggesting that dream time is necessary to many people's mental health.

Dement had subjects sleep in his laboratory. As long as the subjects were showing light or deep sleep, he let them alone. Once an REM period began, however, Dement would wake them up immediately. When the subjects would go back to sleep, their cycles would (as is almost always the case) begin at Stage 1, proceed through Stage 4, and from thence to REM. At this point in their cycle, Dement would wake them up again. His subjects therefore got all the *deep sleep* they normally would—but they got in very little *dreaming* because dreams are associated almost entirely with REM periods.

Many of Dement's subjects became cranky, annoyed, impulsive, and hostile when deprived of dreaming for several nights. They seemed to have considerable difficulty remembering things they had learned the day before (animals deprived of REM sleep also show poor memory for tasks unless given adequate REM sleep).

After his subjects had been dream-deprived for several days, Dement let them sleep without interruption. He reports that most of them showed greatly increased REM periods—as if the subjects were trying to "catch up" on all the dreaming he had deprived them of.

However, further experiments by Dement and other scientists have shown that not all people respond to REM deprivation in the way that Dement's first subjects did. In fact, some people can tolerate a week of dream-deprivation without showing too many ill effects. But, according to Robert Hicks, both humans and animals respond to REM-deprivation by becoming more aggressive when stressed. And animals deprived of REM sleep become more sensitive to pain. Not all psychologists agree with Hicks, however, so the actual effects of dream deprivation are still a matter of some debate.

Dream Content

If you are like most people, your first dreams of the night will tend to be rather dull and trivial—mostly having to do with things that you have done during the day. In later REM periods, however, your dreams will probably become more unusual, more vivid, more colorful, easier to remember, and sometimes more anxiety-provoking. During any one REM period, you are likely to experience a *sequence of related dreams*, or to run through the *same dream two or three times*. Mostly, though, you will dream about things that are of some interest or importance to you.

The connection between dream content and REM sleep is not entirely understood. But there does seem to be a close relationship between the *direction* in which your eyes move and what you are dreaming about. For instance, if you dream you are watching someone walk up a hill, your

Lucid dreaming (LOO-sid). Lucid means "clear." Lucid dreaming is that in which you maintain a low level of consciousness and sometimes can control the outcome of your dream.

REMs will be predominantly up and down. But if you dream you are at a tennis match, your eyes will mostly dart back and forth from right to left.

Question: If dreams are primarily a "right hemisphere" activity, would you expect to carry on lengthy conversations (or write a book) in most of your dreams?

Lucid Dreaming

In most of your dreams, things are more likely to *happen to you* than they are to happen because you consciously *want them to*. In recent years, however, psychologists have reported a number of techniques by which some individuals seem to be able to control both the content and the outcome of their dreams. And other scientists have developed ways of helping people maintain "conscious awareness" that they are dreaming even while the dream is taking place.

As an example of how you can "control the destiny of your dreams," consider a report by Rosalind Cartwright published in *Psychology Today* in December, 1978. Cartwright states that, by holding discussions with people before they went to sleep, she was able to train people to influence the outcome of their dreams. Apparently, when some individuals "want" their dreams to have happy endings, their right hemisphere often obliges.

The act of maintaining some low level of consciousness during REM periods is often called **lucid dreaming**. According to Stanford psychologist Stephen P. La Berge, lucid dreaming is most likely to occur during the last dream cycles of the night. La Berge states that, during a lucid dream, you are aware that your "experiences" are dreams rather than reality, and you can remember the dream quite well after you have awakened. Sometimes you can even evaluate what was happening during the dream, and take an active role in resolving the conflict that occurs during a lucid dream.

In 1981, La Berge reported results of a study of four people—two women and two men—noted for having frequent lucid dreams. These four individuals were trained (while awake) to move their eyes in a certain pattern and to clench their fists as a signal that they were "aware they were dreaming." Scientists then measured EEG patterns, eye movements, and fist clenchings while the four subjects slept in the laboratory for sev-

Table 3.1   A comparison of incubus and anxiety nightmares

	Frequency in Average Person	Occurs in Cycle	Stage of Sleep	Conditions Favoring Occurrence	Vocalizations and Movement	Content of Dream
Incubus Nightmare	Extremely rare	1,2	Stage 4	Sleep deprivation	Scream, sleepwalking	Cat-Animal suffocating dreamer
Anxiety Nightmare	Not uncommon	5,6,7	REM Sleep	Dream deprivation	None, usually	Falling, fleeing, mild fear

eral nights. Each morning the subjects would report whether or not they had experienced a lucid dream, and also whether they thought they had signaled that the dream had occurred.

According to La Berge, the subjects reported 27 lucid dreams while being observed in the laboratory. In 22 of these cases, the subjects believed they had been able to signal that they were aware they were dreaming. And indeed, this turned out to be the case. The special "eye movements and fist clenchings" occurred only during REM sleep periods, and only on those nights when the subjects reported having been aware that they were having a lucid dream.

Judging from La Berge's research, with the proper training you might learn how to exercise some control over the content of your dreams—and even be aware that you are doing so. However, the most vivid (and disturbing) type of dream that you are ever likely to have is one that you seldom have much influence over—the *nightmare*. Let us now examine these terrifying dreams in some detail.

Question: How might the differing abilities of the two hemispheres help explain lucid dreaming—that is, the fact that one part of your mind can be unconsciously dreaming while another is aware that a dream is taking place?

Nightmares

Imagine yourself comfortably sleeping in your bed, unaware of everything around you. Then you begin to sense—deep down inside you—that something has gone very wrong. Slowly, almost dimly, you regain enough consciousness to realize that you are suffocating, that some heavy weight is lying on your chest and crushing your lungs. Suddenly you realize that your breathing has almost stopped, and you are dying for air. Ter-

rified, you scream! At once, you seem to awaken. You see a black, cat-like beast crouched on your chest. Its saliva-drenched lips hover over your mouth as if it were sucking the very life out of your lungs. You try desperately to move, but you are paralyzed. A feeling of doom falls on you like a heavy blanket.

Suddenly you start to resist. Your pulse begins to race, your breathing becomes rapid, and you push futilely at the thing that is choking you to death. Your legs tremble, then begin to thrash about under the covers. You sweep the bedclothes aside, stumble to your feet, and flee into the darkness. You run clumsily through the house, your arms outstretched blindly in front of you, the cat-like animal in hot pursuit.

And then, all at once, you find yourself in your living room. The lights come on, the cat-beast instantly retreats to the shadows of your mind, and you are awake. You are safe now, but you are intensely wrought up and disturbed. You shake your head, wondering what has happened to you. You know that *something terrible occurred*, but you can hardly remember what it was. You are still disturbed, of course—but probably not nearly as upset as anyone who happened to be watching while you stumbled about the house blindly, muttering loudly to yourself.

Stage 4 Incubus Nightmare

The cat-beast dream is a classic example of the **incubus** nightmare, or *night terror*. According to Anthony Kales, a scientist at the Penn State Medical School, incubus attacks occur to but one person in several hundred. However, night terrors seem to run in families and thus may have a genetic basis. If someone else in your family has a history of night terrors, you are 10 times more likely to experience incubus nightmares than would ordinarily be the case.

Sleep, Drugs, and Altered States of Consciousness

Unlike most other dreams, the incubus nightmare begins during Stage 4 (deep) sleep and *not* during an REM period. The attack itself apparently begins when the pulse becomes *abnormally slow* during deep sleep, and breathing almost ceases. One of the lower centers in the dreamer's brain subsequently "panics" and responds as if the person were being suffocated.

According to Ernest Hartmann, the brain produces epileptic wave patterns during night terrors. Occasionally there are rhythmic movements of the tongue and other parts of the body that seem similar to the onset of a mild *grand mal* seizure. Hartmann points out, however, that victims of night terrors are not epileptic. He notes further that just reassuring them of this fact often helps to reduce the number and intensity of the attacks.

Night terrors can be dangerous. In the April 1981 issue of *Psychology Today*, Hartmann reports the case history of a man who experienced an incubus attack while sleeping in his car by the side of a major highway. The man "sleep-drove" his car onto the highway and crashed into another automobile, killing three people. Hartmann admits this is an extreme case, but believes that night terrors are always a *potentially* dangerous experience for those few people who experience them (and for others who are around when the attack occurs).

Anxiety REM Nightmare

By far more common than the incubus attack is the **anxiety nightmare**, which typically occurs late in the sleep cycle at the end of a very long REM period. If you have an anxiety nightmare, your body will seldom be aroused to a panic state. In fact, there will really be little change in your body's *physiological responses* during the nightmare. It is, therefore, the *psychological content* of the dream itself (being chased, falling, witnessing frightening events) that leads to the anxiety attack.

If you experience this sort of dream, you will usually awaken from it rather readily. You will seldom sleepwalk, and while you may talk or mumble a bit, you are not likely to scream. Unlike a night terror—which you seldom remember afterward—you probably will recall in vivid detail what happened to you in a nightmare. And, as distressing as the experience might seem to you, this type of dream is a fairly mild event compared to the incubus nightmare.

Incubus attacks are most frequent when your physiological need for *deep sleep* is greatest. Nightmares, however, occur when your psychological need for *REM sleep* is greatest. Thus incu-

Incubus (INN-cue-bus). From the same Latin word that gives us "incubate," meaning "to sit" or "to lie" on something. The incubus is an evil spirit said to lie on people while they sleep, and often to have sexual intercourse with women at night.

Anxiety nightmare. A disturbing dream that typically occurs during REM sleep, particularly during the last stages of the nightly sleep cycle. Often involves dreaming that you are about to fall from some height, or that you must flee from some enemy.

bus attacks occur following sleep deprivation, while nightmares occur following dream deprivation (see Table 3.1).

In his book *The Sleeping Pill*, Ernest Hartmann notes that various illnesses and high fevers often reduce the amount of REM sleep you experience. So do sleeping pills. Thus anxiety nightmares often occur when you are recovering from sickness, or just after you have stopped taking sleeping pills. Hartmann warns that taking drugs to help you sleep can be dangerous. For once you stop using the drug, your REM sleep increases tremendously, and you may have almost constant anxiety nightmares for several nights in a row. You may then return to the pills—not to put yourself to sleep, but to reduce your REM periods and hence get rid of all those disturbing anxiety nightmares.

Sleep and dreams are a type of altered consciousness that most of us experience every evening. Now that we have talked about them briefly, suppose we look at some other types and then try to determine what *causes* your conscious awareness to shift from one state to another.

Question: One of the most common anxiety nightmares is that of "running through molasses"—trying to escape something terrible, but not being able to move. What happens to your muscles during REM sleep that might explain the commonness of this type of anxiety nightmare?

Altered States of Consciousness

Psychologists generally assume that everything you feel or experience is reflected by the functioning of your body—particularly by the way in which your nervous system reacts. When your brain is alert (beta waves), you are consciously alert. When your brain sleeps (delta waves), you become almost totally unconscious. And when your brain waves speed up during sleep, you quite frequently dream. If your nerve cells fire at a faster-than-normal rate, you may experience great anxiety, fear, or pain—or great pleasure. If

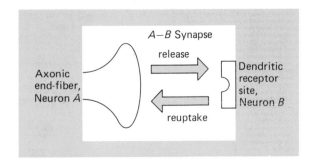

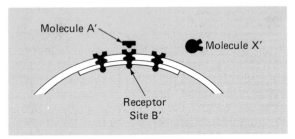

Fig. 3.3. Chemical transmitters released by axonic end-fibers of neuron A find a receptor site on the dendrites (or cell body) of neuron B causing B to fire. The transmitters then break up, and the pieces are taken up by A and put together again. **(top)**

Fig. 3.4. The "lock-key" hypothesis states that a transmitter molecule (the "key") must be the right size and shape to fit into a given receptor site (the "lock") on neuron B. In this drawing, molecule A fits receptor site B and thus can "unlock" neuron B and cause it to fire. Molecule X, however, has the wrong shape and thus cannot "unlock" neuron B. **(bottom)**

your neurons fire more slowly than usual, you may feel relaxed, peaceful, dreamy—or even mildly "down" and a bit depressed.

In short, when some change occurs in the *speed* at which important parts of your brain take in and process information, there is usually some corresponding change in (1) the way you think and feel about yourself; and (2) how pleasant or unpleasant you perceive the world around you to be.

Direct and Indirect Methods of Altering Consciousness

Drugs are a *direct* method of speeding up or slowing down neural firing—a quick if sometimes deadly way that people have chosen for a great many centuries. In just a moment, when we look at the effects of drugs on human behavior, we will find that there is a chemical compound that can affect your brain almost any way that you wish— *but usually at a cost of some kind.*

In the past, religion, philosophy, and mental discipline offered the only non-drug or *indirect*

ways to alter the state of your brain—but usually these methods are effective only after you have undergone long training and practice. Today we have much more efficient ways of educating or conditioning our brains, including the use of highly sophisticated electronic gadgets. However, before we can discuss the rather abnormal brain states that drugs and discipline can bring about, we first must delve a little more deeply into the manner in which your brain functions under more normal conditions.

The Molecules of the Mind

From a biochemical standpoint, your whole body is little more than a bag of complex molecules kept in place by your skin and skeleton. You take in such molecules as oxygen and food, digest or "process" them, and return the molecules in altered form back to the environment as waste products. If you don't get enough of the right kinds of chemical inputs, or get too much of the wrong kinds, you die.

The cells in your body are bags of chemicals too, kept together by a cellular "skin" or membrane. Your cells take in oxygen and food from your blood and excrete wastes back into the blood. The neurons in your brain are highly specialized in the way they function, but primarily they are *cells* that stay alive by maintaining a delicate balance between the chemicals inside the membrane and the chemicals that must remain outside if the neuron is to survive. But neurons do more than excrete waste products—they **secrete** very complex substances which affect everything that happens in your brain.

As you know from reading Chapter 2, when a neuron fires, a wave of electrical energy sweeps down the axon. This action potential generally does little in and of itself, except to cause the neuron to *secrete more molecules.*

Nerve cell *A* usually cannot stimulate nerve cell *B* by shocking it *electrically*. Rather *A* must stimulate *B* *chemically*—by releasing neural transmitters into the synaptic space between *A* and *B*. The more frequently neuron *A* fires, the more transmitter molecules it launches into the synaptic space—and the greater the likelihood that *A* will cause *B* to fire.

Receptor Sites

The dendrites and cell bodies of neurons seem to have tiny "gaps" or **receptor sites** that are particularly sensitive to neural transmitters. If a transmitter molecule from *A* lands on one of these receptor sites on neuron *B*, it triggers off a chemical reaction that causes *B* to fire. An action potential then pulses down *B*'s axon, causing *B*'s axonic end-fibers to release neural transmitters at the synapse between *B* and *C*.

If a transmitter molecule from neuron *A* doesn't land on a receptor site—*or if the sites are already filled by other molecules*—the transmitter will rapidly break down chemically and lose its effectiveness. And even if the transmitter molecule *does* find a receptor site on *B*, it will usually break down quickly—so another transmitter molecule can take its place and cause *B* to fire once more. The broken pieces of the transmitter will, *in either case*, mostly be taken up by *A*'s axon, put together, and used again (see Fig. 3.3).

Of course, you are not directly aware of all the chemical activity that goes on inside your brain. Yet it is exactly true that you cannot lift a finger, see a sunset, solve a problem, or even remember your own name unless you can somehow control the transmitter substances in your brain.

"Lock and Key Hypothesis"

Transmitter molecules come in many different shapes and sizes, but each neuron seems to secrete just one specific type of molecule. There also seem to be many different kinds of receptor sites.

Generally speaking, only one type of transmitter molecule will "fit into" a given receptor site. When a molecule of the right size and shape from *A* lands on the proper receptor site on neuron *B*, the transmitter "unlocks" *B* and causes *B* to fire. And just as a key of the wrong shape won't unlock your front door, a molecule with the wrong size or shape won't fit into *B*'s receptor sites and make it fire (see Fig. 3.4).

The belief that *specific transmitters* will only fit into *specific receptor sites* is called the **lock and key hypothesis** of synaptic transmission. As we will see, this hypothesis helps explain why various drugs can affect *highly specific parts of the brain*.

Function of the Synapse

The neurons in your cortex are so incredibly tiny that 20,000 of them could fit on the head of a pin. The synaptic space *between* neurons is, of course, much smaller yet. Indeed, several transmitter molecules placed one atop the other are enough to bridge the gap between most neurons.

The major purpose of the synapse seems to be this: It helps control the flow of information through your nervous system. With certain minor exceptions, neurons "fire" in just one direction— from the cell body to the axon. Thus in the illustration we have been using, *A* can cause *B* to fire, and *B* can cause *C* to react. But *C* can't fire *B*, and *B* can't fire *A*.

Secrete (see-KREET). The cells in your body manufacture many types of chemicals that are released or secreted into the blood or onto your skin. Cells in glands at the corners of your eyes secrete tears onto the surface of your eyes.

Receptor sites (re-SEPT-er sights). Only certain small spots or sites on the dendrites or soma seem to be sensitive to the transmitter chemicals. If nerve cell *B* is to be stimulated into firing by nerve cell *A*, the transmitter molecules must cross the synaptic space and reach one of these receptor sites.

Lock and key hypothesis (high-POTH-ee-sis). The theory that neurons secrete many types of transmitters, each of which can fit into just a limited number of receptor sites. If a transmitter "key" fits into a receptor "lock," it unlocks the neuron and causes it to fire.

Excitation. A neuron is said to be "excited" when it "fires"—that is, when it produces an action potential. The more action potentials it produces, the more "excited" the neuron is.

Inhibition. The opposite of excitation. Anything that prevents neural firing is said to inhibit the neuron.

Information about the world around you enters your body through such sensory receptors as your eyes and ears. Your receptors respond by sending messages to your brain along *input pathways* in your nervous system. But to get from your eye to your brain, a visual input must pass along several neurons in A-B-C fashion, crossing many synapses in the process. When you respond to these inputs, messages from your brain flow down *output pathways* in A-B-C fashion, again crossing several synapses before they reach your muscles.

Input and output pathways are one-way streets that carry neural messages in just one direction. The synapses act as traffic cops that prevent the messages from going the wrong way.

The *amount* of traffic passing along a neural pathway is determined by the number of transmitter molecules each neuron secretes. Anything that causes your neurons to fire faster—and hence release more transmitters—will increase the number of messages the pathways carry.

Drugs such as marijuana, alcohol, heroin, cocaine, and LSD can influence your brain in a variety of ways. But chiefly they act by either speeding up or slowing down the frequency with which *specific neurons fire*. And, as surprising as it may seem, a drug-induced change in the *speed* at which your nerve cells release transmitter molecules may cause a profound change in the *quality* of your conscious experience.

To appreciate why a *quantitative* change in neural firing can bring about a *qualitative* change in your conscious experience, you need to know something about neural **excitation** and **inhibition**.

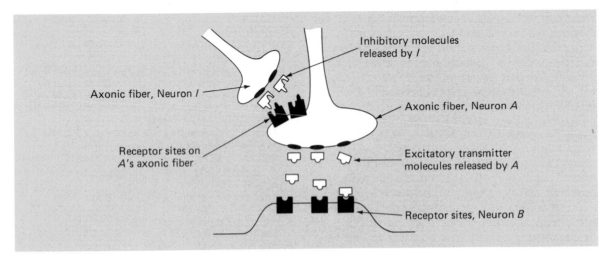

Fig. 3.5. Transmitter molecules released by neuron A's axonic fibers find receptor sites on neuron B and thus "excite" B into firing. But inhibitory transmitter molecules released by neuron *I* inhibit A from releasing more transmitters. Thus, when *I* "fires," it serves to inhibit A from exciting B.

Excitation and Inhibition

Suppose that, later on today, you are sitting quietly in your chair, reading. Suddenly you get an urge to eat an apple lying on the table beside you. So you decide to reach out and take the apple in your hand. Both the "urge" and the "decision" are communicated from one part of your brain to another by electro-chemical means.

The motor centers in your cortex transmit the order "reach for the apple" by sending an output message to the muscles in your arm telling them to get to work. The motor nerves that make synapse with your arm muscles respond by dumping transmitter chemicals into those "neuro-muscular" synapses. These transmitters cause *chemical reactions* in your muscles so they extend and contract in just the right way for your arm to be guided toward the apple.

Now, let's add some complications. Suppose that, just as your hand nears that big red fruit, you notice something that greatly disturbs you. For crouched just behind the apple is a huge, hairy black spider that you recognize as a tarantula! Suddenly a great many nerve cells in your brain that were sitting back resting will shift into emergency gear. These neurons will begin dumping a great many transmitter chemicals into a great many synapses all over your nervous system!

Your first impulse may be to jerk back your hand as quickly as you can. But any quick movement on your part might disturb the spider and make it attack. So what you really should do is to

freeze for a moment before you slowly retract your hand. (And then maybe you should exit from the scene as gracefully but as rapidly as possible.)

Excitatory and Inhibitory Synapses

At the instant you spotted the spider, your hand was in the process of *reaching out* for the apple. How do you go about explaining to your hand that you've suddenly changed your mind, and that it should *freeze*? The problem is that your motor nerves have already dumped a rather large supply of transmitter molecules into their synapses. So how does your brain recall those molecules once they've been launched into the synaptic space?

Actually, your brain will do three things at once. For each muscle that (when chemically stimulated) will cause your hand to reach out, there is another muscle that will make your hand pull back. So first, your brain will order the "pull-back" muscles to get *excited* and rescue you. Your neurons will obey this first order by releasing transmitters into the synapses that control the "pull-back" muscles.

Second, the motor centers in your cortex will *stop* sending output messages to the "stretch-out" muscles, so that no further transmitters are released into those synaptic canals.

But third, your brain goes one step farther. There are many neurons in your brain that can *inhibit* other nerve cells from firing. Whenever your brain needs to "shut down" neural transmission, it simply orders the inhibitory neurons to do their job.

How does this inhibition work? We're not entirely sure, but the most likely way is shown in Fig. 3.5. Here, neuron *A* makes synapse with *B*, as usual. Transmitters released by *A*'s axonic end-fibers cross the *A-B* synapse, find receptor sites on

B, and cause *B* to fire. However, as Fig. 3.5 shows, if neuron *I* happens to fire, it releases molecules which prevent *A* from releasing its transmitters. In this figure, *I-A* is an **inhibitory synapse**, while *A-B* is an **excitatory synapse**.

Excitation and inhibition are not just chemical events, however. They also exist at the intrapsychic and the social/behavioral level. To show you how changes in your body chemistry can affect both your mind and your behavior, let us explore the subject of *drugs*.

Drugs

A **drug** is usually defined as any substance that can affect the structure or functioning of your body. Actually, that definition doesn't mean very much because almost any chemical will have some kind of effect on you—if you take a large enough dose, or take it the wrong way. For instance, water is not usually considered a drug, but if you get too much of it in your lungs, you may drown.

A more useful definition is the one we will use in this book: A drug is any chemical which, when taken in relatively small amounts, *significantly increases or decreases cellular activities somewhere in your body*.

Most of the drugs we will discuss in this chapter have their main effects on neural firing,

"DR. GOTTSCHALK, I JUST HAD THIS REMARKABLE DREAM, AND I WAS WONDERING IF YOU COULD COME RIGHT OVER AND ANALYZE IT."

Inhibitory synapse (inn-HIBB-it-tory), **excitatory synapse** (ex-SIGHT-tah-tory). Neuron *A* causes *B* to fire when *A*'s axonic fibers release transmitters into the *A-B* synapse. This is an excitatory synapse. Neuron *I* can inhibit *A* from releasing transmitters, however, if *I* releases inhibitory molecules onto *A*'s axon. The *I-A* connection is an inhibitory synapse.

Drug. A chemical which significantly alters cellular activities somewhere in your body. For the most part, drugs increase or decrease cellular functions.

Neurological (new-roh-LODGE-eye-cal). From the word "neuron." Having to do with the functions of neurons.

usually by altering the rate or *speed* at which your nerve cells release synaptic transmitters. There are other ways that drugs can affect neural responses, but changing the rapidity of neural firing is perhaps the most common. Some drugs—such as caffeine—tend to increase the rate at which your neurons fire. Other drugs—such as sleeping pills—have an inhibitory effect on neural firing.

However, the actual effects a particular drug will have on a particular person are often complex and hard to predict. And, in order for you to guess how a drug will influence someone, you must know as much about the person's genetic background, past history, and present social environment as you know about the chemical composition of the drug itself. Thus a drug that affects you one way might affect another person in quite a different manner. And a pill that would have little influence on you when you were happy and content might cause you to experience great depression if you took it when you were "feeling down in the mouth."

Although we cannot always guess accurately how a particular drug will affect a given person, we can categorize drugs according to whether their **neurological** effects are fairly specific or rather general. Chemicals such as caffeine affect almost all the nerve cells in your brain the same way—they speed up the release of neurotransmitters at excitatory synapses. But other drugs—such as pain-killers—tend to inhibit neural transmission in many parts of your brain while having little or no effect on the rest of your nervous system. Still others—such as alcohol—seem to inhibit some synapses while exciting others.

Thus, in categorizing drugs, we will find it useful to ask three questions:

1. Does the drug have a specific or a general effect on neural transmission?
2. If the effect is general, does the chemical tend to increase or to inhibit neural firing?
3. If the effect is specific, does the drug mostly affect *inputs*, *cortical processes*, or *outputs*?

The Coca God, worshipped by natives in Colombia and South America.

system, which controls such involuntary activities as breathing, heart rate, and so forth. We will have more to say about your autonomic nervous system in Chapter 13. For the moment, all you need to know is that psychic energizers speed up many of your bodily processes that are controlled by synaptic transmission.

"Uppers" are also called **stimulants**, because they chemically stimulate your neurons into firing more often. As your nerve cells release more transmitters into the synaptic canals, your whole body speeds up its tempo. As a result, any or all of the following responses may occur:

1. Your heart beats more quickly.
2. Your mouth becomes dry.
3. Blood rushes to the surface of your skin.
4. The pupils in your eyes open or **dilate**.
5. You breathe more rapidly.
6. Your hair stands on end.
7. Your digestion is shut down.
8. Your appetite vanishes.
9. Your urine flow and bowel movements are inhibited.
10. You may become sexually excited if the environment or your own thought processes encourage you to do so.
11. Your muscles become tense, and your reaction times are speeded up.
12. You typically wake up and become alert, but often find it difficult to concentrate.

Caffeine is perhaps the most common "upper" in our society. Less common—and considerably more dangerous—is a class of drugs called by such names as **amphetamines**, pep pills, or **speed**. Amphetamine itself is often referred to as Benzedrine. Two other similar but more powerful drugs are Dexedrine and Methedrine. Since they all increase neural activity, any or all of these "uppers" can be referred to as *speed*.

Like any other drugs, "uppers" can be dangerous. For example, continued use of amphetamine (or any other type of "speed") can produce symptoms that are much the same as the severe mental disorder called paranoid schizophrenia we mentioned earlier in this chapter.

That is, where in the brain does the drug produce its effects?

Let us begin by looking at drugs that influence almost every one of your 15 billion nerve cells.

Drugs Affecting General Activity Levels

One of the most common effects a drug can have is to change your activity level. You normally walk at a certain pace, talk at a certain speed, sleep a certain amount each 24 hours. If you cared to make precise physical measurements of your own behavior, you could fairly readily determine what your own general level of activity would be in most situations. When you swim, ski, play tennis, jog, or dance, this level increases. The more active you are physically, the more rapidly *most* of your neurons must fire. Anything that increases your activity level also causes more transmitters to be dumped into the excitatory synapses in your brain and also in the synapses between your motor nerves and your muscles.

"Uppers"

"Uppers," or **psychic energizers**, are drugs that typically facilitate or increase synaptic transmission. "Uppers," therefore, usually make you more physically and mentally active. They do this by affecting nerve cells in your **autonomic nervous**

"Downers"

Drugs that slow down or inhibit neural activity go by the general name of "downers." The strongest "downers" in general use are the **barbiturates**, which are sometimes called "sleeping pills" because they depress neural activity so much that they often put a person to sleep.

The **tranquilizers** are both more specific in their effects and usually less powerful than the barbiturates. Tranquilizers affect the nervous system in several different ways. However, many of them act by exciting those neurons (such as *I* in Fig. 3.5) which *inhibit* other nerve cells from firing.

The general effects of "downers" are the opposite of those produced by "uppers." That is, "downers" slow the beating of your heart, take blood away from the surface of your body, and retard the rate at which you breathe. They also cause your pupils to close or constrict, and generally make it more difficult for you to react quickly to any emergency. Some "downers" are relaxing because they make it more difficult for you to move your muscles—it is hard for you to experience blind panic and the urge to flee when you are so relaxed that you can barely move.

"Downers" have physical and psychological side effects that range from mildly unpleasant to downright deadly. Wisely used, these drugs can be of considerable medical help. When abused, these chemicals can lead to depression and other severe types of mental disorders. And, as we will soon see, in the US "downers" are particularly likely to be abused by women.

Drugs Affecting Sensory Input

Information about the world around you comes to you through your sensory receptors. As we will see in later chapters, if you were totally cut off from the outside world, you would rapidly stop being a normal human being. But not all of the sensory messages that reach your brain bring pleasant news—some involve the experience of *pain*, a highly complex psychological experience we will discuss more fully in Chapter 17.

In part, pain is a *sensory input* signaling that something has gone wrong with the functioning of your body. Pain commands your attention because "it hurts." And because "it hurts," humans have long made use of various chemicals in order to rid themselves of pain. Some of these drugs— such as aspirin—have their **analgesic** or pain-killing effects by *blocking out* the neural messages before they can reach your brain and thus before you perceive them as "hurting." Other drugs— particularly those derived from the opium poppy— are analgesic because they inhibit the *processing* of the painful inputs in various neural centers in your brain.

Aspirin is perhaps the most common pain-killing drug known to humans. It is probably the only drug that everyone reading this book will have tried at least once. Aspirin occurs naturally in the bark of the willow tree and was first **synthesized** in 1860. Some 12 million kilograms (27 million pounds) of aspirin are consumed annually in the United States—enough to treat 17 *billion*

Psychic energizers (SIGH-kick). Drugs that speed up neural firing, that "turn on" the nerve cells by stimulating them to fire more often.

Autonomic nervous system (aw-toh-NOM-ick). That part of the nervous system which controls involuntary activities such as breathing, heart rate, digestion, and so forth. See Chapter 13.

Stimulants. Psychic energizers that stimulate neurons to produce more action potentials.

Dilate (DIE-late). To open, or expand.

Amphetamines (am-FETT-ah-meens). A type of stimulant or "upper." Also called "speed."

Speed. Any powerful neural excitant, stimulant, or "upper." In moderate doses, speed can pep you up, and make you feel good if you are depressed. After a while, you may begin to feel "jangly" and nervous, and you can't relax or go to sleep.

Barbiturates (bar-BITT-your-rates). Neural inhibitors that come from barbituric acid, often used as sleeping pills. Not to be confused with narcotics (from the Greek word **nark**, meaning "to benumb" or "to paralyze"), most of which come from opium or alcohol. Narcotics are more effective as pain-killers than are barbiturates, but both types are habit-forming.

Tranquilizers (TRAN-quill-eye-zers). Drugs that help people relax and become less afraid of things.

Analgesic (an-al-GEE-sick). From the Greek words meaning "no pain." Technically speaking, any drug that reduces pain without causing a loss of consciousness.

Synthesized (SIN-thuh-sized). Complex drugs like aspirin are often "manufactured" by plants or animals as part of a natural process. But all drugs are chemical molecules that can be made artificially or synthetically in a laboratory (if we are smart enough to figure out how to do so). It is much cheaper to make drugs like aspirin synthetically than to grow the millions of willow trees we would need to yield enough "natural" aspirin to drive away our headaches.

Opiate (OH-pee-ate or OH-pee-at). Any of the narcotic drugs that come from the opium poppy. Almost all opiates are habit-forming.

Morphine (MORE-feen). A product of opium. Morphine is a dream- or sleep-inducing drug and, like all opiates, is a powerful pain-killer.

headaches. As potent a pain-killer as aspirin is, though, it is also a deadly poison that must be treated with respect. Perhaps 20 percent of the deaths by poisoning that occur in the United States each year are due to an overdose of aspirin. And, when taken in large doses by a pregnant woman, aspirin may either kill the unborn child or cause it to be badly deformed.

The Opiates

Aspirin is a mild pain-killer. In case of severe pain, a more potent medicine—such as an **opiate**—is needed. *Opiates* are derived from opium, a drug used for centuries as an analgesic in the Near and Far East. When the seed pods of the opium poppy are slashed, a sticky resin oozes out. This resin is collected by hand, heated and rolled into balls, and then smoked in tiny pipes as opium.

In 1806, **morphine** was first synthesized from opium. Since morphine can be injected di-

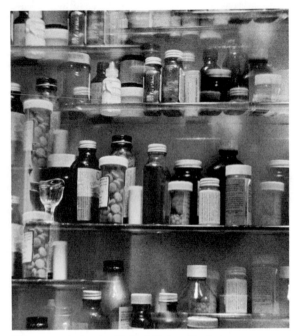

More people in the United States die from an overdose of legal drugs such as aspirin than from illegal drugs such as heroin.

rectly into the body in controlled amounts, and since it lacks some of the side effects of opium, morphine rapidly gained wide use in medical circles.

No one really knows why the opiates reduce or kill the experience of pain. It seems likely, however, that these drugs stimulate inhibitory neurons which then "turn off" the synapses in your brain which are involved in processing the painful inputs (see Fig. 3.5).

The Opioid Peptides

Morphine has one terrible side effect: It is very *addictive*. The exact biological mechanism underlying addiction is still not fully understood. However, there is considerable evidence suggesting that natural pain-killers produced by the body itself may be involved. These naturally occurring analgesics have many names, including **enkephalin**, **endorphin**, and **opioid peptides**. And when you learn how these natural analgesics work, you will understand a bit more about how they may be involved in morphine addiction.

During the 1970's, scientists both in Great Britain and in the United States isolated the first of these natural pain-killers, *enkephalin*, which is one of the endorphins. They found enkephalin in the brains of both rats and human beings. When enkephalin—or any other endorphin—is injected into the bodies of rats, it appears to reduce

pain at least as much as does morphine. However, the effects of the endorphins on the human body and on mental processes are complex and—as we will see at the end of this chapter—perhaps a little surprising.

Solomon Snyder and his associates at Johns Hopkins University were among the first to identify enkephalin. Snyder believes that all of us have a certain amount of this analgesic chemical present in our bodies at all times. The amount of enkephalin your body normally produces is sufficient to protect you from many of the ordinary aches and pains of life. When you experience severe pain, however, you are likely to turn to stronger medicine, and morphine is one of the strongest yet available.

Opiate Addiction

If, for medical reasons, you were to take morphine, it would act much as enkephalin does. That is to say, morphine would: (1) block neural transmission in your brain's pain centers; and (2) stimulate certain nerve centers involved in experiencing pleasure. But, according to Snyder, morphine also *inhibits the production of the endorphins*. Thus, when you take morphine for any length of time, your body stops manufacturing its natural pain-killers almost entirely.

If you use morphine daily for a month or so, you are likely to become *addicted to the drug*. Then, if you don't get your "daily fix," you feel miserable, you ache all over, you are depressed, and you may even experience convulsions. Why? Because, when you stop taking morphine, your body needs several weeks before it can replenish its supply of the endorphins. During this period of time, your body has no defense against pain. Thus even the slightest cut or bruise will be **excruciatingly** unpleasant. Little wonder, then, that so few morphine addicts withdraw from using the drug voluntarily.

When enkephalin was first discovered, Snyder hoped that it might be useful in treating morphine addiction. After all, if we could find some way to get the body to manufacture large amounts of endorphins, we could probably reduce the **withdrawal symptoms** that occur when an addict is cut off from morphine. However, research reported in 1976 by Eddie Wei and Horace Loh suggests that enkephalin is as addictive as morphine. If this is indeed the case, history will have repeated itself.

Late in the 1800's, scientists hunting for a non-addictive opiate (to replace morphine) stumbled upon **heroin**, which is also made from opium. Heroin is several times more powerful than morphine as a pain-killer, and at first heroin was touted as a solution to "the morphine problem." So, in the early 1900's, morphine addicts were given heroin instead. Unfortunately, heroin soon proved to be even more addictive and dangerous than morphine. Because of its addictive qualities, heroin is seldom used as an analgesic in the United States today—except by the million or so drug addicts who take it as regularly as their funds allow them to.

Local Anesthetics

Laughing gas, or nitrous oxide, is another example of a pain-killer that once enjoyed great medical popularity but which is not used much today. First discovered in 1799, nitrous oxide was often employed by dentists and surgeons as an analgesic because it made their patients so "happy" that tooth-pulling and minor surgery didn't seem to hurt very much.

The effects of laughing gas were often unpredictable, however, and dentists soon began using **procaine** or Novocain instead. Both procaine and Novocain are synthetic forms of **cocaine** that kill pain by *inhibiting neural transmission* wherever they are injected into the body.

Cocaine is a moderately strong drug made from the leaves of the coca plant. Cocaine, or "coke," is notorious for the rush of pleasure or **euphoria** that it gives almost immediately after a person takes it (usually by sniffing). Frequent use of cocaine can lead to a variety of problems, however, including severe damage to the nose and throat.

Cocaine was first used as a local anesthetic in the late 1800's by a Viennese doctor named Carl Koller. Sigmund Freud, who also lived in Vienna, learned of Koller's work and began experimenting with the drug. Freud found it such a pleasurable medication that he recommended it to his patients as a substitute for aspirin. When he saw the bad effects cocaine occasionally had, though, he changed his mind.

Americans were much slower to use cocaine "recreationally" than were Europeans. According to a 1979 government report, some 10 million people in the US now use cocaine fairly regularly, and another 5 million people have tried it at least once. In the March 1982 issue of *Scientific American*, Craig Van Dyke and Robert Byck estimate that cocaine sales run more than 30 billion dollars a year in the US alone. These scientists suggest that cocaine is not *physically* addictive, but is severely habit-forming. Surprisingly enough, Van Dyke and Byck also report that even experienced users could not tell the difference between sniffing cocaine and sniffing a **placebo**. Van Dyke and Byck believe that the effects of cocaine depend as

Enkephalin (enn-KEFF-ah-linn). A natural pain-killer discovered in the brain by scientists in the United States and Great Britain.

Endorphin (en-DORF-in). The general class of pain-killers produced in the brain. Enkephalin is one of several different endorphins.

Opioid peptides (OH-pee-oid PEP-tides). A peptide is a specific type of small molecule. The endorphins are all peptides that resemble opiates such as morphine. Thus the endorphins are a class of molecules called opioid peptides.

Excruciatingly (ex-CREW-she-ate-ting-ly). From the Latin word meaning "to nail to a cross." Anything that is excruciating is extremely painful.

Withdrawal symptoms. Those physical and psychological changes that accompany giving up a drug after you have become addicted to it. Vomiting, fever, loss of appetite, compulsive shivering, and hallucinations often accompany withdrawal from narcotics such as heroin.

Heroin (HAIR-oh-in). An opiate derived from morphine. Very addictive, or habit-forming.

Procaine (PRO-cane). Like Novocain (NO-voh-cane), a synthetic form of cocaine.

Cocaine (KO-cane). A "local" pain-killer made from leaves of the coca plant. Usually taken by "sniffing" the drug in powder form. Continued use of the drug leads to considerable damage of tissues in the nose and throat.

Euphoria (you-FOR-ee-ah). From the Greek word meaning "good feeling," hence a rush of pleasure.

Placebo (pla-SEE-boh). From the Latin words meaning, "I please." A harmless substance, such as a sugar pill. In drug experiments, any neutral or inactive substance given to subjects to make them think they are taking "the real thing."

Hallucinogens (hal-LEW-sin-oh-jens). Drugs that affect sensory input neurons, or "processing" neurons, and hence "trick" you into seeing or hearing or feeling things that really aren't there.

much on the user's past experiences, expectations, and present environment as on the drug's effects on body chemistry and neural transmission.

According to Van Dyke and Byck, deaths from "recreational" use of cocaine are rare. However, in large doses cocaine can cause panic and even convulsions.

Drugs Affecting Central Processing

Analgesics reduce pain in one of two ways: They either prevent painful inputs from occurring, or they keep the inputs from stimulating the "pain centers" in your brain by inhibiting neural transmission. Which is to say that analgesics "work" because they prevent you from experiencing the world (and your body) as it really exists.

Hallucinogens

The **hallucinogens** are a class of drug that work in quite a different way. Rather than affecting inputs, hallucinogenic drugs act on the central

Table 3.2. *Comparison of various symptoms of schizophrenia with those induced by PCP, sleep deprivation, and LSD*

Symptom	Acute Schizophrenia	PCP	Sleep Deprivation	LSD
Faulty mental association	+ + + +	+ +	+	+ +
Overinclusive thoughts	+ + + +	+ +	+	+ +
Dreamy withdrawal	+ + +	+ + + +	+ + + +	+ + + +
Emotional problems	+ + + +	+ +	+ +	+ + +
Attention disorder	+ + +	+ + +	+ + + +	+ + +
Depersonalization	+ + +	+ + + +	+ + +	+ + +
Delusional thinking	+ + + +	+	+	+
Visual hallucinations	0	+	+ + + +	+ + + +
Auditory hallucinations	+ + + +	0	+	0
EEG changes	0	+ + +	+ + + +	+ +
Response to isolation	+ +	+ +	+	+ +

Adapted, by permission, from a table in E.F. Domino, ed., *PCP (Phencyclidine): Historical and Current Perspectives*. Ann Arbor, Mich.: NPP Books, 1981.

processing areas of the brain that try to "make sense" out of these sensory messages. And, by speeding up activity in some brain centers and inhibiting activity in other centers, hallucinogens make you experience or perceive the world as it actually *isn't*. **LSD, mescaline, psilocybin**, and **PCP** are perhaps the best-known hallucinogens in our society, although a wide variety of other drugs also fall into this category.

LSD

LSD is an artificial or synthetic chemical not found in nature. It was first made in a Swiss laboratory in 1938. However, its rather profound effects on human behavior were not appreciated until five years later. In 1943 Albert Hofmann—the Swiss scientist who had first synthesized LSD—accidentally licked some of the drug off his fingers. About half an hour later, knowing that something unusual was happening to him, Hofmann decided to stop work and bicycle home from the lab. Wobbling and weaving all the way, he finally made it. But by the time he reached his house, everything he saw looked so terrifying, Hofmann was sure he had gone mad.

Because LSD caused people who took it to experience some of the symptoms associated with **schizophrenia** (see Table 3.2), Hofmann believed that the drug might be useful in brain research. Therefore, he suggested that it be given to people with mental disorders. LSD was first tried with patients in a Swiss mental hospital and, as is often the case, a few of these patients did seem to get better. Whether this improvement

was due to the drug or to the special attention the patients got was never proven, however.

In the 1950's, LSD was occasionally used in psychotherapy in the United States, particularly in the treatment of alcoholism. However, in the late 1960's, a study by A.M. Ludwig and his associates showed that about 75 percent of alcoholic patients given psychotherapy got well whether or not LSD was used in their treatment. Similar research by other scientists suggested that LSD was of little value in treating *any kind* of mental disorder. Writing in the January 1981 issue of *The Sciences*, Harvard psychiatrist Lester Grinspoon states that the use of LSD in therapy *may* have potential at some time in the future. But the issue is still very much in doubt.

Mescaline and Psilocybin

Mescaline is a chemical found in buttons on the peyote cactus. It can also be produced in synthetic form in a laboratory. The hallucinogenic effects of mescaline have been known for centuries to American Indians, who at times have eaten peyote buttons as part of their religious ceremonies.

Less well known is a drug called *psilocybin*, found in a mushroom that grows wild in certain parts of the world. Psilocybin also produces hallucinations and also has been used in religious ceremonies.

PCP

PCP, also known as Angel Dust, has replaced LSD and mescaline as the most abused hallucinogen in the United States. Discovered in 1956 by Victor Maddox and Graham Chen in Detroit, PCP was used for a time as an anesthetic for both humans and animals. However, it was banned for human use after tests showed that in large doses it produced convulsions, uncontrollable rage, **coma**, and death.

In his 1981 book on PCP, Edward Domino notes that PCP acts as a **dissociative anesthetic**. That is, the drug doesn't make patients unconscious. Rather, it "disconnects" them from their bodies—and from their environments. One male subject who took PCP in an experiment reported that his legs were "ten miles long," while a female subject said, "I feel like the head of a pin in a completely black atmosphere." Domino believes that PCP inhibits neural activity in the *processing areas* of the brain. And, by doing so, it induces psychological symptoms similar to those reported by people suffering from a variety of mental disorders (see Table 3.2).

One of the greatest dangers of PCP seems to be the unpredictability of its effects—sometimes it causes euphoria, sometimes fear, sometimes rage, sometimes severe depression, and sometimes a complete loss of reality. In 1980, almost 50 percent of the patients admitted to mental hospitals for drug-related problems suffered from PCP **psychosis**. However, as Domino notes, by the spring of 1981 abuse of PCP seemed to be falling off markedly.

No one really knows why the hallucinogens affect people as they do. But, according to Edward Domino, hallucinogenic drugs seem to influence neural processing in two important ways. First, they decrease the brain's ability to *screen out* many types of sensory inputs. And second, the drugs seem to disrupt the brain's attempts to *integrate complex stimuli*. Let us look at both effects in more detail.

First, as we will see in Chapter 8, there are parts of your nervous system that allow you to gate out unimportant sensory inputs and pay attention only to those sensory messages that you wish to focus on. Hallucinogens, however, seem to open up the sensory gates and let almost all inputs come through with equal intensity. People who take LSD or PCP often appear to become confused and frightened by this onslaught of uncontrollable inputs. Terrified by this loss of sensory control, the drug-taker may withdraw from the world in order to try to "make sense out of sensory experience."

Second, people who are "high" on hallucinogens often cannot put complex inputs together to

LSD. Common name for d-lysergic acid di-ethyl-amide (dee-lie-SIR-gick A-sid die-ETH-ill-A-midd). Also called "acid." Synthetic hallucinogen first synthesized in Switzerland.

Mescaline (MESS-ka-lin). An hallucinogen found in the peyote (pay-YO-tee) cactus.

Psilocybin (SILL-oh-SIGH-bin). An hallucinogenic drug that comes from a wild mushroom.

PCP. Common name for phencyclidine (fenn-SIGH-kli-deen). Also called "Angel dust."

Schizophrenia (skitz-zoh-FREE-knee-uh). A severe mental disorder involving disordered thought processes. There are several types of schizophrenia. See Chapter 23.

Coma (KO-mah). An abnormal form of sleep usually caused by accident or disease.

Dissociative anesthetic (diss-SOH-see-ah-tive ann-ness-THET-tick). To dissociate means "to pull apart." A dissociative anesthetic is a drug that kills pain by separating the mind from the body.

Psychosis (sigh-KO-sis). A very severe form of "mental illness" which often requires hospitalization. Schizophrenia is a type of psychosis.

Cannabis (KAN-ah-biss). The common hemp plant, from which come such drugs as marijuana (also spelled marihuana) and hashish. In the Western world, the most widespread species is **cannabis sativa** (SAT-ee-vah), which grows wild in most of the continental US.

make a unified experience. For example, if you have taken LSD, you may not be able to match the sight of a friend's face with the sound of the friend's voice because the hi-fi distracts you. So you end up perceiving your friend as singing instead of talking—or see your friend's face whirling around inside the loudspeaker. This type of experience may be amusing—or terrifying.

Hallucinogens cause little physical damage to the body. Their danger comes from their effects on mental processes and behavior. One of the most frequent problems associated with use of these drugs is that the user "loses control" of his or her flow of thoughts and emotions. This sort of experience is often called a "bad trip." In an interview in the July 1981 issue of *OMNI*, Albert Hofmann notes that almost everyone who takes LSD has a bad trip now and again. And Edward Domino believes that almost anyone who takes a sufficiently large dose of PCP—or who takes small doses regularly—is likely to need medical or psychological help.

Marijuana

Marijuana is a product of the hemp or **cannabis** plant, a weed found in abundance in many parts of the world. The "active ingredient" in marijuana is a chemical that goes by the complex name of delta-9-trans-tetrahydrocannabinol—which we can gladly abbreviate as **THC**.

Patients suffering from Glaucoma, an eye disease, can legally use marijuana because no better treatment is presently known for this condition.

As Solomon Snyder points out in his book *Uses of Marijuana*, cannabis has a long and interesting history. A century ago cannabis was almost as commonly used for medicinal purposes as aspirin is today and could be purchased without a prescription in any drug store. Cannabis became illegal in the US in 1937, but scientific evidence suggests that it still might be useful as a medicine. It seems particularly effective against diseases caused by tension and high blood pressure, menstrual bleeding, and glaucoma (a build-up of pressure within the eyeball). But its most important use may be that of helping relieve the nausea that cancer patients often experience when given **chemo-therapy**.

Very little is known about how cannabis affects the central nervous sytem, for it is chemically very different from the opiates, from all other known hallucinogens, and from cocaine. In small doses cannabis can produce a pleasant change of mood. In larger amounts it can produce mild hallucinations similar to those brought about by a small dose of LSD or mescaline. In very large doses it can induce vomiting, chills, and fever—as well as the bad-trip "loss of control" caused by hallucinogens.

Is Marijuana Dangerous?

In the spring of 1982, the National Academy of Sciences released a study on the dangers of marijuana. According to this report, there is no evidence that cannabis causes permanent, long-term health effects in humans, but a number of shorter term reactions to the drug "justifies serious national concern." The scientists conducting the NAS study state that there is no conclusive evidence the drug is addictive, that it leads to use of "harder" drugs, affects the structure of the brain, or causes birth defects. But it does affect motor coordination, short-term memory, oral communication, and may disrupt sperm production in males and ovulation in females.

All drugs have their dangers. But most of the other "recreational" drugs seem considerably more damaging than cannabis. Indeed, in 1973 a Presidential Commission on Marijuana and Drug Abuse came to the following conclusions on the subject:

1. Alcoholism is our worst drug problem.
2. Heroin dependence is our second worst problem.
3. *Legal* use of "downers," particularly by housewives, is our worst "hidden" drug problem.
4. Cannabis use is a minor problem compared with the abuse of alcohol and other drugs.

Drugs Affecting Motor Output

Almost all of the "uppers" and "downers" affect motor outputs as well as sensory inputs and central processing. However, many drugs have their major influence on muscular reactions.

Perhaps the best known of these drugs is **meprobamate**, also called Miltown or Equanil. When meprobamate was first introduced, it was called a "psychic" tranquilizer. Later research indicated it does not affect central processing all that much, but rather increases the output of inhibitory molecules at the neuro-muscular synapses, thus lowering the level of muscular activity.

Alcohol

As the Presidential Commission suggested in 1973, alcoholism is by far the most abused drug in the United States today. Alcohol is partially or wholly responsible for more than 100,000 deaths each year, and it is involved in some half of the automobile accidents on American highways. Alcohol abuse costs the country billions of dollars each year in medical care and in time lost from work. And at least 25 percent of the admissions to US mental hospitals involve alcohol abuse.

Alcohol affects the brain in many ways, but two effects seem most important. First, alcohol

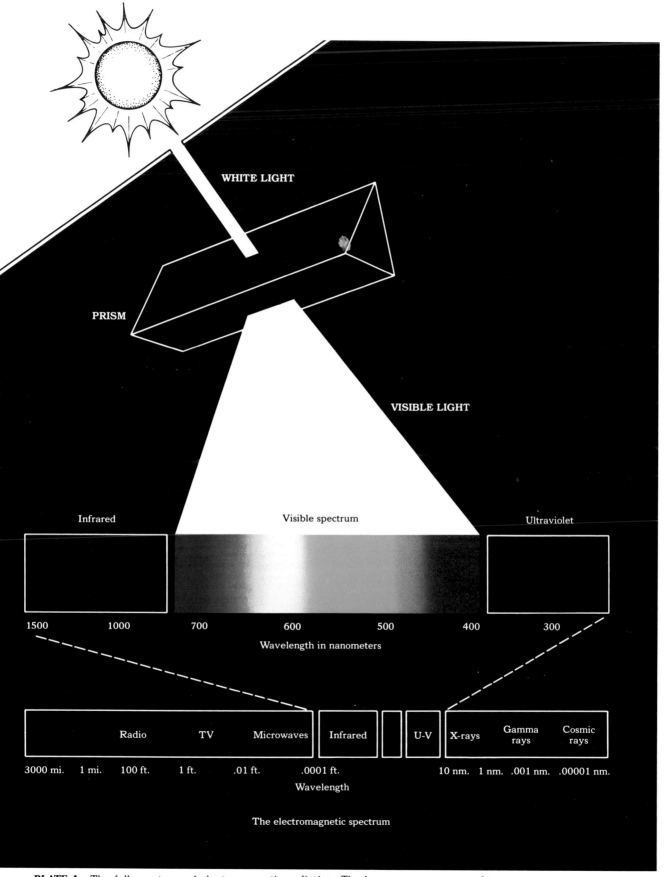

PLATE 1 The full spectrum of electromagnetic radiation. The human eye can see only the narrow band extending from 400 to 700 nanometers in wavelength. A nanometer is the equivalent to one-billionth of a meter (one meter = 39.37 inches). (From Rathus, 1981)

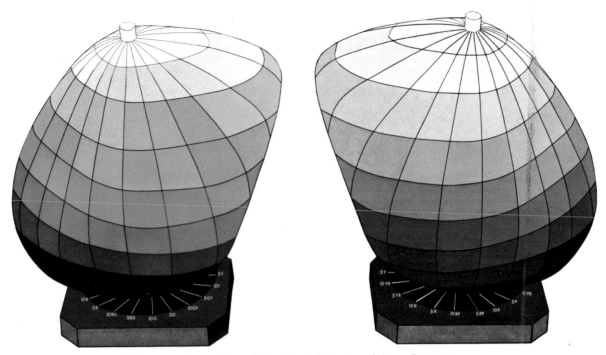

PLATE 2 The purple-blue to yellow color solid on the left is viewed from the green side. The yellow to purple-blue range on the right is viewed from the red side. (Munsell Color, Macbeth Division of Kollmorgen Corporation)

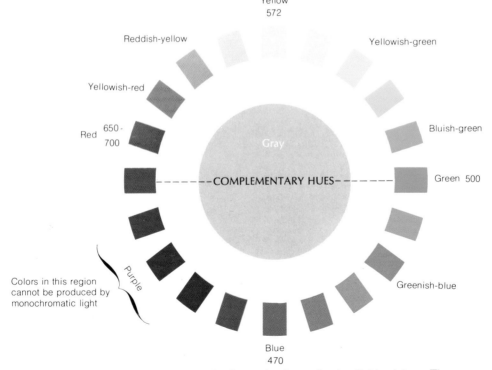

PLATE 3 The color circle illustrates the facts of color and color light mixture. The color names and their corresponding wavelengths (in nanometers) are given along the outside of the circle. Complementary colors are those colors opposite each other in the circle (such as reddish-yellow and greenish-blue); they will result in gray when mixed. The mixing of any two other wavelengths gives us an intermediate color. By proper mixing of three wavelengths equidistant in the circle (such as blue, green, and reddish-yellow), we can produce all color sensations. (From Bourne and Ekstrand, 1976)

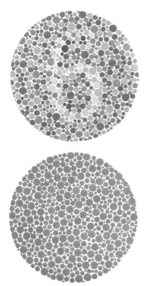

PLATE 4 These two illustrations are from a series of color-blindness tests. In the top plate, people with normal vision see a number 6, while those with red-green color-blindness do not. Those with normal vision see a number 12 in the bottom plate; red-green blind people may see one number or none. These reproductions of color recognition tests cannot be used for actual testing. The examples are only representative of the total of 15 charts necessary for a complete color recognition examination. (American Optical Corporation from their AO Pseudo-Isochromatic Color Tests)

PLATE 5 Look at the design on the cover of this book. A person with normal color vision would see all the colors. At the top of this page the cover design is reproduced as it might look to someone with red-green color-blindness; and in the middle as a person with yellow-blue color-blindness might see it. At the bottom is a black-and-white reproduction of the cover design as a totally color-blind person might see it.

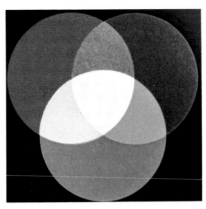

PLATE 6A Additive color mixture. By shining a light of a single wavelength onto a white surface, we will see the color that corresponds to that wavelength because the surface reflects only that wavelength to our eyes. However, if two lights of different wavelengths are shined on the surface together, the surface reflects both wavelengths which add together to produce an additive mixture. In fact, the complete color spectrum can be produced by mixing three properly chosen wavelengths in correct proportions. (Inmont Corporation)

PLATE 6B Subtractive color mixture. Now if we mix paints (instead of colors) the color we see is produced by subtraction. For example, when yellow paint is mixed with blue paint, the yellow paint absorbs or subtracts non-yellow wavelengths from the blue paint, leaving the wavelengths between yellow and blue—resulting in green. As this plate shows, we can produce a variety of colors by subtractive mixtures of three properly selected paints. (Inmont Corporation)

PLATE 7 Vincent van Gogh's "The Starry Night" (1889) illustrates the painter's imperfect sensory perception. Look at the concentric rings of color around the "starry lights." (Oil on canvas, 29x36¼" Collection, The Museum of Modern Art, New York. Acquired through the Lillie P. Bliss Bequest)

PLATE 8 Jan van Eyck's "The Madonna of Chancellor Rolin," a fifteenth-century painting showing the property of linear perspective. (Shostal Associates, Inc.)

PLATE 9   Georges Seurat's *Port-en-Bassin, Entrance to the Harbor.* A Nineteenth-century French painting which illustrates both linear and aerial perspective. (From Price, 1982)

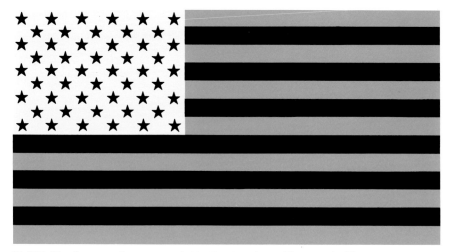

PLATE 10   Stare at the center of this flag for about 30 seconds. Then look at a white wall or sheet of paper. You will see a negative after-image in the colors complementary to those shown here.

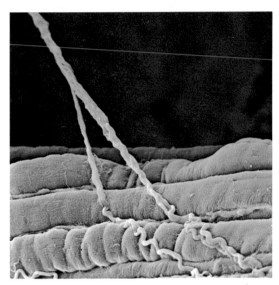

PLATE 11 Photograph of the nerve-muscle synapse. Axonic fibers (upper left) reach down to make a synapse with thick muscle fibers. (Photograph by Lennart Nilsson from *Behold Man.* ©1973 by Albert Bonniers Förlag, Stockholm, published by Little, Brown & Company, Boston, 1974.)

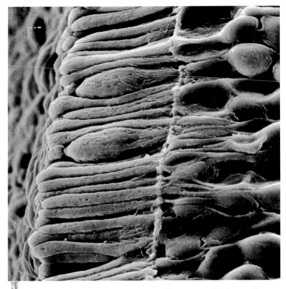

PLATE 12 The rods are the slim, pencil-shaped cells on the left of the photograph; the cones are the two fat cells squeezed in between the rods. Light enters the retina from the right; the back of the eye (choroid coat) is to the left in this photograph. (Photograph by Lennart Nilsson from *Behold Man.* ©1973 by Albert Bonniers Förlag, Stockholm, Published by Little, Brown & Company, Boston, 1974.)

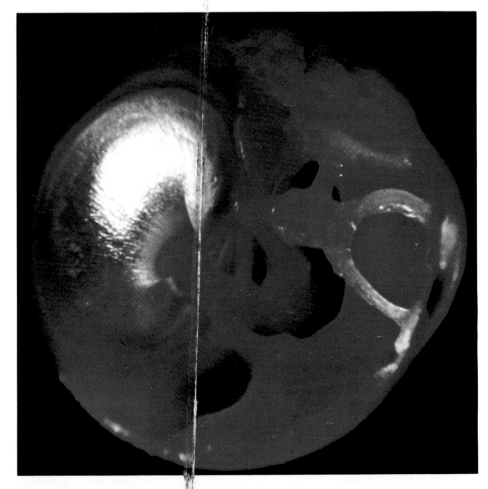

PLATE 13 A cross section of the middle ear. The hammer is connected to the eardrum which is the bright spot in the middle of the photograph. The stirrup, seen on the right, is connected to the oval window. The anvil connects the hammer to the stirrup. (Photograph by Lennart Nilsson from *Behold Man.* ©1973 by Albert Bonniers Förlag, Stockholm, published by Little, Brown & Company, Boston, 1974.)

PLATE 14 A cross section of the fovea, which is a pit in the center of the retina where vision is clearest. The two black bands to the left are supporting cells that help process visual inputs. The third band of cells from the left is made up of rods and cones. Light enters from the left; the back of the eye (choroid coat) is to the right. (Photograph by Lennart Nilsson from *Behold Man.* ©1973 by Albert Bonniers Förlag, Stockholm, published by Little, Brown & Company, Boston, 1974.)

PLATE 15 A cross section of the retina showing all ten layers. The rods and cones are at the bottom. (Photograph by Lennart Nilsson from *Behold Man.* ©1973 by Albert Bonniers Förlag, Stockholm, published by Little, Brown & Company, Boston, 1974.)

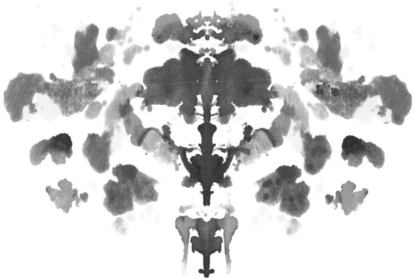

PLATE 16 This water color is similar to the colorful inkblots used in the Rorschach test. A psychologist can gather data about an individual's personality by asking that person to report what he or she sees in the inkblots.

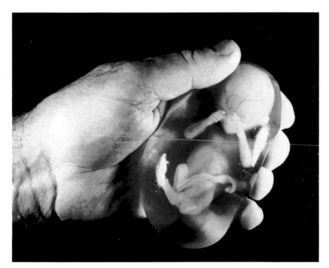

PLATE 17 A human fetus, about twelve weeks old. Even at this age, though, it already shows many human features. (From Baron, Byrne, and Kantowitz, 1980)

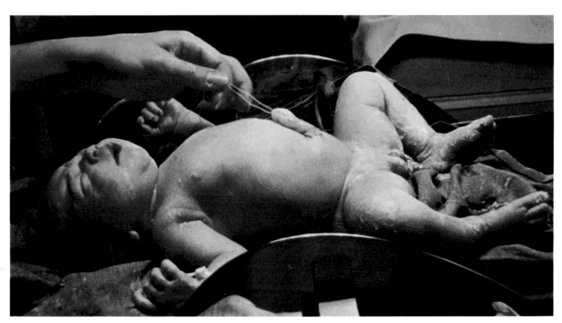

PLATE 18 A healthy human child, moments after birth. (From Baron, Byrne, and Kantowitz, 1980)

kills nerve cells—but in a highly selective fashion. In the January 30, 1981 issue of *Science*, Charles Golden and his associates report that alcohol tends to destroy brain tissue *primarily in the dominant hemisphere*. The behavioral changes associated with chronic drunkenness tend to support Golden's findings. For example, the slurred speech, the inability to think logically and to plan effectively, and the emotional outbursts shown by many alcoholics all suggest that alcohol disrupts the dominance normally shown by the left hemisphere. Indeed, Golden and his colleagues believe that these symptoms result from the right hemisphere's attempts to take over the functions lost through destruction of tissue in the left hemisphere.

Second, alcohol appears to affect the same inhibitory synapses in the brain that are blocked by cocaine and morphine. Consumed in larger amounts, however, alcohol disrupts motor coordination—presumably by making it difficult for the person to inhibit many types of muscle movements.

We will have much more to say about alcoholism in Chapter 23, when we will consider chronic drunkenness as a mental disorder. For the moment, all we need do is to note the problems associated with alcohol consumption. A study released early in 1982 by the Survey Research Center at The University of Michigan shows that consumption of marijuana, PCP, LSD, and heroin is *decreasing* in high school students. However, consumption of alcohol is on the increase in this age group.

Drugs and Mental Processes

For the most part, we take drugs because certain chemical compounds make us feel better than we do without the drugs—or because we *believe* that the drugs will make us feel better. And beliefs often can have just as strong an influence on the "drug experience" as does the biochemistry of the drug itself.

For example, in the December 1981 issue of *Psychology Today*, G.A. Marlatt and D.J. Rohsenow report that most of the "social effects" of alcohol may be due to people's *expectations* about the drug. Subjects who drank tonic water but thought it was alcohol showed most of the "classic" symptoms of intoxication, while subjects who drank alcohol but thought it was tonic water failed to get "high." More specifically, men who thought they had consumed alcohol became less anxious in social situations. They also became more aggressive and sexually aroused. Women who consumed tonic water thinking it was alco-

THC. An abbreviation for tetra-hydro-cannabinol (TET-trah HIGH-dro kan-NAB-uh-nol). Marijuana contains many chemicals, of which THC seems the main one that induces a "high."

Chemo-therapy (KEY-moh-THER-a-pee). Treatment that involves giving a person drugs or other chemicals to help the person get better.

Meprobamate (mepp-pro-BAMM-ate). A drug that acts to relax the muscles.

Trance state. A state of partly suspended animation or the inability to function normally. A sleep-like state in which the body moves slowly, if at all, while the mind is usually focused narrowly on a single thought. See Chapter 17.

hol became more anxious in social situations and less aggressive. The women *reported* they became sexually aroused, but physically they actually became less so.

Marlatt and Rohsenow also tested alcoholics by giving them tonic water but telling them it was vodka. The alcoholics experienced the same "craving" for alcohol after the tonic water as they typically did when consuming alcohol. They did *not* report this craving after drinking vodka they thought was just tonic water.

Marlatt and Rohsenow conclude that the setting in which alcohol is consumed and the drinker's expectations are even *more* influential in determining the drinker's reactions than are the physical effects of the alcohol itself. Put another way, the effects that your thought patterns have on your body are at least as important as the effects that your body has on your mental processes. Indeed, there is now evidence that what you think and feel and do may *change your body chemistry* as much as your body chemistry changes what you think and feel and do.

Shock, "Getting High," and the Endorphins

Almost all descriptions of "getting high" have two important aspects to them: (1) The person feels no pain; and (2) the person feels detached from his or her body and from ordinary reality. Oddly enough, these experiences may well be like those brought about by great shock—and with the release of massive amounts of enkephalin and other endorphins inside the brain.

Writing in the December 20, 1980 issue of *The Lancet*, William McDermott of the Harvard Medical School speculates that the onset of intense shock may lead the brain to create an abnormal amount of one or more of the endorphins. The sudden release of all this "natural pain-killer" apparently puts the organism in a **trance state** similar to that occasionally achieved by Eastern mystics. This altered state of consciousness is also akin to the euphoria caused by some drugs,

"Runner's high" is apparently caused by a massive release of endorphins.

and to the insensitivity to pain associated with hypnosis.

What led McDermott to this conclusion was a passage from the journals of David Livingstone, a noted surgeon who spent many years exploring the wilds of Africa. In the journal, Livingstone describes what he experienced when he was attacked by a large male lion:

> I heard a shout. Starting and looking half round, I saw the lion just in the act of springing upon me. I was on a little height; he caught my shoulder as he sprang and we both came to the ground below together. Growling horribly close to my ear, he shook me as a terrier does a rat. The shock produced a stupor similar to that which seems to be felt by a mouse after the first shake of a cat. It caused a sort of dreaminess in which there was no sense of pain nor feeling of terror, though [I was] quite conscious of all that was happening. It was like what patients partially under the influence of chloroform describe, who see all the operation but feel not the knife . . . The shake **annihilated** fear, and allowed

no sense of horror in looking round at the beast. The peculiar state is probably produced in all animals killed by [other animals]; and if so, is a merciful provision by our benevolent Creator for lessening the pain of death.

McDermott notes that there is currently no scientific proof that the endorphins are associated with the sort of trance state Livingstone experienced when the lion attacked. However, in the March 6, 1981 issue of *Science*, Barbara Herman and Jaak Panksepp state that *decreasing* the amount of enkephalin in an animal's brain seems to *increase* its sensitivity to pain and to social isolation.

At the human level, Alan Gintzler notes in the October 10, 1980 issue of *Science* that there is a significant increase in endorphins in a woman's brain just before she gives birth to a child. In 1981, several scientists reported that the endorphins seem responsible for the "high" that runners often experience. And, as we will see in Chapter 17, when you are hypnotized—or when you are given a placebo you *think* is a pain-killer—your brain may secrete more endorphins than usual.

If we follow William McDermott's line of reasoning, it is tempting to speculate that *almost all altered states of consciousness* are probably associated with an abnormally large release of natural pain-killing chemicals within the brain. Sometimes you secrete endorphins because of the drugs you have taken. But, just as often, you secrete them because of your *expectations* about how the drugs will affect you. Thus *some* of the effects of alcohol, the opiates, marijuana, and cocaine are due to biochemical changes these drugs cause at various synapses. But *other* effects of these drugs are caused by the types of neural transmitters and inhibitors your brain secretes in response to what you *think* the drugs ought to be doing to you.

To restate a point we have already made, your mental processes have as much influence on the behavior of your neurons as the behavior of your neurons has on what you think and feel.

We have already described the electrochemical functions of the *individual neuron*. In the next chapter we will look at how *groups of neurons* cooperate in order to help you cope with the pleasures and pains of life.

Summary

1. **Consciousness** is a **primitive term** that is defined as your ordinary state of mental functioning.
2. Certain experiences—such as falling asleep, dreaming, and taking various drugs—can lead to unusual or **altered states of consciousness**.
3. When you relax, or fall asleep, many of your

nerve cells fire at much slower rates than normal. Whenever you are extra-alert, or extremely excited, many of your neurons fire at much faster rates than normal.

4. Your body has certain **diurnal rhythms** that involve altered states of consciousness, the most obvious one being the **sleep-waking cycle**.

5. The four stages of sleep run from light sleep **(Stage 1)** to deep sleep **(Stage 4)**. Following Stage 4, you typically go into **REM sleep**, during which you will have one or more dreams.

6. Each sleep cycle is about 90 minutes long, including an REM period of about 10 minutes. Stage 4 (deep) sleep predominates during the first and second sleep cycles of the night. REM periods and **dreaming** increase during later cycles.

7. During REM sleep, most of the **voluntary muscles** in your body are paralyzed—except for those that control eye movements.

8. Dreaming seems to be primarily a function of the right hemisphere.

9. **Short sleepers** tend to be conventional and ambitious, while **long sleepers** tend to be shy and passive.

10. Dream deprivation makes both animals and humans respond to stress by becoming more aggressive.

11. Some people have **lucid dreams** in which they can control the content and outcome of their dreaming.

12. There are two main types of nightmares: **anxiety REM nightmares** and **incubus attacks**. Incubus attacks take place during Stage 4 sleep and occasionally are followed by sleepwalking.

13. Neurons have **receptor sites** on their dendrites and cell bodies that are particularly sensitive to **neural transmitters**.

14. The **lock and key hypothesis** states that, if a specific transmitter molecule "fits" a specific

---

Annihilated (an-NIGH-ih-late-ted). From the Latin word meaning "to reduce to nothing." To annihilate something is to kill or destroy it.

---

receptor site, it "unlocks" the neuron and makes it fire.

15. Your brain contains both **excitatory** and **inhibitory synapses**.

16. **Drugs** such as the **opiates** that inhibit sensory inputs can sometimes reduce the intensity of painful stimulation.

17. Your brain produces a variety of natural pain-killers called the **endorphins**.

18. **Morphine** inhibits endorphin production. Withdrawal from morphine is painful because your body has no endorphins to protect itself.

19. Experienced **cocaine** users apparently cannot tell the difference between sniffing the drug and sniffing a **placebo**.

20. Drugs that affect **cortical processing** can also alter the experience of pain, change moods, and cause you to **hallucinate** or misinterpret your sensory inputs.

21. **PCP** is a **dissociative anesthetic** that disconnects people's minds from their bodies.

22. **Marijuana** affects motor coordination, short-term memory, oral communication, sperm production in males, and ovulation in females. But there is no conclusive evidence that it causes long-term health problems.

23. Experienced drinkers cannot tell the difference between **alcohol** and tonic water.

24. The brain reacts to shock and stress by secreting endorphins. In large amounts, the endorphins can bring about a **trance state** or **euphoria**.

25. Your mental processes have as much influence on the behavior of your neurons as the behavior of your neurons has on what you think and feel.

(Continued from page 53.)

"Well," said the Bureaucrat, puffing nervously on his pipe. "Back from the Amazon so soon?"

"It's been 18 months," said Dr. Susan Ogdon.

"Ah, yes. Well, time certainly flies, doesn't it?" The Bureaucrat carefully inspected the faces of the two psychologists sitting in his office. They seemed tanned and relaxed. He wished that he could go buzzing off to tropical climes any time he wished. "And how were the pot-smoking natives? Still lost in the 'Stoned Age,' I suppose?" He chuckled over his little joke.

Roger Ogdon smiled wanly. "The natives are decent human beings, just like you and me. Some of them do smoke marijuana, of course, but I doubt theirs is any more of a 'Stoned Age' than ours."

"Um, yes," said the Bureaucrat, quickly swallowing his chuckle. "And what were the results of your study?" In fact, he had a copy of the Ogdons' report lying on his desk in front of him. But he had only found time to skim the first page or so. Besides, he preferred to hear such things first-hand. "I trust you didn't come up with anything too radical?"

Susan Ogdon sighed. "No, our results were about the same as those that Vera Rubin and Lambros Comitas found in their study of marijuana use in Jamaica, and that Paul Doughty and his colleagues at the University of Florida found in their work in Costa Rica."

The Bureaucrat frowned. "Oh, you read those studies, did you?" He wondered why scientists were always checking out the literature when it seemed that tackling a problem with a fresh mind might be so rewarding. He stirred his cup of coffee and took a small sip to perk him up a bit.

"Well," said the woman, "We began by looking at the ways in which our natives used marijuana. They chew it, smoke it, brew it as tea, and use it in cooking."

"Oh, my," said the Bureaucrat. "That much, eh?"

"Yes," Roger Odgon responded. "And they give it to their children as a medicine, so they start using cannabis at a very early age. But, of course, not all the natives use it."

"Good," the Bureaucrat said. "That means that you could find a control group of non-users, I presume?"

"Yes," said Susan Ogdon. "We found 30 men who were long-time, heavy pot smokers, and 30 who had never used it at all. The users smoked an average of 8 'joints' a day, except that they call them 'spliffs' instead of joints. And, as we note in our report, they refer to pot as 'ganja,' just as the Jamaicans do. It has much more THC in it than does the pot that usually finds its way to the US."

"Excellent!" said the Bureaucrat, reaching for his pipe. "And the non-users were similar to the users in all respects other than the use of this 'ganja'?"

Roger Ogdon nodded. "They were of about the same height, age, occupation, and educational background. And the men in both the experimental and control groups were heavy smokers of tobacco."

The Bureaucrat refilled his pipe and lit it. "Well, if the groups were that similar, then any differences in their mental or physical health most probably were due to the fact that one group smoked marijuana, and the other didn't, right?"

"That's what we presume," said the woman.

"And what was the major difference?" asked the Bureaucrat. "Something startling, I presume?"

Susan Ogdon laughed softly. "Very startling. The ganja smokers weighed, on the average, seven pounds less than did the non-smokers."

The Bureaucrat frowned. "Seven pounds?" he asked. He rubbed his stomach and wondered if he shouldn't lose a little weight. Perhaps those diet pills his wife was taking would help. Then a stray thought popped into his mind. "Wait a minute," he said. "I thought pot-smoking gave you 'the blind munchies.' How come the ganja smokers weighed less, not more, than the natives in your control group?"

Roger Ogdon answered. "It's a cultural thing, I suppose. Here the myth is that pot makes you hungry. In the Amazon, they believe it calms your stomach. As I'm sure you know, our feelings and behaviors often reflect our cultural backgrounds and social biases."

"Everyone knows that," responded the Bureaucrat. "But stop teasing me. What else did you find? Surely the ganja smokers had poorer health . . ."

"No," said Susan Ogdon. "Not at all. We took X-rays of their lungs. Both groups showed fairly normal tissue, except that the men who *didn't* smoke ganja had a bit more scarring of the lungs. But then, as we said, both groups were heavy tobacco smokers as well."

The Bureaucrat put down his pipe. "Well, imagine that. But what about genetic damage?"

Susan Ogdon responded. "The ganja smokers all had parents and grandparents who had been heavy smokers. You'd expect some genetic problems from that, wouldn't you? Yet the ganja smokers actually showed slightly fewer genetic abnormalities than did the men in our control group."

"Oh, my," replied the Bureaucrat as he poked a nasal inhaler up one of his nostrils and inhaled deeply. "I don't think the Deputy Assistant Secretary is going to like your data at all. But that's his problem, now isn't it?" He put the inhaler back in his desk before continuing. "Well, what about personality differences between your experimental and control group subjects?"

"None," said the woman. "We found no significant differences in personality, intelligence, tendency toward mental illness, or brain-wave recordings between the two groups."

The Bureaucrat reached in a desk drawer and extracted a small, white capsule. He had spent the morning in a conference with the Deputy Assistant Secretary, and the meeting had not been particularly pleasant. A mild "downer" might help soothe his nerves, he told himself. He swallowed the pill and then picked up the thread of the conversation. "But what of the social consequences? What of motivation? Some scientists insist that pot-smoking decreases the desire to work and to get along in society. Did you find that was true in the Amazon?"

"Of course not," Roger Ogdon replied. "The smokers had no more trouble getting or holding a job than did the non-smokers."

"But how long had the pot smokers been puffing on this 'ganja'?" asked the Bureaucrat.

"On the average, about 18 years," said Susan Ogdon.

"And all that ganja didn't even affect their sex lives?" the Bureaucrat said with a gasp.

Roger Ogdon laughed. "Not that we could tell. Or at least not that their wives or girl friends noticed. More objectively, the men in both groups had normal amounts of male hormone."

"But wasn't there an article in *Science* back in 1979 suggesting that marijuana may affect the sex hormones?"

"There are several such studies in the literature," Roger replied. "And I have no doubt they are accurate reports of what reputable scientists found in their own laboratories. So the issue surely is in doubt. Perhaps there's a difference between the effects of marijuana in the lab and in real life settings. All *we* can say is that the men we studied had normal amounts of male hormone, even after smoking pot for an average of 18 years."

"Oh, my," said the Bureaucrat. He couldn't imagine how he'd explain this to the Deputy Assistant Secretary. His stomach rumbled. He patted it gently, then helped himself to an antacid tablet he had tucked away in his desk for just such emergencies.

"You aren't going to object to our publishing the results of our study, are you?" Susan Ogdon asked.

The Bureaucrat smiled. "No, surely not. As you obviously know, your findings really aren't all that surprising, given the results of the Jamaica and Costa Rica studies."

"But what about your Deputy Assistant Secretary?" she questioned.

"Well," responded the Bureaucrat, "I take my cue from Winston Churchill. He once said, 'The truth is incontrovertible. Panic may resent it; ignorance may deride it; malice may distort it; but there it is.'" The man chuckled for a moment. "Leave the Deputy Assistant Secretary to me. Besides, rumor has it that he will be leaving for another position shortly. So let the truth prevail."

"'And the truth will set you free,'" replied Roger Ogdon, smiling.

"Let's hope so," said the Bureaucrat. "But the truth is, I still don't understand why some of the natives smoke ganja, and others don't."

"Individual choice, we presume," Roger Ogdon replied.

The woman nodded. "Yes, and perhaps some difference in their sensitivity to pain."

"Pain?"

"Look," Roger Ogdon continued. "Those men work 10 hours a day or more in the fields, doing very difficult manual labor. They use cannabis as a pain-killer. They probably produce less per hour when they're stoned, but they seem to be able to work longer."

"Then what do they do at night, when they want to relax?" asked the Bureaucrat?

Roger Ogdon laughed. "They drink alcohol."

"No kidding?" responded the Bureaucrat. "Perhaps they're not so different from us after all. But that's what we wanted to find out about, and that's why we supported your research. Please do publish it, wherever you wish. And, in conclusion, let me say that it's been a real pleasure to work with you two."

The Bureaucrat shook their hands and walked the two psychologists to the door. Then he returned to his desk, gathered up his papers, and put them in his briefcase. He tossed in a box of aspirin, and then glanced briefly at his watch. It had been a long, hard day, and he hoped that his wife would have a martini waiting for him at home.

Then a sad thought crossed his mind. "Pity about those natives having to work so long and hard in the fields," he said aloud. "I suppose they need a little something too, just to get them through the day." He picked up his pipe and tucked it into his briefcase. "Ah, well, different smokes for different folks."

Recommended Readings

Arkin, A.M., J.S. Antrobus, and S.J. Ellman, eds. *The Mind in Sleep: Psychology and Psychophysiology* (Hillsdale, N.J.: Erlbaum, 1978).

Barker, J.L., and T.G. Smith, Jr., eds. *The Role of Peptides in Neuronal Function* (New York: Dekker, 1980).

Domino, E.F., ed. *PCP (Phencyclidine): Historical and Current Perspectives* (Ann Arbor, Mich.: NPP Books, 1981).

Drug Abuse Council. *The Facts about "Drug Abuse"* (New York: Free Press, 1980).

Garfield, Patricia. *Creative Dreaming* (New York: Simon & Schuster, 1974).

Hartmann, Ernest. *The Sleeping Pill* (New Haven, Conn.: Yale University Press, 1978).

Horne, J.A. "Restitution and human sleep: A critical review," *Physiological Psychology*, Vol. 7, 1978, pp. 115–125.

Structure and Function of the Brain

4

Did You Know That . . .

Many early Greeks believed the mind was located in the heart?

Many people once believed you could read someone's personality by studying the bumps on the person's head?

There are four main sections or lobes in each of your cerebral hemispheres, and that each lobe has quite different functions?

If you electrically stimulate certain parts of your frontal lobes, your arms and legs will twitch and move about whether you want them to or not?

About 80 percent of the murders committed each year involve people related to or friendly with each other?

Most murderers and their victims are under 30 years of age?

British studies suggest that young boys who commit violent acts are very likely to be "heavy" TV watchers?

Males who watch pornographic films of women being raped often become more aggressive and hostile toward women?

A rat shocked in a confined space will almost always attack anything handy?

Removal of a small part of a monkey's brain can cause it to become hypersexual in its behavior?

Some scientists believe that much human violence is due to hidden brain damage?

There apparently is no simple cure for the violence we find in the world?

"The Riddle of Rage"

"Peace," the young woman said as she got into the car. "Nice of you to give me a ride."

"No trouble at all," the older woman said as she put her car in gear and drove off down the dusty road. "My name's Elsie Smith. What's yours?"

"Jennifer Ahearn," the younger woman responded. "But my friends call me Jeff."

Mrs. Smith nodded cordially. "Pleased to meet you, Jennifer. Don't get many hitchhikers up here in the backwoods of Manitoba. Where are you headed?"

"To the Hutterite colony, about 15 miles away," Jennifer responded. "Are you going that way?"

Mrs. Smith nodded. "Drive right past there." Then, taking her eyes from the road for a second or two, the woman looked Jennifer over. Noticing the young woman's slacks, the beads around her neck, and her loose-flowing hair, Mrs. Smith chuckled. "Well, you sure don't *look* like a Hutterite."

"I'm not," Jennifer replied. "I'm just visiting."

"What you plan on doing with them folk?"

"I'm going to study their peaceful ways," Jennifer replied earnestly. "It's my Action Project for the summer. I'm majoring in psychology, and we're supposed to spend our summers either working in a laboratory or out in the field somewhere. Last summer I worked at a clinic, you see, and that's why this year I decided to come live with the Hutterites."

Mrs. Smith pursed her lips. "No, I reckon I don't see."

Jennifer Ahearn frowned. "At the clinic we mostly worked with battered women and abused children. I got sick to my stomach seeing wives with black eyes and broken bones, and kids whose bodies were covered with bruises and whip marks. The 'aggressive instinct' at work, you know."

Elsie Smith shook her head in dismay. "Were you able to help the women and children very much?"

Nodding positively, Jennifer said, "Oh, yes. We helped as much as we could. But we were just cleaning up after the damage had been done, if you know what I mean. We couldn't *prevent* violence, just fix things up afterward."

"So?" Mrs. Smith said, steering her car deftly around a large pothole in the road.

"So, I studied up on violence and aggression. And then I read an article by Gertrude Huntington in *Natural History* on the Hutterites. They fled to America from central Europe because they refused to join the army and fight in wars. They may be the most peaceful people in the world."

"They are peaceful, I'll give them that," Elsie Smith said.

"And my professor, Dr. Sackoff, says there simply is no child abuse among the Hutterites, and practically no violence of any kind. That's why I decided to come study them for the summer."

"To see if maybe you can learn how to prevent wife beating and child abuse back where you live, eh?"

Jennifer laughed. "You got it! I figure the Hutterites must have a secret of some kind. I want to learn what it is and then teach other people how to live in peace the way the Hutterites do."

Mrs. Smith was silent for a few moments. Finally she said, "What does your teacher back at the university—Dr. Sackoff, you said?—what does she say about this project of yours?"

The young woman shrugged. "Well, when I told her I was sure I could find a way to end war and violence on earth, her enthusiasm wasn't exactly overwhelming. But finally she agreed to my coming up here. She said, if nothing else, it ought to be a 'learning experience.'"

Elsie Smith roared with laughter. "Yes, dear," she said, "It really ought to be that." Then she stopped the car at the side of the road. "See that big white building over there between the trees? That's the Hutterite 'long house,' as they call it. Just walk straight down that path, and you can't miss it."

Jennifer Ahearn gathered her gear together and got out of the car, then turned to smile at Mrs. Smith. "Thanks so much for the ride," she said.

"Oh, you're welcome, dear," the older woman replied. "And I just hope that you like what you learn from the Hutterites." Then, with a laugh, she put the car in gear and roared off down the dusty road.

"Children are born with stubborn natures, Miss Ahearn," the Hutterite woman said as she shook a birch switch at her son to warn him he was misbehaving. "Like my Donny, here, all children are willful and selfish. They're born aggressive, and inclined to misbehave." Then the woman smiled warmly at the boy. "Of course, Donny's only three yet, and that's very young. But I don't doubt he'll need many a switching before his will is broken."

Jennifer frowned. "That's what you send them to kindergarten for, then? To break their wills?"

"Certainly," the woman said. "What else should a child learn at Donny's age other than to obey the will of God, and of the group? But kids naturally want to fight, and do things on their own. That's their evil tendencies showing through. So we break their wills in kindergarten to teach them to be obedient, loving, God-fearing, and peaceful."

"You mean," Jennifer said, "You teach them to understand right from wrong, and to be ethical. That way they will grow up wanting to be peace-loving citizens."

The woman shook her head. "No, Miss Ahearn. Doesn't matter what they *want* to be, or whether they *understand*. They're too young to do anything but memorize, and act like we tell them to act. So we teach them to obey the rules."

"But if they don't think the right thoughts . . ."

The Hutterite woman laughed heartily. "That's the trouble with you 'outsiders.' You keep talking about what goes on inside the mind. Oh, wrong thinking is bad, I agree. But if you keep your thoughts to yourself, what does it matter? *Thinking* bad is not a sin. But bad *behavior* is a sin, because everybody can see that you're transgressing the law. And that goes against God's will."

Jennifer Ahearn was puzzled. "But don't you ever have aggressive impulses? I mean, when Donny here misbehaves, don't you ever get angry and feel like hitting him until he acts the way he ought to?"

"Hit a child in anger? You must be kidding," the woman said. "Why, that's against our rules. A couple of licks with a birch switch is enough, anyhow. We punish a child to teach him a lesson, not to make ourselves feel better."

"But doesn't your anger ever get out of control . . . ?"

The woman grinned. "I'm not saying I don't *feel* anger down inside me. But it doesn't matter. If I tried to harm Donny in any way, the rest of the group would keep me from doing so." She sighed deeply. "That's one of the great joys of living among the Brethren. They keep you walking the straight and narrow path, even when you might be inclined to stray from the true way."

"And the true way is . . ."

"The way of the God of love," the woman said immediately. "The way of truth. We follow the example set by our martyrs, who were burned at the stake or died of starvation rather than fight in wicked wars. We forsake all worldly things, and all the sinful and corrupt ways of you outsiders. Because, as we learn in our schools, 'It is better to die the bitterest death, yea ten deaths, than to forsake the truth.'"

Jennifer's face flushed in anger. "I may be an 'outsider,' but I'm not sinful and corrupt. I love God and peace as much as you do."

The Hutterite woman snorted in amusement. "Not likely, Miss Ahearn. Look at your clothes! You wear pants, like a man. Sinful! And you should cover your head with a scarf and a cap, instead of letting your hair flow free like a harlot's!"

"But it's too hot to wear a scarf and a cap today," Jennifer replied angrily.

"Humph," the woman said. "You can't expect to be comfortable in *this* world and in the hereafter both."

"And as for the slacks I'm wearing, they're *sensible*! Back at school, *all* the girls wear slacks, so you'll just have to forgive me . . ."

The woman frowned. "Can't forgive wicked behavior, no matter where it occurs. Of course, I *understand* you didn't grow up here in the colony. And so your will wasn't broken when you were young, and you don't know the godly way to dress. 'By their fruits ye shall know them,' God says in the Good Book. God judges you by what you wear, and what you do, because those are the fruits you bear to others. Your trouble is, you just weren't taught obedience when the time was right. But now you've been here a while, and you ought to be learning."

"I came here to learn how to stop child abuse, and how to teach people to love each other," Jennifer said. A tear rolled down one cheek. "I don't see what wearing a scarf and cap has to do with stopping war and aggression. Besides, I don't look good in floppy old clothes like the ones you're wearing."

"Pride goeth before a fall, Miss Ahearn," the woman replied, clucking her tongue as she did so. "You must learn to submit yourself to the will of the group, to God's way, if you want to be pure of heart and give up your evil, aggressive behaviors."

"I am *not* evil and aggressive!" Jennifer shouted.

"Stubborn, stubborn, stubborn," the woman said. "You're worse than Donny, here. And he's only three." The woman pulled her son to her and hugged him. After a moment she sighed again. "But then, maybe our way is just too difficult for you to learn, you being a woman and all that."

"I can learn anything I want to learn!" Jennifer said loudly.

The woman shook her head in disagreement. "No, still full of sinful pride, because your will wasn't broken at the right time. But there's hope for you, I think."

"Hope?"

The Hutterite reached out and patted Jennifer tenderly on the arm. "Yes, hope. Come live with us, and learn the true path to peace. It will be hard, I know. But we'll help all we can, Miss Ahearn. We'll tell you when you're right and wrong, we'll guide your behaviors as we would a child's. And you'll get your reward in the hereafter."

"You'll *guide* me along the path to peace?"

"Oh, yes," the woman said. "It won't be easy because, like a child, you place your own needs above those of the group. But submit yourself to the will of the colony, and we'll wring the disobedience and aggression from your heart. And then we'll help you discover what love and peace are all about."

"You'll *tell* me what I have to do . . . ?"

The woman patted Jennifer's arm again. "Of course we'll tell you! That's why we live together, to tell each other when we stray from the path of God. Learning to live in peace isn't something you can do on your own. You need someone observing you each minute of the night and day, to correct your misdeeds and show you the proper way to dress and act."

And then a saintly smile lit up the Hutterite woman's face. "Come live with us, Miss Ahearn, and you'll be the most fortunate of women. For here there are always a hundred helpful eyes watching you."

(Continued on p. 105.)

The Mind-Body Problem

What makes you tick?

A simple-sounding question, perhaps, but one that humans have debated (sometimes violently) for a great many centuries. Most of the time, when people raise this question, they are asking, "Who are you?" That is, they are asking what biological, psychological, and social events have made you into the person that you are today. (To anticipate a bit, we will spend most of the rest of this book trying to answer *that* particular question.)

But there is an even more basic problem hiding behind the innocent-appearing phrase, "What makes you tick?" Namely, what do we really mean when we use the pronoun YOU? At this deeper level of analysis, the question becomes not "WHO are YOU?" but "WHAT are YOU?"

Are you merely a biological machine, a body full of complex clockwork run by a motor called the brain? Or are you a unique psychological or spiritual identity that happens to inhabit a certain body the way you also happen to inhabit a certain house, apartment, or dorm room?

Put this way, the original question becomes, "Does your mind run your body, or does your body run your mind?" (Or, to raise a more disturbing thought, are they both perhaps controlled by outside forces that neither your mind nor your body is entirely aware of?)

This kind of questioning may seem odd to you, or even downright stupid, if you've never encountered it before. For, if you are like most people, you probably *assume* that your mind controls your body. After all, YOU make up your mind to go to the store, so your legs carry you there. YOU decide to have dinner, so your hands get the food and your mouth eats it. From this viewpoint, your "psychological" mind gives the commands that your "biological" body executes.

But consider the following troublesome facts: First, you spend about one-third of your life asleep, yet your body continues to function beautifully even when your mind is unconscious. Who runs your body when your cortex takes a nap?

Second, if you take a couple of drinks, or smoke some pot, YOU become **intoxicated**. It is easy to understand how the chemicals in alcohol and cannabis can affect the ticking of your nerve cells, but how can *physical* reactions in your brain cause the *psychological* or *spiritual* YOU to get high?

And third, if your mind controls your body, *how does it do so?* When you drive a car, you sit in the driver's seat, you push on the pedals with your feet, and you turn the wheel with your hands. If you consider your body to be a biological machine "driven" by your mind, where does the driver "sit," and how does your purely spiritual or psychological "mind" pull the biological strings that make your neurons fire and your muscles move?

What and Where Is Your Mind?

The question, "What and where is the mind?" has puzzled people at least since the time of the early Greek philosopher Plato. Yet we still do not have one simple, agreed-upon answer to what the mind

"AS PART OF THE NEW DE-EMPHASIS ON VIOLENCE, PLAY UP THE LINE THAT HE'S FIGHTING EVIL BECAUSE HE HATES EVIL, INSTEAD OF FIGHTING EVIL BECAUSE HE LOVES TO FIGHT."

Intoxicated (in-TOCKS-uh-kay-ted). From the Latin word *toxicum*, meaning "poison." A toxic substance is one that is dangerous or harmful to life. In everyday speech, to be intoxicated is to be drunk, stoned, or "high" from drinking or smoking a toxic chemical such as alcohol or marijuana.

Mind-body problem. The foremost problem in psychology. Namely, where and what is the mind, and how does it function? How does it affect the behavior of the body, and how does the body affect the behavior of the mind? (See Chapter 5).

Sophisticated (so-FISS-tic-kay-ted). A group of philosophers called Sophists lived in Greece several hundred years before Christ was born. The sophists were very good at winning arguments, more through their ability to "shoot the bull" effectively than through logical thinking. Our English words "sophomore" and "sophisticated" come from "Sophist."

Homunculus (ho-MUN-cue-lus). The Latin word *homo* means "man." A homunculus is a "small man," such as a dwarf or midget.

is, and how it manages to interact with the body. For buried away within the question "What is the mind?" is a psychological nettle that stings almost everyone who attempts to grasp it. Philosophers call this nettle the **mind-body problem**, and it has to do with the complex relationship between your mental and your physical processes—and where inside your body those "mental" processes take place.

As you will see, we still don't know as much as we'd like about the mind's relationship to the body. But we do assume that mental activities take place (for the most part) inside the head. Ancient humans, however, were not quite so wise and **sophisticated**.

Aristotle's "Radiator Theory"

For example, Aristotle—a Greek scholar who lived long before the birth of Christ—believed that our minds (or souls) reside in our hearts. From his observations of animals being slaughtered and of humans wounded in battle, Aristotle knew that the heart was in constant motion— beating, beating, beating. If you pierced a man's heart with a sword or arrow, the man almost always died. The brain, on the other hand, was quiet. No matter how much you poked or prodded it, the brain *simply did not respond*. Many early Greeks considered the brain to be little more than a radiator where blood was pumped to be cooled off when a woman or man flew into a "hot rage."

The Homunculus Theory

Another view, supposedly held by the early Egyptians, was that a "little man" lived inside each person's skull. This **homunculus** (to use the Latin word for "little man") supposedly peered out through your eyes and listened through your

Descartes

M.J.P. Flourens

Paul Broca

ears. Once the "little man" decided how to *process* or react to incoming sensory information, he pulled the strings that operated your muscles much as a puppeteer pulls the strings that make marionettes behave.

Nor was this *homunculus theory* as ridiculous as it may have seemed at first. Ancient people knew that if you looked directly into a friend's eyes, you would see a "little man" or "little woman" looking out at you (try it—it works!).

Furthermore, the theory established our superiority over lower animals. If you stare into a dog's eyes, you will see a human face looking out at you, not a dog's. So "little men" obviously pulled the strings for animals as well as for humans. (What the dog sees when it looks into your eyes is a question the early theorists apparently forgot to ask.)

Even today, the homunculus theory has its believers. How many TV commercials have you seen in which "little men" or "little women" chase about the human body causing headaches or stomach upsets?

Question: If a "little man" pulls the strings that move your muscles, who pulls the little man's strings?

Descartes' Theory of Separate Substances

Three centuries ago the French philosopher **Rene Descartes** offered one of the first modern solutions to the mind-body problem. Descartes believed that mind and body were made of *separate substances*.

According to Descartes, your body—whose actions are purely mechanical—is composed of *physically measurable* substances such as blood and guts. Your mind is supposedly a ghostly something that exists *spiritually* or *psychologically*, but has no physical existence.

Descartes thought that mind and body were *coupled*, like man and wife. The mind did not control the body directly, nor did the body control the mind. But, like a married couple, mind and body were very closely related and they did *interact* with each other. The brain (which was physical) was the most important part of the body because it was the "marriage bed"—that is, *the point of maximum interaction between mind and body*.

Rene Descartes knew precious little about the functioning of the brain, for modern biology didn't exist at the time that Descartes lived. But he was one of the first scientists to insist that the seat of consciousness (YOU) lay within the skull, and thus he turned the mind-body problem into the mind-brain problem.

Question: Suppose we could transplant your brain into another body. How would your personality be affected by the operation? Would "you" go with your brain, or stay with your body? And if "you" went with your brain, how would it affect your feelings and behaviors if your new body were of the opposite sex?

Phrenology

By the year 1800 medical doctors were convinced of the psychological importance of the brain, but they could not begin to unlock its secrets because they knew so little about chemistry and electricity. So the medical profession studied the brain as best it could—by poking and cutting at this magnificent organ as if it were a lump of muscle tissue.

As we said in Chapter 2, most of us are right-handed (and left-brained). Because we do most of our heavy labor with our right hands, the muscles in our right arms are slightly larger and better developed than are the muscles in our left arms. Any time you exercise a particular muscle, it swells a bit. Now, if your brain reacted like muscle tissue, then the more you used it, the larger it should grow. Right?

Well, that's what a European medical doctor named Franz Joseph Gall said around the year 1800. Gall spent considerable time studying people in jails and insane asylums. He found (or so he thought) that most pickpockets and thieves had a "bump" on their skulls just above their ears. He then tried to relate this *physical* characteristic with the thieves' *personality* (or behavior). From Gall's point of view, thieves differ from honest people because thieves continually exercise the psychological habit of "acquiring" other people's property illegally. Therefore, Gall reasoned that the part of their brains associated with "acquisitiveness" would surely be largest because it got the most exercise!

And as this "acquisitiveness center" of the brain swelled and grew from all that exercise, it would presumably *push outward on the skull*, causing a bump. And since the thieves that Gall studied had bumps over their ears, then shouldn't it be true that the brain tissue immediately under this bump was the location of the "acquisitiveness center"?

Now, suppose you adopted Gall's rather odd viewpoint. How would you go about determining anybody's personality? Obviously, all you would have to do would be to "read the bumps" on a person's skull!

Gall gave the practice of bump-reading a very fancy name, **phrenology**, which he made up from the Greek words meaning "to study the mind" (see Fig. 4.1). He went around Europe hunting for people with special talents or **psychological traits**, and then tried to find a bump that matched each trait. For instance, Gall placed the trait of "destructiveness" just behind the ear because he found bumps there (1) in a medical student who was "so fond of torturing animals that he later became a surgeon"; and (2) in a man who worked as an executioner and who apparently enjoyed his work immensely.

Phrenology became very popular in the United States during the early 1800's since it seemed to offer practical-minded Americans an easy way to improve themselves. But the phrenology fad didn't last very long for at least two reasons: First, Gall never could give his clients a workable set of "mental exercises" to reshape their personalities. And second, the bumps *didn't seem to change* no matter what the client did.

Rene Descartes (ren-nay day-cart). Usually considered the greatest of French philosophers. He was born in 1596 and lived until 1650. A world-famous scholar who made many great contributions to physics, mathematics, psychology, and philosophy.

Phrenology (free-NOLL-oh-gee). Reading the bumps or depressions on a person's skull in order to make guesses about the person's psychological abilities. Phrenology, which was invented by Franz Joseph Gall, doesn't work very well.

Psychological traits. Distinguishing qualities of character. A trait is a particular mental ability or skill, or a psychological peculiarity of some kind.

Pierre Flourens (pee-air flu-rans). A noted French medical scientist who, in the early 1800's, made many brilliant discoveries about how the brain works.

Extirpation (ex-tir-PAY-shun). From a Latin word meaning "to pull up by the roots." To extirpate means to destroy, usually by taking something out or cutting something away. In medical terms, to extirpate is to remove a part of the body or brain by surgery.

Question: *What sort of experiment could you perform to test the correctness of Gall's hunches about the brain?*

Science versus Phrenology

In the long run, however, it was the scientific method that effectively bashed phrenology over the head. **Pierre Flourens**, the great French physiologist, demolished most of Gall's claims in the 1820's by performing actual *experiments* on brains instead of merely reading bumps on people's skulls.

Gall had located the "bump of amativeness" (or sexuality) on the back part of the head, in areas that we now know are associated with visual sensory inputs. What would happen, Flourens asked, if this part of the brain were destroyed? Presumably, the person's sex life would also be destroyed—or at least greatly changed. As a surgeon, Flourens was occasionally called upon to remove this part of a patient's brain in order to save the person's life. But on recovery from the operation, these patients seldom showed decreased sexual activity. They might be partially blinded, but they could still make love (and did)! In fact, Flourens found he could remove large areas of the cortex from badly wounded patients without destroying the psychological traits that Gall said were lodged in those areas of the brain.

Because Flourens knew little or nothing about electricity and chemistry, his primary means of studying the brain was by cutting out parts of it to see what effects this **extirpation** had on people's behaviors. Since patients with brain damage had trouble taking care of themselves, Flourens decided that the cerebral hemispheres were the seat of perception, intelligence, and all *voluntary activity*. Which is to say that Flourens

The Mind-Body Problem

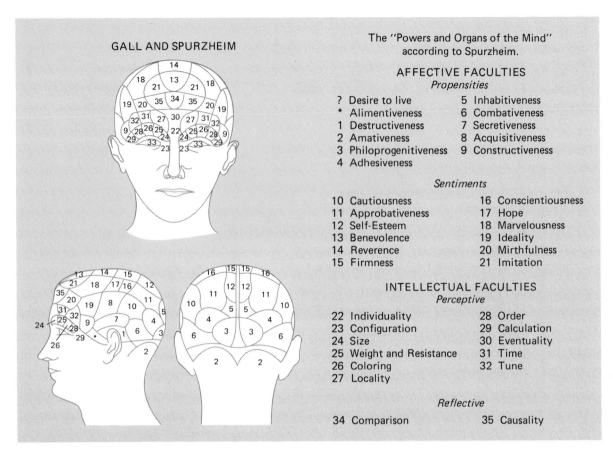

GALL AND SPURZHEIM

The "Powers and Organs of the Mind"
according to Spurzheim.

AFFECTIVE FACULTIES
Propensities

?	Desire to live	5	Inhabitiveness
*	Alimentiveness	6	Combativeness
1	Destructiveness	7	Secretiveness
2	Amativeness	8	Acquisitiveness
3	Philoprogenitiveness	9	Constructiveness
4	Adhesiveness		

Sentiments

10	Cautiousness	16	Conscientiousness
11	Approbativeness	17	Hope
12	Self-Esteem	18	Marvelousness
13	Benevolence	19	Ideality
14	Reverence	20	Mirthfulness
15	Firmness	21	Imitation

INTELLECTUAL FACULTIES
Perceptive

22	Individuality	28	Order
23	Configuration	29	Calculation
24	Size	30	Eventuality
25	Weight and Resistance	31	Time
26	Coloring	32	Tune
27	Locality		

Reflective

34	Comparison	35	Causality

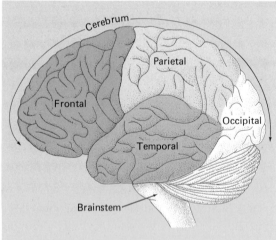

Fig. 4.1. Gall's map of psychological traits. **(top)**
Fig. 4.2. The four lobes of the brain. **(bottom)**

believed that the hemispheres were "the seat of the mind." And perhaps in reaction against Gall's wildly incorrect ideas, Flourens decided that psychological traits or abilities had no *specific locus* or homesite within the brain.

It took a lunatic to prove Flourens wrong.

The Speech Center

In 1831 there came to an insane asylum near Paris a young Frenchman whose only mark of madness was that he wouldn't talk. He could communicate by making signs, but he refused to write or speak. Although he appeared to be normal in all other respects, he was put into the insane asylum because the French authorities decided that no sane man would refuse to talk to his fellow beings. The doctors could find no cure for his silence, so the man remained in the hospital for 30 years.

In April of 1861 the man caught an infection and was put under the care of Paul Broca, a noted French surgeon. Broca examined the man carefully, determined that the man's vocal cords were perfectly sound, and that the patient was intelligent enough to be able to speak. Five days later—unfortunately for the man, but perhaps fortunately for millions of other patients—the man died of the infection.

Broca put the man's body to **autopsy** at once and discovered a mass of scar tissue in the *left hemisphere* just about where the man's temple would have been. Broca assumed, rightly, that this site in the brain must contain the neural tissue that controls speech.

Gall had assumed that *each part of the brain* had a highly specific function—and Gall was proven wrong by Flourens. Flourens had assumed that there was *no specific locus within the brain* for specific psychological functions or traits. But Flourens was proven wrong by Broca, who correctly located the speech center in the left half of his patient's brain.

And for the next century, the battle seesawed between these two viewpoints. On the one hand, there were many scientists who believed that there must be a specific center or site in your brain for each type of behavior you are capable of. On the other hand, there were many other scientists who were convinced that almost every part of your brain participated in producing each thought or action that you experience.

As is usually the case in such scientific free-for-alls, the truth actually lies somewhere between these two extreme viewpoints.

The Lobes of the Brain

Let us return once more to that magic mirror that allows you to inspect your own brain. If you could look into that mirror, you would probably first notice the huge, deep valley between the left and right hemispheres of your brain. But if you inspected your brain a little more closely, you would see that each hemisphere is actually divided into *sections* (see Fig. 4.2).

Viewed from the top, as we mentioned earlier, your hemispheres look much like a mountainous landscape—there are dozens of smoothly rolling hills which are separated by steep-sided valleys. Some of the valleys are so large that they seem to separate the cerebrum into definite areas or sections, which we call **lobes**.

There are four main sections or lobes in *each* cerebral hemisphere:

1. The **frontal lobe**, which lies just under the skull in the region of the forehead.
2. The **temporal lobe**, which lies under the skull just above each ear, in the general region of your temple.
3. The **parietal lobe**, which lies under the top center of your skull.
4. The **occipital lobe**, which lies at the back of your head, just above your neck.

It was tempting to Broca to assign highly specific psychological traits or functions to each of these lobes and, as we will see, Broca was partially correct in doing so. But as much as he learned about the brain from his surgery and his autopsies, he didn't know enough to help hundreds of his patients who were sick or dying from

Autopsy (AW-top-see). A careful inspection of a dead body to determine why the person died.

Lobes. Rounded bumps that typically project out from the organs of the body. Each half of your cerebrum has four main lobes or projections.

Frontal lobe. The part of your cerebrum which lies just above your eyes. Experiments suggest this part of your brain may be involved in decision making, among many other things. The motor cortex is part of the frontal lobe.

Temporal lobe (TEM-por-all). Part of your cerebrum that lies just above your ears. It seems to be involved in hearing, in speech production, and in emotional behavior, among many other things.

Parietal lobe (pair-EYE-uh-tall, or puh-RYE-uh-tull). Part of your cerebrum at the very top of your brain. Sensory input from your skin receptors and muscles comes to this part of your cerebrum.

Occipital lobe (ox-SIP-it-tall). The lower, rear part of your cerebrum just above the back of your neck. The visual input area of your brain, among other things.

brain disease. For, like all of his colleagues at that time, Broca did not understand that the nerve cells work electro-chemically.

What the scientists of the 1860's obviously needed was an *electrical* method of investigating brain reactions. And in 1870 they got just that—but it took the violence of a major war to give it to them.

The Electrical Probe

The Franco-Prussian War between Germany and France reached its climax late in the summer of 1870 near the small French town of Sedan. The immediate political consequences of that war have long since been forgotten—even by most German and French citizens. But a discovery that two German doctors made on the battlefields outside the sleepy little village of Sedan changed the course of modern medicine.

G. Fritsch and E. Hitzig were trained as medical doctors. When the Franco-Prussian War broke out, Fritsch and Hitzig both entered the armed forces of Germany. During the battle of Sedan, Fritsch and Hitzig wandered among the wounded men, helping those whom they could. Some of these soldiers had skulls blown open by cannon fire. Nothing could be done to save these men, all of whom were unconscious and dying. But perhaps, thought Fritsch and Hitzig, these soldiers could contribute priceless medical information to the world in their final moments of life.

In 1870, biologists were already speculating that electrical currents might flow through the brain. What would happen, Fritsch and Hitzig asked themselves, if they provided *electrical stimulation* to the brains of the dying soldiers? So they did just that. And, as inhumane as their actions might seem after the fact, the experiments performed by Fritsch and Hitzig on the battlefield led to important insights on brain functions. Indeed, their work has probably helped millions of brain-damaged patients.

Fritsch and Hitzig soon found that if they applied electrical stimulation to an area at the top rear of the *frontal lobe*, just where it joins with the parietal lobe, the arms and legs of their human subjects would show repeated, jerky movements. Once the war was over, Fritsch and Hitzig continued their experiments (using animals) and reported they had discovered what seemed to be a "motor output center" in the cortex of both frontal lobes.

Fritsch and Hitzig had also pioneered a new tool for investigating the functioning of the brain and for curing some of its ills—the *electrical probe*.

Mapping the Cortex Electrically

If someone stuck a pin in your arm, you would experience pain. Surprisingly enough, though, if someone stuck a pin directly into your exposed cortex, you probably wouldn't *consciously* experience any discomfort at all.

With certain minor exceptions, there simply are no "pain receptors" in the brain. (There *are* pain receptors in the skin covering the brain, however.) Because brain tissue is insensitive to pain, patients undergoing brain operations are often conscious, so they can help the doctor locate whatever damaged section might need to be removed or treated. During such surgery, the doctor may stimulate various parts of the patient's cortex electrically and ask what the patient feels the moment the current is turned on.

What would you experience if you were willing to let a scientist "map" your *entire cortex* with an electrical stimulator? Well, the most dramatic results of all would surely come if the scientist touched the probe to your *motor output area* (motor cortex), which lies at the rear of each frontal lobe (see Fig. 4.2). Stimulation of the nerve cells in the motor cortex in your left hemisphere would cause the muscles on the right side of your body to twitch or jerk—even though you didn't *consciously will* these muscles to move. Stimulation of the motor cortex in your right hemisphere would, of course, make the muscles on the left side of your body move involuntarily.

When the probe was applied to the *occipital* lobe at the back of your head, you would see brief flashes of light or "shooting stars."

If the scientist stimulated parts of your *temporal* lobe, you would hear brief bursts of sounds.

And if the probe were touched to parts of the *parietal* lobe at the top of your head, you would feel odd "prickly" sensations in your skin.

Strangely enough, however, the scientist could apply the probe to large areas of all four lobes without your experiencing *anything at all*!

Sensory, Motor, and "Silent" Areas

The physiologists who first mapped the brain electrically concluded that your cerebral cortex has three general types of areas:

1. *Sensory input areas*, where nerve axons carrying messages from your sense organs make synapse with dendrites of cortical neurons. We will discuss these areas in detail beginning with Chapter 6.
2. *Motor output areas*, which contain nerve cells whose axons reach out to make contact with the muscles and glands of your body.
3. *"Silent" areas*, which have no function that can be determined directly from electrical stimulation.

The early physiologists were surprised to find that *most of the surface area of the cortex* is "silent" to an electrical probe. At first, these early scientists assumed that the silent areas were where memories—or *associations* between sensory inputs and motor outputs—were located. So these silent parts of the cortex were nicknamed the **association areas**. But many lines of evidence now suggest these are the cortical *processing areas*. For it is in these regions that incoming sensory information is processed and evaluated, and where "command decisions" seem to be made.

The Birth of Psychology

When electrical probing of the brain first began, many early *biologists* were convinced that they were about to resolve the mind-body problem in favor of the body. These scientists presumed that they would be able to find a specific locus in your brain that matched each unique hope, fear, dream, thought, hatred, and desire you might ever experience. (Had they been able to find such specific brain sites, then biology would have swallowed up psychology, and you would be reading a book quite different from this one.)

Imagine the frustration of these scientists, then, when electrical stimulation of much of the brain failed to elicit any "mental" responses at all. The biologists were convinced that "the mind" was lurking somewhere in that 1.3 kilogram (3 pound) mass of neural tissue inside the skull, but somehow the most important parts of human experience kept eluding (and still elude) their needle-like probes.

In a sense, both intra-psychic and social/behavioral psychology grew out of the successes and failures of the early biologists. For while these scientists failed to solve the mind-body problem to everyone's satisfaction, they did demonstrate that the *scientific method* could be successfully applied to the study of human behavior.

In the late 1800's, then, a group of scholars who called themselves *psychologists* started applying the scientific approach to the study of what humans thought and did. Some psychologists began to develop "mental probes" to map out the mind as the biologists had mapped out the brain. Other psychologists tried to measure and record the visible behavior of the human organism as precisely as the biologists had measured and recorded the electro-chemical behavior of cortical neurons. Still others started studying the effects of the social environment on human thoughts and actions.

Out of this sudden burst of scientific activity, there emerged three quite different ways of answering the question, "What makes you tick?" These three are the *biological*, the *intra-psychic*, and the *social/behavioral* approaches to psychology. Each of the three has its own strengths and weaknesses, and its own contributions to make in answering the mind-body riddle.

To help us put all three approaches in perspective, let us first look at them briefly, then dis-

> **Association areas**. Those parts of your cortex which, when stimulated electrically, do not yield any sensory experiences. Although the functions of these "silent areas" of your cortex are not fully understood, we assume that they are involved in cortical processing—that is, in evaluating incoming sensory information and in storing memories.
>
> **Physiological psychology** (fizz-ee-oh-LODGE-uh-cal). That part of psychology which looks upon humans primarily as being biological organisms. Physiology is that division of biology dealing with the activities and processes of living systems. *Physio* means "of the body." *Psycho* means "of the mind."

cover how each attempts to explain a pressing human problem—the occurrence of such *violent behaviors* as war, rape, and murder.

The Mind-Body Problem: Three Theoretical Viewpoints

The Biological Viewpoint

As we have noted, psychology partially grew out of the sciences of medicine and biology. That area of psychology concerned with studying how bodily functions affect behavior is called **physiological psychology**. This old and highly respected field is now sometimes referred to by such new names as *biological psychology, psychobiology,* or *biopsychology.* Some physiological psychologists work primarily with animals, while others usually work with human subjects.

For the most part, physiological psychologists are interested in the *interactions* between body processes and behavior. That is, they study how changes in your biology are related to changes in your behavior.

At times, a biopsychologist may induce a change in an organism's behavior and then look for changes in the organism's body. For instance, the scientist might teach a dog to perform a trick and then study what happens in the dog's brain as a result of the change in its performance. Mostly, though, the physiological psychologist is likely to alter the functioning of the brain in some way to see how the organism's behavior changes *as a consequence.* For example, if you stimulate parts of a cat's motor cortex, the animal's legs will move. If you stimulate other parts of the cat's brain electrically, the animal will fly into a rage.

Perhaps because biopsychologists tend to "do something physical" to an animal and then note its behavioral changes, these scientists occasionally talk as if biology *causes* psychology. Not all physiological psychologists take this restricted, biological view toward the mind-body problem, of course. But many of them do occasionally speak as if they believed the interaction between brain and mind was a one-way street—as if physical events in your nervous system were the *major cause* for all the subjective experiences in your mind. This is a viewpoint that the intra-psychic psychologists object to strongly.

The Intra-Psychic Viewpoint

At the beginning of this chapter, when we asked where the "essential, psychological YOU" resided, we were speaking in intra-psychic terms. That is, we were asking about the location of your own subjective world, of your own stream of consciousness, or of your *mind*. Traditionally, the intra-psychic or mental viewpoint has dominated the psychological sciences, just as it dominates most of the material in this book.

From an intra-psychic standpoint, YOU are a conscious entity separate from but somehow related to your body. That is, your mind has *voluntary control* over your body (brain), and not the other way around. Our legal system takes this intra-psychic point of view, for the laws of the land don't view you as a machine. Rather, they hold YOU responsible for your actions.

Scientists who study what the "inner woman" or "inner man" is really like will usually admit that your genes help determine what your mind is like. And they realize that a brain-damaged person such as Joe (whom you met in Chapter 1) cannot be expected to act and think exactly as normal people do. But from a strictly "mentalistic" viewpoint, the condition of your body merely *sets limits* to what your mind can accomplish. Within these biological limitations, YOU are presumed to become whatever YOU decide you should be.

The social and behavioral psychologists, however, offer many important reasons why the intra-psychic viewpoint simply cannot explain everything that we know about human beings.

The Social/Behavioral Viewpoint

As the poet John Donne said, you are not an island unto yourself. Rather, you grew up around other people who helped determine your ideas, your values, your joys, your disappointments, your speech, and your behaviors. However, because the biological and the intra-psychic viewpoints have dominated our thinking for so many centuries, it has taken us a very long time to realize the importance of the social and physical environments we live in.

Those psychologists who emphasize the strong influence that the outside world has on what we think and do typically have adopted the social/behavioral viewpoint as their solution to the mind-body problem. For the most part, these scientists are referred to as *social psychologists*.

As we will see in Chapters 25–27, social psychologists are interested in many aspects of human behavior. They spend much of their time, however, studying how your attitudes and behaviors are affected by the actions of the *groups* and *organizations* you belong to. In social psychology, your family is considered a "group," while the school you attend is an organization.

From the strict *social viewpoint*, your body creates your mind at birth and has a minor influence on it thereafter. But the outside world creates all your important attitudes and behavioral reactions while you are growing up. From this social viewpoint, therefore, if you want to change your mind, you must first change your environment (or the way that it treats you).

Behavioral psychology goes a step farther. To a behaviorist, your thoughts, feelings, and emotions are *subjective* events. Because these mental experiences take place inside the privacy of your own mind, they cannot be seen or measured directly by a scientist. However, your *behavior* is something that most certainly can be seen and recorded by a scientific observer. *What you do*—the movements you make and the things you say—are non-mental events. Your behavior therefore can be treated as an object and hence can be measured *objectively*—just as one can measure the "behavior" of such other objects as a falling stone, an ocean wave, or a neuron firing. And because behavioral psychologists prefer to study human behavior objectively, they tend to ignore your subjective (mental) experiences and focus instead on what you do and say.

Behaviorists admit that your actions are determined partly by your biological inheritance. But they note that one of the main ways your genes influence your behavior is by making you particularly sensitive to your environment. For example, many behavioral studies suggest that you seem to be "biologically programmed" to seek pleasurable inputs and avoid painful inputs. And since these pleasures and pains come to you primarily from your *social and physical environment*, behaviorists believe that all of your mental and physical reactions are the *consequences* of external inputs.

Most behaviorists suggest, therefore, that if you want to change your own behavior, you typically must first change the behavior of the people in the world around you.

Question: What strong similarities do you see between the social and the behavioral solutions to the mind-body problem?

Which View Is Correct?

Despite occasional arguments psychologists may have on the subject, very few of them hold rigidly to just one of the three viewpoints we have described. Instead, psychologists use whatever view seems most appropriate or useful in solving whatever human problem they happen to face at the moment. Different psychologists may *emphasize* the value of one viewpoint or another, but almost all psychological theories make reference to biological, intra-psychic, and environmental influences.

We need to learn as much as we can about all three points of view, for no one of them *all by itself* can explain the rich complexity of human experience. To demonstrate this point as vividly as possible, let us now study one aspect of human behavior—*violence*—as seen from the social/behavioral, the intra-psychic, and the biological points of view.

Violence: Three Theoretical Viewpoints

To many people, the most terrifying form of violence is murder. If you have ever walked the empty streets of a big city late at night, surely you have feared that some madman might leap out of the shadows to attack you. And if you have seen the results of some particularly bloody massacre on TV, surely you have wondered why the police don't do a better job of protecting innocent people from such criminals. But, as Donald T. Lunde points out in his fascinating book *Murder and Madness*, the facts about violent death are probably quite different from your fantasies and fears.

To begin with, you are quite right to worry about violent death, for at least 20,000 Americans are murdered annually. In fact, more of us in the US were killed by other Americans in the last four years than were killed in Vietnam during the entire war there. According to Reynolds Farley, of the University of Michigan Populations Studies Center, there were 21,000 murders in the United States in 1978. And by 1981, the number of murders was even higher. There are also at least 30,000 rapes and more than 300,000 cases of violent assault per year in this country.

In a way, however, you may be much safer on the streets than in your own home, and better off with strangers than with people you know and love. For almost 80 percent of the murders committed each year involve people related to or friendly with each other, and about 40 percent of the killings occur in homes or apartments.

Per capita (purr KAPP-it-tah). A Latin phrase that means, roughly, "to take an average" or "to count heads." If a city of 1,000 people has one murder per year, and a city of 10,000 people has ten murders per year, the per capita murder rate is the same in both cities.

Daytime is safer than night, for few murders take place during business hours. In Philadelphia, as Lunde reports, two-thirds of the killings occur on weekends, most of them on Saturday night between 8 P.M. and 2 A.M. And perhaps because we're around friends and family more during summer holidays and at Christmas, the murder rate peaks in July and in December. For a variety of reasons, the South is more dangerous than the North. Some 44 percent of all recent murders occurred in the southern states, while the lowest murder rate **per capita** is found in New England.

Some Violent Statistics

As far as violence is concerned, young people are much more dangerous than are older people. For instance, less than 10 percent of the murderers are over 50, and the average killer is about *20 years of age*. It is also true that older people are murdered a lot less than younger ones, for most murder *victims* are under 30 years of age.

As you might suspect, men are three times as likely to kill someone as are women. But women are frequent victims. One-fifth of all the people killed in the US are women murdered in their own bedrooms (usually shot to death by husbands or lovers). When a woman is the murderer, she is most likely to kill a husband or lover by stabbing him to death or shooting him in the kitchen.

According to Lunde, race plays an important part in murder. In some 90 percent of all killings, the victim and the murderer are of the *same race*. However, black men are 10 times as likely to be victims as are white women. Indeed, as Reynolds Farley notes, murder is now the fourth most common cause of death for black males in the United States.

When cross-racial murders do occur, whites are much more likely to kill blacks than vice versa. Blacks are more likely to use knives as murder weapons than whites, while whites are more likely to use guns.

No matter what their race, however, murderers under 15 and over 50 use guns almost exclusively. And, in at least one-third of the cases, the victim seems to have *precipitated the killing*—either by taunting or goading the murderer, or by pulling out a weapon first.

Despite common views on the subject, there is only the slimmest connection between murder and mental illness. Less than 4 percent of convicted murderers in recent years were judged criminally insane in courts of law. A patient released from a mental hospital is no more likely to commit a murder than is the average person—*unless* the patient was hospitalized for being violent. And then the patient is only slightly more likely to commit a crime than is anyone else.

But if we cannot blame most acts of violence on insanity, what is it that causes people to kill each other? Probably each of us has her or his own answer to this question, but most of the explanations will fall within the social/behavioral, intra-psychic, or biological viewpoints. Let's see what each point of view has to say about violence.

Question: *Knowing these statistics, what things could you do to decrease the likelihood that you would either commit a murder or be a murder victim?*

Social Determinants of Violence

Does the society you grow up in affect the probability that you will harm another individual? Do some cultures repress violent behaviors, while other cultures reward or encourage rape, assault, and murder? Perhaps so. For many research studies suggest that the attitudes held by the majority of people within a given society have a marked effect on the level and type of violence found within that society.

In the United States, as we just mentioned, there are more than 20,000 murders a year. The majority of these deaths stem from gunshot wounds. About 51 percent of all American murders are committed with pistols or hand guns, while rifles and shotguns account for another 15 percent or so of the recorded **homicides**.

The city of Detroit has a population of about two million people who, according to police estimates, own an average of one gun per person. In 1981, there were some 700 murders in Detroit, the majority of these being deaths from firearms. By contrast, during the same year, there were fewer than 150 murders in *all* of Great Britain—a land of some 50 million people. And there were only 7 murders by handgun. Americans, in general, take a fairly positive attitude toward the private ownership of hand guns, and almost all of our police are armed. In Great Britain, hand guns are illegal. Not even the police wear pistols, except on rare and very special occasions.

Does the fact that British society takes quite a different attitude toward guns and violent behavior help explain why there are 100 times as many murders (per capita) in the United States each year as in Great Britain? Or should we point the finger of shame at television and other cultural influences instead?

Effects of TV on Violence

In 1969 the US Senate, worried about the impact of TV violence on the personality development of young children, asked the Surgeon General to undertake an extensive study on this subject. In 1972, after an expenditure of one million dollars in research funds, Dr. Jesse Steinfeld (the Surgeon General) reported some interesting findings.

Is there violence on television? Yes, indeed. In 1967, according to the National Commission on the Causes and Prevention of Violence, a staggering 94.3 percent of cartoon shows contained violent episodes. That same year, 81.6 percent of all prime-time entertainment shows on TV contained violence. The Commission estimated that a normal child, growing up during the 60's and 70's, would have watched at least 20,000 incidents of violence on television by the time she or he was 19. By the 1980's, the amount of violence on TV had declined somewhat, in part perhaps because many cultural and religious groups had protested against this type of show. Still and all, in 1981 more than two-thirds of *all* programs still featured episodes of violence.

So television certainly does expose us to violence, but how does this exposure affect us? According to Dr. Robert M. Liebert, a psychologist who helped prepare the Surgeon General's report, "The more violence and aggression a youngster sees on television, regardless of his age, sex or social background, the more aggressive he is likely to be in his own attitudes and behaviors." Dr. Liebert came to this conclusion after reviewing more than 50 scientific studies covering the behavior of 10,000 children between the ages of 3 and 19.

Belson's London Study

By 1982, many other scientists had published experiments whose results tended to confirm some—but not all—of Liebert's conclusions. For example, in 1978 William Belson reported that young British men who are "heavy" watchers of TV violence are much more likely to commit aggressive acts than are boys who view such violence only occasionally.

The several hundred subjects in Belson's study were selected by **random sample** from all parts of London. Belson interviewed and observed the young men for some 10 hours to determine how many violent TV programs they had viewed in recent years. He then divided the boys in two groups—the "heavy watchers" and the "occasionals"—and studied them further.

Surprisingly enough, there were no obvious social, physical, or educational differences between the boys in the two groups. But when Belson asked the boys to report secretly how many acts of violence they had *actually engaged in* during the six months, he found rather shocking results. The "heavy watchers" reported having performed a much larger number of violent acts than did the "occasionals." (Some of the acts reported, incidentally, were dropping lighted matches into a shopper's bag, busting open pay telephones, kicking other boys in the crotch, and beating on automobiles with hammers.)

One important point about Belson's work: Some 50 percent of the boys in the study did not report *any violent acts at all*. A mere 12 percent of the boys were the "active" aggressors—and most of them were "heavy" watchers of violence on television. But each of these "actively" violent young men reported having performed *at least 10 acts of serious violence* in the six months before being interviewed.

Eron's Chicago Circle Studies
In the February 1982 issue of the *American Psychologist*, Leonard D. Eron answers some of the questions raised by Belson's research. Eron and his colleagues at the University of Illinois at Chicago Circle have studied violence in children for more than two decades. In their most recent work, they have found that TV has an effect on aggressive behaviors not only in boys, but in girls as well. But *which* boys and girls does TV affect most, and why?

Eron states that aggressive children have certain common characteristics. First, they tend to be disliked by other children. Second, they indulge in active aggressive fantasies. Third, both aggressive boys and girls prefer masculine activities. Fourth, they are low achievers in school. And fifth, they enjoy watching violence on TV and often identify strongly with the violence they see on the television screen.

The *parents* of these aggressive children have certain things in common, too. First and foremost, Eron says, "Those parents who punish their children physically and express dissatisfaction with their children's accomplishments and social behaviors have the most aggressive children." Both the mothers and fathers of aggressive boys also tend to be aggressive themselves. The younger and less educated the father, the higher his son's aggression. And the lower paying the father's job, the more aggressive his daughter is likely to be.

Homicides (HOMM-ah-sides, or HOME-uh-sides). From the Latin words meaning "man" and "to kill." Generally speaking, homicides are the killing of one human being by another.

Random sample. To make sure that they don't bias or prejudice their results, scientists often select their subjects by "drawing names out of a hat," or by choosing their subjects in some other "random fashion." A sample is a small part of a larger population.

Pornographic (pore-no-GRAF-fick). From an ancient Greek term meaning "writing about prostitutes." Pornography is any written, visual, or other material that is designed to be sexually arousing.

Eron believes that one of the main reasons some children are aggressive is that they have poor models, both in their parents and in the programs they watch on television. Furthermore, these young people apparently cannot differentiate between the fantasy violence they watch on the tube and aggressive behaviors in real-world situations. In his 1982 article, Eron reports that he and his colleagues gave "reality training" to a group of aggressive children in order to help them learn the difference between televised fantasy and reality. The technique involved teaching children the "tricks" that TV producers use in filming their programs. The children were also exposed to the sorts of attitude-change procedures we will describe in Chapter 27. Eron states that the "aggression therapy" was apparently successful. He concludes, "There are simple instructional procedures that can be used by parents and teachers to counteract the negative effects television is having on our children."

Question: *Given the fact that parents of aggressive children tend to be punitive, rejecting, and of low educational status, how likely are they to use the sorts of instructional procedures that Eron has developed? What sorts of things could be done to encourage the parents to learn and use these techniques?*

Violence and Pornographic Films
On American television—and in American movies—violence and sexual aggression are often combined. And it is almost always a male who takes out his violent and aggressive feelings on a female.

In a report in the December 1, 1980 issue of *Behavior Today*, Edward Donnerstein describes what happened when he showed 120 male college students **pornographic** films and then made the subjects angry. Next, Donnerstein gave the subjects an opportunity to display aggression toward other males and females (who were actually actors assisting Donnerstein in the research). According to Donnerstein, if the movies were merely erotic, the students showed little or no increase in

Donald Lunde

As Donald Lunde points out, cultural traditions help determine violence. Police officers in England carry handguns only on rare occasions. Do these photos of police in England (**top left**) and the United States (**right**) help explain why there were less than ten handgun murders in all of England in 1981? During the same period, there were more than 10,000 handgun murders in the United States.

aggression. However, if the films depicted males raping women, the amount of real-life hostility the student-viewers showed toward women increased dramatically. Aggression toward other males increased slightly, but not as much as toward women.

In a subsequent experiment, Donnerstein showed male students two "rape" films—one that showed the woman as "enjoying" the experience, and another that depicted the woman as being greatly hurt and feeling badly humiliated by the experience. Donnerstein reports that subjects who saw the film showing the rape as an "enjoyable experience" became much more hostile and aggressive toward women than did students who saw the woman as being hurt by the rape.

Donnerstein notes that today's aggressive-erotic films almost always show women as enjoying rape and violence. Thus these films reinforce "the myth that women want to be raped. The men perpetrating the violence are not depicted as **deviants**, but as handsome, all-right guys. So the effect may be to reduce many men's inhibitions to be aggressive toward women."

The "Body Language" of Victims

Some people get mugged frequently; others never do. Is there any connection at all between the actions of the *victim* and the aggression the *criminal* shows toward that victim? Psychologists Betty Grayson and Morris Stein believe there is. In the August 1980 issue of *Psychology Today* they report that the way you walk may (in part) determine whether a mugger will select you as a victim—or leave you alone.

Grayson and Stein began by secretly filming 60 people as they walked along the streets of New York City. Then the psychologists showed these films to 65 prisoners who had been convicted of assault and asked the prisoners to rate the "walkers" in terms of their "muggability." Grayson and Stein state that there was an exceptionally high level of agreement among the prisoners as to which of the "walkers" would make easy targets, and which would not.

Grayson and Stein then inspected the films carefully to analyze the way in which the pedestrians walked. Those individuals with high "muggability" scores tended to walk in a dreamy, exaggerated way. Their strides were either very long or very short, and they acted as if they were in conflict with themselves. Grayson and Stein believe that the *body language* of the victims was a loud and clear signal to the **assailant**, "Here is an easy target."

It takes two to tango, and it takes both a victim and an assailant for a violent crime to take place. The Grayson and Stein research suggests that the victim picks the aggressor as much as the other way round.

Violence: A Multi-Determined Behavior

If we put together the various studies on violence, it seems probable that the most likely "candidate" for aggressive behaviors would be a young person who grew up in a family that approved of violence, whose parents watched violent TV shows and discouraged the young person from expressing any sympathy for the victim of aggression. And, judging from the little research so far reported, the victim would most likely be someone confused about life, whose parents had not taught the person much about self-control and getting along with others.

But are social factors the only—or even the major—determinants of violent actions? Is all aggression learned by "imitation," or is the situation much more complex than that?

Bowling Green University psychologist J.P. Scott has studied aggression in man and animals for a great many years. Scott believes that violence is usually multi-determined. That is, aggres-

Deviants (DEE-vee-ants). To deviate is to depart from the average or norm. A sexual deviant is someone whose sexual actions depart so much from the average that the person is considered *abnormal*.

Assailant (ass-SAIL-ant). From a Latin word meaning "to leap upon." An assailant is someone who attacks another person violently, either physically or psychologically.

sive attacks almost always have biological, intra-psychic, and social/behavioral causes.

Scott says that, at the human level, societal factors are usually the most important of all. He points out that males in our culture are encouraged to leave home when they reach sexual maturity, but typically do not form new family ties until several years afterward. Perhaps this is why, in the United States, violent crimes are most likely to be committed by single or divorced males between the ages of 16 and 25.

It is likewise true that these men commonly come from a proverty-stricken background and from homes broken by desertion, divorce, or death. Furthermore, as Scott notes, unmarried young men occasionally organize into groups whose main purpose is that of making war or terrorizing others. The street gangs found in many big cities—and the groups of young men who engage in riots—are good examples of "terrorist organizations." (And while Scott does not say so in his articles, these same men are the ones most likely to become victims of violent crime as well.)

Scott believes that we will not do away with violence and aggression until we create societies that promote peace, stability, and positive interpersonal relationships—particularly among disadvantaged young people in all cultures.

But do we need to teach "peaceful thoughts and behaviors" to *all* people, or are there some individuals whose "inborn personalities" are such that they are likely to become violent—or victimized—no matter what social environment they grow up in?

Intra-Psychic Determinants of Violence

In the later chapters of this book, when we discuss a topic called *personality theory*, we will find that many psychologists view violence as a mental trait or characteristic that is determined by a person's subjective outlook on life. From this intra-psychic position, personality traits are produced both by one's biological inheritance and by what happens during certain critical stages in a person's early development.

Intra-psychic psychologists typically believe that we are born with certain innate response

Fig. 4.3. A raccoon and a hooded rat remain far apart in cage before shock. **(top left)**

Fig. 4.4. Two seconds after receiving a shock, the animals move toward each other. **(top right)**

Konrad Lorenz

patterns—called **instincts**—that are passed along to us genetically by our parents. Our childhood environments, particularly our interactions with our mothers and fathers, shape or mold these instinctual thoughts and behaviors into what we call our *minds*. (As we will see, not all psychologists believe that humans are born with instinctual behavior patterns.)

As we mature, our minds become more and more capable of acting on their own, and we become more and more capable of achieving our personal, subjective goals—within the limits set by our bodies and our cultures.

Many social/behavioral psychologists theorize that we are born without any strong tendency either to be violent or non-violent—we thus become what our environment *teaches* us to become. But according to many intra-psychic theorists, we are born with an aggressive instinct that we must somehow *learn to control*. Thus one of the major functions of civilization is that, at its best, a civilized society trains us to **repress** our aggressive instincts.

Konrad Lorenz

As evidence to support their view, intra-psychic theorists often point to the research of **Konrad Lorenz**, a German scientist who got his ideas about human aggression from spending many years studying the behavior patterns of wild animals. One of the first things Lorenz noted was that instinctual behavior patterns in lower animals are primarily controlled by: (1) such internal physiological factors as hormone levels; and (2) environmental inputs which seem to "release" the instinctual response. During mating season, for example, most male animals will immediately at-

tack another male that wanders into their territory. However, this aggressive behavior occurs only when the amount of male hormone is very high, and when the first male sees, hears, or smells another male. Furthermore, this aggression is almost never directed toward females or infants.

Lorenz believes that while aggressive instincts first evolved in lower animals, the tendency toward senseless violence has reached its peak in human beings. Human males, for instance, often attack other individuals (including women and children) whether or not the attackers have high levels of male hormone. Humans also kill each other out of hatred, prejudice, politics, or "just for fun"—and not, like animals, only when the victim intrudes into the killer's home territory.

Despite Lorenz's very creative research on aggression in animals, however, it is still an open question whether or not human beings are *born* with an aggressive instinct that we must learn to control. But in seeking further data on this matter, it might help if we asked the following question: Do animals ever show the kind of "vindictive nastiness" that we see too often in humans—both on television and in real life?

Pain and Aggression

Psychologist Nathan Azrin and his colleagues, working at the Anna State Hospital in Illinois, fell into the study of violence quite by accident. Azrin is a behavioral psychologist who believes in the importance of rewards and punishments in determining behavior, and he wanted to see if he could train two rats to become "more social." In his research, Azrin defined *social behavior* as "moving toward each other." And Azrin presumed that the more he could reward the rats for "seeking each other's company," the more social behavior they would show.

Azrin and his group began by putting the two rats in a "shock box" (see Figs. 4.3 and 4.4). The psychologists planned to shock the animals and then reward them for moving toward each other by turning the electricity *off*. To the great surprise of Azrin and his group, however, they never got the chance to reward the rats for "social movements." For the moment the shock went on, the two animals turned on each other and attacked each other violently.

Wisely enough, Azrin *et al.* abandoned their original objective and began to study aggression.

First, the psychologists had to make sure they knew what they were studying. Think about it for a moment. How would you go about defining *aggression* in a rat? Azrin *et al.* found that the animal had a characteristic posture: As soon as the rat was shocked, it would stand up on its hind legs, face another rat, open its mouth, bare its front teeth, and then strike out at the other animal with its forepaws. Oddly enough, if another rat (or some similar object) was not present, the shocked animal would show none of this behavior, but would keep its mouth closed and would cling with all four paws to the metal grid on which it stood.

Second, Azrin and his group had to determine whether it was really the *shock* which was causing the aggression, and not some incidental factor they had overlooked. The psychologists tested the relationship between shock and violent behavior by varying the strength or *intensity* of the electrical current. They found that: (1) the stronger the shock, the longer the aggression lasted; and (2) the more frequently the shock was given, the more vigorous and vicious the animal's attack was. Furthermore, the rats did not ever seem to get used to or **habituate** to the shock. The animals would display the attack behavior several thousand times a day if the experimenters shocked them that often.

Azrin *et al.* also showed that this aggressive response was instinctual and not learned, for animals raised from birth in complete isolation from

Instincts. Inherited desires or behavior patterns. An innate reflex is a highly specific stimulus-response pattern that is inherited. For instance, if a mother touches her infant's cheek, the infant will reflexively turn its head as if to suckle. An instinct is a less specific behavioral pattern. For example, the "maternal instinct" is the set of behavior patterns women are supposed to inherit that makes them *want* to take care of their infants. The maternal instinct is not a reflex since the mother presumably will respond to **any** need that the infant expresses. Many psychologists doubt that humans inherit such ill-defined desires or instincts.

Repress. To block out or to forget something deliberately.

Konrad Lorenz (CONE-raht LOR-rents). A noted German biologist who became famous for his studies of animal instincts. Lorenz believes that humans have stronger killer instincts than any other animals, but not all psychologists agree with Lorenz. Technically speaking, Lorenz should be called an *ethologist* (ee-THOL-oh-gist)— that is, a scientist who is interested in the biological basis of behavior. Lorenz received the Nobel Prize in 1973 for his ethological research.

Et al. (ett-all). From the Latin term *et alia*, meaning "and others." Scientists like to give each other credit. If an experiment was performed by Smith and Jones, it is usually referred to as "the study by Smith and Jones." But some experiments are performed jointly by a dozen or more scientists. Rather than writing Smith, Jones, Johnson, Ginsburg, Washington, Lee, Brodsky, Blanc, and Gonzalez each time we speak of the study, we usually say "Smith *et al.*" Usually—but not always—the first name listed is that of the "senior scientist" who had the greatest responsibility for the research.

Habituate (hab-BITT-you-ate). To become accustomed to a place or to a given stimulus. The first time you handle a snake, you may be very frightened. But if snake-handling becomes a habit, your fears may habituate.

other rats still demonstrated the violent attack pattern when they were first shocked. Rats that lived together from birth attacked one another just as often as they attacked animals that were complete strangers. And since both males and females aggressed against members of either sex, Azrin concluded that neither sexual competition nor attraction was responsible for this reaction.

Azrin believes that it was the *pain* of the shock that brought the instinctual behavior pattern into readiness. But it was the *sight* of another animal that "released" the innate response.

Question: Why does the research of Azrin et al. *support the notion that violence is almost always triggered off by the presence of a "victim"?*

Violence Induced by Frustration

Is there something special about the *physical* pain caused by electrical shock that triggers off aggressive behavior, or would a *psychologically* painful stimulus do just as well?

In their next series of experiments, Azrin and his group found that almost any situation which caused the animal psychological discomfort or *frustration* would set off an attack. If a hun-

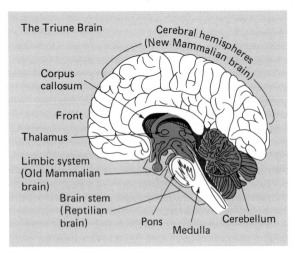

Fig. 4.5. The triune brain.

gry pigeon is rewarded with a piece of grain each time it pecks at a button, it will soon learn to peck the button vigorously. If, after it has been pecking away for some time and earning its corn, you suddenly stop giving it the reward, the pigeon will typically first attack the button. Then it will peck viciously at any other object (such as another pigeon) that happens to be handy. Obviously, "psychological pain" or frustration can lead to violence as readily as can electric shock.

Fortunately, as Azrin *et al.* found out, there is a way to prevent violence from being the natural consequence of frustration and pain. The aggressive **syndrome** usually does not occur if the frustrated animal is given the alternative of *escaping* rather than *attacking*. A rat cooped up in a small box with another animal will attack because it apparently has no alternative. The same rat, if shocked in an open field, will flee from the pain rather than take out its frustration on nearby objects. The attack behavior will also not occur if the animal is given the opportunity to *avoid* the pain or frustration in the first place, or if the animal can end or *terminate* the pain through a peaceful gesture.

Question: From an intra-psychic viewpoint, why might violence be expected to occur more frequently in crowded, big-city slums than in suburban areas? And why would riots be more likely to take place during times of high unemployment than when jobs are easy to get?

Frustration-Aggression Hypothesis

Perhaps the greatest modern contributor to the intra-psychic viewpoint was Sigmund Freud, the Viennese psychiatrist who developed an intra-psychic theory of personality called psychoanaly-

sis. As we will see in later chapters, Freud believed that there is a childish part of our personalities which demands immediate gratification of all its wishes. Whenever this "child" in our minds is frustrated, it may either throw a temper tantrum or display other immature forms of emotion.

Using Freud's basic idea, several psychologists jointly derived what they call the **frustration-aggression hypothesis**. According to this theory, frustration occurs whenever you are (1) highly motivated; and (2) encounter a barrier of some kind that prevents you from reaching a much-desired goal. The barrier may be physical, psychological, or symbolic. If you cannot get around the barrier, you experience frustration, and your behavior typically becomes less logical and more strongly emotional than would usually be the case. According to the hypothesis, aggression is *always* caused by frustration. But a frustrated person may aggress in a great many ways.

Is the frustration-aggression hypothesis correct? Is violence *always* a product of frustration? Well, what about people like Joe who suffer brain damage in an accident? For the most part, Joe was a placid and unemotional individual. But at times he did throw rather violent temper tantrums. Did the damage to Joe's neurons merely cause him to be more easily frustrated than you and I, or did the damage somehow set off "rage attacks" in Joe's brain much like the *grand mal* seizures experienced by people with epilepsy?

To answer that question, we must turn to the "third viewpoint" to discover what scientists know about violence and the brain.

Biological Determinants of Violence

We are not entirely sure what takes place inside the brain of an animal (or human) who flies into a rage and attacks someone else. However, certain parts of the brain do seem to be heavily involved in aggressive behavior, and certain chemicals do appear to inhibit violent reactions while other chemicals excite them. Before you can understand the neuro-chemistry of aggression, though, you will need to know a bit more about the parts of your brain.

The Triune Brain

Dr. Paul D. MacLean is a noted neuro-physiologist who serves as chief of brain evolutionary research at the National Institute of Mental Health. MacLean believes that the human brain evolved over millions of years from the brains of lower animals. But this evolution took place in three main stages, says MacLean, and thus the human brain has three main parts. MacLean calls this belief the **theory of the triune brain**.

According to MacLean, the first animals to develop a true brain were the ancient reptiles. This *reptilian brain* still exists inside your head, says MacLean, in the form of your **brain stem** (see Fig. 4.5). The stem of your brain sits atop your spinal cord, and reaches up to your cerebrum much as the stem of a mushroom reaches from the roots of the plant up to the big, fleshy cap.

Your brain stem includes such neural structures and the **pons** and the **medulla**, which help control such vital activities as walking, breathing, swallowing, and adjusting your heart rate. The brain stem also is the main pathway for conducting messages between your brain and your spinal cord.

Over millions of years, the ancient mammals evolved from the reptiles. And in the evolutionary process, MacLean says, many additional neural structures got tacked onto the reptilian brain. MacLean calls these "tacked on" nerve centers the *old mammalian brain*. The most important parts of this old mammalian brain are the **thalamus**, the **hypo-thalamus**, and the **limbic system**. Your *thalamus* acts as a giant switchboard which routes sensory inputs to the proper areas of your cortex, and transmits output commands from your cortex to the muscles you want to move. As we will see in Chapter 11, your *hypothalamus* is intimately involved in the process of motivation. And we will discuss the *limbic system* in detail in just a moment.

According to MacLean's theory, as the mammals themselves evolved (from rat to cat to elephant to monkey), they acquired the huge cerebral hemispheres that make up the major part of the human brain. MacLean calls this the *new mammalian brain*, which is composed of the cerebrum (and the cortex), the corpus callosum, and the **cerebellum**.

Functions of the "Three Brains"

Although MacLean typically speaks in evolutionary terms, he notes that your "reptilian brain" is incredibly more complex than the brain of any snake or lizard. And your "old mammalian" brain is likewise much more developed than, say, the brain of a rat or cat. Small wonder, then, that your thoughts and feelings and actions are so much more complicated than either a snake's or a rat's.

MacLean tends to assign certain psychological functions to the three types of brain. For instance, he believes that the brain stem controls certain inherited types of behaviors, such as walking and breathing. This part of your nervous system (and of your behavior patterns) presumably

Syndrome (SIN-drome; rhymes with "BEEN home"). A group of symptoms or signs typical of a particular disease or reaction pattern. The aggressive syndrome varies from one animal to another. In cats, for instance, it usually includes spitting, scratching, biting, arching of the back, flattening of the ears, baring of the teeth, twitching of the tail, and so forth.

Frustration-aggression hypothesis. A theory put forth by several psychologists which asserts that frustration is always followed by aggression. Although aggressive behavior obviously does result from some types of frustration, aggressive reactions apparently have other causes as well.

Theory of the triune brain (try-YOUN). A theory by Paul MacLean that there are three main divisions of the brain, each of which evolved from the brains of ancient animals. The brain stem evolved from the reptilian brain, the middle parts of the brain (thalamus, limbic system) evolved from ancient mammals, and the cerebrum evolved from more recent mammals. Each of the three parts of the brain supposedly controls different behavior patterns. Not all scientists agree with MacLean's theory.

Brain stem. The lower area of the brain that connects the spinal cord with the middle parts of the brain.

Pons, medulla (me-DULL-ah). Neural centers in the brain stem that control vital activities such as walking and breathing.

Thalamus, hypothalamus (THALL-ah-mus, HIGH-poh-THALL-ah-mus). Neural centers in the middle part of the brain. Your thalamus is a giant switchboard which routes input messages to various areas of the cortex. Your hypothalamus influences emotions and motivated behaviors (see Chapters 11–13).

Limbic system (LIM-bick). A related set of nerve centers in your brain that influences your emotional behavior.

Cerebellum (ser-ee-BELL-um). From the Latin word meaning "little brain." A large center of neural tissue at the rear of the brain, just below the occipital lobe, that coordinates muscle movements (among other things).

is determined by your genes and functions entirely at an unconscious level.

The old mammalian brain also operates at an unconscious, instinctual level. But most of the activities it controls are involved in satisfying bodily needs and in expressing emotions. This part of your nervous system is, however, capable of learning new response patterns and thus is not restricted entirely to expressing inherited behaviors.

It is your "new brain," however, that gives you the capacity for learning to speak, to think creatively, and to deal with the rich array of informational inputs that come to you from the complex world you live in. It is also true, MacLean says, that your cortex and your cerebral hemispheres are capable of coordinating the activities of the two more "primitive" areas of your brain.

Not all scientists agree with MacLean's notions of how the three main parts of the brain evolved. But to show you how they operate—and how your cortex exercises control over the lower centers in your brain—let us now look more closely at what goes on in your limbic system.

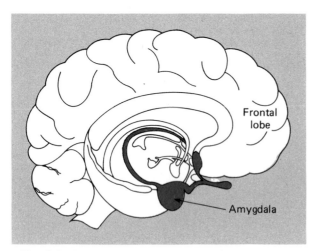

Fig. 4.6. The limbic system in color, showing the amygdala.

hol. But we can remove the animal's cortex surgically while leaving the limbic system intact. How do you think a cat would react if we used a surgical knife rather than a drug to free the limbic system from cortical inhibition?

To begin with, this "de-cortex-ed," or **decorticate**, animal gets along surprisingly well, considering that it has been deprived of more than 10 percent of its brain. There seems to be no basic change in the animal's personality—friendly cats remain friendly, and aggressive felines remain aggressive. However, even *very slight pain or frustration* is enough to set these animals into an explosive, violent rage.

Question: How does MacLean's belief that alcohol makes you "regress" to a more primitive brain agree with the data on the social and psychological influences on alcoholic behavior discussed in Chapter 3?

The Limbic System

The Latin word *limbus* means "border," and the limbic system is so named because it makes up the "border" or inner surface of both your cerebral hemispheres. There are identical limbic systems in both your hemispheres, but since they are usually in close touch with each other (via the corpus callosal bridge), we can consider them as one unit.

Just as each of your cerebral hemispheres is divided into sections—the four lobes—so your limbic system has several parts or structures to it (see Fig. 4.6). One of these structures is the **amygdala**, which is buried deep within the temporal lobe on each side of your head. The amygdala is a nut-shaped group of neurons that gets its name from the Latin word for "almond." Since the amygdala in each of your temporal lobes has a decided influence on how violent you are, and on your sex life, it is well worth studying.

Cortex vs. Limbic System

Under normal circumstances, your cortex maintains control over the primitive, emotional reactions that are set off by activity in your limbic system. But what happens when you take a drug that reduces the ability of your "new brain" to dominate the two more primitive brains? According to the triune brain theory, you would regress to a more "animalistic" way of behaving. The theory assumes, for instance, that drunks act in a childish, aggressive manner because alcohol knocks out cortical control of the limbic system.

Support for this assumption comes from experiments on cats. It isn't easy to get a cat drunk because most animals tend to refuse alco-

Sex and Aggression

Next, what do you think would happen if we "reversed" the kind of operation just described? That is, what would happen if we removed parts of the limbic system in animals but left most of the cortex intact? Heinrich Kluever and Paul Bucy were probably the first scientists to perform this operation. Their experimental animals were rhesus monkeys, a species of **primate** noted for its vile temper and its readiness to aggress. Kluever and Bucy surgically removed the temporal lobes from both hemispheres in their animals—thus taking out the amygdalas and other parts of the limbic system.

After the monkeys had recovered, their personalities appeared to have changed rather profoundly. They were gentle and placid in almost all circumstances, even when attacked by another animal. They also became markedly *oversexed.* The males would attempt to mount anything handy, including inanimate objects. The females would attempt to have sex even with such strange "partners" as water faucets.

Later studies confirmed the Kluever and Bucy experiment by showing that removal of the amygdala in ferocious animals like the lynx or the wolverine makes them relatively tame.

Stimulating the Amygdala

Given the results of the Kluever-Bucy experiment, what do you think would happen if you could somehow *stimulate* the amygdala in a normal cat electrically? The answer is not particularly surprising. If you insert a long, thin needle electrode into a cat's amygdala and turn on the current, the animal flies into a rage. Its hair stands on end, its back arches, it spits and screams, and it will usually attack anything nearby (including the experimenter).

There are at least two explanations for this rage response. First, the electrical stimulation may cause the animal *intense pain* and the cat merely responds as did Azrin's rats. Second, the current may actually trigger off an unconscious *aggressive reflex* which may or may not cause the animal to feel pain. The first explanation seems more likely, however, since recent studies show that pain-killing drugs such as morphine and enkephalin have an *inhibitory effect* on neural activity in various parts of the limbic system. It is also true that the *precise rage response* the animal makes is dependent on what objects are present in its environment when you stimulate its brain, and how it has learned to respond to ordinary rage in the past.

Now, knowing how cats respond to electrical stimulation of their limbic systems, what do you think would happen if someone stuck a needle electrode in *your* amygdala and turned on the current? More to the point, perhaps, why would anyone wish to do such a thing?

Brain Damage and Violence

Some humans—acting perhaps like monkeys without limbic systems—seem to be placid and even-tempered even in the worst of situations. Others of us, however, seem to fly off the handle at the slightest provocation. Could it be that individuals who are particularly bad-tempered might suffer from some subtle damage to their amygdalas?

Vernon Mark and Frank Ervin—two noted neuro-physiologists who worked together in Boston for many years—believe that senseless human violence is almost always associated with some form of brain damage. Mark and Ervin studied many patients who were hospitalized because they had killed or maimed others in "fits of rage." Some of these patients also had epileptic-type seizures, and EEG recordings often suggested the presence of scar tissue in their amygdalas.

When drugs and psychotherapy failed to reduce the number of violent attacks these patients had, Mark and Ervin decided to remove the damaged amygdalas surgically. Some of the patients showed a dramatic improvement following the operation. Unfortunately, many of the patients either were unchanged in their behaviors, or became even worse.

"Psycho-surgery"

Physicians call operations such as the removal of the amygdala **psycho-surgery**, because the pur-

Amygdala (a-MIG-dah-lah). An almond-shaped nerve center in your temporal lobe that is part of your limbic system. Removal of the amygdala makes a monkey rather unemotional and easygoing, but has other effects as well.

Decorticate (de-CORT-uh-cate). An animal or human whose cortex has been removed, usually through surgery.

Primate (PRIME-ate). From the Latin word *primus*, meaning "leader" or "first in line." Biologically speaking, primates are the "top animals"—humans, the monkeys, and the apes. The rhesus (REE-sus) monkey is a primate; so are you.

Psycho-surgery (SIGH-ko-SIR-jurr-ree). Operations performed on the brains of people or animals in order to get them to change their thoughts or behaviors. Biological surgery in order to achieve a psychological "cure" of some kind. As many psychologists have noted, psycho-surgery is seldom all that effective. And what effects it does achieve may not be due to the surgery.

pose of the surgery is to "cure" patients of inappropriate *thoughts or behaviors* that seemingly cannot be removed by pills or medication.

But before we routinely chop up people's brains in order to "make them behave," there are several dangers we should take note of. First, Mark and Ervin have been able to demonstrate clear-cut brain damage in but a *small fraction* of the patients they have studied. Second, as we noted, not all the patients were improved after the surgery. And third, not all scientists have been successful in their attempts to repeat the Mark and Ervin research.

Karl Pribram, a noted neuro-surgeon at Stanford, points out that there is no doubt at all that a damaged amygdala can lead to episodes of violent rage in human beings. But, according to Pribram, we would be very wrong to assume that the reverse is true—*that episodes of violence are a universal sign of scar tissue in the amygdala.* In fact, *most* assaults and aggressive behaviors seem to caused by psychological and social factors, not by brain damage.

Psycho-surgery, then, not only doesn't work very well in most cases, but seems to be aimed at the wrong goal—that of changing the *brain*, rather than changing the violent person's *mental processing* or *social environment*.

Furthermore, the moral questions raised by such operations are complex and often frightening. Pribram reminds us too of another factor that we must always consider in evaluating research such as that performed by Mark and Ervin. Even if a patient does cease being violent after psycho-surgery, we cannot be certain that it is the *surgery* that was responsible for the behavioral change. It may be that the changed *attitudes* of the patient's family, friends, and the medical staff after the operation caused the decrease in aggression. If we *expect* psycho-surgery patients to behave more maturely after parts of their brains are removed, the patients may *respond* to our expectations even if the surgery itself was not particularly successful.

Question: *What kind of experiment could you perform to determine if it were the removal of the amygdala that decreased the patient's violent episodes, or merely the fact that the patient had had an operation of some kind?*

Violence and the Mind-Body Problem

What Causes Violence?

By now, you will understand that your answer to that question depends on your solution to the mind-body problem.

If you take the social/behavioral viewpoint, you will see violence as stemming primarily from the "models" we see in our own family settings and on TV, as well as from the effects that environmental rewards and punishments have on our attitudes and behaviors.

If you take the intra-psychic viewpoint, you will think of violence as a personality trait, an in-

stinctual emotional response to a frustrating or painful situation.

If you take the biological viewpoint, you will look upon violence as caused primarily by electrical activity in the limbic system and other more "primitive" parts of the brain.

If you take an even broader view, however, you will see that there really is *no single cause for violence*. Behavior is always *multi-determined*. Your thoughts and actions are always affected by your biological inheritance, your past experience, and what is going on in your present environment. To give up any of the three main viewpoints toward the mind-body problem would be to short-circuit your understanding of why you think and act as you do.

As we will soon see, however, the major conflict among the three viewpoints comes not so much in explaining "what makes you tick," as it does in suggesting how to repair the human clockwork when it gets violently out of adjustment. Or to put the matter another way, your *theoretical viewpoint* toward people almost always determines the type of *treatment* you think they should have in order to "tick better."

We will begin our discussion of theories and therapies in the next chapter.

Summary

1. The complex set of interactions among brain, mind, and environment is often referred to as the **mind-body** problem.
2. The ancient Greeks thought the mind resided in the heart. The ancient Egyptians believed that a **homunculus** inside the skull pulled the strings that made the body move. **Descartes** stated that mind and body were made of **separate substances** that interacted like husband and wife.
3. In the early 1800's, Franz Joseph Gall developed a technique for "reading the bumps on the head," which he called **phrenology**. Phrenology failed when Pierre Flourens showed he could remove large parts of the brain without removing the "psychological traits" Gall said were located in those parts. Paul Broca first located the **speech center** in the left hemisphere in 1861. We now know that some behaviors are mediated by specific sites in the brain, but others are not.
4. Each cerebral hemisphere is divided into four parts—the **frontal lobe**, the **temporal lobe**, the **occipital lobe**, and the **parietal lobe**.
5. The frontal lobe contains the **motor cortex**. If the motor cortex is stimulated electrically, the person's muscles move or jerk.
6. The temporal lobe contains nerve centers that influence speech, hearing, and emotions. Electrical stimulation to the temporal lobe causes people to hear sounds or noises.
7. The occipital lobe is the visual center of the brain. If the visual input areas in this lobe are stimulated, the person "sees stars."
8. The parietal lobe receives sensory inputs from the skin and muscles. Electrical stimulation to this lobe can cause "prickly feelings" that seem to come from the skin.
9. Large areas of the cortex are silent to electrical probing. These so-called **association areas** are presumably the parts of the cortex where information processing and decision-making occur.
10. That area of psychology concerned with studying how body functions affect behavior is called **physiological psychology**, **biopsychology**, or **psychobiology**.
11. Violence is caused by many factors, including social, intra-psychic, and biological influences.
12. The US is a "violent society" in that we experience more murders and assaults per year than do countries such as England. Most murderers—and their victims—are young.

Most murders involve people who know each other. Some two-thirds of all murderers use a gun.

13. The violence on TV may serve as a **model** for some but not all young people.

14. Males who watched **pornographic** films in which women seem to enjoy rape became more hostile toward women. If women were depicted as being hurt by the rape, the males became much less hostile and aggressive.

15. The **body language** of mugging victims may signal their weakness to their assailants.

16. **Frustration** most often leads to **aggression** when the organism cannot escape from the painful situation.

17. According to the **theory of the triune brain**, the **brain stem** evolved from the reptilian brain, the **old mammalian brain** evolved into the lower centers of the cerebrum such as the **limbic system**, while the **new mammalian brain** evolved into the **cerebrum** and **cortex**.

18. Emotional behavior is correlated with electrical activity in the limbic system, a related set of neural centers that include the **amygdala** in the temporal lobe. Stimulation of the amygdala is often followed by aggressive attacks. Removal of the amygdala leads to a marked reduction in aggressive behavior in animals, but not necessarily in humans.

19. **Psycho-surgery** is an attempt to change thoughts and behaviors by removing parts of the brain. It seldom is effective.

20. Behavior is **multi-determined**. There is no one unique solution to the problem of violence in today's world because almost all violence involves biological, psychological, and environmental factors.

(Continued from p. 84.)

"Peace," Jennifer Ahearn said as she slipped demurely into the chair in front of Professor Rosalind Sackoff's desk.

"Looks more like 'pieces' to me, Jeff," Dr. Sackoff said. "Pieces of this and that, which you dragged out of a trunk of old clothes you found in the attic. Where did you get that Mother Hubbard dress, not to mention that black polka-dot scarf tied around your head?"

"Oh, this is the typical dress of a Hutterite woman," Jennifer said quietly. "I thought you might like to see how they dress."

Rosalind Sackoff laughed. "Whatever happened to blue jeans and T-shirts?"

Jennifer shrugged. "They made me change."

"*Made* you change?"

The young woman nodded. "That was the price I had to pay in order to learn the secret of their peaceful ways."

"Well, don't keep me in suspense," Dr. Sackoff said. "You know how I adore secrets."

Jennifer stared at her hands for a moment or two. "The Hutterites *are* peaceful, you know. They are totally opposed to violence of any kind. No wars, no wife beatings, no child abuse. They live together in almost total harmony."

"Okay, I'll give you that," Rosalind Sackoff said. "But what's their secret? Do they put Miltown in the water, or Pheno-barb in the potato salad?"

"No, they don't believe in drugs of any kind," Jennifer replied. "Not even painkillers. They believe that discomfort is a part of life, and you've just got to get used to it."

Dr. Sackoff shrugged. "So it must be yoga. They sit in the lotus position all day long to achieve oneness with the Universal Spirit."

Jennifer shook her head. "No, they work all day long. Every day. Sometimes they work 16 hours a day, or more. Happily. Contentedly. Peacefully."

A grin creased Rosalind Sackoff's face. "Well, if working 16 hours a day is their secret, it's one I'd like all my students to learn."

"No, their 'secret,' as you put it, is something else."

"Okay, Jeff, I give up. What do the Hutterites do that makes them so nonviolent?"

Jennifer Ahearn sighed. "They brainwash their children."

"They *what*?"

"They call it 'breaking the will.' It isn't really 'brainwashing,' of course, because they don't isolate the kids. But it is a pretty severe type of mental indoctrination, as far as I can tell. They train the child for years and years to do exactly what the group wants the child to do. They make the child give up all its own desires, and force it to obey the Hutterite rules and regulations. And since they have very strict rules against any behavior that would harm another person, they all turn out to be peace-loving."

Dr. Sackoff stared intently at the young woman. "And how do the Hutterites accomplish this miracle? I mean, if it's all that easy, I've known a couple of kids I wouldn't mind trying the technique on."

"Oh, no," Jennifer said. "You couldn't. You see, everyone in the group has to agree on what's right and what's wrong. Everybody has to think the same thoughts and feel the same feelings. And each of them has to give up his or her individuality in order for the system to work."

"Sounds like what we have to go through in order to get tenure," Professor Sackoff said with a laugh. "But seriously, Jeff, how do they manage to achieve such uniform value systems? Do they beat self-discipline into the kids, or something?"

"No," Jennifer replied. "And that's maybe the most terrifying thing about their child-rearing techniques. As far as the Hutterites are concerned, there *is* no self. There is only the group. They don't teach their kids self-discipline, because no one is allowed to decide what is right or wrong. Only the group can do that. All the individual is allowed to do is to obey the will of the group."

Rosalind Sackoff frowned. "No self-discipline at all? Don't they have any feelings of guilt or shame when they break the rules?"

"They don't teach self-guilt," Jennifer said, "Because they believe it's only natural for people to want to misbehave."

"But who punishes you when nobody else is around and you misbehave?

Jennifer Ahearn smiled wanly. "You're *expected* to sin when nobody is watching you. In her article in *Natural History*, Gertrude Huntington describes how her teen-aged daughter reacted to the Hutterite children's lack of self-guilt. The girl was very angry because her parents, the Huntingtons, expected her to be 'good' even when no adults were around. But the other children didn't have to behave when they weren't being observed by adults. And, of course, the kids *did* misbehave occasionally when they were off by themselves."

"Because that was what the group expected them to do."

"Of course," Jennifer said.

"And so the *real* purpose of the group is to watch you continuously so that your evil nature doesn't assert itself," Dr. Sackoff said.

Jennifer nodded in agreement. "Makes a weird sort of sense, doesn't it?"

"Eternal vigilance is the price of peace, eh?"

"Yes, but vigilance by the 'hundred friendly eyes always watching you,'" the younger woman said.

The older woman sighed deeply. "That's a pretty expensive price to pay, at least from my biased point of view."

"But it *works*!" Jennifer said loudly. "They have no child abuse, no women battered to bits by their husbands, no murders, and no violence at all."

"And, if I remember correctly, they also don't have any real art, music, science, or literature to call their own. Would you give up Shakespeare and Beethoven and all the miracles of modern medicine in exchange for cutting the murder rate to zero?"

Jennifer Ahearn stared quietly at her hands for a few seconds. "I don't really know."

"Would you give up self-awareness, free will, and the ability to choose things for yourself? Would you surrender all individuality as the price for everlasting peace?"

After a moment, Jennifer said, "I haven't figured that one out yet. You see, their system does work, for them, at least. And it does turn out the most peace-loving kids in the world. And you know something?"

"What?"

"After a while, when I got used to the rigid sex-roles, and the loss of privacy, I sort of got to like it. A little bit, anyhow. I mean, I felt very safe, and very secure, and very much a part of the group. But . . ."

"But you aren't about to go back, are you?"

Jennifer shook her head. "No, it was a nice place to visit . . ."

"But you wouldn't want to live there?" Dr. Sackoff said, laughing.

"Not just yet. But I did get to know myself—and other people—a little better while I was there."

"It was a real learning experience, eh?" the professor said.

"It was that," Jennifer said, smiling. "And it gave me a lot of things to think about."

Rosalind Sackoff grinned. "Good. And generous me, I'll give you the whole semester to figure out how to achieve the Hutterite goals without paying the penalty they do. In 20 pages or less, typewritten, double-spaced, and with lots of references, of course."

Jennifer laughed. "Of course," she responded, getting up from her chair and heading for the door.

"Peace," Dr. Sackoff said.

Jennifer turned and looked thoughtfully at the woman. "Yes, peace," she said finally. And then she opened the door and went out.

Recommended Readings

Belson, William. *Television Violence and the Adolescent Boy* (London: Teakfield, 1978).

Cater, Douglass, and Stephen Strickland. *TV Violence and the Child: The Evolution and Fate of the Surgeon General's Report* (New York: Russell Sage, 1975).

Lunde, Donald T. *Murder and Madness* (New York: Charles Scribner; San Francisco: Freeman, 1975).

MacLean, Paul. "A mind of three minds: Educating the triune brain," in *Education and the Brain*, 77th Yearbook of the National Society for the Study of Education, Part II (Chicago: University of Chicago Press, 1978).

Mark, Vernon H., and Frank R. Ervin. *Violence and the Brain* (New York: Harper & Row, 1970).

Valenstein, Elliot S. *Brain Control: A Critical Examination of Brain Stimulation and Psychosurgery* (New York: Wiley, 1973).

Zillmann, Dolf. *Hostility and Aggression* (Hillsdale, N.J.: Erlbaum, 1979).

General Systems Theory 5

Did You Know That . . .

The better the predictions that a scientific theory makes about future events, the more accurate it probably is?

The most important reason for accepting or rejecting a scientific theory is usually its usefulness?

According to General Systems Theory, you are a "living system"?

All living systems are capable of learning how to alter their behaviors in order to get the inputs they want?

When you "decide" to do something, you typically make use of "feed-forward" and "feedback"?

The "mind/body" problem is one of the oldest and most important in the whole field of psychology?

Early in this century, the behaviorists denied the "mind" existed?

Mental problem solving and creativity may involve a "dialogue between the two hemispheres of the brain"?

Learning to help others often means learning to change yourself first?

"The System Is the Solution"

"Well, Tom," Dr. Donald Severeid asked, "How are you doing with Patti?"

Tom Watson smiled broadly. He was a graduate student in educational psychology with a strong love for young children. Thus when Dr. Severeid had offered him the chance to work with a severely retarded child named Patti, Tom had jumped at the opportunity. "Things are going beautifully."

"But when you first saw her, you thought there would be real problems. Remember?"

A serious expression wiped the smile off Tom's face. "Yeah, I know. When I met Patti, all I could see were the things she did wrong. I thought she was little more than an animal."

"A pig, as I recall," Severeid said.

"Well, she *was* a pig then," Tom replied defensively. "She was four years old, but she acted like a spoiled two-year-old. She was fat from over-eating, she couldn't talk very well, and she had a mean streak in her that was a mile wide."

Professor Severeid frowned. "A *mean streak*?"

Tom nodded. "Every time she got angry at you, she'd pinch you as hard as she could. And that young lady has *strong* fingers."

"I thought we had agreed to be objective about Patti's problems, Tom. Wouldn't it be better to say that her response to stress and frustration was to display aggressive behavior?"

"What's the difference?" Tom asked.

Dr. Severeid sighed. "To say that she has a 'mean streak in her' implies that you can actually see inside her mind. And having looked, you have *perceived* an innate personality characteristic you call 'meanness.' In truth, all you can say *objectively* is that she responds to stressful inputs by pinching you. This 'mean streak' business is simply your theoretical way of trying to explain why she acts as she does."

Tom Watson nodded. "I see what you're getting at. But if I really love the kid—and you know I do—does it really matter how we describe her?"

"Of course it does," the professor said. "If you say she has a mean streak, therapy consists of trying to 'change her personality.' But if you say that pinching is a 'learned response to frustration,' then you try to teach her better ways of handling stress. Which technique do you think would work best with Patti?"

Tom sighed. "I *know* which way works best. I tried lecturing her, and appealing to her pride, and she just pinched harder. Then I did what you suggested, and taught her how to get what she wants without pinching."

"And?"

"And she doesn't pinch much anymore. Particularly when I remember to reward her when she behaves well."

Dr. Severeid smiled. "Yes, of course. Good for you, Tom. And what else have you done? What about her over-eating? Did you work on her 'piggishness,' or did you try to find out what was causing her to ingest all that food?"

Tom laughed in response. "You're right again. Her parents had scolded her for eating too much, and her reaction was to eat more. So I didn't really work on 'piggishness' as such."

"What did you do?"

Tom leaned back in his chair. "Well, I looked at her behavior in terms of inputs, outputs, and consequences. I decided that she just hadn't learned how to get what she wanted, so she grabbed everything in sight and stuffed it in her mouth. And when her parents fussed at her, they were merely rewarding her inappropriate behaviors."

"So?"

"So I taught her the names for food, and to say 'please' when she wanted something and 'thank you' when she got it." Tom Watson frowned thoughtfully. "I must say that she learned much faster than I thought she would, given the fact that she was born with such a damaged brain. I guess nobody had tried the right sort of treatment with her before, and maybe we just blamed her for being brain-damaged instead of blaming ourselves for not finding a way to help her effectively."

Dr. Severeid's face brightened into a smile. "Nice insight, Tom. But what about self-control?"

"Well, after I taught her to ask for things politely, I started to delay giving her the food for a few seconds. She learned to handle the delay because she could always see the reward she was waiting for, and she knew she'd get it if she just waited a moment or two longer."

"And what about her screaming? Didn't that bother you a lot at the start of treatment?"

Tom grinned. "Yeah, it bothered everybody. I remember once I took her to the supermarket, to help her learn the names of some new foods. And we had this slight disagreement about what to do next. I wanted to go home; Patti wanted to stay. I started pulling, and she started screaming. Three women came over and bawled me out for hurting the little darling." Tom smiled wistfully. "Patti pinched all three of them. I think they got the message."

"I'm sure they did," Dr. Severeid replied in an amused tone of voice. "But how did you handle the screaming response, Tom?"

The young man laughed. "One day when we were heading home from a walk, we took a shortcut across the football field. Not a soul in sight. Patti decided she didn't want to go home, so she started yelling. I just sat down, covered my ears, and let her scream. Every once in a while, when she was catching her breath, I'd tell her quietly that we'd go home when she stopped the noise. It took 20 minutes or so before she calmed down, but finally she gave in. Funny thing, she hasn't screamed at me much at all lately."

Professor Severeid nodded. "Extinction of a learned response. If you don't reward her for screaming, she eventually stops it. A bit wearing on the ears, but it works." After a moment, the man went on. "Have you tried extinguishing any of her other inappropriate behaviors?"

"A couple of them," Tom said. "Mostly having to do with soiling her pants. You know, her doctor said that she might be too retarded to learn how to control her bowels, but that's not her problem at all. She's got too much control! When she gets tired of working on food names, she begins to whine. If I don't stop right away, she cries, 'Oh, oh! B.M.!' And then she dumps. Takes about 10 minutes to clean her up, and by then I don't feel like doing much of anything except go home."

"How are you handling the soiling response?" the professor asked gently.

"I asked her doctor if I could put her back in training pants. He agreed. Now when she cries, 'Oh, oh! B.M.!' I just let her sit in her own mess for a while and continue the lesson. She hasn't tried that little trick on me now for a couple of weeks."

Dr. Severeid nodded soberly. "Well, Tom, it sounds like you're making real progress. I wonder if you wouldn't like to bring Patti over to show to my class. You might talk with her parents and, if they approve, you can give her a lesson in that demonstration room with the one-way mirror. The class can watch what you're doing without Patti's seeing them. And afterward, they can ask you questions about your work."

A week or so later, Tom escorted four-year-old Patti into the demonstration room. As the door clicked shut solidly behind them, Tom led her over to the table and dumped a bag of goodies on the table.

"Food," Patti said, pointing at the bag.

"Yes, food," Tom responded, pulling two chairs up to the table. He looked at the mirror-like window set in one wall. The students in Dr. Severeid's class presumably were behind the glass, watching. They could hear Tom's voice—and Patti's—through a loudspeaker. He nodded briefly at the students and then turned his attention to the little girl.

Holding up a piece of sweet cereal so that Patti could see it, Tom asked, "Patti, would you like this?"

"Oh, yes," Patti squealed delightedly.

"Ask for it politely, by name, and you can have it."

Patti frowned. "Froot Loop," she said, and reached for the sweet.

"No, ask for it politely, and I'll be happy to give it to you."

"Please Tom can I have the Froot Loop?" she said, struggling to get the words right.

"Patti, you can have anything at all if you ask for it nicely," Tom said in an encouraging tone of voice, giving her the piece of cereal.

Patti devoured the sweet greedily. "More!" she cried.

Tom ignored her and pulled a fresh green grape from the bag of goodies. "What is this, Patti?"

"I want it," was the girl's eager reply.

"Tell me what it is, and ask for it politely, and you can have it. Now, what is it, Patti?"

"Groop," said Patti.

"That's good, very good. You said it almost right. Grape, Patti, grape. Now you say it."

"Grape," she squealed, and grabbed for the piece of fruit.

"Say 'please,' Patti."

"Please give me the groop."

Tom could hear some muffled giggles from the other side of the one-way mirror. He tried a little harder. "Please give me the *grape*."

"I want it!" Patti wailed.

"I'll give it to you when you ask politely," Tom said, fearing that the students wouldn't appreciate what a great improvement even this behavior was over the way she had acted before he had started working with her.

"Please give me the grape, Tom," Patti said, all sweetness and smiles.

Tom handed her the grape. "You're doing beautifully, Patti. Just keep it up so that everyone will know know smart you really are." He reached in the bag again and pulled out a small cookie, knowing it was one of her favorites.

"Cookie!" Patti squealed with delight. "Gimme."

"Yes, you're right. It's a cookie. But you have to ask for it, and then when I give it to you, you have to wait 30 seconds before you eat it. Okay? If you can wait for 30 seconds, you can eat that cookie, and another one too!" He pulled another cookie out of the bag. "Now ask for it politely . . ."

"Please, please, can I have the cookie?" She held out her hand.

"Okay," Tom said, placing the bit of cookie on her open palm. "Now just hold it there safely until I say 'Go.'" He started counting off the seconds. "One, two, three . . . that's marvelous, Patti. You're really doing beautifully . . . twelve, thirteen, fourteen . . . You're a good girl, Patti. You're really learning self-control. Now just a little longer . . . twenty-eight, twenty-nine, thirty, EAT!"

Patti gobbled the cookie down at once. Tom smiled and gave her the second cookie, which she pushed into her mouth even before she had finished the first.

"Good girl, Patti," Tom said. "You did just beautifully. I bet you could wait 40 seconds next time, couldn't you?"

Patti nodded, still munching on the cookies.

"Okay, now it's time to learn a new word. Again Tom reached into the bag and pulled something out. It was a tiny sweet pickle. "Do you want this, Patti?"

Patti turned up her nose. "Don't like. Wanna go home."

Tom panicked. "No you don't. You want to learn some new names today, don't you? This is a pickle, Patti. A sweet pickle. Say 'sweet pickle' and I'll give you a bite."

Patti turned away from him. "Don't like."

"You'll get us both in a pickle if you don't behave, Patti. Tell you what, if you try to say 'sweet pickle,' I'll give you another cookie? Okay?

"Wanna go home!" Patti shrilled.

"Not yet, darn it. We've got a lot of work to do, and . . ."

"Oh, oh! B.M.!" Patti screamed.

There was a strange noise, and a contented look spread over the little girl's face.

Tom ignored the whole episode. "Okay, Patti, just a little longer, and then we'll go home, okay? Now, please try to say 'sweet pickle.' Please?"

Patti squirmed uncomfortably in her chair. A peculiar and rather upsetting smell arose from her vicinity.

"Don't like. Wanna go home," she said, rather softly.

"I know. I'll take you home just as soon as you try to say 'sweet pickle.' So please, Patti, try to say it. I'm really proud of what you've done, and I want you to look good. So try, Patti, try."

The smell got worse.

"Sweat puckle."

"That's close. Very close." He patted her on the back. She squirmed again, and the odor became more intense. "Sweet pickle. Just say it right once, and we can go home."

"Sweet buckle."

The stench was now so bad that Tom was feeling a bit sick. But then he remembered the students watching him. Since they couldn't smell anything through the mirror, they didn't know what he was putting up with. So he tried again.

"One more time, Patti. You're doing really good. Just say 'sweet pickle,' and we'll go home right now. And I do mean now."

"Sweet pickle," Patti said, smiling brightly.

"Beautiful, Patti. I knew you could do it. Here's the cookie." He gave her the reward, and gathered up what was on the table and stuffed it into his bag. "And now let's get out of here," he said, gagging a bit as he spoke.

Grabbing the little girl by the hand, he led her to the door. He reached for the knob and pulled hard. The door wouldn't budge. Tom tried again. And again. The door didn't move even a fraction of an inch. It was obviously locked from the outside.

Tom turned toward the mirror. "Hey, you guys. The door is locked. Somebody come open it before I die of asphyxiation."

There were noises from the other room, and soon other noises outside the door. Patti began to cry softly, and the stink became unbearable.

Moments later, Tom heard a muffled voice outside the room. "The door is locked, and we haven't got a key. You'll just have to stay there until we can find the janitor."

"Well, hurry up!" Tom yelled.

"I wanna go home," Patti wailed, and pinched Tom's arm.

"Listen," Tom said angrily. "You do that once more and I'll pinch you back right where it will hurt the most." He reached down, his fingers threatening painful revenge.

Patti screamed in terror. "Oh, oh! B.M.!"

"Oh, oh," Tom moaned. "Sweet pickle!"

(Continued on page 131.)

How To "Tick Better"

In the last chapter we asked, "What makes you tick?" And we found that "ticking" is *multi-determined*—that your attitudes, your feelings, and the things you say and do are influenced by physiological, mental, and environmental factors. In this chapter, we ask you, "What do you have to know or do in order to tick *better*?"

The answer to that question turns out to be surprisingly complex. For in order to help yourself, you often must learn how to understand, deal with, and help other people. And in order to deal successfully with others, you typically must have some understanding of—and control over—your own thoughts and actions.

It is at this very practical level of trying to help ourselves (and others) that most of us run into difficulty. For most of us have never been trained to look at human behavior *systematically*, much less *objectively*. That is, most of us have not learned how to identify—and deal with—the biological, intra-psychic, and social influences on our thoughts, emotions, and behaviors. Put more precisely, most of us have never acquired a **holistic** or *unified* theory of human nature.

The major purpose of this chapter, then, is to give you a *theoretical perspective* that may enable you to see yourself and others in a more unified way. And once you learn to *perceive* the world differently, you may find new ways to *reshape* that world to bring it closer to your heart's desire.

Scientific Theories

All sciences, including psychology, are built on **theories**. Scientific theories are summaries of what we *know* about a given topic. And since they gather past knowledge together in a structured form, they help us predict future events. Thus theories are extremely handy things to have around, for they give you a framework for understanding yourself and the world around you. But as necessary as these theoretical explanations may be, they can mislead you if you don't remember one fact—theories are merely *approximations to the truth*.

To put the matter another way, even our best scientific explanations are *limited in their usefulness*. For theories are merely verbal or mathematical descriptions of the world, and the world is far too complicated for the simple words and mathematical symbols we presently have available to us. Thus all theoretical frameworks are somewhat *incomplete* and somewhat *inaccurate* descriptions of real-world systems.

But we cannot live without theories because they help us organize what we know about ourselves and the rest of the world. And theories not only give meaning to the facts we already have available to us, they also tell us what we should do in the future to learn more about a variety of subjects. The question then becomes, how should we pick and choose among the many psychological explanations of human behavior available to us?

Judging a Scientific Theory

Scientists have many different **criteria** by which they judge theories. Some scientific scholars want a theory that leads them to further research and to exciting new ways of perceiving the world. Other scientists prefer **hypotheses** that tell them which facts have practical importance, and which don't seem very valuable at the present. Still other scholars—mostly those who are politically active—desire theories that reinforce their notions about how people ought to behave in a variety of situations.

There is, therefore, no one set of guidelines that all scientists agree upon when it comes to judging the "goodness" of a theory. However, most scientists do admit that the following four criteria are quite important:

Holistic (ho-LISS-tick). From an old English word *hool*, meaning "whole." A holistic theory is one that assumes that "the whole is greater than the sum of its parts." Put another way, you are more than a collection of organs and cells, for you have properties (such as consciousness) that cannot be explained in terms of the actions of your parts.

Theories (THEE-or-rees). From the Latin word meaning "to behold, or view." A "theorem" (THEE-or-em) is a scientific or mathematical statement whose truth has been proven, or at least assumed. A theory is a set of related theorems, thus a collection of statements about some aspect of science. Generally speaking, a theory is a set of assumptions about the way the world (or a part of it) works. A theory is also a collection of facts, or data. It is thus a *viewpoint* that is capable of being disproved by additional factual evidence. A theory that is incapable of being *disproved* is, scientifically speaking, not worth the paper it's written on. The word "theater" comes from the same Latin word as does "theory," and a theory presents the same condensed view of things that a play or movie does.

Criteria (cry-TEER-ee-ah). Plural of *criterion* (cry-TEER-ee-on). From a Latin word meaning "to judge, or decide." The criteria for success in school usually include good grades, the ability to read and write effectively, to think logically, and so forth.

Hypotheses (high-POTH-ee-seize). Plural of hypothesis. An hypothesis is a guess or conjecture about the world or some part of science or mathematics. Generally speaking, a good theory gives you many new hypotheses that you can then test experimentally.

1. How accurate is the theory?
2. How complete is the theory?
3. How elegant or impressive is the theory?
4. How useful is the theory?

Let us look at these four criteria one by one.

Accuracy

In order to test the accuracy of a theory, we usually follow the *scientific method*. That is, we use the theory to *make a prediction* about something, and then we run experiments or make observations to see how accurate the prediction was. If the theory does a good job of predicting, we tend to accept or believe in the theory. If it does a poor job of predicting, we probably should either revise the theory, or switch to another one.

Completeness

Some theories give us detailed descriptions of one limited part of the world, while other theories give us broad descriptions of "the whole big ball of wax." Psychology has both types of theories.

For example, *perceptual theories* are an attempt to describe one small part of your life—how you take in information about your world and process it so that it makes sense (see Chapters 6–10).

Motivational theories are a way of describing another limited aspect of your life—your goals, and how you attempt to reach them (see Chapters 11–13).

Learning theories treat yet another small segment of your psychological world—how you acquire new thoughts, attitudes, and behaviors, and how you remember them (see Chapters 14–17).

Developmental theories are a bit more complex. These theories attempt to describe where all your perceptions, motives, habits, and memories come from—and how they develop over the span of your life (see Chapters 18–20).

Personality theories are even more complicated, for they try to lay out in systematic terms not only how you became the person you are, but also how you might go about changing yourself (see Chapters 21–24).

Social theories are ultimately the broadest of all, for they try to tell us two important things: First, how individuals react to each other; second, how social systems (such as groups and organizations) grow and develop (see Chapters 25–27).

In psychology, then, our theories run from the simple to the complex. But what we need in addition is a sort of "master viewpoint" that would let us put all these individual theories together into one comprehensive whole. By far the most holistic or unified of the "master viewpoints" is *General Systems Theory*. We will talk more about this approach in just a moment.

Elegance

The noted French physicist Paul Dirac once said, "It is more important to have beauty in one's [theoretical] equations than to have them fit the data." Some scientific theories may impress you because they are particularly simple or **elegant**. Other theories may impress you because they match the world as you see it. For example, if you stand on the beach and look out at the ocean, the world surely *looks* flat. We now know that "looks are deceiving." But up until 1520—when Ferdinand Magellan and Juan del Cano sailed around the world—most people refused to question the "flat earth" theory because it fit what they saw.

Other viewpoints are impressive because they tell us what we want to hear. For instance, consider the very strange theory of intelligence dreamed up 100 years ago by Paul Broca—the noted French scientist who discovered the "speech center" in the brain. Broca began with an incorrect assumption, namely, "the bigger the brain, the brighter the person." He then performed a rather sloppy study of the *size* of human brains. Broca concluded—incorrectly—that males had larger brains than females, and that whites had larger brains than blacks. Broca then announced that he had *proven* that men were more intelligent than women, and that whites were innately smarter than blacks.

Actually, there is no known relationship between "brain size" and "intelligence" in humans. But because what Broca said confirmed what many French citizens believed anyhow, his work was accepted as "fact" rather than "theory."

If you are like most people, you will tend to prefer beautiful, elegant, simple theories that reinforce your own observations and prior beliefs. And once you have accepted a theory because it impresses you favorably, you may find yourself reluctant to give it up even when newly discovered facts show that it is less accurate or complete than another theory.

Usefulness

Although not all scientists agree, one of the most important criteria by which a theory is typically judged in real-life situations is this one: How useful is it to you?

The *usefulness* of a theory can be measured in many ways. At a personal level, a theory can give you emotional pleasure because it offers new insights into the world and the people you live with. If you are a practicing scientist, and a theory suggests new and exciting experiments to perform, then it may be useful to you professionally. Personal theories tend to be loosely stated, such as "fat people are jolly," or "spare the rod and spoil the child." Scientific theories tend to be more formal and mathematical, such as Einstein's famous equation, $E = mc^2$.

However, the ultimate joy for most of us is that of reaching our own personal goals. In the long run, therefore, you will most likely adopt the personal or scientific theories that give you the best predictions about yourself and others—and thus give you sufficient control over yourself and your environment so you can get what you want from everyday life.

You already have a great many *personal* theories about human behavior that you probably believe in rather strongly—but that you're aren't conscious of believing in. One of the major purposes of this book, then, is to make you aware of the personal theories you already hold. But a second major purpose is to impress you with the usefulness of various *scientific* viewpoints that you might wish to consider adopting.

Of all the broad-scale psychological theories available to us, **General Systems Theory** is one of the most comprehensive and elegant. Even more important, the General Systems approach is one of the most useful in helping us change ourselves—and others.

So let us spend a few pages describing General Systems Theory, and then discuss both its good points and its failures.

General Systems Theory

If you are like most people, you will marry and raise a family sometime in your future life. Perhaps you are already doing so. In either case, at some point after the birth of your first child, you probably will give considerable thought to what your child's future might be.

So, imagine that you are sitting beside a crib, and in that crib is your own first child. The infant is now a healthy six weeks old. Chances are good that, as you look as this marvelous youngster, you will perceive it (theorize about it) in several ways. First, you will see it as being *your* child— that is, you will *assume* the infant is an extension of your own mind and body. Second, you will see it as being a normal *human being* which, according to most theoretical (and moral) viewpoints, you ought to love and help as best you can.

But just for a moment, stand back and—like a physician judging your infant's state of health— look upon this child of yours as being a **living system**. This child has biological needs that must be met if it is to survive. No matter how much you may love the child, if you do not give it food, air, and water—and if you do not protect it from germs and other physical dangers—the child will die before it can reach maturity.

First and foremost, then, your infant is a *biological system* that requires certain inputs from its environment in order to maintain that miraculous internal process we call "life."

But infants are more than mere biological machines. For each human being is a unique *psychological system* as well, and each of us is a part of such larger *social systems* as groups, organizations, and societies.

Thus, in order for you to best meet *all* the needs of your infant—biological, social, and psychological—you may have to *perceive* this tiny child as being much, much more complicated than you had ever dreamed it was. And to help it survive, you must come to *understand* how the child interacts with you and the rest of its environment. But to achieve these goals, you may need one or more scientific theories about human life to guide you.

Question: In some present-day cultures with very high rates of infant mortality, parents understand very little about germs and disease. The parents thus see no reason for boiling their drinking water or keeping their children clean.

Elegant (EL-ee-gant). From a Latin word meaning "to select, or elect." To be elegant is to be graceful and dignified in appearance or manner. An elegant theory is one that is a simple way of defining and solving scientific problems. Given a choice between two competing theories, most scientists will prefer the one that has the fewest loose ends hanging about, or that is the shorter or more "refined."

General Systems Theory. A holistic view of the biological, psychological, and sociological sciences. According to General Systems Theory, humans are living systems made up of sub-systems (cells, organs). But humans are themselves sub-systems of such larger social systems as the group, organization, and society. In order to understand yourself, then, you must learn how your own sub-systems affect you, and how you affect (and are affected by) the groups, organizations, and societies to which you belong.

Living system. The cell, organ, organism, group, organization, and society are all examples of living systems. All systems are made up of related parts (sub-systems), are open to the environment (have inputs and outputs), act as if they were motivated to achieve goals, are controlled by feed-forward, expectancies about consequences, and feedback, and are capable of a certain amount of self-control.

Why would it be difficult for you to reduce the number of infant deaths in these cultures without first changing the parents' "theoretical viewpoint" toward dirt and germs?

What Is Life?

What does it mean—in practical terms—to view your infant as a *living system*? Before we can answer that question, we must first define a few terms.

A Pattern of Interactions

As we noted earlier, *primitive terms* such as "life" are terribly slippery things to define. Life is a *process*, not a lump of coal or a piece of concrete reality. An instant after you die, much of your body will still be *physically* what it was the moment before. But because most of your organs would no longer be actively interacting with each other, you would be dead rather than living. From a systems point of view, then, life is determined by a *pattern of interactions* among the various parts of your body.

This pattern of interactions *among* your body parts is so complex that we understand very little about how the miracle of life occurs. Indeed, we don't really know all that much about how any *one* part of your body takes care of itself, much less how it communicates with other parts. But at least we have learned some of the *biological characteristics* that all living things seem to possess. We know, for example, that biological systems function as if their *major purpose* in life was that of *survival*.

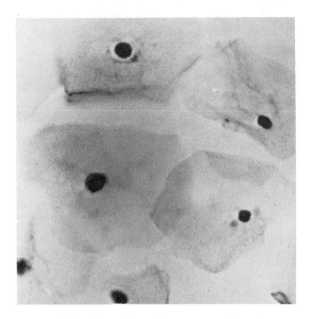

Various types of systems; a cell, an organ, an organism, and a group. All systems have certain characteristics in common.

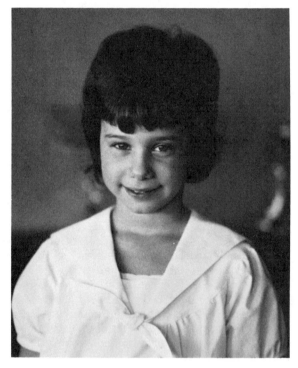

Goal-Oriented Behaviors

Oddly enough, as soon as we use the word "purpose," we have switched from a biological to a psychological viewpoint. For "purposes" imply actions and behaviors, and it is difficult to discuss *behavior* in purely physiological terms.

So we might note that, *psychologically speaking*, all living systems possess certain specific characteristics too. For instance, from the tiniest cell to the largest animal, all living things behave as if they were *goal-oriented*, which is to say that all living systems have ways of achieving the inputs (or goals) that they require to sustain life.

Motivation and Emotion

If you observe your child carefully, you will soon note an interesting fact. The infant cries when it is hungry, but it stops crying when it is full. Why? The child cries because it experiences hunger and is motivated to reduce its hunger pangs. It stops crying when the food it has eaten reduces its hunger and thus its motivation.

As we will see in Chapters 11–13, the term *motivation* almost always refers to goal-oriented behavior. Hunger is a type of motivation that the infant experiences as a painful event (input). The crying is the child's way of expressing (outputting) its *emotional feelings* about its need for food.

When deprived of something needed for life—or when kept from achieving a goal—almost all living systems show *agitated movements* that we typically call "emotional behavior." *Emotion*, therefore, is another psychological characteristic of all living systems.

Learning

The first time a newborn infant cries for food, it usually does not stop its agitated actions until long after it has begun to eat. After a few days or weeks, however, the newborn child will often cease its crying as soon as its mother or father appears. For it has *learned* that the arrival of a parent (or whoever feeds the child regularly) means that food is at hand. Eventually the infant learns to cry in one way when it is hungry, and in another way when it is wet or cold or wants to be played with.

Of all the psychological characteristics of life, *learning* is probably the most important. For without the ability to change, to adjust, and to grow, we surely wouldn't survive for a very long time.

Life is a process, then, with many different biological and behavioral aspects to it. But this process of life occurs only in **systems**, so before we can appreciate fully what life is, we must define the second word in the term "living systems."

Question: How does the infant's ability to learn to cry in "different tones of voice" aid its survival? What would happen if the parents responded the same way no matter how the infant cried?

What Is a System?

What do you think of when a person says, "I have a system"? Probably you will imagine some technique or series of steps that the person has in mind for achieving a particular goal. But what do you think of when a friend of yours says, "I want to beat the system!" Now you will probably see "the system" as being a social organization of some sort.

An Organization of Related Parts

The key word in defining the term "system" is *organization*. Technically speaking, a system is *an organization of related parts*. And for the parts of

> **System**. From the Latin word meaning "to bring together, or combine." A system is a set of parts that are related to each other in some way, that are in communication with each other, or that have ways of affecting each other. The system itself is *always* greater than the sum of its sub-systems. Living systems are open to the environment—that is, they take in energy and information from the world, and give energy and information back to the environment.

a living system (such as your infant) to be "related," these parts must be in some kind of *communication* with each other. As an example, the organs in your body communicate with each other in many different ways. Your heart pumps food and oxygen to your brain, while your brain sends neural messages to your heart telling it when it should become excited and pump blood faster, and when it should relax and pump slower. Your heart thus communicates *energy* to your brain, while your brain communicates *information* to your heart.

Inputs, Processes, Outputs

In order to survive, each living system must take in such things as food and water from its environment. The system then uses (or *processes*) what it gets, and releases its wastes back to the environment. One of the major characteristics of living systems, therefore, is that they have *inputs, internal processes, and outputs* (see Fig. 5.1).

Information vs. Energy

Generally speaking, there are two major types of inputs, internal processes, and outputs: those having to do with *energy*, and those having to do with *information*.

When you eat supper, your body takes in food, which it then digests or processes internally. Later, your body will release energy (and matter) back to your environment—in part through waste products, in part through behavior.

As you read this book, you are "inputting" information of one kind or another. You process this information as you evaluate it, try to understand it, and as you file the material away in your memory. And you output that information by talking or responding in new ways.

Most inputs, internal processes, and outputs involve *both* energy and information. You learn what to eat, and what not to eat. And you need food in order to learn new habits that will help you survive.

Controlling Your Inputs

Think back again to your infant lying in its crib. We have already said that it is strongly goal-oriented, and that its major goal is that of survival.

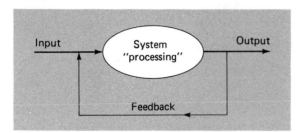

Fig. 5.1. The inter-connection of input, output, and feedback.

But how does an infant survive? By now, perhaps you can see that no living system (including both you and your infant) can survive unless that system can somehow *control its environmental inputs*.

Almost all of your goals in life can be expressed in terms of getting the inputs you need in order to thrive and survive. That's what motivation and emotion are really all about. When you need something from your environment, you typically experience a painful emotion. When you satisfy that need, you typically experience a pleasurable emotion. Motivation and emotion thus are internal, psycho-biological processes that help you *choose* those behaviors that will satisfy your input needs.

Now think a little bit further. In order to control your *inputs*, you usually must control your *outputs*. That infant of yours needs food in order to survive. It soon learns that it is more likely to get food (rather than a fresh diaper) if it cries in one tone of voice when it is hungry, but in another tone of voice when it is wet. Crying is thus *information* about its internal energy needs that the infant *outputs* to its environment. By controlling its crying, your newborn child influences what sorts of inputs it gets from you and from other people in its world.

Question: How does an infant reward its parents when they help satisfy the child's needs?

Controlling a Living System
Generally speaking, systems are controlled by their inputs. Some of these inputs concern energy; others concern information. But how do you (as a living system) achieve the inputs that you need in order to satisfy your needs?

As we noted earlier, you get the inputs you want by learning how to control your outputs. But to achieve this miracle, you must make use of three processes that you may not have given much thought to. First, you must be able to plan a series of actions (outputs) that presumably will yield the inputs that you desire. You then execute

the plan by telling your body the *sequence of behaviors* it must perform. In systems terms, this "sequence" is called **feed-forward**.

But how do you know that this sequence will yield the reward you desire? Because you are able to *guess the consequences* of most of the things you do. *If* you eat, *then* your hunger will be satisfied. *If* you pick up a crying baby, *then* most likely it will quit crying.

And how did you learn that food satisfies hunger? Because your body and your environment give you **feedback** about the results of your actions. And if the consequences of your behavioral outputs aren't those you predicted (or desired), then you do something else until you get the inputs you wanted in the first place.

"Feed-forward," "predicting consequences," and "feedback" may seem rather strange concepts to you at first. But they are really just new terms for ideas that you probably are already familiar with. So let us look at these concepts in a bit more detail, because you will need to understand them if you are to make much sense out of General Systems Theory.

Feed-forward
How do you get a computer to solve an equation for you? The first thing you do is to feed the machine information about the *sequence* of steps it should follow in order to generate a solution to the equation. The computer then carries out your commands "one step at a time" until it completes the task you have given it. The "programming" input that you initially give the machine is called "feed-forward" because you tell the computer *now* what you want it to accomplish during some *future* (forward) time period.

Living systems too make use of "feed-forward" in order to plan and execute a series of responses that will lead them toward some goal. Suppose you are reading a book when you suddenly "feel hungry." So you decide to go get an apple from the refrigerator. But your "mind" can't accomplish this goal on its own—your body must do the actual moving (and eating). Thus when you "make up your mind" to get the apple, parts of your cortex decide on a *sequence of movements* that will get your body up from the chair and moving toward the refrigerator in the kitchen. Your cortex next "feeds forward" the sequence of commands to the lower centers of your brain. These lower centers then execute the movements without any conscious effort on your part.

Whenever you read the term "feed-forward" in this book, then, you will know that we are referring to *future behaviors designed to achieve some goal*.

Predicting Consequences

Telling your body what movements it must make to get you an apple from the refrigerator is but a small part of the process of satisfying your hunger needs, however. All along the way, your brain must generate predictions about what the actual consequences of your actions will be. For example, why do you want an apple when you feel hungry? Because you have learned that eating an apple reduces your hunger pangs. Drinking a glass of water or standing on your head are behaviors that just don't have the consequences devouring an apple will have.

Many psychologists believe that one of the main purposes of your brain is that of predicting what the results of your actions will be. Indeed, these scientists view your brain as an incredibly complex computer that does little more than the following three things:

1. Your brain measures your internal needs and the demands placed on you by your environment.
2. Your brain then plans behaviors (sequences of outputs) that will meet these needs in a predictable manner.
3. It then compares the actual consequences of your actions with what it expected and adjusts your outputs accordingly.

Feedback

How did you learn that standing on your head doesn't usually reduce your hunger pangs? Well, perhaps once when you were starving, your brain told your body to stand on its head because it predicted this output might help. But your stomach growled just as loudly as before. This painful *feedback* from your gut informed your brain that the first plan it fed forward to your muscles didn't get the job done. So your brain generated another plan which, when fed-forward and executed, got you an apple and reduced your hunger.

Feed-forward is defined as a planned sequence of outputs that your brain predicts will move you toward some goal. Feedback is information about whether those outputs actually did or did not get the job done. From a General Systems viewpoint, *all* your motivated activities involve planning (feed-forward), predicting (guessing consequences), and adjusting (using real-world feedback to stay on target).

Question: Does your brain predict the actual consequences *of your actions, or does it generate predictions about* what kind of feedback *your behaviors will yield?*

Feed-forward. A series of commands or orders that you issue (usually all at once) that are to be executed in sequence at some time in the future. The "rules and regulations" issued by any group or organization are feed-forward in that the rules tell the members of the group or organization what behaviors are allowed, what behaviors are forbidden, and what the *consequences* of obeying or disobeying the rules will be. Your own personal "code of ethics" (conscience) is also a type of feed-forward in that this code tells you what sequences of actions to perform in certain situations in the future.

Feedback. Information about a system's present or past performance which is fed back into the system to control the system's present or future actions. If you ask a friend, "How do I look?" you are asking for feedback on your present appearance. If your friend says, "You look great!" you are likely to continue to dress as you presently have. If your friend says, "Terrible," you may use this feedback to correct the way you dress in the future—or to find a new set of friends!

Self-control. Living systems have the ability to make use of feed-forward and feedback in order to grow, mature, change, learn, and hence achieve their goals more effectively. Self-control is the ability to change your outputs voluntarily so that you can gain the present or future inputs you desire. Children learn self-control when they discover that reducing their temper tantrums and impulsive actions will yield them rewards they can't otherwise get.

Self-Control

At first glance, it may seem that General Systems Theory views you (or at least your brain) as being little more than a giant computer. Not so, because your brain is but a small part of YOU. There's also the rest of your body, *and* your mind, *and* your environment. Systems Theory is useful in part because it takes into account—as no other theory does—the biological, psychological, and social/behavioral factors that determine what you think and feel and do.

And Systems Theory goes much farther, for it is built on the assumption that even complex machines lack one critical ability that you share with all other living systems—the ability to choose among various goals and *voluntarily* change your actions in order to achieve whatever goal you pick. To put the matter another way, you are capable of exercising voluntary **self-control**— but machines aren't.

Like all other human beings, you weren't born with very much innate self-discipline—but you were born with the capacity to *learn it*. That is to say, you inherited the ability to see that the best way to satisfy your biological, psychological, and social needs is to control your biological, psychological, and social outputs. And to control your outputs, you need informational inputs that will tell you (1) what your actions should be in the future (feed-forward); and (2) what you have been doing right and wrong in the past (feedback).

To a great extent, what we call *personal development* is little more than the study of how people learn self-control. Much of what you will do as a parent is to give your children informational inputs about what they should do, what they could do, and what they are presently doing. You also need to teach your children how to predict the consequences of their actions. Your children can then learn how to plan and execute their own sequences of output behaviors in order to satisfy their own unique input needs. But the key to meeting needs is *self-control*. For as your children learn to control their own thoughts and actions, they learn as well how to get what they want from you—and from the rest of their environment.

From a General Systems Theory viewpoint, then, one of the *main tasks of a parent* is to discover what inputs children need so that they can discover how to control and change their thoughts, values, and actions. For it is only in this way that children can achieve what the humanists call **self-actualization**.

Let us pause for a moment to summarize what we have learned about "living systems," and then finish our study of General Systems Theory.

The Living System: A Summary

Living systems have the following characteristics:

1. Living systems behave as if they were goal-oriented.
2. They frequently show emotional reactions associated with achieving (or not achieving) their goals.
3. Living systems are capable of learning.
4. They are made up of organized parts that are in some kind of communication with each other.
5. They have inputs, internal processes, and outputs. Some of these inputs, internal processes, and outputs are informational. Others have to do with energy.
6. Living systems are capable of self-control—that is, of learning to change their internal processes and outputs in order to achieve the inputs (goals) they need.
7. They acquire self-control by discovering how to plan their actions (feed-forward), predict the consequences of their behaviors, and how to use feedback to stay on target as they move toward satisfying their needs.

Systems within Systems

Now that we have gotten the definitions out of the way, let us view YOU through the eyes of General Systems Theory—both to add to your understanding of yourself, and to demonstrate why you must learn as much about relationships *among* systems as you do about individual systems themselves.

Biological Systems
The Cell
Every cell in your body is a living system. Cells are made up of complex molecules, but these molecules do not exhibit the property of *life*. Only when these molecules interact with each other in very complicated ways does the property of life *emerge* in the living cell.

Like other biological systems, the cell is affected by its genetic inheritance and by any damage that it may have sustained in its past history. In a sense, then, each cell in your body is as much a unique, individual living system as you are yourself.

The Organ
One cell isn't enough to keep a heart going—any more than one person is enough to keep a group going. The various types of cells in your heart play quite different biological roles. Yet, working together, they manage to keep the blood pumping through your body.

Your heart itself is an **organ**—an *organ*ized group of individual cells. But it is also a system in and of itself. You can learn a great deal about hearts by studying the behavior of individual cells. However, if you want to view the heart as an *organ*, you must also look at the way these cells cooperate. That is, you must study the *relationships among cells*. For if the cells did not relate to each other in some way, they would not be organized enough to form a system as complex as your heart.

Cells make up organs, but your heart is more than a random collection of different types of cellular systems. And when we shift our perspective—our *level of analysis*, so to speak—from the cell to the heart, we find that the heart has properties that we could not have predicted no matter how thoroughly we understood the functioning of its individual cells.

The major **emergent properties** at the organ level seem to be those of *cooperation* and what we might call *role specialization*. A single-celled organism—such as the **amoeba**—lives and dies in solitary splendor. It reproduces by splitting in two, but these two offspring don't cooperate or even associate with each other as two human brothers or sisters might. Rather, each amoeba does almost everything on its own.

Any system that acts entirely on its own must play many roles—such as food gatherer, warrior, and reproductive agent. Heart cells, however, *specialize*. Some of them are built for working, others for support and protection, still others for circulating food and oxygen. A few nerve cells inside the heart act as "organ regulators" by controlling the rate at which the organ beats. And because each of these many types of cell is specialized for a single task, the heart cells must *cooperate* with each other—or die.

It is this *cooperation* (born of *specialization*) that allows the heart cells to create a more complex system—the organ.

Question: How long would a "General Hospital" survive if its staff was made up just of kidney specialists? What other "medical roles" are needed in order to keep the hospital functioning smoothly?

Psychological and Social Systems
The Organism

Each organ in your body is a complex living system with its own types of inputs, internal processes, and outputs. Indeed, your organs are so complicated that medical doctors often specialize in treating the diseases of just *one* organ system.

But your body itself is an **organism**, a much more complex living system than any one of its component organs. A "family physician"—someone who treats the *whole body* (and often the mind as well)—must not only understand the behavior of your heart and liver and brain, but the *relationships among them as well*.

YOU, as a living organism, are surely something more than a heart, a liver, a brain, and a few other organs loosely thrown together inside your skin. For YOU have properties (such as perceptions, thoughts, memories, and attitudes) that your individual organs simply do not possess. Your heart is not "conscious"—and never will be—because *consciousness* is a characteristic that emerges only at the level of the organism.

Question: Your brain is an organ. Can you list the various "specialized roles" apparently played by your left hemisphere? By your right hemisphere?

The Group

You do not live your life in social isolation, as does the amoeba. Rather, you share your existence with, and are dependent upon, other human beings. To put the matter in more technical terms, organisms form **groups** in much the same way that your individual organs unite to form organisms such as yourself.

From the standpoint of General Systems Theory, the group is a kind of *super-organism* with emergent properties that are unique to it.

Self-actualization. A term from *humanistic psychology* that means "the act of becoming the best person you possibly can become." The process of actualizing, or achieving, your own goals or your own ideal state of personal development—usually by learning that you must help others achieve their own goals so they can help you achieve yours too.

Organ. From the Greek word meaning "tool, instrument, or parts that work together." An organ is thus a means of accomplishing something. Your heart is an instrument for pumping blood. Your brain is a tool for processing informational inputs.

Emergent properties (ee-MER-jent). From a Latin word meaning "to rise, or come out of concealment." When you put the pieces of a jigsaw puzzle together, the "picture" emerges. But you cannot usually predict what the *whole* picture will look like just by looking at a single piece or two. Thus the visual properties of the picture emerge from concealment only when the pieces are put together in a *systematic* way.

Amoeba (ah-ME-bah). A very primitive, simple, single-celled organism that looks more like a moving blob of gelatin than it does like a "real" animal.

Organism (OR-gan-ism). A living system capable of getting along on its own. You are an organism. Your heart is a living system, but is not an organism because it can't ordinarily function on its own without the rest of your body (or some artificial support system).

Groups. Sets of individuals considered as single entities. A group is a *super-organism* in much the same way that your body is a sort of *super-organ*.

Sexual reproduction is one such property. It takes two people to tango, and it takes both a male and a female human being to produce that new living system we call an infant.

Spoken language is another property that emerges at the level of the group. Cells and organs communicate with each other chemically and electrically. Members of family groups communicate with each other using verbal and nonverbal signals. *Speech*, then, is a system of informational inputs and outputs that emerges at the level of the group.

Question: How many different "roles" would you like your own child to learn as it grows up? How do you plan to help the child learn these roles?

The Social Organization

You started life as a single cell that divided billions of times to form new cells. In a sense, then, you began as the simplest form of living system, but grew in complexity until you developed into the adult organism that you presently are.

Now, did you ever stop to ask yourself how all those billions of cells in your body managed to form the highly structured body you now inhabit? Why didn't you turn out to be a sack full of individual cells—each striving to go its own way and do its own thing?

The answer seems to lie in the fact that living systems are made up of *organized* parts. The first few cells you started life with were bound together in a tight little ball of tissue (see Chapter 18). As these cells began to multiply, they also began to specialize and take on *different roles*. Some of the cells grew together to form your brain. Other cells organized themselves to form your heart, your skin, your stomach, and your blood vessels.

A heart cell does not have the freedom to behave like a liver cell, nor can your liver start acting like your brain if you are going to survive for very long. Your **genes** keep your cells and organs from "misbehaving" by specifying what role each should play. That is, your genes *specify in advance* what inputs each of your cells and organs will be sensitive to, and what kind of output they will give to each type of input received. Your genes thus provide your cells and organs with *biological feed-forward*—a set of genetic "rules and regulations" designed to keep all the parts of your body in touch with each other, and striving toward the common goal of keeping you intact and healthy.

Social organizations are much like your body. They typically start small and develop slowly into highly complex systems. And since social organizations don't have "genes" to guide them, they must have *formal* rules and regulations to control their functioning. Being able to write these "rules and regulations" down in some formal language can aid an organization in many ways. Thus *written language* is a property that probably emerged when people first began to form large organizations.

It is also at the level of the organization that formal **social roles** first appear, including those of "teacher," "student," "parent," "worker," "manager," and "police officer" (see Chapter 25). As perhaps you can guess from the titles we usually assign these roles, they are actually a set of *expected outputs*. Thus knowing a person's social role allows you to predict the consequences of your own actions toward that person. Why? Because the role tells you something about the response (feedback) you can expect from the individual *if* you behave in a certain way.

Individual organisms who play the role of "teacher" are expected to act and think in one way, while organisms who play the role of "student" are expected to produce quite a different set of behavioral outputs. From an *organizational* point of view, however, it often doesn't matter which organism fills which role—any more than it matters to you which of your cells becomes a part of your liver and which becomes brain tissue.

All you care about—and all the system cares about—is that all the roles are filled, and all the goals are met, so that you (and the organization) can survive.

Question: *Does an organization have the ability to control its outputs* voluntarily?

Societies and Cultures

You are a complex system composed of cells and organs—but you are also a member of groups, organizations, and societies. That is to say, you are made up of living biological systems, and you help make up complex social systems.

A group is a simple social system composed of organisms like you (and hence of collections of cells and organs).

An organization is a fairly complex social system made up of groups and individuals.

A society or culture is an extremely complex social system that is composed of formal organizations, each of which plays its role in supporting the society.

Although organizations sometimes act as if they were free to work toward any goals their members wished, the fact is that no complex social organization can long endure without the strong support of the rest of society. Thus, the better an organization fulfills its cultural expectations, the better off the society, the organization, and each individual member thereof will be.

Question: *A scientific experiment usually consists of changing the inputs to a system and then noting what changes occur in the system's outputs. What would be the easiest system to study scientifically—a cell, an organ, an organism, a group, an organization, or a society? Which science seems most advanced these days—biology, psychology, or sociology? Why is this so?*

The Mind/Body Problem: A Systems Approach

Now that we've covered General Systems Theory in outline form, let's see where it came from historically, and how it handles that most difficult of issues, the mind/body problem.

In a 1977 article in *Science*, George L. Engel states that one of the major failings in the field of psychiatry today is the lack of a good solution to the mind/body problem. And until a worthy answer is found, Engel says, **psychiatry** will remain "a hodgepodge of unscientific opinions, assorted philosophies and 'schools of thought,' mixed **metaphors**, role diffusion, propaganda, and politicking for 'mental health' and other esoteric goals."

On the one hand, there are those psychiatrists who emphasize mental processes to the near exclusion of the body—or of the social environment. These psychiatrists tend to focus on "what goes on inside your head," not on the ways in which inputs from your body (and the people around you) influence your thoughts and feelings. On the other hand, there are those psychiatrists who try to reduce all mental activity to biochemical and electrical events inside your brain, without taking into account the strong influence that your mind has on your body—and on your environment.

Dr. Engel—who is a professor of psychiatry at the University of Rochester—believes that General Systems Theory may be a useful new way of solving the mind/body problem.

Introspectionism

As we noted in an earlier chapter, the conflict between "mentalists" and "biologists" has a long history in the behavioral and social sciences. At the turn of the century, psychology was defined as "the science of mind" by most scholars. The dominant approach to studying people was to get them to **introspect**—that is, to look inside their minds to analyze their own mental experiences.

Structuralism

The **structuralists** were probably the first "mentalists" in psychology. Taking their cue from physics, the structuralists assumed that the "mind" was constructed of "mental atoms" just as a lump of coal is made up of carbon atoms. By "introspecting" their own inner experiences, the early structuralists assumed they would be able to identify what this "atom" of the mind actually was. In a typical experiment, they might sound a musical note and have subjects try to analyze their mental experiences when they heard the tone. The structuralists hoped all subjects would break the tone down into the same mental components. Alas, they did not. The search for "mental atoms" failed because introspectionism is too subjective a technique for most scientific purposes.

Next in line historically were the **functionalists**, who also believed in "introspecting," but who thought it equally important to measure behavioral responses. William James, who founded the first psychological laboratory in the US some 100 years ago, was the first American functionalist. According to James, the purpose or *function* of both your mental processes and your behaviors was to help you adapt to your environment. Because the functionalists were more interested in "processes" than in "structures," James and his

Genes (pronounced as "jeans"). A single "word" in the genetic code that determines the structure and function of your body. When you were conceived, a set of genes from both your mother and father combined to form your own unique "biological language" that described the body you would be born with.

Social roles. A role is a stereotyped or systematic way of behaving or thinking about something. When you say, "The good guys always wear white hats," you are describing a social role both in terms of the actor's behaviors and style of dress. A social role is thus a set of feed-forward instructions telling you how to act if you wish to play a certain part or role in society.

Psychiatry (sick-KY-ah-tree). A branch of medicine dealing with the "healing of the mind." Psychiatrists take the M.D. degree first, then specialize in an applied form of psychology usually by working in a mental hospital. Psychologists take the Ph.D. degree, and practice many different specialties. Some psychologists also work with patients who have mental problems. Because of the psychiatrists' medical background, they often take a more biological view of mental illness than do psychologists (who cannot legally prescribe pills or other medications).

Metaphors (MET-ah-fors). From the Greek word meaning "to transfer, or change." A metaphor is a figure of speech in which one object takes on the properties of something else, or in which one object is compared with something else. To say that "Freedom of speech is the most precious diamond in Liberty's crown" is to transfer (metaphorically) the value of a jewel onto the ability to say what you think. A mixed metaphor is an inappropriate or contradictory comparison, such as "Freedom of speech is a pig in a poke floating like a cloud on the blue American sky."

Introspect (inn-tro-SPECT). To "inspect" what's going on within your own mind. To attempt to perceive and analyze your own mental processes.

Structuralists. An early "school" of psychology started by the German scientist Wilhelm Wundt (VILL-helm Voondt). The structuralists attempted to model psychology after chemistry; thus they hunted for the "atoms" or "elements" that composed the mind.

Functionalists. Early American psychologists—particularly John Dewey (1859–1952) and James R. Angell (1869–1949)—who were more interested in the functions of the mind than in its structures. Dewey proposed that psychology should study "what mind and behavior *do*."

followers had a great impact on psychology—particularly in the field of education. Many of the contributions that the functionalists made are still valid and useful. However, as a *theoretical approach*, functionalism fell out of favor when psychologists began searching for more objective ways of studying human behavior than asking people to describe their subjective experiences.

In the final analysis, *introspectionism* failed for three reasons:

1. Your "conscious experiences" are private events and thus cannot be measured directly by an outside observer. You can *tell* a psychologist about the things you are conscious of, but you cannot *show* the psychologist what you are experiencing.

2. You are not directly "conscious" of many of the activities that go on inside your head. As you

G. Engle   William James   John B. Watson   B.F. Skinner

learned in Chapter 2, what we generally call "consciousness" is primarily a property of your left hemisphere. Your right hemisphere has its own form of consciousness, but under normal circumstances your left hemisphere seems not to be *directly aware* of what goes on in the right half of your brain. Nor are you conscious of the activities of the lower centers of your brain, such as your limbic system. Thus how can you "introspect" about mental processes you simply aren't directly aware of?

3. Your conscious mind can no more "stand back and watch itself in operation" than you can *objectively* observe yourself as you give a speech, play tennis, or make love. If you've ever been surprised by a movie or a video tape of yourself, or shocked by how your voice sounds on a recording, you know full well that you don't see and hear yourself as others do.

"Introspecting," therefore, is at best a very limited tool for discovering either the structures or the functions of the mind—perhaps because it only deals with those internal processes you are directly conscious of.

Watson's Behaviorist Revolution

In 1913, John B. Watson began the behaviorist revolution by throwing out the concept of "mind" entirely. To Watson, people were like simple adding machines—a stimulus input came along, pressed a button in their brains, and out popped a response of some kind. Watson believed that inputs are controlled by the environment, while response outputs are shaped *entirely* by genes and past learning. People, he said, have no more voluntary control over their actions than does an adding machine. And just as you wouldn't bother asking an adding machine to explain its actions, you shouldn't bother asking people to tell you why they did what they did.

According to Watson, your thoughts, feelings, and behaviors are completely determined by forces beyond your conscious control. You may *believe* that your mental processes influence your actions, but that belief is a mere illusion with no scientific substance to it. And since psychologists can study stimuli and responses objectively, Watson said, why should they bother trying to look at the "internal processes" that come between input and output?

This very mechanistic approach to psychology probably disturbed more people than it pleased, particularly the **humanists** and the **psychoanalysts** whom we will discuss in later chapters. But Watson's approach did force the "mentalists" to pay a bit more attention to environmental stimulation and to the effects of learning on thoughts and behaviors.

Thought as "Silent Speech"

The major problem with Watson's brand of behaviorism is this: You know full well you have a mind, even if Watson couldn't inspect it or measure its internal processes directly. You know too that "what goes on inside your head" *does* have a meaningful relationship to how you behave. Thus, you may ask, how could Watson explain thinking, problem-solving, and creative activities if he denied the existence of the mind?

Watson's solution to this problem was a clever one. You don't think "in your head," Watson said. Rather, you "speak silently" by moving your lips and vocal cords *very slightly* in response to some environmental input. Thus, in Watson's view, *thinking* to yourself is really a form of *talking* to yourself. By taking this extreme approach, Watson made mental activities *measurable* because he claimed they were really just muscle movements. Now Watson didn't need the concept of "mind," because he had converted internal mental processes into external muscle twitches.

Evaluating Watson

Watson was both right and wrong in his beliefs. Studies do show that many people make slight movements of their vocal cords and lips while "thinking." But, according to Watson, you would be *unable to think* if we paralyzed your muscles. And most research suggests that you are quite capable of continuing to process information "mentally" even when a drug such as **curare** paralyzes your lips and vocal cords. Furthermore, Watson never could explain the "silent voice" that seems to guide many types of problem-solving and creative thought. Thus Watson's behavioral theory fails because it doesn't describe the world as accurately as it should.

Watson did have an excellent idea of how the brain "feeds forward" a complex sequence of motor commands. But he missed the boat on two important counts. First, he failed to see that the brain can *anticipate* the consequences of actions before it actually executes them. And second, Watson denied the importance of *feedback* in shaping human thoughts and behaviors. It thus fell to Harvard psychologist B.F. Skinner to take the next step in the behaviorist revolution—that of adding "feedback" and "consequences" to the human equation.

Skinner's Contributions

B.F. Skinner took Watson's half-formed ideas on behaviorism and made them work in real-world situations by demonstrating that organisms are particularly sensitive to the consequences of their actions. If a hungry pigeon gets a piece of corn when it pecks a button in a training box, this "positive feedback" encourages the pigeon to repeat the response that yielded it the corn. But if the feedback is negative instead of positive, the pigeon will try some other response instead of continuing to peck at the button. In Skinner's view, organisms use external feedback to guide their actions through long sequences of goal-oriented behaviors.

"Behavior is determined by its consequences," is one of Skinner's best-known sayings. And with this slogan as his motto, Skinner developed one of the most impressive *technologies* of behavioral change the world has ever known (see Chapter 15).

"Having" a Poem

Psychologists often describe human behavior in terms of whatever complicated machines are popular in their times. Watson lived and died before computers were commonplace, and he "processed" all of his laboratory data using simple adding machines. Small wonder, then, that he

Humanists. A "school" of psychology that probably started with Alfred Adler (see Chapter 23). Humanists tend to emphasize the *differences* between humans and other members of the animal kingdom, and to believe that people are capable of *self-actualization*, or of achieving their own unique goals. According to Dr. Stanley Krippner, Director of the Institute of Humanistic Psychology in San Francisco, the major thrust in humanistic psychology today is General Systems Theory.

Psychoanalysts (sigh-ko-ANN-uh-lists). Psychologists or psychiatrists who are followers of Freud's theoretical position (see Chapter 23).

Curare (cure-RAHR-ree). A paralyzing drug obtained from a variety of South American plants. Curare paralyzes the voluntary muscles, but not the nervous system.

Procreative (PRO-cree-ate-tive). To procreate something means to make a copy of that thing. When you have children, you procreate yourself.

viewed people as mechanical puppets whose control buttons were pushed by environmental inputs and whose actions were entirely determined by genes and past experience.

Skinner was one of the first psychologists to make extensive use of programmable computers in his laboratory. So we shouldn't be surprised to learn that Skinner views the human organism as a computer whose behavioral "programs" can be altered by real-world feedback. And, like Watson, Skinner has his own unique, mechanistic explanation of such "mental acts" as creativity and problem solving.

Skinner admits that "mind" exists, but states that mental processes are entirely unmeasurable. He therefore focuses entirely on *observable behaviors*. He does not study "thinking," he studies verbal responses; he does not study "creativity," he investigates creative reactions to external inputs. Thus "thought processes" and "mental creativity" become, for Skinner, *learned behaviors* that are entirely under environmental control.

"You do not *write* a poem," Skinner said in a speech in the mid-70's, "You *have* a poem, much as a woman *has* a baby." A pregnant woman does not create an infant by an act of will—the **procreative** process takes place automatically and without her conscious direction. And, according to Skinner, the "creative process" occurs in much the same way. The environment stimulates you to put words down on paper, and past experience and your present environment "shape" your words without any conscious effort on your part. Thus you have no more "voluntary" control over the shape of your poem than a pregnant woman has conscious control over the shape her infant is born with. In Skinner's view, therefore, people are not *born* creative. Rather, they are *programmed* to give creative responses by past and present environmental inputs.

Skinner's solution to the mind/body problem pleased neither poets nor introspectionists, both of whom insisted that the creative process is shaped as much by conscious **volition** as it is by direct environmental stimulation. However, as Skinner points out, there is one seemingly fatal flaw to this argument: Mental activities ordinarily cannot be observed and measured by anyone except the person doing the "thinking" or "creating."

Evaluating Behaviorism

What are we to make of Watson and Skinner? To begin with—as we will see in many later chapters—the behaviorist tradition has given us highly effective ways of changing ourselves and of helping others do likewise. Thus we would be foolish to reject behaviorism out of hand. However, the fact remains that "things go on inside our heads" which influence our behaviors—even if we cannot prove the existence of our mental processes to the behaviorist's satisfaction.

Scientists such as George Engel believe that we need a new "model of the mind," one that views humans as complex bio-psycho-social *systems* rather than adding machines or simple computers. Systems are controlled by environmental inputs, influenced by feedback, and capable of learning. So the systems approach fits loosely within the behaviorist tradition. However, as we have seen, *living systems* also have measurable "internal processes." And they are capable of self-control—that is, they can monitor and evaluate their own actions and voluntarily change their own behavioral programs.

According to Dr. Engel, General Systems Theory seems to provide a comfortable middle ground between the warring camps of the "mentalists" and the behaviorists. To show how this might be the case, let us describe in systematic terms how you might go about writing a poem or solving a difficult mental problem.

Problem Solving and Creativity

Of the many types of thought processes that psychologists study, two are of particular importance. One is often called *problem solving*, while the other involves artistic or intellectual *creativity*. A variety of studies suggest that both types of "thinking" may consist of some sort of "silent conversation" between the two hemispheres.

Problem solving usually occurs when you are trying to discover a path to a *particular* mental or behavioral goal—that is, when you can specify in advance what a solution might look like. Under these circumstances, your left hemisphere seems to generate a "trial sequence" of *neural commands* that might get you to the goal. These neural commands are probably sent to your motor cortex just as if you were going to speak out loud. But your speech muscles apparently are inhibited from moving while you "think"—presumably because, as a child, you learned to inhibit lip movements while you were reading silently or solving problems "in your head."

Whether you speak out loud or think silently, then, your left hemisphere sends commands to your motor cortex. But it also surely sends an "information copy" of its neural commands to your right hemisphere. Your right (monitoring) hemisphere could then *anticipate* the results of these actions, and pass along its expectancies to your left hemisphere.

Evidence supporting this view of problem solving comes from recent studies on split-brain patients that we discussed in Chapter 2. As you may recall, Roger Sperry and his associates showed pictures just to the right hemisphere of one patient, then asked the left hemisphere to state what the right had seen. The left (verbal) hemisphere then engaged in a guessing game in which it apparently received "emotional clues" from the right as to the correctness of its guesses. Thus, in problem solving, the left hemisphere apparently *proposes solutions* which the right hemisphere *evaluates*.

During *creative* or artistic activities, however, your right hemisphere might take the lead. It presumably would have sensed some perceptual pattern that it wished your left hemisphere to reproduce in word or deed. Your left hemisphere would then generate behavior patterns until it hit upon the one that most closely resembled what the right hemisphere was thinking about. Evidence to support this view is primarily **anecdotal**. But artists and composers often talk about an "inner voice" that guides their creative activities. And many mathematicians have said their best insights "broke through to consciousness" as a completed pattern.

In most situations, of course, your hemispheres work together as a team. But, theoretically speaking, most scientific and artistic *insights* might well begin as "perceptual patterns" in your right hemisphere. And your artistic and scientific *behaviors* may be little more than your attempts to express these patterns in the language of the left hemisphere.

Watson and Skinner deny the importance of "mental processes" in determining behavior in part because they view "mind" as a *thing*, not as a system made up of sub-systems. If we adopt the systems viewpoint, however, we can describe mental processes as "communications between sub-systems in the brain." And we can measure such processes *objectively*, using the experiments performed on split-brain patients as our guides. Thus, as Dr. Engel said, General Systems Theory does appear to offer a solution to the mind/body problem that allows us both to focus on behavioral outputs and to measure the internal processes associated with those behaviors as well.

Now that we have given you an outline of General Systems Theory, it is time to evaluate it briefly using the criteria we mentioned on p. 13. As you will see, while there are many things to be said in its favor, there are also several problems associated with adopting the "holistic" approach to psychology.

Strengths of Systems Theory
Accuracy
Most psychological theories are *qualitative* rather than *quantitative*. That is to say, psychologists tend to describe things in words rather than in the sorts of mathematical symbols used by physicists, chemists, and biologists. It was perhaps for this reason that our first great psychologist, William James, described physics as a "hard-headed" science, but called psychology a "soft" science. Hard or soft, theoretical insights about human behavior can certainly be useful. But, as James noted, it is not very easy to judge the accuracy of most psychological theories because they are based more on hunches than on **empirical** data.

Briefly put, General Systems Theory is probably as accurate as any other broad-scale theory in that "soft" science we call psychology. However, it is not as precise as many "mini-theories" that attempt to explain just a small part of human thought, emotion, or behavior.

Completeness
As Dr. Engel pointed out in 1977, the General Systems approach seems by far the most complete psychological theory presently available. General Systems Theory therefore does not *disprove* or *displace* any of the other theories in psychology— it merely helps pull many of them together into a more coherent whole.

Impressiveness
Just how impressive General Systems Theory is to you will depend on your own prior assumptions about what a theory should do. Writing in the June 1979 issue of *Contemporary Psychology*, Harvard psychologist Brendan Maher states that

"Those who seek universal, coherent, elegant formulations in the grand manner" will find the systems approach to their liking. However, if you prefer a simpler view of human nature—or a more complex one—you may not find the General Systems Theory very impressive at all. Whatever the case, it is not important that you *believe* the theory—just that you understand it well enough to translate the material in this book into terms that make sense to you.

Usefulness
General Systems Theory may be useful to you in at least three ways:

1. It offers you a more objective ("hard" science) understanding of yourself than do most other theories.
2. It can give you a better technology for personal change than do most other approaches.
3. It is a very optimistic theory indeed.

Objective
First, General Systems Theory offers an *objective* understanding of human behavior. That is, the theory is based on a large number of controlled experiments aimed at discovering *how* people change their thoughts and actions when you alter their stimulus inputs. *Subjective* theories about human nature are typically built more from feelings and attitudes than they are from empirical data. Thus General Systems Theory may be useful to you because it offers you a different explanation of your thoughts and behaviors than would a theory based primarily on subjective feelings.

In the "hard" sciences, you typically begin by trying to discover new input-output relationships. Once you've established these relationships, you then go on to the delightful task of theorizing about *why* a given input is so regularly followed by a specific output. Technology, in the "hard" sciences, is primarily a matter of using information about input-output connections either to maintain a system's old outputs or to establish new ones.

From a General Systems Theory point of view, we should look at people's *abilities,* not their *disabilities.*

Better Technology

From a technological point of view, you don't always have to understand *why* a system changes in order to *get* it to change. Indeed, in many cases, you can help systems acquire new responses without ever knowing for sure which "internal processes" **mediated** this learning.

General Systems Theory yields a stronger "technology of change" because it helps you find the inputs you need in order to alter your own outputs (and those of other systems).

Optimistic

General Systems Theory is very optimistic about the *changeability* of living systems. We are all affected by our social environments, and all cultures have certain prejudices about human conduct built into them. As an example, our society has dozens of "folk sayings" that seem to tell us that people cannot change very much no matter how hard they try. One such saying is, "You can't change human nature." Others are "You can't teach an old dog new tricks," "Leopards never change their spots," and "You can lead a horse to water, but you can't make him drink." All of these sayings seem designed to convince you that human change is difficult if not impossible.

From a General Systems Theory standpoint, however, *change is always possible* (at least theoretically). A system will *always* change its internal processes and its outputs *if* you are bright enough to find the input that will cause the change you desire. If you desire change, then—in yourself, in someone else, or in a group, organization, or society—it is up to you to discover the inputs that will do the job. And if change doesn't occur, you can't fault "human nature." Instead, you must blame yourself for not finding the way to achieve your goals.

Question: What inputs do you think you could give an "old dog" to help it acquire a new set of "tricky" outputs?

Problems with General Systems Theory

In order to evaluate *any* theory, you must know both its strong points and its weaknesses. We have already mentioned some of the benefits involved in taking the systems approach to psychology. Now, let us discuss some of the problems you may encounter in trying to look at yourself and others from this new viewpoint.

Some New Insights Are Painful

Suppose your child doesn't learn as fast as you wish it to. If you adopt a "human nature" explanation of the child's slowness, you might blame it on "fate" or "bad genes." But if you adopt the General Systems viewpoint, you may face a serious **dilemma**. For you will have to face the fact that many of the unpleasant things that happen to you are at least partially your own fault. To put the matter in different terms, when you look at yourself in objective terms, you may grow painfully dissatisfied with your past actions. Under these circumstances, you may be tempted to reject your new insights since they will force you to make some fundamental changes in the ways that you think and behave.

Attitude Change Is Not Always Enough

All of us occasionally must own up to a very thorny problem—the fact that our attitudes don't always agree with our actual behaviors. For example, the parents of many retarded children will tell you that they prefer to reward their child's progress rather than merely punish it when it does something wrong. And yet, if you measure the *actual performance* of the parents in real-life settings, you may find that they are more likely to be **punitive** than rewarding.

As we will note in Chapter 27, psychologists have made many scientific studies of what happens when a person's attitudes come in conflict with that person's actual behavioral outputs. For the most part, people tend to reduce this type of conflict by producing complicated **rationalizations** for their actions—and then go on behaving just as they always had. If you tend to react in this manner, you may not care much for General Systems Theory. For it continually reminds you that changing your internal processes (such as attitudes) isn't enough. You must keep working until you change your behavioral outputs as well.

Helping Others Means Changing Yourself First

From a General Systems viewpoint, people need each other—desperately. For we all require feedback from our environments if we are to change, grow, or achieve the highest level of personal satisfaction. And other people are usually our best source of feedback, since they see our *actual behavioral outputs* rather than our intentions.

According to the systems view, your own personal growth will occur most readily when the feedback you get from others is rewarding or encouraging. That being the case, what can you do if most of the feedback you receive is critical or punishing rather than **positively reinforcing**?

Mediated (ME-dee-ated). From a Latin word meaning "to take the middle position." If you mediate a dispute, you help the people arguing with each other come to some resolution of their conflict—usually by taking a position that is between the positions held by the parties having the dispute.

Dilemma (dye-LEMM-uh). From a Greek word meaning "involving two assumptions." When you are "caught between the devil and the deep blue sea," you face a dilemma. That is, you must choose between two equally unpleasant alternatives.

Punitive (PEW-nih-tive). To be punishing is to be punitive.

Rationalizations (rah-shun-nall-eye-ZAY-shuns). From the Latin word meaning "to reason, or compute." To explain something in rational terms is to make it seem reasonable. To rationalize, however, is to offer "logical excuses" for what you wanted to do anyhow—to explain your emotional impulses in reasonable terms. Freud considered *rationalization* to be a mechanism by which the ego defended some of its more neurotic actions (see Chapter 23).

Positively reinforcing. To reinforce something is to make it stronger. To positively reinforce a behavior is to strengthen the probability that it will be repeated. When you reward someone for acting in a particular way, you reinforce the likelihood that the person will behave that way again whenever the circumstances are right. Generally speaking, "positive reinforcement" and "reward" mean the same thing (see Chapter 15).

How can you get the important people in your life to treat you in a more encouraging and rewarding manner?

The answer is this: First you must learn how to give positive reinforcement to the people around you! If you do not "reflect back" to others information about the good things that they are doing, can you really expect them to give you the sort of encouragement that you need from them?

The Biblical "Golden Rule" has been around for many thousands of years, and it is an excellent theoretical statement of how people *ought* to behave. But most of us are far better at preaching the Rule than at practicing it—perhaps because we seldom bother to measure the *actual consequences* of what we do. General Systems Theory—like many other viewpoints—accepts the Golden Rule as a goal well worth achieving. But unlike most other approaches, the systems approach offers a step-by-step *technology* for putting the rule into practice.

Learning Is Time-Consuming

Before you can begin to make use of *any* psychological theory, you must first learn as much as you can about the "nuts and bolts" which hold the theory together. Put another way, in dealing with any science you must learn facts first and practical applications later.

By now you probably understand that, from a General Systems Theory point of view, all psychological processes *begin with inputs*. If you

Reward and punishment are two types of feedback.

They have quite different consequences.

want to "make sense" out of what goes on inside your head, therefore, you may find the most sensible approach is to start by learning some of the "nuts and bolts" facts about what your senses actually do for you.

Now that we have described and evaluated General Systems Theory, let us next turn our attention to *sensory psychology*—the scientific study of inputs to the mind/brain.

Summary

1. Science is a mixture of facts and theories. The facts describe the world in very concrete or **empirical** terms. A **theory** organizes these facts in order to describe the world in words or mathematical **symbols**.
2. Scientists judge theories by at least four **criteria**: Accuracy, completeness, impressiveness, and usefulness.
3. The better the predictions a theory makes about future events, the more accurate it probably is.
4. Some theories describe in detail a limited part of the world. Other more **holistic** theories can sometimes tie several simple theories together to give us a more complete picture of the world.
5. Impressive theories tend to be both elegant and simple.
6. For many scientists, the most important criterion for accepting or rejecting a scientific theory is its usefulness.
7. **General Systems Theory** is an attempt to analyze the world in terms of the **living systems** that inhabit the world.
8. Living Systems:

a. Are goal-oriented, their major goal being that of survival.
b. Show emotional reactions associated with achieving or not achieving their goals.
c. Are capable of learning and adapting.
d. Are made up of organized parts that are in some kind of communication with each other.
e. Have **inputs, internal processes**, and **outputs**.
f. Are capable of self-control—which is to say they can alter their outputs in order to achieve the inputs they desire.
9. In order to achieve self-control, systems make use of **feed-forward**, **predicting consequences** of their actions, and **feedback**.
10. Feed-forward is a **sequence of responses** the system can make at some future time. Feedback is information about the system's past or present performance.
11. The **cell** is the smallest living system, which is made up of non-living **molecules**. It is the organization of these molecules which gives the **emergent property** of "life" to the cell.
12. When cells cooperate with each other—and

take on different **role specializations**—they can combine to form **organs**.

13. The **organism** is a collection of specialized organs which cooperate to produce the emergent property of **consciousness**.
14. Organisms form **groups** by learning how to communicate and cooperate with each other.
15. Groups form **social organizations** in which **formal rules** and written language typically emerge.
16. Social organizations can combine to form such complex **social systems** as societies and cultures.
17. The **mind/body problem** is one of the oldest problems in psychology—and one of the most important.
18. Early in this century, the **structuralists** and the **functionalists** tried to describe "the mind" by using **introspection**—the act of looking inward at your own mental processes.
19. Introspectionism failed because mental events are not objectively measurable, and because you cannot "introspect" your unconscious processes.
20. The behaviorists deny the importance of mental processes, and tend to focus on measuring behaviors instead. By emphasizing the great influence feedback has on behavior, the behaviorists developed a most impressive **technology** of personal change. However, the behaviorists have problems explaining how people "think" their way through problems.
21. From a General Systems Theory point of view, both **problem solving** and **creative thinking** may involve a **dialogue between the hemispheres**.
22. General Systems Theory seems to be a reasonably accurate and complete theory. It can be useful in three ways: It offers an objective viewpoint of the world; it yields a strong technology of personal change; and it is optimistic about the possibility of change.
23. The problems associated with adopting General Systems Theory include the fact that some new insights are painful, the theory requires you to change both your behaviors and your attitudes, helping others often means changing yourself first, and you must learn many facts before you can use the theory.

(Continued from page 112.)

The party was marvelously noisy. There were a great many people on hand, all to help Patti's parents celebrate their "lucky seventh" wedding anniversary. Dr. Donald Severeid and his graduate student, Tom Watson, sat quietly in a corner, ignoring the turmoil. They knew very few of the other guests.

"I still don't believe that you took Patti back to the table and continued her lesson after you found out the door was locked," Dr. Severeid said, taking a sip from his glass. "Surely that was above and beyond the call of duty."

Tom Watson gave a bemused groan. "It was either that, or sit down on the floor and cry. Especially since it took them 45 minutes to find the janitor."

"Has she stopped the voluntary 'soiling' behavior now?"

"It was a case of 'one-trial learning' on both our parts," Tom responded. "I never threatened to pinch Patti again, and she never soiled her pants to try to control me."

Dr. Severeid nodded "hello" to Patti's mother as the woman walked through the room headed for the kitchen. "What about her self-control with food? Can she really hold a cookie in her hand for several minutes without eating it?"

"You won't believe this, Dr. Severeid, but we've timed her at 30 minutes by the clock. Of course, she did grind the cookie up a bit with her fingers, but she didn't eat a bite of it before I told her to. That's why I asked Patti's parents to invite us to the party tonight. I figure we've been giving Patti and her parents a private class in systems technology. You know—teaching them about inputs, outputs, feedback, and consequences. And I wanted you to help grade their final examination."

"Final examination? What do you mean?"

Tom leaned back in his chair. "Well, it used to be that her parents could either have a party, or Patti, but not both. Once the food was put out, she'd run screaming from plate to plate, grabbing everything in sight and stuffing it into her rosebud mouth. She'd even snatch food from the guests. But she's learned so much self-control that tonight she's going to be allowed to show off."

"How so?" Professor Severeid asked.

Tom grinned. "She's going to pass a tray of goodies among the guests. If she doesn't snitch any food, she gets to eat whatever she wants. Her parents and I have been practicing with her for several days now. They've learned a great deal about how to handle Patti, and I'm sure she'll make it."

At that moment, Patti's mother came into the room. "Listen, everybody," she said loudly. "Patti is going to serve you some food. Please help yourself to anything you want." The little girl came into view holding a large platter heaped high with delicacies. "But please don't encourage Patti to eat anything, because she has promised to wait until you've all been served before she eats."

Patti smiled and, at her mother's direction, walked up to an elderly woman and offered the plate to her. The woman beamed, took a little sandwich, and patted the girl on her cheek. Patti walked to the next guests, a young couple, and presented the plate to them. Both the man and the woman took something to eat from the platter and thanked Patti warmly.

Then she was in front of Tom. "Can you have a cookie, please?" she said, giggling just the smallest amount.

"Thank you very much, Patti. You're doing beautifully."

Patti offered Dr. Severeid the plate and, after he thanked her, moved to the next bunch of guests. Watching her actions carefully, the professor sighed softly. "Amazing progress for a little girl we all thought was too badly retarded to learn very much."

Tom smiled paternally. "She's an amazing person. I suspect we were the ones who retarded her progress, really. As long as we viewed her as being 'incurably brain-damaged,' or 'piggish,' or 'mean,' there wasn't much we could do to help. But when we took a broader view . . ."

"When you saw her as a living organism, imbedded in a social system . . ."

"Then we realized we first had to change the way we treated her, in order to get her to grow and develop as she always could have. Patti can probably learn anything we're smart and patient enough to teach her."

Professor Severeid nodded in agreement. "It's like the telephone company says, Tom. Sometimes 'the system is the solution.'" The man thought for a moment, then continued. "Her parents are the most important part of the system, of course, and they've obviously changed considerably."

"Oh, they have. I think they understand that, for the most part, Patti just responds to their inputs. So they helped Patti rehearse for tonight, and they give her lots of love and encouragement. And they're making a big sacrifice for me tonight."

The professor looked puzzled. "What do you mean?"

"Although it's one of Patti's mother's favorites, there's one item of food she promised me wouldn't be on the menu tonight."

"What's that?" the older man asked.

Tom grinned. "Sweet pickles."

Recommended Readings

Engel, George L. "The need for a new medical model: A challenge for biomedicine," *Science*, 196 (1977), pp. 129–136.

Miller, James G. *Living Systems* (New York: McGraw-Hill, 1978).

Morton, Adam. *Frames of Mind: Constraints on the Common-Sense Conception of the Mental* (Oxford, England: Clarendon, 1980).

Pribram, Karl H. "Problems concerning the structure of consciousness," in Globus, G.G., Grover Maxwell, and Irwin Savodnik, eds., *Consciousness and the Brain* (New York: Plenum, 1976).

Simon, Herbert A. *Models of Thought*. (New Haven, Conn.: Yale University Press, 1979).

2

Sensation and Perception

Introduction to Sensory Psychology: "Touch", Taste, and Smell

6

Did You Know That . . .

Your skin is primarily sensitive to warm, cold, pressure, and, in a complex way, to pain?

Some 95 percent of your skin is hairy?

Muscle receptors tell your brain where your arms and legs are, and what they are doing?

Special receptor cells in your inner ear help you detect "up" from "down"?

Your sense receptors primarily detect *changes* in your environment?

Even the best steak doesn't *taste* much different from old shoe leather?

There are only four basic taste qualities: sweet, sour, salty, and bitter?

The best way to smell the aroma of wine is to "chew" it with your mouth open?

A woman's sensitivity to tastes and odors varies with her menstrual cycle?

Sex-related odors can change the way many women *perceive* other people?

"How To Build a Better Robot"

The mile-long chunk of rock hung suspended in the dark of outer space like a frayed cigar floating quietly on the surface of a huge black lagoon. The little NASA space ship circled the asteroid-rock twice, and then dropped toward it slowly for a landing. The ship's directional jets hissed nervously as it twisted this way and that, now slowing its speed a bit, now correcting its slippery course through space with just the briefest puff of gas from one of the many jet nozzles protruding from its sides.

The space ship was millions of kilometers from earth, probing the ring of asteroids that girdled the distant sun like the belt around a fat man's belly. But this belt was a circle of rocks flung far out in space, sandwiched somewhere between the orbits of the planets Mars and Jupiter. A few of the asteroids were large enough to be seen by telescope from earth, but most of them were so small that you had to be right on top of them to detect them.

No one knew where the asteroid belt had come from—probably from some planet that had blown up a billion years ago. And only a few scientists really cared one way or another. But everybody knew and cared that some of these hunks of celestial garbage were loaded with valuable metals. And that's what the little NASA space ship was out here for—to search for such earth-rare metals as radium, uranium, and plutonium. The National Aeronautics and Space Administration had a long-time need for these radioactive substances.

Major Jack Amundsen watched the dials and displays on the ship's control panel cautiously. The asteroid toward which he was guiding his craft was not all that large. But if the space ship's radioactive detector was right, it contained a chunk of uranium big enough to make the NASA brass back in Houston very happy indeed—and to earn him a very accelerated promotion. And Amundsen was the sort of man who found promotions very accelerating indeed.

As the ship inched in for a landing on the cigar-shaped rock, Amundsen switched on the landing lights. For the most part, the asteroid's surface seemed pitted with cracks and craters. But almost in the center, running around the rock like an equator, was a shallow groove that appeared to have a reasonably flat bottom. Amundsen dropped the little ship down into the depression carefully and, when the ship made contact, pressed a button on his control panel. Immediately, high-speed drills in the ship's legs chewed their way into the hard rock underneath and effectively bolted the ship to the asteroid. Only then did Major Amundsen lean back in his command chair and relax.

"Pretty good piloting, don't you think, Mark? Bet you couldn't do half that good."

Robot XSR 5 Mark III/21, sitting next to the Major, turned its head from the control panel. Its metallic eyes sparkled as if in amusement.

"You know, Major, that I am not programmed for landings except in emergency conditions. I am an exploratory space robot, not a pilot robot." The machine's voice was so musical that it almost sounded human.

"Then go explore. And don't let any meteorites puncture your space suit." The Major smiled at his little joke, for the robot wore no space suit at all.

Raw space was dangerous to man, as the deaths of several US and Russian astronauts had proved only too dramatically. The NASA brass had split down the middle on how to overcome the dangers. Some administrators wanted all exploration done by machines. But some space experts insisted that machines were not flexible enough to meet the challenge of unknown conditions.

So an odd sort of compromise occurred. Humans would go into space, but would be mostly confined to the ship. As their companions, the astronauts would have advanced and highly complex robots to perform all the dangerous work outside the ship.

At first, Amundsen had resented the robot, wishing it were flesh and blood rather than metal and plastic. But during the long trip out, the Major had grown to accept Mark as being "almost human."

Mark lumbered clumsily into the space lock, pumped the precious air back into the ship, then moved slowly down a ladder onto the surface of the asteroid. Being a robot, Mark did not need much protection from the vacuum and cold of space. But Mark did need a searchlight and a radiation detector to help discover the substances that NASA was after.

As the robot moved away from the ship, the needle on the radiation detector hinted that the lode of uranium should be a few hundred meters ahead and very close to the surface. Mark moved cautiously, testing each step, the balance sensors in his head working overtime as he attempted to remain upright while walking weightlessly up the side of the small depression into which the ship had settled.

"How are you doing?" came Amundsen's gruff voice over the radio.

"Major, all is well. The stick-tite shoes grip the surface of the asteroid tightly, my walking reflexes function well; I have not stumbled once." The robot rounded a boulder and stopped, directing the light fastened to its head toward the mouth of a cavern near where it was standing.

"Major, the uranium appears to be buried inside a cave. May I descend?"

All hazardous procedures had to be approved by the human pilot.

"You may descend," came the Major's quick response.

Mark III/21 moved slowly into the mouth of the cave, stopping each few feet to daub a spot of fluorescent paint on the rocks. The paint marks would help guide the robot back to the surface should it lose its way inside the cave. Then Mark moved onward. The deeper underground the robot went, the more wildly the needle on the radiation detector danced. When the robot had pushed its way more than 300 meters into the ground, it came to the top of a large, hollow chamber in the cave.

As the robot crawled to the bottom of the chamber, the detector needle jumped off the dial. Mark stopped and swung around, the light on its head flooding the chamber with brightness. Then the robot knelt, put its tools down beside it, and picked up a handful of black, soft, somewhat sticky material. Under the light, the soft stuff looked like pitchblend, one of the most common ores containing uranium.

"Major, we have apparently struck paydirt, if I may use that phrase."

Back at the space ship, Amundsen was sitting at the control console waiting for news. When he heard what Mark said, he grinned.

"That's great, Mark, super great. Just gather up a sample in your bag and then . . ."

And then their world nearly ended.

Coming up from their blind side at a high speed, one of the asteroid's smaller brothers smacked into the rock's mid-section, just a few hundred meters from the ship. The asteroid shuddered like a punching bag hit by a world champion heavyweight. The smaller rock then bounced off into space again, leaving its devastation behind for the Major and the robot to handle as best they could.

Amundsen had been knocked from his seat when the crash occurred, and he thrashed about in midair momentarily. Because there was no gravity on the ship, objects knocked loose by the collision floated about the cabin lazily. The Major grabbed at a seatbelt and pulled himself to the control console. A quick glance at the dials and lights assured him that the ship was intact and safe. But the robot?

"Mark!" he called into the microphone. "What happened? Are you all right?"

The answer was slow in coming, and the robot's voice seemed distorted, fluttery, and very unmusical.

"Major, I survive, but barely. A rock hit my head. My light is gone. My vision circuits are inoperative. I am blind. I have lost contact with the bottom surface of the large chamber I was in. I float. Rocks and other objects float by me. What am I to do?"

The Major thought a while, picturing the robot tumbling about in the hollow underground bubble like a piece of meat in a bowl of stew.

"Reach out your arms and legs and wait until you make contact with one of the chamber walls."

"I obey, Major," the robot said. A minute or so later, it reported success, but in a doleful tone of voice. "I have touched the wall, Major. But what do I do now? My light is gone, and I cannot see. I cannot find the trail markers. I cannot find the tiny entrance to this large chamber. I have but three hours' power left in my batteries. How do I find my way back to the ship, Major?"

The problem was serious. Amundsen was under strict orders not to leave the ship even if the robot became endangered. He could return to earth safely without Mark, but when the robot's batteries were exhausted, its heater would no longer function. Then its delicate "brain" circuits would freeze and warp. For all practical purposes, the robot would be "dead." NASA would be furious at the loss of a multi-million dollar piece of equipment, and Amundsen would have lost a . . . friend?

Amundsen retraced the robot's path in his mind's eye. Always Mark had reported going down, down, deeper into the ground. Suddenly the solution seemed obvious.

"Mark, just keep moving upward. If you move upward, you'll get to the surface eventually and I can pick you up then with the ship. No sweat at all, really, Mark. Just keep moving upward."

"Major," said the robot after a while. "There is no gravity here and I do not know in which direction I am pointed. Major, which way is up?"

(Continued on page 155.)

The Senses

According to popular opinion, there are but five senses—vision, hearing, taste, smell, and touch. But there is also "common sense," which is unfortunately rare; "non-sense," which is unfortunately common; and the "sixth sense," which some people claim warns them of impending disaster (and which as we will see in Chapter 10 may be ordinary "horse sense").

In truth, there are *more* than five senses, no matter how you wish to define the word. For example, in this chapter you will discover that what most people call "touch" is not just one sense but several: (1) pressure; (2) temperature; (3) feedback from your muscles that lets you know where your arms and legs are; and (4) detection of changes in motion. To make matters even more complex, you will also find out that taste is both simpler and more complicated than you might have imagined, and that smell has a decided effect on your sex life. And, in case you have any doubts, some of these facts are guaranteed to be sensational!

In order to help you "make sense" of your senses, let's begin by seeing what sorts of sensory information a robot would need in order to survive in outer space. For if you can understand what inputs a complex machine would need, perhaps you'll understand better what sorts of sensory experiences you require in order to survive on the planet Earth.

Project "Robot"

A few years from now, our first real inter-planetary space ships will blast off from earth and take *people* out to one or more of the planets. As you know, the US space program is directed by the National Aeronautics and Space Administration. Let us suppose that, some time in the future, NASA decides that the environments on the other eight planets are so hostile that *robots* should be sent out first to investigate—to test things out to make sure that human beings can survive in space suits if and when we do arrive.

For many reasons, NASA further concludes that the robot ought to be man-sized. It should be mobile, and it should carry its own protection against the elements. The robot should also have a means of sensing and measuring its environment, and a way of sending messages back to its home base to report the data it gathers.

Now, let us further assume that you are hired by NASA to help with "Project Robot." Your first assignment is to worry about what kind of *sensory inputs* the robot should have. So you begin by asking yourself, "What kinds of sensory stimulation are humans sensitive to, and what use do we make of the information that we get from our bodies and the world around us?"

Sensory Coherence

The robot that you will design will have a purpose of some kind. That is, it will have to execute certain commands, maintain itself in reasonable order, and be able to move about in one fashion or another. All of these actions require that the robot be in touch with both the external world as well as its own body functions. And in this respect, the robot is little different than you are. For if you are to survive, you must be able to interact with your environment and know what's going on inside your own body.

The *major purpose* of sensory inputs, then, is to give you a **coherent** picture of both your internal and your external environment so that you can decide how to achieve your goals in life (including that of survival). You can be the brightest person ever born, but if you don't get the proper inputs (or don't use them correctly), you won't be around for very long.

Getting the proper inputs is not too difficult for most of us—we have only to open our eyes and ears and "take in the world." But how do you *make sense* out of these inputs? Well, that's one of the chief functions your brain serves—to tie together sight and sound and touch and smell and taste into one *coherent whole.*

To "make sense" of an input may seem easy—after all, your brain performs this task routinely millions of times a day. But think about the *sensory process* for a moment. Suppose you look at a bright red sports car passing by. You "see" the car because of light rays which are reflected to your eyes from the automobile. But your brain is not sensitive to light. So somehow your eyes must *translate* or **transduce** those light rays into a pattern of neural messages which your eyes then send to your brain. Your brain momentarily "stores" these neural signals while it checks its memory banks, and "recognizes" the pattern as one it has experienced before. Your brain then combines the *sight* of the car with the deep rumbling *sounds* its engine is making (and perhaps the *smell* of the exhaust) and somehow produces a coherent mental image—that of a bright red sports car.

Sensory psychology deals with each of the various types of inputs you can detect—sight, sound, smell, taste, and "touch." *Perception* is the process by which your brain puts these inputs together to make a coherent experience. We'll have more to say about perception in a later chapter. For the moment, let's first try to figure out what your sensory inputs *really are*, and how your brain *detects* what's going on inside your body and in the outer world.

"WHAT I LIKE ABOUT THIS OFFICE IS I CAN SEE THE CITY, BUT I CAN'T HEAR IT OR SMELL IT."

Coherent (ko-HERE-ent). Anything that is coherent is logically consistent. When you put all of your sensory inputs together—sight, sound, taste, smell, and "touch"—you are able to *perceive* the world in a logical manner.

Transduce (trans-DOOSE). To transduce is to change something from one form into another. Your eyes transduce light waves into neural energy which is sent to your brain as a sensory input message.

The Skin

What is your most important sensory organ? Your eyes? Your ears, perhaps? Before you answer, think of the many blind people you know who get along quite well in this complex world. And think of how many deaf people manage to survive without being able to hear. But have you ever known anyone *without a skin to cover their flesh and bones*?

As you can perhaps now realize, your skin is the *most important sensory organ* that your body has. For it not only gives you sensory information, it gives you physical protection from the elements as well. Thus, when your boss at NASA assigns you the task of deciding what kind of covering the robot should have, you are rather pleased. Because you have been asked to design one of the most critical parts of the robot's body.

To start matters off, you ask yourself a very important question: "What purpose does the skin serve?" A little thought convinces you that your skin answers many needs. It keeps your vital organs inside where they belong, and keeps the outside world outside where it belongs. It stretches as you gain weight and shrinks when you shed a few pounds. Your skin also helps regulate your internal temperature, for it has several layers to it that help insulate you against the cold. And when you get too hot, your skin has sweat glands that release water which cools you by evaporation.

Most important, however, your skin is filled with *receptors* that let you know what the world around you is like. If you had no skin receptors, you wouldn't know when you had hurt yourself. You also wouldn't know when you were touching something, and whether what you touched was hard or soft, cold or hot. How long could you survive without this kind of sensory knowledge?

But would *your* skin serve a robot's specialized needs? After due consideration, you conclude that you can't tell what type of covering the robot ought to have until you know more about what this robot is going to have to do. So you begin to think about what types of *sense organs* the robot is going to need in whatever skin it gets.

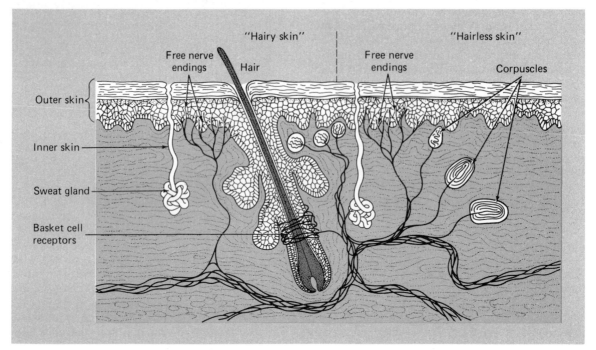

Fig. 6.1. A schematic diagram of the skin. Basket cell receptors are found only in hairy skin. Corpuscles are found primarily in hairless skin. Free nerve endings are found in both hairy and hairless regions.

The Skin Receptors

If you like to experiment on yourself, please go find several small objects—things like a pencil, a glass, a rubber band, a ring, a key, a piece of cloth—and put them on a table near you. Now, close your eyes and *feel* each object. Begin by just pressing the palm of your hand down on the objects.

What can you tell about these small objects without fingering them? That they are hard or soft, large or small, that they have points or sharp edges or rounded **contours**—and that is about all you can tell. A pencil or key is hard, a rubber band or an eraser yields when you press on it and hence feels soft.

But to ask what may at first seem a stupid question, *how do you know what is hard and soft?*

The Pressure Receptors

When you touch an object gently, you depress or deform your skin. Very sensitive nerve cells detect this *deformation of your skin* and fire off a message to your cortex. This input message moves down the axons of the receptor cells until it reaches your spinal cord, then moves up the cord to the stem of your brain. From your brain stem, the message flows through several "lower centers" and finally works its way up to your cor-

tex. But only when the input arrives at your cortex do you realize *consciously* that your skin has encountered a foreign object of some sort.

Now, with the fingers of one hand, gently pinch the palm of your other hand. You will notice that the skin on your palm feels fairly thick. Next, gently pinch the skin on your forearm. The skin is much thinner there. But the major *physiological* difference is that the skin on your forearm has hairs on it, while the skin on your palm does not. Some 95 percent of the skin on your body (whether you are male or female) is *hairy* skin. Only the palms of your hands, the soles of your feet, your lips and mouth, your eyeballs, some parts of your sex organs, and a few other scattered areas are made up of *hairless* skin.

Now, pick a single hair on your arm and pull it gently. You will probably experience a "pressury" feeling. Tap the hair gently (without touching your skin). You will experience much the same sensation of *pressure* as when you pulled on the hair.

Hairless skin contains tiny receptor cells that are called **encapsulated nerve endings**. Some of them look much like small onions and are known as **corpuscles**. The corpuscles are more-or-less round in shape, much like small onions. And, if you were to cut one open, you'd find that these "onion-shaped" corpuscles have many layers to them (see Fig. 6.1).

Hairy skin has a few encapsulated nerve endings in it. But it also has a unique type of

Introduction to Sensory Psychology: "Touch, Taste, and Smell"

touch-receptor neuron buried at the base of each hair. The fibers of these nerve cells are woven around the bottom of each stalk of hair. Whenever the hair-stalk is pushed or pulled in any direction, the nerve fibers are squeezed so that they fire off a "pressure" message to your brain. These hairy-skin receptors are called **basket cells** because they look like a wicker basket wrapped around the bottom of the hair stalk.

Both hairy and hairless skin also contain receptor neurons called **free nerve endings**. "Free" in this case means that they are not attached to any particular place (see Fig. 6.1). The free nerve endings are very simple nerve cells whose fibers spread out freely like the branches of a vine just under the outer layers of your skin. Since the free nerve endings are found everywhere on the surface of your body, they are by far the most common sort of skin receptor that you have.

All three types of receptors—the encapsulated nerve endings (including the corpuscles), the basket cells, and the free nerve endings—yield a simple "pressure sensation" when they are stimulated. (As we will see, however, some of the free nerve endings manage to do a bit more than that.)

Primary Sensory Qualities

Now, go back to the objects that you were feeling on the table near you. Close your eyes and have someone place first a *wooden* object and then a *metal* object in your hands. You can tell wood from metal in two ways: (1) The wood is usually softer than the metal; and (2) the wood will feel warm while the metal feels cold.

Your skin receptors give rise to two qualitatively different sensory experiences—*pressure* and *temperature*. The encapsulated nerve endings in the hairless regions and the basket cells around each hair are primarily *pressure receptors*. The free nerve endings detect both *pressure* and *temperature*.

It may come as a surprise to you that these two sensations (plus pain, which we will discuss later) are the *only primary sensory qualities* that your skin can tell you about. However, most psychologists believe that all the information you get from your skin about the world around you is merely a *combination* of pressure sensations and temperature sensations—plus, occasionally, the experience of pain (see Chapter 17).

Complex Pressure Sensations

Next, rub the palm of your hand over your clothes, the surface of the table, the cover of this book, the upholstery of a chair, or the top of a rug.

Some objects feel smooth to your touch, others feel rough. How does your skin tell you which is which if it can experience *just* pressure and temperature?

The answer comes from this fact—when you move your hand across a surface, you stimulate many receptors at once. If the surface of an object is rough, parts of your skin "stick" as you rub your palm across the object. This "sticking" causes your skin to wrinkle a bit and, where your skin is wrinkled the most, the receptors fire vigorously. But where your skin is unwrinkled and smooth, the receptors hardly fire at all. Your brain perceives this *pattern of incoming sensory information* as "roughness" or "smoothness."

If the robot you are helping build for NASA is going to stroll about the surface of some distant planet, you will want it to be able to bend over, pick something interesting off the ground, and examine it. If you put pressure receptors of some kind in the robot's fingers, you will be able to tell if the object is hard or soft, or rough or smooth, simply by decoding the *pattern of signals* from the robot's pressure receptors.

You could also put temperature detectors in the robot's fingers and learn whether the object was hot or cold.

But hot or cold in relation to what?

The Temperature Receptors

When you first crawl into a bathtub of hot water, it may seem that you are going to be boiled alive before the bath is over. The water feels intensely hot, and your skin turns lobster red as your brain orders an increase in the flow of blood through

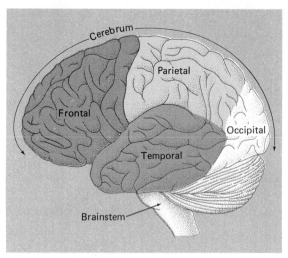

Fig. 6.2. The lobes of the brain.

your skin to help cool things off. If you manage to stay in the tub for a while, the water feels cooler and cooler (even if you keep the temperature of the water as hot as when you first crawled into the tub). When you get out, the air in the bathroom may seem surprisingly cool to your naked skin.

"Hot" and "cold" are *relative* terms that, in your body's case, are always related to *whatever your skin temperature is*. Anything you touch that is *colder* than your skin will seem cool to you. Anything you touch that is *hotter* than your skin will seem *warm*. The warmer or colder the object is in relation to your skin temperature, the more rapidly your temperature receptors will fire.

Question: Given the fact that hot water seems cooler to you after you have been soaking in it for a while, do your receptors seem to respond to temperature itself, or to changes in temperature?

The Somatic Cortex

The messages that your skin receptors send to your brain tell you four things:

1. The *location* of the experience—that is, what part of your body is detecting the sensations.
2. The *quality* of the experience (that is, pressure or temperature).
3. The *quantity* or strength of the experience (intense pressure or weak, slightly warm or very cold).
4. The *duration* of the stimulation—whether it is brief or continuing.

Let's see why all four of these things are important. Suppose you are walking along barefooted and you step on a tack. As you probably well know, you realize almost instantly *what part*

of which foot has been punctured, *how intense* the wound is, and whether the tack is *still* in your foot or has fallen out. How do you become conscious of all this information so quickly?

Well, think for a moment about the NASA robot that you were helping design. If you wanted the robot to *localize* its skin sensations, how would you hook its skin receptors up to the robot's brain? Probably you would want to put in a direct "telephone line" between each receptor and a *specific* part of the "brain." Each receptor would, in effect, have its own "telephone number." The robot could tell where the stimulation was coming from simply by checking to see which telephone line the message was coming over.

In a sense, your nervous system is "constructed" in much the same way. For each receptor cell in your skin is connected to a specific region in the *sensory input areas* in your **parietal lobes** (see Fig. 6.2). Thus your brain can tell the location of any stimulation on your body by noting *where* the input message arrives in the parietal lobe.

You may recall from Chapter 4 that the parietal lobe in each of your cerebral hemispheres is located at the very top center of your brain. The front edge of the parietal lobe is immediately adjacent to the *motor output area* at the rear of the frontal lobe. The cortex at this front edge of the parietal lobe is often called the **somatic cortex**. "Soma" is the Greek word for "body," and it is to this part of your cortex that all of your body or *somatic receptors* send their sensory messages. Receptors in the left side of your body send their inputs primarily to the somatic cortex in the right half of your brain. The receptors in the right side of your body send their messages to your left somatic cortex.

The Deep Receptors

If you made the NASA robot much like yourself, it could tell the hardness, smoothness, and temperature of an object it had picked up just by noting what its "skin" receptors were signaling. But what about the object's size, shape, and weight?

Pick up a pencil, close your eyes, and roll the pencil around in your hand. You can tell at once what size, shape, and weight the pencil has. But it is *not* your surface or skin receptors that give you this information, for we could anesthetize all the nerves in the skin of your hand and you would still be able to tell the size, shape, and weight of the pencil.

The muscles, joints, tendons, and bones in your hand (and in much of the rest of your body, too) all have sensory receptors in them. These are called **deep receptors**, to distinguish them from the *surface receptors* in your skin. Whenever you contract a muscle in your hand, a tiny nerve cell buried in that muscle sends a feedback signal to your somatic cortex saying that the muscle is in operation. The heavier an object is, the harder your muscle must work to lift the object and hold it steady. And the harder the muscle pulls or contracts, the more vigorously the tiny receptor neuron buried in the muscle fires—and the more intense feedback you get.

Distribution of Receptors

If you were building a robot, you would surely want its *fingers* to be more sensitive to pressure and temperature than, say, the middle of its *back*. For robots (like people) would seldom be called upon to make fine discriminations or judgments about objects with the "skin" on their backs. So you would probably wish to put *more* sensory receptors in the robot's fingers than on its back.

There are more pressure receptors in your fingertips, your lips, your eyeball, and on the tip of your tongue than elsewhere on your body. Thus the skin on your back and buttocks contains but a fraction of the number of receptors per square centimeter of tissue that the skin on your lips contains.

Generally speaking, the distribution of the sense receptors in your body is just about the same as you would logically decide should be the case for your robot. Those parts of your body you use most to make sensory discriminations have the most pressure receptors, while those parts that you use least have fewer receptor neurons.

Motion-Change Detectors

By working out electronic circuits that would operate much the way the neural circuits in your body operate, you could fairly easily design a robot that would be able to pick things up, measure them with its fingers, and keep track of where all its arms and legs were in the process. But what if your robot fell over and ruined its vision tubes? How would you get it upright and walking again? How would it know which way was up?

Contact receptors in the soles of your robot's feet might be helpful, but they would not tell the robot whether its head was bent over or upright. You could add position detectors in the robot's "muscular" system that could monitor the location of all its limbs and its head. But even these receptors would not be enough, for the robot still could not tell "up" from "down" just by getting feedback about where its arms and legs were.

Parietal lobes (pair-EYE-uh-tull, or puh-RYE-uh-tull). That part of each cerebral hemisphere located at the very top of the brain. Sensory input from the skin receptors and the muscles comes to this part of your cerebrum (see Chapter 4).

Somatic cortex (so-MAT-ick KOR-tecks). The outer layer of the parietal lobe is called the parietal cortex. The front section of the parietal cortex receives sensory-input messages from the skin and muscle receptors. This front section is called the "somatic cortex."

Deep receptors. Your brain must have some means of determining the movement, position, and condition of the various parts of your body. Each of the muscles, joints, tendons, and bones of your body has special receptor cells that fire whenever the muscle (joint, tendon, or bone) moves or is damaged in any way. Your brain sends out command messages (feed-forward) telling your muscles to move, for instance. The deep receptors provide informational feedback to your brain as to whether the movement has actually occurred.

Your own body solves this problem of location and movement in space with a special set of "motion-change" detectors inside your ears. To understand how these receptors work, however, you need to remember what Newton's *law of inertia* is all about.

Law of Inertia

The law of inertia states that a body at rest tends to remain at rest, while a body in motion tends to continue to move. As an illustration of how the law works, let's look closely at what happens to your own "body" when you are riding as a passenger in the front seat of a car. Now, suppose that the car is stopped at a red light. When the light turns green, the driver hits the gas pedal and the car leaps forward rapidly. But your body is not directly connected to the frame of the car itself. Thus when the car accelerates, your body will "tend to remain at rest." So you are pushed back rather roughly into the seat cushions and you feel a great surge of acceleration as the car picks up speed. If the car stops suddenly, your body "tends to continue to move" and (if you forgot to buckle your seat belt) you are thrown into the dashboard or the windshield. It is the law of inertia, then, which makes it important that you wear some kind of restraint when riding in an automobile or an airplane.

Two Types of Motion

Whether you are considering robots or people, there are two basic types of motion that a "body" must be sensitive to: (1) straight-line or linear movements; and (2) rotary or circular movements. Buried away inside each of your ears are two types of receptor organs that detect *changes* in the motion of your body. One type of receptor responds to changes in "straight-line motion."

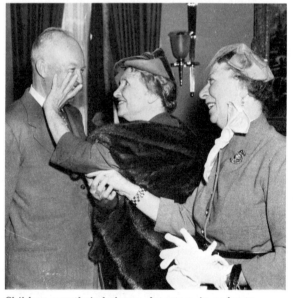

The other type responds to changes in "circular" motion. Both types of receptor organs function by obeying Newton's law of inertia.

Linear Motion-Change Detectors

The "flip-flop" movements that your body makes when an automobile speeds up or slows down are usually straight-line or linear movements. The detectors in your ear that sense *changes in linear motion* are two small organs called the **saccule** and the **utricle**.

Children use their balance detectors in order to learn how to maintain an upright posture. **(top)**

In zero gravity conditions, your balance detectors can't tell you "up" from "down." **(bottom left)**

Helen Keller, blind and deaf from childhood, met Dwight D. Eisenhower at the White House in 1954. She "listened" to what the then President was saying by placing her fingers on his lips. **(bottom right)**

Both the saccule and the utricle are made up of Jello-like or gelatinous tissue filled with tiny stone-like particles—rather as if someone had made a bowl of cherry Jello and put in just the pits instead of the cherries. When your head begins to move in a straight line, the saccule and utricle flip-flop in your inner ear the same way that your body flip-flops in an automobile. The "rocks in your head"—that is, the bits of stone in the saccule and utricle—increase the quivering of Jello-like material.

Hair cells buried in this gelatinous tissue are pushed or pulled this way and that by all the quivering in the saccule and utricle. The *basket nerve cells* at the base of each hair cell are stimulated by the flip-flopping and signal your somatic cortex that your body is starting or stopping a straight-line (linear) movement.

Rotary Motion-Change Detectors

Any *change* in rotary motion your body makes is detected by the **semi-circular canals** in your ear. These three canals are positioned at right angles to each other inside your ear so they can detect changes in circular motion in any of the three dimensions of space.

When you turn your head, the fluid in the semi-circular canals accelerates more slowly than does the rest of your head. This fluid presses against a small mound of gelatinous tissue at the base of each canal. When this Jello-like tissue is pushed one way or the other, hair cells in the gelatin are twisted or pulled. The *basket nerve cells* at the base of each hair then signal your somatic cortex that your head has either stopped or started some kind of rotary motion.

Centrifugal Force

If you have ever been to a carnival or amusement park, you may have ridden on a "loop-the-loop" roller coaster. If you have taken one of these frightening yet thrilling rides, you may have asked yourself why you didn't fall out of the car when it turned you upside down at the top of the "loop."

The answer is, **centrifugal force**. Centrifugal force tends to throw any object in the roller coaster car *away* from the center of the rotation. As the car makes the loop, therefore, centrifugal force plasters you firmly against your seat cushion despite the fact that you are upside down.

Centrifugal force is actually an example of Newton's law of inertia, and your motion-change detectors respond to centrifugal force just as they do to any other form of movement. If you could stand up in the roller coaster car just as you reached the top of the "loop," your head would be pointed straight at the earth. Yet the bottom of the car would seem "down" to you, while the earth itself would seem to be "up."

Some of the more creative thinkers at NASA have designed wheel-like space ships that we

might use to visit the planets. During the journey, the wheel would turn just rapidly enough to create an artificial gravity so that the men and women on board could walk comfortably around the inside of the outer wall of the wheel—with their heads pointed to the center of the wheel. Since the motion-change detectors in the travelers' ears couldn't tell the difference, centrifugal force presumably could make a pleasant substitute for gravity.

Adaptation and Habituation

Your brain is your main organ of survival. And if you are to survive, you must usually pay more attention to *changes* in your environment than to stimuli that *remain constant* for a period of time.

There are at least two ways in which your nervous system adjusts to constant inputs: First, by what we will call **receptor adaptation**; and second, by what we will refer to as **central habituation** to a stimulus input. Receptor adaptation occurs in the receptor neurons themselves, while central habituation occurs in your brain.

As an example of *receptor adaptation*, consider what happens when you first sink into a tub of water that is 20° warmer than your skin. As you know, your "warm" receptors will immediately begin firing vigorously. But as you remain lying in the tub, your skin temperature itself warms up. After a short period of time, your free nerve endings will fire less vigorously because the tempera-

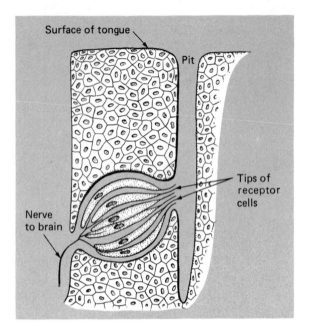

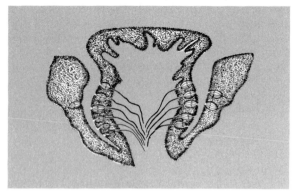

Fig. 6.3. A single taste bud. **(left)**
Fig. 6.4. A papilla in the tongue. **(right)**

ture of your skin is now much closer to that of the water. Because your skin and your free nerve endings have *adapted* to the heat, the water will now seem much less hot to you.

As an example of *central habituation*, think of what happens when you move into a house beside a busy highway. At first, you will probably notice the sounds of the traffic almost continuously. But, after a few days, your brain will stop paying much attention to the continual drone of the passing cars and trucks. Indeed, you may be surprised when a visiting friend asks how you can stand the noise. But in this case, it is your *brain* that has changed its way of responding to a constant input, not the receptors in your *ears*.

In general, we use the term *adaptation* whenever your receptor cells themselves slow down or reduce their firing rates in response to a constant stimulus. We use the term *habituation*, however, to refer to your brain's tendency to ignore sensory inputs that seem of little interest or importance.

Adaptation and habituation are complex subjects that we will discuss often in this book. For the moment, however, you should remember that the human body has a great ability to adjust to the world around it, but this adjustment hinges on your body's being able to notice and react to what is *changing* in the environment.

Question: *When you have been soaking in a hot tub for a while, can you make the water "feel" warmer just by paying attention to it? When you have lived in a house by a noisy*

highway for a while, can you hear the traffic just by paying attention to it? What do your answers to these two questions tell you about the differences between receptor adaptation and central habituation?

A Window of Skin

Your skin senses are among the most important senses that you have, surely as critical to your survival as are vision and hearing. And yet, perhaps because you seldom use them for communication or artistic expression, you may have overlooked their complexity, their beauty, and their incredible usefulness.

As an example of your skin's importance, consider the story of Helen Keller. She was born a normal child, but an illness when she was 19 months old left her deaf and blind. Although she had learned to say a few words before the illness, she soon stopped speaking. For the next several years of her life, Helen Keller was little more than an animal, trapped in a black and silent cage, completely unable to communicate with those around her.

When Helen Keller was 6, however, her parents appealed to Alexander Graham Bell for help. Bell, the inventor of the telephone, recommended as a teacher a young woman named Anne Sullivan. Within a month Miss Sullivan had taught Helen to make sense of the myriad sensations her skin receptors poured into her brain. Helen learned how to "talk" using her fingers, and how to "listen" when someone "wrote" on the palm of her hand. Later she learned to "read speech" by placing her fingers on the lips of the person who was speaking.

Helen Keller's skin was her only window to the world, but she "saw" through this window with exceptional clarity. When she would meet

Introduction to Sensory Psychology: "Touch, Taste, and Smell"

someone for the first time, she would run her hands over the person's face to find out what the person "looked like."

If you would like to learn "skin language," do as Helen Keller did. The next time you are alone with a very good friend or relative, have this person sit quietly while you close your eyes and explore the person's face with your fingers. Do not speak. Simply move your fingers gently around the person's eyes, ears, nose, lips, and hair. What kind of a person is this? What does the person *feel* like?

Every scrap of knowledge you have about the world around you, including the images you have of people you love and hate, first came to you as a pattern of neural inputs that your sense organs sent to your brain for processing. If you understand where your inputs come from—that is, how your receptor neurons react and why they function as they do—you will certainly be able to build a better robot if you ever have to. But, more important, you will also come closer to understanding your own internal psychological processes—and your behavioral outputs—than if you choose to ignore the "input side" of your own body's functioning.

Taste

Your skin is an important "input organ" in part because it protects you from things in the outside world that shouldn't get inside your body. But there are times when you *must* "input" certain items—such as food and water—if you are to survive. And much as it may surprise you, your skin helps you determine what to eat and drink—and what not to. For, as we will soon see, receptor cells in the skin that line your tongue, mouth, and nose are responsible for mediating those sensory qualities that we call "taste" and "smell."

Let's look first at what taste is all about. Pick your favorite food and imagine it in your mind's eye. Let's say that you picked a steak—three inches thick, wrapped in bacon, and cooked just the way you like it. Now, ask yourself what may seem a very stupid question: Why does the steak *taste* good to you?

Whatever reasons you come up with, chances are they're partly wrong. For even the best of steaks has almost no *taste* at all—at least if we speak technically and we restrict "taste" to the sensory qualities that come from the skin receptors in your tongue. Steak *smells* good; it *looks* good; it has a fine *texture* to it that you enjoy chewing. And if it comes to your table sizzling hot, steak both *sounds* good and has just the right *temperature*.

Taste buds. The taste buds are found scattered across the surface of the tongue. Each bud contains two or more hair cells, which are the taste receptors. When chemicals in the food you eat (or liquids you drink) come in contact with these hairs, the buds send "tasty" signals to your cortex.

Papillae (pap-PILL-eye, or pap-PILL-ee). The bumps on your tongue that contain the taste buds.

But none of these sensory qualities has anything to do with the *taste* of steak. In fact, if we could block out all the other sensory qualities except those that come from your taste receptors, you'd find that you could hardly tell the difference between the taste of steak and that of old shoe leather.

The Taste Receptors

Your **taste buds** contain the hair cells which are your taste receptors. The taste buds are your body's "poor relations" (see Fig. 6.3). Impoverished in almost every sense of the word, your taste buds are scattered in nooks and crannies all across the surface and sides of your tongue. Mostly, however, they are found clumped together in bumps on your tongue called **papillae** (from the Latin word meaning "nipples"). If you stick out your tongue and look at it, you will see the papillae very clearly.

Most of the papillae have grooves around their sides, like the moats or canals that circled old European castles. The taste buds line the sides of the papillae, like windows in the outer wall of a castle (see Fig. 6.4).

Taste buds are made up of several receptor cells. Each of these cells has a hair at one end which pokes out into the "moat" around the papillae much as the hairs on the skin of your arm stick out into the air. When you eat or drink something, the liquids in your mouth fill up the moats around the papillae, and various molecules in the food stimulate the hair cells *chemically*. The cells then fire off their sensory input message to your brain, and you experience the sensation of taste.

The chemical processes that lead to the experience of taste are not entirely known. But it appears that the food molecules fill in specific *receptor sites* on the hairs and receptor cells, much as the transmitter molecules in the synaptic canals find receptor sites on the dendrites and cell bodies of the neurons in your brain.

Certain types of food molecules fit into one receptor site but won't fit into others—much as a key will fit some locks but not others. When a molecule fits into a taste receptor site, it causes the receptor cell to fire. Your brain then figures

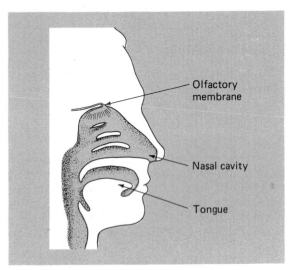

Fig. 6.5. The nasal cavity in cross section.

out what kinds of chemicals are present in your mouth by noting which receptors have been "unlocked," or stimulated.

Taste Qualities

There are only four basic taste qualities: **sweet**, **sour**, **bitter**, and **salty**—a paltry few *primary* qualities compared to the richness of the sensory experiences you get from vision, hearing, and smell. The noted psychologist E.B. Titchener once estimated that you can discriminate about 3,000 different tastes. However, all of them appear to be *mixtures* of the four basic taste qualities.

The number of your taste receptors is limited, too—a fraction of the number of receptor cells found in your eyes, ears, or nose. And yet, as impoverished as your tongue may seem in terms of sensory richness, it plays a very important role in your life for, along with your nose, your tongue acts as *guardian of your stomach.*

Some tastes are innately pleasing; others seem acquired. For instance, newborn infants will usually drink milk shortly after birth, but will spit out sour or bitter substances. The liking for sweet or slightly salty substances thus seems "built into your genes," but a fondness for beer or for "gin and tonic" would seem to be a learned response since infants don't care much for such tastes.

Some people are very insensitive to the taste of certain foods—you must really saturate their tongues with these foods for these people to detect the substance at all. This **taste blindness** is far from rare, and seems to be caused by some inherited deficiency in the chemical composition of the person's saliva. However, the taste-blind individual can usually detect the substance rather

easily if you first dissolve the food in the saliva of a person with normal taste sensitivity.

Taste is a necessary but, as we noted, not a particularly rich "sense." For the truth is, most of the food qualities that you ascribe to your tongue really should be credited to your nose.

Question: *When you catch a cold, and your nose is clogged but your tongue is not affected, why does food suddenly lose its "taste"?*

Smell

Your nose has two cavities or open spaces inside it (see Fig. 6.5). The roof of each of these nasal cavities is lined with a thick covering called the **olfactory membrane**, which is really a type of skin. Embedded in this membrane are millions of receptor cells called **olfactory rods**. At the base end of each of these rods is an axon that runs directly to your brain. At the front end is a branched set of dendrites. These dendrites stick out of your olfactory membrane to make contact with the air as it passes through your nasal cavity en route to your throat and lungs.

The stimuli that excite your olfactory rods are complex chemicals in *gaseous form* that are suspended in the air you breathe. These gaseous molecules appear to lock onto specific receptor sites on the receptor cell hairs. This "locking on" causes the olfactory rod to fire off an input message to your brain.

To be truthful, no one yet knows exactly how these chemicals "excite" your olfactory rods. We are sure, however, that most of the odors your nose detects come from gaseous molecules that are heavier than air. Unless the air is stirred up, these heavy molecules tend to collect at ground level. If you want to "smell better," then, you might try putting your nose down close to the floor—where the majority of the odors around you actually congregate!

"Chewing" the Wine

When you breathe through your nose, air is forced up into your nasal cavities. But only a small portion of this air reaches your olfactory rods. When you chew and swallow your food, air is pushed up to the very top of each nasal cavity and stimulates your olfactory rods. You sniff a flower because this action forces the "smelly" molecules in the blossom up to the olfactory membrane where you can best detect these chemicals.

Most whiskey companies employ professional tasters who judge the quality of their products. These tasters take small sips of the alcohol and roll it around in their mouths while making chewing motions. This "mouthing" of the liquid can force the odor-laden air up the back entrance to the nasal cavity toward the olfactory membrane. Tea and coffee tasters test their products the same way.

If you order a bottle of wine at a good restaurant, the wine steward will open the bottle and give you the cork to sniff. If the cork if moist—and if it smells "sweet" and fresh—the wine is probably good. But if the cork smells "sour" or "putrid," the wine may have turned to vinegar, and you should ask for another bottle instead. If the cork smells fine to you, nod to the steward and she or he will pour a little of the wine into your glass. If you swirl this sample of wine around in your glass, you will release the odor molecules into the air inside the glass. You may then sniff the wine to make sure that it smells as good as the cork did.

The next stage in this pleasant ritual comes when you sip a bit of the wine sample in order to "taste" it. Actually, you should "chew" the wine and roll it around in your mouth the way that professional whiskey tasters do before you swallow it. If the wine suits your taste (actually, if it suits your smell), you may nod approvingly to the wine steward, who will follow the ritual of filling your guests' glasses before he or she fills yours.

Hormones and Sensory Acuity

Speaking olfactorily, some people smell better all the time, and you smell better some days than others. Which is to say that olfactory sensitivity varies considerably from one individual to another, presumably because of inheritance. Complete loss of the sense of smell occasionally occurs in older persons. And, according to John Amoore of the University of California Medical Center in San Francisco, many of us lack the ability to smell specific substances. Amoore found that 47 percent of the people he tested could not smell the urinous odor, 16 percent were "blind" to malty smells, 12 percent couldn't detect musky odors, and 3 percent could not smell sweat. These "smell blindnesses" apparently are present from birth.

Judging from Amoore's research, your genes influence your ability to detect various odors. But recent experiments suggest that your olfactory thresholds are also influenced by the amount of sex hormones present in your body. **Hormones** are chemicals secreted by various glands in your body that have a profound influence on your growth and behavior. As we will see in Chapter 12, the sex hormones are created primarily in the sex organs and serve to regulate sexual development and behavior.

Sweet, sour, bitter, and **salty**. The four basic taste qualities. All the thousands of different tastes of food are combinations or mixtures of these four simple tastes.

Taste blindness. The inability to taste one or more of the four basic taste qualities. Actually, it should be called "tastelessness," since "blindness" ordinarily refers to vision and not to taste. However, "lack of taste" is a term we use to refer to someone whose attitudes or opinions don't agree with ours; thus we use "taste blindness" to refer to those individuals whose tongues don't function as ours do.

Olfactory membrane (oal-FACK-torr-ee). "Olfaction" (oal-FACK-shun) is the process of smelling. The olfactory membrane is a layer of tissue at the top of each nasal cavity that contains the receptors for smell. There are two olfactory membranes in your nose—one inside each nostril.

Olfactory rods. The actual smell receptors. The olfactory membrane contains about 5 million olfactory rods.

Hormones (HOR-moans). Chemicals from various body glands that affect both growth and behavior.

Modalities (moh-DALL-it-tees). From the Latin word meaning "measures" or "manners." A modality is a way of doing or arranging something, or a type of sensory experience. Vision is one sensory modality; taste is another.

Acuity (ack-CUE-it-tee). The ability to detect very weak stimulus inputs, or to make fine sensory discriminations—that is, to judge very small differences between quite similar stimuli.

Testosterone (tess-TOSS-tur-own). One of the male sex hormones, secreted primarily by the testes (TESS-tees) or testicles (TESS-tickles) of the male. Masculine behavior patterns are strongly influenced by the presence of testosterone in the body.

Berkeley psychologist Frank Beach reports that before and during menstrual bleeding, a woman's body is almost totally deprived of sex hormones. As a consequence, during menstruation most women become less sensitive to inputs in *all* their sensory **modalities**. In fact, only in the middle of their menstrual cycle are women usually as sensitive to sensory inputs as men are all the time. However, women who are "on the pill" maintain a continuously high hormone level. Hence their sensory **acuity** also remains high.

Beach and many other psychologists have noted as well that men are more sensitive to some odors just after receiving injections of the male sex hormone **testosterone**.

Men may be somewhat better at *detecting* odors than women. However, in the July 1981 issue of *Psychology Today*, William Cain reports that women appear to be superior at such tasks as *identifying* and *remembering* smells. Cain asked 102 men and 103 women subjects to name and identify 80 different odors. Cain exposed the subjects to the smells a total of five times. As Fig. 6.6 shows, the women were superior to the men on each of the tests. Cain believes that this superiority is a matter of experience, however, for *all* the subjects showed improvement over time. And by the fifth test, the men were performing as well as

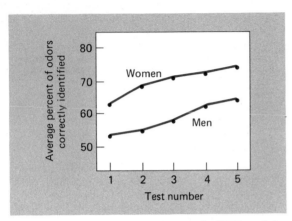

Fig. 6.6. Outcome of an experiment by William Cain, who tested men and women on their ability to learn 80 odors. The ability of both women and men to come up with the correct names improved over time. But, on the average, women correctly identified more items on the initial test and maintained this superiority in four later trials.

the women had at the start of the experiment. In present-day American society, Cain says, women are more likely to deal with foods, perfumes, and other "smelly" objects than men are.

Question: *William Cain notes that learning to give a "verbal label" to an odor helps considerably in identifying it at a later time. Why might attaching a name to a smell help you remember it?*

Smells and the Menstrual Cycle

The relationship between smells and sexual behavior is a complex but very interesting one. To begin with, the menstrual cycle itself seems to be controlled in part by olfactory inputs. There are many "old wives' tales" suggesting that women who live together tend to have menstrual periods that are "in synch" with each other. In 1971, Martha McClintock tested this folk belief by studying the menstrual cycles of 135 women living in a dormitory at Wellesley College. McClintock found that, as the college year progressed, the menstrual cycles of good friends and roommates did in fact become more similar.

An explanation for this "menstrual synchrony" may come from research reported in 1977 by California psychologist Michael Russell and his colleagues. Russell believes that when we sweat, the **apocrine glands** under our arms release sexual substances. To test this notion, Russell and his group asked a woman with a very regular menstrual cycle to wear cotton pads under her arms daily. The experimenters then rubbed

portions of these pads on the upper lips of female volunteers who agreed not to wash their faces for several hours afterward. A "control" group of volunteers was treated with pads not containing human sweat. The women in the control group maintained their normal menstrual cycle. However, the menstrual cycles of the women who smelled the sweat pads daily became strikingly similar to those of the women who had donated the sweat.

It would seem, then, that the mere *smell* of certain natural sexual substances is enough to strongly influence the menstrual cycle.

The Sweet Smell of Sex

It has long been known that both male and female animals secrete chemicals that attract the opposite sex. But what about humans?

Naomi Morris and Richard Udry have studied the relationship between smells and sexual intercourse for more than a decade in various groups of married women. In 1968, Udry and Morris reported that many of the subjects in their first study were more likely to engage in intercourse—and to achieve orgasm—during the middle of their menstrual cycles than at any other time. The women's hormone production (and hence her sensitivity to smells) is, of course, greatest in mid-cycle. But how could an increase in olfactory acuity account for an increase in sexual behavior?

Copulins

In 1974, Richard Michael and his colleagues at Emory University reported that female monkeys secrete chemicals called **copulins** that are sexually attractive to males. More recently, Michael has discovered that these same copulins are produced by human females. Michael believes that the peak production of copulins occurs in the middle of the menstrual cycle.

Although some scientists have criticized Michael's work, a study reported in 1978 by Morris and Udry does seem to support the belief that women release chemicals that act as **aphrodisiacs**. Morris and Udry asked 62 married women to rub one of four different perfumes on their chests before going to bed at night. Only one of the four perfumes contained copulins, and the women were not told which perfume was which. The women used a different perfume each night, and kept records of their sexual activities and of their menstrual cycles.

Morris and Udry report that only 12 of the 62 couples showed the expected "peak sexual activity" at the middle of the woman's menstrual cycle. It would seem, then, that while human females do secrete copulins, these sexual attractants do not affect all men in the same way.

Question: *How might differences in* olfactory sensitivity *help explain the Morris and Udry data?*

Exaltolide

Do men secrete copulin-like substances too? The answer seems to be a qualified "yes." In 1952, a French scientist named J. LeMagnen reported that women seem to be particularly sensitive to the odor of a chemical named **exaltolide**. This musky fragrance—which is found in many well-known perfumes—is excreted in human urine, but men produce about twice as much of it as do women.

Sexually mature women can detect the smell of exaltolide readily, particularly in the middle of their menstrual cycle when their hormone levels are highest. Men are relatively insensitive to the odor. Women who have had their ovaries removed—and hence are no longer producing female sex hormones—are as insensitive as are males. But even a woman without ovaries becomes highly sensitive to the smell shortly after receiving an injection of female sex hormone.

Although LeMagnen believes that the smell of exaltolide is sexually attractive to women, the

Apocrine glands (AH-poh-krin). Glands in your armpits that, when stimulated by sex hormones, release a "smelly" type of sweat.

Copulins (KOPP-you-lins). Chemicals released by female animals (including women) that act as sexual attractants for many males. Thus they are chemicals that stimulate organisms to copulate or engage in sexual activity.

Aphrodisiacs (AFF-roh-DEE-see-acks). Sexual stimulants. The Greek goddess of sexual love and beauty was Aphrodite (AFF-roh-DEE-tey). The Romans called her Venus. According to the famous Greek poet Homer, Aphrodite "overcomes all mortal men and immortal gods with desire." Thus anything to eat, drink, or be merry with that raises the passions—among other things.

Exaltolide (ex-ALL-toe-lide). A chemical compound released in urine. Men secrete twice as much exaltolide, on the average, as do women. Supposedly an aphrodisiac for women, but not for men (who cannot detect its smell).

matter has not as yet been proved scientifically. It does seem clear, however, that sex-related odors can change the way in which women perceive and feel about other human beings.

In the late 1970's, J.J. Crowley and his colleagues at Hatfield Polytechnic in England reported they had been able to influence the judgments that women students made about political candidates. Crowley and his group presented a large class of psychology students with printed information about six people who were competing for a student government position. Three of the candidates were men, three were women. The psychology students were asked to judge each candidate in terms of her/his personality and fitness for office.

While the members of the class were making their judgments, they were asked to wear paper masks—supposedly to keep their classmates from noticing their facial expressions. In truth, some of the masks had been coated with small amounts of sexual attractants. One third of the masks contained exaltolide, and one third contained copulin-like chemicals. The final third contained no attractants at all, so the students who wore these masks made up the "control group" in this experiment.

Crowley reports that the male psychology students were seemingly not affected at all by the "smelly" masks. The sex-related odors did alter the judgments of the women students, however. Those women exposed to exaltolide tended to favor the more assertive and aggressive of the six candidates for office. Those women exposed to copulins, however, preferred the shy and unaggressive candidates. The odor inputs thus apparently affected the *feelings* that the women students had concerning the office-seekers.

"MY COMPLIMENTS TO THE FOOD TASTER."

The sense of smell affects not only what you eat and drink, but also influences sexual attractiveness.

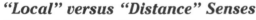

"Local" versus "Distance" Senses

Smell and taste are often called **chemical senses** because the stimulus that excites the receptors in your tongue and nose are *complex chemical molecules*.

But there is a very important difference between taste and smell—whatever your tongue tastes must ordinarily be brought to your mouth, while your nose can detect stimuli that are some distance away.

The skin senses, including taste, are *local* receptors—that is, they give your brain informa-

tion about the exact point on your body that is being stimulated. Olfaction, hearing, and vision are *distance* receptors—that is, they typically tell your brain what is going on some distance away from the surface of your body.

However, to borrow a phrase from the world of high-fidelity music, taste and smell are essentially **monaural** or "mono" senses. It may take you some time to locate the body of a mouse that had the misfortune to die in some out-of-the-way corner of your home, or to find in July an egg that was hidden too well at Easter. Why? Because your nose doesn't give you good *directional cues* as to the location of the "smelly" stimulus. Your eyes and ears, on the other hand, are strictly "stereo." Standing quite still in the middle of a strange room with your eyes closed, you can point out rather precisely the location of some noisy object like a ticking clock. And if you cover your ears but open your eyes, you can see a clock even if it's on a tower miles away.

If you wish to find out why your eyes and ears are so much better than your tongue and nose at helping you judge the *location* and *distance* of a stimulus object, "lend an ear" and "see" what you find out about yourself in the next chapter.

Summary

1. Your skin is your window to a great part of the outside world. **Receptor cells** in your skin provide sensory inputs to your **somatic cortex (parietal lobe)** telling your cortex what your body is doing, what your skin is touching, and whether the outside world is warm or cold.

2. The **corpuscles** in the hairless regions of your skin, and the **basket cells** in the hairy regions, detect pressure. The **free nerve endings**—found in all skin—detect both pressure and temperature.

3. Any object warmer than your skin will be sensed as warm. Any object cooler than your skin will be sensed as cold.

4. The **deep receptors** in your muscles, joints, tendons, and bones tell your cortex the position and condition of various parts of your body.

5. Buried away in your inner ear are your motion-change detectors—the **saccule**, the **utricle**, and the **semi-circular canals**. The saccule and utricle sense changes in straight-line or **linear motion**. The semi-circular canals respond to changes in circular or **rotary motion**.

6. Receptor **adaptation** is a slowing down of the firing rate of your sensory receptors which occurs when the receptors are stimulated at a constant rate. Central **habituation** is a process that occurs in your brain when you no longer pay attention to a **constant stimulus input**.

7. Taste and smell are called "chemical senses" because the receptors in the nose and tongue are stimulated primarily by complex chemical molecules.

8. The primary receptors for taste are the receptor cells in the **taste buds**, which are located in mushroom-shaped bumps called **papillae** on the surface of the tongue.

9. The four basic taste qualities are **sweet**, **sour**, **bitter**, and **salty**.

10. Taste is a very simple sense, with but four basic qualities. Smell is much more complex. Most of the "taste" of food is really the smell of the food rather than its taste.

11. The smell receptors are the **olfactory rods**, which lie on the **olfactory membrane** inside each of the two nostrils.

12. Women are more sensitive to all types of sensory inputs in the middle of their **menstrual cycles**—when their **hormone level** is high—than at any other point in the cycle. The sensory acuity of males is not cyclical as it is in women. However, men do become more sensitive to sensory inputs immediately after an injection of male sex hormone.

13. Women who are housed together tend to experience similar menstrual cycles. This **menstrual synchrony** seems to be caused by chemicals that the women release in their sweat.

14. Women (and many female animals) release chemicals called **copulins** that can be sexually attractive to some males. Both men and women release a chemical called **exaltolide** in their urine, but men produce twice as much of it as do women.

15. Exaltolide has a musky odor and is used in many perfumes and aphrodisiacs. Men are generally insensitive to the smell of exaltolide, but women are fairly sensitive to its odor—particularly in the middle of their menstrual cycle. The odor of exaltolide can affect the way women perceive or feel about other humans.

16. Smell and taste are both **monaural** (single) senses in that they seldom help us locate objects in space very well.

Chemical senses. Taste and smell are called the chemical senses because the stimulus input that sets them off is a chemical molecule of some kind.

Monaural (mon-R-al). Sound produced by a single source, as through just one loudspeaker.

(Continued from page 140.)

Major Jack Amundsen turned down the volume on the radio link between him and the robot. Mark III/21 was trapped somewhere in the very heart of the asteroid, clinging to the walls of a cave that had no top or bottom as far as the robot could sense. Amundsen could rescue Mark easily, quickly, if he could only find some way to let the robot know in which direction it should move to get out of the cave. But how could he tell Mark which way was "up" on an asteroid that had no gravity?

But what is gravity, after all, but a force that keeps the human race glued to the earth? Were it not for gravity, the Major reminded himself, the centrifugal force created by the earth's rotation would have flung us all into outer space long ago. Could he perhaps substitute one force for the other?

"Listen, Mark," the Major said on the radio. "I'm going to try something. Our space ship is bolted to this cruddy piece of rock. If I aim the positioning jets just right, I can probably set the whole asteroid spinning slowly like a top. If it does, your direction detectors will start operating again."

The robot was silent as Amundsen calculated what to do. The ship was parked almost dead center on the asteroid. If the positioning jets could generate enough sideways power—that is, create enough thrust at right angles to the surface of the asteroid—the asteroid would start to rotate. Amundsen turned on the jets and watched the dials on his control console. Slowly, ever so slowly, the huge piece of cosmic debris started to rotate like a wheel.

"Major, I feel it moving. The loose rocks that were floating around in the cave are falling to the floor of the chamber. Your idea worked." Mark's voice was as unemotional as ever, but Amundsen could swear the robot was smiling electronically.

"Major, my sensors are now functioning. I now know which way is up. I shall return to the ship shortly."

Amundsen suddenly panicked. "Wait a minute, Mark! Which way are you moving?"

"Up, Major, ever upward," came the calm reply.

"Stop, Mark! You're going the wrong way! Your sensors are giving you the right information, but you're interpreting it incorrectly. What seems to be 'up' to you is actually the center of the centrifugal rotation, the center of the asteroid. To get up to the space ship, you've got to move in the opposite direction of what seems up to you right now. It may seem screwy to you, Mark, but you've got to walk *down* in order to get *up*."

"But Major, my reflexes are all wrong. I see the logic of what you say, yet my motion detectors indicate that I would be going in an inappropriate direction if I move downward. Help me, Major. I cannot decide which way to go."

Major Amundsen grinned. Wait till he told the boys back in Houston about this! There were some things that a robot couldn't handle after all!

Amundsen pressed the button on his microphone and issued a command:

"Robot XSR 5 Mark III/21, this is your superior officer, Major Jack Amundsen, speaking. I hereby order you to continue moving in what seems a downward direction until you reach the surface of this asteroid and can then return to the space ship."

"Yes, Major. I hear and will obey."

Major Jack Amundsen breathed a sigh of relief, and then said gruffly, "Listen, Mark, be careful. The asteroid is whirling around fairly rapidly. So when you get to the surface, use your stick-tite shoes to keep from flying off into outer space."

Amundsen paused to think of what had happened to him and his robot companion, then laughed out loud. "And Mark, may the centrifugal force be with you!"

Recommended Readings

Boring, E.G. *Sensation and Perception in the History of Experimental Psychology* (New York: Appleton, 1942).

Dethier, Vincent. "Other Tastes, Other Worlds," *Science*, 201 (1978), pp. 224–228.

Hopson, Janet. *Scent Signals: The Silent Language of Sex* (New York: Morrow, 1979).

Keller, Helen. *Story of My Life* (New York: Airmont, 1970).

McBurney, Donald H., and Virginia B. Collings. *Introduction to Sensation/Perception* (Englewood Cliffs, N.J.: Prentice-Hall, 1977).

Uttal, William R. *The Psychobiology of Sensory Coding* (New York: Harper & Row, 1973).

Uttal, William R. *The Psychobiology of Mind* (Hillsdale, N.J.: Erlbaum, 1978).

Hearing and Seeing 7

Did You Know That . . .

You can locate sounds in the left-right dimension better than in the up-down dimension?

Three little bones in your middle ear act like sound amplifiers?

The two most important attributes of a sound wave are its frequency and its amplitude?

Your hearing is most sensitive to about the same range of frequencies as produced by the human voice?

Animals can often hear higher frequency sounds than can humans?

Loss of hearing can produce behavioral symptoms similar to those of paranoia?

Visual acuity is best in a part of your eye called the "fovea"?

Each of your eyes has a blind spot almost in the middle of your visual field?

The retina of the eye is sometimes considered to be an extension of the brain?

You can have better than 20/20 vision?

About 1 person in 20 is partially color-blind?

"The Eyes and Ears of the World"

"Okay, dear, which kid do you want?"

Judy Jones looked around the room. There were children of all ages, all sizes, all colors. Some were playing together, some were fighting, some were sitting quietly in corners minding their own business. Judy glanced quickly at Mrs. Dobson, the woman who had asked the question, and then gazed back at the dozens of children packed into the room.

"How about that little girl over there, in the pink dress?" Judy asked, pointing her finger at a dark-skinned, handsome girl who was playing with several other youngsters. "She looks adorable."

Mrs. Dobson turned to see which child Judy was pointing to. "Oh, Arabella. Sorry, dear, but somebody's already working with her. The pretty ones are always picked first, you know. Pick an ugly one instead, if you want my opinion. They're starved for love, and they need your help just as much as the cute ones do."

Judy was shocked at Mrs. Dobson's bluntness, but guessed the woman might be right. Judy inspected the room carefully, then spotted a little boy with red hair sitting by the window, looking at a magazine. He was by far the most unattractive child in the room. His eyes were watery, his hair uncombed, his skin covered with brown blotches and blemishes. His face was lopsided, and his head seemed too large for his body. Not only that, but he was white. Judy, a black student at a college near the Children's Home, had hoped to work with someone of her own race.

"What about him?" Judy said, pointing again.

"Oh, that's Woodrow Wilson Thomas. Ten years old. Nice little fella, but ugly as home-made sin."

"Home-made sin?" Judy asked.

"Sorry, dear. It's a saying I got from my mother," Mrs. Dobson replied. "Appropriate enough in his case. Woodrow is a bastard, you see."

Judy was shocked. "You mean, he's nasty?"

"No, dear," came the calm response. "I mean bastard in a technical sense. A love child, a natural-born child, the offspring of an unwed mother. I read his record a couple of years back. His mother was 16 when she got pregnant, and she didn't quite remember who the father was. Maybe somebody in the family, for all we know. Anyhow, the mother got rubella—that's German measles—while she was carrying poor little Woodrow, and he just didn't turn out right. They thought of putting him up for adoption when he was born. But he was so ugly, they figured nobody would take him. So they kept him for a while."

"For a while?" Judy asked, beginning to sympathize with the little boy more and more.

"Yes, 'for a while.' Woodrow not only got off to a bad start in life, he didn't grow up very well either. The record says he crawled and walked at a normal age, but his speech was very retarded. Made animal noises and grunts instead of talking words. Still does, poor little fella. Doesn't understand much when you talk to him, and he won't usually do what you tell him to do. When you try to get through to him, he just stares at you with those watery eyes, and then he looks out the window while you're trying to say something. No wonder his folks put him in the Home here so the state could take care of him. Retarded, that's what Woodrow Wilson Thomas is."

Judy turned the matter over in her mind. "Do you think there's anything I can do for him? I mean, it's part of an assignment for my psych class. We're supposed to show that we can help a retarded or emotionally disturbed child. Can I help Woodrow?"

Mrs. Dobson sighed. "I don't see why not. There must be something you can do. We're so overcrowded here, and we've got such a small staff, I reckon nobody's worked with that child for two or three years. He's no trouble, you see. Doesn't have temper tantrums or act up. Never plays with the other kids, or gets into difficulties. He just sits by the window and looks at his books and magazines all day long."

"Well, if he can read magazines at his age, he can't be all that retarded."

Mrs. Dobson laughed. "Read? Don't be foolish, dear. He just looks at the pretty pictures, and smiles. One day, a year or so ago, I saw him puzzling over a picture like he was trying to figure out what it was. So I asked him what he saw. He just ignored me. Maybe you can get through to him, but I don't promise. But you should learn a lot, and he won't give you any trouble."

Judy accepted the challenge. She went over to the window and tried to talk to Woodrow, but he didn't seem to want to listen. Finally, in desperation, she tugged on his shirt and pulled him over to a nearby table. Woodrow seemed happy to come along with her.

"Now, Woodrow, we're going to draw some pictures. You like pictures, don't you?"

The boy's watery blue eyes drifted toward the window.

Judy pulled on his shirt again until he looked back at her, then she picked up a crayon. She drew a crude picture of a cow while Woodrow watched, seemingly interested. She gave him the crayon and motioned to him that she wanted him to draw. Woodrow took the crayon carefully in his right hand, then looked up at Judy, a puzzled stare on his face.

"Draw a cow, please, Woodrow," Judy said, making scribbling motions with her hand and pointing to the drawing she had just made.

Woodrow smiled serenely as he touched the crayon to the paper. Within three minutes, he handed back to her a crude but recognizable picture of a cow. Judy was so pleased that she wrote the letters C-O-W beneath the drawing. Woodrow took the scratch paper back and copied his own version of the letters underneath those Judy had written.

Judy was thrilled by his response. She got out some of the textbooks she had brought along and hunted through them until she found other pictures for Woodrow to draw. He made a horse, and an auto, and a house. When Judy wrote their names on the scratch paper, Woodrow copied the letters as carefully as he could.

When her time with Woodrow was up, and she had to catch the bus back to the college, Judy kissed Woodrow on the forehead.

"I don't care if you are retarded, young man. You're going to learn to read. I just know you are!"

Then she gathered up her textbooks and rushed off.

In her excitement at wanting to tell the other students how well things had gone, Judy failed to notice that she had left her algebra textbook behind. Woodrow picked it up and began to look through it. Although it didn't have any real pictures in it, he found the book utterly fascinating.

The next week, when Judy came back to the State Home for the Retarded to be with Woodrow again, he solemnly presented her with a sheet of scratch paper. On one side were childish drawings of a cow, a tree, a car, and a house, each correctly labeled several times over. On the other side, in very poor but legible script, were written out the first two review problems at the end of the introductory chapter of the algebra textbook.

"My God," said Judy when she saw them, "You've done the algebra correctly!"

(Continued on page 180.)

The "Social" Senses

In the last chapter, we discussed "touch," taste, and smell. And we pointed out that these sensory **modalities** are important for several reasons—they help you locate your body in space, they protect you from harm, and they assist you in finding the "energy inputs" you need in order to survive. But neither man nor woman survives by bread alone, for you need other people as much as you need food and water. Thus you cannot view yourself merely as a "unique individual"—you are also a "unit" in various social systems that enhance the quality of your life.

As we mentioned in Chapter 5, however, the sub-systems of any system must be in *communication with one another*, or the system will soon collapse. Perhaps we could use our skins and our chemical senses to "talk" with each other, as some animals do. But, for many reasons, humans communicate primarily through the written and spoken word, through music, and through pictures and visual symbols. Vision and hearing, then, are the two main "social senses," because these sensory modalities allow us to pass along information from one person to another.

Hearing and vision are much more than mere "channels of social expression"—of course—they are also rich sensory experiences in their own right. But as we look at these two modalities, we should keep in mind that our social systems would disintegrate if we could not see and hear each other. Thus the survival of society *as we presently know it* depends almost entirely on written and spoken communication. So, if you want to learn about people and how they get along with each other, you first must discover something about the *sensory channels* that carry human communications.

Hearing

From a physiological point of view, what do your eyes and ears have that your skin, nose, and tongue lack? One answer is—*separation*.

Let's first compare hearing with olfaction. If you block one of your ears with cotton, your ability to localize the *position* of sounds diminishes

"Sound coming from two speakers far apart *horizontally* sounds three-dimensional. **(top left)** Sound coming from speakers close together sounds one-dimensional, **(top right)** as does sound coming from speakers that are spread apart *vertically* **(bottom left)** because the ear cannot locate up-down differences as well as it can locate left-right differences."

considerably. But if just one of your nostrils is stopped up when you have a cold, you could locate a rotten egg just about as rapidly as if both your nasal chambers were operating unimpaired.

One important difference between hearing and smell, then, is this: Your ears are some 15 centimeters apart; your nasal chambers are separated by less than a single centimeter.

If you would like to demonstrate to yourself the importance of the "space between your ears," you might try a musical experiment. Find a **stereo** with two *movable* speakers. Put the speakers as

far apart in the room as you can. Now put on your favorite stereo record and sit between the two speakers with your eyes closed. You will hear music coming at you from all directions, but some sounds will seem to be on your left, while others seem to be on your right.

Next, put the two speakers right next to each other and repeat the experiment. Now, the music is compressed, pushed together, cut down in size to a *point source of sound*. In short, the stereo music will now sound monaural or "mono."

Your ears are like the two speakers spread far apart. Your nose and tongue are like the two speakers put close together.

Localizing Sounds

In a sense, your ears are similar to the microphones used to record music. To get a stereo effect, the record company must use at least two mikes that are some distance apart. When a band performs, each mike "hears" a slightly different version of the music.

Suppose the lead guitarist in the band is on the left. The mike on the left would then "hear" the guitarist much more loudly than would the mike on the right. If the drummer is on the right, then the right microphone would pick up the sounds of the drum more loudly than would the mike on the left.

Record companies typically make a *completely separate* recording of what the left mike "hears" and what the right mike "hears." These two different records make up the two channels of stereophonic music that are pressed on stereo discs or dubbed on tapes.

By keeping the two channels separate during both recording and playback, you can maintain left-right relationships. That is, when you hear the record, the sounds made by the lead guitarist come primarily from the left speaker. The drummer's beat, however, will come to you mostly from the right speaker.

Your ears are just far enough apart so that you can readily detect left-right differences in sound sources. Sound waves travel at about 1,200 kilometers an hour (750 miles/hour). If a cricket

2 meters to the left of your head chirps loudly, the noise will reach your left ear a fraction of a second before it reaches your right ear. And since the insect is closer to your left ear than to your right, the noise will be louder when it reaches your left ear than when it finally gets around your head and reaches your right ear.

Your brain *interprets* the difference in the auditory inputs from your left and right ears to *mean* that the cricket is to your left. But, as we will soon see, your brain can be fooled in such matters if you know how to go about it.

The farther apart your ears are, the more precisely you can detect the location of a sound—because there is a greater difference in what your two ears would hear. When a recording company sets its microphones 3 meters (10 feet) apart, they are effectively increasing the *apparent* distance between your ears to 3 meters—particularly if you listen to the music with stereo headphones.

Now go back to your stereo set and put one speaker on the floor and the other as high up in the air as you can directly above the first (see Fig. 7.1). Sit with your head upright between the two speakers. When you play music now, it will seem strangely "mono," for each of your ears is the *same distance from both speakers*. In fact, you may find that you tilt your head to one side without realizing it, as your brain attempts to turn monaural music into a stereo message that carries much more interest and information.

Your ears can detect the location of sounds spread out in the *left-right* dimension rather well. But your ears do very poorly in locating sounds in the *up-down* dimension.

Question: Why might it help to "cock your head to one side" when trying to locate the source of a sound over your head?

The Auditory Stimulus

Hearing is a *vibratory sense*. That is, the **auditory** receptors in your ears are sensitive to *vibrations* of the molecules in the air around you. These vibrations usually come in waves, which we call "sound waves." Thus the stimulus for hearing (or

"K, C, ⊒..."

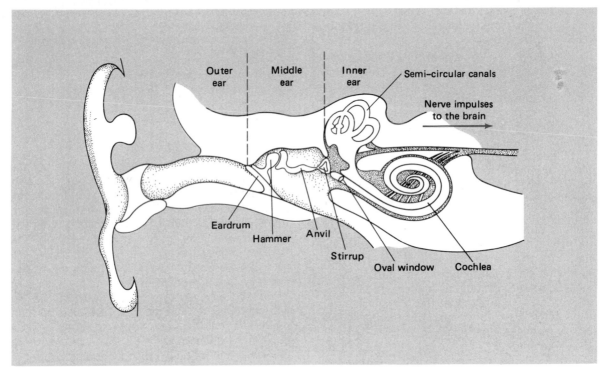

Fig. 7.1. Structure of the human ear.

"audition") is usually a vibratory wave of some kind. (Words such as "audition," "audio," and "auditorium" all come from the Latin word *audire*, meaning "to hear.")

Imagine yourself seated a couple of feet above a very quiet pool in a forest. You take a stone and toss it in the center of the pond, and what happens? Wave after wave of ripples circle out from the center until they strike the edges of the pool. If you looked closely, you would see that when one of the waves reached the shore, it "bounced back" in a kind of watery echo.

The sound waves that stimulate the *auditory receptors* in your ear are not very different from the ripples that you create by dropping the rock in the pond. Whenever any fairly rigid object is struck forcibly, it tends to *vibrate*. As this object vibrates back and forth, it "makes ripples" in the molecules of air around it. These "ripples" are really *sound waves*. That is, they are waves of energy that pass through the air just as the ripples pass across the surface of the water when you throw a stone in the pond. When these *sound waves* reach your ear, they set your eardrum to moving back and forth in rhythm with the vibrating object. Other parts of your ear then translate the vibrations of the eardrum into *patterns of neural energy* that are sent to your brain so that you can "hear."

Parts of the Ear

Your ear has three main divisions: (1) the outer ear; (2) the middle ear; and (3) the inner ear.

1. The **outer ear** is that fleshy flap of skin and other tissue sticking out from either side of your head. Your outer ear tends to "catch" sound waves and direct them into a narrow tunnel called the **auditory canal**. At the inner end of this auditory canal is your *eardrum*, a thin membrane stretched tautly across the auditory canal like the skin on a drum. The eardrum separates your outer ear from your middle ear.

2. The **middle ear** is a hollow cavity in your skull which contains three little bones called the **hammer**, the **anvil**, and the **stirrup** (see Color Plate 13). If you were to inspect these three little bones under a microscope, they would look much like the real-world objects they are named after. One end of the hammer is connected to the eardrum, so that when your eardrum moves, it pulls the hammer back and forth rhythmically.

The hammer transmits this "wave" of sound energy to the anvil, making the anvil move back and forth. The anvil pulls the stirrup back and forth in similar fashion.

The stirrup is connected to another membrane stretched across an opening called the **oval**

window. As the stirrup moves, it forces the membrane on your oval window to wiggle back and forth in rhythm too.

The three little bones and the two membranes act as the *amplifiers* in your own biological stereo system. By the time the sound stimulus has reached your oval window, it is many times louder or stronger than it was when it first struck your eardrum.

Your middle ear is like a bubble of air trapped inside your skull bone. When you go up in an airplane, the air pressure around you decreases but the pressure inside your middle ear remains the same. This pressure difference would rupture your eardrum were it not for the **eustachian tube**, which connects your middle ear to your throat. When you swallow, the tube opens momentarily, allowing air to escape from your middle ear. Each time your ears "pop" on a plane ride, your eustachian tube has opened briefly to reduce the pressure difference between air in your middle ear and the air outside.

3. The oval window separates the middle ear from the **inner ear**. Your inner ear is a fluid-filled cavity that runs through your skull bone like a tunnel coiling through a mountain. This inner ear of yours has two main parts: (1) the **cochlea**; and (2) the motion detectors we discussed in Chapter 6 (the saccule, the utricle, and the semi-circular canals).

The cochlea gets its name from the Latin word for "snail shell," which is just what your cochlea looks like. Your auditory receptors are hair cells which are part of the **organ of Corti** inside your cochlea. Input messages from the hair cells pass along the auditory nerve to the lower centers of the brain, which relay them up to the temporal lobe of your cortex. Generally speaking, you are not *consciously aware* of hearing anything until the auditory message reaches your cortex.

Frequency and Amplitude

Sound waves have two important *physical* aspects: Their **frequency** and their **amplitude**.

The frequency of a musical tone is related to how *high or low* the tone sounds to your ear. Put more precisely, the psychological *pitch* of a tone is primarily determined by the physical *frequency* of the sound wave.

The amplitude of a musical tone is related to how *loud or soft* the tone sounds to you. Put more precisely, the subjective *loudness* of a tone is primarily determined by the objective *amplitude* of the sound.

Outer ear. The fleshy outer part of the ear. Also called the auricle (AW-rick-cull), the pinna (PIN-nah), or the auditory meatus (me-ATE-us). The outer ear catches sound waves and reflects them into the auditory canal.

Auditory canal (AW-dit-tor-ee). The hollow tube running from the outer to the middle ear.

Middle ear. Contains the hammer, anvil, and stirrup. Lies between the eardrum and the oval window.

Hammer, anvil, and **stirrup** (STIR-up). Three small, connected bones in your middle ear that make sounds louder.

Oval window. The thin membrane lying between your middle and inner ears. The stirrup is connected to one side of the oval window, the basilar membrane (BASS-sih-lar) which supports the organ of Corti is connected to the other.

Eustachian tube (you-STAY-shun). A narrow canal connecting the middle ear to the throat. Opens briefly when you swallow to allow the air pressure in the middle ear to equalize with the pressure of outside air.

Inner ear. A fluid-filled "worm hole" in your skull that contains both the motion detectors (the saccule, utricle, and semi-circular canals) and your receptor neurons for hearing.

Cochlea (COCK-lee-uh). The snail-shaped portion of your inner ear that contains the basilar membrane.

Organ of Corti (KOR-tie). A highly complex structure lying on the basilar membrane that contains the sensory receptor cells for hearing.

Frequency. In auditory terms, the number of times a sound source vibrates each second. The frequency of a musical tone is measured in Hertz.

Amplitude (AM-plee-tood). From the Latin word meaning "muchness." We get our word "ample" from the same Latin source. Amplitude is the amount of sound present, or the strength of a musical tone. Literally, the "height" of a sound wave.

"Pitch" and "loudness" are terms that describe *psychological* attributes of the subjective experience of hearing. "Frequency" and "amplitude" are terms that describe the *physical* characteristics of the auditory stimulus.

Pitch and Frequency

If you drop a stone in a deep pond, you set up just one big wave that moves out from the point at which the stone hits the water. But if you drop several pebbles in, one after the other, you set up a *series of waves*. If you dropped in 10 pebbles each second, you would set up 10 waves a second (under perfect conditions). The *frequency* of the waves would then be 10 per second.

When you pluck a string on a guitar, you are doing much the same thing as dropping a rock in a pond. For the string creates sound waves that have *exactly the same frequency* as the number of vibrations that the string makes per second. Your ear detects these sound waves, and your brain turns them into musical tones. The *faster* a particular string vibrates, the *more* "waves per second" it creates—and the *higher* the pitch of the tone will seem to be when you hear it.

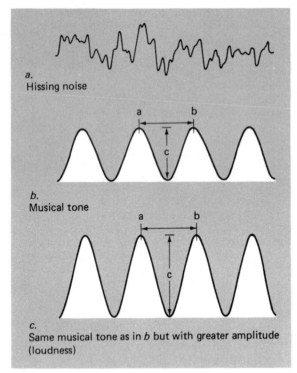

a.
Hissing noise

b.
Musical tone

c.
Same musical tone as in b but with greater amplitude (loudness)

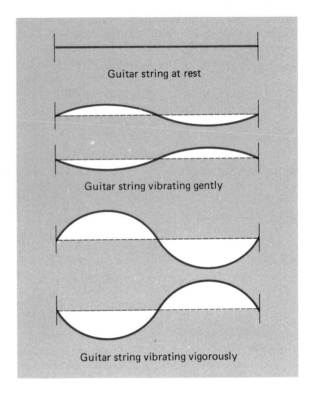

Guitar string at rest

Guitar string vibrating gently

Guitar string vibrating vigorously

Fig. 7.2A. A sound wave "cycle" or "Hertz" is measured from peak to peak. **(top left)**

Fig. 7.2B. A vibrating guitar string. **(top right)**

If you plucked the "A" string on a guitar, it would vibrate 440 times per second. This number is called the *frequency* of the musical tone "A." In technical terms, we would say that this tone has a frequency of 440 "cycles per second," or 440 **Hertz** (440 Hz). In general, the thinner and shorter a string is, the higher the frequency at which it vibrates—and the higher the pitch of the tone that it makes.

Amplitude and Loudness

The loudness of a tone is determined primarily by the tone's *amplitude*, not by its frequency. If you happen to pluck the "A" string of the guitar *very gently*, it vibrates 440 times per second. But if you plucked the string *as hard as you could*, it would still vibrate at about 440 Hz. If it didn't, you wouldn't hear the note as being an "A."

But surely something different happens, for the more energetically you pluck a string, the louder the note sounds. The answer is that the string moves *further up and down* during each vibration—but it still vibrates at about 440 times per second (see Fig. 7.2). In similar fashion, if you gently drop 10 pebbles per second into a pond, you create 10 very small waves. But if you throw 10 pebbles per second into a pond as hard as you can, you create 10 very large waves. In either case, however, there are still just *10 waves per second*.

In technical terms, the "bigger the wave," the greater its *amplitude*. And the greater the amplitude that a sound wave has, the louder it will sound to your ear.

The Range of Hearing

What kinds of musical tones can your ear hear?

Your range of hearing is, roughly speaking, from *20 Hz to about 20,000 Hz*. But you are not equally sensitive to all frequencies within this range. Your hearing is best from about 400 to 4,000 Hz. Human conversation ranges between 200 and 800 Hz. The lowest tone a bass singer can produce is about 100 Hz, while the highest tone most sopranos can produce is about 1,000 Hz. Thus your ear is "tuned" to listen to other people speak (and sing).

There seems to be a general rule that holds *across animal species*: The smaller the cochlea, the higher the animal's range of hearing is likely to be. The dog can hear notes at least as high as 25,000 Hz, while the bat is sensitive to tones as high as 100,000 Hz. Elephants, on the other hand, probably have a hearing range that cuts off at about 7,000 Hz.

Question: *If you wanted to design a whistle that could be used for calling dogs but that couldn't be heard by human beings, what frequency range would you want to investigate?*

Deafness

What difference would it make to your life if you became deaf?

Hearing is the major channel for *informal* social communication. Our customs, social graces, and moral beliefs are still passed down from one generation to another primarily by word of mouth rather than in writing. And most of us (textbook writers included!) prefer the informal transmission of knowledge that comes from talking to the formality of the written word.

Bone Deafness and Nerve Deafness

When people grow older, the three small bones in the middle ear often become brittle and thus do not work properly. Since the hammer, anvil, and stirrup serve to *amplify* the sound waves as they come into the ear, you usually become deaf when these bones malfunction. This type of **bone deafness** can usually be corrected if you are fitted for a hearing aid, a device that acts like a miniature hi-fi set and "turns up the volume" electronically

Hertz (hurts). The frequency of any wave, such as a sound wave. Used to be called "cycles per second," or cps. Named for the German scientist Heinrich Hertz who made the first definitive studies of energy waves.

Bone deafness. A form of hearing loss caused by damage to the three bones of the middle ear. Often occurs naturally in old age. Usually can be helped either by use of a hearing aid or, occasionally, by surgery.

Nerve deafness. A form of hearing loss caused by damage to the hearing receptors or to the auditory nerve. Nerve deafness can seldom be helped either by surgery or by use of a hearing aid.

Spectrum (SPECK-trum). From the Latin word meaning "to look," from which we also get the words "specter" (ghost) and "spectacle." The word "spectrum" means a set or array of related objects or events, usually a set of sights or sounds.

Paranoia (pair-ah-NOI-ya). A severe type of mental disorder characterized by delusions of grandeur and suspicions that people are whispering about you or trying to control your behavior.

(see Fig. 7.3). Some severe types of bone deafness can be corrected by surgery.

Many types of infection can attack the hair cells on the organ of Corti. If your receptor cells were permanently damaged for any reason, you would suffer from **nerve deafness**. If only a small section of your basilar membrane were affected, you would lose the ability to hear just high notes, or low notes, or even notes in the middle of the auditory **spectrum**. If the damage to your nerve cells was widespread, however, you might become totally deaf for *all frequencies*. Nerve deafness can seldom be corrected either by surgery or by a hearing aid.

There are two major causes for nerve deafness—disease, and exposure to extremely loud sounds. The jet engines on modern airplanes create ear-splitting sounds, which is why people who work around jets wear protective earphones. The sound levels in many factories can cause damage too if the workers are exposed to the noise for too long a time.

Question: *The sound levels produced in rock concerts often equal that of jet engines. What conclusions can you draw from this fact concerning the risk factor that rock musicians face in terms of possible hearing loss?*

Deafness and Paranoia

According to Philip Zimbardo, older individuals who slowly lose their hearing may be reluctant to admit their growing deafness. For to do so, Zimbardo says, would be to admit that they are "growing old." Thus many older people with hearing losses tend to blame their hearing problems on the behavior of others rather than on their own faulty ears. This "blaming behavior" often takes the form of a mild **paranoia**, in which older peo-

165

The Auditory Stimulus

Fig. 7.3. Some kinds of deafness can be helped with hearing aids. **(top left)**

Many older people maintain good hearing. Those who don't often become paranoid and suspicious. **(top right)**

ple grow highly suspicious that others are whispering about them behind their back.

In the June 26, 1981 issue of *Science*, Zimbardo and two of his associates report the results of a study they performed on "experimental deafness" at Stanford. The psychologists began by hypnotizing some of their subjects and telling them that they would have severe difficulties hearing other people talk. This sort of temporary hearing loss under hypnosis is completely reversible (see Chapter 17). Zimbardo and his colleagues then asked the temporarily hard-of-hearing subjects to work together in discussion groups with normal subjects. The tasks the discussion groups had to accomplish were, for the most part, the sort of "problem-solving exercises" that psychologists often ask subjects to engage in. The experimental subjects were given personality tests both before and after the problem-solving sessions.

Zimbardo and his colleagues report that most of the temporarily deaf students showed marked signs of mild paranoia. That is, the subjects became convinced that the other members of their discussion groups were "talking ill" of them, or were trying to do them harm. They also became more hostile, confused, agitated, irritable, and less creative. Zimbardo believes that the tendency to blame other people for one's own faults may explain many personality disorders, including some types of paranoia.

Question: If you don't "speak up" around a person with hearing problems, how might your own behaviors increase the deaf person's feelings of paranoia?

Language Learning, Deafness, and Feedback

If you are telling someone a story or teaching someone a lesson, you typically will watch your listener's face. And the person who is listening will usually respond with a smile or a nod of the head to indicate understanding or agreement with what you have said. This *feedback* from your listener is of critical importance in shaping your own verbal behavior. For communication is best when it is a two-way street. You give out a message. It is received by a listener who, in turn, sends you back a message evaluating or responding to what you have said.

Learning to sing, dance, play the guitar, or drive a car—all these complex motor tasks require *feedback*. Children who are born deaf—or partially deaf—have trouble learning to *talk* because they cannot *hear* what noises their voices are making. Without the auditory feedback from their vocal cords, children can never learn to shape their spoken words properly, because they simply do not know *what their own voice sounds like*.

Until scientists discovered how necessary some kind of feedback is in learning to talk, we often thought that partially deaf children were dumb or stupid. Occasionally we mistakenly confined these children to homes for the mentally retarded—although many of them had very high intelligences. Fortunately, now that hearing tests for young children are much more common than they used to be, we are less likely to confuse partial deafness with mental retardation.

Question: Suppose that a very bright but partially deaf child is mistakenly put in a home for the mentally retarded. Would anyone be likely to try to train the child to read? Under some circumstances, could the child perhaps learn to read on his or her own?

Vision

Psychologically speaking, hearing is a far more complex sense than is "touch," taste, or smell. But when it comes to "richness" of sensory experience, vision is perhaps more complicated than all the other sensory modalities put together. More of your brain tissue is devoted to processing visual inputs than to any other sense. Thus, when it comes to getting information about yourself and the world around you, the "eyes surely have it."

Because vision dominates so much of our lives, psychologists have studied it in greater detail than they have the other senses. As a result, we know more about how and why you see than we do about how you experience the rest of your sensory world.

Vision has often been called "the sense of wonder." To appreciate how your ability to see influences your thoughts and behaviors, however, you need to understand at least three things:

1. What the visual stimulus (light) is like.
2. How your eye converts light into a sensory input to send to your brain.
3. How your brain interprets this incoming sensory information.

The Visual Stimulus

The stimulus for vision is *light*, which is a very small part of the **electro-magnetic spectrum**. The electro-magnetic spectrum also includes X-rays and radio waves.

The smallest, most elementary unit of light is called the **photon**, which gets its name from the Greek word meaning "light." The flame from one match produces millions of photons. A flashlight produces a great many more photons than does a match. Thus, in general, the *stronger* the light source, the *more* photons it produces in a given unit of time (such as a second).

When you turn on a flashlight, photons stream out from the bulb at an incredible speed or **velocity**. To give you a better "feel" for this speed, consider the fact that the velocity of sound waves is about 1,200 kilometers per *hour* (750 mph). The speed of light, on the other hand, is about 300,000 kilometers per *second* (186,000 mph).

If you could travel as fast as a photon, you could zoom all the way around the world *seven times* in just a second, and you could go to the moon and back in less than three seconds.

Wave-Lengths of Visual Inputs

The bulb of a flashlight produces photons in *waves*—much as the string on a guitar produces

Electro-magnetic spectrum. The entire range of frequencies or wave-lengths of electro-magnetic radiation ranging from gamma rays to the longest radio waves. Includes the visible spectrum.

Photon (FO-tohn). A tiny packet of energy which is the smallest unit of light. According to William Uttal, under ideal circumstances, your eye is so incredibly sensitive that it can detect a single photon.

Velocity (vee-LOSS-sit-tee). The speed at which an object or wave moves. From the Latin word meaning "to be quick." The velocity of natural objects such as photons tends to be **constant** under normal conditions.

Visible spectrum (SPECK-trum). When you look at a rainbow in the sky, you see the array (spectrum) of visible colors that make up sunlight. For most purposes, "rainbow" and "visible spectrum" can be considered the same things.

sound waves when the string vibrates, or the wind produces waves on the surface of the ocean. If you want to understand how scientists study light waves, learning something about ocean waves first might be of help.

If you wanted to, you could take a boat out on the sea and actually measure the distance *between* one ocean wave and another. And if you did so, you would find that the distance between the crests of the waves was remarkably consistent. On a calm, peaceful day, as the waves moved slowly and majestically, the distance *between* waves would be rather large. But on windy, choppy days, this wave-length would be rather small. Thus, if you knew the strength of the wind, even without going out on the water, you would have some notion of what the length between the crests of the ocean waves would be.

Much the same sort of consistency holds for the wave-length of light and what color it appears to be. If you will turn to Color Plate 1, you will see a rainbow-like display called the **visible spectrum**. The blue colors have very short wave-lengths. The reds, at the other end of the spectrum, have much longer wave-lengths. The colors between red and blue have wave-lengths that fall between these two extremes. Thus if you know what *wave-length* a visual input has, you will know what *color* it ordinarily will appear to be.

However, the distance between the crests of light waves is much, much smaller than the distance between any two ocean waves. The wave-length for red is so short that it takes about 38,000 "red waves" to make an inch (2.5 centimeters). The wave-length for blue is much shorter—it takes about 70,000 "blue waves" to make an inch.

Scientists seldom measure the wave-length of light in fractions of an inch, because the figures are just too clumsy to use. Instead, scientists

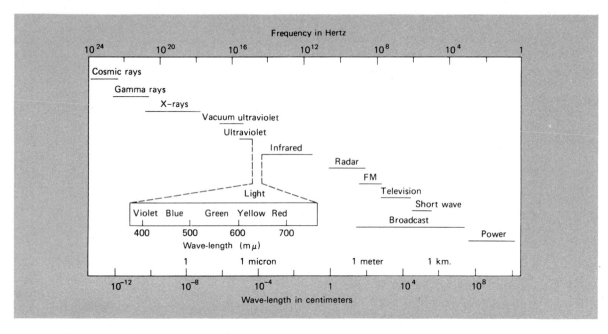

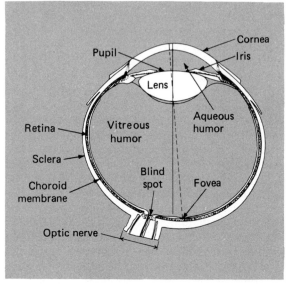

Fig. 7.4. The visible spectrum. **(top)**

Fig. 7.5. A diagram of the eye. **(left)**

measure wave-lengths in **nanometers**. The Greek word for "dwarf" is *nanos*. From this fact, you can perhaps guess that the nanometer is a "dwarf" or fraction of a meter. In fact, there are one billion nanometers in each meter (39.37 inches).

Amplitude of Visual Inputs

The physical wave-length of a light stimulus usually determines the color that it will appear to you, such as blue or red. But some blue lights are bright, while others are dim. The physical intensity of a light determines how bright it will seem, and *intensity* can be specified in terms of the height or **amplitude** of the wave.

If you measured the *length* between crests of ocean waves on a calm day, you might find that the wave-length was about 6 meters (20 feet). The *height* of each wave, however, might be no more than 1 meter (3.28 feet). During a storm, the wave-length might still be 20 feet, but the height of each ocean wave might now be 3 to 4 meters (10 to 13 feet).

In similar fashion, a dim blue light might have a wave-length of 423 nanometers. If you "turned up the intensity" of this blue light until it was so bright it almost blinded you, it would still have a *wave-length* of 423 nanometers—but the *amplitude* of each wave would be many times greater.

When you make a light brighter, you *amplify* the height of each light wave—just as when you turn up the volume on your stereo set you *amplify* the height of each sound wave the machine puts out.

The *psychological color* of a visual input, therefore, is determined primarily by its *physical wave-length*. And the *psychological brightness* of a visual stimulus is determined primarily by the *physical amplitude* of the light wave.

The Visible Spectrum

In a manner of speaking, light waves are much like X-rays and radio waves—except that X-rays have such short wave-lengths that they are invisible to your eye, and radio waves have such long wavelengths that you can't see them. As Fig. 7.4 suggests, the only waves you can *see* lie between 400 and 760 nanometers. We call this range of waves the *visible spectrum*.

Below 400 nanometers lie the **ultra-violet rays** that are used in "black lights" and in sun lamps. These rays have a very damaging effect on the complex chemicals in your eye that help you see, which is why you shouldn't look directly at "black lights"—and why you should wear dark glasses when you sit under a sun lamp.

Beyond the red end of the visible spectrum (760 nanometers) lie the *heat rays*. If you stare at a heat lamp for too long, you may not only warm up your face, but you may "cook" parts of your eyes as well.

Why does a psychologist interested in human behavior bother with such technical measures as wave-length and amplitude? For two reasons, really.

First, because visual inputs *stimulate* people to act and respond, and the more precisely we can specify the *stimulus* that evokes a certain reaction, the better we can understand the *behavior* itself.

Second, because we are often interested in individual differences. If we show *exactly the same* visual stimulus to two people, and they report *different* psychological experiences, we know that these reports are due to differences in the people and not to some variability in the physical stimulus itself. We will have more to say about this point when we discuss color-blindness later in this chapter.

The Eye

What physiological processes occur when you see? These processes are so complex that we still don't understand them completely.

In some ways your eye is like a color TV camera (see Fig. 7.5). Both are essentially "containers" that have a small hole at one end which admits light. The light then passes through a lens that focuses an image on a **photo-sensitive surface**. In both your eye and in the color TV camera, the "hole" can be opened to let in more light, or closed to keep light out. And in both, the lens can be adjusted to bring near or far objects into focus.

In the case of the color television camera, the light coming through the lens falls on an electronic tube that contains several complex chemicals. These chemicals are photo-sensitive—that is, they react chemically when struck by photons. The camera then produces several different im-

Nanometers (NAN-oh-meters). A nanometer is one-billionth of a meter, or about 1/40,000,000,000th of an inch.

Amplitude (AM-plee-tood). The height of a light wave or sound wave. Generally speaking, the greater the amplitude of a sound wave, the louder the sound; the greater the amplitude of a light wave, the brighter the light source will appear to be.

Ultra-violet rays. Light waves that are "beyond the violet" end of the visible spectrum. These are the rays that produce "tanning" when you sun-bathe.

Photo-sensitive surface. Light waves can set off rather dramatic reactions in some chemicals. These light-sensitive chemicals are said to be "photo-sensitive." The film in a camera reacts to light— hence, film is photo-sensitive. The inner surface of your eye contains pigments (colored chemicals) that are also photo-sensitive.

Cornea (CORN-ee-ah). From the Latin word meaning "horn-like." We get our words "horn" and "corn" (the kind of blister you get on your foot) from this same Latin source. The cornea is the tough, transparent tissue in front of the aqueous humor.

Aqueous humor (A-kwi-us). The watery substance between the iris and the cornea that keeps the front of your eyeball inflated to its proper size and provides nutrients to the cornea.

Pupil (PEW-pill). The opening in the iris through which light passes into the eye.

Iris (EYE-riss). The colored or pigmented area of the eye. When you say that someone has brown eyes, you really mean the person has brown irises. The Greek word for "rainbow" is *iris*.

Vitreous humor (VITT-tree-us). From the Latin word meaning "glass." The vitreous humor is a clear, glass-like substance in the center of the eyeball that keeps your eye in its proper rounded shape. Light must pass through the vitreous humor before it strikes your retina.

ages which, when properly combined on a TV set, reproduce the scene in vivid color.

In the case of your eye, light first passes through the **cornea** and the **aqueous humor**. The cornea helps focus light rays as they enter your eye. The aqueous humor is a watery substance that helps nourish your cornea and keeps your eyeball filled out in its proper shape.

Once through the aqueous humor, light enters your inner eye through an opening called the **pupil**. The **iris** is the colored part of your eye which, by expanding and contracting around the pupil, controls the amount of light admitted inside your eye.

Just beyond the pupil is the lens. The purpose of the lens in your eye—like the lens in a camera—is to allow you to *focus clearly* whether you are looking at something close or far away. As you change your point of focus from a near object to something several feet away, muscles inside your eye pull on the lens to change its shape and thus refocus the light.

The lens *focuses* the image of what you are looking at and *projects* this image through the **vitreous humor** onto the inner surface of your eyeball—just as the lens in a camera focuses the

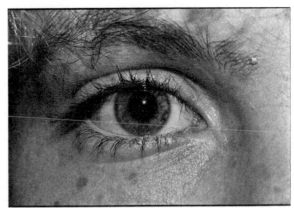

In a sense your eye works much like a T.V. camera does, except that your eye typically sees more of a given scene.

image or picture and projects it on the film in the back of the camera.

The vitreous humor is a transparent, jello-like substance that, like the aqueous humor, acts to keep your eyeball "inflated" in its proper, rounded shape.

The inner surface of your eyeball is called the **retina**, from the Latin word meaning "net" or "network." Your retina is a network of millions of cells that—like the picture tube in the TV camera—contain several photo-sensitive chemicals.

The Retina

In a sense, your eyeball is a hollow sphere whose shell has three layers.

The outer layer—which contains the cornea—is called the **sclera**. The sclera is really the "skin" of your eyeball. Like most other skin tissue, the sclera contains *free nerve endings* that are sensitive to pressure, temperature—and pain.

The middle layer of the "shell" of your eye is a dark lining that is called the **choroid membrane**, or coat. The choroid coat contains blood vessels and dark pigment cells. The blood vessels supply the visual receptors with food and oxygen. The dark pigment cells absorb stray rays of light that might otherwise interfere with your vision.

The third layer is the *retina*, which is really the inner surface of your hollow eyeball.

The Fovea

Your retina contains the *receptor cells* that translate the physical energy of a light wave into the patterns of neural energy that your brain interprets as "seeing." There are two special parts of your retina that you should know about. The first is called the **fovea**. The second is your **blind spot**.

Fovea is the Latin word for "small pit." The fovea in your eye is a tiny pit in the center of your retina where your vision is at its sharpest.

The *blind spot* is a small area of your retina near the fovea which is, for all practical purposes, totally "sightless." We will discuss the blind spot in greater detail later in this chapter. The reason that this part of your eye is sightless, however, is that it has *no receptor neurons* in it. (See Color Plate 14.)

While your eye is like a TV camera in some ways, there are many differences between the two. The camera is large, bulky, clumsy to operate, and requires an external power source of some kind. Your eye is small and, in a sense, self-powered. The photo-sensitive plate or picture tube in a camera is flat, while the retina in your eye is *curved* to cover almost the entire inner surface of the eyeball.

But perhaps the major difference between your eye and a TV camera is the way that each mechanism *translates* light waves into patterns of electrical energy. The picture tube in a black-and-white TV camera contains just one kind of photo-sensitive chemical, while the tube in a color camera has several such chemicals. Your eye is something like a combination of the two, for it has both black-and-white detectors and a separate set of color detectors.

The Rods and Cones

The receptor neurons for vision are the **rods** and **cones**. Their names are fairly descriptive of their shapes. In the human eye, the rods are slim, pencil-shaped nerve cells. The cones are thicker and have a cone-shaped tip at their "business" end. (See Color Plate 12.)

Both the rods and cones contain chemicals that are very sensitive to light. When a beam of light strikes a rod, it causes the *bleaching* or breakdown of a chemical called **rhodopsin**, or visual purple (the Greek word *rhod* means "rose-colored"). In ways that we still don't entirely understand, this bleaching action causes the rod to respond electrically. This visual input message passes up through the lower centers of your brain and eventually reaches the occipital lobe (see Fig. 7.5). At this point, you become "consciously aware" that you have actually seen something.

Your rods are *color-blind*. They "see" the world in blacks and whites no matter how colorful the world actually is. Your rods respond much like a "fast but grainy" black and white film you might use in your camera responds. That is, they need less light to operate than the cones do, but they give a less detailed picture of the world than the colorful view provided by your cones.

For the most part, the rods are located in the outer reaches or **periphery** of the retina. There are about 120 million rods in each of your eyes.

Your cones contain several types of photo-sensitive chemicals which break down when struck by light waves. This chemical reaction triggers off an electrical response in your cones which passes along the optic nerve until it reaches the visual input area in your occipital lobes.

The cones are your *color receptors*. There are a few cones in the periphery of the retina, but most of the cones are bunched together in the center of your retina near the fovea. The fovea contains no rods at all, *only cones*. There are between six and seven million cones in each of your eyes.

Since your cones are located *primarily* in the center of your retina, this is the part of your eye that is *most sensitive to color*.

When you look at something straight on, the light waves coming from that object strike your fovea and stimulate the cones, giving you clear color vision. When the same object is at the outer edges (periphery) of your vision, the light waves from the object strike primarily the rods in the periphery of the retina. Since the rods are color-blind, you will see anything that appears at the edges of your visual world as lacking or very weak in color.

Structure of the Retina

If you were called upon to design the eyes for a NASA robot, the odds are that you would never think of making the robot's retina like yours.

Retina (RETT-tin-ah). The photo-sensitive inner surface of your eye. Contains the visual receptor organs.

Sclera (SKLAIR-ah). The tough outer layer of the eyeball.

Choroid membrane (KOR-oid). The dark, middle layer of the eyeball that contains blood vessels and pigment cells.

Fovea (FOE-vee-ah). The tiny "pit" or depression right at the center of your retina that contains only cones, and where your vision is at its clearest and sharpest.

Blind spot. That small part of the retina near the fovea where blood vessels and nerve pathways enter and exit from inside the eyeball. The blind spot contains no visual receptors.

Rods. The needle-shaped visual receptors that mediate black and white vision.

Cones. The visual receptors that mediate color vision. They also respond to black and white visual stimuli. Located primarily in and near the fovea.

Rhodopsin (ro-DOP-sin). From the Greek word meaning "reddish-purple." We get our words "rose" and "rhododendron" from this same Greek source. Rhodopsin is a purple-colored, photo-sensitive pigment found in the rods.

Periphery (pair-IF-er-ee). From the Greek word meaning "to move around the outside." The periphery is the outer edge of any closed surface, such as a circle.

Peripheral nervous system (pair-IF-er-al, or purr-RIF-er-al). Those neurons that lie at the outer edge of your body, such as your skin receptors.

To begin with, your retina has *ten distinct layers*, with the rods and cones making up the *back layer*. The tips of your rods and cones—which contain the photosensitive chemicals that react to light—are actually pointed *away* from the outside world. For light to strike your rods and cones, it must first pass through *all nine other layers of your retina* (see Color Plate 15).

The receptor cells in your *skin* are a part of your **peripheral nervous system**. That is, they are nerve cells which lie outside your brain and spinal cord. Since the retina evolved directly from the brain, however, it is considered by most authorities to be a part of the central nervous system.

The top layers of your retina contain a great many "large neurons" that are very similar in structure to those found in your cortex. These "large neurons" begin processing visual information right in the retina, before sending messages along to your visual cortex (in the occipital lobes at the back of your brain). Your retina is the *only receptor organ* in your body that processes inputs so extensively before sending them along to the cortex.

The top layers of your retina also contain the tiny blood vessels that serve the retina. Surprisingly enough, light must pass through these "large neurons" and the blood vessels before it can stimulate the rods and cones. Fortunately,

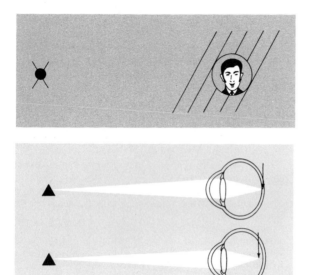

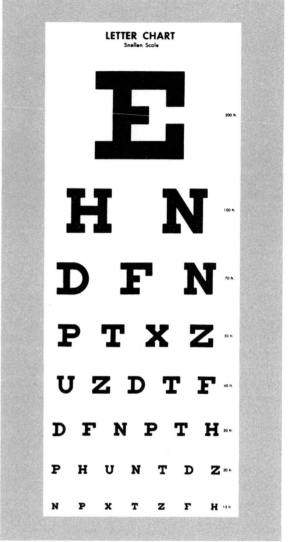

Fig. 7.6. Close your left eye and stare at the crossed dot with the book held about 6 inches away. The face should disappear. **(top left)**

Fig. 7.7. A normal, near-sighted, and far-sighted eye. Notice where the image ends at the arrow in each case. **(bottom left)**

Fig. 7.8. The Snellen chart. **(right)**

these neurons and blood vessels are pushed aside at the point of the fovea. This fact helps explain why the fovea looks like a "pit," and why vision is clearest at this point.

The Blind Spot

It is probably hard for you to imagine that each of your eyes has a spot that is, for all practical purposes, *totally blind*. This fact means that there is actually a "hole" in your visual field where you see nothing at all.

Why this hole in your visual field? Well, your eyeball is hollow like a balloon, and your retina is *inside* the eyeball. The blood vessels that feed your rods and cones must somehow get into this balloon, and out again. And the axonic end-fibers from the "large neurons" must somehow get through the walls of the eyeball if they are to reach their destinations in your brain.

All these axons meet at a point near the fovea to form the *optic nerve*, which exits from your eye at the *blind spot*. There are no receptors

at this point in your retina—only axonic fibers and blood vessels—and so the part of your visual world that falls on the blind spot is not recorded in your brain.

You are usually unaware of the blind spot because your brain "cheats." That is, it fills in the hole by making the empty spot in your visual world look like whatever surrounds it. You can prove this to yourself by following the instructions given in Fig. 7.6. If you look at the picture from just the right position, the man's face disappears. But notice too that the spot where the man's face should be is filled in by your brain with the lines that surround the man's picture.

Your brain is constantly *making assumptions* about the world around you and filling in details which are not actually there. That is to say, sometimes your brain creates imaginary inputs where real ones don't actually exist, and sometimes it blocks out real inputs it doesn't wish to deal with. Thus we all have *psychological* blind spots which can greatly affect our perception of the world. We will have much more to say about this point in later chapters.

Optical Defects

Many distortions of your visual world are caused by misinterpretations made by your brain, but quite a few distortions stem from physiological problems with the eye itself.

For example, the chances are one in four that you either wear glasses or should wear them to help you overcome correctable visual difficulties. For the most part, these problems come from slight abnormalities in the *shape* of your eyeball.

Near-Sightedness and Far-Sightedness

If your eyeball is *too long*, the lens tends to focus the visual image a little *in front* of your retina rather than clearly on it. You then see *near* objects rather clearly, but distant objects appear fuzzy and blurred to you. We call this condition **near-sightedness** (see Fig. 7.7).

If your eyeball is *too short*, the lens tends to focus the visual image *behind* the retina rather than directly on it. Close objects are therefore indistinct to you, but *far* or distant objects are usually in clear focus. We call this condition **far-sightedness**. While other physiological problems can also cause near- and far-sightedness, these optical defects are usually the result of an eyeball that is too long or too short (see Fig. 7.7).

If you watch carefully in the next movie you attend, you may notice something like the following: A woman standing close to the camera is talking with a man some distance away. When the woman is speaking, the camera focuses on her face, which you see clearly—but the image of the distant man is blurred and fuzzy. *This is the way that the near-sighted person typically sees the world* (see left photo next page).

Now, as the dialogue in the movie continues and the man begins to speak, the camera shifts focus (but not position). Suddenly the woman's face, which is close to the camera, becomes blurred—but the distant image of the man sharpens and becomes distinct. *This is the way the far-sighted person typically sees things in the world* (see right photo next page).

The lens in your eye operates much the same as does a camera lens, changing the focus from far to near as the occasion demands. As you

Near-sightedness. If your eyeball is too long, your lens may focus the visual image so that you see near objects clearly, but see distant objects as being fuzzy. Near-sightedness is usually correctable with glasses.

Far-sightedness. If your eyeball is too short, your lens may focus the visual image so that near objects seem fuzzy to you, but distant objects are clear. Usually correctable with glasses.

Old-sightedness. A type of far-sightedness associated with aging and caused by a hardening of the lens. Also called *presbyopia* (prez-bee-OH-pee-ah).

Astigmatism (as-STIG-mah-tism). A visual defect caused by imperfections in the shape of the cornea. Usually can be corrected with glasses.

Snellen chart (SNELL-en). A visual test devised by a Dutch eye doctor named Herman Snellen. The chart usually has a big "E" at the top, with lines of progressively smaller letters underneath.

grow older, however, your lenses become brittle, and you cannot focus back and forth between near and far objects as well as when you were young. This condition is called **old-sightedness**, or *presbyopia*. The solution to this problem is *bifocal glasses*. The upper part of the lens gives a clear picture of distant objects, while the lower half of the lens allows the person to see near objects clearly.

If your cornea were irregularly shaped, you might suffer from a common visual defect called **astigmatism**. Fortunately, you can usually overcome this problem by wearing the proper prescription glasses.

Visual Acuity

When you go to an eye doctor to be tested for glasses, or when you apply for a driver's license, you will be given one of several tests to determine how accurately your eyes *discriminate* small objects. Your ability to discriminate such things as the small print in a phone book is called your *visual acuity*.

One very common visual test is the **Snellen chart** (see Fig. 7.8), which presents letters of different sizes for you to read. A person with normal vision can barely read the largest letter on this chart at a distance of 200 feet (60 meters), and can just make out the next largest letters standing 100 feet away.

If you took this test yourself, you probably would be asked to stand 20 feet away from the Snellen chart. If you could read the "normal" line of letters at this distance, we would say that you can "see at 20 feet what the normal person can see at 20 feet." Hence, you would have 20/20 vision.

If you stood 20 feet away from the chart and could only read what the normal person can easily see at 100 feet, your vision would be 20/100,

A view of a scene as a nearsighted person sees it. **(top left)** The same scene as viewed by a farsighted person. **(top right)**

When your eyes are dark-adapted a bright light can be blinding. **(bottom left)**

which is fairly poor. But if you could make out the very small letters on the bottom line when you were standing 20 feet away, you would be able to read letters that normal people can discriminate only when they are *10* feet away from the chart. In this case, you would have 20/10 or superior visual acuity.

Visual Sensitivity

In order to discriminate objects in your visual world, you typically depend on your cone vision. Under normal circumstances—in daylight, for instance—your *visual acuity* depends primarily on your cones.

The reflexes of your eye are so arranged that the visual image of anything you want to inspect closely will fall on your fovea, where there are millions of tiny cones packed together in an area about the size of the head of a pin. During daylight hours, when there is plenty of illumination, your color vision dominates and you can easily make out the details of objects in your visual world.

But at night or in any dim illumination—when you are often more interested in *detecting* faint sources of light than in *discriminating* fine details—your rods come into play. Your rods are much more sensitive to light than are your cones—which is to say that the rods are better light detectors than the cones are. Your cones, however, are better than your rods at "seeing things in fine detail."

Visual Adaptation

When light strikes one of your rods or cones, the light causes the photo-sensitive chemicals in your receptors to *bleach*. Bleaching is a chemical reaction in which molecules *break apart* because they have been struck by a beam of light. It is this "breaking up" of the photo-sensitive molecules which causes your rods and cones to become electrically excited and to send input messages to your brain.

Your eye replaces the "broken down" photo-sensitive molecules fairly rapidly. If it didn't, you'd only "see" until all the light-sensitive chemicals in your eye were exhausted.

As you might guess, your eye can replace these "visual chemicals" more rapidly in the dark than in bright illumination. And the larger your supply of these photo-sensitive molecules, the more sensitive your vision becomes. Thus after you have "adapted" to the darkness for a while, your ability to detect faint light sources is much better than when you've been sitting in bright sunlight.

Dark adaptation is caused by at least two things. First, you must have a surplus of rhodopsin (visual purple) in your rods and a surplus of various other photo-sensitive chemicals in your cones. And second, according to psychologist William Uttal, darkness causes certain neural changes in the rods and cones themselves that help you to see better under conditions of dim illumination. These neural changes in the rods and cones appear to be similar to those that occur in your skin receptors when you sit in a tub of warm water for a period of time.

As an example of dark adaptation, consider what happens when you walk into a darkened theater. For the first few minutes, you can barely make out the shapes of the people sitting around you. But after your eyes have "adapted" to the dim illumination—and hence have built up a large store of photo-sensitive chemicals—you may notice that you can see quite well.

Your cones adapt more quickly in darkness than do your rods. Your cones become almost as sensitive as they are ever going to get in a matter of 10 minutes or so. Your rods continue to adapt for 30 minutes or more. Because they build up a larger "surplus" of photo-sensitive chemicals, your rods are a thousand times better at *detecting* weak visual inputs when fully dark-adapted than are your cones.

Question: *How long do you think an airplane pilot should be required to adapt to the dark before she or he is allowed to fly at night?*

Night-Blindness

Some people do not see at all well at night. Usually this defect is caused by some disability of the rods. Night-blindness may have many causes, but a lack of Vitamin A is perhaps the most common one. Vitamin A is necessary for the build-up of rhodopsin (visual purple) in the rods.

Even if your vision is perfectly normal, however, you may have difficulties seeing at night unless you've received special training. For under very dim illumination, your cones don't function very well. And when you try to stare at something in the dark, your visual reflexes work against you.

In daylight, your eyes automatically focus the image of an object on your fovea—where your visual acuity is best in good illumination. But your fovea contains only cones, hence it is "blind" at night. So when you stare directly at an object in dim light, the object may "disappear" because you're trying to see it with your cones. And the harder you try to focus the image of the object on your fovea, the less you will be able to see it!

If you want to see something at night, don't try to look directly at it. Instead, remember that your rods are most numerous in the *periphery* of

your retina. So you should try to stare at the object "out of the corner of your eye," so that the object's visual image will fall on the periphery of your retina. That way, you can look at the object with your rods, not your cones. And that way, you can actually see better in dim illumination.

Question: *Why do most objects look less colorful at twilight than at bright noon? (Hint: Remember the distribution of cones in the retina.)*

Color Vision

One of the main problems in studying your senses is this: Scientists tend to use two quite different languages in describing sensory processes. Theoretically speaking, we should use the language of physics to describe the physical properties of sensory inputs, but we should employ psychological terms to describe the effects that these inputs have on living systems such as yourself. The difficulty comes from the fact that we sometimes confuse the two languages, and thus end up confusing ourselves as well.

For example, perhaps you've heard the old **conundrum**, "If a tree fell in a forest and no living thing was around to hear it fall, would the tree make any sound?" To a physicist, the answer is clearly *yes*. For in physics, "sound" is a physical event described in terms of the frequency and amplitude of the sound source. But to a psychologist, the answer is clearly *no*. For in the behavioral sciences, "sound" is a stimulus that has reality only when it is *processed* by a living system of some kind. To a psychologist, then, "sound" is a behavioral process measured in terms of subjective pitch and loudness.

We run into the same two types of descriptive languages in the field of color vision. To a physicist, "red" is a light wave that has a certain frequency—about 700 nanometers. But to a psychologist, "red" is an internal process of some kind that may or may not be associated with a physical event. For instance, close your eyes momentarily and picture a luscious, ripe tomato "in your mind's eye." Did it look red to you? Probably so. But the "input" that caused you to "see" the tomato surely wasn't a light wave with a frequency of 700 nanometers!

More to the point, perhaps, suppose you happened to glance at a ripe tomato out of the corner of your eye in very dim twilight. What "color" would it be? Unless you have a very vivid imagination, it probably would look gray to you, not red—despite the fact that the light rays coming from the tomato would still have a wave-length of about 700 nanometers. Why? Because in dim illumination, you tend to focus objects on the periphery of your retina. Thus you would "see" the object with your rods, not with your cones. (To a physicist, of course, the tomato would still be "red" no matter what color you saw the tomato as being.)

As you learn more about your own ability to "see color," you might keep this fact in mind—to a physicist, *color resides in objects* (or, more precisely, in the light waves the objects generate or reflect). But to a behavioral scientist, *color is an internal psychological process*. For the most part, there is a very close connection between the physical attributes of a stimulus and the psychological experiences that the stimulus creates inside your head. That's why it is very important that you learn something about the physical aspects of various stimuli. As we will see, however, there are times when your eyes (and brain) respond to inputs in ways that cannot be explained in purely "physical" terms.

Question: *How would you go about describing the color "red" to someone who was totally color-blind?*

Hue

In *physical* terms, when you speak of the color of something, you are really talking about that object's **hue**, or the wave-length of light that the object produces or reflects. Each wave-length of light in the rainbow (visible spectrum) produces a unique *hue*. The psychological experience of *color* is closely associated with the physical *hue* or wave-length of the stimulus object.

If your color vision is normal, you will *perceive* four of the hues in the visible spectrum as being "psychologically pure colors." Red, green, blue, and yellow are the four **primary colors**. Psychologically speaking, these four colors seem to be "pure" in that they don't appear to be *mixtures* of other more primitive colors.

Other hues, however, produce colors that are clearly "mixtures" rather than being "psychologically pure." For example, most people see orange as being a mix of red and yellow, and most of us view chartreuse as a mixture of green and yellow. Both orange and chartreuse appear in the rainbow, and thus each has a specific wave-length and a unique hue. But to the human eye, these are "mixture colors" rather than "primary colors."

Most of the familiar colors appear on what psychologists call the *color circle*, which is made by joining the ends of the rainbow (see Color Plate 3). Arranged around the outer edge of this circle are all of the spectral colors you can see, and each point on the circle has a unique hue and wave-length. But any color on the circle can be created *psychologically* by mixing two or more of the primary colors (red, blue, green, and yellow).

Saturation

Hue alone is not enough to explain all of the colorful visual experiences that you have. For example, what two primary colors mixed together make pink? Red and blue? Red and yellow? No, pink is not a mix of any two colors, but rather is a weak or *diluted* red. The vividness or richness of a color is what we call **saturation**.

Saturated colors are rich-looking and strong. Desaturated colors are weak and diluted. For example, suppose that you poured red food coloring into a fishbowl filled with tap water. The water would become deep red—a highly saturated color. Now suppose you pour in a lot more tap water. What happens? The ruby red soon becomes a pale, *desaturated* pink.

The hues around the outer edge of the color circle were carefully picked to be the most saturated possible. As you move inward toward the center of the circle, the colors become less and less saturated until you reach gray, which has *no hue at all*.

Complementary Colors

Any two colors that are opposite one another on the color circle are *complementary*. If you mix two complementary colors in more-or-less equal amounts, you get a completely desaturated gray. Thus if you add green to a red, the red becomes less and less saturated until it becomes gray. However, the red *never turns green* until it has passed through gray.

If you mix two colors that are close to each other on the circle, you get a "mixture color," not a gray. Thus if you add yellow to red, the red turns orange first and then finally becomes a slightly reddish yellow—without first passing through gray.

Lightness

Look at the *color solid* shown in Color Plate 2. As you can see, this solid figure is really a three-dimensional "color circle." The hue changes as you go around the figure, while saturation decreases as you move from the outer edge toward the center of the figure. But there is a third dimension to this figure aside from hue and saturation. This third dimension is called *lightness*. The "north pole" of the solid is pure white. The "south pole" is pure black. Gray lies in the very center of the solid. The "lightness" of a visual stimulus, then, ranges from white to gray to black.

By definition, black and white are completely desaturated colors. And like gray, black and white are "colors," but not "hues."

By making careful use of color, saturation, and lightness—or their physical attributes—we can describe almost any color experience you have in very precise terms.

Question: *Can you guess just from looking at the figure shown in Color Plate 3 why the color solid is "lop-sided" rather than being a perfect sphere? (Hint: Think about the comparative richness or saturation of yellows and blues.)*

Color-Blindness

Suppose you wanted to determine whether other people "saw the world" in the same colorful way that you do. How would you go about finding out?

Well, you might just show a variety of objects—a rose, a lime, a blueberry, and a lemon—to a random sample of subjects and *ask* them what colors the objects were. But even if everyone in your sample announced that "the rose is red-colored," how would you know that the subjects actually *saw* the rose as being the same color you did? Red, after all, is a *subjective experience*, not a physical dimension. One way to bring some objectivity to your experiment might be to show your subjects a rose and then ask them to *mix three colored lights* until they just matched the redness of the rose. You could pick almost any three colors from the spectrum for your "mix colors," of course. But let's say that you picked red, blue, and a greenish-yellow. You could then use these same three "mix colors" when you asked your subjects to match the green of a lime, the yellow of a lemon, and the blue of a berry.

(Actually, there are two types of color mixtures—additive and subtractive. *Additive mixtures* are combinations of light, as you might get if you focused several slide projectors on the same movie screen. Color Plate 6A shows what an additive color mixture looks like. If you mixed paints together instead of lights, you'd get a *subtractive color mixture* as shown in Color Plate 6B. Since it is easier to control the intensity of the stimulus using lights rather than paints, psychologists

Hue (rhymes with "few"). The colors of the rainbow, or of the visible spectrum. Technically speaking, "color" includes not only the hues of the rainbow, but all the mixtures of hues plus blacks, whites, and grays. Black and white are not considered hues, although technically they are "colors." Pink (red + white) is a color; its hue, however, is red.

Primary colors. The four colors that seem to be "psychologically pure" to most people with normal vision. The primary colors are red, green, blue, and yellow.

Saturation (sat-your-RAY-shun). The intensity or richness of a color. Pink is a weak (desaturated) red. The colors of the rainbow are about as saturated as any colors can be.

Partially color-blind. A person who is "red-weak" sees red, but not very well. A "red-blind" individual usually sees yellows and blues quite well, but is entirely blind to the color red. Because the person is blind to just one (or perhaps two) color, the color-blindness is "partial."

often use additive mixtures in their research rather than subtractive.)

Color Weakness

If you tested enough people using an additive color mixture technique, you would soon find that a few of your subjects needed an abnormally large amount of red in order to reproduce the redness of a rose. These people would be *red-weak*. That is, they *see* the color red, but it appears much weaker to them than do the other three primary colors (green, blue, and yellow). If you asked a red-weak individual to mix red and blue to match the purpleness of a plum, this person would mix in much more red than would a subject with normal "red vision."

A few other subjects might need an unusually large amount of greenish-yellow to match a lime-colored light. These people would be *green-weak*. If you asked a person with normal color vision to mix green and blue to match a turquoise-colored light, the person might mix the two colors in equal proportions. A green-weak individual, however, might well need 80 percent green and 20 percent blue to get a "subjective match" for the turquoise-colored light.

Most *color-weak* individuals show a deficiency either to red or to green—or to both these hues.

Partial Color-Blindness

About 5 percent of the people in the world are almost totally blind to one or more hues on the color circle, although they can see most of the other hues perfectly well. The majority of these **partially color-blind** people are *men* for, color-blindness is an inherited deficiency that seldom affects women.

Karl M. Dallenbach

The partially color-blind person can reproduce all of the colors she or he can see by mixing just *two* basic hues. The main types of partial color-blindness involve a red-green deficiency or a blue-yellow deficiency.

Although there are several kinds of red-green blindness, a person who suffers from any one of them will see the world amost entirely in blues and yellows (plus black and white). A bright red fire engine will look a dull yellow to such a person, while grass would appear to be a desaturated blue.

The rare individual who is blue-yellow blind sees the world entirely in reds and greens (plus black and white).

Although the exact mechanism for partial color-blindness is not fully understood, psychologists assume that the cones are somehow responsible. There appear to be several different types of cones, each of which may be responsive to different wave-lengths. The person who is partially or totally blind to red stimuli, for instance, may have been born with few if any of the cones that respond to wave-lengths in the red end of the visible spectrum.

There are many different theories of color vision that attempt to explain why some people see colors normally, while other people don't see colors as they should. To date, none of the theories has proved itself fully acceptable to all psychologists.

Color-Blindness Tests

Odd as it may seem, many partially color-blind individuals reach maturity without knowing that they have a visual defect. For instance, Karl Dallenbach, a psychologist who spent his professional life studying sensory processes, learned of his red-green blindness in an introductory psychology class.

Students in this particular class were seated alphabetically to make checking attendance easier for the teacher. Dallenbach was in the front row. During a lecture on vision, the professor wished to demonstrate an old color-blindness test called the **Holmgren wools**. The test consists of a large number of strands of colored wool that the subject is asked to sort into various piles according to their hues. Dallenbach was tapped for the honor of being a subject simply because he was right under the teacher's nose.

When asked to sort all the reds into one pile, Dallenbach included all the wools with a greenish hue as well as those that were clearly red. When asked to sort all the greens, he included the reds.

At first the teacher thought that Dallenbach was playing a joke, but subsequent tests proved that he was red-green blind. Like most partially color-blind people, Dallenbach had learned to compensate for his handicap while growing up. Since everyone said that grass was green, he saw it as being somehow different from red roses—although, under controlled conditions, Dallenbach could not tell the color of grass from that of most red roses.

Despite this visual problem, however, Dallenbach went on to become a noted psychologist. But perhaps because of his red-green blindness, Dallenbach specialized in the study of taste and smell—not of color vision.

The Holmgren wools are but one (and perhaps the least accurate) of many different tests for color deficiencies. Most of the other tests contain hundreds of tiny dots of colors. These dots are so arranged that a person with normal vision sees letters, numbers, or geometric figures in the dots. A person with partial color-blindness, however, sees only a random jumble of dots or a different number than would the normal person. An example of this sort of color-blindness test is shown in Color Plate 4.

Question: *Red and green were picked as the colors for our traffic signal lights before we realized that millions of drivers are "blind" or "weak" to these two hues. How might we slightly alter the traffic-light colors to make it easier for drivers with red-green deficiencies to tell the difference between a "stop" light and a "go" light? (Remember, these drivers can see blue and yellow quite well.)*

Total Color-Blindness

Only about one person in 40,000 is totally color-blind. A few of these totally color-blind individuals were born with normal vision, but lost the ability to see hues as a result of disease. Others became totally color-blind because their cones were poisoned by such pollutants as lead or carbon disulfide. Many of these people can recover at least some of their color vision if given proper therapy—including large doses of Vitamin A.

Most totally color-blind people, however, suffer from **albinism**—an inherited condition involving a lack of pigment throughout their bodies. Like the albino rabbits and rats, these people have colorless hair, pink-white skin, and pinkish irises. Since the photo-sensitive chemicals in the cones are, in fact, *pigments*, albino people lack functional cones and *cannot see color at all*.

All albino humans have foveas that are *totally blind*, so the albino must learn to defeat the usual reflexes that tend to focus images in the area of the fovea. Most albinos develop rather jerky eye movements that prevent their visual images from focusing in on the fovea. But even so, their visual acuity is well below average. For if they look straight at something, it disappears from their sight.

Since albino individuals have only rod (or night) vision, they find normal day illumination

> **Holmgren wools** (HOLM-grin). A color vision test devised by a Swedish scientist named Alarick F. Holmgren. The test consists of strands of colored wool yarns that the subject must sort according to their hues. The test is seldom used these days.
>
> **Albinism** (AL-bin-ism). From the Greek word meaning "white." Albino individuals suffer from an inherited condition that prevents their skin and eyes from developing the normal pigments that color our skins and allow our cones to respond to colored stimulus inputs.

blindingly bright. They usually compensate by learning to keep their eyelids half-closed, or by wearing dark glasses even when they are indoors. Put more accurately, they use their *brains* to help them perceive the world in situations where their visual inputs are somewhat imperfect.

Sensory inputs are but the first stage of that marvelous process called *perception*. We will discuss perception in detail in Chapter 9. But first, suppose we see what might happen if you were totally cut off from all stimulus inputs—a condition known as *sensory deprivation*.

Summary

1. Hearing is a **stereo** sense. Because your two ears are several centimeters apart, sounds reach each of your ears at slightly different times and at slightly different loudnesses. Your brain analyzes these differences and converts them into an understanding of whether the source of the sound is to the left or right.

2. While your ears discriminate left-right differences in sounds very well, they do not discriminate up-down differences at all well.

3. When sound from any source arrives at your ear, the sound passes through the outer and middle ear until it reaches the hair cells in your inner ear. The middle ear contains three bones—the **hammer**, **anvil**, and **stirrup** that amplify sound waves. The **eardrum** separating the outer from the middle ear is connected to the hammer. The stirrup is connected to the **oval window**, which separates the middle from the inner ear.

4. The inner ear is a snail-shaped space called the **cochlea**. The hair cells that are the true **auditory receptors** lie on the **organ of Corti**, which runs through the cochlea.

5. Sound waves have both frequency and amplitude. Frequency is measured in **Hertz**, or Hz. The greater the frequency of a musical tone, the higher it generally sounds. The larger the

amplitude of a sound, the louder it will usually seem to be.

6. **Bone deafness** is a hearing loss caused by improper functioning of the bones in your middle ear. Bone deafness can usually be corrected with a properly fitted hearing aid or, in some cases, with surgery.

7. Nerve deafness results from damage to the hair cell receptors. This form of deafness can seldom be corrected.

8. Children born deaf have problems learning to speak because they cannot hear the sound of their own voice.

9. The stimulus input for vision is light, which is made up of waves of very tiny energy particles called **photons**. Whenever you strike a match or turn on a lamp, you produce millions and millions of photons.

10. The **frequency** of a light wave helps determine the color the light will appear to be. The **amplitude** (intensity) of the light wave generally determines how bright it will seem.

11. The **visible spectrum** (or rainbow of colors) runs from blue through green, yellow, and orange to red.

12. The **wave-lengths** for the visible spectrum run from 400 **nanometers** (blue) through 760 nanometers (red).

13. Beyond the blue end of the spectrum lie the

ultra-violet ("black light") rays and the X-rays. The wave-lengths of these waves are less than 400 nanometers. Beyond the red end of the rainbow lie the **heat waves**. The wave-lengths of these waves are more than 760 nanometers.

14. The eye is something like a color TV camera. Light enters your eye through the **cornea** and **aqueous humor**, then passes through the **pupil**, the **lens**, and the **vitreous humor**. The light then strikes your **retina**, which is the **photosensitive** inner surface of the hollow eyeball.

15. Muscles attached to your lens help focus the visual input so that it falls squarely on your retina.

16. The retina contains your **visual receptors**—the **rods** and **cones**. The cones are sensitive to all the colors, including whites and grays. The rods see the world only in shades of gray.

17. In the center of your retina is a small pit called the **fovea** that contains only cones. Your vision is at its sharpest when the visual image falls on the fovea.

18. Near the fovea is the **blind spot**, which contains no visual receptors. The optic nerve, which runs from your retina to your brain, exits from the eyeball at the blindspot.

19. **Near-sighted** people typically see close objects more clearly than they do far objects. **Far-sighted** people typically see distant objects more clearly than they do objects that are close to their eyes.

20. **Old-sightedness** is a condition caused by hardening of the lens. It often can be corrected with **bi-focal** eyeglasses.

21. A person with normal **visual acuity** (keenness of vision) is said to have **20/20 vision**. This means that the person can see at a distance of 20 feet (6 meters) what the average person can see at a distance of 20 feet.

22. When you sit in the dark, your rods and cones adapt to this decrease in light intensity. **Dark adaptation** is mostly complete in about 30 minutes or so. Your rods are more sensitive at night (or in dim illumination) than are your cones. If your rods malfunction, you may suffer from **night-blindness**.

23. Colors have **hue** (red, green, blue, yellow) and **saturation** or richness.

24. Black, white, and gray are completely **desaturated colors**. The black-white axis of the **color solid** runs from white to gray to black, and is called **lightness**.

25. If a person can see a color, but only when it is very intense, the person is said to be **color-weak**.

26. If a person cannot see a particular color no matter how intense it is, that person is said to be **partially color-blind**.

27. Men tend to be "color-weak" and "partially color-blind" more frequently than women.

28. The most common form of partial color-blindness is the failure to see reds and/or greens as people with normal color vision do.

29. **Albino** humans and animals lack the pigments necessary for normal color vision. They therefore see only with their rods and are **totally color-blind**. They are also totally blind in their foveas.

(Continued from page 159.)

Dear Judy Jones:

I was going through some of my stuff today, packing it all up, when I found this old sheet of scratch paper. It had a cow on it, and a horse and an automobile. On the back was a couple of algebra problems, written out in long hand. My ticket to the world, I always used to call it. Reminded me that I hadn't written you a letter in some time, so maybe I ought to catch you up with the news.

I'm going to college! Can you believe it! That's what I was packing for, when I found the scratch paper. Bet you never thought, the first time you saw this ugly boy, Woodrow Wilson Thomas, that he'd be going off to college someday. I don't remember that first day you came to the Home too well, maybe because I didn't know the words to remember things with back then. But the algebra book, that is something I sure won't ever forget. I guess I learned how to read with that book. And your help too, and then Mrs. Dobson's. She told me later you had a real argument with her. She thought I was retarded, but you insisted I must just be deaf. Then there was a doctor checking me out, and the hearing aid that the State bought me. Did I ever tell you, the first day I had the hearing aid, I just sat and listened to the birds all day long? Can you imagine not knowing what a bird sounds like until you're 10 years old?

Anyhow, as you know, it took me a couple of years to learn how to talk like normal people do. Still not too good at it, I guess. But I went to school, and I caught up, and now I'm going to college. I still can't believe it. I guess I did pretty good in high school, except maybe in English. But real good in math. Good enough to get a scholarship. How 'bout that? I'm going to study math in college. Hope to be a teacher some day. My complexion has cleared up a lot since you saw me last, and maybe I'm not so ugly any more. Anyhow, I've got me a girl friend. Sort of.

It's been so long, maybe you're married now and have kids of your own. If you do, I bet you'll have their ears checked out early, won't you?

Anyhow, I just wanted to let you know how things are going, and about the college bit. I guess if it hadn't been for you, I'd still be at the Home, sitting in the window, looking at the pretty pictures in the magazines. I guess I really owe the world to you, Judy Jones. So I thought I'd write and say thank you.

Best,

Woody

Recommended Readings

Braginsky, Dorothea D., and B.J. Braginsky. *Hansels and Gretels: Study of Children in Institutions for the Mentally Retarded* (New York: Holt, Rinehart and Winston, 1971).

Meadow, Kathryn P. *Deafness and Child Development* (Berkeley: University of California Press, 1980).

Uttal, William R. *A Taxonomy of Visual Processes* (New York: LEA, 1981).

Van den Brink, G., and F.A. Bilsen, eds. *Psychophysical, Physiological and Behavioural Studies in Hearing* (The Netherlands: Deft University Press, 1980).

Wasserman, Gerald S. *Color Vision: An Historical Introduction* (New York: Wiley-Interscience, 1978).

Attention and Input Control

8

Did You Know That . . .

Your brain receives millions of inputs at any one moment, but is aware of but a few of these at any given time?

You are more likely to pay attention to stimuli having to do with food when you are hungry than when you have just eaten?

Inputs flow into your brain along two different routes?

The reticular activating system keeps your cortex alert?

Human subjects who were deprived of inputs experienced hallucinations, distortions in their body images, and long "blank periods" in which they couldn't really think at all?

One scientist who immersed himself in a tank of warm water for several hours believed that he had returned to the womb?

Sensory isolation has been used to help people stop smoking, lose weight, and reduce their consumption of alcohol?

Autistic children appear to suffer from an inability to screen out most inputs voluntarily and selectively?

"Womb Tanks and REST"

Philip Cassone laughed when they shut the door. This was going to be a cinch, no doubt about it. Imagine those crazy psychologists wanting to pay him $20 a day for just doing nothing!

Plus room and board!

He just might stay here for weeks, maybe for months. Let them go bankrupt, as far as he was concerned.

The bed Phil was lying on was narrow but comfortable. The long cardboard tubes into which his arms were stuck were annoying, but Phil was sure he could adjust to them with little difficulty.

The goggles covering his eyes let in some light. But he couldn't make out any details of the room he was in, except that the walls were painted black. He knew the room was small, though—maybe 2 meters wide by 3 or 4 meters long. Big enough to live in if you didn't move around very much, and the crazy psychologists were paying him for not moving.

All Phil could hear was the quiet, gentle, soothing whirr of an air-conditioning unit. Black as a tomb, that's what the room was.

Phil yawned, stretched a little on the narrow bed, and relaxed. A lead-pipe cinch, that's what it was going to be. He drifted gently off to sleep.

Some time later, Phil awoke. He had a moment of panic when he couldn't remember just where he was. But then he smiled and relaxed.

"Inside the little black box," he said to himself. That's where he was. He must have slept for, oh, maybe 3 hours. Or was it more like 4 or 5? Phil couldn't tell exactly, and that bothered him a bit.

How long had he been in the room so far? Maybe 6 hours? How much had he earned? Maybe 5 dollars? Not bad for just sleeping.

A few minutes later, Phil decided that he needed to go to the bathroom, so he yelled out, "I want to go to the john." There was a microphone in the room that carried his voice to the crazy psychologists in the next room. *If* they were still there, like they said they would be. They could talk to him too, over a loudspeaker hanging on the wall, but so far they hadn't said anything at all.

The door opened and someone came in and touched him on the shoulder. Phil hopped out of bed and almost fell flat on his face. Funny he should be so clumsy. Maybe he was still half asleep. He spoke several times to the person leading him, but got no answer. After he had urinated, he was led back to the little black room by his silent escort. Strange the man wouldn't talk to him . . . if it was a man.

Phil lay down on the bed again and started to contemplate the world. He thought about his school work; he thought about his family; he gave serious attention to several girls he had encountered in recent weeks. And then, when he ran out of things to think about, he started over again.

It was all getting pretty boring. Maybe he'd only stay in the room for a few weeks after all, until he had earned enough money to make a down payment on that car he had seen in the showroom. What did that car look like anyway? He could barely remember . . .

"Phil, are you awake?"

The voice sounded remote and at first he couldn't be sure that he wasn't imagining it.

"Hello, Phil, are you awake?"

He told the crazy psychologist he was, but his own voice sounded odd and hollow to him.

"Okay, Phil, I want to give you some tests now. Are you ready?"

Phil said he was.

The psychologist's voice came out of the black haze again. "All right, let's start with the letter H. How many words can you think of that begin with the letter H? Don't use verbs and don't use proper names. Go ahead and start now."

H? What begins with H? Hell, for one thing. And Horse and House and Heart and Hurt and Help. And Hungry. Am I hungry? Maybe that was what was wrong. What will they give me for dinner? Maybe a hamburger. Oh, yes. Hamburger begins with H. And Horse. No, I said that. Horsemeat in the Hamburger . . .

What else? Celery? No that doesn't begin with an H. Helpless? Honda. No, that's a proper name. Hello out there. Happy? No, that isn't a word, is it? More a state of mind, really. Head! Yes, Head would do. ·

Then Phil thought and thought, but nothing else popped into his head. Finally he asked, "Is that enough?"

"If that's all you can think of, that's fine, Phil."

He smiled and relaxed. That ought to show them.

My God, it's quiet, he said to himself a few moments later. The silence seemed to stab at his eardrums like an ice pick. How could silence be so loud, so overwhelmingly bright?

And the colors, the sparks of colors. Banners of different colors waving back and forth. The wallpaper was wiggling, writhing, pulsating, just the way it did that time he had foolishly taken that drug his friend Van had given him.

Oh, what in the world was that sound? A dark green clunking noise. Could it be the air conditioner? Sounded more like an elephant stomping around. Clunk, clunk, clunk. My God, it was a herd of elephants!

The elephants changed color. Now they were sort of black, with pink and blue and purple . . . elephants moving . . .

No, the elephants are standing still, aren't they? It's the picture that's moving, and the elephants are like cutouts in a moving picture. There they go, over the hill . . .

"Hey. You people listening in. Do you know there's a herd of elephants marching around in here?"

Why didn't the crazy psychologists answer?

And the quiet again. How long has it . . .

"Now, Phil, we have a series of records you can listen to if you wish. Would you like to hear them?"

Records? Why not? Maybe some good rock . . .

But no, it's a voice talking about ghosts. Who the hell cares about ghosts? Dullsville. But at least it's a voice, talking . . .

Yes, play it over one more time. This is getting interesting. Yes, play it again, Sam . . . It sure sounds more sensible this time round. Yes, ghosts are for real. Why hadn't he realized that before? Yes, play it just one more time . . .

"Hey, you people. What time is it? Why don't you answer? Don't you know I can't stay in here too long? Why don't you say something? It's been at least 24 hours, hasn't it? I've earned my 20 bucks, now tell me what time it is . . ."

Floating . . . looking down . . . Who was that strange person lying on that little bed down there with the cardboard tubes on his arms? Maybe he was dead and nobody knew it . . .

. . . There's that dark green clunking sound again. They must be letting something else into the room. Last time it was elephants. Wonder what it is . . .

My God, it's a spaceship! It's only six inches long, but it's a real spaceship. How did they manage that? It's buzzing around the room like Darth Vader chasing Luke Skywalker . . .

"Hey, you crazy psychologists, what are you trying to pull? Get that spaceship out of here! Shooting at me, that's what it's doing. It's shooting laser beams at me!"

"Ouch! Oh, my God, I'm hit! Hey, you stupid people, stop that! If you don't stop that, I'll have to come out right away. You know that. What are you trying to do, make me quit? I can't take this much longer. Darth Vader is going to kill me with his laser beams . . .

"Why won't you help me? If you don't do something right now, I'm coming out. Don't you understand, it's your fault!"

Philip Cassone angrily stripped the tubes from his arms and jumped off the bed. He jerked the door open and stumbled into the room next door where two startled psychologists sat working at a table containing recording equipment.

"You bastards ruined the experiment. You made me come out. Now aren't you sorry you let Darth Vader get at me?"

And then Phil started to cry.

(Continued on page 204.)

Input Control

Now that you know something about how your body *receives* stimuli from the outside world and *translates* these sensory inputs into neural messages, it's time to ask four important questions:

1. Millions of stimuli **impinge** on your receptors at any given instant in time, but your mind pays conscious attention to only a few of these stimulus inputs. What biological, psychological, and social factors determine whether an input is important enough to break through to your conscious awareness?
2. How does your brain *select* the inputs your mind wishes to attend to, and how does your brain *screen out* those stimuli your mind isn't interested in at the moment?
3. How does your mind react to **input overload**—that is, to situations when your brain receives *too many stimuli all at once*? And how does your mind react to **input underload**—that is, to situations when your brain receives *too few stimuli* for your mind to do its work properly?
4. How do psychologists explain the fact that what is an *overload* situation to some people is "merely normal" or even an *underload* situation to many other individuals?

Let us begin our discussion of *input control* by trying to answer these questions as best we can. And then, armed with this knowledge, we can better appreciate a fascinating if little-understood psychological disorder called "juvenile autism."

" I CAN UNDERSTAND MY MOTHER AND MY FIRST-GRADE TEACHER BEING THERE, BUT THERES ALSO A TV ANNOUNCER WHO DOES DOG FOOD COMMERCIALS, AND A SECOND-STRING CATCHER FOR THE DETROIT TIGERS."

Impinge (im-PINJ). From a Latin word meaning "to drive in." To impinge on something is to touch, affect, or enter it.

Input overload. A condition that results from too much sensory stimulation. Often leads to stress (see Chapter 12).

Input underload. Also called "sensory deprivation" or "sensory isolation." A condition that results from too little sensory stimulation.

Attention. The act of applying your mind to a thought or sensory input. Your brain receives inputs over many sensory channels, but usually can attend to but one input at a time. The act of choosing which input to be aware of is called attention.

Attention

HELP!!

Chances are, if you were just skimming through the pages of this book, your eye would be strongly attracted to the word "help" that appears above. But why would you be more likely to look at this word than at any other word printed on this page?

If you could answer this question *completely*, you would know as much about the process of **attention** as any psychologist in the world. So, let's see what sort of answer you might give.

Stimulus Factors

Generally speaking, you will attend to a stimulus input if the *stimulus object* itself makes a strong "contrast" with its surroundings. This contrast may be in stimulus *intensity*, *size*, *shape*, *color* (or some other quality, such as pitch), *location*, or *duration*. For the most part, the more intense or different a stimulus is from its surround, the greater the contrast and the more likely it is that you will become consciously aware of (or react to) the input.

The word "help" is: (1) in color; (2) printed in large type; (3) centered in the middle of the page with lots of white space around it; and (4) set off by exclamation points. Little wonder, then, that your eye is attracted to this word much as iron is attracted to a magnet.

Intra-Psychic Factors

FOOD!!

Stimulus factors help explain why you attend to some stimuli and not to others. But psychological factors are equally important. *Motivation* is one of these factors. For example, if you happen to be hungry right now, you are much more likely to notice the word "food" than the word "study." However, if you have just had a

H. W. Magoun

Your brain is like a T.V. control room, in that you have inputs coming in over many different sensory channels. When you choose to "pay attention" to one channel, your brain typically supresses the inputs on all other channels temporarily.

large meal, but are faced with an important exam tomorrow, you might well pay more attention to the word "study" than to "food." Your attention, therefore, varies from moment to moment *according to your own unique set of needs*.

As you will learn in the next chapter, you tend to "see what you expect to see." If a friend tells you that someone dropped a contact lens on the floor, you will be on the lookout for something that reflects the light. And you may well notice the lens nestled in the carpet when—without prior warning—you might have stepped on it unwittingly. Thus *expectancy* plays an important role in directing your attention toward some inputs and away from others.

Past experience also plays its part in directing your attention. A *novel stimulus*—that is, one that you've not seen before—is often more likely to attract your eye than one that you are very familiar with. However, a stimulus that may be quite novel to you can be "old hat" to someone else. Thus "novelty" is an attentional factor that differs from person to person (and from time to time, of course, depending on your motivational state).

Perhaps the most important intra-psychic factor of all, however, is that of *change*. As we noted in Chapter 6, both your brain and your receptor organs seem constructed to pay maximum attention to stimulus inputs that represent some kind of *physical or psychological change*. We will

have more to say about this point when we discuss "habituation" a bit later in this chapter.

Question: *Why is it that, when you first learn a new word, it seems to pop up all over the place, even in material you have read before?*

Social Factors

SEX!!

As we stated earlier, past experience plays a large role in directing your attention. However, you *learn to attend* to some stimuli—and not to others—depending on the society in which you are brought up. What you attend to (and what you ignore) is therefore determined in part by social factors.

For example, each culture has its own set of "ideal standards" that you internalize when quite young. And you are more likely to attend to a stimulus that matches one of these cultural ideals than one that doesn't. In the US in the 1980's, for instance, Robert Redford probably rates close to a "10" on most people's scale of masculine beauty. Thus, in the US you are more likely to pick someone with a Redford-like handsomeness out of a crowd than someone with "ordinary looks." In the orient, though, a different set of standards applies. Most orientals, therefore, might not notice Redford in a crowd of Americans but might instantly pay attention to someone who met their own criteria of beauty.

Judging from the use of sex-related stimuli in advertising, the nude (or nearly nude) human figure would seem to have a "high attentional value" in our culture. In a poverty-stricken country, however—where clothes were hard to come by—a naked body might well attract less interest than would someone who was well-dressed.

Question: *In what kind of society would a call for help not have a very high attentional value?*

Sensory Channels

In a sense, your brain is rather like the control room of a television station. The director of a TV show usually sits in front of a bank of video monitors, each of which shows a different scene. The director must select—from instant to instant—which of the channels to send out on the air.

In similar fashion, inputs arrive at your brain over *a number of sensory channels*. But at any given moment in time, you typically "pay attention" only to the inputs coming in on one channel. These inputs continue to arrive at the lower centers of your brain, however, even when your cortex is not "watching that channel." For example, when you are concentrating on studying for a test, you may not hear the hi-fi playing softly in the background. However, if you closed your eyes momentarily, you probably would become aware of the music almost immediately.

Part of the problem of explaining attention, therefore, is trying to figure out *which sensory channel* is likely to become prominent at any given instant in time. And, as you might suspect, which "channel" you pay attention to is determined primarily by the physical properties of the stimulus, as well as by the intra-psychic and social factors we discussed above.

Habituation

As we mentioned in Chapter 6, your receptor organs tend to *adapt* to constant stimulation. When you first put a new ring on your finger, the pressure receptors in your skin fire rapidly. But within seconds, the receptors' firing rate slows dramatically. If you wear a tight ring for some time, you hardly notice it is there. However, when you remove the ring, your skin receptors again fire rapidly for a brief period of time because of the *change in stimulation*.

Your brain *habituates* to constant stimulation in much the same fashion. When you move to a new town, the water may taste noticeably unusual to you. After you've lived there for a while, the water will probably taste "ordinary" to you, and thus you will pay little or no attention to it.

The amount of habituation that occurs in any given situation also depends on stimulus, intra-psychic, and social factors. It is much easier for your brain to block out a weak and psycholog-

ically unimportant input than, say, the cry of a baby or the throbbing pain of a toothache.

Both attention and habituation are *learned processes*. A newborn infant's attention is controlled almost entirely by the intensity and complexity of the stimuli around it. The infant must *learn* to block out some inputs and focus in on others, a process that typically takes months if not years. And, as we will see, the child that fails to learn how to screen out inappropriate stimuli often suffers severe psychological problems.

Arousal

The factors that direct your attention from one input to another have long been well known. However, it has only been in fairly recent years that we have begun to understand the *physiological mechanisms* that allow your brain to focus on one stimulus while blocking out almost all others.

The classic research on the physiology of attention was performed by H.W. Magoun and his colleagues at UCLA. Magoun was interested in the problem of **arousal**—that is, the biological and psychological mechanisms that wake us up and keep us functioning at a peak level of performance. Magoun and his associates not only discovered what most of these mechanisms were, they gave us considerable insight into the factors controlling conscious attention as well.

Input Control

Prior to Magoun's work, psychologists generally assumed that sensory information reached your brain in only one fashion. First, external stimuli *impinged* on sensory receptors such as the free nerve endings in your skin. The receptor neurons were excited by this external energy and fired off a message that went up your spinal cord to the somatic sensory cortex in your parietal lobe. This informational input let your brain know which receptors had been stimulated, and how intense the stimulation was. Your brain then processed this message and, if you needed to respond, the motor centers in your frontal lobes caused your muscles to move.

This view of sensory functioning was correct as far as it went, but it pictured the sensory

Arousal. Certain parts of the brain seem particularly involved in waking an organism up or in increasing an organism's activity level. Magoun (mah-GOON) and his colleagues discovered that electrical stimulation delivered to a part of the brain stem called the reticular system greatly increased the arousal level of their animal subjects.

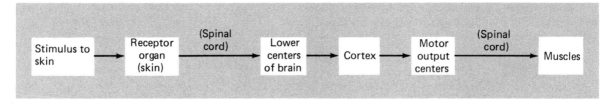

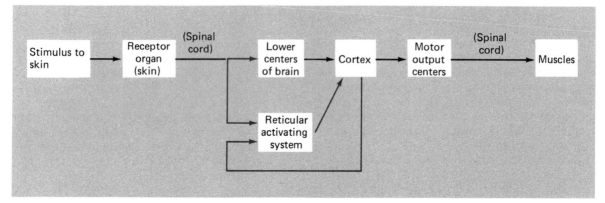

Fig. 8.1. Until recently, scientists believed a stimulus input passed up your spinal cord to your cortex, which processed the input and sent command messages to your muscles. This is the "straight-line sensory system." **(top)**

Fig. 8.2. We now know that sensory input messages "split" at the top of the spinal cord. Unless activated by the reticular system, the cortex does not respond to the message coming through on the "straight-line" system. But activity in the cortex can inhibit or enhance activity in the reticular system as well. **(bottom)**

pathways as being "one-way streets." That is, it assumed that information flowed in *one direction only*—from receptors up to the brain and then out from the brain to the muscles (see Fig. 8.1).

What Magoun (and later, many other scientists) showed was this: Incoming information actually reaches your cortex through *two* quite different pathways. Magoun also proved that your cortex exercises considerable *control* over what information gets through to it, and over what messages are blocked out in lower centers and thus never reach conscious awareness.

Magoun proved that the sensory routes to your brain are "superhighways" where messages flow in *both* directions (see Fig. 8.2). These neural pathways also have "toll booths" spotted here and there to keep out unwanted travelers. The road map for this maze of inter-connected pathways is far from being completely drawn, but we can at least sketch in some of the landmarks.

Two Important Sensory Pathways

As far as "input control" is concerned, almost all of your sensory modalities operate in similar fashion. So let us see what happens when a free nerve ending in your skin responds to an external stimulus. The process begins when the receptor cell "fires," and sends a patterned burst of electrical energy up your spinal cord to your brain stem (the "stem" of the cerebral mushroom). Up to this point, only one input route is involved.

In your brain stem, however, the road to your cortex "splits" into two pathways. One road

leads directly to the somatic sensory cortex in your parietal lobe. This route is called the **straight-line sensory system**; it lets your brain know what part of your body has been stimulated and how strong the stimulation is.

A second road leads into the **reticular activating system**, which gets its name (like the retina) from the Latin word for net or network. The reticular system is a network of cells that begins at the top of your spinal cord and runs up through the brain stem to the lower parts of your cerebrum. The reticular system acts as an *alerting system* for the rest of your brain—rather like the bell on your telephone. When the reticular system is activated, it rings up your cortex to let it know that an important message is coming through on the straight-line sensory "telephone."

The message from the free nerve endings in your skin will usually reach your somatic sensory cortex *whether or not* your reticular system is aroused. However, unless the reticular system "rings the bell" and activates your cortex, your brain appears to *ignore* any information that comes through on the straight-line system. And your brain acts in this fashion whether the message comes from your skin, your eyes, your ears, or from any other sensory channel.

The Reticular Activating System (RAS)

Magoun's experiments demonstrating the function of the **RAS** (*reticular activating system*) were performed on animals rather than humans. So let us talk about cats first, and people second.

Suppose we implant an electrode in the RAS of a cat. Then we let the animal continue its daily life. But, occasionally, we deliver a small amount of electrical current to the cat's RAS. What happens?

If we stimulate the cat's RAS when it is awake and moving about, it reacts as if it had "heard something." That is, the animal suddenly becomes tense and alert, as if its environment had suddenly *changed* dramatically and it ought to pay attention to what was going on around it.

If we wait until the cat goes to sleep, a short burst of electrical energy delivered to the RAS causes the cat to open its eyes and jump up, rather as if someone had stepped on its tail.

If we cut or surgically remove the cat's RAS, it lapses into deep sleep from which it seldom if ever recovers. If we shake the cat violently, it will wake up momentarily and move around for a minute or two. But even if it were starving to death, the animal would soon lie down and drift off to sleep.

Next, suppose we put a recording electrode in the somatic sensory cortex of the cat whose RAS we had removed. Then we pinch the animal's tail. The signal coming from the electrode would show that the neural message from the the cat's tail does in fact reach the animal's brain. So the animal's straight-line sensory system is still functioning properly. But since there is nothing to *arouse* the animal's brain—to *alert* it that information is coming through that needs to be acted on—the cat remains asleep.

The Human RAS

Your own RAS functions much as does a cat's. As you know, we can record the electrical activity that occurs in your brain while you are asleep. Recordings taken from human volunteers suggest that information from almost all your sensory receptors does indeed *reach your cortex* while you are unconscious. But falling asleep involves "turning off" the alarms of the outside world. That is, when you are asleep, neural activity slows down in your RAS, but not in your straight-line sensory system. As you drift into Stage 1 or 2 sleep, then, some part of your brain *inhibits* the

Straight-line sensory system. The sensory input pathways that lead from the body's receptor neurons rather directly to the sensory regions of the cortex.

Reticular activating system (ree-TICK-you-lar). The information contained in sound waves goes from your ear to your temporal lobe by way of the auditory nerve (a straight-line sensory system). The *meaning* of the sound is carried by the auditory nerve. However, auditory inputs are also passed along to the reticular activating system in your brain stem. If the auditory stimulus seems important enough, your reticular system turns on or "activates" your cortex so that you pay conscious attention to the message coming in on the auditory nerve.

RAS. Abbreviation for "reticular activating system." When Magoun and his associates made their first discoveries, they spoke of the "ascending reticular system," which they abbreviated ARS. The name was changed for perhaps two reasons. (1) Most important, it was later found that the reticular system "descends" as well as "ascends"—that is, it sends neural commands down toward the receptor neurons, in addition to sending messages up to the cortex. (2) Amusingly enough, ARS is close to the British word "arse," meaning "ass." For a time, the reticular system was referred to as "Magoun's ARSe."

Coma (KO-mah). A loss of consciousness due to disease or any other type of brain damage.

firing rates of the neurons in your RAS so that the RAS won't bother your cortex except (as we will see) in cases of real emergency.

Anything that affects neural activity in your RAS also affects your consciousness. Many of the sleep-inducing drugs have their inhibitory effects on the synapses in the RAS (see Chapter 3). And if an accident of some kind damaged your RAS, you would lapse into a **coma** from which you might never awaken—despite the fact that the rest of your brain was in perfect condition.

Stimulus "Blocking"

Since it sits atop your spinal cord—and extends up into your lower brain centers—your RAS is in a perfect position to act as a toll booth or *gate* through which incoming sensory information must pass if it is to have an effect on your cortex (see Fig. 8.3). If the incoming message is trivial or routine, the RAS will allow your cortex to ignore the stimulus by "blocking it out" before it reaches consciousness. But if the message seems important, the RAS *alerts* the higher centers of your brain and they pay attention to what is coming through on your straight-line sensory system.

What do we mean by *important* messages? Experiments with animals suggest that your RAS can *learn* which stimuli need your instant attention—and which stimuli are unlikely to be threatening or to require a response.

As you read this book, your receptor cells are sending millions of messages per minute through to your brain on the straight-line sensory

Normal people can "screen out" competing stimuli and pay attention just to what they want to see or hear.

Fig. 8.3. The reticular activating system. **(left)**

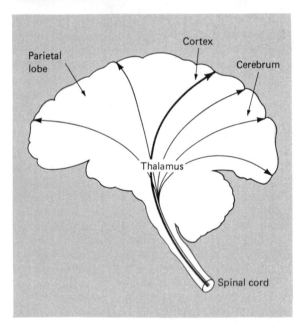

system. But your RAS is (presumably) telling your cortex that it needn't bother with most of this sensory input. For instance, until you read this sentence, you probably were not consciously aware that your shoes (or socks) are full of feet, or that your clothes are pressing in on various parts of your skin. Your RAS has *learned* that these signals don't need your attention while you read.

But a sudden *change* in the pattern of incoming stimulation (as when a friend shouts "help!") is recognized by the RAS as being important information, and it alerts your cortex that an *emergency message* is coming through. Your attention then shifts from vision (occipital lobe) to hearing (temporal lobe). The words your friend shouts at you are immediately processed by your cortex, and you respond appropriately to the emergency input.

People who live next to a railroad track—or to an airport or highway—soon *habituate* to the sounds of the passing traffic. But friends who come to visit are often kept awake at night by these noises until their own RAS's learn to ignore them. And if, in a given family, it is the wife's job to take care of the children, she will awaken at night to a child's whimpering while the husband's RAS screens out these stimuli and lets him continue to sleep soundly.

The important point to remember is that the RAS tells the cortex that a message is important—but *not what the message actually is*. The "content" of the message is handled by the straight-line sensory system.

Question: *Suppose you are reading something interesting when a friend says something to you. Why do you often have to ask your friend to repeat what was said, even though you know that your friend said something important?*

Cortical Influence on the RAS

The road between the cortex and the RAS is, as we suggested earlier, a two-way street. Early studies on the RAS showed that it had a marked influence on activity in the cortex, but later experiments showed that the cortex has ways of affecting the RAS as well.

Whenever you choose to concentrate or focus your attention on something, your cortex tells your RAS not to bother it for a while. Your cortex exerts this control directly by *inhibiting* neural activity in the RAS. On the other hand, if you decide to cram for an exam by studying all night, your cortex is usually able to keep itself awake by continuing to *stimulate* the RAS—which feeds this stimulation back to the cortex itself.

Stimulus Hunger

Your body has certain physiological needs that you are often painfully aware of—a need for food, air, water, sleep, and for a certain range of comfortable temperatures. Thanks to recent research, we now know that your nervous system also "needs" a certain optimum level of *incoming sensory stimulation* in order to function properly. Psychologists often refer to this need as **stimulus hunger**, for when you are deprived of inputs for any length of time, you tend to seek *stimulation* much as you look for food when you are hungry.

The *optimum* level of stimulation that you need varies from moment to moment. When you must "process" stimuli that are *too intense* or *too numerous*, you may suffer from what psychologists call *input overload*. And when the level of stimulation falls *below optimum*, you may experience a condition called *input underload*. We will discuss the effects of input overload in just a moment. First, let's see how you might respond when your environment is so bleak that you get "hungry for sensory stimulation."

Sensory Isolation

Whether you realize it or not, you spend much of your time and energy trying to *predict and control your sensory inputs*. And little wonder that you do, since you can't survive unless you can gain some measure of control over what your environment gives to you. For most of your biological needs can only be satisfied by energy inputs, and most of your intellectual and social needs can only be satisfied by informational inputs. Indeed, even the "joys of doing" can be considered inputs, since it is usually the feedback from your muscle movements (or the effects your actions have on your environment) that you find rewarding.

As you know by now, sensory psychology is primarily the study of *inputs*. Sensory psychology thus can tell you a great deal about "what makes you tick." For you can't begin to grasp what goes on inside your head unless you can identify, measure, and to some extent control the stimulus inputs that prompt your head to tick the way that it does.

If you still doubt the important effects that inputs have on your *mental processes*, ask yourself this question: What would happen to you if, as you were reading these lines, you suddenly lost *all* your sensory inputs?

That is, what would you *experience mentally* if something unexpectedly blocked off all incoming information from both your body and the outside world? What if you couldn't hear, see, smell, taste, or feel anything at all? How would you know where your arms or legs were? How would you discover whether you were wearing clothes or not, or whether it was hot or cold where you were? How would you react if you couldn't determine whether any parts of your body were moving, or whether you were standing up or lying down?

Consequences of Input Underload

Whenever you are deprived of the inputs you want or need in life, several things happen to your body and mind. To begin with, your motivational systems are aroused. If you get no food, you become hungry. If you are deprived of informational inputs, you will hunger for intellectual stimulation. If you are cut off from other people, you will surely yearn for the sight of a familiar face.

The second important consequence of input underload has to do with your values. The hungrier you become, the more important food becomes to you, and the better the food will taste when you finally get it. Furthermore, the greater your deprivation, the more likely it is that you will work for food, and the more probable it becomes

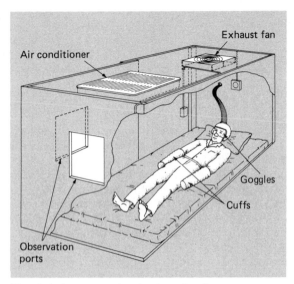

Fig. 8.4. A sensory-deprivation chamber.

that you will eat new or unusual items. In short, the *greater your need*, the *more flexible and changeable you are likely to become* in your attempts to satisfy that need.

The third consequence of input deprivation, highly related to the first two, has to do with the voluntary control you have over your thoughts and actions. Although you may not realize it, your mind and body are so constructed that they *cannot operate normally if you are cut off from your environment.*

You can't make hamburger if you don't have meat to grind, and you can't digest food until you've swallowed it. Nor can you think about things for very long if you don't have sensory inputs to process. Thus, under conditions of severe sensory deprivation (input underload), you might well lose voluntary control of your thought processes. And if, at this point, someone were to give you inputs aimed at changing your values and behaviors, you might well accept these inputs as uncritically as a starving person might accept rotten food.

"Brainwashing"

During the 1930's and 1940's, strange rumors began circulating in the scientific world that the Russian and Chinese governments were using some form of sensory deprivation on prisoners. The term **brainwashing** apparently was first applied to these techniques by journalist Edward Hunter in his 1951 book *Brain-Washing in Red China*. Hunter took the term from the Chinese words *hsi nao*, which literally mean "to wash the brain."

According to Hunter, "brainwashing" typically involved isolating a prisoner from almost all normal sensory inputs for a period of time. This isolation seemed to "soften the person up," allowing the authorities to "wash out all the old thoughts" from the prisoner's mind. The authorities could then replace the old values with new ones more acceptable to the Communist way. The "brainwashing" technique also involved *rewarding* prisoners for becoming more Communistic in their thoughts and actions, and *punishing* them when they resisted change.

The reports on "brainwashing" in China and Russia had one immediate effect—Western governments became worried that the Communists had discovered some kind of psychological magic. The Canadians were perhaps the first to react. As early as 1951, the Canadian government commissioned a group of psychologists at Donald Hebb's laboratory at McGill University to investigate the effects of sensory isolation on *attitude change*. While the experiments were supervised by Hebb, the actual work and planning were done by four of Hebb's students and associates— W. Heron, W.H. Bexton, T.H. Scott, and B.K. Doane.

Although this research itself was not classified as secret, the first explanation that Heron and his colleagues gave for performing the research had nothing to do with brainwashing. Rather, the Canadian psychologists stated that they were interested in studying the effects of monotony and isolation on watch-keeping and other such tasks. In fact, this "pretend" reason for the research is fascinating in and of itself.

For centuries, people have often reported undergoing very peculiar psychological experiences when they were accidentally caught in isolation (input underload) situations. Shipwrecked sailors would, upon rescue, often describe the weird and wonderful *hallucinations* they had while adrift in the middle of the ocean. Pilots flying thousands of feet above the earth reported what was called a "break-away" effect. After the pilots had been cruising along at high altitudes for several hours, they seemed to lose contact with the earth—and with reality. Sometimes they would break out in cold sweats. At times they would feel that they could no longer trust their eyes or their instruments. And they often reported seeing strange objects flying around them. Many such episodes ended in crashes. And if the pilots did succeed in landing the plane, they were often psychologically unfit to fly again.

At a more earthbound level, truck drivers rumbling along deserted highways late at night sometimes reported seeing jackrabbits larger than their trucks.

In all of these "sensory underload" situations, the person affected was obviously *deprived* of the normal amount of information she or he had come to depend on in everyday life.

The McGill Experiments

When Heron and his colleagues at McGill decided to study sensory deprivation, they began by building a small **isolation chamber** (see Fig. 8.4). They then paid students $20 a day to lie on a small bed, their arms inside cardboard mailing tubes. The students' eyes were covered by **transluscent** goggles, and their hearing was masked by a noisy air conditioner.

The students were fed and watered when necessary, but were asked to remain as motionless as possible during the course of the entire experiment.

Prior to undergoing the sensory deprivation, the students were given a battery of tests and questionnaires. The subjects received similar tests while in the isolation chamber, and after the deprivation experience had ended.

While they were in the chamber, the students were exposed to a series of propaganda messages read in a rather boring monotone. These messages concerned such supernatural events as mental telepathy, ghosts, and those noisy spirits called **poltergeists**.

In order to make sure that any changes in the subjects' attitudes or behaviors were due to the isolation and not merely to exposure to the propaganda, Heron and his colleagues hired a separate group of students to serve as a *control group*. These students simply sat in a quiet room and listened to the propaganda speeches through earphones without undergoing any real sensory isolation.

Intellectual Impairment and "Blank Minds"

The results of the McGill experiments were somewhat surprising. To begin with, Heron and his colleagues had expected that most of the subjects would be able to withstand the isolation for several days. In fact, almost half of the students quit during the first 48 hours.

Those who stayed showed considerable intellectual impairment during the sensory deprivation itself and for some hours afterward. Simple problem-solving exercises often seemed beyond the students' mental capacities. Furthermore, they had difficulties with motor coordination, and they did not adapt well to new situations.

Not all of the isolated subjects lasted long enough to be exposed to the dull and repetitious

Brainwashing. A term used by the mainland Chinese to denote a "cleansing of the mind" of thoughts and beliefs disapproved by the government. Brainwashing always involves isolating the individual from her or his normal inputs. In the US the word is sometimes incorrectly used to refer to any situation in which one person tries to trick another into changing or conforming.

Isolation chamber. Any small room or large container in which a person can be deprived of most of his or her sensory inputs for a period of time.

Transluscent (trans-LOO-scent). Any material that transmits light but not patterns. Milk is transluscent because you can see light through it, but not objects. Water is transparent because you can see both light and patterns through it.

Poltergeists (POLE-ter-guy-sts). From the German words meaning "noisy spirits." Perhaps you have read about old houses where the dishes suddenly fall off the shelves or where strange noises come from the attic or basement. Supposedly, poltergeists are responsible for such frightening experiences.

propaganda messages. But those who did usually asked to hear the speeches again and again and again. These subjects were also much more profoundly affected by what they heard than were the students in the control group.

Of equal interest were the subjective reports the subjects gave of their experiences while in the "black box." At first they thought a great deal about their various personal problems. But, as time went on, they found such organized thinking more and more difficult. They could no longer concentrate on much of anything, so they just relaxed and let their minds drift.

Eventually most of these subjects experienced "blank periods" during which they simply could not *think* at all. They were conscious—which is to say that they were not asleep. But their minds simply were not functioning in a logical fashion. During these periods, their emotions often ran wild.

All of the students found the sensory deprivation very stressful and even very frightening.

Hallucinations

About 80 percent of the McGill subjects reported some form of *visual hallucination* despite the fact that they were all wearing blindfolds. Often the first symptom the students experienced was a lightening of their visual fields, followed by the appearance of dots or lines all around them. Next, the students would "see" geometric figures that duplicated themselves like wild wallpaper patterns.

Very vivid, cartoon-like scenes were usually the next step in the hallucinatory sequence. Often these scenes looked like something out of a Walt Disney movie. For instance, one student reported seeing a line of squirrel-like animals with sacks

Fig. 8.5. An iron lung used to force air into the lungs of polio victims who cannot breathe for themselves.

over their backs marching "purposefully" over a hill.

For reasons no one yet understands, the *content* of these hallucinations seemed beyond the mental control of the subjects. One student, for example, could see nothing but eyeglasses, no matter how hard he tried to think of something else. Presumably some part of his brain—perhaps the right hemisphere—was producing these vivid scenes.

Many subjects reported disturbances in what might be called their *body images*. For example, one student had the impression that his body had turned into *twins*. That is, he was convinced that there was another body lying on the bed with him, and that his own body partially overlapped this "twin." A second student stated that his mind seemed to leave his body and roam around the cubicle. Occasionally this "free mind" would look back at the "body" lying quietly on the bed to see what it was doing.

Still other students had "floating" feelings as if their bodies had somehow overcome gravity and were hanging suspended in midair.

Distance Perception

The students' abilities to judge distances and to see the world in three-dimensional depth were markedly disturbed both during and after the iso-

lation experience. According to one unpublished account, a rash of minor driving accidents occurred among the students soon after they had left the deprivation chamber. Most of these accidents involved parallel parking—when backing into an empty parking space, the students apparently could not judge where their cars were in relation to other objects.

Once this problem became known, the McGill experimenters warned the students not to drive a car for a period of several days after their isolation period was over. Most of them complied, but one subject reportedly took the warning about *cars* only too literally. This man was learning to be a pilot and wanted to get in some flying time. So he asked a friend to drive him to the airport and then the man took off in a light plane. To his dismay, once he was airborne he found he simply could not perceive up from down. Fortunately, the control tower was able to talk to him by radio and brought him down safely.

Other Deprivation Studies

Once the results of the McGill experiments were made public, psychologists in many laboratories in the United States began paying students to stay inside "black rooms" too. The results of these studies soon showed a common trend—the reactions a subject showed to sensory deprivation were mostly a function of what the subject's personality was like prior to entering the isolation chamber.

For example, students judged as being "normal and healthy" tended to *underestimate* the length of time they had been isolated. However, subjects who were judged as being "somewhat psychologically disturbed" before isolation often *overestimated* the length of time they had been in the cubicle. These subjects also broke off the experiment more readily than did subjects with apparently stronger or more mature personalities.

Almost everyone who underwent sensory deprivation reported wild flights of fancy, at least during the first stages of isolation. Although the content of these fancies varied widely from one person to another, the experiences were all similar to "tripping" on LSD or mescaline. However, the subjects seldom reported having sexual daydreams. As one subject put it, "I was surprised I couldn't **conjure** up more than I did."

In general, the greater the state of deprivation, the less the subjects were able to tolerate the isolation. If the subjects were allowed to move around freely (in a totally dark room), they could often stand the experience for several days. But if they were forced to remain lying motionless on a bed, the subjects quit much sooner.

The shortest stays of all were reported by a group of scientists who asked their subjects to lie inside an iron lung—that is, a small tank-type **respirator** used by some victims of polio (see Fig. 8.5). Most of these subjects were terrified at being trapped inside such a narrow space and demanded to be released after spending but a few hours in the iron lung.

Lilly's Womb Tank

The man who put himself through the most complete sensory deprivation of all was probably John C. Lilly, a psychiatrist who immersed himself in a tank of water for many hours at a time.

Before entering the tank, Lilly donned a diving helmet so that he could breathe underwater. Then he submerged himself, hanging absolutely motionless between the surface of the water and the bottom of the tank. Since Lilly kept the water at his body temperature, he had little or no sensory input from his skin receptors. Since he didn't move, he received no feedback from his muscles. And since the diving mask blocked out vision and hearing, Lilly was almost completely isolated from *all* types of sensory stimulation.

Lilly has only recently commented in any detail on what he experienced during his stay in this "womb tank." He does note that after he had been in the water for an hour or so, he had tremendous urges to move—to twiddle his fingers or twitch his nose. He had to exercise very strong

"CRITICALLY SPEAKING, I'D SAY IT'S A RATHER ORDINARY HALLUCINATION, WITH LITTLE DRAMATIC CONTENT, AND ONLY LIMITED VISUAL AND AUDITORY ORIGINALITY."

Conjure (KONN-jurr). From the Latin word meaning "to conspire" or "to swear together." As commonly used, to conjure is to employ a magical spell to "call up" an image or spirit. A "conjure woman" is a witch who often conspires with your imagination to make you think she has worked some kind of magic.

Respirator (RESS-pirr-ray-torr). A mechanical device that helps people breathe, often by pressing rhythmically on their chests.

Restricted Environmental Stimulation Therapy. Also called REST. Use of sensory isolation in order to reduce stress and motivate people to change their attitudes and behaviors.

willpower to resist the desire to move. After two or three hours, however, the urges left him. Then he seemed to slip down into a "warm, dark cave." The cave soon became a "black tunnel with a strange blue light dimly visible in the distance."

When Lilly finally came out of the water, a few hours later, he felt that he had been "born again."

Isolation as a Therapeutic Tool

Because your brain needs a certain level of inputs in order to function effectively, you might well consider a "womb tank" or a "deprivation chamber" something to be avoided at all costs. And you might also assume that sensory isolation can only be used to harm people.

But most scientific techniques can be used for good as well as for harm. Beginning in the 1960's, many psychologists started employing **Restricted Environmental Stimulation Therapy** (or REST) as a type of *treatment* with certain populations of people who needed rather special help.

Drinkers, Smokers, and Over-eaters

One group of individuals for whom sensory isolation has proved useful are those people who need "extra motivation" to change their personal habits. Canadian psychologist Peter Suedfeld has performed a series of experiments in which he has put clients in very restricted environments. Some of these people were overweight and simply could not keep to a diet. Others were heavy smokers who found it almost impossible to give up cigarettes no matter what kind of therapy they tried.

Suedfeld's clients typically remained in a sensory deprivation chamber for 24 hours or so. During this period of time, Suedfeld played recorded messages aimed at convincing them either to lose weight or to stop smoking. The clients were then given "booster sessions" two months later in which they again spent some time in the chamber. Suedfeld reports considerable success.

195

John C. Lilly   Peter Suedfield

A subject of Peter Suedfield in a sensory deprivation chamber.

For example, all of the smokers on which he tried the technique reported a significant reduction in their "craving" for cigarettes, and the majority were able to give up smoking for at least a period of several months.

In another set of studies, psychologists G. David Cooper and Henry Adams worked with a group of 60 people who were heavy social drinkers. Half of the group were men, half were women. The drinkers voluntarily spent some three hours in a sensory deprivation chamber similar to the one used in the McGill studies described earlier in this chapter. After the subjects had been in the cubicle for 90 minutes, they heard an anti-alcohol message. For half the subjects, this message was *confrontational*. The subjects were told, "If you need alcohol to feel sociable, you're in trouble." The other half heard a supportive message that said, "You don't really need to use alcohol as a routine part of your life-style."

Cooper and Adams also tested several *control groups* of people who had similar drinking problems. One control group heard the messages, but not while in sensory deprivation. A second control group spent time in the deprivation cubicle, but heard no messages. Yet a third control group was given no treatment at all.

According to a 1981 report by Cooper and Adams, the experimental subjects who heard the confrontational message while in the cubicle cut their subsequent drinking by about 60 percent. The subjects who heard the supportive message did less well, but both groups maintained their reduction in alcohol consumption for at least six months without further treatment of any kind. The subjects in the three control groups, however, continued to drink about as much as they did prior to the study.

Judging from these studies, it seems likely that sensory deprivation is effective in helping people change their thoughts and behaviors for

two reasons: First, deprivation increases the *attention* that a subject pays to a propaganda message. And second, it increases the *acceptability* or social value of that message.

Tanking

John Lilly's experiments with his "womb tank" apparently convinced him that almost anyone could benefit from spending time in a water-filled deprivation chamber. Lilly calls this experience "tanking," and believes it is particularly effective in combating the bad effects of stress. In a 1981 article in *Omni*, Lilly states that sitting in a dark, warm tank for a few hours a day is "a sublime way of 'mending the ravelled sleeve of care.'" Lilly goes on to say that, "The tank is an awareness tool, like meditation . . . . [it] assists in a very simple function. It allows us to expand our awareness of our internal state of being, of our internal flow."

Some people who have "tanked" do report feeling better. But despite this fact—and Lilly's claims—there is little scientific evidence that tanking is a psychological **panacea** or "cure-all." And many scientists believe that tanking presents more dangers than benefits. For example, Connecticut psychologist David DePalma states that tanking "is open to abuse because tankers are extremely vulnerable to suggestion and manipulation when they come out." DePalma is particularly opposed to letting people "tank" unless they do so under the supervision and guidance of professional therapists.

Most psychologists view tanking as a form of REST treatment. And properly used—as part of a treatment plan supervised by experts—tanking or any other form of REST may indeed be a valid and useful form of treatment for people with real behavioral or mental problems. Until Lilly and other advocates of tanking provide scientific proof of its effectiveness, however, most psychologists will probably remain skeptical about its usefulness with the general public.

For some types of emotionally disturbed children, however, less severe types of sensory isolation may well turn out to be highly effective forms of treatment.

Autistic Children

The proper use of REST techniques in psychological treatment can best be illustrated by describing how sensory deprivation is used with **autistic** children. Let us describe *autism* first, and mention previous ways of treating this severe mental disorder. Then, perhaps, you will understand why using sensory isolation with autistic children seems so promising.

Juvenile Autism

Autism affects but 5 children in 10,000. Some 95 percent of these children are boys. But of all the types of children diagnosed as being "mentally ill," the autistic child is surely one of the most difficult to work with. He is frequently non-verbal, avoids contact with others, and usually averts his eyes when you attempt to speak to him. Australian psychiatrist J. Randle-Short has listed 14 symptoms of juvenile autism (see Fig. 8.6). Randle-Short suggests that any child who shows at least 7 of these 14 symptoms is very likely to be autistic.

There are many different viewpoints as to the cause of juvenile autism but, generally speaking, they fall into the familiar trio of "biological, intra-psychic, and social/behavioral."

Bernard Ritvo, who takes a biological view toward the problem, believes that autism is an inherited disorder of the brain. There is a fair amount of evidence to support Ritvo's view. Autism does seem to "run in families," and autistic children apparently do have more of a chemical called **serotonin** in their brains than do normal children. The best guess so far is that the excess of serotonin affects the way that these children *process sensory inputs*. Despite his research on the *biological causes* of autism, however, Ritvo has not as yet found a *medical treatment* that will reduce the amount of serotonin in the brain. Nor has he discovered any pill or surgical technique

Panacea (pan-ah-SEE-ah). From the Greek words meaning "all healing." A panacea is a remedy that supposedly cures everything.

Autistic (aw-TISS-tick). A severe mental disorder that usually appears in children between one and three years of age. There are at least 14 different symptomatic behaviors that characterize autism (AW-tism). The most profound of these are reduced speech, social isolation, and occasionally self-destructive behaviors.

Serotonin (ser-oh-TONE-in). A transmitter chemical found in the brain that, in excess, can cause symptoms similar to those produced by LSD.

that "cures" (or even helps) autistic children in any long-lasting way.

Bruno Bettelheim, who looks at autistic children from an intra-psychic standpoint, states that autism stems from the child's failure to develop a true "self-concept" because he has been badly treated by his parents. To escape parental punishment and stress, Bettelheim claims, the child "goes into hiding" somewhere in the dark recesses of his mind. Bettelheim's ideas seem correct—as far as they go. And Bettelheim *has* helped some autistic children recover—at least to some extent. But his type of treatment takes a long time and is not uniformly successful.

UCLA psychologist Ivar Lovaas, a behaviorist, believes that autism is actually a set of *inappropriate behaviors* the child learns from his social environment. Support for Lovaas's position comes from the fact that he has been able to teach many autistic children to behave in a more normal fashion. He has been less successful in teaching these children to talk, however, than he has been in merely reducing their inappropriate responses. Thus Lovaas—like Ritvo and Bettelheim—seems to have but part of the answer to the riddle of autism.

Each of the three viewpoints—the biological, the intra-psychic, and the social/behavioral—has added to our understanding of the autistic condition. However, none of these approaches *taken individually* has yielded a type of treatment that is broadly effective with a wide range of autistic children. Let us see what might happen, however, if we put these viewpoints together in a *systematic* way.

The General Systems Approach

From a General Systems point of view, juvenile autism is thought to result from a *combination* of biological, psychological, and social factors. The autistic child presumably is born with a physiological disorder which is made worse by the child's early social environment. This combination of genetic disability and inappropriate early experience apparently so stresses the child that

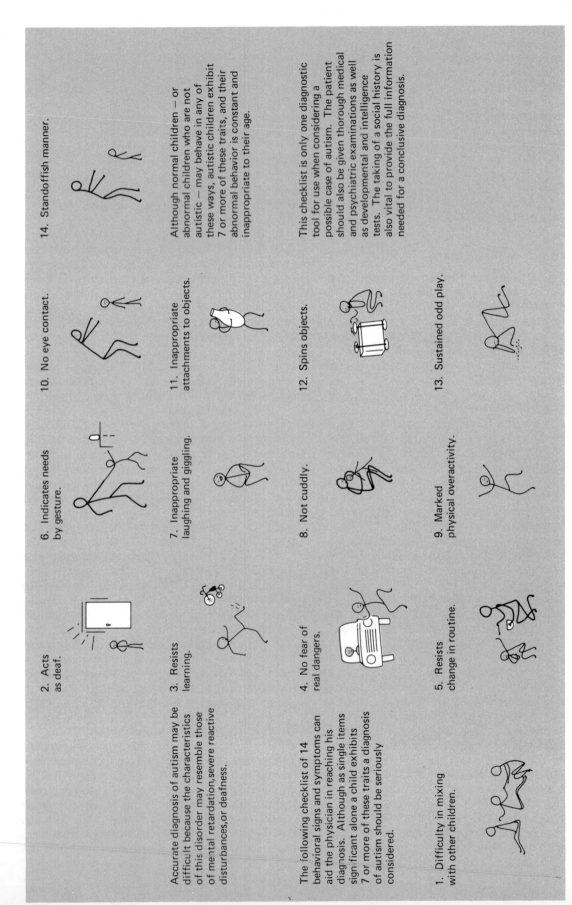

Fig. 8.6. Infantile autism diagnosis.

he fails to learn the sorts of self-control skills that most normal children develop rather readily.

Most studies of autistic children suggest that the *biological problem* involves an innate inability to "screen out" competing inputs. Perhaps an excess of brain serotonin is responsible for the problem, perhaps not. However, this much seems clear: Because the child cannot block out distracting stimuli, he does not learn to "focus his attention" in a normal fashion. And because the autistic child cannot shut out distracting inputs, his world is probably like a disco gone wild—full of blaring sounds and blazing lights that stress the child almost beyond belief.

The *intra-psychic response* the autistic child makes to the stress associated with all this input overload is that of blocking out *almost all incoming stimuli*. And because the child cuts himself off from most of the outside world, he experiences difficulty in developing language, social skills, and self-discipline.

The *social problem* has to do with a pattern of parental care. If the autistic infant is given gentle, non-demanding support during its early years, the child may eventually learn to screen out competing inputs in a normal fashion. However, if the child's parents demand too much of him at too early an age, they may unwittingly force him to retreat deep inside himself as a measure of self-protection. And the more the parents pressure him "to perform normally," the deeper the child will probably retreat.

There is a fair amount of scientific data supporting the view that autism results from the stress associated with input overload. The most important evidence of all, however, comes from the use of input *underload* as a way of helping these children develop the social and psychological skills they so obviously lack. Suppose we look at the scientific data first, in order to put the therapy into proper perspective.

We will begin by discussing how normal infants learn to view the world, and then talk about how they respond to visual overload.

Visual Processing in Infants

Marshall M. Haith and his colleagues at the University of Denver have made extensive studies of the ways in which infants learn to process visual inputs during the first weeks of life. According to Haith, a 4-week-old child is not mature enough to process such complex visual stimulus patterns as the human face. Therefore, the very young infant typically gazes away from its mother's face about 80 percent of the time, and only fixates on her face about 20 percent of the time. By 9 weeks of age, however, the normal infant has learned how

to handle complicated visual inputs and gazes directly at its mother's eyes and mouth almost 90 percent of the time that it can see her.

At this point in the child's development—as we will see in Chapter 20—the mother typically aids the child's social development in two ways. First, she engages in "mutual gazing" with the child, and starts responding to its facial expressions. Second, she attempts to get the infant to "follow her eyes" as she gazes away from the child (and rewards the child when it looks where she is looking). The mother then uses "gaze following" as the first step in teaching the child voluntary self-control and other social skills.

Autism as a Response to Input Overload

For a child to learn to process the complex visual inputs associated with "gaze following," the infant must be able to *selectively block out other inputs*. This "selective screening" of sensory inputs seems to involve both hemispheres of the brain, as well as the reticular activating system (RAS). The left hemisphere is involved since both "gaze following" and self-control seem to be voluntary (left hemisphere) activities. The right hemisphere and the RAS are involved because—as the evidence already presented in this chapter suggests—they are the parts of the brain that do much of the "selective screening" of sensory inputs.

Now, given this knowledge, what do you think would happen if an infant were born with a physiological problem that prevented the child from learning how to "gate out" stimulus inputs in a normal fashion? For one thing, the infant's left hemisphere would surely be bombarded with stimuli that the child simply couldn't handle. The child would experience the type of stress associated with severe *input overload*. And the child might well respond in the only way that he could—by "isolating" his left (dominant) hemisphere in an attempt to *shut off almost all incoming stimuli*. Psychologically speaking, the child might then "retreat" to his non-verbal right hemisphere in an attempt to reduce the tension and anxiety associated with the overload his left hemisphere was experiencing.

Put another way, the autistic child might well impose a form of sensory isolation *on himself* as a response to stress.

Autism and the Right Hemisphere

Brain scans of autistic children taken both here and in England have shown that autistic children have relatively inactive left hemispheres, and studies of neuro-physiological activity in these children's brains suggest that they process most inputs with their right hemispheres. The hyper-

Bruno Bettelheim   Marshall Haith

After spending time in sensory isolation autistic children are often more willing to learn new skills.

emotionality and lack of speech shown by most of these children also indicate that the right hemisphere has somehow become "dominant" in the autistic child. Additionally, as psychiatrist Bernard Rimland reports, at least 10 percent of these children show amazing mathematical, artistic, or musical talents. These traits, of course, are those typically associated with the right hemisphere.

All the evidence gathered so far, then, suggests that autistic children have "retreated" to their right hemispheres as a response to stress associated with input overload. But this "flight from the left hemisphere" is probably as much due to parental demands as to an innate inability to screen out competing stimuli.

Patterns of Parental Care

As we will see in Chapter 20, in our society the mother typically trains the infant in such left-hemisphere tasks as speech and self-control. The father, on the other hand, usually engages the child in such right-hemisphere skills as sports, singing and dancing, and other types of patterned physical play. If the mother over-stresses the infant, the child is usually slow to develop language and social skills. If the father ignores the child, the youngster often fails to develop the proper motor coordination and control of his or her physical movements.

For a number of years, Donald E.P. Smith and I—along with our colleagues at Michigan—have worked fairly intensively with autistic children. We find that most of them come from middle- or upper-class homes in which the mother has very high expectations about how her children should perform. We suspect that, in most cases, the mother quite inadvertently over-stimulates the autistic infant by demanding that he learn to "pay attention" and engage in "gaze following" at a very early age. Most children probably would thrive on this sort of maternal care. But an infant who lacked the usual capacity for blocking out strong inputs might well be highly stressed by the mother's demands—and might "block off his left hemisphere" in self-defense.

Smith and I believe as well that the fathers of autistic children do not, by and large, engage the infant in the normal amount of physical play during the child's early years. Both our own observations and a study of the scientific literature suggest this to be the case. Thus the autistic child usually fails to receive the sort of training that would aid the development of right-hemisphere skills. When the child "retreats to the right hemisphere" to block off the stress associated with the mother's demands, therefore, he goes from the frying pan into the fire. He lacks access to his left hemisphere, and his right hemisphere is too under-developed to allow him to cope with the world in a normal fashion.

Smith and I believe that the parents of autistic children should not be blamed for their child's condition. These parents are, by and large, loving and concerned individuals who are as puzzled by their child's reactions as have been most experts. Many of these parents have other children who turned out to be quite normal when given the same type of early care as the autistic child. Little wonder, then, that most of these parents view autism as an innate disability over which they have little control.

Once Smith and I decided that autism was caused by input overload, we attempted to develop a treatment plan to help these children learn speech and self-control. Most prior therapy for autistic children has involved the use of massive stimulation to "break through" the psychological barriers the child uses to block off external inputs. We have taken the opposite tack. With the help of our colleagues, Smith and I have devised a way of using input underload rather than input overload.

The REST Cure

In a study reported in 1981, Donald Smith used restricted environmental stimulation to reduce **maladaptive** behavior patterns in autistic children. Therapy consisted of putting the child into a dimly lit, quiet room for a brief period each time the child showed any inappropriate behaviors. Smith calls this procedure **time-out**, but the treatment is very similar to REST. Whatever name you wish to call this type of treatment, the results it achieved were very encouraging.

In one case, an 11-year-old autistic girl had engaged in more than 500 self-injurious actions (face slapping and head banging) *each school day* prior to treatment. When she was given "time-out" after each attempt to hurt herself, however, her self-injurious behaviors dropped to zero in just 20 days. In another case, a 10-year-old autistic boy who screamed loudly in class and who soiled his pants 20–30 times a day was given similar therapy. Again, after Smith put the boy in a quiet room briefly each time he misbehaved, the incidence of inappropriate behaviors dropped to zero. In both cases, the children maintained the self-control skills they had learned during the "REST cure" even when this "time-out" treatment was no longer given.

Peter Suedfeld and his colleagues in Canada, and Marshall Schechter and his associates in Oklahoma, have reported similar success with autistic children. However, both of these groups used *complete isolation* for two or more days rather than using the "time out" procedure.

The "Phonic Ear"

The use of REST techniques seems quite effective in helping autistic children reduce *inappropriate* behaviors. However, Smith and I wished to go one step farther and train these children in such *positive* behaviors as social speech. So the next thing we tried—with the help of our associates—was an input-control device called the "Phonic Ear."

Smith and I suspected that one of the reasons autistic children fail to learn to talk is this: When they block out almost all stimuli to protect themselves from stress, they also gate out the *sound of their own voices.* Thus they fail to learn speech because they get no auditory feedback from their own vocal cords. But Smith and I suspected we could get them to listen to their own voices if we could find some means of helping

them screen out distracting inputs *electronically.* As we reported late in 1981, the "Phonic Ear" allowed us to do just that.

The "Phonic Ear" consists of two parts—a set of earphones connected to an FM radio, and a highly directional wireless microphone that broadcasts to the radio over short distances. We used the "Ear" first with a nine-year-old autistic boy named Greg who had been practically **mute** for most of his life. We put the earphones on Greg's head, showed him how to control the loudness of what he heard, and then *gave the microphone to the child.* Now Greg could listen to whatever *he* wanted to hear—and screen out all other sounds—merely by turning the volume to an input level he found comfortable and then pointing the microphone at whatever he wished to hear.

Prior to treatment, Greg had kept his fingers stuck in his ears most of the time he was in the classroom. His teacher had responded to this "ear-plugging" behavior by pulling his fingers away from his head and then shouting in his ear. His teacher—a very humane woman, really—was merely following "customary practice" in such cases. Like the noted psychiatrist Bruno Bettelheim, this teacher believed that autistic children were "hiding deep inside their minds." Thus she had been taught that the only way to get through to the child was to "force him out of hiding" by over-stimulating him.

Greg's teacher had predicted that he would pull the "Phonic Ear" from his head as soon as we put it on him. In fact, he seemed to love the device. Indeed, the only problem we had with Greg was getting the earphones off him at the end of each training session.

"Sit in Chair"

As soon as we put the earphones on Greg, many of his inappropriate behaviors disappeared. He began noticing his environment almost imme-

---

Maladaptive. The French word "mal" means bad. Maladaptive behaviors are those inappropriate actions that hinder development, or disrupt social relations.

Time-out. A behavioral form of therapy that involves putting a child in a special place (usually a room with minimal distractions) rather than physically punishing the child whenever he or she displays maladaptive behaviors. The child must remain in the time-out chamber for a specified amount of time, usually 5–20 minutes, each time the child misbehaves. Research suggests that this type of treatment is far more effective in reducing maladaptive behaviors than is spanking, criticizing, or threatening the child.

Mute. An inability to speak or communicate with sounds. In fact, most autistic children are not entirely mute. They seldom talk, however, and usually when they do, they merely imitate the sounds of others or answer a question with a single word or two.

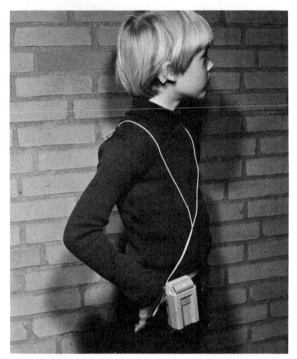

The "Phonic Ear" was developed so that deaf children could hear their teacher anywhere in a schoolroom. Recent research with autistic children involves giving the teacher's microphone to the autistic child so that the child can control his own auditory inputs.

diately and, more important, began to "test it out" with the microphone. He dashed into the bathroom, flushed the toilet, and listened to the rumbling noises. Then he pointed the microphone at his teacher and paid close attention to her for a while. Eventually he began listening to himself as he struggled to force a few sounds out of his own mouth. And much to his teacher's relief, Greg seldom uttered his customary high-pitched screams while he was wearing the "Phonic Ear."

The second day, when Greg came to school, he walked up to his teacher and said, "Duph . . . Duphie." We assume he was trying to say his teacher's name (Debbie) although, prior to wearing the earphones, Greg had seldom approached the woman voluntarily or tried to communicate with her verbally. That second day, however, while Greg was wearing the "Phonic Ear," he seemed more interested in listening to himself than to others.

The third day, Greg entered the classroom with a smile on his face. He walked up to his teacher and said, "Hello, Debbie." Then he strolled over to his chair, pointed at it, and said, "Sit in chair." Next, he sat down in his chair and began to work. By the end of the week, Greg was

speaking in complete sentences—even when he wasn't wearing the "Phonic Ear." And, according to his mother, he was now speaking spontaneously at home—something he had seldom done before.

Self-Control

For a normal child to learn those skills associated with "self-awareness" and "self-control," the child must not only be able to talk to others, but to him- or herself as well. For self-talk allows the child to plan its own behavioral outputs and monitor the consequences of its actions. Because the autistic child "retreats to his right hemisphere" to prevent stressful overload, however, he lacks access to the motor output centers in his left hemisphere. And because he never learns to talk out loud, he never acquires the inner speech associated with "self-awareness" and "self-discipline."

When we put the "Phonic Ear" on an autistic child, we apparently decrease the input overload enormously. Because the child can now screen out stressful inputs electronically, he no longer needs to "turn off" his left hemisphere. And once the child gains access to the motor output centers in his dominant hemisphere, he gains voluntary control over his speech and other behaviors—perhaps for the first time in his life.

Question: *Why does the fact that Greg learned to speak in complete sentences in a week or so suggest that he had already acquired language, but just couldn't produce it voluntarily?*

Further Research Needed

Several other autistic children besides Greg have been treated with the "Phonic Ear." So far, all of them have shown a marked reduction in inappropriate behaviors after wearing the device, and most of them have also shown a marked increase in spontaneous speech. We will need to perform a great deal more research, however, before we can demonstrate conclusively that autism is best viewed as a response to input overload, and that it is best treated with input underload.

Question: *If autistic children don't have a "functional" left hemisphere, are they likely to experience conscious awareness as would a normal child?*

Isolation versus Stimulation

If there is one point that research on autism teaches us, it is this: If you are to survive in this complex world, you must be able to *choose* the input level you need. At times you may well need a stimulating environment to keep you on your toes. But at other times, when the world threatens to overload your neural circuits, you must be able to block out most inputs to keep from being overwhelmed by stress. If you can't *choose* to screen out some inputs, while voluntarily focusing your attention on others, you may experience great difficulty in coping with your environment.

But what factors—past and present—influence your "choice" in such situations? As it turns out, there are several things we must consider if we are to understand why you select the inputs you do. In the next two chapters we will discuss one of them—an internal process called *perception*. Then, in Chapters 11–17, we will show how *motivation* and *learning* help shape what you choose to think about and do.

Summary

1. The process of **attention** determines which of the millions of inputs your brain receives you actually become **consciously aware** of.
2. Attention is influenced by such **stimulus factors** as the intensity, size, shape, color, location, and duration of the input.
3. Attention is influenced by such **intra-psychic** factors as needs, expectancy, novelty, and change.
4. Attention is influenced by such **social factors** as prior learning and cultural norms.
5. Your sensory receptors **adapt** to constant stimulation by firing less frequently. Your brain **habituates** to constant stimulation by suppressing or ignoring various inputs.
6. For your brain to function at its peak, it must be physiologically **aroused**.
7. Inputs flow along two important pathways to your cortex: the **straight-line sensory system**; and the **reticular activating system**, or **RAS**.
8. Sensory information reaches your cortex along the straight-line system even when you are asleep or unconscious. However, you usually do not become aware of these inputs unless your cortex is aroused by your RAS.
9. Damage to the RAS leads to unconsciousness or **coma**. Stimulation of the RAS leads to alertness and focused attention.
10. Your RAS **blocks out** trivial stimuli, but **alerts** your cortex to important inputs coming through on the straight-line system.
11. Your cortex can **suppress** activity in the RAS when you need to concentrate, but can stimulate the RAS when you need to remain alert.
12. When deprived of incoming stimuli, your brain suffers from **stimulus hunger**, or **input underload**.
13. In the 1950's, American scientists became alarmed by reports of **brainwashing** techniques used by foreign governments. At McGill University, researchers paid male student volunteers to lie blindfolded in a tiny room or **isolation chamber** for as long as they would stay. The results of these **sensory deprivation** experiments were as follows:
    a. The subjects soon lost much of their ability to "think straight."
    b. They began having hallucinations.
    c. The longer and more severe the deprivation, the worse the subjects performed.
    d. The subjects became so desperate for inputs that they accepted uncritically much of what they were told by the experimenters.
14. In an attempt to get complete sensory isolation, John C. Lilly immersed himself in a **womb tank** filled with warm water and floated there for hours on end. While in the water, Lilly felt as if he had returned to the womb.
15. **Restricted Environmental Stimulation Therapy**, or **REST**, has been used successfully to help people stop smoking, lose weight, and reduce their drinking.
16. **Tanking** is a voluntary form of REST in which you submerge your body in a tub of warm water while isolated from most inputs for an hour or so. There is no good evidence that tanking is either very harmful or very helpful.
17. **Autism** is a mental disorder that affects mainly boys. Autistic children are **non-social**, **non-verbal**, and often engage in **maladaptive** or **self-destructive** behaviors.
18. **Autistic children** process information primarily with their **right hemispheres**, and often are highly creative. They also appear to have an excess of **serotonin** in their brains.
19. The use of **REST** techniques helps reduce maladaptive behaviors in autistic children.
20. Autistic children seem to suffer from **input overload** caused by an innate inability to **screen out** stimuli voluntarily. Treatment with a device called a **Phonic Ear** which allows them to block out stimuli electronically has increased verbalization in several autistic children.

(Continued from page 184.)

A few hours after he got out of the "black room," Philip Cassone returned to the laboratory to take some more tests. The psychologists explained that they were giving him the tests to find out how soon he had recovered from the effects of the sensory deprivation.

When he took the tests again, Phil did much better than when he had taken them in isolation. Although, to be truthful, he still didn't seem to be as sharp as he usually was. Obviously some of the effects were still lingering on. But the psychologists assured him that within a few days he would be as good as ever.

"How did I do as a subject?" Phil asked the man in charge when the tests were done.

"Let's see," the man said, putting down his pipe and checking the records. "You stayed in for about 26 hours. That's about average. Not bad at all."

Phil was annoyed. He had hoped to do much better than average. He turned to leave in disgust, when he spotted a tape recorder sitting on one of the tables.

"Did you record my voice?" Phil asked.

The psychologist put his pipe in his mouth and nodded gravely.

"Could I listen to some of it?"

The man picked a tape up off the table, put it on the machine, and started the tape in motion.

Phil was shocked to hear the way his voice came out. "Do I really sound like that?"

When the psychologist again nodded soberly, Phil paid even closer attention to the tape. He heard himself demand to know what time it was, heard himself insist that the psychologists talk to him, listened to his scream that if they didn't say something right away he was coming out.

And then he heard a door open and his voice come faintly from a distance . . . "You bastards ruined the experiment. You made me come out."

Phil blushed. "Did I really call you guys bastards?"

Again the psychologist nodded his head slowly in agreement.

Phil groaned. It was the first time he had ever called a professor such a name— at least to his face. "I must have been deprived of my senses to have done something like that," Phil said.

The psychologist just puffed on his pipe and smiled.

Recommended Readings

Lovaas, O.I. *The Autistic Child: Language Development through Behavior Modification* (New York: Irvington, 1977).

Smith, D.E.P., Mary Olson, Frances Barger, and James V. McConnell. "The effects of improved auditory feedback on the verbalizations of an autistic child," *Journal of Autism and Developmental Disorders*, Vol. 11, No. 4 (1981), pp. 449–454.

Solomon, Philip, ed. *Sensory Deprivation* (Cambridge, Mass.: Harvard University Press, 1961).

Suedfeld, Peter. *Restricted Environmental Stimulation: Research and Clinical Applications* (New York: Wiley, 1980).

Visual Perception 9

Did You Know That . . .

A person born blind who gains sight as an adult has great difficulty in recognizing people's faces?

You probably learn to judge distances by moving about?

You tend to see all objects as appearing on a background of some kind?

You typically group objects together according to such principles as proximity, closure, and continuity?

Infants usually prefer to look at human faces rather than at random visual patterns?

Infants only 10 days old will mimic the facial expressions of adults around them?

Blind children are slow to build up an adequate concept of themselves?

The pupils of your eyes often open wider when you are staring at something of interest to you?

Your brain may suppress inputs that disturb or annoy it?

You see what you expect to see?

"Great Expectations"

The Professor was sitting on a large box, cursing like a trooper and sweating like a stallion. There were several other boxes stacked nearby, all of them covered with address labels. On the smallest label of all there was just room for

> Dr. M.E. Mann
> Dept. of Psych.
> Univ. of the Mid-West, USA

Moments before, a group of porters had unloaded the boxes from an ancient pickup truck and trundled the cartons inside the airport, dumping them near the Customs office. And that is where Professor Mann now sat, sweating and cursing.

Outside the airport the African sun shone fiercely, roasting any man or beast foolish enough to venture forth unprotected. Even inside the airport building the temperature was nearly 40° C, reason enough for the Professor's clothing to be soaked with sweat. The cursing was no doubt due to the fact that Dr. Mann was going home royally frustrated.

A small, dark man walked briskly out of the Customs office and headed toward Mann. Despite the heat, his expensive suit and silk shirt and tie looked as crisp and elegant as if he were ready to pose for a fashion ad.

"Ah, my dear Professor, all is in order, all is in readiness," the man said in an elegant tone of voice. "I assure you that we will tuck your boxes of scientific equipment on the plane as gently as a mother tucks a child into bed. Let no one say that the Republic of Lafora treats visiting scientists shabbily." The elegantly dressed man smiled radiantly. "And now, perhaps we might repair to what passes for a cocktail lounge in this ancient airport. I am certain that the limited budget of the Ministry of Science and Technology can be stretched to provide us with a glass or two of cheer while we await the arrival of your jet."

Mann's response was sharp and unprintable.

"Ah," the small man replied. "You are still angry because we cannot approve your venturing into our back country to complete your research. But surely, my dear Professor, you understand my country's position. We are responsible for your safety, and the tribes that you wish to study are still little more than savages."

The Professor made a savage remark.

"No, no," the small man continued hastily. "We could not in good conscience let you go among those tribes unprotected, for they would surely murder you. Your research grant is not of sufficient magnitude to allow you to hire a private troop of soldiers to protect you. And, as you know, all of our military personnel are required at our borders at this dangerous time in our nation's existence. Now, come and have a drink and soothe yourself while we wait . . ."

Mann interrupted. "Oh, come off it, Freddie. All this formality and politeness is just a cover up for the truth. It's prejudice. Pure and simple prejudice. You're a city-born, Oxford-educated, wealthy, sophisticated man. You hold two cabinet posts in the Laforan government. You've been wined and dined in half the capitals of the world, but I'll bet a year's pay that you've never broken bread with one of your backland natives. If they occasionally do wipe out one of your tax collectors or military types, I don't doubt they've been provoked into doing so. But *murderers*? No, that's pure, superstitious prejudice on your part. I've talked to those natives, and many of my anthropologist friends have been out there. You don't understand the backlanders, so you're afraid of them. You shouldn't be. The truth is that they're frightened to death of you city people."

The sharply dressed Minister of Science and Technology began to sweat a little. "My dear Professor, I took your case to the highest authorities in my government, and the answer was no. Absolutely not. What more could I do?"

"You could have pleaded my case with the President himself, that's what," the irate American continued.

"Our great leader is too busy to concern himself with such trivial matters. As you no doubt are aware, we are threatened by enemies on all sides. Even though you are a noted scientist from a country that has long supported our freedom and independence, I would not dare bother the President with such minor problems at this time."

Mann laughed sharply. "That's hogwash! You still see the world in terms of absolutes, in blacks and whites. You wouldn't dare turn down my request if your native prejudice wasn't so great that . . ."

The scream of a shrill siren interrupted them. A large black automobile screeched to a halt in front of the airport, and out popped a huge man dressed in the uniform of a Laforan general. The big man came striding into the building at top speed. Then, catching sight of the Minister and Mann, the General rushed up to them.

"Ah, Freddie," said the General, "Thank God I found you. We have a terrible emergency on our hands. Perhaps you can help."

Freddie said, "Of course," and then quickly introduced General Chambro, head of security for the Republic of Lafora, to Professor Mann.

"Charmed, I'm sure," the General said, bowing slightly to acknowledge the American's presence. Then he continued in an excited tone of voice, "Freddie, the Snake is coming!"

Freddie looked puzzled. "The Snake?"

"Yes, on the next airplane. We just got the message from our agents in Paris. They're sure he's coming to kill the President! You must help us figure out what to do!"

"Well, why don't you just arrest this 'Snake' as soon as he gets off the airplane?" asked the American in a matter-of-fact tone of voice.

"I'm afraid you don't understand," the General said, giving Dr. Mann a withering look. "The Snake is the most dangerous terrorist in the world, responsible for some of the foulest political assassinations you could imagine. The problem is, we simply don't know what the Snake looks like! Not a jot or tittle of information about this assassin do we have. Is he young, old, tall, short, fat, skinny? All we know is that he usually kills his victims by injecting snake venom into them with a fang-shaped needle. The victim dies in horrible convulsions. And to arrange to arrive on this plane! No wonder they call him the Snake!"

Freddie paled visibly during the General's speech. Turning to the American, he said quietly, "There is something you don't understand, Dr. Mann. This particular flight brings to Lafora almost a hundred of the biggest munitions dealers in the world. They are wormy characters, all of them. But we need them because, as you know, we refuse to accept military supplies from any of the major powers. So we spread the word that we wished to buy guns, and chartered a special plane to bring in from Europe anyone interested in selling us weapons. That is one of the reasons I am at the airport now, to greet these men. If we treat them badly . . ."

The General interrupted. "And we cannot check out their passports because most of them travel with forged papers."

"What about giving them a lie detector test?" Freddie asked.

"They wouldn't submit to such a test, of course," said the General contemptuously.

"The lie detector measures emotionality, not truthfulness," the American added. "And I'd guess that your 'Snake' isn't exactly the sort who would lose his cool very readily."

"Too true," said the General, and mopped his face again. "But we must find some way of separating the Snake from—er, the worms, or we are in grave danger."

Freddie cleared his throat and ventured a question. "Professor Mann, you are an expert in the field of perceptual responses. You told me you wished to give certain tests to our backland natives that would tell you about their minds even if they did not understand the purpose of the tests, and even though you could not speak their language. I don't suppose that now . . ."

Professor Mann was suddenly all business. "Yes, Freddie, it might work. We could set up my equipment right here in the airport and test each person as they got off the plane. I would have to draw up some new stimulus cards, but that shouldn't take long. Of course, I don't guarantee anything. The error rate is really very high, you know, and I could easily make a dreadful mistake. But if you're really desperate, perhaps it's better than nothing."

The General looked confused. "I don't understand . . ."

Freddie turned to the military man and said, "You aren't expected to understand—this is a matter for scientists such as Dr. Mann and me. We will screen the men on the plane with the Professor's equipment. You have your soldiers standing by, looking as innocent as possible. When we detect the Snake, we will give you a signal and you must move in for the arrest at once. More than that, you need not know."

"But what will we tell the arms dealers?" the General wailed. "They will want an explanation . . ."

"We will say that Paris has reported an outbreak of a highly infectious eye disease, and we must check each person on the flight to make sure they are not carrying the illness," Dr. Mann said brusquely. "I will put on a white uniform and be very efficient about it all."

At this final comment, Freddie smiled broadly. "You are a positive genius, my dear Professor. We will do just what you say!" And then he turned to some porters standing idly by. "Here, you men! Help us open these crates and set up this equipment!"

(Continued on page 229.)

Perceiving the World

Your eyes are more than "the windows to your soul." Unless you are visually handicapped, your eyes are also the main sensory route by which you acquire information about the outside world. Thus the bulk of perceptual research deals with vision—as does the material in this chapter. So let us begin by asking, "How do you perceive the world around you visually?"

Visual Inputs

When light strikes the retina in your eye, it triggers off a wave of neural activity that passes along the optic nerve to your brain. Sensory inputs from your eyes, however, have little *meaning* in and of themselves until they are *processed* by your brain. The study of perception, then, is really the study of how your brain *processes stimulus inputs*.

When sensory inputs arrive in your central nervous system, they set in motion a complex chain of neural events. First, the inputs are given a preliminary sort of processing by such lower brain centers as your reticular activating system (see Fig. 9.1). Next, the inputs are passed along to the *sensory input areas* in your visual cortex. As Fig. 9.2 shows, your visual input areas are in your occipital lobes.

From the visual input area, the message is next sent to your "association cortex" for handling. It is here, presumably, that many of your *memory circuits* are located. That is to say, most evidence suggests that your association cortex contains **neural traces** of your past experiences. When these memory circuits fire, they help you recall or reconstruct what you have seen and heard and felt in the past.

Your cortex scans or compares both the "memory trace" and the present sensory input. If the two are similar enough, your brain "recognizes" whatever you are looking at as something it has encountered in the past. If no memory trace exists that matches the incoming sensory message, your brain "recognizes" that whatever you are "seeing" is new, different, and has no identifiable name or verbal label.

Perception: Three Different Views

Psychologists are not entirely in agreement as to where the process of **perception** begins and ends. Some scientists believe that perception is primarily a matter of the **registration** of inputs somewhere in the brain. This "registration" or reception of inputs may take place in the lower brain centers, but primarily occurs in the sensory cortex. We might call this the **registration theory of perception**.

Other scientists hold that you don't really "perceive" something until you recognize what it is (or realize that you haven't experienced this input before). These psychologists believe that perception is a matter of building up a **schema** or "mental representation" of an object in your mind. We might call this the **recognition theory of perception**.

Still other psychologists define perception as a process which involves not only registration and recognition, but *responding* to the input as well. These scientists insist that an input has no real meaning unless you *know what to do about it*. (The "response" you make to the input may be either mental or behavioral.) As you can guess, we refer to this viewpoint as the **response theory of perception**.

We might compare these three definitions of perception to the process of "watching" a television program about air pollution. Does *watching* mean that the program merely appears on the TV screen and you "see" it? Or does *watching* mean that you recognize what the program is all about—that the content of the program is somehow "meaningful" to you? Or does *watching* imply that you not only "get the message," but that you know what to do about it as well? (Perhaps you will become aroused enough to write your Senator, or perhaps you will merely wish to change the channel.) If you now substitute the word "perceiving" for "watching," you will see where the problem in defining the process of *perception* actually lies.

Perhaps we would do best to view perceiving as a complex operation that has at least three parts to it—registration, recognition, and responding. Sometimes you can recognize a stimulus input without responding. And (as we will see), sometimes you can respond to an input before you consciously recognize it. In either case, however, there's one thing we can be sure of: Perception *begins* with registration. If the input never reaches your nervous system, we can't really call it an "input," can we?

Question: If a tree falls in a forest, and nobody is around to hear it fall, does the tree make any perceptible sound?

Perception—An Active Process

Generally speaking, perception is a very *active process*. You do not simply sit at home waiting for the world to come to you. Instead, you go out into the world. You challenge it, and you attempt to find out what it and you are all about.

One of the main reasons that you engage in all this activity is that your sensory receptors *lie* to you constantly, and your brain knows it. Your eyes are particularly bad about lying—which is to say that the world is full of visual **illusions**. And if you are to survive, you have got to find a way to *perceive* the difference between illusion and reality. Perhaps an illustration about flying will help you perceive the fact that your eyes really do "lie" to you quite frequently.

Neural traces. Most psychologists believe that inputs leave traces of themselves as they pass through your nervous system. These "traces" are stored as memories and can be recalled at will. For a further explanation, see Chapter 16.

Perception (per-SEP-shun). The act of registering inputs, of recognizing them or knowing what they mean, and of knowing how to respond to them.

Registration. When a woman checks in at a hotel, she "signs the hotel register" to let people know she is there. When an input "registers" on your mind, you are aware that the input has arrived, but not necessarily what the input is or what it means.

Registration theory of perception. The belief that the perceptual process is primarily a matter of how inputs "register" on the brain or mind.

Schema (SKEEM-mah). You recognize an apple as being an *apple* whether you see the fruit from above, from the side, or cut in half. You also recognize it as an *apple* whether it is green, yellow, or red—or even just a black-and-white drawing in a book. "Appleness" is the "schema" or set of related percepts that allows you to recognize the apple under these various conditions, but may also include strategies for relating to or responding to apples.

Recognition theory of perception. The belief that you don't really "perceive" an apple until you have matched the present input to your "schema" of "appleness" and thus know the *meaning* of what you see.

Response theory of perception. The belief that schemas (and hence perceptions) always include your knowledge of how to respond to what you perceive.

Illusions. Misperceptions. Sometimes the visual or auditory stimulus is such that it tricks you into seeing or hearing incorrectly. The cause of the illusion usually is in the stimulus itself, or the way that the receptors in your eye or ear respond to that stimulation, or to the way your brain reacts.

Plane and Fancy Vision

Suppose it is a beautiful spring day, far too nice to work or to sit in class. While you are trying to decide how best to enjoy this gorgeous gift of nature, the phone rings. A friend of yours has somehow come up with an invitation to go flying, and you're invited too.

An hour or so later you find yourself standing beside a plane not much bigger than a delivery van. Rather small, you think—but then you're comparing it in your mind's eye with the huge jetliners at the other end of the airport.

Moments later you are inside, comfortably strapped in a very large seat. The pilot starts the engine, and the plane moves smartly away from the hangar. It then bumps along the taxi strip heading toward the end of the runway.

You pass very close to a firetruck parked by the edge of the taxi strip. The truck is large and red and shiny. Then the pilot calls the control tower on the radio, gets permission to take off, checks the engine, and turns the plane onto the end of the runway.

For just a moment you sit there, the plane shaking eagerly as if anticipating its chance to go

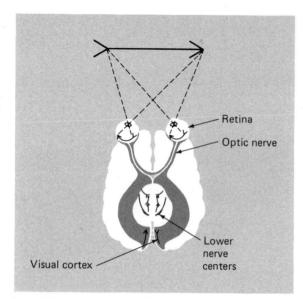

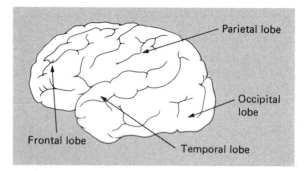

Fig. 9.1. The pathways of vision. Note that part of each path crosses over from one eye to the opposite part of the brain. (top left)

Fig. 9.2. The visual input area is in the occipital lobe. (top right)

Fig. 9.3. The same numbers seen from the ground and from the air. The numbers do not change, but your perception of them does. (middle right)

Perception begins with recognition. After you recognize this as a photo of a boy standing on some steps, you'll perceive it quite differently. (bottom left)

Objects such as planes look like toys when viewed from great heights. (middle right)

Is this a hill or a crater in the surface of the moon? Now turn the page upside down and look again. (bottom right)

roaring down the narrow ribbon of concrete that stretches for a mile in front of you. The number "25" has been painted in large numerals on the runway, obviously an identification of some kind. Oddly enough, the tops of the numbers seem compressed and small from where you are sitting in the plane, yet you know that this can't be so.

And then the pilot releases the brake, guns the engine, and you are rolling faster and faster down the runway. As you pass the numbers painted on the concrete, you see that they were normal size after all. Your eyes were just playing tricks on you (see Fig. 9.3). A second or two later the pilot pulls back on the control wheel and the plane leaps eagerly skyward.

Airborne . . .

A "Topsy-Turvy World"

You climb steadily upward for a few minutes, then the pilot dips one of the wings and turns around in a slow, lazy circle over the airport. Down below you see the firetruck. Why does it now look so tiny and artificial, like a toy that a loving parent would hide under a Christmas tree? And the people—they look more like bugs crawling on the ground than like human beings.

The pilot flies over a near-by town. You see a traffic circle below, the streets radiating out from the center like spokes from the hub of a wheel. A small lake is nestled close to the traffic center. You happen to know that the lake is almost perfectly round, but from the plane it looks oddly distorted. Maybe it's the height that makes it look so funny.

Next you pass a large warehouse with a name written on top of it in very large letters. Surprisingly enough, you can't read the name very easily because, from where you sit, the letters are upside down.

¿NMOD ƎPISDN ƎƆNƎ⊥NƎS SIH⊥
WHY IS IT SO DIFFICULT TO READ

A Strange "Vision" of the World

A few miles farther on, the plane encounters a bank of thick, fleecy clouds. Although you feel rather uneasy about this turn of events, the pilot steers the plane into the clouds apparently without a second thought.

Suddenly the world around you goes gray, and you can't see a thing. You look straight down, hoping for some glimpse of the ground below, but the swirling gray is featureless. After a few seconds your eyes begin to hurt from the strain of trying to focus on pure nothingness. But you keep on looking down because you feel safer when you can see the land below.

Panorama (pan-or-RAH-mah). From the Greek words *pan*, meaning "all," and *horama*, meaning "view." A panorama is thus a "view of everything," such as you get from the top of a mountain on a very clear day.

Hallucination. Caused by incorrect processing of normal incoming sensations, and hence are a fault of the cortex (and not of the receptors or the external stimulus). If you look at an oddly shaped cat and "see" it as a dog, that is an illusion. If you look at empty space (when you're drunk or "high") and think you see a dog, that is an hallucination.

Then the cloud begins to break up a little, and just for a second you see a patch of ground through a hole in the cloud. Is that a big hill you're looking at? But you know there aren't any hills that size in this area! Then the hole in the cloud gets larger, and you see that the "hill" was really a huge gravel pit. Odd that a "pit in the ground" should look like a mountain the first time you saw it.

Perhaps sensing your uneasiness, the pilot lets down below the cloud and heads back to the airport. The tower gives you permission to land, and the pilot circles the airport, then lines the little plane up for a straight-in approach to the runway. As the plane glides down closer and closer to the ground, you notice again that the numbers on the runway seem bigger at the bottom than at the top.

A bit of dirt blows into your left eye, so you close it and begin rubbing it. And you suddenly realize that with one of your eyes shut, you have a very difficult time deciding exactly how near you are to the ground. For some reason, with one eye shut, the wide **panorama** ahead of you seems flat, almost like a painting.

You are rather puzzled by the way your eyes have been acting. Did the altitude somehow affect your vision?

The answer is no—it wasn't the altitude at all. Sometimes it takes an unusual or abnormal situation to help you understand what your eyes are doing *all the time*. Let's see what was going on.

Illusions

When Philip Cassone (see the story for Chapter 8) insisted that he saw a herd of elephants lumbering around the tiny "black room" he was lying in, Phil was suffering from an **hallucination**. As real as the elephants seemed to him at the time, they existed only in his imagination. In more technical terms, Phil's experience was not triggered off by visual inputs—his eyes did not *see* elephants at

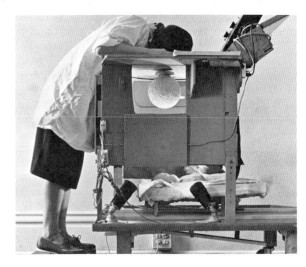

Fig. 9.4. Infants tested in Fantz's apparatus looked at the simple face longer than they did at the design with randomly placed facial features. **(top left)**

Fantz's equipment for observing infant's eye movements. **(right)**

all, but his brain *perceived* memory traces that it confused with reality.

A true hallucination, then, is *not* dependent on stimulation from the external world. But this *imagined reality* may be so striking that you accept the hallucination as if it were a a meaningful input instead of being a distorted product of your own mind.

On the other hand, sometimes the neural circuitry in your brain so distorts the incoming sensory message that you *misperceive* something in the world around you. Such faulty perceptions, as we have noted, are called *illusions*.

Some illusions are due to your *expectations*. For example, suppose you see a spider crawling on the wall just before you get into bed. As you lie quietly, trying to sleep, a loose thread from the pillow case gently touches your cheek. You may sit up instantly, sure that you have "felt" a spider crawling on your face.

Other illusions are apparently caused by odd imperfections in our sensory apparatus. As the famous painter Vincent van Gogh reached the end of his life, he began depicting shining objects (such as the sun) as if they were surrounded by concentric rings of color. For a long time, art critics were convinced that van Gogh had "broken through to a new level of reality" by letting his imagination run free. If this were the case, then we might say that van Gogh was *hallucinating* the circles around the sun that he so often painted.

But as Dr. T.C. Lee of Georgetown University points out in a 1981 article in the *Journal of the American Medical Association*, it's possible that van Gogh was merely "intoxicated" from taking **digitalis**. Apparently Van Gogh told his physician he feared he was epileptic, and in van Gogh's time

digitalis was often used in treating epilepsy. Digitalis causes visual disturbances that include halos and the predominance of the color yellow. Most of van Gogh's late paintings are filled with bright yellows and swirling halos (see Color Plate 7). These facts suggest that, rather than "breaking through to a new level of reality," Van Gogh just painted the world the way digitalis poisoning made him perceive it.

We will have more to say about perceiving illusions in a moment. First, let's look at how perceiving reality develops from childhood on.

The Development of Perception

One of the most nagging questions in all of psychology is this: Which aspects of any human experience are learned, and which are innate? As we will say many, many times in this book, *all behaviors are multi-determined*. That is, everything you think, do, and feel is influenced by: (1) your **genetic blueprint**; (2) your past experiences; and (3) your present environment. Thus your perceptions—as well as your emotions and your behaviors—are a product *both* of your genes and of what you have learned about yourself and the world around you.

There are some aspects of perception, however, that appear so early after birth that they can be considered *primarily* innate. And there are other parts of the perceptual process that clearly appear only when the infant has had a fair amount of "worldly experience." As we discuss this issue in detail, however, you should keep the following two points in mind: First, an infant begins to learn about the world around it *even before it is born*.

And second, all learning is based on a set of innate responses that the infant has available to it at birth. Perception, then—like all other parts of human experience—is truly multi-determined.

Innate Aspects of Perception

Almost a hundred years ago William James stated that an infant probably perceived the world as a "blooming, buzzing confusion." While it may be true that the **neonate** experiences its environment as a blurred and noisy mess, some aspects of visual perception appear so early in the child's life that they are surely "built-in" by the infant's genes.

Dr. Al Yonas of the University of Minnesota's Institute of Child Development believes that many aspects of visual perception are controlled by the child's genetic blueprint. Yonas has shown that a three-week-old infant will blink and recoil slightly from a black triangle moving toward it—even when no physical contact occurs. However, this same baby will be unresponsive when the triangle moves away from it. Yonas also notes that early visual development tends to be better in female infants, those who are above-average in size, and those born after their due dates. These facts are better explained in terms of genetic inheritance than in terms of early visual experience.

Face Perception in Infants

In a previous chapter, we mentioned the fact that scientists had recently shown that infants only 10 days old will mimic the facial expressions of adults. This research suggests there is something rather special about the human face—at least from an infant's point of view.

Look at Fig. 9.4. One drawing is that of a face with the nose, eyes, and other features in their proper places. The other drawing has the same elements, but they are oddly scrambled. Now imagine a very young infant lying comfortably on its back looking up at these figures. Which do you think the baby would spend more time looking at—the normal face, or the scrambled one?

Psychologist Robert L. Fantz photographed the eye movements of young babies using the apparatus shown below. Fantz found that the infants he measured spent much more time looking at the normal than at the scrambled face. This finding suggests that the child has innate response patterns built into its brain which allow it to recognize what the human face looks like.

Fantz also found that babies seem to prefer to look at simple round objects rather than at two-dimensional drawings of the same objects. Fantz believes that infants may have an *innate appreciation of depth*, but points out that his ex-

Digitalis (did-jit-TAL-is). A natural substance found in the leaves of the foxglove plant that stimulates the heart.

Genetic blueprint. The "feed-forward" instructions contained in your genes that tell your body and brain how to develop once you are conceived. While you are in the womb, your body and brain are "built" from this set of instructions just as a house is constructed from an architect's drawings or blueprints.

Neonate (KNEE-oh-nate). From the Latin words meaning "newborn." Your "natal day" is your birthday.

Contours. The edges or outer shape of any object. Your eye and brain have innate elements that allow you to detect contours of objects at birth.

perimental results may also mean that babies learn about faces and depths very early in their lives.

"My Mother's Eyes"

In the last chapter, we mentioned the research that Marshall Haith and his colleagues had performed on "eye contact" in young infants. Haith found that three-week-old infants fixated on the *center* of the mother's face (her eyes, nose, mouth) only 22 percent of the time. Most of the time, the infant tended to fixate on the *edge* of the woman's face. Apparently the human face is too complex and too stressful for these very young children to "process" successfully.

By the time the infants were seven to nine weeks old, however, they gazed at the center of the mother's face almost 90 percent of the time. And they looked at her eyes almost twice as much as at her nose or mouth. Haith believes that newborn infants are innately attracted to *edges* or **contours** of objects in their visual world. By seven weeks of age, however, the baby is sufficiently experienced so that it can begin to perceive the human face as a unified *percept* or *schema* rather than as a "collection of parts."

Haith also notes that a seven-week-old infant is more likely to gaze at its mother's face when she is talking to the child than when she isn't. But Haith also points out that the baby is more likely to gaze at the mother's *eyes* when she is talking than at the mother's *mouth*. Haith believes that the sound of the mother's voice speeds up the infant's visual development—perhaps by soothing the child's fears and helping it overcome the stress associated with input overload. The infant responds to the soothing sounds by gazing at the mother's eyes more often. The mother usually interprets increased "eye gazing" as a sign the child is "paying attention," and thus talks to it (and cradles it) more frequently. Haith concludes that visual perception in the human infant is as

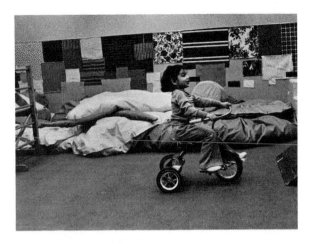

Fig. 9.5. The "visual cliff." **(left)**

Blind children apparently have an excellent concept of "physical space" even though they cannot visualize it. **(right)**

strongly influenced by auditory and skin-receptor inputs as it is by visual stimuli.

Question: *Haith's research seems to contradict Fantz's belief that infants are born with the ability to recognize the human face. How might you resolve this contradiction? (Hint: How old do you think Fantz's infants might have been when he tested them?)*

The Visual Cliff

Another intriguing bit of evidence concerning the innate properties of perception comes from a series of experiments pioneered by Eleanor Gibson, one of America's best-known perceptual psychologists.

One day several years ago, Gibson found herself eating a picnic meal on the rim of the Grand Canyon. Looking straight down into that deep and awesome riverbed, she began to worry about the safety of the children around her. Would a very young child be able to perceive the enormous drop-off at the end of the cliff, or would the child go toddling right over the edge if no adult were around to restrain it?

Gibson was really asking two very important questions about perception. First, are babies born with an *innate ability to perceive depth*? And second, do infants have a *built-in fear mechanism* that would make them retreat from sharp drop-offs even without having been trained to do so?

Once Dr. Gibson had returned to her laboratory at Cornell University, she attempted to answer both these questions. And to do so, she designed an artificial **visual cliff** on which she could test infants safely (see Fig. 9.5).

Running down the middle of the apparatus was a raised plank of wood painted in a checkerboard pattern. To one side of the plank was a sharp drop-off. On the other side was a normal "floor" an inch or so below the center plank. The entire apparatus was covered with sturdy glass so that the infant could see the cliff but could not fall off it.

When an infant was tested, it was put on the center board and allowed to explore freely. Very few of the infants crawled off onto the "cliff" side, although most of them freely moved onto the "floor" side. Even when the child's mother stood at the side of the apparatus and attempted to coax the child to crawl out over the "cliff," most infants refused to do so. Instead, they began to cry loudly. If the mother stood on the "floor" side of the box, the infant would crawl toward her willingly.

A variety of newborn animals—lambs, kittens, puppies, and rats—have been tested on the visual cliff too. For the most part these animals showed an almost immediate perceptual awareness of the "dangers" of the cliff. Gibson concludes that most higher species have behavioral mechanisms built into their brains at birth that tend to protect them from the dangers of falling from high places.

However, not all infants, nor all species, react to the visual cliff as did the babies in Dr. Gibson's studies. Dr. Nancy Rader of UCLA points out that there are great individual differences between infants in their response to the visual cliff. Some babies seem to be *visually-oriented*. These infants recoil with fear from the sight of the cliff. Others tend to be *touch-oriented*. These children apparently trust their skin senses more than their eyes, and crawl right out on the glass covering the cliff as long as it offers firm support. Thus the issue of whether infants are born with an innate fear of heights is far from settled.

Developmental Handicaps of the Blind

Some innate visual tendencies are so subtle that we tend to overlook them—except when we observe the development of the child who is born blind. In her book *Insights from the Blind*, Selma Fraiberg points out that the blind youngster has two severe problems to overcome: (1) learning to recognize its parents from sounds alone; and (2) acquiring a healthy *self-concept* or perceptual "schema" of oneself.

Fraiberg notes that a normal eight-month-old child will reach out its arms the moment it hears its mother's voice—*anticipating* the sight of the parent even before she appears in the child's view. The blind baby does not show this reaching response until much, much later. The blind infant *hears* and *feels*, but cannot "integrate" these sensory experiences very well to form a unified schema of *mother*. Vision, then, is particularly important to a youngster because sight allows the child to pull the other sensory modalities together in its mind.

Blind children are frequently retarded in their speech development. They talk later and more poorly than do sighted children. Much of this speech retardation seems due to their slowness in recognizing the *permanence* of objects in the world around them (see Chapter 20). Blind children also have problems "imagining" things while young and do not identify readily with a doll or with a character in a story their mother reads to them. And they often do not learn the correct use of "I" and "you" until they are five or six.

Fraiberg concludes that blind youngsters cannot *picture* themselves as objects that exist separate from their environments. And since they cannot *visualize* themselves as independent entities, they are slow to develop any real notion of "self."

In brief, *seeing* yourself may be the easiest and most natural way of building up a perceptual schema of your own *self*.

Question: Blind children apparently "process" most inputs with their left (auditory) hemispheres, while the autistic children we discussed in Chapter 8 tend to "process" most inputs with their right (visual, pattern-perception) hemispheres. Can you explain why both types of children might have problems developing a "self-concept," and learning the proper use of "I" and "you?"

Innate or Learned?

The question of which aspects of vision are learned and which are innately determined may

Visual cliff. An apparatus constructed by Gibson and Walk that gives infants the illusion of great depth.

Congenitally (kon-JEN-it-tally). From the Latin words meaning "to bring forth." A "congenital" defect is one present at birth. The defect may be innate (caused by genetic damage) or may be caused by trauma the infant experiences in the womb or during the birth process.

Nature-nurture problem. One of the major controversies in psychology is over the amount of behavior that is inherited ("nature") and the amount that is learned through experience ("nurture"). For a more complete account of this controversy, see Chapter 18.

never be entirely solved. For instance, while children blind from birth are sometimes slow to develop social and verbal skills, they usually are able to move around in the world fairly readily. Indeed, according Barbara Landau and her associates at the University of Pennsylvania, **congenitally** blind children perceive *physical space* (as distinct from "visual space") about as well as sighted children do.

Landau and her group tested Kelli, a $2\frac{1}{2}$-year-old girl who was blind from birth, on a variety of tasks. They found that when Kelli was allowed to explore a room on her own, she could thereafter take the shortest path *from* any spot *to* any spot in the room. Landau and her colleagues believe that Kelli could "perceive" the physical layout of the room even if she couldn't "see" the room visually. Apparently, then, infants are born with an innate ability to *create three-dimensional space in their minds*. But even with this inborn tendency, they still need "worldly experience" if they are to learn to perceive "objects in space."

Explaining Visual Illusions

As this brief discussion of the **nature-nurture problem** in vision has shown, perception is indeed multi-determined. With this thought in mind, suppose we now try to explain those illusions you had on your airplane journey. As we do so, we will try to show you how your genetic blueprint, your past experiences, and your present environmental inputs *all work together* to provide you with an amazing "window to the world."

Size Constancy

As you might guess, it takes considerable time and experience for your cortex to build up the necessary neural circuitry so that you can interpret incoming sensory information accurately. For example, when you were a baby, lying in your crib, your parents dangled toys in front of you. As you reached out a tiny hand to grasp the brightly

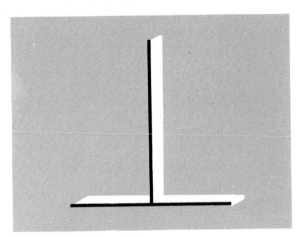

Fig. 9.6. Bisection illusion.

colored objects, you began learning about *distances*.

When someone gave you a teddy bear to cuddle, it was so large that it filled all of your visual world. A day or so later you saw the teddy bear far across the room, and now it occupied only a small fraction of your visual world. Because the bear's image took up so *little space on your retina*, it surely looked smaller to you. Had it shrunk in size?

But no, when you crawled over to it, the bear seemed to grow and grow in size until, when you reached it, the bear was as large as ever. Was this some kind of magic?

When your mother was far away from you, she seemed to be smaller in size than the teddy bear sitting next to you. Yet when your mother came close and handed you the bear, it was obvious that she was much larger than the bear.

Without ever sitting down to think about such things, you eventually learned that *objects remain constant in size whether they are near you or far away*. This important principle of visual perception probably seems so obvious to you now that you can't remember having learned it.

And yet if you hadn't worked out the principle of **size constancy** in your early years, how could you cross a busy street? For instead of seeing cars rushing down on you from all directions, the automobiles might seem to be stationary. And instead of seeing them as moving, you might perceive them as ballooning up in size rather than seeing them as approaching you. And you might view the cars as dwindling in size rather than perceiving them as speeding into the distance.

In short, during your early years you learned that, in many ways, visual size and distance are closely related. When you look at a fire engine a block or so away, the *amount of space* its image occupies on your retina is smaller than that of a toy fire engine up close to you. But you see the distant firetruck as being large and far away, while you perceive the toy as being small and close up.

The principle of size constancy breaks down in extreme cases, primarily because you haven't had the proper sorts of experiences. When you look down at people and cars from a great height—either from the top of a tall building or from an airplane—the objects below often lose reality. People seem like cardboard cut-outs and automobiles seem like toys.

Visual Depth and Distance

Your visual receptors are located in the retinas of your eyes. The retina is, for all practical purposes, little more than a flat, two-dimensional movie screen on which the lens in your eye projects images of the world around you.

Yet, when you look at the world, it doesn't seem to be flat and two-dimensional to you. The world is *three-dimensional*. It has *depth* to it. A blank movie screen has but two dimensions—left/right and up/down. But when you project a first-rate movie on the screen, suddenly a third dimension appears in the picture—depth. How does this near-miracle occur? Suppose we look at a case history or two of blind people who recovered their sight late in life, and then discuss how most people learn to perceive depth.

The Case of S.B.

Like most other psychological experiences, **depth perception** is partially learned and partially due to innate factors. Obviously you wouldn't see *anything* unless you were born with healthy eyes and visual cortex, but what would your world be like if you had been born blind and only now opened your eyes? The answer may surprise you.

Some years ago, British psychologist Richard L. Gregory reported the case of a man who had been blind from infancy, but whose vision was restored at age 52. This patient—whom Dr. Gregory calls S.B.—was an intelligent person whose vision had been normal at birth. At age 10 months, S.B. developed a severe infection of the eyes that left his corneas so badly scarred that he could not see objects at all.

Enough light leaked through his damaged corneas so that S.B. could just tell day from night, but he saw the world much as you would if someone cut a ping pong ball in two and placed the halves over your eyes. S.B.'s corneal scars were so bad, in fact, that for most of his life no doctor would operate on him. Nonetheless, S.B. led a pleasant and very active life. He went places by himself, waving his white cane in front of him to let people know he was blind. He often went for rides on a bicycle, with a friend holding his shoulder and guiding him.

S.B. spent considerable time making wooden objects with rather simple tools. He had an open-faced watch that let him tell time by feeling the positions of the hands. He took care of animals and knew them all by touch, sound, and smell. And he always tried to imagine what things looked like. When he washed his brother's car, he would vividly try to picture what color and shape it really was. When S.B. visited the zoo, he would get his friends to describe the animals there in terms of how different they were from dogs and cats in his home.

S.B.'s Operation

When S.B. was well past his fiftieth year, he prevailed upon a surgeon to attempt an operation in which his damaged corneas were removed and new ones were **grafted** on in their place. The operation was a great success but, as Dr. Gregory reports, S.B. was anything but happy with the results. When the doctor first removed the bandages, S.B. looked straight into the doctor's face—and saw nothing but a blur. He knew that what he saw had to be the doctor's face, because he recognized the man's voice. But it was several days before he could begin to tell one person from another merely by looking at them, and he never became very good at identifying people visually.

Nonetheless, his progress in some areas was rapid. Within a few days S.B. could successfully navigate the halls of the hospital without running into things. He could tell time by looking at the face of a very large clock. And he dearly loved to get up early in the morning and sit at his window watching the traffic rumble by on the street far below his hospital room.

But there were problems. S.B. rapidly learned the names of the colors red, black, and white, but he had trouble identifying most other colors. He could judge horizontal distances fairly well when looking at objects whose size he was familiar with. But heights of any kind always confused him. One day his nurses found him crawling out the window of his fourth-floor hospital room, presumably because he wanted to inspect more closely the automobile traffic in the street below. He looked at the ground 12 meters (40 feet) beneath him and thought it to be no more than 2 meters (6 feet) away.

Prior to the operation, S.B. had crossed even the busiest intersection alone without the faintest

Size constancy (KON-stan-see). Your brain gets a rough idea of the physical size of an object by noting how large a visual image the object casts on your retina. Generally speaking, the larger the visual image, the larger the object will be. However, an object very close to you will cast a much larger image on your retina than will the same object if it is far away from you. If the object is very familiar, your brain will interpret any change in the size of the retinal image as a change in the distance the object is from you. This is the principle of size constancy. If the object is unfamiliar, you may overestimate its size if it is up close, and underestimate its size if it is far away from you.

Depth perception. The ability to see the world in three dimensions. The ability to judge visually how far away from you an object is.

Grafted. Joining parts of one organism to another is called "grafting." In corneal grafts, part of the donor's cornea is surgically removed and transplanted to the eye of the recipient. If the corneal graft "takes," the grafted tissue will function more-or-less normally.

fear. He would plunge into traffic waving his white stick in front of him, and somehow the river of cars and trucks would part for him much as the waters of the Red Sea parted for Moses in Old Testament times. But after S.B. got his vision back, he was absolutely terrified of crossing a street. Dr. Gregory states that it usually took two people holding his arms to force him across an intersection.

Often when S.B. saw a familiar object for the first time, he would be unable to identify it until he closed his eyes and felt it. Then he knew it by touch. And once he "had the picture in his mind," he could recognize it visually after he had looked at it a few times.

But objects that he hadn't (or couldn't) run his hands over before regaining his sight always gave him problems. The moon, for instance, puzzled him greatly. The full moon he could make out, but the quarter moon he had expected to be wedge-shaped, rather like a large slice of pumpkin pie. And when S.B. looked at Fig. 9.6, he saw the horizontal and the vertical lines as being the same length. How do they look to you?

S.B.'s Depression

Immediately after his operation, S.B. was very enthusiastic and happy. He loved bright colors (although he couldn't always give their right names), and he enjoyed being able to see the faces of people he knew. But then he began to get depressed. He complained bitterly about the ugliness in the world around him—houses with the paint coming off, buildings with dirty walls, people with blemishes on their faces. He would spend hours sitting in his local tavern watching people in the mirror. Somehow their reflections seemed more interesting to him than their real-life images.

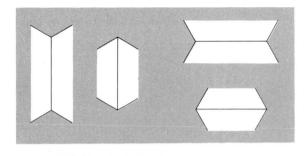

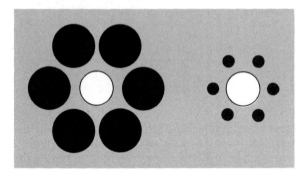

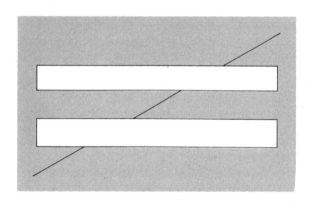

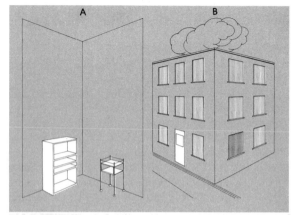

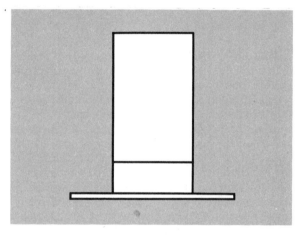

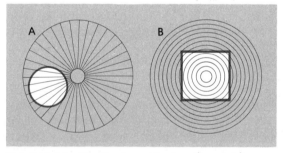

Often S.B. would withdraw from human contact and spend most of the day sitting in darkness, claiming that he could "see" better when there was no light.

There have been no more than half a dozen confirmed cases of people who have gained sight as adults. According to Gregory, depression and unhappiness are common consequences of their getting back their vision. In part, the unhappiness and sad feelings come from the discovery of how hard it really is "to see," and in part they stem from the slow realization of how much in life the person missed.

We should note, however, that not all patients who recover sight late in life have the same problems—or the depression—that S.B. experienced. One woman who recovered her sight in 1980 had no problem at all seeing and naming colors the moment her bandages were removed. Nor did she become unhappy with her newfound

Fig. 9.7. The Mueller-Lyer illusion. **(top left)**

Fig. 9.8A. The corner where the walls meet is the same height as the edges of the walls. **(top right)**

Fig. 9.8B. The outside corner of this building is the same height as the other edges. With the illustration on the left the Mueller-Lyer illusion is formed.

Fig. 9.9. Are the center dots in both figures the same? **(middle left)**

Fig. 9.10. Top hat illusion. **(middle right)**

Fig. 9.11. Is the diagonal line straight? **(bottom left)**

Figs. 9.12A (left) and 9.12B (right). The backgrounds in these two figures distort the colored circle and square. **(bottom right)**

sight. These facts suggest that S.B.'s early illness may have damaged his rods and cones more than Gregory imagined, and that many of the difficulties that S.B. had in perceiving the world were due to retinal damage rather than to an inability to learn to see the world correctly so late in life.

Mueller-Lyer Illusion

Cases such as that of S.B. demonstrate the critical influence that your early life experiences have on shaping how you will see the world when you have grown up. For during your childhood years, you learn the "rules of visual perception" even though you are far too young to know what words like "visual" and "perception" really mean.

Look at Fig. 9.7A. Doesn't the vertical line on the left look shorter than the vertical line on the right? And doesn't the bottom line with the arrowheads (Fig. 9.7B) seem much shorter than the upper line with the "V's" on each end? Yet if you measure the lines in both these figures, you'll see they are exactly the same length.

Why does one line look longer than the other? Richard Gregory believes that this illusion is based on your perception of corners. If you are reading this book indoors, look at one of the corners of the room you're in. Notice that the angles the wall makes with the floor or the ceiling form lines much like those in the "V" figure. If you are sitting outdoors, look at the corner of a building. You will see that the angles made by the roof and the ground are similar to the same lines in the "arrowhead" figure (see Fig. 9.8A and 9.8B).

Question: *It is rather simple to train a pigeon in a laboratory to peck at the shorter of two lines in order to get a bite of food. How might you use this procedure to test whether pigeons are as fooled by the Mueller-Lyer illusion as humans are?*

Circles and Straight Lines

The Mueller-Lyer illusion points up an interesting fact—you seldom see an object *all by itself*. Instead, you almost always see an object *in context*, or in relationship to the other objects around it. In the Mueller-Lyer illusion, for example, the two horizontal lines have "tails" at either end that affect your perception of the lines themselves.

Now look at Fig. 9.9. The two center dots are exactly the same size, but they surely don't look the same!

Look also at the "top hat" drawing (Fig. 9.10). Is the hat taller than it is wide? If you think so, take out a ruler and measure the distances. The "bisected line" drawing (Fig. 9.6) shows the same sort of illusion.

Diagonal (die-AG-oh-null). If you were standing straight up, then leaned over at an angle, your body would be diagonal to the floor. The "slant mark" (/) on the typewriter is a diagonal line.

Taboo (tab-BOO). Sometimes spelled "tabu." Any object or behavior that is prohibited because it is illegal or immoral. The most common form, found in almost all cultures, is the incest taboo—the strong belief that you are not supposed to have sexual experiences with close relatives.

The apparent straightness of a line can easily be affected by whatever objects the lines seem to penetrate. In Fig. 9.11, the **diagonal** line crossing the two bars seems to be three disconnected lines. In fact, as you can determine by using a ruler, the line is absolutely straight. Oddly enough, the illusion disappears for most people if they turn the drawing around so that the line is straight up and down.

A circle drawn in the middle of a "wheel," such as that in Fig. 9.12A, somehow looks lopsided. A square drawn in the middle of concentric circles (Fig. 9.12B) looks warped. These figures—like the lake you observed from the air earlier in this chapter—are good illustrations of how difficult it is for your eye to follow a line that is interrupted by other lines.

A "straight line" and a "circle" are not things that you simply "see." Rather, they are *concepts* that your cortex *perceives* after taking many things into account. Straightness and circularity are *percepts* that are affected by feedback from your eye muscles as much as by input messages from your retina.

You grew up in a world of straight lines, corners, and sharp angles. But suppose you had lived as a child in an environment where straight lines were **taboo**? How would now perceive the Mueller-Lyer illusion?

The answer is—you probably wouldn't see the illusion at all. The Zulus—a tribe of primitive people in South Africa—live in what Richard Gregory calls a "circular culture." Their huts are round mounds with circular doors. They plow their fields in curved lines, and even their toys and tools lack straight edges. When shown the Mueller-Lyer illusion, the typical Zulu native sees one line as being only very slightly longer than the other. Some illusions, such as that shown in Fig. 9.12B, affect the Zulu hardly at all.

Clues to Visual Distance

Your eye inspects the world in front of you and reports to your brain what it sees. Your brain takes into account not only the visual sensations coming from your retinas, but also the way your eyes move in their sockets, the sounds your ears

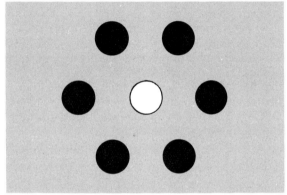

Fig. 9.13. The railway line illusion. The two colored lines are the same length; do they look that way to you? **(top left)**

Fig. 9.14. We know the man and building are not the same height, so we assume the building is far away from us and the man close. **(top middle)**

Fig. 9.15. Seen in a haze, buildings and other objects seem to be further away. **(top right)**

Fig. 9.16. Irradiation illusion. **(bottom left)**

Because the Zulus have what Richard Gregory calls a "round culture," they are little affected by straight-line illusions such as the Mueller-Lyer. **(bottom right)**

report, the smells around you, your bodily posture, and all the memories it can dredge up. Once your cortex has fitted all these inputs into a perceptual schema, then and only then does it decide what it is you are looking at.

An automobile passes you on the street. You know that it is about 9 meters (30 feet) away from you because you remember what size cars ought to be, how long it takes you to walk 9 meters, and how the visual image of the car will change as you walk toward it.

The *apparent size* of an object gives you a good notion of how far away the object is. But there are other clues that your brain uses, even though you are often unaware of what these clues are.

Linear Perspective

If you stood in the middle of a railroad track and looked down the roadbed, the rails would seem to come together in the distance. Your mind tells you that the rails don't actually converge at the horizon, but your eye insists that they do. And if you draw two identical lines between the tracks, the top line seems to be longer (see Fig. 9.13). Can you figure out why?

And when you stand at the end of a runway at an airport, looking down toward the other end, can you understand why the tops of the numbers painted on the runway look "scrunched up?"

This apparent *convergence* of parallel lines as they approach the horizon is called **linear perspective**—one of the cues your brain uses to judge distance. And, as Fig. 9.14 shows, linear perspective also affects your judgment of the *size* of objects in the distance.

Oddly enough, it took artists a long time to realize that they had to make use of linear perspective in their paintings if they wanted to reproduce distances effectively. In some paintings, such as those by Persian artists in the sixteenth and seventeenth centuries, an almost complete lack of linear perspective gives the painting a curiously flat, distorted, unreal appearance. (See Color Plate 9.)

Question: If an artist paints a scene that lacks linear perspective, does this mean that the artist actually does not see perspective in his or her own visual world? How could you prove experimentally that your answer is correct?

Aerial Perspective

Anyone who has grown up in a smog-ridden city knows that there are often days when you can't see more than a block or two away. But there are parts of the world still blessedly free from this aerial pollution. In some of our deserts, for instance, the air is often so clear that visibility is practically unlimited. The city dweller who first visits these regions is sometimes shocked at how badly she or he actually judges distances in clean, fresh air. A mountain peak that appears to be no more than 5 or 10 kilometers away may actually be more than 80 kilometers down the road.

The more hazy and indistinct a remote object seems to you, the further away it appears to be—a fact that psychologists refer to as the **aerial perspective** of an object (see Fig. 9.15).

Light and Shadow

Often we use the *lightness* of an object to give us some notion of its size or distance from us. For reasons we still don't understand, dark objects often appear to be smaller than light-colored objects. For example, look at the 7 dots in Fig. 9.16. Although it doesn't look like it at first glance, the distance *between* the dots is exactly the same as the size of the dots themselves.

Sometimes we make judgments about the visual world from what we *don't* see, instead of from what we do see. Look at Fig. 9.17, a simple representation of the word "shadow." Notice that each of the six letters in this word is printed in full. Now look at the next word. Here there are no

Linear perspective (LIN-ee-er per-SPECK-tive). "Linear" has to do with straight lines, such as the horizon (the line between earth and sky). "Perspective" means "viewpoint." Parallel lines (such as railroad tracks) appear to meet at the horizon. If you were drawing a realistic picture of railroad tracks, you would want to draw them so that they "met" at the horizon in your picture.

Aerial perspective (AIR-ee-ull). Literally, the "way you see an object through the air." Fuzzy objects seem distant; clear (distinct) objects seem close.

Convergence (kon-VERGE-ence). Means "to come together" or "to turn or move toward one another." Parallel lines converge at the horizon. You can demonstrate "eye convergence" if you get a friend to cooperate. Hold up one of your fingers about half a meter in front of the person's nose and ask the person to focus on the tip of your finger. Now slowly move your finger right up to the person's eyes. As your fingertip nears the person's nose, the person's eyes will turn toward each other.

letters, just the shadows themselves. But look carefully. Doesn't your eye actually *see* the forms of the letters as if they were really there? And what about the five black figures in Fig. 9.18? Can you see the word "fly" spaced between the figures? And after you recognize the word "fly," can you perceive the drawing as just a collection of odd-shaped black figures? Why not?

You also make use of shadows in judging whether you are looking at a mountain or at the hole left when somebody dug up the mountain and carted it away. Photographs of the craters and hills on the moon and on Mars are fairly commonplace now. When you look at one of these photographs, you automatically make an assumption about how the sunlight is falling on the landscape. If you make the *wrong assumption*, then your brain will show you a hill instead of a crater.

Question: S.B. often mistook shadows for real objects. Why do you think this was the case?

Convergence

Humans are essentially two-dimensional animals, bound to those parts of the surface of the earth that our two feet can walk on. We judge distances rather well—if they are no greater than we can walk or run or ride. But we judge heights rather poorly, at least in comparison with animals such as birds and fish that move readily through all three dimensions of space.

When you look at something in the distance, both your eyes point straight ahead. When you look at something up close, however, both your eyes turn inward, toward your nose. The amount of strain that this **convergence** creates in your eye muscles is noticed by your brain, which uses this cue as an index of how far away the object is.

SHADOW SHADOW

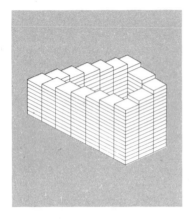

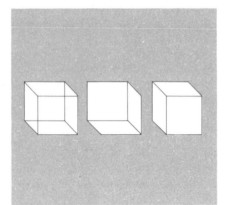

Fig. 9.17. If you look closely you will see that the word on the right is made up of shadows, not real letters. Look at the illustration at the left. **(top left)**

Fig. 9.18. A perception illusion. **(top right)**

Fig. 9.19. The magic stairs. **(middle left)**

Fig. 9.20. The Necker Cube. **(left)** It can be seen as projecting up or down in three dimensions in the first cube. In the other two cubes the perspective is stabilized. **(middle)**

Fig. 9.21. Do you see two profile faces? Or a wine glass? **(middle right)**

Fig. 9.22. Do you see an old lady or a young girl? **(bottom left)**

To judge how *distant* an object is, you have merely to let your eyes converge and notice the strain on your eye muscles. But to judge *height*, you usually have to move your head up and down or crane your neck. For most of us, the neck muscles are poorer judges of distance than are the eye muscles.

Question: Why are pilots usually better at judging heights than are non-pilots?

Perspective Reversals

Look at the "impossible figure" in Fig. 9.19. Do the stairs go up or down, or both ways? What is there about the perspective of this figure that "fools" your eyes?

Now look at Fig. 9.20, the famous Necker Cube. Does it project upward or downward? Actually, it projects either way and, if you stare at it long enough, it will "reverse its perspective" from time to time. However, the frequency with which the Cube changes perspective may depend in part on what sort of person you see yourself as being. Judith and Bruce Bergum at Texas A&M showed the Cube to 128 students and asked them how frequently the Cube "changed directions." The Bergums reported in 1981 that students who had a high reversal rate tended to perceive themselves as being more: (1) creative and original; (2) enthusiastic and optimistic; and (3) excitable and appreciative than did students with a low reversal rate.

Can you learn to make the Cube reverse its perspective at a faster rate? Perhaps so. The Bergums note that architecture students at Texas

A&M tended to have much higher reversal rates on the Cube than did business students. The Bergums believe that architecture students were probably rewarded by their teachers for being able to "change perspectives" rapidly, while students in business administration were probably expected to take a much more stable view of the world. Thus it seems likely that, with training, you can learn to make the Cube "reverse perspective" as frequently or infrequently as you wish.

Question: How else might the Bergums' findings be explained? (Hint: Are students with a "creative, unstable view of the world" more likely to study architecture or business?)

Figure-Ground Relationships

The perception of a single object in visual space is fairly well understood by psychologists. You seldom get the chance to look at just one object, however. For usually your visual world is crowded with all manner of things to look at and admire.

And you typically see all the things in the world as having some kind of *relationship* with each other. The simplest form of this relationship is that of **figure-ground**. Even such a simple percept as that of a fluffy white cloud dancing alone in the clear blue sky is usually that of a *something on a something*, a figure or object on a background.

Whatever you focus on—or pay most attention to—is usually said to be the *figure*, for it appears to stand out in your visual world. Psychologists call anything that stands out from its background a **salient** figure. As the object becomes more complex, however, you may have difficulty telling figure from background.

Look at Fig. 9.21, for instance. Which do you see: (1) two shadow-faces looking at each other; or (2) a fancy wine glass? These two stimulus patterns are so related to each other that either one can be figure *or* ground. If you stare at the illusion for a few seconds, you will find that it is almost impossible to see *both* patterns at once. Rather, first you see one, then the other. And the percepts alternate rather rapidly.

Question: Why do you think you can't see the Necker cube as projecting up and down at the same time?

Expectancy

As we said earlier, you usually see what you *expect* to see. When a novelist writes a mystery story, the writer often gives the reader hints as to

Figure-ground. If you look closely at a book lying on a table, the book is the stimulus figure, the table is the background. Whatever you focus on visually is the figure. Whatever surrounds this object is its ground.

Salient (SAY-lee-ent). A word much beloved by psychologists. From the Latin term meaning "to leap or jump out." Something is salient if it is important or very noticeable. In figure-ground relationships, the figure is almost always salient.

who did what to whom. But often the clues are so stated that the reader gets quite the wrong impression or *expectancy*. For many readers, half the fun of reading a mystery is trying to outguess the author as the story proceeds. The other half comes (once the piece is finished) in going back over the tale trying to discover how the author led the reader astray.

With that thought in mind, look at Fig. 9.22. As you can see, it is a drawing of an *ugly old woman* with her chin buried in a fur coat. Look at it carefully and try to figure out what kind of an old woman she is. Is she happy or sad? And what is this old woman thinking of?

The artist who drew the picture claims she is dreaming of her daughter. And if you look carefully at the picture again, you will see the face of the old woman change into that of the daughter. The mother's nose becomes the chin and the jawline of the younger woman's face. The older woman's left eye becomes the daughter's left ear, and the mother's mouth becomes a necklace around the daughter's neck.

Several experimenters have shown this picture to groups of college students. If the students are told to expect a picture of an *old woman*, most of them discover the mother's face before finding the daughter's. But if the students are told they will see a drawing of a *young woman*, they tend to see the daughter's face easily but often have trouble "finding" the picture of the mother.

Question: Were you "fooled" by the ending to the story that begins this chapter? If so, can you discover the "false clues" that gave you the wrong expectancy?

Visual Grouping

As you look out at the world, your mind makes use of several psychological principles in trying to bring some kind of order to its percepts.

Proximity and Closure

As an example of one such perceptual principle, you tend to *group things together* according to how close they are to each other. In part (1) of Fig.

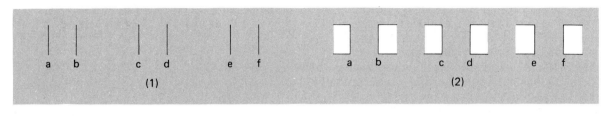

(1)   (2)

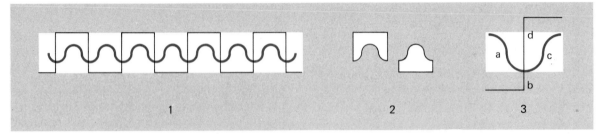

1   2   3

Fig. 9.23. Which lines seem to relate in each of these pairs? **(top)**

Fig. 9.24. The Principle of Continuity. **(middle)**

Fig. 9.25. How do you "group" these circles? **(left)** Why do you group the circles in **A** in Fig. 9.25 differently than you do those in **B**?

Fig. 9.26. What is the shape of these drawings? **(bottom left)**

Fig. 9.27. The same picture frame head-on and at an angle of 45 degrees is no longer visually the same. **(bottom right)**

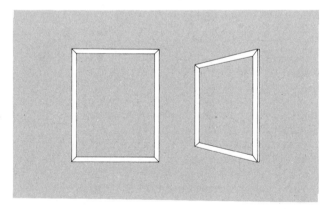

9.23, you probably see three "pairs" of lines. You will group *a* and *b* together because they are close to each other.

In part (2) of the figure, however, things have changed. Now *b* and *c* seem to go together—to form a rectangle of some kind. Indeed, if you stare closely at the *b-c* rectangle, you will see rather faint, *imaginary* lines as your brain attempts to fill in or close up the open figure.

Part (1) illustrates the principle of **proximity**, or physical closeness. Part (2) illustrates the prin-

ciple of **closure**—that is, your brain's tendency to join broken lines together to make a closed figure of some kind.

Continuity and Similarity

A third perceptual principle is that of **continuity** and is illustrated in part 1 of Fig. 9.24. In this illustration you will probably see a wavy line superimposed on a square-cornered line. If we now break up the pattern somewhat differently, as in part 2, you see not two lines but two closed figures joined together. Why do you think this is so? And, if you wish, you may even break the figure up into a different set of components, shown in part 3.

Once you have learned what the parts of the figure can be, you can perceive it many different ways. But, at the beginning, your eye tends to follow the wavy line because it is *continuous*.

A fourth principle of perceptual grouping is that of **similarity**. Fig. 9.25A shows a series of 25 circles arranged in a square. If you fixate on this figure, you will notice that sometimes you "group" the circles together in bunches of fours, or nines, or sixteens. And sometimes you see five horizontal rows of circles, sometimes five vertical columns. In such **ambiguous** situations your brain tests out various percepts, attempting to see which fits the stimulus pattern best.

In Fig. 9.25B, the situation is much less ambiguous. Here, you see a cross formed of Xs, while the empty circles group themselves into squares of four circles each.

When you look out into a cloud from an airplane, your brain is faced with a similar but even more difficult perceptual situation. For a cloud has no firm structure at all—whatever patterns you see in such *ambiguous* situations are those which your brain actually imposes on incoming sensory information.

Gestalt Principles

Early in this century a group of German psychologists began a detailed study of the perceptual principles outlined above. These scientists eventually decided that the brain was so organized that it tended to see **Gestalts**, which is the German word for "good figures" or "good forms."

To these Gestalt psychologists, a circle was a "better" or more natural figure than an ellipse. Hence, the Gestalt psychologists said, you tend to see the object on the left side of Fig. 9.26 as a round half-dollar turned slightly away from you rather than as a coin that has somehow been squashed into an elliptical shape. To make the "form" of the coin a better Gestalt, your brain projects the image into three dimensions.

The Gestalt theorists explained most of **shape constancy** in terms of the brain's *innate desire* to force all percepts into better or more natural shapes. For example, look at Fig. 9.27, which shows what an empty picture frame looks like when you see it: (1) head-on; and (2) rotated away from you about 45 degrees. In the drawing of the rotated frame, the edge of the picture frame nearest you actually is longer than the edge farthest away from you. But chances are that you *still perceive the picture as being square*. In Gestalt

Proximity (procks-IM-it-tee). That which is close. If you live a block from the fire station, you live in the proximity of the fire station. Objects that are proximate (close to each other) tend to be perceived as units.

Closure. "To complete" or "to close." If you glance very quickly at a circle that has a tiny gap in it, you may very well see the circle as being closed, or complete.

Continuity (con-tin-NEW-it-tee). From the word "continue" or "continuous." Things that are connected together in time or space have continuity. Your own stream of consciousness has a certain continuity or connectedness, in that one experience follows the other without a noticeable gap or "blank period of consciousness."

Similarity. Objects that are physically like one another tend to be perceived as units or wholes.

Ambiguous (am-BIG-you-us). Anything that is vague or indefinite. If you ask someone to go on a date, and the person says "maybe yes, maybe no," the person has given you an ambiguous answer.

Gestalts (guess-SHTALTS). A German word that is difficult to translate. Literally, a Gestalt is a "good form" or "good figure." Also means the tendency to see things as "wholes" rather than as jumbled bits and pieces.

Shape constancy. The tendency to "see" an object in its correct shape even when you view it from an odd angle. When you look at a coin tilted away from you, you will most likely see the coin as being round—although its visual image is really that of an ellipse.

Trapezoid (TRAP-ee-zoid). A four-sided figure with two sides that are parallel. In the drawing of the picture frame "tilted away from you" on this page, notice that the left and right sides of the frame are parallel, but the top and bottom sides are not. The picture frame—as viewed from this angle—is a trapezoid.

terms, your brain projects the figure into three dimensions in order to perceive the picture frame in its "best form."

The Ames Distorted Room

Adelbert Ames, a US psychologist who began his professional life as a painter, took advantage of *shape constancy* to produce a number of very amusing illusions which illustrate the Gestalt principles of perception. The best-known of these illusions is Ames's "distorted room," shown in Figs. 9.28A and 9.28B.

When looked at head-on, the "distorted room" appears quite normal—until you see three people standing in the room. And then you know that something is very definitely wrong.

The windows in the room look "square," as the Gestalt theorists would predict. But in fact, the windows are really **trapezoids**, like the window frame on the right in Fig. 9.27. But your brain assumes that windows ought to be rectangular, hence your brain "sees" them as being rectangles.

In order to keep the windows looking like rectangles, your brain must produce *distance distortions* that make one of the men in the room look much larger than his smaller companions.

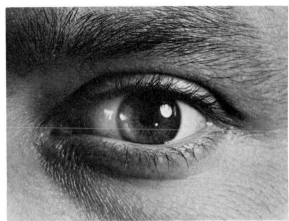

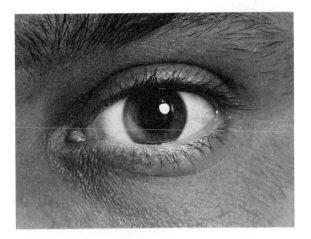

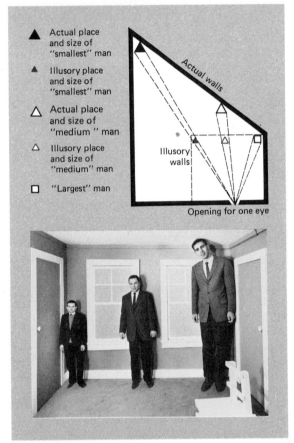

▲ Actual place and size of "smallest" man

▲ Illusory place and size of "smallest" man

△ Actual place and size of "medium " man

△ Illusory place and size of "medium" man

□ "Largest" man

Actual walls

Illusory walls

Opening for one eye

Your pupil usually dilates (opens) as in the photo at the left, when you are looking at something of interest, and closes a bit, as at the right, when you are not. **(top)**

Fig. 9.28A. A diagram of the Ames "distorted room" as seen from the top. **(middle left)**

Fig. 9.28B. The Ames "distorted room" as seen from the front. The man on the left is really the same height as the other two men. **(middle left)**

Fig. 9.29. The teapot pouring liquid and the teacup can be fused visually so that the tea seems to flow into the cup. **(bottom left)**

Given the choice between preserving "good form" (the shape of the windows) or "size constancy" (the size of the men), your cortex typically votes in favor of good form—just as the Gestalt theorists predicted.

Are Gestalts Innate?

The Gestalt position was that all the really important aspects of your visual experience are determined by your genetic inheritance, not by what you have learned. However, most recent experiments suggest that even the tendency to see "good form" is influenced by past experience as well as by present environmental inputs. The fact that S.B. did not perceive the world as the Gestalt psychologists would have predicted is perhaps evidence enough that perception is indeed multi-determined.

Pupil Responses

Perception is an exceptionally complex process. Inputs from your eyes go to your brain and are processed. But once your cortex "perceives" something, it can send commands back to your eyes that affect what you perceive *next*. Now that we have discussed simple eye-to-brain illusions, let's look at some complex perceptions that are created *after* your cortex has made its initial response to a visual input.

One of the major purposes of your visual system is to gird you for *action*. When you walk out of a darkened movie theater, your pupils decrease in size rapidly to keep you from being blinded by the sudden increase in light. Your brain didn't have to *learn* how to make your pupils close under these conditions—the response is *innate*. And at dusk, when the sunlight dims, your pupils automatically open up or *dilate*. The wider your pupils open, the more light comes through and the better you can see and react to objects in your visual environment. Again, this response is determined by your genes, not by previous learning.

Your pupils also dilate when you look closely at some object, even though there is no change in illumination. The harder you stare at the object, the wider your pupils will open. *What* you choose to inspect closely, of course, is determined primarily by your past experience. So *this* type of pupil dilation is influenced by what you have learned about the world.

Psychologist Eckhard Hess made use of this information to test a hunch of his. Hess reasoned that you stare more at something you are really interested in than at something you dislike or are bored by. So he showed pictures of many different objects to the college students he used as subjects in his experiments.

Hess found that women typically had much larger pupil openings when he showed them pictures of babies or nude males than when he showed these women pictures of landscapes or nude females. Men, on the other hand, usually had wider pupils when shown pictures of nude females than when shown photographs of babies, landscapes, or nude males.

Hess's research suggests that you can often discover a person's *real* interests simply by noting when the person becomes "wide-eyed."

Question: Is the tendency for women to become "wide-eyed" when looking at babies or nude males learned, innate, or both? How might you prove your answer is correct?

Visual Suppression

On very rare occasions your cortex is forced to choose between two quite different visual inputs.

Imagine a large black box with two eyeholes in one side. There is a wooden partition inside the box that divides it in half. Thus, when you look through the holes, your left eye sees quite a differ-

Suppresses (sup-PRESS-es). To inhibit or to put down.

Dilemma (die-LEM-mah). A problem that has two or more equally good solutions. To be "caught on the horns of a dilemma" is the same thing as being "caught between the devil and the deep blue sea," in that any solution you pick is equally good—and equally bad.

ent scene than does your right eye. How would your brain handle this odd situation?

Generally speaking, there are two types of responses your brain makes when faced with conflicting visual inputs. Most of the time your brain simply **suppresses** or rejects one of the pictures and *concentrates* on the other. But on rare occasions, your cortex may *combine* the two inputs into one.

If we show a different scene to your left eye than to your right, which scene will your brain suppress? If your vision is clearer in one eye than in the other, your cortex will almost always pick the scene that it sees best. But if both your eyes are in good shape, your brain faces a **dilemma**.

If your left eye is looking at a teacup, while your right eye is looking at a teapot that is pouring liquid from its spout, your brain may actually fuse the two scenes together so that you see a pot pouring tea into a cup (see Fig. 9.29). If one of your eyes sees a baby hanging in mid-air, while the other sees a woman holding out empty arms, your brain may superimpose one scene on the other so that you see the woman holding the child.

But suppose the two pictures are so different that they can't be fused? Then your brain typically concentrates on whichever scene it finds *more interesting*, and suppresses the other scene almost completely. In many cases this suppression takes place so rapidly that you are simply not aware that you are being shown two different objects or photographs.

Research suggests that you are more likely to suppress unpleasant or frightening scenes than you are to block out pleasant or stimulating scenes.

Question: Suppose you need to determine whether a group of workers has unconscious prejudices about female supervisors. How might you use photographs of male and female supervisors—presented in the "black box" apparatus—to help determine the workers' underlying attitudes?

Predicting Is Prejudging

You can "see" at birth, but you must learn to make *sense* of what you see. That is, you must learn to *perceive* the meaning and value of the rich variety of visual inputs that come your way, and you must learn how to respond to what you see. Without either your innate reflexes, or learning how to put them to best use, you simply could not survive.

But learning always carries with it the burden of prejudice. When your brain predicts what will happen to you next, it is *prejudging* the situation more on the basis of its past experience than on the basis of present inputs.

Given the data on how perceptions are built up, we probably should examine our viewpoints constantly to make sure that we aren't being fooled by the thousands of illusions that populate our worlds.

We will examine some of the effects of prejudice on perception in the next chapter.

Summary

1. Much of what you know about the world comes to you through your eyes. The study of **perception**, therefore, often focuses on visual perception.

2. Visual inputs have little meaning until they are **processed** by the lower centers of your brain and by your cortex. This "processing" includes comparing the present input with **neural traces** of your past experiences with similar inputs.

3. Some psychologists believe that perception is the process by which inputs are **registered** on your brain or mind. Other psychologists hold that perception is a matter of building up a **schema** or "mental representation" of objects in your world. The schema then allows you to **recognize** these objects when you see them again. Still other psychologists believe that perception involves not merely registration and recognition of inputs, but knowing how to **respond** to them as well.

4. When you *misperceive* an input, you are likely to experience an **illusion** or faulty percept. When you mistake a "mental image" for an input, you are likely to experience an **hallucination**.

5. Perception is influenced by your **genetic blueprint**, your past experience, and your present environment.

6. Psychologists do not agree on how much of the perceptual process is determined innately, and how much is learned. This is called the **nature-nurture** controversy.

7. Some aspects of visual perception occur so soon after birth that they seem *primarily* determined by your genes. Three-week-old infants will recoil from objects moving toward them; 10-day-old infants mimic the facial expressions of adults around them; and babies prefer to look at pictures of human faces rather than mixed-up drawings of facial features.

8. Three-week-old infants tend to look away from their mothers' faces, but seven-week-old babies are experienced enough to gaze directly at the mother's eyes and mouth.

9. Most (but not all) infants will avoid a **visual cliff**.

10. **Blind children** are slow to develop language and a **self-concept**, but do seem to have an innate appreciation of **physical space**.

11. As you grow up, you learn about **size constancy**. Thus, if you know what an object is, you will probably interepret both its size and its distance correctly.

12. Humans who lose their sight in childhood but regain it as adults often have severe problems adjusting. They must learn to recognize visually objects that they had only touched or heard about. They do not perceive visual illusions in the same way that normally sighted humans do.

13. Past experience seems to influence a variety of visual illusions. The **apparent size** of an object tells you its distance. **Linear perspective**, **aerial perspective**, **convergence**, and **light and shadow** also give you clues which allow your brain to perceive the world in **three dimensions**, or depth.

14. Some illusions involve **perspective reversals**. Research suggests that students who have a high **reversal rate** perceive themselves as being more creative, enthusiastic, and excitable than do students with low reversal rates.

15. **Figure-ground** relationships have a strong influence on perception. You tend to see **salient** objects as "figure" rather than as "background."

16. **Gestalt** principles of perception include the following:
    a. You tend to see incomplete or "open" figures as being closed because closed figures make better Gestalts.
    b. You tend to force percepts into the best possible visual forms (**shape constancy**).

17. **Expectancy** has a strong influence on perception. For the most part, you see what you expect to see.

18. You tend to group things together perceptually according to the principles of **proximity, closure, continuity**, and **similarity**.

19. Your **pupil size** is primarily determined by visual reflexes that you had when you were born. However, your pupils open wider when you look at something interesting than when you look at something boring.

20. When your two eyes are shown different scenes, your mind may **suppress** one of the scenes, or it may **fuse** the two together to make a "Gestalt." You are more likely to suppress threatening scenes than pleasant ones.

21. Your visual mechanisms seem designed to help you **predict and control future inputs**.

(Continued from page 208.)

The last of the male passengers came out of the little airport waiting room sweating profusely and shaking his head. "Bunch of bloody nonsense," the man muttered to himself as he passed by the elegant figure of the Laforan Minister of Science and Technology.

Freddie glumly watched the man depart. They had held the passengers of the special Paris jet in a quarantine waiting room, letting them pass one by one through the office where Professor Mann had inspected their eyes. Mann had agreed to signal Freddie if the tests detected the Snake, but no signal had come.

And now the waiting room was empty, save for a number of attractive but overdressed young women and one rather forlorn-looking matron cradling a baby in her arms. Freddie was confident that the pretty women were girl friends of the munitions dealers. The matron was probably a wife of one of the dealers—although why a man would bring a wife and child to Lafora on a business trip, Freddie wasn't sure.

Freddie sighed. It seemed certain that Dr. Mann's tests had failed him—and failed the Republic of Lafora as well. The former fault he could tolerate. The latter came close to treason, and he mentioned this point to the US Professor.

"What have you done, and why didn't it work?" Freddie demanded.

Mann looked annoyed at the Minister's bluntness. "First I showed a series of drawings to each man and measured the size of his pupils while he was watching. One of the drawings was of a snake. I had thought that our friend the assassin would show a larger pupil size to this drawing than to any other. Three of the men did so, but they failed the second test."

"Which was . . . ?"

"A suppression test. I have a variety of drawings—a pile of money, guns, airplanes, a picture of your President, a number of animals, and a snake striking at something with dripping fangs. I had the men look into my little black box that shows one drawing to the person's left eye, another to the right eye. And then I simply asked them to report what they saw. I figured most of the men would suppress the image of the snake, since most people are afraid of snakes."

Freddie snorted inelegantly. "But wouldn't the Snake see through your little tricks?"

"Perhaps, although I figured that, at the very least, he'd hesitate or be a little confused. But every man on the plane suppressed the picture of the snake without a moment's hesitation."

"And so your oh-so-scientific tests have failed," Freddie said glumly.

"No, Freddie, we're not through yet. There are still people in the waiting room."

Freddie looked around. "Just women and children, my dear Professor. We might as well let them go."

"You'll do nothing of the kind. Send them along for the eye checks, or their boy friends are going to be rather suspicious, don't you think?"

Freddie paused to consider the matter. As he did so, the matron approached them hesitantly and spoke to Freddie. "Excuse me, sir, my little boy is not feeling well. I'd like to get some warm milk for him and change his diaper. I wonder if you would allow us to go on through to the ladies' room?"

Before Freddie could respond, Professor Mann said loudly, "Right after you have your eyes checked, Madam. Part of the health inspection, you know. Now if you'll just look into this black box and tell me what you see . . ."

"Of course," the matron said, "if you'll promise to hurry."

The woman turned to Freddie and handed him the infant, which immediately set up a lusty bawling. Freddie's nose crinkled at the moist little bundle he had been handed, and he held the child clumsily and with obvious distaste. "Hurry it up, will you?" he said loudly to the Professor.

"Here's the first picture. What do you see?"

The matron leaned back a bit. "It's a gun of some kind," she said. "I don't approve of guns, you know."

"And how about this second picture?"

The matron glanced into the eyeholes in the black box, then leaned forward a bit. "Why, it's a snake—a big, black, ugly snake."

Freddie glanced up immediately. The Professor smiled at him with wide-open eyes.

"And now we'll try another test entirely. When I say 'Now,' I want you to look into the apparatus and tell me as quickly as you can what you see. All right?"

"Certainly," said the matron demurely, as Professor Mann adjusted the slides inside the box.

"Now."

The woman leaned forward to look. She paused for several seconds, then responded. "That's odd, very odd indeed. I seem to see two things at once. First I see that snake again, and then I see a picture of the Laforan President, and then . . . then I see the snake biting the President. Now why would I see something like that?"

Freddie knew perfectly well why. He moved the infant to one arm and signaled vigorously with the other. Two large guards swooped down on them at once.

"Arrest this woman and search her baggage carefully," he told the guards.

General Chambro hurried up to them, a worried look on his big, round face. "Freddie, you've gone mad! This woman can't be the Snake!"

"How can you be sure, if you don't know what the Snake looks like?" the Professor asked, as the guards removed the matron from the scene.

"Yes, my dear General," Freddie said, a smile on his face. "I'll bet you a month's pay that Professor Mann has snared the Snake for us. The perceptual tests are positive."

"Perceptual tests be damned," said the General loudly. "Killing is a man's business, and everybody knows that the Snake is a man . . ."

"And that's why nobody ever caught her," replied Professor Mann. "She gave you a beautiful illusion to fool yourselves with. Down through history the snake has always been a symbol of masculine sexual power and ruthlessness. Take the primitive tribe that I had hoped to visit, for instance. The chief warrior has a snake carved on the staff he carries. And if you look closely at those gold buttons that cover your uniform, General, you'll find the snake symbol on them all."

The General inspected his buttons, then frowned.

Professor Mann continued. "But of course the Snake did give you one clue to her identity—isn't poison a woman's weapon? Or was it just your minds she was attempting to poison?"

Freddie grinned, the General sputtered in protest, and the Professor added a footnote. "I'll offer one more suggestion. Look through those baby things very closely. What more unlikely place to carry snake venom than in a child's rattle?"

A few moments later the guards reported that they had found a tiny hypodermic needle and a small bottle of white liquid inside the bottle of milk that the woman carried.

General Chambro was beside himself with happiness. He embraced Professor Mann in a huge bear hug, then hurried off to tend to military matters.

"He smells a promotion, I'm sure," said Freddie caustically.

"Helping catch the Snake won't hurt your image any either, now will it, Freddie?"

"My dear Professor Mann, you speak with a forked tongue. But you are right, of course. The President will be very pleased . . ."

"And as for me?"

Freddie frowned. "Whatever do you mean?"

"What about those 'murderous savages' that I want to visit? Are you still afraid that they might do me in? Well, if I can catch a snake for you, can't I manage to handle a few frightened primitives?"

"Well, my dear friend . . ."

The Professor interrupted. "You're still showing your prejudices, Freddie. You get very, very angry at all the whites in this world who judge a man by his skin color rather than by his true capabilities. Yet your view of women is just as biased and as distorted as their view of skin color. Isn't it about time you saw through some of your own illusions?"

Freddie smiled. "You psychologists! Ah well, I suppose that I might just mention to the President what your part in this afternoon's activities was. And our President is a very generous man indeed."

Freddie looked around and saw a couple of porters lounging near one of the doors.

"Here, you men! Get this equipment packed up again, then take it outside and put it back on the truck. Professor Mann will need it in the back country."

The American smiled softly. "Thanks, Freddie. I do appreciate your changing your mind. And now, how about that drink you promised me two hours ago?"

They walked off, arm in arm, headed for the cocktail lounge. The porters began to load up the heavy crates with the perceptual apparatus. The boxes were covered with address labels. On the largest label of all, written in scrawling print, was:

> Dr. Mary Ellen Mann
> Department of Psychology
> University of the Mid-West
> USA

Recommended Readings

Coren, Stanley, and Joan S. Girgus. *Seeing Is Deceiving: The Psychology of Visual Illusions* (Hillsdale, N.J.: Erlbaum, 1978).

Fraiberg, Selma. *Insights from the Blind: Comparative Studies of Blind and Sighted Infants* (New York: Basic Books, 1977).

Gregory, Richard L. *Eye and Brain: The Psychology of Seeing*, 3rd ed. (New York: World University Library, 1977).

Haber, Ralph Norman, and Maurice Hershenson. *The Psychology of Visual Perception* (New York: Holt, Rinehart and Winston, 1973).

Haith, Marshall M. *Rules That Babies Look By: The Organization of Newborn Visual Activity* (Hillsdale, N.J.: Erlbaum, 1980).

Kaniza, G. *Organization in Vision: Essays on Gestalt Perception* (New York: Praeger, 1979).

Sommer, Robert. *The Mind's Eye: Imagery in Everyday Life* (New York: Delacorte, 1978).

Thresholds, ESP, and Subliminal Perception

10

Did You Know That . . .

Some people once feared advertisers could control people's minds by flashing "hidden messages" on movie screens?

Many sensory messages get through to the lower centers of your brain and affect your behavior without your being conscious of what these stimuli are?

Some people repress awareness of emotional, sexual, or threatening stimuli, while others actively seek out such sensory inputs?

A recent survey suggests that more people in the US believe in ESP than in God?

English teachers are much more likely to believe in mental telepathy than are psychologists?

Belief in ESP tends to increase during crises and disasters, but decreases when times are good?

Most experiments supposedly demonstrating that ESP exists either have a "fatal experimental flaw" or have data that were "fudged" by the experimenter?

"It's All in Your Mind"

"Al, Baby, you've simply got to come see this horse!" Vince said in an excited tone of voice. "It's the most super-incredible, absolutely impossible animal that ever lived!"

"Now, Vince, calm down," Al said.

"No, seriously, Al," Vince continued as excited as before. "It's the find of the century! It's the Houdini of Horses, the Einstein of Equines. And I found it at a farm just outside of town!"

Al shook his head in mock dismay. "Listen, Vince, sit down, relax, and try to get a grip on yourself. I'm sure this horse that you've discovered is an amazing animal, but . . ."

"But nothing!" Vince said loudly. "This is positively the most spectacular scientific discovery of the century, and you want me to relax! All we've got to do is to come up with a thousand bucks . . ."

Al groaned loudly. "Not another quick and dirty way to fame and fortune, Vince."

Paying no attention to his college roommate, Vince looked around the apartment. "Now, we can sell my stereo for maybe 600 bucks. And we ought to be able to get a couple of hundred for your electric typewriter . . ."

"*My* typewriter! You keep your hands off my typewriter."

"That's 800 bucks already. I hate to hock the furniture, but that sofa . . ."

"*My* sofa . . ."

"That sofa ought to bring in 50 bucks at least from the Salvation Army. Which gives us just 150 bucks more to scrape up."

"Whoa, there, old buddy," Al said loudly. "Before you go selling off everything we own, sit down and talk to me in very simple terms. Begin at the beginning, and don't leave out a single detail."

A puzzled look spread over Vince's face. "Beginning? What do you mean?"

Al shook his head. "Well, I gather you've discovered some type of horse . . ."

"Sure, Al. Harry the high-IQ Horse. He belongs to this farmer named Bill Nagler— at least until we can buy him."

"And how did you discover this amazing animal?" Al asked.

Vince grinned. "Well, I was touring the back country on my snowmobile this afternoon. And I saw a sign outside this farmhouse that said, 'Harry, the Talking Horse. Let Him Answer Your Questions for $5.'"

"So you coughed up the cash . . ."

"Yeah, man. I knocked on the door of the farmhouse, and this big, ole weather-beaten guy answered. Said his name was Nagler, and that he bought a young stallion at the State Fair last summer. Used the horse around the farm, of course, and got the impression that the beast was pretty smart. Then a couple of weeks ago, he discovered that the damned animal could count."

"Count?" Al asked in a wary tone of voice?

"Yeah," Vince said. "Nagler was fussing at his son for being so stupid. Told the boy he was so dumb he couldn't add two and two. And Harry the Horse just lifted up his front paw . . ."

"Hoof, you mean." Al said.

"Hoof, schmoof, what difference does it make? Anyhow, Harry the Horse lifted up his hoof and tapped on the ground four times." Vince looked at Al, who seemed unimpressed. "Two plus two equals four, Al."

Al stared at Vince skeptically. "I know that, Vince. What I don't know is that the horse was actually 'counting.'"

"Oh, that was just the beginning. But Nagler was so impressed that he started asking Harry the Horse more questions. Like, 'What is the square root of 36?' And damned if the animal didn't tap its hoof 6 times."

"Most impressive, I'm sure," Al said, his voice heavy with sarcasm.

"It certainly was," Vince continued. "So then Nagler started experimenting. He painted a big board with the alphabet, a calendar, and the numbers from 1 to 100 on it. He stuck this board at an angle against the barn wall so that Harry could point at it with his paw, er, hoof. Then he asked Harry what day it was, and Harry pointed to Wednesday, then to the number 19, and then to the month of November."

"And sure enough, it was Wednesday the 19th of November."

"Right on, man. And when Nagler asked Harry who was president of the United States . . ."

"The horse spelled out R-E-A-G-A-N."

Vince nodded enthusiastically. "You got it, man. Incredible!"

"Did you actually *see* Harry perform, or did this Nagler guy just tell you what Harry had done when you weren't around?"

Vince looked annoyed. "What kind of nerd do you think I am? Of course I saw Harry perform. I asked him what the square root of 49 was . . ."

"And he pointed to 7, I suppose?"

"Sure. And he spelled Reagan's name for me. And my own name, too! That horse knew who I was, Al! Do you think he could read my mind?"

"If he could read your mind, Vince, I'm sure the horse would have spelled out Debbie's name, or Thelma's, or the name of any of the other women you're chasing after when you're not chasing fantasies instead."

"Al, baby, this horse is no fantasy. He's for real, a genuine genius. You've got to come see this animal for yourself. Then you'll agree with me that we've got to buy the beast right away, while he's still for sale cheap."

Al laughed. "Vince, you never learn, do you. Last month, you were into tanking. Going to hock your hi-fi to buy a womb tank and rent it out during exam week. The month before, it was acupuncture. There was this oriental gentleman who was going to sell you some needles and show you how to make a fortune sticking pins in people. For a price, of course. You're a sucker for a con game, Vince, and you know it."

Vince smiled sheepishly. "I know I've gone off on tangents in the past, Al. But this is for real. Just hop in the Jeep with me right now, and let's drive out to Nagler's place. The roads are snowy, but they aren't that bad. And if you can prove to me that Harry the Horse is a fake, I promise to do all the cooking *and* wash the dishes for the rest of the semester."

"You're on," said Al. "And if you get dishpan hands, you can always tell people you got them from horsing around."

Half an hour later, the two students pulled up in front of Nagler's farm. After Vince had introduced Al to Mr. Nagler, and given the man 10 dollars, the farmer escorted them to the barn and began to put Harry the Horse through his paces. The animal spelled out the president's name, and the name of the governor of the state. He got Al's first name without difficulty, but somehow couldn't dredge up his last name until Vince pointed out the first letter and began coaxing the horse. Then he slowly spelled Al's last name too. Nagler rewarded the animal by giving it a lump of sugar.

"Pretty impressive, eh?" Vince said.

"Downright amazing, in its own way," Al replied in an odd tone of voice.

"Ask him something else, something hard," Vince said enthusiastically.

Al thought for a minute. Then a very big smile crept across his face. "Of course!" he said loudly. "Now I remember!"

"Remember what?" said Vince.

"The question I have to ask," Al said slyly.

"So, ask it."

Al nodded. "Okay, Harry. Tell me this. What equation did Einstein make famous?"

The heavy-set farmer frowned. "Who is this person 'Eye-son-stine?'"

"He was a famous physicist," Vince replied. "Hey, Al, baby, that's a pretty rough question to ask a dumb horse. I don't even know the answer myself."

"Let the beast try to answer anyhow," Al insisted.

The farmer stroked the horse's neck and pointed his finger at the "answer board" with the alphabet and numbers on it. The horse raised its right front hoof, tentatively pointed toward the board, and then paused, hoof in the air. After a few seconds, the animal snorted and put its hoof back on the barn floor.

"I think you've stumped the beast," Vince said, frowning.

Al smiled happily. "No, I think I've got him Stumpfed."

(Continued on page 248.)

Subliminal Advertising

In 1956, a public-relations executive named James Vicary held a press conference that set New York City on its ear. At that conference, Vicary announced to the press that he had discovered a new advertising technique that (so he claimed) would revolutionize America's buying habits. According to Vicary, the technique was so powerful that almost no one would be able to resist it. And it was so subtle that most Americans would never realize that their behaviors had been affected.

What Vicary did was to project "secret messages" on the screen of a movie house in Fort Dix, New Jersey. The messages themselves said "Drink Coke," and "Eat Popcorn." These hidden advertisements were flashed on the movie screen (by means of a slide projector) while the audience was watching a feature film. The "secret messages" were **super-imposed** on top of the movie at such rapid speeds—less than 1/100th of a second—that the audience wasn't *consciously aware* that they were being exposed to hidden advertisements.

According to Vicary, sales of both Coca-Cola and popcorn rose dramatically. Vicary explained his results by claiming that the "secret ads" stimulated the *unconscious* portions of the mind. Thus, he said, people in the audience purchased Coca-Cola and popcorn because their conscious minds couldn't resist the demands their unconscious minds made.

Vicary called his technique **subliminal advertising**. Within a few days after the 1956 press conference, the newspapers and magazines were full of anguished articles denouncing Vicary for having thrust a new and terrible method of "mind control" upon an unwilling world.

Vicary's Claims versus the Awful Truth

In point of fact, *subliminal advertising* was neither new nor an effective way of pushing people around without their knowledge. As we will see, the technique had been tried many times earlier—and had been abandoned because, as an *advertising*

Super-imposed. "Super" means above, or over. Vicary flashed his ads on the same movie screen that was showing a feature movie; thus his ads were "super-imposed" on top of the movie.

Subliminal advertising (sub-LIMM-in-al). "Sub" means below, while "limen" (LIME-en) means threshold. Subliminal ads are those shown to you at a speed so fast that you are not consciously aware of them because they are "below your perceptual threshold" or perceptual limen.

Charlatans (SHAR-lah-tans). From an old Italian word meaning "someone who makes pretense to knowledge or power the person doesn't really possess." There are presently several companies in the US who market devices that whisper such messages as "Don't Shoplift" and "Work Harder," which are used in some stores and businesses. The companies claim installing the device reduces shoplifting and increases productivity, but refuse to offer scientific proof that it is the *whispered message* that causes the behavioral change. Can you think of other reasons why installing such a device might temporarily increase productivity or decrease shoplifting?

technique, it simply didn't work very well. Indeed, after the press conference, many scientists tried to repeat Vicary's study in other movie houses—but failed to get the same results.

To tell the awful truth, there has never been a well-controlled, *scientific* study demonstrating that "hidden advertisements" can affect people's buying behaviors in real-life settings. However, "negative results" seldom get splashed about on the front page of newspapers, nor highlighted on prime time television. And so subliminal advertising still crops up in horror movies (such as "Agency"). As Eric Lander noted in *Omni* in 1981, the technique is presently marketed by several **charlatans** who claim that it can reduce shoplifting and increase productivity but who cannot offer scientific proof to back up their claims.

To understand what subliminal advertising is all about, where the idea came from, and why it doesn't work very well, you will first need to discover what *thresholds* are all about.

Question: James Vicary did not use "control groups" in his study of subliminal advertising, nor did he test the effects of using different feature films. What kinds of control groups do you think he should have used in order to be sure that it was the "hidden messages" that caused the increase in sales? (Hint: Would the audience have bought more Coke even without the hidden ads *had the feature movie been "Lost in the Desert" than if it had been "Lost in the Arctic"?*)

Thresholds

What does the word "threshold" mean? If you find yourself on the threshold of a dream, you are still awake—but you are just on the *verge* of entering

"Is THIS A RERUN, OR DÉJÀ VU?"

or obtaining your dream. If you stand on the threshold of a room, you are obviously in the doorway—neither entirely *in* the room nor all the way *out* of it. The threshold, then, is a *halfway point* between two places or states of being.

But a threshold is also a *barrier* of sorts that you have to cross in order to get from one place or state into another. Some thresholds are low and hence easy to cross over, while others are higher and thus difficult to negotiate.

A *sensory input* from the outside world must pass over at least two neural thresholds before you become conscious of the stimulus—and must negotiate yet a third neural threshold before you respond to the input. Let's examine these three thresholds in detail.

1. The **physiological threshold**. A stimulus must possess enough *physical energy* to excite your receptor neurons. If the stimulus is strong enough, it will cause your receptors to fire and hence send a message to the lower centers of your brain. But if the stimulus is not strong enough, your receptors will fail to respond, and the message will never be sent. A whisper may be far too weak too excite the hair cells in your cochlea, but a shout will almost always get through at least to the lower parts of your brain.
2. The **perceptual threshold**. The mere fact that a stimulus is physically strong enough to reach the lower centers of your brain doesn't mean you will become conscious of the input. For unless the message is *psychologically important* to you, your reticular activating system may block it out. At any given moment, thousands of stimulus inputs reach the lower centers of your brain. If you had to pay conscious attention to them all, you'd never get anything done. Generally speaking, then, only meaningful stimuli are strong enough to attract your attention and hence cross your *perceptual threshold* into conscious awareness.
3. The **behavioral threshold**. Just because you are aware of an input doesn't mean that you will respond to it in any measurable way. If a stranger shouted a dirty word at you, you might choose to ignore it. If the same stranger shouted "Help," you might decide to take action.

These three thresholds are so inter-related, you may have trouble telling where one begins and the other leaves off. For instance, how cold does a room have to be in winter before you *consciously perceive* the chill? And how much colder does it have to get before you *take action* by putting on a coat or turning up the heat? How long must you go without food before you *consciously realize* that you are hungry? And once you take action, how much food must you eat before you notice that you're "stuffed" and hence stop eating?

Perhaps if you learn how physiological, perceptual, and behavioral thresholds are actually *measured*, you will better understand how to tell them apart.

Question: *What relationship do you see between these three thresholds and the three theories of perception (registration, recognition, and response) mentioned in the last chapter?*

Behavioral Thresholds

Probably the most famous behavioral threshold in history is described in the old phrase, "the straw that broke the camel's back."

Suppose that you decided to run a scientific test to see if, indeed, adding one more straw to a camel's maximum load would "break its back." What might happen? To begin with, you'd probably learn almost immediately that these old stories are mostly exaggerations. Any reasonably intelligent camel you used as a subject would simply lie down, roll over, and refuse to get up long before the weight you put on its back was sufficient to do it any real harm. So you'd probably have to settle for trying to discover how many straws it took to make the animal "lie down and roll over." Therefore, you'd start piling on the hay to see what would happen.

Individual straws don't weigh very much, so you could load thousands of them on the animal's back before it collapsed. Then—at least according to the saying—there would come a critical point in your experiment. Suppose you had put 999,999 straws on the camel and it was still standing upright. Now you add one additional wisp of hay, and down the beast would go.

The camel's *behavioral threshold* would obviously be 999,999 straws.

Question: *There are many types of behavioral thresholds. For instance, we noted in Chapter 4 that a rat confined in a small box will attack anything handy if it is shocked or sufficiently frustrated. What kind of experiment could you set up to determine the "frustration-aggression" threshold in rats? Could you determine the same sort of behavioral threshold for people—or for nations?*

Perceptual Thresholds

Next, suppose you wanted to determine what would be the smallest amount of light you could see under the best of conditions. At first blush, it

Thresholds, ESP, and Subliminal Perception

might seem that you would be measuring your *physiological threshold* for vision, but that wouldn't be the case. For "seeing" implies "conscious awareness." And if you are *conscious* of seeing the light, then you would be working with a perceptual threshold. We will discuss physiological thresholds in just a moment. Right now, let's see how you could test your own perceptual threshold for a very weak visual stimulus.

One way would be to get a light bulb whose brightness you could increase or decrease merely by turning a knob of some kind. Then you could sit in a dark room for 30 minutes (to give your eyes a chance to adapt). Next you might start turning up the intensity of the bulb until you first became aware that the light was on.

The point at which you could just make out (consciously) that the bulb was shining faintly would be one measure of your *visual perceptual threshold*. Turn the light down a little, and you can't see it. Turn the knob up a bit and you have no trouble seeing the light all the time.

But there would be a point—a halfway point—between seeing and not seeing, which you could determine by using the bulb-knob apparatus. This halfway point is your perceptual threshold (at least at the moment you tested it).

By definition, then, the visual perceptual threshold is that intensity of stimulus—that brightness of a light—that you *can* consciously see half the time and that you *can't* see half the time at the moment of testing.

Question: *How would you go about testing your auditory threshold, or your threshold for the taste of salt?*

Two Important Points

A couple of points about thresholds will probably occur to you at once. The first point is that the way we define them is quite **arbitrary**. There's no reason why we couldn't have decided that the perceptual threshold is that stimulus strength which you could consciously perceive 25 percent of the time, or 75 percent of the time, or even 38.729 percent of the time. However, European scientists in the 1800's picked the 50 percent point and, for the most part, that definition has stuck.

The second point about thresholds that might set you wondering has to do with their *stability*. Let's go back to the camel. Suppose you decided to test the animal just after it had run a long race across the desert, and the beast was very tired. Under these conditions the camel might collapse if you piled no more than 800,000 straws on its back. However, suppose you tried

Physiological threshold (FIZZ-ee-oh-LODGE-eye-cal). "Physiological" means having to do with the nervous system, or with neural firing. If a stimulus is strong enough to excite your receptor organs and make them fire, it has crossed your physiological or biological limen.

Perceptual threshold. If an input message is strong or important enough to break through to conscious awareness, it has crossed your perceptual threshold.

Behavioral threshold. If you respond to an input you are conscious of, the stimulus has crossed your behavioral threshold.

Arbitrary (AR-bih-trary). Any decision that you make purely by whim or by personal preference is an arbitrary decision. To arbitrate is to settle a dispute, or to make a decision about something.

Signal detection theory. Your nervous system is "noisy," which is to say that there is a lot going on at any given time inside your brain that can affect what you perceive and how you respond. If you are told that a very weak stimulus input may occur during the next minute, you may "detect" it even if it doesn't occur. In fact, you are really responding to "noise" in your nervous system because of your *expectancy* that a signal would occur, and thus what you reported was a "false alarm" and not a real "input." "Signal detection theory" is a mathematical way of predicting the likelihood that a given response is a "false alarm" or a true stimulus input.

your experiment with the animal after it had rested for a couple of weeks. Then it might be able to tolerate 1,100,000 straws with no great strain.

Thresholds differ. They differ from person to person, from day to day, even from moment to moment. Indeed, thresholds vary so much that some psychologists prefer to use what is called **signal detection theory** instead. However, the concept of the threshold still has great usefulness in most areas of psychology. So, to continue with the camel, if you counted up the number of times the animal's behavioral threshold was *exactly* 999,999 straws, the number of times it was 999,998, and so on, you could put the figures on a graph like the one in Fig. 10.1.

By looking at the curve, you can tell that most of the time the camel's "fall down" threshold was very close to 999,999 straws. Once you knew this fact, you could begin working out ways to keep the animal from collapsing. Making sure the camel was in good health would be one way. Keeping its load well below 900,000 straws would be another.

Question: *If someone you know gets angry very easily, how might you use the threshold concept to help reduce the number of temper tantrums the person throws?*

The Limen

Perceptual thresholds are much like behavioral thresholds—the *weaker* the stimulus with which you are presented, the *lower* the probability that you will perceive the input on any given test trial.

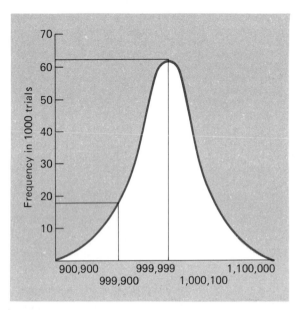

Some habits, such as riding a bicycle in traffic, become so habitual you can "respond without awareness."

Fig. 10.1. "The number of straws it takes to break a camel's back" from one day to the next. The number of times that it took exactly 999,999 straws is called the **frequency** with which that event occurred (out of 1000 trials). The threshold was 999,999 some 62 times, while it was 999,900 some 18 times. **(top left)**

Fig. 10.2. The two-point threshold experiment using electric stimulation on the skin of a subject's back. **(bottom left)**

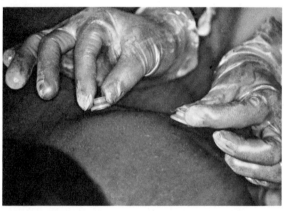

Suppose, while you are wearing earphones, we present you with a musical tone. This tone is so soft that, out of 100 trials, you are consciously aware of the tone only *once*. What can we say about this auditory input?

If the tone were *right at* your auditory threshold, you would be aware of it half the time, or 50 times out of 100. A tone that you hear only once in 100 trials, therefore, is obviously far *below* your usual threshold.

The Latin word for threshold is **limen**. Thus, speaking technically, the very weak tone is "below your perceptual *limen*," or **subliminal**.

A subliminal stimulus is one so weak that you would be conscious of it much less than 50 percent of the time. But it still would be strong enough so that *occasionally* it might break through to consciousness.

As you will soon learn, the word "subliminal" almost always refers to a stimulus that is *below* your perceptual threshold but *above* your physiological threshold. For instance, even the faintest of stimuli may contain enough physical energy to excite the rods and cones in your retinas and hence cross the *physiological* limen. But it takes a great deal more energy for a stimulus to cross your conscious *perceptual* threshold.

Physiological Threshold

More than a century ago a European scientist named Suslowa noticed something rather odd when he was attempting to determine the **two-point threshold** of his experimental subjects (see Fig. 10.2). Since Suslowa's work is important to understanding both the physiological threshold and subliminal perception, let's discuss this research in some detail.

Suslowa had two pointed pieces of metal through which he could pass a weak but mildly painful electrical current. He would touch these points, or electrodes, to the skin of a blindfolded male subject and turn on the current. Suslowa then asked the subject whether he could feel *both* the points separately, or whether they were so close together that the mild stimulation seemed to come from a *single spot* on the subject's skin.

Quite frankly, this kind of research is very boring for most subjects. And sometimes, just to keep the subject alert, Suslowa would touch the man with but *one* of the electrodes. Thus, sometimes Suslowa touched two points to the man's skin, sometimes just one. On any given trial it was the subject's task to perceive whether he had been stimulated with "one point" or with "two."

Suslowa was interested in mapping out skin sensitivity, and was one of the first scientists to do so. But what we remember him most for was the following discovery: On those trials when his subjects insisted that they couldn't *consciously* tell whether it was one point or two, his subjects "guessed" the right answer *far more often* than chance would allow.

To appreciate how intriguing this discovery was, perhaps we should restate what Suslowa did. When he gave his subjects a **supra-liminal** stimulus—that is, when the two points were far enough apart—they were conscious of experiencing two points. And they reported this fact willingly. But when the two points were very close together, the stimulus was *subliminal* because the subjects couldn't consciously tell if Suslowa had used one point or two. However, when Suslowa forced the subjects to *guess*, they were surprisingly accurate.

The subjects themselves could not account for the fact that they were responding with such accuracy to a subliminal stimulus. But we now know that this stimulus was *above* the physiological threshold, but *below* the perceptual threshold. And, indeed, that is the definition of any subliminal stimulus—an input that is strong enough to reach the lower (unconscious) centers of your brain, but not strong enough to break through to conscious awareness *even when you try your best to perceive it*.

Responding without Awareness

How is it that you can guess accurately about something that you can't really perceive? At first, psychologists thought that it was a matter of *attention* (see Chapter 8). Your behavior is often influenced by environmental events that you pay little or no conscious attention to. For example, have you ever been driving a car along a highway while you were thinking about something important? And then you suddenly "woke up" to the fact that you had been paying no attention at all to the car? Yet somehow you managed to stay on the road, slow down at the right moments, and speed up when necessary. How is it that you didn't have an accident?

Limen (LIME-en). The Latin word for threshold.

Subliminal. Below the *perceptual* limen, but above the *physiological* limen.

Two-point threshold. Also called the "two-point limen." The distance apart that two points must be (when touching your skin) so that you can perceive them as being "two" instead of "one" exactly 50 percent of the time.

Supra-liminal (SUPP-rah-limm-in-al). Above the threshold. Our words "supreme" and "super" come from the same Latin word as does "supra."

Reflexive (re-FLEX-ive). A response that is automatic and often unconscious. May be learned or unlearned.

Responding without awareness. A set of rather automatic responses that you engage in while thinking about something else. The stimuli you respond to (without being conscious of what they are) are all supra-liminal. That is, you **could** become aware of them if something called your attention to them.

After you have been driving for a while, most of the motor skills necessary to keep the car on the road become automatic. That is, the responses that your hands make on the steering wheel and your feet make on the pedals are so *overlearned* that they become **reflexive**.

The stimuli that you respond to when you are driving are almost always *supraliminal*. But you have made these responses so often that you can perform them rather well unconsciously. We call this ability **responding without awareness**, and it is a very common experience for most of us.

"Responding without awareness" always involves a reflexive response to stimuli that are *above both your sensory and your perceptual thresholds*. That is, you *could* perceive the stimulus inputs you are responding to if your attention were called to them.

Subliminal Perception

Subliminal perception is quite different from responding without awareness. For subliminal perception involves reacting to stimuli that are *above* your physiological thresholds but *below* your perceptual thresholds. In fact, these stimuli are so weak that even if your brain worked overtime trying to detect them, it simply couldn't do the job.

How, then, does subliminal perception work?

The answer is—not very well. The neurological road from your receptors to your cortex contains many gates and barriers. Each time a sensory input must cross a synapse, there is a chance for very weak stimuli to be gated out or rejected. And, as you might imagine, there are some inputs strong enough to get through to the very lowest centers of your brain—but no higher. You are

Elliott McGinnies

never conscious of them, but they can affect your behavior in very slight ways.

For instance, in Chapter 7 we mentioned that your eye makes many reflexive movements. When a point of light suddenly appears at the edge of your visual field, you automatically turn your eyes toward the light. This reflexive movement is controlled by the lower visual centers of your brain. If the pinpoint of light is bright enough, you will *consciously* see it after you look in its direction.

But suppose the light stimulus is just strong enough to reach the lower centers and set off the reflexive movement, yet is not strong enough to reach your cortex. Now you would *respond* to the light, but you couldn't *see* it no matter how hard you tried. So if someone asked you if you *saw* anything, you would truthfully say "no." However, you would be *consciously aware* that your eyes had moved (although you wouldn't know why). Thus, if someone asked you to *guess* whether a light had been there or not, the fact that you knew your eyes had moved might lead you to say "yes."

So there are times when you can respond correctly to stimuli that are far too weak or *subliminal* for you to perceive consciously. You might keep this point in mind as we continue our discussion of subliminal perception.

Perceptual Defense and Perceptual Vigilance

One of the most interesting sets of studies on subliminal perception were the "dirty word" experiments performed in the 1950's and 1960's by Elliott McGinnies and several other US psychologists.

McGinnies began by determining the *perceptual threshold* for ordinary words. He did this by showing students words such as "table" and "chair" at faster and faster speeds. With each sub-

ject (and for each word) McGinnies was able to calculate an exposure time so rapid that the subject would perceive the word *exactly 50 percent of the time* (and not perceive it 50 percent of the time).

For a word such as "whale," this perceptual threshold might be about 100 **milliseconds**. For an emotionally laden word such as "whore," however, the threshold was typically much *higher*— 200 milliseconds or more.

McGinnies believed that his subjects were *unconsciously defending* against perceiving such "disturbing" words as "whore." He called this effect **perceptual defense**.

Many psychologists objected to McGinnies' studies, claiming that he had not *controlled* for all the outside influences he ought to have taken into account. For instance, we know that the more common a word is, the *lower* its perceptual threshold will be. You can recognize the word "cat" in a much shorter time than you can recognize the word **concatenation**. In the 1950's, words such as "whore" seldom appeared in print, so the students might well have been relatively unfamiliar with the printed form of the word.

We also know that, in some circles, speaking such "dirty" words out loud is unacceptable— particularly if both sexes are present. McGinnies' critics speculated that if a male student were presented with the word "bitch," he might indeed recognize it but be afraid to say it in public. Instead, he might say "botch" or "batch" or "butch." And he might keep on doing so until he clearly saw it was "bitch." These critics guessed that male students would be more likely to report "dirty" words if the psychologist testing them were male than if the psychologist were female. And, as further experiments showed, the critics were quite right.

The critics also noted that a few students actually had *lower* thresholds for "dirty" words than for "clean" words. How might this finding be explained?

The answer given by McGinnies is that while most people *defend* against sexual stimuli, a few of us are vigilantly searching the world around us for anything that might be slightly smutty. McGinnies called this *lowered* threshold **perceptual vigilance**.

Whether a person tends to seek out, or to defend against, sexual stimuli seems to be a matter of each individual's own past experience and moral upbringing. But even when the criticisms against this line of research are taken into account, there still seems to be fairly good evidence that something like perceptual defense or vigilance does occur in many people.

Unconscious Censoring

Presuming that the *perceptual defense* experiments are valid—and the bulk of experimental studies suggest they are—how can we explain them? How can you *defend* against perceiving a word until you actually *see* it?

One explanation comes from Sigmund Freud, who was probably the greatest personality theorist of modern times (see Chapter 21). Freud theorized that you have a **censor** operating somewhere within your mind. The censor's chief task is to prevent sexual or other types of threatening impulses or memories from breaking through to consciousness to embarrass you. According to Freud, this censor acts as a "mental gate" through which all your thoughts and memories must pass before you become aware of them.

If you want to call up some simple, pleasant image from your storehouse of memories, this image should get past your censor with no difficulty. However, whenever you are prompted to remember some psychologically upsetting event, your censor goes into action. It simply screens out offending material by *increasing the threshold* that the memory must cross in order to become conscious.

Your censor may also attempt to screen out incoming *sensory* information, but stimulus inputs are usually too strong for your censor to handle. However, if the disturbing stimuli are weak enough, the censor may in fact be able to raise your perceptual threshold sufficiently to screen them out too.

Physiological "Screening"

When Freud first postulated his theories more than 70 years ago, he used "mentalistic" explanations (such as *censor*) because scientists were fairly ignorant of how the nervous system operated. Now, in the 1980's, there is a fair amount of physiological experimentation to support Freud's early notions.

In one of the "dirty word" experiments, for instance, psychologist Robert McCleary hooked his subjects into a polygraph or "lie detector" before testing their visual thresholds. McCleary found that when he showed his subjects "dirty words" at speeds far below their perceptual thresholds, the subjects denied seeing the stimuli. But the subjects often showed emotional responses *on the polygraph record* even when they insisted that they hadn't the foggiest notion what the word was. And, just as McCleary had predicted, these "emotional reactions" did not show up on the polygraph when the stimuli used were words such as "table" or "chair."

Milliseconds (MILL-ee-seck-unds). The Latin word *milli* means "thousands." A millisecond is therefore a thousandth of a second.

Perceptual defense. The act of suppressing or repressing threatening stimuli.

Concatenation (kon-KAT-tee-nay-shun). A fancy word meaning "a chain of events," or "things that are linked together."

Perceptual vigilance (VIDGE-ill-ants). The opposite of perceptual defense. The lowering of a perceptual threshold.

Censor (SENN-sor). From the Latin word meaning "to assess, or tax." When the lower centers of your brain assess an input as being highly emotional or threatening, they may reflexively cut it out of your conscious awareness.

Subsequent experiments by both Canadian and US psychologists have confirmed McCleary's early research. But still the problem remains—how can you react to the emotional content of a stimulus when you don't consciously know what the input is?

We aren't entirely sure, of course. But the answer may lie in the way that the two hemispheres of the brain "process" information. If you are right-handed, your right hemisphere generally recognizes *visual patterns* much better than does your left. When you attempt to perceive a word flashed on a screen at a very high speed, you will most likely be aware of the *pattern* of the letters before you can read the letters one by one. Thus it seems possible that your right hemisphere can recognize the "shape" of an emotionally charged word long before your left hemisphere becomes conscious enough of the word to say it out loud. And since your right hemisphere controls many of your unconscious emotional responses (including many reactions picked up by the polygraph), the right half of your brain could easily defend against (or even seek out) weak emotional stimuli before they broke through to consciousness in your left hemisphere.

Whatever the case, the experimental evidence does suggest that you are capable of reacting to subliminal stimuli—that is, to sensory inputs that you can't consciously perceive.

Is Subliminal Advertising Effective?

To return now to the question with which we started: Need we worry about men and women of evil intent who might practice "mind control" using subliminal advertising?

The answer appears to be *no*. Subliminal inputs *can* influence your behavior—but only under three rather rare conditions: First, you must be in a position where all the *supra*-liminal inputs available to you don't give you the information you need to make a decision. Second, you must be highly motivated to make use of even the weakest of "hunches." And third, as we will show in a moment, there must be little or no cost to you for "guessing" at the correct answer.

When you are forced to guess the answer to difficult or tricky problems, or when it is urgent that you pay attention to all subtle stimuli which you might usually ignore—then, and only then, will you make use of sensory inputs that lie below the threshold of conscious awareness.

We will have a few more choice words to say about subliminal advertising at the end of this chapter. For those words to make much sense, however, we must first take a small detour through the realm of *para-psychology*.

Psi Phenomena

Both subliminal perception and "discrimination without awareness" have sometimes been used as explanations of **psi phenomena**, or dimly understood "powers of the mind." Many people believe that, under certain special conditions, the human mind can **transcend** the laws that control the physical world. If this were true, you might be able to control objects by "willing" them to move, or you might be able to "read someone's mind" or "perceive objects or events that were out of your sight."

There are many types of psi phenomena. Four of the best-known are mental telepathy or **ESP**, clairvoyance, precognition, and psycho-kinesis.

1. **Mental telepathy** is the technical term for "reading someone's thoughts."
2. If you could see through walls, as Superman does in the comics and movies, you would have to do so by *extra-sensory* means, since your senses are incapable of this feat. **Clairvoyance** is the term we use to describe the possible perception of external objects or events without normal sensory stimulation.
3. **Precognition** is the ability to perceive future events before they happen.
4. If you could influence the movement of physical objects simply by wishing them to move, you would be demonstrating a power called **psycho-kinesis**, or **telekinesis**. Literally speaking, psycho-kinesis is the power of "mind over matter."

Who Believes in Psi?

The study of psi phenomena makes up a field called **para-psychology**, or the investigation of events that are beyond the normal boundaries of behavioral science.

In 1978, New York psychologists Mary Monnet and Mahlon Wagner asked more than 1,100 US college teachers if they believed in ESP. Overall, 16 percent thought ESP was an established fact, while 49 percent believed it probably was a real-life occurrence. About 24 percent of the teachers denied ESP existed, while the rest thought it "merely an unknown." Teachers in the humanities, arts, and education were the most enthusiastic supporters of ESP—about 75 percent believed in it. Only 5 percent of the psychologists thought ESP to be an established fact, and only 29 percent thought it was likely.

The general public, however, is more likely to accept ESP as an "established fact." A 1978 Gallup poll found that more than half the US population believed in ESP. And, according to R. Wuthnow's survey in the same year, more people in the US believe in extra-sensory perception than believe in God!

How can we explain the **discrepancy** between what the general public believes, and what psychologists will accept as factual? The answer probably lies in the *experimental method*, which we discussed in some detail in the early chapters of this book. If you (or one of your friends) has had what seemed to be a psi experience, chances are good that your belief in ESP will be fairly strong. But the *science of psychology* can accept "super-natural" explanations only when all natural explanations have been ruled out. And, as we will see, most experiments purporting to "prove the existence of ESP" have not been as well controlled as they might have been.

Demonstrating that an event can be explained in normal scientific terms often calls for great ingenuity. So let us see why psi experiments are so difficult to design, and how their results are sometimes misinterpreted.

ESP Experiments

Suppose you volunteered to participate in a para-psychological experiment. You might be shown a pack of ordinary bridge cards so that you could make sure that—like all other bridge decks—this one contained 52 cards divided into four suits. The experimenter would then shuffle the cards thoroughly and place the deck face down on the table between the two of you.

The experimenter might then pick up the cards one by one in such a manner that he or she could see the card, but you couldn't.

You would then be asked to "read the experimenter's mind"—that is, to guess the *suit* of the card that the para-psychologist was looking at. Since there are four suits in the deck, you would have *one chance in four* of being right with any given card. If, the first time you tried this experiment, you guessed the suit correctly 13 times out of 52, you would have done no more than would normally be expected *by chance alone*.

Undaunted by your first experience, you try again. And this time you guess all 52 of the cards correctly! Surely this is evidence that mental telepathy occurred, isn't it?

The answer is—not yet. First you must show that you had no *sensory* cues to help you out. Thousands of studies similar to this one have been performed in the past—and almost all of them are useless from a scientific point of view. Why? Because the experimenter failed to appreciate how likely it is for *subliminal perception* and *responding without awareness* to occur in this type of situation.

Question: How many times would you have to guess the suit correctly before you might begin to suspect that something para-normal had occurred?

Miller's Harvard Study

More than 30 years ago psychiatrist James G. Miller trained Harvard college students to "guess" correctly the symbols on a deck of cards even though the students could not consciously see the symbols and were not aware that they were being trained or "conditioned."

Miller got students (all males) to volunteer for what they thought was an ESP experiment. He then asked each of them to sit in front of a glass screen fixed on the wall like a mirror. The student was supposed to stare at the glass screen and to "project" on the screen the mental image of whatever card he thought Miller was looking at. Miller would stare at the card, remind the student to look at the screen, and then ask him to guess the card. If the student was right, he was rewarded. If he was wrong, the student was given a mild shock.

To most students' great surprise, they were able to "guess" the symbols with incredible accuracy—although their accuracy disappeared if Miller omitted *either* the reward for correct responses *or* the punishment for incorrect responses.

Had Miller demonstrated a high level of ESP among Harvard students? Not quite. What the student didn't know was that the glass screen was really a one-way mirror. In the next room, Miller had a slide projector aimed at the back side of the mirror. When he pressed a button, the projector in the next room would throw on the mirror a very faint image of the card that Miller was looking at.

The projected image was so weak that it was well below the student's *conscious* threshold. Yet when Miller *motivated* the students highly

Psi phenomena (SIGH fee-NOMM-ee-nah). "Psi" is a Greek letter that often stands for psychology, or "the mind." "Phenomena" is the plural of "phenomenon," which comes from a Greek word meaning "to show, or appear." A phenomenon is thus anything that "shows" or happens. Psi phenomena are events that happen because of mental powers, not because of physical actions.

Transcend (trans-SEND). To go beyond the normal limits or thresholds.

ESP. Abbreviation for extra-sensory perception. Perceptions are ordinarily triggered off by sensory stimuli—that is, by inputs to your eyes, ears, and so forth. If you could perceive something without making use of these sensory inputs, you would experience extra-sensory perception.

Mental telepathy (tell-LEP-uh-thee). The Greek word *tele* means "far off," or "at a distance." The word "television" means "seeing at a distance." The word "telephone" means "speaking over a distance." The Greek word *pathos* means "experience" or "emotion." Mental telepathy is therefore to experience something at a distance through mental or emotional communication rather than by physical means.

Clairvoyance (clair-VOY-ants). From the French words meaning "clear-sighted." The ability to see things hidden from normal sight.

Precognition (pree-cog-NISH-shun). Cognition is the intellectual process by which knowledge or ideas are gained. Precognition is knowing or perceiving something before the event actually occurs.

Psycho-kinesis (SIGH-ko-kin-EE-sis). The Greek word *kinesis* means "movement," or "to move." *Psyche* is the Greek word for "mind." Psycho-kinesis is the ability to move things mentally (by willing them to move) rather than by touching them physically.

Telekinesis (TELL-ee-kin-EE-sis). To move things at a distance through thought power instead of physical power. Another word for psycho-kinesis.

Para-psychology. That part of psychology concerned with the study of ESP and other para-normal happenings.

Discrepancy (diss-KREP-an-see). A difference between two things or viewpoints.

enough, they were able to make use of sensory information so subliminal that it never reached consciousness. As you might guess, none of the students reported actually *seeing* the picture of the card as it flashed on the screen.

In a second part of the experiment, Miller switched from studying subliminal perception to studying responding without awareness. At first, each student was shown very weak stimuli as before. But, while the experiment was in progress, Miller gradually increased the intensity of the projected images until they were well *above* the conscious threshold.

Most of the students continued to stare at the "blank" screen without being aware that the symbols had become as visible as the numbers on the door to the experimental laboratory. At this stage of the experiment, of course, the students were "guessing" the cards with 100 percent accuracy—but they still thought they were "reading Miller's mind." Miller then told them what he was doing and, naturally enough, the students immediately "saw" the symbols quite clearly.

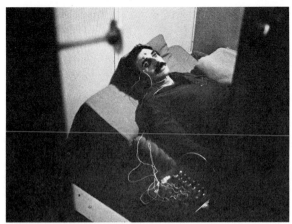

At the American Society for Psychical Research, a subject is in an altered state of consciousness in a dark, soundproof room while stimulus pictures, randomly chosen, are displayed six doors away. The subject is asked to describe the pictures. The subject's brain waves, eye movements, and muscle tension are being monitored.

Miller's explanation of what the experiment was all about did not please all of the students, however. Some of them insisted afterward that they had guessed correctly using *mental telepathy*, and that Miller was trying to "trick" them into believing that they hadn't really used ESP after all!

Question: *Why did motivation play such an important part in getting the students to perform well? (Hint: Suslowa's subjects guessed correctly only when he forced them to do so.)*

Kennedy's Stanford Study

At about the same time Miller was working at Harvard, J.L. Kennedy at Stanford was studying what he called **unconscious whispering**. Kennedy asked two students at a time to participate in his study. One of them was to look at a card from a special deck and to "send" the other student a mental message about the card. The "receiver" student guessed out loud what card the "sender" was looking at. The sender would then tell the receiver whether the guess had been right or wrong.

Kennedy used a wooden reflector in his experiment that "funneled" very faint sounds from the sender's mouth to the receiver's ear—much as a long narrow hallway "funnels" echoes from one end to another. Kennedy could wipe out these faint sounds by taking away the reflector. He found that when the reflector was in place, many of the receivers had incredible success in "guessing what card their senders were looking at. How-

ever, the instant Kennedy removed the reflector, the guesses would drop back to chance level.

Kennedy observed very carefully just what his successful senders were doing. He noted that, in many cases, the sender would make a *characteristic sound* for each different type of card that the sender looked at. For example, if the sender was looking at a heart, she or he might make an "ahem" sound. If the card was a spade, the sender might inhale sharply.

The receiver apparently soon learned what faint sounds were associated with which cards. As you might expect, though, neither senders nor receivers were aware of this "unconscious whispering."

Some of the students turned out to be very good "unconscious" senders and receivers. In general, those subjects who were strong believers in ESP were good at the task, while those people who had a firm disbelief in ESP were unable either to send or to receive successfully.

Question: *How would Freud explain the fact that the "disbelievers" were so poor both at sending or receiving the "unconscious whispers"?*

Schmidt's Precognition Study

Neither Miller's nor Kennedy's experiments disproved the existence of ESP, nor were they aimed at doing so. Rather, both studies showed how difficult it is for anyone to perform a cleanly designed, well-controlled investigation of a topic that is by definition almost beyond the boundaries of modern science.

As Miller and Kennedy both noted, one of the difficulties with ESP studies is that the experimenter must make sure that there is *no possible way* the information the subject is trying to "receive mentally" could be received by normal sensory pathways. Thus the experimenter must control for "unconscious whispering" and other such sensory clues.

Another problem with ESP studies is that the experimenters themselves may unconsciously "cheat" while recording the results of the study. As Kennedy notes, "human beings . . . are not trustworthy recording devices," particularly when they *hope very strongly* that the results will turn out a specific way.

In 1969, physicist Helmut Schmidt reported a study on *precognition* that seemed to overcome the objections to ESP studies raised by Miller and Kennedy. Schmidt built a *random generator*—a machine that would randomly turn on one of four colored lights. Beneath each light was a button that the subject could press. It was the subject's task to predict which light the machine would turn on, on any given trial, by pressing the appropriate button.

Since the machine did not make its random selection until *after* the subject had pressed a button, there was no way that either Schmidt or the subject could know which light would turn on—except through *precognition*. Thus there was no way that either Schmidt or his machine could have given the subjects "unconscious clues."

In his first experiment, Schmidt used three subjects who made more than 60,000 guesses. They guessed correctly far more often than chance would allow. In a second experiment, the subjects could guess either which light would turn on, or which one wouldn't. Again they did far better than chance.

Criticisms of Schmidt's Studies

Do Schmidt's studies *prove* that precognition exists? No, not necessarily. A lengthy discussion of the pros and cons of Schmidt's work appears in the July 1980 issue of the **Zetetic Scholar**, a journal that offers "independent scientific review of claims of **anomalies** and the para-normal." Although some psychologists believe that Schmidt's research is fairly encouraging evidence, others are less convinced. As James Randi points out in the *Zetetic Scholar*, Schmidt's work has not as yet been properly observed by other scientists, nor has his work been **replicated** successfully by other researchers. Randi also points out that in

Unconscious whispering. The act of making sounds you are unaware of making that give clues to other people about what you are seeing or thinking.

Zetetic Scholar (zeh-TET-ick). A journal of information and debates about psi phenomena. Published twice a year by Marcello Truzzi, editor, Department of Sociology, Eastern Michigan University, Ypsilanti, Michigan 48197. Individual issues cost $8.00 each.

Anomalies (a-NOMM-ah-lees). From a Greek word meaning "abnormalities." Anomalies are things that don't fit too well within a given framework or theory.

Replicated (REPP-plee-kate-ted). To repeat something (such as a scientific experiment) exactly. In fact, it is almost impossible for a scientist in one laboratory to replicate *precisely* an experiment performed in another lab. The conditions simply are too different. Therefore, when scientists say they have replicated a study, they mean that they have repeated it "more-or-less exactly."

Occult (ah-CULT). From a Latin word meaning "hidden."

almost all of the famous ESP studies, subsequent investigations by skeptical scientists have either exposed a fatal defect or have uncovered evidence that the experimenter might have "fudged" the data.

Does ESP Exist?

Do all these objections mean that ESP is no more than a figment of people's imaginations? No, not at all. But extra-sensory perception seems at best to be a kinky, slippery, undependable thing that happens rarely, unpredictably, and for the most part uncontrollably. And to the great frustration of all scientists interested in the subject, ESP seems to occur much more frequently in "real life" than in the laboratory.

If the *scientific evidence* doesn't generally support a belief in ESP, though, why do many people ignore the "scientific facts" and continue to place very strong faith in the para-normal? Early in 1981 Barry Singer and Victor Benassi offered a number of intriguing answers to this question in an article in the *American Scientist*.

Belief in the Occult

Singer and Benassi have spent many years studying **occult** beliefs in college students. In their article, they make three important points. First, the students tended to believe whatever they saw in print or on TV—particularly if they thought the source of the information was "scientific" or a "documentary." Second, when the students were asked to give examples of "scientific sources" and "documentaries," they listed *Reader's Digest*, the *National Enquirer*, and movies such as *Star Wars*. Third, as Singer and Benassi note, most newspapers, magazines, and TV programs report stories about para-normal events *without demanding scientific proof that the event occurred.*

The "floating woman" is actually suspended by a complex set of metal rods. As Singer and Benassi have shown, many people prefer to believe in "magic," even when the tricks are exposed to them.

Singer and Benassi believe that the popular press prefers "spectacle" to "scientific fact." For example, you have probably read stories about psychics who have supposedly used their "occult powers" to help the police find lost children or identify murderers. In fact, as Roger Depue (chief of the behavioral science unit at the FBI Academy) notes, there simply is no evidence supporting the claims made by any of these psychics. However, few if any newspapers or TV programs have reported Depue's statements.

In truth, there is good experimental evidence that psychics are no better than the average person in guessing the solutions to crime. In 1978, the Los Angeles Police Department (LAPD) tested 12 psychics to see what clues they could give as to the identity of the "Hillside Strangler." Not only did the psychics disagree among themselves, but the suggestions they gave turned out to be no closer to the truth than those of policemen or night school students who were also asked to guess the identity of the killer. Singer and Benassi note that the LAPD studies received little or no mention in the newspapers or on TV.

Intuition versus Experimental Evidence

Singer and Benassi give another important reason why belief in ESP may be so strong. To begin with, they cite a number of scientific studies showing that people tend to trust **intuitive** judgments rather than experimental evidence. Almost everyone has dreamed about something that eventually came true. But is this proof of *precognition*? No, because people have hundreds of similar dreams that don't come true. But we tend to forget those unfulfilled dreams and just remember the ones that "proved out." As Singer and Benassi put it, "A

rare event is seen as one that seldom occurs, regardless of the number of opportunities for its occurrence. As a result of our natural tendency to misunderstand the probabilities involved in a match of dreams and reality," we are more likely to explain the dream as precognition than as mere chance. And we do so, of course, because we often tend to trust our intuitive feelings more than scientific data.

Next, Singer and Benassi point out that many people resist giving up their belief in ESP no matter how strong the experimental evidence against it. In one of their most recent studies, Singer and Benassi had a magician perform various "psychic tricks" for introductory psychology students. Even when the students were told in advance that the performer was a magician—and even when they admitted that what they saw could easily have been "mere tricks"—*more than half the students* insisted that the magician's "tricks" were proof that ESP exists!

ESP and Motivation

Singer and Benassi state that belief in the paranormal tends to rise during wars and other disasters, but tends to fall during good times. Apparently, then, people turn to ESP for simple explanations of complex events that are beyond their control. Perhaps accepting the supernatural gives most people a feeling that they have greater control over their destinies than is actually the case.

And, as Singer and Benassi note, belief in ESP seldom costs a person very much. For people seldom adopt superstitious explanations when the stakes are high or when they know from personal experience that other approaches work better. You might ask an **astrologer** to help you select a date for a fancy party. But if you're going into a business partnership with a person, you are more likely to check that individual's credit record and talk to a lawyer than merely to consult an astrologer. As Carl Sagan put it in 1979, "A people going to war may sing over their spears in order to make them more effective. If there ever have been people who felt they could defeat an enemy in war merely by singing and who therefore dispensed with spears, we have not heard of them; they were, undoubtedly, all dispatched."

According to Singer and Benassi, we turn to the supernatural primarily when we are *highly motivated* to explain something, and only when it will cost us little no matter what explanation we come up with.

Question: *In Kennedy's Stanford experiment, why did only those subjects with a strong belief in ESP pay attention to the "unconscious whispering"?*

"Magic" versus "Scientific Facts"

As we noted in Chapter 3, uncertainty is stressful. And, as we will see in Chapter 13, there are two major ways of controlling stress. The first method is to look reality in the face, and then change your perceptions and behaviors to fit the observable facts. The second method is much easier—it merely requires you to make up some magical explanation for whatever is giving you stress.

For example, if you don't always understand why you buy the things you do, it's much easier to blame "hidden persuaders" such as subliminal advertising than to study your own buying behavior objectively. And if you want to increase productivity among your employees, it's much simpler to rent a black box that whispers "Work Harder" than it is to try to motivate your workers.

In similar fashion, explaining para-normal events in terms of ESP takes much less effort than does learning all the facts about thresholds and responding without awareness. And performing

Intuitive (inn-TOO-it-tive). Technically, the act of gaining direct knowledge without rational thought. Loosely speaking, to be intuitive is to act on your feelings or hunches without being able to defend your acts rationally.

Astrologer (ass-TROLL-oh-jer). From the Greek words meaning "star gazer." An astrologer is someone who gives people advice based on the position of the stars and planets at the time the person was born. There have been many scientific studies of astrologers, all of which tend to show their advice is little more than intuitive guesses.

well-controlled scientific experiments always requires more thought and effort than does running a sloppy study that serves merely to confirm your prior beliefs.

Your own personal motivation is thus the key to understanding how you try to control your inputs, and what explanations you give for the way people think, feel, and behave. It is to the study of *motivation*, then, that we next turn our attention.

Summary

1. Despite claims that the use of "hidden messages" increases sales, there is no scientific evidence that **subliminal advertising** works in real-life situations.
2. A **threshold** is a point half-way between two places or states of being.
3. As stimulus inputs pass through your nervous system, they must pass three main types of thresholds:
   a. An input must be physically strong enough to cross your **physiological threshold**; that is, to excite your receptor organs so they send the input to the **lower centers of your brain**.
   b. If an input is strong or important enough, you become conscious of it. That is, the input crosses your **perceptual threshold**. Many stimuli evoke responses in lower brain centers, but not in your cortex. Thus you may occasionally respond **reflexively** to inputs you never become conscious of.
   c. If an input you become aware of requires action, it will pass your **behavioral threshold** as you respond to it.
4. On rare occasions, a stimulus may evoke a response from your lower brain centers, but not in your cortex. Thus you may occasionally respond **reflexively** to inputs you aren't consciously aware of. This type of input is called a **subliminal stimulus**, because it is below your perceptual threshold and cannot be perceived no matter how hard you try.
5. The lower centers of your brain—and perhaps your right hemisphere—often respond to stimuli that your left hemisphere ignores. You *could* become conscious of these inputs if someone called your **attention** to them, but generally you are not because you are thinking of other things. The act of reacting unconsciously to stimuli you *could be aware of* is called **responding without awareness**.
6. Some people are emotionally aroused or upset by certain types of stimuli, such as "dirty words." Some part of the brain apparently unconsciously raises the perceptual thresholds for these stimuli, an act called **perceptual defense**.
7. Other people may seek out presumably threatening or arousing stimuli, an act called **perceptual vigilance**.
8. **Psi phenomena** are events or experiences that seem to transcend the laws of nature as we know them. "Psi" includes such talents as **mental telepathy** or **ESP, clairvoyance, precognition**, and **psycho-kinesis** (or **tele-kinesis**).
9. The study of psi phenomena is often called **para-psychology**.
10. Most teachers in the humanities believe in ESP, but few psychologists do.
11. Many ESP experiments are better explained in terms of **subliminal perception** and **responding without awareness** than in terms of **occult** powers.

12. There is little scientific evidence that **psychics** can predict the future or help identify murderers.
13. People apparently explain events in terms of the para-normal only when (1) they wish a simple explanation for highly complex events; (2) they are strongly motivated to do so; and (3) there is little cost to them for doing so.

(Continued from page 234.)

"Stumpfed?" Vince said. "I don't get it."

"You will," Al replied. Then he turned to the farmer. "Would you mind if Vince and I talked to the horse for a minute or two in private?"

William Nagler grumbled, but left the students alone in the barn.

Once the older man had gone, Al turned to his roommate and said, "Okay, Vince, now ask Harry the Horse what the square root of 49 is."

Vince nodded, and turned to the handsome animal. "Okay, Harry, let's show this doubting Thomas how good you are. What's the square root of 49, Harry?" The horse lifted its hoof and moved it slowly to the answer board with the alphabet and numbers painted on it. Vince leaned forward in excitement, his eyes riveted on what the animal was doing. The hoof continued to move down the line of numbers. And each time it moved a bit closer to 7, Vince became more excited. Finally, when the hoof was poised over the 7, Vince nodded excitedly. And down came the hoof on 7.

"Seven come 11," Vince cried excitedly. "See, I told you Harry is a genius."

"Sure, Vince. If the horse is so smart, ask it what the square root of 3249 is."

"Gee, Al, that's a toughie, even for a horse like Harry. I don't even know the answer myself."

Al nodded sagely. "That's why I'm asking, Vince. Just go ahead and try."

Vince asked the horse the question. The animal raised its hoof, moved it tentatively toward the answer board, hesitated, and then put its hoof back on the ground.

"Stumped again," Vince remarked.

"No, Stumpfed again," said Al.

"Why do you keep saying 'Stumpfed?'" Vince asked. "Who or what is 'Stumpfed?'"

"Professor Carl Stumpf, of the University of Berlin. That's who."

Vince scratched his head. "What's this Stumpf cat got to do with Harry the Horse?"

Al grinned. "Back in 1904, Professor Stumpf and one of his students—a young man named Oskar Pfungst—solved a mystery that had all of Berlin on its ear. There was a German named Herr van Osten who owned a horse . . ."

"A horse?"

"Yep, a horse named 'Clever Hans.' This horse was supposedly so bright that it could do fractions, multiply 3-digit numbers in its head instantly, tell you the day and year you were born, and read German fluently. It could also answer any questions you cared to ask it about music, art, science, or history."

"So," said Vince casually, "Maybe there have been other talking horses before Harry. So what? So maybe Harry is even a direct descendant of this 'Clever Hans.' What's that got to do with our buying Harry from Mr. Nagler?"

"So, listen, buddy. 'Clever Hans' was the rage of Berlin. Physics professors, medical doctors, zoologists, and mathematicians came to see him, but none of them could explain how the horse managed to solve the problems he did. The newspapers claimed it was telepathy, or something paranormal."

"Well, I told you Harry can read my mind."

Al shook his head. "It's not your mind Harry is reading, Vince. It's your behavior the animal is paying attention to. That's what Stumpf and Pfungst proved beyond a shadow of a doubt."

Vince scratched his head again. "I don't get it."

"You don't, but Stumpf and Pfungst did. They proved that 'Clever Hans' could only answer questions that people around him knew the answers to."

"So? That just means he's reading people's minds."

"No," replied Al. "When Pfungst put blinders on Hans so he couldn't see the person asking the question, Hans failed miserably. And if Harry the Horse could read my mind, he'd know that the equation Einstein made famous was $E = mC^2$. And that the square root of 3249 is 57. I knew the answers to those questions, but you and Mr. Nagler didn't. If Harry the Horse could read my mind, why didn't he get those answers?"

"Maybe you just give off bad vibes, at least as far as mental telepathy is concerned."

"No, maybe I just *don't* give off the right kind of non-verbal cues. You see, Stumpf and Pfungst proved that 'Clever Hans' was merely moving his hoof in response to very subtle behavioral cues that people gave him. I watched you carefully, Vince. You gave the same sorts of cues to Harry, and so did Mr. Nagler."

Vince became angry. "What do you mean, I gave him cues?"

"When you ask Harry a question, you look directly at him and speak in a very firm tone of voice. Harry then raises his hoof and points it at the answer board. You nod your head very slightly and then lean forward a bit. Harry moves his hoof toward the board, and you nod again. The closer his hoof comes to the correct number or letter, the more excited you get. And when the animal's hoof is right over the answer, you nod your head vigorously. Down goes the hoof, you give a cry of happiness, and then reward the horse with a pat on its head or a lump of sugar."

"You mean this stupid animal is just picking up on my non-verbal behavior?"

"You got it right, Vince."

"And he's not a genius after all?"

Al smiled. "Well, he's obviously bright enough to know how to get pats on the head and sugar from the people around him. That isn't too dumb a trick, now is it?"

"But that kind of trick isn't worth a thousand bucks, I guess."

"You got it, buddy," Al said, nodding his head in agreement.

Vince frowned. "Where'd you learn about 'Clever Hans' and this Stumpf character?"

"In my intro psych class, Vince," Al replied. "You know, it's funny. Biologists and physicists and chemists are darned bright people, but they almost always get taken in by 'mind readers' and 'talking horses' and other quack examples of ESP."

"Why's that?"

"Because they've never been trained to look at *behavior*. That is, they don't know how to look at what people and horses *actually do*. Instead, they tend to make up supernatural explanations for things and then they 'see what they expect to see.'"

"Yeah, but my physics prof said last week that psychology wasn't really a science, it was just 'common sense.'"

Al grinned. "What do you think, Vince?"

Vince considered the matter for a moment, then smiled broadly. "I guess psychology is more like 'horse sense,' isn't it?"

"You got it right, baby," Al replied.

Recommended Readings

Benassi, V.A., P.D. Sweeney, and G.E. Drevno, "Mind Over Matter. Perceived Success at Psychokinesis," *Journal of Personality and Social Psychology*, Vol. 37 (1979), pp. 1377–1386.

Hardy, Alister, Robert Harvie, and Arthur Koestler. *The Challenge of Chance* (New York: Random House, 1974).

McConnell, James V., R.L. Cutler, and E.B. McNeil. "Subliminal Stimulation: An Overview," *American Psychologist*, Vol. 13 (1958), pp. 229–24.

Randi, James. *Flim-Flam: The Truth about Unicorns, Parapsychology, and Other Delusions* (New York: Lippincott & Crowell, 1980).

Wuthnow, R. *Experimentation in American Religion* (Berkeley, Calif.: University of California Press, 1978).

3

Motivation

Introduction to Motivation 11

Did You Know That . . .

Motivation can be viewed as a series of questions about *why* you do what you do?

Some psychologists consider the need for "self-actualization" the most mature need of all?

Stimulation of a rat's "feeding center" will cause the animal to eat huge amounts of food?

Stimulation of a rat's "satiation center" will cause the animal to refuse almost all food?

Colleges often discriminate against overweight students?

Fat people tend to be "plate cleaners"?

More lower-class than upper-class persons in the US are overweight?

Some husbands seem to push food on their wives to keep the women fat and faithful?

Almost anyone can lose weight by using a technique called Behavior Modification?

"By Bread Alone"

Thelma Green shook her plump face in dismay. "It's a dirty shame the way they treat people who are a trifle overweight," she said. "They don't consider our problems at all, and we've got lots."

Annette Holmes smiled and nodded encouragingly. Thelma Green certainly did have "lots"—about 280 pounds of "lots." But Annette liked the woman and, because Annette was a therapist at the Weight Control Clinic, she wanted to help Thelma shed some of those pounds if she could. So Annette just nodded and smiled and waited to see what Thelma had in mind.

"Take, for instance, clothes." Thelma Green picked at the blouse she was wearing. "Who makes good-looking clothes for somebody as fat as me? Potato sacks are what they sell us, and we have to buy them because there's nothing else available."

Annette looked carefully at Thelma's clothes. They didn't look all that bad. The woman was neat in her appearance despite her size. But Annette continued to nod her head.

"And anyhow, what kind of wardrobe can you have when you shoot up or down 30 pounds every six months?" Thelma continued. "I'm like a yo-yo. I gain a little, so I don't fit most of the things I have. And then I go on a crash diet, and I lose 40 pounds, and I *still* don't fit my clothes because now they're too big for me. I tell you, I've been on so many diets I think I'll puke if I ever see another bowl of cottage cheese!"

"Diets don't do all that much good, it's true," Annette said. "It's not losing pounds that is the difficult part, as you know. It's learning how to eat sensibly so that you reach and maintain a reasonable weight that's so terribly hard for most over-weight people."

"Why is that?" Thelma asked plaintively.

Annette warmed to her subject. "Starving yourself is a just a short-term change in behavior. And you pretend that when you've lost a few pounds, you've solved your basic problem. But you haven't really made any fundamental changes in your eating habits, your exercise habits, or in your self-image. If you want to keep your weight down permanently, you have to learn to eat sensibly, and keep on eating that way. Most overweight people just aren't motivated to make that drastic a change in the way they live and think and feel."

"But I don't eat all that much," Thelma replied, an edgy tone in her voice. "I just can't understand why I stay so heavy."

Annette smiled. "Look, Thelma. Fatness is caused by just one thing—you take in more calories than you burn up. Some people eat too much. Other people eat fairly sensibly but exercise too little. But the real problem is that most people don't *measure* what they're doing. So they never face the fact that they're inputting too much and outputting too little."

"That can't be my problem," Thelma said a bit testily. "Because I know what I eat, and it's very little, I assure you. No breakfast at all, and I have a very light lunch. I eat a sensible dinner, and that's it. Maybe 1,500 calories per day. But I gain weight on that, so maybe there's something wrong with the way my body utilizes food, or something."

Annette sensed the woman's impending anger and backtracked a little. "Well, I suppose that could be the difficulty. Have you seen a doctor yet?"

"I've seen a dozen," Thelma said unhappily. "They've put me on a dozen differ-ent diets, they've given me pills, and they've given me hundreds of lectures. Hasn't helped a bit. I saw one guy last week. He told me I had a possible heart problem, that something might be wrong with my kidneys, and that I was going to die if I didn't lose 100 pounds right away. I asked him how I was going to shed those pounds, and he said that any dummy knew how to lose weight. Then he gave me another diet and said it would be my fault if I got sick and died because I was too stubborn to lose weight."

"So how did you react to this news?" Annette asked.

Thelma pulled out a handkerchief and dabbed it at her eyes. "I got so discour-aged and depressed I went home and cooked a huge meal to make me feel better."

Annette had heard that one before. She just wished medical doctors would look at the actual consequences of the "little lectures" they gave their patients. Perhaps they'd lecture less and give their patients emotional support more often. "Well, I can understand your reaction to what your doctor said," Annette said, smiling warmly. "But it does seem as if you ought to try to learn how to eat better so that you can get back into shape medically as well as socially. Suppose we start off by taking a baseline of what you really eat . . ."

"It isn't much, I told you that."

Annette smiled again. "I know, but we want exact figures. Here's a form I'd like for you to fill out. Please record everything you eat and drink. Put down the time, the place, the amount, who else is present, what you're doing, and how you feel. That will give us a good baseline or starting point. Once we have those data, we can talk seriously about how to help you learn some new eating and exercise habits."

"Fifteen hundred calories a day, it's no more than that. And I still gain weight!"

Annette nodded. "Perhaps, but you may be surprised. What I want you to do next is to decide how much you'd like to weigh a year or so from now. Then make a list of all the benefits and gains you'd receive if you got down to that weight."

"Well, my clothes would fit better," Thelma responded. "And I could go bowling again, and there's my friend Shirley in Miami I want to impress . . ." Her voice trailed off pensively.

"Very good thoughts!" said Annette. "Please put all those things down on your list, and any others you can think of. And come see me again on Friday at this same time. We'll have our dietician see you then."

Thelma Green gathered herself together and stood up. "Do you really think there's any hope for me?" she asked softly. "Can I really get things under control?"

Annette looked the woman squarely in the eye. "Certainly there's hope. You can do it—if you really want to."

"I really want to," Thelma said. "I really do."

Three days later Annette got an urgent telephone call. "I don't believe it!" Thelma wailed. "I wrote down everything I ate and drank, just like you said I was supposed to do . . ."

"The baseline, yes . . ." said Annette. "That's good."

"No, it's terrible! Absolutely terrible! I added it up, and I'm taking in 5,000 calories a day. Can you believe that?"

"I can believe it," Annette said, thinking of the woman's size.

"Listen," said Thelma, "I want to go on a 1,000 calorie-a-day diet right away. Do you hear, right now!"

For just a second, Annette panicked. Cutting down from 5,000 to 1,000 a day would surely be too big a change. So Annette stalled a bit. "Listen, Thelma, you said you didn't eat much breakfast or lunch and had just a light dinner. When are you taking in all those calories?"

"At night, after dinner, sitting in front of the boob tube," the woman replied. "I snack and snack and snack. About 3,000 calories worth an evening, to tell you the truth."

Annette nodded to herself, then spoke again into the phone. "And how do you feel when you're snacking?"

"Bored," came the reply. "I had a bad day at work yesterday, and I got depressed, and I came home and started dinner and just kept on eating all night long."

"Well," said Annette, "What happened at work that got you so depressed?"

Thelma paused a moment before replying. "To tell you the truth, one of the women I supervise screwed up a report, and when I told her to get her ass in gear and do it over again, she threw the report in my face. I'm just trying to be helpful, and she throws a temper tantrum like a three-year-old."

Annette frowned. Weight control therapy seemed so simple when you first went into it. Just help people learn to eat correctly, right? But very often you had to help people clean up their emotional problems before you could teach them to control their overeating. Annette suspected she'd have to teach Thelma some new job skills so that she wouldn't get depressed at work and then overeat when she came home.

"Listen," continued Thelma, "I've gone through the kitchen and thrown out all the junk food I could find. But now there's practically nothing left to eat. I'd go to the grocery store right now, but I don't know what to buy or how to cook low-cal stuff. Can you help me?"

"Of course I can help," Annette responded. "That's what I'm here for. Tell you what. I'll come over and we can make up a shopping list. Then we can have a light dinner somewhere and go to the grocery store."

Thelma snorted loudly. "Go to the store *after* you eat?"

"Certainly," Annette replied. "That way you cut down on impulse buying. I'll bring over a really good diet plan I have, and we can work it out, and then go shopping. I'll bring over a nice exercise plan too."

"Exercise?" Thelma said in a shocked tone of voice. "I don't go for that stuff very much. Except for bowling, which I've given up for the duration."

"Why?"

Thelma sighed. "Well, I used to belong to this bowling league, and I really did like it. But I got so big I didn't fit my bowling clothes any more. And then we usually had three or four drinks, and you know how many calories there are in alcohol. And, well, to tell the truth, sometimes when I got a little snockered I had these arguments with my buddies . . ."

Annette could see it all quite clearly. Thelma simply didn't know how to get along very well with people. So she avoided company and stayed home by herself and got depressed and watched the tube and snacked. "Listen," Annette said, "You should go back to bowling even if your clothes don't fit. You can tip the bartender to give you a glass of icewater with lots of cherries and orange slices in it, and everyone will think you're drinking gin. And we can do some role playing so that you'll learn how to handle any social situations that might bother you. Okay?"

"Okay," came the reluctant response.

"But we're going to have to get you on a regular exercise program too."

"None of that crazy jumping around stuff, do you hear?"

Annette grinned. "Of course not. We'll start with walking. Just walking. For instance, you tend to eat when you first come home from work, right?"

"Right."

"Well, we can interrupt that habitual behavior by having you walk for 10 minutes when you get home. That way . . ."

Thelma suddenly sounded excited again. "That way I don't associate eating with getting home from work, right? Hey, that's great. And you know I live in an apartment house, so even if it's raining I could just walk up and down the stairs for a while. Probably meet a lot of my neighbors for the first time, too. Might be fun . . ."

"Of course it will be," Annette said enthusiastically. "Tell you what. Why don't you go for a walk and meet me at the parking lot in a quarter of an hour. Then we can make out the diet and go grocery shopping."

"Okay, it's a deal. But listen, no grapefruit and no cottage cheese, or I'll upchuck right there in the supermarket."

Annette laughed. "Okay, but no cookies and no potato chips either."

Thelma moaned softly and hung up the phone.

A month later, Annette sat quietly in her office, a worried look on her face. For the first time ever, Thelma had missed an appointment. She had asked to see Annette at 9 P.M., because she was going bowling right after work. Annette had agreed, because Thelma was doing beautifully. She had lost 22 pounds in four weeks, which was amazing. She was walking at least 30 minutes each day, and she had made several new friends while marching up and down the apartment stairs. Now it was nearly 11 P.M., but where was Thelma?

Annette reviewed the situation mentally. Thelma had gotten many insights into her own personality in the process of trying to lose weight. As Annette had guessed, Thelma tended to be rather bossy and punishing to her friends. But during their role-playing exercises, Thelma had learned how to express affection and gratitude openly instead of converting it into criticism.

She also was doing much better on the job. Before treatment, Thelma had ignored the people she supervised unless they goofed up. Now she spent most of her time helping them set goals for themselves and letting them know when they were showing progress. So she seldom came home depressed, and she had so many invitations to visit her friends that she almost never spent the evening alone watching TV.

Annette dialed Thelma's number again, but there still was no answer.

Of course, the woman still had a long way to go—both physically and psychologically. She had a terrible self-image, and she wouldn't use cosmetics at all. "I don't deserve to look good," Thelma had said. "No one as fat as me deserves to look anything but ugly."

Annette had solved the problem by teaching Thelma how to use lipstick and rouge, and by getting her to write down daily at least one good thing she thought about herself. But Thelma frequently got depressed when she felt she "wasn't getting anywhere," so the two women had talked at length about Thelma's real goals in life.

The one thing that Thelma wanted was the respect and affection of others. Her feelings about Shirley, the friend who lived in Miami, were an example. "Shirley's a doll," Thelma had said. "She's stuck by me through thick and thin. Mostly thick, of course, given my size. Anyhow, what I want to do most is to lose 100 pounds, and fly to Miami without telling her I'm coming. I've seen that scene a thousand times in my mind's eye. Shirley opens the door, and she is thunderstruck. 'Hi, Shirl,' I say to her. 'It's the new me.'"

What better motivation? Annette had asked herself. So, at her suggestion, Thelma had started putting away $2.00 in her piggy bank every day that she stuck to her diet. Half the money went for cosmetics, but the other half she put in the bank to pay for the projected trip to Miami. But Thelma still had a few dozen pounds to lose before she flew south.

Annette gave Thelma's number one last try. After three rings a discouraged and somewhat intoxicated voice answered.

"Thelma? This is Annette. What's happened?"

After a moment's silence, Thelma sobbed, "Oh, Annette. I'm so sorry. I'm just no damned good. I just don't deserve to get better."

The crisis, Annette thought. It almost always happens when the person is right on the brink of success.

"Look, Thelma, I want to come over to see you. Right now."

"You better hurry, honey," came the tearful reply. "There may not be much left to see if you don't."

(Continued on page 277.)

Motivation: Fact and Theory

As David Edwards of Iowa State University notes, **motivation** isn't really an "area in psychology." Rather, it is a series of questions that we ask as we try to explain *why* people act as they do. Different psychologists tend to ask quite different sorts of questions. Therefore, there are about as many definitions of *motivation* as there are psychologists. Almost all behavioral scientists agree, however, that humans have needs, and that the study of needs makes up a large part of what we call "motivation." So, suppose we begin this chapter by asking several questions about needs.

First, what *kinds* of needs do you have? Obviously, you have a biological requirement for things such as food and water. But can we explain everything you do in terms of your attempt to satisfy these basic *physical* wants? Or do you have intra-psychic and social needs that are (in their way) as strong as your need for food and water? If so, what are these psychological and social needs? Do they vary much from person to person, or do all people develop about the same sort of motives at the same stage in life? In short, *what kinds of needs motivate you*?

Second, *where* do your motivations come from? Your basic needs are surely instinctual, but what about your social and intra-psychic mo-

tives? Are they also determined (even in part) by your genetic blueprint? Or are they entirely imposed on you by your culture and your past experiences? In brief, how much of your motivation is *innate*, and how much is *learned*?

Third, what are the various *mechanisms* by which you satisfy your wants? Are all your behaviors aimed at reducing stress and pain? Or are you motivated primarily by the promise of pleasure? That is, do you eat to reduce your hunger pangs, or because food tastes so good?

Last, but not least, does your mind do anything more than yield to your body's itches and urges? Or can you voluntarily *choose* among a variety of behaviors in any given situation? Put more simply, can we explain your motives entirely in terms of blind biological drives, or is motivation a matter of your consciously selecting among various behaviors available to you at a given time?

These are some of the thorny questions you must try to answer when you try to explain *why* people do what they do. Little wonder, then, that the field of human motivation is at the same time one of the most fascinating yet one of the most frustrating areas in all of psychology.

Suppose we begin by looking at some early definitions of this slippery concept called motivation.

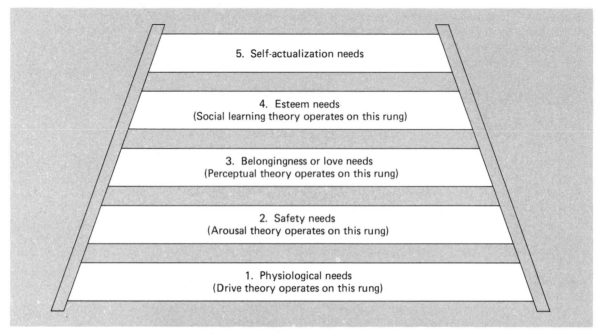

5. Self-actualization needs

4. Esteem needs
(Social learning theory operates on this rung)

3. Belongingness or love needs
(Perceptual theory operates on this rung)

2. Safety needs
(Arousal theory operates on this rung)

1. Physiological needs
(Drive theory operates on this rung)

Fig. 11.1. Maslow's hierarchy of needs.

Abraham Maslow

Motivation and Self-Movement

The word *motivation* comes from the Latin term meaning "to move." Ancient scholars were fascinated by the fact that some objects in the world seem to be *self-movers*, while other objects remain stationary unless *acted upon* by some outside force. The ancients assumed that self-initiated motion was caused by a *spirit* inside the object—a "little man" of some kind—that pushed or impelled the object into action. Whenever the "spirit was moved," so was the object or body that the spirit inhabited.

Nowadays, we assume that only living systems are capable of self-initiated movement. But to tell the truth, some of our theories of motivation (and of life itself) are still based on the idea that there is a **homunculus** deep inside us which pulls our strings and keeps us on the go. "Mind," "soul," "cosmic force," and **libido** are just a few of the terms we use to refer to this inner spirit or power that pushes us along life's path.

It was not until about the sixteenth century that Western scientists gained enough knowledge of physics to explain the "behaviors" of such **inanimate** objects as rocks and rivers in purely *mechanical* terms. That is, it was not until a few hundred years ago that we managed to get the **animus** out of inanimate objects. And once scientists had made this giant intellectual step, they began to wonder if the actions of *living* organisms couldn't also be understood in physical or non-spiritual terms. Many of our theories of motivation are thus based on the belief that human activities are just as mechanical as are the movements of bedbugs and bacteria. The best-known of these mechanistic approaches are *drive theory* and *arousal theory*.

Opposed to these biological viewpoints are a variety of psychological and social theories which stress the importance of intra-psychic and environmental influences on behavior. But these approaches are limited too, in that most of them neglect the importance of biological needs.

Fortunately, there is one holistic theory which more-or-less encompasses the biological, the social, and the intra-psychic approaches to motivation. Although it, too, is far from being complete, let's talk about that approach first, and then explain drive theory and arousal theory. Finally, we will attempt to show the real complexities of motivation by discussing one very human problem in some detail—that of why some people over-eat.

Maslow's Theory of "Self-Actualization"

According to Abraham Maslow, human needs can be placed on a **hierarchy**, or ladder. This hierarchy runs from the simplest physiological motives up to the most complex of intra-psychic and social desires. As you develop in life, you move up the ladder until you reach the top rung, which Maslow calls **self-actualization** (see Fig. 11.1).

Maslow assumes that you start life at the lowest level of the motivational hierarchy. That is, he believes you are born with innate reflexes that help you satisfy your basic biological needs. Once you are blessed with biological life, however, you must secure some control over your physical environment. Thus, almost immediately after birth, you begin to move up to the second level of the motivational hierarchy, that of safety needs.

The next two rungs of the ladder involve the social environment. You need people to love, and you need people to love you. Part of these needs are satisfied by your family, but there are also

Motivation (mote-tie-VAH-shun). From the Latin word *motivare*, meaning "to move." Motivation is defined in many different ways, the most common being that it is a series of questions that you ask about *why* people think, feel, and behave as they do.

Homunculus (ho-MUN-cue-lus). From the Greek and Latin words meaning "little man." See Chapter 4.

Libido (lib-BEE-doe). From the Latin word meaning "desire" or "lust." According to Freud, the libido is a set of unconscious instincts that provide the energy for all our thoughts and actions. See Chapter 21.

Inanimate (inn-ANN-ee-mate or inn-ANN-uh-mutt). The word "animate" comes from the Latin term meaning "breath" or "spirit." "Animate" also means "to move about in a spirited fashion." Animate objects are those that have an internal source of motivation or movement power. Inanimate objects are those that move only when acted upon by some external motivator or mover. Our word "animal" comes from the same Latin source.

Animus (ANN-ee-muss). The Latin word meaning "spirit."

Hierarchy (HIGH-er-ark-key). To make a hierarchy is to list things (or people) in order of their importance. See Chapter 14.

Self-actualization. The process of becoming the best possible person you can become, of achieving your own goals in life. See Chapter 21.

work groups and various social organizations you can join. Not only can these groups offer you rewards for performing well, but also they can help you learn what self-respect is all about.

If you are fortunate, you will finally reach the top rung of Maslow's hierarchy and achieve *self-actualization*. This term is difficult to define. Put simply, it means reaching your own greatest potential, doing the things you do best in your own unique way, and then helping those around you achieve these goals too. But you can only get to this final stage of human development by first solving the problems associated with the four lower levels.

Now that we have outlined Maslow's theory in broad terms, let's look at what he says in more detail.

Maslow's Hierarchy of Needs

Maslow states that there are five primary levels on the ladder of human motivation.

1. *Biological needs.* Bodily needs come first, which is to say that you must always satisfy your physical wants or you won't live long enough to take care of any psychological or social needs you may have. You cannot take the next step up the motivational ladder unless, and until, your primary biological needs are met. (As we will soon see, *drive theory* operates at this rung of the ladder.)
2. *Safety needs.* Neither man nor woman lives by bread alone. Once an infant's basic needs are satisfied, the child is ready to explore its physi-

"AS A MATTER OF FACT, I COULD GO FOR SOME SALTED PEANUTS."

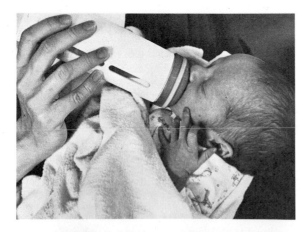

According to Maslow biological needs such as food are the most basic of all. **(top left)**

As children gain emotional security they begin to explore their physical world. **(top right)**

According to Maslow all people have "belongingness" needs that are innately determined. **(middle left)**

Maslow states that "esteem" needs are high on the hierarchy, but that gaining the esteem of others eventually teaches you the greater importance of "self-esteem." **(bottom left)**

Maslow states that "self-actualization" or desire to reach the limits of your own potential, is at the top of the needs hierarchy. **(bottom right)**

cal environment. But as we will show in later chapters, young children typically don't explore unless they feel secure. A predictable world is, generally speaking, a much safer environment than one which is unpredictable. Thus one reason that you "move about" in your environment is to reduce your uncertainty about what the world has to offer. With this knowledge, you can choose sensibly among the various physical inputs that you

need to sustain life. And once you know what to expect from the world, you can move on to the next rung of the motivational ladder. (Arousal theory operates in part at this stage of development.)

3. *Belongingness* and *love needs*. Once you have gained control over your physical environment, you can then turn your attention to social inputs. As the poet John Donne once said, "No man is an island, complete to itself." Donne knew quite well that, to be a *human* being, you must have other people around you. Thus, according to Maslow, you have an innate need for affection and love that can only be satisfied by other people. You thus must **affili-**

ate with others, and identify yourself with one or more like-minded individuals. When you identify with someone else, you learn to perceive part of the world as that person presumably does. (As we will learn in Chapters 12 and 13, perceptual and emotional theories of motivation apply primarily to the first three rungs of the ladder.)

4. *Esteem needs*. One reason you need other people is this: They can help you set your life's goals. That is, they offer you *models* or **feed-forward** on what your future behavior might (or should) be. Groups also offer you external **feedback** on how close you are coming to achieving your targets in life. And the better you get at reaching your goals, the more esteem you will likely have for yourself (and the more esteem you will probably get from others). According to Maslow, "esteem needs" are just as important for *human* life as food and water. (Social learning theory and the various theories of social motivation we will discuss later in this book operate at levels 2, 3, and 4 of the hierarchy.)

5. *Need for self-actualization*. Until you have achieved self-esteem, you probably will not feel secure enough to become a "fully-actualized person." That is, unless you have confidence in yourself, you will not dare to express yourself in your own unique way, make your own special contribution to society, and thus achieve your true inborn potential. Perhaps you will become an artist, a scientist, a teacher, a politician, a religious leader, or someone concerned with keeping the gears of business turning smoothly. Or perhaps you will prefer to spend most of your time making sure your own children live happy and productive lives. Whatever the case, you are not likely to discover what your own innate potential is until you have satisfied most of your basic physiological and social needs. And once you have achieved self-actualization for yourself, Maslow says, you will find you have a strong urge to help others get where you have gotten. And to do *that*, you will need to teach others the lessons you learned as you worked your way up the four lower levels of the motivational hierarchy. (The many theories of personality and human development discussed later apply to all the rungs of Maslow's ladder, but primarily to the fifth rung.)

Question: *How far up the ladder would a frequently abused child be likely to climb? Or a student whose teachers gave him or her nothing but criticism?*

Affiliate (aff-FILL-ee-ate). From the Latin word meaning "to adopt as a son." To affiliate means to join with or become a part of. According to many psychologists, you have an instinctual need to be with other people. Sometimes called "Need-Affiliation."

Feed-forward. The act of specifying future outputs or behaviors. Your genes are a type of biological feed-forward. Laws and organizational rules are a type of social feed-forward. See Chapter 5.

Feedback. Information on present or past outputs or behaviors. See Chapter 5.

Criticisms of Maslow's Theory

Like all theories in psychology, Maslow's *hierarchical* approach to human motivation has been subjected to many criticisms. As we will see in a later chapter, Maslow based his theory on the study of highly successful people in the Western world. Thus, his viewpoint is most applicable to middle- and upper-class individuals in our present society. But this theory may not apply to other cultures, nor even to all segments of our own society.

More than this, Maslow's is one of many "stage" theories. That is, Maslow presumed that *all* humans move up through five clearly definable steps as they mature. Whether there are actually *five* rungs to the motivational ladder, or 15, or 150, is something that Maslow never really proved. Furthermore, he assumed that you must somehow "conquer" the problems associated with each lower rung before you could move on to a higher one. This assumption is, at best, highly debatable.

Nor does Maslow tell us what physiological and psychological mechanisms underlie the types of human needs he describes. For example, he admits you need food, but he doesn't describe how your body senses and responds to this need. And he states that you strive for self-esteem and self-knowledge, but he doesn't say how you manage to learn what these concepts are all about.

Last, but not least, other than the case histories Maslow offers, there simply is no *experimental* evidence proving that Maslow's approach is correct. Indeed, it is rather difficult to imagine how one might put many of Maslow's notions to a critical test.

Strengths of Maslow's Theory

Despite these criticisms, Maslow's approach has many strengths to it. To begin with, it is one of the few theories that emphasizes the importance of *individual choice* in determining behavior. That is, Maslow views the human organism as being capable of choosing between alternative courses of action. True, many of the things you do are influenced by your biological state and your social

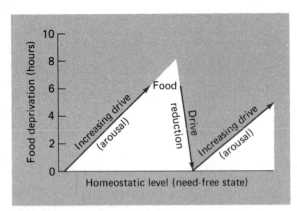

Fig. 11.2. A simple diagram of drive theory using food deprivation as an example.

chologists tried to explain all human behavior in terms of physiological processes. Rather than assuming that people (or animals) are capable of self-determined actions, these psychologists theorized that organisms are *driven* or pushed into motion much the way an automobile engine is cranked into activity when you turn the ignition key or step on the starter.

At its simplest, the physiological approach to motivation is often called **drive theory**. As David Edwards notes, Clark Hull was one of the first great drive theorists. Hull assumed that *biological* needs are the ones that rule your life. Biological pain arouses or *drives* you to movement, while reducing your drives gives you biological pleasure and rewards those movements that led to the drive reduction. Hull made the concepts of drive and drive reduction the cornerstones of his theory of learning (see Chapter 15).

You do have other motives than biological pain and pleasure, of course. But drive theorists such as Hull assume that you *learned* these needs by associating them with your attempts to reduce the physical arousals that propel you along life's highway.

Homeostasis

The key concept in understanding drive theory is that of **homeostasis**. The term itself comes from a Greek word meaning "home state" or "normal condition." To a drive theorist, your body is like an automobile engine. To keep a car's engine in a state of fine tune—its "normal condition"—you need to take constant care of it. That is, you must give the engine oil, water, fuel, and lubrication. And you must protect it from damage. To keep your body in "fine tune"—or *homeostasis*—you must also give it the things it needs to function properly. These needs include food, water, air, a given range of temperatures, and protection from germs and accidents.

Whenever the engine in your car departs from its normal condition, red lights blink on the dashboard telling you what is wrong. Perhaps you need to add oil, or buy some fuel. Whatever the case, those lights will continue to flash until you satisfy the engine's needs. In similar fashion, whenever your body runs low on food or water, warning signals go off inside you telling you something is wrong. That is, you experience hunger or thirst. And you go on being hungry or thirsty until you satisfy your body's need—and return your body to its usual *homeostatic* condition.

"Homeostasis," then, simply means the innate biological urge you have to keep your bodily processes in a balanced or need-free state.

environment. But given these limitations, you still are able (in Maslow's view) to exercise voluntary choice in most situations.

Second, Maslow's hierarchy is by far the best-known of the *holistic* approaches to the study of motivation. That is, his is one of the few theories which gives relatively equal value to biological, intra-psychic, and social/behavioral influences on behavior. Drive theory—which we will discuss momentarily—does a good job of explaining how organisms react in situations of extreme deprivation. Arousal theory incorporates the best aspects of drive theory and adds a number of its own strengths. However, none of these narrow theoretical viewpoints can begin to explain the enormous complexities of even the simplest of human activities, such as eating.

Suppose we first take a quick look at drive and arousal theory. Then we will discuss a highly specific problem—that of **obesity**—and show how drive and arousal theory simply cannot explain why we eat as we do. Finally, to make the matter both more interesting and more practical, we will use what psychologists know about human motivation to develop a highly workable recipe for *losing weight*.

Now that we have set the stage, let's see what drive theory is all about.

Drive Theory

As we noted, physics became a science when physicists began to explain the motions of inanimate objects in terms of fairly simple *equations*. For the past century, many psychologists have attempted to imitate the "hard" sciences by reducing the complexities of human motivation to fairly uncomplicated *biological* equations. Instead of dealing with the mind—with such intra-psychic events as thoughts and feelings—these psy-

Primary Needs and Drives

Most drive theorists refer to those things you absolutely must have to survive as **primary needs**. These basic needs include such things as air, food, water, and a proper temperature. Whenever you run short of one of these things, built-in mechanisms in your body detect that need. As the need increases, the firing rates in various neural centers in your brain start to increase. This increased neural activity creates a **primary drive** inside you that arouses you to action. When your arousal is great enough, you are *driven* to seek out whatever you need.

Generally speaking, the longer you are deprived of something you need, the faster your nerve cells will fire. And the more aroused your nervous system becomes, the greater the primary drive you will experience. And the stronger the drive becomes, the more "motivated" you are to reduce that drive.

For example, you have a "primary need" for food. The longer you are deprived of food, the greater your primary drive (hunger) becomes, and the more aroused or driven you are to find something to eat. If you go hungry long enough, your aroused movements will probably bring you into a position to satisfy your need. Once you do so, the "hunger centers" in your brain stop firing. At this point, your drive level decreases, your arousal (motivation) disappears, and your normal homeostatic *balance* is reinstated. (See Fig. 11.2 for a diagram of drive theory using food deprivation as an example.)

Intra-Psychic and Social Needs

You need to take in food in order to maintain your normal homeostatic "good biological health." But *what* you eat depends in large part on what drive theorists call your learned or **secondary needs**. Other psychologists refer to these as "intra-psychic needs" and "social needs."

Primary (biological) needs are innately determined. But secondary needs presumably are learned through some association with the satisfaction of a primary need. For example, suppose you "get hungry for a steak." According to drive theory, this *specific hunger* is an acquired, secondary drive. At some time in the past when you were hungry, you ate a steak. This behavior reduced your hunger drive, and you were thus rewarded for consuming a steak. As a consequence, when you get hungry in the future, you are more likely to "want" a steak than some food you've never eaten before.

To summarize, the drive approach to motivation is what we might call a biologically oriented, *one-level* theory. It is biological in orientation because physiological needs are presumed to be primary—all other motives are said to be acquired or learned. And the theory operates on only one level because it claims that the feelings, perceptions, emotions, and social behaviors of the organism are learned *because* they are associated with the reduction of primary (biological) drives.

Question: What position do drive theorists appear to be taking with regard to solving the mind-body problem?

Criticisms of Drive Theory

Many objections have been raised to the simple form of drive theory that we have just outlined. Three of the major objections are as follows:

1. Not all psychologists agree with drive theorists that intra-psychic needs are *learned*. For instance, most young animals (including children) seem to have an innate desire to explore their environment. This "exploratory drive" apparently is specified by the genetic blueprint, but it is difficult to think of "exploration" as being a *biological* need. Indeed, although we have some notion of the physical mechanisms which underlie the hunger drive, we simply don't know what part(s) of the brain control "exploration." Thus, to many psychologists, it seems more appropriate to consider exploration an innately determined *intra-psychic* drive.

2. In similar fashion, not all psychologists believe that social needs are merely acquired by asso-

---

Obesity (oh-BEE-sit-tee). From the Latin words meaning "to over-eat." Obesity means fatness; an obese (oh-BEESE) person is someone who weighs *at least* 25 percent more than the person's "ideal weight."

Drive theory. The belief that all our really important needs are physical, such as food, air, and water. Hence a biologically oriented theory that assumes intra-psychic and social/behavioral needs are learned.

Homeostasis (home-ee-oh-STAY-sis). The tendency to move toward a need-free or drive-free condition. Any action that an organism makes to reduce drives is called a "homeostatic behavior."

Primary needs. Things that the body must have in order to survive; physical needs, such as food, air, and water. Unlearned or innate needs.

Primary drive. Whenever your body is deprived of something necessary for life, an urge or desire for that "something" builds up which "drives" you to hunt for what you need. Associated with each primary need is a related primary drive. Food is a primary need; hunger is the associated primary drive.

Secondary needs. The need for food is a primary, unlearned need. The need for steak (instead of for chicken or chop suey) is acquired, as is the need for a Cadillac instead of a VW. Drive theorists assume that most social needs are secondary needs.

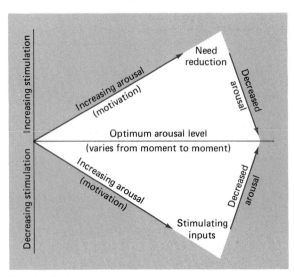

Fig. 11.3. A simple diagram of arousal theory.

ciation with the reduction of some biological drive. For example, most newborn animals seem to have an innate urge to identify with a "mother figure." And as we will see in later chapters, most female animals (including human mothers) readily develop an intense "social bond" with their infants immediately after birth. Thus mother-infant behaviors seem to be specified by the genetic blueprint. However, we don't know what biological mechanisms underlie these instinctual needs. And it is difficult to think of these highly motivated social behaviors in terms of "homeostasis."

3. Drive theory equates an *increase* in neural excitation with an *increase* in motivation. Yet, as we learned from the sensory deprivation experiments, sometimes a *decrease* in excitation can cause an *increase* in psychological arousal.

As we will see, the scientists who raised these objections often were "driven" to create competing motivational theories of their own.

Arousal Theory

In the late 1950's, Elizabeth Duffy (and others) made a telling criticism of classical drive theory. Duffy had spent many years studying the exploratory drive in animals. Her work convinced her that arousal is not always caused by a lack of such things as food, air, or water. For we have intra-psychic *informational needs* that are as innate and as highly motivating as are our life-sustaining or *energy needs* (see Chapter 5). And the "boredom" associated with a marked *decrease* in neural excitation can be as arousing or motivating as

the *increase* in neural firing typically associated with food deprivation (see Chapter 8).

This objection led Duffy and other scientists to create a new approach to motivation called **arousal theory**. The basic **postulates** of this position can be summarized as follows:

1. Homeostasis isn't really a point of *zero* neural excitation, but rather is a point of **optimum** stimulation.
2. This optimum point may *change* from time to time, depending on your biological condition.
3. A *decrease* in optimum stimulation may be as arousing or motivating as an *increase*.

Boredom and Homeostasis

Arousal theory had its beginnings not only in Duffy's work on the exploratory drive, but also in the sensory deprivation experiments we described in Chapter 8.

The concept of *boredom* was always a difficult one for the drive theorists to handle. For example, consider the hunger drive. Technically speaking, any balanced diet should satisfy all of your biological needs for food. Therefore, from a drive theory point of view, you might well be expected to eat the same menu at every meal. But eating *exactly the same foods* at every meal gets boring, so you tend to vary what you consume. Yet, according to classical drive theory, you should eat primarily those foods you've eaten most often in the past. And it's difficult for a drive theorist to explain why you should ever eat something entirely new to you while old (and satisfying) foods are available.

In similar fashion, lying quietly in a sensory deprivation chamber theoretically should be a very pleasant thing—if all of your biological needs are being met. However, as you know, most subjects put in "womb tanks" were highly motivated to seek increased sensory arousal. Yet, according to classical drive theory, a *decrease* in excitation is always rewarding while an *increase* in neural firing presumably is always painful or punishing.

The conclusion Duffy drew from these points is as follows: You do not have a single "homeostatic level" that is set at birth and never varies thereafter. Rather, your need for stimulation changes according to your past experience and present conditions.

Optimum Arousal

According to Duffy, the optimum level of stimulation you need *varies from moment to moment*. There is good reason why this is so. If your sensory inputs become too constant, your receptors "turn off" and leave you with little or no stimulation at all. And if your inputs vary too much, your environment becomes too unpredictable.

Thus you need a certain amount of *stability* in the world around you—just as the homeostatic model would predict. However, you also need a certain amount of *variability* in stimulation. According to Duffy, your "point of optimum arousal" will fluctuate from moment to moment in response to the level of inputs that you receive from your environment. But this optimum point will always lie somewhere between complete stability and complete unpredictability. (Fig. 11.3 illustrates how we might diagram arousal theory.)

Question: In Chapter 3, we noted that certain drugs such as LSD lead to a stressful experience called "loss of personal control." In Chapter 8, we noted that sensory deprivation can cause a panic-inducing experience in which subjects can no longer control their thought patterns. How might both these unpleasant situations be related to a need to predict and control your inputs?

Problems with Arousal Theory

Arousal theory was a noticeable improvement over drive theory in that Duffy could explain a number of motivational situations that early drive theorists had difficulties with. But the arousal position remained a one-level, biological theory that reduced motivation to what seemed to be purely physical processes.

In particular, neither position was able to explain the incredible complexity of even the simplest of human behaviors. To see why this was the case—and to show why many psychologists prefer a broader view of motivation—suppose we look in considerable detail at an important American problem, that of people who overeat.

Obesity: A Holistic Approach

There are four billion people living on earth at the present time. At least a third of these people don't get as much of the right things to eat as they should, and hence are undernourished or suffer from **malnutrition**.

There are more than 230 million people in the United States. Perhaps because we are the richest, most powerful nation on earth, only a relatively small percentage of our population is badly undernourished. Hunger *is* a very real problem for some people living in poverty-stricken rural and slum areas. But many more Americans suffer because they eat too much, not too little.

Arousal theory. A one-level, biologically oriented theory in which motivation comes from some departure from a norm or optimum point of neural excitation. Any increase or decrease in neural firing moves the organism away from this optimum point and hence is arousing.

Postulates (POSS-tew-lates or POSS-tew-lutts). To postulate is to make a guess about something, or to insist that something exists or is very important. Postulates may or may not be facts.

Optimum (OPP-tee-mum or OPP-tuh-mum). From the Latin word meaning "best." Literally, the most favorable point or condition.

Malnutrition (mal-new-TRISH-shun). The French word *mal* means "bad," or "sickness." Nutrition is the whole process of eating food, digesting it, and turning it into energy that your body can use. Malnutrition comes from not having enough food to eat, or from eating the wrong kinds.

Overweight. Scientists have worked out an "ideal weight" for people, depending (mostly) on their age and height. Anyone who tips the scales at 10 percent more than this "ideal" is usually considered to be "slightly overweight," and anyone more than 25 percent above this "ideal" is usually considered to be "noticeably overweight." The definition of "overweight," however, varies considerably from one expert to another.

Calories (KAL-or-rees). The Latin word *calor* means "heat." The caloric (kal-LOR-ick) content of anything is the amount of heat it will generate when burned. Your body "burns" food when it converts what you eat into energy to keep you alive. Rich, sweet, fatty foods have lots of calories (that is, a high caloric content). Water has no calories at all. Fat burns; water doesn't.

Dietitians estimate that from 10 to 25 percent of the American public is **overweight**.

The average family doctor treats more than 10 patients a month who want to lose weight. Perhaps 1 in 20 of these patients has a *physical* problem that is responsible for the fatness. And with these patients, the medical profession can often be of considerable help. The other 19 out of 20 people are fat simply because they take in more **calories** than they use up, and their bodies store the surplus energy as fat tissue. And with these patients, medical science has not done particularly well.

At a 1972 meeting on the topic of fatness, Dr. Alvan Feinstein of the Yale Medical School reported that the success rate of most *medical* weight-loss programs is "terrible, much worse than in cancer." The situation hasn't changed much since 1972. Experts now estimate that only some 12 out of 100 patients who seek a *physician's* help actually lose weight, and that 10 out of these 12 gain back their excess pounds within a year or two.

Presuming that your own weight is normal, why should you worry about such things? First, because fatness could happen to you someday, and probably has already happened to several of your friends or relatives. Second, because fat people are a very discriminated-against minority.

Marshall R. Jones

The Biology of Hunger

Marshall Jones, who has spent most of his career studying problems of motivation, points out an interesting fact: Motivated behaviors are often *related sequences of responses*. And to understand behavioral sequences, you must answer the following questions:

1. Why does a given behavioral sequence begin? That is, what inputs prompt the thought or get the action going?
2. Why does the behavior go in a particular direction once it begins?
3. Why does the thought or behavior eventually come to an end? That is, once a behavioral sequence has begun, what brings it to a stop?

Eating is a motivated behavior—but so are over-eating and under-eating. Therefore, to understand why you eat as you do, we must answer three critical questions: Why do you start eating? Why do you prefer steak and ice cream to fried worms and boiled monkey brains? And why do you eventually stop eating?

As we will see, drive theory and arousal theory offer partial answers to these questions. But they have little to say about why you select the foods you choose to consume, much less why you eat when you're not really hungry.

Question: From a motivational point of view, fat people might be overweight for at least four reasons: (1) They eat too frequently; (2) once started, they don't know when to quit; (3) they prefer rich, fat-laden foods; and (4) they don't burn up enough energy through exercise and physical labor. Would you think that different forms of therapy would be needed depending on what combination of these four behaviors the person engaged in?

Problems Overweight People Face

If you are overweight, you have difficulty buying attractive clothes. You also have difficulty getting out of many chairs and getting into some small cars. Getting a job can also be a problem, since many employers are hesitant to hire overweight individuals.

Fatness can even affect your academic career. Several years ago, H. Canning and J. Mayer made an interesting study of the effects of obesity on high school students. These scientists report that school counselors are less likely to write letters of recommendation for fat students than for normals. Canning and Mayer also found that college admissions committees discriminate against fat students during interviews. Faced with two students with equally good grades and equally high test scores, college committees tend to accept the non-obese student and to shut out the one who weighs too much.

Unfair? Of course it is. So is our society's discrimination against people with dark skins or slanted eyes. Of course most of us realize that you had little to say about your skin color—but fatness is primarily a *voluntary choice*, isn't it?

No, in a very strange way, you are not entirely responsible for how much you weigh. First, there is a strong genetic component in fatness, and you are no more to blame for inheriting "fat genes" than for inheriting a certain skin color. Second, the psychological and social influences on fatness or thinness are just as important as the genetic factors. So if you happen to be snacking on something delicious, perhaps you'll want to put the food aside while we look at the biological, intra-psychic, and social/behavioral influences on **gluttony**.

Blood Sugar Level

When you eat a dish of ice cream for dessert, how does your body make use of this fuel? To begin with, your digestive system breaks the food into tiny molecules, most of which contain sugar. Blood containing these energy-rich molecules flows to almost every part of your body and passes sugar on to any cell that might be "hungry." A few hours after you have eaten a large meal, your blood contains a great many sugar molecules. However, if you starve yourself for 24 hours or so, your blood would contain relatively few of these energy particles.

Here is our first clue as to what the *hunger drive* is all about. To maintain its homeostatic balance, your body needs a certain level of sugar in its blood. And when this level drops below a certain point, you experience hunger "pangs" and are aroused to seek out food. Therefore, if we could somehow control the molecules floating around in your bloodstream, might we not be able to control your sensation of hunger directly?

From a purely biological point of view, the answer is a probable yes. Under normal conditions, your body secretes a chemical called **insulin** which stimulates your body to digest sugar. If we let a hungry rat eat all that it wants, then take a blood sample from the animal a little later, we would find a lot of sugar molecules in the rat's blood. If we now inject the animal with insulin, its blood sugar level drops—and to our surprise the rat will soon begin to eat again (even though it had a very large meal just minutes before).

Somewhere in your body, then, there must be a "sugar detector" that lets your cortex know how many sugar molecules are floating around in your bloodstream. Recent research suggests that this "detector" is located in a central part of your brain called the **hypothalamus**.

The Hypothalamic "Feeding Center"

Sitting right at the top of your *brain stem* is a neural center called the **thalamus**. The thalamus is a sort of "central switchboard" through which sensory inputs pass before being relayed to your cortex. The word "hypo" means "below" or "beneath." The hypothalamus is a bundle of nerve cells lying just under the thalamus that exercises rather strong control over many of your physiological motivations and emotions (see Fig. 11.4).

One small part of your hypothalamus contains neurons that are particularly sensitive to the amount of sugar in your blood. When the blood sugar level drops too low, the cells in this region of your hypothalamus begin to fire more rapidly—and you typically begin to feel hungry.

If we put a metal electrode into this part of a rat's brain and stimulate the cells electrically, the rat will begin to eat at once (even if it has just had a big meal). If we stimulate this hypothalamic **feeding center** continuously, the rat will eat and eat and eat—until it becomes so obese that it can barely move around. If we continue the electrical stimulation even when food is not present in the rat's cage, the animal will often gnaw on anything handy—including air.

If we destroy this "feeding center" in the rat's hypothalamus, the animal often refuses to eat at all and will die of starvation unless we force-feed it.

Does this one "feeding center" in the hypothalamus control all aspects of eating behavior? Certainly not. To begin with, even the "dumb rat" knows better than to over-eat continuously, no

Gluttony (GLUT-tone-ee). From the Latin word meaning "to gulp or swallow." A glutton (GLUT-tun) is someone who enjoys over-eating. A "glutton for punishment" is someone who "eats up punishment with pleasure."

Insulin (IN-sull-in). A hormone secreted by the pancreas (PAN-kree-uss), which is a small organ near the stomach. Insulin makes it easier for the cells in your body to take in sugar molecules. People whose bodies do not secrete enough insulin may suffer from a disease called diabetes (die-uh-BEET-ease). Diabetics (die-uh-BETT-ticks) have to control the amount of sugar they eat, and may have to take daily injections of insulin.

Hypothalamus (HIGH-po-THALL-ah-muss). A very important neural center lying just under the thalamus. The hypothalamus influences many types of motivated or emotional behavior, including eating and drinking.

Thalamus (THALL-uh-muss). Sensory messages from your eyes, ears, skin, nose, and tongue all pass through the thalamus before being passed on to your cortex (and other higher centers of your brain). The thalamus is thus a sort of "giant switchboard" in your brain.

Feeding center. That portion of the hypothalamus which, when stimulated electrically, causes an organism to engage in eating behaviors.

Endorphin (en-DORF-in). A class of chemicals secreted by the body that act as "natural pain killers." See Chapters 3 and 17.

matter what we do to it. If we give rats the continual hypothalamic stimulation mentioned earlier, the animals will become very, very fat. But eventually they will reach a cut-off point beyond which they will not go. Their weights will stabilize at this point and we cannot induce them to become much fatter.

(You will probably be pleased to know that, when we stop prodding the rat's brain with electrical stimulation, the animal will typically go on a "crash diet" and return to its normal body weight.)

Stress and Over-Eating

As we noted in Chapter 3, your body produces a natural pain-killer called **endorphin**. According to R.L. Atkinson of the University of Virginia, endorphin may be related to fatness.

A number of experiments show that when you are stressed, endorphin secretion increases dramatically. In the May 1981 issue of *Science 81*, Atkinson reports that endorphin not only kills pain, it also increases the production of insulin. The insulin then reduces the blood sugar level, causing you to feel hungry. So you eat—in response to the stress, not because you really need more food. But the food you consume causes your body to release even more insulin, which again lowers your blood sugar level. And soon you are caught in a stress-related cycle in which the act of eating causes you to eat some more.

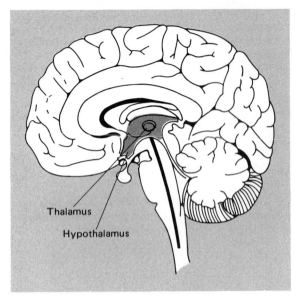

Fig. 11.4. The hypothalamus and thalamus.
A hypothalmic, hyperphagic rat. **(right)**

R.L. Atkinson believes that many people are overweight because their bodies produce too much endorphin. As of 1982, Atkinson had shown that a chemical which reduces the endorphin level in rats caused the animals to lose weight. Whether or not this chemical will be of help to humans, however, is something that Atkinson is still testing.

Problems with "The Hunger Drive"

Drive theory can explain rather readily why you start to eat. As the sugar content in the blood reaching your brain *decreases*, electrical activity in your hypothalamic "feeding center" *increases*. Your cortex translates this neural input into the psychological experience of "hunger pangs." And you go looking for a decent meal, just as drive theory would predict. But why do you stop eating once you've begun? Why don't you munch away for hours and hours?

Because, you say, as soon as you start eating, the sugar content in your blood goes up dramatically and your "feeding center" turns off. That explanation would surely fit drive theory, but it happens not to be so. For eating behavior doesn't have a simple explanation, even at a biological level.

If you ate a big steak right now, it would take several hours for the meat to be digested and assimilated into your bloodstream. It takes only 10 to 20 minutes for you to eat the steak, though. Thus you actually *stop eating* long before that steak can greatly affect your blood sugar level. In

fact, if you're a quick eater, your "feeding center" may still be signaling "eat—eat—eat!" at the top of its neural voice at the very moment when you push yourself away from the table, so stuffed with food that you can't imagine ever being hungry again.

So a lowered blood sugar level can turn *on* your hunger. But what physiological mechanism turns it *off*?

The Hypothalamic "Satiation Center"

As arousal theory points out, homeostasis is really a *balance* of forces, rather than being a point of zero excitation. Thus for every physiological function that pushes you in one direction, there is another function which tends to pull you back toward an optimum level of existence.

So if there is a "feeding center" in your hypothalamus that causes you to *start* eating, wouldn't you guess there might also be a center that, when stimulated, causes you to *stop* eating? It is called the **satiation center**, and it is also located in your hypothalamus, close to your "feeding center."

Suppose we implant an electrode in a rat's hypothalamic "satiation center." Then, just as the hungry animal starts to eat, we pass a weak electrical current through this "satiation center." The animal will suddenly refuse its meal. And if we continue the stimulation for a long enough time, the animal will come close to starving itself to death.

On the other hand, if we surgically remove the rat's "satiation center," the animal will become **hyper-phagic**. That is, the animal will go on an eating jag and will become as obese as the rats whose "feeding centers" were electrically stimulated. But as you might already have surmised, eventually the animal will reach its "obesity limit" and will taper off its wild consumption of food.

Under normal conditions, your "satiation center" functions *symmetrically* with the "feeding center." When your blood sugar level goes up, the neurons in your "feeding center" *decrease* their response rate and the nerve cells in your "satiation center" *increase* their firing rate. When your blood sugar level falls, your "feeding center" turns on and your "satiation center" turns off.

Furthermore, your "satiation center" seems sensitive to inputs from your digestive system as well as from your blood sugar level. In the August 12, 1980 issue of *Science*, R.D. Myers and M.L. McCaleb report that receptor cells in the stomach are connected directly to the "satiation center." When Myers and McCaleb injected food into the stomach of rats, these receptors sent messages to the hypothalamus which caused neurons in the "satiation center" to increase their firing rate. The Myers and McCaleb research is important because it may tell us why you stop eating before your blood sugar level falls—the mere presence of food in your stomach may cause your "satiation center" to start responding (and thus decrease your hunger pangs).

So now we know why you start eating and stop eating, don't we?

Sadly enough, we've learned only part of the answer. For what do you think would happen if we surgically removed *both* the "feeding center" and the "satiation center" from a rat's hypothalamus? Would the animal starve, or would it become obese?

The answer is, some animals will starve, but many will continue to eat pretty much as they did before the operation. So there must be systems in the brain other than the "feeding" and "satiation" centers that strongly influence eating behaviors.

The "Swallow Counter"

One mechanism for turning off eating behavior is what we might call the **swallow counter**.

A young rat eats almost continuously. As it grows up, however, it soon learns to associate the intensity of its hunger pangs with the amount of food that it ought to eat. When the rat has been deprived of food for a couple of hours, it eats a

small amount. But when it has gone without eating for 12 hours, it will consume a great deal more food. The question is, how does the rat know how much food it actually needs?

Research indicates that some part of the animal's brain actually *counts* the number of swallows the animal makes as it eats. When the rat has had enough to satisfy its *present* state of hunger, it stops eating. And it stops *before* there is much of a change in its blood sugar level, or in the firing rates in its "feeding" and "satiation" centers. So learning plays as much of a role in turning the hunger drive on and off as do the centers in the hypothalamus.

Stellar's Experiments

But even the "swallow counter" doesn't give us the whole answer to the puzzling question, "Why do you stop eating?" For example, experiments by Eliot Stellar and his associates at the University of Pennsylvania suggest that people are able to control their food inputs even if they can't "count" what they're swallowing.

Stellar and his colleagues asked students to swallow a tiny plastic tube that pumped liquid food directly into their stomachs when the students pressed a lever. The students could not see, smell, taste, chew, or swallow the food. But they somehow learned to control the amount they consumed just as readily as if they were drinking it from a glass. Perhaps the most interesting result of these experiments was the fact that the students were completely unable to explain to Professor Stellar how they managed this feat!

Stellar's experiments suggest that your stomach "knows" things about your eating habits that your "feeding" and "satiation" centers are only dimly aware of. For example, when you've packed your stomach with a huge meal (or with liquid), the muscles in your stomach are stretched out or distended. The feedback nerve cells in your stomach would surely let your brain

---

Satiation center (say-she-A-shun). Our word "satisfied" comes from the Latin words *satis*, meaning "enough," and *facere*, meaning "to do" or "to make." Satiation is the condition of being completely satisfied. The "satiation center" is that part of the hypothalamus which, when stimulated electrically, causes a hungry animal to stop eating—that is, to behave as if it were already satisfied.

Hyper-phagic (HIGH-purr-FAY-gick). From the Greek and Latin words meaning "big eater" or "over-eating." A rat that ate too little and became dangerously thin would be *hypo-phagic*.

Swallow counter. That part of the brain that supposedly measures the amount of food an organism takes in. No one really knows where or what it is.

Walter B. Cannon

Hilde Bruch

Elliot Stellar

Albert J. Stunkard

Stanley Schachter

know how inflated your stomach was, and then your cortex could inhibit or block out the input messages from your "feeding center" even before your blood sugar level changed.

It is possible that Stellar's results could be explained by appealing to the research just cited by Myers and McCaleb. That is, perhaps the liquid food merely stimulated the stomach receptors that are connected to the "satiation center." However, research by Walter Cannon suggests a different mechanism is involved.

Cannon's Experiments

Long before the "feeding center" had been discovered, physiologist Walter Cannon performed a very important experiment on hunger. He got a student volunteer to swallow a balloon attached to a long hose. Once the balloon was inside the man's stomach, Cannon pumped air through the hose and inflated the balloon until it pushed firmly against the walls of the subject's stomach. (Fortunately, the man suffered little or no pain from this procedure.) Now, whenever the man's stomach contracted at all, the balloon was pinched and air was forced up the tube. By measuring the air pressure in the hose, Cannon got an excellent reading of when the man's stomach muscles churned about.

Cannon found that "stomach contractions" began an hour or so before the man would normally have eaten a meal. As lunch time approached, for instance, the man's stomach began to contract more and more vigorously—and the man reported an increased interest in food. An hour or so after the man's usual lunch time, the stomach contractions almost stopped—*despite the fact that the man hadn't eaten a thing*. The man's subjective experience of hunger also decreased.

If you eat lunch every day at 12 noon, your "feeding center" and other parts of your brain begin to *anticipate* when they will have to go to work. An hour or so before noon, your brain starts sending neural signals to the muscles in your stomach telling them to "wake up" and get ready to start performing. The muscles contract in response to these signals, and your stomach "growls."

Other parts of your brain notice the growling (and the input signals coming from your "feeding center") and decide you're probably hungry. The closer the clock gets to noon, the more vigorously your stomach muscles respond.

Oddly enough, if you once get past the lunch hour without eating, your stomach will often calm down just as it does after you have eaten. Then your hunger pangs will decrease, only to rise again as supper time approaches.

Question: *Why do both your hunger "pangs" and your stomach contractions tend to decrease after lunch even though you didn't eat anything?*

The Hunger Habit

The hunger pangs that come from stomach contractions are **conditioned**. But almost any conditioned habit can be unlearned if you go about it the right way. If you stop eating *entirely*, your subjective experience of hunger will rise to a maximum in three to five days as the centers in your brain and the muscles in your stomach continue to anticipate meal after missed meal. By the end of five days of *complete* starvation, however, your body will have started to learn that food simply isn't going to be coming along as it once did. Your stomach contractions will slow down and eventually cease almost entirely, and your subjective experience of hunger will drop to a low ebb. However, if you go on a diet and "eat just a little" at each regular meal time, your "habitual" stomach contractions will take a very long time to change, and you may experience biting, gnawing hunger for weeks on end.

If you wish to break the hunger habit in order to gain better control over your own food intake, you might be wise to do so slowly—by putting yourself on a very irregular eating schedule. If you vary the times at which you eat, the number of meals each day, and the amount you consume at each meal, you will slowly train your body not to be hungry at specific times of the day. Once you have lost the hunger habit, you will find that dieting is somewhat easier.

Obesity and "Body Signals"

In 1959, psychiatrist A.J. Stunkard repeated parts of Cannon's balloon experiment with 37 obese and 37 normal subjects. That is, he asked these subjects to swallow balloons that would let him record their stomach movements. Then, for several hours, he frequently asked the subjects whether or not they *felt* hungry.

Stunkard found that, when their stomachs were *not* contracting, both fat and normal people were much alike—about 38 percent of them reported they were hungry. When their stomachs *were* contracting, however, the groups were markedly different. About 71 percent of the normals said they were hungry, while only 48 percent of the fat subjects said they were hungry. No matter what kinds of reports they gave, however, both groups of subjects showed about the *same number* of stomach contractions during the experiment.

There are at least two explanations for Stunkard's results. The first is that fat people have *defective sensory input*. That is to say, their stomachs contract, but the receptor cells in their stomachs don't let their brains know what is happening. Further research reported by Stunkard in the early 1970's casts doubt on this possibility. For Stunkard has now proved that fat people can very easily be *trained* to recognize their own stomach contractions.

Conditioned (konn-DISH-shunned). When an organism is trained to give a particular response to a specific stimulus, we say that it has been conditioned to respond to that stimulus. As we will see in Chapter 15, there are several types of conditioning. Psychologists often use the words "learning" and "conditioning" as if they were the same.

The second explanation seems more probable—fat people simply don't *listen* to what their bodies are trying to tell them. Psychoanalyst Hilde Bruch reported in 1961 that her obese patients literally did not know when they were physiologically hungry. Dr. Bruch suggests that, during childhood, these patients were not taught to discriminate between hunger and other arousal states such as fear, anger, and anxiety.

Perhaps fat people simply label almost *any* state of physiological arousal as hunger. And so they eat whenever they are angry, anxious, upset, or annoyed. To understand what Dr. Bruch was talking about, we must look more closely at hunger as a "mental experience."

Question: As we noted earlier, R.L. Atkinson has recently shown that rats tend to over-eat when stressed because endorphin increases the amount of insulin in their blood. How might you use Atkinson's laboratory studies to explain Bruch's clinical findings?

Intra-Psychic Influences on Obesity

Consciously or unconsciously, many parents train their children to be over-eaters. Sometimes the parents are overweight themselves and, without realizing it, over-feed their children in order to make the children like themselves. Other parents may believe that "fatness" and good health are pretty much the same thing. If the usual reward that the parents offer the child for good behavior is an extra helping of pie or cake, the child will soon learn that over-eating is a very effective way of winning approval. Food then takes on the *symbolic meaning* of love and acceptance. Later, as an adolescent or young adult, the person may feel a yearning to "raid the refrigerator" whenever she or he feels rejected or disappointed by life.

Data to support this view come from an additional series of studies by Hilde Bruch, who found that many overweight people felt unwanted, inadequate, and insecure as children. According to Dr. Bruch, these subjects began over-eating not only to gain attention from their parents, but also because eating too much made them feel big and important to themselves.

Schachter's Studies of Obesity

If fat people eat to satisfy symbolic needs—or because they cannot tell the difference between hunger and some other form of arousal—then one would expect eating behavior to be primarily under the control of internal or intra-psychic drives.

Columbia psychologist Stanley Schachter disputes this view—at least as far as fat people are concerned. Schachter believes that normal people eat when their bodies tell them to—that is, when their stomachs contract and their "feeding centers" are active. However, according to Schachter, obese people *don't listen to their bodies*. Rather than being driven to eat by internal cravings and desires, overweight individuals are simply abnormally sensitive to the world around them. In one set of studies, Schachter and his group showed that fat subjects tend to "eat by the clock," not by how much their stomachs are contracting. In another study, Schachter showed that fat people tend to be "plate cleaners" who eat everything set before them whether they need it or not. Normal people, on the other hand, pay attention to their stomachs and eat what they need even if this means "leaving a little something on the plate."

Fat people are also more affected by the taste of food than normals, according to Schachter. When offered food of average or above-average taste, fat individuals eat a great deal more than do normals. When offered food of below-average or miserable taste, however, fat people eat a great deal less than normals do. Obese individuals are also less likely to perform physical labor for food, or to suffer mild amounts of pain to get to eat, than are normals.

When we see someone who is grossly overweight, we often assume that their problem is that they are greedy, psychologically immature, or that they must have a physiological difficulty of some kind. That is, we *attribute* their obesity to some sort of "character defect." But if Schachter is right, the major cause of obesity may be *external* rather than *internal*, for we often forget the strong effects that our culture has on our eating habits.

Let us now look briefly at how the social environment influences what, when, and how people eat.

Question: Why would a drive theorist have difficulties explaining the results of Schachter's studies? Why wouldn't Maslow have the same difficulties?

Social/Behavioral Influences on Obesity

The social world you live in plays a great part in controlling what you eat—and when you eat it. In some cultures where food is or has been scarce, being fat is a sign of wealth. In other societies, "eating regularly and frequently" is not only a habit, but a status symbol of sorts.

For example, European farm workers often have five or six "regular" mealtimes per day. When they are working in the fields 12 to 14 hours daily, they need all this fuel to stay healthy. But many of them continue to eat just as frequently when they move to the city and take jobs in offices. They may even continue their five meals a day when they move to a new country.

A recent study by A.J. Stunkard shows that farm women from central Europe who immigrate to the United States are four to five times more likely to be overweight as are women from the same background whose families have lived in the United States for several generations.

People from different **social classes** in the US have quite different types of eating habits. Men and women who belong to the wealthiest or "upper class" tend to be thinner, healthier, and to live longer than do men and women of the so-called "lower class."

Many upper-class women jokingly remark that, "You can't be too thin or too rich." A recent study of 1,660 adults living in New York City tends to confirm this view. Some 32 percent of the men and 30 percent of the women in the lower classes were found to be obese. However, only 16 percent of the men and 5 percent of the women in the upper class were overweight. Four times more upper-class women were "thin" than were women in the lower class. And the chances that an upper-class individual will go on a diet are two to three times as great as the chances that a person from any other social class will start to lose weight voluntarily.

Fat Wives and Insecure Husbands

Many of our social needs are pressed upon us by the people around us. Thus we may over-drink or over-eat because individuals we love may be *rewarded* in various ways when we are drunk or fat.

Richard B. Stuart worked for many months with married women who were complete failures at losing weight. Stuart eventually began to suspect that the women's husbands were partially responsible for keeping their wives **corpulent**. To test his hypothesis, Stuart asked these couples to make tape recordings of their dinner-table conversations.

Stuart found that, although all the women were on diets and their husbands knew it, the husbands were 12 times more likely to *criticize* their wives' eating behaviors than to praise them. The men were also four times more likely to offer food to their wives than the wives were to offer food to the husbands. These "food-pushing" husbands fell roughly into four groups:

1. Some husbands enjoyed demonstrating their masculine power by coaxing or forcing their wives to become fat. If the wife was overweight, the husband sometimes found this a useful fact to bring up in family arguments. The man could win almost any battle by calling the woman "a fat slob." Stuart believes the husbands realized (perhaps unconsciously) that if their wives lost weight, they would begin losing more arguments.
2. Other husbands viewed dinner time as being the main social event of the day. When the wives refused to eat very much, the husbands saw this as a rejection of themselves and the rest of the family group.
3. Some men had lost any sexual interest in their wives. They seemed to want to keep their wives fat as an excuse for their "playing around" with other women. Stuart's data also indicate that the husband lost sexual interest first, and then began rewarding the woman for over-eating, rather than losing interest after the wife was already fat.
4. Other husands apparently feared their wives might be unfaithful to them if the women were too attractive. These men encouraged their wives to over-eat in order to keep their wives fat—and therefore faithful.

Question: *Do you think even a superb therapist could help these women change their eating behaviors unless the husbands were somehow motivated to solve their own psychological problems?*

How To Lose Weight

Like almost everything else you do, your eating behavior is *multi-determined*. That is, you eat not just because you've been without food for a while, but also because: (1) your blood sugar level has fallen; (2) your stomach is contracting; (3) your "feeding center" has increased its neural activity; (4) your "satiation center" has decreased its neural activity; (5) your "swallow counter" has been silent for a while; (6) your regular dinner time is approaching; (7) you smell food in the air and hear other people talking about "what's for lunch"; (8) because your mother and father

Social classes. A way of grouping or classifying people according to their occupations, incomes, family histories, where they live, and their social relationships. There are three general classes. About 5 percent of the US population is said to be "upper class." These people are mostly very rich. About 40 percent of the US population is considered to be "middle class." These people are white-collar workers, middle-level executives, or professional people. About 55 percent of the population is said to be "lower class." These people are blue-collar workers, who perform unskilled or semi-skilled jobs and who have less education and (usually) smaller incomes than do members of the other two classes.

Corpulent (KOR-pew-lent). From the Latin word *corpus*, or "body." We get our words "corpse" and "corporation" from the same Latin source. To be "corpulent" is to have too much body—that is, to be somewhat obese.

thought that fat babies were healthy babies; and (9) because food and eating have a variety of symbolic values for you.

Obviously, then, if you want to lose weight, your dietary program must take into account not just the calories you consume and how you burn them up, but your *motives* and *mannerisms*, as well as the behavior of the people around you.

If you wish to embark on a well-rounded weight-loss program, the first thing you should do is to have a physical check-up. That way you can make sure that you are not that one American in 20 who is under- or overweight because you have a physical problem of some kind. If you want to gain or lose more than 5 to 10 kilograms (11 to 22 pounds), you probably should do so under medical guidance. Your physician may wish to prescribe drugs to help control your appetite, and may also send you to see a registered dietician.

However, diets and pills are only the first step in a long journey. The real problem usually lies in learning enough about yourself to recognize what internal and external *stimulus inputs* affect your eating behavior. You must somehow *measure* these inputs—and their consequences—and then change the way you react to these inputs.

Using Behavior Modification To Lose Weight

If you wish to lose weight, you might consider using *behavior modification* to help you do so, for a variety of studies show that the behavioral approach yields the best long-term results as far as weight loss is concerned. Many behavioral therapists recommend a program which has nine steps to it:

1. Begin by recording *everything* you eat and drink for a period of a week or so. Psychologists call this "taking a **baseline**." Your own

For the most part, we are a diet and weight conscious people. We try many different methods of weight control from fad diets to carefully monitored programs.

baseline should include a record of where you eat, the events that occurred just before you started eating, what you thought about just before you ate (and afterward). And, *most important*, you should note who is around when you eat and what their response is to your food intake. Is anyone in your life (other than yourself) rewarded by your being too fat or too thin? In brief, your baseline should be a measure both of *what you eat* and the psychological and social *consequences* of your eating behaviors.

2. Write down all the rewards and pleasures that will come to you if you gain better control over your eating behavior.

3. Break the hunger habit by changing your meal times to a very irregular schedule several weeks before you begin your diet. (If you are underweight and eat irregularly, you may wish to force yourself to eat on schedule in order to help build up the hunger habit so that your stomach muscles will begin urging you to eat more.)

4. Increase your physical activities to help you burn off excess fat. If you are out of shape, begin by walking a few minutes each day and work up from there. *Don't* push yourself to do too much at any one time. Pick the forms of physical exertion you like best, and *keep a record* of what you do so that you can note your progress. A 1982 doctoral study at The University of Michigan suggests that *only those people who keep behavioral records* are likely to maintain an exercise program once they begin it.

5. Once you have your baseline material available, you may want to talk things over with a psychologist. You may be using your fatness as a psychological defense, or as a substitute for healthier behaviors. Unless you solve your own psychological problems first, you are not likely to be particularly successful at losing weight.

6. Habits are difficult to change, and you will

probably need all the help you can get. So you may find it wise to involve as many people as possible in your program. If someone close to you unconsciously wants you to remain fat, you may well have to find some substitute reward for this person if you are to gain her or his active and willing participation in your weight-loss program.

7. When you start your program, make a large chart or graph on which you record each aspect of your daily routine. Post the graph in a prominent place so that everyone can see your progress and comment on it. Have someone give you regular rewards (money, special privileges, a gold star on your chart, or a verbal pat on the back) each time that you meet your daily goal. Give yourself a bonus for meeting that goal every day for a whole week. This graph is perhaps the *most important part* of any weight-control program, for it gives you immediate feedback on your progress. Learning to eat correctly is a matter of establishing voluntary self-control over your actions. And without feedback, you will find it almost impossible to acquire the self-discipline you will need both to get your weight down and to *keep* it down.

8. Don't expect too much too fast. Unless you change your diet drastically, your average weight loss or gain will be about two pounds a week. Because your weight fluctuates from day to day, it is good to keep track of what you eat

and the exercise you do *in addition* to charting your weight each day.

9. Don't think of your program as being a "weight-loss" program, or you probably won't maintain your gains. Rather, think of it as your way of finally learning how to eat properly.

Losing Weight Means Knowing Yourself

Long-term weight loss may be difficult to achieve because it is affected by so many different parts of your life. If you set realistic goals for yourself, you can probably achieve them. And as you see the first small effects of your program take place, you will probably be encouraged to continue. The old saying that "nothing succeeds like success" has a great deal of psychological truth to it. So do your best to arrange your program so that—at least at the beginning—there is little or no chance you can fail.

However, if after the first few days your graph shows that things aren't going as they should, don't hesitate to make adjustments in your schedule. And keep on making changes until you find something that works for you.

Even if you are one of the lucky majority of people whose weight is more-or-less normal, you still might wish to try to gain or lose a few pounds as an experiment on yourself. For once you have put yourself through this kind of psychological analysis, you will have achieved something even more important than gaining voluntary control over your own eating behavior—you will have learned a great deal more about your own motives, desires, habits, needs, and drives than reading a textbook can ever teach you.

The Concept of Choice

Now that we've given you an overview of the field of motivation, perhaps you can understand several things about this fascinating part of psychology better than when you started the chapter. To begin with, perhaps you can now see why a simple question such as, "Why do some people overeat?" is so difficult to answer. For even when we attempt to study the simplest of behaviors, there are biological, intra-psychic, and social influences that we always must take into account. It remains true, then, that there are no easy answers to complicated problems.

At first blush, it might well seem that we know more about the *biology* of hunger and eat-

" I JUST <u>LOVE</u> THESE FAD DIETS. I'M ON FOUR OF THEM RIGHT NOW."

ing than we do about the intra-psychic and social/behavioral factors. In a sense, that's true, for there have been many more experiments on the physiological variables that affect eating than there have been on the psychological and social aspects of the problem. But few of these physiological studies do us much good when we try to help *human beings* change their eating patterns. There are at least three reasons why this is the case.

First, most of the laboratory studies have used animal subjects rather than humans. We know little or nothing about the intra-psychic processes of the white rat, and next to nothing about the social influences of one rat's actions on the amount of food that another rat eats. And even if we did know more than we do, we couldn't be sure that the knowledge we gained using rats as subjects would *generalize* to the level of human beings.

Second, most of the laboratory studies on the biology of hunger have used subjects who were severely deprived of food. Indeed, much of this research has dealt with animals who were near starvation. Little wonder, then, that the animals seemed preoccupied with obtaining food. However, few obese humans in our culture ever reach this state. As University of Washington psychologist Robert C. Bolles has pointed out, physiological mechanisms tend to dominate behavior in cases of extreme deprivation—but not at any other time in an organism's life. Given a crisis of some kind, your body may well "take over" your behavior. Most of the time, though, you "pick and choose" what you want to do because your physiological needs are almost always being met on a regular basis. Bolles believes that most eating and drinking—in humans as well as rats—is "secondary." That is, these behaviors are not really related to any *immediate biological need*. Thus most behaviors simply cannot be explained by drive theory, arousal theory, or any other "narrow" psychological viewpoint.

Third, *medical intervention* has a very low "cure rate" when it comes to helping people lose weight. The behavioral program outlined above is much more effective because it pays attention to a wide range of intra-psychic and social factors that influence eating behavior. And if these factors are most influential in helping people lose weight, they are also likely to be involved in causing people to over-eat in the first place.

You Help Choose What "Moves You"

Robert Bolles believes that motivation is best described as a "response selector mechanism." He notes that the organism is always active, always doing something—even if that "something" is just day dreaming or watching television. Thus you are always *turned on* (behaviorally speaking) both to your external world and to your internal thoughts and needs.

According to Bolles, you "behave" when you (1) respond to external stimulation; or (2) commit yourself to some course of action. In extreme situations, your responses will probably be governed primarily by your body needs. But in most circumstances, you will *select* the one thing you want to do "right now" from a long list of possible actions. And the factors that most influence (but do not totally determine) what you select are your past experiences and your present social environment.

Behavior is multi-determined. And one reason that statement is true is that your motives—your choices of what to do—are strongly affected by your physiological state, your emotions, your thoughts, your memories, your gender, your past upbringing, and the people and things presently around you.

What "moves" you? According to Bolles, you move yourself. True, many of your actions are fairly predictable—but only if we know a great deal about who you are, what you have experienced in the past, and what your present environment is like. The study of motivation, then, boils down to knowing as much as we can about you and your own set of personal choices.

To repeat our opening quote from David Edwards, motivation is a set of questions you ask in order to determine *why* you do what you do. As you must realize by now, those questions are so numerous and so complex that you may never answer them to your complete satisfaction. However, the study of human behavior remains a delightful and rewarding journey for most people. And a journey of a thousand miles begins with the motivation to take the first step.

Summary

1. **Motivation** is not so much an area in psychology as a series of questions about *why* people do what they do.
2. Many "why" questions involve human **needs**—what kinds of needs do you have, are these needs **learned** or **innate**, what are the **mechanisms** by which you satisfy your needs, and do you exercise any voluntary **choice** over your behavior patterns.
3. Motivation implies **movement**. Ancient

scholars differentiated between objects that were **animate** or "self-movers" and those that were not. In a sense, the study of motivation is the study of "what moves you."

4. According to Maslow, human needs can be placed on a **hierarchy** with five levels: **biological, safety, belongingness, esteem, and self-actualization**. Although there is little scientific proof supporting Maslow's view, it is one of the few **holistic** theories of motivation.

5. **Drive theory** focuses primarily on biological needs. Clark Hull assumed that associated with each physical need was a **primary drive**. Whenever your body lacks something needed for life, the appropriate drive increases, causing you pain and thus motivating you to satisfy that need and return your body to **homeostasis**.

6. Hull assumed that **secondary needs** or social needs were learned by being associated with the pleasures that accompany primary **drive reduction**.

7. Criticisms of drive theory include the fact that you have **information** needs as well as **energy needs**, and the fact that some social behaviors seem innately determined rather than being learned.

8. **Arousal theory** was developed by Elizabeth Duffy to counter the criticisms of Hull's drive theory. Duffy assumed that homeostasis is a point of **optimum arousal**, and that a decrease in sensory inputs can be as arousing as an increase in biological drives.

9. Human behavior is too complex to be explained by any narrow view of motivation. As an example, **obesity** is influenced by a great many different biological, intra-psychic, and social factors.

10. At a biological level, the **hunger drive** is affected by **blood sugar level**. When you go without food, your **hypothalamic feeding center** detects a decrease in blood sugar molecules and motivates you to eat. Stress increases the production of **endorphin**, which stimulates your body to produce **insulin** which also decreases your blood sugar level. Thus you may over-eat because of stress.

11. Your **hypothalamus** also contains your **satiation center** which, when stimulated, causes you to stop eating. Hunger pangs are also affected by your **swallow counter**, by your knowledge of how much you have already eaten, and by **conditioned stomach contractions**.

12. Intra-psychic influences on obesity include the fact that some parents train their children to be fat, thus giving over-eating a **symbolic** value.

13. Schachter has shown that fat people pay little attention to their biological needs. They "eat by the clock," are "plate cleaners," and over indulge in good-tasting food but reject poor-tasting food.

14. Social/behavioral influences on obesity include the fact that in some cultures fatness suggests wealth, and that some **social classes** place more of a premium on thinness than do others.

15. Stuart has shown that **insecure husbands** often reward their wives for remaining fat.

16. **Behavior modification** offers an excellent method for losing or gaining weight. The technique involves taking a **baseline** of present food input, **establishing goals**, increasing **exercise**, keeping precise **records** of food-related activities, and establishing personal and social **rewards** for progress.

17. According to Robert Bolles, **drives** affect behavior primarily in times of severe deprivation. For the most part, humans appear to be able to **choose** which behavior patterns are most satisfying to them. The study of motivation then may be trying to discover why you **select** the specific responses that you make in any given situation.

(Continued from page 257.)

The crisis, Annette thought as she rushed up the stairs to Thelma's apartment. People like Thelma could stand anything except success achieved through self-discipline. And if you didn't catch them right away . . .

A bedraggled-looking Thelma answered the door and quietly invited Annette in. Her eyes were moist and puffy from crying. "Listen, Annette," she said when they were seated. "I'm terribly sorry about tonight. I just sort of lost control, you know?"

"I know," Annette replied.

"I mean, it was a rotten day at the office. I jumped all over people, and they were nasty to me in return. I knew what I was doing wrong, but I just couldn't stop myself. Anyhow, I went bowling after work, and I was feeling so damned rotten, I decided to have just one little drink. Just one, you know . . ."

Annette nodded. "I know."

"And then before I knew it I was on my fourth Tom Collins, and I bowled really lousy, and I told one of my friends to go to hell." Thelma started weeping. "I mean, I *knew* I was hurting people, and I just couldn't seem to stop."

"Yes, we all do that sometimes," said Annette quietly.

"Then I got so mad at myself I just ran out to the car and started driving. I couldn't bear to face you right then. Does that make sense to you?"

"Of course."

"I must have driven for three hours anyway. I kept hoping the car would run out of gas way out in the country somewhere, and I'd just die or something before anybody found me." Thelma sighed. "But finally I just gave up and drove back here. And then you called."

"I'm glad I did."

Thelma nodded, trying to smile a bit. "So am I, Annette. I think I finally figured it out, what went wrong. But I want your advice on it."

"Of course," said Annette, brightening considerably.

"It sounds screwy, I know, but I think I got depressed because I was doing so well. You know what I mean?"

Annette nodded. "I know exactly."

"I mean, I've lost 22 pounds in a month, I've done better at the office—except for today—and you've helped me like nobody else ever has. But *I* was the one who did it, you understand? I mean, *you* didn't resist all those hunger pangs in the middle of the night, *I* did. And *you* didn't have to do all that exercise, *I* did."

"I know," Annette said reassuringly. "And you really did beautifully."

"That's the trouble!" Thelma cried. "I lost weight, I did better on the job, I've got my friends back, I look better, I feel better, I'm happier than I've been in years."

Annette smiled. "And that's the problem, isn't it?"

"Of course," Thelma said in a weary tone of voice. "I kept asking myself, why did I have to wait so long to make all these changes? Why did I need you to help me do what should have been obvious? And I kept thinking about all of the wasted times in my life, the people I'd hurt because I didn't know any better."

"You've got a lifetime left to make up for it," said Annette.

"Oh, I know. And I suppose I will. But even that isn't the real problem, is it?"

Annette grinned broadly. "No, Thelma, it isn't."

"I mean, the problem is, I *know* I can change myself. I've already done it. So I guess I could do some more, right?"

"Right," said Annette. "You've got both the motivation and the technique."

Thelma nodded. "That's the scary part. Now that I can do just about anything I want to do, what the hell do I really want to do?" Thelma giggled a bit. "I mean, as long as I was failing, I could blame it all on God, or my parents, or just about anybody. Now I've got nobody to blame except myself. I finally have all the freedom anybody could ask for. That's frightening."

"Of course," said Annette. "Because there's no freedom without responsibility. Freedom's pretty expensive, when you stop to think about it."

Thelma laughed. "Well, I guess I can afford it now." She shook her head, as if in wonderment. "You know, I guess I must be the happiest person in town. No, that's wrong. I must be the happiest person in the whole wide world."

Now it was Annette's turn to cry a bit. "Can I be number two?"

Thelma reached over and squeezed Annette's hand tightly. "Sure. And thanks for everything, you know?"

"I know," said Annette, wiping her eyes with a tissue.

Thelma released Annette's hand and leaned back in her chair. "Listen, we've got some things to plan. I've been thinking about getting a new job in a year or so, after I've lost another hundred pounds or so. But you know what I want to be?"

"No, tell me."

Thelma grinned. "An airline stewardess."

"You're kidding!"

Thelma nodded. "They're so slim and trim, you know. I've wanted to be just like that, all my life. And now maybe I can be." She paused for a second. "And there's another thing about being a stewardess, you know."

"What?"

Thelma roared with laughter until she almost cried again. "Well, it sure would beat buying my own ticket to Miami!"

Recommended Readings

Beck, R.C. *Motivation: Theories and Principles* (Englewood Cliffs, N.J.: Prentice-Hall, 1978).

Bennett, William, and Joel Gurin. *The Dieter's Dilemma* (New York: Basic Books, 1982).

Bolles, R.C. *Theory of Motivation* (New York: Harper & Row, 1975).

Deci, Edward L. *The Psychology of Self-Determination* (Lexington, Mass.: Lexington Books, 1980).

Maslow, Abraham. *The Farthest Reach of Human Nature* (New York: Viking, 1971).

Stuart, Richard B., and Barbara Davis. *Slim Chance in a Fat World* (Champaign, Ill.: Research Press, 1972).

Sexual Motivation 12

Did You Know That . . .

Until recently, we knew more about how your heart and liver function than about the biology of your sex organs?

The first scientific studies of the human sexual response were probably performed by psychologist John B. Watson in 1917?

Watson lost his professorship for undertaking his pioneering studies of human sexuality?

The sex life of animals is controlled primarily by hormones?

Male insects may perform their sexual functions better if the female first bites the male's head off?

A female fetus may be born with male sex organs if the mother is exposed to excessive amounts of male hormone during pregnancy?

No matter what your sex, you have both male and female sex hormones in your body?

You have "pleasure centers" in your brain which, when stimulated electrically, make you "feel good"?

"The Mating Game"

Clare Wilson put down her library book and smiled warmly at her fiance, Bill Meyer. "I think we should have a girl first. And don't you think that Christine would be a nice name for her?"

Bill's eyes opened slightly, but his gaze never strayed from the TV set. He was watching the US Open Golf Tournament, and didn't really want to be disturbed. One of his favorite golfers, Jack Nicklaus, was two strokes ahead of the other players, and Bill was trying to give Nicklaus some moral support. Nicklaus sank a difficult 30 foot putt on the fourteenth hole, and the crowd cheered. "You drive for show, but you putt for dough," Bill said approvingly.

"You won't mind if our first child is a girl, will you, dear?"

Bill glanced quickly at Clare, then looked back at the television. "I don't think I have much choice in the matter," he said.

"Oh, I know that. But if it *is* a girl, you won't mind, will you?"

Bill sighed. It was difficult to concentrate on the golf tournament when Clare wanted to talk about things. "I don't really care, Clare. But how will you feel if she turns out to be a boy?"

Clare shrugged her shoulders. "We'll name him Christopher, and try again."

With a sly grin on his face, Bill replied, "I don't mind that 'trying again' business at all."

Clare laughed. "Sex. That's all you men ever think about, isn't it?"

"Way to go!" Bill said loudly, as Jack Nicklaus hit a ball that flew 250 yards through the air before landing in the middle of the fairway on the fifteenth hole.

"Well, isn't it?" Clare demanded.

"Isn't it what?" Bill asked.

"Sex," Clare said, a touch of laughter in her voice. "Isn't that all that guys ever think about?"

Bill shook his head in dismay. "You brought the topic up, not me. I was just sitting here, minding my own business, watching a golf tournament on the tube."

"I did *not* bring the topic up," Clare said, teasing Bill a bit. "I was talking about what we were going to name our first child. And you had to go and drag sex into the discussion."

"Well, how in the world are you going to have kids if you don't have sex first?" Bill asked.

Clare raised an eyebrow. She knew Bill was trying to concentrate on the golf tournament, but she enjoyed twitting him a bit when he got too involved in sports. Besides, this was a very important issue between the two of them—at least as far as she was concerned. So she said, "Having children is primarily a matter of love and commitment, not sex. It means getting married, building a stable relationship, and taking a responsible role in life."

A TV announcer extolling the virtues of a new automobile interrupted the tournament. Bill stood up, pretended he had a golf club in his hands, and began taking practice strokes. "*Right* down the middle," he said as he hit a phantom golf ball down an imaginary fairway.

"Bill, I know that you're really into golf. But I do wish you'd listen a bit more attentively when I'm trying to have a serious discussion with you," Clare said.

"Sorry about that," Bill replied, a touch of guilt in his voice. He stopped pretending he was playing golf, sat back down in his chair, and smiled at Clare. "Now, let's see. You were talking about sex . . . ."

"I was *not* talking about sex, Bill Meyer! I was talking about our *relationship*. You're the one who dragged the conversation into the gutter."

"The gutter!" Bill said in dismay.

"That's right," Clare replied, delighted that Bill was giving her his full attention now. "I asked if you would object to calling our first child Christine, and you said . . ."

"I said that having children involves having sex first. Which it does. But, okay, I apologize for not paying attention. Now, tell me, why do you think we ought to have a daughter before we have a son."

Clare smiled happily. "Because, the way my career is going, I'll have more time to spend with our first child than with the second. So, Christine ought to be the first, because I want to make sure that she grows up to be a completely liberated young woman. And that will take a lot of work on my part."

Bill gazed back at the television set. Pleased to see that Nicklaus was still ahead of the other golfers, he looked back at Clare. "I'm not supposed to play much of a role in bringing up our daughter, I gather."

"Oh, of course you'll play a part," Clare said. "An important part, too. But you're such a *traditionalist* when it comes to women, Bill. Sometimes I suspect that you think our only purpose in life is cooking and having babies . . ."

"Keep 'em barefoot and pregnant, huh?"

"There you go, talking about sex again," Clare replied in mock seriousness. "Anyway, that's why I want to make sure that Christine picks up her social values from me instead of from you. You can train Christopher, when he comes along. But Christine is going to be my responsibility, since I want her to break free of the usual social constraints that you men impose on women."

"Constraints?" Bill muttered. "I never met a woman yet I could constrain in any way imaginable."

"Don't be silly," Clare replied. "You are perfectly aware that women are not allowed to do most of the things that you men do."

"Like what?" Bill said, his gaze wandering back to the golf tournament again.

"Like, be president of the United States, or be chairperson of General Motors, or win the Heisman trophy in college football . . ."

"Well, we've got a woman on the Supreme Court now."

Clare gave him an annoyed look. "One out of nine, and you think we ought to be satisfied. A token appointment to keep the natives from getting restless. The occasional woman senator, the infrequent woman mayor or governor . . ."

"Way to go!" Bill cried, as one of the golfers sank a very long putt. In his excitement, he stood up and started swinging an imaginary golf club again.

"See what I mean?" Clare responded. "You don't take the women's equality movement as seriously as you take that golf tournament you're watching. Which reminds me. Why don't you pay as much attention to women's golf as you do to the men's tours?"

"Because they won't let me play in the women's tournaments. Although, the way my game is going lately, I'm not sure I could win even playing against the ladies."

"You see!" Clare said teasingly. "You think women are inferior to men, even on the golf course. Typical, chauvinistic male attitude. And that's why I want to make sure that I'm the one who trains our daughter, Christine. If I didn't, you'd dress her up in frilly clothes and hair ribbons, and make her think her only purpose in life was to attract young men."

A commercial featuring Joe Namath flashed on the television screen. Bill smiled, remembering the time that "Broadway Joe" had stirred up so much controversy by starring in a pantyhose commercial. Then he turned his attention back to Clare. "Well, our daughter Christine would look a lot better in frilly dresses and hair ribbons than our son Christopher would."

"So, you would *constrain* our daughter from dressing any way that suits her, eh? See what I mean about the typical male attitude?"

Bill thought a moment. "No, I don't care how Christine dresses. That's up to her."

"And me," Clare said.

"And you," Bill agreed. "But what about Christopher? How are you going to rear him?"

Clare gave the matter some thought. "Well, I want him to be healthy and happy, of course. And I do want him to realize that his sister is his equal. But aside from that, he's chiefly your responsibility."

"You don't want to make sure he learns how to cook and sew and change diapers?"

Clare paused. "Well, those would be useful skills, I suppose. And I do think that a man and woman should share responsibility for household chores. But I'm sure you'll want him to learn how to play golf, and football, and those sorts of things too. I'd go along with that, just so Christine is free to participate in sports too."

"Wouldn't you prefer for Christopher to grow up wanting to stay home and cook and run the vacuum and take care of our grandkids? While his wife earned the money by being chairperson of G.M.?"

Clare frowned. "If he *wanted* to do that sort of thing, I suppose I wouldn't object. Not too much, anyhow." Then her face brightened. "Besides, if our daughter-in-law is chairperson of G.M., they could afford to hire a maid, and Christopher could do whatever he liked."

"But suppose he really *wanted* to be a househusband."

"Well, I don't really know," Clare said, realizing that the conversation had reached a delicate turn. "I just can't imagine that any son of mine would want to stay home and do the household chores."

Joe Namath appeared on the television set again, talking sincerely about another product. Bill thought about Namath for a moment, then said, "Well, what if Christopher was so liberated that he wanted to wear dresses and pantyhose?"

"Don't be silly!" Clare said in a shocked tone of voice.

"Aren't you the one who's being conventional now? I mean, you think it's okay if our daughter Christine wears slacks and sneakers and T shirts . . ."

"Of course it's okay, because she'll be liberated from the traditional feminine role . . ."

"But our son Christopher can't be liberated enough to wear pantyhose . . ."

"That's not 'being liberated,' that's being *abnormal*."

Bill grinned. "And you're the one who said that men can do anything they want, while women are constrained by the wicked, chauvinistic males in our society."

"That's absolutely true, Bill, and you know it. Men are free, and women aren't."

"But Christopher can't wear pantyhose, right?"

"No son of mine would *want* to wear pantyhose!"

"Why not, Clare? Why not?"

(Continued on page 296.)

The Scientific Study of Sexuality

Sex has always posed something of a problem for the psychologist, both at a theoretical level and, as we will see, sometimes at a personal level as well.

As far as theory goes, it would seem that sexual needs should be explainable in the same terms as are any of the other biological needs. However, there is a crucial difference: You cannot live without air, water, food, elimination, and the proper temperature. But you could readily (if not pleasantly) live out your entire life without engaging in any reproductive behavior whatsoever. Without air, a person dies within minutes. But at one time or another in your life, you may go for weeks, months, or even years without having any sexual contact with another person.

The major difference between sex and other physical needs is this—food, air, and water are necessary for the survival of the *individual*, but sex is necessary for the survival of the *species*.

For reproductive activities to occur, two more-or-less compatible individuals must find each other and adjust to each other's needs—at least momentarily. Men and women breathe the same way, drink the same way, eat the same way. But their sexual behaviors are typically quite different, and so presumably their sexual motivations are different too. For this reason, human sexuality seems to involve learning to satisfy the desires of your partner in order to meet both your own needs and those of society and the human race.

In higher animals, species survival depends not only on getting the male and female together so that mating can occur, but also on keeping one or both parents around to care for the young until they are large enough to face the world on their own.

An adequate theory of sexuality, then, must explain not only the differing sexual desires and responses of male and female, but maternal and paternal activities as well. We will talk about "parenting" behaviors in later chapters. But, given the complexity of sexual behaviors, perhaps you can understand why none of our theories about sex really explains all we need to know.

The Objective Study of Sex

The *theoretical* issues facing the psychologist interested in sexual behavior are only a small part of the difficulties involved in studying this complicated subject, however. Consider the *practical* problems for a moment.

In our society, at least, sexuality intrudes into almost everything we do. It is a major topic of conversation; it is the presumed cause of many crimes; it leers at us from movie screens and winks at us from television tubes. Sex is no longer something for private consumption. Rather, it is marketed with a commercial shrillness once reserved for automobiles and breakfast cereals.

And yet, for all the noise, we really know less than we should about human sexuality. Medical science has, until very recently, avoided any serious study of biology of sexual behavior. Until the last decade or so, we knew more about the functioning of your heart and liver than we did about the normal functioning of your sexual organs. And the reasons for this ignorance were social and psychological, not biological.

Until the last decade or so, sexual knowledge for the average young person consisted mostly of whatever "facts of life" were passed on by the person's parents or **peers**. Formal training about sexuality is compulsory in the schools of some foreign countries, but not in the US. Many states have attempted to make "sex education" available here, but not with any great success. For example, in 1978 the State of Michigan undertook a survey of parental attitudes toward sex education. The vast majority of parents stated that young people should receive their sex educations at home, not at school. However, more than 80 percent of these same parents reported that they had never once discussed the technical aspects of sexual behavior with their own children.

Early Research on Sexuality

In the first half of this century, a few scientists tried to bring human sexual behavior into the laboratory, to study it as objectively as other scientists studied the digestion of food. Almost without exception, however, these pioneers were rejected by their scientific colleagues for daring to perform experiments on what most people believed was an intensely private aspect of human life.

Back in the early 1900's, psychologists at Cornell asked their graduate students to record their **introspections** during sexual activities (as well as at other times). And Clelia Duel Mosher, a physician who taught at Stanford from 1910 until 1929, made an extensive study of sexuality in college women. However, the Cornell data never appeared in print, and Mosher's results were first published in 1974, almost 35 years after her death.

Watson's Physiological Studies

The most famous of these early investigators was John B. Watson, who started the **behaviorist** tradition in psychology. Watson believed that sexual behavior was a very important aspect of the human condition. In 1929, he wrote that sex "is admittedly the most important subject in life . . . And yet our scientific information is so meager. Even the few facts that we have must be looked upon as more or less bootlegged stuff." Since the medical sciences had studiously ignored the subject of human sexuality, Watson set out in 1917 to investigate the matter himself—at first hand.

Watson tackled the issue directly—by constructing a set of instruments to measure the physiological responses of a woman during sexual arousal. Since Watson's wife refused to participate in such a project, he used his female laboratory assistant as a subject. Watson fathered what were probably the very first reliable data on the female sexual response. And since it was a topic he could obviously study with pleasure, he acquired several boxes of scientific data. Unfortunately for all concerned, Watson's wife eventually discovered why her husband was spending so much time in the laboratory, and she not only sued him for divorce, but also confiscated the scientific records!

Although Watson was one of the brightest and most creative men of his time, his academic career was ruined by this episode. He had to resign his professorship at Johns Hopkins University, and most of his friends and colleagues deserted him. The Baltimore newspapers reported the divorce in lurid detail, and the judge presiding at the trial gave Watson a severe tongue-lashing—calling him, among other things, an expert in *mis*behavior.

After the divorce, Watson married his assistant. But he still could not find a job at any other college or university. In desperation, he took a position with a large advertising agency and stayed with it the rest of his professional life. Although he continued to write books and scientific papers, he considered himself a ruined man and soon slipped into the solace of alcohol. He died in 1958, at the age of 80.

Sex Research in Columbia, Missouri

In 1929 Watson wrote that, "The study of sex is still fraught with danger. It can be openly studied only by individuals who are not connected with universities." As H.W. Magoun pointed out in the November 1981 issue of the *Journal of Sex Research*, Watson's warning was not an idle one. In 1929, a young man named O. Hobart Mowrer was an undergraduate at the University of Missouri in Columbia. As part of a project for a sociology class, Mowrer gave out a questionnaire on "The Economic Aspects of Women" to some 600 Missouri students. Three of the questions Mowrer included in his survey concerned attitudes toward extramarital sexual relations.

When the newspapers discovered what Mowrer was doing, they raised a furor. The townspeople in Columbia circulated a petition demanding that the "people responsible" for this outrage be fired. The state legislature agreed, and the president of the university responded by firing the professor who had taught the course. Mowrer fortunately survived the incident and went on to a distinguished career in psychology. In 1954 he became President of the American Psychological Association.

Kinsey's Interviews

Watson's influence on the scientific study of human sexuality was profound, but largely indirect. One of Watson's students, Karl Lashley, did undertake some work in the area. But Lashley's major contribution came when he got a noted biologist interested in studying sexual responses—a biologist named Alfred Kinsey.

The first survey of US sexual behavior based on an adequately large segment of the public did not come until 1948, when Kinsey and his associates published their monumental volume, *Sexual Behavior in the Human Male*. The Kinsey group asked many thousands of men to talk about every aspect of their sexual lives, and a surprisingly large number responded to the questions without apparent shame or evasion. Since Kinsey depended on volunteers, it may be that his sample was fairly **biased**. For one can never be sure of what goes on in the life of a man who won't talk about his experiences. Nonetheless, Kinsey did show that a large group of normal-appearing US males regularly engaged in a wide variety of sexual practices that "nice people" were not even supposed to know about.

In later years, Kinsey and his group published a similar book about female sexual behavior. And, in the late 1970's, scientists at the Kinsey Institute reported a study of **homosexual** activities. (As we will note in a later chapter, the major

Peers (rhymes with "beers"). From the Latin word for "equals." People who belong to the same group in society, especially when membership in that group is determined by age, grade, or status. The US Constitution guarantees that if you are to be tried in a court of law, the jury must be made up of your "peers," that is, people similar to you.

Introspections (in-troh-SPECK-shuns). To introspect means "to look inward." Your own personal inner thoughts and feelings. See Chapter 5.

Behaviorist. A psychologist who emphasizes the objective measurement of *response outputs* rather than attempting to determine thoughts, attitudes, or introspections. See Chapter 5.

Biased (BUY-est). From a Latin term meaning "to cut or go against the grain." In psychological terms, to be biased is to have preconceived notions about a situation, or to perceive things as you want to see them, not as they actually are. A "biased sample" is one not selected randomly, but rather selected according to some (often unconscious) scheme.

Homosexual. Sexual activities between two (or more) males, or between two (or more) females. As opposed to *heterosexual* (HETT-er-oh-sex-you-all) activities, which occur between a male and a female. Homosexual behaviors are frequently found in lower animals and, according to Kinsey, take place more often among humans than "prudish people" are willing to admit. Freud—and most other scientists who have studied human sexuality—believe that homosexual activities are as "normal" and as "genetically determined" as heterosexual behaviors.

Perverts (PURR-verts). From the Latin word meaning "to turn the wrong way, or to corrupt." Anyone who takes her or his sexual pleasures in a manner not approved by society is considered a pervert—at least within that particular society.

Gynecologist (guy-nuh-COLL-oh-jist, or jin-nuh-COLL-oh-jist). The Greek word *gyne* means "woman." A medical doctor whose specialty is treating the reproductive problems of women is called a gynecologist.

conclusion of this study was that homosexuality in humans is primarily determined by the genes. Thus the belief that a "homosexual orientation" is mostly a matter of choice—or of early experiences—seems to be wrong.)

Perhaps Kinsey's most significant contribution was this: When his books were published, a great many people who thought themselves **perverts** or mentally ill discovered that, compared to almost everyone else, their sex lives were really rather tame.

Masters and Johnson's Research

Still and all, the writings of Kinsey and many others all sprang from conversations and case histories rather than direct observations—people were asked to *talk* about their sex lives while the scientists recorded what the people *said*. It was not until the 1950's that William Masters and Virginia Johnson began to study what people actually *did*.

Masters was trained as a **gynecologist**—that is, a physician who has specialized knowl-

"HEY, GUYS — WAKE UP!"

Alfred C. Kinsey

Virginia Johnson and William Masters

edge of the female reproductive system. Johnson received her training in social work and psychology. They started their work in St. Louis, using female prostitutes as paid subjects. Following Watson's lead, Masters and Johnson made recordings of their subjects' bodily reactions while the women experienced various simple types of sexual arousal (chiefly **masturbation**). Later, they studied the physiological changes that accompany sexual excitement in males, as well.

When Masters attempted to present his early data to a gathering of US gynecologists, the majority of these physicians refused to support his research and urged him to give it up. Many of the best-known medical journals would not publish his findings, and political pressure prevented his getting governmental support for his work.

Thus the first public discussion of Masters and Johnson's research was delayed until 1962, when they presented their findings to an enthusiastic audience at a meeting of the American Psychological Association.

The Physiology of Orgasm

The Masters and Johnson research has challenged many of the old superstitions concerning sexuality. Prior to their studies, it had been thought (primarily by male scientists) that women achieved different types of sexual climaxes depending on the manner in which they were excited or aroused. Masters and Johnson found that a woman's body undergoes the same characteristic changes no matter what type of stimulation brings the woman to orgasm. Although the woman's *feelings* might vary considerably from one sexual experience to another, the *biological changes* associated with orgasm almost always occur in the same sequence.

Sex Therapy

Masters and Johnson also pioneered new types of therapy with men and women who had various types of sexual problems. For instance, many women suffer from **frigidity**—that is, the inability to achieve climax. Until recently, most psychologists and psychiatrists assumed that the major cause of frigidity was **repression**. That is, the woman's feelings of guilt and anxiety concerning the sexual act were so strong that she simply could not relax and let nature take its course. Therapy usually consisted of helping the woman talk through her early sexual thoughts and experiences in the hope that she would gain some insight into what was really bothering her.

Masters and Johnson believe that frigidity is often caused by ignorance and clumsiness on the part of both the woman and her partner. By teaching these women and their partners to pay greater attention to the *physical indicators* of sexual arousal, Masters and Johnson have been able to help many patients for whom the usual "talk" therapies were not particularly effective.

Men often suffer from the opposite sort of problem—they achieve their own climax so quickly that their partners are left unsatisfied. By training the women to monitor the man's state of sexual arousal, Masters and Johnson have achieved nearly 100 percent success in their treatment of this problem, called **premature ejaculation**.

Sex: A Multi-Determined Behavior

Sexual behavior has much in common with the eating behavior we discussed in the last chapter. First, both types of activity are based on physiological needs. Second, both have important intra-psychic or personal aspects. And third, both are greatly influenced by the environment and by social rewards and punishments. Thus both sex and eating are multi-determined behaviors. In the case of food-taking, however, the intra-psychic and social/behavioral factors are often ignored or misunderstood. In the case of sex, it is often the *physical* or *mechanical factors* whose importance is frequently neglected.

We will look at sexuality from an intra-psychic and an environmental standpoint in several later chapters. For the moment, let us see how your body chemistry influences both your sexual motivation and your sexual behavior.

The Physiology of Sex

In almost all forms of animal life, sexual behavior is greatly influenced by fluids secreted in several different glands or organs within the animal's body. Glands are small chemical factories that release their products either into the bloodstream, onto the tissues surrounding the gland, or even into the outside world. Some of these chemicals have primarily a local effect. For instance, the tear glands in your eyes secrete that clear but romantic liquid which, in small quantities, lubricates the movement of your eyes in their sockets. In larger amounts, your tears tell the world that you are sad or unhappy and thus are involved in *emotional responses*.

Other types of glands secrete their products directly into your bloodstream, and thus have their primary effects some distance away from the glands. These "action-at-a-distance" chemicals are called **hormones**, from a Greek word that means "to stir up, to attack, to set in motion."

Hormones

You have two **adrenal glands**—one atop each of your kidneys. Your adrenals secrete more than 20 different hormones that influence both your growth and your behavior. The majority of the adrenal hormones regulate such bodily functions as digestion, urine excretion, and blood pressure. And, as we will see in the next chapter, these hormones also play a large role in your response to stress. However, several of these chemicals also have a direct effect on your sex life. These are called the *sex hormones* (see Fig. 12.1).

Sex hormones are also produced by your **gonads**, or sex glands—the testes in the male, and the ovaries in the female. From the time of your conception onward, your adrenals and your gonads worked together to provide your body with the chemicals it needed to develop into—and to remain—a sexually mature adult.

Masturbation (mass-tur-BAY-shun). To bring oneself to sexual climax by hand, by rubbing against something, or occasionally through fantasy. Also called "self-abuse," "playing with yourself," "the solitary vice," and other terms.

Frigidity (frih-JID-it-tee). Sexual coldness or unresponsiveness in the female. The inability of a woman to enjoy sex or to achieve orgasm.

Repression (ree-PRESH-un). To inhibit thoughts, desires, or actions.

Premature ejaculation (PREE-mat-chur ee-jack-you-LAY-shun). "Premature" means "to arrive too early" or "to *explode* too soon." To ejaculate is to discharge semen (SEE-men) at the moment of a male's orgasm. When a male reaches sexual climax before the female has achieved satisfaction, he has ejaculated prematurely.

Hormones (HORR-moans). Complex chemicals secreted by various glands that affect growth and behavior.

Adrenal gland (add-DREE-nul). A small gland at the top of the kidney that secretes many different hormones, including those that affect sexual growth and behavior. You have two adrenal glands—one for each of your kidneys.

Gonads (GO-nads). The primary sex glands—the ovaries in the female and the testes in the male. The ovaries produce the egg cells that are fertilized by the sperm secreted by the testes.

Androgens (ANN-dro-jens). From the Greek words meaning "producer of males." There are several male hormones; collectively these are known as androgens.

Estrogens (ESS-tro-jens). The Latin word *estrus* (ESS-truss) refers to the period in a female's reproductive cycle when she is fertile and hence capable of becoming pregnant. Estrogens are the hormones that generate or bring about estrus.

Progesterone (pro-JEST-ter-own). One of the several female sex hormones.

Genitals (JEN-it-tulls). From the Latin word meaning "to beget, to reproduce, to generate children." The external sex organs, or *genitalia* (jen-it-TAIL-ee-uh).

Male hormones are called **androgens**. The two main types of female hormones are known as the **estrogens** and **progesterone**. Whether you are a woman or a man, however, your adrenals and your gonads produce *both* male and female hormones. As we will see, though, it is the *relative amount* of these two types of hormones that is important.

Primary and Secondary Sex Characteristics

Biologists differentiate between two types of sex characteristics—primary and secondary. When scientists speak of *primary sex characteristics*, they mean the actual sex organs themselves—the ovaries, vagina, uterus, and clitoris in the female, and the penis and testes in the male. Additionally, those parts of the reproductive organs in either sex that can be seen by the naked eye are often called the *external genitalia*, or **genitals**. Male-female differences in *primary* sex characteristics are usually present at birth.

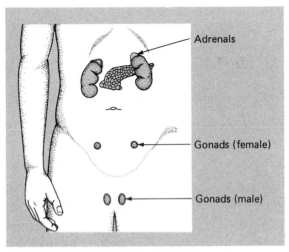

Fig. 12.1. The location of some major endocrine glands.

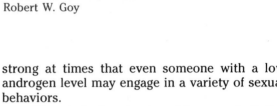

Robert W. Goy

The *secondary sex characteristics* are those that appear at **puberty**—the growth of facial hair and deepening voice in the young man, the development of the breasts and broadening of the hips in the young woman. The appearance of both primary and secondary sexual characteristics is controlled almost entirely by *hormones*.

If a young boy's adrenals and testes *overproduce* androgens—or *underproduce* estrogens—he will experience early puberty. That is, his voice will change and his beard will begin to grow sooner than expected. But if the boy's glands *underproduce* androgens or *overproduce* estrogens for some reason, his puberty will be delayed. His body may then take on feminine characteristics—a high voice, overdeveloped breasts, and a lack of facial hair.

If a young girl's adrenals and ovaries *overproduce* estrogens—or *underproduce* androgens—the girl will come to sexual maturity earlier than expected. If the reverse is true, her puberty will be delayed, and she may even develop such masculine secondary characteristics as flat breasts, excess facial hair, and a low voice.

Androgens and Sexual Behavior

From a behavioral point of view, estrogen and progesterone seem to be correlated with childbearing and child-rearing. It is the androgens—in both men and women—that tend to promote *sexual behavior itself*. Thus a man or a woman with a low androgen level is likely to experience a low *biological* sex drive. However, as we will see, cultural inhibitions can suppress sexual behavior even in someone with a high androgen level. And stimulation from the environment may be so strong at times that even someone with a low androgen level may engage in a variety of sexual behaviors.

Thus, in both animals and humans, both the strength of the sex drive—and the types of behaviors that the organism produces—are *always* affected both by genes and by social factors.

Gender

As we will see in a later chapter, your sexual **gender** was determined at the moment of your conception. The sperm cells of the male are normally of two types—the X sperm and the Y sperm (see Chapter 18). If an X sperm from the father unites with (fertilizes) the egg carried by the mother, the child will be a female. However, both the type of genitalia that the **fetus** is born with and its behaviors are influenced by the hormones present in the fetus's body while it is in the womb.

The March 20, 1981 issue of *Science* includes a number of articles on the effects of hormones on gender in humans and animals. According to these papers, both male and female hormones can be found in most fetuses while they are in the womb. It is the *balance* of the hormones during certain **critical periods** which biases the fetus toward male or female behavior patterns.

Generally speaking, the critical period for most species is just when the central nervous system is beginning to develop. If androgens predominate during this critical time, the fetus will develop male genitalia. In addition, various parts of the brain involved in masculine behavior patterns will be activated, while the brain centers that mediate feminine behavior patterns will be suppressed. If estrogens predominate during the critical period, of course, the fetus will develop female genitalia and behaviors while the brain centers that control masculinity will be suppressed.

Innately Determined Sexual Behavior

It took scientists a long time to realize that the genetic blueprint for most animals includes *both* male and female response patterns. Recent studies by Robert Goy and his colleagues at Wisconsin have rather dramatically shown this to be the case, though.

For example, suppose that a mother monkey is carrying a fetus conceived from an X sperm. If all went well, the baby monkey would be female. However, in one experiment, Goy and his group injected a monkey mother with male androgens during a critical developmental period. The baby was born with male genitalia—even though subsequent tests proved the infant had been conceived by an X (female) sperm. As this female infant grew up, she showed male patterns of play and social behavior.

Other scientists **castrated** male rats at birth and gave them injections of female hormones at that time. When they became adults, the rats displayed a complete set of female behavior patterns.

Hormones are just one of the factors which influence adult sexual behavior patterns. Personal experience is just as important and, in the case of humans, perhaps even more so. As Robert Goy notes in the May 18, 1981 issue of *Newsweek*, "It looks as though what the hormone is doing is predisposing the animal to learn a particular social role. It doesn't insist that it learn that role; it's just making it easier. The hormone doesn't prevent behavior from being modified by environmental and social conditions."

Hormones and Behavior

The sex hormones not only provide an initial "behavioral bias" during fetal development, they also *motivate* adult animals to perform the sex act itself. The female white rat, for instance, is sexually receptive to the male only when her estrogen level is high. If her ovaries are removed, she will not mate unless given injections of estrogens.

If the testes of an adult male rat are removed by castration, the male will continue to mate with receptive females for a few weeks until the androgens already present in his body are depleted. But during this period, his interest in females gradually wanes and eventually vanishes—unless he is given injections of male hormones.

Sexual behavior in most lower animals is **cyclical** and usually tied to a particular part of the year. Most of the time, the amount of hormone

Puberty (PEW-burr-tee). The onset of sexual maturity, when the person becomes physically capable of sexual reproduction. Usually between the eleventh and the fourteenth year, the female's ovaries begin producing eggs and menstrual (MEN-strew-ull, or MEN-strull) bleeding begins. At about the same age, the male's testes begin producing semen and ejaculation becomes possible.

Gender (JEN-durr). The *physical* characteristics associated with being male or female. Gender *behaviors* are those controlled primarily by the physical characteristics of the person, such as pregnancy and nursing in females. As differentiated from "sex roles," which are learned social behaviors or thought patterns. A man with effeminate behavior patterns is of the male gender, but may play what society considers to be a feminine sex role.

Fetus (FEE-tuss). An unborn child, still carried in its mother's womb. More precisely, the unborn child after it has taken on human characteristics (during the final six months in the womb).

Critical periods. There are certain times during the developmental sequence when the fetus or child is maximally sensitive to certain types of chemicals or to various psychological experiences. These are called "critical periods." See Chapter 20.

Castrated (KASS-trait-ted). From a Latin word meaning "to cut to pieces." Literally, to cut off the testes. Two centuries ago, boys with good voices were occasionally castrated prior to puberty so that they would retain their pure, high voices. These singers were called *castratos* (cass-TRATT-toes) and often played women's roles in operas (and in real life).

Cyclical (SIGH-klick-call, or SICK-lick-all). Anything that repeats itself, or that goes in a full circle. The seasons of the year (winter, spring, summer, fall) are cyclical. During her fertile years, the human female ordinarily has a menstrual cycle that repeats itself about every 28 days.

present is very low. Thus such environmental stimuli as the sight or smell of a receptive partner don't trigger off sexual responses. However, at one or more times during the year, the passing of the seasons will stimulate the production of sex hormones. When the hormone level is high enough, the animal responds to sexual stimuli in its environment—and we say that the organism is now *motivated* sexually.

The Praying Mantis

One of the reasons that lower animals don't mate "out of season" is that their brains contain *inhibitory circuits* that prevent sexual behavior from occurring except when hormone levels are high. We will discuss sexual inhibitions in humans momentarily. For the moment, though, consider the case of the male praying mantis, whose sex life is fraught with difficulties that most human males would shudder to contemplate.

The praying mantis is an insect several inches long that looks for all the world like a twig with a head and legs. The female mantis spends her time stalking other insects—including the much smaller male. When she comes close to another insect, her heavy forepaws slash forward, crushing the prey and dragging it back to her well-formed jaws.

Daniel Lehrman has shown that the reproductive cycle of doves is highly complex. Hormones "release" instinctive behavior patterns in each sex which, in turn, stimulate the production of additional hormones in the opposite sex. **(top)**

The brain of the praying mantis contains primarily inhibitory neural centers. **(left)**

During most of the year, the female mantis would as happily consume the male for dinner as she would a beetle or a butterfly. But during the mating season—when her hormone levels are sufficiently high—she will allow the male to come close to her without immediately attacking him. However, hunger is usually a stronger drive than sex, even during the mating season. So the male mantis's best chance for success lies in waiting until the female has just caught an insect. The male then stealthily approaches the female from behind and attempts to mount her while she is distracted by more important things. If he misses

in his first attempt, his cause is lost—and he typically ends up as the main course of her meal.

But even if he finds the proper position on his first try, his troubles are far from over. For, during the act of copulation, his head comes dangerously close to hers. And should she notice him, she is very likely to reach up and bite his head off for dessert.

Luckily, this little romantic by-play has a happy ending. For the nervous system of insects is quite different from that of humans. A headless insect can live for several hours, and the brain of the male mantis is made up almost entirely of *inhibitory* centers that (among other things) decrease the animal's sexual functions. Once the male has literally "lost his head," he copulates much more vigorously and effectively than when his brain is present to repress him.

The male's inhibitory centers are necessary to keep him out of the female's range during most of the year. But not even the seasonal increase in male hormones can knock out the inhibitory activity of his brain as effectively as does one crunch of the female's jaws! In this case, then, a *behavioral* response helps overcome *biological* inhibition.

Mating and Nesting in Doves

The complex interplay between hormones and environmental stimulation is nicely illustrated in a classic series of studies by Daniel Lehrman and his colleagues at Rutgers.

Lehrman and his group studied mating and nesting behaviors in the ring dove. During the mating season, the male ring dove approaches the female and dances around her. At one point in his ritual, he bows low in front of her and utters a characteristic "coo" sound. Under normal circumstances, the female accepts the male's advances, and the two subsequently mate. Both birds then build a nest. When the female lays her eggs, both birds sit on them and care for the **fledglings** after they hatch.

If the male ring dove is castrated, he shows no interest at all in the female and simply won't mate. If he is subsequently injected with androgen, he will perform the "bow-coo" dance and mate, but he won't help with nest-building nor will he sit on the eggs. If the male is now injected with estrogen, he will help the female construct the nest, but he won't hatch the young. If he is also given progesterone, the male will complete the sequence and care for the fledglings as well.

As far as the female dove is concerned, it is the *sight* of the male's dance and the *sound* of his voice which triggers off estrogen production. The increase in estrogen causes her to mate, gather materials for the nest, and then lay her eggs. The *act* of nest-building causes her ovaries to secrete progesterone, which encourages her to hatch the eggs and care for the young.

As Lehrman notes, in the case of the ring dove, sexual behavior affects hormone production as much as hormone production affects sexual behavior.

Primate Sexual Behavior

The **primates**—humans, monkeys, apes, and chimpanzees—show much more complex sexual behaviors than do the lower animals. In the higher species, for instance, the sex drive is less frequently seasonal and not as closely tied to the female reproductive cycle. The female rat will mate only during that part of her cycle when her eggs are ready to be fertilized by the male. The human female is fertile only a few days out of her 28-day reproductive cycle, but her receptivity to the male is determined more by *psychological* factors than by the types of hormones her body is producing at any given moment.

The male rat will usually attempt to mount females only when they are at the receptive point in their cycle—when the female releases **copulins** into her urine. The male monkey may try to

Fledglings (rhymes with "HEDGE-lings"). From an Old English word meaning "capable of flying." Fledglings are young birds that are just at the point of being able to fly.

Primates (PRIME-eights). The highest or "prime" order of mammals. Includes humans, apes, chimpanzees, monkeys, and several more primitive monkey-like animals.

Copulins (COPP-you-lins). Chemicals released by females that have a sexually arousing effect on males. See Chapter 6.

Impotence (IM-po-tents). The inability of a male to achieve erection, or to sustain the erection long enough to achieve orgasm and ejaculation.

Repressive. To repress is to deny consciousness to your own unacceptable thoughts. To be repressive is to force others to deny expression of their thoughts that you may consider improper. Repressive actions almost always involve punishment, criticism, or both.

mount female monkeys at any point in their cycles—and will often attempt to mount younger or less aggressive males as well. When an older, stronger monkey becomes aggressive toward a younger male, the weaker animal may often protect himself by assuming the posture of a receptive female and allowing the dominant animal to mount him and to attempt to copulate.

In humans and monkeys, sexual behavior is predominantly under the control of the *brain* rather than the hormones. Birds and rats can be induced to mate out of season or cycle if injected with the proper hormones. However, hormone injections are not an effective therapy for frigidity in most women or for **impotence** in most males.

In humans, most sexual inhibition appears to be learned—primarily during the person's early life. If the child's parents are **repressive**—if they punish the child whenever it touches its genitals or when it asks questions about sex—the child's sex life as an adult may be marked by shyness, fears, or even outright distaste for sexual matters. Thus, no matter how high the person's androgen levels may be, learned inhibition may prevent the individual from leading a very active sex life.

Almost anything learned can be unlearned, however, and most people can overcome their sexual inhibitions if given careful guidance and suitably rewarding experiences.

Why should the brain be so full of inhibitory centers? In Chapter 11, we pointed out that it is as important to know why a behavior *stops* as to understand why it *starts*. If there were not some way to *turn off* a behavioral pattern once it began, you might be so rewarded by what you were doing that you would continue this pattern indefinitely. By putting the brakes on motivated behaviors once they have served their purpose, inhibitory centers free you to go on to other activities.

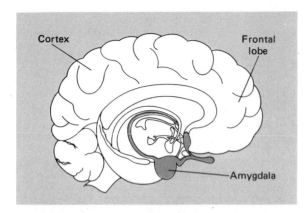

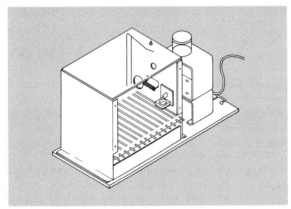

Fig. 12.2. The colored areas are part of the limbic system. **(top left)**

Fig. 12.3. James Olds (right) and Peter Milner discovered that stimulating certain parts of a rat's brain seems "rewarding" to the animal. **(top right)**

Fig. 12.4. A single-lever rat box. **(left)**

Question: *Orgasm seems to have at least two functions. Can you guess what these two functions seem to be?*

Why Sex?

With all of the cultural taboos and inhibitions on sexual activity, you might legitimately wonder why people bother with it at all! Reproductive behavior is, as we said earlier, necessary for the survival of the species, but not for the survival of the individual. Yet nature seems to have worked out a way to motivate members of both sexes to *want* to reproduce themselves. For sexual stimulation usually creates within the individual a great amount of intense *sensory pleasure*.

But, as scientists, we may legitimately ask the question: What is the biological basis of this pleasure? Or, to put the matter another way, why in the world does sex "feel so good"?

The Pleasure Centers

When physiological psychologists first began sticking electrodes into the brains of rats and other animals, they found that stimulation of a few parts of the **limbic system** (see Fig. 12.2) caused the animals to react as if they had experienced sharp, biting pain. This discovery was, at first, surprising—because, as we saw earlier, the brain has no pain receptors *as such*.

These scientists suspected that they had tapped into what are now called the "avoidance centers" of the brain. So they began to map out as many different regions of the brain as they could, trying to find out how extensive these "avoidance centers" really were. As it turned out, these centers are not very extensive at all. You can stimulate more than 99 percent of the brain electrically without getting an avoidance reaction from the animal. However, this search paid unexpected dividends when, in the early 1950's, two psychologists working in Canada discovered that sometimes electrical stimulation of the brain can have *pleasurable* consequences.

Olds and Milner's Discovery

James Olds took his doctorate in psychology at Harvard in 1952. Then, because Olds was interested in the biological processes underlying motivation, he went to McGill University in Montreal to work with the noted physiological psychologist, Peter Milner.

Olds and Milner implanted electrodes in the "avoidance areas" in the brains of white rats, then let the animals run about on the top of a table (see Fig. 12.3). When the rat would move toward one particular corner of the table, Olds and Milner would turn on the current. The rat would stop, then turn around and move in the opposite direction. The animal subsequently avoided that particular corner of the table even if it was not given any more electrical stimulation.

However, one day Olds and Milner made a glorious mistake—they stuck an electrode in the wrong place in one rat's brain. When this animal started moving toward one of the corners of the table, they turned on the electrical current as usual. But this rat stopped, sniffed, and then moved a step or two *forward*!

Olds and Milner assumed that the current wasn't strong enough to have any effect, so they turned up the juice and stimulated the animal again. And once again, the rat twitched its nose rather vigorously, and then moved several more steps forward. The more that Olds and Milner stimulated the rat's brain, the more eager it became to get to the corner. Finally, the animal reached the corner, sat down, and refused to move! It is to their credit that, instead of thinking the rat was "sick" or "abnormal," Olds and Milner realized at once that they had discovered a part of the rat's brain where electrical stimulation was obviously very *rewarding*.

We now know that there are dozens of **pleasure centers** in the brains of most mammals (including humans) which, when stimulated electrically or chemically, will give the animal the subjective experience of *pleasure*.

Pleasure or Compulsion?

In animals such as the white rat, neural excitation in these "pleasure centers" causes a strange and oddly *compulsive* set of behaviors to occur. Suppose we rig up a small, rat-sized box with a single metal lever in it (see Fig. 12.4). The lever is connected to an electrical stimulator so that every time the rat presses the lever, the animal stimulates one of the "reward centers" in its own brain. Will the rat press the bar very often?

The answer is yes—very often indeed. Under these conditions, a rat will bang away on the lever as often as 100 times a *minute*. It will continue to do so hour after hour after hour—until it collapses in exhaustion. The rat will then sleep for a while until it regains its strength. But as soon as it wakes up, it starts pressing the lever again. And, if we offer this rat the chance to bar-press as a reward for problem-solving behavior, it will learn highly complicated mazes just to get a few whacks at the lever.

Limbic system (LIM-bick). A related set of neural centers in the brain that influence emotional behaviors. See Chapter 4.

Pleasure centers. Various areas of the brain that, when stimulated electrically, seem to be rewarding to the organism or give it "mental experiences" akin to pleasurable sensory inputs. Stimulation of the pleasure centers in rats causes them to engage in compulsive behaviors. Stimulation of similar areas in the human brain gives mildly pleasurable experiences, but does not cause compulsive behaviors.

Obviously, something about the electrical stimulation of the "pleasure centers" is highly *motivating* to a rat. But is the motivation that of pleasure, or that of yielding to a "compulsion"?

Two Types of Pleasure

Until the discovery of the "pleasure centers" by Olds and Milner, sexual behavior had always posed something of a problem to motivational theorists. Knowing nothing about the "pleasure centers" in the brain, early drive theorists assumed that pain *reduction* was the chief motivational force underlying all behavior.

But sexual excitement is almost entirely a matter of pleasurable *arousal*—the more stimulated an organism is, the more pleasure it feels. How, then, could an *increased* drive level be associated with pleasure rather than with pain? Wasn't this rather like hitting yourself over the head with a hammer because it felt so good when you stopped?

At first, drive theorists assumed that electrical stimulation of the "pleasure centers" merely triggered off a set of *compulsive behaviors*. However, later experiments with humans proved that the drive theorists were wrong. At least at the human level, stimulation of the "pleasure centers" does indeed yield a very pleasurable feeling.

We now know that there are two distinctly *different* types of pleasure: (1) the generalized feeling of relief when pain ceases; and (2) the sensory thrill associated with what we might call "pleasurable inputs." For example, food not only reduces hunger, it tastes good as well. Therefore, there must be a direct connection of some kind between the taste receptors in your tongue and the "pleasure centers" in your brain. Once Olds and Milner had shown the way, psychologists began looking for just those connections.

Specific and Generalized Pleasures

Current animal research indicates that some parts of the rat brain are associated with sexual pleasure, while other parts are associated with eating or drinking pleasures. Stimulation to still other brain areas seems to give the rat a "general

In humans, sexual behavior is predominantly under the control of the *brain* rather than just hormones.

glow of satisfaction" that isn't tied to any specific physiological drive yet known.

If we implant an electrode in those "pleasure centers" related to eating behavior, the rat will bar-press compulsively *only* if it is hungry. If we feed the rat first, it will ignore the lever for several hours until its hunger drive mounts a bit. If we implant the electrode in those parts of the brain connected with drinking behavior, the rat will bar-press only if it is thirsty.

Oddly enough, once the rat begins bar-pressing, it typically prefers electrical stimulation to either food or water. Perhaps direct brain stimulation yields stronger rewards than do food and water. Or perhaps the electrical current triggers off *both* pleasurable feelings and compulsive behaviors. The answer to this problem awaits further study.

Drives and Pleasures

Now, let us extend the animal research to the human level. The neural pathways running from your tongue and nose to the "food-reward areas" in your brain were built in by your genetic blueprint. But these pathways only become *functional* when you are hungry. Thus the lower your blood sugar level becomes, the easier it is for the taste and smell of food to excite the "food pleasure centers" in your brain.

Food deprivation, therefore, does two things almost simultaneously: First, it creates a painful "hunger" drive. Second, it increases the possibil-ity that your "pleasure centers" can be stimulated by sensory inputs from your nose and mouth.

In similar fashion, a build up of sex hormones both motivates an organism to seek out sexual stimulation and makes that stimulation pleasurable. If we put an electrode in one of the "sex reward centers" of a male rat's brain, we find that the animal will bar-press much more vigorously if it has been sexually deprived than if it has copulated recently. More than this, if we castrate the rat, we find that it presses the lever less and less frequently on the days following the operation. Apparently, as it uses up all the male hormone left in its body after castration, it finds the electrical stimulation less and less pleasurable.

We can restore the castrated rat to its original high performance level, however, by giving it an injection of androgens. Within a short period after the injection, it begins to press the lever vigorously.

The same sort of effect occurs at the human level. Injections of androgens almost always lead to an increased interest in—and willingness to participate in—sexual activities in *both* men and women. At this point, the similarity between rat and human ends, though. Rats injected with sex hormones almost always engage in sex if given the opportunity. But in humans, sexual behavior is also strongly affected by moral codes, social standards, and learned inhibitions. Thus, no matter how deprived the man or woman—nor how strong the drive—sexuality at the human level is determined *primarily* by intra-psychic rather than biological factors.

Human Pleasures

When Olds and Milner first reported their results, many people feared that governments might seize upon electrical stimulation of the brain as a new way to control people against their wills. Some writers warned that big corporations might implant electrodes in the brains of all their workers and pay off these employees in jolts to their "pleasure centers" instead of paying the workers in cold cash.

However, these fears proved to be groundless. For the "compulsiveness" that one can create in a rat with brain stimulation seems to be lacking in humans. Those women and men who have volunteered to have their "reward centers" tickled with electricity have all reported the experience as being mildly pleasant—but something they could take or leave.

For example, when the "food-pleasure centers" of the subjects' brains were stimulated, they often reported things like, "Oh, that was nice, rather like eating a good meal. But I'd rather have steak and French fries." Or, "Yes, that felt good, and it did have a sexual flavor to it somehow. But nothing like the real thing."

Pleasure in humans is obviously a more complex experience than it is in the lower animals. The androgens, estrogens, and progesterones shape our bodies, bias our brains, and energize our behaviors. Pleasure is the neural carrot that nature dangles before us to entice us down the path of biologically appropriate behavior. The pain of deprivation is the chemical club that nature applies to our backsides to urge us onward. But overriding these biological motivations are the neural commands that come from the higher centers of our brains.

The pattern of sexual activity that we find physiologically rewarding grew out of the millions of reproductive experiments that nature has conducted since life first appeared on earth. But only humans have brains complex enough to understand that societies must survive as well as species, to conduct our own scientific studies on the subject of sexual behavior, and to realize that unlimited population growth may sometimes be a disaster rather than a blessing.

Nature points us in a given direction and pushes us along. But, as we will see in later chapters, the beliefs and attitudes of our parents and friends—and the "rules and regulations" of the groups we belong to—provide us with our road maps, stop signs, and detours. Our higher brain centers, with their inhibitory powers, are the battleground for this war between nature's nudges and society's strictures.

Just how we individual foot soldiers learn to cope with the stresses and strains of this constant warfare is a matter to be covered in the next chapter.

Summary

1. **Sexual motivation** is difficult to study scientifically for many reasons, not the least of which is **social pressures** against the objective measurement of sexual behaviors.
2. Sexual needs have a **biological basis**, but differ from hunger and thirst in that they are necessary for the survival of the specific individual.
3. Early research on **human sexuality** usually met with resistance from society. John B. Watson studied the female sexual response, but lost his professorship because of his research.
4. Alfred Kinsey published the first **scientific survey** of US sexual behavior in 1948. While his findings were disputed, he did show that many people engaged in a wider variety of sexual behavior than many people had imagined.
5. The first studies of actual **human sexual behavior** were made by Masters and Johnson. They found that the female goes through the same physical sequences no matter how she reaches climax. They also found ways of helping people with **sexual problems** achieve happier lives.
6. In lower animals, sexual behavior is controlled primarily by the **sex hormones**—the **androgens** in males and the **estrogens** and **progesterone** in females. These hormones are secreted primarily by the **adrenal glands**.
7. Both male and female sex hormones are found in both sexes. It is the relative amount of these hormones that determines **primary** and **secondary sex characteristics**.
8. The **androgens** tend to promote sexual behavior in both males and females. The **estrogens** and **progesterone** help determine whether the behavior pattern shown will be male or female.
9. It is the **relative balance of sex hormones** during **critical developmental periods** which biases the fetus toward male or female behavior patterns. A female monkey injected with androgens prior to birth will develop male behavior patterns at adulthood.
10. Sexual behavior is **cyclical** in lower animals, but not in humans and some of the higher **primates**. Lower animals don't mate "out of season" primarily because **inhibitory centers** in their brains suppress sexual behavior except when hormone levels are high.
11. The brain of the male **praying mantis** contains chiefly inhibitory centers. The animal copulates much more readily when the female **decapitates** the male during mating.
12. The sexual behavior of the **ring dove** is controlled by a complex interaction between hormone levels and the **mating behaviors** of the male and female dove.
13. Sexual behavior is strongly influenced in lower animals by **pleasure centers** in the animals' brains. Electrical stimulation of these centers leads to **compulsive behaviors** in the rat, but not in the human.
14. Electrical stimulation to the **food-related**

pleasure centers is most effective when the animal is hungry. Stimulation of the **sexual pleasure centers** is most effective when the animal's hormone levels are high. Thus stimulation is most effective when the animal's **motivation** is at a peak.

15. There are two types of pleasure: **generalized relief** when pain ceases; and **sensory thrill** associated with "pleasurable inputs."

16. Sexual behavior is **multi-determined** and, in humans, is more affected by intra-psychic and social factors than by hormone level or other biological influences.

(Continued from page 283.)

"Why not, Clare?" Bill Meyer asked his fiancee. "You assume that our daughter Christine would *want* to wear men's clothes. So why wouldn't our son Christopher *want* to wear dresses and pantyhose?"

Clare Wilson frowned as she considered the matter. "Well," she said finally. "I guess I see what you're getting at. I know only too well the sort of stupid male prejudices against women my daughter will face. Maybe I've never given much thought to what sorts of social constraints my son will have to put up with."

"Right on," Bill said. "You women are convinced that men have locked you into a rigid social role of some kind. Well, men are at least as locked into a male 'role model' as women are—and maybe more. It has always ticked me off that women demanded the right to wear men's clothes, and heaven help the man who got upset. Yet if a man appears on television dressed in pantyhose, you think he's a disgrace of some kind."

Clare grinned. "Yes, and so do you."

"Not if he's making as much money as Joe Namath did," Bill said, laughing. "But the point is, why do you approve of women who take on male characteristics, but get upset when a man acts in a feminine way?"

Clare paused for a moment. "It is odd, isn't it? I guess I see men as being socially superior in some strange way. When women dress like men—or act in a traditionally masculine way—they're just trying to improve their status in society. But when a man acts like a woman . . ."

"Then he's giving up status," Bill said. "And that does seem unnatural to all of us. But if men and women are *really* equal, then . . ."

" . . . Then both men and women should be free to act as they wish," Clare said thoughtfully. "Yes, I can understand the logic behind that point. And maybe it's the same thing with blacks or any minority group. We can understand when they dress and behave like the dominant group in society. We even encourage them to take on the values of white, middle-class Americans, and think it's great when they do."

Bill nodded. "But saints preserve any white, middle-class person who tries to act or talk 'black.' Unless they're doing it as an obvious joke, we see 'black talk' by whites as being abnormal because it involves a voluntary loss of social status."

Clare sighed. "I guess we won't really be an unprejudiced society until we allow all people to act and feel any way their genetic makeup dictates, eh?" After a moment's hesitation, she continued. "But how can we be sure it's our genes, and not our social prejudices, that make us feel that a particular behavior is either normal or abnormal? There *must* be some way to tell the difference."

Bill glanced at the television screen. Jack Nicklaus was still ahead in the golf tournament, but Calvin Peete was only one stroke behind going into the seventeenth hole. "You mean, like, men are more interested in sports while women are more interested in library books and opera and stuff like that."

"Now, Bill," Clare said teasingly. "You know that women are just as sports-minded as men are."

"No, they're not," Bill replied, refusing to be baited by Clare's comment. "There's never been a culture in the history of the world where that was true. My psych prof was talking about that just a few days ago. Young male monkeys rough-house three times as much as female monkeys do. Same thing with all the primates. The males are almost always bigger, stronger, and more physically active. Now, don't get me wrong. Women are *good* at lots of sports—better than men at olympic swimming, for instance. And maybe at long distance running, too. And they're better at skills that require fine-motor coordination. But, on the average, men are just more interested in physical challenges than women are."

Clare smiled. "And you think that's a genetic difference between men and women?"

Bill nodded. "Sure, just like their sexual interests are different."

"There you go again, Bill."

"Oh, come off it, Clare," Bill replied, having temporarily forgotten the golf tournament. "Women are just as interested in sex as men are. It took me a long time to realize that, but it's true. It's just that men and women are concerned about different aspects of the sexual experience."

"I should hope so."

"I should hope so too. If we weren't, we wouldn't have families and children," Bill replied.

"What do you mean?"

Bill thought a minute. "Well, somebody's got to make sure that sex occurs, so there will be children. And maybe that's the man's job. And maybe that's part of what sports and social aggression are all about. But historically speaking, at least, it's been the woman's job to see that the children were fed and taken care of properly. And you've got a biological advantage over men in that department, you must admit."

Clare straightened her shoulders. "Now, Bill . . ." she said demurely.

"It's true, and I'm glad of it," Bill said in a playful tone of voice.

"But that still doesn't give you the right to talk about sex all the time," Clare said, trying to regain control of the conversation.

"You talk about it all the time, too, Clare. Only you call it 'commitment,' or 'our relationship,' or 'feelings.' But it amounts to the same thing."

"It does *not* amount to the same thing," Clare replied.

"Yes, it does. To a man, sex is an act that leads to child-bearing. So the man thinks most about how to get the woman to 'do it.' But to a woman, sex is an act that leads to child-rearing. And to make sure that the man is around to help take care of the kids, she's got to get some kind of commitment out of the guy so that he doesn't run off after every skirt he sees. So she thinks about how to get a loving relationship going. But it's still sex she's thinking about and talking about."

"And you think that sort of psychological difference is *genetic*?"

"I don't know of any data on the subject, but it seems logical to me."

Clare considered the matter. "But what about the women's equality movement? Are we wrong to try to get men to do those things—like cooking and changing diapers—that have always been foisted off on women by the dominant males?"

Bill laughed. "Well, we can share the labor of taking care of the kids, but we can't share the labor pains, if you know what I mean."

"Ouch," said Clare, a hint of laughter in her voice.

"And I suspect that men are at least as good at taking care of kids as women are—maybe better."

"Better? What do you mean?" Clare said in surprise.

"Just last week my psych professor quoted a recent study showing that infants are more relaxed when held by their fathers than by their mothers. Maybe learning how to cradle a football in your arms teaches you how to cradle a baby, or something like that."

Clare sighed. "Okay, so you don't object to men and women sharing the burden of child-rearing. That's progress, at least. But how do we get men to treat women like equals in *all* situations?"

"You can only do that if you give men something they want in return."

"Like . . . ?"

"Oh, like a lot of things. Like not demanding that we see the world from your viewpoint unless you're willing to look at things from the male point of view too. Like not demanding that a male 'commit' to a woman, and then telling him he's got a dirty mind when he wants sex in return. Maybe even admitting that you're as interested in the sexual *act* as men are."

"I'll have to think about that for a while," Clare replied. Then she stood up, walked over to Bill, and put her arms around him. "What you're saying is that even if the equality movement succeeds, there will always be some differences in the way that men and women act and feel. Just because their genders are different."

"*Vive la difference*," Bill said.

Recommended Readings

Goy, Robert W., and Bruce S. McEwen. *Sexual Differentiation of the Brain* (Cambridge, Mass.: MIT Press, 1980).

Katchadourian, Herant A., and Donald T. Lunde. *Fundamentals of Human Sexuality*, 2nd ed. (New York: Holt, Rinehart and Winston, 1975).

Masters, William, and Virginia Johnson. *Human Sexual Response* (Boston, Mass.: Little, Brown, 1966).

Pomeroy, Wardell B. *Dr. Kinsey and the Institute for Sex Research* (New York: New American Library of World Literature, 1973).

Emotion, Stress, and Coping

13

Did You Know That . . .

Your emotional reactions are controlled in large part by your autonomic nervous system?

Most people find it difficult to tell the difference between hunger, fear, anger, and sexual arousal just on the basis of their bodily changes during these emotional states?

William James believed that, when you see a snake, you know you're afraid because you run away, not that you run away because you're afraid?

Some people believe that whatever happens to them is due to chance, and that they have little control over their own destinies?

Animals can be trained to be "hopeful"?

Direct methods of coping with stress are usually more effective than indirect or defensive methods?

Pills are not a particularly effective way of dealing with depression on a long-term basis?

There is "good stress" as well as "bad"?

"The Stress of Life"

Charlie lay quietly on his back, staring at the bare light bulb dangling from the ceiling. Its glaring white light seemed bright as the tropical sun. Charlie wondered whether he would get a sunburn the way he did that day in Vietnam when he lay on the beach for too long.

"Get up and turn off the light," said one part of his mind in a bright, arousing tone of voice.

"Don't!" said another part of his mind in heavy, demanding tones. "A sniper might get you if you move. Movement is forbidden!"

Charlie recognized that voice of authority, so he remained motionless, except for his eyes. They turned stealthily, inspecting the room for perhaps the hundredth time that hour. There was a religious picture on one wall, a painting that his mother had given him. On the other wall was a photograph of Gail, his girl friend. He avoided gazing in that direction. But mostly there was just dirty wallpaper everywhere he looked.

"Get a new room," Gail had said. "This one stinks."

"Stay where you are," the heavy voice in his head had said to him. Charlie stayed, and Gail had gone off mad.

"Come home and live with us," his mother had pleaded. "There's plenty of room, and we miss you."

"You want to go through *that* again?" the voice had asked him. Charlie knew he hadn't the strength to go through "that" again with his mother, so he kept the room. It was small and safe and quiet. It folded itself around him snugly like a blanket. Why leave?

For several months, in Vietnam, Charlie had lived in a tiny cubicle in the barracks. He always felt safe there. Then his best friend, Red, went out on patrol one night and came back in a canvas bag.

"Go to his funeral. You owe him that, at least," the soft-spoken voice had urged him.

"Stay where you are," the heavy voice had said. "Red should have stayed in bed."

So Charlie stayed in bed for a while. The sergeant ordered Charlie to get up, called him a "dirty dogface" and a "coward," but he just tuned the man out. There were snipers out there. The sergeant should have known that.

Eventually they took him to a hospital outside Saigon and put him on a ward with lots of crazy people who shouted and screamed all day and all night. Charlie had found a dark, friendly corner and refused to come out.

"Those crazy people will kill you," the voice had said. "Don't go near them!" Charlie stayed in his corner until they flew him back to the States.

Right after the plane took off, they flew into the sunrise. Charlie had stared at the sun for half an hour, until the man sitting next to him pulled down the shade and told him he'd ruin his eyes. The sun hadn't been much brighter than the bulb dangling from the ceiling in his room, but he had left the blind pulled the rest of the trip.

After Charlie got home, things got brighter for a while. His parents came to see him, as did Gail, and the doctors convinced him he could "make it" out there in the world. The heavy voice had gone on vacation for months and months, and Charlie got a job and rented a room and saw a lot of Gail.

His mother didn't like Gail, of course. Not good enough for him, she said. But then, no girl was good enough for his mother. To tell the truth, he wasn't good enough for her himself. She'd told him that often enough—usually just after she had smacked him across the mouth for saying or doing something she didn't approve of. "Don't you ever try that again," she'd say. And then she'd usually hit him again, "Just to make sure." Half the time Charlie never knew quite what it was he had done wrong.

Charlie had volunteered for the Army more to get away from the sound of his mother's voice than to serve his country or to see the world. And all he saw were people getting killed, and all he heard was the sergeant screaming at him not to act like the dirty dogface he was. All the Army was for him was a series of hurdles he had to jump to avoid getting snarled at by his sergeant.

The phone rang. It had been ringing all day. He ignored it. Probably just more bad news anyhow.

Gail had been good news, at least when he first got back from 'Nam. They had enjoyed each other immensely, despite his mother. He kept telling Gail that she was the only good thing to happen to him in his entire life. She kept him from thinking of Red, and of 'Nam, and of his mother. When she smiled, she lit up his world like sunshine. But then came that rainy day when the sun had vanished into the clouds.

The phone rang again, and a faint but excited voice inside his head urged him to answer.

"Don't touch that phone!" the heavy voice suddenly demanded. "It's not safe to talk to people. You know that. All they tell you is lies."

"So here I lie," Charlie said aloud. And alone. He had tried to explain to Gail why he had to live alone, at least for a while. She had talked him into going to see Dr. Smith, because she said it wasn't healthy to live that way. He had seen the psychologist a couple of times, and rather liked him. But the heavy voice told him it wouldn't do any good, that Dr. Smith would end up sniping at him like all the rest. So

Charlie had missed the last couple of appointments. Better not to do anything than to make a mistake, and have people hurt you.

Take Gail, for instance. She had given him everything. Everything. Sometimes he was so happy he just couldn't believe it, and he kept waiting for the heavy voice to come tell him it was all a fake. And it turned out to be a fake, just as he had feared, although the voice hadn't warned him.

Gail didn't love him. She couldn't, not when she had shouted and screamed at him and then slapped his face. And just because she had caught him with Cynthia. Charlie hadn't wanted to take Cynthia to dinner, but his mother had insisted. Cynthia was "her" kind of young woman. Something had told him not to give in to his mother's demands, but she cried and acted hurt, so he gave in.

Charlie heard a knocking sound at the door.

"Don't move!" the heavy voice said.

The knocking got louder.

"Don't answer!" the voice demanded. "It might be a trick."

"Trick or treat," Charlie chuckled softly to himself. He had treated Cynthia to dinner, and his mother had tricked him. He hadn't wanted to invite Cynthia home to his room, but she had rubbed against him and coaxed him. And then she had demanded that he show her where he lived.

So he showed her everything—his bed, his body, his wounds, where he really lived.

"Oh, do it! Do it!" Cynthia had cried.

"Oh, how could you do it!" Gail had cried, when she opened the door and turned on the light and saw Charlie and Cynthia naked on the bed.

And then Gail had screamed at him and slapped him.

He had forgotten that Gail had a key to his room. And he should have known that his mother had set the whole thing up with Cynthia. Then she had probably called Gail and told her he was sick and needed her. Sniped again.

Cynthia had giggled about it all, so he threw her out and locked the door behind her. And then he crawled into bed and pulled the covers over him. How long ago was that? Two days? Three? Well, it didn't matter. He wouldn't be going out again, ever.

Someone knocked at the door again, and called his name.

"Ignore it!" commanded the voice inside his head. "There's nothing but snipers behind that door. Do you want to end up in a canvas bag?"

Charlie heard the sound of metal scraping on metal, like a key going into a lock. Then the door opened.

Gail. And Dr. Smith. He could barely make out their faces.

"Close the door," he said in a heavy tone of voice. "I can't cope with snipers."

And then he pulled the covers over his head.

(Continued on page 317.)

Emotions

In Chapter 11, we noted that the term "motivation" came from the Latin word *motivare*, meaning "to move." There is another common psychological term which comes from the same Latin source: "emotion." The dictionary gives many definitions of "emotion," most of which have to do with *agitated movement* of some kind. And most of this "agitated movement" has to do with goals. You often feel joy and happiness when you reach a goal. You often feel angry and frustrated when you perceive a barrier between you and a goal. And you may experience pain and depression when you believe you cannot possibly get what you want or need. Most of the *scientific definitions of emotion*, though, tend to emphasize rather a limited part of emotional experience.

To many biologically oriented scientists, emotion is primarily a *physical reaction* that involves rather special parts of your nervous system. To these psychologists, the purpose of your

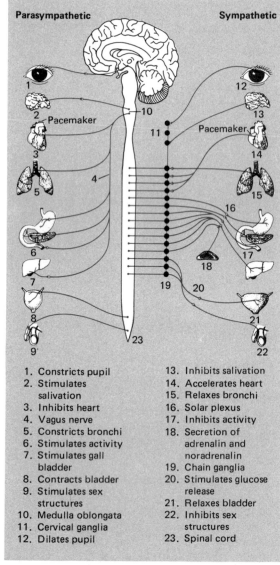

Parasympathetic   **Sympathetic**

1. Constricts pupil
2. Stimulates salivation
3. Inhibits heart
4. Vagus nerve
5. Constricts bronchi
6. Stimulates activity
7. Stimulates gall bladder
8. Contracts bladder
9. Stimulates sex structures
10. Medulla oblongata
11. Cervical ganglia
12. Dilates pupil

13. Inhibits salivation
14. Accelerates heart
15. Relaxes bronchi
16. Solar plexus
17. Inhibits activity
18. Secretion of adrenalin and noradrenalin
19. Chain ganglia
20. Stimulates glucose release
21. Relaxes bladder
22. Inhibits sex structures
23. Spinal cord

Fig. 13.1. Schematic layout of the autonomic nervous system.

emotions is to arouse your body for some kind of specific action (such as fighting or fleeing), or to depress physical responses so that your body can repair itself.

To other psychologists, emotion is primarily an *intra-psychic experience* that involves "inner feelings" rather than physiological reactions (or overt behaviors). Some of these experts divide emotions into various types of mental experiences, such as fear, anger, love, hate, and lust. Other intra-psychic psychologists view feelings as being **bipolar**. That is, these scientists view the emotions as being either "pleasant" or "unpleasant."

Still other psychologists perceive emotions as being *behavioral responses*. They do not speak of fear, but rather of fearful reactions to some external stimulus. They talk not of depression, but rather of massive inactivity or unresponsiveness.

Cutting across this debate about what emotions *are* is the age-old controversy about where emotions *come from*. Some psychologists believe that emotions are primarily *innate*; thus all people in all cultures should share similar emotional reactions. Other behavioral scientists view the emotions as being mostly *learned reactions* acquired through experience. These psychologists believe you had to be carefully taught to love the things you love, and to hate the things you despise.

There is one point about emotions, however, that almost all psychologists agree upon. Namely, that emotions—whatever they are, and wherever they come from—can be quite *stressful* to the body and mind. Which is to say that, for the most part, your feelings involve the expenditure of physical, mental, or behavioral energy. Learning to cope with your emotions, therefore, typically requires you to learn how to handle the stresses and strains of life.

In the first part of this chapter, we will look at your emotions from the biological, intra-psychic, and social/behavioral viewpoints. Then we will discuss the "nature-nurture" controversy concerning the origins of your emotions. And last, but surely not least, we will talk about stress and coping.

The Physiology of Emotions

Those psychologists who view emotionality as primarily a biological event tend to focus on *arousal* and *depression*. Thus these scientists often perceive emotional reactions as being your body's way of preparing to respond to some kind of physical or psychological challenge. Perhaps you are in danger. Then you must prepare yourself either to fight or to get out of the threatening situation. Or perhaps you are hungry and discover some food. Then you must calm yourself down so that you can consume and digest your meal in comfort. In either case, your physiological reactions are likely to be *reflexive*. That is, your emotional responses will take place without your conscious **volition** or desire. You don't have to "will" your sweat glands to secrete water or your teeth to start chattering when you are frightened or cold. Nor do you have to consciously direct your stomach to start digesting the food you've just eaten. These activities are handled for you *automatically* by the unconscious parts of your brain and nervous system.

Autonomic Nervous System

That part of your body which controls your emotional reactions is called your **autonomic nervous system**. (see Fig. 13.1). It is connected to most of the glands and many of the muscles in your body.

Your autonomic nervous system has two major parts or divisions: (1) the **sympathetic nervous system;** and (2) the **parasympathetic nervous system**. In general, activity in your sympathetic system tends to excite or *arouse* you much as an "upper" drug might. Activity in your parasympathetic system tends to *depress* or slow down many of your bodily functions, as would a "downer." Your sympathetic and parasympathetic nervous systems work together in a *coordinated* fashion to control your bodily activities. When you need to be aroused, your sympathetic system speeds up and your parasympathetic system slows down. When you need to relax and "vegetate," your parasympathetic system increases its neural activities while your sympathetic system slows down. It is the *joint action* of the two systems which allows you to respond appropriately to most of the physical and psychological challenges you meet in life.

Sympathetic Nervous System

Your sympathetic nervous system consists of a group of 22 *neural centers* lying on or close to your spinal cord. From these 22 centers, axonic fibers run to all parts of your body—to the sali-

vary glands in your mouth, to the irises in your eyes, to your heart, lungs, liver, and stomach, and to your intestines and genitals. Your sympathetic nervous system is also connected with your sweat glands, your hair cells, and with the tiny blood vessels near the surface of your skin.

Whenever you encounter an emergency of some kind—something that enrages you, makes you suddenly afraid, creates strong desire, or calls for heavy labor on your part—your sympathetic nervous system swings into action in several ways:

1. The pupils in your eyes open up to let in more light.
2. Your heart pumps more blood to your brain and muscles and to the surface of your skin.
3. You breathe harder and faster.
4. Your blood sugar level is elevated.
5. Your digestion is slowed down to a crawl.
6. Your skin perspires to flush out the waste products created by the extra exertion and to keep you cool.
7. The sympathetic nervous system also controls orgasm and ejaculation during sexual excitement.

In short, activity in your sympathetic nervous system prepares you for fighting, for fleeing, for feeding—and for sexual climax.

Question: *Why do people often get red in the face when they get angry?*

Parasympathetic Nervous System

Your parasympathetic nervous system connects to most (but not all) parts of your body as does the sympathetic. In general, parasympathetic

"I THINK WE CAN RULE OUT STRESS."

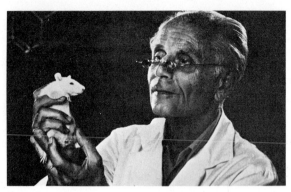

Hans Selye

stimulation produces physiological effects that are the *opposite* of those induced by sympathetic stimulation. Activity in your parasympathetic system does the following things:

1. It closes down or constricts the irises in your eyes.
2. It decreases the rate at which your heart beats.
3. It slows down your breathing.
4. It lowers your blood sugar level.
5. It increases salivation, stimulates the flow of digestive juices, and promotes the processes of excretion.
6. It retards sweating.
7. It induces penis erection in the male and nipple erection in the female during sexual activity.

Generally speaking, activity in your parasympathetic nervous system *conserves* or builds up your body's resources. For this reason, the parasympathetic is often referred to as the *vegetative* nervous system.

Question: *Heroin causes the pupils to narrow to mere pinpoints, even when the person is sitting in relative darkness. Which part of the autonomic nervous system does heroin affect most?*

Homeostatic Balance

Increased neural excitement in the sympathetic system tends to *inhibit* activity in the parasympathetic, and *vice versa*. But the two systems are not really **antagonists** or competitors. Rather, they function together smoothly in a coordinated fashion to maintain an optimum balance between over-arousal and under-arousal.

For instance, parasympathetic stimulation is necessary for erection to occur. However, orgasm and ejaculation are controlled by sympathetic excitation. Thus sexual activity must begin with relaxation (parasympathetic stimulation) but typ-

ically goes on to arousal and climax (sympathetic stimulation). Too much sympathetic arousal or inhibition early in the sex act can lead to impotence in the male and disinterest or frigidity in the female. And too much parasympathetic stimulation will prevent orgasm in both sexes. Normal sexual activity thus requires you to maintain a *balance* between parasympathetic and sympathetic stimulation.

It is this *balanced coordination* of the two systems that, to a major extent, led the early physiologists to theorize about *homeostasis* (see Chapter 11). And it was this same interplay between the two systems that drove early psychologists to create drive theory.

There is one major *difference* between the two systems, however—the sympathetic nervous system is connected to your adrenal glands, while the parasympathetic system is not.

The Adrenal Glands

You may recall from the last chapter that you have two adrenal glands, one sitting atop each of your kidneys. As we mentioned, your adrenals produce hormones that influence sexual development and that monitor bodily functions such as urine production. But these glands also produce two chemicals that are referred to as the "arousal" hormones. The old names for these two hormones are **adrenalin** and **nor-adrenalin**. These days, the terms "epinephrine" and "nor-epinephrine" are more common.

When epinephrine and nor-epinephrine are released into your bloodstream by your adrenal glands, these hormones bring about all of the physiological changes associated with strong emotions such as fear, anger, hostility, and sexual aggressiveness. That is, these two hormones act to prepare your body to meet an emergency by increasing your blood pressure and heart rate, speeding up your breathing, widening the pupils in your eyes, and increasing perspiration.

As you might guess from this description, the release of epinephrine and nor-epinephrine is under the control of your *sympathetic* nervous system, whose activities the hormones imitate or mimic. When you encounter an arousing situation, your sympathetic nervous system goes into action first, mobilizing your body's energy resources and also causing the secretion of the two "arousal" hormones. As you secrete epinephrine and nor-epinephrine, these hormones continue the arousal process by chemically stimulating the *same neural centers* that the sympathetic nervous system has stimulated electrically.

But the hormones also increase the firing rate of the nerve cells in the sympathetic nervous system itself. This stimulation causes you to secrete more of the hormones, which increases activity in the sympathetic system, and so on until the emergency has passed or you collapse in exhaustion.

Why should you have two separate arousal systems? The answer seems to be this: Sympathetic arousal is quick—an "emergency alarm" that mobilizes your body almost instantly. But at times you need *sustained arousal*. It is more efficient for your body to maintain an aroused state by means of the adrenal hormones than by continuous activity in your sympathetic nervous system.

Selye's General Adaptation Syndrome

The noted Canadian scientist, Hans Selye, first outlined the three states that your body seems to go through when its resources must be mobilized to meet situations of excessive physiological *stress*. According to Selye, your biological reaction to stress almost always follows the same adaptive pattern. Selye calls this pattern the **General Adaptation Syndrome**, or GAS. According to Selye, the GAS has three main stages or parts.

Suppose you suffer from a severe physical or emotional *trauma*. Your body will immediately respond with what Selye calls the **alarm reaction**, which is the *first stage* of the General Adaptation Syndrome. During this stage, your body and mind are in a state of *shock*. Your temperature and blood pressure drop, your tissues swell with fluid, and your muscles lose their tone. You don't think clearly and, as we will see in a later chapter, your ability to file things away in Long-term Memory may be disrupted.

The second part of the GAS is the **stage of resistance**, or *countershock*. During this stage, your body begins to repair the damage it has suffered, and your mind begins to function more clearly. A small gland in your brain releases a complex hormone known as **ACTH**. The ACTH acts on your adrenal glands, causing them to release their own hormones. These adrenal hormones counteract the shock in several ways, chiefly by raising your temperature and blood pressure. However, you pay a price for resisting the shock, for your body uses up its available supply of ACTH and adrenal hormones at a rapid pace. If the stress continues, your adrenal glands will swell as they strive to produce enough hormones to neutralize the stress.

During the first two GAS stages, your sympathetic nervous system is intensely aroused. However, if the emergency continues for too long, an

Antagonists (ann-TAG-oh-nists). The Greek word *agonistes* means "competitor." An antagonist is someone who is opposed to, or competes with, a certain viewpoint or position. A protagonist is someone who is in favor of or who defends a certain position.

Adrenalin (uh-DREN-uh-lin). One of the two "arousal" hormones released by the adrenal glands. Also called epinephrine (EP-pee-NEFF-rin).

Nor-adrenalin (NORR-uh-DREN-uh-lin). The second of the two "arousal" hormones released by the adrenals. Injection of adrenalin or nor-adrenalin into the body causes a rise in blood pressure and pulse rate, an increase in the breathing rate, and a general speeding up of bodily functions. Also called nor-epinephrine (NOR-EP-pee-NEFF-rin).

General Adaptation Syndrome (SIN-drome). A "syndrome" is a set of related symptoms that defines a particular disorder or behavior pattern. Selye's (SELL-ye) GAS is an attempt to describe the characteristic way in which the body responds to stress, particularly that caused by disease or physical trauma. As is true of most people trained in the medical sciences, Selye takes a biological view of emotionality.

Alarm reaction. The first stage of Selye's GAS, in which the bodily defenses are rapidly called into play. Similar to a "shock" reaction.

Stage of resistance. The second stage in Selye's GAS. A type of "countershock" during which the body tries to repair itself while continuing to react in an aroused manner.

ACTH. Adrenocorticotrophic (add-DREEN-oh-CORT-tih-coh-TROF-fick) hormone. For obvious reasons, almost always abbreviated as ACTH. A hormone released by cells in the pituitary (pit-TOO-ih-tarry) gland in the brain. ACTH stimulates cells in the "cortex" or head of the adrenal glands to release "arousal" hormones. "Trophic" comes from a Greek word meaning to nourish. Thus ACTH is a hormone that "nourishes" or stimulates cells in the adrenal cortex.

Stage of exhaustion. According to Selye, if the first two stages of the stress reaction last too long, the body's resources are exhausted, the parasympathetic system takes over, and all physiological functions slow down dramatically. If the stress lasts too long, the organism may collapse or die.

overwhelming *counter-reaction* may occur in which your parasympathetic system takes over. You may fall into the third state—the **stage of exhaustion**. During this state, you go into shock again because your body has been over-stimulated for so long that it is depleted of ACTH and adrenal hormones. Further exposure to stress at this time can lead to depression, insanity, or even death.

Selye believes that many "diseases of adaptation"—high blood pressure, arthritis, and some types of ulcers—are caused by excessive stress.

The James-Lange Theory of Emotion

The most famous physiological theory of emotionality is surely the one Harvard psychologist William James first proposed in 1884. According to James, your body always takes the lead in emotional situations. To James, your "feelings" are merely mental responses to the changes that have *already occurred* in your nervous system, muscles, and glands.

To illustrate James's viewpoint, suppose you are walking through the woods one day and you almost step on a huge rattlesnake. Chances are, you will momentarily go into shock. Then, almost immediately, your heart will start pounding, your hair will stand on end, and you will breathe more rapidly. And, if you are wise, you will slowly back away and then run for your life. Moments later—usually after you are out of danger—you will notice these physiological reactions and realize that you are scared.

You may think that you saw the snake, became frightened, and then ran. But according to James, this is not the case. For he presumes that your bodily reactions precede and thus *cause* your feelings. As James put it, "We are afraid because we run; we do not run because we are afraid."

In 1885, the noted Danish physiologist Karl G. Lange independently proposed much the same sort of explanation of emotional behavior. For that reason, this viewpoint is often called the **James-Lange theory of emotions**.

The Cannon-Bard Theory

As you might guess, the James-Lange approach led to a lot of highly emotional debate and, happily, a lot of useful research as well. For example, in 1937 physiologist Walter B. Cannon pointed out the following objections to the James-Lange theory. First, James-Lange assumed that your feelings are dependent upon activity in your sympathetic nervous system. However, people who (through accident or disease) have lost use of their sympathetic systems still feel emotions and show emotional behaviors. Second, the bodily changes associated with emotion generally occur *after* the "feelings and behaviors" have started, not *before* they take place. Third, the same physiological changes occur in very different emotional states—and in non-emotional states as well.

Cannon believed that emotional inputs were processed almost simultaneously by two different parts of the brain, the *thalamus* and the *hypothalamus* (see Chapter 11). According to Cannon, the thalamus controlled emotional *feelings*, while the hypothalamus controlled *bodily responses*. Thus, Cannon said, you would experience conscious "fear" of a snake even if your body were totally paralyzed because "fear" and "running" are mediated by different centers in your brain.

P. Bard advanced almost the same viewpoint in 1937 as well. For that reason, this approach to the explanation of emotionality is often called the **Cannon-Bard theory**.

Other Physiological Viewpoints

As it turned out, the same sorts of criticisms that Cannon leveled against James and Lange were also raised against the Cannon-Bard theory. In 1960, Karl Lashley noted that people with damaged thalamuses still experienced emotional feelings, and people with damaged hypothalamuses still showed emotional responses. At about the same time, other scientists showed that both the *limbic system* (see Chapter 4) and the right hemisphere (see Chapter 5) were involved in mediating emotional feelings and behaviors.

By the 1970's, a number of theorists had made a very telling point against *all* the biological theories of emotion. The point is this: Bodily reactions do play an important role in *creating* and *sustaining* emotions. However, our feelings are so frightfully complex that we simply can't *reduce* them to mere hormonal and neural activity. To gain a more complete understanding of emotionality, therefore, we must look at intra-psychic variables as well.

Intra-Psychic Aspects of Emotionality

Intra-psychic psychologists believe that the biological psychologists have put the cart before the horse. That is, they believe that how you *perceive* and *feel* about a situation determines your bodily reactions rather than vice versa. And those psychologists with an intra-psychic viewpoint can marshall a fair amount of evidence to support their beliefs.

For example, can you tell the difference (subjectively) between your emotions? That is, can you differentiate between such emotional states as hunger, fear, anger, and sexual arousal? Most surely, you can. But you apparently do so on the basis of intra-psychic cues rather than biological states. For, with minor exceptions, the physical changes that occur in your body are *pretty much the same* no matter what type of emotional upheaval you are undergoing.

There is some recent evidence that your adrenal glands produce more epinephrine when you are afraid, but secrete more nor-epinephrine when you are angry. However, both hormones are released to some degree in *all* arousal situations. Thus we cannot tell *objectively* whether you are angry or afraid just by measuring the relative amounts of epinephrine and nor-epinephrine floating around in your bloodstream.

When human volunteers have been injected with large amounts of epinephrine or nor-epinephrine, they often report feeling as if they were "about to become emotional," but they can't say why. The "arousal" they experience does not seem "real" somehow, because it isn't focused or directed toward any given object. Many of the volunteers described the experience as "cold rage."

Question: Some people report that they are most easily aroused sexually when they are hungry, or immediately after a frightening experience or a violent argument. Why might this often be the case?

Types of Emotions

How many different types of emotions can you experience? If you made a list, you'd probably include love and hate, lust and revulsion, joy and sadness, anxiety and calmness, guilt and relief, anger and friendliness, fear and security, elation and depression. Now, notice several important things about this list.

First, these emotions tend to come in *pairs*. One member of each pair seems to involve arousal, while the other seems to involve inhibition or depression. And one member typically seems to be a positive emotion, while the other seems to be negative. These facts have tempted several psychologists to arrange the emotions on a set of scales that run from +1 to 0 to −1. On this sort of measuring device, "utter joy" would rate a +1, "indifference" would be a zero, and "utter sadness" would be a −1. Love would be placed at the positive end of the scale, while hate would be at the negative pole.

POSITIVE				NEGATIVE
AROUSAL				INHIBITION
+1.0	+0.5	0	−.5	−1.0
JOY	INDIFFERENCE			SADNESS
LOVE	INDIFFERENCE			HATE

All attempts to put emotions on such simple scales have failed, however. Joy is much more than sympathetic arousal, and sadness involves more than an increase in activity in your parasympathetic system. Nor does it make much sense to describe love as a positive form of hate, or hate as a negative form of love.

The second important point about our verbal descriptions of emotions is this: Words are at best poor descriptions of complex psychological processes. Is your love for peanut butter the same sort of intra-psychic experience as your love for your mother or for your country? And when you

say you're "somewhat afraid of spiders," is that merely a weaker form of the fear someone else feels when he or she says, "I loathe and despise those creepy-crawly things!"? Perhaps you see what the problem really is. Namely, we seldom experience emotions in a vacuum. Rather, emotions are tied to specific events, situations, and objects. Thus it seldom makes much sense to talk about "love" in abstract terms. Rather we should probably speak of "the love *of*" something, or "the love *for*" something.

Feeling Tone

The third point concerning "emotional pairs" has to do with what psychologists call **affect**, or *feeling tone*. Some emotions are not only positive and arousing, they give us a pleasant feeling as well. Other emotions are not only negative and depressing, they are also downright unpleasant. But again, things are not as simple as they seem. Some loves make us happy; others are frustrating and unrewarding. Some hatreds are depressing; others stimulate us to pleasurable accomplishments.

Writing in the 1980 *Handbook of Clinical Neuropsychology*, Karl Pribram takes account of the **paradox** that the concept of "feeling tone" seems to create. Pribram believes that there are two types of positive affect, which he calls *gratification* and *satisfaction*. There are also two types of negative affect or feeling tone, which Pribram calls *distress* and *dissatisfaction*.

According to Pribram, you experience "gratification" whenever your needs are satisfied or your physiological drives are reduced. The feelings that accompany this gratification are relief, calmness, and tranquility. "Satisfaction" goes

Julian Rotter   Curt Richter

beyond mere calmness, however. For it occurs when you reduce your uncertainty about things. The feelings associated with satisfaction are those of delight, relish, joy, and exhilaration.

To illustrate the difference between "gratification" and "satisfaction," imagine what you might feel if you lost your job and had to accept food from friends in order to survive. Eating the food would gratify your hunger drive, but leave you unsatisfied because you would still be very uncertain about your future. And if you got a job, you might be satisfied even though you had to go hungry (ungratified) until your first paycheck arrived.

The two negative feeling tones are "distress" and "dissatisfaction." Pribram believes that "distress" is the feeling you get when a drive increases, or when you experience some painful stimulus or situation. Pain, agitation, and unpleasant arousal are the feelings associated with "distress." "Dissatisfaction" occurs when you lose control over events or when you experience uncertainty about the future. Anxiety, dread, and perplexity are unpleasant feelings associated with "dissatisfaction."

Although Pribram cites a fair amount of clinical data to support his views, there are no *experimental studies* that firmly support his theory. And there is one important point that Pribram does not discuss—the fact that different people react to the same situation in quite different ways. As Julian Rotter has shown, not all of us find satisfaction in "gaining control over events," or experience dissatisfaction when we can't "control our own destinies." Rotter believes that the positive or negative affect you feel in any situation will be dependent on what he calls your **locus of personal control**.

Locus of Personal Control

Some people believe they are **autonomous**. That is, they seem convinced they are masters of their own fates and take responsibility for what happens to them. They see their own *locus of personal control* as being *inside* themselves, and they believe that whatever rewarding inputs they get from their environments are due to their own actions. Julian Rotter calls these people **internalizers**.

On the other hand, many people believe that they are helpless pawns of fate, controlled by *outside forces* over which they have little if any influence. These individuals feel that their *locus of personal control* is external rather than internal, and that all the good and bad things that happen to them are due to chance rather than to their own actions. Rotter calls these people **externalizers**.

According to Rotter, *externalizers* usually believe that God or "fate" controls whatever happens to them. When faced with an external threat of some kind, these people either block off the stressful inputs, ignore them, or become depressed. These individuals might well not feel "dissatisfaction" at losing a job if friends (or the government) guaranteed them food and shelter.

Internalizers, on the other hand, don't believe in fate or "luck." They feel that "getting ahead in the world" is primarily a matter of what you do, not what accidents befall you. When threatened, internalizers tend to face the matter directly, or to remove themselves to temporary safety.

Pribram's description of the "two types of affect" seems to fit internalizers, but not externalizers. However, as we will see in Chapter 23, there are no "pure" personality types. Concepts such as "locus of control" are useful, but we must not make the mistake of thinking that everyone in the world must be either a "pure" externalizer or a "pure" internalizer. Many of us are "internalizers" in some situations and "externalizers" in others.

Locus of Organizational Control

Psychologists Patricia and Gerald Gurin have found that many individuals have an *internal* locus of control as far as their personal lives are concerned, but have an *external* locus of control on the job. These people are quite effective in handling their own personal stresses—they know how to cope in many day-to-day activities, and how to face the strains of living with their relatives and close friends. But many of these individuals work for large organizations and lack the social or managerial skills to achieve their goals on the job. Thus, while at work, they see themselves as puppets pushed around by forces they don't really understand. Locus of *personal* control, therefore, includes a somewhat different set of attitudes and behaviors than does locus of *organizational* control.

But both ways of perceiving and interacting with the external environment seem to be learned. And it is often the *social environment* itself—rather than any innately determined personality pattern—which determines whether you will become an internalizer or an externalizer.

Question: What kind of therapy could you give externalizers to convince them that—under certain conditions, at least—they could "control their destinies"?

Social/Behavioral Influences on Emotion

The next time you are in a crowd of people, try to pick out someone who is obviously quite happy. Once you've identified this individual, try to figure out what makes you sure the person is actually experiencing an emotion you call "happiness." In truth, you can never be sure what goes on inside an individual. All you can do is to *theorize* about the person's internal states by looking at the person's facial expressions and bodily movements. And, whether you realize it or not, you typically use your knowledge about the *situation the person is in* to help you guess at what the individual is feeling.

Many people believe they can guess your emotions merely by noting your facial responses. In fact, about all you can tell from facial expressions and bodily posture is whether the person is relaxed or agitated. (Most people believe they can guess your emotions by watching your face. However, as Daniel Goleman notes in the August 1982 issue of *Psychology Today,* your body language tells more about your true feelings than do your facial expressions.)

People from different cultures express their emotions in quite different ways. In some countries, a funeral is celebrated with laughter, dancing, and drinking. In other societies, death leads to sorrow, crying, and depression. In China, white is the color associated with grief. In the US, we mourn by wearing black clothes or armbands. Thus you cannot understand the emotion that a person is feeling unless you know something about the complex interactions that exist between the individual and her or his environment.

Richter's Hopeful Rats

Psychiatrist Curt Richter became interested in the consequences of emotional stress early in his long and productive scientific career. He saw many people literally fold up and die when they found themselves under too great pressure from their social or physical environments. The stress

Locus of personal control (LOW-cuss). The word *locus* means "location" or "place." According to Rotter, some people believe they control their own destinies, and thus have an internal locus of control. Others act as if their actions were almost entirely under the influence of external sources.

Autonomous (aw-TON-oh-muss). From the Greek word meaning "independent," or "self-directed." If you make your own decisions, you are autonomous. If you obey other people's orders, you are not.

Internalizers (in-TURR-nuh-lie-zers, or IN-turr-nuh-lie-zers). According to Julian Rotter, people who think they control their inputs (or gain reinforcers) by what they do, not by what fate hands them.

Externalizers (EX-turr-nuh-lie-zers). People who, according to Rotter, believe their inputs (or reinforcers) come to them by chance, or "by God's will," rather than by some action on their own part.

Hypertension (HIGH-purr-TEN-shun). A state of almost continual arousal or tenseness. Can lead to strokes, heart attacks, and other physical illness.

the environment caused was often purely psychological—but it was the patient's body as well as the patient's mind that often collapsed. So Richter began a fascinating series of experiments in which he measured—as best he could—the biological consequences of various highly threatening situations.

Since any abnormally stressful environment is potentially harmful to the organism, Richter worked with rats rather than with human beings.

One of Richter's experimental situations involved a large tub filled with water. He would throw a rat into the water and let it swim until the animal was so absolutely exhausted that it would have drowned if it had not been rescued. If the water was at room temperature, the average rat would swim about 80 hours (without rest) until it went under. If Richter made the water too cold or too hot, however, the rat would give up after no more than 20 to 40 hours. If he blew a jet of air into the animal's face while it was swimming, the rat became exhausted even more quickly.

After the experimental animals had met all these challenges, Richter would inspect various parts of their bodies to see what physiological changes had taken place. His early work was instrumental in the development of drugs that have helped thousands of human patients survive the devastating effects of psychological stress and **hypertension**.

Death by a Whisker

One of Richter's most fascinating findings came about almost by accident. Richter noticed that, when he threw most of his rats into the water, they always swam around the sides of the tub in

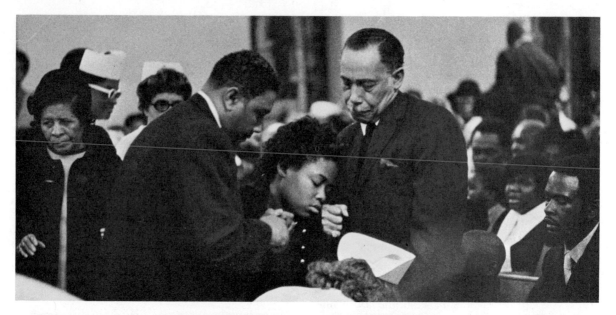

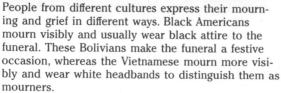
People from different cultures express their mourning and grief in different ways. Black Americans mourn visibly and usually wear black attire to the funeral. These Bolivians make the funeral a festive occasion, whereas the Vietnamese mourn more visibly and wear white headbands to distinguish them as mourners.

the same direction. Some animals always swam clockwise, some always counter-clockwise. But once they had "picked" their direction, they never changed it.

Richter knew that many insects and other lower animals show the same sort of "circling" behavior if you cut off one of their "feelers" or **antennae**. An ant that has lost its left antenna will

tend to circle to the left, and a lobster deprived of its right "feeler" will circle to the right. Richter wondered if there might not be some connection between the length of a rat's whiskers and the direction in which it swam in the tub. Perhaps rats always turned their heads toward the side where their whiskers were the shortest.

And so Richter asked his assistants to cut the whiskers off one side of a rat's face and toss it into the tub. When they did so—to everyone's surprise—the animal paddled around frantically for a minute or two. And then it sank straight to the bottom of the tub like a stone. The de-whisk-

Emotion, Stress, and Coping

ered rat would have drowned in two minutes (rather than 80 hours) if they hadn't rescued it.

Now, this finding simply didn't make sense to Richter. Obviously a rat doesn't depend on its whiskers to keep it afloat. What could be wrong? So Richter asked his assistants to show him what they had done to the rat while clipping it.

The Traumatic Black Bag

For the most part, the white rat found in psychological laboratories is a gentle rodent that can be handled without gloves. But rats have sharp teeth, as Richter's assistants knew only too well. If the rat becomes frightened, it will sharpen its keen teeth on any handy object—including the fingers of a lab assistant.

To avoid being bitten when clipping the rat's whiskers, Richter's assistants had nearly smothered the animal inside a black bag. To get the rat out of its cage, they had held the mouth of the bag up to the open cage door. Perhaps because the animal thought it could escape easily, or because it was attracted to darkness, the rat had jumped right into the thick black sack. The assistants then grabbed the animal tightly through the cloth and peeled back the top of the bag until the rat's head was exposed. Holding the rat's body firmly inside the bag, the assistants proceeded to clip the whiskers from one side of its face with a large, noisy clipper. Then they held the sack over the tub and dropped the frightened **rodent** into the water in the tub.

Little wonder that the rat sank to the bottom almost at once!

Richter soon found that it was the *trauma* induced by the handling—and not the whisker clipping at all—that so over-stimulated the animal's fear responses that it went straight into the stage of exhaustion. The parasympathetic nervous system simply took over and clamped down on all activity. The rat's heart slowed down almost to a complete stop, and the animal soon lost consciousness and sank.

It was from these and related studies that Richter concluded that "death by a whisker" was brought about by parasympathetic rather than sympathetic over-stimulation. But the cause of the death was not merely *environmental*. It soon turned out that "beliefs" and past experiences were also responsible.

Learning To Be Hopeful

Can your beliefs kill you? Perhaps so. For one of the most interesting findings Richter made was this: If he pulled the de-whiskered rat out of the water even seconds before it was about to drown— and let it sit on a table for a minute or two—the

Antennae (an-TEN-knee). The antenna of a TV set is the metal rod or wires put up to catch television waves. The antennae (or antennas) on an insect are the "feelers" that stick out of its head. Most insect antennae contain touch and olfactory receptors that help it "feel out the world" around it.

Rodent (ROH-dent). From the Latin word meaning "to gnaw." Rodents are a class of small, gnawing animals such as mice, rats, squirrels, and beavers.

animal would make a remarkable recovery. Once it had rested and gathered its wits together, it seemed to realize that it could, in fact, survive this traumatic situation. And so, if Richter then tossed it back into the water, the rat would swim for many hours.

Those two or three minutes out of the water were enough to give the rat momentary *hope*. If it were given several gentle, playful exposures to the black bag before having its whiskers clipped, it swam about 80 hours after being dumped into the tub. And if it were "rescued" several times during the first few minutes it was swimming, the rat apparently gained excellent control over its autonomic nervous system. It then managed to swim even better than did rats that hadn't been trained in this way to withstand stress.

Hope springs eternal. But it only "springs" when your body, mind, and your social environment cooperate. So, now that we've looked at various limited explanations of emotionality, suppose we turn to a more holistic view.

Question: How might you explain Richter's results in terms of turning "externalizers" into "internalizers"?

Emotion: A Holistic Approach

Emotional experiences seem to have four rather distinct aspects:

1. The bodily changes associated with arousal and relaxation.
2. Emotional behaviors such as fighting, loving, or running away.
3. The feedback that your environment gives you when you express an emotion verbally, or behave in an emotional way.
4. The subjective feelings that give a distinctive personal flavor to the emotion.

Some theorists emphasize just one aspect of emotionality, or believe that one is much more important than the other. In truth, however, emotion almost always involves *all four aspects*. Thus any attempt to describe emotions as *just* physiological reactions, or *just* intra-psychic feelings, is likely to give an incomplete picture of what emotions are all about.

Because the first three aspects of emotional arousal can be studied relatively easily from an objective viewpoint, we have a fair amount of hard data about them. But feelings such as love and hate are private events that occur within your mind. We can investigate these intra-psychic states only indirectly, by asking you to tell us what you are experiencing. However—as psychologists learned very early in their scientific study of emotions—whenever you stop to analyze your own feelings, they tend to change, diminish, or disappear entirely.

The difficulty in studying the intra-psychic aspect of emotionality is complicated by two additional facts. First, many people are rather bad at pinning precise labels on their emotional states. And second, individuals who are quite good at discriminating one emotion from another can't always identify the internal and external cues that triggered off the emotional response. However, the mere fact that inner feelings are hard to investigate scientifically doesn't mean that we can ignore them.

From a holistic approach, your emotions always involve a complex set of interactions between your body, your mind, and your environment. The need for taking this broad-scale view of emotionality can best be shown if we now look at the *stress* that your emotions can cause you, and at the ways that you might *cope* with that stress. As you will see, the "coping techniques" that various psychologists advocate typically depend on whether they view emotions from a narrow or from a holistic standpoint.

Coping

During your lifetime you have met many challenges, experienced many stressful situations, and worked your way through many emotional experiences. That is to say, you have *learned to adjust* to the problems that you face in life. Psychologists often speak of "learning to adjust" as **coping** with the world.

Your problems typically come to you as *inputs*, which you must *process* in some way and then *react* to. There are many different ways of *coping*, but they all involve making some change in your "input-output relationships." Thus some methods of coping involve changing, controlling, avoiding, or even denying certain inputs. Other coping strategies involve changing the way in which you "process" or think about problem-related inputs. Still other methods of coping in-

volve altering your outputs—that is, changing the ways in which you respond or behave when the problem occurs.

But whether you attack the problem by working on your inputs, your internal processes, or your outputs, you will typically choose one of two major ways of adjusting—**defensive coping** or **direct coping**.

Defensive coping typically involves protecting yourself by getting away from the threatening inputs. Direct coping involves meeting the challenge head-on.

Defensive Coping

Most forms of defensive coping involve either mental or physical *escape* from the traumatic situation. You either flee from the problem and in the future avoid going near the stress-inducing situation—or you block out the threatening inputs and deny that the inputs are stressful. Many of the **defense mechanisms** described by Sigmund Freud are types of defense coping.

Freudian Defense Mechanisms

As we noted in Chapter 10, if you are threatened by sexual thoughts or stimuli, you may repress them by not paying attention to them until they become incredibly strong. *Repression*, then, is a type of defensive coping.

Hysteria is the unconscious blocking off of input messages from one or more of your sense receptors. Hysterical blindness is perhaps the most common form of hysteria in our society. During battles, soldiers who see their best friends shot down may become psychologically "blind." Their eyes still work—but their minds refuse to process any incoming visual stimuli. By refusing to see anything at all, these men defend against having to witness more deaths.

Reaction formation, *projection*, and *displacement* are also forms of defensive coping. The mother who hates her child, but finds this hatred stress-inducing, may adjust to the situation by forming an entirely different reaction to the child. That is, she may repress the hatred and *react* to the child with far too much love. Or she may *project* her feelings onto the child by telling herself that she really loves the child, but the child hates her. Or she may *displace* her feelings by kicking the cat when she really wants to kick the child.

Fixation and *regression* are forms of defensive coping that involve going back to old ways of behavior or refusing to learn new ways. A growing child may become *fixated* at an immature level if it is punished each time it tries to take the next step up the developmental ladder. Or if the individual does learn to act in an adult way, but experiences great stress, the young person may *regress* to a much more childish (but safe) way of behaving.

We will discuss the Freudian defense mechanisms again in Chapter 21.

Depression

Depression is not a Freudian defense mechanism, but it is surely one of the most common types of defensive coping. Stress almost always involves an increase in sympathetic nervous system activity. One way to counter this arousal is somehow to increase activity in your parasympathetic system. For some people, this means learning how to relax and "stay cool" in the face of danger. But other people go a bit too far—they seem to turn their parasympathetic systems up to "maximum volume." They *give up*—both physiologically and psychologically. And, like Richter's rats, these individuals fall into such a deep depression that they are incapable of dealing with any of life's problems.

Geneticist Lowell Weitkamp believes that depression is inherited. In the February 1982 issue of *Discover*, Weitkamp suggests that depression is linked to the **immune reaction**, and thus probably is controlled by a specific group of genes. However, Weitkamp's only scientific proof is that depression "tends to run in families." Other geneticists are skeptical of Weitkamp's ideas, as are psychologists who point out that depression is typically a response to such events as the death of a loved one or the loss of one's job. Thus, at best, the *tendency* to react to stress in a depressive way may be inherited. But the "trigger" for the depression is usually environmental or personal stress.

Pills and Depression

As we will see in Chapter 17, people who adopt a defensive method of coping often turn to alcohol and pills as "chemical crutches" to help them live with their problems. Pills are a *defensive* method of coping because they don't involve any fundamental change in the way you face the world. Rather, you "pop a pill" and go on making the same mistakes that you always made. And you may even be encouraged to do so by your family physician, who may prefer a *medical* solution to what is really a *psychological* disorder.

But, as Stanton Peele points out in the August 1981 issue of the *American Psychologist*, the use of drugs *alone* to treat depression has not been very effective. Although many patients welcome the temporary relief that comes from taking anti-depressants, the patients are still left with unresolved personal and social problems. According to Peele, **chemotherapy** is best viewed

Coping (KO-ping). From Latin and Greek words meaning "to strike." To cope with something is to fight against it successfully.

Defensive coping. A way of dealing with stress-related problems by running away from them physically or psychologically, or by walling yourself off from reality, or becoming depressed. According to Freud, all types of defensive coping are "unhealthy adjustments to reality."

Direct coping. A way of dealing with stress-related problems by facing the issues and solving them. Direct coping involves identifying the stressful inputs, then figuring out ways of handling them in a step-by-step manner. Both defensive and direct means of coping are "life styles" that are learned, usually at an early age. Adults can usually learn new ways of coping if given the proper help.

Defense mechanisms. According to Freud, your ego or self must mediate between the demands of your unconscious instincts (your id) and the demands of society. To protect itself, your ego typically makes use of various psychological strategies, called defense mechanisms. See Chapter 21.

Immune reaction. To be immune to something is to be able to protect yourself from that something. If you are immune to a given disease, your body has ways of rejecting the germs that cause that disease. Hay fever is an immune reaction your body makes as it tries to reject pollens produced by various plants when they are in flower.

Chemotherapy (KEY-moh-THER-ap-pee). Psychotherapy is treatment that involves the use of psychology. Chemotherapy is treatment that involves the use of drugs or other chemicals.

as a temporary crutch to help people survive while they learn new and more *direct* methods of coping with stress.

Direct Coping

Most forms of *direct coping* involve at least three steps:

1. An *objective analysis* of what your problem is, how it came into being, and how you are presently responding.
2. A clear statement of how things might be better—that is, a precise description of what your *ultimate goal* or adjustment would be.
3. A *psychological road map*, or list of new approaches to life that you might use to help you reach your goal.

Direct coping is not always easy, and it is often very time-consuming, for it requires that you "stand back" and look at things as unemotionally as you can. When you are caught up in the middle of a frightening or stressful situation, you may have neither the motivation nor the self-control to think things through rationally. Thus you may find it helpful to seek professional help if you wish to learn how to deal with stressful inputs in a direct manner (see Chapter 24).

Direct coping also requires that you set clear-cut goals, and then move toward these goals a step at a time. People in stressful situations— such as those who want to lose weight—aren't

Pilots begin work on the ground using flight simulation rather than real airplanes.**(top left)**

The man having an encounter with the firemen is experiencing "bad stress" while the woman hurdler could be experiencing "good stress."**(right)**

always willing to set realistic goals or take the slow-but-steady approach to solving their problems. And there are many individuals who believe the best way to learn how to cope is to jump right into the middle of things. The experimental data, however, suggest otherwise.

"Sink or Swim" Learning

In 1980, Lt. Col. William Datel reported an interesting set of experiments performed during the 1970's on Army recruits at Fort Ord, near Monterey in California. Each year, thousands of recruits are given their basic training at Fort Ord. Most of the recruits find the situation fairly stressful. They have little privacy, they are punished (often severely) for any mistakes, they are not allowed to talk back or argue with orders, and they are restricted to camp for the first several weeks of their stay at the camp.

Many recruits survive this stressful ordeal rather well. But many young men and women fall by the wayside. Some try to escape the situation by "going AWOL"—that is, by being absent without leave. Others become ill or depressed. A few commit suicide.

When Colonel Datel was asked to help find better methods of providing basic training, he first analyzed the situation psychologically. The basic philosophy in most army camps is that recruits must be "tempered in the fire of experience." Thus many army training methods are devised to arouse the maximum amount of stress in the recruits—and then throw them into waters of experience to see if they sink or swim.

Direct methods of coping—like all other habits—are usually best-learned when you are

rewarded for progress rather than being punished for failure. Knowing this, Colonel Datel set up an experimental unit at Fort Ord that trained a random selection of recruits using **positive reinforcement** rather than punishment. These men earned "points" for everything they did well, but were not penalized for their mistakes. The recruits in this experimental unit could trade in the points for any rewards they wished—including the privilege of going into town the first night they were at the camp.

Colonel Datel followed his experimental recruits both while they were at Fort Ord and throughout their next several years in the Army. He compared their progress with that of a "control group"—namely, an equal number of recruits who went through the regular stress-oriented basic training at Fort Ord.

Datel's first finding was that almost none of the men in the experimental program went "AWOL." This result alone saved the Army many thousands of dollars. Datel also found that his experimental subjects got better marks on such skills as rifle marksmanship and map reading than did recruits in the "control group." Furthermore, when the experimental subjects went into combat in Vietnam, they performed better under enemy fire than did the "control group" recruits. And more of the experimental group reenlisted at the end of their term of duty than did members of the "control group."

Despite Datel's data, the Army abandoned much of the experimental program a few years after Datel had set it up. Most military commanders apparently still believe that "sink or swim" techniques are the best way to help recruits learn to cope with stress.

"Step-by-Step" Learning

In recent years, the Federal Aviation Agency collected data that tend to confirm Colonel Datel's research. The FAA, however, made more creative use of their findings than did the military.

The FAA is charged with testing the nation's airline pilots to make sure that they have the skills needed to fly commercial aircraft. Twice a year, each commercial pilot must fly a "test run" with an FAA inspector. For many years, these inspectors used to create highly stressful situations for the pilots—usually by turning off the plane's engines or by disabling the plane in some unusual way while it was in their air. The **rationale** for this sort of testing was that pilots must learn to expect the unexpected. They can hardly hope to save the lives of their passengers in emergency situations unless they have experienced those situations and learned how to cope with them.

The "emergencies" that the FAA inspectors threw at their test pilots, therefore, were often dangerous ones. Most of the pilots did beautifully, but a few buckled under the stress or didn't recognize what had gone wrong until too late. In one such situation, an FAA inspector "killed" two engines on a jetliner just as the pilot was trying to land at New Orleans. The plane went out of control and crashed into a large motel.

After this disaster, the FAA changed the stress-testing techniques they used. Rather than dumping pilots into dangerous water without warning, the FAA identified as many types of emergencies as they could. They then created a step-by-step training procedure in which pilots start with the simplest type of emergency and slowly work up to the more dangerous situations. The pilots take most of this training on the ground—using computerized **flight simulators** rather than real airplanes. Once the pilots experience success in the simple problems, they are allowed to move up to progressively more stressful tasks. And they usually are not challenged with a situation while "in the air" until they have proved they can handle that emergency in the simulator.

According to the FAA, flight safety has increased measurably since they have adopted their new techniques.

Positive reinforcement. The use of a reward of some kind to strengthen a learned response. See Chapter 15.

Rationale (rash-oh-NAL). From the Latin word meaning "to think." Your rationale for doing something is your logical explanation of why the action is necessary.

Flight simulators (SIMM-you-lay-tors). When you pretend to be happy, you "simulate" happiness. A flight simulator is a machine that "pretends" to be a real airplane cockpit. It contains all the equipment found in a true cockpit, but is connected to a computer that "fakes" the experience of flying.

Eustress (YOU-stress). From the Greek word *eu*, meaning "good." Euphoria is "good feelings," eulogy means "to speak good" of someone, eugenics means "good genes," and the eucalyptus tree gets its name from "good shade."

Question: Almost all pilots succeed in learning how to handle stress when trained by the step-by-step method. Why does this fact help support Stanton Peele's contention that drugs alone *are not the best way of helping people learn to cope with stressful situations?*

Eustress

In an interview with Hans Selye, published in the March 1978 issue of *Psychology Today*, the man who "invented" the concept of physiological stress talks at length about **eustress**, or "good" stress.

According to Selye, not all stress is bad. We shouldn't try to avoid all stress, for that would be impossible. Rather, we should recognize what our typical response is to stress—and then try to adjust our lifestyles to take advantage of what that typical response is.

Selye believes that some of us are what he calls "turtles"—that is, we prefer peace, quiet, and a tranquil environment. Others of us are "racehorses," who thrive on a vigorous, fast-paced way of life. The optimum amount of stress we may require to function best is what Selye calls *eustress*.

In a sense, Selye has done little more than adapt the "Arousal Theory" of motivation to his own terms. But his point remains valid. The problem with Selye's approach is this—he assumes that you are born a "turtle" or a "racehorse." Thus, from Selye's point of view, there is little you can do about changing your response to stress other than trying to compensate for the genes that Nature gave you. Few psychologists agree with Selye on this issue.

Society depends on eustress, for cultures are kept going by motivated people who are willing to learn how to cope with each other—and with their own individual needs and personalities.

Thus emotionality is necessary for life. The problem comes in discovering ways to make your emotions helpful to you rather than harmful. Needless to say, the more you know about your feelings, the better off you will be. And that means not only discovering what your emotions *are*, but learning effective ways of *handling them* as well.

Now that we have explored the stressful aspects of motivation, perhaps it is time we coped with the laws of learning.

Summary

1. **Emotion** comes from the same Latin word as does **motivation**. Emotion has to do with **agitated movement**, most typically that associated with achieving or failing to achieve **goals**.

2. Some scientists view emotions as being primarily **bodily reactions**. Others see emotion as a **bipolar intra-psychic experience**. Still other psychologists define emotion primarily in terms of **learned behavioral responses**. In truth, emotion is all of these things and much more.

3. **Biological psychologists** tend to focus on **arousal** and **depression** as being the main components of the emotional response. These physical reactions are controlled in large part by the **autonomic nervous system**.

4. The autonomic nervous system has two parts, the **sympathetic** and **parasympathetic nervous systems**.

5. Your sympathetic nervous system arouses you to handle such activities as fighting, fleeing, feeding—and sexual climax.

6. Your parasympathetic nervous system acts to depress or slow down those bodily functions that are aroused by sympathetic system activity. The parasympathetic is sometimes called the **vegetative nervous system**.

7. The sympathetic and parasympathetic systems generally have opposite effects on your reactions, but the two actually operate together in a **coordinated manner**. Working together, they influence much of what you do and feel.

8. Once you become excited or emotionally stirred up, your sympathetic system causes the release of **epinephrine** and **nor-epinephrine**—the **arousal hormones** secreted by the **adrenal glands**.

9. The arousal hormones have much the same excitatory effect on **biological reactions** (such as blood pressure and pulse rate) as activity in the sympathetic system itself. The sympathetic system arouses the body almost immediately. The arousal hormones give you **sustained arousal**.

10. In his **General Adaptation Syndrome** the-

ory, Hans Selye suggests that your body goes through three rather distinct stages when stressed:

a. The **alarm reaction**, in which your body's defenses are mobilized by activity in your **limbic system**, sympathetic system, and through secretion of epinephrine and nor-epinephrine.

b. The **stage of resistance**, which occurs if the stress continues for very long. During this stage, your adrenal glands secrete **ACTH**, a hormone that helps neutralize the effects of stress.

c. The **stage of exhaustion**, which comes about if the emergency continues for too long. During this stage, your body may use up all of its ACTH and fall into **shock**. If the stress continues, you may experience depression, insanity, or death.

11. According to the **James-Lange theory of emotions**, your "feelings" are merely responses to changes that have already occurred in your body and in your behavior. The theory states that you are "afraid because you run, not that you run because you are afraid."

12. The James-Lange theory fails because "feelings" generally precede physical or behavioral emotional responses, and the same biological changes occur in many different emotions.

13. According to the **Cannon-Bard theory of emotions**, your **thalamus** controls "feelings," while your **hypothalamus** controls bodily responses.

14. The Cannon-Bard theory fails because emotional bodily responses are now known to be controlled by the **limbic system** and the **right hemisphere**.

15. Biological explanations of emotion tend to fail because subjects given arousal hormones experience "cold" emotions that have no meaning. Emotional responses thus seem tied to specific situations and intra-psychic experiences, and are not merely physical reactions.

16. Many intra-psychic psychologists tend to put emotions in **pairs** on **psychological scales**. The "pairs" include such feelings as love-hate

and joy-sadness. There is no evidence that all emotions can be put on such simple psychological scales.

17. Karl Pribram theorizes that **affect**, or "feeling tone" has two major dimensions. The first is "positive affect," which includes **gratification** and **satisfaction**. The second is "negative affect," which includes **distress** and **dissatisfaction**. There is no real experimental evidence to support Pribram's views.

18. Julian Rotter believes people respond to psychological pressures in different ways, depending in part on their own personal **locus of control**.

    a. People who believe they are **autonomous**—that is, who believe they control their own fates—are aroused by threats and try to overcome them. Rotter calls these people **internalizers**.

    b. Individuals who see themselves as being controlled primarily by external forces may face threats passively, waiting for some outside agency to protect or take care of them. Rotter calls these people **externalizers**.

13. Some individuals have an internal locus of personal control, but have an external **locus of organizational control**. These individuals cope well with their personal problems, but believe that their careers are influenced by external forces over which they have little control.

14. Curt Richter found that stressing rats before putting them into a tub of water caused the animals to **give up** and sink at once. However, if he gave them **hope**, they swam longer than usual.

15. Generally speaking, there are two main ways of adjusting to stress—**defensive coping** and **direct coping**.

16. Defensive coping strategies include such **Freudian defense mechanisms** as **repression, hysterical blindness, projection, reaction formation, displacement**, and **regression**. Another method of coping with stress defensively is **depression**.

17. Direct coping methods involve **problem analysis**, **goal setting**, and moving toward the goal in a **step-by-step manner**.

18. **Authoritarian** groups and organizations—such as the military—foster an external locus of control by training their members to handle stress in a **sink or swim** fashion. The "step-by-step" method, however, usually yields better results.

19. All motivation is based on stress of some kind. Selye calls the amount of stress you need to function properly **eustress**, or good stress.

(Continued from page 301.)

"Get up, Charlie."

Dr. Smith's voice was loud, but somehow not as heavy and as threatening as the voice inside Charlie's head usually was.

"I can't get up. I can't cope with things out there," Charlie said dully, pulling the covers more tightly over his head.

"Of course you can," Gail said. She seemed to be crying. He wondered why she wasn't still angry at him.

When Charlie didn't respond, Dr. Smith tugged gently at the covers. "Open up in there and come on out. You can make it, Charlie. Just try it and see."

"Don't move!" the heavy voice warned him.

"I won't," Charlie responded.

Dr. Smith thought Charlie was talking to him. "Won't is very different from can't, Charlie. You can make it if you want to."

"Do something, please!" Gail said to Dr. Smith.

Charlie thought she was talking to him. "I'm too tired to do anything," Charlie said.

"Too tired of what?" Dr. Smith asked.

"Hurdles," Charlie said finally. "Too many hurdles for this dogface to jump, and too many snipers trying to hit you."

Gail sobbed and sat on the bed beside him.

"Hurdles. That's it, of course. And dogs," Dr. Smith said, pulling up a chair. "Listen to me, Charlie. I want to tell you a story."

"Go away," Charlie said. Gail thought he was speaking to her and sobbed again.

Dr. Smith tugged on the blanket again, exposing a bit more of Charlie's face. "Once upon a time, Charlie, there was a psychologist named Martin Seligman. He worked with dogs."

"I was a dog once," Charlie said. "A dirty dogface. I couldn't make it as a dog, either. They sent me to a hospital."

Again the gentle tug on the blanket. "Seligman made his dogs jump a hurdle, Charlie, just like you said. The hurdle separated two chambers in a large wooden box. Seligman taught the dogs to jump the hurdle when he sounded a signal. If they jumped into the other chamber right away, they were safe. If they didn't jump when the signal came on, they got shocked."

"Snipers don't give signals," Charlie said.

"Seligman did," Dr. Smith continued. "When he first put a dog in one of the chambers and gave the signal, the dog ignored it. Then came the shock. The dog bounced around, hunting for a way out."

"There is no way out," Charlie mumbled.

"Yes, there is. Over the hurdle," Dr. Smith said. "After the dog had jumped around for a while, it accidentally went over the hurdle. And found it was safe."

Charlie pulled the blanket up again. "It's not safe anywhere."

"Yes, it is," Dr. Smith continued. "The dog soon learned to jump the moment the signal came on. And it always avoided the shock."

"That sounds cruel," Gail said. "Why are you telling Charlie stories like that?"

"It's a cruel world," Charlie said. "Even for dogs."

Dr. Smith tugged the blanket down once more. "And even dogs can learn, Charlie. Listen. Once the dog had gotten the message, it never forgot. Even when Seligman turned off the electric current, the dog continued to jump, and jump, and jump. There wasn't any shock to hurt it, but it just kept right on trying to avoid something that wasn't there any more."

"Why did it do that?" Gail asked.

"The signal had become stressful and arousing," Dr. Smith said. "Jumping reduced the dog's conditioned fear and hence turned off the stress."

"Safer to jump," Charlie said.

"Smarter to learn when you don't have to be afraid," replied Dr. Smith. "But Seligman found a way to help the dog cope. He simply made the hurdle so high that the dog couldn't possibly jump over it. Then he turned on the signal."

Gail seemed distressed. "But the dog couldn't escape . . ."

"That's right," the psychologist said. "It tried to leap over the barrier, but couldn't. It kept trying to jump for several minutes while the signal sounded. Eventually it realized that the shock was gone forever. So it stopped being afraid of the signal. Then, when Seligman lowered the barrier and turned on the signal, the dog ignored it. The dog had learned a better way of coping with its fear than by blindly jumping the instant the signal came on."

"Avoid these people!" the voice inside Charlie's head signaled.

Dr. Smith pulled the blanket down to expose a bit more of Charlie's face. "Listen. We all go around avoiding things that we really ought to face up to, because they no longer have any power to hurt us. But that's not the most important lesson in Seligman's research."

"Then why talk about it?" Gail asked.

"Because of what he did next," Dr. Smith said, avoiding a direct answer to Gail's question. "Next, Seligman took an untrained dog and put it in the chamber, but he started with the hurdle up so high the animal couldn't jump it. Then he turned on the signal and the shock."

"No way out," said Charlie.

Emotion, Stress, and Coping

Dr. Smith nodded, and pulled the blanket completely away from Charlie's grasp. "That's right. The poor dumb beast leaped all around the place. It whined, and it crapped on the floor, but it couldn't find a way out. So what do you think it did?"

"Hid in a corner," Charlie said, struggling for control of the blanket.

"Gail, take hold of the blanket, please," Dr. Smith said. She pulled the cover toward her.

"Hide!" cried the heavy voice inside Charlie's head.

"No, it couldn't hide," said Dr. Smith. "The best the dog could do was to stand on its tippy-toes with its eyes shut. That way it got the least amount of shock possible. It couldn't escape, so it learned to cope by shutting off as much of the outside world as it could."

Gail looked at the psychologist. "It hid inside its own mind, you mean."

"And it never came out," said Charlie, covering his face with his arms.

"That's right. At first it wouldn't come out," Dr. Smith said. "Not even when Seligman lowered the barrier and gave it a chance to get away. The dog still went up on its tippy-toes when the signal went on."

"Even though it could see the other side of the chamber?" Gail asked.

"Safer on the inside," Charlie mumbled.

Dr. Smith nodded, and shook Charlie by the shoulder. "Come out from in there."

"No!" cried the voice.

"But why wouldn't the dog jump when Seligman gave it a chance?" Gail asked.

Dr. Smith laughed. "Why doesn't Charlie jump into your arms, now that you've come back to him? You faced the facts about what his mother did to him, and you adjusted. Why can't Charlie make the same jump to freedom?"

"Because!" Charlie moaned as he squirmed about on the bed.

"Because," Dr. Smith continued, "like Seligman's dog, Charlie was punished for all his attempts to find a way out. So Charlie just gave up and stopped looking. The stress signal comes on, and Charlie instantly goes up on his mental tippy-toes because that's the way he's learned to minimize the pain. 'Learned helplessness' is what Seligman calls it."

"Leave me alone," Charlie cried.

A puzzled look crossed Gail's face. "But surely if Seligman coaxed the dog . . ."

"Seligman tried that, but it didn't work. He tried offering the dog food, too. The dog just closed its eyes." Dr. Smith shook the young man's shoulder a bit roughly. "Listen, you in there, you've got to learn to stand on your feet instead of on your tippy-toes."

Gail persisted. "But how did Seligman get the dog to cope?"

"Grab Charlie's other arm, please," Dr. Smith said, pulling the young man to his feet with Gail's help. "We're going for a walk into the real world."

"Help!" cried the heavy voice.

"Better help than helplessness," Dr. Smith said, propelling Charlie through the door.

"You didn't answer my question," Gail said as the three of them walked clumsily down the apartment house stairs.

"Oh," said Dr. Smith. "Seligman put a rope around the dog's neck and dragged it across the hurdle to freedom. Had to do it 40 to 50 times before the dog got the message that jumping was safe."

As they reached the front door, a car on the street outside backfired. Charlie pulled back violently. "Snipers! It's not safe out there!" he cried.

Dr. Smith grabbed him firmly by the collar. "Listen, Charlie. You can make it out there. I promise you that."

"Can't!" cried the heavy voice.

"Yes, you can," Dr. Smith said, pulling him forward.

"Yes, you can," Gail urged, pushing from behind.

The three of them tumbled out onto the street. It was a bright, clear, summer day. Pulling and shoving, coaxing and caressing, Gail and Dr. Smith got him moving.

Like a couple of tugboats towing a heavy barge, they plowed slowly down the side-walk toward a little park a couple of blocks away.

"You're making it!" Dr. Smith said.

"You're doing great!" said Gail.

Once inside the park, they moved down a wooded pathway. And then they came to a large tree trunk that had fallen across the path. Dr. Smith bounded across the barrier with ease, but Charlie balked.

"Stop!" cried the heavy voice.

"Jump, Charlie," urged Dr. Smith. "You can make it."

"Can't!" Charlie moaned.

Gail leapt lightly over the obstacle. "Look, Charlie, if I can do it, you can too."

"Jump!" cried Dr. Smith.

"Jump!" Gail coaxed.

Charlie leaned forward, tripped, hopped, skipped, and clumsily jumped over the tree trunk.

"You did it!" Gail said, grabbing Charlie in her arms.

He held on to her tensely, panting, shaking with fear.

"And you can do it again, any time you want," said Dr. Smith, patting him on the back.

A few seconds later, after he got his breath and stopped trembling like a frightened puppy, Charlie looked up. The sky was blue, the sun was shining, and there wasn't a single sniper in sight.

"Any time you want to," Gail reminded him, kissing his cheek. Her smile matched the radiance of the sun.

Charlie relaxed a bit, then frowned, then almost managed a grin. He listened carefully for the heavy voice, but all he heard were birds singing. After a while, he shrugged his shoulders. "Maybe I can," he said.

Recommended Readings

Baum, Andrew, and Jerome E. Singer, eds. *Advances in Environmental Psychology,* Vol. 2: *Applications of Personal Control* (Hillsdale, N.J.: Erlbaum, 1980).

Garber, Judy, and Martin E.P. Seligman, eds. *Human Helplessness: Theory and Applications* (New York: Academic Press, 1980).

Rotter, Julian. "External control and internal control," *Psychology Today*, Vol. 5, No.1 (1971), pp. 37–42.

Plutchik, Robert, and Henry Kellerman, eds. *Emotion: Theory, Research, and Experience*, Vol. 1: *Theories of Emotion* (New York: Academic Press, 1980).

Selye, Hans. *The Stress of Life*, rev. ed. (New York: McGraw-Hill, 1978).

Selye, Hans, ed. *Selye's Guide to Stress Research*, Vol. 1 (New York: Van Nostrand, 1980).

4

Learning
and
Memory

Conditioning and Desensitization

14

Did You Know That . . .

Although a Russian named Ivan Pavlov is usually given credit, a US psychologist named E.B. Twitmyer was apparently the first to experiment with what we now call the "conditioned response"?

Pavlov was able to train dogs willingly to withstand considerable pain to get food?

Animals put in conflict-inducing situations often display behaviors that, if they were human, would lead us to assume the animals were "mentally ill"?

The so-called "lie-detector" doesn't really detect lies?

A person with an abnormal fear (called a "phobia") can sometimes be helped by the same sort of conditioning techniques Pavlov used with his dogs?

You can overcome "fear of exams" if you follow a technique called "desensitization"?

Learning how to relax "on cue" is often a first step in learning how to overcome your fears?

The most effective forms of therapy usually involve changes in attitudes and emotional responses as well as changes in behavior?

"The Leningrad Connection"

"First of all, I'm only here because my wife wanted me to come," Kevin Lynn said to psychologist Dr. Nancy Wagner. "I have this little problem, I guess. Not really a problem exactly, just my own way of doing things. It doesn't hurt anybody but me, so what's the difference? I mean, what's to get excited about? Do you see what I mean?"

A spark of veiled amusement lit up Dr. Wagner's dark blue eyes. "No, Mr. Lynn, I don't see. But I'm sure I will if you tell me more about it."

Kevin Lynn ran a nervous hand through his thick black hair. "Well, it's a sort of very personal problem, if you know what I mean. Nothing really abnormal, or anything like that. But it cuts close to the skin, and I'm not exactly eager to talk about it. And really, when you stop to think about it, it's as much my wife's problem as my own."

The man had a bright, glib way of talking, but Dr. Wagner sensed that he shared his wife's concern. So she nodded encouragingly and said, "Marital problems almost always involve both husband and wife. So why don't you tell me more about what's troubling the two of you?"

Kevin Lynn began to sweat a little. "Gee, you know, some things are very personal. Now, don't take this wrong, because I don't want to hurt your feelings. But . . . I mean, isn't there a *male* doctor I could talk to? I mean, there are some things . . ."

Dr. Wagner smiled reassuringly. "Mr. Lynn, I can't blame you for being reluctant to talk about sexual matters. But don't you think that women are often more understanding of a man's sexual problems than other men are? And I'm sure that you're right in thinking that it's as much your wife's responsibility as yours. So just relax for a moment, lean back in your chair, and get comfortable. And then see if you don't want to tell me what's troubling you."

Lynn stared at the woman for a moment or two, then followed her suggestion. He sighed deeply as he let himself go limp. Then he began to talk.

"I don't satisfy her, Dr. Wagner. At least, I can't usually make it, well, *worthwhile* for her without a little something extra to turn me on." His voice dropped to a halting whisper. "I guess if I told you how screwed up I really am, you'd be pretty shocked."

Nancy Wagner smiled. "It depends on what it takes 'to turn you on.' The last man I worked with was impotent unless he took his teddy bear to bed along with his wife."

"You're kidding!"

"No, not at all."

Kevin Lynn giggled. "Well, maybe I'm not so bad off as I thought. And it's not that I *have* to have them, it's just that it's usually better that way . . ."

"Have what?"

The man sighed again. "The whips. I like the touch of a whip when it's bedtime. The cutting edge, you might say. Gives me the power to get up and go, stirs my blood a bit. So when we got married, I bought my wife a couple of small whips—tiny ones, really—and asked her to use them on me. At first, she didn't want to. She said it hurt her more than it did me. But when she gave in and tried them for a while, it was good, really good."

Kevin Lynn paused, remembering old times. "But now, she's read some stupid book, and she says I need help because I'm a masochist." He spat it out like a dirty word, MASS-oh-kist. "I guess that's pretty weird, isn't it? A guy who needs pain to get sexually excited?"

"It's a great deal more common than you probably realize. Pick up any of the underground newspapers and see how many 'personal' ads talk about whips and leather clothes and 'the need to be disciplined.'" Dr. Wagner smiled gently at the man. "And we may be able to give you more help than you suspect."

Lynn's voice quickened. "Gee, do you really think so? I mean, this book my wife read, it says I feel guilt and anxiety because I unconsciously think sex is dirty. So I've got to be punished first, to pay in advance for my sinful deeds and pleasures. Otherwise, I can't relax and do what comes naturally." He paused. "Is that what you think is wrong with me?"

The woman cleared her throat. "Mr. Lynn, there are many different views on what causes masochism. Some therapists believe that the real problem is *sadism*— or the desire to hurt other people. According to this view, people who can't tolerate the thought of hurting others may turn their desires inward. They hold their own hostile impulses in check by making other people hurt them instead."

Kevin Lynn shook his head firmly. "I don't like to hurt anybody. I just like to be hurt, you know?"

"I know," Dr. Wagner said. "Well, to continue, some psychologists believe that masochism is related to castration anxiety, that the man invites his wife to hurt him slightly as a way of warding off her attempts to castrate him."

"My wife doesn't think that way! Besides, I was into whips before I met her."

"Good point. Anyhow, still other psychologists think the problem is basically one of being *trained* to like or accept pain when you are very young."

Lynn frowned in confusion, not knowing quite what to think. "What do you believe, Doctor?"

The woman smiled. "There's a lot to be said for all those views, and just because one might be right doesn't mean that the others are wrong. Some types of therapy focus on understanding your past. Other therapies are oriented toward helping you change your future."

"Which would be best for me?"

Dr. Wagner frowned. "Ideally, we'd want to try both types of treatment at the same time. Masochism is sometimes a symptom of unconscious anxiety that needs to be uncovered if you're to learn to cope with and avoid similar difficulties in the future. In recent years, however, psychologists have found that many types of masochism are the result of improper learning when the person was young. In these cases, we 'condition' you to learn more appropriate ways of responding."

"How does this conditioning stuff of yours work? Do you have to whip me, or something?" Lynn's voice was eager and a bit mischievous.

The woman smiled. "No, we assume that some time early in your life you were rewarded for hurting yourself or being hurt by someone else. Probably there were sexual overtones to the experience, and that's how you were shaped into needing pain to stimulate you. Perhaps one time you were terrified of something that involved sexuality or your own sex organs, and you got hurt, and somehow your anxiety was greatly reduced. Then pain would become associated in your mind with fear-reduction. For example, did your parents have frequent fights?"

Lynn's face reddened in embarrassment. "Oh, I wouldn't say they were *frequent* . . ."

Dr. Wagner nodded. "I'm not trying to insult your parents, Mr. Lynn. But when a child's parents have a fight, the child may become terrified. If the child gets hurt, and the parents stop fighting in order to give love or affection to the child, then the child might unconsciously be conditioned to seek pain in order to reduce fear and anxiety."

"I don't seem to recall anything like that," Lynn said, still slightly embarrassed.

"This sort of conditioning could happen when you're so young that you don't remember it as an adult," Dr. Wagner said.

The man shrugged his shoulders, more at ease now. "Well, if you say so. But how do we start? Do I lie on a couch, or something? Or maybe a bed of nails?"

Dr. Wagner laughed warmly. "No, we'll talk about the origins of your masochism later on. But first, you will have to decide what you most urgently need help with right now."

Lynn thought for a moment, then said softly, "I guess my relationship with my wife comes first."

"All right, perhaps we can retrain you to enjoy sexual pleasure with your wife without having to suffer pain first."

An impish look crept over the man's face. "Couldn't we just train my wife to be a sadist? I mean, wouldn't that be just as quick?"

The woman laughed again. "I doubt she'd agree. Anyway, do you want your problem to control you, or do you want to control your problem?"

"Yeah, I guess you're right. What do we do first?"

"First, we teach you how to relax, and how to listen to your body. You see, pain has probably become a conditioned signal for sexual arousal in your case. If you skip the whips, you probably become nervous about whether or not you'll be able to perform sexually, am I correct?"

Lynn began to sweat a little. "Yeah, you got it right."

"Well," said Dr. Wagner, "Anxiety is controlled by your sympathetic nervous system. That's the part of your body that handles excitement. Unfortunately, erection is controlled by your parasympathetic nervous system, that part of your body which is involved in relaxation."

"So you're saying that I can't feel sexy unless I'm relaxed?"

Dr. Wagner nodded. "At the beginning of things, yes. And the more anxious you become about not being able to perform, the more your sympathetic nervous system turns on and the more difficult it is for your parasympathetic system to do its job."

The man nodded. "Yeah, that makes sense, in a strange kind of way."

"So we teach you how to handle your anxiety by learning how to relax. Then we'll make a list of all the situations that make you tense, beginning with things that aren't really all that disturbing and working up to things that make you break out in a cold sweat even just thinking about them."

"We'll make a little list, eh?"

The woman agreed. "That's right. And then, when you learn to differentiate between the signals your body gives when you're relaxed—and those signals your body gives when it's tense—you'll know how to relax whenever you want to. Next, we'll start talking about the items on that list, starting with the simplest and working up to the most disturbing. If we can teach you to talk about these things while you're calm and cool and collected, then they won't make you very anxious any more. And if you're not anxious . . ."

" . . . then I can make love to my wife without needing the whips, you mean."

Dr. Wagner smiled. "That's right."

Kevin Lynn pondered the matter for a long time. "Well, I guess it might work. How do we begin?"

"It's simple. First, stretch out your legs and make them as rigid and as tense as you can. Go ahead, do it now. Do you feel the tension?"

"Sure. It almost hurts."

"Good. Now, relax your legs completely. Relax your feet and your ankles and your thigh muscles. There. Now tense them up again. That's right, tense, tense, tense. Feel the tension? Okay, now relax again, just go completely limp. Now, can you tell the difference between tension and relaxation?"

"I sure can. There's a world of difference."

"Good," said the woman. "Next, we'll do the same thing with your arms, and then with your head and neck muscles. We want to get you to the point where you can discriminate tension from relaxation. Then you can command your body to relax any time you want to, and the muscles in your body will respond automatically."

Lynn grinned. "If I could do that . . ."

"Then your immediate problem would be solved, and you could go on to find out how the masochism got started."

"That sounds like a painfully slow process."

Dr. Wagner laughed lightly. "I thought you liked pain, Mr. Lynn."

Kevin Lynn favored her with a broad smile. "Okay, Dr. Wagner. You've got a deal."

(Continued on page 341.)

The Innate Reflex

Some time about the beginning of this century, a young man named E.B. Twitmyer began work on his doctoral dissertation in psychology at the University of Pennsylvania. Twitmyer was interested in *innate reflexes*—those automatic behavior patterns that are wired into your brain circuits by your genetic blueprint. And most particularly, he was interested in the **patellar reflex,** or knee-jerk.

You can elicit the patellar reflex in either of your legs rather simply (see Fig. 14.1). When you are sitting down, cross one leg on top of the other, leaving your uppermost leg hanging freely. Now, reach down with the edge of your hand and strike this leg smartly just below your kneecap. At this point, your patellar tendon runs close to the surface of your skin. Whenever you tap on this tendon, the lower half of your leg will swing forward involuntarily.

Twitmyer's Experiment

Twitmyer believed that the patellar reflex might be influenced by the emotional or *motivational state* a subject was in when the reflex was set off. So he rigged up a small hammer that would strike the subject's patellar tendon when he let the hammer fall. Twitmyer didn't bother telling his subjects when he was about to stimulate their reflexes—he merely dropped the hammer and measured how far their legs jerked. But his subjects soon complained that the hammer blow often caught them unaware. Couldn't he ring a bell as a warning, so that they wouldn't be surprised? Twitmyer agreed, and began sounding a signal to announce the hammer drop.

One day when Twitmyer was working with a subject whose knee had been hit hundreds of times, he accidentally sounded the warning signal without dropping the hammer. As promptly as clockwork, the subject's knee jerked *despite the fact that his tendon hadn't been stimulated*. Although Twitmyer didn't realize it at the time, he had just discovered the **conditioned reflex**, a response pattern upon which a dozen different psychological theories would later be built.

However, Twitmyer did appreciate the fact that he was on to something important, and he dropped his original research plans in order to investigate his discovery. He established some of the conditions under which this new type of reflex occurred, and reported his findings at the 1904 meeting of the American Psychological Association.

Sadly enough, the psychologists to whom Twitmyer spoke paid little attention to what he had to say. Discouraged by the frosty reception his ideas received, he dropped his laboratory research and became a clinical psychologist instead. And so credit for the discovery of the *conditioned reflex* passed by default to the famous Russian physiologist, Ivan Pavlov.

"YOU MUST CLEAR YOUR MIND. YOU MUST CONCENTRATE. YOU MUST FOCUS. THEN YOU WILL FIND IT IS AN EASY MATTER TO HIT A LOW, OUTSIDE FAST BALL."

Patellar reflex (pat-TELL-are). The patella is the knee bone. If you strike your leg just below this bone, the lower part of your leg will jerk. This "knee-jerk," or patellar reflex, is an automatic response over which you have little volitional control.

Conditioned reflex (con-DISH-shunned). A learned response pattern in which a stimulus is bonded or connected to a response. The "conditions" for acquiring the reflex usually involve pairing a "neutral" stimulus (such as a bell) with a stimulus that innately sets off a reflexive response (such as striking the patellar tendon). Also called a "conditional reflex."

Pavlov's Conditioning Studies

Ivan Pavlov, who lived from 1849 to 1936, is perhaps Russia's most famous scientist. After taking his medical degree in 1883, he traveled in Europe, studying with various other scientists. In 1890, Pavlov founded the Institute of Experimental Medicine in Leningrad, which he directed the rest of his life.

Pavlov's early interests were in the physiological processes of *digestion*, and he chose dogs for his experimental animals. He trained the dogs to lie quietly on operating tables or in leather harnesses while he studied what went on inside their digestive tracts before and after the dogs had eaten a meal. His experiments proved for the first time that the nervous system coordinates *all* digestive responses. Because of the pioneering nature of his work, Pavlov was awarded the Nobel Prize in 1904—the first Russian to be so honored.

Psychic Stimulations

Digestion actually begins in the mouth, when you produce *saliva* that starts breaking up food particles chemically. Pavlov soon found a way to measure the amount of saliva that the glands in the dog's mouth produced. While the dog was in a harness, Pavlov would give food to the dog, then count the number of drops of saliva that these glands secreted. Dogs do not have to be trained to salivate when given food—they do so reflexively, or automatically. Salivation is therefore an innate *response* or reflex that is elicted by the *stimulus* of food in the mouth.

Pavlov wanted to determine the neural pathways that connected the stimulus receptors in the dog's mouth with its salivary glands, but his research was often interrupted by peculiar responses the animals would make. After an animal had gotten accustomed to being fed in the harness, its salivary glands would often "juice up" *before* it got the food. In fact, an experienced dog would usually start salivating if one of Pavlov's assistants merely rattled the food dishes in the sink or walked toward the dog carrying a plate.

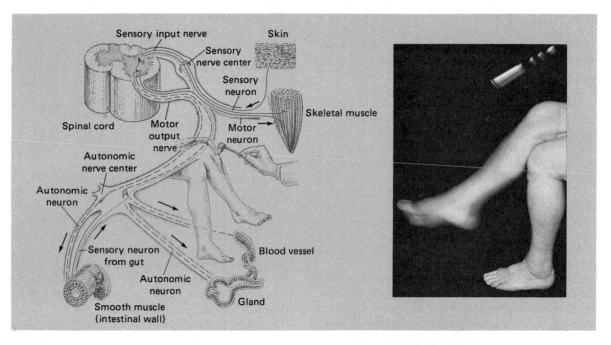

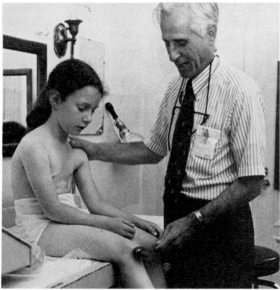

E. B. Twitmyer. **(bottom right)**

Fig. 14.1. The patellar reflex, or knee-jerk. **(top)**

Tapping the patellar tendon with a hammer elicits the "knee-jerk reflex." **(middle left)**

Pavlov's first experiments at the physiological department of the Soviet Military Medicine Academy. **(bottom left)**

Pavlov called these "unusual" reactions **psychic stimulations**, and they infuriated him because they "got in the way" of his regular research. He did his best to ignore them because he wasn't interested in anything "psychological." However, the psychic stimulations refused to go away. And so, in 1901, Pavlov began to study them systematically, hoping to get rid of these "annoyances." He told his friends that this work surely wouldn't take more than a year or two to complete. In fact, Pavlov spent the last 34 years of his life determining the properties of these "psychic stimulations."

Unconditional Stimulus-Response Connections

If you blow food powder into a dog's mouth, the animal will salivate reflexively. This response is determined by the dog's genetic blueprint. Pavlov called the food an **unconditional** or **unconditioned stimulus** (UCS) because the food's power to evoke salivation is not *conditional* upon the dog's having learned the response. The salivation *reaction* is also innately determined. Therefore, Pavlov named it the **unconditional** or **unconditioned response** (UCR) since it too is not *conditional* upon learning.

We might diagram this innate input-output connection as follows:

$$\text{UCS (food)} \xrightarrow[\text{connection)}]{\text{(innate stimulus-response}} \text{UCR (salivation)}$$

Conditional Stimulus-Response Connections

One of the first things that Pavlov discovered in his research was this: If he sounded a musical tone just before he blew the food into the animal's mouth, the dog would soon come to salivate almost as much to the music alone as it would to the tone *plus* the food powder. Apparently the animal learned to "associate" the *sound* of the music with the *stimulus* of the food. Thus the tone took on many of the psychological properties the food had. And thus each time the tone sounded, the dog *anticipated* it would be fed, and so it salivated to the tone just as it did to the food.

This sort of *conditioning* occurs in people as well as in dogs. The smell of bacon frying in the morning is enough to set your mouth to watering, but only because you have learned to associate the *smell* of the meat with how it *tastes*. In similar fashion, the clang of a dinner bell is often enough to set your stomach rumbling because your stomach muscles have been *conditioned* to expect food shortly after the bell sounds.

Technically speaking, this kind of learning involves an *association between stimulus inputs*. In the case of Pavlov's dog, the association is between a **neutral stimulus** (the tone) and an un-

Psychic stimulations. Pavlov's original name for the conditioned response or conditioned reflex.

Unconditional (unconditioned) stimulus. Abbreviated UCS. You are born with certain innate responses, such as the patellar reflex. These reflexes are set off (elicited) by innately determined (unconditioned or unlearned) stimuli. The blow to your patellar tendon is an unconditioned stimulus that elicits the unconditioned response we call the knee-jerk. The term "unconditional" is used to describe these stimuli because their ability to elicit the response are not *conditional* on learning.

Unconditional (unconditioned) response. Abbreviated UCR. Any innately determined response pattern or reflex that is set off by a UCS. The knee-jerk is a UCR.

Neutral stimulus. Any input that does *not* set off a particular *un*conditioned reflex. A stimulus whose power to elicit a particular response is gained through learning. Since dogs don't normally salivate whenever a musical tone sounds, the tone is a "neutral stimulus" as far as the salivation response is concerned.

Conditional (conditioned) stimulus. Abbreviated CS. The CS is the "neutral" stimulus which, through frequent pairings with an unconditioned stimulus, acquires the ability to elicit an unconditioned response.

conditioned stimulus (the food). We might diagram this associative learning as follows:

$$\text{Neutral S (tone)} \xrightarrow[\text{connection)}]{\text{(learned stimulus-stimulus}} \text{UCS (food)}$$

But the food powder "unconditionally" elicits the salivation *response* in the dog. So every time we pair the tone with the food, the dog salivates. Rather rapidly, then, the "neutral" tone takes on much the same ability to elicit salivation that the food has.

Pavlov called the tone a **conditional** or **conditioned stimulus** (CS) because its power to call forth the salivation response is *conditional* upon its being paired with the food powder. We can diagram the situation as follows:

$$\text{CS (tone)} \xrightarrow[\text{connection)}]{\text{(learned stimulus-stimulus}} \text{UCS (food)} \xrightarrow[\text{connection)}]{\text{(innate stimulus-response}} \text{UCR (salivation)}$$

Once the dog has learned the connection between the tone and the food, you can present just the tone alone—without giving the dog food—and the dog will salivate. In similar fashion, once you have learned to associate the aroma of bacon with its taste, the mere *smell* of the meat will set off your salivary glands even if you don't eat any of the bacon.

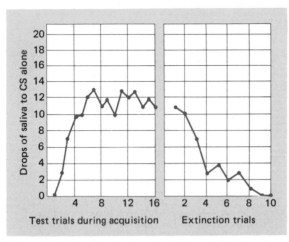

Fig. 14.2. The charts show first the acquisition of conditioned salivation in a trained dog, and then extinction.

Question: Is the odor of bacon more likely to cause you to salivate when you're hungry or when you've just finished a large meal?

The "Conditioned Response"

But what can we call the salivary response when it is triggered off by the tone alone? Surely it is no longer an *un*conditioned response because there is no innate connection between a "neutral" musical tone and salivation. Pavlov named this *learned* reaction to the neutral stimulus a **conditional** or **conditioned response** (CR). *Conditioning* is the term Pavlov used to describe the process by which the previously "neutral" stimulus (CS) gains the power to elicit the conditioned response (CR).

Once the conditioning process has taken place, we can diagram the situation as follows:

	(learned stimulus-response connection)	
CS (tone)	$\longrightarrow$	CR (partial salivation)

The type of training developed by Pavlov is called by many names: classical conditioning; reflex conditioning; Pavlovian conditioning; **respondent conditioning**; and stimulus-response (S-R) learning. Generally speaking, when psychologists use the term *conditioning*, they refer to some situation in which a *previously neutral stimulus* gains the power to elicit a *response* in a reflexive or mechanical fashion. So when we say that you have been "conditioned" to do something, we mean that you have learned to respond rather automatically to a particular stimulus.

Perhaps the most important point about conditioning is this: Because the learning is reflexive, you need not be *aware* that it has taken place.

Question: Can you figure out how you were conditioned *to believe that, in our society, men shouldn't wear pantyhose?*

Factors Affecting Conditioning

During the many years that Pavlov studied the conditioning process, he made a number of interesting discoveries about the factors that affect this type of learning:

1. The more frequently the CS and the UCS are paired, the stronger the CR becomes. For example, the more often a tone is associated with food powder, the more drops of saliva the tone will elicit. And the more frequently the CS and UCS are paired, the better the animal will remember the learning later on.
2. Conditioning is fastest when the CS is presented *immediately* before the UCS. For example, the optimum time interval for conditioned salivation in the dog is about half a second. If the tone is presented too long *before* the food— or is presented *after* the food—little or no learning occurs. However, the optimum time interval varies from animal to animal, from species to species, and from situation to situation.
3. Conditioned responses are *unlearned* just as easily as they are learned. Suppose you train a dog to salivate—that is, you establish a CS-CR connection in the animal between a tone and salivation. Now you present the dog with the tone *without* giving it the food. You would find that the animal salivates less and less on each trial. Finally, the response would be **extinguished** completely.
4. An "extinguished response" is not completely *forgotten* (see Fig. 14.2). Suppose you condition a dog, then extinguish the response. Then you pair the CS with the UCS for a second round of training trials. The dog will now acquire the conditioned response much more quickly than it did the first time around. Apparently the original conditioning has left a "trace" of some kind that makes relearning easier.
5. In similar fashion, suppose you extinguish a dog's conditioned salivation response and then let the animal sit in its cage for two weeks. Now you bring it back to the lab, hook it up in its harness, and again sound the tone. What will happen? As you might guess, the dog will have *forgotten the extinction* and it will again salivate. Psychologists call this **spontaneous recovery** of a previously extinguished response.

Conditioning and Desensitization

6. The mere passage of time can act as a conditioning stimulus. When Pavlov fed his animals regularly each half-hour, they began to salivate a minute or so before the next feeding was due even though there were no *external stimuli* such as dish rattles to give them cues that it was almost time to eat.

Question: *Pavlov believed that the mere pairing of the CS and the UCS was sufficient for conditioning to occur—whether or not the subject wished to learn or found the experience rewarding. Look back over the past couple of pages. How many times have the terms "CS" and "conditioned stimulus" been paired? Are the two terms now associated in your mind? Were you conscious that you were learning? And the next time you watch television, look closely at the commercials. Do the advertisers seem to be using Pavlovian techniques to get you to like or remember their products?*

Pavlov's Masochistic Dog

Pavlov believed that learning was always accompanied by the establishment of new neural connections in the brain—a position held by most psychologists today. Having made this initial point, Pavlov then moved into the field of mental health. He wondered why a few people—called **masochists**—seemed to enjoy or seek pain. Many psychologists believed that *masochism* was the result of some deep-seated "flaw" in the individual's personality. Pavlov suspected that this "love of painful inputs" might be the result of simple conditioning. To settle the matter, Pavlov trained a dog to withstand extremely painful stimuli by using a "step-by-step" learning technique.

First, Pavlov carefully marked off an area of skin on the dog's front leg. Then he stimulated this area with a weakly painful CS, and *immediately* gave the dog food. The strong unconditioned salivation response appeared to *inhibit* or suppress any avoidance response the dog might have made to the tiny amount of pain.

Then, day after day, Pavlov carefully increased the intensity of the painful CS, each time pairing it with food. At no time did the animal respond as if it were being hurt. Indeed, the dog seemed more than willing to be put in the training harness and given the pain—since the pain soon became a conditioned signal that food would shortly be forthcoming.

Once the dog was fully trained, it would passively withstand incredible amounts of painful stimulation delivered to its front leg. However, if Pavlov applied the painful CS to any other part of the dog's body, the animal would instantly set up

Conditional (conditioned) response. Abbreviated CR. Any reaction set off by a CS. A bright light (UCS) flashed in your eye causes your pupil to contract (UCS). If someone frequently rings a bell (CS) just before turning on the bright light (UCS), the sound of the bell (CS) would soon gain the power to make your pupil contract. Once this conditioning has taken place, the UCR (contraction) becomes a CR that can be elicited by the CS. Since pupil contraction can now be set off *either* by the CS or the UCS, the contractive response is *both* a CR and a UCR. In many cases, however, the CR looks slightly different from the UCR.

Respondent conditioning (re-SPOND-dent). Pavlovian conditioning is called by many names, including "classical conditioning," "reflex conditioning," and "stimulus-response conditioning." These terms are often used more-or-less interchangeably, although some psychologists attach slight differences to the various terms. See next chapter for comparison of respondent and "operant" conditioning.

Extinguished (ex-TING-guished). To "extinguish" a response is to reduce the frequency of a learned response either by withdrawing the reward that was used during training, or by presenting the CS many times without the UCS. In fact, it is the "bond" or "connection" between the CS and the CR that is extinguished.

Spontaneous recovery. The recurrence of a previously extinguished response after a passage of time in which no further training occurs.

Masochists (MASS-oh-kists). Masochism (MASS-oh-kiss-em) is a sexual deviation in which pleasure is derived from pain. The pain may be psychological or physical, and may be self-inflicted or inflicted by others. The term comes from the name of the Austrian novelist Leopold V. Sacher-Masoch, whose stories frequently featured scenes in which sexual pleasure was associated with painful stimulus inputs.

Discrimination training. Teaching an animal to discriminate—that is, to react differently to fairly similar stimuli. If you can tell the difference between two things, you know how to discriminate between them.

a great howl and attempt to escape from its training harness.

Pavlov concluded that when he touched the CS to the dog's front leg, the animal did not in fact *feel* any pain because all responses except salivation were suppressed by the strength of the pain-salivation neural connection. Apparently, in dogs, as well as in humans, "You can't do more than one thing at a time." And whatever response is strongest tends to suppress most other responses that could be made to the *same stimulus*.

The parallel between Pavlov's masochistic dogs and those humans who seek pain or humiliation in order to gain pleasure (often sexual) is rather remarkable. But as important as these experiments might have been to the discovery of a "cure" for masochism in humans, this research was regarded with considerable distaste by most other scientists.

Discrimination and Generalization

Perhaps the most interesting "mental health" experiment Pavlov conducted had to do with **discrimination training**. Pavlov began by showing a

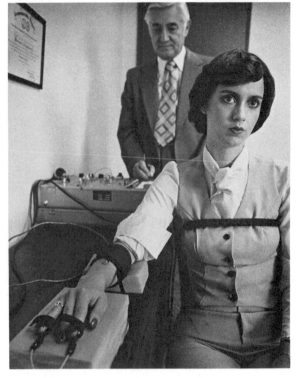

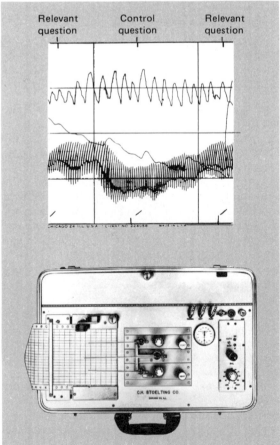

Relevant question | Control question | Relevant question

Children are conditioned—and can be unconditioned—to fear animals. **(top left)**

The polygraph, or "lie detector," actually measures emotional responses, not "lies." **(right)**

Fig. 14.3. A polygraph machine and record; the midpoint indicates a control question. **(bottom left)**

dog a drawing of a circle, then giving it food immediately. Very soon the dog became conditioned to salivate whenever it saw a circle.

Pavlov then tested the animal by showing it drawings of figures such as an ellipse, a pentagon, a square, a rectangle, a triangle, and a star. He found that the salivary response *generalized* to stimulus inputs other than the original CS (the circle). As you might suspect, this **generalization** followed a specific pattern—the more similar the other figure was to a circle, the more the animal salivated.

Pavlov then trained the dog to *discriminate* between the two stimuli by always giving food to the dog when the circle appeared, but never giving it a reward when he showed it the ellipse. Soon the dog learned to salivate *only* when the circle was shown.

After Pavlov had established that the dog could discriminate between a circle and an ellipse, he tried to fool the animal. On subsequent trials, he presented the dog with ellipses that were closer and closer to being completely round. Eventually the animal's nervous system was strained to the breaking point, for the animal could not perceive the difference between the positive CS (the circle) and the negative CS (the ellipse).

Overcome by stress, the animal broke down, snapped at Pavlov and his assistants, barked loudly, urinated and defecated, and tried very hard to get out of the restraining harness. If a human being had displayed the same behavior patterns, we probably would say the person was **neurotic** or "unable to cope."

How different Pavlov's two "mental health" experiments were! In the first case, an animal learned to give a *normal* response to a very abnormal stimulus input. In the second study—even though it received no painful stimulation at all—the dog gave an *abnormal* response to a very "normal" set of stimuli.

These two studies convinced Pavlov that "mental illness" was learned and was mostly a matter of mixed-up brain signals. (Pavlov took a purely biological view toward the causes of mental illness. As we will see in later chapters, there are intra-psychic and environmental influences that are at least as important.)

Conditioned Emotional Responses

Once Pavlov had shown the way, a number of US psychologists began experimenting with conditioning procedures using humans rather than animals. John B. Watson, the father of behaviorism, was perhaps the first to study how emotional responses (such as fear) get established in children.

Watson and Little Albert

In one of Watson's most famous experiments, he and his second wife (Rosalie Rayner) conditioned a boy named Albert to fear a white rat. At the beginning of the study, Albert was unafraid of the animal and played with it freely. While Albert was doing so one day, Watson deliberately frightened the child by sounding a terrifying noise behind him. Albert was startled and began to cry. Thereafter, he avoided the rat and cried if it was brought close to him. (This sort of experimentation is now forbidden by the American Psychological Association's Code of Ethics.)

In Pavlovian terms, Watson and Rayner had set up a *bond* between the sight of the rat (CS) and an arousal response in Albert's autonomic nervous system (CR). Once this S-R bond was fixed, the fear response could also be elicited by showing Albert almost any furry object.

Fears *generalize* to stimuli similar to the CS. Fear or anxiety also generalizes to any random or accidental stimulus cues that happen to be present when the conditioning or sensitization takes place. The burnt child not only dreads the fire, it also fears stoves, pots and pans, ovens, pictures of flames, and even stories about the great Chicago fire.

Generalization (jen-ur-al-eye-ZAY-shun). *Stimulus* generalization is the tendency to make the same response to two similar stimuli. If a monkey has been trained to lift its right paw when you turn on an orange light, it may also lift its paw when you turn on a yellow or a red light. *Response* generalization is the tendency to make a slightly different reaction to the same stimulus. If you hold down the monkey's right paw when you turn on the orange light, the response may generalize to the left paw instead.

Neurotic (new-ROT-tick). Abnormal or unusual behavior patterns are sometimes referred to as being "neurotic." A neurosis (new-ROW-sis) is a relatively mild form of mental disorder. As we will see in Chapter 23, however, psychologists do not agree on the causes and cures of neurotic behaviors.

Polygraph (PAHL-ee-graff). *Poly* means "many." A polygraph is a machine that makes a graph of many different responses simultaneously. Sometimes called a "lie detector," but it records emotional responses, not "lies."

Measuring Emotional Responses

Words are *stimuli*, just like bells and musical tones. If you were chased by a bull when you were a child, you probably experienced great fear. And you would still show some *conditioned autonomic arousal* even now if you read the word "bull," saw a picture of one, or were asked to think about one.

The Polygraph

We could *measure* your fear reaction by attaching you to a **polygraph**, a machine often called a "lie detector" (see Fig. 14.3). The polygraph would record your pulse, blood pressure, breathing rate, and the amount of sweat produced on the palms of your hands.

As you know, arousal of your sympathetic nervous system would lead to an increase in sweating, an acceleration in heart rate, and a change in the way you breathe. If we showed you an emotionally "neutral" stimulus, your polygraph record would remain calm and regular. If we then presented you with a picture of a large bull, or said the word aloud, the graph would note a sudden sharp *change* in your autonomic activity. We would then *assume* that you had experienced some emotional arousal, such as that associated with fear, anxiety, or guilt.

As David Lykken points out in his 1981 book *A Tremor in the Blood*, the polygraph is an *emotion detector*, not a "lie detector." It is useful to police agents because suspected criminals often lie and are afraid of being found out. For instance,

Fig. 14.4. A polygraph records a person's emotional responses to stimulus words.

suppose someone has been murdered by being strangled with a silk scarf of an unusual color. Presumably only the murderer would recognize the scarf. The police might show this scarf to several suspects, all of whom might deny ever having seen the scarf before. But if one of the suspects showed a strong emotional reaction on the polygraph, the police would be justified in questioning this suspect further (see Fig. 14.4).

As Lykken notes, the polygraph could only work as a "lie detector" if there were a distinctive *guilt response* that almost everyone made when they were lying, but didn't make when they were telling the truth. And for *everyone* to make the same sort of guilt response, it would have to be genetically inherited. Lykken concludes there is no such "innate guilt reaction." Instead, there are only **conditioned emotional responses**, which the "lie detector" does pick up. But since not everyone is conditioned in early life to react to emotion-arousing situations in the same way, the polygraph is far from being infallible.

For instance, some criminals feel no anxiety or guilt whatsoever concerning their crimes. If they then "lie" about what they have done, their polygraph records will suggest innocence rather than guilt. On the other hand, a person may show violent emotional reactions to a stimulus such as a colorful scarf without having committed any crime. For these and other reasons, polygraph records are not admitted as evidence of guilt in a court of law.

Counter-Conditioning

Many forms of psychotherapy are based on *breaking* S-R bonds instead of establishing new ones. Once Watson and Rayner had demonstrated (in 1920) that a child could be conditioned to fear furry things, it was even more important to show that fear conditioning could be "cured" using the same techniques that caused it. And, in 1924, another student of Watson's—Mary Cover Jones—did just that. She used a method now called **counter-conditioning**. This technique is based on the fact that you can't give two incompatible responses to the same CS.

Suppose that, at some time in the future, your own two-year-old son accidentally became conditioned to fear small furry animals. You might try to cure the boy the way Mary Cover Jones did—by attempting to attach some response other than "fear" to the conditioning stimulus. The sight of a white rat would presumably upset your son, but the sight of food when he was hungry would surely make him happy and eager to eat. If you could somehow *bond* the "rat" stimulus to the "happy" response, your child would obviously become counter-conditioned to like the rat rather than fear it.

You might begin the counter-conditioning procedure by bringing a white rat into the same room with your son while you were feeding him. At first, you would want to keep the animal so far away from your son that he could barely see it out of the corner of his eye. Since the animal wouldn't be close enough to bother him, he probably would keep right on eating. Then, step by step, you might bring the rat closer.

Since your son could not cry and eat at the same time, the CS-CR fear response would gradually *extinguish*. At the same time, the strength of the CS-CR "pleasure of eating" bond would increase. Eventually, your son would be conditioned to give a new response to the animal that was *counter* to his previous reaction. That is, he would now respond to the rat with pleasure rather than with fear. When Mary Cover Jones followed this procedure (actually using a white rabbit instead of a rat), she found that children soon learned to play with animals that had previously terrified them.

The important point about counter-conditioning is this: It almost always involves breaking an inappropriate S-R bond by attaching the old "S" to a new and more appropriate "R."

The Case of Anne M

In a sense, Watson and Rayner created a **phobia** about rats in little Albert. *Phobias* are intense, irrational fears about people, places, things, or situations. Usually these fears are so strong that the person with the phobia cannot control her or his reactions even when the person clearly realizes that the terror is illogical and unreasonable. Phobias are sometimes created from a single emotion-charged encounter with the object dreaded.

Just as likely, they can come about because of a series of highly unpleasant interactions.

As an example of how phobias can be learned—and then unlearned—consider the case of Anne M., a middle-aged woman living near Cleveland. Anne M. shared a house with her mother, upon whom she was very dependent emotionally. One day the two women got into a quarrel at their home. At the end of the argument, the mother ran out into the street. Anne followed her mother to the door—just in time to see the older woman get hit and killed by a passing car.

As a consequence of witnessing the death of her beloved mother—and because she felt partially responsible—Anne developed a phobia about moving vehicles. She retreated to the security of the house and refused to come out. She closed the curtains on all the windows, for even the sight of an automobile or truck was enough to throw Anne into a violent panic reaction. Finally, her withdrawal from the rest of the world became so severe that she had to be hospitalized in a nearby mental institution.

Once in the hospital, Anne refused to leave. Her therapists tried to explore her guilt feelings and her anxieties about death. But even after years of treatment, Anne M. still panicked whenever she looked out of the hospital window and saw an automobile passing on the road.

Desensitization Therapy

At this point, two psychologists then at The University of Michigan—David Himle and Clayton Shorkey—attempted a form of counter-conditioning called **desensitization therapy**.

In their first talks with Anne M., Himle and Shorkey drew up a **hierarchy of fears**—that is, a list of disturbing *stimuli* arranged from least to

Conditioned emotional responses. Almost all fears, loves, hates, and social attitudes are learned through conditioning, usually in childhood. Racial, religious, and political beliefs are also typically acquired by the same type of conditioning process that Pavlov used with his dogs. Argumentation and logic seldom serve to "decondition" emotional responses. Try counter-conditioning instead.

Counter-conditioning. A method of extinguishing a conditioned emotional response, typically by attaching the old stimulus to a new type of response. Desensitization is a type of counter-conditioning in that it involves attaching a relaxation response to the feared stimulus, thus breaking the previous bond between the feared stimulus and emotional arousal.

Phobia (FOE-bee-uh). From the Greek word for "fear." A phobia is a strong and often unusual fear of something.

Desensitization therapy (DEE-sen-suh-tie-ZAY-shun). When you acquire a conditioned fear of cats, you have become *sensitized* to cats and thus become anxious or afraid each time you see one. Desensitization therapy, as developed by Joseph Wolpe (WOHL-pee), involves training you to relax whenever you see a cat. Once this form of counter-conditioning is complete, your fear of cats will have been "desensitized."

Hierarchy of fears (HIGHER-ark-key). To make up a hierarchy is to list things (or people) in order of their importance. A hierarchy of fears, as used in desensitization therapy, is a list of dreaded stimuli running from the most feared to the least feared.

most frightening. The act of actually riding in an automobile was the most frightening thing Anne could think of. Getting into a parked automobile was somewhat less disturbing. Thus sitting in a car ranked *lower* on the hierarchy than did riding. Walking past a car was even less threatening, but was still more likely to induce panic than just seeing a car or truck through a window. Merely imagining what a car looked like evoked very little fear, so this item was at the bottom of the hierarchy.

When Himle and Shorkey began treating Anne M., first they got her to relax as much as possible. Once she was quite comfortable, they asked her to imagine seeing a car out of the window. Very rapidly she could tolerate seeing a car "in her mind's eye" without feeling any anxiety at all. Then they asked Anne M. to gaze out a window briefly, and got her to relax again. Soon Anne M. was able to look at cars out the window whenever she pleased.

At this point in her treatment, Anne M. had been conditioned to handle the lowest items on her fear hierarchy. For the stimulus of "seeing a car through the window" now elicited the conditioned response of *relaxation* rather than the conditioned response of *panic*.

Next, Himle and Shorkey asked her to imagine walking out the front door of the building and approaching a car. Once she could manage this imagery, they got her to leave the hospital building and actually touch a parked automobile out-

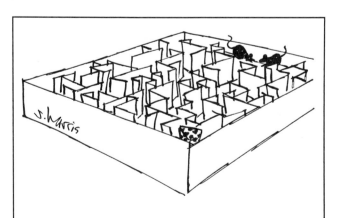

"YOU CAN'T MISS IT. GO DOWN TO THE CORNER AND MAKE A LEFT, THEN ANOTHER LEFT, A RIGHT..."

Joseph Wolpe.

Fig. 14.5. A patient and Dr. Joseph Wolpe during systematic desensitization. Note that the patient's index finger is raised to indicate that she is visualizing the scene required by the therapist. **(top left)**

Fear of heights can be "desensitized" using counterconditioning procedures. **(bottom left)**

3 patients being "desensitized" to a fear of dogs by learning to relax in the presence of the feared animal. **(bottom right)**

side. When she was relaxed enough to handle this real-life problem, they encouraged her to get inside the car and take a short ride.

At the end of just 10 training sessions, Anne M. was driven out of the hospital grounds onto a nearby highway on a short excursion—a trip that caused her little or no discomfort. Thereafter, with no further therapy, Anne M. began taking part in more of the social activities on the ward, including short visits to points of interest near the hospital. Once she saw that she could tolerate these brief trips, she spontaneously began visiting friends who lived in nearby towns.

The final test of Anne's desensitization came when she was invited to spend a few days with some relatives who lived several hundred miles away. Anne had to make the trip by bus. When she

felt she was relaxed enough to handle this experience—which might well have rated right at the top of her original hierarchy of fears—she packed her bag and caught the bus.

Ironically, the vehicle broke down while on the expressway and Anne and the rest of the passengers had to sit by the side of the road for more than an hour while traffic buzzed furiously past them. However, Anne handled the situation without any panic and reached her destination safely. Thanks to the help of Drs. Himle and Shorkey—and the staff at the hospital—Anne M. no longer had a phobic reaction to moving vehicles.

Curing a "Blood Phobia"

S.H. Kraines has reported a somewhat simpler form of desensitization therapy involving a young medical student who feared the sight of blood. This young man, whom Kraines calls J.M., seriously considered giving up the study of medicine because each time the student walked into an operating room, he keeled over in a dead faint.

Kraines first attempted to determine the causes for this response and tried to change the man's attitude toward medicine—but he also tried a step-by-step deconditioning treatment. J.M. was told to walk into the operating chamber during an operation and then immediately to walk out. On the second day J.M. went into the room, counted five, and then walked out. On the third day J.M. stayed a full minute before leaving. On subsequent days, he remained for longer and longer times.

Two weeks later, when J.M. was supposed to stay but 10 minutes, he got so interested in the operation that he remained until it was completed. Thereafter, Kraines reports, J.M. had no trouble at all—even when called on to assist in operations. His "blood phobia" appeared to be gone for good.

Question: Some college students become so aroused and frightened when forced to take an examination that they become violently ill. How might desensitization therapy be used to help them?

Desensitization: Pro and Con

Dr. Joseph Wolpe, now at Temple University in Philadelphia, is usually given credit for having popularized desensitization training. Wolpe believes that the secret of its success comes from never over-stimulating the patient or letting the phobic reaction get so strong that it cannot be counteracted by voluntary muscular relaxation (see Fig. 14.5). Wolpe and his colleagues achieve this goal by always starting with the least-feared item on the hierarchy and working up the scale. They also stop treatment momentarily whenever the client shows the slightest sign of distress.

Cognitive Desensitization

Cognitive and attitudinal changes often occur during desensitization training. That is, the patient frequently reports *perceiving* the once-feared situation in a new and less frightening light. Wolpe and many others believe that these perceptual changes are the *result* of learning to handle disturbing stimuli in a relaxed fashion—that the lack of muscular tension leads to or induces the change in the patient's attitudes.

But many other therapists insist that Wolpe has put the cart before the horse. These psychologists believe that cognitive changes occur *first*

Cognitive (COG-nuh-tive). From the Latin word meaning "to think."

Cognitive desensitization. Pavlov and the early behavioral psychologists dealt entirely with *external* stimuli and *observable* responses. During the 1960's, psychologists discovered that Pavlovian techniques could be used to condition (or decondition) inner processes, such as thoughts and feelings. Desensitization seems to occur just as rapidly if the patient *thinks* relaxing thoughts (a cognitive process) as if the patient actually relaxes (an observable response).

and thereby allow the patient to relax in the presence of the dreaded stimulus. As evidence, these therapists cite research suggesting that you need not start at the bottom of the fear hierarchy and work up gradually to the most disturbing item. Rather, you can pick items at random and expose the patient to them—as long as the patient doesn't become too disturbed by the procedure. Furthermore, many studies show that purely *mental* relaxation can be as powerful in helping cure phobias as is *muscular* relaxation. The use of mental rather than muscular relaxation is sometimes called **cognitive desensitization**.

Desensitization or "Natural Extinction"?

A survey of the literature suggests that *any* technique which keeps the patient in the "presence" of the feared object (or situation) for an extended period of time will help extinguish the fear. Desensitization may be effective, therefore, simply because it is an elegant way of getting patients to remain near the things they are afraid of until a sort of "natural extinction" takes place. And the more "cognitive" forms of counter-conditioning may work because they require the patient to think about the feared objects or situations until the same sort of natural extinction occurs. We will return to this point momentarily.

Psychoanalysis versus Desensitization

While admitting that desensitization therapy can be effective with simple phobic reactions, psychoanalysts believe that many phobias represent a person's attempts to *suppress* or defend against inappropriate or threatening impulses.

For instance, a woman who cannot make a normal heterosexual adjustment might become phobic about—or *sensitized* to—pointed objects because they symbolize the male sexual organ to her. Or a young man who hates his parents and wants to kill them might develop a phobia about guns and knives. His fear then serves to keep him away from weapons he might use if his hatred ever got out of control. Unfortunately, the psychoanalysts note, his phobia also serves to keep him from facing what may be a basic flaw or weakness in his personality.

The psychoanalytic view is that the phobia is simply a *symptom* of an underlying personality problem that cannot be helped merely by curing the *symptomatic behavior*. Merely curing the symptom—without first changing the personality structure that gave rise to the phobic reaction—won't work because other more devastating symptoms will take its place. (As we will see in Chapter 24, there is not much scientific evidence to support this fear of "symptom substitution.")

Wolpe's Response

Wolpe's reply to these criticisms is twofold. To begin with, he believes that the symptom is usually what really bothers the patient. A man may continue to fear guns and knives long after his parents are dead and buried. Talking through his hatred for the long-gone parents may give the man considerable insight into his problems, but research suggests it usually does very little to help him overcome his gun phobia.

In the second place, Wolpe holds that what the analysts call "the underlying problem" is typically an attitude or perception that was *learned* by the same laws of conditioning as was the phobic reaction. Men aren't born with an instinctive hatred of their parents. It takes years of careful training—usually on the part of the parents themselves—to achieve that. If a therapist feels that a patient's perceptions of her or his parents should be changed, conditioning techniques offer a fast and reliable methodology for doing so.

Which Changes First: Attitudes or Behaviors?

Must you always change your attitudes first, if you want to change your behavioral outputs? Or do most attitudinal changes result from your first changing the way you behave?

In retrospect, Wolpe and the psychoanalysts appear to be caught up in yet another battle over the "mind-body" problem we discussed in earlier chapters. And the truth seems to be that attitudes and behaviors change more-or-less simultaneously. It is difficult if not impossible to prove that a change in one always *causes* a change in the other.

Wolpe is a physician who places much faith in biological processes and little faith in what goes on inside the mind. The cognitive psychologists are convinced that intra-psychic changes are the ones to aim for—and thus often neglect both biological and social inputs. And the psychoanalysts can often uncover suppressed emotions, but don't always know how to help patients alter their emotional *outputs* or responses efficiently. None of the groups looks at the *whole* patient—from a biological, intra-psychic, *and* a social/behavioral point of view.

In fact, there really is little sense in fighting over which form of therapy is best, since all types of treatment have their uses. Indeed, it is likely that psychoanalysts unconsciously make use of some forms of conditioning while treating their patients, although they may not realize that they are doing so. For example, when they get their patients to "talk through" a fear time and time again, they actually are allowing a sort of natural extinction to occur. In similar fashion, many behaviorists don't stop at removing the symptomatic behaviors—they try to determine how and when the phobia was learned as well. And then they use desensitization techniques to "decondition" the emotionality connected with those early experiences.

Sometimes, in the heat of defending our theoretical positions, we all lose sight of the prime goal—namely, to get the patient back to normal as quickly and as surely as possible. And to do that, we surely should make use of any type of treatment that "works," no matter how revolutionary that therapy may seem when first introduced. We will raise this issue again at the end of the next chapter, after we have looked at a different form of learning called *operant conditioning*.

Summary

1. The **conditioned reflex** was discovered by Twitmyer, but credit for its discovery is usually given to Ivan Pavlov, who developed most of the conditioning techniques and terminology still in use.
2. Conditioning involves pairing a **neutral stimulus** (the CS) with an **unconditioned stimulus** (the UCS). The UCS already has the power to elicit the **unconditioned response** (the UCR). If the CS is paired with the UCS enough times, it *conditionally* takes on the power to evoke a reaction similar to the UCR. This "similar" reaction is called the **conditioned response** (the CR).
3. In Pavlov's research, he paired a bell (CS) with food powder blown into a dog's mouth (the UCS). The food naturally evoked salivation (the UCR). Once the bell had been paired

Conditioning and Desensitization

with the food for several trials, sounding the bell *without food* caused the dog to salivate (the CR). The CR differed from the UCR in several ways, one being that it was almost always weaker.

4. Psychologists often use the term **conditioning** to mean **learning**.

5. All learning or conditioning is built on—or is an adaptation of—**innately determined stimulus-response connections**, the UCS-UCR bond.

6. Conditioning is sometimes referred to as strengthening S-R or **stimulus-response bonds**. The stronger the bond, the more likely it is that the conditioned stimulus will elicit the desired conditioned response.

7. The more frequently the CS and the UCS are paired, the stronger the **S-R bond** becomes.

8. Conditioning proceeds fastest when the CS is presented immediately before the UCS.

9. Conditioned responses are unlearned just as easily as they are learned. Unlearning proceeds fastest when the CS is presented several times without being followed by the UCS. Once the S-R bond is broken, the response is said to be **extinguished**.

10. An extinguished response is not totally forgotten. If the CS is again paired with the UCS, **relearning** usually takes much less time than did the original learning. Furthermore, extinguished responses often show **spontaneous recovery** after some time has passed.

11. **Internal stimuli** (such as muscle tension) can serve as a CS just as well as can bells or musical tones. The passage of time can also serve as a conditional stimulus.

12. Pavlov conditioned dogs to withstand pain by pairing a weak painful stimulus with a strong UCS, such as food. The food evoked salivation. Soon the painful stimulus also evoked salivation rather than escape.

13. If an animal is trained to respond to an orange light, this response may **generalize** to other similar stimuli, such as a red or yellow light. However, with the proper training, the animal can usually learn to **discriminate** among similar stimuli and give different responses to each.

14. If this discrimination becomes too difficult, the animal may show such **neurotic** responses as biting, barking, and defecation.

15. Watson and Rayner conditioned a boy called Little Albert to fear a rat by pairing the sight of the rat with a frightening noise. Mary Cover Jones **deconditioned** this sort of fear by pairing the sight of the animal with food.

16. The **polygraph** or "lie detector" measures **conditioned emotional responses**, not "lies" or "guilt."

17. Many psychologists believe that most human **phobic reactions** are conditioned in the same manner that Watson and Rayner created a fear response in Little Albert.

18. Joseph Wolpe showed that conditioned fears can be **desensitized** or extinguished through **counter-conditioning procedures** that involve pairing the feared stimulus with relaxation. The patient makes a **hierarchy of fears** ranging from least feared to most feared. The patient learns to relax in the presence of stimuli low on the hierarchy of fears first, then **step-by-step** moves up the hierarchy.

19. Although **desensitization** (counter-conditioning) has enjoyed considerable success with many types of anxious patients, some psychologists believe that the technique merely removes the **symptom** and does not cure the **underlying cause** of fear. When one symptom is removed, they say, another will replace it. There is little scientific evidence to prove that this occurs.

20. Some psychologists believe that **attitudinal changes** occur first, and that behaviors change as a consequence. Other psychologists believe that behavior changes first, and attitudes follow. The data suggest that a change in either is likely to cause a change in the other.

21. Perhaps the best form of therapy is one that treats *all* of the patient's problems, whether the problems be biological, psychological, or social.

(Continued from page 328.)

"Well, what do you think about the desensitization program so far?" Dr. Nancy Wagner asked two months later.

Kevin Lynn grinned mischievously. "You really ought to ask my wife. After all, she's the one who whipped me into coming to see you."

Dr. Wagner clucked her tongue. "I thought the problem was that your wife *wouldn't* whip you."

"Just kidding," Kevin Lynn said. "Actually, it's going pretty well even without the whips." Then he paused, and a crimson blush spread over his pale face. "Except for the other night."

"Oh," replied the woman. "What happened the other night?"

"Nothing happened," Lynn said quietly. "That was the trouble."

Dr. Wagner nodded sympathetically. "Why don't you tell me about it, and then we'll pick up where we left off on the hierarchy."

Lynn sighed. "Let me relax a minute first." He tensed various parts of his body, then let them go limp. "Still feels good when I do that. But it just didn't work the other evening."

"What was the situation?" the woman asked. "Tell me what you were doing, what your wife was doing, and how you responded."

"She was lying in bed, watching television, eating some candy. Chocolates, I think." Lynn stopped abruptly. "Funny, suddenly I'm tense all over."

Dr. Wagner smiled reassuringly. "Relax for a moment. Completely relax. Okay?"

"Okay," said the man.

"Now, shut your eyes and listen to your body while I talk. The moment that you feel any tension, lift your right hand. Understand?"

"Okay," said the man, exhaling loudly.

"I want you to imagine your bedroom. Look at the chairs, and the dresser. Any tension?"

The man shook his head.

"Now look at the bed. Any tension yet?"

"Maybe a tiny bit. No big deal, really."

Dr. Wagner nodded. "That's progress. A month ago, you felt tense just thinking about the bed. Okay, now imagine your wife is lying in the bed. She's turned on the TV and is watching some program. Is that unusual?"

"Happens all the time, although I can usually give her a reason to turn the TV off—if I really want to."

Dr. Wagner grinned. "But that's a different kind of tension, so you just relax now. Keep your eyes closed, and imagine your wife watching the TV. Just as you walk into the bedroom and start to approach her, she reaches into a box of chocolates . . ."

"Stop," the man said. "That did it. I could feel it then."

"Chocolates," said the woman. "Why does that bother you?"

Lynn shook his head. "Haven't the foggiest." He sighed. "Oh, well, the tension seems to be gone now anyhow."

"Good," Dr. Wagner said. "Tell me if it returns. Now, what happened after you saw your wife eating the candy?"

"Hum," said the man, trying to remember. "We talked a bit, kidded around a bit. She was smoking a cigarette, but when I sat down on the bed, she went to put it out, and knocked the ashtray over . . . ."

Dr. Wagner leaned forward. "Suddenly you're sweating."

"The tension started just then," the man said.

"Relax. Just go limp, really limp."

Kevin Lynn sighed deeply, and then nodded when his muscles seemed relaxed.

"Stop me if the tension starts again," Dr. Wagner said. "Now, there seem to be four stimuli that, put together, cause the tension. You just stay as relaxed as you can while I name them. First, your wife in bed. Second, she's watching television. Third, she's eating chocolates. And fourth, she knocks over the ashtray."

"Stop," Lynn said. "There it is again."

"Well," the woman said. "It seemed to be the ashtray that you really reacted too. Now, I want you to relax deeply again. Go deep down inside your mind, and look for something about an ashtray. Did you ever knock one over?"

The man shook his head. "Not that I remember."

Dr. Wagner continued. "Well, did you ever see someone else knock one over? Your mother, perhaps, when you were a small child."

"Stop," Lynn said. "I feel tense again. Not much, but a bit."

"Just relax. Be calm," the woman said. And when the man sighed, she went on. "Okay, the ashtray is the clue. Did your mother smoke?"

Lynn shook his head. "No, but my father did." He stopped. "Oh, wow, I'm tense again."

"Relax, relax as deeply as you can," the woman said. "We're getting close now. I want you to push your memory as hard as you can. I want you to think of a time when you and your mother and your father were together, and your mother was eating chocolates and watching television."

Kevin Lynn groaned loudly. "Oh, my God, it's all coming back to me now."

"Good, good," said Dr. Wagner. "Just go limp, really limp, and then tell me what you remember. If you get too tense, just relax, and don't worry about it."

"Incredible," said the man. "I completely forgot about it until now. I must have been nine or ten. Mom was watching television. She loved the tube. She used to say it was her only friend." He paused for a long time. "Funny, I wonder if she meant that she and my father didn't get along too well in bed."

"You're tensing up again," Dr. Wagner said. "Just relax."

Lynn sighed. "I guess I can finally think about things like that now. Anyhow, she made me stand in the corner in the bedroom, while she watched the tube. Seems like I was always standing in the corner for one reason or another. Anyway, this particular night, she was eating chocolates and watching the tube, and I really had to . . . to . . ."

"Urinate?" asked the woman.

"Yeah," the man said softly. "So I was squirming a bit, you know, trying to hold it back, and she got very upset because I was . . . " He shifted nervously in his chair.

"Touching your genitals?"

"That's right. I guess most kids do that, don't they, when they have to urinate?"

Dr. Wagner nodded her agreement. "They certainly do. Most natural thing in the world." She paused to think, then continued. "Now, I want to ask you a question, but I want you to relax deeply first. Okay?"

"Okay, I'm relaxed."

"Did your mother threaten to whip you when you touched your genitals?"

Lynn groaned again. "Oh, Lord, yes. All the time when I touched myself."

"Relax," commanded the woman. "It's all right. Now, tell me what happened next."

He paused. "You know something, this is getting pretty painful."

"I know. We can stop now if you like, and go on some other time."

Lynn shook his head. "No, let's go on. We might as well get it all out in the open. Okay, I was standing in the corner, squirming around and touching myself, and my mother was watching the tube and eating chocolates and threatening to whip me if I didn't behave. Then my father came into the room, and . . ."

"You're tensing again."

"I can handle it," the man said gruffly. "Anyway, my father came into the room, and I guess they must have had another argument. Now that I think about it, they had lots of arguments. But this one was a lulu. Scared the hell out of me . . ."

"Very understandable," said the woman, soothingly.

"Yeah, well, I remember he called her a fat slob, and she said, uh, . . ."

"Relax," the woman said. "Take it easy."

Lynn nodded. "She said all he wanted to do was to, you know, mess around."

Dr. Wagner nodded.

"Then they started calling each other dirty names, and shouting at each other, and my father got pretty mad, I guess. He probably had been drinking a little, you know?"

"I know," said Dr. Wagner.

The man sighed. "Anyhow, she said something about how he wasn't good enough for her, that he didn't deserve her, and . . ."

Dr. Wagner leaned forward. "Relax, Kevin. You're very close to the heart of the problem now."

"He must have screamed at her, or something. I remember I got really scared and tried to get away—to the bathroom, I guess." Lynn stopped. "There's something else, though, something I can't recall . . ."

"Are you fairly relaxed?" Dr. Wagner asked.

"Yeah," said Lynn. "I guess so. Why?"

Dr. Wagner smiled. "When your father screamed at your mother, what did she do?"

"Oh, my God," the man said. "Of course! I remember now! She threw the ashtray at him, but she missed, and . . . and . . ."

The woman nodded. "I know, it hit you instead, didn't it?"

"That memory hurts," the man said softly. "It hurts like hell."

"Of course it hurts," Dr. Wagner said. "And it would have gone right on hurting all the rest of your life if you hadn't dredged it up and faced it squarely. I think you're doing beautifully."

Lynn frowned. "But I still don't see the connection completely. So my mother hit me with an ashtray. So what?"

Dr. Wagner sighed. "You've got the wrong connection, I suspect. See if you can remember what happened after the ashtray hit you."

The man suddenly gasped for air. "Oh, my, that did it. That really did it. I had forgotten that part entirely."

"Relax as best you can, and tell me about it," she said.

"Okay. I remember I screamed, and they stopped arguing. My mother rushed over to me and grabbed me up. She kissed me and hugged me to her breast and said she didn't mean it. She said she'd make it up to me." Lynn stopped. "Oh, my," he said a moment later. "It all makes sense now."

Dr. Wagner nodded again. "Yes, it does, doesn't it? You got afraid and very tense, then you got hurt, and that stopped the argument and the fear. And then your mother hugged you and kissed you. One-trial conditioning, I'd say."

"Oh, my," the man said hoarsely.

The woman sighed deeply. "I think we've done enough for today. We can put the scene into the hierarchy the next time you're here. Shouldn't take too long to desensitize you to the whole thing. Okay?"

Kevin Lynn smiled. "Okay. But right now, I'm going home and break every ashtray in the house. And throw out all the chocolates."

"And the whips?"

"Yeah. Especially those. And then I'm going to kiss my wife, and . . ."

"And?"

Lynn grinned. "And then I'm going to show her I love her in the best way I know how."

"No sweat," said the woman.

"No pain," said the man.

Recommended Readings

Kendall, P.C., and S.D. Hollon, eds. *Assessment Strategies for Cognitive-Behavioral Interventions* (New York: Academic Press, 1981).

Lazarus, A.A. *Multi-Modal Behavior Therapy* (New York: Springer, 1976).

Lykken, David T. *A Tremor in the Blood* (New York: McGraw-Hill, 1980).

Pavlov, Ivan. *Conditioned Reflexes* (Oxford: Clarendon Press, 1927).

Wolpe, J., and A.A. Lazarus. *Behavior Therapy Techniques* (London: Pergamon Press, 1966).

Cognitive Maps and Operant Conditioning 15

Did You Know That . . .

Most of the teaching techniques used in US classrooms are derived from laboratory experiments with animals?

E.L. Thorndike's law of effect states that S-R connections are strengthened by rewards?

Chimpanzees seem to have the same sort of insight (or "Ah ha!") experiences during learning as do humans?

If you use an effective educational technology, you can teach a pigeon to bowl in a couple of hours or so?

B.F. Skinner believes that rewards increase the probability that an organism will repeat the response it has just made?

Most complex behaviors appear to be sequences of simple responses that have been "chained" together?

The speed with which an organism responds is frequently dependent on the schedule of reinforcement the animal receives?

Most of the animals you see performing on TV and in shows are trained using techniques developed by Skinner and his associates?

"That'll Learn You!"

I am writing this because I presume He wants me to. Otherwise He would not have left paper and pencil handy for me to use. And I put the word "He" in capitals because it seems the only thing to do. If I am dead and in hell, then this is only proper. However, if I am merely a captive somewhere, a little flattery won't hurt matters.

As I think about it, I am impressed most of all by the suddenness of the whole affair. At one moment I was out walking in the woods near my home. The next thing I knew, here I was in a small, bare room, naked as a jaybird, with only my good sense to stand between me and insanity. When the "change" occurred—whatever the change was—I was not aware of even a momentary flicker between walking in the woods and being here in this room. He must have a technology available to Him that is very impressive indeed!

As I recall, I was worrying about how to teach my introductory psychology class some of the more technical points of Learning Theory, when the "change" came. How far away life at the University seems at the moment! I hope the Dean will forgive me if I am now more concerned about where I am—and how to get out of here—than about cajoling undergraduates into understanding Pavlov or Skinner.

Problem #1: Where am I? For an answer, I can only describe this gray, windowless room. It is about 20 feet square and 12 feet high. The ceiling glows with a soft white light, and the spongy floor has a "tingly" feel to it suggesting it may be in constant vibration.

The only furniture in the room are "lumps" that resemble a table and chair. On the table I found a rough sort of paper and a stick of graphite which I have sharpened into a sort of pencil. My clothes are gone. The suit was an old one I won't miss, but I am worried about what happened to my watch. It was one of those fancy digital things, and quite expensive.

The #1 problem still remains, however. Where in the hell am I—if not Hell itself!

Problem #2 is a knottier one—*why* am I here? I have the usual quota of enemies, but even the Dean isn't powerful enough to arrange for something like this. And I surely am not rich enough to kidnap. So, where am I, and why? And who is He?

There is no sense in trying to keep track of time. This room is little more than a sensory deprivation chamber, and I haven't the faintest notion of what hour or even what day it is. Well, it can't be that important. If He wasn't bright enough to leave me my watch, He can't complain that I don't keep accurate records.

Or is that the problem I'm supposed to solve?

Nothing much has happened. I have slept, been fed and watered, and have emptied my bladder and bowels. The food was waiting on the table when I awoke last time. I must say that He has little of the gourmet in him. Protein balls are not my idea of a feast. However, they will serve to keep body and soul together (presuming, of course, that they *are* together at the moment).

But I must object to my source of water. While I was asleep, a small nipple appeared on the wall. It produces a sweetish liquid when I suck on it. But drinking this way is a *most* undignified behavior for a full professor to engage in. I'd complain to the Management if only I knew to whom I should complain!

Following my meal, the call to nature became a little too strong to ignore. Now, I was adequately toilet-trained, and the absence of indoor plumbing is most annoying. However, there was nothing much to do but choose a corner of the room and make the best of a bad situation. However, I have at least learned why the floor vibrates, for the excreted material sank out of sight moments later. Clever technology, but bothersome, since I have to sleep on the floor. I will probably have nightmares that the floor will gulp *me* up too, all in a piece.

You know, this place seems dreadfully quiet to me.

Suddenly I have solved two of my problems. I know both where I am and who He is. And I bless the day that I got interested in sensory psychology and the perception of motion.

The air in this room seems to be filled with dust particles. This fact became important when I noticed that the dust seemed to pile up along the floor against one particular wall. At first I thought there might be an air vent there. However, when I put my hand to the floor, I could feel no breeze whatsoever. Yet even as I held my hand there, dust motes covered my hand. I tried this same experiment everywhere else in the room, but this was the only spot where the dust coated my hand.

But if ventilation was not responsible for the dust, what was? Suddenly there popped into my mind some calculations I had made when NASA first proposed building a wheel-shaped satellite and then set it to spinning slowly in space. Centrifugal force would substitute for the force of gravity, and the outer shell of the wheel would appear to be "down" to anyone inside the wheel. It immediately occurred to me that dust would move in a direction *opposite* to the rotation of the wheel, and thus airborne particles would pile up against any wall that impeded their flight.

It also seemed that the NASA engineers had overlooked one important fact. Namely, that humans are at least as sensitive to angular rotation as they are to the

Cognitive Maps and Operant Conditioning

pull of gravity. As I figured the problem then, if a man aboard the wheel moved his head a few feet toward or away from the center of the doughnut-shaped satellite, he would have sensed the angular rotation of the wheel. Rather annoying it would have been too, becoming dizzy every time you sat down or stood up.

With this thought in mind, I climbed atop the table and jumped off. Sure enough, I immediately felt dizzy. My hypothesis was confirmed.

I am aboard a wheel-shaped spaceship!

The thought is incredible, but in a strange way comforting. At least now I can postpone worry about heaven and hell and start worrying about other things. And, of course, I know who "He" is. Or rather, I know who He *isn't*, which is something else again. Since no country on earth has a space station like this one, He must be an alien!

I still have no notion of *why* I am here, however, nor why this alien picked me of all people to bring to His spaceship. One dreadful thought did occur to me, though. Maybe He's an alien scientist—a biologist of sorts—out gathering specimens. Is He going to cut me open to see what makes me tick? Will my innards be smeared over a glass slide for hundreds of youthful Hims to peer at under a microscope? Brrrr! I don't mind giving my life to Science, but I'd rather do it a day at a time.

Good God! I should have known it! Destiny will play her little tricks, and all jokes have their cosmic angles.

He is a *psychologist*!

Had I given the matter thought, I would have realized that whenever you come across a new species, you worry about behavior first, physiology second. So I have received the ultimate insult—or the ultimate compliment, I don't know which. I have become a laboratory specimen for an alien psychologist!

This thought first occurred to me when I awoke after my latest sleep (which was filled with frightening dreams). Almost at once I noticed that one of the walls now had a lever of some kind protruding from it. Underneath the lever was a small hole with a container beneath the hole. When I accidentally depressed the lever, it made a loud clicking noise. Immediately a protein ball popped out of the hole and fell into the container. For just a moment I was puzzled. This seemed so strangely familiar. Then, all at once, I burst into wild laughter.

This room is a gigantic Skinner Box!

For years I have been putting white rats in an operant chamber and making them press a lever to get a pellet of food. And now, after all those experiments, I find *myself* trapped like a rat in a Skinner Box! Perhaps this is hell after all, and He is just following the Lord High Executioner's advice to "let the punishment fit the crime."

Anyhow, it didn't take me long to discover that pressing the lever would give me food only at rather lengthy intervals. The rest of the time, all I get is a click for my efforts. Since I am never quite sure when the proper interval has passed, I stomp over to the lever and press it whenever I think it's getting close to dinner time. Just like my rats always did. And since the pellets are small and I never get enough of them, occasionally I find myself banging away on the lever with all the compulsion of a stupid animal. But I missed the feeding time once and almost starved to death (so it seemed) before the lever next delivered food. About the only consolation to my wounded pride is that I've already lost an inch or so around my waist.

At least He doesn't seem to be fattening me up for the kill!

I have been promoted. Apparently He has decided I'm intelligent enough to handle the Skinner Box. So I've been promoted to solving a maze.

Can you picture the irony of the situation? All of the classic laboratory apparatus is being thrown right in my face. If only I could communicate with Him! I don't mind being subjected to tests nearly as much as I mind being underestimated. Why, I can solve puzzles hundreds of times more complex than the ones He's giving me. But how can I tell Him?

As it turns out, the maze is much like the ones I have used. It's rather long, with 23 choice points along the way. I spent half an hour wandering through the thing the first time. Surprisingly enough, I didn't realize what I was in, so I made no conscious attempt to memorize the correct turns. It wasn't until I reached the final choice point and found food that I recognized what was expected of me. The next time I made fewer errors, and was able to turn in a perfect performance fairly rapidly. However, I'm embarrassed to state that my own white rats could have learned the maze somewhat sooner than I did.

Now that I am very sure of what is happening to me, my thoughts have turned to how to get out of this situation. Mazes I can solve easily, but how to escape apparently is beyond my intellectual capacity. But come to think of it, there was precious little my own experimental animals could do to get out of my clutches.

And assuming that I am unable to escape, what then? After He has finished putting me through as many paces as He wishes, where do we go from there? Will He treat me as I treated most of my rats—that is, will I get tossed into a jar containing chloroform? "Following the experiment, the animals were sacrificed," as we so politely put it in our journal articles. This thought doesn't appeal to me very much, as you can imagine. But perhaps if I seem particularly bright to Him, He may use me for breeding purposes, to establish a colony of His own. Now, that might have possibilities . . .

Oh, damn Freud anyhow!

And damn Him too! I had just gotten the maze well learned when He changed it on me. I stumbled about like a bat in the sunlight for quite some time before I finally got to the goal box. I'm afraid my performance was pretty poor. What He did was to reverse the whole maze so that it was a mirror image of what it used to be. Took me only two trials to discover the solution. Let Him figure that one out if He's so smart!

My performance on the maze reversal must have pleased Him, because He's added a new complication. He's trying me out on a "jump stand." I sit on a little platform facing three doors across an empty space. If I jump to the right door, I get food. If I pick the wrong one, I fall into a pool of icy water. And if I don't jump at all, He shocks the devil out of me until I do!

I suppose I could have predicted what He would do next if I had been thinking in the right direction. The trouble is, I've been out of graduate school for too long. I took my first advanced course in learning theory from a strict Behavioral Scientist. "Dr. B-S," we called him. He was convinced that rats learned a maze mechanically, by relying entirely on stimulus-response bonds. The professor for my second course was a confirmed "mentalist," who insisted that rats learned a maze by creating a "cognitive map" of the apparatus in their minds. "Dr. Cog," we called him. And oh! the delicious battles he and "Dr. B-S" used to have when they debated in public.

The conflict between the two reached a peak when one of Dr. Cog's students started working with the Oddity Problem. Imagine yourself sitting meekly on a jump stand, staring at three doors across a water-filled gap. The two outer doors are white, the middle door is black. You try jumping at each of the white doors, and end up in the drink. So you leap toward the black door in the middle and find a nice meal of protein balls awaiting you. Thereafter—whether the black door is on the right, the left, or in the center—you jump toward it as quickly as you can. And you are always rewarded.

Now, the question is, *how* did you learn this trick? Dr. B-S insisted that you had "acquired the habit" of approaching the black stimulus and avoiding the white stimulus. But Dr. Cog contended that you learned to go to the "odd" color—in this case, black. This explanation infuriated Dr. B-S, who insisted that *oddness* is a "mental concept" rather than a true stimulus and that rats weren't capable of "conceptualizing."

Dr. Cog then proposed a Grand Theoretical Test. Namely, he would now show a rat two black doors and one white door and see what it did. If the rat had merely learned "to approach the black stimulus," it would leap wildly toward one of the black doors. But if it had learned to "approach the odd-colored door," it would jump to the white door instead *even though it had never before been rewarded for approaching white*. Dr. B-S scoffed, since rats obviously weren't bright enough to "think in concepts."

So, what do you think happened? Most of the rats Dr. Cog tested jumped to the white door the first time they saw it! Dr. B-S was furious, and Dr. Cog chortled smugly for weeks on end. Dr. Cog then rubbed salt in Dr. B-S's wounds by testing his rats on two doors with vertical stripes and one with horizontal stripes. And then on the reverse. Each time, most of the animals picked the "odd" stimulus. The results were so impressive that Dr. B-S threw up his hands in dismay and went to Hawaii on sabbatical to observe the native life there. When he returned, he began studying biofeedback in humans, and never touched a rodent again.

What has all this got to do with me? Well, He must be a simple behaviorist, like old Dr. B-S. The last time He put me on the jump stand, I found myself facing two blue doors and a yellow one. I realized what was up instantly, and leapt toward the yellow. Success! Immediately He tested me with two yellow doors and a blue one. I jumped to the blue, and heard what I can only describe as a cosmic roar of frustration. I gather He wasn't very happy with what I had done.

Next up were two red doors and a green one. I "went for the green," and had no more than landed safely when the whole apparatus started to shake as if someone had kicked it in anger!

The next thing I knew, I was tossed rather roughly back in my cage. Since nothing has happened for an hour or so, I presume He's off sulking somewhere because my actions didn't confirm His expectations.

I suppose I should have realized it before now. Theories are typically born of the equipment one uses. If Skinner had never invented his blasted box, if the maze and the jump stand had not been developed, we probably would have entirely different theories of learning today than we now have. For if nothing else, the type of apparatus you use *reduces* the types of behavior that your subjects can show—and your theories only have to account for the kinds of responses that show up in laboratory situations.

But if He has a problem, I have a worse one. What should I do next, now that I know what He expects of me? Should I help Him confirm his narrow notions about behavior—and about the new species He's testing? Or should I prove to the monster that I'm more "cognitive" than He thinks I ought to be?

I'm sure He will shortly snatch me back for a final test. When I face those different-colored doors, should I perform "stupidly" like the intelligent human being I really am, or should I perform "intelligently" by acting like the dumb rat He wants me to be?

What am I anyhow? A man, or a mouse?

(Continued on page 363.)

Learning Theories

During the many years that you have gone to school, you must have had contact with dozens of different teachers. Some of them probably were strict **disciplinarians** whose "learning theory" had two parts. First, that knowledge had to be *pounded* into your head through constant repetition. And second, that it was better to correct your mistakes than to reward your progress. Holding a lesson book in one hand and a stick in the other, these teachers probably "drilled" you until you could spew back from memory whatever material the teacher believed you should learn. If you survived their classes, you surely acquired a large number of facts. But the constant threat of punishment may also have conditioned you to hate anything associated with school.

Other teachers may have been more concerned with creating an academic environment in which your inborn intellectual potential could grow and blossom like a flower seed planted in

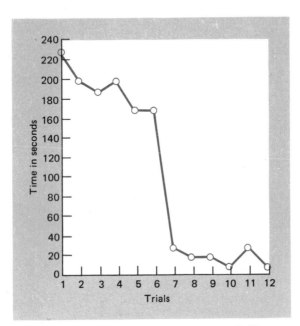

Fig. 15.1. The seventh trial shows a remarkable improvement in the time it took one of Thorndike's cats to open a puzzle box.

E. L. Thorndike   E. C. Tolman

fertile soil. These teachers probably gave you a great deal of encouragement but little or no academic guidance. And while you may have enjoyed their classrooms, the important question is whether you can acquire the basic skills of life in such unstructured settings.

Is there a "best way" to educate all people? Should students be treated like Pavlov's dogs—drilled and conditioned until they have acquired the proper response for any stimulus they are likely to encounter? Or should pupils be considered **cognitive**, self-motivated creatures who will learn everything they need to know if given a rich intellectual environment?

As you will soon see, the history of psychological learning theories—and the history of educational practice in the US—sometimes resembles a battle plan between these two opposing viewpoints.

Thorndike's Theories

In a sense, it all began with E.L. Thorndike, a giant of a figure in psychology who influenced educational practices here almost as much as Pavlov did in Russia. Thorndike spent most of his academic career at Teachers College, a part of Columbia University in New York City. He helped create some of the very first intelligence and **aptitude** tests. He was a strong supporter of educational research. And, with the help of C.L. Barn-

hart, he developed a series of dictionaries for school children that is still widely in use.

Thorndike believed that humans were descended from the lower animals and hence *learned the same way* as did cats and rats. So in 1890 he undertook some of the first laboratory studies ever performed on how animals learn. His early work involved putting cats inside a "puzzle box." If the cat could figure out how to unlatch the door to the box, it escaped and was given a bit of food as a reward.

At first the cat typically showed a great deal of what Thorndike called "random behavior." It sat and scratched or licked itself, it mewed and cried, it paced the box, or it bit at the bars and tried to squeeze between them. Eventually, the cat would accidently bump into the latch. The door would fly open, and the animal would rush out and be fed.

In subsequent trials, the cat spent more and more time near the latch and got out of the box sooner and sooner. Eventually the cat learned what was required of it. The moment it was placed in the box, it would hit the latch, escape, and claim its reward.

When Thorndike plotted on a graph the amount of time it took the cat to exit from the box on each trial, he came up with something that we now call a "learning curve" (see Fig. 15.1). Similar experiments on monkeys, chickens, and even humans yielded the same-shaped curves, a finding that confirmed Thorndike's original theory that animals and humans solve such simple tasks in much the same manner.

Trial-and-Error Learning

Thorndike believed that animals learn to escape from puzzle boxes by **trial and error**. That is, they perform various behaviors in a blindly mechanical way until some action is *effective* in getting them out of the box. Ineffectual actions such as sitting and scratching bring the animal little satisfaction. So these responses rapidly drop out of the animal's behavioral **repertory**. But those actions that gain the animal's release and lead to food are very *satisfying*, so these responses become strongly connected to the stimuli in the puzzle box. The "satisfying" responses thus are much more likely to occur whenever the animal is next put in the box.

Thorndike's Laws of Learning

The results of his puzzle box experiments led Thorndike to formulate two basic laws of learning: (1) the **law of exercise**; and (2) the **law of effect**.

In part, the *law of exercise* states that the S-R connections you make are *strengthened* by practice or repetition—in short, that practice makes perfect.

The *law of effect* holds that S-R bonds are also strengthened by the "effects" of what you do. These effects may be either "satisfying" or "punishing." Thorndike defined *satisfiers* as situations you willingly approach or do nothing to avoid. And he defined *punishers* as situations you typically avoid or do nothing to approach.

If the response you make to a stimulus somehow gives you pleasure or satisfaction, the connection between the S and the R will be appropriately increased. This is the first half of the "law of effect," and it holds today just as it did when

"You had it wrong, kid. It's meditation in the dressing room and biofeedback in the ring."

Thorndike first announced it. The second half of the law has to do with the effects of punishment on learning. Early in his career, Thorndike stated that "punishers" weakened or broke S-R bonds. But he changed his mind on this point later, when laboratory research proved that punishment *suppresses* responses temporarily rather than breaking S-R connections. By then, however, many teachers had used Thorndike's laws of learning to justify a "disciplinarian" approach in the classroom.

Cognitive Theories of Learning

As we noted in Chapter 9, we often see what we expect to see. This principle holds in scientific investigations as well as in ordinary life. Thorndike surely *expected* his cats to learn by trial-and-error methods before he began his work. Indeed, as **Gestalt** psychologist Wolfgang Koehler pointed out, the puzzle box could hardly be solved in any other way.

Koehler was trained at the University of Berlin. He believed that animals were capable of greater intellectual accomplishments than random solutions to puzzle boxes. He thought that, given the chance, they could discover *relation-*

351

Fig. 15.2. Sultan in action.

ships between objects and events. The animals could then act on these relationships to gain whatever ends they had in mind. Much of Koehler's research involved presenting various "intellectual" problems to chimpanzees, to see what kinds of solutions they might come up with.

Learning by Insight

Koehler's most famous subject was a particularly bright chimpanzee named Sultan. First Sultan learned to reach through the bars of his cage with a stick and rake in a banana. After Sultan had mastered this trick, Koehler set the animal the much more difficult task of putting two sticks together to get the food. The banana was moved farther away from Sultan's cage, and the chimp was given two bamboo poles. When the two poles were fitted together, they were just long enough to gather in the reward (see Fig. 15.2).

At first Sultan was confused. He tried to pull the fruit in with one stick and then with the other, but neither would reach. Despite the fact that this approach didn't get him the banana, Sultan repeated the behavior again and again. When the chimp abandoned the banana and (perhaps in frustration) retreated into his cage to play with the sticks, Koehler decided the animal had failed the test. So Koehler went home, leaving Sultan to be observed by an assistant.

Not long after Koehler left, Sultan happened to hold one stick in each hand so that their ends were pointed toward each other. Gently, he pushed the tip of the smaller one into the hollow of the larger. *They fitted.* Even as he joined the

two sticks together, Sultan was up and running toward the bars of his cage. Reaching through with the double stick, he touched the banana and started to draw it toward him.

At this point fate played Sultan a nasty trick for which Koehler was most grateful—the two sticks came apart! Annoyed at this turn of events, Sultan gathered the sticks back into the cage, pushed them *firmly* together, tested them briefly, and then "liberated" the banana.

These actions proved—at least to Koehler's satisfaction—that Sultan actually understood that *joining the poles together* was an effective way of lengthening his arm. Koehler used the term **insight** to refer to this very rapid "perception of relationships" that sometimes occurs in humans and animals. He believed that *insight* involved a sudden restructuring or reorganization of the organism's perceptual world into a new pattern or *Gestalt*.

As you might imagine, Ivan Pavlov did not take gladly to Koehler's experiments. As soon as the chimpanzee work appeared in print, Pavlov leapt to the attack. From his sanctuary in Leningrad, Pavlov issued one **vitriolic** criticism after another. First he accused Koehler of being a "mentalist," which Koehler surely was. But Pavlov also unjustly criticized Koehler for performing "sloppy" experiments. (To Pavlov, a "sloppy" study was one in which the CS and the UCS could not readily be identified.) Since Koehler was much more interested in learning how animals solved real-life problems than in specifying CS's and UCS's, he ignored Pavlov's comments. But thanks to Koehler's work, Pavlov soon found himself assailed by a barrage of experiments from the US. Unfortunately for Pavlov, few of these studies yielded results that could easily be fitted into the Russian scientist's theory of conditioning.

Tolman's "Cognitive Maps"

One set of studies came from E.C. Tolman and his associates at the University of California, Berkeley. During the height of the Pavlov-Koehler controversy, Tolman and his group published a series of articles showing that rats apparently were much more "insightful" than either Thorndike or Pavlov thought they ought to be.

In most of Tolman's experiments, the rats were given considerable training in very complicated **mazes**. Although the animals could reach the food reward at the end of the maze by a great many pathways, one path was typically much shorter than the rest and was preferred by the animals. When that pathway was blocked, however, almost all of the rats would instantly shift to the next most efficient way of getting to the food.

If at any time the experimenter moved the reward from one part of the maze to another, the rats responded immediately as if they had some kind of **cognitive map** of the maze. That is, the rats acted as if they understood a great deal about the *spatial relationships* involved in getting quickly from one part of the maze to another.

The experiments by Tolman and other Gestalt psychologists clearly demonstrated that *some* rats, in *some* situations, acted as if they had "cognitive maps" of their environments. Monkeys, chimps, and humans show a great deal more cognitive activity than do rats, however. So Gestalt theorists typically used primates as their preferred laboratory subjects. Because Pavlov, Thorndike, and the early behaviorists focused entirely on S-R bonds, they weren't interested in "mental processes." The rather mechanical behavior patterns of the lower animals appealed greatly to the behaviorists, and so they chiefly stuck to their rats, cats, and dogs. Thus it took a bird-brained pigeon to show the narrowness of Pavlov's views, and to map out a kind of common ground between the Thorndikeans and the Tolmaniacs.

Question: An "insight" is often defined as a sudden rearrangement of the elements in a pattern to form a new concept. How might you combine the behavioral and the cognitive approaches to help someone acquire new insights? (Hint: You have to learn the elements in a pattern before you can rearrange them.)

Operant Conditioning

The learning theories of Pavlov, Thorndike, and Tolman have all been applied in classroom situations. But the theoretical approach most frequently followed in schools today is surely that called **operant conditioning**, which was developed by B.F. Skinner. We will compare operant conditioning with the other theories of learning later in this chapter. First, let's see why it is so powerful a method for teaching new behavior patterns to both pigeons and people.

Teaching a Pigeon To Bowl

Suppose that, as a final examination in one of your psychology classes, your instructor gives you a common, ordinary pigeon and tells you that if you want to get an A in the course, you must teach the pigeon to bowl!

After you recover from your surprise, you take stock of the situation. The apparatus you can use is a large box with a wire screen over the top of it. Inside the box is a small bowling alley with a

Insight. The power or act of seeing into a situation or into oneself. Clear and immediate understanding of the solution to a problem that presumably does not involve trial-and-error learning.

Vitriolic (vitt-tree-OLL-ick). A biting, scathing verbal attack on someone or something. From the Latin term meaning "caustic."

Mazes (MAY-zizz). A network of pathways and blind alleys between a starting point and a goal, used chiefly to study learning and problem-solving in animals and humans. The first maze for laboratory animals was built by psychologist W.S. Small in 1900, and was similar to a famous maze made of hedges at Hampton Court Palace in England that has delighted millions of visitors.

Cognitive map. Some psychologists (such as Thorndike and Pavlov) believe that animals learn each section of a maze by trial and error. Other psychologists believe that animals acquire a "mental map" of the maze and can "think" their way through to the goal—rather than respond reflexively (and unconsciously) to the specific stimuli in each section. In fact, animals such as rats seem to do a little of both.

Operant conditioning (OPP-per-rant). Skinner's technique for "shaping" responses by rewarding successive approximations to a goal.

tiny ball at one end and pigeon-sized bowling pins at the other (see Fig. 15.3). In one corner of the box is a metal cup into which you can drop food pellets from the outside. Just above the food cup is a small bell. Fortunately, the pigeon has already been trained to run to the food cup to get the pellets whenever you ring the bell.

Your instructor tells you that if you can teach the pigeon to bowl in a matter of two hours or less, you pass the exam and get your A reward. Keeping in mind all of the practical knowledge on learning theory you have acquired so far in this book, how would you go about educating your pigeon in order to satisfy your instructor, yourself, and, of course, the bird?

Pavlov's Approach

If you played the game according to Pavlovian rules, what would you do? Well, you might begin by ringing the bell and then pushing the pigeon toward the ball, hoping that an S-R connection of some kind would be established in the bird's nervous system. In fact, the pigeon would surely resent such an intrusion into its life space. Instead of learning to bowl when you rang the bell, it probably would learn to peck at your hand viciously. For Pavlovian conditioning is almost always built on *already-established unconditioned responses* (UCS's). If dogs did not salivate naturally when given food, how would you go about teaching them to salivate when you sounded a buzzer?

If the pigeon already knew how to bowl, you could probably train it to give this response on command when you rang the bell. But you could read everything Pavlov wrote—in Russian or in

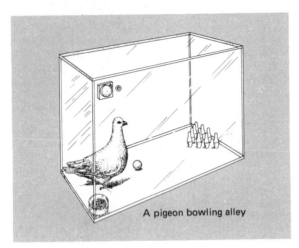

Fig. 15.3. A pigeon bowling alley.

English translation—without learning much about how to get a bird to bowl in the first place.

Cognitive Approach

If you turned to Tolman and the Gestalt theorists instead, you might decide to give the pigeon plenty of experience in the bowling box itself before you started the training. Once the animal had acquired a cognitive map of the apparatus, it would surely learn how to bowl much faster. But the relationship between striking the ball and knocking down the pins is an insight that comes hard to most pigeons—unless you facilitate matters a little along the way. And not even Koehler offered much practical advice about how this facilitation should be accomplished.

Trial and Error Approach

If you looked to Thorndike for help, you still might have troubles. You could utilize the law of effect by waiting until the pigeon accidentally happened to knock the ball down the alley. You could then ring the bell and give the bird some food, and this reward would increase the chances that the bird would *repeat* its actions in the future. But how long would you have to wait until the pigeon *by accident* hit the ball straight down the alley the first time? The problem with Thorndike's approach, then, is that he doesn't give you a very efficient way of bringing about *the very first response*.

All of these components—*reward*, *exercise*, *repetition*, and *unlearned* or *innate responses*—are necessary if you are to train the pigeon and pass your exam. But putting them all together into a workable educational system took the genius of Harvard professor B.F. Skinner, who surely quali-

fies as being our most influential living psychologist.

B.F. Skinner's Techniques

According to Skinner, whenever you wish to change an organism's behavior, you always begin defining *precisely* what it is you want to accomplish. For instance, to get your A, you must train the pigeon to bowl. But what do we mean by "bowling"? Do we have some objective, clear-cut, agreed-upon way of measuring the response pattern we call "bowling"? If so, then we know when to *terminate* the training, and we know when you've passed the exam.

Terminal Response or Goal

Bowling is obviously a complex *set of responses* that ends when the pigeon has whacked the ball down the alley toward the pins. Thus your goal must be that of getting the bird to hit the ball in the proper direction.

Skinner calls the *final* step in any chain of behaviors the **terminal response**. When the organism has performed this final act, the chain of responses is *terminated*—usually by a reward or punishment of some kind. Thus when the pigeon finally "bowls," you will ring the bell and give it a pellet of food. And when the pigeon "bowls" regularly, you will terminate the training and receive your A.

The single most important thing about the terminal response, however, is that it must be *measurable*. As you will soon see, pigeons *can* be trained to bowl in two hours or less if you go about it the right way. However, how long do you think it would take to train a bird to be a "good sport"?

Question: College catalogues often state that the goal of higher education is to turn students into "creative individuals" who are "good citizens" and "productive members of modern-day society." What might B.F. Skinner say about the measurability of such terminal responses?

Taking a Baseline

Once you have a well-defined goal to work toward, you are ready to tackle the second stage in Skinner's analysis of behavioral change—determining what the organism is doing *before* you begin to train it. Skinner refers to these "prior responses" as the organism's **baseline behaviors**.

In order to determine the *baseline behavior*, you measure what the organism is already doing, and plot its responses on a graph or record of some kind. Skinner calls this "taking a baseline." Like the terminal response, the baseline behaviors must be stated in objective, measurable terms. Clever animal trainers (or people educators) always take advantage of the response patterns that the organism brings to the training situation. You always build new learning on old, according to Skinner.

Successive Approximations

When you are sure of: (1) the organism's baseline behaviors and (2) the terminal behavior that you hope to achieve, you are ready to move from (1) to (2). Skinner suggests that you do so in a step-by-step fashion called **successive approximations to a goal**.

Neither people nor pigeons typically make dramatic changes in their behaviors in large, insightful jumps. We *can* do so occasionally, as the Gestalt theorists showed. But most of the time we change slowly, bit by bit, millimeter by millimeter. And we usually need to be coaxed and encouraged whenever we must acquire a new way of doing things. That is, we typically need to be rewarded or **reinforced** for each tiny step that we make toward the goal or terminal response. (We will have more to say about the importance of reward momentarily.)

The technique of *successive approximations to a goal* is the heart of the Skinnerian system. But mastery of the step-by-step technique calls for rather a penetrating insight on your own part. Namely, you must realize that even the faintest, feeblest movement toward the goal is *a step in the right direction*, hence one that you must vigorously reward. Most people unfamiliar with Skinner's techniques seem unable or unwilling to analyze behavior in these terms. This fact may explain why most people would not be able to train a pigeon to bowl in two hours or less.

Behavioral Analysis

If we apply the Skinnerian *behavioral analysis* to the problem of getting your pigeon to perform, we can perhaps see how the technique works.

The terminal behavior your instructor has set is that of "bowling." But how shall we define it? Humans usually pick up the bowling ball in their hands and roll it down the alley. However, Mother Nature has given the pigeon wings instead of arms, and feathers are poor substitutes for fingers when it comes to lifting a heavy ball.

But could we teach an armless man to bowl? Couldn't the man kick the ball down the alley, or even butt it with his head? Do you really care how he manages it, so long as the ball zings down the alley and hits the pins?

One of the purposes of getting you to "take a baseline" of the pigeon's normal response pat-

Terminal response. Also called "terminal behavior pattern" or "terminal goal." The final step in training an organism, or the last response that the animal makes in a chain of learned behaviors.

Baseline behaviors. The behavior patterns of an organism before training begins. According to behavioral therapists, you must always build upon the client's strengths (the good behaviors) and select out of these "baseline behaviors" those actions that can be shaped toward the terminal response. Entering behaviors also include problematic or inappropriate actions, but these should be ignored (or at least not rewarded) in the hope that they will thereby be extinguished.

Successive approximations to a goal. Rewarding any incremental (in-kree-MENT-tal) response that will lead the organism toward the terminal response. That is, reinforcing any slight behavioral change (increment) that represents a step in the right direction.

Reinforced. Concrete with steel rods inside it is called *reinforced* concrete, because the steel strengthens the concrete. Positive feedback reinforces an S-R bond by making it more likely that the response will occur again the next time the stimulus input appears.

terns is this: It forces you to see what the bird *already* does that you can make use of during training. If you observe pigeons for a while, you will notice they use their beaks much as we use our hands. So if you can train the bird to hit the ball with its beak, you surely have taught the animal to "bowl" within the stated definition of the problem. And you surely should get an A on your exam.

Now that you know what your goal is, you can begin to take advantage of the baseline behaviors the pigeon already shows. At the start of training, the bird merely moves around nervously, inspecting its new environment. The final response that you want from the animal is that of striking the ball with its beak so that the ball travels down the alley and hits the pins. To make this terminal response, though, the animal must be standing *near the ball*. So your first task would seem to be that of getting the pigeon to move to where the ball is. But how to do it?

If you were training your child to bowl, you would probably explain to the child—in English—what you wanted it to do. Then, when the child first approached the ball or picked it up, you would tell the child it was doing well. But pigeons are non-verbal—they don't even speak "pigeon English." So how can you give your bird feedback to let it know when it's doing something "on target"? The answer is: You *reward* each step it makes toward the goal. But you give the bird food rather than a verbal pat on the back.

Two Functions of Reward

Reward or positive reinforcement has at least two functions. First, it gives you pleasure, usually by satisfying some need or reducing some drive or

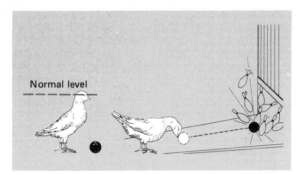

Fig. 15.4. Whenever the pigeon's head bobs below the normal level that it keeps its beak at, you "ring the bell" and reward the pigeon. Then, step by step, you reward it for moving its head lower and lower. Finally, the bird's beak will be on the floor, where the ball is.

deprivation state. But rewards also have an *informational* aspect to them, for they give you feedback as to how well you are doing, and how close you are coming to a goal. Positive reinforcement, then, *increases the probability* that an organism will *repeat the response* that led to the appearance of the rewarding stimulus.

As we noted a few pages back, your pigeon has already been trained to go to the food cup when it hears the bell ring. Thus you can use the *sound of the bell* as a rewarding input whenever you want to let the pigeon know instantly that it has made a step in the right direction toward the goal of bowling.

"Shaping" a Pigeon To Bowl

With these preliminaries out of the way, you would be ready to start passing your final examination. You know your goal; you know the bird's entering behavior; the animal is deprived of food; and you have an effective reinforcer available. What is your next step?

Actually, as Skinner points out, the next step is up to the bird. As it wanders around the box excitedly, at one time or another it will *accidentally* move toward the bowling ball. If you have the insight to recognize this simple movement as being "a step in the right direction"—and if you ring the bell *at once* and reward the animal with food—you will have no difficulty in training the bird to bowl. But if you insist the bird doesn't *deserve* a reward until it scores a strike, it may take you years to pass the exam—if you ever do.

Presuming that you do sound the bell the first time the bird moves tentatively in the general direction of the ball, how does the pigeon respond? By running to the food cup to claim its reward. After eating the food, it will pause for a

while near the food cup. But when pausing doesn't ring the bell, it will usually begin its random trial-and-error movements around the box again. Once more, as soon as it heads toward the ball, you sound the bell. And again the bird runs to the food cup and eats.

The fifth or sixth or tenth time the pigeon repeats this response, a very strange event often occurs. The bird behaves as if it has experienced a "flash of insight" into what is happening. That is, the pigeon acts as if it had discovered that it can actually control *your* behavior! All it has to do to *force* you to give it food is to move in a given direction.

Once your pigeon has learned the connection between *doing something* and *being rewarded*, you can go much faster with your training. Each time that you sound the bell, the pigeon will dash to the food cup, then return at once to where it was the instant the bell rang. Now, on each successive trial, you merely wait until the animal accidentally moves one step nearer to the ball before you ring the bell. In a matter of minutes, the bird will be hovering over the bowling ball.

The Beak and the Ball

Once the bird is standing *over* the ball, you must find a way of getting the animal's beak *down to floor level*. Again, you go back to the natural responses that the animal makes. As pigeons move, their heads bob up and down. Sometimes, then, the bird's beak is closer to the ball than at other times. An experienced animal trainer will soon perceive the bird's downward head movements as "good responses," and begin to reward them (see Fig. 15.4).

After several such reinforcements, the pigeon begins to return from the food cup holding its head a little lower than before. If you demand that the bird depress its head an additional inch or so each subsequent trial, you can get it to touch the floor with its beak in minutes.

Question: Do you imagine that, at any time during training, the pigeon gains a cognitive awareness that it is "learning to bowl"?

On to the Goal

By now the pigeon's beak is close to the floor, and the bird is moving about near the ball. Within a few moments, its beak will touch the ball "accidentally." The skilled animal trainer now rings the bell joyously, knowing that victory is near. When the bird returns from claiming its reward, it typically takes a second swat at the ball. When again the bell sounds, the pigeon scoots back and forth from food cup to ball, whacking the ball each time it comes close to it.

Now it is up to you to shape the bird's "whacking responses" so that the animal knocks the ball straight down the alley instead of merely hitting it in any random direction. Such **shaping** should take only a few minutes, for at first you reinforce only those whacks that aim the ball in the general direction of the pins. Then you selectively reward those hits that are closer and closer *approximations* to your stated goal. The pigeon soon learns that it will be fed only when it strikes the ball so that it rolls straight down the alley and hits the pins.

An experienced pigeon-handler can usually shape a hungry pigeon "to bowl" in less than an hour. (Training the animal to get a good score takes a little longer.)

Analysis of Skinner's System

There are several fairly subtle points about the Skinnerian system that are sometimes over-looked:

1. Skinner differentiates between two "unpleasant" types of inputs which have entirely different effects on behavior. The first is *punishment*, which is a painful input that the animal learns to avoid. The second is **negative reinforcement**, which is the termination of a painful "drive state" such as extreme hunger. As we will see, negative reinforcement affects behavior in much the same way that positive reinforcement does.

The difference between punishment and negative reinforcement is best seen in their *consequences*. Punishment *disrupts* behavioral sequences. It may occasionally suppress certain responses, but it does so only *temporarily*. And punishment seldom "wipes out" inappropriate behaviors. Thus those teachers who threaten to punish you *unless* you perform correctly often teach you little more than to avoid them (and all academic settings).

Negative reinforcement, on the other hand, *strengthens* a behavioral sequence just as positive reinforcement does. Negative reinforcement is an input that *reduces* discomfort, while punishment is an input that *increases* pain or displeasure. Punishment leads to active avoidance and other types of emotional behaviors. Negative reinforcement, however, leads to approach behaviors and to learning.

The next time you visit a "marine world" of some kind, ask the animal trainers how they teach porpoises to perform in public. You'll find the trainers use reinforcement almost ex-

Shaping. To "shape" a response is to bring it about using successive approximations to a goal. Thus *shaping* means "training an organism using operant conditioning techniques."

Negative reinforcement. Technically speaking, "positive" reinforcement is the *onset* or appearance of a stimulus input which "satisfies" an organism in some way. "Negative" reinforcement is the *termination* of a stimulus situation which the organism would ordinarily avoid. "Punishment" is the *onset* of a painful stimulus that the organism would ordinarily avoid, thus punishment is *not* (repeat *not*) the same thing as negative reinforcement. Punishment suppresses behaviors temporarily, or teaches an organism to avoid an unpleasant situation. Negative reinforcement strengthens behaviors by reducing a drive or terminating an unpleasant stimulus.

Chained. To write the word "cat" on a typewriter, you must first hit the "c" key, then the "a" key, then the "t." You will have made (at least) three different responses that are chained together to achieve the goal of typing the word "cat." Behaviorists believe that complex human behavior patterns are mostly long chains of related responses that must be learned one at a time.

clusively. If you punish a porpoise, it sulks in a corner for days. But if you give it food, you reinforce it both positively and negatively. First, the food tastes good. Second, it slightly reduces the animal's natural hunger. Animals don't hold trainers responsible for getting hungry. They do hold trainers responsible for the punishment they inflict, though. And if you punish a "killer whale," the consequences may be more disastrous for you than for the whale!

2. Notice that in teaching the pigeon to bowl, *no punishment* was necessary to get the animal to perform. The pigeon obviously *can* learn. If it fails to do so, the fault presumably lies with the teacher (or with the learning environment) and not with the student.

3. You control the *timing* of the reinforcement—but the pigeon determines whether it wants the reward you offered it. If the reinforcement is meaningful and satisfying to that particular bird, then the animal will work. But if you offer the animal something it doesn't want or need—or if you expect too much work for the amount of pleasure that you give the bird in return—it is free to rebel and ignore you. (Surprisingly enough, pigeons appear to enjoy this type of training. Once they have learned the task, they will "bowl" again and again with but a minimal amount of encouragement.)

4. "Bowling" is obviously a very complicated set of responses that the animal has to learn in a *particular order or sequence*. You got the bird to learn one simple thing at a time, never demanding too much. You always encouraged the "right" things the pigeon did, and you ignored (or certainly didn't punish) its mistakes. And by doing so, you **chained** the sequence of re-

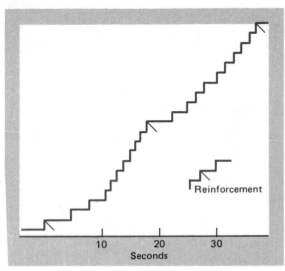

Fig. 15.5. A cumulative record of a pigeon trained to peck a button on a 10 to 1 fixed-ratio reinforcement schedule. Each vertical movement of the graph represents one press of the lever. Note that the pigeon responds more quickly just prior to a reinforcement than just afterward.

sponses together from its first approaching step to its last whack at the ball. However, the experienced pigeon will perform its bowling routine so smoothly and efficiently that it is not easy for us to see the various *individual responses* that have been chained together during training.

Question: If you can train a pigeon to bowl without using punishment, would it be possible to teach a child how to read and write without criticizing or spanking the child when it makes a mistake? Why aren't more children taught this way?

Schedules of Reinforcement

According to Skinner, at the beginning of training you should reward *each and every move* the bird makes toward the goal. However, once the pigeon has mastered a given response in the chain, you may begin slowly *fading out the reward* by reinforcing the response **intermittently**. Continuous reinforcement is necessary at first, both to keep the animal eager to perform and to let it know that it is doing something right. However, once the pigeon learns what that "something" is, you may begin reinforcing the response every second time, then every third or fourth time, then perhaps every tenth time. If you fade out the reward very gradually, you can get a pigeon to make a simple response (such as pecking a button) several thousand times for each reinforcement.

During the fading process, the exact *scheduling* of the reward is crucial. If you reinforce *exactly* every tenth response, the bird will soon learn to anticipate which response will gain it food. As soon as it makes this tenth response and feeds, it will take a "rest break" because it knows that its next response never brings it any goodies. Skinner calls this **fixed-ratio reinforcement**, because the ratio between the number of responses required and the rewards given is fixed and never varies.

If we make a **cumulative record** of the time intervals between each response the animal makes, we would find that it responds slowly just after a reinforcement, but more and more quickly as it approaches that response it knows will gain it the reward (see Fig. 15.5).

We can get the pigeon to respond at a more or less *constant* rate by tricking it a bit—that is, by rewarding it on a **variable-ratio schedule** rather than on a fixed-ratio. Instead of reinforcing *exactly* the tenth response, we vary the schedule so that sometimes the third response yields food, sometimes the seventh, sometimes the eleventh, sometimes the twentieth—or any response in between. A hundred responses will yield *about* 10 rewards, but the bird will never know when the next reward is coming. When trained on variable-ratio schedules, pigeons respond vigorously and at a fairly constant pace.

We could also reward the pigeon using **interval reinforcement**. That is, we could reward the first correct response the bird made after (let's say) an interval of 2 minutes had passed. Generally speaking, however, *ratio* reinforcement is easier to use than is *interval* reinforcement.

Question: Do the slot machines in Las Vegas pay off on a fixed ratio or a variable ratio? Why?

"Shaping" Responses

"Shaping" any organism's responses is more of a psychological art than a science, and some people are much better behavioral artists than are others. Skinner says that you should reward each successive step toward the behavioral goal you have in mind. But there are thousands of different response chains that might lead from the animal's baseline behaviors to the terminal goal. Unfortunately, Skinner doesn't tell you which one to pick, nor how to judge which pathway is best.

Lion tamers at the circus—as well as teachers at dog and cat "obedience schools"—often make use of Skinnerian principles in teaching their beasts to perform dazzling tricks. But some lion trainers are much better at putting the "big cats" through their paces than are other animal-handlers, just as some instructors are much more effective than others at rewarding successive approximations to educational goals. As you might guess, there is still considerable debate about what behavioral traits you need in order to become an effective "shaper."

Question: Which parts of "shaping" seem to be left hemisphere traits? And which might be right hemisphere or "perceptual" traits?

Operant versus Respondent Conditioning

Skinner calls the type of learning he studies **instrumental conditioning**, or operant conditioning. Skinner chose the term "operant" because he believes that the organism must learn to *operate* on its environment in order to get the reinforcers that it desires. Stated in General Systems Theory terms, the system must somehow change its behavioral outputs until it finds one that is instrumental in bringing it the rewarding inputs that it needs.

Skinner refers to Pavlovian training as **respondent conditioning** because Pavlov taught

Intermittently (in-turr-MITT-tent-lee). If it rains on Monday, is clear on Tuesday, but rains again on Wednesday and Thursday, then it has rained intermittently during the week. If you reward a rat each third time that it presses a bar, you are giving the animal intermittent reinforcement.

Fixed-ratio reinforcement. If you reward a rat for *exactly* each third bar press that it makes, the ratio between responses (bar presses) and reward is fixed.

Cumulative record (CUE-mew-luh-tive). From the word *accumulate*, meaning "to acquire." As you grow older, your years are cumulative—that is, you never lose a year once you've lived through it. A cumulative record is an increasing graph or record of all the responses that an animal has made in a certain time period. The record shows the number of responses the animal has made, the time between each response, and each reinforcement the animal receives.

Variable-ratio schedule. A schedule of reinforcement that involves rewarding the animal for *approximately* every third (or fifth or one-hundredth) correct response that it makes.

Interval reinforcement. Fixed-interval reinforcement involves rewarding the first response an organism makes after, say, 60 seconds. Variable-interval reinforcement involves rewarding the first response an organism makes, say, after *approximately* 60 seconds.

Instrumental conditioning. Also called "operant conditioning." A type of learning in which the organism must learn which of its responses will be instrumental in yielding a reward.

Respondent conditioning. Also called "classical conditioning" or "Pavlovian conditioning." So named because the organism always responds to presentation of the CS with the CR.

Elicits (ee-LISS-sits). To elicit is to pull out, to evoke, to stimulate into action. In Pavlovian conditioning, the stimulus that elicits the CR is always identifiable. The important bond is the one between the stimulus and the response.

his animals to *respond* in a specific way to a specific stimulus (see Fig. 15.6).

Elicited versus Emitted Responses

There are many differences between operant and respondent conditioning. Surely one of the most obvious ones is this: Pavlovian (respondent) learning is always tied to a unique and specific stimulus, while operant conditioning is not. Food powder blown into a dog's mouth **elicits** the salivary response. Pairing the bell with the food gives the bell the power to elicit the same sort of salivation—whether the dog likes it or not. The important point is that neither dogs nor humans go around salivating unless they are stimulated to do so by a highly specific sensory input. Respondent conditioning thus involves setting up involuntary, *elicited* responses to specific stimuli.

On the other hand, pigeons (and people) perform all kinds of actions that don't seem to be "elicited" or pulled out of the organism automatically. Rather, says Skinner, we typically **emit** or produce a wide variety of behaviors rather freely. Those activities that are reinforced, we tend to repeat. Those behaviors that aren't reinforced tend to drop out of our *behavioral repertory*.

"MY PROBLEM HAS ALWAYS BEEN AN OVERABUNDANCE OF ALPHA WAVES."

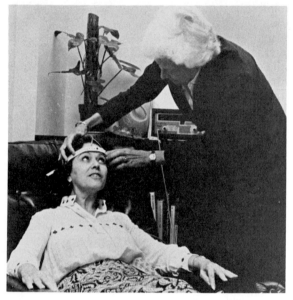

Most animals used in movies and professional shows are trained using operant conditioning (reinforcement) techniques rather than punishment. **(above)**

Fig. 15.6. The rat in a specially designed Skinner box is being rewarded for responding correctly in a learning experiment. **(top left)**

Fig. 15.7. This woman, using biofeedback, can reduce the pain of a migraine headache by learning to lower the temperature of her forehead. **(left)**

Stimulus-Response Connections

Respondent conditioning involves attaching a *new stimulus* to an *already-established response*. Thus the important association in Pavlovian conditioning is that between the CS and the UCS. Once this connection is made, the connection between the CS and the CR follows rather automatically.

Operant conditioning, however, involves attaching a *new response* to *already-present stimulus inputs*. Thus the important association is between the *response* itself and the *feedback* the response generates.

Pavlov didn't train his animals to respond in a new way. He merely taught them to give the same old salivation response to a new stimulus (the bell). Skinner, however, almost always teaches organisms to respond in ways they never

have before. But they learn these new responses without Skinner's having to add new stimuli to the situation, as Pavlov did.

Voluntary versus Involuntary Muscles

Respondent conditioning typically involves those *involuntary muscle groups* controlled by the autonomic nervous system and the lower brain centers. Most emotional learning—such as acquiring a fear or a phobia—involves Pavlovian conditioning. The fear response is *already present* in the organism's repertory. All respondent conditioning does is to attach the involuntary fear reaction to a *novel stimulus*.

Operant conditioning typically involves *voluntary muscle groups* controlled by the cortex and the higher brain centers. Motor skills, such as sewing or playing football, are usually the result of some type of operant conditioning. For acquiring a new motor skill almost always involves learning a new way of responding to stimuli that were already present in your environment.

The subtle differences between operant and respondent conditioning are probably of greater interest to learning theorists than to anyone else. For almost all real-life learning involves both types of conditioning. And both kinds of conditioning are built on the innate response tendencies that most organisms are born with.

Question: Suppose, using operant techniques, you trained a dog to press a bar to get food. Do you think that, at some time during the training, the animal might learn involuntarily to salivate at the sight of the bar?

Biofeedback

For many years, psychologists believed that it was nearly impossible to use Skinnerian techniques to help organisms gain voluntary control over their autonomic responses. Recently, however, a number of experiments using a technique called **biofeedback** have challenged this view.

Biofeedback in Medicine

Suppose you were a physician trying to treat a 40-year-old woman suffering from hypertension, or high blood pressure. And further suppose the woman was so sensitive to drugs that you couldn't use any kind of medication to help lower her blood pressure. What could you do to help?

You might begin by teaching her the "relaxation techniques" we discussed in the previous chapter. But surely it would help if the patient had some way of knowing when her blood pressure was rising, and when it was falling. You might then hook the woman up to a machine that gave her *visual feedback* about a specific *biological* response (her blood pressure). If she *saw* the pressure was rising, she could "go limp" and try to think relaxing thoughts. And if she *saw* the pressure was falling, she could try to remember what she was thinking so she could repeat that calming thought in the future.

In their 1980 book *Biofeedback*, David Olton and Aaron Noonberg report considerable success in training hypertensive patients to gain voluntary (operant) control over heart rate and blood pressure. Olton and Noonberg have also found biofeedback useful in treating asthma, epilepsy, stomach disorders and migraine headaches. In all these cases, the secret of success lies in finding some way of giving patients new types of feedback about their involuntary bodily processes. During a migraine attack, for instance, patients often have abnormally cold hands and an unusually warm forehead. By using machines that provide visual feedback on their skin temperatures, patients are often able to warm up their hands

Emit (ee-MITT). The important association in operant conditioning is between the response itself and the reward that follows. If a rat is trained to press a lever only when a light is turned on, the rat is said to "emit" the response *in the presence of* the light stimulus. However, the light doesn't really elicit the bar-press response. It merely serves as a "discriminative" stimulus that lets the rat know that if it now emits a response, that response will be rewarded.

Biofeedback. Literally, biological feedback. Any mechanism that feeds back information on biological performance, such as an EEG machine. See Chapter 3.

and cool down their foreheads voluntarily. This operant control of skin temperature frequently helps reduce the severity of the headache (see Fig. 15.7).

Olton and Noonberg note that the use of biofeedback is in its infancy in medical circles. But they believe that operant technology will surely be widely employed in the future to help sick people gain voluntary control over many of their physiological responses. And how odd it is that a laboratory technique developed in order to train pigeons would turn out to have such usefulness for humans.

Skinner's Approach: An Evaluation

B.F. Skinner has developed what is clearly the most advanced technology the world has ever known for helping people change their behaviors. As powerful as the Skinnerian system is, however, it suffers from the same narrowness of view that afflicts most other psychological theories.

For one thing, Skinner views the organism as being a *passive receptor* of stimuli from the outside world. You have no "free will" because your actions are determined primarily by your past experience and your present environment. "People have assumed from the beginning of time that they initiate their own actions," Skinner said in an interview printed in *The New York Times* on September 15, 1981. "To suppose this is a great mistake." Instead of your *selecting* your own behaviors, he says, the environment does this for you. Skinner thus banishes all of motivational and cognitive psychology from what he calls "the scientific study of behavior."

Nor does he give much **credence** to biology. "I don't deny the importance of genetics," he said in the *Times* interview. However, Skinner believes that the only thing your genes do for you is to "program" you to respond to environmental inputs in an operant manner. Skinner thus dismisses most of physiological psychology from his system.

And because he pays most attention to the effects that the environment has on *individual organisms*, Skinner has added little to social psychology. He believes the study of group processes and other social variables is mostly a waste of time. For from Skinner's viewpoint, "scientific psychology" consists entirely of the study of the effects that the outside world has on the measurable behaviors of *individual* organisms.

Skinner and Self-Control

Skinner takes a very pessimistic view of the world these days, primarily because he views organisms as *passive* rather than *active living systems*. He looks at people from the outside in, and refuses even to guess at "what goes on inside the mind." He talks about feedback, but not about feed-forward. He measures biological rewards such as food, but ignores most psychological and social reinforcers. And he refuses to deal with such concepts as perceptions, cognitions, and self-awareness. Thus he fails to understand the importance of such "systems properties" as **self-control**.

When Skinner trains a pigeon to bowl, *he* determines what the goal of the training will be. *He* measures the entering behaviors of the bird, and *he* selectively reinforces approximations to the goal. The bird *behaves*; Skinner *monitors* these behaviors and *gives the animal feedback* in order to shape its responses. Because Skinner can tell you what he is doing as he goes along, he can describe both the terminal response and the approximations in measurable terms. Thus he doesn't need to talk about what goes on inside the pigeon's mind, and he can legitimately claim that such intra-psychic concepts as "thinking" and "self-control" aren't needed in order to explain behavior.

However, humans are more complex systems than are pigeons, and you can use operant techniques to change your own outputs *voluntarily* in a wide variety of ways. The problem for Skinner is that this sort of self-determined change is difficult to explain in purely operant terms.

Cognitive Behavior Modification

Given the history of our science, Skinner's demand that psychologists deal with measurable events was certainly a step in the right direction. And surely the techniques of *behavior modification* he developed in the 1940's and 1950's have given us powerful tools to help us change ourselves. However, even Skinner's own students seem to have passed him by. By the 1960's, several psychologists had shown that operant techniques could be used to shape thoughts and perceptions as well as overt actions. Intra-psychic events thus became "inner behaviors" that obeyed the same operant principles as did such "overt behaviors" as bowling and pecking a button in a Skinner box. Simple operant technology thus evolved into **cognitive behavior modification**, and behavioral therapists started shaping their patients' thoughts and feelings as successfully as they shaped muscle movements.

More than this, the cognitive behavior modifiers have learned that they can teach their patients to *modify their own thoughts and actions*. It is this self-determined change that Skinner has the most difficulty in explaining, for he denies the concept of "self" entirely.

As we noted, no one living has contributed more to psychology than has B.F. Skinner. But, in a sense, you demonstrate the narrowness of his viewpoint each time you have a creative insight, experience the joy of learning, think through a problem, or voluntarily control your thoughts, feelings, or behavioral outputs in order to achieve some personal goal.

Summary

1. Until recently, **disciplinarian** teachers used **repetition and punishment** to train their pupils, while **humanistic** teachers gave their students encouragement but little intellectual guidance. Both approaches stem from early **theories of learning**. The disciplinarians took their cue from Pavlov and Thorndike, while the humanists followed the lead of the **Gestalt** and **cognitive** theorists.
2. E.L. Thorndike assumed that humans learn in much the same way that animals do. His studies with cats in a **puzzle box** led him to believe that most new behaviors come about by **trial-and-error learning**.
3. Thorndike stated that learning is influenced by two laws:
   a. The **law of exercise** states that the more frequently an animal repeats an **S-R bond**, the stronger it becomes.
   b. The **law of effect** states that stimulus-response (S-R) bonds are strengthed if the effect of the response is to yield the animal a reward. Early in his career, Thorndike also stated that punishment "broke" S-R bonds, but he recanted that view later on.
4. Thorndike, like Pavlov, believed that all learning is mechanical or **reflexive**. **Gestalt psychologists**, such as Wolfgang Koehler, as-

sume that animals are capable of thinking about what they do and of solving problems mentally (through **insight**) rather than just through mechanical trial and error.

5. According to Tolman, animals do not learn a maze by acquiring hundreds of S-R connections. Rather, they make a **cognitive map** of the maze which guides their behavior.

6. B.F. Skinner, a behaviorist much like Thorndike, developed **operant conditioning**—a method of training organisms that differs from **Pavlovian** or **respondent conditioning**. Operant technology is by far more effective in the classroom (and elsewhere) than are either Pavlovian or Gestalt techniques.

7. Pavlov believed that the CS **elicits** or pulls the CR out of the animal involuntarily. Skinner believes that animals **emit** responses freely and the environment rewards some of those responses but ignores or punishes others.

8. According to Skinner, **reinforcement** tends to increase the probability that an organism will emit the same response the next time it is free to do so.

9. Training an organism by operant (Skinnerian) techniques consists of several steps:
   a. First, the **terminal response** or goal of the training must be stated in measurable terms.
   b. Second, the **baseline behaviors** (what the organism is doing before intervention begins) must be measured precisely.
   c. Third, those baseline behaviors that seem directed toward the terminal response are **rewarded**. All other responses are *ignored*.
   d. Each small step toward the goal is reinforced—a technique called **shaping**.

Credence (KREE-dense). From the Latin word meaning "to trust, or believe." To give credence to something is to trust in its value.

Self-control. A property of living systems. The ability to control your inner processes and outputs voluntarily in order to gain those inputs you desire.

Cognitive behavior modification. The use of Skinnerian techniques to modify or change inner processes (thoughts, feelings) as well as behavioral outputs.

10. Generally speaking, **variable ratio reinforcement schedules** yield smoother **cumulative records** (response curves) than do **fixed ratio schedules**.

11. **Punishment** temporarily *suppresses* behaviors, but does not usually **extinguish** them. Punishment differs from **negative reinforcement**, which rewards a response by terminating an unpleasant drive or stimulus.

12. Generally speaking, Pavlovian or respondent conditioning involves those **involuntary muscles** controlled by the **autonomic nervous system** or the **lower brain centers**.

13. Generally speaking, operant conditioning involves those **voluntary muscles** controlled by the **cortex** and **higher brain centers**.

14. The proper use of **biofeedback** can allow you to gain voluntary control over such involuntary responses as your heart rate, skin temperature, and so forth.

15. Although Skinner claims that all behaviors are directly controlled by environmental inputs, he has problems explaining **voluntary self-control** in purely operant terms.

16. In the 1960's, many behavioral psychologists adapted Skinner's techniques to the shaping of thoughts and feelings, a technique called **cognitive behavior modification**.

(Continued from page 349.)

FROM: Experimenter-in-Chief, Interstellar Labship PSYCH-192
TO: Director, Bureau of Science

Thlan, my friend, this will be an informal memo. I will send the official report along later, but I wanted to give you my impressions first.

The work with the newly discovered species is, unfortunately, at a standstill. Things went well at first. We picked what seemed to be an average but healthy animal and began testing it with our standard apparatus. I may have told you that this new species looks much like our usual laboratory subject, the White Rote. So we gave it a couple of the "toys" that the Rotes seem fond of—thin sheets of material made from woodpulp and a tiny stick of graphite. Imagine our delight when this new specimen made exactly the same use of the materials as have many of the Rotes. Could it be that there are certain innate behavior patterns to be found throughout the universe in the lower species?

The answer is of little importance, really. Your friend Verpk keeps insisting that the marks the Rotes make on the sheets are an attempt at communication, but that is, of course, utterly impossible. (Why did you saddle me with this idiot anyway when there are so many reasonable-thinking scientists available?) At any rate, this "scribbling" behavior did give us hope that the new species would behave according to accepted theory.

And at first this was the case. The animal solved the Bfian Box problem in short order, yielding as beautiful data as I have ever seen. We then shifted it to mazes and jump stand problems, and the results were equally pleasing. The animal clearly learns by forming conditioned reflexes linking stimuli with responses in purely mechanical fashion.

Then, just to please Verpk, we tested it on the Oddity Problem. Now you and I both understand that lower organisms are not that bright, even if some cognitive theorists (whom I shall not name) disagree. For a few terrible trials, it seemed that those nameless theorists might be right! Which is to say that the animal *appeared* to react correctly even to stimuli it had never seen before! What an annoyance that would be since we are committed to "protecting" species intelligent enough to form concepts.

Ah, well, not to worry. The Oddity Problem apparently overloaded its simple brain circuits, for the organism soon broke down and became quite ill. Probably just as well, since this species is obviously unsuited for further experimentation.

I am not sure what to do next, either with this specimen or the world from which we took it. One of the students has nursed the animal back to some sort of health, and wishes to keep it as a pet. Verpk, however, suggests we put it back where we found it, and that we begin a crash program to see if these organisms really are concept-formers. Stupid suggestion, but I pass it along anyhow. My own belief is that we should sacrifice the animal and study its anatomy carefully to determine if it really is related to the White Rote.

But that is not why I write. Since this new species tends to break down readily under stress—much like Lavpov's Wogs—I see little sense in wasting our time in this part of the universe. We will not serve either our race or our glorious theories by studying what is clearly another stupid species.

The question is, then, should we stay here and continue our work as Verpk insists, or should we look for healthier and more normal animals elsewhere? And if we depart, should we first destroy the "home colony" so that these pests cannot be used in unscientific ways by those cognitive theorists whom I refuse to name?

Since all lower species are under your protection, we need your advice. My hope is that you will let us seek out new colonies and test our theories with *healthy* animals. For it is only in this fashion that science as we know it progresses.

Respectfully yours,
Iowyy

Recommended Readings

Birbaumer, Niels, and H.D. Kimmel, eds. *Biofeedback and Self-Regulation* (Hillsdale, N.J.: Erlbaum, 1979).

Davis, Hank, and Harry M.B. Hurwitz, eds. *Operant-Pavlovian Interactions* (Hillsdale, N.J.: Erlbaum, 1977).

Gatchel, R.J., and Kenneth P. Price, eds. *Clinical Applications of Biofeedback: Appraisal and Status* (New York: Pergamon Press, 1979).

Hall, John F. *Classical Conditioning and Instrumental Learning: A Contemporary Approach* (Philadelphia, Pa.: Lippincott, 1976).

Koehler, Wolfgang. *Gestalt Psychology* (New York: Liveright, 1947).

Skinner, B.F. *Walden Two* (New York: Macmillan, 1960).

Skinner, B.F. *Reflections on Behaviorism and Society* (Englewood Cliffs, N.J.: Prentice-Hall, 1978).

Memory 16

Did You Know That . . .

You have not one memory, but many different kinds of memories?

Your eyes momentarily store an "exact photo" of what you see, but your brain "forgets" most of what your eyes see?

Your Short-term Memory is limited to about seven items?

Your Long-term Memory consists in part of "mental file cards" that allow you to reconstruct past events rather than remember them exactly?

Amnesia typically involves forgetting "what" but not "how to"?

People suffering from aphasia sometimes can read the word "hymn," but not the word "him"?

When you learn, you seem to "re-program" your own brain?

Some scientists believe that, when you learn, your brain manufactures new "memory molecules"?

Some experiments suggest these "memory molecules" can be transferred from one organism to another by injection?

"Where Is Yesterday?"

"Custard cups?" Bill Plautz said in a shocked tone of voice as he unpacked the groceries. "You and Tom bought 32 glass custard cups?"

"Sure," Devin Eckhoff replied, a happy smile on his face. "They were only a dime apiece."

"You two paid 10 cents *each* for 32 glass custard cups?" Bill continued in an outraged tone of voice. "And you took the money out of our *grocery* budget?"

"Sure," Tom Laine said, sitting down at the kitchen table. "Better than taking it out of the beer budget."

Mike Keller looked up from his math book. "The four of us share and share alike in this apartment, Tom. So how could you and Devin spend $3.20 plus 16¢ sales tax for glass dishes, particularly when you know I don't even *like* custard!"

"The cups aren't for custard," Devin said. "They're for the worms."

"Oh," said Bill, his voice dropping a full octave on that single word. "Why didn't you say so?"

"You didn't ask," Tom responded.

Bill rummaged through the grocery bag a bit more. "And what is this tiny piece of beef liver for? Are we supposed to make a meal of this?"

"No, but the worms will love it," Devin said. "They don't eat very much, you know."

Mike sighed. "Neither will we, if you guys whoop off all our grocery money on worm dishes and beef liver."

"Well," Tom said. "You know we all agreed to work together on the research project that's required for our lab course in animal behavior."

"Yeah," Devin continued. "And we all agreed we'd try to condition planarian flatworms, to see if they could learn."

"Nobody's done it before, remember?" Tom said excitedly.

"I still don't see why we have to do this research project in our kitchen," Bill said, continuing to put away the food that Devin and Tom had bought.

"Because Professor Sauermann hates flatworms," Devin replied. "So he won't let us work in the animal labs."

Mike groaned. "That's no way to get an A on our project, you know. Doing research that Sauermann doesn't approve of."

"Our worm project is going to be so fantastic, he's bound to approve of it eventually," Tom said. "It might even make us famous!"

"Humph," Bill said, reaching the bottom of the grocery bag. "And what, may I ask, are these tiny camel's hair brushes for? Are we going to paint the worms different colors, or something?"

"We need the brushes to transfer the worms from the cups to the training trough," Devin replied. "You can't just pick 'em up with your fingers, you know. They're slippery little rascals, and they're only about an inch long."

"Speaking of worms, where are we going to get them?" Mike asked.

Tom laughed. "We're going to 'liberate' them from the pond in front of the biology building. I was over there yesterday. There are hundreds of the wee beasties crawling around in the muck at the bottom of the pond."

"And what about the training trough?" Mike asked.

"That's my department," Bill replied. "I'm working in Dr. Eastrum's chem lab this semester. He's got a dandy block of plastic he isn't using, and I can borrow his tools to gouge a tiny trough into it. And I've tucked away a couple of thick brass pins I can insert at either end of the trough to use as electrodes to pass shock through the water in the trough."

Devin frowned. "We still need a shock source of some kind."

"Dr. Calvin was showing me through the Psych Department Museum the other day," Mike replied. "They've got boxes and boxes of junky old equipment stuck away in the back room. One entire box was filled with strange metal devices that Dr. Calvin called 'Harvard inductoriums.'"

"Called *what*?" Tom asked.

"Inductoriums," Mike replied. "They're an old-fashioned contraption invented at Harvard around the turn of the century. Psychologists used it to shock undergraduates in verbal learning studies, or something."

"Do you think it would work with worms in a water-filled trough?" Bill asked.

"Probably," Mike replied. "And think how impressed Dr. Sauermann would be if we told him we gave our planarians a 'Harvard education.'"

Devin laughed, then turned serious. "All right, you guys. It's time we got organized. Mike, you go over to the Psych Building and see if you can scrounge one of those inductoriums when nobody's looking. And Bill, you go over to Eastrum's lab and get that trough put together."

"What about you and Tom?" Mike asked.

Tom grinned. "We're off to the biology pond to free 32 flatworms from their muckish existence."

"What are you going to do if somebody catches you?" Bill asked.

"Oh, we'll worm our way out of it somehow," Devin replied.

"I found a couple of fat ones," Tom said, carefully brushing two flatworms off a leaf into the bucket of water that he and Devin had beside them.

"Great," Devin replied.

"Hey, what are you two guys doing?" a male biology student asked, walking up to the pond.

Tom looked up at the young man. "Gathering specimens for an experiment."

"What kind of specimens?"

"Flatworms," Devin said casually.

"Oh, platyhelminthes," the biology student said knowingly. "What are you going to do with them?"

"We're going to train them in a conditioning trough," Devin replied.

The biology student shook his head in dismay. "Don't be silly. Worms can't learn."

"How do you know that?" Tom asked.

"Because I was reading Libbie Hyman's classic work on platyhelminthes just last week, and she says they can't learn. That's why," the student replied.

"Why can't they?" Devin responded. "They've got brains and a primitive nervous system. They've even got synapses."

The biology student laughed. "Who cares about synapses? If worms could learn, a zoologist would have done the study already. And then it would be reported in Hyman."

"Well, did any zoologist you know of ever try to condition a planarian?" Tom asked.

"Of course not," the student replied. "It would be a waste of time, because organisms that simple are incapable of forming associations."

Devin looked at Tom, and then grinned broadly. "Well, judging from the specimens I've seen today, I'm not sure that even biology students are capable of learning."

The biology student shifted uncomfortably on his feet. "Does the Chairman of the Biology Department know you're stealing our worms?"

"No," said Tom. "But we'll be sure to give the Biology Department credit when we publish our study proving planarians can learn."

"Yeah," Devin continued. "We'll mention you guys in a worm-sized footnote."

"Well, now, let's see," Bill said, laying out all of the equipment on the kitchen table. "We've got the worms . . ."

"Thirty-two fat and healthy specimens, housed in individual custard cups," Tom remarked in a happy tone of voice.

"We've got the trough gouged out of the plastic block that I swiped from Eastrum's laboratory. It's precisely 8 inches long, half an inch wide, and half an inch deep."

"And it's filled to the top with pond water," Mike added.

"Water, courtesy of your old buddies, Devin and Tom, who risked life and limb to steal it from the biology building pond," Devin remarked.

"The electrodes at either end of the trough are connected to a 6-volt battery by means of a Harvard inductorium," Bill continued.

Mike interrupted him with a laugh. "Professor Calvin thought I was crazy, you know, borrowing such an *old-fashioned* piece of equipment."

"And we've got Tom's goose-necked study lamp to provide light to shine on the worms as the conditioning stimulus," Bill said.

"How many groups are we going to run?" Mike asked.

"Four," Bill said. "An experimental group that gets the light paired with the shock, and three control groups. With the experimental animals, we turn the light on for two seconds, then shock them. The light is the CS, the shock is the UCS."

"What's the CR?" Tom asked.

"The 'scrunch' the worm makes when we shock it," Bill said.

Devin asked, "How are we going to prove to Professor Sauermann that the experimental animals have learned?"

Mike replied. "On each trial, we observe the worm to see what it does during the two seconds after the light comes on and before the shock starts. At the beginning of training, the animal shouldn't respond much to the light at all."

"Oh, I see," Devin said. "But as we train the animal, it should start 'scrunching' to the light more and more frequently."

"That's right," Tom said. "Because the light becomes a signal that the worm is about to get blasted. So it 'scrunches' in anticipation of the shock."

"But do we really need *three* control groups?" Mike asked plaintively, thinking of all the work involved.

Bill grinned. "Absolutely. We've got to prove it's the *pairing* of the light and shock that causes any change in the way the worms respond. So the first control group gets light, but no shock. The second group gets shock but no light. And the third group gets both light and shock, but they're not paired. The response rate to the light should increase significantly in the experimental subjects, and decrease in the three controls groups."

"Okay, who does what when?" Devin asked.

"Mike and I will train two groups each day," Bill said, "And you and Tom can train the other two groups. We'll switch groups daily, to equalize the work."

"And when you and Mike are working, Tom and I can go play racquetball," Devin remarked.

"Yeah," Tom said, grinning. "And ever since Devin got hit in the eye with a ball, you should see him 'scrunch' whenever I serve him a zinger."

"Hey, man, you've got me conditioned!" Devin laughed.

They flipped a coin, and Bill and Mike won the honor of starting first. So while Devin and Tom went off to the racquetball courts, Mike and Bill settled down to work. Mike put a healthy planarian in the trough, and then told Bill to get ready. When the worm was crawling steadily in a straight line, he called out, "Now."

Immediately Bill switched on the light. Two seconds later, he turned on the shock for half a second. The Harvard inductorium buzzed noisily.

"Boy," Mike said. "You should have seen that baby scrunch."

"Before or after the shock?" Bill asked.

"After the shock," Mike replied. "He sort of wiggled his nose for a fraction of a second when the light came on. But he didn't scrunch at all until you zapped him."

"Okay," Bill said. "We'll put down, 'Trial 1, W for Wiggle.'"

"Get ready for the next trial," Mike said moments later. And when the worm was again moving steadily in a straight line, he said, "Now!"

And again, Bill turned on the light for two seconds, and then the shock.

"Not even a wiggle that time," Mike announced. A few seconds later, he told Bill, "Ready . . . . Now!"

Bill applied the light and the shock.

"A scrunch!" Mike said excitedly. "A good, clean scrunch."

"Great," said Bill. "Let me observe the next worm while you run the light and shock."

"Sure," Mike replied. Then, as he waited for the worm to turn around at the end of the trough and start moving steadily again, he continued. "Do you *really* think these funny little critters are capable of learning?"

Bill thought a moment. "The worms will answer that for us, Mike. The important question is whether Devin will ever learn to wear goggles when he plays racquetball with Tom."

Mike sighed. "Oh, well. Maybe if worms can learn, humans can too." Then, noticing the planarian was again moving majestically down the trough, he said, "Ready . . . . Now!"

(Continued on page 385.)

Memory

What time is it?

A simple question you probably are frequently asked. And how do you respond? Probably you look at your watch, or at a clock, and you give the answer almost automatically. If you are **bilingual**—that is, if you speak another language besides English—you will answer the question in whatever language the question was asked in.

"What time is it?" A simple question, true. But we know very little about how your brain processes such inputs, and we know even less about how your brain responds so appropriately. If we explore this question further, though, you might well gain an even greater respect for—and understanding of—the complexities of both your mind and your nervous system.

Memory Systems

To answer any question, you must make use of your **memory**. If someone asks you the time, you must first recognize that someone has spoken to you. Next you must check your memory banks to make sure you recognize the language the person has used. Then you must realize that you have been *asked a question* to which you should respond.

But while your brain is "checking all these things out," *it must have some way of remember-*

Bilingual (buy-LING-wall). From the Latin words *bi*, meaning "two," and *lingua*, meaning "tongue" or "language." The term "lingo," meaning the slang words used by a particular group of people, also comes from the Latin word *lingua*. For that matter, so does the word "slang."

Memory. From the Latin and Greek words meaning "to be mindful, or to remember." Your memory is your store of past experiences, thus the seat of your ability to recreate or reproduce past perceptions, emotions, thoughts, and actions.

ing what the original question was. If you had no way of holding the question in some kind of "temporary storage," you'd end up realizing that someone had asked you something without being able to remember what the question was.

We really don't know precisely where in your brain memories are stored. But consider this important fact: You can lose your ability to recall *immediate* events, yet still be able to remember things that happened years ago. Thus a different part of your brain apparently is involved in *temporary storage* of the question, "What time is it?" than is involved in *answering* the question itself.

Question: Suppose you are reading an interesting book when someone nearby asks you something. Have you ever responded with "What did you say?" and then, even before the question could be repeated, given the correct answer?

Memory Sub-Systems

In point of fact, you don't have just one "memory system," you have several "memory sub-systems." And they typically perform their functions *in sequence*. Whenever a new stimulus comes to your attention, your *receptors* appear to hold on to the stimulus pattern for a fraction of a second while some part of your brain "looks the stimulus over" to see if it is familiar to you. If you recognize the input, another part of your brain then takes over and "memorizes" the most *salient* or important parts of the stimulus for a few seconds while the rest of your brain decides what to do with the incoming message.

Sensory Information Stage

What time is it?

When the image of those words first impinges on the retinas in your eyes, your rods and cones respond by sending a characteristic *pattern of nerve impulses* along your optic nerve to the visual centers of your brain.

Suppose that we flashed the words "What time is it?" on a screen for exactly one-tenth of a second. How long would your rods and cones continue to respond after the words had disap-

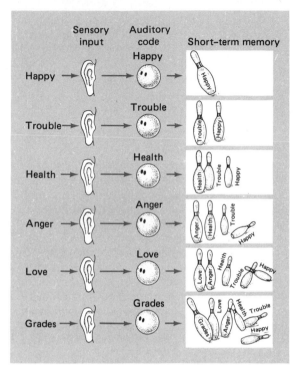

Fig. 16.1. Short-term Memory storage.

peared? The answer is—it depends. If you had been sitting in absolute darkness for several minutes, the words *What time is it?"* would hang suspended in your visual field for quite some time. However, if you were sitting in a lighted room, the next thing you looked at would erase the phrase "What time is it?" from your retina. Under normal conditions—as you look from one object to another in your visual world—your eye holds on to each stimulus pattern for but a fraction of a second before that pattern is replaced by yet another visual input.

Your memory *begins*, then, in your receptors—in what psychologists call the **Sensory Information Storage** stage of information processing. When your eye briefly "stores" a visual input, it records the scene in amazing detail, much as a photograph would. However, by the time this visual information reaches your brain, and you become aware of what you are looking at, much of the rich detail is lost.

To put the matter another way, your *eye* has a "photographic memory," but your *brain* doesn't. For as soon as the lower centers in your brain receive the input, they begin "processing" or "analyzing" the message for its meaning and importance. These lower centers promptly reject any trivial part of the input.

Short-Term Memory

While the lower centers of your brain are judging the *importance* of the incoming message, other parts of your brain make a preliminary interpretation of what the stimulus input *means*. While this "interpreting" is going on, your brain must be able to put the stimulus input on "hold" for a few moments. So your brain *codes* the input and tucks it away in your **Short-term Memory** while the input is being processed. Generally speaking, anything coded for Short-term Memory has a very brief lifetime—probably no more than 30 seconds or so.

"Coding" for Short-term Memory often involves translating visual stimuli into sounds. For instance, suppose we flash the letters *aqvom* on a screen for half a second and ask you to remember them. Then, 15 seconds later, we ask you to repeat what you saw. If you make a mistake, you are most likely to substitute a letter that *sounds like* the one you missed instead of a letter that *looks like* the one you forgot. That is, you are more likely to substitute *c* for *v* than *w* for *v*, despite the fact that *v* looks more like *w* than *c*.

Your Sensory Information Storage system records (momentarily) a more-or-less exact copy of the stimulus pattern. Your Short-term Memory holds the *auditory representation* of this pattern for a few seconds longer, while the rest of your brain is deciding how best to respond to the stimulus. But much of the complexity of the stimulus pattern is lost in the short-term storage process. To prove this fact to yourself, read the following sentence rapidly and then look away from the page for a few seconds and try to remember exactly what the stimulus sentence was:

Который час?

Chances are, unless you are familiar with the Russian language, you had a difficult time trying to remember what you actually saw. You surely sensed at once that the sentence was written in a language other than English. But could you "see" in your mind's eye each of the letters in that strange (to us) alphabet that the Russians use? Or was it more or less a jumbled blur?

Question: *Would a camera have any more difficulty photographing the phrase in Russian than in English? Why does this fact suggest that your Short-term Memory stores items in* sounds *rather than as* visual stimuli?

Familiar Items

Now glance quickly at the following stimulus sentence and then look away and try to visualize exactly what it says:

What time it is?

When this phrase appeared in Russian, your Short-term Memory couldn't "code" the words very well because (chances are) you couldn't say them aloud. But when the phrase appeared in English, you remembered it very well, because you knew the *sounds* of the words. Generally speaking, *familiar items* are much easier to "code into sounds" than unfamiliar items. Your Short-term Memory can hold a familiar item for 30 seconds or so. Less-familiar items (such as the phrase in Russian) tend to drop out much more rapidly.

Question: Look again at the "stimulus phrase" one paragraph above. Does it really say what you remembered it as saying? If you didn't perceive it correctly, what does this fact tell you about your Short-term Memory?

Sensory Information Storage. The first stage of memory storage. Your sensory receptors hold a more-or-less exact copy of an input for a fraction of a second before that copy is "erased" by the next input.

Short-term Memory. As incoming stimulus messages are passed to the brain from Sensory Information Storage, some part of the brain translates them into an auditory code or representation of the input and "remembers" them for a few brief seconds. You typically hold no more than about seven items at a time in your Short-term Memory.

Long-term Memory. Your store of permanent memories. Inputs that are important enough to survive your Short-term Memory are transferred to long-term storage by some biological mechanism we don't yet understand. Salient features of an input are stored according to various categories. Long-term memory also includes an auditory representation of the input and information on how to reproduce the item in writing or speech.

Limited Capacity

Your Short-term Memory ordinarily cannot store more than six or seven items simultaneously. At the moment that your brain inserts an item into Short-term Memory, that item is strong and clear and easy to recall if you do so *immediately*. But shortly thereafter, your brain tucks away a second item, and then a third item, and a fourth. Although only a few seconds have passed, you will now have much more trouble trying to recall what the first item was.

By the time your brain has pressed five or six new items down on top of the first, that original item has lost most of its strength and has faded away. The new items appear to *interfere with* or erase the ones in front of them—just as each new visual pattern you look at wipes clean the stimulus you were looking at just a moment before (see Fig. 16.1).

While you are holding an item in Short-term Memory, you can recall it more-or-less at will. However, once the item drops out of "temporary storage," it is likely to be gone forever—unless your brain decides to make a *permanent record* of the stimulus input.

Long-Term Memory

If you stroll along a busy street, you may see a thousand different people in one short hour. Most of their faces will fade from your memory almost immediately. Yet some things (and faces) you remember vividly—or at least you think you do.

For example, think of the last long trip you took. Can you recall *right at this instant* the exact date and hour that the trip began and ended? Chances are that you can't. But if you actually take the time to think about the details—and per-

haps write them down as you go—you'll find that you can *reproduce* a surprising amount of detail about that trip, even though it may have occurred months or years ago. However, if you inspect those memories carefully as they pop back into consciousness, you'll find they are *qualitatively* quite different from the immediate memory you have of a face you've just seen.

In fact, your recollection of things that happened long ago usually is hazy and incomplete at first. The reason for this haziness was explained more than 100 years ago by Hermann Ebbinghaus, one of the earliest and greatest investigators of human memory. Ebbinghaus proved that you typically don't *remember* complex events. Rather, you recall a few "high points" and then *reconstruct* the experience piece by little piece (see Fig. 16.2).

Reconstruction versus Exact Recall

Your Sensory Information Stage memory is a more-or-less *exact copy* of the original sensory input. Your Short-term Memory is rather like an "instant replay" on television—a few seconds of highlight action that you can recall with considerable clarity for a brief period of time thereafter. But it is the *auditory coding* of the input, and not all the rich sensory detail, that you can replay at will until the sounds fade away into obscurity.

Your **Long-term Memory** seems to be much more complex, for it stores many different aspects of your experiences. First, it records certain *salient features* of your sensory inputs and files these according to various *memory categories*. Second, it creates an *auditory representation* of the input. And third, Long-term Memory records information on how to *reproduce* the items you've filed away—that is, how to write and say things aloud.

Hermann Ebbinghaus

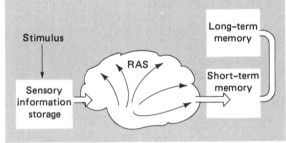

Fig. 16.2. Short- and Long-term Memory flow chart.

Look at the people in this photo for a few seconds, then look away. How long do you think you can remember their faces? **(top)**

When you draw on your Long-term Memory, it then *reconstructs* the event from the associations and auditory representations it has in its files. However, Long-term Memory usually does not allow you to *relive* experiences in any great detail.

Item Storage and Retrieval

Your Long-term Memory is practically limitless—rather like a huge library with billions of books stashed away on the shelves. You add thousands of new volumes to that library every day of your life, but you never seem to run out of shelf space for new arrivals. Nor do you seem to lose track of

most of the items that you've filed away in this brain-library of yours. Still, most of us complain that we have lousy memories. Why?

To appreciate how your Long-term Memory works—and why it often fails to function the way you would like it to—you must first discover the answers to five important questions:

1. What *part* of your immediate psychological experiences do you file away, and which parts do you discard?
2. What psychological and biological mechanisms are involved in storing items in your Long-term Memory?
3. Once an item is placed in your permanent memory bank, how do you go about recalling

it? That is to say, what is the process of **item retrieval** all about?

4. What *changes* in memory occur over time?
5. What causes you to forget things?

As you will see, we have but partial answers to these questions. But by drawing on a wide variety of research sources, we can at least give you a "feel" for how your permanent memory banks function.

Memory Categories

In the November-December 1980 issue of *American Scientist*, Harold Goodglass notes that humans tend to tuck items away in Long-term Memory in terms of several rather specific categories. We can best illustrate these categories by asking you to consider how you might go about filing the word "chair" in your memory banks.

1. *Identity*. First and foremost, you would try to remember the word itself, "chair." But, as you will see, you rapidly split up this category in a variety of ways.
2. *Class*. A chair is a piece of furniture. Thus you would file this item not merely as a word unto itself, but as part of a larger class which would include such other items as "table," "couch," "bed," and "lamp."
3. *Attributes*. A chair is soft or hard, large or small, metal or wood, upholstered or plain. You may enjoy chairs, or hate them. Your memory of a chair, then, includes some notion of the various physical and psychological attributes that a chair has.

"WHEN YOU'RE YOUNG, IT COMES NATURALLY, BUT WHEN YOU GET A LITTLE OLDER, YOU HAVE TO RELY ON MNEMONICS."

Item retrieval. You retrieve items from long-term storage by checking various "categories" under which the item might be filed. If you cannot find the right entry point (or category) to retrieve the item, you will not ordinarily be able to remember it. The item is still in your memory files; you merely don't know where it is located.

Clangs. A technical term meaning "words that sound alike," such as worm, squirm, term, and so forth.

Mnemonics (knee-MON-icks). From the Greek word meaning "mindful." A mnemonic is any device or "trick" that helps you remember things.

4. *Context*. You expect to see a chair in a living room, not inside a bathtub. But you may also remember a specific chair in a rather unusual context, such as an electric chair in a prison, or your mother's chair in her bedroom.
5. *Function*. You associate the word "chair" with certain verbs denoting its function, such as "sit," or "recline."
6. *Sensory Associations*. The word "chair" will be paired with the *sight* of typical chairs, with the *smell* of leather and wood, the *feeling* your skin has when you sit on a chair, and perhaps with a squeaking *sound* that old chairs make when you lean back too far in them.
7. *Clangs and Visual Patterns*. You not only file the *concept* of a chair away in your memory, but also certain salient features of the word itself, such as its *sight and sound*. Thus "chair" will be stored according to its **clangs**, or "sound-alike" words (bear, pear). It will also be filed according to the visual pattern the letters c-h-a-i-r make, the initial letter of the word, the number of syllables in the word, and so forth.
8. *Reproductive Information*. Your Long-term Memory also includes information on the muscle movements needed to *say* the word "chair," to *write* it, to *draw* a picture of a chair, and so forth.

These eight "memory categories" are by no means the only ones having to do with *item storage* in Long-term Memory. But they are perhaps the most important ones, and those most studied by psychologists.

Mnemonics

If nothing else, the eight categories listed above may give you some notions about how to improve your memory. There are a variety of **mnemonics**, or "memory tricks," that psychologists have developed to help people remember things better. Some of these devices involve training you to *associate* whatever you want to recall with something already well-established in your memory banks. Other mnemonics require you to use one

As in the Loftus study, here is the same vehicle approaching the corner where, at one time there was a stop sign; at another time a yield sign.

Elizabeth Loftus

or more of the eight categories in trying to memorize a specific item.

For example, if Mr. Bird looks like an owl, you can make an easy connection between his face and his name. Or you might pick out one salient feature about his background and try to associate that with his name. Something like, "Mr. Bird flew into town three years ago," could do the trick.

If you have a list of terms you must memorize, you might write a poem that includes all the items in the proper order. Or you could take the initial letter of each term and memorize the letters themselves. Recalling the letters at a later time would then give you a clue as to the terms themselves.

Psychologist Laird Cermack lists a great many helpful mnemonics in his 1978 book *Improving Your Memory*. Among other things, he urges you to: (1) pay very close attention to the most important features of what you want to memorize; and (2) organize your thoughts in a logical way. For, as Ebbinghaus noted more than a century ago, the more salient and meaningful an experience is, the more likely it is that you will be able to recall it at a later date.

Forgetting

As Sigmund Freud once said, you learn about the normal by studying the abnormal. In the field of memory research, that certainly is the case. For we have discovered a great deal about *memory* by studying *forgetting*. And we have learned an amazing amount about *item storage* in normal people by investigating the difficulties that brain-damaged people have in *retrieving* even the simplest items from long-term storage.

Let's look at the most common types of "dis-remembering" in some detail.

Neural Decay

The sensory information storage system in your receptors provides you with sharply etched neural impressions of the world around you. But this pattern of neural firing is quickly destroyed in one of two ways—either the receptor neurons adapt to the input (and hence the neural pattern *decays*), or the next visual input "erases" the first input.

Once an input reaches your brain, it may be put into Short-term Memory. But your Short-term Memory is very limited because, as new items are plugged into "temporary hold," older items decay and you thus forget them.

Neural decay is perhaps the simplest type of forgetting.

Interference

New memories interfere with old ones, and vice versa. There are two main types of "memory interference." The first has to do with *item storage and recall*. The second has to do with the fact that new inputs can actually distort or *transform* old memories.

The **serial position effect** is an example of how learning one thing can interfere with storing and recalling other items. Suppose you are asked to memorize a list of 20 ordinary words. You look them over for a minute or so, and then try to recall them from memory. Chances are you will remember the words at the beginning and end of the list much better than the words in the middle. Research suggests that the items at either end of the list *interfere* with your ability to recall the words in the middle. In short, the *position* of the item in the series affects how readily you can remember it later on.

Nor is an item safe from interference once it has been tucked away in your long-term memory banks. In an elegant series of studies, Elizabeth Loftus has shown that what you learn today may actually distort your memory of what happened to you yesterday. In one experiment, Loftus showed films of auto accidents to people, and then asked them questions about what they had seen. If she asked her subjects, "About how fast were the cars going when they *smashed* into each other?", her subjects gave much higher estimates of speed than did subjects who were asked, "About how fast were the cars going when they *collided*?" Apparently, the use of the word "smashed" somehow *changed* the subject's memories of what they had seen!

A week later, Loftus asked these same subjects if they had seen any broken glass in the films. In fact, there was no broken glass. But more of the subjects exposed to the word *smashed* "remembered" seeing broken glass than did those exposed to the word *collided*. Again, the question that Loftus used to pull the memory out of long-term storage seemingly *changed the memory itself*.

In another experiment, Loftus showed half her subjects a series of photos involving a car. One photo showed the automobile approaching a yield sign. The other half of the subjects were exposed to the same series of photos, except that the car was shown approaching a stop sign. Loftus then asked the "yield sign" subjects what the car had done *at the stop sign*. Almost half of these subjects subsequently insisted that the sign had said "stop" instead of "yield."

In brief, what Loftus and other psychologists have demonstrated is this: Items filed in your memory banks can be radically changed by new inputs—even though you are *unaware* that the change has taken place.

Question: *How might the way a lawyer phrases a question affect the answer a witness might give when testifying in court?*

Serial position effect. When you memorize a list of items, they interfere with each other in Long-term Memory. Typically, you will recall items at the start and end of the list better than those items in the middle positions of the series.

Rejection and Repression

The lower centers in your brain scan each incoming stimulus pattern and reject inputs that are meaningless or unimportant to you. Although you are usually unaware of it, this "screening out" of trivial items goes on constantly and is a very necessary part of the forgetting process. (Can you recall *exactly* what the skin on your back felt like 20 minutes ago? How often do you need to recall such items?)

If a given stimulus input is threatening or disturbing, the emotional centers in your brain may *repress* the stimulus and hence make it very difficult for you to remember later on. Repression is thus an unconscious but perhaps "deliberate" form of forgetting.

Cataloging, Filing, and Retrieval Errors

Any item in Short-term Memory that is of real importance to you is processed for Long-term Memory. This processing usually involves cataloging the item in terms of the eight "memory categories" listed above. Your brain also seems to make a "mental index card" for each category under which that experience will be filed. You use these index categories when you try to *retrieve* an item from your memory storage banks. These "mental index cards" occasionally get catalogued in the wrong way, mis-filed, or even totally lost.

Cataloging errors seem to occur most frequently when you have to learn too many things at once. For example, if you are introduced to a dozen unfamiliar people at a party, you may well make some mistakes as you try to attach the right names to the proper faces. If you met one new person a day for a dozen days, you would have a better chance of getting the "file cards" filled out correctly.

Your memory also *mis-files* things occasionally, and thus you will have trouble locating it in your memory banks. The more similar two items are, the more likely it is that one of them will be filed in the place supposedly reserved for the other.

Old experiences are often hard to *retrieve* because you have to scan the millions of similar index cards you've made since then to recover that one unique memory. Brand new experiences are sometimes hard to remember because you have such a limited number of cues as to their location in your long-term files.

According to a 1980 survey made by Elizabeth and Geoffrey Loftus, most people think that Long-term Memory is much like a "video recorder," and that you can *always* recover an item if you try hard enough. As the Loftuses note, though, the experimental data don't support this viewpoint. Indeed, a large number of scientific studies suggest that most of us totally forget much of what we've experienced in the past. And, judging from the bulk of the laboratory studies on this subject, once an item is lost, it's probably gone forever.

Amnesia

Memory is the process by which information is stored in your brain. *Amnesia* is the process by which this information is physically erased from your memory banks, blocked off from easy access, or prevented from being stored in the first place. Amnesia has both biological and psychological causes.

Forgetting "What" but Not "How to"

There is an odd quality to amnesia that has always fascinated scientists. Amnesia due to brain damage seems to affect both verbal and non-verbal material, and it affects all the sensory modalities equally. However, amnesiacs are more likely to forget language skills than motor skills. For example, they may be unable to *say* the word "car" when you show them a picture of one, but will still be able to drive fairly well.

Although amnesia patients typically have difficulty learning new words and concepts, they apparently can do so under the right circumstances. In the October 10, 1980 issue of *Science*, Neal Cohen and Larry Squire report that they were able to teach a number of amnesia patients to read new words *reflected in a mirror*. Although the patients didn't recognize that some words were repeated 20 times or more, they did increase their ability to mirror-read and retained this ability over time. Cohen and Squire believe their study supports the old belief that amnesia affects your ability to remember "what" happened, but not your ability to "know how" to do things.

Retrograde and Anterograde Amnesia

As we will see momentarily, memory storage does not occur instantaneously. Rather, it takes some 30 minutes or so for your Long-term Memory to file an item away. Any physical or psychological *trauma* that occurs to you during this half-hour-long **consolidation period** can prevent the item from being recorded in your memory banks. This type of forgetting is called **retrograde amnesia**, because a shock to your nervous system *now* can erase the memory of something that happened *several minutes earlier* (see Chapter 1). Memories already in long-term storage usually aren't affected by retrograde amnesia since they are already "consolidated."

Severe brain damage and the diseases associated with old age, however, can cause a somewhat different type of forgetting, called **anterograde amnesia**. If you suffered from anterograde amnesia, you could retrieve *old* items with ease, but you no longer would be able to convert *new* items from your Short-term Memory into long-term storage. Thus you would forget the incidents of your daily life shortly after they occurred to you. But you would still be able to remember most things that had happened to you before the anterograde amnesia set in.

Question: *Retrograde amnesia caused by a blow to the head seems to erase memories of what happened 20 to 30 minutes prior to the trauma. Why does this fact suggest that memory storage is basically a* physiological *process?*

Psychological Amnesia

Psychological amnesia, caused by an emotional shock, is really a form of repression. Witnessing a terrible automobile accident can cause you to "block off" all your memories of that fateful day. The items are still in your long-term storage banks, however, and you could probably retrieve them if you tried hard enough to do so (or underwent psychotherapy).

Aphasia

In his 1980 *American Scientist* article, Harold Goodglass defines **aphasia** as impairment in the ability to use or remember language. In right-handed individuals, aphasia typically results from damage to the left hemisphere of the brain. The exact type of language impairment the person suffers depends on what part of the left hemisphere is affected.

Goodglass notes that some aphasic patients can understand the spoken names of American cities and can locate them on a map, but may totally fail to understand names of common body parts. Other patients can understand nouns but not pronouns. For instance, one patient Goodglass describes could read the word "hymn" quite readily, but not the word "him." Still other patients can produce most verbs with ease, but can't produce nouns and adjectives.

Aphasic patients are better at naming things they can see than things they smell or words they hear. They are also better at remembering objects they can touch and feel (ball, spoon) than objects they experience at a distance (cloud, moon). They can occasionally write words they cannot say, or speak words they cannot write. There are many types of aphasia. All of them, however, seem related to one or more of the "eight memory categories" we described earlier.

Types of Aphasia

Those patients who cannot *name* objects readily are said to suffer from **anomic aphasia**. When shown a picture of a fork, an anomic aphasic cannot say "fork." But the person may say something like, "You eat with it," or "I have one at home." One woman suffering from this problem described her daughter's marriage this way: "And then she, you know . . . . dum-dum-dedum" (humming the wedding march). According to Goodglass, most anomic aphasia results from damage to the border area between the temporal and the parietal lobes.

Damage to the rear portion of the temporal lobe can cause a type of problem called **Wernicke's aphasia**. If you showed a picture of a chair to someone with this disorder, the person couldn't say "chair" at all and might well use some made-up term like "chossi" instead. But the person also might substitute a name from the *class* of objects like chairs and say "stool" rather than "chair." A person with this problem obviously has difficulties *locating* an item in long-term storage.

According to Goodglass, damage to the upper portion of the temporal lobe may lead to **conduction aphasia**. If you showed the picture of the chair to someone with this disorder, the individual would typically make repeated efforts to get close to the word, but to no avail. The person might say, "Flair . . . no, swair . . . fair." Thus the person obviously knows the *sound* of the word, but simply cannot reproduce it correctly. Conduction aphasics also seem to know the first letter, the number of syllables, and the sound of the first syllable in the word. Thus they can *locate* the word in their memory banks, and they know the sound and shape of the item. They simply cannot *reproduce* the word unless you say it aloud for them first.

Someone with damage to the "speech center" located between the temporal and frontal lobes is likely to suffer from **Broca's aphasia** (see Chapter 4). A person with this disorder has problems naming numbers and letters, but does reasonably well with colors. The individual often can recognize a word if shown it for a long time, but has difficulty pronouncing it. Thus the person

Consolidation period. The period of time (20 to 30 minutes) which it takes your brain to file an input or experience away in Long-term Memory. Any trauma that disrupts your nervous system during the consolidation process will probably prevent that input from being put in permanent storage.

Retrograde amnesia (RETT-tro-grade am-KNEE-see-ah). "Amnesia" comes from the Greek word meaning forgetfulness. When you are hit on the head, you are likely to forget most of the things that had happened to you for 20 to 30 minutes prior to the blow—but you may very likely remember things that happened immediately after the trauma. The amnesia is "graded" because you will very likely forget *everything* that happened immediately before the trauma, *most* of what happened five minutes before, and *some* of what happened 20 minutes before. The term *retro* means "after the fact."

Anterograde amnesia (an-terr-oh-grade). Memory disorder usually caused by trauma or brain damage involving inability to transfer items from Short-term to Long-term Memory. You can recall things prior to the trauma quite well, but not what happened to you an hour ago.

Aphasia (ah-FAZE-ya). An impairment in the ability to use or remember language.

Anomic aphasia (a-NOM-ick). Memory disorder marked by the inability to recall the names of objects.

Wernicke's aphasia (WERR-nick-ease). Memory disorder marked by the inability to locate an item precisely in long-term storage. Person often substitutes the class of the item for the item's correct name.

Conduction aphasia. Memory disorder in which you can find the item in memory, but cannot reproduce the item in speech without prompting.

Broca's aphasia (BROH-ka's). Memory disorder in which you cannot recall the "shape" or "sound" of an item, even though you may recognize the item as being familiar.

might say "tssair" rather than chair. These patients seem to have little memory of the "shape" of the word or the number of syllables it has.

"Tip-of-the-Tongue" Aphasia

Even people with normal memories sometimes show a momentary type of forgetting called "tip-of-the-tongue aphasia." For example, have you ever tried to retrieve a name from memory, and been quite confident that you knew the word you were looking for? Yet somehow you couldn't reproduce the item when first you tried? Studies of college students who experience this type of momentary aphasia suggest that the students know the sound and shape of the word, its meaning, and the letter it starts with. When told the name, they immediately recognize it as being the word they were searching for.

Question: What does "tip-of-the-tongue" aphasia tell you about the types of mnemonics that might be useful in helping you remember names?

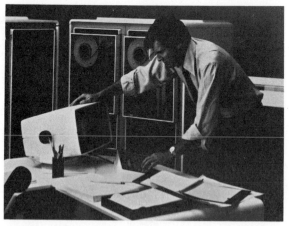

In some ways, your brain functions like a biological computer. **(left)**

Fig. 16.3. As complicated as modern-day computers are, their memory banks are much more limited than those in your brain. **(right)**

Three Stages of Item Retrieval

Based on his extensive study of memory disorders, Harold Goodglass concludes that you probably go through three distinct stages when you are shown an item (such as a picture of a chair) and asked to retrieve the item's name from long-term storage. In the first stage, you *recognize* the item and search through your memory banks for its "file card." In the second stage, you hunt for the *auditory representation* of the item's name. In the third stage, you attempt to discover the set of *motor commands* that will permit you either to speak or write the name.

Those aphasic patients who cannot reproduce a word at all apparently suffer from a breakdown in stage one of the retrieval process: They simply cannot find the right "file card" and often do not recognize the word when you say it aloud for them. Patients who say "stool" for "chair" can get close to the right card, but must settle for the *class* of the item rather than for the item itself.

Aphasic individuals who recognize the word but who say "air" for "chair" apparently suffer from a breakdown in the second stage of item retrieval. They can retrieve the item itself, and they can get close to the *sound* of the word. Indeed, they can often repeat the word when told what it is. But they cannot generally find the correct "auditory representation" on their own.

Some patients recognize the stimulus word, can tell you what other words it sounds like, and indicate in a variety of ways that they know the meaning of the word and most of its attributes. They simply cannot write the word or say it aloud. Goodglass believes these patients suffer from a

breakdown in the third retrieval stage. They can find the "file card" and its "auditory representation," but they have lost access to the "motor commands" that would allow them to reproduce the word as language.

Judging from evidence Goodglass presents, these three different stages of item retrieval are *mediated by different parts of the temporal lobe*. Just how your brain manages to work through all three stages so rapidly when you're asked to name an item, no one really knows. But, as we will see, scientists suspect that changes in your brain's *synapses* are intimately involved in storing items in Long-term Memory.

The Search for the Engram

Logic suggests that, whenever you learn something, there must be a *physical change* of some kind in your brain associated with storing that item away in your permanent memory banks. We call that physical representation of a memory an **engram**.

We *assume* that there must be a different engram for each tiny bit of information you have ever learned, and that your brain therefore is jam-packed with many billions of engrams. But we have no real proof for these assumptions, and no one has ever been able to put a finger on an engram or view one under a microscope. About all we can say is this: On the basis of the laboratory data gathered so far, different sorts of engrams appear to be stored in different parts of your brain.

The "search for the engram," as it is sometimes called, has occupied the attention of thousands of scientists for the past century or so. When scientists first discovered the amazing amount of electrical activity that occurs in the brain (see Chapter 4), they speculated that the engram might be an electrical loop or circuit of some kind. As long as the electricity flowed in its proper pathway through the brain, the engram was maintained. Early computers were built on this memory model. The problem was that if you shut off the electricity even for an instant, the computer lost its memories and couldn't retrieve them even when it was turned on again (see Fig. 16.3).

Years ago, Ralph Gerard and his colleagues tried the same experiment with animals—that is, they turned off all the electrical activity in a hamster's brain to see if this would wipe out the animal's memories. When bears, hamsters, and other beasts go into the deep sleep associated with hibernation, their brain temperatures drop considerably and most electrical activity ceases. So Gerard and his group trained a hamster, then put it to sleep and cooled its brain down until they could no longer detect any electrical responses at all. Later they warmed the animal up again and checked to see what it would remember. The answer was, it could recall *almost everything*. The electrical-current hypothesis had failed, and scientists had to look elsewhere for the engram.

Synaptic Switches

Computers store memories in a variety of ways. One memory device used in computers is a simple switch, which can be left in either an open or closed position. When a message passes through the computer, the switches can route the information from one point to another—much the way the switches in a railroad yard can route a train from one track to another. If you ask a computer a simple question, such as "what is $2 + 2$?", the computer routes your question through a series of switches until the final destination, "4," is reached. Switches are not very complicated mechanisms. But given enough of them, the computer can store almost *any* information, no matter how complicated.

Most scientists believe that the *synapses* in your brain function in much the same way that the switches in a computer do. When someone asks you a question such as "What is your name?", the message must cross over a number of synaptic switching points before you can answer it. If you could rearrange the functioning of these synaptic connections—opening some neural switches and closing others—you could send the message to any part of your brain that held the right answer (see Fig. 16.4).

It is generally agreed that the engram—that physical representation of whatever you remember—must involve some functional change

at the synapse. But there is not much agreement (or solid data) about how you go about shifting the switches in your brain. Many scientists appeal to Thorndike's *law of exercise*, described in the last chapter. And a number of experiments do suggest that if you force a neural message to cross a certain synapse again and again, it is thereafter much easier for the message to take that particular route. Why this might be so, no one really knows. But some scientists believe that a *chemical change* must take place at the synapse when you learn something, and that the chemicals actually "throw the synaptic switch."

The Biochemistry of Memory

Perhaps the first person to speculate in public that chemicals might be involved in memory storage was Ward Halstead. In 1948, Halstead advanced the theory that **RNA** and protein molecules might be the *engrams* that scientists had sought for so many years.

At about the same time, Swedish biologist Holger Hydén said much the same thing. However, Hydén believed that RNA, not protein, was the chief candidate. During the 1950's, Hydén and his colleagues taught various tricks to rats, then looked at the chemical composition of the animals' brains. Hydén and his group theorized that the brain of a trained rat should be *chemically different* from the brain of an untrained rat. Their research tended to support this belief. For they found noticeable changes in the amounts of RNA in the brains of trained animals (as compared with the brains of untrained rats).

Subsequent experiments in laboratories both here and abroad have generally confirmed the view that an organism's brain chemistry is *subtly altered* by whatever experiences the organism has. More important, it now appears that different types of psychological experiences can give rise to quite different sorts of chemical changes.

Whenever an *action potential* sweeps down the axon of a neuron, the cell responds by suddenly increasing its production of several chemical molecules, including RNA. The more vigorously a neuron fires, the more RNA it produces. And the more RNA a nerve cell produces, the

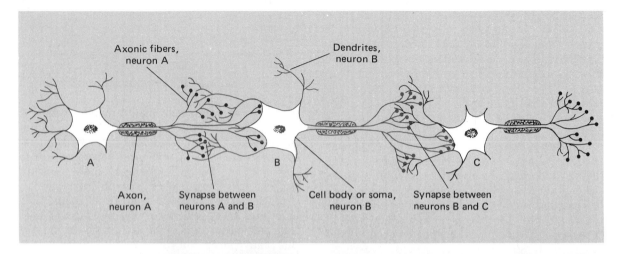

Ward C. Halstead

Senility is a problem many elderly people must face. **(bottom right)**

Fig. 16.4. Three neurons in a row. The axonic fibers of A make synapse with the dendrites and cell body of B, and the axonic fibers of B make synapse with the dendrites and cell body of C. **(top)**

more protein it typically manufactures as well. In short, nerve cells are not only generators of electrical activity, they are very efficient chemical factories too.

Chemical "Erasers"

You are not consciously aware of all the chemical changes taking place in your brain as they occur, of course. But if the changes didn't come about, you probably wouldn't be "aware" of anything at all! For example, what do you think might happen if, while you were studying for an exam, someone injected into your brain a chemical that destroyed RNA? How might that injection affect your ability to learn?

This question was first asked by E. Roy John. In the mid-1950's, John taught a cat a rather difficult task involving visual perception. Once the cat had learned the task and was performing very well, John injected **ribonuclease** into the animal's visual cortex. After the ribonuclease injection, the cat performed as if it had never been trained at all.

Memory Loss in Old People

One of the symptoms associated with **senility** is the type of *anterograde amnesia* we discussed earlier. That is to say, most senile patients are much better at recalling events that happened years ago than they are at learning new things. Psychiatrist D. Ewen Cameron spent many years trying to help older patients in several hospitals in Canada and the United States. His studies were, for a time, aimed at discovering whether or not the *body chemistry* of his patients was measurably different from that of other individuals who were just as old, but who were not senile.

In one of his experiments, Cameron found that senile patients had more *ribonuclease* in their bloodstreams than did non-senile oldsters. Cameron guessed that this enzyme might be destroying brain RNA as fast as the senile person's neurons could manufacture it. And if RNA were involved in helping the brain store away long-term memories, then too much ribonuclease would *wipe out the engrams* before they could become permanent. If so, Cameron thought he might be able to help his patients by *lowering* the amount of ribonuclease in their bodies.

Cameron tried two different types of chemical therapy. First, he injected his patients with large amounts of yeast RNA, hoping that the ribonuclease would attack this foreign RNA rather than the RNA produced by the patient's brains. While this approach seemed to help *some* senile patients recover *part* of their memory functions, the yeast RNA was often impure and gave Cameron's patients fevers. Next Cameron tried giving his subjects a drug that was supposed to increase the *production of brain RNA*. Again, he was fairly successful—but only with people who had not slipped too far into senility. And once the patient was taken off the drug, the person's memory often began to deteriorate again.

Cameron died of a heart attack before he could complete his work. A group of scientists in Italy repeated his research and reported at least partial success, but no one in America seems to have picked up where Cameron left off. However, in the January 1982 issue of *Developmental Psychobiology*, Michael Warren reports that "elderly" mice who were good at problem-solving had more RNA in their brains than did equally old mice who had difficulties with the same tasks. Warren notes that keeping the mice in "exciting environments" increased their brain RNA levels, while confining the mice to "sensory isolation chambers" decreased the amount of RNA in their brains. Warren believes that older humans who maintain an active life in stimulating circumstances need not fear a decline in their mental abilities.

Drugs and Memory

As we noted earlier, your long-term memories take time to form or *consolidate*. Anything that disrupts normal brain function during this consolidation period will interfere with your ability to remember. A number of chemicals, including some antibiotics, have been shown to disrupt memory consolidation in animals if the drugs are given either before or immediately after training trials.

The other side of the memory coin is perhaps a bit more intriguing, however. For it is also true that anything that *facilitates* or speeds up your brain activity during the consolidation period will make it easier for you to form engrams.

Ribonuclease (RYE-bo-NEW-klee-aze). An enzyme (protein) that breaks up, or destroys, RNA. Ribonuclease is found in most living cells.

Senility (see-NILL-uh-tee). From the Latin word *senex*, meaning "old" or "old man." Senility is the loss of physical and mental ability that sometimes accompanies advanced age. Our word "senior" comes from the same Latin source.

We usually think of strychnine as a poison. In fact, it is a neural excitant. In large doses, it causes convulsions and eventual death. In very small doses, strychnine increases neural firing rates much as does the caffeine found in coffee or cola drinks.

If you inject a rat with a tiny amount of strychnine just *before* you train it on a simple task, the rat typically will learn the problem faster. The explanation usually offered for this effect is that strychnine makes the animal more active and alert to its environment; hence it learns faster. However, you can cause a similar "memory facilitation" by giving the strychnine a few minutes *after* the animal has been trained. Now, when you retest the rat on the same problem a day or so later, the animal injected with strychnine will remember the task much better than will a rat injected with salt water.

How can a post-training injection speed up *learning*? It can't, for the rat given the strychnine takes just as long to *learn* the task as does the animal injected with salt water. What the drug apparently does is to make the animal's brain more active during the *consolidation period* following training. And the more active the animal's brain is *following the experience*, the more of the experience it remembers later on. However, the strychnine must be given within 30 minutes or so after the training, or the "facilitation effect" does not take place. A rat injected two hours after training remembers no better than does an uninjected animal.

Memory Transfer

The strongest but most controversial evidence that the engram may be a chemical molecule comes from the so-called "memory transfer" experiments. Since I was personally involved in many of these studies, I hope you will forgive me for writing about them in the first person.

In 1953, when Robert Thompson and I were graduate students at the University of Texas, we attempted to train common flatworms using Pavlovian conditioning techniques. We used light as the CS and shock as the UCS, and were able to show that the animals could make the same sorts

Robert Thompson

Jessie Shelby

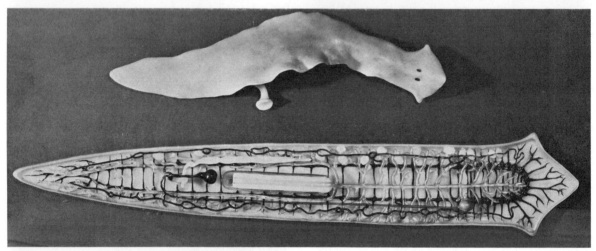

Fig. 16.5. A water-filled training trough for planarians. **(top right)**

Fig. 16.6. The fresh-water planarian has a true brain, a simple nervous system, a food-tube in the middle of its body instead of a mouth, and can regenerate any missing part of its body. **(middle)**

Fig. 16.7. RNA from a conditioned donor being injected into a recipient planarian. **(bottom left)**

of conditioned associations as did Pavlov's dogs (see Fig. 16.6).

The simple **planarian** flatworm we used in our studies reproduces both sexually and asexually (see Fig. 16.5). That is, a flatworm may mate with another planarian and subsequently lay eggs. Or its body may split in half, following which both head and tail sections will **regenerate** into complete worms.

The flatworm is also the simplest animal to possess a true brain and a synaptic-type of nervous system. It was this fact that got Thompson and me interested in working with these animals. In 1953, the synaptic theory of memory storage was just becoming popular. We reasoned that if synapses were important for learning, the flatworm should be capable of learning. Since our conditioning data convinced us this was the case, Thompson and I published our findings in 1955.

Regenerated Memories

When I came to The University of Michigan in 1956, my students and I continued where Thompson and I had left off. Daniel Kimble and Allan Jacobson helped with the first study, which involved training worms and then cutting them in half. We retested both heads and tails a month later, after they had completely regenerated all their missing parts. To our surprise, *both halves* of the worm remembered. We concluded that there was not one engram, but several—scattered throughout the animal's body.

Shortly thereafter, E. Roy John and William Corning discovered they could "erase" a freshly cut tail's memories by exposing it to ribonuclease while it regenerated. Subsequent experiments in Russia and in Turkey suggested that a strong solution of ribonuclease could erase memories even in uncut planarians.

Memory Transfer by Cannibalism and Injection

All of these experiments led me to believe that memory formation somehow involved the creation of new molecules, and that RNA played some part in the process. But how to prove it?

About 1960, it occurred to me that if two worms learned the same task, the chemical changes that took place inside their bodies might also be identical. If this were so, it might not matter how the chemicals got inside the worms. Provided the right molecules were present, the worm should "remember" whatever its chemical engrams told it to remember. Our attempts to test this odd notion took us not to the heart of the matter, but to the worm's digestive system.

In 1960 Reeva Kimble, Barbara Humphries, and I classically conditioned a bunch of "victim" planarians, then chopped them in bits and fed the "trained" pieces to untrained cannibalistic flatworms (our experimental group). We fed untrained victims to another group of cannibals (our control group). After we had given both groups of cannibals a couple of days to "consolidate" their meals, we trained both groups. To our delight, the planarians that had eaten educated victims learned much faster than did the worms that had consumed their untrained brethren. We seemed to have "transferred an engram" from one animal to another.

A year or so later, we extracted RNA from trained worms and injected it into untrained worms. These worms showed a "transfer effect," but worms injected with RNA from untrained planarians did not. (see Fig. 16.7)

In 1964 scientists working in the United States, Denmark, and Czechoslovakia reported similar success using rats rather than worms. And by 1982 several hundred successful memory transfer experiments had been reported in the

Planarian (plan-AIR-ee-ann). A very simple, inch-long flatworm that lives in ponds and streams throughout the world. A much-loved experimental animal used by certain simple-minded psychologists (and thousands of high school students competing in science fairs).

Regenerate (ree-JEN-er-rate). From the Greek and Latin words meaning "to regrow, or replace." Simple animals can often replace large parts of their bodies, including their brains.

Validity (vall-LID-uh-tee). Strong, believable, trustable facts are "valid" facts. The validity of a set of experimental results is the "trustability" of those results.

Reliability (ree-lie-uh-BILL-it-tee). Reliable friends are those people you can count on when the going gets tough—whose behavior toward you never varies. Reliable experiments are those that can be repeated again and again with the same results.

scientific literature. However, we are still far from proving conclusively that memories are coded in RNA, or that engrams can be transferred from one animal to another.

Are Memory Transfer Studies Valid?

To begin with, there is the nagging question of **validity**. That is, when you inject an animal with chemicals taken from a trained donor, are you really transferring *specific memories* or are you merely giving the animal molecules that excite its brain activity as do caffeine and strychnine?

Jessie Shelby and I apparently answered that question for planarians some time ago. We first trained donor worms to go either to the light or the dark arm of a simple, water-filled T-maze. We then fed the donors to untrained cannibals. As we had expected, we got a highly specific "transfer effect." That is, the cannibals learned fastest when trained to go to the same-colored arm as had the donors they ate. However, the most interesting results came from a group of cannibals fed "conflicting instructions." These planarians ingested a "worm stew" made up of some donors trained to go the light-colored arm and of some donors trained to go to the dark arm of the maze. The "conflicting engrams" these cannibals digested made learning more difficult than if they had ingested nothing at all.

Several other laboratories soon showed much the same sort of stimulus-specific transfer using rats and goldfish.

Are Memory Transfer Studies Reliable?

An equally important question has to do with the **reliability** of the transfer effect. In 1970 James Dyal questioned everyone who had attempted transfer experiments with rats and other higher animals. Dyal found that a number of well-known scientists had been *unable* to repeat the memory transfer experiments successfully. However, positive results were reported by more than 100 scientists in a dozen different countries.

Still and all, many scientists remain highly skeptical of this research, perhaps with good reason. For despite the apparent validity and reliability of our studies, we never were able to prove that each memory you form is "coded" by an RNA molecule. Nor could we ever figure out a humane way of testing the transfer effect with humans.

Unraveling the "Memory Code"

Suppose your nerve cells *do* manufacture a unique new set of molecules for each of your memories. What a different world we could create if we could unravel this "memory code!" If we can ever devise *safe* drugs that would speed up learning, we might make college a more effective, less boring experience. And should we find ways to synthesize memories in test tubes, students who "dropped chemicals" might be getting a higher education rather than merely "getting high."

Summary

1. When sensory inputs arrive at your receptor organs, they are held momentarily in what is called **Sensory Information Storage**—an exact copy of the stimulus itself.

2. While your brain is interpreting the input, it typically **codes** the input by translating it into sounds. This **auditory representation** of the input is held briefly in **Short-term Memory**, which has a capacity of about seven items. The "hold time" for an item in Short-term Memory seems to be a minute or so at most.

3. Items drop out of Short-term Memory very rapidly as they are replaced by other incoming stimuli.

4. Important inputs move from Short-term Memory into **Long-term Memory**, which is the permanent "memory bank" of your brain.

5. Your long-term memories seem to be filed by **categories**, so that you can **retrieve** items readily. These categories include the item's name or **identity**, its **class, attributes, context, function**, and various **sensory associations** related to the item. In addition, you record the **sound** and **visual pattern** of words or of the auditory representation of the item.

6. Your Long-term Memory also stores information on how to **reproduce** items—that is, how to say, write, or draw them.

7. Once you understand how your memory files items, you can use **mnemonics** or "memory tricks" to help you remember things.

8. There are many types of **forgetting**:
   a. An input to Sensory Information Storage either **decays** rapidly, or is "wiped out" by the next input.
   b. Items in your Short-term Memory **interfere** with each other, and thus are continually forgotten.
   c. Items in your Long-term Memory **interact** with each other, and thus old items can be distorted or changed by new inputs.
   d. Some inputs are **rejected** by the lower centers of your brain because they are meaningless or unimportant, while other inputs are deliberately (if unconsciously) **repressed**.
   e. Your Long-term Memory also suffers from **cataloging, filing**, and **retrieval** errors.

9. Amnesia is a type of memory loss caused by brain damage or emotional trauma. Amnesia typically involves forgetting "what" you have experienced, but not "how to" do things.

10. It takes about 30 minutes for your brain to **consolidate** an item in Long-term Memory. Interruption of the consolidation process leads to a type of forgetting called **retrograde amnesia**.

11. Brain damage can also cause **anterograde amnesia**, in which new items are no longer translated from Short-term to Long-term Memory.

12. **Aphasia** is an impairment in the ability to use or remember language. There are several types of aphasia, but all seem to stem from damage to the **temporal lobe**.

13. According to Goodglass, retrieving the name of an item from long-term storage involves three steps:
    a. You must **recognize** the item and search your memory banks for the item's "file" or identity card.
    b. You hunt for the **auditory representation** of the item's name.
    c. You try to discover the set of **motor commands** that will permit you to say or write the name.

14. The physical representation of a memory is called an **engram**. No one knows what the engram really is, but remembering does seem correlated with rearranging the **synaptic switches** in your brain.

15. Recent studies of the biochemistry of memory suggest that molecular changes may occur in

your neurons whenever you learn something. The molecules involved in memory formation may be **RNA** and/or **protein**.

16. A series of controversial studies suggests that memories can be **transferred** from one animal to another under some circumstances. However, there is some question as to whether these experiments are **valid** and **reliable**.

(Continued from page 368.)

"Look at those learning curves!" Mike Keller said, as he finished plotting the data of their planarian experiment on graph paper.

"How'd they come out?" Devin Eckhoff asked. He was too engrossed in the latest issue of *Penthouse* to look for himself.

Bill Plautz picked up the curves that Mike had drawn. "Amazing. The experimental animals initially responded to the light about 20 percent of the time. But after 150 trials, their response rate went up to 92 percent."

"What about the control groups?" Tom Laine asked, momentarily putting down his copy of *People*.

"They all started off with an initial response rate of 20 percent, just like the experimental worms," Mike replied. "But all three control groups showed a marked decrease in responding over the 150 trials."

"So, what next?" Devin asked.

Bill cleared his throat. "We write the experiment up and turn it in to Dr. Sauermann."

"And pray for a good grade," Tom said, going back to his magazine.

"Yeah, I know that," Devin continued. "But what do we do next with the worms? I mean, we've got the equipment, and the animals, and the custard cups . . ."

"Yeah," said Mike. "We ought to be able to think of *something* outrageous to confound the scientific world with next."

For a few moments, the four of them sat in silence, each lost in thought. Then suddenly Tom looked up from his magazine. "Hey, guys, look at this!"

"What is it?" Bill asked.

"It's an ad for a home permanent, that's what," Tom replied.

"Just what you need," Devin said slyly.

Tom threw the magazine on the kitchen table. "You're still angry with me because I beat you at racquetball this morning. But look at the ad and tell me what ideas it gives you."

Devin picked up the magazine. "The ad shows two absolutely gorgeous young ladies. That gives me lots of ideas."

"They're identical twins," Mike said, looking over Devin's shoulder to inspect the ad. "One has an expensive, beauty-parlor permanent, and the other has a $1.79 home permanent."

"Yes, but what does the headline on the ad say?" Tom asked.

Bill replied. "It says, 'Which twin has the home permanent?' But what's that got to do with worms?"

"Well," said Tom. "I've been doing a little reading on planarians."

"You mean you actually *read* that book by Hyman that you got out of the library?" Mike asked in an amused tone of voice.

"Sure," Tom answered. "And Hyman says that if you cut a planarian in half, the head will grow a new tail, and the tail will regenerate a new head. And the regenerated halves are *identical twins*, just like the two gorgeous twins in the ad. Doesn't that give you an idea for a new experiment?"

"What do you have in mind?" Mike asked.

Tom grinned. "Well, suppose we conditioned a worm, then cut it in half and let both pieces regenerate into whole planarians. Which half would retain the original training?"

"Which twin has the memory, eh?" Bill said.

"Right," said Tom.

"That's an easy question," Devin responded. "The head would remember. After all, it keeps the original brain. The tail has to regrow an entire new nervous system when it regenerates."

"Yeah," said Mike. "But wouldn't it be amazing if the tail showed any retention at all of the conditioning even though it had to grow a new head and brain?"

"That sure would upset those biology students," Devin said, a happy smile on his face. "I can just hear them now. 'If tails could remember, a zoologist would have done the study years ago.'"

"It's not mentioned in Hyman's book," Tom said.

Bill shook his head. "It's really a nice idea, Tom. Very creative. But I don't think anybody would believe us if the tails remembered."

"Particularly not Dr. Sauermann," Mike added.

Tom thought the matter over for a moment. "I guess you guys are right. The scientific world just isn't ready for my brilliant insights yet."

Mike laughed. Bill snickered. Devin grinned, and picked up his copy of *Penthouse* again. But as he turned the pages, he asked, "Racquetball, anyone?"

"Sure," said Tom. "Go get your racquet. But if I cut you in half with my sizzling serve, I hope you don't regenerate into identical twins."

"Then you'd have twice as much trouble beating me," Devin replied.

Tom gathered up his equipment, then noticed that Devin was still reading his magazine. Tom crumpled a piece of paper into a ball and threw it at his roommate.

"Scrunch, scrunch," Devin said as he ducked. He put down the magazine and stood up. "I'll get my goggles too."

Recommended Readings

Anderson, J.R., and Gordon Bower. *Human Associative Memory: A Brief Edition* (Hillsdale, N.J.: Erlbaum, 1980).

Cermak, Laird S. *Improving Your Memory* (New York: McGraw-Hill, 1976).

Fjerdingstad, Ejnar, ed. *Chemical Transfer of Learned Information* (Amsterdam: North-Holland Publishing Company, 1970).

Fromkin, Victoria A., ed. *Errors in Linguistic Performance* (New York: Academic Press, 1980).

Norman, Donald A. *Memory and Attention: An Introduction to Human Information Processing*, 2nd ed. (New York: Wiley, 1976).

Hypnosis, Pain, and Placebos

17

Did You Know That . . .

Many of the "patent remedies" sold as medicine don't cure anything, but can make you mildly drunk or stoned?

Perhaps half of the "cures" supposedly caused by pills or medicines are actually brought about by a psychological factor called the "placebo effect"?

People who respond well to placebos tend to have had punitive parents?

Hypnosis was discovered in the 1700's by a famous "quack" named Anton Mesmer?

The French government once banned hypnosis because it supposedly made women too easy to seduce?

Sigmund Freud rejected hypnosis because it didn't seem to help cure "mental illness"?

People with rich fantasy lives often make good hypnotic subjects?

A hypnotized person may, under certain special conditions, commit murder or engage in other anti-social acts?

Some psychologists believe that hypnosis is an altered state of consciousness, while others believe hypnosis is only a form of role-playing?

You can learn how to reduce pain by using certain "cognitive strategies"?

"Mesmer's Magic Wand"

"Are you sure you want to do it in class?" Brian Healy asked.

"Why certainly," Assistant Professor Don Powell replied, staring intently at his teaching fellow. "Hypnotic suggestion is a legitimate demonstration of mental functioning, a tool used extensively by respected members of the medical and dental professions. Isn't it time that hypnosis was taken out of the closet and brought into the open? It isn't a cure-all; it isn't a parlor trick; it isn't a mysterious force. It's merely mind over matter." Powell smiled. "Besides, the students will love it."

"I don't doubt that at all, Professor Powell," the teaching fellow said. "But what if something goes wrong?"

"What could possibly go wrong?"

Brian Healy thought for a moment. "Well, what if the person you hypnotize doesn't come out of the trance? Who'd want to be hypnotized for life?"

"Nonsense!" Powell snorted. "I suppose at one time or another, some hypnotist must have experienced problems in bringing a subject back from a deep hypnotic trance. But I've never run across a fully authenticated case where that happened.

What we do know is that if you don't wake a person up deliberately, the person drops off into a restful, normal sleep, and in a short time wakes up naturally. And with no physical ill effects, I might add emphatically," Powell added emphatically.

"Okay, you're the boss," Healy said. "But what if nobody in the class can be hypnotized? What would you do then?"

"Change the subject, probably," Powell said, perhaps a little too truthfully. "But it won't happen. In a class of 100, I'd expect roughly 15 students would not be hypnotizable at all, that about 65 would go into a light or medium trance, and that 20 would be capable of achieving a really deep hypnotic state. The subject's prior attitudes are the main controlling factor anyhow. If you think you can't talk when you're hypnotized, you won't talk no matter how much the hypnotist coaxes you. If you think you can't stop talking when you're in a trance, nothing will shut you up."

"Sounds like my mother-in-law. Nothing can shut her up either."

"Brian, no personal problems, please! We must approach this demonstration seriously. Hypnotism isn't a joke of some kind. It's a serious psychological tool. We are following in the great tradition of Braid, Charcot, and Freud. Just do as I tell you, and everything will turn out fine."

And, of course, it did. Professor Powell began the class with a lengthy discussion of the history of hypnotism, beginning with Anton Mesmer and his animal magnetism, and concluding with recent experiments on the effectiveness of hypnotherapy. Much of the class was entranced. Next, he attempted to hypnotize all 100 students at once. Much of the class was tranced.

Then, as his final demonstration, Dr. Powell asked for a volunteer who might want to test out her or his mental powers. An alert, eager, wiry young man immediately stuck up his hand.

"What is your name, please?" Powell asked the volunteer.

"Elvis McNeil," the young man said, running one of his hands through his wavy hair.

"All right, Mr. McNeil. I'm going to put you into a trance, if I can. And then we're going to open up the pathways to your mind. We're going to unshackle all the latent mental powers you've always suspected you had. We're going to prove to you that your own mind—as untrained and untutored as it may be in its present state—can move mountains."

The young man began nodding in almost too-eager agreement, so Powell changed to rather a cautious tone of voice. "We won't do anything that could possibly harm you, of course. But there is always the possibility that you may feel a little foolish afterward. Is your ego big enough to withstand the laughter of your fellow students?"

"Gee, Professor Powell, I think my ego only has problems when people *don't* laugh at me," the intense young man said, carefully adjusting his glasses. "I'll go along with anything you want to try."

Powell smiled. "Excellent, my boy, excellent. Now just sit in this comfortable chair right here in the middle of the stage and start relaxing. Are you comfortable?"

Elvis McNeil nodded as he settled into the chair. Dr. Powell then pulled out a long, sharp hatpin and sterilized it over the flame of a match. "Would it hurt you if I jabbed this pin into one of your fingers?"

Elvis tensed a bit. "Of course it would. I thought you said it wouldn't hurt!"

"Since we won't try it until you're fully hypnotized, I guarantee you that you won't feel a thing. It's just a test to see if you're really in a trance. You won't mind, will you, as long as it's a scientific test of sorts?"

"Not if it unleashes the latent powers of my mind," McNeil said solemnly.

"Good," Powell replied, pulling a gold watch on a long chain out of his pocket with a flourish. "Now, Mr. McNeil, I want you to stare at this mystical timepiece that was given to me by my grandfather. See it swing back and forth before your eyes? Look at it closely, Mr. McNeil. Watch as it moves back and forth, back and forth, back and forth."

McNeil stared intently at the glittering gold watch.

Powell continued in a soft, crooning tone of voice, almost as if he were singing. "Your eyelids are getting heavier and heavier. Your eyelids are like lead, sinking slowly down over your eyes. You are getting sleepier and sleepier and sleepier. Soon you will be fast asleep, deep asleep. Soon you will see nothing but what I tell you to see. And you will hear nothing but the sound of my voice. Go to sleep, Mr. McNeil. Sleep. Deep, deep, deep sleep."

McNeil's eyes closed. He sat rigid, unmoving.

"Are you asleep?"

McNeil's head nodded slowly.

"Deeply, completely asleep?"

Again the young man's head nodded, almost mechanically.

"Hold your hand out, Elvis. That's right, straight out in front of you. Your hand is made of steel, isn't it? Impenetrable, painless steel. You can't feel a thing in your hand, Elvis. See, I can touch it, and you can't feel my touch, can you?"

"No."

"That's right, no pain at all. I can even stick this pin in your hand and it will cause you no pain at all. You can't feel a thing, remember. Now I will stick the pin in—like this!—and it didn't hurt at all, did it?"

The class gasped as Powell plunged the sterilized hatpin half-an-inch into the young man's hand. But McNeil didn't react. Instead, he shook his head slowly and whispered, "No, it didn't hurt at all."

Professor Powell removed the pin, inspected McNeil's hand, and put a small bandage over the tiny wound. Then he turned to the class and said, "So, you see, pain is ultimately controlled by the cortex. Your brain can turn pain off or turn it on, depending on the circumstances. Under hypnosis, you can be made to perceive things that aren't there, and you can be made *not* to perceive even very strong stimuli. Mr. McNeil here is obviously a very good hypnotic subject. So now let's put matters to a further test."

Powell motioned Brian Healy to come toward him. "Now, Mr. McNeil, you surely remember what my teaching fellow, Brian Healy, looks like. Right?"

McNeil nodded slowly.

"Well, in a moment, Mr. NcNeil, I'm going to ask you to open your eyes. But when you do so, Mr. Healy will be totally invisible to you. You simply won't be able to see Mr. Healy no matter where he is or what he does. Do you understand?"

Again the slow nod.

"Good. Now, please open your eyes."

Elvin McNeil blinked a couple of times and looked around cautiously.

"You can see me, right?" Powell asked, putting an arm around Brian Healy's shoulders. "But is there anyone else up here on the stage with me? Do you see anyone else here but me?"

McNeil said, "Only me. There's just you and me on the stage, Professor Powell."

"Right, absolutely right. You're a very perceptive person, McNeil. Now then, I want to help you open up the channels of your mind and tap the secret powers that lie dormant inside your skull. I want to give you the faith of a mustard seed, the faith that moves mountains and turns the physical world into your mental slave, to do with as you wish. Would you like to learn those secrets, McNeil?"

Although he was still apparently in a deep trance, Elvis became excited. "Yes, yes," he cried loudly. "I want to learn the secrets of the universe! That's what I came to college for in the first place!"

"Then you should have taken this course sooner, right? Well, now, Mr. McNeil, let's begin by teaching you how to levitate objects—that is, how to make things fly through the air just by willing them to do so." Powell moved very close to the young man. "We'll begin with that empty straight chair on the other side of the stage. Do you think you can get it to float upward merely by giving it the mental command to rise?"

McNeil looked dubious. "If you say so . . ."

"Good. Good," Powell said, motioning Brian Healy to grab hold of the empty chair, which was some 5 meters away from McNeil. "Now, Elvis, all you have to do is to concentrate. Concentrate with all the hidden power in your cortex. Order the chair to rise. Do so now. Talk to the chair—give it commands out loud, and then watch what happens when your concentration becomes deep enough!"

McNeil took a deep breath. "All right, chair, you're going to rise. You're going to go sailing up into the blue like a toy balloon. Rise. Rise!"

As the young man spoke, Healy began to lift the chair slowly from the floor. "Rise! Rise!" McNeil cried again.

The chair "rose" an inch or two each time McNeil urged it upward.

"Holy Moly, Professor Powell, it's working! What a trip!"

The chair suddenly dropped back onto the floor.

"You're not concentrating, McNeil. Keep your mind on the business at hand."

"Sorry, sir," McNeil said, and took another deep breath. "Okay, chair, let's float some more. Up, up and away!"

In Brian Healy's strong hands, the chair rose a foot off the stage.

"That's right, chair, keep going. Higher, higher, higher!"

The class began to giggle just a bit, not sure of what was going on. Healy lifted the chair until it was at the level of his waist.

"Don't stop now, get it on up there!"

Healy raised the chair above his head. Small beads of sweat began to pop out on his forehead. The chair was heavier than he had thought it would be.

"Higher! Higher!" McNeil screamed.

Quickly, Professor Powell interrupted. "That's high enough for the first time around, McNeil. We don't want to strain your cortex, after all. Why don't you tell it to dance instead?"

"Sure. I can do it. I know I can! Okay, chair, I want you to shake, rattle, and roll."

Healy twisted the chair over his head rhythmically, following the beat of some distant drummer.

Suddenly McNeil burst out laughing. "It's a rocking chair! That's what it is. A crazy chair that dances because I've got rock in my head!"

"Be serious, McNeil, or you'll ruin everything," Powell warned him sternly.

As if in sympathy, the chair came crashing down onto the stage, and Brian Healy collapsed into it.

The class went wild with applause. McNeil beamed, confident the clapping was for him. Brian Healy stood up and took a bow, but Elvis appeared not to notice it and just smiled happily at his fellow students.

"And now, Mr. McNeil, I want you to wake up, to recover completely from the trance, as soon as I count to three," Professor Powell commanded. "Ready? One, two . . . THREE! You're awake!"

McNeil shook his head, then looked around slowly.

"Do you feel okay? Good," said Powell, not waiting for an answer. "And can you see Mr. Healy now?"

Elvis McNeil looked at the teaching fellow, then nodded. "Of course. He's right here on the stage with us."

"And how do you feel?"

"Fine, fine. But what happened? How did I get this bandage on my hand?"

"That's where I injected you with the secret powers. Don't you remember making the chair dance in the air?"

McNeil looked puzzled. "Oh, yes. I remember. How did I do that, Professor Powell?"

"Mind over matter, my boy. Concentration, that's what does the trick. Thank you very much for your assistance."

At that point, the bell rang, ending the class. Several students crowded around Professor Powell to ask questions. After he had answered as many as he could, he and Brian Healy headed back toward the office.

"What do you think the after-effects will be for poor Mr. McNeil?" Healy asked.

"After-effects?" Professor Powell said. "Why there won't be any. Elvis will find out what really happened, and he'll be embarrassed for a while. He's one of those students who takes psychology thinking that it's magic, or something. Now perhaps he'll see that the only way to unleash the powers of the mind is to study like crazy, learn all the facts about human nature, and then discover how to apply the facts wisely. Hypnosis is a marvelous tool, for some things. I think we proved that in class. But it's not a miracle cure for acquiring personal power or for gaining mystical control over the world. Besides, we proved another point that's even more important— you perceive what your mind wants you to perceive. Beautiful demonstration, didn't you think so?"

Brian Healy scratched his head. "Sure, Professor Powell. Sure."

(Continued on page 404.)

Mind over Matter

The field of medicine has always attracted its share of quacks and **charlatans**—that is, disreputable women and men with little or no medical knowledge who promise quick cures at cheap prices. The reasons why quackery thrives even in modern times are not hard to find.

To begin with, pain seems to be a chronic human condition. At a 1979 conference on pain sponsored by the National Institutes of Health, Dr. John Bonica described how widespread pain is in the US. According to Bonica, 50 percent of all Americans *annually* experience "acute or chronic pain needing therapy." Bonica estimates that the cost of dealing with pain in the US exceeds 50 billion dollars *each year*.

The second reason that charlatans are still with us is that many people lack the training necessary to evaluate medical claims. Given the choice between (1) a reputable physician who says a cure for cancer will be long, difficult, expensive, and may not work at all; and (2) a **patent remedy** salesman who says that five bottles of his "snake oil" will cure not only cancer, but tuberculosis, syphilis, warts, and bad breath as well, some individuals will opt for the bottles of snake oil.

Some patent medicines actually work. But the "snake oil" remedies sold by quacks are mostly bad-tasting concoctions that are highly laced with alcohol or narcotic drugs. People often drink them to drown their pains in the rising tide of pleasant intoxication. Little wonder that "snake oil" is a popular cure-all for minor aches and hurts!

The Correlation Illusion

Another reason that quack cures remain popular is what we might call the "correlation illusion." We all learn in school that if event B always

follows event A, then B and A are *correlated*. That's true. But we then go on to presume that A somehow *causes* B to take place. That is, we infer a *causal connection* between two events merely because they are "co-related." Yet if there is one point you should learn about **statistics** from this text, it is this: "Correlations don't imply causality."

To make this point clearer, suppose that you overindulge at dinner and wind up with a nasty stomach ache. A friend of yours offers you a sure-fire cure—dried frog eyes mixed with chicken blood! You hold your nose, swallow a spoonful of the dreadful medicine, and go to bed as quickly as you can. The next morning the stomach ache is gone. A miracle? No, for chances are you would have felt much better anyhow after a good night's sleep. And yet, the mere fact that (1) you took the medicine, and (2) the pain later went away, might give you the *illusion* that A had caused B to happen. So the mere fact that two events occur together frequently—i.e., the two events are correlated—doesn't prove that one causes the other. (For more information on this point, see the Statistical Appendix to this book.)

Question: *What connection do you see between Pavlovian conditioning techniques and how the "correlation illusion" occurs in the human mind?*

The Placebo Effect

By far the most potent reason that quack medicines still are sold around the world has to do with what psychologists call the **placebo** effect. A placebo is a pill made of sugar or ordinary flour. It does no harm at all, but when prescribed by a physician, the placebo may actually reduce pain

Anton Mesmer became the rage of Paris in the late 1700's when he convinced people that "magnetic fluids" could heal illnesses. Rich Parisians flocked to Mesmer's salons to touch injured parts of their bodies to metal rods that stuck out of tubs filled with "magnetic fluids."

given a drug called **naloxone**. Naloxone *counteracts* the effects of the body's natural pain-killers, the **endorphins** (see Chapter 3).

Those subjects taking naloxone consistently reported a *worsening* of their pain after taking the drug. As Fields notes, the naloxone apparently "wiped out" the endorphins that the body usually releases when painful stress occurs.

Those subjects taking the placebo fell into two sub-groups. About a third of the patients got almost immediate relief from the sugar pill. Fields calls these people "placebo reactors." The other two-thirds experienced little or no decrease in pain, and thus were "placebo non-reactors." Once Fields had identified the two sub-groups, he gave them both naloxone. The "reactors" reported an immediate *worsening* of their pain, but the "non-reactors" didn't.

Fields believes his study proves that one of the main effects that placebos have is this: They cause the brain to release a sudden surge of endorphins. But the "placebo effect" is only likely to work in certain people—namely, those of us who have been *conditioned* to secrete endorphins when stressed much as Pavlov's dogs were conditioned to secrete saliva when the bell rang.

Question: *Given the data so far, what percentage of the general population would you guess are "externalizers"?*

Placebo Abuse in Hospitals

Several studies suggest that placebos are just as effective as narcotics in relieving the severe pain associated with abdominal surgery. But the sugar pills work only with one-third of surgery patients, presumably the same one-third of the general population who are "placebo reactors." Given the fact that narcotics are always dangerous, you might imagine that most hospital personnel would prefer to give sugar pills to "reactors" rather than morphine. However, as James Goodwin and his colleagues at the New Mexico School of Medicine discovered, this is seldom the case.

In 1979, Goodwin and his group reported that the medical staff gave placebos almost exclusively to those patients the staff thought were *faking pain*. As one physician put it, "Placebos are used with people you hate, not to make them suffer but to prove them wrong." Sadly enough, the fact that a third of the patients given placebos felt relief seemed to prove to the medical staff that many patients are "pain fakers."

Goodwin states that alcoholics were most often given placebos, primarily because the staff judged them to be "undeserving of real pain killers." Patients who failed to respond to normal

and promote healing. How can a "sugar pill" help you recover more speedily from an illness? There are several reasons, some psychological, some biological, some a mixture of both.

Expectancy and "Locus of Control"

As we noted in Chapter 8, you see what you expect to see. You also *feel what you expect to feel*. If you are convinced that taking a pill will reduce your pain, chances are that you will *perceive* whatever pain you have as being less intense after you swallow that pill. Thus one reason that placebos "work" is that they alter the way you "process" pain signals coming from your body.

Another reason that sugar pills are effective has to do with the way you respond to your environment. As we noted in Chapter 13, Julian Rotter has shown that people he calls "externalizers" believe their destiny is controlled by outside forces. "Internalizers," on the other hand, see themselves as being responsible for what happens to them. In the April 1981 issue of *Psychology Today*, Joan Duncan and James Laird report that placebos are particularly effective with those individuals who are sensitive to external cues and social pressures. Apparently, then, you are more likely to respond to a placebo if your "locus of personal control" is external rather than internal.

Placebos and Endorphins

In 1978, Howard Fields and his associates at the University of California in San Francisco asked volunteers to rate how much pain they experienced after having a tooth pulled. Half the volunteers were given placebos. The other half were medication were also likely to be given placebos, apparently because the staff felt guilty that standard medical techniques hadn't worked with these patients. Goodwin notes as well that patients who appear to "enjoy narcotics" are also likely candidates for placebos, primarily because they "frustrate" the doctors and nurses.

Fortunately, as Goodwin notes, placebo *abuse* is a fairly rare event in most hospitals. Unfortunately, its *correct use* occurs just about as infrequently, presumably because most medical personnel haven't been taught how powerful a pain-killer placebos can be with some patients.

Question: *Which group do you think would make better hypnotic subjects, "placebo reactors" or "placebo non-reactors"? Why?*

Anton Mesmer and the Discovery of Hypnosis

One of the most famous quacks in all of medical history was a man named Anton Mesmer. Born in 1734 in a tiny Austrian village, Mesmer took degrees in theology and medicine at the University of Vienna (where Freud later taught). At the time that Mesmer began his medical practice, the prevailing view toward mental illness was that insanity was due to an imbalance of certain body chemicals called **humors** (see Chapter 23). Mesmer rejected the humoral theory in favor of the

Charlatan (SHAR-lah-tan). From the Italian word meaning "to chatter" or "to talk noisily." A smooth-talking salesman of worthless medicines is a charlatan or quack.

Patent remedy (PAT-tent REMM-uh-dee). A packaged drug or medicine or "secret composition" whose name may be protected by a "patent" or "trademark." Many patent remedies are put out by reputable drug companies and are quite useful. Others, particularly those sold by a quack or charlatan, are worthless.

Statistics (stah-TISS-ticks). A branch of mathematics dealing with the collection, analysis, and interpretation of scientific data.

Placebo (plas-SEE-bo). From a Latin phrase meaning "to please." A harmless drug given for its psychological effect especially to satisfy the patient or to act as a control in an experiment.

Naloxone (nah-LOX-own). A drug that counteracts or antagonizes the effects of morphine and the endorphins.

Endorphins (en-DORF-ins). Natural pain-killers secreted by the body. See Chapter 3.

Humors (YOU-moors). From the Latin word meaning "fluids" or "moisture." According to early Greek medical men, the body secreted four different humors: black bile, yellow bile, blood, and phlegm.

Agitations (adge-jit-TAY-shuns). From the Latin word meaning "to drive" or "to turn over in the mind." To agitate (ADGE-jit-tate) is to stir up, or to move quickly to and fro. To shake or quiver.

even more "humorous" notion that the mind was strongly affected by magnetic radiation from outer space.

"Cures" by Magnetism

Mesmer lived at a time when magnetism and electricity were new and exciting physical forces, and people still believed that the stars and planets radiated "magnetic fluids." Little wonder, then, that Mesmer thought that magnets could focus these "celestial fluids" on a sick person's body and thus restore the person to health.

One of Mesmer's first patients was an hysterical woman who complained of various pains, convulsions, and **agitations**. When Mesmer "magnetized" her stomach and legs, the woman's pains vanished for several hours. Mesmer became so successful at these "magnetic cures" that he took to wearing odd clothes and soon announced that, through his techniques, "the art of healing reaches its final perfection."

Mesmer never guessed that his "cures" might be due to the *power of suggestion*. But this explanation did occur to Mesmer's colleagues at the University of Vienna. They investigated his techniques and decided his "cures" were a product of imagination rather than magnetism. Mesmer was thereafter expelled from the university, fled Vienna, and set up shop in Paris.

Mesmer's "Grand Crisis"

Paris in the 1780's was friendlier to Mesmer than Vienna had been, and he soon opened a healing

"HE TOLD ME TO TAKE THREE PILLS TWICE A DAY, OR TWO PILLS THREE TIMES A DAY, OR 42 PILLS ONCE A WEEK. I THINK IT'S A PLACEBO."

According to the famous French scientist Charcot, hysterical women made the best hypnotic subjects. **(top)**

Fig. 17.1. An example of hypnotic induction. **(left)**

salon that had in its center a huge tub containing "magnetized water." Twisted, oddly shaped rods stuck out from all sides of the tub. Mesmer made his patients sit holding hands in a closed circle around the tub so that the rods could touch the injured parts of their bodies. The rods supposedly directed the "magnetic fluids" toward the wound and thus promoted healing.

To help things along, Mesmer dressed in a long purple robe and walked around the tub, touching his patients with a wand. He frequently urged them to yield themselves up to the magnetic fluids that surrounded them, saying they would be cured if only they could focus on the heavenly powers within their sick bodies. Some of the patients apparently went into trance-like states. They would sit or stand as if frozen in place, apparently unseeing and unhearing.

Mesmer had, in fact, discovered *hypnosis*, but made no real scientific study of what the hypnotic state was like or what really induced it. Instead, he urged his clients "to reach farther into their minds." By continually pushing his patients psychologically, Mesmer drove many of them to reach what he called a "grand crisis," something we would call a *grand mal* convulsive seizure. Mesmer was convinced that the "grand crisis" was responsible for the cures his clients reported. Other medical doctors were not quite so sure.

Mesmerism, the name soon given to the technique for inducing a trance state, became the rage of Paris. The French government offered Mesmer a reward of 20,000 francs to reveal the secret of his "cures." When he refused, the government appointed two committees to investigate his techniques. Benjamin Franklin, then the US ambassador to France, was a member of one. The committees were unanimous in their public reports—Mesmerism was a hoax, and the cures were due to suggestion and imagination rather than to magnetism. The committees also sent a secret report to the French king, warning that the "grand crisis" was probably habit-forming and dangerous to your health. Furthermore, they told the king, women seemed to be particularly susceptible to the "grand crisis" and could easily be seduced while in this state.

So Mesmerism was banned on moral as well as medical grounds. Mesmer's star fell from public view. He soon retired to Versailles, a town near Paris, where he lived another 30 years—presumably basking in the magnetic radiations of the celestial bodies and, perhaps, occasionally trying to Mesmerize a peasant or two.

Question: *What similarities do you see between the "cures" Mesmer achieved and those claimed by Lilly for "tanking" (see Chapter 8)?*

Mesmerism (MEZZ-mur-ism). The first name given to hypnosis, or hypnotism (HIPP-no-tism, but often mispronounced HIPP-*mah*-tism).

Hysteria (hiss-TARE-ee-ah). From the Greek word meaning "wandering womb," because women were supposedly more prone to this mental disorder than were men. Hysteria involves denial and over-emotionality. See Chapter 23.

Suggestibility. The state of following suggestions, of doing what you are told to do. If someone dares you to eat frog eyes, and you do, you are probably quite suggestible. The French anatomist Charcot (shar-KOH) believed hypnosis was merely a matter of some people's being highly suggestible.

Hypnosis

Until fairly recently, most scientists considered hypnotism more of a parlor trick or black magic than a legitimate psychological phenomenon. However, a few dauntless physicians and psychologists over the years did try to study hypnosis objectively.

James Braid, a Scottish physician, gave *hypnosis* its present name in 1842. He took the term from the Greek word for "sleep." After attending a session held by a wandering Mesmerist, Braid became convinced that magnetic fluids had nothing to do with the effect. Rather, Braid felt, it was an abnormal or intense form of sleep that the hypnotist induced by somehow affecting certain centers in the subject's brain.

Shortly thereafter, Jean Charcot, a noted French professor of anatomy, began work in this field. Charcot soon reported he had found a close connection between **hysteria** and hypnosis. Other French scientists disputed Charcot's claims, believing that the hypnotic state was a result of **suggestibility**, not hysteria, although there seemed little doubt that hysterics often made good hypnotic subjects.

Freud and Hypnosis

It was into this sea of controversy that Sigmund Freud stepped in the winter of 1885. Freud went to Paris in 1885 to study for a few months with Charcot. The experience marked a turning point in his life. Prior to this visit, Freud had viewed mental illness as a *physiological* problem. Thus he had used massage, baths, rest, and electrical stimulation with his hysterical patients. When he returned to Vienna in 1886, he began thinking of insanity as having primarily *psychological* causes.

Following Charcot's lead, Freud used hypnosis to suggest to hysterics that their symptoms would vanish. But he soon ran into difficulties. For while the patients' symptoms did disappear, they usually came back again. Furthermore, Freud soon discovered that not all of his patients could be hypnotized. And those that could be hypno-

tized often became so dependent on his suggestions that they could not function in society unless they were under his hypnotic spell (see Fig. 17.1).

Renouncing hypnosis as a useless therapeutic tool, Freud instead developed psychoanalysis, which we will describe in a later chapter. But as Freud's influence grew, his negative opinions about hypnosis tended to discourage people from investigating the technique. It thus was not until the 1930's—when American behavioral psychologists took up the subject—that hypnosis again became a subject deemed fit for study in scientific laboratories.

Suggestibility

What is hypnosis? Braid thought it a form of sleep. But the early behaviorists believed it was a state of narrowly focused attention in which the hypnotized person somehow becomes extremely *suggestible*. Clark L. Hull, the noted learning theorist, made a lengthy study of suggestibility and hypnosis. Hull was hunting for some simple test that would quickly tell who would be a good hypnotic subject. Perhaps because he looked at behavior rather than at a person's "fantasy life," Hull was unable to find any one trait that was a sure-fire index of hypnotizability.

Suggestibility and Fantasy

Theodore X. Barber has recently developed a Suggestibility Scale that he uses in his research. The major questions on the Scale have to do with your ability to *imagine* yourself in a variety of unusual situations. One of the primary traits that the Scale seems to measure is the ease with which you can create mental fantasies.

In the January 1981 issue of *Psychology Today*, Barber reports that many women who are excellent hypnotic subjects—and who score high on his Scale—seem to have spent much of their adult lives lost in a world of fantasy. Most of these women began to fantasize early in life, as an escape from an unhappy childhood. As children,

Clark Hull

Theodore X. Barber

they tended to have imaginary companions, and almost all of them believed their dolls and stuffed animals were actually alive. The majority of these women reported they sometimes had orgasms solely through sexual fantasy. But despite the fact that they spent "at least 90 percent of the time" lost in fantasy, these women were all quite successful. All were either college students or graduates. One was a psychiatrist, another a psychologist, and all but one were married or had steady boyfriends.

Barber's research suggests there is a high correlation between the ability to "fantasize" and the ability to be hypnotized. As Barber notes, however, the fact that you are "suggestible" or are "addicted to fantasy" doesn't mean you can't live a happy and productive life.

Imagination and Parental Punishment

Data gathered by Ernest Hilgard and his associates at Stanford tend to support Barber's views on the close connection between suggestibility and fantasy. Hilgard's research suggests that the response you make to a hypnotist is partially determined by the type of upbringing you had. If your parents were inclined to punish you severely and frequently when you were young, chances are that you will be able to "go under" in an hypnotic trance rather easily. Hilgard gives three reasons why this may be the case. First, continual punishment can *condition* you to respond to authority automatically and without questioning what you are told to do. Second, you may learn to escape parental wrath by retreating into your own imagination. And third, you may find you can prevent punishment by learning to play various social roles. We will have more to say about this last point in a moment.

Question: Julian Rotter reports that most externalizers had punitive parents. Why isn't this fact particularly surprising?

Effects of Hypnosis

One of the fascinating aspects of hypnosis is that people often seem to do things while hypnotized that they couldn't (or wouldn't) do otherwise. For example, studies show the following effects of hypnosis:

1. Subjects in a deep hypnotic trance can be made to act as if any (or all) of their sensory inputs have been cut off completely. They also can be made to respond to sights, smells, sounds, tastes, or tactile stimuli that aren't really there.
2. Subjects may perform what seem to be incredible feats of strength, such as lifting objects that weigh several hundred pounds.
3. Subjects gain great voluntary control over their muscles. For instance, you can tell a woman to make her body rigid as a board, then put the woman's head on one chair, her feet on another, with nothing in between. Now you can sit on the woman's unsupported stomach without having her buckle underneath your weight.
4. Hypnotized subjects can often learn long lists of words with apparent ease and may recall past events with what seems to be surprising clarity.
5. If the hypnotized subject is particularly susceptible, you may tell the person that you are going to touch a very hot poker to the person's arm—and then merely touch the subject with the point of your finger. Within a few hours a blister-like welt may appear just where you put your finger to the subject's flesh.
6. Under certain circumstances, you may talk a shy, very proper young woman into taking off all her clothes in public, command the leader of an anti-violence movement to shoot one of his best friends, or get a secret agent to divulge confidential government material.

But as impressive as these feats may seem, there is a strange quality of *role-playing* to them that demands further investigation and discussion.

Under hypnosis, a slightly built young woman can be made to lift an object weighing 135 kilograms (300 pounds) when ordinarily she would refuse to consider picking up even half that weight. Has hypnosis suddenly made her as strong as Mr. Universe? No, not at all. Women in peasant societies lift heavy weights as a matter of daily routine. And what would this same young woman do if she walked out of her house one day and saw that the wheel of the family car had come to rest on top of one of her children?

Hypnosis then does not make you any stronger than normal. But it can *motivate you to perform as if your life depended on it.*

Anyone can pretend to be blind—actors on stage do a credible job of it all the time. And anyone can pretend to see things or people who aren't physically present—many children have imaginary playmates with whom they hold long conversations daily. But only a very few subjects can "raise blisters" when hypnotized. As it turns out, however, these individuals are all prone to getting rashes and blister-like cold sores when emotionally upset. When they are under hypnosis, they apparently "do their biological thing" on command. The ordinary subject, even in a deep trance, cannot match this performance.

Question: *Would externalizers or internalizers be more likely to commit anti-social acts* on command?

Anti-Social Behaviors

As Theodore X. Barber notes, we all perform anti-social acts occasionally if we think we can get away with them. We also act in unusual ways if some *higher authority* has told us to do so. A modest young woman will only disrobe in public if the hypnotist convinces her that it is proper to do so. A non-violent young man can be talked into picking up a gun (loaded with blanks) and firing it at a friend, but only if the hypnotist convinces him the friend is about to murder his mother or rape his sister. And secret agents have been made to "tell all" under hypnosis, but only when the agent believed that he or she was acting under legitimate orders to do so.

In short, you will perform under hypnosis only those acts that you *would perform normally*—if the situation were right, and if your motivation were high enough. But even these factors are usually not enough. If you are to violate society's laws when hypnotized, you will usually do so only when your desire to please the hypnotist is intensely strong—as strong as it might be to please authoritarian parents. And, of course, if you have a burning need to obey someone's commands or suggestions, you probably will do so whether or not you are hypnotized.

According to Barber, hypnosis imparts no magic powers to the subject or to the hypnotist, nor does it enhance your physical or mental abilities. It merely increases your motivation to do things you might not ordinarily do.

There are two seeming contradictions to Barber's view of hypnosis, one having to do with memory, the other having to do with pain. Let us look at memory first.

Hypnotic age regression. To regress to an earlier age under hypnosis. To return to an earlier time when a hypnotist tells you to do so. Many psychologists believe that when you regress hypnotically, you are just "role-playing" because you wish to please the hypnotist.

Hypnotic Age Regression

The early behaviorists were particularly impressed with the rapid access that hypnosis seemed to give to a person's early memories. They soon found that, while in a deep trance, subjects apparently could "relive" certain events of childhood. When told to "go back" to her fifth birthday, for instance, a young woman might begin to talk in a very childish voice. She would then recount in detail who was at her party, what presents she got, what her parents said and did, and even what she dreamed later that night.

A few hypnotic subjects went much farther. When pressed to do so, some of them reported detailed conversations they thought had occurred between their mothers and fathers while they themselves were still being carried in their mother's womb. Other subjects recounted events that happened to them centuries before, when they were seemingly *living in a different body.* The "memory feats" these people performed under **hypnotic age regression** seemed fabulous indeed to those early psychologists who had not yet discovered the connection between hypnosis and fantasy. The police were even more impressed.

Because of the research on hypnotic age regression, many police agencies now routinely make use of hypnosis in criminal investigations. In particular, the police hypnotize witnesses to help them recall details of events that seem lost to ordinary memory. In the April 1978 issue of *Human Behavior*, Martin Reiser of the LA Police Department claims that in 77 percent of the cases where hypnosis was used, "important information was elicited from witnesses and victims that was not available by routine interrogation."

However, most psychologists now take rather a dim view of the use of hypnosis by the police. In a recent interview, Ernest Hilgard states, "It is well-known that hypnotists may implant memories, so that the hypnotized person accepts them as his [or her] own." And Martin Orne, past president of the International Society of Hypnosis, notes that what people remember under hypnosis is often *completely inaccurate.*

Generally speaking, the US courts also are skeptical of the use of hypnosis in aiding recall. Most judges will not admit as evidence any testimony obtained under hypnosis, and to date no

Martin Orne

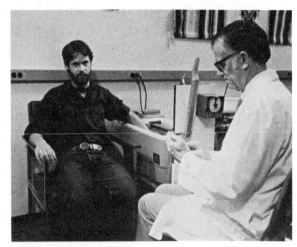

Fig. 17.2. Ernest Hilgard measuring the pain response of a subject whose arm is immersed in ice water.

one has been convicted of a crime solely on the basis of what a witness remembered while in a hypnotic trance.

Question: As we noted in the last chapter, Elizabeth Loftus has shown that the questions you ask someone about an event can actually transform the person's memories. What problems does Loftus's research raise about the use of hypnotism by various police agencies to "recover forgotten memories"?

Hypnotic "Role-Playing"

Martin Orne has been studying hypnotic age regression for more than 30 years. In the 1950's he published a series of studies suggesting strongly that hypnotic age regression was chiefly a matter of rather excellent *role-playing* on the part of the hypnotic subject.

Orne put several college students into deep hypnotic trances and regressed them back to their sixth birthdays. He then asked the students to describe what had happened to them that day. The students responded magnificently, piling one insignificant detail on top of another. Orne was more impressed with their inventiveness than with their accuracy, however. For in many cases he had independent descriptions (from the students' parents and from other sources) of what had actually happened. As it turned out, the students were woefully inaccurate—they mixed up events from many different birthday parties, they included events they had read about in novels, or they simply made up things that never happened.

In a few cases, Orne obtained actual records of psychological tests the students had taken when they were children. He then regressed the students back to their childhood years through hypnotic trance and re-administered the same tests. Their answers as hypnotized adults were stylized attempts to act childish, and were noth-

ing like the answers they had actually given at that age. Orne then allowed the students to inspect their early records as closely as they wished. Then he once more regressed them back to their childhoods. Now the students responded to test items as they *actually had* when at that early age—a feat they could not accomplish until they looked at their test records.

Orne believes that hypnosis is mostly a matter of highly motivated role-playing. When you allow someone to hypnotize you, Orne says, you temporarily "submit" to the hypnotist just as you would to punitive parents. When the hypnotist suggests you are six years old, you try very hard to respond appropriately because you have been trained to want to please anyone you "submit" to. If you can't remember exactly what you did and said when you were six, then you "fake it" as best you can.

Question: If someone offered you $1,000 to withstand a painful jab with a needle without flinching, would you be sufficiently motivated to take the offer?

Hypnosis and Pain

More than a century ago, a number of British physicians reported they had used hypnosis during hundreds of operations with great success: They claimed that the patients experienced no pain at all and suffered no ill effects. However, scientific investigations of these claims turned up a most intriguing point. Quite often the hypnotized patient did indeed show evidence of experiencing terrible pain during these operations. But afterward, when the patients were out of the trance, they denied having felt anything at all! The scientific commissions reported that hypnosis didn't reduce pain, it merely prevented the patients from remembering the unpleasantness afterward.

The effect of hypnosis on pain is a complex one. As Ernest Hilgard has shown with a series of experiments performed at Stanford, a subject under hypnosis may both experience pain and simultaneously *not* feel it.

In one of his experiments, Hilgard asked 20 volunteers to hold their arms in ice water for 45 seconds. The water was painfully cold—as the subjects reported only too willingly if they were not hypnotized. Hilgard then "suggested" that they try consciously to control their experience of pain, and most of them were able to do so. They now reported much less pain than before.

Next Hilgard hypnotized the subjects and suggested they would feel *no pain at all* from the ice water. While their arms were in the water, Hilgard asked them if they experienced pain. The subjects told him, "Some, but not much." Then Hilgard asked them to move a finger on the hand *not* in the water if the subjects *really* felt the pain at some "unconscious level." Most of the subjects immediately did so. Thus *consciously* the subjects were suppressing the pain, but at some deeper level, they apparently knew the pain was really there (see Fig. 17.2).

"Hidden Observers"
Hilgard believes that hypnosis is an *altered state of consciousness* in which your consciousness can "split." One part of you acts in a hypnotized fashion and experiences no pain if the hypnotist tells you not to. But another part of your mind—which can communicate by gestures during the trance—remains unhypnotized and perceives the discomfort your conscious mind is repressing. Hilgard calls this part of the mind the subject's "hidden observer."

As we will see in Chapter 23, this "splitting of the mind" is very similar to the "split personalities" that are occasionally found in mentally disordered individuals. Usually, when one personality "takes over," it temporarily *suppresses* any other personality patterns the person has. According to Hilgard, this same *personality split* may occur in normal individuals during hypnosis.

Is Hypnosis an "Altered State of Consciousness"?
Both Martin Orne and Theodore X. Barber disagree with Hilgard's definition of hypnosis as an "altered state of consciousness." They point out that Hilgard's subjects may be unconsciously "faking" the presence of a *hidden observer*, just as

Analgesic (an-al-GEE-sick). Any substance that reduces or "kills" pain. See Chapter 3.

people unconsciously "fake" any experience that they think the hypnotist may want them to have.

In fact, both Orne and Barber seriously doubt whether "hypnosis" actually exists! In a recent paper, Barber points out that Hilgard seems to define hypnosis in rather a circular way. "How do you know a man is in a hypnotic trance? Because he responds to suggestions. And why does he respond to suggestions? Because he is hypnotized!" According to Barber, hypnotism is actually made up of equal parts of "role-playing" and learning how to control the way in which you *perceive* your sensory inputs.

"Conscious Strategies" for Controlling Pain
Over the past 20 years, Barber has conducted a series of studies in which he has taught people *conscious strategies* for reducing the intensity of pain. Some of these strategies are more effective than others, but the best of them seem to reduce pain at least as much as does an hypnotic trance.

For example, in one study, Barber asked subjects to immerse their hands in extremely cold water. Some of the subjects were told to try various "cognitive strategies" for reducing their discomfort. That is, they were told to do such things as the following:

1. Imagine their hands were so numb they couldn't feel pain at all.
2. Concentrate on other things.
3. Reinterpret the stimulation as being non-painful.
4. "Disassociate" themselves mentally from the pain.
5. Not let themselves be bothered by the ice water.

Another group of subjects was given similar instructions while hypnotized. By all measures of "painfulness," the *cognitive strategies* for reducing pain were at least as effective as was hypnosis.

Barber concludes that, since hypnosis is no better as an **analgesic** than is "mental discipline," perhaps we should discard "hypnosis" entirely as a psychological concept. Not all psychologists agree with Barber, and the matter is far from settled.

But it seems clear that, before we can make up our minds about what hypnosis is or isn't, we must face squarely a problem that we rather delicately ignored in Chapter 6—namely, what is *pain*?

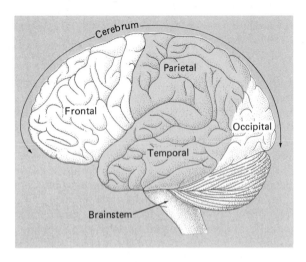

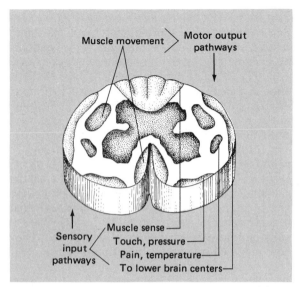

Fig. 17.3. The cerebrum, showing the parietal lobe. **(left)**

Fig. 17.4. The spinal cord in cross section. **(right)**

Pain

A century ago, most sensory psychologists believed there were four unique psychological experiences you could get from stimulating your skin—warmth, cold, pressure, and *pain*. Each of these four experiences was thought to be mediated by a specific type of receptor or nerve ending buried somewhere in your skin.

But further study turned up some troubling facts. There did seem to be receptors that were primarily concerned with temperature sensations, and other receptor cells that seemed to mediate the experience of pressure. But no one ever found a nerve ending that was *solely concerned* with the sensation of pain.

Investigations of the parietal lobe uncovered parts of the somatic cortex that, when stimulated electrically, gave rise to the experience of pressure or temperature. But no one ever found a part of the parietal lobe whose stimulation produced *pain* (see Fig. 17.3). Nor could a "pain center" be found anywhere on the surface of the cerebral hemispheres.

No special receptor organs, no special "input area" on the cortex—what an **enigma** pain seemed to be! But if no one could figure out how the pain signal got started in the skin—or where it ended up in the brain—there was no doubt at all about how it got from the "non-existent receptors" to the "invisible locus in the brain!" For it had long been known that pain sensitivity was quite well represented in the *spinal cord*.

Spinal Pathways

Your spinal cord contains *input* pathways that run from your body to your brain, and *output* pathways that run from your brain back to your body (see Fig. 17.4). Certain types of diseases that affect the spinal cord often give rise to continuous and vicious pain that can be relieved only by *cutting* some of the sensory pathways going up the spinal cord from the skin receptors. So pain obviously is an "input" message of some kind. But, as we have found in recent years, even the spinal cord data are more complex than they seem to be at first glance. And if you are to understand why pain hurts as it does, and why hypnosis and "cognitive strategies" can sometimes reduce or alleviate the pain, we must take another (very quick) look at how your skin receptors operate.

Fast and Slow Fibers

The basket cells and the encapsulated nerve endings in your skin send their messages to your brain primarily by way of special pathways in your spinal cord. The nerve cells in these pathways are **insulated**. That is, the axons of these cells have a layer of fat wrapped around them. Because this layer of fat insulates the electrical impulses that pass along the axon, the speed with which the neural messages flow is *faster* in these fibers than in nerves that lack this fatty insulation. Insulated fibers are called **fast fibers**.

The free nerve endings, on the other hand, send their messages up your cord *slowly* by way of uninsulated axons. Since neural messages travel 30 times slower in your uninsulated nerve tracts than in the "fast fibers," the uninsulated neurons are called **slow fibers**.

If you implanted an electrode in the *fast fibers* of someone's spinal cord and stimulated these nerve cells directly, the person would report "pressury" feelings. If you stimulated the *slow fibers* instead, the person might report feeling pressure or temperature changes. But if the current was *intense* enough, the person might well report feeling pain. However, if you stimulate both fast and slow fibers simultaneously, the person will feel no pain no matter how intense the slow-fiber stimulation is. Apparently slow-fiber activity turns pain on, but fast-fiber activity somehow turns it off!

These facts suggest that skin pain is not a special "sense" all on its own. Further research has confirmed this view. Indeed, we now realize that pain is a highly complex psychological *experience* that is affected by many factors. Some of these factors are psychological, some physiological, others are biochemical. Some have to do with memory and conditioning, while others are strongly influenced by stress and motivation.

We will discuss all these factors in a moment. But if you wish to understand why painful inputs often "hurt," you must first discover why they sometimes don't!

Pain Insensitivity

In the 1960's, there began to appear in the medical literature reports of seemingly normal individuals who experienced no pain at all! These rare individuals had the usual sensitivity to pressure and to temperature, but *no amount of stimulation* to any part of their body caused them any kind of sensory unpleasantness. One such male, treated by neurologist Kenneth Magee at The University of Michigan Medical Center, was named Joseph B. All his life Joseph B. had thought the people around him were "sissies" because they complained of having "pains." Joseph B. enjoyed visiting dentists—if he had the time. If he didn't, having his teeth pulled with a pair of pliers was fine with him. And while he enjoyed eating, drinking, and sex, Joseph B. didn't experience discomfort from any form of sensory over-stimulation—even when kicked in the testicles.

The problem that patients such as Joseph B. pose is this. These people apparently have activity in both their fast and slow fibers, so why don't they feel pain?

"Spinal Gate" Theory of Pain

In 1965 Ronald Melzack of McGill University and Patrick Wall of University College in London put all these odd facts together and created a comprehensive theory of what pain is—and isn't. Melzack and Wall believe that there is a kind of neurological "gate" in your spinal cord that determines whether or not you will feel an incoming sensory message as painful.

Enigma (ee-NIGG-mah). From the Greek word meaning "to speak in riddles." Winston Churchill once said, "I cannot forecast to you the action of Russia. It is a riddle wrapped in a mystery inside an enigma."

Insulated (IN-sue-lay-ted). From the Latin word meaning "island," or "to isolate." Telephone wires have rubbery insulation around them to keep the message traveling down one wire from mixing with the messages on an adjacent wire. The axons of some nerve cells have a fatty insulation called *myelin* (MY-uh-lin) around them to keep sensory messages from "jumping wires."

Fast fibers; slow fibers. Neural messages travel along axonic fibers at different speeds, depending on the thickness of the fibers and the amount of myelin wrapped around the axon. Uninsulated fibers are "thin and slow"; sensory inputs travel along slow fibers at a speed of about 3 meters (10 feet) per second. Some insulated fibers are so thick and fast that messages flow along the axons at about 100 meters (300 feet) per second or more.

Spinal gate. To gate something out means to keep something from entering. Melzack and Wall believe there is a nerve center in the spinal cord that "gates out" some sensations and lets others through to the brain. No one has yet located this "spinal gate" precisely nor determined exactly how it works.

According to Melzack and Wall, it is the *relative amount* of neural activity at the point of the **spinal gate** that controls the sensation of pain. The same message coming through on the slow fiber tracts will "hurt" or "not hurt" depending on how active your fast fibers are at that moment. If your fast fibers are completely silent—as when they are damaged or cut—almost any stimulation of the slow fibers will cause you considerable pain. But if your fast fibers are firing at a very high rate, you simply won't feel pain no matter what your slow fibers are doing.

Activity in the fast fibers, then, tends to *inhibit* or "close the gate" on the experience of pain (see Fig. 17.5). The question now becomes, what controls activity in your fast fibers? As we will see, part of the answer may be chemical. But part is surely psychological.

Question: *If you stick your hand into a bowl of very cold water, you will first feel the pressure of water on your skin. Then, a fraction of a second later, you will feel that the water is very cold. And then, a moment after that, you will experience pain. How might you explain these facts in terms of the Melzack-Wall "spinal gate" theory of pain?*

Substance P and the "Spinal Gate"

To date, no one has discovered a "spinal gate" anywhere in the nervous system. But by 1980, a number of scientists had speculated that the "gate" might be *chemical* rather than *biological*.

More than 50 years ago, biochemists discovered in the nervous system a complex neural

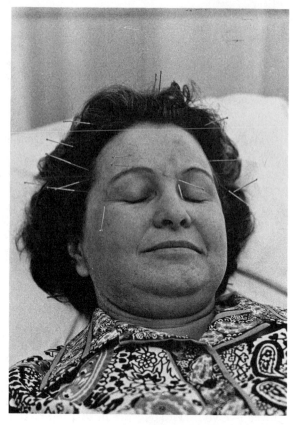

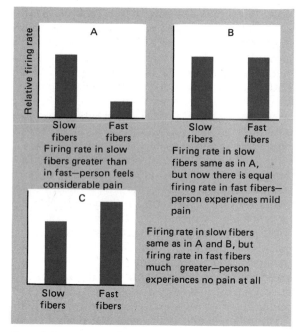

One of the reasons that acupuncture "works" seems to be that sticking needles in people causes their bodies to release large amounts of endorphins. **(left)**

Fig. 17.5. How the "spinal gate" operates. **(right)**

Ronald Melzack

transmitter they called Substance P. For half a century, no one knew precisely what Substance P did. However, recent research by Thomas Jessell at the Harvard Medical School suggests that Substance P may be the main transmitter for pain in the human nervous system.

The data linking Substance P to pain are of two types. First, food seasonings such as paprika and red peppers can cause intense pain when in-

gested in large quantities. They also cause the release of Substance P in the *slow fibers* of the spinal cord. Second, as Thomas Jessell has recently shown, the endorphins appear to *inhibit* the release of Substance P. Jessell suggests that Substance P "opens the spinal gate" to pain, while the endorphins close it.

And so we are back where we started from. For the question now arises, what controls the release of endorphins?

Question: *Although there are no data on the subject, would you guess that people like Joseph B. who don't feel pain have much Substance P in their bodies?*

Mind over Matter

Consider these facts. The endorphins mediate the experience of pain. But whether or not your body secretes endorphins in any given situation depends on your personality and your present environment, not on the amount of Substance P in your slow fibers. If you have been *conditioned* to release endorphins when you are stressed, then you have acquired a psychological way of "closing your spinal gate" when you feel pain.

Research shows that you are likely to secrete large amounts of endorphins in the following situations: when you are highly stressed; when you are hypnotized; when you "submit" to someone who tells you not to feel pain; when you undergo **acupuncture**; when you take a placebo, when you consciously focus your mind on blocking out painful inputs, and when you are strongly motivated to "forget" painful events. Therefore, you cannot understand pain—or the effects of placebos and hypnosis—unless you know something about what kind of person you presently are and how you were *trained* to respond to the world. For it is during your childhood that you typically learn those mental skills that allow you to control pain voluntarily when you are an adult.

Transmitter. A chemical released by axonic end fibers into the synapse that sets off an action potential in the next neuron in line. See Chapter 3.

Acupuncture (ACK-you-punk-ture). The Latin word *acus* means "needle." Acupuncture is an ancient Chinese form of medicine that involves puncturing the body with needles either to "cure" an illness or to reduce pain. Recent studies suggest its main effect is to cause the release of endorphins.

We have spent the first part of this book studying such mental processes as sensation, perception, memory, and motivation. Let's next look at how you put these processes together to develop your own unique pattern of personality.

Summary

1. According to the National Institutes of Health, 50 percent of all Americans experience severe **pain** annually.
2. Physicians have known for centuries that a **placebo** can be very effective in reducing pain—if the patient *believes* that the placebo is some powerful medicine.
3. Placebos work, in part, because they cause the release of **endorphins**, particularly in "externalizers" (people who believe themselves controlled by fate rather than by free will).
4. **Hypnotism** was first discovered by Anton Mesmer in the late 1700's, who thought he had "cured" his patients by putting them in a **trance state**.
5. Sigmund Freud used hypnosis to "remove symptoms" from **hysterical patients**, but abandoned the technique because it didn't always work.
6. Clark Hull and the early behaviorists believed that hypnosis was a state of narrowly focused attention in which the subject became extremely suggestible.
7. T.X. Barber has shown that people with rich **fantasy lives** often make good hypnotic subjects.
8. Ernest Hilgard believes that people with **punitive parents** often resort to fantasy as a way of escaping psychologically from parental wrath.
9. Under hypnosis, you may perform **anti-social acts** and many unusual feats of mind and body—but nothing that you wouldn't do anyhow if **highly motivated**.
10. Subjects undergoing **hypnotic age regression** often act as if they had access to **repressed** or forgotten memories. Most of these experiences can be explained as a type of **role-playing**.
11. Hilgard believes that, under hypnosis, the mind "splits" and that painful inputs not experienced by the conscious mind are felt by a **hidden observer**.
12. Barber believes that hypnosis is not an **altered state of consciousness**, and that Hilgard's data can better be explained in terms of role-playing.
13. A century ago, pain was thought to be a sensory input similar to pressure, temperature, sights, and smells. Recent studies suggest that pain is a **complex mental experience** rather than a sensory input.
14. Pressure sensations are carried up your spinal cord by **fast fibers** that are insulated by fat. Temperature sensations are carried by uninsulated **slow fibers**.
15. If stimulation from the slow fibers is greater than the stimulation from the fast fibers, the brain usually experiences pain. If the stimulation from the fast fibers is greater, the brain usually does not experience pain.
16. According to the **Melzack-Wall theory of pain**, the brain may at times inhibit or depress messages flowing through the **spinal gate**. The brain can thus shut off painful inputs by turning off the "spinal gate."
17. Pain seems to be mediated in the spinal cord by a neural transmitter called **Substance P**, which is inhibited by the **endorphins**. Since the endorphins are released by stress and other psychological experiences, whether you feel pain ultimately depends more on perception, motivation, past training, and your personality than on sensory inputs.

(Continued from page 391.)

Assistant Professor Don Powell and his teaching fellow, Brian Healy, were correcting exam papers in Powell's office when a loud knock at the door interrupted their work.

"Come in!" Powell cried.

When Elvis McNeil walked through the door, the psychologist paled momentarily. Recovering quickly from his shock, Powell forced a broad smile. "Come in, come in, Mr. McNeil. Sit down! Make yourself comfortable! Why, we haven't seen you for several days! Wherever have you been?"

McNeil sat confidently in the chair that Powell had indicated. "Reading, sir. Reading everything I could find about the powers of the mind."

Powell seemed a little flustered. "Er, well, yes. Interesting. Very interesting. We were afraid that you were angry with us—with Mr. Healy and me—about the little hypnosis demonstration we put on in class. I do hope you haven't stayed away from class because of some juvenile embarrassment . . ."

"Embarrassment? Of course not, sir! The very opposite."

"Then you aren't angry with us?"

"Certainly not, Professor. I came to thank you—and to ask for your help. You see, I've always been convinced that I had a strong mind, that I had hidden talents which I simply couldn't bring out into the open and gain control of."

Powell and Healy looked at each other uneasily.

"Yes, Professor Powell," McNeil said, leaning toward the psychologist. "Even before I took your class, I had searched through all the occult literature. I had answered ads in magazines that offered to make me a mental giant if I would purchase a set of their long-suppressed secrets. I had read the life histories of the mystics and tried to tap the power of the stars through astrology. But none of it worked very well. And then . . . and then, you opened the doors to my perception! You transported me to the pinnacles of power!"

Powell glanced sternly at Brian Healy, who was struggling valiantly to suppress a grin.

"Yes, well, I'm sure that's one way to look at it," Powell said hurriedly. "No harm done, then . . ."

"Oh, no. No harm at all. You see, I was sure I could really make the chair float around and dance without any help from you, if only I could find the key that would unlock my latent mental energies. Hypnosis did it, as you saw for yourself. So I've been reading all the books I could find on using hypnotism to unleash cortical forces. You really set my synapses to tingling!"

Brian Healy made a noise suspiciously like a muffled giggle.

"The trouble is," Elvis McNeil continued, not perceiving the reactions his words were evoking, "The trouble is, I can't seem to regain the powers that I had while hypnotized that day in class. I mean, I've tried and tried and tried. I've talked to one chair after another, and none of them will float—not even a centimeter. I feel I'm getting extremely close to the real mental break-through I've always searched for. But I can't seem to make that final step. That's why I'm here."

"Yes?" said Professor Powell suspiciously.

"Sir, how much would you charge to hypnotize me again, and bring back the power?"

The psychologist was stunned. "Well," he said a few moments later. "Well, well. We'll have to think about that one for a while."

Elvis McNeil said hurriedly, "I can't afford much, but I'll pay whatever I can. Anything, anything to get that mystical magic back under my voluntary control!"

Powell gave the young man a wide-eyed look. Then he shook his head, almost sadly. "Yes, well, I do think we'd better have a long talk about mysticism and magic, McNeil. In private." Powell reached for his desk calendar. "Could you come see me tomorrow afternoon, say about 4 o'clock?"

"Certainly, sir. Any time you name."

"And let's keep our mouths shut about all this, shall we? I mean, we wouldn't want to let everybody in on the secret, now would we?"

"Certainly, sir. Anything you say."

"And in the meantime, I want you to go to the library and check out a book called *LSD, Marihuana, Yoga and Hypnosis* by Theodore X. Barber. Read it through carefully, particularly the section on hypnosis. Read it very, very carefully indeed. And if you're behind in any of your studies, use those latent mental powers of yours to catch up quickly. Okay?"

"Okay."

"And see me tomorrow at 4 P.M. sharp."

"Yes, sir. I can hardly wait!"

After Elvis McNeil had left the office, Professor Powell sat staring at the wall and tapping a pencil nervously on his desk. Then he turned to his assistant and said, "You know, Brian, when we teach this course next semester, instead of having a class demonstration on hypnotism, what would you think about showing a movie on the subject? I mean, maybe that's a fine way to demonstrate that while hypnosis can be useful, if improperly used it can cause, er, unexpected problems."

Brian Healy scratched his head. "Sure, Professor Powell. Sure."

Recommended Readings

Barber, Theodore X. *LSD, Marihuana, Yoga and Hypnosis* (Chicago: Aldine-Atherton, 1970).

Bowers, Kenneth S. *Hypnosis for the Seriously Curious* (Monterey, Calif.: Brooks/Cole, 1976).

Fromm, Erika, and R.E. Shor, eds. *Hypnosis: Developments in Research and New Perspectives*, 2nd ed. (New York: Aldine, 1979).

Hilgard, Ernest R. "Hypnosis and Consciousness," *Human Nature*, Vol. 1 (January, 1978), pp. 42–49.

Smith, W.L., Harold Merskey, and S.C. Gross. *Pain: Meaning and Management* (New York: SP Medical & Scientific Books, 1980).

5

Maturation
and
Development

Physical Growth and Development

18

Did You Know That . . .

Each human being starts life as a single cell with 46 chromosomes (which contain the person's genes)?

You became a male or a female because of the influence of just one of these 46 chromosomes?

Children who are badly malnourished during infancy may become permanently retarded if they are not given special attention and a stimulating environment?

If a newly hatched goose follows a human being rather than its own mother, it will (as an adult) be sexually attracted to humans rather than to other geese?

An infant develops control over its head muscles long before it develops control over the muscles in its legs and feet?

Most infants are mature enough to imitate facial expressions just an hour after birth?

Many parents of children born with genetic defects reject or badly distort the scientific information they are given about their children?

With the proper training and encouragement, even severely handicapped individuals can be helped to reach their genetic potential?

"Where Sex Leaves Off"

Dr. Martin Mayer stared at the classroom, terrified. Through his thick-lensed glasses, the bright young faces seemed distorted, larger than life. The students swarmed around the room in constant motion, like bees defending their hive. High school students, Mayer said to himself, have more energy than they know what to do with. How in the world could he have let himself in for something like this?

The man standing at the front of the classroom beside Dr. Mayer smiled mechanically. "All right, young people. Let's settle down now and listen. We have a special guest today, someone famous in the field of genetic psychology, or the study of inherited behavior patterns. He's come all the way from Mid-American University to give the annual Science Lecture this afternoon. And since he arrived earlier than we had expected, we've prevailed upon Dr. Mayer to address all the biology classes today. Isn't that kind of Dr. Mayer?"

Kind? They hadn't really given him the chance to refuse. At the University, he taught only small graduate seminars. These bubbling, excited high school students were at least 10 years younger than the men and women who elected his classes at the university. What could he say to these youngsters that he hadn't already planned to cover in his formal address later that afternoon? A sinking feeling in the pit of his stomach began working its way up his digestive system.

The biology teacher droned on. "Dr. Mayer has published more than 100 articles in various scientific journals, and he is co-author of the famous *Handbook of Behavior Genetics*. I'm sure you'll want to give him your closest attention. And now let's welcome Dr. Mayer with a nice round of applause."

The students clapped loudly, and one or two even whistled. Dr. Mayer blinked twice. The co-author of the famous *Handbook of Behavior Genetics* was frankly petrified. Every face in the class was focused on him now, waiting expectantly. His wife, Elizabeth, would have called it a "pregnant pause." What had she told him, just before he got on the plane? "If you get stuck for something to say, just talk about sex. They'll listen."

Dr. Mayer adjusted his glasses on his nose. "With your permission, students, I'd like to talk about sex."

Their immediate rapt attention gave him all the permission he needed.

"As a scientist, I'm interested in sex—in all its aspects. Among lower animals, sex is primarily a matter of hormones and instincts. Among humans, it can also be an act of love. But among both humans and lower animals, sex is the beginning of life, not just the living end of things. For life starts where sex leaves off. And scientists who study the beginnings of life, as I do, must consider the biological as well as the social and moral consequences of the sexual act."

Mayer smiled at the students wanly. "A few months ago, I read Aldous Huxley's novel, *Brave New World*, for the third time. Huxley was a renegade, an artist born into a family of famous scientists. Late in his life, he studied the effects of hallucinogens like mescaline on human perception. But before he got interested in drugs, Huxley studied genetics. He was particularly interested in the social consequences of sexual behavior.

"Huxley came to the study of genetics naturally, for his grandfather had defended Charles Darwin's theory of evolution against attack by religious leaders in the 1860's. Darwin believed that animals mated rather freely, and their genes mixed rather randomly. When a male lion had sex with a female lion, neither of them was trying to create a super-lion. They were just following their blind instincts. Some of their lion cubs were, by chance, bigger and stronger than others, and these cubs survived. The weak cubs died because the environment in which they lived favored big, strong lions."

Mayer glanced at the students. They were still listening raptly, so he continued. "Humans are different, of course. We have the ability to select quite deliberately which of our offspring will survive simply by controlling the environment our children live in. And that ability puts us in a moral bind that lions don't have to face."

Mayer paused to take off his glasses and clean them. "Sometimes I think it would be great just to be a lion, so I wouldn't have to worry about the consequences of having sex."

Several of the students laughed.

"Control of the environment is perhaps the most difficult problem facing us at the moment," Mayer said once his glasses were adjusted. "But Huxley saw that an equally difficult social issue would pop up in the near future. What would happen, he asked in *Brave New World*, if we could control the genetic process itself?"

Mayer frowned gently. "When two human beings—or two lions—mate, the sperm from the male unites with the egg borne by the female. One of the primary functions of the genetic message inside each sperm and egg cell is that of telling the cell how to grow and develop into an adult organism. The genes, then, are a kind of 'computer program' that instructs the cell in what its future behavior should be like."

Now the scientist smiled. "Ever ask yourself why you turned out to be a human instead of a lion? The answer lies in the genes you inherited from your mother and father. Human genes have different instructions in them than do lion genes. And you developed blue eyes—or brown ones—because your parents and grandparents' genes passed along 'biological instructions' that programmed your cells to turn out as they did. You had no choice in the matter—just as you will pass on your genes for eye color or skin color to your children whether you or they like it or not.

"But what if we could *change* your genes before you started creating the next generation? That is, what if we could *re-program* your genetic computer? Aldous Huxley was bright enough to see that, when scientists learned enough about genes, we could probably do just that."

Mayer shook his head. "See what I mean about the consequences of sex? Well, someday soon, we can go to a young married couple and say, hey, what kinds of kids would you like to have? Do you want a big, blond football player for a son? Would you prefer a small, dark-skinned daughter as beautiful as the Queen of Sheba? Or would you rather your daughter became a physicist, a sort of Alberta Einstein? And is there any reason why she couldn't be both beautiful and exceptionally bright? And would you like for your son to have big hands—not so he could catch a football, but so he could play the piano like Van Cliburn?"

Some of the students frowned, a fact that pleased Mayer immensely, so he kept on talking. "That's part of what *Brave New World* is all about. What I'd like to ask you today is the same question—when that great day comes and we know how to reprogram the genes of our children, what kind of kids would you like to have?"

The class sat silent, as if this was an idea they didn't really care to give much thought to.

"You," Dr. Mayer said, pointing to a young girl sitting in the second row. "How are you doing in biology?"

The girl blushed and the class giggled. Obviously biology wasn't one of the girl's better subjects.

"Are you getting an A+ in biology?"

The girl shook her head.

"Do you have to study more than you'd like in order to get grades that aren't as good as you wish?"

The girl nodded her agreement.

"Wouldn't it have been nice if your parents had 'spliced up your genes' to make you a 'brain,' so you could breeze through the biology book and learn it all very quickly? Wouldn't that help?" Mayer asked in a joking tone of voice.

"But then I wouldn't be *me*," the girl wailed. "I'd be somebody else!"

Mayer turned quickly to a small, handsome young man sitting toward the back of the class. He had a guitar case lying beside his chair. "You, there, you're pretty good on the guitar, aren't you?"

"I'm just learning," the young man said shyly.

"But you'd like to be able to play as well as Segovia, or some of the popular rock stars, right? Did you know that the best guitar players seem to have much better finger coordination than average players have? The ability seems to be inherited, and all the practice in the world won't make you a performing genius if you don't have the right genes to start with. Don't you wish now that your parents had fixed up your finger genes before you were conceived?"

"Sure," the boy said quietly.

"You're smaller than average, too," Dr. Mayer continued. "Does that ever bother you, maybe just a little?"

The boy nodded slowly.

"Well, wouldn't you like your kids to be taller than average? Wouldn't you want to see a genetic engineer to splice up your genes before you start having a family?"

One of the boys in the middle of the room interrupted. "But if everybody wanted their kids to be bigger than average, what would happen to the average?"

The class laughed.

"That's pretty unnatural, isn't it?" one of the girls asked.

"Of course it's unnatural," Mayer shot back. "Lions can't do it and neither can elephants. But the way 'gene splicing' is going these days, we'll soon be able to plan these things. Before you marry, you'll probably spend a lot of time deciding what your first house or apartment is going to look like. Don't you think you ought to spend just as much time planning what kind of children you'll have?"

"But you can't change human nature," the guitar-playing boy said.

"Ah, but you can," Mayer said. "Education is always an attempt to change human nature. But education starts too late in many cases, because you can't teach a child anything until after it's born. With genetic control, though, we can start 'educating' the child even before it's conceived."

One of the girls started to interrupt, but Mayer continued. "Nowadays, if you have ugly children, your friends and neighbors don't blame you for it because you couldn't do anything to change how they looked. But if your kids are badly dressed, or if you don't send them to school, that's a *conscious choice* and people hold you responsible. In the future, when we can re-program genes at will, the world will hold you responsible for how pretty your children are—and for what native abilities they have. The lion can have sex without worrying about it. You can't. You'll have to decide whether you want your kids to be geniuses or just average types."

"But if everybody wanted their kids to be Einsteins, who'd collect the garbage?" complained a young man sitting in the front row.

"Beautiful question," Dr. Mayer said. "If there's a shortage of strong-bodied people who like to collect garbage, will the government require you to have kids who have an instinctive love for gathering up other people's trash?"

"I don't want anybody telling me what kinds of kids I've got to have," a young black student said. "Probably they'd try to make them all into robots."

"Hey, man, you're making *assumptions*," said another. "I mean, is garbage-loving an interited tendency?"

"Magnificent!" Dr. Mayer cried. "As far as we know, it's not. But maybe it could be. What kinds of *behaviors* do you think we can engineer into your children's genes?"

After a moment's pause, the guitar-playing boy responded. "You already said that finger coordination was inherited."

"Right. But someone born with the ability to move her or his fingers quickly probably could become a great violinist as well as a great guitarist. Or would be great at sewing or repairing computers. How would you feel if you had your future son's genes arranged so that he had superb finger coordination and he wanted to become a football player instead of a musician?"

"I'd send him to Notre Dame," said a large young man with an apparent interest in sports.

"Good idea," said Mayer. "But what other innate skills would you want to program into your future son to push him toward music? An inborn sense of rhythm? Is that something you inherit, or do you learn it from your parents? You, young lady," he said, pointing again to the girl in the second row. "What musical talents do you think are inherited, and which ones are learned?"

"I think you're trying to make us think too much," the young woman replied. "Why can't we just have kids and let them grow up the natural way, like our parents did?"

Mayer smiled. "For the same reason that we can't pretend that nuclear bombs don't exist. Genetic engineering is going to happen whether you like it or not, so you might as well start thinking about how it might affect you. As for me, I can't do anything about changing my children's genes because they're already born. But I can study behavior genetics in my lab so that your kids, or your grandchildren, can make decisions I couldn't make. But meanwhile, I've got a great big problem and it has to do with sex."

The class, which had become rather noisy during the discussion, suddenly quieted down again. Mayer smiled at how well things were going. His wife, Elizabeth, had given him very sound advice.

"Someday in the future, as Huxley pointed out, we'll have genetic engineering and we will be able to order our kids from a catalog. But we already know that some diseases and maybe even some types of insanity have a genetic component. The facts are that some people carry the *wrong kind of genes*. If we were lions, nature would take care of things—lions with the wrong genes just don't survive in lion environments."

Mayer frowned. "The problem is, we're humans, and we tend to keep people alive no matter what's wrong with them, and no matter how much it costs. If we were 'natural' about things, the way lions are, we'd just let these people die when they were young. Until we have genetic engineering, and we can change these bad genes into good ones, what can we possibly do to protect ourselves from bad genes?"

The guitar-playing boy stuck up his hand. "Well," he said quietly, "Why don't we just pass a law saying that people with bad genes can't have kids?"

The class exploded in anger.

(Continued on page 429.)

Human Growth and Development

In the previous 17 chapters, we have discussed YOU in bits and pieces. That is, we have studied the biological and psychological *sub-systems* that make up your body and mind. These sub-systems included your neurons and the various parts of your brain, your sensory inputs and perceptions, and your motives and memories. In the next six chapters, we will put these bits and pieces together to form a bigger picture of what you are like and where you came from. And, as we promised in Chapter 5, we will soon see that *the whole is greater than the sum of its parts*. Put another way, YOU have "emergent properties" that your various sub-systems lack.

There are two traditional ways of presenting the scientific material on human growth and development. The first approach—typically called **developmental psychology** or *child psychology*—involves discussing how various *aspects* of your personality grow and mature over time, particularly during your younger years. The second method—often called the **life span approach**—usually traces the maturation of a "typical" individual from birth through middle-age to old age and death.

The developmental approach often takes an experimental view of the early years that is firmly anchored in scientific data. But it tends to focus more on such processes as perception and emotion than on the growth of the entire individual. The life span approach tends to look primarily at the "whole person" as she or he passes through various stages or "life crises," and it is often more applied than scientific in its orientation. But in paying attention to "wholes," the life span method sometimes fails to break human behavior down into its component processes.

Rather than adopting just one way of presenting the material on how humans grow and mature, we will use both approaches. In Chapters 18, 19, and 20, we will look primarily at "bits and pieces." That is, we will discuss *physical, social/ emotional*, and *cognitive* growth and development, with an emphasis on the early years of life. Then in Chapters 21, 22, and 23, we will focus on the "whole person," which is to say that we will study how your own unique *personality* develops from birth through old age.

Before we can adopt either approach, however, there are certain rather important issues that we must discuss if you are to understand the complexities involved in studying how YOU got to be what and who YOU are.

Developmental Themes

There are four major themes that run through all the literature on developmental psychology:

1. The infamous *mind-body problem* bedevils the developmental area as much as any other part of psychology.
2. What part of your personal growth is determined by your genes, and what part by experience? Here, again, the *nature-nurture* controversy rears its head.
3. Should we study those aspects of your personality that *change* over time, or those aspects that are *unchangeable* and consistent throughout your life?
4. Should we focus on *individual differences* or *human similarities*?

Let's begin by looking at each of these four grand themes briefly.

One of the major themes of developmental psychology is individual differences vs. human similarities. All children develop in much the same way, yet each child has his or her unique way of responding even to such simple situations as riding a rocking horse.

Mind/Body Problem

If you haven't read Chapter 5 by now, it might be to your benefit to do so before you tackle the material on developmental and personality psychology. Many developmental psychologists attempt to *reduce* all human growth and maturation to changes in the functioning of the nervous system. Other psychologists tend to focus almost entirely on changes in *measurable behaviors*, particularly those brought about by changes in the environment. Still others look primarily at "the growth of the mind." If you adopt a holistic solution to the mind/body problem, you will probably be interested in all three of the classical viewpoints (biological, social/behavioral, and intra-psychic).

Nature-Nurture Controversy

There probably is no issue more violently debated in developmental psychology than the question of what is learned and what is innately determined about human growth and maturation. In truth, as we have noted so many times before, *everything* you do or think or feel is influenced both by your genes and by what you have experienced in the past. Thus the issue really boils down to determining how nature and nurture *interact*. As you will see, however, many psychologists still adopt rather extreme positions that are not always strongly supported by the experimental data.

Change versus Consistency

Generally speaking, those psychologists who view behavior as being primarily learned tend to emphasize *human change*. However, some of them believe that your basic personality and behavior patterns are pretty much fixed during the first years of your life, while others assume that you are capable of "developing" up to the moment of your death. Nor is there universal agreement as to what aspects of your personality change, nor how and why those changes come about.

Those scientists who focus on human *consistency* often emphasize the importance of the genetic blueprint in determining why individuals grew up to be the people they are. These psychologists assume that since all humans tend to have similar bodies and basic needs, they all should develop in much the same way. However, other theorists presume that psychological consistencies are due primarily to the fact that a person was reared in a relatively consistent environment.

In the long run, you may learn more about yourself (and others) if you look both at what parts of your personality change over time, and which of your traits appear to be long-lasting.

Similarities versus Differences

You are YOU—a unique living system. You have your own psychological needs and personality traits that differ in many ways from anyone else's. But like most other humans, you probably have two arms and legs, a nose and mouth, two eyes and ears, hair, and skin. Even your values and opinions are probably similar to those of your family and friends. From an objective point of view, then, you dress and walk and talk like most other humans, and you think, feel, and react to most situations as does almost everyone else in the world.

So, what is more important about you—the fact that you are unique, or the fact that you share most of your thoughts, feelings, and behaviors with all other humans?

As we will see, some psychologists who study the human personality tend to emphasize the ways in which people are similar. These scientists assume you go through the same *developmental stages* that everyone must pass through, and that you experience the same *life crises* that all humans presumably experience. Other psychologists are more impressed by the fact that there are striking differences across individuals.

Developmental psychology. The study of human growth and maturation, particularly during the childhood years, that focuses on how various aspects of the body and personality develop. Often called "child psychology" as well.

Life span approach. The study of the development of a "typical" individual from conception and birth through the various maturational stages to old age and death.

Nucleus (NEW-klee-us). From the Latin word meaning "kernel," as in the phrase, "This statement has a kernel of truth to it." The nucleus is the heart or center of any system. The sun is the nucleus of our solar system. The yolk is the nucleus of an egg. The center portion of a living cell is called the nucleus, which usually contains the genes that direct the cell's functioning.

Chromosomes (KROH-moh-sohms). From the Greek words *chromo*, meaning "colored," and *soma*, meaning "body." The genes of a cell are strung together like strands of colored beads. These "strands" are the chromosomes.

These scientists note that even if you passed through nearly the same stages as did most other people, you did so at your own speed and in your own way. And even if you encountered life crises similar to those of the person living next door, you surely solved your difficulties in your own unique fashion.

Actually, as you might guess, by far the *most important aspect* of your own development is the fact that you are like others in some ways, but different from everyone else in the world in other ways.

The Four Themes

We will encounter these four "grand themes" constantly as we look at the material on human growth and development. Indeed, part of the delight in studying this area of psychology is that of learning not only how various theorists and researchers have tried to handle these themes, but in discovering what your own beliefs have been in the past (and perhaps acquiring a few new ones before you finish the next six chapters).

That said and done, suppose we now take a look at *physical growth*. In Chapter 19 we will discuss *social* and *emotional* development. And in Chapter 20, we will delve extensively into *cognitive* growth and maturation.

Genetic Development

Like all other human beings, you began life as a single cell (see Fig. 18.1). This egg cell—produced in your mother's reproductive organs—looked much like many other human cells. That is, the egg cell was a tiny round blob of material with a dark **nucleus** in its center. The nucleus contains what we might call the "managers" of the cell—its **chromosomes** (see Fig. 18.2).

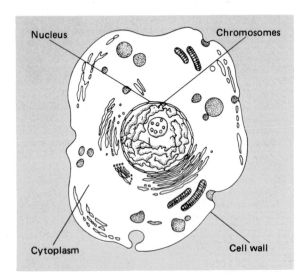

Nucleus
Chromosomes
Cytoplasm
Cell wall

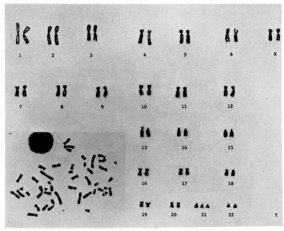

Genes are composed chiefly of DNA molecules such as the ones shown in this model. **(top right)**

Fig. 18.1. A cell. **(top left)**

Fig. 18.2. Humans have 23 pairs of chromosomes, shown on the left as they might appear in a living cell. The 23rd pair is either XX or XY and determines the person's sex. If the 21st pair has an extra member, as shown on the right, the person will suffer from trisomy-21, or Down's Syndrome. **(left)**

Fig. 18.3. Cell reproduction. **(bottom)**

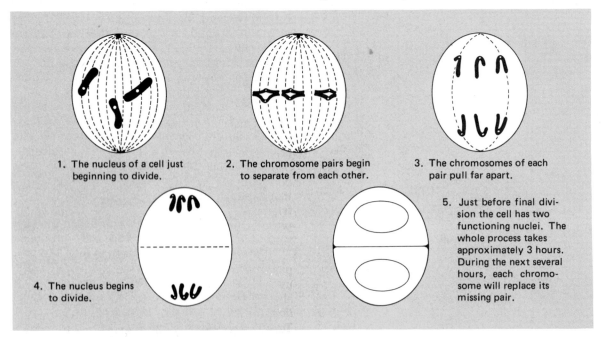

1. The nucleus of a cell just beginning to divide.

2. The chromosome pairs begin to separate from each other.

3. The chromosomes of each pair pull far apart.

4. The nucleus begins to divide.

5. Just before final division the cell has two functioning nuclei. The whole process takes approximately 3 hours. During the next several hours, each chromosome will replace its missing pair.

Most of the cells in your body contain 23 *pairs* of chromosomes. If you looked at them through a microscope, each of these 46 chromosomes would seem to be a long strand of colored beads. These 46 chromosomes are composed chiefly of a substance called **DNA**, which is an *acid* because of its chemical composition. It is a *nucleic* acid because it is found chiefly in the nucleus of the cell. Your genes are composed chiefly of DNA molecules.

DNA controls the functioning of the cell by making a substance called RNA, another nucleic acid. RNA carries the "instructions" from the DNA in the nucleus out to the **cytoplasm** or work area of the cell. It is in the cytoplasm that the proper proteins are put together which keep the cell (and you) alive. These "instructions" are really a form of cellular *feed-forward*, for they are a series of biochemical commands telling the "workers" in the cytoplasm what proteins to produce next (see Chapter 5).

DNA. An abbreviation for deoxyribonucleic acid. The genes are composed chiefly of DNA molecules. You developed into a human being rather than a rat or a flatworm because the DNA in your genes is quite different from the DNA in rat or flatworm cells. See Chapter 16.

Cytoplasm (SIGH-toe-PLASS-em). The Greek word *kyto* means "hollow vessel" or "cell." Our word *plasm* comes from the Greek word meaning "plastic," "formable," or "fluid." Cytoplasm is the fluid-like substance surrounding the nucleus of a cell, as the white of an egg surrounds the yolk.

Trisomy-21 (TRY-so-me). From the Greek words *tri*, meaning "three," and *soma*, meaning "body." The modern term for mongolism, or Down's syndrome. A relatively common form of birth defect in which the facial features of the person somewhat resemble Oriental or Mongolian characteristics. Some form of mental retardation is often associated with trisomy-21, although the person's intellectual development is often as "retarded" by poor teaching techniques as by physiological fault.

Turner syndrome (SIN-drome). A "syndrome" is a collection of symptoms all having (presumably) a common cause. Turner's syndrome is the collection of symptoms associated with a woman's having a single X 23rd chromosome, rather than the normal XX 23rd chromosome.

Cellular Division

Cells reproduce by dividing (see Fig. 18.3). When a cell divides, its nucleus splits in two and half the DNA present goes into one of the daughter cells, while the other half of the DNA goes into the other daughter cell. (The term "daughter" is used even if the child will develop into a son rather than a daughter.) But as cell division takes place, the nucleus must *double* the amount of DNA present so that each daughter cell will have its full complement of 46 chromosomes the moment the split occurs. Since the daughter cells have exactly the same DNA, the two cells are "identical twins."

The only exception to this rule is in the case of the sperm and unfertilized egg cells. When an egg cell is produced through division, the original 23 chromosome pairs split in half *without doubling*, so that the egg cell contains exactly half the chromosomes it needs to survive and multiply. But since the sperm and egg have *different* DNA when they unite, they form a cell that is *unlike* any cell in either the mother's or father's body.

X and Y Chromosomes

The sperm cell, like the egg cell, contains only 23 chromosomes (see Fig. 18.4). The only way the sperm cell can survive is by mating with an egg cell to make up the 23 *pairs* of chromosomes every human cell needs to function properly. But the sperm cell is somewhat different from the egg. Its twenty-third chromosome can be either the large X type or the smaller Y type. The twenty-third chromosome of the egg cell is *always* a large X type.

If an X-type sperm is the first to enter the egg cell, the fertilized egg will of course have an XX twenty-third chromosome pair—and the child will be female. If a Y-type sperm fertilizes the egg, the twenty-third chromosome pair will be of the XY variety and the child will be a male.

There are slightly more male children born than female, a fact which could have several explanations. The human male might produce slightly more (or slightly more vigorous) Y sperms than X sperms, or the female body might be slightly more receptive to Y sperms than to the X type. Generally speaking, however, the chances of a man's fathering male or female children are about equal.

Chromosomal Abnormalities

The human reproductive process is a very complicated one indeed, and sometimes it breaks down. Occasionally the twenty-first chromosome pair does not divide properly, and the child is born with *three* twenty-first chromosomes rather than the normal pair (see Fig. 18.5). This **trisomy-21** condition leads to a type of mental, physical, and behavioral deficiency called *Down's syndrome* (see Fig. 18.6).

Sometimes the twenty-third chromosome pair does not divide properly and the child ends up with but a *single* twenty-third chromosome— always an X-type—or with one or more *additional* X or Y chromosomes. In what is called **Turner syndrome**, the child's cells contain but a

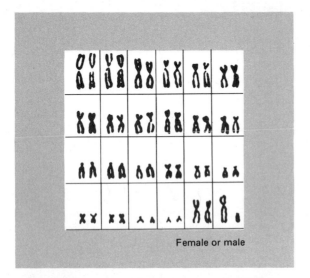

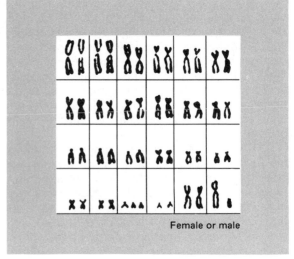

Female or male

Female or male

Fig. 18.4. Human chromosome cells. Only the 23rd pair differ—XX for female, XY for male. (**top left**)

Fig. 18.5. Trisomy-21. Note the three chromosomes instead of the usual 21st pair. (**top right**)

Fig. 18.6. A child suffering from Down's syndrome, or trisomy-21. (**bottom left**)

single X chromosome. Individuals who experience this chromosomal problem have female genitalia but lack ovaries. If given injections of female hormones at puberty, they develop the normal behavioral and physical characteristics of an adult female.

A child with an XXY twenty-third chromosome will be physically a male—with penis and testicles—but with strong feminine characteristics. This condition—known as **Klinefelter's syndrome**—occurs in about one child out of every 900 born.

About one boy in 1,000 has two Y chromosomes and one X. There are marked if subtle differences between the XYY and the XY male. The XYY male is typically taller than average, and tends to reach sexual puberty a year or more be-

fore the normal XY male does. About half of the XYY males suffer from moderate to severe acne—a much higher percentage than is found among normal men. Homosexual and many other abnormal patterns of sexual behavior are much more frequent in XYY males than in XY's. And, for reasons we still don't understand, the XYY condition appears primarily in white males.

Research reported in Europe in the 1960's and 1970's suggested that an abnormally large number of XYY males turn up in hospital wards reserved for the criminally insane. Some scientists at first believed that the extra Y chromosome actually *caused* the criminal behavior to occur. However, current thinking takes a different view. The extra *male* chromosome causes the boy's adrenal glands to secrete abnormal amounts of androgen during his development. This excess male hormone seems responsible both for the early onset of puberty and for the acne.

However, as we learned in Chapter 12, the androgens are also the "major motivators" of human behavior, and excess amounts of male hormone typically lead to an increase in *impulsive behaviors*. Most XYY males who get into trouble with the law appear to come from lower class families in which the parents apparently lack the social skills needed to teach such an impulsive child how to control himself. XYY males born to middle or upper class families seldom show this lack of self-discipline, and thus seldom end up in prisons or mental hospitals.

In summary, then, the XYY male is at risk only if he is born to parents who fail to give him adequate training in self-control during his early years. It is thus the *interaction* between genes and social environment that causes the problem, not the genes alone.

Question: *Some XYY males accused of crimes have asked to be pardoned, claiming their genetic disability "made them do it." If you were on the jury, what would your thinking be?*

The Beginnings of Life

At the moment that you were conceived, you were no more than a single egg cell locked away in your mother's body (see Fig. 18.7). But within 24 hours after your conception, that original egg cell had grown large enough to divide into two daughter cells. During this and all subsequent cell divisions, an identical set of 23 chromosome pairs went into each daughter cell. So, if the original cell you started life with had any form of chromosomal abnormality (such as the XYY condition), this abnormality would be passed along to every cell in your body.

At this point in your life, you might have become *identical twins* (see Fig. 18.8). Usually the first daughter cells remain close together and develop into a single individual. Sometimes, for reasons not clearly understood, these first cells separate and each eventually creates a complete human **embryo**. Since the daughter cells were identical, the twins will be identical too.

Fraternal twins are much more common. Occasionally a woman will produce two (or more) eggs during her fertile period. If both egg cells are fertilized, they will both begin independent growth at the same time, and the woman will produce fraternal twins nine months later. Since these two egg cells were fertilized by *different sperms*, they are no more identical than are brothers and sisters born to the same parents at different times.

If the two daughter cells remain linked after the first division, each of them will divide once more within a second 24-hour period. Within a third 24-hour period, all four of these cells will divide again. While this cell division goes on, the group of cells travels slowly down a tiny tube to the mother's womb. About nine days after fertilization, the rapidly forming human being attaches itself to the wall of the womb. At this point in your own life, you were about 0.5 millimeters (0.02 inches) in size.

Klinefelter's syndrome (rhymes with "MINE-belter"). A set of related physical characteristics (syndrome) found in males who have an extra X chromosome.

Embryo (EM-bree-oh). An unborn child from the time of conception to the second or third month of development, when the child takes on vaguely human form and is thereafter called a fetus. From the Greek word meaning "to swell within." Oddly enough, the German word sauerkraut ("swollen cabbage") comes from this same Greek term.

Fraternal twins (fra-TURN-al). Twins born from two fertilized eggs. Fraternal twins are no more alike than are brothers or sisters born at different times. From the Latin word meaning "brothers," from which we get the word "fraternity."

Ectoderm ECK-toh-durm). *Ekto* is the Greek word meaning "outer." *Derma* is the Greek word for "skin." A dermatologist (durr-mah-TOLL-oh-jist) is a medical doctor who specializes in treating skin diseases. A hypodermic is a needle that injects fluids under (hypo) the skin (derma).

Mesoderm (ME-so-derm). The "middle skin." The Greek word *mesos* means "in the center."

Endoderm (EN-doh-durm). The "inner skin." The Greek word *endon* means "inside" or "within."

Cellular Differentiation

Some two weeks after your life started, a remarkable change occurred in the tiny cluster of cells that made up your rapidly forming body. Up until this point, all of your cells were pretty much identical—because the "feed-forward" commands from the chromosomes were identical. But as we noted in Chapter 5, living systems are made up of sub-units that perform *different roles* in keeping the system alive. Thus, 13 to 14 days after fertilization, some of the chromosomes began feeding out slightly different sets of "command" instructions, and the cytoplasmic chemical factories in these cells began to produce slightly different proteins (and other materials).

As these new proteins and other molecules appeared, they forced the cells to *differentiate*—that is, to change shape, size, and function.

Fetal Development

By the fourteenth or fifteenth day of your life, you were made up of three clearly different groups of cells (see Fig. 18.9). One of these groups developed into what we call the **ectoderm**, a technical term that means "outer skin." Eventually these cells became your skin, your sense organs, and your nervous system.

Another group of cells, on instructions from their chromosomes, developed into what we term the **mesoderm**, or "middle skin." These cells eventually became your muscles, bone, and blood.

Yet a third group of cells received instructions to become **endoderm**, or "inner skin." These cells turned into your digestive system.

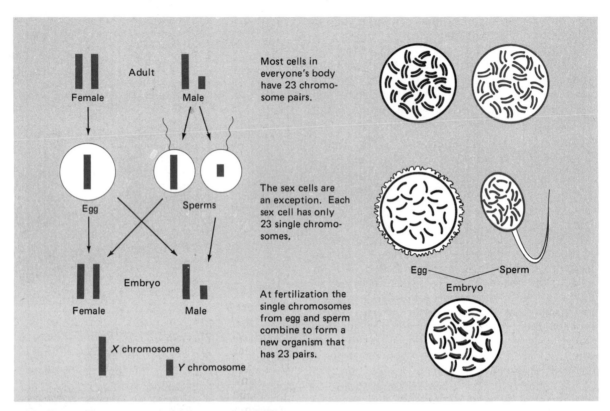

Most cells in everyone's body have 23 chromosome pairs.

Adult
Female
Male

Egg
Sperms

The sex cells are an exception. Each sex cell has only 23 single chromosomes.

Embryo
Female
Male

At fertilization the single chromosomes from egg and sperm combine to form a new organism that has 23 pairs.

I X chromosome

▮ Y chromosome

Egg — Sperm
Embryo

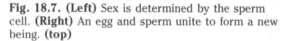

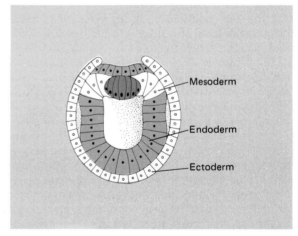

Mesoderm
Endoderm
Ectoderm

Fig. 18.7. (Left) Sex is determined by the sperm cell. **(Right)** An egg and sperm unite to form a new being. **(top)**

Fig. 18.8. Identical twins—such as these two—have identical sets of genes, and hence are very similar to each other. Fraternal twins, however, are no more alike than would be brothers and sisters born at different times. **(bottom left)**

Fig. 18.9. The embryo at about 2 weeks showing the three kinds of "derm." **(bottom right)**

At the moment this differentiation into the three "derms" occurred, you were a hollow ball about 2.5 millimeters (0.1 inch) in size, and technically you were then an *embryo*. It was not until six weeks later—some two months after your life started—that the three types of cells arranged themselves into vaguely human form, and the embryo thus became a **fetus**.

The Placenta

Developing cells—like developing children—are *unusually sensitive* to the environments they find themselves in. Luckily, as you grew within your mother's womb, you were protected from most of the chemicals in her body by an organ called the **placenta**. The placenta acted as a screen or barrier which blocked out most of the substances in your mother's blood that might have harmed your cells.

Illnesses, such as the German measles, can cause the pregnant woman's body to secrete chemicals somewhat different from the usual. If these chemicals (or the germs that cause them) infiltrate the placenta, they can upset the normal development of the fetus. If a woman has German measles during the third month of her pregnancy, for instance, the child is often born badly retarded. Narcotic drugs, such as morphine, also pass through the placenta and can set up an addiction in a fetus long before it is born. The presence of the morphine apparently keeps the fetus from developing the normal amount of endorphins. At the time of its birth, the child suffers rather frightening withdrawal symptoms until its cells can start producing endorphins in the usual quantities.

Effects of Physical Deprivation

Your genetic blueprint specified in rather general terms what you would be like and how you would grow. But this blueprint is always brought to life by orders from the DNA molecules in each cell. And, depending on circumstances, your growth and development can either be speeded up or retarded.

If a pregnant woman is forced by circumstances to undergo starvation, her body protects the fetus as much as it can by giving the unborn child almost all the resources the woman's body has available to it. Still, the child may be born much smaller than usual. If the child receives ample food immediately after birth, it usually catches up to the size its genetic blueprint had set for its normal development.

The same kind of catching up often occurs if a growing child is deprived of nourishment for brief periods by war or poverty. As an example, consider a study on Korean children reported late in 1975 by Myron Winick, Knarig Katchadurian Meyer, and Ruth C. Harris. During the Korean conflict in the 1950's, many very young children in that Asian country were separated from their parents and were placed in orphanages. Most of these youngsters suffered from severe malnutrition before they entered the institutions. After the hostilities ended, some of these children were returned to their war-shattered homes. But many others, whose parents were dead or missing, were placed in foster homes in the United States. Winick and his colleagues studied the physical

and intellectual development of several hundred of these Americanized orphans.

On the average, these children were so malnourished when they entered the orphanage that they fell far below other Korean children as far as height and weight were concerned. After several years of good care in the United States, however, *all* of these children were taller and stronger than the average child who remained in Korea.

Of even greater interest are the data that Winick *et al.* gathered on school achievement and intelligence. Previous studies had shown that the Korean children who were returned to their own home environments suffered rather severe mental and social retardation. This retardation continued through young adulthood. In marked contrast, the Americanized orphans had intelligence test scores that were, on the average, 40 to 50 points higher than those of the children who stayed in Korea. Indeed, their US foster homes were apparently so stimulating that the orphans had IQ's and school achievement scores that averaged slightly better than those of native-born US children of the same age.

It would seem that your genes *set limits* for your physical and intellectual development. But it is the environment you were reared in that determines *where within these limits* your actual growth will fall.

Neonatal Growth and Development

In general, as soon as the newborn child's muscles, sense organs, and nerves are fully formed, the child begins to use them. But much of the human nervous system is not fully developed until the child is a year or two old—and some parts, such as the corpus callosum, continue to mature for at least the next 20 years.

As the noted child psychologist Arnold Gesell pointed out long ago, there are two general patterns of bodily development. The first is from *head to foot*. The second is from *near to far*. The underlying principle explaining both patterns has

Children can only learn new motor skills—such as walking—when neural pathways between their muscles and their brains mature and become functional. **(top left)**

Oriental infants react to physical restraint (such as bundling) much more passively than do black or white infants. **(top right)**

Using twins, Gesell showed that early training on motor skills such as climbing stairs appears not to speed up physical motivation. **(bottom left)**

(such as crawling or grasping) always suggests that the brain centers have just become connected to the muscles involved in the new motor skill.

Effects of Early Training

Children develop at different speeds, in part because of their environments, but also because they follow different genetic schedules. Most children begin to walk between 12 and 18 months of age. No matter how much coaxing and practice the parents may give their six-month-old child, it will not walk much sooner than if the parents had simply let the child alone.

In many primitive cultures, infants spend the first year or so of their lives bound to a board or bundled tightly inside a bag carried on their mothers' backs. These children are released from their restraints only for an hour or two each day, so they have little chance to practice motor skills. Yet their muscular development is not retarded, and they creep, crawl, and walk at about the same ages that children do who are not restrained. (As we will see in a later chapter, however, oriental

to do with maturation of the connections between the central nervous system and the muscles. The motor centers in the brain (see Chapter 4) send long nerve fibers out through the spinal cord to connect with the muscles in various parts of the body. Since the head muscles are closer to the brain than are the foot muscles, the head comes under the control of the motor centers long before the feet do (see Fig. 18.10). And since the muscles in the trunk of the body are closer to the spinal cord and brain than are those in the hands and feet, the shoulder and hip muscles come under control sooner than do those in the fingers or toes. The appearance of a new motor skill children react to "bundling" rather more passively than do black or white infants.)

Many years ago, in his research on identical twins, Arnold Gesell showed that practice is not necessary for early motor development. In most of these studies, Gesell encouraged one twin to practice a skill (such as climbing stairs), while confining the other twin to a playpen. Training usually began well before either twin could be expected to display the skill and proceeded until the "experimental" twin had clearly mastered the desired behavior pattern. At that point, Gesell removed the "control" twin from its playpen and tested it. The usual finding was that right from the first trial, the "control" twin could perform the task almost as well as the "experimental" twin.

There are two exceptions to Gesell's findings. The first has to do with special skills—such as swimming, skating, or playing a musical instrument. These behaviors need practice and guidance, and a child left to develop on its own usually does not do well without special training. The second exception has to do with the *attitude* the child takes toward physical activities. A child who is encouraged to explore its environment is more likely to become active and physically outgoing than a child who is confined to a playpen. Thus learning and physical development *always go hand in hand*.

"MOM AND DAD —IT'S BEEN GREAT GROWING UP AS A WOLF BUT WELL, I UNDERSTAND I'VE BEEN MISSING OUT ON A LOT': PIZZA, STEREO, SATURDAY AFTERNOON MOVIES, BLUE JEANS..."

Critical-period hypothesis. The belief that there is a best time for a child to experience certain things or learn certain skills. Trying to train a child before or after this critical period is supposed to be like picking an apple before it is ripe—or after it has turned mushy and rotten.

Imprinting (IM-prin-ting). To imprint is to make a permanent impression on something. In psychological terms, imprinting refers to the very rapid and long-lasting learning that occurs during the first day or so of a young animal's life, when it attaches itself emotionally to the first moving object that it sees or hears.

Critical Periods

There is some evidence that the best time for a child to learn a given skill is at the time its body is just mature enough to allow mastery of the behavior in question. This belief is often called the **critical-period hypothesis**, the belief that an organism must have certain experiences at a *particular time* in its developmental sequence if it is to reach its most mature state.

Imprinting in Animals

There are many studies from the animal literature supporting the critical-period hypothesis. For instance, Nobel Prize winner Konrad Lorenz discovered many years ago that birds, such as ducks and geese, will follow the first moving object they see after they are hatched. Usually the first thing they see is their mother, of course, who has been sitting on the eggs when they are hatched. However, Lorenz showed that if he took goose eggs away from the mother and hatched them in an incubator, the freshly hatched birds would follow *him* around instead.

After the goslings had waddled along behind Lorenz for a few hours, they acted as if they thought he was their mother and that they were humans, not geese. When Lorenz returned the goslings to their real mother, they ignored her. Whenever Lorenz appeared, however, they became very excited and flocked to him for protection and affection. It was as if the *visual image* of the first object they saw moving had become so strongly "imprinted" on their minds that, forever after, that object was "mother" (see Fig. 18.11).

Imprinting reaches its strongest peak 16 to 24 hours after the baby goose is hatched. During this period, the baby bird has an innate tendency to follow anything that moves, and will chase after its mother (if she is around), a human, a bouncing football, or a brightly painted tin can the experimenter dangles in front of the gosling. The more the baby bird struggles to follow after this moving object, the more strongly the young animal becomes imprinted to the object.

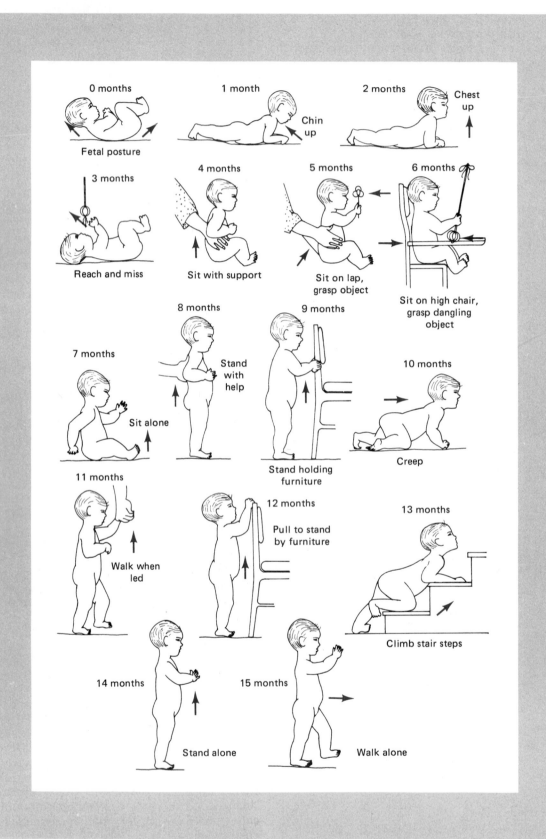

Fig. 18.10. Motor development in an infant.

Once the goose has been imprinted, this very special form of learning cannot easily be reversed. For example, the geese that first followed Lorenz could not readily be trained to follow their mother instead. Indeed, when these geese were grown and sexually mature, they showed no romantic interest in other geese. Instead, they attempted to court and mate with humans.

During the past 20 years or so, scientists have devoted much time to the study of *imprinting*, as it is now called. Imprinting takes place in many (but not all) types of birds, and it also seems to occur in mammals such as sheep and seals. As we will see in a moment, there is still considerable debate about whether anything like imprinting occurs in humans.

Question: *Goslings show unusually large amounts of REM sleep during the first 24 hours after they hatch. Can you explain why? (Hint: See Chapter 3.)*

Innate Fears

If a goose is hatched in a dark incubator and is not allowed to see the world until two or three days later, imprinting often does not occur. At first it was thought that the critical period had passed, and hence the bird could never become imprinted to anything. Now we know better. The innate urge to follow moving objects does appear to reach a peak in geese 24 hours after they are hatched, but it does not decline thereafter. Rather, a second innate urge—that of *fearing and avoiding new objects*—begins to develop. Some 48 hours after hatching, this fear overwhelms the urge the bird has to follow after anything that moves.

Question: *How might you get unimprinted birds to imprint even 72 hours after hatching? (Hint: What are the effects of tranquilizers on fear responses?)*

Mother-Infant Bonding in Humans

Once Lorenz and other **ethologists** had demonstrated imprinting with birds, scientists began hunting for similar effects in humans. Among the first to report success were Marshall Klaus and John Kennell, professors of pediatrics at Case Western Reserve University in Cleveland.

In their 1976 book *Maternal-Infant Bonding*, Klaus and Kennell state that there is a critical period in the first hour or so of life during which an infant can *bond* with its mother. This bonding takes place only if the mother and child are in close physical contact during the "sensitive period," according to Klaus and Kennell. Supposedly, the "bonding" increases the mother's love for her child and makes her more attentive to the

Ethologists (ee-THOLL-oh-gists). Scientists who study the biological underpinnings of behavior, particularly those involving "instincts." Ethology is a part of zoology, not of psychology. Behavioral scientists working in the same field are usually called "comparative psychologists," because they compare the behaviors of different animal species (including humans).

infant's need. Indeed, Klaus and Kennell believe that the mother is likely to neglect or abuse the child later in life if the "bonding" fails to occur.

Klaus and Kennell have presented such a large amount of evidence supporting their beliefs that most medical societies now recommend that mothers be given their infants to cradle immediately after birth—a practice that few doctors approved of prior to the Klaus-Kennell research.

Not all scientists are all that impressed with the notion of "bonding" in humans, however. In the April 1982 issue of *Psychology Today*, Michael Lamb reviews all the experiments purporting to show that "bonding" occurs. Lamb is a professor of psychology, psychiatry, and pediatrics at the University of Utah. He believes that most of the "bonding" studies have such serious flaws that they offer little support for the position taken by Klaus and Kennell. "Taken together," Lamb says, "the studies . . . show no clear evidence for any lasting effect of early physical contact between mother and infant on subsequent maternal behavior. The most that can be said is that it may sometimes have modest short-term effects on some mothers in some circumstances."

Lamb notes that there are no known *ill effects* from early mother-infant contacts. But he fears that those mothers who were not allowed to hold their children immediately after birth may feel that they are somehow "inadequate parents." That simply isn't so, Lamb says, and offers as proof the fact that most adoptive mothers are at least as loving as are "bonded" mothers. Thus the question of whether any form of imprinting occurs in human infants has not as yet been completely decided.

What Newborn Infants Can and Can't Do

Over the past century, developmental psychology has swung back and forth between the two extremes stated in the nature-nurture controversy. Almost 100 years ago, William James stated that the newborn's sensory world was a "blooming, buzzing confusion." Taking a very strong "nurturist" position, James saw the neonate's mind as a "blank piece of paper." It was only when *experience* wrote on this piece of paper that the young child's mind began to form and develop.

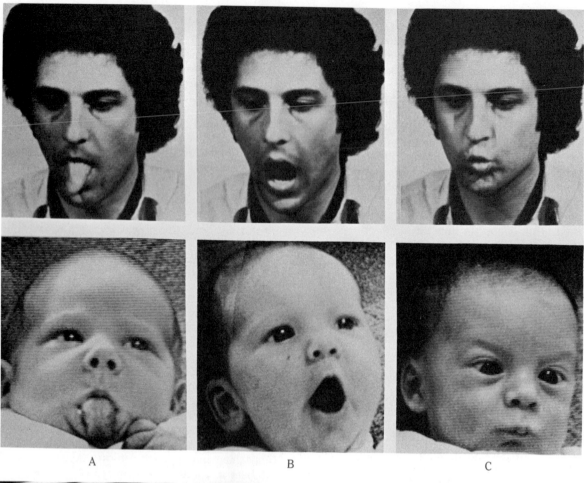

Sample photographs from videotape recordings of 2-to-3 week old infants imitating (A) tongue protrusion, (B) mouth opening, and (C) lip protrusion demonstrated by an adult experimenter. **(top)**

Fig. 18.11. Konrad Lorenz "mothering" his goslings. **(left)**

However, as Maya Pines points out in the February 1982 issue of *Psychology Today*, we now know that, almost from birth, an infant can sort out stimuli, remember, and predict future inputs. Neonates apparently can recognize their own names by two weeks of age, and they can distinguish among colors by the time they are three months old. They seem to develop depth perception by the fourth month of life.

In the January/February 1982 issue of *Science 82*, Richard M. Restak writes that, "Infants arrive less wet behind the ears than we thought." He goes on to state that, "Only moments out of the womb, infants are capable of a wide variety of behaviors." Their eyes are alert, and they turn their heads in the direction of any voice they hear. They prefer female voices to male, but apparently search their visual world to locate the source of *any* human voice. They move their arms and legs in synchrony to human speech—but not to random noise or many other sounds (such as tapping). Furthermore, they respond to *any* human language, but not to artificial sounds and broken-up speech patterns. They recognize their mother by the time they are two weeks old, but are more playful and alert in the presence of their father than of the mother.

Restak notes as well that a two-week-old infant apparently can integrate sights, sounds, and touch into a meaningful pattern or *schema*. The "mother" schema is particularly powerful. British researcher Genevieve Carpenter tested two-week-old babies in four different situations: (1) the mother speaking to the child in her own voice; (2) a strange woman speaking to the infant; (3) the mother speaking in the strange woman's voice; and (4) the strange woman speaking in the mother's voice. The babies responded most positively to the first situation, thus demonstrating they can recognize their own mothers very early in life. However, the infants cried or became frightened by the third and fourth situations. Carpenter believes that the sound of the mother's voice coming from another woman's face "disrupted the infant's expectations" because this situation didn't fit the infant's schema of what its mother should sound like.

Expressive Imitation

According to Andrew Meltzoff of the University of Washington, an infant can imitate some facial expressions *one hour after birth*. But because such newborn children are difficult to work with, Meltzoff and his colleagues have performed most of their research on two-week-old babies.

In an elegant series of studies begun in 1977, Meltzoff has shown that two-week-old infants will stick out their tongues or open their mouths fully the first time they see these facial expressions in the adults around them.

Meltzoff's experiments seem particularly well-controlled. The adults whose expressions the babies imitated were all strangers to the infants. The infants' responses were filmed and then judged by scientists who did not know what expression the baby was supposed to be imitating. Furthermore, Meltzoff did not tell the children's parents what he was up to. (In one early study when the parents were told, the mothers trained the infants to stick out their tongues before bringing them to the lab. As one mother put it, "I didn't want my baby to fail his first test.")

Meltzoff has also shown that two-week-old infants can *remember* facial expressions for brief periods of time. In one study, he stuck pacifiers in the babies' mouths and then exposed them to adults who either opened their mouths or stuck out their tongues. A few minutes later, when the pacifier was removed, the infants still gave the proper imitative response.

Nature or Nurture?

"No longer can we look upon a newborn as a lump of clay ready to be molded by the environment," says T. Berry Brazelton, who is chief of the Child Development Unit of Children's Hospital Medical Center in Boston. "We've come a long way in our understanding of just how marvelous a creature a human infant really is."

Brazelton's remarks are similar to those made by many scientists who are increasingly impressed by the range of responses that neonates possess. However, as we will see in the next several chapters, the *innate reflexes* that an infant has at birth constitute but a tiny fraction of the behaviors displayed by any normal two-year-old. True, these "innate behavioral programs" are important, for all the child's future thoughts and actions are built on these unlearned response patterns. But it still remains true that the most important thing that "nature" gives to any child is the capacity to *learn from experience*.

Thus, the nature-nurture controversy will never be settled. But as long as scientists argue about what is innate and what is learned, the more we will learn about factors that control human growth and development. And the more likely it is that we will be able to correct genetic or developmental problems before they occur.

Genetic Counseling

The importance of the nature-nurture controversy perhaps becomes clearest when we consider those children who are born with genetic defects, such as trisomy-21 or *Down's Syndrome*. Some day in the future, perhaps, we will be able to correct such problems with genetic surgery. At the moment, medical treatment is of limited value, so we must rely on *psychological* treatment instead. And, as many researchers have shown, this treatment must be aimed as much at the parents as at the child.

What would you do if you knew that you might carry defective genes, and thus there was a good chance that you might pass on genetic problems to your own children? Judging from the evidence at hand, you might well cope with this problem *defensively*, mostly by denying that it really existed (see Chapter 13). Princeton sociologist James Sorenson has made a study of parents who knew they were carriers of defective genes and who sought genetic counseling about the risks they ran in having children. Early in 1973, Sorenson reported that almost all of these parents waited to ask for help until *after* they had already had at least one child who suffered from genetic damage. Furthermore, these parents tended to spend more time and money trying to *disprove* the initial medical **diagnosis** than they did in trying to find out how to help the child (and themselves).

Sorenson notes as well that about half the couples he studied either forgot, rejected, or badly distorted the scientific information they were given. In many cases, this new information seemed to cause a dramatic change in the parents' own evaluations of themselves. It also led to frequent marital problems. When only one parent carried the defective genes, the parent often developed severe and chronic feelings of guilt and shame. The other parent often came to have strong negative emotional feelings toward her or his partner. When both carried some kind of "genetic misfortune," Sorenson says, the situation was likely to produce a sense of being a *doomed family*—a feeling on the part of both partners of having lost control of their lives. And the sad thing is that, while this feeling exists, neither parent is likely to search out those psychological treatment plans that might help them and their children.

Moral and Ethical Issues

In recent years, medical scientists have developed a number of methods for testing the fetus while still in the womb in order to determine if it has a genetic disability. While these tests are far from being perfect, they often can give the parents some notion of what the odds are that the child will be born normal or handicapped.

The decisions that the parents must make if it seems the child will be badly disabled are difficult ones indeed. Some parents opt for abortion if the genetic problem is a severe one that may cause the infant to die within a few months or years after birth. Other parents, who are opposed to abortion on moral or religious grounds, are at least warned far in advance of the child's birth about the problems they may encounter. But, in either case, the stress on the parents may indeed be severe.

In many cases, the parents may prefer not to be told the bad news. Other parents may insist on knowing. But doctors occasionally make mistakes, and a doctor in the state of New York was recently held legally responsible for the care of a child born with a defect after he had assured the parents the child would be normal. There are even several law suits now pending against physicians who failed to warn women over 35 that they stood an increased risk of having a Down's Syndrome child.

The moral and ethical issues involved in genetic counseling are many and complex. However, the good news is that both medical and behavioral scientists are making progress in discovering ways of helping both handicapped children and their parents.

Helping the Handicapped

Twenty years ago, the Down's Syndrome child was often looked upon as a burden that God had visited upon its parents. The child's physical growth would be retarded, and it presumably would be mentally and emotionally handicapped all its life. At best, given some training, the child might be able to learn how to take care of a few of its needs. The major question the parents faced was whether to institutionalize the child, or try to keep it at home.

Now, thanks to pioneering work at the University of Oregon and many other places, we know that these children can be helped considerably. They need a highly stimulating environment, and much more careful training than a "normal" child. If this training is begun in the first year of life, though, the Down's Syndrome child often achieves a near-normal level of intelligence and is capable of learning most of the self-care skills that normal children acquire.

We do not yet know the best ways to help children whose physical, psychological, or social development is retarded because of genetic problems. But we are more likely to help them if we look at their *capabilities* rather than at their *disabilities*. Handicapped children are different from normal children, but "different" surely doesn't mean "inferior." And the more we learn about how *all* children grow and develop, the more likely it is we will be able to help both normal and handicapped children reach the maximum potential that their genes will allow.

Summary

1. There are two traditional ways of studying the growth and maturation of humans—the **life span approach** and **developmental psychology**. The first looks at the changes that occur in a "typical" individual from birth to death. The second studies various aspects of personality change, mostly in the younger years.

2. There are four main themes in developmental psychology—the **mind/body problem**; the **nature-nurture controversy**; **change versus constancy**; and **similarities versus differences**.

3. You began life as a single **egg cell** that contained 23 **chromosomes**. At the moment of

fertilization, one of your father's sperms penetrated the egg and added 23 chromosomes of its own.

4. Since all the cells in your body are **daughters** of this original cell, the **nucleus** of every cell in your body (with certain minor exceptions) has 23 **pairs of chromosomes**.

5. These chromosomes contain the **genes**, made up of **DNA** molecules, that govern the functioning of each cell. The DNA sends "command messages" via **RNA** to the **cytoplasm** of the cell telling it what kinds of proteins and other molecules to manufacture.

6. If an **X sperm** unites with the egg, the 23rd chromosome will be **XX**, and the child will be born a female. If a **Y sperm** unites with the egg, the 23rd chromosome will be **XY**, and the child will be born a male.

7. Shortly after fertilization occurs, the fertilized egg begins to divide to make other identical cells. Should these first daughter cells become separated, each will form two **embryos** that develop into **identical twins**. Should the mother carry two eggs at once, each may be fertilized (by different sperms) and the mother will give birth to **fraternal twins**.

8. Sometimes the chromosomes of the mother and father contain **genetic defects**. If the child's cells contain but a single X chromosome, the child will suffer from **Turner's syndrome**. A child with an **XXY 23rd chromosome** becomes an infertile male and is said to suffer from **Klinefelter's syndrome**. A child with an **XYY 23rd chromosome** becomes a normal-appearing male but may have difficulty learning **impulse control**.

9. If the child's cells have three **21st chromosomes** rather than two, the child will suffer from **Down's Syndrome**.

10. Two weeks after fertilization, the cells begin to **differentiate** or take on different roles. The three main types of cells are **ectoderm**, **mesoderm**, and **endoderm**.

11. During pregnancy, the fetus is protected from the mother's body by an organ called the **placenta**.

12. If the mother is starved during pregnancy, the child may be born smaller than usual. If the

Diagnosis (die-ag-NO-sis). From the Latin term meaning "to recognize something by its signs, or to distinguish one thing from another." Medical doctors diagnose a disease by distinguishing the symptoms of that disease from all other types of illnesses.

infant is given ample food, however, it will usually "catch up" to the size its **genetic blueprint** originally specified.

13. If the infant is reared in a poor environment, it may become physically and mentally retarded. However, if it is given ample stimulation later on, it will usually "catch up" to its original **genetic potential**.

14. Physical development in the infant typically proceeds in a **head-to-feet, near-to-far pattern**. The muscles controlling the head and neck become mature much sooner than those needed for walking or climbing.

15. Children cannot be taught to walk before their leg muscles are mature. However, if a child is prevented from walking at the time it would normally do so, it doesn't appear to suffer much **physical retardation**.

16. Baby geese (and the young of other animals) often **imprint** on the first moving object they see or can follow. Whether imprinting or **affectionate bonding** actually occurs in humans is not yet decided.

17. The **critical-period hypothesis** states that the "best time" for learning to occur is when the organism is first ready to make a response.

18. Only moments after birth, infants can **imitate** facial gestures, **search** visually for the source of human voices, and **move their limbs in synchrony** with the human voice. By two weeks, babies **recognize** their parents and form perceptual **schemata**.

19. Parents whose children are born with genetic defects often avoid or distort **genetic counseling** about how to help their children reach their maximum potential.

20. Most children with genetic defects can overcome many of their problems if we give them the environmental inputs they need to counteract their genetic limitations.

(Continued from page 413.)

When the class calmed down a bit, Dr. Martin Mayer continued. "That's a very interesting approach," he said, nodding at the guitar-playing young man. "I presume you mean we could identify men and women who are carriers of the wrong kinds of genes, and prohibit them from having kids. Not from getting married or from having sex—but from raising a family."

"You're asking us to play God with human souls!" said one of the girls. "That involves religion, not genetics."

"We certainly must take religious views into account," Dr. Mayer said, polishing his glasses again. "But sex is also a matter of economics. Any of you students grow up on a farm?"

Several of the young people held up their hands.

Mayer put his spectacles back on his nose. "Well, I guess your daddies have a few cows around to give milk and to supply meat, right? And probably they buy the best breeding stock they can afford, because good cows give more milk and more butter fat than poor cows. And good bulls produce stronger offspring with better meat on them than do puny bulls. One good bull can service a whole lot of cows through artificial insemination. Even a scrawny little cow will have better offspring if her eggs are fertilized with genes from a first-rate bull. Perhaps we should do the same with humans. Maybe only the President should be allowed to have children."

"If only the President of the United States can have kids, he's going to be one busy daddy," one of the girls said laughing.

"Doesn't seem fair somehow," the boy sitting next to her said. "You've gotten rid of half the bad genes by using just one prime bull, but what about the scrawny cows? They're still passing along their scrawny genes to their kids. Why not have just one big mother cow that's as good as the bull?"

"Good idea," Mayer continued. "Just because a first-rate cow has good genes in her egg cells doesn't mean that she has to be burdened with carrying the calf until it's ready to be born. It's a waste of her time. So we've worked out a deal. After we inseminate the prime cow artificially, we let the fertilized egg grow for a few days, and then we remove the embryo and transplant it into the body of a scrawny cow and let her do all the work of carrying the little calf until it's ready to be born. A few months later, the scrawny cow gives birth to a super-calf with superior genes."

"Why bother?" a student asked.

"Financial reasons," Mayer responded. "Once we remove the embryo from the super-prime cow mother, she starts producing new eggs right away, which also can be fertilized artificially and then transplanted to the body of another inferior cow. That way, one super-momma can produce lots of superior calves each year instead of just one or two. It's still too complicated a technique for general use, but when the cost comes down, it's sure going to make a lot more money for the farmers."

"I know what you're going to say next," said the guitar-playing boy. "If it works with cows, why not try it with humans?"

"You've got to be kidding," one of the girls said. "I wouldn't want to carry somebody else's baby."

"Not even for a million dollars?" Mayer asked. "Suppose a rich lady offered you a million dollars if you'd let her doctor transplant the embryo into your body. That way you could carry the child for her while she went off on a fancy vacation somewhere. Then, when the child was born, she could pick the child up at the hospital and give you the million dollars. How would you like that?"

"If I carried the baby, it would be mine, and no rich lady could take it away from me," the girl replied.

"Yeah, but what if the government decided you couldn't have kids," one of the boys said.

"Why couldn't I have kids, I'd like to know?"

"Because the government said you didn't have the right kind of genes, stupid. Just like my daddy decides which of his cows can have calves and which can't," the boy added rather smugly.

"But I've got great genes!" the girl said. "And no government is going to tell me I don't! And even if they did, I'd just get Dr. Mayer to engineer my genes so they were the right kind. So there," she concluded, making a face at the boy who was tormenting her with his comments.

"What's the right kind of genes?" asked another girl.

"Yes, it all boils down to that decision, doesn't it?" Mayer said. "As Aldous Huxley pointed out in *Brave New World*, the day will surely come when we can engineer genes—if we know what kinds of kids we want to have. We can judge what kinds of cows we want because we value meat and milk production. But what do we value most in humans? Size? Strength? Intelligence?"

"That old Einstein wouldn't have done so well as a fullback for the Dallas Cowboys," an athletic young man said.

"I don't even want to talk about this, it scares me so," another girl said. "It's abnormal and immoral. It could never happen in the United States."

"That's probably what the cows thought a few years ago," said one of the boys.

"Well," said Mayer, "Maybe it won't happen here, but the possibility of genetic engineering won't disappear just because we refuse to talk about it. In fact, just the opposite. But let's get back to that point about who should carry the baby. Is there any reason why a woman should have to go through a lengthy pregnancy? In *Brave New World* the embryos are grown in bottles rather than in their mothers' bodies. When they are ready to be born, the babies are uncorked like a bottle of fine wine. Maybe the day will come when each home has a mechanical incubator in it. You would watch your child's development before birth just the way you watch a plant grow and flower."

"That's outrageous," said the girl in the second row. "I don't want my baby born in a machine."

"You'd destroy the warm, maternal feeling a woman has when she's carrying her own baby," said another.

"I wouldn't love my baby if I didn't carry it myself," said another girl.

"And how would my baby feel if it learned that it had developed in a machine instead of inside me?" said another. "It just wouldn't love me as much."

"Do you really think that maternal love is dependent on carrying the baby yourself?" Mayer asked.

"Of course," said the girl in the second row. "You just wouldn't take care of the baby as well if it weren't for that special feeling of closeness you get when you're carrying the child. It just wouldn't be *yours*, and you wouldn't love it as much."

A girl in the middle of the room suddenly stood up, tears filling her eyes. "I'd like to say something. A woman doesn't have to carry a child, or give birth to it, in order to love the baby and see that it gets the best care and attention. And whether a child is born in a bottle or from its mother's body doesn't affect the love it has for the person who brings it up. Maybe you ought to remember that I'm adopted. My mother couldn't have children, so she and my father adopted me when I was just two weeks old. And they love me very, very much, both of them."

The class was absolutely silent for several moments. Then the bell rang.

"Thank you very, very much," Dr. Mayer said, a smile on his face.

Recommended Readings

Ambron, Sueann Robinson. *Child Development*, 3rd ed. (New York: Holt, Rinehart and Winston, 1981).

Brim, Orville G., Jr., and Jerome Kagan, eds. *Constancy and Change in Human Development* (Cambridge, Mass.: Harvard University Press, 1980).

Gould, James L., and Carol Grant Gould. "The Instinct to Learn," *Science 81* (May 1981), pp. 44–50.

Liebert, R.M., and Rita Wicks-Nelson. *Developmental Psychology*, 3rd ed. (Englewood Cliffs, N.J.: Prentice-Hall, 1981).

Mussen, P.H., John Janeway Conger, and Jerome Kagan, eds. *Readings in Child and Adolescent Psychology: Contemporary Perspectives* (New York: Harper & Row, 1980).

Social and Emotional Development

19

Did You Know That . . .

Death and love are two important areas of human existence seldom studied scientifically?

Even though all their other needs are met, infant monkeys will die if not given something to "love"—that is, something to cling to and rub against?

A human infant, if separated from its mother, may fall into a profound depression?

If a female monkey does not engage in "sex play" with her peers when young, she may refuse to mate as an adult?

Much of what we call "maternal" and "paternal" instincts are really learned behavior patterns?

Monkey mothers raised in isolation often destroy their own offspring?

Mothers who treat their children inconsistently, or unresponsively, can predispose the children to later psychological difficulties?

Girls separated from their fathers by divorce tend to become more promiscuous in their early sexual behavior than do girls reared in intact homes?

"Love Me, Love Me Not"

"Now, admit it. Isn't this the cleanest, most modern nursery you've ever seen?" The Director of the nursery, who was leading the tour, hardly waited for his guests to answer. "Spotless, absolutely spotless. We want to make sure that the infants are completely protected from dirt and disease. And I dare say we're succeeding."

The Director was showing the kitchen to his visitors, two women and a man. "The best of all possible baby foods, served in absolutely sterile containers. Each portion contains special vitamins and minerals, prepared by cooks wearing face masks so that no germs ever contaminate the food. Isn't it beautiful?" the Director asked, an angelic smile on his face.

Then he moved forward. "Let's go into the observation room. We can watch the children through the glass. You understand that we can't let you actually go into the sleeping room with the children themselves. That is, unless you're willing to scrub down first in the shower and put on one of our freshly laundered white uniforms. We can't have you transmitting some disease to these poor little babies, now can we?" The Director uttered a small, brief, high-pitched laugh.

Through the glass window the visitors could see the nursery room. Each of the infants had its own little bed made up with immaculately white sheets. Waist-high wooden partitions stood between each of the cribs, giving every infant almost complete privacy.

"Why do you have the cribs separated that way?" one of the women visitors asked.

"Ah, an interesting question," replied the Director. "We want to minimize the transmission of disease, you see. Should one of the infants contract an ailment, the others are too far away to be readily infected. The partitions are covered with a special white paint, and we wash them down with disinfectant once a week. Nothing but the best, I assure you!"

One of the infants was crying lustily. A nurse came into the room and picked the child up, holding it close to her starched white uniform. Although the woman cradled the infant in her arms for some time, it continued its loud, gulping cries.

"Why is that child crying so much?" asked one of the visitors.

The Director smiled confidently. "A new arrival, just separated from its mother. Takes them a while to get used to new surroundings, of course. After a few days—a couple of weeks or so—they calm down and begin to enjoy their healthy new environment. After all, we've rescued many of them from very unsanitary home conditions."

"Why was it necessary to separate the children from their mothers?" asked one of the women.

"Mostly because the mothers had to go to the hospital for a while, either because of illness or for an operation. So it's not at all surprising that the children should be a little upset at first. 'Parting is such sweet sorrow,' you know. They all cry a fair amount when they first arrive, but look at them now! They aren't making much of a fuss, now are they?"

It was true. Most of the infants lay in their cribs unmoving, staring at the white ceiling with wide-open eyes. Large tears rolled gently down one child's cheeks. The nurse stopped by its crib, offered it a play toy, but the child merely continued its gentle weeping.

"You see, before we took over, the children were raised in filth, real filth. Noise, grime, germs—that was their steady diet. Many of them took sick and died. Now, it's different. Those kids must have the most unpolluted environment on earth. Isn't it great?"

One of the visitors looked at the Director with raised eyebrows. "What's your sickness rate now?"

The Director cleared his throat. "Oh, I think we're doing quite well, all things considered."

"What do you mean, 'all things considered'?"

The Director's voice squeaked slightly as he responded. "Well, remember that these kids all come from bad home environments. Mothers sick, families mostly broken apart at the seams. You've got to keep that in mind. You'd expect a lot of illness in those situations anyhow, wouldn't you?"

"What kinds of symptoms do the children show?"

The squeak in the Director's voice grew more pronounced. "Well, you see, it's really odd. They don't eat. That's the main problem. Maybe when we sterilize the food, we take all the taste out or something. And they catch a lot of colds. We don't really understand why. Probably a bug or something that's going around, but I'm sure we'll lick it."

"What do you plan to do?"

"Well, first we're going to wash the whole place down again with disinfectant, and then . . ."

(see page 449)

Science and Social Taboos

Science is, to some extent, the fine art of asking questions and then trying to find reasonable and reliable answers. Sometimes the questions are safe and obvious: Why does the sun give off heat and light? Why is grass green? Why does lemon juice taste sour? The answers to these questions are often complex and highly mathematical, but they seldom offend anyone.

Occasionally, however, scientists manage to pose a problem that many of us would rather not have investigated objectively: What are the actual consequences of war? What happens when we show violence on television? What are the effects of giving pornography to children? Our culture gives us *socially acceptable* answers to these questions. Thus the scientists who wish to peer further into the matter—or to obtain experimental data rather than collect opinions—frequently find themselves outcasts.

There are many areas of human behavior that are partially or entirely restricted from scientific investigation. One such is death, which is a *partially* restricted area. For while we can study what happens to people when they are dying, we obviously cannot hasten the process merely to see how the person might react.

Another taboo area is love. As we noted in Chapter 12, sexual love is a topic much discussed but seldom studied in the laboratory. But its non-sexual aspects are often ignored by scientists too, perhaps because we fear that the magic of love would somehow disappear if we analyzed it in factual terms.

A related "forbidden topic"—at least until very recently—is that of parent-child relationships. John B. Watson, the first behavioral psychologist, believed that parents should not give much love or affection to their children for fear of "spoiling" the child. But Watson never bothered to test out his belief in any scientific way. Other psychologists have stated loudly that the *primary task* of a parent is to give "love" to the infant. But these psychologists have not always defined "love" in measurable terms. Nor have they performed controlled studies in which parents were required either to "love" or to "hate" their infants for long periods of time. And as hard-hearted as that viewpoint may seem, we are not likely to discover how parents' behaviors affect the child's growth and development until we *do* perform scientific experiments on living children. But societal **mores** and our own gut feelings usually prevent us from undertaking such experiments.

Such information as we have gathered on the subject suggests that many of our long-cher-ished notions about love and infant care are reasonably accurate—but a great many more are mere flights of human fancy. In this chapter we will examine some of these findings, and then draw such conclusions as we can about *social and emotional development in children*.

Love

Let us begin with an apparently simple question— what is love? The usual belief (in our society) is that love is an emotion. That is, love is an *internal state or process* that almost everyone experiences. Love certainly is an emotion, and it obviously has its intra-psychic aspects. This side of love has been written about for centuries by some of the wisest poets and novelists the world has known. When Elizabeth Barrett Browning wrote, "How do I love thee? Let me count the ways . . ." she told us as much about the subjective experience of love as any psychologist could.

However, love can also be approached objectively. For example, we may look at maternal love and say that it is an instinctual, biological response strongly influenced by the female's hormones. Or we may look at an individual's behavior and *assume* that only someone in love would act in that fashion. We can then study "loving behaviors" quite objectively, and draw conclusions about what internal processes *mediate* these behaviors. These objective investigations of love will never *replace* our subjective, poetic examination of this glorious condition—nor is there any reason why they should. But once we realize that love is, *in part*, a response to some living or inanimate object, we can make certain statements about love that we could not make otherwise.

For example, taking this viewpoint we can see that, like all behavior, loving responses must be affected by a person's genetic blueprint, past experience, and present environment. We can also state that loving behaviors will *tend to increase* if they are followed by satisfaction and reward, and that they will *tend to decrease* if followed by pain, punishment, or lack of reinforcement. We do not usually think in these terms, and yet the data suggest that loving behaviors are as influenced by internal secretions and external stimuli as are eating, breathing, and speaking. By taking an objective view toward love, we may lose a bit of the magic and mystery. But we surely gain a great deal in terms of understanding what the emotion called love is all about.

Question: How would your solution to the mind/body problem influence what aspects of "love" you decided could be studied scientifically?

Parental Love

In this chapter we will pay particular attention to the love that an infant shows toward its parents, and the attraction that mothers and fathers feel toward their children. Since most of this research has involved mother-child relationships, we will look at this type of love most closely.

We will find that "mother love" is not merely a mystical emotional bond, determined by the genes, and neither is "father love." In fact, both types of love are *patterns of interactions between parent and child*. Some of the behaviors involved are innately determined. Others are learned. The task for scientists studying maternal love is to determine which is which.

Society demands that parents love—or at least care for—their children. So social factors surely influence both paternal and maternal love. But these social influences always *interact* with biological and intra-psychic factors. For instance, in his book *The First Relationship: Infant and Mother*, Daniel Stern describes how mother and child form a **social dyad** almost immediately after the infant's birth. Stern has a laboratory at New York Hospital's Payne Whitney Clinic. For many years, he has filmed the reactions of mothers to their newborn children. He then slows the movies down and analyzes them "frame by

frame." Stern reports that both the mother and her infant appear to have an "inborn mutual readiness" to respond to each other. This "readiness" apparently is a genetically determined *social behavior* in both the mother and the child. But it is also a pattern of interaction that society strongly reinforces once it occurs.

Louis Sander, a psychiatrist working at the University of Colorado Medical Center, has also filmed parents interacting with very young infants. And he too tends to analyze these films in slow motion. In one such film, a mother hands her eight-day-old infant to its father because the child is restless. The man takes the child and holds it casually while continuing to talk. Both father and infant appear to ignore each other, but the child soon stops crying and falls asleep. However, as Richard Restak notes in the January/February issue of *Science 82*, a frame-by-frame analysis of the movie reveals a different story. The father looks down several times at his baby, who returns the gaze. But touching is as important as looking. The father cuddles the infant closely while glancing at it. The baby clasps the little finger of the man's hand and, at that very instant, drops off to sleep.

Perhaps it is not as glamorous to study interactive patterns as it is to study "love." But, as Robert Emde notes, we are more likely to understand these natural parental-child patterns if we look at them objectively. Emde is a psychiatrist at the University of Colorado Medical School. His studies suggest that the infant triggers off maternal and paternal behaviors in the parents as much as parents set off innate responses in the child. He sums up the matter this way: "For years, theories described how mothers shaped babies, but we are now beginning to appreciate how much babies shape mothers." And how they shape their fathers, too, as Emde also points out.

The question then becomes, what are the crucial variables that determine parental/child patterns of interactions? And do the responses the parents give to the child shortly after its birth have any strong influence on the child's later social and emotional development? In truth, we cannot yet give definitive answers to these questions, primarily because the needed research has yet to be done. We cannot separate 100 human infants from their parents merely to see how *parental*

"THERE'S ANOTHER HEREDITARY DISEASE THAT RUNS IN THE ROYAL FAMILY. YOUR GRANDFATHER WAS A STUBBORN FOOL, YOUR FATHER WAS A STUBBORN FOOL, AND *YOU* ARE A STUBBORN FOOL."

Margaret and Harry Harlow in a laboratory with monkeys. **(top)**

Fig. 19.1. Baby monkey in a cheese-cloth blanket. **(left)**

Fig. 19.2. Baby monkey with surrogate cloth monkey. **(right)**

deprivation influences the manner in which the children grow up. Nor can we take 100 neonates and deliberately give them to "terrible parents" just to see if the children grow up to be any different from infants reared in loving environments. But we can isolate *monkey* infants from their mothers in the hope that these studies will tell us how to care better for human children whose mothers desert them.

Thus, before we return to parental love at the human level, we first must take a brief detour through a primate laboratory in Wisconsin.

Love in the Laboratory

The scientist who has conducted the best long-term laboratory experiments on mother-child relationships in primates is surely Harry Harlow, who did most of his work at the University of Wisconsin. Professor Harlow did not set out to study love—it happened by accident. Like many other psychologists, he was at first primarily interested in how organisms learn. Rather than working with rats—as many other psychologists have done—Harlow chose to work with monkeys.

Since Harlow needed a place to house and raise the monkeys, he built the Primate Laboratory at Wisconsin. Then he began to study the effects of brain lesions on monkey learning. But Harlow soon found that young animals reacted somewhat differently to brain damage than did older monkeys, so Harlow and his wife Margaret (also a psychologist) devised a breeding program and tried various ways of raising monkeys in the laboratory.

The Harlows soon discovered that monkey infants raised by their mothers often caught diseases from their parents, so the Harlows began taking the infants away from their mothers at birth and tried raising them by hand. The baby monkeys had been given cheesecloth diapers to serve as baby blankets. Almost from the start, it became obvious to the Harlows that their little animals developed such strong attachments to the blankets that, in the Harlows' own terms, it was often hard to tell "where the diaper ended and the baby began" (see Fig. 19.1). Not only this, but if the Harlows removed the "security" blanket in order to clean it, the infant monkey often became greatly disturbed—just as if its own mother had deserted it.

The Surrogate Mother

What the baby monkeys obviously needed was an artificial or **surrogate** mother—something they could cling to as tightly as they typically clung to their own mother's chest. The Harlows sketched out many different designs, but none really appealed to them. Then, in 1957, while enjoying a champagne flight high over the city of Detroit, Harry Harlow glanced out of the airplane window and "saw" an image of an artificial monkey mother. It was a hollow wire cylinder, wrapped with a terrycloth bath towel, with a silly wooden head at the top. The tiny monkey could cling to this model mother as closely as to its real mother's body hair (see Fig. 19.2).

The surrogate mother could be provided with a functional breast simply by placing a milk bottle so that the nipple stuck through the cloth

at an appropriate place on the surrogate's anatomy. The cloth mother could be heated or cooled. It could be rocked mechanically or made to stand still. And, most important, the surrogate would not "protest" when it was removed from its "child."

While still sipping his champagne, Harlow mentally outlined much of the research that kept him, his wife, and their associates occupied for many years to come. And, without realizing it, Harlow had shifted from studying monkey learning to studying primate social and emotional development.

Five Types of Social Love

Harlow believes that there are five types of social love—that is, the love of one organism for another. These five types appear in a definite developmental sequence:

1. First comes the love an infant shows for its mother—or for her surrogate or substitute.
2. Out of this infant-mother love grows what Harlow calls "peer love," the affection of young organisms for other youngsters their own age.
3. When children reach puberty, they can experience a new dimension in their emotional development—that of heterosexual love, which Harlow believes develops from peer love. As we will see, this third type of love is possible only if the organism has learned certain behavior patterns while playing with its peers.
4. The fourth type of love is available (under normal circumstances) only to females, for it is the affection that a mother shows to her infant.
5. Males—under the right conditions—may demonstrate the fifth type of love, which Harlow calls "paternal love."

Question: What kinds of information about the social and emotional development of humans (and other species) can best be obtained from "real life observations," and what kinds can best be obtained in a laboratory?

Infant-Mother Love

During the first two weeks of its life, warmth is perhaps the most important thing that a monkey mother has to give to its baby. The Harlows discovered this fact by offering infant monkeys a

James Prescott   John Bowlby

choice of two types of mother substitutes—one wrapped in terrycloth and one that was made of bare wire. If the two artificial mothers were both the same temperature, the little monkeys always preferred the cloth mother. However, if the wire model was heated, while the cloth model was cool, the baby primates picked the wire substitute as their favorite for the first two weeks after birth. Thereafter they switched and spent most of their time on the more comfortable cloth mother.

Why is cloth preferable to bare wire? Something that the Harlows call **contact comfort** seems to be the answer. Infant monkeys spend much of their time rubbing against their mothers' skins, putting themselves in as close contact with the parent as they can. Prolonged "contact comfort" with a surrogate cloth mother appears to instill confidence in baby monkeys and is much more rewarding to them than is either warmth or milk.

According to the Harlows, contact comfort creates *trust* in infant monkeys. If the infant is put into an unfamiliar playroom without its mother, the infant ignores the toys no matter how interesting they might be. It screeches in terror and curls up into a furry little ball. If its cloth mother is now introduced into the playroom, the infant rushes to the surrogate and clings to it for dear life.

After a few minutes of contact comfort, the infant apparently begins to feel more secure. It then climbs down from the mother substitute and begins tentatively to explore the toys, but often rushes back for a deep embrace as if to reassure itself that its mother is still there and that all is well. Bit by bit its fears of the novel environment are *desensitized* (see Chapter 14), and it spends more and more time playing with the toys and less and less time clinging to its "mother."

Question: How might you explain "trust" in terms of the infant's need to predict and control its environmental inputs?

Nurturance in Human Infants

Why is "contact comfort" so important? According to neuro-psychologist James W. Prescott, sensory stimulation of the infant's receptor organs is necessary for the infant's brain to develop properly. Prescott works at the National Institute of Child Health and Human Development. In 1978, he undertook a survey of child-rearing practices in a variety of human cultures. Prescott noted that in some societies parents give their offspring very little *physical affectional stimulation* or "nurturance," as Prescott calls it. In 36 of the 49 cultures Prescott studied, there was a strong connection between "lack of physical affectional stimulation in infants" and violence in adults. Prescott believes that children reared in these circumstances develop a pattern of brain functioning that predisposes them to violence.

Whether a lack of nurturance causes a child's *brain* to develop in an abnormal fashion is still a matter of dispute. But several studies do support the notion that poor nurturance can affect a child's social and emotional development. For example, scientists at the University of Colorado have studied three generations of families who abused their children. The Colorado scientists found that although the abused infants received adequate care and food, they were deprived of touching, physical affection, and sensory stimulation. In most cases, the abused children grew up to be as violent and as abusive as their own parents had been.

Psychiatrist Henry Massie reported similar findings in 1978. Massie, who works at the University of California Medical School in San Francisco, showed home movies of mother-infant interactions to a group of impartial judges. The judges tried to guess which of the children had become psychotic later in life, and which children had grown up to become normal individuals. The movies, of course, had been taken years earlier, before anyone knew how the children would turn out.

At first the judges concentrated on observing the responses of the children themselves. But they soon found that all the infants behaved the same way. That is, the infants in both groups touched, gazed at, and responded to their mothers in similar fashion.

However, the judges could tell at once which child would become psychotic by watching *how its mother treated it.* The mothers whose infants grew up to be normal touched the infants often, held them close, gazed at them frequently, and seemed very strongly attached to the children. The mothers of the children who later became psychotic, however, gave "low quality" nurturance. Since there was no observable difference in the way that the infants reacted to the mothers, Massie concludes that it was the quality of sensory stimulation the mother gave to her infant that *predisposed* the child to become either normal or psychotic at a later stage in its development.

Question: Although Prescott believes that poor "nurturance" causes the child's brain to develop abnormally, what other explanations can you think of?

Good Mothers and Bad
According to the Harlows, once a baby monkey has become *emotionally attached* to its mother (real or surrogate), the mother can do almost no wrong. In one of their studies, they tried to create "monster mothers" whose behavior would be so abnormal that the infants would desert the mothers. The Harlows designed four types of "monster mothers," but none of them was apparently "evil" enough to impart fear or loathing to the infant monkeys. One such "monster" occasionally blasted its babies with compressed air. A second shook so violently that the baby often fell off. A third contained a **catapult** that frequently flung the infant away from it. The most evil-appearing of all had a set of metal spikes buried beneath its terrycloth. From time to time the spikes would poke through the cloth, making it impossible for the infant to cling to the surrogate.

The baby monkeys brought up on the "monster mothers" did show a brief period of emotional disturbance when the surrogates first rejected the infants. But as soon as the surrogates returned to normal, the infant would return to the "monster mother" and continue clinging, as if all were forgiven. As the Harlows tell the story, the only prolonged distress created by the experiment seemed to be that felt by the experimenters!

There was, however, one type of surrogate that uniformly "turned off" the infant monkeys. S.J. Suomi, working with the Harlows, built a terrycloth mother with ice water in its veins. Newborn monkeys attached themselves to this "cold momma" for a brief period of time, but then retreated to a corner of the cage and rejected her forever.

Anaclitic Depression
In order for the child to build up expectancies about the world around it, that world must present certain regularities and certainties. *Too much regularity* can cause problems too—if this regularity is suddenly disrupted before the child is mature enough to respond appropriately. For

Contact comfort. The pleasure that a young animal gets in rubbing its body against a soft, "woolly" object, or from clinging tightly to its mother's body. Unless a young primate gets enough contact comfort, it fails to develop "trust," and its social and emotional maturation is likely to be retarded.

Catapult (CAT-ah-pult). From the Greek words meaning "to throw against." An ancient military device for hurling stones at an enemy. Our modern version of the catapult is the slingshot.

Anaclitic relationship (ann-ah-KLITT-ick). A strong, non-sexual love; the loving dependency and trust of a young child for its mother. The emotional attachment that builds up between a child and its mother.

Anaclitic depression. A type of passivity or apathy that very young children show when they are separated from their mothers for any great length of time. During the first two or three weeks of the separation, the child may be highly emotional. If the mother does not return, the child falls into an apathetic condition known as anaclitic depression.

instance, a child cared for by a mother with consistent behavior patterns rapidly builds up an emotional *attachment* to its mother, for it learns that much of what is pleasant and satisfying in its world comes to it through inputs from its mother. Psychologists call this an **anaclitic relationship**, the phrase coming from the Greek word meaning "to lean on."

J.A. Bowlby has studied infant-mother attachments for a great many years. And, according to Bowlby, disturbing the anaclitic relationship can be dangerous. If it is the mother who *always* feeds the child, the infant soon builds up a schema that incorporates both "food" and "mother." When food appears, the child expects its mother to be there too, because it is not yet mature enough to discriminate food from mother. If the infant is suddenly separated from its mother during the first few months of its life, Bowlby says, the child may have considerable difficulty adjusting to its altered circumstances.

Evidence supporting Bowlby's beliefs comes from research by psychiatrist R.A. Spitz. He studied the reactions of infants 6 to 12 months old who, for various reasons, had been separated from their mothers and put into institutions or foster homes. In their new environments, these infants received at best impersonal care. Almost as soon as the infants were institutionalized, they began showing signs of disturbance. They became quite upset when anyone approached them. They lost weight, became passive and inactive, and had trouble sleeping as well.

Spitz calls this condition **anaclitic depression**. The first sign of this disorder is a type of behavior that he describes as "a search for the mother." Some babies quietly weep big tears; others cry violently. None of them, Spitz says, can be

According to Harlow, peer love develops out of infant-mother love and develops into heterosexual attraction.

quieted down by any type of intervention, although at the initial stage of the depression they still cling tightly to any adult who picks them up. If the mother does not return in three to four weeks, the infant's behavior changes. It withdraws, lies quietly on its stomach, will not play if offered a toy, and does not even look up if someone enters the room. The baby becomes dejected and passive, refuses food, loses weight, and becomes more susceptible than usual to colds and other ailments.

Spitz believes that anaclitic depression might well account for some types of mental retardation, since the children he studied seemed to show considerable physical and intellectual impairment during and immediately after their periods of depression.

Maternal Deprivation in Humans: A Case History

Children who enter a hospital for treatment are, quite naturally, very prone to anaclitic depression since they usually must be isolated from their mothers, sometimes for an extended period of time.

That this depression may affect the child's behavior in rather unusual ways was shown in a study by Clayton Shorkey and John Taylor while they were at Michigan State University. Their patient was a 17-month-old girl who suffered severe burns. The little girl was placed in isolation as soon as she was admitted to the hospital. The first day the infant was fairly quiet, but on subsequent days she cried lustily and tossed her limbs about in a violent, agitated manner.

To treat the child's burns, the nurses applied a drug called silver nitrate. The child reacted to this apparently painful treatment by crying. The doctors also began a series of skin grafts, but discontinued them when the infant's physical condition grew markedly worse. After a month of treatment, the little girl refused to eat. More than this, she became extremely upset whenever she was approached by any of the nursing staff.

At this point Shorkey and Taylor were called in to help. They observed that the nurses would frequently interrupt the painful silver nitrate treatment by talking to the girl, singing, and playing with her toys. The more the nurses attempted to give the child love, the more violent the infant became in her rejection of their attention and affection. Indeed, it almost appeared that the staff members were making the child worse, not better.

Conditioning Therapy

Shorkey and Taylor reasoned that the infant had been *conditioned* to expect hurt rather than love whenever a nurse appeared on the scene. Treatment, then, should consist of helping the child build up a new set of conditioned expectancies so that she would be able to predict ahead of time what was going to happen to her.

Shorkey and Taylor instituted the following changes: Whenever the nurses were to bathe the girl's bandages with silver nitrate, they first turned on bright white lights. The nurses were instructed to wear green medical garments during the "treatment condition" and were not allowed to talk with or handle the infant unnecessarily and did not play with her. But when the nurses wanted to socialize with the child, they were told to turn on red lights. During this "social condition," the nursing staff wore distinctive red garments, and they spent as much time as possible playing with the girl, rubbing the unburned parts of her body, talking to her, and giving her food.

By the end of the second day, the infant began responding differently to the two treatment conditions. She continued to cry—but briefly—when the white lights were on and she was doused with the painful silver nitrate. But when the red lights were on, her crying ceased and for the first time in several weeks she lost her fear of the staff members. By the fourth day the infant began entering into little games with the staff. By the end of two weeks, she was playing happily during the "red light" condition. At this point, the doctors resumed the skin grafts. By the end of six weeks, the little girl was well enough to be discharged from the hospital.

The Mother's Reactions

An interesting sidelight to this case involves the behavior of the child's mother. At first she refused to follow the new rules, since she insisted the infant would recognize her as "mother" no matter what she was wearing and no matter which lights were on when she entered the room. To the woman's surprise, the child continued to react with lusty crying whenever she saw her mother while she was dressed in normal clothes. When the mother was persuaded to wear red clothes and to see the girl only when the red lights were on, the infant rapidly adjusted and responded to her mother in a positive, accepting fashion.

Shorkey and Taylor studied the little girl for a period of two years after her discharge from the hospital. They report she showed no detectable problems in either her physical or psychological recovery from the trauma. They also note that the child was placed in her grandmother's care after she left the hospital because the child's mother had indicated that her daughter's injury might not have been entirely accidental—a point we will return to later in this chapter.

Question: How does the Shorkey-Taylor research reinforce the belief that parents must provide their infants with consistent stimulus inputs?

Infant-Mother Love: Learned or Innate?

A number of studies suggest that the love an infant experiences for its mother is due to an intense "bonding process" that develops during the first days of the child's life. Some scientists believe that this bonding is a form of *imprinting*, similar to that found in birds and other lower animals. However, as we noted in the last chapter, there is little good evidence that this is the case.

Peer. From a Latin word meaning "equals." Your peers are the people of your own age and social station whom you grew up with.

Stereotyped (STAIR-ee-oh-typed). Any activity that is repeated automatically, without thought and without variation, is said to be stereotyped.

Judging from Daniel Stern's research, mentioned earlier in this chapter, most infants are born with a readiness to respond to the adults around them. If they are "nurtured" in a loving and stimulating way, they soon grow strongly attached to whoever takes care of them. However, the *strength* of the attachment process is influenced by rewards and punishments. And the infant will "attach" to *any caretaker*, not just to its biological mother (and father). Thus the "ability to bond" is determined by the genes, but the bonding itself is shaped primarily by the adults who care for the child, and the manner in which they treat the infant.

Peer Love

The first type of "love" that Harlow mentioned was the love of an infant for its mother (or for whoever nurtures it). This infant-parent relationship helps the child develop expectancies about the world around it, and stimulates the child to grow both physically and psychologically.

The second type of love is affectionate bonding between two or more young organisms. **Peer** love, as it is called, seems to be necessary for the child to develop mature *social responses*. Let us again return to the Harlows' work to see why this is the case.

Monkeys raised on cloth surrogates appear to be fairly normal in their behavior patterns—at least while they are isolated from their peers. However, when the Harlows put *groups* of surrogate-trained monkeys together, they soon found they had a problem. Although these animals had never seen other monkeys during their entire lives, they responded to one another with excessive amounts of aggressive behavior. Eventually this hostility waned and then disappeared, but the animals' social behavior remained unusual, to say the least.

Many of these monkeys showed the kinds of **stereotyped** activities one finds in certain types of patients in mental hospitals. That is, the monkeys made oddly repetitive movements that seemed to have no function, or they froze into bizarre postures, or they would stare into space for hours on end. Sometimes, while a monkey was looking blankly out of its cage, one of its arms would rise slowly as if not really attached to the monkey's body. The Harlows refer to this as a **floating limb response**, and note that it is also seen in human patients who suffer from **catatonic schizophrenia**. If the monkey noticed its limb while it was "floating," the animal often jumped away in fear or even attacked its oddly behaving limb.

As the Harlows point out, these infant monkeys had been raised in *partial* social deprivation. They had their surrogate mothers, and they often interacted with their human keepers. But the animals had never experienced the pleasures of socializing with other growing monkeys. Little wonder they didn't get along well with each other.

Sex and the Isolated Monkey

The Harlows put the partially deprived monkeys together so that they might breed and hence provide more baby monkeys for experiments. But the animals refused to cooperate. Even when the Harlows introduced an experienced, normally raised male into the colony, he was a complete failure as far as impregnating any of the females was concerned.

As we noted in Chapter 12, the sex life of lower animals (such as rats) is determined almost entirely by their hormones. When their gonads say "go," the animals are ready and able to respond. In primates, however, hormones are not the only determining factor. Heterosexual love appears to grow out of peer love, and if the monkey has no peers to respond to when young, it doesn't respond sexually as an adult.

During much of peer group play, normally reared young monkeys chase each other and "rough-house" a great deal. Some of this playful behavior ends with the immature male attempting to mate with the young female. Apparently, this "play-mating" is a necessary step in learning adult sexual behaviors. For, as Harlow puts it so well, unless a female monkey is *chased* by her age-mates when she is young, she will very likely remain *chaste* all the rest of her life.

Peer Deprivation in Monkeys

The presence of peers is necessary—but not sufficient—for normal emotional and social development in monkeys. In one of their best-known experiments, the Harlows tried to reproduce a human type of *anaclitic depression* in normal infant monkeys. These young animals were raised from birth in a large group with their mothers present. Then, for a period of several weeks, the mothers were taken away, leaving the infants to get along as best they could together.

As you might expect, the tiny monkeys went through much the same sort of anaclitic depression as human infants. At the time of their separation, the baby monkeys searched actively for their mothers and cried loudly. Soon, however, they began to withdraw. Even though they had their peers to romp about with, they stopped playing and socializing. Instead, the babies huddled in corners alone, each clinging to its own body, each lost in its individual bleak-brown thoughts.

Once the mothers were re-introduced, the infants went through a momentary period of frantic activity, most of which was aimed at clinging so tightly to the mother that she could never leave them again. Peer play soon became re-established and the infants recovered normally.

In a further set of studies, the Harlows showed that it is not merely the loss of maternal "magic" that leads to severe depression. Rather, it is the deprivation of whatever form of social stimulation the organism is *accustomed to* at the time of separation that throws it into a state of hopelessness. Monkeys raised from birth in the presence of other infants their age (but without any mothers present) appear to grow up fairly normally. When these infants are isolated from their peers, however, they too fall into an anaclitic depression, just as if they had been separated from their mothers. When reunited with these peers, they engage in the same intense clinging as would an infant given back to its mother.

Question: The anaclitic depression occurs not merely because the infant is separated from its mother, but because its expectancies are grossly violated. How might this fact help explain adult depressions caused by loss of job, friends, or loved ones?

Mother-Infant Love

Peer love grows out of the love an infant has for its parent(s), and heterosexual love grows out of peer love. These three types of love, therefore, are based on *experience* as much as they are on *instinct*.

But what about maternal love? Isn't this a natural, normal, innately-determined type of emotionality that would appear no matter what the mother's prior experience had been?

Judging from the data, the answer seems to be "no." In one study, the Harlows were able to find ways of getting female isolates pregnant (despite their lack of interest in mating) by confining them in a small cage for long periods of time with a patient and highly experienced male. When these isolated females gave birth to their first monkey baby, however, they turned out to be the "monster mothers" the Harlows had tried to create with mechanical surrogates. Having had no contact with other animals as they grew up, they simply did not know what to do with the furry little strangers that suddenly appeared on the scene. These motherless mothers at first totally ignored their children, although if the infant persisted, the mothers occasionally gave in and provided the baby with some of the contact comfort it demanded.

Surprisingly enough, once these mothers learned how to handle a baby, they did reasonably well. Then, when they were again impregnated and gave birth to a second infant, they took care of it fairly adequately.

Maternal affection was totally lacking in a few of the motherless monkeys, however. To them, the newborn monkey was little more than an object to be abused the way a human child might abuse a doll or a toy train. These motherless mothers stepped on their babies, crushed the infant's face to the floor of the cage, and once or twice chewed off their baby's feet and fingers before they could be stopped. The most terrible mother of all popped her infant's head into her mouth and crunched it like a potato chip.

We tend to think of most mothers—no matter what their species—as having some kind of almost-divine "maternal instinct" that makes

"DON'T YOU REALIZE, PETER, THAT WHEN YOU THROW FURNITURE OUT THE WINDOW AND TIE YOUR SISTER TO A TREE, YOU MAKE MOMMY AND DADDY VERY SAD?"

Floating limb response. People (and monkeys) suffering from some mental disorders seem at times to lose voluntary control over the movements of their arms and legs. The person's arm may rise "as if it had a mind of its own," without the person's being conscious of why the arm is making this "floating" kind of movement.

Catatonic schizophrenia (CAT-uh-TONN-ick SKITS-oh-FREE-knee-uh). *Schizophrenia* comes from the Greek words meaning "split mind." Someone whose mind is "split away from reality" is said to suffer from a severe form of mental illness, or schizophrenia. *Catatonia* means "under tension" or "contracted." A mentally disturbed person who "freezes" his or her body into strange positions has contracted the muscles abnormally.

---

them love and take care of their children no matter what the cost or circumstance. While it is true that most females have built into their genetic blueprint the *tendency* to be interested in (and to nurture) their offspring, this inborn tendency is always expressed in a given environment. The "maternal instinct" thus is strongly influenced by the mother's past experiences.

Question: What does the Harlows' research tell us about possible causes of child abuse in humans?

Infant versus Maternal Bonding

We often speak of a "maternal instinct," but seldom of an "infant instinct." Yet the data available so far suggest that the attachment an infant has for its mother (or other caretaker) is much stronger and much more under genetic control than the "instinctual love" a mother presumably has for her child. In his 1980 book, *Parent-Child Interaction*, Hugh Lytton notes that almost all human infants show attachment, but that many mothers (and fathers) fail to do so. Thus infant bonding is less influenced by experience than is maternal bonding.

Lytton found as well that young children often were more sensitive to how their parents treated them than vice versa. Children who were rewarded for complying with their parents' demands were much more likely to comply in the future. However, the fact that a child complied when it was rewarded did not usually make the parents more positively reinforcing toward the child in the future. Generally speaking, Lytton says, parents were much more likely to correct or punish a child for bad behavior than they were to reward a child for appropriate actions. And the parents continued this behavior no matter how ineffectual their actions were.

Judging from Lytton's research, it would seem that attachment increases the reward value of a parent's behaviors. However, maternal (or

Mothers tend to talk to and gaze at their infants more than fathers, but fathers tend to touch their children and engage them in physical play more than do mothers. **(top)**

Fatherless boys can often learn the "adult male role" from teachers, counselors, and other surrogate fathers. **(left)**

paternal) bonding apparently does not make the child's behaviors all that much more rewarding to the parents.

Paternal Love

The noted anthropologist Margaret Mead once said that "fathers are a biological necessity but a social accident." But data gathered by devel-

opmental psychologists tend not to support Dr. Mead's viewpoint. As Drs. Ross Parke and Douglas Sawin report in the November 1977 issue of *Psychology Today*, fathers contribute significantly to an infant's social and emotional growth, although the father's contributions are often quite different from the mother's. While the father is just as capable of taking care of an infant as the mother, the father's chief role (at least in our society) seems to be that of *playmate* to the child.

Parke and Sawin studied the responses of fathers to their infants and found that—when given the chance—fathers were just as likely to nurture and stimulate their children as were the mothers. In fact, fathers were more likely to hold the infants and to look at them. Furthermore, the fathers were just as likely as the mothers to interpret correctly the cues the infants gave. However, in most real-life settings, the fathers were less likely to feed and change the child's diapers. This difference in parental behaviors seems due to cultural roles, however, and not to innate differences in male-female "instincts."

Harvard pediatricians Michael Yogman, T. Berry Brazelton, and their colleagues found that fathers talked to their infants less than mothers. However, fathers were much more likely to touch or hug the child. The fathers primarily engaged in rough-and-tumble play with their children, while the mothers were more likely to play conventional games, such as peek-a-boo. Brazelton notes that, "When several weeks old, an infant displays an entirely different attitude—more wide-eyed, playful, and bright-faced—toward its father than toward its mother." One explanation for this, Brazelton says, is that the fathers apparently *expect* more playful responses from their children. And the children then respond to the father's expectations.

Oregon psychologist Beverly Fagot studied 20 male and 20 female nursery school teachers. In the November 1981 issue of *Psychology Today*, she notes that the male teachers were more physically affectionate toward the children than the female teachers. The men were also more likely to comment favorably on the children's activities and to join in their play. Thus the notion that mothers are more suitable companions or teachers for young children than fathers apparently is incorrect, for mothers and fathers apparently influence different aspects of the child's development. In most studies of the child's reactions to its parents, the data suggest that children respond more positively to the father than to the mother. They are more likely to pick the father as a preferred playmate, and apparently feel more at ease among strangers if the father is an involved parent than if the mother is the sole caretaker. The father's contribution, then, is often that of physical and social stimulation, while the mother's is more verbal training and general nurturance.

Paternal Deprivation

Given the fact that a father's influence on his child is more strongly social and emotional than intellectual, what would be the result of the father's absence during the child's early years? Would boys react differently to paternal deprivation than would girls?

Several studies reported in the 1950's suggested that boys reared without fathers are less aggressive, more dependent, and have more "feminine" interests and behavior patterns than boys who are brought up in normal families. And in a 1980 study, psychiatrist James Herzog reports that "father deprivation" is particularly harmful to boys 18 to 24 months of age. He states that these children tended to have recurring nightmares

about monsters, which he interprets as being a sign of "displaced aggression." Father-deprived boys from ages two to five tended to be hyperactive and more aggressive "than normal." We should note, however, that Herzog did not compare these fatherless boys to a comparable set of boys from intact families. Apparently, he merely *assumed* that any "unusual" behaviors the boys showed were due to paternal deprivation.

Psychologist Joseph Pleck reviewed these studies in the September 1981 issue of *Psychology Today*. Pleck states that most of them are of questionable value because they have major experimental flaws. He concludes that boys who grow up without a "male identity figure" present are neither more nor less "masculine" than boys reared in intact families. Nor are they badly affected in most other ways. In their 1971 book *Boys in Fatherless Families*, Elizabeth Herzog and Cecilia Sudia report that boys who grow up in fatherless homes turn out to be just as normal and well-adjusted as boys reared in intact families. The only exception to this finding is a slight increase in delinquency and in school disciplinary problems among fatherless boys. However, this same increase is found in both boys *and* girls reared by a single parent of *either* sex.

Given the fact that fathers tend to engage in more physical play with their children than mothers, one might expect that fatherless boys would show *some* effects from paternal deprivation. The Harlows' experiments suggest that, during physical play, young monkeys learn something about self-control and the limits of aggression. Perhaps, then, it isn't surprising that the only proven effect of paternal deprivation on boys seems to lie in the realm of aggression and "disciplinary problems."

Father-Daughter Relationships

Research reported by E. Mavis Hetherington suggests that young girls may also need their fathers if they are to grow up in a fashion our culture views as normal. Dr. Hetherington began by observing the activities of three types of girls—those whose mothers were divorced when the girls were very young; those whose fathers had died when the girls were very young; and those who had grown up in normal family situations. None of the girls had brothers. Although few of these young women had noticeable behavior problems, and all were doing reasonably well in school, there were marked differences in the way these adolescent girls reacted to the males in their environments.

According to Hetherington, girls reared by divorced mothers sought more attention and praise from males than did girls in the other two

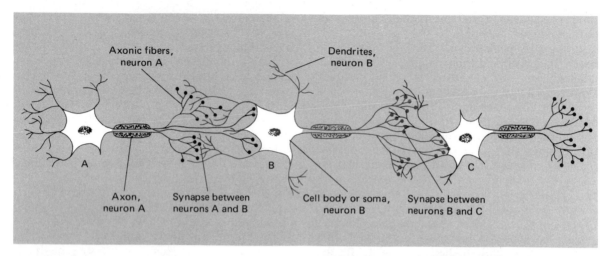

Axonic fibers, neuron A

Dendrites, neuron B

A

B

C

Axon, neuron A

Synapse between neurons A and B

Cell body or soma, neuron B

Synapse between neurons B and C

Mavis Hetherington

Fig. 19.3. Scientists have shown that a stimulating environment causes neurons to build up an increased number of synaptic connections. **(top)**

Fig. 19.4. A baby "therapist" comforts a monkey reared alone. **(left)**

Research suggests that girls reared in fatherless families often react to young men differently than do girls who grow up with their fathers present in the home. **(right)**

groups. They were also more likely to hang around places where young males could be found—gymnasiums, carpentry and machine shops, and the stag lines at school dances. In marked contrast, girls with widowed mothers tended to avoid males as much as possible. These fatherless girls stayed away from typically male gathering places, some of them remaining in the ladies' room the entire evening during dances and other social events. These differences apparently were not due to popularity, for both groups of girls received equal numbers of invitations to dance when they were actually present in the dance hall.

All three groups of girls appeared to have similar and quite normal relationships with other girls and women, but not with men. Girls reared by divorced mothers dated earlier and more frequently than did the others, and were more likely to have engaged in sexual intercourse. By contrast, girls with widowed mothers tended to start dating much later than normal and seemed to be sexually inhibited.

Hetherington concludes that girls apparently need the presence of an adult male during their formative years in order to learn appropriate responses to men when the girls reach puberty.

Question: Would you expect father-deprived girls to be as active in sports as girls reared in intact homes?

Love and Psychotherapy

As Harry Harlow noted, the development of loving behavior patterns does seem to go through several stages. The infant loves its mother, then its peers, then enters into heterosexual love, then loves its own offspring. The critical point to note, however, is how dependent all of these forms of love are on the organism's *interactions with its environment.*

Given the great influence that the people around a child have on its social and emotional development, it is understandable that infants who grow up in abnormal environments are likely to end up with abnormal thoughts and behavior patterns. If parents and peers are absent—or if the child's father and mother are punitive, inconsistent, or unresponsive—the child will very likely need psychological help at some stage in its life.

But what kind of help? How do you teach someone to love?

We will attempt to answer some of these questions *at the human level* in later chapters. But we might mention how the Harlows attempted to solve similar problems with *monkeys* who were raised in social isolation (on terrycloth surrogates).

When the Harlows introduced these animals into normal monkey groups, the isolates responded with fear and withdrawal. When their terror of others had habituated, the isolates reacted with hostility and aggression. The Harlows figured that even these isolates might learn to love, but who could best act as a therapist for a socially withdrawn animal?

Because the Harlows reasoned that *contact comfort* was the key to turning an isolated monkey into a normal one, they selected as their "therapists" socially normal female infants who were only three to four months old (see Fig. 19.3). The isolates were all males. The "therapists" remained with their natural mothers except during "therapy hours." Since these young female monkeys were all much smaller than the male isolates, the Harlows believed the babies would not threaten the isolates as much as would an adult animal—or a human. Then, too, persistence in therapy often yields rich rewards, and there are few things in life as persistent as a baby monkey in search of contact comfort.

So the Harlows built a "mental hospital" in which they could control the interactions between the isolates and the baby-therapists. At the beginning, the babies were allowed contact with their "patients" for two hours a day. At their first meeting, the typical male isolate (who had not yet learned to be aggressive) retreated to a corner of the "hospital" cage, hugged himself, and rocked back and forth, doing his best to ignore the infant. The infant's response was to approach the isolate and try to cling to him. Although the isolate rejected the "therapist's" overtures again and again during the first day or so, gradually his fear of the tiny stranger extinguished. The isolate stopped retreating from the infant and soon let her satisfy her need for contact comfort by clinging to his body.

Within a few days, the isolate was clinging to the infant with the same apparent pleasure that the infant derived. Within a few weeks, the isolates and "therapists" were playing together enthusiastically. Gradually, over time, most of the isolates' abnormal behaviors disappeared. By the time therapy had continued for six months, the isolates appeared to have recovered completely from their initial period of social deprivation. At this point the isolates could be introduced into normal monkey groups and could make a successful adjustment.

Question: How might we use the Harlows' research to design new types of psychotherapy for disturbed human children?

Learning about Love

The scientific study of social and emotional development has taught us many things about love that we never knew before. In our society, apparently, we presume that human maternal and paternal "instincts" are so strong that society itself does not have to worry about the rights of the child. Indeed, until fairly recently, children were considered to be the *property* of their parents—to be loved, beaten, or even sold into slavery if the mother and father desired. Little wonder society ignored what really went on in family settings since "parental instincts" were thought always to be healthy and good.

And because society assumed that punishment was an acceptable way to socialize children, we paid little attention to child abuse until fairly recently. We were particularly late to realize that, if these abused children managed to survive, grow up, and become parents themselves, they would very likely harm their own children as they had been harmed.

We are just beginning to learn the *scientific facts* of social and emotional development. We still do not know what aspects of social maturation are primarily controlled by the genes, and which are more strongly influenced by experience. Nor do we yet understand as much as we should about helping children overcome the sometimes crippling effects of early emotional trauma. But the data do suggest that the best way to make sure a child grows up to be socially normal and emotionally healthy is for both parents to give it wise and attentive love.

Summary

1. Love is an **emotion**—an internal state or condition—that cannot be measured directly. But we can measure **loving behaviors** and discuss them objectively.

2. Mother and newborn child form a **social dyad**. Evidence suggests that both mother and child have an **inborn mutual readiness** to respond to each other. Further studies suggest that the infant **shapes** parental responses as much as parents shape the child's reactions.

3. From their studies of laboratory monkeys, Harry and Margaret Harlow identified five types of social love:

   a. **Infant love**—the love an infant has for its mother (or for whoever nurtures it).
   b. **Peer love**—the love a child has for others its own age.
   c. **Heterosexual love**—the sexual love an adult has for his or her mate.
   d. **Maternal love**—the love a mother has for her offspring.
   e. **Paternal love**—the love a father has for his offspring.

4. A newborn monkey clings to its mother because she gives it warmth, food, and **contact comfort**. Warmth is the most important input during the first two weeks of a monkey's life. Thereafter, contact comfort, or "rubbability" is more important.

5. A young monkey will cling to any warm, "rubbable" object if deprived of its mother.

6. Contact with the mother (or her **surrogate**) appears to give the infant the **trust** it needs in order to mature socially and emotionally.

7. According to James Prescott, sensory stimulation of the infant's receptor organs is necessary for proper development of the brain. Children deprived of **physical affectional stimulation** or nurturance may be predisposed to violent behaviors as adults.

8. Children who are treated inconsistently or who are given minimal stimulation by their mothers seem predisposed to suffer later psychological problems.

9. Maternal contact also allows the infant to build up **perceptual expectations** about its world. When its expectancies are grossly violated, the infant falls into an **anaclitic depression** and may die if not returned to its mother.

10. If an infant monkey grows up without having other young monkeys to play with, it never develops peer love and does not know how to respond in social situations. Sexual love grows out of peer love. Young monkeys deprived of the pleasure of their peers do not mate in the usual fashion as adults.

11. Both the **paternal instinct** and the **maternal instinct** are greatly influenced by learning and early experience. **Infant attachment** is much more under the control of the **genetic blueprint**.

12. Female monkeys raised on surrogate mothers often treat their first infants cruelly.

13. When given the opportunity, human fathers seem as interested in and as responsive to their infants as mothers. Fathers tend to engage more in rough-housing and **physical contact** with their children.

14. Mothers tend to talk to their children more than fathers, but **touch** and play with the children less.

15. Early studies suggested that boys who grow up without fathers often show very "feminine"

behavior patterns, but later experiments contradict these early findings. The only consistent result is that fatherless boys tend to be more **aggressive** than normal.

16. Girls who grow up without fathers may either be strongly attracted to adult males or tend to avoid them, depending in part on whether the girls' mothers were divorced or widowed.

17. Monkeys raised on surrogate mothers can learn to get along with other monkeys if given **contact comfort therapy** by normal monkey infants.

18. Our early experiences strongly affect our social and emotional development. Fortunately, with the right kind of training, we can usually overcome the many problems associated with growing up in poor social environments.

(see page 433)

You see, Señores, we do the best we can. But we have little money, and we have tradition to fight. So it is very difficult . . ."

The Superintendent of the jail shrugged his shoulders with an eloquence that could only come from practice. He was showing his visitors—two women and a man—the jail's kitchen. A fat, contented-looking little child, perhaps 18 months old, waddled across the floor and sat down by its mother, who was shelling beans.

"Look at that poor child," one of the women said. "Just look at the dirt on its face! And the rags that it's wearing! Can't you at least provide the children with adequate clothing and keep them clean?"

Again the Superintendent shrugged. "Señora, we try. But the government does not give us money to buy clothes for the children. You see, they are not here officially. It is the mother who is in jail, not the child. But it is our custom not to separate the little ones from their mothers, and who am I to go against such tradition? The mothers would complain loudly if I did. And the fathers as well—if we knew who the fathers were!"

The fat little child got to its feet and started to walk again, but soon stumbled and fell to the floor. Almost before the first cry was out of its mouth, its mother scooped it up and pressed it to her breast.

The visitor persisted. "But the dirt. At least you can do something about that!"

A smile crept across the Superintendent's dark, heavily wrinkled face. "Dirt? Señora, these women come from huts with dirt floors. They are not from what you would call the best classes of society. We merely keep them in jail. We are not equipped to teach them to be ladies!"

"But cleanliness is next to godliness!"

"Señora, the padre will tell you that even the godliness of some of these women is in rather grave doubt."

The child stopped its crying, but tears still ringed its eyes. The mother brushed the tears away with a dirty rag, then dangled a bunch of beans in front of the child's face, teasing it. The baby reached for the beans, but missed, so the mother continued the little game. On the second try, the child caught the beans and pulled them away from its mother. Both of them laughed.

"Just listen to them," one of the women visitors said, shaking her head in disgust.

"Yes, it's apparent that we must do something to save these children from such an unhealthy and unwholesome environment," said the male visitor. "We should be shirking our duty if we left these poor little babies to grow up in a jail!"

"What do you think would be best?"

The man thought for a moment. "Well, what do you think of building a nice, clean orphanage or hospital for them? We could paint the walls white, and . . ."

Recommended Readings

Harlow, H.F., M.K. Harlow, and S.J. Suomi. "From Thought to Therapy: Lessons from a Primate Laboratory,".*American Scientist*, Vol. 59, No. 5 (September-October 1971), pp. 539–549.

Kagan, Jerome, Richard B. Kearsley, and P.R. Zelazo. *Infancy* (Cambridge, Mass.: Harvard University Press, 1978).

Lerner, R.M., and G.B. Spanier, eds. *Child Influences on Marital and Family Interaction: A Life-span Perspective* (New York: Academic Press, 1978).

Maccoby, Eleanor E. *Social Development: Psychological Growth and the Parent-Child Relationship* (New York: Harcourt Brace Jovanovich, 1980).

Parke, Ross D., and Douglas B. Sawin. "Fathering: It's a Major Role," *Psychology Today* (November 1977), pp. 109–112.

Tiger, Lionel, and Robin Fox. *The Imperial Animal* (New York: Holt, Rinehart and Winston, 1972).

Cognitive Development 20

Did You Know That . . .

Jean Piaget, perhaps the most respected child psychologist of this century, published his first scientific paper when he was 10?

According to Piaget, cognitive development is the study of how children acquire knowledge?

Piaget believed there were three kinds of knowledge, knowing "how," "what," and "why"?

According to Piaget, a child's mental development passes through four distinct stages or periods?

Language learning is one of the most complex aspects of cognitive development?

During the time you were learning to speak your mother probably taught you the use of "social contracts" as well?

Chimpanzees have been taught 100 or more words of an artificial language called "Yerkish"?

Many early theorists believed that a child would "explode" from surplus energy if it didn't release this energy in play?

Piaget believed that play is "a child's work"?

"Play's the Thing"

"Harry, you've got to get rid of those two snot-nosed little girls."

"What?" said Harry Smith, a shocked look on his face. "I know you're the boss around here, Dr. Jensen, but I can't just make those two children disappear, you know."

"I don't care what you do," Dr. Jensen said as the two men walked toward one of the old stone buildings at the orphanage. The Iowa summer was in full bloom. The sky was a brilliant blue, the sun was blinding hot, and waves of heat pounded at the men from all directions. "We're up to our adenoids in kids as is. You know that. We've got them jammed into every nook and cranny as is. Nice, normal kids with a chance for adoption someday. We can't be putting up with God's rejects."

The heat got to Harry a bit. "Don't call them that. They're human beings, just like you and me."

Dr. Jensen's sudden, sharp laughed sounded almost like a bark. "Human, yes. Like you and me, no." The man stopped a moment to wipe his sweaty brow. "Look, Harry, I know you think I'm being hard-nosed about all this. But try to see the situation from my point of view. I'm trying to run a decent home for the hundreds of orphans that the sovereign state of Iowa dumps in my lap. We've got twice as many youngsters as we can handle. The blond, blue-eyed, good-looking kids we can place right away. The average, run-of-the-mill types maybe we can place, maybe we can't. But the snot-nosed idiots are losers from the word 'go' and there's no sense in kidding ourselves about it."

"They're not idiots," Harry replied angrily. He started walking toward the nearest building, leaving Dr. Jensen to catch up with him.

"Hey, wait up," the man said. "I know that technically they're not idiots, because they've got IQ scores above 20. That means they're imbeciles, not idiots, but you know what I mean."

"They're not imbeciles, either. They're disadvantaged human beings," Harry replied, walking even faster.

"Yes, they are imbeciles, Harry. They're scrawny, bawling, ugly little critters with runny noses and IQ scores below 50 points. They sit in their beds all day long, whining and rocking back and forth. Nobody in their right minds would want to adopt those two, and you know it. They're dumb, ugly, and about as lovable as runty pigs with diarrhea. You just get rid of those two so we can make room for kids with some kind of future."

The two men had reached the front of the old stone building and paused for a moment in the shade of the doorway.

Dr. Jensen put his hand on the younger man's shoulder, then continued. "Harry, you're like most kids fresh out of college. You're full of all kinds of optimistic hopes about how to change the world and make things better. But this orphanage isn't college, Harry. It's the cold, cruel world of hard facts. Those two little girls you're so taken with haven't a ghost of a chance. They're severely retarded, and they have miserable personalities. They're doomed to live out their shabby little lives in state institutions, as guests of the taxpayers of the great state of Iowa. So they might as well get a head start."

"But surely there's something we can do, Dr. Jensen."

"There's nothing we can do except make the best of a bad situation. Those two little girls are God's mistakes. They never should have been born. But they were, and you and me together, working full time, couldn't turn them into normal human beings."

"But . . ."

"But nothing, Harry. We hired you straight out of the university to help us take care of orphans until we can find a home for them. There's only one home those two girls are ever going to know, and it's down the road a piece."

Harry frowned. "You mean the State Home for the Retarded?"

Dr. Jensen nodded sadly. "That's it. That's where they're going to end up anyway, so they might as well get a head start. And give us room for kids we can do something with."

"But the State Home doesn't have a nursery! They've got no facilities for taking care of children that young."

"That's their problem, not ours. You write out the transfer papers and take the girls over there. And you do it right away."

"I . . ."

Dr. Jensen paused, then shook his head in dismay. "I know this is tough on you, Harry. But you've got to get used to making tough decisions if you're going to stay in this business. You've got to learn to spend you time working on problems you can do something about, instead of wasting your efforts on lost causes like those two runty little girls. We've got too little money and too many kids, and the taxpayers frankly don't seem to give a damn. So get them transfered, and don't shed any tears over the matter. Believe me, you'll see worse things than this if you stick in this business for any length of time."

Harry looked the older man directly in the eye. Maybe it was true. Maybe there wasn't anything he could do. "All right, Dr. Jensen. I'll do it."

The older man smiled knowingly, then walked inside the building. Harry followed reluctantly. It was cool and dark inside the stone walls; the air had the musty smell of a cluttered closet. *Skeletons*, Harry said to himself. *We are the keepers of the skeletons in one of society's closets. No wonder so few people come to see the children. People are embarrassed by these kids. Who wants to adopt a skeleton?*

Dr. Jensen paused at the door to his office. "Now you get those transfer papers ready, and I'll sign them. Okay?"

"Okay," Harry said, reluctantly but with a note of resignation in his voice. "But I don't think the women at the State Home will know quite what to do with those two young girls."

"Like calls to like, Harry," Dr. Jensen responded. Then he barked out another laugh. "And you never can tell. Those ladies at the State Home may know more about helping their own kind than you and me put together."

(Continued on page 471)

Cognitive Development

In the previous two chapters, we discussed the biological and social/emotional development of children. But young people have minds as well as bodies and behaviors, and watching the intellectual growth of a child can be at least as fascinating as observing the age at which an infant walks and the social responses it makes to its parents and peers. Thus it is to *cognitive* development that we now turn our attention.

At the beginning of Chapter 18, we listed four major "themes" that cut across child psychology. One was the mind/body problem. At first blush, it might seem as though cognitive psychologists would uniformly resolve this issue in favor of the "mind." After all, we can hardly speak of "cognitive" development unless we are willing to admit that there *is* a mind—or at least that children have "internal processes" that we can somehow follow over time. As we will see, however, there are many scientists working in this area who equate "cognitive development" with the growth of speech and problem-solving *behaviors*. So the mind/body problem remains an important issue even in the field of cognitive psychology.

The second theme—the nature-nurture controversy—is probably of far greater importance, however. Are human infants born with an innate ability to think and process language, or are these skills almost entirely learned? Are there basic "structures of the mind" which are part of a child's genetic blueprint, or are thinking and reasoning "programmed" into a child by its social environment? As we will soon discover, there are almost as many different viewpoints on this topic as there are psychologists working in the area.

The third theme had to do with developmental *consistency*, and the fourth with *individual differences*. In the field of cognitive development, these topics show up primarily in the "stage theories" of mental growth. Some psychologists believe that all children must pass through specific "stages" of mental maturation. These theorists assume that the growth pattern for all children should be *consistent across developmental stages*, and thus pay little attention to individual differences. Other psychologists hold that these "stages" are primarily the result of social influences. These theorists believe that the consistencies we see in children are features of the cultures the children grow up in, not of the children themselves. Thus these psychologists tend to be more interested in an individual child's rate of development than in the fact that the child matures in ways similar to other children in the same environment.

We will touch on these issues again in the next chapter, when we discuss *personality*. But you should keep all four themes "in mind" as we now look at the cognitive development of the child.

Jean Piaget

Jean Piaget was one of the most respected figures in child psychology. When Piaget died in September, 1980, at age 84, Harvard psychologist Jerome Kagan called him "the most influential developmental theorist of this century, if not of all time."

For some 50 years, Piaget was a professor at the University of Geneva and director of the Rousseau Institute. Trained as a zoologist, Piaget began publishing his scientific observations at the ripe

Jean Piaget

Now, how did this miraculous change occur? That is, how did you develop from a passive "bundle of biological reflexes" into the infinitely complicated, self-directed human being you are today? Was your mental maturation determined primarily by your genes, by your environment, or, more likely, by an *interaction* between the two?

Piaget was, in his own way, an interactionist. Indeed, he often called himself "the man in the middle" of the nature-nurture controversy. He believed that you were born with certain *innate mental structures* that determined the shape of your cognitive development. These structures provided both your *motivation* to interact with your environment and guided the growth of your knowledge about the world. However, according to Piaget, you were not "taught" by the people around you. "The child is the teacher," Piaget said. By this, he meant that you *constructed* your own semblance of reality using the mental tools you were born with. Thus you needed your environment in order to grow mentally, but the pattern of your development was determined by your genes.

Now that we have briefly outlined Piaget's position on the nature-nurture controversy, let's see what he thought about the pattern of cognitive development and what stages you went through as you matured into an adult.

old age of 10. It was not until his college years, however, that he began what he called his search for a "theory of knowledge," a search that led him to study the intellectual development of children.

Piaget was a gentle, wise man who loved children and wanted to figure out how their "mental structures" grew and developed. But he also loved science, art, and religion. When he was 20, Piaget wrote a novel, *Quest*, about a young man named Sebastien who searches for answers to such questions as, "Who am I?" and "What is the meaning of life?" The answers Sebastien discovers in the novel eventually became the basis for much of Piaget's later theorizing about cognitive development. Indeed, most of Piaget's research on children appears to be little more than a life-long attempt to confirm the insights he had while still a very young man.

Mental Development

The basic psychological problem Piaget tried to solve can be stated fairly simply. When you were born, you were little more than a bundle of biological reflexes. You took in food, you excreted wastes, and you responded in a reflexive way to a variety of stimuli. But you did not "think," solve problems, or have any real understanding of who you were or what the world was really like. Now, many years later, you are a conscious, self-directed, mature human being. You speak a complex language, you are capable of understanding the strange symbols of mathematics and nuclear physics, and you can create new things (such as poetry and music) if you wish to. You engage in **altruistic** behaviors that often benefit others more than they benefit you. You probably have a firm sense of what is right and wrong, and how to make many things in the world better than they presently are (including yourself).

Equilibrium

At heart, Piaget was really an "information processing theorist" long before such a label even existed. That is, he saw the mind as a kind of computer that used sensory inputs to construct an internal representation of the outside world. However, ordinary computers are *passive* instruments that must be "programmed" by external sources. To Piaget, the child's mind is an *active* computer that continually changes or reprograms itself. It does this by *abstracting* reality—that is, by searching for general laws that will allow it to understand the basic principles which govern the behavior of people and objects in the world around it.

Computers process data because they are built to do so. Thus their motivation is supplied by external sources. Children, however, are motivated by an inner biological drive that Piaget calls the process of **equilibrium**. In Chapter 11 we discussed the concept of *homeostasis*, which is the body's innate tendency to move toward a need-free state. Whenever you lack something (such as food), a physical drive occurs that motivates you to search for whatever will bring your bodily processes back into balance. In a sense, the cognitive process of "equilibrium" is little more than homeostasis applied to mental rather than biological needs.

According to Piaget, you are born with the ability to construct an abstract representation of the world in your mind. But your attempts to do so are necessarily inaccurate, particularly when you are young and inexperienced. Whenever you compare your abstraction with the real world, and the two *do not match*, you experience "disequilibrium." A sort of "cognitive drive" is created in your mind that motivates you to change your inner representation until your abstractions again match reality. At that point, your cognitive drives are reduced and you achieve a new (but higher) state of equilibrium. Thus, to Piaget, cognitive development is a process of creating ever-more-accurate abstractions, and achieving ever-more-advanced states of mental equilibrium.

Because of the emphasis that Piaget placed on the process of equilibrium, he saw all other forms of psychological and social motivation as flowing from this innate cognitive need. In this respect, he is much like drive theorists who viewed personal and social needs as "secondary"—that is, as being acquired through association with primary needs. (And in this respect, too, most of the arguments raised against drive theory apply to Piaget's concepts of equilibrium as well.)

Structures of the Mind

You were born with certain *innate reflexes*, which allowed you to respond automatically to inputs from the outer world during your first days of life.

"WHAT'S THE BIG SURPRISE? ALL THE LATEST THEORIES OF LINGUISTICS SAY WE'RE BORN WITH THE INNATE CAPACITY FOR GENERATING SENTENCES."

Altruistic (al-true-ISS-tick). From the Latin word *alter*, meaning "other." To be altruistic is to have a genuine concern for the welfare of others, to place the well-being of someone else above your own happiness or prosperity.

Equilibrium (ee-kwill-LIB-bree-um). Piaget believed people are motivated by an innate desire to match actual sensory inputs with their own abstract representations of reality. Any mismatch results in disequilibrium, which "drives" the person to change her or his mental structures to bring them into accord with reality.

Schemata (ski-MAHT-tah). Plural of "schema." Schemata are mental structures that represent reality in some abstract manner. Similar to "perceptual schemata" that allow you to recognize and respond to sensory inputs (see Chapter 9).

Organization. One of the two invariant mental functions that guide the development of schemata and other mental structures. Organization is the innate tendency to create complex structures out of simple ones.

Adaptation. The second unchanging mental function. The innate tendency to adjust to the world either by assimilating inputs or accommodating to them.

The sucking reflex is a good example, since all infants suck and swallow without having to be taught how to do so. At birth, however, you began modifying these inborn reflexes because of your experiences with the outside world. As we pointed out in Chapter 15, new learning is always built on old, and *conditioned* reflexes are but adaptations of *innate* reflexes.

In much the same fashion, says Piaget, you were born with certain "mental reflexes," or innate cognitive structures that allow you to process sensory inputs (and therefore represent reality) in a crude sort of way. At birth, however, you begin to adapt these inborn mental structures as you construct your own "inner programs" for processing reality. Your motivation to re-program your cognitive structures comes from your innate need to achieve equilibrium, which is upset whenever your current view of the world doesn't match reality. Disequilibrium, therefore, "drives" you to modify your mental structures so they represent the world more accurately.

In Piaget's terms, each "mental program" you have for processing inputs or thinking about the world *is a schema* (see Chapter 9). The history of a child's cognitive development is that of creating ever-more-complex **schemata**, or mental structures.

Functions of the Mind

According to Piaget, there are two mental *functions* that guide your cognitive development, **organization** and **adaptation**. These functions are *invariant*, in that they do not change during your entire life.

Put more simply, your schemata or mental *structures* change as you grow and develop. You do not perceive yourself now in the same way that you did 10 or 20 years ago. Thus your "self-schema" has changed over time, and will continue to change in your future years. But the mental *functions* which guide the growth of your "self-schema" remain the same throughout your entire life. These "functions" are organization and adaptation.

Organization is the mental function which allows children to create complicated mental structures out of simple ones. For example, during the first weeks of its life an infant learns what its mother smells like, looks like, feels like, and sounds like. Each of these sensory modalities is, at first, a unique if rather simple schema. Eventually, as the infant matures, it integrates these simple percepts into a far more complex mental structure, the "mother schema." Piaget believed that the tendency to organize simple schemata into more complex ones is inherited.

Adaptation is the infant's innate tendency to adjust to the world by processing information in one of two ways. The child may either try to incorporate inputs into already existing schemata, a process Piaget calls **assimilation**. Or, if the inputs simply will not fit the child's present view of reality, the child may be forced to change, add to, or reorganize its present schemata. Piaget refers to this process as **accommodation**.

Assimilation

Piaget was first and foremost a biologist. Thus many of his notions of cognitive development are analogies to biological processes. For example, consider the process of digestion. You eat food, and your stomach breaks the food down into small particles. Your blood distributes these particles to the cells, which assimilate these particles by incorporating them into the structure of the cell. Biological assimilation thus involves changing energy inputs to make them part of your body.

The process of cognitive assimilation works in much the same way. According to Piaget, when you "code" an input in order to store it your mind, you break the input up in much the same way your stomach breaks food down into tiny particles. You then incorporate the "coded" input into already existing mental structures, just as the cells assimilate food particles into already existing cellular structures. Cognitive assimilation thus involves *changing* sensory inputs to make them part of your mind.

For instance, a newborn infant tends to suck any small object that is put in its mouth. It soon builds up a mental schema related to "suckability" and assimilates all small objects into this category whether they really fit there or not. Thus when it encounters any new small object, the child often pops the object in its mouth at once.

In a sense, Piaget's notion of assimilation is much like the process of "coding" inputs into various categories for storage in Long-term Memory that we discussed in Chapter 16.

Accommodation

Sometimes a given input simply will not fit within the schemata a child already has available. For instance, suppose an infant finds a small red pepper and pops that into its mouth. Very rapidly, the child will discover it must create a new schema, that of "not suckable." Any new experience which conflicts with already existing mental structures causes the child to resort to the process of accommodation—that is, to altering its schemata to make them fit reality.

To restate matters, assimilation is the mental function that allows you to change *inputs* so that they fit your present schemata or other mental structures. Accommodation is the mental function that allows you to change your *schemata* so that they match the reality represented by your present inputs.

When you employ the process of assimilation, you often analyze inputs and thereby discover *similarities* across objects and experiences. For example, an apple and a banana don't look much alike, but both can be fitted within the schema "fruit." Thus the two objects are similar in that you can eat both of them. Accommodation is, in part, the process by which you discover *differences* between various sensory inputs. An apple and a red rubber ball may look alike, but one is edible while the other isn't. When you were growing up, you accommodated to the sight of an apple and a rubber ball by creating a different schema for each input.

Both assimilation and accommodation are invariant processes that guide your cognitive development from birth to death. That is to say, you typically first attempt to "code" inputs according to the mental categories that you already have created. If the inputs simply won't fit, you accommodate to reality by changing the way in which you perceive or "process" the inputs.

Piaget's Language

Piaget's theory of cognitive development is one of the most complex and difficult to understand in all of psychology. Some of the reasons for this difficulty have to do with the language he uses. To begin with, Piaget writes in highly technical French, and even the best translations of his writings are barely adequate. For instance, one word he uses constantly is **epistemology**, which the dictionary defines as "the study of a theory of the nature and grounds of knowledge, especially with reference to its limits and validity." And much of Piaget's research is epistemological in that it is aimed at discovering how *children come to know themselves and the world around them*. But it is not always clear just what Piaget means by this term.

Writing in the July 1978 issue of the *American Psychologist*, Piaget said:

> If we want to study cognitive functions and pursue a developmental point of view in order to study the formation and transformations of human intelligence (and this is why I specialized in child psychology), then the problems must be formulated very differently: How is knowledge acquired, how does it increase, and how does it become organized or reorganized?

Piaget answers his question thus:

> Indeed, we see at once that these are epistemological solutions stemming from empiricism, apriorism, or diverse interactionism, which are more or less static or dialectic. In short, it is impossible to avoid epistemological problems in this kind of research—epistemological problems that concern epistemology in movement, or genetic (psychogenetic) epistemology.

It takes a great deal of patience (and wisdom) to translate such thoughts into simple English.

Second, Piaget often twists words a bit to make them suit his own purposes. As we mentioned, "epistemology" means the study of how people come to "know." But to Piaget, "knowing" has several meanings. There is "knowing how" and "knowing what" and "knowing why." And it is not always easy to "know" which meaning Piaget has in mind at any given moment. Or take his use of the word "assimilation." At one level, he uses it to refer to analyzing and coding inputs in order to fit them into cognitive categories. But Piaget sometimes invests the term with much more complexity. Consider a child who picks up a stick and declares, "This is a magic wand." Piaget claims the child has *transformed* its perception of the piece of wood into a wand in order to suit the child's momentary needs. But since Piaget claims the transformation process is reversible, the child can transform its perception of a wand back to that of a stick of wood at will. In biology, the process of "assimilation" simply is not that reversible.

Despite the problems concerning Piaget's use of language, there is no doubt that his descriptions of how children mature contain many brilliant insights. So let us look at the four devel-

Assimilation (ass-sim-il-LAY-shun). The process of adaptation by which inputs are altered in order to fit into present schemata or mental structures. "Coding" an input into memory categories for long-term storage is a form of assimilation. So is "pretending" that a stick is a magic wand, for you alter the input to fit your present needs.

Accommodation (ack-komm-oh-DAY-shun). The process of adaptation by which mental schemata are changed or added to in order to match them to reality. If a given input won't fit into any present schema, you accommodate by creating a new one.

Epistemology (ee-pis-tee-MOLL-oh-gee). The scientific study of how people acquire knowledge. According to Piaget, all children have an innate desire to learn about themselves and the outer world. Thus the study of child development, to Piaget, was epistemological (ee-pis-tee-moh-LODGE-eye-cal) in that it was the study of how the child's perception of reality changes over time.

Sensory-motor period. The first of Piaget's developmental stages. The infant begins with innate reflexes and action schemata, which it correlates with sensory inputs to develop more complex schemata that combine sensory inputs with actions.

opmental stages Piaget says children go through. After that, we can evaluate his contributions, pro and con.

Piaget's Four Developmental Stages

According to Piaget, there are four major stages of cognitive development:

1. The sensory-motor period.
2. The pre-operational stage.
3. The stage of concrete operations.
4. The stage of formal operations.

Each of us goes from one stage upward to the next at slightly different ages. But the *average age* at which children attain each maturational level might well be similar in all cultures.

Sensory-Motor Period

The first of Piaget's four stages is called the **sensory-motor period**, which begins at birth and usually ends when the infant is 18 to 24 months old. It is during this time that the infant builds up its intial schemata, most of which involve the objects and people in its world.

For the first month or so of life, the infant "knows its world" solely in terms of its innate reflexes, which serve to keep it alive. But, within a month or so, the infant begins to form crude "action schemata" which let it explore and respond to its world. To Piaget, both innate reflexes and "action schemata" are examples of "knowing how," but not of "knowing what" or "knowing why."

Through the processes of assimilation and accommodation, these initial action schemata develop and become organized into more complex mental structures. The infant begins to asso-

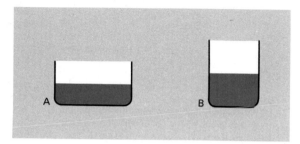

Fig. 20.1. Conservation of quantity according to Piaget.

ciate sensory inputs with muscular movements. For example, it gazes at its hands as it grasps for a toy, and thus connects visual inputs with sensory feed-forward and feedback. Eventually it can reach for the toy without looking at its hands as it does so.

According to Piaget, the infant has no real concept of **object permanence** ("knowing what") during the first few months of its life. A six-month-old child will typically follow an object with its eyes as the object moves across its field of vision. But if the object disappears, the infant shows no disappointment, nor does the child appear to anticipate the object's reappearance. Playing "peek-a-boo" with a child this young is often a frustrating task because the infant seems not to realize what the game is about. When the child reaches eight months of age (on the average), though, it will reach for an object hidden from view provided that the infant has seen the object being hidden. Peek-a-boo then becomes a fun game.

By the time the child is 18 months of age or so, it will search for something it hasn't seen hidden—an indication, according to Piaget, that the child now realizes that an object can exist independent of the child's own involvement with the object. According to Piaget, this is the beginning of *symbolic thought*, for the child maintains the symbol of the object in its mind even when the object is out of sight.

Pre-Operational Stage

During the sensory-motor period, the infant responds to its environment directly and rather automatically. But, as the child acquires sophisticated language, it passes to the second, or **pre-operational stage** of development, which runs from about age two to seven. Language gives the child the ability to deal with many aspects of its world symbolically, by talking and thinking about objects rather than having to manipulate them directly. Piaget believes that language also

allows the child to *remember past events* and hence to anticipate their happening again.

The pre-operational stage is also marked by what Piaget calls **egocentric reasoning**. By "egocentric," Piaget doesn't mean "selfish." Rather, he means that the child cannot readily *differentiate itself from its environment*. Early in this period, the infant presumes that the world is merely an extension of its own mind. Thus, a child may believe that the purpose of nighttime is to make it easier for the child to sleep, or that the sun shines primarily to give the child light and warmth. Later, it imagines that everyone else perceives the world as it does because the child cannot see things from any perspective other than its own.

The pre-operational stage is also marked by perception-bound thinking. That is, the child realizes that objects have permanence, but it struggles with the fact that objects can undergo *transformations* without being destroyed or physically changed. If you turn a sock inside out, then back again, the child is surprised to see that the sock remains the same. For when its *perception* of the sock changed, it assumed the sock had been altered too. Put another way, the child knows "how" and "what," but doesn't know "why" objects behave as they do.

Because the child doesn't realize that transformations are reversible, it cannot **conserve** physical properties such as quantity and length (see Fig. 20.1). For instance, if you fill two identical, tall thin glasses with water, the child will agree both glasses have the same amount of water in them. But suppose you empty the water in one glass into a wide container. You "know" the fat glass holds the same *quantity* of water as does the tall thin glass because you can "conserve quantity" in your mind. But, to a four-year-old, the tall glass now seems to have more liquid in it because the child doesn't realize that the process of pouring didn't *alter* the quantity of liquid in any way. If you now pour the water back into the tall thin glass, the child is surprised because it can't yet grasp the fact that transformations are reversible.

The pre-operational child is also unable to conserve length. If you lay two sticks of equal length before the child, it will agree that they are the same. If you move one stick forward a bit, the child may insist that the stick you moved is now longer than the other.

Not until the child is four or five years of age does it seem capable of dealing with abstractions—such as love and hate, up and down, large and small. The child can think—it can use language to generate expectancies—but it cannot reason. Reasoning, to Piaget, is the mental manipulation of abstract symbols, the process of "knowing why." Thus, when asked why a balloon flies, the pre-operational child may respond, "Because it is red and has a string hanging from it." This is a "what" answer, not a "why" answer.

The pre-operational stage is a transition period. As the child acquires more complex language and mental structures, it moves into the stage of concrete operations.

Question: *Piaget seems never to have used shaping techniques (described in Chapter 15) to teach a child to conserve quantity. How might you go about using successive approximations of pouring just a little bit of water back and forth from tall to wide glasses to see if children could be taught conservation of quantity at a young age?*

Stage of Concrete Operations

By the time a child reaches the age of 6 or 7, it typically enters into what Piaget calls the **stage of concrete operations**. Now it can conserve both length and quantity, because it can perform these transformations mentally. But it usually cannot conserve weight until its ninth or tenth year. If you place two identical rubber balls in front of a young child, it will assure you that they weigh the same. But if you now cut one ball in pieces, the child may announce that the cut-up pieces don't weigh the same as does the intact ball. According to Piaget, the child's answer suggests that it actually *perceives* weight in quite a different way than older children and adults do. However, once the child learns to conserve weight, it finally realizes that the whole is equal to the sum of its parts.

The concept of *number* is another acquisition the child usually makes during the stage of concrete operations. Suppose you lay out 10 pennies in two rows on a table, and show them to a child still at the pre-operational stage:

$$0\ 0\ 0\ 0\ 0$$
$$0\ 0\ 0\ 0\ 0$$

The child will see at once that the two rows are identical and that they both contain the same number of pennies. But suppose you widen the spaces between the pennies in the bottom row:

$$0\ 0\ 0\ 0\ 0$$
$$0\quad 0\quad 0\quad 0\quad 0$$

The pre-operational child will now state that the second row has more pennies, despite the fact that the child can count the coins in each row

Object permanence. According to Piaget, a very young infant does not realize that an object has an existence independent of its own perceptions of the object. Once the infant is capable of symbolic thought, it builds up complex schemata involving the object and then realizes the permanence of the object.

Pre-operational stage. The second of Piaget's developmental stages, from about 2 to 6 or 7 years, during which time a child learns to speak and to manipulate its world symbolically.

Egocentric reasoning (EE-go-SEN-trick). According to Piaget, young children cannot differentiate themselves from the external world. Thus they see the world from a self-centered viewpoint.

Conserve. In Piaget's terms, to "conserve" something is to realize that an object is not necessarily transformed when it changes in some way. To Piaget, the mental process involved in transforming inputs was always reversible. But a child must be fairly mature to realize that this is the case.

Stage of concrete operations. The third of Piaget's developmental stages, from about 7 to 12 years, during which the child learns to visualize a complex series of operations. It can perform this series "in its head," but cannot state the abstract principle that explains why the operations succeed.

Stage of formal operations. The final stage of intellectual development, which is reached about the age of 12 and continues thereafter. According to Piaget, it is at this stage that the individual can handle such abstract concepts as truth, honor, and personality. The individual also "reasons" in a deductive manner and tests his or her deductions against reality.

with no difficulty. Piaget emphasizes that *counting* is not the same thing as the *concept of number*, a schema the child usually attains only during the stage of concrete operations.

It is during the stage of concrete operations that the child begins to visualize a *complex sequence of operations*. A five-year-old child can walk to school without getting lost—that is, it can perform a series of complex operations in order to reach a goal. But it is usually after age six that the child gains the ability to draw a map showing the route it takes from home to school. And it is only at this point that the youngster realizes that anyone else could follow the map as well. Now the child begins to give up its egocentric view of the world, because it can see things from other perspectives than its own. However, it cannot describe the *abstract principles* involved in map making (or anything else) until it reaches the stage of formal operations.

Stage of Formal Operations

The last of Piaget's four periods of intellectual development is called the **stage of formal operations**, which begins about age 12 and continues through the rest of the person's life. Prior to the twelfth year of its life, Piaget says, the child is limited to thinking in concrete, or non-symbolic, terms. Only in the final, mature stage can the young person think in completely abstract terms. At this level of development, people can solve

In the sensory-motor stage, the infant builds up simple schemata of the world. For instance, it may respond to all objects as if they were "suckable" until experience teaches it otherwise. **(top left)**

In the preoperational stage, children begin to acquire language. They begin to give names to objects, and thus can manipulate some aspects of the world "in their minds" once they have encountered the object in real life. **(top right)**

In the stage of concrete operations, children learn to conserve quantity when they discover that transformations are reversible. That is, the quantity of water doesn't change when you pour it from one container into another. **(bottom left)**

In the stage of formal operations, young people can reason and think in abstract terms. Thus, they "test the world" by planning and executing various types of experiments. **(bottom right)**

problems in their minds by isolating the important variables and manipulating them mentally or perceptually. Now at last the individual is able to draw meaningful conclusions from purely abstract or hypothetical data.

It is only at this stage that the person can play the "what if" game. If you ask a 10-year-old girl what she would be like if she had been born in China, she will reply that the question is silly because she was born in the US. A 15-year-old will take the question seriously, though, because she can mentally put herself into situations she's never experienced. If she knows Chinese children, she can deduce the fact that she'd probably be like them in many ways. She can also make hypotheses about the world on her own, and attempt to test them in her own way.

It is during the stage of formal operations that the structures of the mind become complex enough to allow the individual to be able to create a personal "theory of knowledge." This theory involves all types of knowledge—"how," "what," and most important, "why."

In a sense, Piaget's *stage theory* is an attempt to explain "why" children develop as they do. Now that we have briefly described his theory, let's see how others have reacted to it.

Piaget and His Critics

One of the major criticisms leveled at Piaget is that many of his ideas were mere adaptations of early work by US psychologist James Mark Baldwin. As Robert Cairns pointed out in *Contemporary Psychology* in 1980, there is some truth to this accusation. For in 1897 Baldwin described the various stages of a child's cognitive development as part of his theory of "genetic epistemology." And he used terms such as "sensory-motor," "pre-logical, logical" and "hyper-logical stages." Cairns notes that Baldwin said the child must *accommodate* to the stimulating environment, as well as *assimilate* events and ideas to which he is exposed."

It is difficult to take this criticism seriously, however. To begin with, Piaget has acknowledged Baldwin's influence. Second, Baldwin was a theorist, not someone who engaged in much actual research, and his theory was both incomplete and untested. Piaget spent almost 60 years testing, refining, and adding extensively to the ideas that Baldwin had published at the turn of the century. Furthermore, Piaget's fame rests primarily on his astute observations of children's behavior, not on his stage theory of cognitive development.

As for the theory itself, however, British psychologist Susanna Millar points out that Piaget makes three basic assumptions which may not be true. The first assumption is that intellectual development absolutely must proceed in 1–2–3–4 sequence, and although the *rate* at which a child matures may be sped up or retarded, but the *sequence of stages* must always be the same. The second assumption is that there are no halfway points between two stages. Just as a child cannot keep its foot for long between two rungs of a ladder, so it cannot linger for long between the pre-operational and operational stages. The third assumption is that all mental development can be described in terms of the logical operations a child employs while thinking. The evidence supporting these three assumptions is, at best, debatable.

The children Piaget spent a lifetime observing were for the most part white, middle-class youngsters reared in normal European homes. His four-stage theory appears to hold in good measure for such children, who do tend to learn conservation of volume about age six, conservation of weight at about age nine, and who typically show an ability to handle abstract operations when they are 12—at which age they are often welcomed into adulthood by religious ceremonies such as the *bar mitzvah* or *Christian confirmation*. But what about children brought up in other cultures, or even in different segments of our own society? Would a child reared in an orphanage or ghetto show the "normal" pattern of cognitive development? Perhaps because Piaget was a biologist first and a psychologist second, he seems to have over-emphasized the importance of the genetic blueprint and under-emphasized the strong role played by the environment in cognitive development. The fact that most children proceed up the maturational ladder rung by rung does not tell us how they *might* develop were we bright enough to discover more effective ways of educating them.

A more telling criticism can be found in David Feldman's 1980 book, *Beyond Universals in Cognitive Development*. Piaget assumed that there were "general structures of the mind" that the child could apply to all situations. Feldman points out that there is little evidence that these "general structures" exist. Rather, the child seems to build up specific mental processes for handling specific types of situations. And the child may do much better in some situations than in others. For instance, a seven-year-old genius may play chess at an adult level, but still may not be able to see the world from other people's point of view. And as we noted in Chapter 8, some autistic children show an amazing ability to deal with mathematical abstractions, but cannot dress themselves or use pronouns correctly. What developmental stage shall we say these children are at?

Another point we might raise is that Piaget "observed" children; he did not "experiment" with them. Thus he missed some of the finer points of human development. For instance, Piaget said that the child does not develop a "mother schema" until it is several months old, because that is what he observed in real-life settings. But, as noted in Chapter 18, laboratory studies show that children develop a "mother schema" by two weeks of age. The criticism here is not merely that Piaget's timetable was wrong, but that he failed to test his theory using the experimental method.

Piaget cared little about such criticisms, though. He was convinced his basic assumptions

Charles A. Ferguson   Jerome S. Bruner

According to Jerome Bruner, mothers often teach their infants social skills while teaching them language.

were correct, and therefore saw little need to test them experimentally. As he put it in *Quest*, the novel he wrote when he was 20, "You would not search for me, had you not [already] found me." Thus Piaget didn't seek the truth empirically—he merely tried to demonstrate to others the wisdom he had already found as a young man.

In 1979, Daniel P. Keating stated in *Contemporary Psychology* that, "The enduring components of Piaget's genius are not likely to be found in the experimental rigor or even the accuracy of the answers he has offered, but rather in the quality, range, and importance of the questions he has raised." Many of the wise questions Piaget asked have surely reshaped the field of developmental psychology. But much of his wisdom is of an earlier age, and is increasingly disputed by the results of *experimental* studies of child behavior. We can make this point most tellingly by describing recent studies of how children acquire and use language.

Language Development

During the first year or so of its life, a child communicates its wants primarily by means of crying, laughing, gurgling, and various gestures. An attentive parent can soon tell what kind of cry means the child is hungry, and what kind means that a pin is sticking the infant somewhere.

Infants come "pre-wired" to pay attention to speech. T. Berry Brazelton, whose research we mentioned in Chapter 18, has demonstrated that an infant less than two days old will cease crying and turn its head to look at you if you "croon" at it. The infant will *not* give this response as readily to anything other than human speech. And, as we also noted earlier, an infant will move its arms and legs in synchrony with the patterns of spoken language, but does *not* respond in a similar way to random sounds or to broken speech. Brazelton

believes that the infant is "innately prepared" to respond to language.

According to Charles A. Ferguson, a **linguist** at Stanford, mothers are also "pre-wired" to speak to their infants in certain highly specific ways. Ferguson studied the behavior of mothers of six different nationalities as they spoke to their infants in their native tongues. He reports that often the baby elicits from its mother behavior she has never exhibited before. He also found that, no matter what the language, the mothers all employed rather a similar type of "baby talk." They tended to use very short sentences, nonsense sounds, and simple phrases. They transformed their language in specific ways, saying "pwitty wabbit" instead of "pretty rabbit." When talking to their infants, the mothers raised the pitch of their voices dramatically. They also engaged in more prolonged eye contact with their infants than they typically engaged in with adults.

There are cultural differences in child-rearing practices, however. And these differences may be more genetic than social. According to a 1979 report by Daniel G. Freedman, European, American, and African children tend to be much more active and irritable than are oriental infants. White and black infants will usually struggle when confined, but oriental and **American Indian** infants accept restraint rather passively. Western mothers tend to "speak" to their babies and demand that they respond. The babies usually react by moving their arms and legs in synchrony with the mothers' voices, and simultaneously gaze at their mothers. Oriental mothers engage in fewer "conversations" with their infants. They typically attract the child's attention by gazing at the infant silently, and the oriental infant responds just as silently by gazing back. When the mother does speak, however, she uses a speech pattern similar to that used by western mothers. And the oriental infant also responds with body movements synchronized to the mother's speech. However, the oriental infant's movements are usually less vigorous than those of western infants. Oriental children continue to be much less active physically during their developmental years than do white or black children.

Freedman believes that these behavioral differences are caused by *genetic factors*, for oriental children born and reared in the US respond like infants in China and Japan, not as American infants do.

Question: *Given the fact that infants seem "pre-wired" to pay attention to high-pitched voices, is it surprising that mothers in all cultures raise the pitch of their voices when talking to their infants?*

Babbling and "Mutual Gazing"

By the time the child is three or four months old, it begins babbling to itself. That is, the infant makes sounds such as "ma," "mu," "da," and "na." Usually by its sixth month, the infant's verbal responses become more complex as it learns to *chain* sounds together: "dadadada." Since almost all children in almost all cultures produce these sounds (and build similar "verbal chains"), we assume that the production of "baby talk" is part of the human genetic blueprint.

But while infants *produce* sounds instinctively, it is up to the child's parents to *shape* these instinctive vocal responses into whatever language(s) the child must learn. And, as Oxford psychologist Jerome Bruner has noted, parents typically teach children to speak by use of "modeling" and by reinforcing successive approximations to correct speech. Bruner has studied language acquisition in children for more than 30 years, and is one of the world's leading experts on the subject. Recently he reported a study in which he made videotape recordings of mothers as they taught their children to communicate both verbally and nonverbally.

Much of the early nonverbal communication involves the eyes. According to Bruner, during the first few months of the child's life, a mother spends much of her time simply trying to find out

Linguist (LING-gwist). From the Latin word meaning "tongue" or "language." A linguist is someone who studies the structure and acquisition of language.

American Indian. Most anthropologists believe that the Indians who inhabited America when Columbus arrived were immigrants from the orient. They apparently came across from Asia—through Alaska—more than 15,000 years ago. There are many genetic similarities between American Indians and present-day Japanese, Mongolian, and Chinese peoples. It is no surprise, then, that oriental infants show similar behavior patterns to American Indian infants.

what the infant is looking at. Then she begins trying to get the infant to look where she is looking. At age four months, only about 20 percent of the children Bruner studied would follow their mother's gaze. But by one year of age, almost all of the children would do so, even if the mother was looking at an object behind the infant's back.

"Shaping" Verbal Responses

According to Bruner, once the mother discovers how to attract the child's attention, she begins to point out objects and give them names. At about 10 months of age, the child can point to objects in response. The mother then begins the "verbal shaping process," which has several parts to it. First the mother points to an object, perhaps a picture of a dog in a magazine. Next she asks the child, "What is that?" At first, the child may not respond, so the mother answers her own question: "That's a dog." The child may now say, "Dog." The mother will usually reward the child at this point, often by smiling and saying, "Yes, that's right. That's a dog." The mother may also hug the child momentarily. Once the youngster can give correct one-word responses, the mother begins demanding increasingly more complex answers to her questions.

Bruner points out that this mother-child interaction is really much more complex than it looks at first glance. For the mother is not only teaching "words" to the child, but also instructing it in social skills. For instance, the mother's voice rises in pitch when she points and asks a question. At first this rising pitch merely attracts the infant's attention. But the child soon learns that this voice pattern means that the mother is demanding a response of some kind. If the child responds inappropriately, the mother gently corrects it—thus modeling the sort of "criticism" that the mother will later tolerate from the child. If the child says "dawg" instead of "dog," the mother will repeat the correct pronunciation of the word and encourage the child to try again.

Bruner also notes that, during language learning, the mother begins making *social con-*

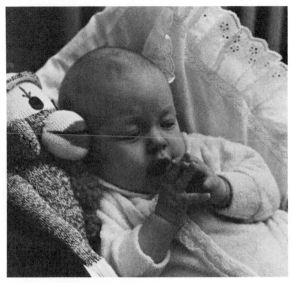

Otto Weininger

Research suggests that fathers help their children learn right-hemisphere skills such as emotional control and pattern perception when engaging the child in rough-and-tumble play. **(top left)**

Piaget says an infant must first learn "how" before it learns "what." That is, the child builds up perceptual schemata of what the world is like by observing the consequences of its own movements. **(top right)**

According to many psychologists, "play is a child's business." **(bottom left)**

tracts with the child that serve as the pattern for adult behaviors. If the child grows restless, the mother may say, "Let's learn two more words, and then we'll go play." If the child requests a cookie, the mother may ask the youngster where the cookies are kept. If the child answers correctly, the mother may give the child permission to go get the sweet. Should the child refuse to do so, the mother may offer to get the cookie if the child will do something for her in return.

When the child fulfills a social contract with the mother, she often praises it by saying some-

thing like, "See how well you did? Aren't you pleased with yourself?" Thus, according to Bruner, while the mother is "shaping language," she is also encouraging the child to monitor the consequences of its actions and to become increasingly less dependent on the mother's actions and judgments.

Question: Piaget always insisted that the child teaches itself by deliberately testing its environment in order to restore "equilibrium." Why might Bruner not agree with Piaget on this point?

Self-Talk and Self-Judgments

The next stage in language development may well come at about two years of age, when the child begins making (and fulfilling) social contracts with itself. And to do this, the child must learn to *talk to itself*. Until the child establishes some sort of "self-talk," it cannot evaluate its own actions *without performing the action first*.

Psychologist Jerome Kagan notes that a 20-month-old infant will happily imitate the actions of an adult model, but a 24-month-old child often refuses to do so. In one of Kagan's studies, a woman assistant "modeled" a chain of three simple behaviors for a watching child. The behaviors mostly involved playing with dolls or toys. Then the child was asked to perform the series of responses. Most 20-month-old infants had little difficulty in repeating the actions that the woman had demonstrated. But two-year-olds often showed signs of distress when called upon to "perform." Some of them cried, others clung to their mothers, while a few threw temper tantrums. Kagan believes that the children "experienced uncertainty" about their ability to get the sequence of actions correct.

Prior to this age, the youngsters apparently merely imitated the behaviors of adults and then waited for external praise or correction. Because they had not established complex self-talk, they could not predict *before performing an action* how well they would do. Once the child establishes "inner language," though, it can evaluate its own actions before performing them (see Chapter 5). Kagan believes that the distress the two-year-old shows when asked to perform is the earliest form of what in older children and adults is called **fear of failure**. But this fear apparently does not appear until the child can use language to rehearse and evaluate its own behaviors before acting them out.

The Father's Role in Language Learning

Traditionally, in most societies, it is the mother who spends the most time with an infant. And it is the mother who is most responsible for nurturing the child. However, the father's role in teaching an infant to speak is also important, although his contributions are likely to be more indirect than direct.

As we noted in Chapter 18, fathers tend to talk to their infants less (and touch them more) than do mothers. According to a recent Harvard study, mothers also speak more softly, repeat words and phrases more frequently, and imitate the infant's sounds more often than do fathers. The fathers, on the other hand, usually play more stimulating games with the child—tapping it rhythmically, tossing it into the air, and introducing it to physically exciting and often creative types of play activity.

Fathers also give the child more confidence. Studies from several different cultures suggest that infants cope better with the appearance of strangers when their fathers have spent consider-

able time with them. A child whose father is an involved parent is thus more likely to *perform verbally in public* than one whose father is uninvolved in caring for the child.

The support that the father gives the mother also influences the child's language development. Sandra Eyres and Carol Gray reported recently in the *American Journal of Nursing* a study they performed in Seattle, Washington. Eyres and Gray observed parents in 193 families just before or immediately after the first-born child arrived. They found that some mothers expected their children to learn and become active early in life. These mothers provided interesting playthings for their infants, spoke to them frequently, and initiated "mutual gazing" not too long after the infant's birth. Other mothers believed that *all* children were passive for many months after birth, and learned little until they were a year or more of age. These mothers spoke to their infants less often and provided fewer playthings than did the mothers with higher expectations. And, as you might imagine, the infants who received the most stimulation developed the quickest and showed the most achievement by age two.

As Eyres and Gray note, the mothers with low expectations about their children tended to come from families with low income and educational levels. However, no matter what the income or educational level of the family, the father's influence was important. The more supportive of the mother and interested in the child the *father* tended to be, the higher the *mother's* expectations for the infant were, and the more mature the child was by age two.

Question: The mother's greatest influence seems to be on the child's verbal and social development, while the father's greatest influence seems to be on the child's perception of rhythmic patterns and on its its creative abilities. How do these facts relate to the various "functions of the hemispheres" discussed in Chapter 5?

The Source of Language Learning

As you know, neural control of speech is usually located in just one of the two cerebral hemispheres. And, in fact, the "speech center" in the left hemisphere is physically a little larger than

Fear of failure. A 20-month-old child will imitate adult behaviors readily. By 24 months, the child gains sufficient linguistic skill to be able to predict the consequences of its own actions before performing them. Thus for the first time the child may experience a fear of failing to perform as it wishes to perform.

Table 20.1.   Rhesus Calls[a]

Roar	Long, fairly loud noise	Made by a very confident animal when threatening another of inferior rank
Pant-threat	Like a roar, but divided into "syllables"	Made by a less confident animal who wants support in making an attack
Bark	Like the single bark of a dog	Made by a threatening animal who is insufficiently aggressive to move forward
Growl	Like a bark, but quieter, shriller, and broken in short sound units	Given by a mildly alarmed animal
Shrill-bark	Not described	Alarm call, probably given to predators in the wild
Screech	An abrupt pitch change; up then down	Made when threatening a higher-ranked animal, and when excited and slightly alarmed
Geekering screech	Like a screech, but broken into syllables	Made when threatened by another animal
Scream	Shorter than the screech and without a rise and fall	Made when losing a fight while being bitten
Squeak	Short, very high pitched noises	Made by a defeated and exhausted animal at the end of a fight

[a]Adapted from figure 2, Rowell, T.E. Agonistic noises of the Rhesus monkey (*Macaca mulatta*). *Symp. Zool. Soc. Lond.* No. 8 (1962): 91–96 by permission of the Zoological Society of London.

the same area of the right hemisphere in most right-handed humans. This size difference between the hemispheres exists to a much lesser extent in the higher primates, but is not found at all in lower animals. It is likewise true that the kind of "dominant hemisphere" found in humans is not present in any other animal species. Furthermore, the vocalizations made by monkeys and chimpanzees seem to be primarily under the control of centers in the *limbic system* (see Chapter 4). Electrical stimulation of the limbic system can call forth all of the vocal responses that monkeys are capable of making (Table 20.1). Destruction of the "cortical speech center" in humans typically leaves them speechless. Destruction of similar areas of the monkey cortex does not affect the animal's vocalizations at all.

It would appear, then, that human brains are uniquely suited for language learning, and hence for reasoning and abstract thought. However, many scientists have recently been successful in teaching chimpanzees to communicate either in "sign language" or by pressing keys on a computer console.

For example, psychologists Sue Savage-Rumbaugh and Duane Rumbaugh have been able to train chimps to use an artificial language called **Yerkish**. To help the animals learn, the Rum-baughs present word-symbols on an overhead projector. The chimps respond by pressing illuminated buttons on a computer console. If the chimps use the word-symbols correctly, they are rewarded. Several chimpanzees have been able to learn 100 or more symbols, and use them as correctly as might a child in the pre-operational stage.

In 1978, the Rumbaughs reported that they had taught two animals, named Austin and Sherman, to communicate directly with each other using Yerkish. In one experiment, Sherman was given a variety of foods that both animals knew the "names" for. Austin could see the foods through a window, but could not obtain them directly—except by requesting the items by punching out a sentence in Yerkish. Austin soon learned to do so, and Sherman usually responded by giving Austin the *specific* food requested. Indeed, the only problem came when Austin would ask for an item (such as chocolate) that Sherman was particularly fond of. In this case Sherman usually would offer Austin something else instead.

More recently, the Rumbaughs have shown that Sherman and Austin could correctly place items into proper "cognitive categories." The Rumbaughs first taught the apes the general meaning of categories such as "tool" and "food."

The animals were then shown specific items (such as a banana or a mechanical lever) and asked which category the item belonged to. In a 1980 report in *Science*, the Rumbaughs state that Austin and Sherman did an excellent job of sorting the items into the correct categories.

Other psychologists have taught apes to use **American Sign Language**, and have claimed that their animals could "create sentences" and "use language in a symbolic way" much as very young children can. However, there is a continuing controversy in the scientific literature about this research. For detailed analysis of "ape language" often suggests that the trainers are *cueing* the animal's responses in various subtle ways much as did the man who owned the famous "talking horse," Clever Hans (see story for Chapter 10).

Can apes speak? The answer depends on how you define "speak." Some apes can surely communicate their needs by way of "signing," or pressing buttons on a computer console. But as Adrian Desmond points out in his 1979 book *The Ape's Reflexion*, the issue is far from settled. Desmond notes that no one has yet proven that ape language has "grammar." Nor is there concrete evidence that apes can manipulate symbols with, say, the sophistication of even a fairly young child. Thus the question of whether apes can use language remains a matter that is still being hotly debated.

Why Study Apes?

Few scientists believe that apes will ever be able to communicate as well as even a six-year-old child. However, as David Premack and Guy Woodruff point out, research on language learning in primates has told us a great deal about the *specific stimulus patterns* needed to help very young infants learn to speak. And this same research may well give us important clues concerning language learning in retarded children. Yerkish is already being taught with some success to severely impaired humans who lack the ability to handle English.

Perhaps a much more important question is this one: Why do *humans* bother to speak at all? What does speech do for us that mere "signing and signalling" couldn't accomplish? There are many answers to this question. But as Piaget noted half a century ago, surely one of the most important functions of language is that of letting children *re-program their own cognitive structures*. By thinking and reasoning—that is, by talking to themselves using symbols to represent the real world—children can "mentally practice" behaviors they will not need until much later in life.

Yerkish (YOUR-kish). Much of the work on language learning in primates has been performed at a research institute named after R.M. Yerkes, a famous animal psychologist. Yerkish is an artificial language named to honor Yerkes.

American Sign Language. One of several "sign languages" used by the deaf to communicate without speaking.

Pre-social. The first of Harlow's two types of play, which includes exploration, parallel play, and instigative (INN-stuh-gate-tive) play in which a child merely imitates the actions of someone else.

But language is not the only way in which young people rehearse for the future. Play is another highly important way of learning adult skills and attitudes while still a child. So let us close this section on cognitive development in children by demonstrating that play behavior is far more than just "fun and games."

Play

The infant is born little more than an animal. If society does not condition it to become human, the child will remain non-verbal, non-social, and "retarded" (at least it will seem retarded from our biased point of view). We typically call this conditioning process *education*, and believe that "study" is more important than "play." Recent studies suggest, however, that a young child may learn as much from seemingly random "play" as it learns in the schoolroom.

Types of Play

There are several types of play, and children seem to pass through them in much the same "developmental stages" as Piaget described. Suppose we describe the types first, and then look at theoretical explanations of what causes playful behavior, and why it is so important.

Pre-Social Play

The first type of play that infants engage in is rightly called **pre-social**. That is, the six-month-old infant plays with a doll dangling from its crib, it plays with bells and rattles and balls and teddy bears, and it plays with its own hands and feet. Only later does it learn the marvelous capacity for play that other people offer.

Psychologist Harry Harlow lists three types of pre-social play—exploration play, parallel play, and instigative play—all of which Piaget would define as belonging to the pre-operational stage.

The infant *explores* its environment by crawling around, inspecting, and playing with anything that drops into its narrow life space. A little later, the child makes the first step toward social contact with its peers by engaging in *parallel play*. Even before an infant is ready to interact with other children, it may choose to play beside them—but not with them. A little later yet, it may engage in activities that are directly instigated by other people—follow-the-leader, mimicking, peek-a-boo. Yet in these behaviors the child does not really interact socially with the "leader." Harlow calls this *instigative play* and believes it is the final step toward true social interaction.

Social Play

As the child passes from the pre-operational to the operational stage of intellectual development, its play becomes more complex and other people begin to become animate partners in its life rather than mere objects to be manipulated. **Social play** seems to be of three major types—*free play, formal play,* and *creative play*.

Of the three, physical free play with other children is perhaps the easiest for the child, and hence often the first to appear. As Harlow points out, this sort of "rough-housing" is also the most disturbing to the middle-class parent who is often afraid that the child will either hurt itself or be hurt by others. Yet this type of activity may help the child learn to tolerate minor frustrations and keep its temper in check.

As the child becomes more verbal, rough-and-tumble play drops off sharply, and formalized play begins. The mock fights of four-year-old boys develop rapidly into games of tag and cops and robbers in which the youngsters must follow *formal rules*. And once the child begins to learn society's "rules and regulations," it can begin predicting the consequences of its social actions *before* it engages in them.

In Piaget's terms, creative play is primarily a matter of *assimilation*—of "pretending" that things might happen that haven't yet happened. The child thus learns to anticipate what kinds of reactions (feedback) might occur if things were different than they presently are. Piaget believes that creative play is the child's way of learning to manipulate symbols rather than objects. He calls it the "high point" of all types of play. He also calls it "a child's work."

But even if "play is work" in some sense, the question becomes *why* children engage in this activity at all. As we will see, there are many explanations.

Biological Theories of Play

Most of us might assume that play is an activity that children fall into spontaneously, and that its major purpose might be that of making children

more pleasant—or of keeping them occupied for a while. However, to a variety of scientists, play has a deeper and more profound importance.

Both Plato and Aristotle suggested that children be given toy tools to play with, to "shape their minds" for future activities as adults. Later philosophers tended to see play as being the "unfolding" of innate or inborn talents and desires, and suggested that children be left alone to determine freely what they wanted to do or become. Nineteenth-century German philosophers believed that play somehow restored the child's physical and mental powers and recommended it as a form of relaxation for exhausted children.

Perhaps the most detailed theory of play came from British philosopher Herbert Spencer. Writing a little more than 100 years ago, Spencer suggested what is now called the *surplus energy hypothesis* of play. Spencer thought that each child was born with an energy-producing machine of some kind inside it. This energy had to be released regularly or the child would simply "explode." Before humans became civilized, Spencer said, children used up most of this energy just in surviving. But modern-day infants are well-cared for, and thus they have surplus energy inside them which finds expression in aimless outbursts of activity. Spencer thought that all art came from play, as did Sigmund Freud. As we will see in the next chapter, Freud incorporated many of Spencer's ideas about psychic energy into his theory of psychoanalysis.

Play and Evolution

Although Spencer's ideas on the purpose of play were influenced by Charles Darwin's books on evolution, it was G.S. Hall who pushed evolutionary theory to what now seem absurd lengths. Hall believed that each child must **recapitulate** (relive) the behavioral history of the human race through its play. For instance, children supposedly love splashing about in water because they are re-enacting their fish ancestors' pleasure in swimming in ancient oceans. Youngsters love climbing trees because our monkey ancestors did such things. Young boys enjoy gathering in groups to go hunting and fishing because early humans had to make their living that way. According to Hall, before the child could become a modern-day adult, it had to *rehearse* or retrace all the ancient behaviors built into its genetic blueprint over millions of years of evolution.

Although Hall's 1904 book on child psychology did have the effect of interesting many psychologists in studying children more closely, his theory has many serious faults. As Susanna Millar points out, it is difficult to explain a modern child's joy in bicycles, airplanes, telephones, and space ships as being a reliving of ancestral experiences.

Darwinian theory was pushed even farther by Karl Groos, who taught philosophy in Switzerland at the turn of this century. Groos believed that play was a generalized instinct which caused a young organism to practice all the other "instincts" it would need to survive as an adult. To Groos, rough-housing was a boy's way of preparing for the pleasure of fighting off other adults to win the hand of his own true love, and even of learning the skills of war.

Groos's books on play did point out several interesting and previously overlooked aspects of play—that it often involves almost all of the natural functions of an organism, and that behaviors (such as random exploring) which may look aimless can still serve important biological functions. But to say that children play because they have an *instinct* to play tells us very little about human behavior and neglects the profound influence that social inputs and feedback have even on children.

Question: *How would a "surplus energy" theorist explain anaclitic depression in infants deprived of their mothers?*

The Purpose of Play

What, then is play, if it isn't blowing off steam or a way of stepping rapidly up the developmental ladder? The truth seems to be that play serves so

many different functions in so many different situations that no one theory can explain its many functions.

In most cultures, play allows children to explore their physical environments, to acquire motor coordination, and to determine their own physical limits. It helps children learn about *aggression*, and how to control their own aggressive behaviors.

Play also allows the child to practice social roles—that is, to build up sequences of behaviors that yield approving feedback from the adults the child must live with. Little wonder, then, that in his book 1979 book, *Play and Education*, Otto Weininger states that play is not only the business of childhood, it is the basic tool for all of early childhood learning. As Weininger puts it, play isn't everything—it's the *only* thing!

As Weininger notes, by exploring both its physical and social environments, the child learns to perceive the world more accurately, to monitor its outputs, and to predict the consequences of its own actions. This perceptual learning is apparently what Piaget means when he speaks of creative play as "symbol manipulation." The child checks and rechecks its perceptions when it plays house or cops-and-robbers or builds castles out of blocks. It also learns to "think through" problems silently (see Chapter 5). Thus, one of the chief functions of play is that of developing such right-hemisphere skills as creativity, rhythmic patterning, and emotional expression. And, as Weininger points out, these skills are seldom taught effectively in most schools.

Play, then, serves to stimulate the physical, emotional, social, and intellectual development of the child. And its hallmark is *pleasure*. Children who laugh while they are fighting seldom hurt one another. Adults who smile as they read textbooks seldom murder authors. Play is, therefore, a useful, necessary, vital part of life—but primarily because it *rewards* children (and adults) for learning the cognitive and behavioral skills they have to learn.

Now that we have studied the "bits and pieces" of child development, suppose we look at how these pieces fit together to form an intact *personality* which grows and develops throughout the entire span of life.

Summary

1. **Jean Piaget** was one of the most respected figures in child psychology. For more than 50 years, he studied **cognitive development** in children. By cognitive development, he meant the child's **search for knowledge**, or attempt to construct an **abstract representation** of the world in its mind.

2. Piaget believed a child is born with certain **innate mental structures and functions** that guide its intellectual growth. The mental structures change over time because of environmental interactions, but the functions remain constant.

3. According to Piaget, a child's motivation to develop comes from an innate drive he called **equilibrium**, a sort of **cognitive homeostasis**. When the child's abstractions of the world don't match reality, it experiences a drive called **disequilibrium**, which motivates it to change its inner representations of the world to bring them into accord with reality.

4. Each "mental program" that a child has for processing sensory inputs is a **schema**. Mental development proceeds as a child develops more and more complex **schemata**.

5. The two **mental functions** that guide development are **organization** and **adaptation**.

6. Organization is the tendency to create complicated mental structures out of simple ones. Adaptation is made up of two opposing processes, **assimilation** and **accommodation**.

7. Assimilation involves **changing inputs** to fit the child's present mental structures. Accommodation involves **changing mental structures** (or making new ones) to make them match present inputs.

8. Assimilation often involves recognizing **similarities** across objects and experiences. Accommodation often involves recognizing **differences**.

9. Piaget was interested in **epistemology**, the study of how knowledge is acquired. Piaget believed there were several types of knowledge, knowing **how, what**, and **why**.

10. According to Piaget, all children pass through four **developmental stages**, each of which grows out of (but is more complex than) the one preceding it:
    a. During the **sensory-motor period** (birth to 2 years), the infant child learns to integrate its various sense impressions into complex **schemata**. In this stage, the child knows "how" and begins to learn "what," but doesn't know "why."
    b. During the **pre-operational stage**, the child learns to speak and to deal with its world in **symbolic terms**, by talking about objects rather than by having to manipulate them directly. But its reasoning is **egocentric**, and it does not realize that objects can be **transformed** without being changed.
    c. During the **stage of concrete operations**, the child learns to visualize a whole series of operations in its mind and to differentiate itself from the outer world. And it learns that the process of transformation is reversible.
    d. During the **stage of formal operations**, the young person gains the ability to think in purely **abstract terms**. That is, the individual now knows "why" as well as "how" and "what."

11. Piaget believes that children pass through these stages at their own individual speeds, but that the stages cannot be reversed or their order changed.

12. Much of Piaget's theory is similar to an earlier theory by **James Mark Baldwin**. However, Piaget elaborated on and provided proof for Baldwin's beliefs.

13. Many psychologists have criticized Piaget's theory, but his fame rests primarily on his **observations of children's behavior**, not on his stage theory.

14. **Language learning** is one of the most complex aspects of cognitive development. Infants come **prewired** to pay attention to speech. They **babble** instinctively, but it is up to the environment to **shape** these sounds into meaningful language.

15. In our society, the mother usually trains the child to speak, and many of her responses to the infant may be innately determined. First, she learns to attract its **attention**, often by using a **high-pitched tone of voice**. Then she asks it questions, **models** the answer, and **reinforces** correct responses.

16. During language learning, the mother also trains the child in the use of **social contracts**.

17. Oriental infants appear to be more **passive** during their early life than are black or white infants. Oriental mothers tend to attract their infant's attention by gazing at it. Western mothers tend to attract attention verbally.

18. The child learns to monitor and evaluate its own performance using **self-talk** about age 2, at which time it may experience **fear of failure**.

19. Western fathers appear to be more involved

in **physical stimulation** of the child than in teaching it to talk. However, children whose fathers are **supportive** of the mother and interested in them tend to develop more rapidly than children whose fathers are uninvolved.

20. Chimpanzees have been taught to "speak" 100 or more words and phrases, but whether their language has **grammar** and whether they can communicate in **symbols** is still a matter of debate.

21. Harlow has listed several types of play:
   a. The first is **pre-social play**, which includes **exploration, parallel,** and **instigative play**.
   b. At a later age, the child engages in various forms of **social play**, including **formal, creative,** and **free play**. Piaget considered creative play to be **pure assimilation**.

20. Piaget said that play was **a child's work,** but Herbert Spencer believed that play was necessary for the release of **surplus energy** within the child.

21. G.S. Hall believed that in play a child **recapitulated** the history of the human race. Karl Groos stated that play gave children a chance to practice all the **instincts** it would need as an adult.

22. Play serves to stimulate the **physical, emotional, social,** and **intellectual development** of the child. Its hallmark is **pleasure**.

(Continued from page 453)

A year or so later, Harry Smith knocked boldly on the door of Dr. Jensen's office. Interpreting the barking noise from within as permission to enter, Harry opened the door and went in. Two young girls followed close behind him.

"Dr. Jensen, I'd like for you to meet two charming young ladies." He pushed a bright-eyed young blonde girl in front of him. "This is Betty Jo, who's five. Isn't she pretty?" Betty Jo giggled and tried to hide her face. "And this is Sally Ann," Harry continued, pulling a healthy-looking brunette around in front of Dr. Jensen's desk. "Sally Ann is awfully advanced for her age, aren't you? Shake hands with Dr. Jensen, Sally Ann."

The brown-haired girl walked boldly around the desk and stuck a tiny hand out toward the older man. Startled, but pleased, Dr. Jensen shook her hand with considerable gravity. "You are a pretty little thing, aren't you?"

"I'm pretty too," said Betty Jo. And, not wanting to be left out, she too extended her hand.

"You're both thoroughbreds, that's for sure," Dr. Jensen said. He turned to Harry. "Where did you find these delightful young ladies?"

"We live with our mummies," Sally Ann replied in a high but pleasing voice.

Dr. Jensen looked puzzled. "Oh, I thought you were coming to live with us here. But if you live with your mothers, you can't be orphans, now can you?"

"Oh, we're orphants, all right," said Betty Jo in a happy tone of voice.

"But we live with our mummies and aunties down the road," said Sally Ann.

"Down the road? What is this, Harry? Who are these children?"

Harry Smith grinned but remained silent.

"Can I sit on your lap, please?" Sally Ann asked. And without waiting for permission, she climbed up on the older man and made herself comfortable.

"Me, too," said Betty Jo, squeezing in as best she could.

Dr. Jensen adapted to this assault on his authority as best he could by putting an arm around each of the girls. He inspected them carefully. They were obviously normal, healthy, lovable kids. There was even something oddly familiar about them. "If you live down the road, why are you here?"

"I told you," Betty Jo said, leaning forward to pick up a pencil off Dr. Jensen's desk. "Because we're orphants, and Uncle Harry says this is where we really belong. In the orphantige." She leaned forward, the pencil firmly in her hand, and began marking up a paper on Dr. Jensen's desk.

"Don't do that, dear," he said, removing the pencil from her grasp. "That's a transfer order I have to sign."

And then it dawned on him. He stared intently at the girls, then shook his head in disbelief. "It can't be, Harry. Say it isn't so."

Harry laughed. "It is so, Dr. Jensen. These are the 'runty pigs with diarrhea' you told me to get rid of."

"But what's happened to them?" he said, catching Betty Jo as she almost wiggled off his lap.

"I did what you told me to do. I put them in one of the wards at the State Home for the Retarded."

"And?"

"And the women there adopted the girls and took care of them."

"My mummy and my aunties take good care of me. They talk to me all the time," said Sally Ann, reaching for a bottle of ink. Dr. Jensen rescued it just as the girl was about to pour it over the top of a stack of papers.

"My mummy takes me walking, and the nurses take me shopping and for rides in the country, and everything!" said Betty Jo, getting down from Dr. Jensen's lap and walking over to Harry Smith. He picked her up and held her in his arms.

"My mummy and my aunties spend all day with me, every day," Sally Ann said, hunting for something else besides the bottle of ink to play with. "Will you play with me all day here at the orphantige?"

Dr. Jensen coughed. "No, dear, we don't have time for that. But Harry, you haven't told me what happened yet. What did you do to these two girls?"

"I didn't do anything. The women at the State Home did it all. There are 30 or so of them in the ward, and each woman took turns taking care of the girls. Can you imagine what it would be like to be a child and to have the undivided attention of 30 women every day of your life? Can you imagine how stimulating it would be to a child to have that kind of social environment? Can you imagine what that might do to your intellectual development?"

"But, Harry, those women are *retarded*!"

"Not so retarded that they don't know how to take loving care of babies, Dr. Jensen. But the nurses and the attendants helped too. It's surprising what a little stimulation will do."

Dr. Jensen removed an ashtray from Sally Ann's grasping fingers, then pulled her tightly to him to keep her out of mischief. "But what about their IQ scores, Harry? Didn't they score below 50 when they were here?"

Harry smiled as he sat down in a chair, still holding on to Betty Jo. "I gave them both tests last week. Would you believe they both scored above 100?"

"You're joking. IQ scores don't vary that much."

Harry chuckled. "They seem to go down a bit after we've kept children here for a while, don't they?"

Dr. Jensen huffed defensively. "That's different. We don't have time to cater to kids very much. Don't have the staff for it. But you can't tell me that living with retarded women will *double* a child's IQ. It just isn't right!" He removed a cigarette lighter from Sally Ann's hands before she could set a pile of papers on fire. "Besides, no professional person would believe it. Not for a minute, they wouldn't."

"Will you take us for walks, and talk to us all the time like our mummies and aunties do?" Betty Jo asked.

"No, you'll live with 20 or so other children your own age in a nice little house. And you'll have a house mother to take care of you, when she has the time. Won't you like that?" Dr. Jensen replied.

"No," said Betty Jo, putting her arms around Harry's neck. "I like my mummy and my aunties best. But Harry says if we're orphants, we ought to be here at the orphantige."

Dr. Jensen rescued a vase of flowers from Sally Ann's grasp before she could turn it over on his desk. "I think we ought to talk this matter over, Harry. I want to see the test scores myself. And I want to talk to the people at the State Home. Meanwhile, I think you ought to leave these lovely children right where they are."

"Kind of embarrassing, isn't it?" Harry replied. "We took a couple of living skeletons and tucked them away, out of sight. And a year or so later, they emerge as living flesh and blood and normal in every respect." He sighed, thinking of the supposedly normal children who had stayed at the orphanage, and who weren't doing nearly this well.

Dr. Jensen grabbed Sally Ann's hand just as she was removing the pen from his shirt pocket. He put the pen in the center drawer of his desk. "I don't know what those retarded women did to these two youngsters, but I suppose we ought to find out. Might be helpful here. Meanwhile, don't you breathe a word of this to anybody. If the word gets out that retarded women are better at rearing kids than our professionally trained staff is, you and I will both be out of a job."

"They're not better mothers because they're retarded, they're better because they spent massive amounts of time with the girls." Harry sighed. "Just think how much progress we could make if we had 30 well-trained staff members for each of our orphans. I dare say we'd do even better than the women at the State Home did with these two."

"Couldn't get the money for that sort of intensive care," Dr. Jensen said. "Waste of state money. Probably couldn't hire enough staff even if we had the money."

"So?"

Dr. Jensen caught Sally Ann just as she was pulling his expensive gold watch out of his pocket. He put the watch back, kissed her on the cheek, and put her down on the floor. "You go with Uncle Harry, dear. He'll take you back to your mother and your aunts. You stay there a while, and maybe later you can come live with us. If we have room."

Harry got up from the chair and took the two girls by the hand. "Mum's the word, eh? Okay, Dr. Jensen. But I have a feeling that we ought to do a little research on the matter. I won't squeal if you can dig up some funds to support a little research."

"You drive a hard bargain, Harry. But if you don't squeal, as you put it, you've got a deal."

Harry nodded. "Tell Dr. Jensen 'goodbye,' girls."

They both turned and waved. Betty Jo then started out the door, but Sally Ann hung back for a moment. She giggled a couple of times, then said, "Did you really call us 'runty pigs with dia-uh-reed-uh?'"

Dr. Jensen pursed his lips. "Oh, my," he said. "What an idiotic thing to say!"

Recommended Reading

Broughton, John M. "The Genetic Psychology of James Mark Baldwin," *American Psychologist*, Vol. 36, No. 4 (1981), pp. 396–407.

Bruner, Jerome S., Alison Jolly, and Kathy Sylva, eds. *Play—Its Role in Development and Evolution* (New York: Basic Books, 1976).

Geber, Beryl A. *Piaget and Knowing: Studies in Genetic Epistemology* (London: Routledge & Kegan Paul, 1977).

Feldman, D.H. *Beyond Universals in Cognitive Development: Publications for the Advancement of Theory and History in Psychology* (Norwood, N.J.: Ablex, 1980).

Flavell, John H. *Cognitive Development* (Englewood Cliffs, N.J.: Prentice-Hall, 1977).

Millar, Susanna. *The Psychology of Play* (New York: Penguin, 1968).

Piaget, Jean. *Adaptation and Intelligence: Organic Selection and Phenocopy* (Chicago: University of Chicago Press, 1980).

Terrace, H.S. *Nim: A Chimpanzee Who Learned Sign Language* (New York: Knopf, 1979).

6

Personality

Personality Theory: Psychoanalysis, Humanism, and Social Learning Theory

Did You Know That . . .

The study of personality involves identifying the distinctive patterns of thought, behavior, and experience that characterize your unique adjustment to life?

All the major theories of personality have their roots in Darwin's theory of evolution?

Freud described your basic instincts as a "cauldron of seething excitement"?

Freud thought that the causes of behavior are often unconscious?

According to Freud, all children go through a "natural homosexual period"?

Carl Jung believed people inherit "racial memories" that he called archetypes?

Alfred Adler believed you are motivated by a conscious desire to achieve superiority?

Erik Erikson states you must pass through eight developmental stages on your way to complete maturity?

Social learning theorists believe that you "construct reality" in your mind, and then use this constructed reality to change the world around you?

We still don't have a personality theory that tells us all we want to know about the human condition?

"The Span of Life"

The afternoon wind, the *breva* as it is called by the natives, ruffled the soft blue waters of Lake Como in the northern part of Italy. It was late September, but a few steamers still chugged back and forth, taking passengers from one end of the pencil-thin lake to the other. Water taxis buzzed back and forth from Cadennabia on the western shore of Lake Como to Bellagio on the eastern bank. Cadennabia and Bellagio are but three miles apart by water, but more than 50 miles apart by road.

Just outside the town of Como, at the southern end of the lake, is the beautiful Villa d'Este, one of the last great hotels in all Europe. Sitting on the hotel's concrete terrace, looking up the lake toward Cadennabia and Bellagio, were three famous scientists. One was a tall, thin, well-dressed man in his 60's, psychologist Jonathan L. Fraser from the University of London. The other man was shorter, younger, and a bit on the heavy side. His name was Donald M. Papas, a biological psychologist from

McGill University in Montreal. The third member of the group was a woman, Joyce Young Sapir, the noted psychoanalyst from Israel.

"Don, why did you invite us here?" the woman asked, as they waited for their drinks.

Donald Papas glanced nervously at the woman. She was short, dark, verging on plumpness. But she had a fiercely handsome face. Joyce Sapir's psychoanalytic research, conducted chiefly at Hebrew University in Jerusalem, had brought her considerable fame.

"Why did I ask you all to come here? Because I have hope, I suppose."

"Hope for what?" Fraser asked. "Not that I'm complaining, you understand. Beautiful spot, and all that."

A waiter brought the three of them drinks. Papas signed the bill, and the waiter vanished silently back into the Villa d'Este. "Yes. Como is one of the most heavenly places in the world, isn't it?"

"I know you Canadians are rich and generous, and I'm sure that Montreal is deadly dull this time of year," Professor Fraser said. "But you never leave your laboratory unless you have some earth-shaking purpose in mind. So, my dear friend and colleague, tell me what you're hopeful about."

Papas stretched out in his metal chair. "Well, as you know, the Foundation is very interested in peace. So they asked me to put together a small International Symposium on Peace and Personality. If either of you had bothered to read the 'Statement of Purpose' I sent along with the invitation, you'd have known that."

"Don't be foolish, Don. We read it—quite carefully, I might add," Joyce Sapir said. "It had all the proper terms in it—all those lovely words so loaded with self-importance that we academics toss around. 'Utilize our knowledge of the structure and dynamics of human personality to reduce international tensions,' for example. But we are hard-nosed types, Dr. Papas, and we aren't that easily tricked by fancy language."

"How can you say that?" Fraser interrupted, a twinkle in his gray eyes. "All that you Freudians have as your stock in trade is fancy language."

Joyce Young Sapir favored the Englishman with a harsh stare. "I am not a Freudian, Jonathan Fraser, I am an Ego Psychologist. We accept many of Freud's ideas, but we have benefited from the criticisms and contributions of Jung, Adler, Erikson—and from his own daughter, Anna Freud."

Fraser snorted. "No matter what you call yourselves, you still deal in fancy fictions instead of facts. If you were objective about things, if you looked at behavior instead of mucking about in the cesspools of the mind, you might actually discover something worthwhile." Fraser was obviously enjoying himself.

Dr. Sapir lit an Israeli cigarette. "I have observed, in my many years of practice, that disturbed people tend to take on the personality characteristics of their pets. You, Jonathan Fraser, have spent so much of your life studying pigeons that you are getting to be something of a bird-brain yourself!"

"Now, now," said Papas. "Let's save the nasty comments for the meeting tomorrow, when the tape recorders can preserve for posterity your so-called peaceful comments."

"Don't try to shush me, Don," the woman said. "Fraser is not a psychologist. He is a behavioral mechanic, just like Skinner. Human beings are subjects, not objects. The richest, most vital part of humanity lies in our subjective experiences. Our outward behavior is a pale copy of our mental activity. To look at us entirely from the outside is to ignore the *causes* of what we do. You cannot understand people merely by measuring their muscle twitches from afar. You must peer deep inside them, learn to appreciate their instinctual urges, bring to light their unconscious thoughts, find the true meaning of their personal experiences. Only when you have stripped away the hidden deposits of the past can you help their egos face reality, and hence achieve self-actualization."

"I've seen more meaningful deposits on the bottom of my pigeon cages," observed Fraser dryly.

"Whoa!" Papas said quickly. "Both of you are looking at people from a very limited perspective. Pigeons behave, and so do men and women. Our nervous systems are similar, and humans respond to rewards and punishments as do birds, rats, and worms. But our differences are just as important as our similarities."

"More important," Joyce Sapir said militantly.

"No, *just* as important," Papas replied. "It is as foolish to say we can learn *nothing* about humans from studying pigeons as it is to say that we can learn *everything* about ourselves from experiments involving animals. That's one of the things I hope we can get some agreement on during the symposium."

"But birds don't have personalities!" the woman said loudly.

"How do you know?" Fraser asked. "Have you ever psychoanalyzed a pigeon?"

"Now, calm down, you two," Papas interposed. "What you are really saying, Joyce, is that one major difference between humans and animals is that humans have symbolic language. Or 'verbal behavior,' if you want the Skinnerian term. The major tool we have for investigating the human mind is the spoken word. We ask people to express their feelings, their experiences, and they must do so in language that we understand."

"Then you really study verbal behavior, and not the human psyche," Fraser said, a grin illuminating his thin face. "Remember what Watson said about the Introspectionists—that they weren't being subjective at all, they were just refusing to be objective."

"Nonsense," the woman said. "We use our intuition to go beyond the language, so that we can tap the meaning that lies latent in the words. We call it 'listening with the third ear.' People tell us what they are like without knowing that they are doing so. Their words are like footprints in soft sand. Speech tells you what kind of prehistoric beasts are roaming the beaches of the unconscious, but you cannot trap the beasts themselves. You must guess at their size and shape and colors from the tracks they leave behind."

"And from their droppings," said the British psychologist.

The woman turned on him angrily. "Jonathan Fraser, you are the most anal personality I have ever met."

"But witty. You must admit that, Joyce," said Papas.

"Freud said that wit was often a form of unconscious or disguised aggression. If we are to study peace, perhaps first we had better dissect Professor Fraser's personality to discover the unconscious roots of his aggression."

"That's easy," Fraser said. "I've been shaped into it. People pay me more attention when I say nasty things about them. And, like most academics, I find attention very rewarding. If you want me to be peaceful, then ignore me when I'm hostile and reinforce me with a smile when I'm polite."

Papas nodded. "Good idea! All we have to do to get rid of war is to establish a 'Smile Corps' and send them out to shape the whole world."

"Nonsense!" said Sapir. "That's utterly superficial. You're dealing with the symptom, not the cause. We could not have survived our early years on earth if we had not fought for our right to survive. But now, our unconscious tendencies to hate and kill are often as useless as our appendixes. We might be better off born without them."

"But that's the point," said Papas. "We *are* aggressive—even pigeons will attack when pained or frustrated—and we have to learn to live with the instinctual parts of our personalities. But we can only do that if we are bright enough to discover who we really are and where we ought to be going."

"And how are we to achieve *that* miracle?" asked Fraser. "Not through psychoanalyzing the whole world, I trust!"

"And certainly not through smiling at people to reward them for polite behavior," said Sapir.

Donald M. Papas adjusted his glasses. "Listen, my children, and you shall hear what I have planned for the First International Symposium on Peace and Personality."

(Continued on page 503.)

Personality Theory

Now that we know how you developed from conception through childhood, we are faced with a number of difficult problems. The first is the fact that psychological growth doesn't end at 12, or even at 30. You continue to change, develop, and mature in a great many ways through your life span. And yet, some parts of your personality do remain the same no matter what your age or stage. We must now look more carefully at which of your behavior patterns are consistent over time, and which aren't.

The second problem is this: If we are to study you scientifically, we must have some way of describing what we find. If you were completely *unique*, we could do little more than paint as accurate a picture of you as possible. But you are similar to other human beings in a great many ways. Thus we must find a basis for comparing your thoughts and actions with those of the people around you.

The third difficulty we will encounter stems from the first two. Some people are more-or-less "normal." That is, they seem to adjust well to the world, they are content with their lives, they stay out of trouble, and make their own contribution to society. But other individuals are unhappy, seem not to adjust well to their circumstances, and seem to take more from the world than they give. What are we to do to help people whose thought patterns are disordered, whose emotions are unusual, and whose behaviors are often harmful to themselves and others?

The first two problems should sound familiar to you, for they make up two of the "four themes of developmental psychology" we listed earlier. In Chapters 18–20, we paid more attention to the other two themes—the mind/body problem, and the nature-nurture controversy. In the next two chapters, we will look more closely at "change versus consistency" and "individual differences versus human similarities."

The third problem—that of abnormal behavior, and what to do about it—we have touched on several times in this book. But, as we pointed out in Chapter 5, how you describe "psychological abnormalities," and what you try to do about them, depends to a great extent on your *theory of personality*. So, suppose we begin this chapter by defining **personality**. Then we can look at several theories that attempt to explain how you ended up with the personality that you presently have. We will save our discussion of abnormal psychology for Chapter 23, and our coverage of psychotherapy for Chapter 24.

What Is Personality?

Writing in the 1981 *Handbook of Behavior Therapy*, Nancy Cantor and John Kihlstrom state that, "The field of personality may be defined as that subdiscipline of psychology which is concerned with the distinctive patterns of thought, behavior, and experience which characterize the individual's unique adjustment to his or her life situation." Your own pattern of personality, then, shows up in the way that you attempt to understand, respond to, and change the physical and social world in which you live.

Different theorists have, of course, emphasized different aspects of personality. Freud, for instance, was primarily interested in the development of the ego, or self, and in conscious and unconscious mental processes. Behavior theorists look primarily at observable responses, while social learning theorists emphasize the influence of the environment on cognitive and behavioral processes. Trait theorists attempt to categorize people according to general modes of thinking or acting, while humanistic psychologists such as Carl Rogers dwell upon the development of self-awareness and self-actualization. But all these approaches are trying to explain why you think, feel, and act as you do. And, as we will see, there are at least four reasons why personality theorists are so interested in you.

Personology

Let us define **personology** as the scientific study of what personality actually is, and how it grows and develops over an individual's life span. According to Nancy Cantor, personologists have four major goals:

1. To describe consistent patterns of individual differences
2. To explain why a person thinks, feels, and behaves as she or he does
3. To predict how a person will act in a new situation
4. To help people change their **dysfunctional** thoughts, feelings, and behaviors

As Cantor points out, some theorists place more weight on one or two of these goals than on others. For example, the Freudian and humanistic psychologists tend to stress "explaining" and "helping." The trait theorists focus on "describing" and "predicting." The social learning theorists and behavioral psychologists emphasize "helping" and "predicting."

Because of their varying goals, these theorists have developed quite different ways of studying the human personality. Freudians tend to look primarily at data gathered from case histories. Trait psychologists utilize various tests and observations. And social learning theorists often perform experiments to determine which environmental inputs affect thoughts and actions. But these differences are chiefly a matter of *relative emphasis* on goals and study methods. For the Freudians, humanistic psychologists, and behaviorists do occasionally make use of psychological tests. And all personality theorists realize the importance of data gathered from scientific experiments.

There is one more important similarity among personologists we should mention. As Cantor notes, almost all theorists are interested in: (1) the general processes that guide and explain personality development; and (2) how individuals differ from the general developmental pattern. As you will see, Freud believed that all people go through specific stages in their psychological growth. But he was also most intrigued by the different ways that specific individuals moved up through these stages. And the trait theorists search as hard for what they call "general personality factors" as they do for specific traits that make you different from all other people.

Now that we have outlined some of the similarities and differences among the major person-

Personality. From the Greek word *persona*, which means "mask." Those distinctive ways of thinking, feeling, and behaving that set you off from all other people. Your own unique way of adjusting to whatever situations you find yourself in.

Personology (purr-son-OLL-oh-gee). The scientific study of what comprises your personality, as well as a description of how your personality develops during your entire span of life.

Dysfunctional (diss-FUNK-shun-al). "Dys" comes from a Greek word meaning bad, or difficult. A dysfunction is an impaired or abnormal way of thinking, feeling, or behaving.

ality theorists, suppose we briefly look at how personology got its start.

Historical Background
As different as psychoanalysis, learning theory, humanistic psychology, and present-day trait psychology may seem, all of them are descendents of Darwin's theory of evolution.

Trait Theory
One of the first people in Great Britain to interest himself in measuring human traits was Francis Galton, who was Darwin's cousin. Darwin had said that evolution was a matter of "the survival of the fittest." In Galton's view, "fittest" meant "intellectually gifted." He assumed that intellectual differences were due primarily to inheritance, not to training. Thus the best way for the human race to survive, Galton said, was to encourage "gifted people" to have more children, and to discourage (or even prevent) "people of inferior intelligence" from reproducing.

In order to determine who should reproduce and who shouldn't, Galton needed an intelligence test of some kind. But how to measure intelligence? Galton spent years testing people's reaction times and sensory thresholds (see Chapter 8). Unfortunately, none of these tests seemed to discriminate very well between gifted and not-so-gifted individuals. Although he failed in his primary objective, Galton's ideas influenced scientists in France, who did devise the first useful intelligence test. As we will see in Chapter 22, *trait theory* really begins with Galton.

Psychoanalysis
While Galton believed that individuals survived because of their superior intelligence, Freud took a more "emotional" view. In 1892, Darwin published a book entitled *Expression of Emotion in Man and Animals* in which he wrote at length about "aggressive instincts." To Freud, *instincts* were the key to survival. He saw "personality" as developing out of a continual war between inherited emotions and the civilizing influences of soci-

"YOU MEAN YOUR BIG SMILE IS BOTTLED-UP AGGRESSION? MINE IS BOTTLED-UP HOSTILITY."

Sigmund Freud

ety. Thus, while trait theory emphasizes the conscious, almost *static* aspects of personality, Freud focused on the unconscious, *dynamic* processes that shape the human mind.

Humanistic Psychology

As we will see, Freud had many followers. One of the most important of these was Alfred Adler, who broke with Freud about 1911. Adler could not accept Freud's view that humans were dominated by blind, irrational urges. Rather, he said, people are motivated by the conscious desire to fulfill themselves as unique individuals. Darwin, Galton, and Freud saw humans as being prisoners of their genes. To Adler—and to most other humanistic psychologists—humans have advanced beyond biological evolution because we can reshape our personalities by an act of will.

Behaviorism and Social Learning Theory

As we noted in Chapter 5, John B. Watson was the first behaviorist. But before he founded behaviorism, Watson too trod in Darwin's footsteps. Darwin got many of his ideas about evolution from studying the plants and animals on the Galapagos Islands off the coast of South America. In his younger days, Watson spent several months observing animal behavior on the Dry Tortugas islands off the coast of Florida.

Darwin emphasized innate reflexes, as did both Freud and Watson. Freud looked "inside the mind" to see what these reflexes were. But Watson rejected "mental processes" entirely. He concluded that stimuli from the external environment "shaped" innate reflexes into learned responses.

Indeed, in his 1924 book *Behaviorism*, he said, "Give me a dozen healthy infants . . . and my own specified world to bring them up in and I'll guarantee to take any one at random and train him to become any type of specialist I might select." To Watson, then, you became who you are because that's what society trained you to be.

Social learning theorists such as Albert Bandura accept Watson's belief in the importance of the external environment in shaping personality. But, like Piaget and Adler, they see the individual as taking an active part in the learning process. Indeed, Bandura believes that people construct cognitive representations of reality in their minds, and then act to transform the outside world to make it conform more closely to what they want it to be. Social learning theorists see the growth of personality as coming from a continual *interaction* between cognitive processes and the external environment.

Static versus Dynamic Theories

Trait theory is "static" in that it holds that the major determinants of personality are the genes. And the genes don't change throughout a person's life. Psychoanalysis, humanistic psychology, and social learning theory are "dynamic," in that these approaches view personality as the result of a continual interplay between biological, psychological, and social forces. We will discuss the dynamic theories in this chapter, and look more closely at the static theories in Chapter 22.

Sigmund Freud

Freud was born in 1856 in what is now Czechoslovakia, but he lived for almost 80 years in Vienna. After taking his degree in medicine in 1881, Freud spent many years in the laboratory studying the human nervous system. He was almost 40 when he married. And since being a laboratory scientist didn't pay much money (then or now), Freud went into private practice in order to earn enough to support a family. Much of his theory of psychoanalysis grew out of the observations he made on these patients.

Around 1885, Freud spent several months in Paris, studying hypnosis with Charcot. Freud's interest in personality theory seems to have begun about this time. As we noted in Chapter 17, he returned from Paris believing that hypnosis might be useful in curing some types of insanity. This view was strengthened by the success that another Viennese psychiatrist, Josef Breuer, had achieved using hypnosis with an hysterical patient. Under hypnosis, Breuer had gotten this patient to relive some early unhappy experiences.

After the patient had "acted out" these childhood miseries, the hysterical symptoms seemed to disappear.

Together with Breuer, Freud developed a technique called **catharsis**, which involves the re-enactment of emotional situations while under hypnosis. During the late 1800's, many European scientists assumed that some type of "psychic dynamo" inside the body produced "energy" which motivated thoughts and behaviors. Breuer and Freud believed that traumatic experiences could *suppress this energy*. But like steam seeping out of the cracks of a boiler, some of this energy did escape—in the form of "abnormal thoughts, emotions, and behaviors." Thus catharsis was supposed to help because it *released* the dynamic forces that had been bottled up inside the patient. And once the "psychic pressure" had been reduced, the energy remaining would again be channeled into normal thoughts and actions.

As we noted in Chapter 17, Freud ultimately rejected hypnosis because it didn't work very well. Instead, he turned to **free association**. That is, he encouraged his patients to talk about all aspects of their past and present lives. And often just "talking through" the patient's problems was enough to bring about catharsis. Additionally, if Freud could get the patient to analyze a traumatic experience in unemotional terms, the patient often gained insight into what aspects of that trauma still bothered the patient. Freud called this technique *psychoanalysis*.

The Unconscious, Preconscious, and Conscious

Why did Freud's patients need his help? Like everyone else, these people had very strong physical needs, particularly a need for sexual expression. Their cathartic ("re-living") experiences suggested to Freud that sexual needs occurred even in newborn infants—if you interpret the word "sexual" in its broadest sense. But most of his patients had been punished for expressing their childhood sexual desires. This punishment appeared to drive their needs "underground," out of the patients' "streams of consciousness." Since the needs had not been satisfied, the energy associated with these needs was still present, lurking unconsciously "in the back of the patient's mind." Catharsis and psychoanalysis brought these hidden needs forward into consciousness.

But where were these lusty, unexpressed desires *hiding* in the mind? Charcot, in his attempt to explain hypnosis, had suggested that there must be different *levels of consciousness* (see Fig. 21.1). Freud took Charcot's idea and made it very much his own. In 1913, Freud divided

Catharsis (kah-THAR-sis). From the Greek word meaning "to purge, or to clean out." If you are constipated and take a laxative to "clean out" your digestive system, you have undergone a physical catharsis. Freud and Breuer (BROY-er) believed that psychotherapy could act as a psychological catharsis to cleanse the mind of bottled-up psychic energy.

Free association. Freud's psychoanalytic method of encouraging people to express their thoughts, feelings, and memories without fear of criticism, to "say whatever comes into mind," and to report whatever emotions they may associate with certain life experiences.

the human psyche into three levels or regions: the *conscious*, the *preconscious*, and the *unconscious* (see Fig. 21.2).

The Conscious Mind

As we noted in Chapter 3, *consciousness* is a primitive term that cannot be defined precisely. Whatever you are aware of at any given instant is what you are "conscious of" at that instant. And, in physiological terms, conscious awareness seems to be a primary property of your left (dominant) hemisphere.

The Preconscious Mind

Long before Freud divided the psyche into three levels, German psychologists had likened consciousness to a cluttered stage in a darkened theater. A narrowly focused spotlight sweeps across the stage, illuminating now this, now that. As you sit in the theater, you see a continual flow of images flash into focus, then disappear into darkness. The narrow beam of the spotlight is your momentary consciousness. The rest of the stage is *potentially* visible to you—if and when the spotlight shines on it. But *at the moment* all you can perceive is what's within the tiny circle of light.

To Freud, your conscious mind included whatever you were aware of or paying attention to at the moment. Your preconscious mind included any sensory input or mental process that *you could become aware of*—if and when the spotlight of awareness shone on it. In physiological terms, the preconscious would be the total range of experiences available to your left (dominant) hemisphere.

The Unconscious Mind

Freud's concept of the unconscious mind is exceptionally difficult to explain in simple terms. Briefly put, the unconscious contains all of those memories, experiences, images, feelings, and motives that you cannot voluntarily bring to consciousness or examine under the light of immedi-

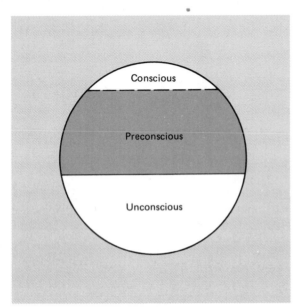

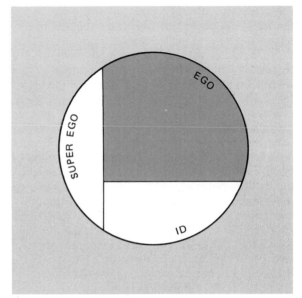

Fig. 21.1. Freud's "levels of consciousness." **(left)**

Fig. 21.2. Freud's "structures of the mind." **(right)**

ate attention. We can define this better by example.

In Chapter 10 we stated that you tend to *repress* unpleasant experiences. That is, you tend to put *blocks* on the spotlight so that it can't shine on some of the messier areas of your "mental stage" that you'd rather not look at. Repressed memories, then, are locked away in the "unconscious" portions of your mind.

As we noted in Chapter 12, you have innately determined reflexes and instincts that affect your behaviors and thoughts *whether you are conscious of them or not*. Your heart beats, your lungs breathe, and your adrenal glands secrete hormones whether or not you're aware of what they're doing. Nor do you have *direct* consciousness of neural activity in the emotional or motivational centers of your brain. "Body language," then, and emotional "feelings" are typically a part of your unconscious mind.

As you discovered in Chapter 16, you tend to file items in long-term memory storage according to certain categories. You cannot recall many of your infantile experiences because you didn't file them in the same "memory categories" you use as an adult. These early memories are "unconscious" because you simply don't know how to retrieve them.

Then there are dreams and flashes of creative insight. You are, by definition, not conscious while you dream, and dreams are often very hard to bring to conscious awareness after they've occurred. Freud thought that the dream was an al-

most perfect example of an unconscious experience. As for insight, it often consists of perceiving a pattern of some kind. Where in your mind did this pattern form if not in your unconsciousness?

By now you may have perceived a pattern yourself. What Freud referred to as the unconscious portions of your mind seem to consist of two things: processes that are mediated by the "lower" centers of your brain; and those that are mediated by your right (nonverbal) hemisphere.

Libido

While Freud was mapping out the *regions* of the mind, he tried as well to determine the psychological processes that energized, focused, moved, and even blocked the spotlight of consciousness.

Freud decided the body continually creates *psychic energy* much as a dynamo continually produces electrical power. Freud called this psychic energy **libido** and believed that it is the motivating force that "powers" *all of your thoughts, feelings, and behaviors*. A build-up of libidinal energy creates a painful drive state that forces you to become aware of some unsatisfied need. You then tend to focus on activities that will allow you to release the pent-up energy and hence reduce the drive. Thus *expending* libidinal energy is associated with sensory pleasure, while *repressing* libidinal energy almost always leads to painful tension and anxiety.

Id, Ego, and Super-ego

An infant is *conscious*, but it doesn't "know" enough to keep itself alive. How then does it survive its first years on earth?

The Id

According to Freud, you were born with a collection of basic instincts or biological drives that are the *source* of your libidinal energy. Freud called this set of instinctual drives the **id**, from the Latin word for "it." These drives are mediated by the lower centers of your brain, such as the limbic system and the hypothalamus. As such, the id is buried at the deepest level of your unconscious mind, far removed from conscious reality. Freud described the id as a "cauldron of seething excitement" which has no inner structure or organization, which operates in illogical ways, and which seeks only the pleasures that come from discharging its pent-up energies.

The id keeps an infant alive because it obeys the **pleasure principle**, which demands the *immediate* gratification of all the infant's needs. Since most of these needs are related to bodily functions—such as hunger, elimination, aggression, and sensual stimulation—the newborn child survives because it is *biologically programmed* to release its libidinal energy in life-sustaining ways.

The Ego

The id helps the infant survive because it is selfish and impulsive. But, as the infant matures, the "real world" begins to make demands on the child—and punishes it severely if the child doesn't respond in socially appropriate ways. As the infant is forced to delay gratification of some of its instinctual needs, it gradually becomes aware that there is a difference between its own desires and those of other people. And, once the child begins to distinguish between itself and the outer world, its **ego** or *conscious self* comes into being.

According to R.M. Goldenson, the ego is a group of mental functions or processes that enable you to perceive, reason, make judgments, store memories, and solve various problems. Your id was present at birth. Your ego developed slowly as you learned to master your impulses, delay immediate gratification of your needs, and get along with others.

Your ego is the part of your personality that is in communication with the external world. For the most part, then, your ego operates at a conscious (or preconscious) level, but it includes some unconscious processes as well. Thus like your id, your ego is subject to the demands of the pleasure principle. But as you mature, your conscious self is more influenced by what Freud called the **reality principle**—the practical demands of daily living. On occasion, however, your ego may be torn between the opposing forces of pleasure-seeking and reality. It often resolves this

Libido (lib-BEE-doh). The psychic energy created by your innate instincts. Psychoanalysis is often called "a hydrolic (high-DROHL-lick) theory of personality" because Freud believed that we are motivated primarily by a need to release pent-up energy. Our innate instincts create energy (libido) which we must express in thoughts and behaviors, much as a pump builds up pressure as it pumps out water. The water (psychic energy) will most certainly spew out somewhere unless it is blocked (repressed). If your upbringing was normal and natural, your psychic energy is expressed in socially approved and healthy thoughts, feelings, and behaviors. But, if you experienced trauma during your early years, the energy is repressed or expressed in unhealthy (neurotic) ways.

Id (rhymes with "kid"). The primitive, instinctual, childish, unconscious portion of the personality that obeys the pleasure principle.

Pleasure principle. Freud's notion that we are all driven to satisfy our needs in childish (instinctual) ways. The reduction of a drive gives us pleasure, the increase in a drive gives us pain. According to Freud, "The id lives by the pleasure principle."

Ego. From the Latin word for "I." That part of the personality which mediates between the id, the superego, and reality. The conscious portion of your mind.

Reality principle. Freud believed that we have to learn that the world has a reality of its own, separate from what we wish it to be. When the ego yields to the demands the world places on it, it is following the "reality principle."

Superego. That part of your personality which "splits off from your ego," and which contains both your own and society's "rules of conduct." The superego has two parts—the stern "conscience," which you acquired from your parents (mostly during the latency period and the genital stage), and the "self-ideal," which you acquired mostly from other people during puberty. The conscience operates mostly at an unconscious level, while the self-ideal operates mostly at a conscious level.

conflict by trying to satisfy your instinctual desires (id) in socially approved ways.

The Superego

There is more to your personality, however, than id and ego, than pleasure principle and reality principle. For, as you grow, the people around you demand that you adopt society's "rules and regulations." To do so, you must build up a *conscience* that keeps you from violating the rules, and an *ego-ideal* that you must strive to attain. Freud called this part of your personality structure the **superego** and regarded it as a part of your ego that splits off and begins to act on its own.

Your superego develops slowly (and unconsciously) during the first five years of your life as you increasingly imitate the thoughts and actions of others—primarily those of your parents. During adolescence and young adulthood your superego matures even more as you come into contact with adults (other than your parents) whom you admire and whose values you take on in part or in whole. For the most part, this socialization process occurs at an *unconscious* level, as your superego gains the power to criticize and supervise both your id and your ego. Your super-

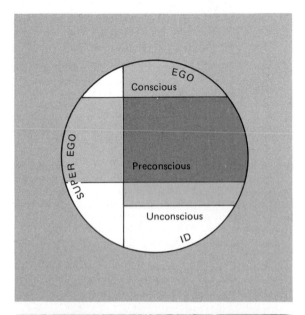

Fig. 21.3. "Levels of consciousness" occupied by the id, ego, and superego. **(top left)**

According to Freud, the ego emerges during toilet training in the anal stage, when the child's parents begin demanding that the child control its instinctual self-gratifying urges. **(top right)**

Freud stated that during the latency period, girls develop an intense love of their fathers (the Electra complex). They resolve this problem by identifying with their mothers. **(bottom left & right)**

ego is thus your "unconscious voice" that helps you discriminate social rights from wrongs without your being aware of why you do so (see Fig. 21.3).

Question: From Freud's point of view, why might some people be unable to give a logical explanation for their hostility toward long-haired men or assertive women?

Psychosexual Development

Freud's notions about personality development came from many sources—from his knowledge of medicine, his studies with Charcot and with Breuer, and from Darwin's theory of evolution. But mostly his theory sprang from his observations of his own patients. Freud was fascinated by the fact that most of his clients seemed to have gone through very similar developmental *crises* as children. Eventually he decided that you pass through various **psychosexual stages of development** which correspond to the maturational stage of your body at various times in your life. Each stage is associated with a unique crisis of some kind.

Oral Stage

The first crisis obviously was that of *birth*, when you were thrust out into the world and became dependent on others to meet your needs. True, you had innate reflexes that helped you survive by creating *libidinal energy* that had to be discharged. But the manner in which you release this energy changes as your body matures. When you were newborn, the brain centers which control your mouth movements were physically the most developed, so you released libidinal energy most easily through such oral activities as sucking and swallowing. Freud called this period—which lasts from birth to about one year of age—the **oral stage** of development.

Freud saw many child-like oral behavior patterns in his patients, such as talking too much, over-eating, excessive smoking, and so forth. He presumed that this "residue of their infantile experiences" remained locked away in their unconscious minds because of some traumatic experience they had while in the oral stage. These patients had problems because they were *still trying to release libidinal energy through adult oral activities*. Therapy for these patients would obviously involve some form of "catharsis" to allow the patients to discharge the libidinal energy that had been repressed while they were still in the oral stage.

Anal Stage

The first developmental crisis you went through was that of birth. The second crisis came when your parents began making demands on you. These demands, Freud said, conflicted with your instinctual need to obtain immediate gratification of all your biological and psychological needs. The second crisis reached a peak during toilet training, when your parents began insisting that you learn to *delay gratification*. Freud assumed you resolved this crisis by creating an "ego" or conscious self that could respond to reality by gaining voluntary control over the release of libidinal energy through anal activities.

Some of Freud's patients were excessively neat, obstinate, and miserly. These three traits make up what Freud called the "anal character," and he saw all three as attempts to punish the mother for the trauma of toilet training. The mother demanded that the child "be clean," so the patient became unreasonably tidy. The mother sat the child on a potty and demanded that the child "produce," so the child rebelled by withholding its feces, and became fixated at the *anal stage*. As an adult, the patient still rebels by obstinately refusing to part with a single penny. Again, catharsis—and giving the patient insight

Psychosexual stages of development (SIGH-koh). Freud's belief that all children must pass through similar periods in the development of their personalities. Each stage has its own crisis, and during each stage the child discharges libidinal energy in a different manner.

Oral stage. The crisis is birth, and the infant discharges libido through oral activities because the neural centers controlling mouth movements are the first to develop. If you experience trauma during this stage, you may as an adult still release libido through such oral activities as over-eating.

Anal stage. The crisis comes during toilet training, when the parents demand that the child learn to delay gratification of its urge to release libido by urinating and defecating "at will." If you experience trauma during this stage, you may as an adult become compulsively neat, and "retain" money as you had to "retain" feces during toilet training.

Phallic period (FAL-ick). The crisis comes from the child's desire to possess the opposite-sex parent which leads to fear or hatred of the same-sex parent. The child discharges libidinal energy primarily through masturbation.

Oedipus complex (ED-ih-pus). A "complex" is a part of the mind that breaks free and begins to function on its own. Freud took many of his analogies from Greek mythology. Oedipus was a young man who inadvertently killed his father and married his mother. Freud believed that all young boys (during the phallic stage) develop an intense incestuous desire for their mothers and a strong hatred for their fathers. But they also fear that if they express their feelings they will be punished (or even castrated) by the father. The boys resolve this crisis both by repressing their incestuous desires (and thereby passing into the latency period), and by introjecting the standards and values of their fathers into the "conscience" portion of their superegos.

Electra complex (ee-LECK-trah). Electra was a Greek woman whose mother killed her father. Electra then talked her brother into murdering their mother. Freud believed that all young girls (during the phallic stage) develop an intense incestuous desire for their fathers and a strong hatred for their mothers. But they also fear that if they express these feelings, they will be severely punished by their mothers. The Electral crisis is resolved later in girls than the Oedipal crisis is in boys, because (according to Freud) the mother is usually kind, while the father is stern and authoritarian. Thus it is difficult for the girl to develop a full-blown hatred for her loving mother. Nonetheless, the girl eventually represses her incestuous desires for the father, passes into the latency period, and introjects the standards and values of her mother into the "conscience" portion of the girl's superego.

into the roots of the problem—seemed to Freud to be the best therapy.

Phallic Stage

At age three or so, your sex organs began to mature, and so did the centers in your brain associated with sexual activity. Thus you acquired a new avenue for discharging your instinctual energies. During this **phallic period**, boys build up a warm and loving relationship with their mothers, which Freud called the **Oedipus complex**. At the same age, girls experience an intense emotional attachment for their fathers, called the **Electra complex**. Freud stated that, during the phallic stage, boys experience incestual desires to possess their mothers and compete with (or even kill) their fathers, while girls come to desire their fathers and fear or hate their mothers.

Freud believed that the phallic stage is marked by frequent masturbation. During the fantasies that accompany this self-stimulation, desires to "possess" one parent and destroy the other break through to consciousness. These fantasies bring about the *crisis* of the phallic stage, for they violate the *incest taboo* found in all societies.

In 1930, Freud wrote that the Oedipus complex "represents the essential part of the content of the neuroses. It is the culminating point of infantile sexuality which, through its after-effects, decisively influences the sexuality of the adult." Men who fail to resolve their yearnings for the mother may delay marriage, or become attached to an older woman as a "mother substitute." Women who postpone marriage may well suffer from a "father fixation." Therapy usually consisted of helping the patient find ways to discharge the libidinal energy that was guiltily repressed during the phallic stage.

Latency Period

According to Freud, you entered the latency period at about age five or six, when you began repressing your infantile sexuality in order to solve the crisis associated with the incest taboo. At this time, you started to move out of the home more frequently, and your friendships with your peers took on greater importance to your emotional and intellectual development. Freud believed this was a *natural homosexual period* during which boys found "heroes" among older male friends and teachers, and girls developed "crushes" on other girls and older women.

Genital Stage

The latency period ends at the onset of puberty. The Oedipus and Electra complexes come to the fore again briefly, but are normally resolved during adolescence. Boys overcome their hatred for their fathers by taking on the fathers' goals and standards. Thus the young men "possess" their mothers symbolically by acting like their fathers. Girls find gratification and fulfillment in the feminine role, Freud said, as a result of both their mother's encouragement and their father's admiration.

During this genital stage, Freud's patients consciously began to hunt for an idealized sort of "life style" in which their main means of discharging libido came through heterosexual activities. Had all gone well during their psychosexual development, the patients would have become fully functioning and self-actualized adults. But all did not go well with many of them. Rather, the problems they faced during their early years were not resolved. These developmental difficulties kept surfacing during their adult years, causing the patients psychological (and sometimes physical) pain. It was this fact that led Freud to state that *most adult personality traits* are determined during the early years of life. To Freud, then, your personality ceased to develop (for the most part) after adolescence.

Defense Mechanisms

Freud's theory of psychosexual development is really the story of how the ego learns to resolve the conflicting demands made by the id, superego, and the reality of the external environment. The ego has several **defense mechanisms** at its disposal to protect itself from being *traumatized* by the stress arising from these conflicts. But the ego is not always aware of what the needs of the id and superego are, because many of these needs are unconscious. The occurrence of **signal anxiety** warns the ego that libidinal tensions have become so strong that it must either handle them or be disabled by stress.

Almost all of the defense mechanisms available to the ego have three characteristics in common:

1. They are ways of trying to reduce stress and anxiety.
2. They involve the denying or distortion of reality.
3. They operate at an unconscious level.

Repression

The most important of the defense mechanisms is undoubtedly *repression*, the process by which the ego blocks off threatening thoughts or desires and thus keeps them from sweeping into the spotlight of consciousness. Most of these experiences have undischarged libidinal energy attached to them in some way. In repressing these experiences, the ego has to use up some of its own energy sources. And the more painful the memory, or the stronger the unacceptable urge, the more energy the ego must expend in order to keep the material repressed. Eventually the ego may run out of steam, and bits and pieces of the repressed material may leak through to consciousness as slips of the tongue, or as symbols in dreams.

Regression

When some of Freud's patients experienced great stress, they fell back into childish behavior patterns. Some of them responded to stress by over-eating or by drinking too much. Freud saw this as a *regression* to an earlier (oral) mode of pleasure. Or when a young male patient encountered heterosexual difficulties, he sometimes would resort to such immature forms of gratification as masturbation or homosexuality. This regression allowed the man to discharge libidinal energy in a "safe" way. But it also prevented him from trying to solve his present interpersonal problems.

Identification

As we noted earlier, people resolve their Oedipus or Electra crisis by taking on the characteristics of their same-sex parent. Freud saw this process of *identification* as the ego's way of defending against incestual feelings. The young girl identifies with her mother out of fear of her mother's wrath—and thereby builds up the unconscious portion of her superego, the "conscience." In adolescence, the girl identifies with other women and thus strengthens the conscious portion of her superego, the "ego-ideal." Freud thus saw the superego itself as a kind of "super" defense mechanism that helped reduce anxiety by allowing the person to release libidinal energy in socially approved ways.

Denial

Many of Freud's patients seemed to be "deliberately" unconscious of certain painful facts. Freud decided that they were practicing *denial*, a defense mechanism by which the ego shuts itself off from certain realities. *Hysterical blindness* is an example of denial (see Chapter 13).

Reaction Formation and Projection

A step beyond denial is *reaction formation*, in which the ego changes unacceptable love into acceptable hate (or vice-versa). If a mother hates her child—a feeling she must deny conscious awareness of—the mother may smother the child with affection. Or the mother's ego may indulge in *projection* by pretending that the child actually hates her. She thus projects her unacceptable emotions onto the child.

Rationalization

Freud found that many of his patients offered him elaborate justifications for what were obviously illogical or immature actions. When he pointed out what they were doing, these patients would usually refuse to confront reality. Rather, they would give him yet another *rationalization* or questionable excuse for acting as they did. This self-justification seemed to allow the patients to reduce any anxiety they had, and yet go right on behaving as they had.

Defense mechanisms. Techniques used by the ego to defend itself against impulses or commands from the id and the superego. See Chapter 13.

Signal anxiety. The internal or intra-psychic feeling that something bad is about to happen—"butterflies in the stomach." A warning to the ego that it is in danger of being overwhelmed by *traumatic anxiety* or stress if it does not find some way of releasing pent-up libidinal energy.

Displacement and Sublimation

Over the years Freud and his followers identified a great many defense mechanisms, of which we have space to mention only the best known. The last of these are *displacement* and *sublimation*.

At birth, the objects of all our instincts are specified by our genetic inheritance. You don't have to teach an infant that food satisfies its hunger, because its body already knows this. But, as the infant grows up, the *objects* of its instincts can change through learning and experience. That is, the child's ego gains the ability to *displace* the flow of libidinal energy from one object to another. But the ego may use this ability inappropriately, as a defense mechanism. If the child gets angry at its mother, it dares not hit her because it will be punished. Therefore, it displaces its anger toward a safe object—such as a doll—that cannot retaliate if the child strikes it.

Sublimation is at once a form of displacement and the most mature of the defense mechanisms. Freud thought that the energy an artist devotes to painting—or a scientist to the laboratory, or a politician to governing—was really energy that had been channeled away from sex or aggression or eating. Although this displacement was socially acceptable and sometimes highly creative, it seldom seemed to satisfy all the id's needs.

As we noted in Chapter 13, the defense mechanisms are really indirect or "defensive" ways of coping with stress and anxiety. By encouraging his patients to bring their unconscious problems to the fore—and thus deal with them at a conscious level—Freud was attempting to get his patients to use a more direct method of coping with their developmental difficulties.

Freud's Influence

Freud's theory has had a tremendous influence on Western thought, in no small part because it forced people to pay more attention to the *unconscious* aspects of human behavior. Prior to his time, psychologists primarily had studied conscious activities or overt behavior patterns. But neither introspection nor the study of condi-

Carl Jung   Alfred Adler   Eric Erikson

tioned reflexes yielded the insights into personality development that Freud gave the world.

Freud was one of the first "drive theorists." He believed that arousal was painful and that pleasure came primarily from the satisfaction of biological drives. Like most other early drive theorists, Freud grew in a repressive and moralistic culture. Little wonder that he saw the effects of punishment more clearly than those of using reward. But by making parents conscious of how they affected their childrens' development, he helped *change* the culture itself into a less punitive one.

But Freud had a little help along the way. People flocked to study with him, and his disciples restructured the fields of psychiatry and personality theory. However, not all of Freud's followers agreed with his emphasis on unconscious biological instincts and the almost unchangeable influence of a child's early upbringing. Among the most important of those theorists strongly influenced by Freud were Jung, Adler, and Erikson.

Carl Jung

Born in Switzerland in 1875, Carl Gustav Jung came from a family of theologians and medical doctors. As a medical student at the University of Zurich, he dabbled in biology, philosophy, archeology, mythology, and mysticism. Jung discovered Freud in 1907 and became something of a disciple until 1912, when Jung developed his own psychoanalytic theory.

Jung could not accept Freud's notion that the goal of "growing up" was to bring the infantile, sexual instincts under control. Rather, Jung said, we are *religious* animals whose unconscious roots go back to the very beginnings of the human race. To Jung, the purpose of our existence is the integration of our conscious perceptions of the outside world with our unconscious, mystical experiences.

Jung believed in the ego, but he said it is made up of our feelings of identity and continuity. That is, your ego is the part of your mind that knows you are the same person today as you were yesterday. But Jung didn't view the ego as striving to mediate between the childish id and the stern superego. Rather, he saw it as a slowly developing structure that pulls together all types of conscious and unconscious activity to form a new "whole." Jung called this integrative process **individuation**, which in many ways resembles what Piaget describes as the "building up of the self-schema." Jung, however, placed a great deal more emphasis on the ego's need to integrate unconscious with conscious processes than Piaget did.

To Freud, the unconscious was primarily the source of our psychic energies. But to Jung, there was not one unconscious but two—the *personal unconscious* and the *collective unconscious*.

The Personal Unconscious

By personal unconscious, Jung had in mind those half-forgotten ideas, wishes, and past experiences that are now so weak they are difficult to bring into consciousness. According to Jung, some of these thoughts and memories may be so closely related that they grow together, or congeal into a **complex** or schema all their own. This complex of associated experiences might then split off from the person's psyche and function independently, with a psychological life of its own. The purpose of psychotherapy, from a Jungian point of view, is often that of identifying these complexes and bringing them back into conscious control.

The Collective Unconscious

To Jung, the collective unconscious houses all of the "racial memories" that each person is born with. In his study of anthropology, Jung noticed that some myths—such as a "great flood," or the creation of the world—seem to appear in *all cultures*. Jung called these myths **archetypes**. He said that, through evolutional processes, the *mental images* associated with these archetypes had become engraved on our genes. Thus, Jung said, each human being is born with some unconscious "mental fragments" of the past history of the human race. The most important archetype of all, however, is that of the *self-concept*, for it encourages us to integrate all of our conscious and unconscious psychological processes into one meaningful whole.

Extroversion and Introversion

Jung's most widely accepted ideas have to do with *extroversion* and *introversion*. Jung thought that we are born with two innate attitudes, one of which leads us to look inward, the other of which leads us to look outward.

Some people seem to be born *introverts*—that is, they spend most of their time looking toward their inner or personal world. Other individuals focus more on the outside environment. Outgoing, highly social individuals are examples of what Jung meant by *extroverts*. Jung believed that you are born with both tendencies, but that one usually comes to predominate. You are usually conscious of which attitude is dominant but, according to Jung, you may not realize that the other attitude often expresses itself unconsciously through your dreams and fantasies.

Jung versus Freud

Freud emphasized the role of biology in personality development. Jung preferred to think that humans could rise above their animal natures. Freud believed that happiness often came from escaping pain or reducing anxiety, and he tended to attract patients who were highly anxious or pain-ridden. Many of Jung's clients were artists, mystics, or wealthy individuals who felt the need for spiritual guidance "outside the church." Freud focused on the early, developmental years, which he saw as determining the entire structure of an individual's personality. Jung worked to a great degree with older patients, and never did offer a complete account of how the personality is formed.

Perhaps the most telling difference of all between the two men, though, lay in their use of language. Freud was a superb writer who was a serious contender for the Nobel Prize in literature. Jung's books and articles, however, were filled with obscure images and symbols. His greatest influence was perhaps not on psychology, but on art and mysticism.

Individuation (in-dih-vid-you-A-shun). The process, according to Jung, by which the ego slowly builds up a self-concept or self-schema by pulling together all types of conscious and unconscious activity to form a unified whole.

Complex. A portion of the mind that splits off and begins to function on its own. To Freud, the superego is a "complex" that splits off from the ego during the latency period. Since it is built on either the Oedipus or Electra complex, Freud called the superego the "heir to the Oedipus complex."

Archetypes (ARK-ee-types). From the Greek words meaning "the original model, form, or pattern from which something is made or from which something develops." The archetypes that Jung referred to are the original models of myths, legends, and stories—instinctual thought patterns passed on genetically from generation to generation.

Alfred Adler

Alfred Adler was born and educated in Vienna. He joined Freud's group a few years after taking his medical degree. Adler's first work was on the living conditions of Austrian tailors, a study that helped confirm his early bias toward the importance of environmental factors in determining personality. But as fascinated as Adler was by Freud's ideas, he was the first to break away from "the master" and form his own group, the Society for Individual Psychology.

Adler disputed Freud's notion that human behavior is dominated by the workings of blind, selfish instincts. Instead, said Adler, people govern themselves by a conscious need to express and fulfill themselves as unique individuals. Rejecting both Freud's theory of biological drives, and Jung's emphasis on intra-psychic mysticism, Adler emphasized the importance of the social environment. He thought that people could shape their own destinies, and that they could build a superior society by satisfying their basic need to transcend their personal problems.

The Creative Power

To Adler, life is a conscious struggle to achieve *superiority*. Thus he denied the importance of sexual instincts and substituted aggressive tendencies in their place. Freud and Jung emphasized the unconscious, unknowable inner influences on behavior. Adler believed that most of us are quite aware of our motives. We see our own *inferiorities*, and we strive to overcome them. We have an instinct for *self-realization*, for completion and perfection, that Adler thought was the driving force of life itself. Adler called this force the *creative power* and thought it was the "first cause" of all behavior.

Table 21.1. Erikson's Stages of Development

Stage	1	2	3	4	5	6	7	8
Maturity								Ego Integrity vs. Despair
Adulthood							Generativity vs. Stagnation	
Young Adulthood						Intimacy vs. Isolation		
Puberty and Adolescence					Identity vs. Role Confusion			
Latency				Industry vs. Inferiority				
Locomotor-Genital			Initiative vs. Guilt					
Muscular-Anal		Autonomy vs. Shame, Doubt						
Oral Sensory	Basic Trust vs. Mistrust							

SOURCE: Reprinted from *Childhood and Society,* Rev. by Erik H. Erikson, by permission of W.W. Norton & Company, Inc. Copyright 1960 © 1963 by W.W. Norton & Company, Inc.

The Inferiority Complex

As children, we learn very early that adults can do things that we cannot. This knowledge creates in all of us an *inferiority complex* that adds to our motivation to succeed. It also creates a drive for *compensation*, the urge to overcome our failures in one part of life by excelling in another. The small, weak boy may try to succeed in his school studies or become a great musician in order to *compensate* for his physical weakness.

Life Style

Adler was an optimist. He believed that you have buried in your genes a basic need to cooperate with others and to work toward building a better society. But you need guidance from the adults around you in order to express this need. For it is only through training and experience that you develop your *style of life*—your own unique way of expressing yourself. In a sense, Adler's "style of life" is equivalent to Freud's concept of the ego. At first, Adler thought this style was fixed early in life. Later, he decided you continue to mature even as an adult. Thus Adler was one of the first theorists to emphasize *life span development.*

Adler's emphasis on the importance of *social factors* in determining personality was, for a time, unique in psychoanalytic circles and helped give rise to what we now call "social psychology." And, by assuring people that they were basically humane, open-minded, and in control of their own destinies, Adler encouraged the development of "humanistic psychology."

Indeed, as humanist Abraham Maslow stated shortly before his death, "Alfred Adler becomes more and more correct year by year. As the facts come in, they give stronger and stronger support to his image of man."

Erik H. Erikson

Freud was trained as a biologist. He emphasized the *psychosexual* side of your personality development, which he saw as being primarily under the control of your genes. Thus once you had resolved the heterosexual crisis that occurs during adolescence, you had reached the peak of personal growth—at least as far as Freud was concerned.

However, other psychoanalysts soon came to believe that there was much more to personality development than the biologically determined psychosexual stages. These theorists saw humans as being *social* as well as *biological* organisms. Following Adler's lead, they believed development continued *throughout the entire span of life*.

Chief among these theorists was Erik H. Erikson, whose **psychosocial theory of development** has had a strong influence on personology. Like most psychoanalysts, Erikson believed the ego was much more important than the id and the superego in shaping the development of your personality. Your ego is the point of contact between you and society. Therefore, Erikson said, the *type of society* that you grow up in is at least as important as your instinctual drives.

Erikson accepted most of Freud's notions on the importance of instinctual drives in young children, but he insisted that it is the *conflict* between instincts and cultural demands that shapes the child's personality. Instincts are presumably pretty much the same from one child to another, but cultures differ remarkably, and they grow and develop just as do human beings.

Freud and Jung emphasized the importance of past history on the maturation of the individual. Erikson, like Adler, emphasized the future. At any given moment in time, Erikson said, your *anticipation of future events* determines how you will behave in the "here and now."

Eight Developmental Stages

According to Erikson, you must pass through eight developmental stages on your way to complete maturity (see Table 21.1). Each of these stages is characterized by its own type of *crisis*, or conflict. Erikson saw these crises as being eight great tests of your character.

1. Erikson called the first developmental stage the "sensory stage," which corresponds to Freud's oral stage. To Erikson, the crisis at the sensory stage is that of learning a basic *trust or mistrust* of other people. At this point in life, the infant is totally dependent on others for its needs. If its mother (or someone else) meets these needs, the infant learns to depend on others in later life. If, for any reason, the mother is inconsistent in satisfying the infant's needs, the infant may carry suspicion and doubt through the rest of its years.

Psychosocial theory of development. Erikson's extension and elaboration of Freudian theory. Freud stated that personality development more or less ends during adolescence. Erikson, who places more emphasis on environmental factors than did Freud, believes that personality development can continue all one's life—that the personality is always a psychological adjustment to social inputs or situations.

Autonomy (aw-TAWN-oh-me). Freedom; self-direction. The autonomic nervous system is usually "free" of conscious direction or control.

2. The second of Erikson's stages, similar to the anal stage, is that of *muscular development*. During toilet training the child learns to control its own muscles and begins to assert its individuality. The crisis here is that of **autonomy**, or the ability to control one's own bodily functions. The child either learns autonomy, or, if it is unsuccessful, develops shame and doubt about its own abilities.

3. The third stage, that of *locomotor control*, is similar to Freud's phallic stage. Now the child attempts to develop its own way of asserting its needs and gaining its rewards. Urged by its instincts to possess its opposite-sex parent (at least in fantasy) and to rival its same-sex parent, the child faces the crisis of inner desires versus society's demands. Erikson believed that if the child could channel its sexual needs into socially acceptable behaviors, the child acquired *initiative*. If not, the child might build up a strong sense of *guilt* that would haunt it the rest of its days.

4. Both Freud and Erikson called the fourth developmental stage that of *latency*. During these (typically) school years, the crisis the child faces is that of *competence* or *failure*. If the child does well in school, it learns that it can succeed and thus becomes *industrious*. If it does poorly, it gains a sense of *inferiority*.

5. At *puberty*, Freud thought, sexual interest returns and the individual must make the final adjustment, that of heterosexuality. Erikson saw the puberty crisis as that of either finding your *identity*, or of developing what he called *role confusion*. You must decide what the future will hold and who you will become. Although the social roles available may vary from one society to another, you must decide which of these roles to adopt. By discovering who and what you want to be, you are able to plan your life as a working, functioning adult.

6. Erikson postulated three final stages of maturation beyond the five that Freud spoke of. The first of these stages, which occurs in young adulthood, presents you with the crisis of *in-*

493
Erik H. Erikson

The second of Erikson's developmental stages is "muscular development." The child either succeeds at self-control and hence learns autonomy, or it fails and develops shame and guilt about its own abilities. **(top left)**

During the latency period, the child either succeeds in school and thus becomes industrious, or fails and develops a feeling of inferiority. **(top right)**

During young adulthood, Erikson said, people face the crisis of "intimacy versus isolation." **(bottom left)**

In maturity, the last of Erikson's developmental stages, people must integrate the fact of death into the pattern of their existence. **(bottom right)**

timacy versus isolation. If you have "found" yourself by now, you can then go on to the delightful task of "finding" someone else to share life's intimacies with. If you fail to resolve your identity crisis, however, you will remain isolated from the closest forms of psychological "sharing" with others.

7. Societies often pass through a period of rapid development, then settle into *complacency* when growth stops and stagnation sets in. Erikson believed that adults often experience the

same "growth" crisis during their *middle years*. Human beings need more than intimacy. We must be productive and helpful to our fellow humans, and we must make a contribution to society. The crisis decision here, then, is that between what Erikson called **generativity** and *stagnation*.

8. Erikson's final stage is that of *maturity*. If you live long enough, you have to face squarely the fact that you are mortal, and that some day you will die. By resolving your prior crises, you gain the strength to *integrate* even death into the pattern of your existence. You come to terms with youself, content with the knowledge that you have done the best that you could under the circumstances. Knowing that your life has been successful, you can die as you lived—with integrity. But, if you fail to solve the earlier crises, you may see your life as having been useless, incomplete, and wasted. And thus you may succumb to feelings of despair at the futility of existence.

Maturity and Old Age

Adler and Erikson deserve a vote of praise for reminding us that people do not stop developing once they reach adulthood. Even today, most personality theorists concentrate on the early years of life, perhaps because children change so dramatically and quickly, perhaps because children are easier to study than are adults. It is also true that childhood development is more influenced by genes, thus is similar from culture to culture. Adult development, however, varies radically from one society to another, because our later years are shaped more by *social learning* than by our *genetic blueprints* (see Chapters 25–27). Whatever the case, we know much more about the mental and physical changes associated with childhood than we do about how older people adapt and develop.

The "growth" crisis that Erikson describes for the middle years is that of generativity versus stagnation. There is a cultural myth in Western society that, like a machine that has worn down from constant use, the older person should become slow-moving, mentally inflexible and rigid, and above all, asexual. Let us look at each of these points in turn.

Physical Changes in Maturity

There is no doubt that most younger people expend more physical energy than do most people in their 40's and 50's. But this change in "body tempo" is probably due more to psychological and social causes than to something like "tired blood." Young people often have neither the skills

Generativity (jen-ur-uh-TIV-uh-tee). To generate is to produce. Generativity is having the power of producing or originating things.

nor the experience to command high-paying desk jobs that require much mental but little physical exertion. And with maturity usually comes the knowledge of how to "husband" your energy, saving it for things you may consider more important than "pure exercise."

Professional athletes often retire in their 30's, not because they are physically incapable of continuing, but because their motivations change. For instance, Maren Seidler is one of America's finest athletes. She holds the women's record in the shotput, and was on the US Olympic team in 1968, 1972, 1976, and 1980. But in 1981, at the peak of her career, she decided to retire. "I've been putting the shot for 16 years, more than half my life," she told *Sports Illustrated* in 1981. "[But] there was no good reason to do it any more. It just seemed silly. The other day in practice I picked up the shot to throw it and instead just laid it back down." *Physically* Seidler could continue for many years to come. *Mentally* she seems interested in going on to other things.

Question: Which of Erikson's crises does Seidler seem to be facing?

Loss of Neurons in Maturity

In the September 1978 issue of *Psychology Today*, Marian C. Diamond attacks a number of myths about what changes occur in your brain as you age. "One persistent bit of folklore about the brain is that we lose a vast number of brain cells as we grow old," Diamond says. She quotes statements in the popular press that you lose "100,000 cells a day after age 30," and that "drinking a single martini will kill 10,000 neurons." All of these reports are nonsense, Diamond says. She has studied the brains of both animals and humans in her laboratory at the University of California, Berkeley, for many years. She concludes that, "In the absence of disease, our studies provide no reason to believe that normal aging in humans produces brain-cell loss until, perhaps, extreme old age."

Diamond further points out that there is considerable evidence that living in an enriched environment promotes good physical and mental health in both humans and animals. "The worst thing we can do is to consign elderly people to sedentary confinement in an unstimulating nursing home." To do so, Diamond says, is to perpetuate the false belief that brain-cell loss and mental deterioration always accompany old age.

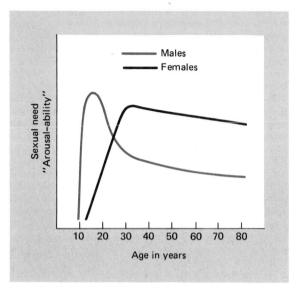

Fig. 21.4. Most psychologists believe that "sexual arousability" reaches a peak in males at about age 18 and thereafter declines, while "arousability" peaks in females at about age 30 and remains fairly constant thereafter.

Learning and Memory in Mature Individuals

One persistent belief in our culture is that "you can't teach an old dog new tricks." Applied to humans, this folk saying implies one of two things: Either (1) older people suffer an age-related memory deficit; or (2) mature individuals find it more difficult to adjust to changed circumstances than do young people. The scientific data tend to support (1) to some extent, but not (2).

As Leonard W. Poon and his colleagues point out in their 1980 book, *New Directions in Memory and Aging*, young people are perhaps more likely to "latch on to new ideas" than are older people. However, older individuals are generally able to learn more quickly those facts or skills that do not directly *contradict* their previous learning. Young people may be capable of taking in information more rapidly, and may have larger Short-term Memories, but older individuals are just as good at making decisions. *Processing speed* thus seems to be the major deficit that uniformly shows up in studies of learning in older people.

In a study of several thousand subjects, Oxford psychologist Patrick Rabbitt reports that most people 70 and older prefer talking to one individual at a time. When part of a conversation group, older individuals apparently cannot process information rapidly enough. Thus they tend to remember what was said, but not who said it—or

they recall who spoke, but not what was said. But Rabbitt also points out that some of the "memory problems" old people seem to have may be due to poor hearing or other physical defects rather than to mental deterioration. He notes as well that 5 to 10 percent of people past 70 have memories just as good as individuals in their 20's.

Perhaps the major "memory" problem that old people have is the *expectations* younger individuals have about memory loss in old age. As Samuel Johnson wrote more than 200 years ago, "If a young or middle-aged man, when leaving a company, does not recollect where he laid his hat, it is nothing. But if the same inattention is discovered in an old man, people will shrug their shoulders and say, 'His memory is going.'" Robin M. Henig confirms Johnson's wisdom in her 1981 book *The Myth of Senility*. Henig notes that older people respond to their environments differently than do younger people, but this fact doesn't mean older individuals are inferior. It merely means that our culture does not equip us to understand the old as well as we understand children and young adults.

Sexuality in Older Individuals

There is not all that much agreement among the experts on how aging affects sexuality, much less *why* these changes occur. The generally accepted view of "sexual arousability" is shown in Fig. 21.4. As you can see, males tend to reach their peak about age 18, then show a sharp drop that continues the rest of their lives. "Arousability" in women, however, tends to peak about age 30 or so and stays relatively high thereafter.

The truth of the matter is that there simply aren't enough studies—made in enough situations—to tell us all that we need to know about sexuality in the later years. It is true that hormone levels reach a peak in the male at about age 18, and fall thereafter. But it is just as true that a 90-year-old male typically has a high enough hormone level to perform the sex act several times a week.

Most research suggests that sexual "arousability" *at any age past puberty* is as greatly affected by intra-psychic and social factors as by hormone levels. Our society has certain "expectations" about sex among older individuals, and those expectations are primarily negative. A study of attitudes among college students—reported in the June 1977 issue of *Psychology Today*—notes that more than half the students believe their parents have sex once a month or less, while about 25 percent of the students think their parents make love less than once a year. (Kinsey's figures suggest that the parents probably have intercourse 3 to 4 times a week, but only 4 percent of the students guessed this was the case!)

On a more positive note, a number of studies do agree on one important point: People who, in their later years, continue to have an active sex life typically look younger, have more energy, and show a greater zest for living than do people who shun sexuality. The older person's *psychological age* thus depends more on the individual's *self-concept* than on the person's *biological age*.

You're as Young as You Feel

"Compared with others your age, do you think you feel older, younger or about the same?" Margaret Linn and Kathleen Hunter asked this question of 150 persons aged 65 or older. They reported their results in the *Journal of Gerontology* in 1979. Those individuals who *perceived themselves* as being younger than others their age were much better off. They had greater self-esteem, they were more satisfied with life, and had better physical health.

What makes you feel younger than your age? According to Linn and Hunter, the crucial variable is *locus of control* (see Chapter 13). Those people with an internal locus of control—who felt "in charge of their lives"—were most likely to feel younger than average. Those individuals who had an "external locus of control" were more likely to view themselves as being older than average.

"Is THIS IT? Is THIS SELF-ACTUALIZATION?"

Linn and Hunter state that feeling younger than others your age may be a defense mechanism of sorts, but "may be necessary for good psychological functioning."

Life Span Development

What can we conclude from all these studies? First and foremost, that personality development thus does not end at 15, as Freud thought the case. Nor does it cease at 30, as popular wisdom sometimes insists. Rather, you seem to be capable of growth and maturity *throughout the entire span of your life*. Whether you will continue to develop, however, depends in large part on your own desire to change—and on how much your social environment encourages you to do so. That point made, let us look at theories of personality that place a greater emphasis on social potential than on biological limitations.

Humanistic Theories of Personality

Freud believed that our destinies lay in our genetic blueprints, and that we more-or-less became what nature intended us to be. To Freud, the social environment could *hinder* your personal development, but it couldn't *enhance* it all that much.

This predominantly physiological view of human nature is rejected by a group of theorists who call themselves **humanistic psychologists**. They see us as being unique, set apart, and above all other life forms. We are not mechanisms wound up and abandoned to tick out our lives as our gene-clocks dictate. Rather, we are masters of our destinies, creative individuals capable of rising above our animal heritage. According to the humanistic psychologists, we are motivated not merely to survive, but to become *better and better*. This process of continual psychological growth and improvement is what the humanistic psychologists call **self-actualization**.

There are many psychologists whose theories fall within the humanistic tradition. Of these, the best known are probably Carl Rogers and Abraham Maslow.

Table 21.2. Abraham Maslow's Whole Characteristics of Self-Actualizing People

They have more efficient perceptions of reality and are more comfortable with it.

They accept themselves and their own natures almost without thinking about it.

Their behavior is marked by simplicity and naturalness and by lack of artificiality or straining for effect.

They focus on problems outside themselves; they are concerned with basic issues and eternal questions.

They like privacy and tend to be detached.

They have relative independence of their physical and social environments; they rely on their own development and continued growth.

They do not take blessings for granted, but appreciate again and again the basic pleasures of life.

They experience limitless horizons and the intensification of any unself-conscious experience often of a mystical type.

They have a deep feeling of kinship with others.

They develop deep ties with a few other self-actualizing individuals.

They are democratic in a deep sense; although not indiscriminate, they are not really aware of differences.

They are strongly ethical, with definite moral standards, though their attitudes are conventional; they relate to ends rather than means.

Their humor is real and related to philosophy, not hostility; they are spontaneous less often than others, and tend to be more serious and thoughtful.

They are original and inventive, less constricted and fresher than others.

While they tend toward the conventional and exist well within the culture, they live by the laws of their own characters rather than those of society.

They experience imperfections and have ordinary feelings, like others.

SOURCE: Condensed from "Self-Actualizing People: A Study of Psychological Health," in *Motivation and Personality,* 2nd ed., by Abraham H. Maslow, Copyright 1954 by Harper & Row, Publishers, Inc.: Copyright © 1970 by Abraham H. Maslow. By permission of the publishers.

Carl Rogers

Carl Rogers taught for many years at the University of Chicago and at the University of Wisconsin. Rogers believes we are born with no self-concept, and no self—but we do have an innate urge to *become* fully functioning and actualized people.

At birth, all we have is a confusing set of sensory impressions, physiological processes, and motor activities. Rogers calls this sum total of our experience the **phenomenal field**. As we mature, the outside world imposes a kind of order or logic onto this field. And, as we become aware of this logic, our *self* emerges and differentiates itself from the phenomenal field. The self is thus the *conscious* portion of experience.

For Rogers, maturation is a matter of distinguishing your own body and thoughts from the objective, outside world. As you mature, your "self" begins to build up expectations about its own functioning—that is, you take on values and make judgments about your own behavior. Some of these values come from your own desires. Other values are imposed on you by the society in

Carl Rogers

which you live. Rogers believes you are most likely to run into developmental problems when society wants you to become something that conflicts with your own internal values or standards. If you yield to the demands of society too much, your psychological experience is distorted and your self-concept suffers accordingly.

According to Rogers, most of your experiences are *unconscious*—that is, below the threshold of awareness (see Chapter 10). But you can bring almost any experience above threshold if you merely give the experience a name or a label. That is, you make an unconscious experience conscious by developing *word-symbols* that allow you to describe (and hence think about) the experience. If a particular event threatens your self-concept, then you may refuse to symbolize this event in words or thoughts. But if you cannot tolerate some of your own behaviors, you will have problems achieving full actualization because you are continually hiding some of your own values or motivations from conscious expression.

When you can accept yourself completely, you become what Rogers calls a *fully functioning individual*. You are open to all experience, and you defend against nothing. You are aware of both your faults and your virtues, but you have a high positive regard for yourself. And, most of all, you maintain happy and humane relationships with others.

Abraham Maslow

Carl Rogers' theory grew out of his long-time work as a psychotherapist. Thus his theory is built in part on the study of abnormal and maladjusted individuals. To a great extent, this statement is also true of Freud's theory, and of Jung's, Adler's, and Erikson's. Abraham Maslow, on the other hand, took his ideas about human behavior from studying highly creative and psychologically *healthy* people. Some of these individuals were his personal friends. Others—such as Lincoln, Einstein, Eleanor Roosevelt, and Beethoven—he studied through books, papers, and letters. Maslow assumed these individuals had achieved a high degree of self-fulfillment or they wouldn't have been so prominent and demonstrated such leadership. By determining the similarities among the members of this noted group, he arrived at the characteristics of a truly "self-actualized" person. A list of these characteristics appears in Table 21.2.

Most psychoanalytical theories focus on what can go wrong during the developmental years. That is, they emphasize the possibility of sickness, not the probability of success. Maslow's approach is different, for he looks primarily at the *healthy side of human nature*. As we noted in Chapter 11, Maslow has created a *hierarchy of needs*, of which self-actualization is the highest. Maslow acknowledges the strength of our physiological instincts, but sees them as being "basic needs" easily satisfied in most civilized societies. But even our drives for food and sex are part of a

Phenomenal field (fee-NOM-me-nall). A phenomenon is an event, a happening, an experience. The sum total of all your experiences (sensory inputs, processings, outputs) is what Rogers calls the phenomenal field.

Lawful. In science, a law is usually an expression of a high, positive correlation between measurable inputs and outputs. A behavioral law usually states that, given a certain input, an organism will respond with a certain specific output. The more powerful the law, the better it predicts the regularities between stimuli and responses, or between inputs and outputs.

more impelling intra-psychic urge—an active "will toward health"—that drives us up the developmental ladder toward self-actualization.

Behaviorism and Social Learning Theory

Freud emphasized the *biological* underpinnings of personality development. The humanistic psychologists—including Adler—emphasize the *intra-psychic* aspects of growth and maturation. True, you need other people, and you learn from them. But, to the humanists, you can become what you want to be, not merely what your parents trained you to be.

Behavioral psychologists take quite a different approach. Generally speaking, they see personality development as being a *set of learned responses*. Thus to B.F. Skinner, you became who you are primarily because that's what your social environment *conditioned you to be*.

Skinner's Behaviorism

The most famous living behaviorist is surely B.F. Skinner, whose principles of behavior change we have mentioned several times earlier (see Chapters 5, 11, 15). And while he hasn't created a theory of child development, as Freud did, we can deduce his position rather readily.

Skinner believes that behavior is, above all else, **lawful**. By this he means that your actions (and hence your thoughts and emotional responses) are predictable because they are primarily under the control of external, measurable influences. You do not eat because you are "hungry," but rather because you have been conditioned to eat in the presence of certain environmental stimuli. Indeed, "hunger" has no meaning to Skinner because it refers to a subjective "inner state" rather than to an objective set of behaviors. To Skinner, then, your "psychic energy" comes not from dynamic forces working deep within your unconscious mind, but from external inputs.

Skinner rejects not only all intra-psychic aspects of personality development, but most biological influences as well. Innate reflexes are always *modified by experience*. Why, then, should we look at genetic dispositions when training and conditioning are much more important determinants of present behavior patterns? The "stage theories" of Freud and Piaget are useless, Skinner says. If "stages" exist at all, they reside in our cultures and not in our genes. Thus, if you wish to study personality development, you should focus entirely on how a given society trains its children. For if you change the pattern of "parenting behaviors" in a culture, Skinner believes, you will completely alter the personalities of children reared in that culture.

Skinner's views often outrage people, particularly the humanistic psychologists, who have frequently debated him in public. For, by denying the usefulness of concepts such as "consciousness" and "self," Skinner seems to make us prisoners of an environment we are incapable of changing.

Do humans have the ability to think, to plan, to scheme, to solve problems "in their minds," and thus to influence their destinies? Actually, Skinner does not deny this possibility entirely. He merely says, as we noted in Chapter 5, that we have no way as yet of measuring thinking. However, we can measure verbal behavior rather precisely. And since the complex vocal outputs that we call "human speech" are obviously learned, why do we need such vague and undefinable terms as "id" or "ego"? Do these concepts really add anything to our understanding of personality development? Or do they merely distract us from our real job—that of measuring behavioral change objectively?

Skinner's major contribution has really been in the field of technology—not in theory. Indeed, Skinner denies that he is a "theorist" in the true sense of the word. But by giving us highly effective ways of changing ourselves, and by emphasizing the importance of the external environment in "shaping" our destinies, Skinner has added much to our understanding of how humans grow and develop. However, by assuming that we make no conscious contribution to our own development, he leaves several important questions unanswered: How did the culture that shaped us develop into what it is? And if we cannot deliberately change the world around us, what forces will determine the society of the future?

One set of answers to these questions comes from **social learning theory**.

Social Learning Theory

As we noted in Chapter 15, in the 1960's the "pure" behaviorism of B.F. Skinner began to give way to "cognitive" behaviorism. For, at that time, behavioral therapists made three important discoveries. First, they found they could use Skinner's techniques to "shape" a patient's thoughts as well as the person's actions. Second, the therapists noted that patients frequently learned how to "self-shape." That is, the person could learn to use Skinnerian techniques to alter her/his own thinking and behaving "at will," without further guidance from the therapist (or anyone else). And third, many patients found ways to "shape" their external environments into helping the patients reach their own goals. All three discoveries, though, suggested that personologists could not hope to explain human development unless they looked at intra-psychic processes as well as at environmental inputs and behavioral outputs. It was this addition of cognitive psychology to behaviorism that led to the creation of *social learning theory*.

According to Skinner, your actions are *directly* controlled by external stimuli. According to social learning theorists such as Albert Bandura, the social environment "shapes" your *cognitive processes*. These intra-psychic processes, in turn, determine how you will behave. Put more simply, Skinner says you react directly to your environment *as it really is*. Bandura says that you react to your *mental constructions of reality*.

In a sense, social learning theory is an interesting mixture of Piaget and Skinner. But, whereas Piaget believed that "mental structures" were determined primarily by the genes, the social learning theorists see cognitive processes as being "shaped" the same way that Skinner says behavior is "shaped." And while Skinner says that the environment *controls* your behavior, the social learning theorists believe that you and your environment *interact*. You first *learn* to construct reality. But, as you mature and gain control over your actions, you can actually *shape your environment* so that it better meets your needs.

Social Learning Theory versus Freud

Freud said that the social environment *brings out* the ego, but *doesn't change it*. For the basic structures of the ego are determined by the genes, not by conditioning. To social learning theorists, the "self-concept" is *entirely learned* and thus varies both from person to person and from culture to culture. But once the self-concept emerges, it **mediates** social inputs and thus can change not only the person's behaviors but the person's environment as well.

Freud believed that abnormal behavior patterns were mere "symptoms" of some underlying abnormal thought process. Thus to cure the symptomatic behaviors, you had to resolve the underlying psychological conflict by giving the patient "insight" into what had caused the problem. Skinner disagreed. He said abnormal behaviors are entirely learned. Thus they can be "cured" by shaping the person to act in a normal fashion. The social learning theorists take a middle position. They see abnormal behaviors as stemming from abnormal thoughts, which were learned. Therefore, you "cure" people by helping them reshape their *cognitions*—including their "self-cognitions"—not merely by teaching them to behave in a different way.

Social Learning Theory versus Humanistic Psychology

Carl Rogers thinks it is both inhumane and immoral to "shape" a child in any way. Rather, he says, you provide a "permissive but encouraging environment" for the child, who is then free to develop in whatever manner he or she desires. Like Piaget, Rogers believes "the child is its own teacher." And should the child come into conflict with society, Rogers believes the child should place her or his needs above society's.

Social learning theorists believe that you must be taught self-control and the techniques of self-change because you have no "innate knowledge" about such matters. Refusing to give you guidance in such matters is both inhumane and counterproductive. Furthermore, you must learn to adopt a "give and take" attitude in your relations with society. For you can best meet your own needs if you help others around you achieve their own goals too.

Maslow believed the "will toward health" was built into your genes. Thus he saw no need to teach you how to achieve "self-actualization." The social learning theorists believe the "will toward health" must be learned—and they provide many effective techniques for helping you achieve "self-actualization" or any other goal you may wish to reach.

Social Learning Theory and Personality Development

In their 1981 article mentioned earlier, Nancy Cantor and John Kihlstrom state that personology is really the study of how cognitive processes are learned by each individual. Some of these processes are directly "shaped" by the society the person grows up in. But others are acquired by the continual "dynamic interplay" between the individual and the social environment.

Thus, to some extent, social learning theorists accept Piaget's description of how the child's mind grows. But there are differences in the two

Social learning theory. A marriage of Skinner's behaviorism and cognitive psychology. Social learning theorists believe that learned cognitive processes mediate behavior. These processes are acquired through reinforcement, but also through such vicarious (vy-KAR-ee-us) processes as imitation and modeling. These cognitive processes are similar to Piaget's schemata.

Mediates (ME-dee-ates). A mediator is a "go-between" who tries to achieve some agreement between two disputing parties. In psychology, your brain "mediates" your mental experiences—that is, it "goes between" inputs from the outside world and your own inner consciousness of those inputs.

Vicarious learning. If you touch a hot stove, you learn *directly* that such stimuli are painful. But if you see someone else touch the stove and shout in pain, you will have learned vicariously (through someone else's experiences) that you should avoid touching hot stoves yourself. Any time that you observe the consequences of someone's behaviors, and then change your own way of responding, you will have engaged in vicarious learning.

positions. For instance, Piaget says the child "*comes* to know" from its interactions with its environment because the child's genes guide its cognitive development through the four stages he describes. However, social learning theorists believe the child "*learns* to know" from its social interactions because the child is innately capable of acquiring new ways of thinking.

Social learning theorists accept much of what Skinner says, as well. But Cantor and Kihlstrom note two important differences between Skinner's view of development and that of social learning theorists. First, Skinner believes you learn only from *direct experience*. Social learning theorists agree that direct experience is important, but they also emphasize the usefulness of **vicarious learning**. That is, you acquire knowledge not only from "doing," but also from observing, and from imitating various "social models." Second, Skinner sees language solely as an *external behavior* that is taught by the environment. Social learning theorists agree that speech is learned. But once learned, it can be internalized. Thus you can deal with the world by manipulating verbal symbols "in your mind" as well as by speaking them out loud. Personology thus involves studying how you learn to *process informational inputs*—that is, think and reason— as well as discovering how you learn to behave.

Generally speaking, social learning theory attempts to use behavioral principles to unify all that we know about sensory processing, perception, cognition, motivation, and learning and memory. But it does so by borrowing the concept of the "self" from Freudian and humanistic psychology. Thus, to a social learning theorist, developmental psychology is really the study of how you *learned* to be you.

Judging a Theory

As we pointed out in Chapter 5, there are four main criteria for judging among scientific theories: accuracy, completeness, impressiveness, and usefulness. How do the theories we have discussed in this chapter stack up against these criteria?

Naturally, each theorist will assume that her or his theory comes out on top. Viewed more objectively, however, we can see some differences. Freudian theory is particularly rich and impressive in its detailed descriptions of how children develop. It is also much more complete than, say, humanistic psychology is. However, social learning theory seems to take more of scientific psychology into account than either the Freudian or humanistic approaches. It also does a better job of predicting future thoughts and behaviors than do the other two. Thus, in a sense, social learning theory is both the most accurate and most complete of the lot.

Psychoanalysis has had the greatest influence on literature and the arts, and that is a very impressive accomplishment indeed. However, the humanistic approach is more impressive to some people because, unlike psychoanalysis, it emphasizes achieving health rather than curing illness. But social learning theory is equally impressive because it tells you *how* to acquire healthy thoughts and actions, rather than merely assuring you that such things "are attainable."

As for usefulness, "you pays your money and your takes your choice." The different approaches have yielded quite different types of psychotherapies, and all are successful in helping some of the people some of the time. We will evaluate therapies in a later chapter. But we might note that none of them *individually* does as well as a *combination* of approaches usually can do.

Someday, perhaps, we will have a master theory that tells us everything about the human personality that we want to know—one that is *holistic* enough to give us "deep understanding" of ourselves as well as the power to predict and control our personal development. But both understanding and prediction imply that we can somehow measure what it is we are trying to comprehend and change. So it is to the *measurement* of human personality (and personality traits) that we must now turn our attention.

Summary

1. The study of **personality** is concerned with identifying the distinctive patterns of thought, behavior, and experience which characterize the individual's unique **adjustment** to his or her life situation.
2. **Personology**, or personality theory, is the scientific study of what personality is, and how it develops over an individual's **life span**.
3. Personologists attempt to **describe** consistent patterns of individual differences, **explain** why people think, feel, and behave as they do, **predict** how a person will act in the future, and **help** people change.
4. There are four major types of personality theory: **trait theory, psychoanalysis, humanistic psychology**, and **behaviorism and social learning theory**. All four have their roots in Darwin's **theory of evolution**.
5. Psychoanalytic theory began when Freud and Breuer developed **catharsis**, a means of releasing repressed **psychic energy**.
6. Freud described three "levels of consciousness," the **conscious**, the **preconscious**, and the **unconscious**.
7. Whatever is in the focus of your **attention** at any given moment is at the level of consciousness. Anything that you *could* become conscious of lies at the level of preconsciousness.
8. Those experiences or processes that you ordinarily cannot bring to consciousness—such as activity in the **emotional** and **motivational centers** of your brain—make up what Freud called the unconscious.
9. An infant is born with a set of **instincts** or **biological drives** that motivate it to live. Freud called these unconscious instincts the **id**. The energy supplied by these instincts is called the **libido**, or **life force**.
10. The id obeys the **pleasure principle**, which means it seeks immediate gratification of its needs by releasing **libidinal energy**.
11. As the infant is forced to learn to delay gratification, its **ego** or conscious self comes into being. The ego obeys the **reality principle** when it takes into account the demands of the external environment.
12. The **superego** has two parts, the stern **conscience** that reflects the demands of society, and the **ego-ideal** that contains the individual's life goals.
13. Each stage in an infant's **psychosexual development** involves a crisis. The crisis during the **oral stage** is that of birth. The infant discharges libidinal energy through such oral activities as **sucking and swallowing**.

14. During the **anal stage**, the crisis is that of learning to **delay gratification**.
15. During the **phallic stage**, boys experience an **Oedipus complex**, or desire for the mother, while girls experience an **Electra complex**, or desire for the father.
16. The **incest taboo** crises associated with the phallic stage are resolved by **repression** of sexuality as the child moves into the **latency stage**, a natural **homosexual period**.
17. The **genital stage** begins at puberty. The child resolves its incestual feelings by taking on the characteristics of the same-sex parent. It also begins to hunt for a **life style**, or ego-ideal, which involves discharging libido through **heterosexual activities**.
18. The ego **mediates** between the demands of the id, superego, and reality by trying to control the release of libidinal energy. The ego experiences **signal anxiety** whenever these demands are not being properly met.
19. The ego protects itself from **trauma** by using **defense mechanisms** such as **repression, regression, identification, denial, reaction formation, projection, rationalization, displacement**, and **sublimation**.
20. Carl Jung believed we are more motivated by **moral** and **spiritual** values than by primitive sexuality.
21. According to Jung, we have two different types of unconscious: The **personal unconscious**, which contains our own individual memories, and the **collective unconscious**, which houses our **archetypes**, or racial memories.
22. Jung believed we have two **innate attitudes**, which he called **introversion** and **extroversion**.
23. Alfred Adler believed the **social environment** was more important in determining personality than the genetic blueprint. He saw life as a struggle to achieve **superiority**, a drive to achieve self-realization. We may **compensate** for an **inferiority complex** by trying to become superior in other ways.
24. Erik Erikson extended Freud's **psychosexual stages** to include the mature years.
25. According to Erikson, every human must pass through eight **developmental stages**, each of which is characterized by its own type of **crisis** or test of a person's character.
26. The **humanistic psychologists** reject most psychoanalytic concepts, emphasizing instead the drive for **self-actualization**.
27. Carl Rogers believes that a **fully adjusted person** can symbolize any experience in conscious verbalizations.
28. Abraham Maslow sees humans as having an innately determined **will toward health**.
29. **Behaviorists** such as B.F. Skinner believe that personality is entirely **learned** by direct experience with the **external environment**. Skinner rejects **thoughts, feelings**, and **motives** because they are not directly measurable. He states that observable behavior is **lawful** and hence predictable.
30. **Social learning theorists** such as Albert Bandura believe that behavior is learned, but that it is mediated by **cognitive processes**. Personality development is thus the study of how people use **vicarious learning** and **social models** to **construct reality** in their minds, and how they employ these constructs to change themselves and their environments.
31. All types of personality theories have contributed to our ability to understand and predict human experience, but no theory is complete in itself.

(Continued from page 479.)

The afternoon sun angled sharply down through the towering mountains onto the waters of Lake Como. Bellagio, on the eastern shore, was bathed in golden light. Cadennabia, just a mile or so directly across the water, had already slipped into twilight. A water taxi buzzing toward Bellagio dipped and tossed in the breeze, its passengers clinging tightly to their seats as the boat plunged through the rough water. And, although the three scientists sitting safely on the terrace of the Villa d'Este didn't know it, they too were about to experience rather a rough passage on their journey toward peace and understanding.

"As I mentioned earlier, I have hope," said Donald M. Papas, the Canadian psychologist. "That is why I agreed to the Foundation's request to lead this First International Symposium on Peace and Personality. And that is why I invited you,

Jonathan, a behaviorist, and you, Joyce, an Ego Psychologist, and ten other personality theorists to come to the conference."

"You really hope to end war throughout the world?" Fraser asked.

"No, I hope to end war throughout psychology. Or, at least, within the field of personality theory."

"An armed truce is about all you can expect of us," Joyce Sapir said.

"I'll settle for that, as a first approximation. I know it's idealistic of me, but I rather hoped that if I could get you all together, talking and listening to each other, we might make some headway."

"Who listens at these conferences?" asked Fraser.

"It depends on who talks," Papas continued. "All of you really have a lot in common—including your individual desires to help people live more peaceful, productive lives."

"To help people achieve self-actualization, you mean," said Joyce Sapir.

"You mean, to help people achieve voluntary self-control over their behavioral outputs," said Fraser.

"There, you see, you're saying almost the same thing, but in different words. It's your language that is at the heart of the problem."

Fraser smiled. "George Bernard Shaw once said that the US and Britain are separated by a common language."

"Exactly!" continued Papas. "In Joyce Sapir's terms, self-actualization means learning enough about your unconscious sensual desires so that you can handle them consciously. Skinner would say that physiological rewards such as food and sex are so strong that we can condition an organism to accept social rewards by pairing praise with food. If you pat a dog on the head each time you give it food, eventually it will find the affection as rewarding as a piece of meat. But isn't that what Freud really meant when he said that a young boy in the latent period learns to act like his father because his mother is more affectionate to him when he does?"

"But humans have an innate need for affection," Joyce Sapir insisted.

"And so do monkeys," responded Fraser. "No, my dear friend, what our sneaky Canadian friend seems to be saying is this—ego psychologists focus on innate needs. You measure these needs indirectly, by asking people how they feel."

"Of course," said the woman.

Fraser nodded. "But you get so involved in hunting for hidden meanings in their verbal responses that you forget verbal responses can serve as *reinforcers*. And reinforcers can be studied objectively. When you praise me, I listen. When you criticize me, I say something nasty in return. It doesn't matter whether or not you *intended* to reward me or punish me, that's the way I react. You analysts measure the unconscious *intent* of the speaker. We behaviorists measure the speaker's *actual* effect on the listener's behavior."

"I see," Joyce Sapir said. "You behaviorists focus on satisfiers instead of needs, because you can *see* environmental inputs. But since you can't measure internal needs or intentions directly, you assume that they just aren't there."

"You're doing beautifully, both of you," Papas said. "But now, let's go a step farther. Skinner defines a reward as anything that increases response rates. He never asks *why* reward has this effect—it just does. And so Skinner studies *how* rewards work. The psychoanalysts and the humanists—like the physiological psychologists—are interested in *why*. But, as the behaviorists learned long ago, insight into the 'whys' of your own motives doesn't necessarily tell you 'how' to change your thoughts and actions and hence achieve inner peace and self-actualization."

Joyce Sapir shook her head sadly. "But knowing 'how' doesn't tell you a thing about *why* people have personal difficulties."

Papas nodded. "True, but to help people best, you have to give them both insight *and* feedback on how well they're doing. Many behavior modifiers will tell you that the person with psychological problems is often the person who ignores feedback. If you can get people to chart their growth or development, they find any positive change in the graph very rewarding indeed."

Joyce Sapir mused a moment, then responded. "Carl Rogers said that we get into trouble when our 'self' or ego loses touch with our biological organism. But if the therapist reflects back to a man what he is really like—if the therapist acts like a mirror—then the person can define himself and, in the process, achieve growth and understanding."

Fraser shook his head in mock dismay. "Don, are you suggesting that Rogers and Skinner were saying almost the same thing?"

"Well, if reflecting back to a man what he's really like isn't giving feedback, I don't know what is," Papas responded. "Rogers says that the feedback should be emotionally neutral, but he calls it 'unconditional *positive* regard.' That sounds suspiciously like positive reinforcement to me."

Joyce Sapir smiled. "And Carl Rogers is one of the most charming, encouraging therapists I've ever met. He almost never has a bad word to say about anyone—except about Skinner, of course."

"Perhaps if Rogers had given Skinner a bit more 'unconditional positive regard,' and Skinner had rewarded Rogers instead of criticizing him, their famous debates would have had a different outcome," Papas said quietly.

"And not nearly as bloody much fun," remarked Fraser. "Don, are you by any chance suggesting that psychologists don't always practice what they preach?"

Papas smiled slyly. "No, merely that we sometimes don't see the forest for the trees. Psychoanalytic theory is a single-minded way of looking at humans—from the inside out. Behaviorism operates from a different point of view—from the outside in. We can't give up one or the other, any more than we can give up either the forests or the trees."

"I can give up psychoanalysis any time I try really hard," Fraser said.

"No, you can't. For the analysts and humanists have identified some very potent reward systems that you really ought to look into," Papas responded.

"But surely some of the personality theorists have come close to achieving a completely integrated theory of human nature," Joyce Sapir protested.

"Sorry, but I can't agree," Papas said. "Freud probably came the closest, but like all the rest, he failed. A complete theory would have to take into account both the physical and psychological aspects of human sensations and perceptions, cognitions and altered states of consciousness, synapses and transmitters, social roles and developmental sequences, needs and motives, rewards and punishments, muscle twitches and ego, instincts and the biochemical basis of learning, memories and forgettings, and even the over-riding urge to achieve self-actualization. And the theory would have to handle all these different viewpoints and levels of analysis in a series of simultaneous equations. I doubt it can be done. But perhaps we *can* build a verbal bridge that will allow us to go back and forth from one level or viewpoint to another. That's what I hope we can do at the Symposium—if I can get all of you to stop carping at each other and use unconditional positive regard instead."

Fraser seemed amused. "Your Bridge of Heavenly Peace will never get off the ground. Carping at each other is far too rewarding!"

"I agree," Joyce Sapir said, smiling. "In my own experience, the need to carp is a basic oral urge, and we all know that professors are uniformly fixated at the oral stage of development. Besides," she added in mock horror, "building a bridge between psychoanalysis and behaviorism would be as senseless as building a bridge across Lake Como, from Cadennabia to Bellagio. Why, it would ruin the view!"

"And put all those water taxis out of business!" Fraser said, turning to watch the little boat as it tossed about in the center of the lake.

"But you'd have fewer seasick passengers to worry about," Papas continued.

Joyce Sapir favored Jonathan Fraser with a smile. "I'd say that our Canadian colleague is as optimistic as Adler and the humanists. How would you say it, Jonathan?"

The British scientist smiled back. "Joyce, I'd simply say that hope springs eternal."

"In the heart of a fool," said Papas, lifting his glass in a toast. "To bridges!"

Recommended Readings

Cantor, Nancy, and John F. Kihlstrom. "Cognitive and Social Processes in Personality: Implications for Behavior Therapy," in C.M. Franks and G.T. Wilson, eds., *Handbook of Behavior Therapy* (New York: Guilford Press, 1981).

Forgus, Ronald, and Bernard H. Shulman. *Personality: A Cognitive View* (Englewood Cliffs, N.J.: Prentice-Hall, 1979).

Gardner, Howard. *Developmental Psychology: An Introduction* (Boston: Little, Brown, 1978).

Jaffe, Aniela, ed. *C.G. Jung: Word and Image* (Princeton, N.J.: Princeton University Press, 1979).

Poon, Leonard W., James L. Fozard, Laird S. Cermak, David Arenberg, and L.W. Thompson, eds. *New Directions in Memory and Aging: Proceedings of the George A. Talland Memorial Conference* (Hillsdale, N.J.: Erlbaum, 1980).

Schafer, Roy. *Language and Insight: The Sigmund Freud Memorial Lectures 1975–1976, University College London* (New Haven, Conn.: Yale University Press, 1978).

Veroff, Joseph, and Joanne B. Veroff. *Social Incentives: A Life-Span Developmental Approach* (New York: Academic Press, 1980).

Personality Tests 22

Did You Know That . . .

The Greek scientist Galen thought your personality was determined primarily by your heart, lungs, and liver?

Harvard psychologist W.H. Sheldon said your personality was determined primarily by the shape of your body?

The first real intelligence test measured "mental age," and was developed by two French scientists?

IQ tests predict academic performance reasonably well, but don't do a very good job of predicting success in later life?

Raymond Cattell believes you have both "fluid" intelligence and "crystallized" intelligence?

Several psychologists have shown that you can sometimes raise your own IQ by taking special training?

Studies show that racial differences on intelligence tests are due primarily to cultural backgrounds and test bias rather than to genes?

Hermann Rorschach believed you would "project your personality" onto vague stimuli such as inkblots?

"Measure for Measure"

"What is this 'Late Bloomer' test of yours, Mr. Flagg? I don't think I've ever heard of it," Jessie Williams said quietly. Tom Flagg had an athlete's physique, a handsome dark-brown face, and a ready smile. But Jessie had learned the hard way that she couldn't always tell the shape of a man's intentions from the shape of his physique. So she was wary of this young graduate student who had just walked into her fourth-grade school room. But she was also quite taken by his appearance.

"The 'Late Bloomer' test was devised by Professor Rosenthal at Harvard," Tom Flagg replied, hoping (for several reasons) to overcome the good-looking young black woman's obvious distrust. "You've been teaching fourth grade for several years, haven't you, Miss Williams?"

"Three years, Mr. Flagg. Exactly three years."

Tom grinned at the woman's precise way of expressing herself. "Well, maybe you've had a kid who seemed real dumb the first few months or so of school. Then, all of a sudden, the kid just took off and bloomed. Like a flower you'd forgotten to water until just then."

"I water all my flowers regularly, Mr. Flagg," Jessie replied. "I don't neglect any of them. Black or white, red or yellow—I hope they all bloom for me as much as they can."

Tom nodded appreciatively. If it wouldn't have prejudiced the results of his experiment, he would have tried to date her. He pulled himself together and resumed the conversation. "Mr. Washington, your principal, told me you were one of the best teachers he's ever seen. So I'm sure all your kids do learn a lot. But aren't you occasionally surprised when one of them does a lot better than you had expected?"

Jessie Williams shook her head. "I expect great things of them all. Maybe that's why I'm not surprised when they do well."

"Okay, said Tom, "I guess my test won't help you any. But maybe you can help me out by letting me give it to your class anyhow. If I don't get to try out the test in enough classrooms, I won't get a good grade on my project back at the university. Even if you don't need the information, I do."

To his surprise, Jessie smiled broadly. "Well, why didn't you say so, friend? I'm always happy to help one of us get ahead. Tell me about these 'Late Bloomers' of Professor Rosenthal's."

"Well, it's really your bloomers I'm interested in," Tom said, and then blushed furiously as he realized what he had said. "I mean, it's a test devised by Professor Rosenthal and his associates at Harvard. They think they've found a way of telling in advance when a school kid is going to show a sudden spurt in intellectual achievement. Rosenthal says the test can also tell when a kid is going to backslide or tread water for a while. The change usually shows up in the kid's grades, although sometimes the IQ blossoms or backslides too."

"Some of our education books say that a child's intelligence is fixed at birth. Don't you believe that's so, Tom?" Jessie asked, a malicious twinkle in her eye.

Tom looked startled. "Well, I suppose that the limits to a person's mind are determined by the genes. But the rate at which people develop intellectually sure varies a lot. And the IQ score you get depends as much on which test you take, who gives it, and how you feel when you take it as it does on how bright you really are. Have you ever given any of your kids intelligence tests?"

"No, Tom. I'm not qualified to do that. I give achievement tests, but the school counselor tests their intelligence."

"But aren't you sometimes surprised at the scores the counselor reports on your kids?"

Jessie Williams smiled slyly. "I just don't pay them any mind."

"What do you do when the parents want to know what the kid's IQ is?"

"I tell them the story of my life, Tom," she said. "I was born in Mississippi, where my father was a tenant farmer. We moved North when I was 6. My first year in school they gave me a test and said my IQ was 87. As you know, that's what you might call 'dull normal.' You just don't learn very much about the world on a tenant farm in the back woods of Mississippi. But I loved school, and I had good teachers, and when I was in the seventh grade, I took another test. This time I got a score of 98. The counselor couldn't understand the change. So he gave me a different test, and I scored 104. He asked me what I wanted to do, and I said go to college and learn how to teach. He told me to forget it, that I'd never make it."

"But you did," Tom said, smiling to reassure her.

"Yes, I did," she said, a strong tone of confidence in her voice. "In high school they gave me another test. This time I tried very hard to impress the woman giving me the test, and I got a score of 111."

"The 'halo effect,' probably," Tom responded. "Good-looking, eager children always score a little higher than uglies do because the tester gives them the benefit of the doubt. And I suspect you were very good looking indeed."

"You needn't flatter me, friend. I've already agreed to help you with your study. Anyway, the counselor said I might just get through college if I worked very hard, although you're supposed to have an IQ of 120 to graduate."

"So you went to the university and got your degree anyhow?"

"No, Tom, it wasn't that easy. My high school grades were excellent but I didn't score too well on the college entrance examination. The university didn't want me. So I went to a community college for two years. I got all A's, and the university finally let me in. My last year there, I took another IQ test. This time I got a score of 122." She paused for a moment, then laughed. "But, of course, by then I knew the kinds of answers they wanted on the test."

Tom shook his head in amazement. His route to the university had been quite different. "And that's why you don't tell the parents what their kids' IQ's are?"

"Right on. Now suppose you tell me what your study is all about."

"Okay," he said. "I'll give the Rosenthal 'Late Bloomer' test to all the kids in your room. When I've scored the results, I'll tell you which kids are supposed to 'bloom,' and which kids are supposed to backslide. Then, six months from now, I'll come back and see if that's what really happened."

A suspicious look crept into Jessie's eyes. "Why are you doing this, Tom? Doesn't sound much like an experiment to me."

"Rosenthal validated the test mostly in white classrooms. I want to see if it predicts for integrated classes as well."

"And you'll come back in six months to see what happened?"

Tom Flagg squared his shoulders a bit. "Well, your class is so important to me, I might just drop around a little more often than that—just to see how things are going."

She favored him with a broad grin. "You do that, Thomas. You do that very thing."

(Continued on page 529.)

Trait Theory

As we noted in the last chapter, Francis Galton was interested in **eugenics**—the "science of improving the human race." He thought the best way to help humanity was to get people who had superior traits to have more children. But he ran into a few difficulties when he tried to get people interested in his project.

Galton's first problem was that of identifying those psychological traits that were somehow **correlated** with "superiority." His second problem was that of finding ways to *measure* these traits. By the time he had solved both of these difficulties to his satisfaction, he had:

1. devised the first intelligence test
2. made the first scientific study of individual differences
3. proven that childhood experiences have an effect on adult thinking
4. developed the first psychological questionnaire
5. undertaken the first behavioral study of human twins
6. helped establish the use of fingerprints to identify people
7. made the first use of statistical correlations in a psychological study
8. written the first book on eugenics
9. measured the sensory and motor capabilities of almost 10,000 people.

Rather an impressive set of accomplishments, even for a man whose IQ was probably about 200. However, Galton's major contribution to **trait theory** surely came from his detailed studies of individual differences.

Individual Differences and Similarities

Galton published his first book on trait theory in 1869. Called *Hereditary Genius*, it was an attempt to prove that intelligence and creativity tend to "run in families." What Galton actually did, of course, was to show that children are more similar to their parents than they are to a random sample of unrelated individuals. And twins are more like each other than they are to distant cousins. Thus trait theory—as defined by Galton and most other psychologists—is partially the study of human *similarities*.

But even twins will differ in many ways. If they are both musicians, one twin may have a

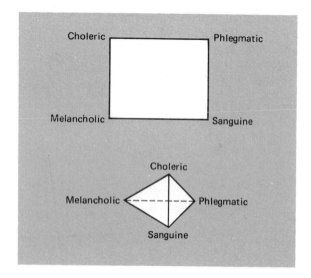

Francis Galton   Galen

Fig. 22.1. Top, Galen's personality traits; **bottom,** Galen's personality pyramid.

finer sense of rhythm than does the other. So trait theory also concerns itself with the study of individual *differences*—what they are, and where they come from.

Galton defined traits as *measurable* and *consistent* patterns of human performance and character. And he assumed that traits were inherited and thus couldn't be altered to any significant degree. Earlier personality theorists tended to agree that traits were inherited, but defined them in quite different ways. Thus even trait theorists have their similarities and differences.

Let's discuss the historical background of trait theory first, and then see what part it plays in modern psychology.

Galen's Humor Theory

Galen was one of the greatest medical doctors the world has known. Although he was born and educated in Greece a century or so after the death of Christ, Galen spent much of his adult life practicing medicine in Rome. His studies of the functioning of human and animal bodies were so excellent that he is often considered the father of modern physiology.

One of Galen's main interests was the various glands in the human body, and the chemicals these glands secreted. Like most other physicians 2,000 years ago, Galen called these glandular secretions the **humors** of the body. Borrowing a notion from the famous Greek physician **Hippocrates**, Galen stated that four of these humors were mainly responsible for human personality.

As far as Galen was concerned, blood was a "humor." If a woman was most influenced by her blood, Galen called her a **sanguine** or "bloody"

person. Sanguine people were supposed to be cheerful, hearty, outgoing, sturdy, fearless, optimistic, and interested in physical pleasures.

The second humor was *phlegm*, the thick, white material that you sometimes cough up when you have a cold. From Galen's point of view, phelgm was cold, moist, and unmoving. If your bodily processes were dominated by too much production of phlegm, you became **phlegmatic**— cold, aloof, calm, detached, unemotional, uninvolved, quiet, withdrawn, dependable, and perhaps just a trifle dull.

Galen believed that the human liver produced two different "humors"—yellow bile and black bile. He called the yellow bile *choler*, because it supposedly caused the disease we now refer to as "cholera." The **choleric** personality was one easily given to anger, hate, and fits of temper—someone who gave in to most of his or her bad impulses.

Black bile was even worse, for it symbolized death in Galen's mind. If your personality was dominated by black bile, you were **melancholic**— that is, you were always depressed, unhappy, suicidal.

To Galen, your biochemistry determined your personality type, and your type determined your traits. It is unclear from Galen's writings whether he thought you had to be entirely one type or the other, or whether you could be a mixture of the four. Assuming mixed personality types were allowed, Galen's scheme might be represented as shown in Fig. 22.1.

As "humorous" as Galen's theory may seem to you, it still lives on today. One of the dominant psychiatric beliefs about mental illness is that abnormal *behavior* is almost always caused by some abnormal *chemical imbalance*. Thus a great many psychiatrists today treat mental illness just as Galen tried to—by giving patients pills that will change their inner chemicals and hence presumably will "cure" their unusual thoughts and behaviors.

Sheldon's Theory of Body Types

The belief that people with certain types of *body structure* are predisposed to have specific *personality structures* has been around a long time. For instance, in one of his most famous plays, William Shakespeare has Julius Caesar say, "Let me have men about that are fat; sleek-headed men and such as sleep o'nights. Yon Cassius has a lean and hungry look; He thinks too much; such men are dangerous." Only in recent days, however, have scientists offered much in the way of *experimental* proof that there might be a correlation between the shape of your body and the structure of your personality.

Around 1940, Harvard scientist W.H. Sheldon stated that there were three major **morphologies**, or body types:

1. the **endomorphs**, who had soft, rounded bodies and big stomachs
2. the **mesomorphs**, who had hard, square, bony bodies with over-developed muscles
3. the **ectomorphs**, who had tall, thin bodies with over-developed heads

Sheldon took these terms from reproductive biology. As you may recall from Chapter 18, shortly after a child is conceived, the growing

Eugenics (you-JEN-icks). From the Greek words meaning "good genes." Literally, the scientific study of the hereditary characteristics of various races.

Correlated (KORR-re-lay-ted). A statistical measure of association, or relatedness. Two variables are correlated if one predicts the other fairly well. Grade point averages and IQ's are correlated because people who get a high GPA tend to have high IQ's. See Statistical Appendix.

Trait theory. The belief that human behavior is determined primarily by underlying or basic personality factors, such as intelligence, reaction time, ability to perceive patterns, and so forth. Most trait theorists believe that these underlying factors are primarily inherited.

Humors (YOU-mors). The Latin word *humor* means "moist, wet, liquid." Galen (GAY-lun) believed that your personality was determined by the fluids secreted by your body. When you were in "good humor," you had good fluids bubbling around inside you.

Hippocrates (hip-POCK-krat-tease). Often called "the father of medicine," Hippocrates lived about 400 years prior to the birth of Christ. Although the best-known physician of his time, and although he wrote the Hippocratic Oath that medical doctors still take when granted their degrees, he made surprisingly little impact on medical science until long after he died (Plato mentions him but twice, Aristotle but once).

Sanguine (SAN-gwin). From the Latin word *sanguis*, meaning "blood." Someone who hopes for the best, or is confidently optimistic, is a sanguine person.

Phlegmatic (fleg-MATT-tick). A watery, slow, unemotional person.

Choleric (KAHL-urr-ick, or koh-LAIR-ick). From the Greek word meaning "bile." Someone readily given to anger, or to losing her or his "good humor."

Melancholic (mell-ann-KOLL-ic). The Greek word *melan* means "black." Melanin (MELL-ann-inn) is the pigment in your skin that darkens when you get a suntan. Melan-choler is black bile. A melancholic individual is someone who is perpetually sad, unhappy, depressed.

Morphologies (more-FOLL-oh-gees). The Greek word *morph* means "shape" or "form." Morphology is the study of biological forms, shapes, or body types. The word also means the structure or form of something, such as the human body.

Endomorphs, mesomorphs, ectomorphs (EN-doh, MEE-zoh, ECK-toh-morffs). Sheldon's three morphologies, or body types, that presumably determine personality traits.

"You did very well on your I.Q. test. You're a man of 49 with the intelligence of a man of 53."

mass of cells develops three distinct layers. The inner layer, called the endoderm or "inner skin," develops into the digestive system and internal organs. The middle layer—the mesoderm or "middle skin"—turns into bone and muscles. The outer layer, or ectoderm, becomes the central nervous system. According to Sheldon, your genetic blueprint usually causes one of these three layers to become predominant—that is, to develop more rapidly and fully than the other two layers:

1. If your endoderm becomes dominant, you develop a roly-poly body and fixate on food. You become very social, enjoy relaxing and lazing about, you talk a lot, and you prefer the "sweet life" of physical comfort.

Gordon Allport

Raymond Cattell

Alfred Binet

Lewis Terman

2. If your mesoderm gains the upper hand during your fetal development, you will have a square, heavy, mesomorphic body. You will be energetic and assertive, courageous and sanguine, and will like sports and power.
3. If your ectoderm comes out on top, your brain will predominate and your body will develop long, thin legs and arms—and a big head. You will be introverted, inhibited, intellectual, and prefer being alone to being in a crowd.

Sheldon's Seven-Point Scales

To test his theory, Sheldon made comparisons of the photographs of 4,000 male college students. He found that most of his subjects were not "pure" body types, however, but mixtures. So he devised seven-point scales for each of the three morphologies and gave numerical ratings to people on each of the three scales. Next he made up a large list of personality traits for each of his three body types. Finally, he interviewed 200 university men to see if their personality traits and body types were associated with each other.

Sheldon reported that sociability was highly correlated with endomorphism, as were 19 other traits. Extroversion was one of 20 traits correlated with mesomorphism, while restraint and passivity were 2 of the 20 traits that were found to a high degree in ectomorphs. Other investigators have found similar but less impressive correlations between behavior patterns and body structure, or type.

Criticisms of Sheldon's Theory

Although Sheldon's findings were confirmed to some extent by other scientists, many questions have been raised about his research. To begin with, he did not really consider the age of his subjects, nor whether they had grown up in poverty or wealth. You may recall from Chapter 18 that Korean war orphans who were reared in the US

were considerably larger and taller than their age-mates who remained behind in Korea in deprived circumstances (it's hard to be a fat, jolly endomorph if you've been starved all your life).

Second, Sheldon never could offer any reasonable explanation of *why* or *how* your body type influenced your thoughts, feelings, and behaviors.

Third, Sheldon didn't employ "blind" testing techniques in his studies to guard against *experimenter bias*. That is, Sheldon rated the body types of his subjects *himself* and also scored their interviews. His findings would be much more impressive had the interviews been judged by someone who was "blind" to what the subjects' body type supposedly was.

Whether or not the *structure* of your body determines your personality remains an open question. However, the scientific evidence gathered so far gives little support to the notion that body type determines psychological traits.

Allport's Theory of Traits

Galton believed that the past determined the present and future. Once you had acquired a trait, therefore, it would last all your life. Galton also believed in the importance of *unconscious processes*. In one of his studies, he tried to give "free associations" to various words, and timed how long it took for him to do so. He found that many of his associations came from his younger years. This finding suggested to him that childhood experiences he was normally unconscious of had a large influence on his thinking as an adult. To Galton, then, your genes and your early experiences were the major determinants of your present and future.

Harvard psychologist Gordon Allport disagreed with Galton's position. Allport believed that the most important traits might be those that look to the future rather than to the past. Like many other humanistic psychologists, Allport saw people as being motivated primarily by the desire to *become*—that is, to change and grow. Allport believed that *conscious* desires control behavior more than do unconscious wishes or instincts. He also said that your values, hopes, goals, and aspirations were more reliable predictors of future experiences than were "mental associations" and the sorts of motor skills that Galton measured in his subjects. For Allport, the important traits were those that *motivated* you. For these tendencies not only provided the structure of your present personality, they guided the destiny of your future as well.

Individual and Common Traits

Allport identified several classes of traits. To begin with, he pointed out the difference between *individual* and *common* traits. No two people are exactly alike. Therefore, all traits are individual and unique. But because all humans have similar genetic heritages, and because our cultures are all fairly similar, our behavior patterns are roughly comparable. All blonds are different, for example, because they are unique individuals. But they do all have light-colored hair. Thus we can talk about "blondness" as long as we remember that the differences among blonds are as important as their similarities.

Cardinal, Central, and Secondary Traits

Within a given individual, Allport said, there are *cardinal*, *central*, and *secondary* traits. If you had just one goal in life—perhaps to make a million dollars—that would be a "cardinal" trait. More common are "central" traits—those few, important values or interest patterns that seem to color almost everything you do. Allport believed that most people have between two and ten central traits. For instance, the noted science fiction writer, H.G. Wells, once said that there were but two themes (central traits) to his life—his interest in promoting world government, and his preoccupation with sex.

According to Allport, cardinal and central traits determine your major motives in life, and thus indicate the sort of person you will *become*. "Secondary" traits are those incidental, learned responses that differ markedly from one person to another—such as a preference for Chinese food, or a strong dislike of crowds.

Criticisms of Allport's Approach

Although Allport has had a great influence on modern trait theory, his approach has often been criticized. The first—and perhaps most important—problem with his theory is that of *consistency*. Presumably, if you have a trait, it should express itself all the time. Yet research shows that people for whom honesty is a cardinal trait will, when under great stress, lie or steal. Indeed, there is *no* trait that seems to affect all behavior in all situations. Allport handles this criticism by noting that traits *interact* with each other, and thus aren't absolutes at all. They predict "typical" behavior patterns, not what you will do in extreme conditions. The fact remains, however, that Allport (like Galton) neglected the importance of the environment in determining thoughts and behaviors.

A second criticism of Allport's approach has to do with the *number* of traits that are needed to explain human behavior. Allport believed that there were perhaps as many as 5,000 traits. Current estimates run as high as 20,000. If the goal of personology is to describe people in fairly simple terms, how can we possibly deal with a list of 20,000 traits, particularly when each trait presumably interacts with all others in unmeasurable ways? One solution to this problem has been offered by Raymond Cattell.

Cattell's Factor Analytic Approach

Raymond Cattell reduced the thousands of traits that Allport had listed to a mere 16. He did this by using a complex statistical technique called **factor analysis**—and by making certain assumptions about human behavior.

Surface Traits and Source Traits

Cattell's first assumption was that there are just a few "common factors" underlying all the traits other scientists had described. And his research soon suggested that many of the traits *clustered together*. From observing people, and from looking at the results of tests he gave his subjects, Cattell identified about 35 of these "trait clusters." To Cattell, though, these were mere "surface" expressions of more fundamental personality patterns. Cattell thus called these 35 clusters of related behaviors *surface traits*.

Factor analysis A statistical device that presumably lets you discover the "underlying factors" that account for correlations or other relationships between variables. Your grade point average is highly correlated with the score that you get on an intelligence test. But a high GPA doesn't *cause* a high IQ, or vice versa. Rather, the underlying factor of *intelligence* presumably accounts for both your grades and your IQ. Factor analysis is one way of trying to determine what basic traits account for a variety of related behaviors.

Table 22.1.	The Sixteen Factors of Personality

1. Schizothymia (aloof, cold) vs. Cyclothymia (warm, sociable)
2. Dull (low intellectual capacity) vs. Bright (intelligent)
3. Low Ego Strength (emotional, unstable) vs. High Ego Strength (mature, calm)
4. Submissiveness (mild) vs. Dominance (aggressive)
5. Desurgency (glum, silent) vs. Surgency (enthusiastic, talkative)
6. Low Superego Strength (casual, undependable) vs. High Superego Strength (conscientious, persistent)
7. Threctia (timid, shy) vs. Parmia (adventurous, thick-skinned)
8. Harria (tough, realistic) vs. Premsia (sensitive, effeminate)
9. Inner Relaxation (trustful, adaptable) vs. Protension (suspecting, jealous)
10. Praxernia (conventional, practical) vs. Autia (Bohemian, unconcerned)
11. Naivete (simple, awkward) vs. Shrewdness (sophisticated, polished)
12. Confidence (unshakable) vs. Timidity (insecure, anxious)
13. Conservatism (accepting) vs. Radicalism (experimenting, critical)
14. Group Dependence (imitative) vs. Self-Sufficiency (resourceful)
15. Low Integration (lax, unsure) vs. Self-Sentiment Control (controlled, exact)
16. Low Ergic Tension (phlegmatic, composed) vs. High Ergic Tension (tense, excitable)

Source: Reprinted from *Personality Theories: A Comparative Analysis* by S. R. Maddi, by permission of Dorsey Press. Copyright © 1973 by Dorsey Press.

Once he had identified this limited number of "trait clusters," Cattell tried to *factor out* the basic relationships among the surface traits. He ended up with a list of 16 factors that he called *source traits*. To Cattell, these 16 source traits are the dimensions by which everyone's personality structure can be measured.

All 16 of Cattell's source traits are *bi-polar*, which is to say that each trait has two extremes, such as "warm-cold," "bright-dull," and "relaxed-tense" (see Table 22.1). Cattell then devised a test which he believed would measure each person's location on all 16 of the source traits. Cattell believed that your scores on this test described your "source traits" in objective, measurable terms. But to paint a complete picture of your personality, he needed additional information.

Criticisms of Cattell's Theory

Cattell took his data about human behavior from three sources: (1) from records of people's lives, and from reports by friends and relatives; (2) from asking people what they thought they were like; and (3) from scores on objective tests such as his "16 Personality Factors Test." Only by analyzing all three types of data, Cattell said, could you give a complete description of an individual's personality and hence *predict* what the person would do in the future.

Cattell's is surely the most comprehensive approach to the study of human traits. But his theory suffers from the same difficulties that all trait or type theories suffer from. First, he assumed your thoughts and behaviors are determined almost entirely by the structure of your personality. However, as we noted earlier, people tend to be more responsive to present environmental inputs than trait theorists assume is the case.

Second, Cattell relied rather heavily on self-reports. But as we will see in future chapters, there is often a great difference between what you *say* your response will be in a given situation and how you *actually behave* when you face that situation in real life. Thus test scores and interviews often do a very poor job of predicting future responses.

Third, Cattell focused almost entirely on adult traits. Although he said that traits were partially learned and partially hereditary, he gave no indication of how traits developed during the early years of life.

Despite these criticisms, however, Cattell and the other trait theorists have had a tremendous influence on the field of *mental measurement*. Since the 1880's, when Galton developed a crude way of measuring individual differences, the use of psychological tests has grown enormously. A majority of these tests spring directly from the assumptions underlying trait theory. So let us continue our study of personality by seeing what some of these tests are like, and how well they "measure up" to what we already know about human behavior.

Measuring Traits

Technically speaking, a trait is a tendency or predisposition to respond to many different stimuli or situations in the same way. If you are kind to almost all of the different people you meet, then you possess the trait of kindness. If you are good at solving all kinds of different problems, and if you adapt rapidly to all types of environmental challenges, then you possess what Cattell called the "source trait" of intelligence.

If we wanted to get an exact *measure* of your kindness, we might dream up a test for this trait—a "kindness scale"—that had 100 questions on it. We could ask things like, "If you saw an injured puppy lying by the side of the road, would you pick it up and take it to the doctor's or just ignore it?" Or, "Do you prefer to pat a person on the back, or kick the person in the seat of the pants?" If the test were a good one, then people who were kind *in real life* would get high scores, while people who were unkind *in real life* would get low test scores. Thus just by knowing a person's score on the "kindness test," you could *predict* the person's behavior in many situations.

Question: What numerical score should the average person get on a 100-point "kindness test"?

Intelligence Tests

Traits such as kindness can be fairly easily measured—provided we can define the trait, and as long as we recognize that kindness might mean one thing in our culture, but something radically different elsewhere in the world.

But what about *intelligence*? How could we go about defining—and measuring—such a complex variable as this? Indeed, is intelligence really a *trait*? Cattell lists it as one of his 16 "source traits," as do other theorists. But not all psychologists would agree, believing that "intelligence" is a *combination* of a great many innate predispositions and learned behaviors. Whatever the case, trait theory got its start when Galton began searching for a way to measure "intellectual superiority." And the crude "intelligence test" he developed helped get the *mental measurement movement* going. So suppose we now look at length at intelligence tests.

Galton's Research

Galton had no clear idea (at least in modern terms) of what intelligence was. But he assumed it had something to do with *processing and reacting to sensory inputs*. So one of the first things he did was to measure how rapidly people could respond to various stimuli. Unfortunately, people

Alfred Binet (bee-NAY). Binet (1857–1911) was a French psychologist who, with Thèophile Simon, developed the first well-known intelligence test.

who were obviously quite intelligent often had slow reaction times, and individuals who were apparently not-so-bright sometimes responded very swiftly. Thus *reaction time* seemingly wasn't a very accurate index of intelligence.

Galton also studied "mental imagery" by asking people to "conjure up a mental picture" of a familiar setting, such as their dinner table. He then scored their responses on a scale from 0 to 100 in terms of how clearly they saw things, how colorful their images were, and so forth. He found rather large differences among individuals in their ability to "see" such things in their minds. First, women and children seemed to do better (on the average) than men. Much to Galton's surprise, some famous scientists—and even some noted painters—did very poorly. More than this, some people did rather well at *visual* imagery, while others were superior at imagining sounds, smells, or even the "touch" of things. Because twins tended to have similar mental imagery, Galton assumed that this trait was inherited. He also presumed that mental imagery was somehow related to intelligence. But his original notion—that the better you were at imagining things, the brighter you were—proved wrong.

Last but not least, Galton measured head size, physical strength, and sensory discriminations in almost 10,000 individuals. He found no significant correlations among these various traits. Thus his measures hardly constituted a test of "general intelligence." But his work did have two rather important consequences. First, he discovered that women were better than men on several of his measures. This finding surprised Galton, since he believed men were superior to women *in all ways*. Second, his work prompted two French scientists to create what was the first *workable* intelligence test.

The Binet-Simon Intelligence Test

One of the people most influenced by Galton's work was a Frenchman named **Alfred Binet**. In about 1890 he became interested in the differences between bright and dull children and tried to devise a simple scale that would allow him to distinguish the smart children from those who would have problems in school.

As we noted in Chapter 5, another French scientist, named Paul Broca, had theorized that *brain size* was related to intelligence, and (at

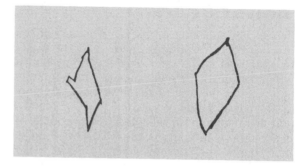

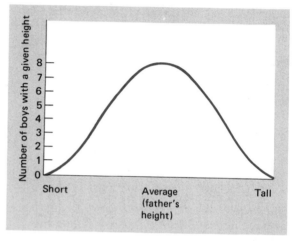

Bead stringing is part of the Stanford-Binet intelligence test. **(top left)**

Fig. 22.2. Drawing of a diamond by a 5-year-old (*left*) and a 7-year-old (*right*). **(top left)**

Fig. 22.3. Bell curve showing the height of 100 boys from one family. **(right)**

first) Binet believed Broca was right. So Binet initially relied on physical measures—such as the size of the child's head or the pattern of lines on the palm of the child's hand. However, none of these scales correlated very highly with the child's performance in school, so Binet abandoned them.

In 1904 the French government asked Binet and a physician named **Thèophile Simon** to devise a test that would allow teachers to identify "retarded" children so that they could be given special attention in school. Binet and Simon pulled together a large number of rather simple problems that seemed to require different mental skills—and then they tried the test problems out on a large number of French school children of different ages. This technique allowed Binet and Simon to select appropriate test items for each age group. They found, for example, that the average seven-year-old could correctly make a pencil copy of the figure of a diamond, but most five-year-olds could not (see Figure 22.2).

If a boy of nine got the same score on the test as did the *average* seven-year-old, Binet and Simon presumed that the boy's mental development was retarded by two years. The boy would thus have a "physical age" of nine but a "mental age" of seven. If an eight-year-old girl did as well

on the test as the average eleven-year-old, then she had a mental age of eleven, although her physical age was but eight.

Later, psychologists in Germany and in the United States put the relationship between **chronological** or physical age and mental age into an equation:

$$\frac{\text{Mental age}}{\text{Chronological age}} \times 100 = \frac{\text{Intelligence}}{\text{Quotient, or IQ}}$$

A girl with a mental age of 6 and a chronological age of 6 would have an IQ of

$$\frac{6}{6} \times 100 = 1 \times 100 = 100 = \text{IQ}$$

By definition, she would be of average intelligence. A boy with a mental age of 7 and a chronological age of 9 would have an IQ of

$$\frac{7}{9} \times 100 = .777 \times 100 = 78 = \text{IQ}$$

A girl with a mental age of 11 and a chronological age of 8 would have an IQ of

$$\frac{11}{8} \times 100 = 1.375 \times 100 = 138 = \text{IQ}$$

The Binet-Simon test did so well at predicting the *academic performance* of school children that intelligence testing became a standard part of educational psychology.

The noted Stanford psychologist, L.M. Terman, made up his own version of the French scale early this century. He called his device the Stanford-Binet intelligence test. Other psychologists soon followed Terman's lead, and now there are hundreds of intelligence tests available.

Most modern intelligence tests don't actually measure "mental age." Instead, they make use of what are called *standard scores*. To understand what a standard score is, though, you first have to know something about what are called *normal distributions* of test scores.

Normal Distributions

Like most other trait psychologists, Binet and Simon were greatly influenced by Darwin's theory of evolution. Darwin had suggested that intelligence is *inherited* in much the same way as eye color, skin color, height, and other physical characteristics. If a man and woman of average height (for their culture) could have 100 male children— so Darwin assumed—most of them would also be of average height. A few would be very tall, a few very short—but most of the boys would be about as tall as their father. If the couple had 100 girls instead of boys, the girls would show the same *distribution of heights*—and would average out much like their mother. If we made a graph of the height of the boys, it presumably would look something like what is shown in Fig. 22.3.

In technical terms, this is called a *normal distribution* of test scores—or a "bell-shaped curve." Many school teachers believe that the scores that students make on a history or mathematics examination should "fit the curve," or be "normally distributed." A few students should get A's, a few should get F's, while most should get C's. The teachers then *write examinations that will give them the results they expect*.

Most intelligence tests are based on this same assumption of normal distribution of scores. Binet and Simon juggled their items around until their test yielded a bell-shaped distribution of "mental ages" for each age level. Modern test-makers do much the same thing, but they work with "standard scores" instead of mental ages. That is, they *standardize* (or "weight") the actual scores on their test so these numbers will "fit the bell-shaped curve." They then assign IQ's "from the curve" rather than from the raw test scores.

If intelligence were a single trait (like height), and if IQ were *entirely determined by your genetic blueprint*, such a procedure might be justified. But are these assumptions really valid?

Théophile Simon (TEY-oh-feel see-MOAN). Simon (1873) was a French physician who became more interested in psychological research than in the practice of medicine. Simon and Binet published their first intelligence test in 1905.

Chronological age (kron-oh-LODGE-uh-cull). Chronos (KROH-nos) was the Greek god of time. Your chronological age is the actual number of years that you have lived.

Is Intelligence a Single Trait?

The results of many psychological studies suggest that intelligence is not a single trait. Rather it is made up of a great many related talents or abilities. Psychologists don't entirely agree on what these "related" talents are, but they often mention such things as the ability to memorize words and numbers, to learn motor tasks, to solve verbal and numerical problems, to evaluate complex situations, to be creative, and to perceive spatial relationships. Indeed, in 1967, J.P. Guilford listed 120 "factors of intelligence," each one representing a different intellectual ability!

If intelligence is really a mixture of many different traits, then there is no reason to expect that IQ's should fit a bell-shaped curve. However, most trait theorists continue to believe that intelligence test scores should be normally distributed. The reason for this belief is simple: There seem to be more people of "normal" intelligence in the world than there are "geniuses" and "mentally retarded" individuals. These facts caused Charles Spearman and Raymond Cattell to rethink the concept of intelligence entirely.

Types of Intelligence

To Charles Spearman, the noted British psychologist, there were but two types of intelligence. He noted that, if you took 10 different intelligence tests, you would usually wind up with 10 different scores. True, the scores probably would be *related* to each other. But which one gives your *real* IQ? And why so many different scores? Spearman decided that each test item actually measured two factors. One he called *general* intelligence, or the "g factor." But each item also measured one or more *specific* types of mental ability, which he called the "s factors." Thus different tests yield different scores because each test tends to emphasize "s" or "g" to a different degree. However, the *mix* of "s" and "g" factors for each test could still fit a bell-shaped curve.

Raymond Cattell agreed that there were two "intellectual factors," but disagreed with Spearman on what they were. Cattell claims you have *fluid* intelligence and *crystallized* intelligence. "Fluid" intelligence is inherited, and involves such talents as the ability to think and reason.

Sandra Scarr   Robert Zajonc

"Crystallized" intelligence involves learned skills such as being able to add and subtract, and the size of your vocabulary. According to Cattell, your "fluid" intelligence sets limits on your "crystallized" abilities. If you aren't innately bright, all the training in the world won't help you get through school. However, if you have a high "fluid" intelligence, and you grow up in a deprived and unstimulating environment, you won't acquire many skills. And you won't get a high score on most intelligence tests, either. From Cattell's point of view, if everyone grew up in the best of all possible environments, "fluid" intelligence would be the major determinant of IQ—and test scores would then "fit the curve" almost exactly.

But what constitutes "the best of all possible environments"? And since we know that many children are reared in unstimulating circumstances, is it ethical to make decisions about their schooling and career opportunities on the basis of IQ? If we believe that intelligence tests primarily measure innate abilities, the answer might be yes. But studies of the effects of early environment on IQ suggest this belief is false.

IQ and Early Deprivation

As we noted earlier, children who are reared in deprived environments often show remarkable improvements in their IQ scores if they are later given the proper intellectual stimulation. One of the first psychologists to make this point was H.M. Skeels. In the 1930's, Skeels shocked many of his colleagues by reporting he had been able to increase the IQ scores of apparently retarded children by putting them in an unusual environment. Skeels took the children out of a dreary orphanage and gave them to a group of retarded women to rear. The first children he studied were two little girls, whose IQ scores rose from below 50 to near normal (see the "story" that opens Chapter 20).

The Minnesota Study

Several recent studies tend to confirm Skeels' findings. Sandra Scarr and Richard Weinberg studied several hundred children in Minnesota who were placed in foster homes. Some of the foster parents were black, but many were white. Most were college graduates with professional jobs or responsibilities. Scarr and Weinberg estimate that, judging from the adopted children's genetic backgrounds, they might have been expected to end up with IQ's well below the national average. Instead, they scored well above average and very close to youngsters brought up in natural homes similar to the ones the orphans were adopted into.

Scarr and Weinberg also report that the younger the child was when adopted, the higher its later IQ score tended to be. Generally, black children adopted into middle-class white homes had about the same IQ's as did white children.

If nothing else, the Minnesota study suggests that orphans placed with concerned, well-educated foster parents do even better than they might have done if reared by their own parents.

Question: *The obvious "control group" for this study would be white orphans reared in black foster homes. Why do you think Scarr and Weinberg were not able to find enough such children to make a meaningful comparison?*

The Milwaukee Study

A similar example of how *changing* a child's early environment can affect the child's IQ comes from a study by Rick Heber and his colleagues at the University of Wisconsin. In 1967, Heber and his associates selected for study 40 infants who were born to black parents living in one of the worst sections of Milwaukee. Blacks in this particular section of town had the lowest average family income and education level in the entire city. They also had the highest rate of unemployment and the highest population density. Although less than 3 percent of the population lived in this area, it accounted for about 33 percent of the children classified as "educable mentally retarded." The mothers of the 40 infants in the Milwaukee Project all had IQ's below 75 and, in many cases, the fathers were absent from the home.

Of these 40 infants, 20 were randomly selected to be in what Heber considered the "experimental" group, while the other 20 were placed in an untreated "control" group. The families of the experimental group infants were given intensive vocational help. They also received training in homemaking and child-care skills as soon as the children were born.

When these "experimental" infants were 30 months old, they were put into a special education center for 35 hours a week. The training at this center focused on the development of language and cognitive skills. The children went to the center almost daily until they were six and could enter school. The families and children in the control group received none of these benefits.

The children in both groups were given intelligence tests frequently. The IQ's of the experimental group youngsters were always 20 points or more above those of control group children. Heber believes that this superiority was due to the special training given the children in the experimental group (and their families).

Question: The experimental group children did not start receiving special training until they were 30 months old. Might the results have been different had the training started earlier? Why?

Dumber by the Dozen?

Galton wanted to get "bright" people to have large families, because he believed that intelligence was determined entirely by the genes. But the studies described above suggest that early environment plays a major role in shaping *functional intelligence*—at least as it is reflected in IQ scores. In trying to discover what this effect is, several experimenters have turned up evidence that Galton's desire for "big families" might not have been such a bright idea.

Lillian Belmont and Francis Marolla examined birth order and IQ scores for almost 400,000 19-year-old Dutch males. Since their subjects included almost all the men born in Holland between 1944 and 1947, the "group" studied was probably representative of Dutch society in general.

Belmont and Marolla found that the more children there were in the family, the *lower their average IQ was*. More than this, the first-born children had a clear-cut advantage over the children born in the family later on. These findings were true for all social classes. It happens that, generally speaking, boys from rich families scored higher than did boys from middle-class or lower-class homes. But within each social class, children from small families scored significantly higher than did children from large families.

The highest IQ's of all were obtained by the first-born child in families of just two children. By far the lowest average scores came from the last-born child in families of 9 children. The difference between these two extremes was more than 10 IQ points.

Robert Zajonc (his name rhymes with "science") explains the Belmont and Marolla data as

follows: Children grow up in quite different intellectual environments, depending on their birth order. The first child is born into a predominantly adult family, for it talks mostly with its two parents (who serve as the child's models). The second child is born into what Zajonc calls a "diluted" intellectual environment. For it not only has two parents but also one slightly older **sibling** from whom it can learn. Since the younger child spends much of its time with the first-born, the second-born doesn't receive the same intellectual stimulation that the first-born did. The third-born has an even more "diluted" environment. And by the time the fifth-born comes along, it is reared primarily by siblings, not by adults.

Question: Generally speaking, the older child in two-child families scored higher than did children with no brothers and sisters. What is there about having a younger sibling that might help improve an older child's IQ?

Can You Raise Your Own IQ?

Most intelligence tests place rather heavy emphasis on *reasoning*—the ability to work your way through a complicated mental task step-by-step. Cattell, Galton, and most other trait psychologists assume that "reasoning" is an inherited ability. Few psychologists doubt that *some* aspects of intelligence are determined by the genes. But is it always the case that people with low IQ's lack the ability to reason? Or is some aspect of that trait learned?

Several years ago, Benjamin Bloom and Lois Broder studied how college students with either low or high IQ's react to mental challenges. Bloom and Broder gave these subjects various problems to work on and asked the students to "talk out loud" as they proceeded. High IQ subjects tended to read the instructions carefully, then diligently eliminated all the incorrect answers. The low IQ students often skipped over the instructions, and lacked the patience to isolate the correct answers when faced with questions that required formal reasoning. The low-scorers didn't seem to carry on an internal conversation with themselves, nor did they proceed through a step-by-step sequence of deductions. If they couldn't see the answer immediately, they felt lost and usually guessed.

Bloom and Broder were convinced that the low-scoring students had never acquired the proper cognitive skills. So they developed a train-

Leona Tyler

Robert V. Guthrie

Early stimulation helps a child develop its intellectual potential. **(left)**

ing program aimed at helping these young people "learn how to think." First, they made the low-scorers *read the instructions aloud*. Many of the students showed immediate improvement, because they were forced to pay attention to what was required of them. Next the students were asked to solve various problems *aloud*. After Bloom and Broder had discussed the student's solution with the student, the experimenters read the correct solution aloud. Then they asked the student to explain what had gone wrong if the student had been incorrect. The students had many difficulties at first, and the instructors had to show tremendous patience. But once the students began to recognize that they actually could learn how to reason, they did so with increasing frequency. Although Bloom and Broder did not re-test the students' IQ's after this training, the psychologists report that most of their subjects got much higher grades in college thereafter.

California psychologist Arthur Whimbey has spent considerable time attempting to help people raise their IQ's. He points out that learning how to reason requires immediate positive feedback and much practice. If you wish to improve your own test performance, Whimbey says, you should work with a trained tutor, and you should use old tests and puzzle books as practice tools. You should think "out loud" as you work, listen to what you say, and try to figure out how you got the incorrect answer if you are wrong. Whimbey notes that following these techniques won't turn you into a genius. But he reports that many of the people he has worked with have increased their test scores by 20 or 30 points.

Question: *If a six-year-old girl wanted to "learn how to reason," would she do better if taught by an adult or by her ten-year-old sister?*

Reliability and Validity of Intelligence Tests

When a psychologist makes up a "trait scale" of any kind, the psychologist has to prove two things to other scientists before they will accept the scale and use it themselves. First, the creator of the test must show that it is *reliable*. Second, the psychologist must provide evidence that the test is also *valid*.

At its simplest, the term "reliability" merely means that a test will yield the same results no matter how frequently you give it. However, Leona Tyler states that—when applied to instruments such as intelligence tests—reliability really means "accuracy." That is, a test is "reliable" if the results it yields are free from *chance effects*.

At its simplest, the term "validity" means that the test measures what it says it does. However, Leona Tyler also notes that modern psychologists take a more complex view of the term. To Tyler, you cannot judge the validity of a test unless you know all the current research showing just what a test does and does not measure. Determining the validity of a psychological scale, therefore, is both a complicated and continuous undertaking.

With these definitions in mind, let's examine both the reliability and the validity of intelligence tests.

Are Intelligence Tests Reliable?

If intelligence were *absolutely fixed* at birth, psychologists would probably have little trouble making up tests that were highly reliable. However, intelligence tests measure *your present level of functioning*, not the underlying factor that Cattell calls "fluid intelligence." Thus your IQ is always affected by your genes, your past experience, and your present situation. If you are unmotivated when you take a test, or you are worried about something or have a toothache, you probably will do more poorly on it than if you were "up" for the exam. In similar fashion, if you grew up in a deprived environment, if you never learned to reason, or if you were the last child in a large family, you probably will not score as high as you would have had your background been different.

Intelligence tests are much more reliable than are many other psychological scales. And when given under the best of circumstances, they are fairly "accurate" in the sense that Leona Tyler uses that term. However, as we noted, no two intelligence tests will yield identical scores. And even if you take the same test several times, your IQ may vary considerably depending on how you feel and what you have learned since the last time you took the test. Thus your IQ *is not a fixed quantity*.

Are Intelligence Tests Valid?

As you must have gathered by now, there is not all that much agreement among experts as to what intelligence is, much less how to measure it. More than 60 years ago, Harvard psychologist E.G. Boring put the matter into perspective when he wrote that, "Intelligence as a measurable capacity must at the start be defined as the capacity to do well on an intelligence test. Intelligence is what the tests test."

As absurd as Boring's statement may seem on the face of it, he spoke with a fair amount of wisdom. For test-builders usually offer their own *carefully limited* definition of what they think intelligence is, and then show that their particular test is valid within those limits. For instance, Binet and Simon assumed that "intelligence" was whatever mental properties were needed to succeed in French schools. Children who scored high on their tests generally got good grades—and were rated as being intelligent by their teachers. Students who scored lower on the Binet-Simon test got lower school grades—and were rated as being less intelligent by their teachers. Binet and Simon then used the correlations between test scores, teacher ratings, and grades to *validate* their intelligence test. And within the limits of their definition, Binet and Simon were correct.

Under certain circumstances, then, intelligence tests do yield "valid" results. First of all, there is a very high correlation between IQ and school grades. Thus we can use intelligence test scores to predict which children will do well in school, and which children will probably get low grades. However, the tests do *not* predict academic performance very well when low-scorers are given the kind of "special training" developed by Bloom and Broder or by Whimbey.

Second, as Tyler notes, IQ's also predict how well people will do in various occupational *levels*. That is, if you have an IQ of 85, you probably will do better in an unskilled or semi-skilled job than you would trying to become a nuclear physicist. However, IQ's don't predict the success that people *within* a given occupation will have. Thus the fact that one nuclear physicist has an IQ of 140 and another has an IQ of 160 doesn't *by itself* tell you which person is most likely to win the Nobel Prize.

Last, but not least, the scores on many intelligence tests can be fairly reliable indicators of what sorts of special training people will need in school and on the job. Thus we would be foolish not to employ test scores in those situations where they are known to be useful. The problem comes, however, when we try to use IQ's to make judgments in situations where they are known *not* to yield valid predictions. And, as we will see, we can also get into trouble when we use IQ's without realizing the various *biases* that are built into the tests.

Question: *How high an IQ do you think you'd get on a test given entirely in Chinese?*

Cultural and Racial Biases

Built into most intelligence tests is a *cultural bias* that we are not always aware of. Binet and Simon, for instance, took many of their basic ideas on intelligence from Paul Broca, who believed that the size of your brain determined the amount of your intelligence. As we noted in Chapter 5, Broca performed some very inexact measurements on brain size and "proved" that men were brighter than women and that whites were smarter than blacks.

Most modern psychologists reject Broca's notions about the superior mental abilities of males and whites. However, a few scientists do still cling to the belief in racial differences. In 1969, Arthur Jensen published an article in the *Harvard Educational Review* entitled "How much can we boost IQ and scholastic achievement?" In this paper—and in many books and articles he published subsequently—Jensen claims that blacks are genetically inferior to whites as far as intelligence goes. Jensen's writings have, to say the least, created a storm of controversy. Let's look at the evidence that Jensen cites, then at the counter-claims.

Jensen begins by quoting a national survey of 81 different studies of black-white IQ's. Accord-

Table 22.2. The Chitling Test [a]

1. A "handkerchief head" is:
   - (A) a cool cat
   - (B) a porter
   - (C) an Uncle Tom
   - (D) a hoddi
   - (E) a preacher

2. Which word is most out of place here?
   - (A) splib
   - (B) blood
   - (C) gray
   - (D) spook
   - (E) black

3. A "gas head" is a person who has a:
   - (A) fast-moving car
   - (B) stable of "lace"
   - (C) "process"
   - (D) habit of stealing cars
   - (E) long jail record for arson

4. "Bo Diddley" is a:
   - (A) game for children
   - (B) down-home cheap wine
   - (C) down-home singer
   - (D) new dance
   - (E) Moejoe call

5. If a man is called a "blood," then he is a:
   - (A) fighter
   - (B) Mexican-American
   - (C) Negro
   - (D) hungry hemophile
   - (E) Redman or Indian

[a] This IQ test was designed by Adrian Dove, a sociologist who is familiar with black ghetto culture. It probably seems as unfair to white middle-class culture as the tests designed by them appear to other culture groups. The answer to all the above questions is C. (Copyright 1968 by Newsweek, Inc.)

ing to this survey, blacks tend to average about 15 IQ points lower than do whites on standardized intelligence tests. Blacks also score somewhat below other disadvantaged minority groups. Jensen also claims that blacks from "upper-status" homes tend to obtain significantly lower test scores than do whites reared in similar circumstances. And, in an attempt to prove that these differences are not merely due to "cultural factors," Jensen makes two further points. First, blacks tend to do even worse on so-called "culture free" intelligence tests than do whites. And second, blacks tends to average 7–8 IQ points below American Indians. And, according to Jensen, American Indians who live on reservations have cultural environments that are typically rated as being far below the environments most blacks are reared in.

Had we not already pointed out that intelligence tests have a built-in bias toward certain cultural values, Jensen's points might deserve serious consideration. However, as Robert V. Guthrie points out in his book *Even the Rat Was White*, the psychologists who constructed most of the widely used intelligence tests were almost all middle-class white males. And most of them shared Jensen's view that intelligence is *primarily an inherited trait*. Thus, if blacks did poorly on standard intelligence tests, the test-makers *presumed* this difference was due to "bad genes" and

not to "bad environments." Guthrie also notes that, until recently, psychologists studying blacks tended to focus on *differences* between the races, not *similarities*. Little wonder, then, that Jensen's views received support from certain scientists (and from certain politicians).

As we have noted many times, *all aspects* of your personality (including your IQ) are determined by the interactions among your genes, your past experiences, and your present environment. Comparing blacks with whites (or any other group of people) is valid *only when the groups have similar past experiences and present social environments*. Many studies indicate that blacks who move from culturally deprived to more stimulating circumstances show a marked increase in IQ's. So do whites, Indians, Koreans, and people of all other nationalities and races. Blacks reared in culturally advantaged environments have higher IQ's than do whites brought up in poor circumstances. Thus intelligence tests, as presently written, probably tend to *underestimate* the innate potential of blacks—and of all other socially deprived groups, including many whites.

The Boston Study
In 1979, Regina Yando, Victoria Seitz, and Edward Zigler reported a study they had made of 304 children in the Boston area. All the subjects were eight years old when the study was made. Half the

children came from upper-class homes, half from lower-class homes. Half the children from each class of home were black, and half were white. The children in each of these four groups were carefully matched for IQ. The psychologists gave each child tests that measured such traits as creativity, self-confidence, autonomy, curiosity, frustration threshold, and dependency.

The results of the Boston study were, in many ways, fairly surprising. To begin with, Yando and her colleagues note that almost all of the differences between black and white children could be accounted for in terms of *social class*. Upper-class children—black or white—were very similar. So were lower-class children. However, disadvantaged children (of either race) were more creative in solving problems, and they were more likely to take risks and persevere at tasks despite frustration. Advantaged children had larger vocabularies and were better at step-by-step reasoning, but were anxious and overly concerned about failure. Disadvantaged black children attending predominantly white schools tended to suffer a loss in self-confidence, but did better academically than their peers in predominantly black schools.

Yando, Seitz, and Zigler also asked the children's teachers to rate each of the subjects. Teacher ratings did, in fact, predict academic skills. However, the psychologists note that these ratings might well have been due to "halo" effects. Thus the fact that disadvantaged children failed to learn some cognitive skills in school might be due to the bias that the teachers showed against youngsters from lower-class homes.

Uses and Misuses of Intelligence Tests

As the Boston study suggests, early experience has a strong effect on functional intelligence. Thus the *performance differences* that Jensen notes between blacks and whites on these tests probably reflect class differences rather than racial differences. So any time we made decisions about people based solely on their IQ's, we are likely to misuse the data the test gives us. For example, in the early part of this century, many noted psychologists (including Yerkes and Terman) used intelligence test scores to support the notion that we should limit immigration to the US primarily to whites from northern Europe. One noted psychologist of that time, H.H. Goddard, gave tests to recent immigrants from southern Europe and the Middle East and announced that "up to 85 percent of them" were feeble-minded. The fact that the tests Goddard used were in *English*, a language most of the immigrants couldn't speak, didn't affect Goddard's conclusions. It is

Hypothetical (high-poh-THET-ee-cal). Any "made up" explanation that you give for events is a hypothetical account of why those events occurred. If you have read Chapter 1, you know that you can measure independent and dependent variables objectively, but you cannot directly measure the intervening variables that presumably account for the relationships between independent and dependent variables. For instance, if a psychologist gives you a particular intelligence test, that's an independent variable because the psychologist could have given you any number of other tests instead. Your test score is the dependent variable. "Intelligence" is the intervening variable that presumably accounts for your score, thus "intelligence" is a hypothetical explanation of why you got the score you did.

also true that for more than 50 years the state of Virginia used IQ's to identify "feebleminded" individuals in state institutions. The people so identified were then forcibly sterilized, "to prevent them from breeding."

Fortunately, most of the more blatant misuses of intelligence tests have now been halted, both by acts of law and by action of the American Psychological Association. For instance, in October 1979, Federal Judge Robert Peckham prohibited the State of California from using intelligence tests to place children with low IQ's in "classes for the mentally retarded." Reviewing all the evidence to that date, Judge Peckham concluded that intelligence tests were culturally biased against minority children. Thus, said Peckham, these tests cannot be used to estimate some **hypothetical** "innate ability," such as "general intelligence."

Most psychologists agree with Judge Peckham's decision to ban the use of IQ's in "segregating" children in schools. Writing in the October 1981 issue of *American Psychologist*, Robert Glaser and Lloyd Bond note that, "Long-standing practices that were generated in the context of older social institutions have been justly criticized. . . . This criticism has stimulated changes that were both necessary and long overdue." But Glaser and Bond go on to state that, "Unfortunately, [the criticism] has also inevitably discouraged the use of tests in situations where they could be beneficial."

When can the use of test scores be beneficial? The entire October 1981 issue of *American Psychologist* is devoted to answering this and other questions related to mental measurement. D.J. Reschly points out that schools still need some method of identifying those children who need special help, and that subjective impressions are even more biased than are mental tests. Lynn H. Fox reinforces this view by demonstrating that tests are better at identifying gifted students from disadvantaged backgrounds than is any other procedure yet developed. Frank Schmidt

The Thematic Apperception Test requires you to look at a picture, and then make up a story to explain what is happening in the picture. **(left)**

Rorschach's ink blot test allows you to project your own feelings and perceptions on to an ambiguous stimulus. **(right)**

and John Hunter report that the use of intelligence tests are valid predictors of on-the-job-performance. Schmidt and Hunter state that the best of these tests "are equally valid for minority and majority applicants and are fair to minority applicants in that they do not underestimate the expected job performance of minority groups."

Thus, intelligence tests do have a place in our society, and it would be foolish not to use them when they are valid, reliable, and do not discriminate against any group of people. However, we must be careful in what conclusions we draw from intelligence test data. In a 1977 paper, Leona Tyler notes that we cannot presently determine what aspects of intelligence are affected by our genetic blueprints, and which aspects are affected primarily by factors such as the environment. Therefore, comparisons of the IQ's of different races tell us nothing at all about such matters as racial superiority or inferiority. She also states that scientists who study such sensitive problems as racial differences have a special responsibility—to take into consideration the social consequences of their research.

Objective versus Subjective Tests

Although intelligence tests have received most of the publicity in recent years, there are many other types of psychological scales that attempt to measure traits or some other aspect of human performance or personality. Some of these tests are *objective*, in that they yield numbers which describe how much of a given trait you possess. Others tests are *subjective*, in that an expert must "analyze" your responses and then give an evalu-

ation of what the responses mean. (In the academic world, a multiple-choice test is usually "objective," while an essay exam is usually "subjective.")

Both types of test have been used for years in the study of human personality. Let's look at both kinds, and then discuss the problems and benefits associated with using them.

Subjective Tests

Suppose that, because you were impressed with Freud's psychoanalytic theory of personality, you wanted to devise a means of getting at the *dynamic* aspects of a person's subjective life. You could hardly ask the person about such matters directly—using a pen-and-paper test—because the most important dynamics are often unconscious and thus the person wouldn't express them openly. But what would happen if you presented the subject with a variety of unstructured or *ambiguous* situations? Wouldn't you expect people to *project* themselves into the task given them? That is, shouldn't people structure ambiguous stimuli according to the structures of their own basic personalities? If they did, then you could easily interpret their responses to these **projective tests** according to psychoanalytic (or any other) principles.

Projective tests are among the most widely used subjective scales. So let's look briefly at several of them.

Word Association Test

The first of these "projective" instruments was the *word association test* devised by Galton more than 100 years ago. It was subsequently revised by Carl Jung for psychoanalytic use in the early 1900's. The test consists of a list of highly emotional stimulus words that are presented to you one at a time. You are asked to respond to each word with the first thing that comes to mind. Sometimes the tester will use a polygraph, or lie detector, to check your physiological reactions as you respond to the words (see Chapter 14).

Both Galton and Jung assumed that if you reacted to a word like "sex" by blocking (refusing to answer)—or if you started sweating, or fainted, or gave a wildly inappropriate reaction such as "firecrackers" or "death"—then you might have sexual problems that a therapist ought to look into.

Question: *What similarities do you see between the word association test and Freud's technique called "free association"?*

The TAT

The **thematic apperception text**, or TAT, was developed by Henry Murray, a US biochemist who became a psychologist through Carl Jung's influence. The TAT consists of a set of 20 stimulus pictures that depict rather vague but potentially emotional situations (see Figure 22.4). You respond by making up a story telling: (1) what led up to the situation shown in the picture; (2) what the people are thinking and feeling and doing

"RORSCHACH! WHAT'S TO BECOME OF YOU?"

Projective tests. According to psychoanalytic theory, people tend to project their own personalities onto vague or ambiguous stimulus inputs. Projective tests—such as the inkblot test and the TAT—are vague stimuli that a psychologist might ask you to describe or talk about, in the hope that you will somehow structure the stimulus in the same way that your personality is structured.

Thematic Apperception Test (the-MATT-tick app-purr-SEP-shun). A "theme" is a story, or the plot of a story. *Apperception* is defined as "the process of perceiving something in terms of your prior experience." The TAT is a set of vague stimulus pictures that you are asked to "tell stories about," presumably because you will perceive or structure the pictures in terms of your own personality. Hence the "themes" of the stories you tell will give the psychologist some clue as to how you perceive the world (in terms of your own prior experiences).

Hermann Rorschach (HAIR-man ROAR-shock). A Swiss psychiatrist (1884–1922) who devised the famous inkblot test.

right then; and (3) what will happen to them in the future. Each story you produce is scored and interpreted individually. The psychologist giving the test usually assumes that you will express your deep-seated needs and personality problems by *projecting* them onto the hero or the heroine in the story.

Inkblot Tests

By far the most famous of the projective instruments is the inkblot test, first devised in the 1920's by Swiss psychiatrist **Hermann Rorschach**. The Rorschach test is a series of 10 inkblots that are given to you one at a time. You look at each inkblot and report what you see—much as you might look at clouds passing overhead and tell someone what "faces" and other things you saw in the clouds. The psychologist then scores and interprets your responses according to one of several methods.

Usefulness of Projective Tests

When used by a sensitive and perceptive psychologist, any one of the projective tests can yield a great deal of information about your personality. However, the bulk of scientific research suggests that most projective tests are neither very reliable nor particularly valid as presently used. Projective tests seem to give us more information about you than we have the wisdom to use. And they provide this information in highly subjective descriptions of what you are like, rather than as reliable, objective test scores.

Question: *It is sometimes said that Rorschach interpretations tell us more about the person doing the "interpreting" than they do about the person who took the test. Why might this sometimes be the case?*

Objective Tests

Objective tests have several purposes. One is to *measure present traits, skills, and knowledge*. Another is to *predict future performance*. A few objective tests attempt to serve both purposes simultaneously.

Achievement Tests

An achievement test is a psychological scale that measures how much you have learned about a given topic. The test does *not* indicate either *why* you learned as much as you did, nor how much you *could have learned* under different circumstances. People with high IQ's will do poorly on achievement tests if they haven't learned much about the topic, or if they once knew the material but now have forgotten it. People with lower IQ's will do well if they have studied the subject thoroughly. Thus achievement tests tell us little or nothing about your motivation or your IQ. They simply measure present knowledge.

Academic achievement tests are useful within school systems, but they don't necessarily give us much information about how well people will do after they have left the academic world. For instance, early in 1981 many city officials in Sacramento, California took a sixth grade math achievement test. The mayor missed 20 out of 25 questions, and the best score made by any of the officials was 80 percent correct. However, dozens of sixth grade students got perfect scores. Presumably the city officials once knew the material, but had simply forgotten it over the years.

Aptitude Tests

In its purest form, an aptitude test attempts to determine whether you possess enough of a certain trait—or certain personality factors—in order to succeed in some job or other situation. Some are fairly simple tests that measure such skills as mechanical or clerical aptitude. Other tests, such as those given to prospective airline pilots, measure a broader range of abilities. Scores on these simple scales tend to predict future performance fairly well.

Unfortunately, many devices that are called *aptitude* tests are really combinations of *achievement* and *intelligence* tests. The Scholastic Aptitude Test is one such, for it tends to measure how much you have already learned about a given academic subject and thus is an achievement test. The SAT also measures—to some extent—how "test wise" you are, and how good you are at solving the types of problems you are likely to face on examinations while in college. Since the SAT correlates rather well with intelligence test scores, it provides a rough measure of your IQ. And since SAT scores are reasonably good at predicting future grades in college, it would seem to be a *valid* academic screening device.

There are, however, several problems associated with scales such as the SAT. One problem is the cultural bias that seems to be built into the test. People from disadvantaged backgrounds tend to do poorly on the SAT, although they may do well if admitted to college. The second problem has to do with coaching. As we noted earlier, both Bloom and Broder and Whimbey have shown that teaching people *cognitive skills* tends to raise their SAT scores. The fact that disadvantaged individuals benefit more from coaching than do advantaged individuals tends to reinforce the belief that the SAT is a biased instrument.

Finally, there is the thorny issue of what SAT scores and school grades actually mean *outside of college*. Harvard psychologist David McClelland noted in 1973 that both your IQ and your SAT scores predict rather well how you will do in medical school. But they tell us little or nothing about how good a physician you will be. For the skills and traits needed to practice medicine successfully and humanely in real-life settings are quite different from those required to get through medical school.

Similar evidence about the limited usefulness of the scholastic aptitude tests comes from a 1963 study by L.R. Harmon. He investigated the professional contributions of physicists and biologists who had taken advanced degrees. He then compared the actual "life's work" of these scientists with their achievement test scores taken when they were still students. Harmon reports no correlation at all between what the scientists actually accomplished in life and their test scores as students.

In a later survey, Michael Wallach and C.W. Wing compared the SAT scores of 500 undergraduates with their achievements outside the classroom. They report that students with low SAT scores tended to achieve just as much as did high scorers. Wallach concludes that, "Testing agencies should perhaps devote less effort to tests and more to helping educators assess achievement in activities that we value."

Personality Tests: The MMPI

Not all objective tests have to do with achievement or aptitude. Some attempt to measure personality traits. The **Minnesota Multiphasic Personality Inventory**, or MMPI, is perhaps the most widely used personality test in the United States today. The MMPI was created to be as reliable as possible—and research suggests that its reliability is indeed fairly high.

In its original form, the MMPI consisted of some 560 short statements that were given to large numbers of people, some of them mental patients, some of them presumably normal. The statements mostly concern psychiatric problems or unusual thought patterns, such as: (1) Someone is trying to control my mind using radio waves; (2) I never think of unusual sexual situations; and (3) I never have been sick a day of my life. When you take the MMPI, you respond to each statement either by agreeing or disagreeing, or by saying that it is impossible for you to respond at all.

As you might expect, the mental patients used in the original sample reacted to many of the statements in quite different ways than did the normal subjects. Depressed or suicidal patients gave different responses than did patients diagnosed as being schizophrenic or paranoid. The authors of the test were able to pick out different groups of test items that appeared to form "depression" scales, "paranoia" scales, "schizophrenia" scales, and so forth. If an otherwise normal individual takes the test and receives an abnormally high score on the "paranoia" scale, the psychologist interpreting the test might well worry that the person could become paranoid if put under great psychological stress or pressure. By looking at the pattern or *profile* of a subject's scores on the different MMPI scales, a psychologist might also be able to predict what areas of the subject's personality needed strengthening.

This approach to the study of personality—judging people almost entirely in terms of their *objective* responses—gives the MMPI a very high reliability. Whether the MMPI is a *valid* index of personality structure is another matter altogether. Under the right circumstances, it probably is. Writing in the October 1981 issue of *American Psychologist*, Sheldon Korchin and David Schuldberg state that the MMPI "has gained and maintained a respected place in clinical practice. . . . There is no question that the test can yield, in the hands of a skilled interpreter, a differentiated picture of important personality characteristics of value to clinical decision-making."

Question: *The MMPI correlates quite highly with diagnoses made by trained psychiatrists. As we will see in Chapter 23, however, there is growing evidence that psychiatrists often make mistakes about what is wrong with a patient. If these diagnoses are questionable, how valid can the MMPI be?*

Minnesota Multiphasic Personality Inventory (mull-tee-FAZE-ick). An objective personality test that yields scores on many different scales. By looking at the *profile* of your test scores, a trained interpreter can often determine those areas in which you are "normal" (that is, like most other people) and those areas in which you might be somewhat abnormal, or might experience problems.

The Future of Trait Theory

In the 1860's, Francis Galton set out to describe and measure all human traits. Now, a century or more later, how is trait theory faring, and what does the future hold for it and the thousands of mental tests that the trait approach has spawned?

In the first part of this chapter, we stated that there is still little agreement among psychologists on what a trait is, much less on how best to measure whatever traits humans possess. Because of this disagreement, as Korchin and Schuldberg note in their 1981 article, "there has been a decided decline and growing criticism of psychodiagnostic testing" in recent years. One criticism that Korchin and Schuldberg cite is that, like trait theory in general, test scores typically ignore the influence the environment has on human thoughts and behaviors. A second objection stems from the social consequences of testing and trait theory—consequences that we are still just beginning to learn about. A third problem is that raised by humanistic psychologists, who are more interested in the meanings people give to their lives than to their test scores. For example, Carl Rogers stated in 1942 that nothing a test score tells you about a patient matters much until the patient discovers the same thing for her- or himself during therapy.

Still and all, Korchin and Schuldberg believe that tests (and newer types of trait theories) will have growing usefulness in the future. They note that the *need* for diagnostic and predictive information about people is even greater now than in the past. What we have to do, they say, is to develop scales that are reliable and valid, but which satisfy ethical, social, and scientific standards better than those tests we have used in the past. They predict we will develop techniques which measure how traits and environments *interact*. They also believe that, in the future, psychologists will give greater weight to people's *own* assessments of their strengths and problems rather than just relying on a battery of test scores. As H.G. Gough put it in 1976, "The personality assessment psychologist must be responsive to himself and to others in a human and intraceptive manner; that is, he cannot be merely a technician or master of a set of methods used in purely [mechanical] fashion."

Like all psychological theories, the trait approach has its strengths and weaknesses. At its best, it reminds us that humans have both similarities and differences. And it gives us ways of measuring both. At its weakest, it tends to put labels on people that they don't always deserve. The problem then becomes, as we will see in the next chapter, that we then respond to the *label* rather than to the *person*.

With that thought in mind, suppose we continue our study of personality by turning our attention to abnormal traits, thought patterns, emotions, and behaviors.

Summary

1. The scientific study of **individual differences** probably begins with Francis Galton, who also devised the first **intelligence test**. Modern **trait theory** has been strongly influenced by Galton.

2. **Type theorists** believe that body type determines traits. Galen (and Hippocrates) were the first type theorists. They assumed that the four main fluids or **humors** of the body (**blood, phlegm, yellow bile, black bile**) were the major determinants of personality, a belief long since discarded by scientists.

3. Sheldon believed that we are all mixtures of three body types, the **endomorph**, the **ectomorph**, and the **mesomorph**. Whichever type you became was determined during your fetal period. Sheldon found correlations between body type and various personality traits.

4. Modern theorists have rejected typologies, focusing instead on traits. Allport believed there were three main types of traits, **cardinal, central**, and **secondary**. Each person presumably has one or two cardinal traits, but up to ten central traits. Allport believed there were at least 5,000 secondary or learned traits.

5. Raymond Cattell believes there are but two types of traits, **surface** and **source** traits. Using **factor analysis**, Cattell determined there are but 16 source traits, which determine some 35 surface traits.

6. A trait is often defined as the tendency to respond to **many different situations in the same way**. Most traits can be measured on **psychological scales**, or **mental tests**.

7. Some psychologists define **intelligence** as a trait, but others do not. Galton devised a crude test, but the first true intelligence scale was the **Binet-Simon** test, which measured **mental age**.

8. **Intelligence Quotient**, or IQ, is often defined as mental age divided by **chronological age** times 100. Most modern intelligence tests measure IQ using **standard scores** rather than mental age. Standard scores are **normally distributed**, which is to say they fit a **bell-shaped curve**.

9. Charles Spearman listed two types of intelligence, a **general** or "g" factor, and several **special** or "s" factors.

10. Raymond Cattell also claims there are two intellectual factors, **fluid intelligence**, which is inherited, and **crystallized intelligence**, which involves learned skills.

11. Children brought up in deprived or **disadvantaged circumstances** generally have lower IQ scores than do children brought up in **stimulating environments**. Making the child's environment more stimulating can often help increase the child's **IQ**.

12. Children brought up in **large families** generally have slightly lower IQ scores than do children brought up in small families. In large families, the **late-born children** usually score lower on intelligence tests than do first-borns.

13. Disadvantaged persons in particular can raise their test scores by learning **cognitive skills**, such as step-by-step reasoning and how to take intelligence tests.

14. Intelligence tests are fairly **reliable**, but there is considerable question about their **validity** since there is no agreement on what intelligence actually is. IQ's do predict **academic achievement**, but most tests **discriminate** against disadvantaged individuals.

15. Arthur Jensen uses IQ data to claim that blacks are **mentally inferior** to whites. However, most studies suggest that blacks and whites from the same **social class** score about the same on intelligence tests. Thus most racial differences on trait tests are caused by **environmental variables**, not genes.

16. Most blatant **misuses** of intelligence tests have now been halted by court action. IQ's do seem useful in identifying children who need special help, and disadvantaged children who are gifted.

17. **Projective tests**, such as the **Rorschach**, the **word association test**, and the **TAT**,

are ambiguous stimuli that you are supposed to "structure" in terms of your own personality. Both the **validity** and the **reliability** of these tests are questionable in most circumstances.

18. **Achievement tests** measure knowledge of a certain subject, while **aptitude tests** attempt to predict future performance. Many aptitude tests actually measure achievement and IQ, however, and thus may be **biased** against disadvantaged individuals.

19. The **MMPI** is a very reliable set of scales standardized on a fairly large population. Many psychologists believe the MMPI is also a fairly valid measure of personality because it correlates well with **psychiatric diagnoses**.

20. The future holds promise that we will develop more accurate and reliable measures of personality traits. But these tests must satisfy **ethical, social**, and **scientific standards** better than those tests used in the past.

(Continued from page 509.)

"Well, Jessie, if I don't get my Ph.D., I can always blame it on you," Tom Flagg said, his smile belying the seriousness of his words.

"Did I mess up your experiment?" Jessie Williams asked in a concerned tone of voice."

"Royally. But luckily, you were practically the only teacher who did."

"None of my bloomers bloomed?"

Tom shook his head. "That wasn't the problem. Just the opposite. *All* of your kids bloomed, black or white, whether the test said they should or not."

"And that's bad?"

"Good for the kids. Bad for my experiment."

Jessie frowned. "Will it really hold you back from getting your doctorate in psychology?"

"No, not at all. As I said, the Rosenthal test predicted rather well for several other teachers." Tom stretched his muscular legs out in front of him. "I just wish that it hadn't."

Jessie looked puzzled. "But I thought you wanted the test to work? I thought you wouldn't get credit for your experiment if it didn't?"

"I couldn't tell you everything about the test, Jessie," Tom said sheepishly. "You see, Professor Rosenthal didn't really make up a test for 'Late Bloomers.' He was interested in people's expectancies instead. He figured if you told a teacher one of her children was going to 'bloom,' the teacher would pay a lot more attention to that child. And the kid would respond to the teacher's expectancies, and would really improve. But if the teacher expected the kid to backslide, she'd pick on the kid's faults and mistakes. Then the kid would become discouraged and wouldn't do well."

"Is that what this Professor Rosenthal found?"

Tom shrugged his shoulders. "In a lot of cases, yes. But it's an iffy sort of thing. Not everybody has been able to replicate Rosenthal's original results, although Rosenthal still insists they're valid."

"And it didn't work with me, did it?" Jessie said, grinning.

"No, it didn't. Not that I'm complaining, you understand. It shouldn't work with really good teachers, because they wouldn't be prejudiced for or against kids just because of their test scores."

"Shower them with love and affection, and you help them all bloom as much as they can."

"Right," said Tom.

"Then why are you concerned if I didn't pay any attention to your test scores, Tom? I'm not suggestible enough for you?"

Tom laughed. "How did you guess?"

"Keep your mind on your experiment. What's troubling you, friend?"

Tom shrugged. "The fact that some teachers were influenced by the faked test scores that I gave them. I can maybe understand why some of the white teachers might be prejudiced in favor of white kids and against blacks—that's part of our culture, though it's changing some now. And maybe I can understand why some of the black teachers would be prejudiced against white kids and biased toward the blacks. Somehow you expect that. But why would white teachers be prejudiced against white kids, and black teachers prejudiced against black kids—just because some silly test said the kids were going to backslide, or do poorly?"

"Brother Thomas, we are all human beings," Jessie Williams said. "Our blood is the same color, our brains are the same size, our bodies are the same shapes, and we all learn our prejudices at our mother's knees. I'm just lucky that I was taught to be prejudiced *toward*, instead of prejudiced *against*. But it's prejudice, just the same."

"You think love is prejudice?"

"Of course. Love is prejudice in favor of life."

Tom swallowed hard. "Well, do you think you might be prejudiced just a little in my direction?"

"It might happen to be so."

"Then maybe I ought to ask you out to the movies tomorrow night."

Jessie grinned. "You do that, Baby. You do that very thing."

Recommended Readings

Gough, H.G. "Personality and Personality Assessment," in M.D. Dunnette, ed. *Handbook of Industrial and Organizational Psychology* (Chicago: Rand McNally, 1976).

Gould, Stephen Jay. *The Mismeasure of Man* (New York: Norton, 1981).

Guthrie, Robert V. *Even the Rat Was White: A Historical View of Psychology* (New York: Harper & Row, 1976).

Jensen, Arthur R. *Bias in Mental Testing* (New York: Free Press, 1979).

Jones, Reginald L., ed. *Black Psychology*, 2nd ed. (New York: Harper & Row, 1980).

Sternberg, R.J., and D.K. Detterman, eds. *Human Intelligence: Perspectives on Its Theory and Measurement* (Norwood, N.J.: Ablex, 1979).

Tyler, Leona A., and W.B. Walsh. *Tests and Measurements*, 3rd ed. (Englewood Cliffs, N.J.: Prentice-Hall, 1979).

Yando, Regina, Victoria Seitz, and Edward Zigler. *Intellectual and Personality Characteristics of Children: Social-Class and Ethnic-Group Differences* (Hillsdale, N.J.: Erlbaum, 1979).

Abnormal Psychology 23

Did You Know That . . .

According to Kinsey, the average white married man aged 21–25 has about four sexual climaxes a week?

Psychologists use the statistical term "two standard deviations from the mean" to describe most forms of unusual or abnormal behavior?

A new diagnostic manual put out by the American Psychiatric Association describes hundreds of different "mental disorders"?

The APA no longer considers homosexual behavior to be a symptom of mental illness?

Most sexual offenders are undersexed, misinformed, and narrow-minded people?

Normal people who pretend to have severe mental problems are usually admitted to mental hospitals, diagnosed as being "psychotic," and have difficulties getting out once they're admitted?

There often is little agreement among psychiatrists as to which type of "mental disorder" a given patient actually suffers from?

When a person develops abnormal behavior patterns, everyone the person has close contact with probably has helped bring about the abnormality?

"I'm Crazy—You're Crazy"

Steve May got out of the car, closed the door, then stuck his head back in through the window. "You really think it will work?" he said for perhaps the tenth time that day.

Dr. Mary Ellen Mann smiled reassuringly at the handsome young man. "Well, it worked for all of Professor Rosenhan's subjects. They all got admitted to the mental hospital without any trouble at all. Getting out's the problem, not getting in. But I'm sure you'll be able to cope beautifully with any problems that may arise. Just get yourself in gear and go convince those people that you're crazier than a bedbug."

Steve thought about the matter for a moment or two. He had willingly committed himself to helping Dr. Mann with her research on the reliability of psychiatric diagnoses. But committing himself to a state mental hospital was a very frightening thought. He supposed that he couldn't really chicken out at the last moment, but still . . . "If they do admit me," the blond young man said, "you're sure that I can prove to them that I'm okay so they'll let me out?"

Dr. Mann snorted as she laughed. "As I told you, Steve, if you get stuck in there, you've got to get out on your own. Oh, I'll come rescue you eventually, have no fears about that." She leaned toward him a trifle. "Or maybe you're afraid that you really are a bit nuts. Is that the problem?"

A rosy flush spread over Steve's face. "Of course not! I'm as sane as you are!"

Dr. Mann snorted even more loudly. "Just don't tell the psychiatrist that, or you may never get out!" Then she smiled warmly. "Good luck, Steve. I really appreciate your helping out with my research this way."

Steve nodded slowly, then pulled his head out of the car window. Dr. Mann waved at him, then put the car into gear and slowly drove off.

Steve turned to look at the hospital. It was a huge, towering, forbidding structure. The thought of spending the next few days—or weeks, or months—in that place frankly scared him. But he had promised . . .

He walked slowly up the path and went slowly through the heavy, wooden door. The lobby inside was cool and almost empty. A nice-looking young woman sat behind a reception desk, filling in a form of some kind on a typewriter. Steve put on his best smile and walked over to her.

"Hello," Steve said.

The woman stopped typing and looked up at him. Her face brightened as she took in his handsome features and his muscular body. "Oh, hello," she said warmly. "What can I do for you? Would you like to see a patient?"

Steve returned her smile. "No, I want to be a patient, if you don't mind."

The woman's smile faded a bit. "Oh," she said briskly. "There's something wrong?"

Steve nodded. "Yeah. I need help. I hear voices."

The woman's smile faded away entirely, as if she had suddenly tucked him into a much less desirable category in her mind. "What do the voices seem to be saying?" she asked.

"They're kind of indistinct," he replied. "Mostly words like 'dull,' 'thud,' 'empty.' You know, things like that."

The woman nodded slowly, mechanically. "And what sex are the voices, male or female?"

Steve smiled wanly. "I can't always tell."

The woman frowned. "Are you in any pain right now?"

"No, not really," Steve said. "But I do think I need your help—for a while, that is, until the voices go away."

Again the woman frowned. "Well, we're pretty full these days. You'll have to see the admitting psychiatrist, of course. But he's very busy right now. And we'll have to fill out a lot of papers, and . . ."

Two hours later, Steve's fingers were almost numb from writer's cramp. He finished all the forms, and then sat patiently in the lobby for another hour or so until the psychiatrist could see him.

The psychiatrist was a pleasant man of about 40 who spoke with such a thick foreign accent that Steve couldn't always understand the questions the man asked him. Steve told the man about his voices—that they were indistinct and that they seemed to be saying 'dull,' 'thud,' and 'hollow.' The doctor nodded sagely, and muttered under his breath. Steve thought the man had said something like, "Existential crisis." Steve smiled inwardly. It was going just like Rosenhan's paper had suggested it would. Almost all of Rosenhan's subjects got the same sort of diagnosis.

Then the psychiatrist started asking questions about Steve's early life. When Steve admitted that he occasionally argued with his father, and that he really got along better with his mother, the doctor nodded sagely again. Steve thought he mumbled something like, "Very significant." And when Steve said that he wasn't always sure what his goals in life were, and that he now and again lost his temper, the psychiatrist muttered something under his breath that sounded suspiciously like, "Poor impulse control."

Aside from the bit about the "voices," Steve answered the man's questions as honestly as possible, just as Dr. Mann had told him to do. At first Steve had been sure the psychiatrist would see through the game, and would announce loudly that Steve was "just faking it." But the doctor apparently took him only too seriously. To Steve's surprise, the psychiatrist never once asked him about his abilities and strengths, or what made him happy. The man obviously couldn't tell that Steve was really normal and healthy, and that thought frightened Steve more than he could admit.

Finally the psychiatrist leaned back in his chair, tapped a pencil on his desk, and stared silently at Steve for a few moments. "Look, Steven, I don't want to alarm you, but I do think I ought to be honest with you. You seem to be suffering from very real psychological problems. You were right to come to us. I'm sure that we can be of help. We'll keep you under observation for a while, and then we'll talk about getting you legally certified . . ."

"Legally certified?" Steve said in a horrified tone of voice.

"Of course. If you are to stay here more than 60 days, which will likely be the case, there are certain legal formalities we have to go through . . ."

"Sixty days! But what if I get better right away—like tomorrow?" Steve protested.

The psychiatrist allowed himself a brief, thin-lipped smile. "As you Americans say, we'll cross that bridge when we come to it." The doctor pressed a button on his desk and, almost immediately, a burly young attendant entered the office.

"Charles, this is Steven," the psychiatrist said. "He will be staying with us for a while. Please check him in and then put him on Ward A-5."

The attendant nodded, then said to Steve, "This way, please."

Steve got up and started to extend his hand to the psychiatrist. But the man was already busy working on the papers that would admit Steve to the mental hospital. So Steve picked up his small bag and followed the attendant out of the office.

"First, we'll check you in and get all your valuables stowed away," the burly attendant said.

"Oh," said Steve, "I'd rather keep them with me."

"Can't. It's the rule," the attendant said. "Got to stow it all away—your money and credit cards and all that stuff. Your watch and rings, too. We can't be responsible, you know. And we'll have to inspect your shaving kit and all your personal gear. No razors, you know, and you can't keep all your clothes either."

"Clothes?" Steve said in an unbelieving tone of voice.

"Belts, stuff like that. Might hurt yourself."

Steve had to hurry a bit to keep up with the attendant. "But surely I can keep my pictures, and my books, and things like that . . ."

"Nope. It's against the rules."

For a moment, Steve panicked. The folly of what he was doing finally struck home. They were taking away all his "cards of identity," all his symbols of power, all his memories and mementoes. They were stripping him of his personality and turning him into a number, a card in a file, a statistic.

"We'll give you a shower and then get you some hospital clothes," the attendant said, opening a huge metal door and then locking it securely after they had passed through.

"But I just had a shower, about an hour ago," Steve protested as they walked down a long, bare corridor. "Do you think what I've got is catching?"

"Don't give me any trouble, man. I don't make the rules." The attendant unlocked another huge metal door at the end of the corridor and banged it shut behind them. They walked down a flight of metal stairs and then the attendant unlocked yet another door that had a small window in it. The window was covered with thick steel bars. The burly attendant told Steve to strip, took his things, and pointed to a shower room. When Steve returned, water still dripping from his hair, the attendant gave him a set of hospital clothes.

"You look fine," the attendant said. "Now, let's get on with it."

They walked down another long, bare corridor to a metal door that bore a small sign, "Ward A-5." Steve shook his head in dismay. They had passed through four locked, steel doors already. If getting into the ward was this difficult, what would getting out be like?

"This is it," the attendant said, unlocking the door and walking into the ward. "Wait here until I find the nurse," the man said, shutting the metal door behind them.

Steve stood staring at the inmates. Several of them were watching a television set, but they didn't seem to respond to the program in any way. One middle-aged man rushed feverishly about the ward, as if looking for something he had lost. A younger man was rocking back and forth in a straight-backed chair. A third man was standing in a corner, quietly urinating.

My God, Steve thought. *You've got to be crazy to stay in a place like this.*

The attendant came up with a nurse, who gave Steve an efficient smile and then showed him where his bed would be. The man in the next bed was curled up in a fetal position, laughing quietly to himself, a serene smile on his face.

Steve stretched out on the narrow bed and stared at the ceiling. "Well, I made it in okay," he said aloud. "But how in the world am I ever going to get out of this place?"

The man in the next bed giggled softly.

(Continued on page 556.)

What Is "Insanity"?

Most of the great personality theorists—Freud, Jung, Adler, Erikson, Rogers, and the rest—based their ideas on the study of mentally disturbed people. Most of these individuals had problems that were *exaggerations* of the mental and behavioral traits that we all have. Therefore, the theorists presumed, the mental patient differs from the average citizen in the *quantity* or amount of madness, not in the *quality* or type of psychological problem. In short, the view of most theorists has been that we are all mildly abnormal, but some of us are more abnormal than others.

But does that view make sense? If everyone **deviates** from the norm one way or another, doesn't the word "normal" lose most of its meaning? And if we can't define the word "normal," what shall we make of the word "abnormal," which literally means "away from the normal"?

There is also the question of *what* about the person is abnormal. Is "insanity" a type of *intra-psychic* problem? If so, we might refer to it as an "emotional disturbance." But if we view "insanity" as caused by some deep, underlying psychological difficulty, we might call it "mental illness." Or if we believe that abnormal thoughts and behaviors are *learned*, then we use terms such as "behavior disorders" or "problems in living" rather than "mental illness." As you will soon see, there is as little agreement on what "insanity" is and what causes it, as there is on how to "cure" it!

All concepts of the "abnormal" spring from a theory of what's "normal," however. So before we can discuss such topics as "mental illness," "behavior disorders," and "insanity," we must first take a good, hard, objective look at the word "normal."

What Is Normal?

Suppose a young married couple named Mary and John Smith are on the verge of divorce. They go to see a psychologist and ask for help. Even before the psychologist learns their names, this counselor knows several things about the Smiths. First, one or both of them is going to be suffering considerable psychological pain, distress, or anxiety. Second, things are probably worse for the couple now than at some time in the past. That is, their way of life has changed from its usual (normal) pattern. Third, they are bright enough to sense this departure from normal and to seek help.

Any deviation from a person's usual way of thinking, feeling, or behaving can be considered a symptom of psychological abnormality—provided that the person was reasonably "normal" (as defined by the person's culture) to start with. Generally speaking, if this deviation is slight, the psychologist is likely to believe that the person suffers from what has generally been classified as a **neurosis**. If the deviation is large, the psychologist may worry that the person suffers from a more severe problem called a **psychosis**.

The *terminology* in the field of clinical psychology is undergoing rapid change right now, a point we will discuss more fully later in this chapter. For the moment, all you need to remember is that some people have relatively minor problems, while others have such major difficulties that they may need to be hospitalized at some point in their lives. It is the psychologist's job, in either case, to help the person solve the problem and return to "normal"—as defined by the society in which the person must live and function.

Sexual Dysfunctions

Mary and John Smith could have many quite different *kinds* of psychological difficulties. Later in this chapter we will describe what some of the more common types are like. But to help us understand what the word "normal" means, let us assume that either or both of them has what a psychologist might call a *sexual dysfunction*.

Suppose that, in their first interview with the psychologist, John complains that Mary is **frigid**, that she consistently refuses him the pleasures of the marriage bed. Mary replies that John is a **satyr**—that is, he has an unusually strong sex drive. She claims that he thinks of nothing else, talks of nothing else, and that he is interested only in her body and not in her mind or personality. (As we will see later, the problem might be the other way around—the wife might desire sex more fequently than the husband. But we will delay discussion of that situation for a moment.)

The psychologist might well assume that the woman was *normal*, but that the man's libido had gotten out of control and was ruining the mar-

Deviates (DEE-vee-ates). To deviate is to turn aside, to go off in an unusual direction, or to move away from the norm or average. Very few people are "right at the norm" on the majority of psychological, social, and political scales. Thus almost all of us are "deviates" in one way or another, even if we typically fail to perceive how deviant we really are.

Neurosis (new-ROW-sis). Also called "psychoneurosis." A mild form of mental disorder that usually does not keep the individual from living a reasonably successful life. Freud thought that the seeds for a neurosis were planted in early childhood.

Psychosis (sigh-KOH-sis). A severe and usually incapacitating form of mental disorder that often requires hospitalization.

Frigid. Frigidity (frih-JID-uh-tee) is a psychological problem experienced by many women who cannot gain sexual pleasure or release as readily as they might wish. Freud believed that frigidity was caused primarily by the woman's repressing sexual thoughts and feelings because she had been taught they were "unacceptable" or deviant for a woman in her station.

Satyr (SAY-teer). An ancient Greek country god supposedly fond of wine, women, and song—but mostly fond of women. Represented in art as a horse or goat.

riage. Or the counselor might assume that the man had a *normal*, healthy appetite for sex, but that the woman was so *repressed* that she could not enjoy one of the finer aspects of marriage. Or the therapist might assume that *both* Mary and John showed symptoms of abnormality. How could the psychologist tell for sure?

Question: *Psychologists always make* assumptions *about what is normal and abnormal for a particular patient. Do you think that male counselors might tend to make different assumptions about John and Mary Smith than would female counselors?*

Cultural Norms

Normality is always defined *within a given context or culture*. No psychologist can come to any meaningful conclusions about the Smiths' problems if the counselor ignores the *social environment* in which the couple lives. That is, before the psychologist can concentrate on the unique aspects of the Smiths' difficulties, the therapist must ask what other people with similar backgrounds are like. How many times do most young husbands expect sex each week? How frequently do most wives desire it? Do husbands typically *wish* to make love more frequently than their wives, or the other way around? And what about the actual *behavior*? How frequently do young married men *actually* achieve sexual climax? And is it always with their wives? And how frequently do young married women actually reach orgasm, and is it always with their husbands?

"I CAN REMEMBER WHEN PARANOIA WAS UNUSUAL."

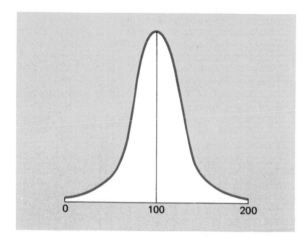

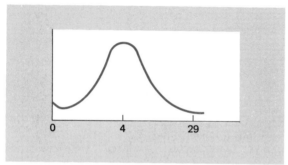

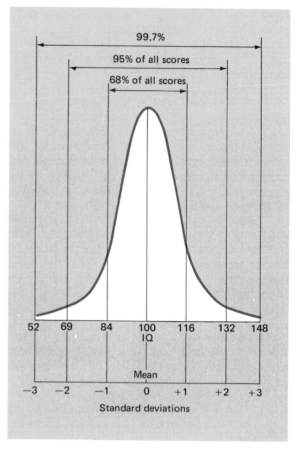

Fig. 23.1. A bell-shaped curve of IQ's. **(top)**

Fig. 23.2. Range of weekly outlets in young married men. **(bottom left)**

Fig. 23.3. Standard deviations tell you what percentage of scores fall within a certain distance from the mean. **(right)**

Sex and the Bell-Shaped Curve

Until Alfred Kinsey performed his pioneering research on human sexuality, no one really knew the answers to these questions. Judging from a rough analysis of the Kinsey data, it would seem that the average white married man aged 21–25 reaches sexual climax about three to four times a week. In Kinsey's rather stilted language, he said that the young, married, white, middle-class US male achieved an average of about four *sexual outlets* per week. (Kinsey thus included in his figures all forms of sexual activity—including masturbation, homosexuality, bestiality, "wet dreams," and extramarital heterosexual contacts.)

Although Kinsey gathered his data more than 30 years ago, recent surveys tend to confirm his findings. Thus we can use Kinsey's results to give us a "social context" in which to consider the Smiths' marital problems—but only assuming that the Smiths are white, middle-class people liv-

ing in the US. Yet there is still a lot more we need to know. If Mr. Smith desired 7 outlets a week, would you consider him abnormal? What if he demanded 17? And would John Smith be "far above normal" if he wanted 77?

Range

As you can see, knowing what the average is doesn't always help. The average score on most intelligence tests is 100. If you get a score of 101, are you "way above average"? Before we could answer, we would have to know the *range* of scores, as well as how those scores were *distributed* over the range. And the best way to find out would be to resort to that favorite psychological tool, the bell-shaped curve.

The range of IQ's on some tests goes from 0 to about 200. And the tests are so constructed that most people's scores are bunched up in the middle of the distribution. Although some 50 percent of the scores lie above the mid-point of the curve—and some 50 percent lie below it—most of the IQ's do not *deviate* very far from this mid-point (see Figure 23.1). Depending on how the mid-point is calculated, it is called the **mode**, the mean, or the **median**. If you are interested in how these terms are calculated, see the Statistical Appendix at the back of this book. However, "mode," "mean," and "median" are merely words that mean the **norm**, or the middle of the range of scores.

In the case of Kinsey's data on the sexual behavior of the (young, white, middle-class) US male, the mean, median, and mode are probably close together. Thus, for our present purposes, we can consider any of them the norm. The actual distribution of outlets per week probably looks something like the graph shown in Figure 23.2.

Now we can see that if Mr. Smith desired 7 outlets a week, he would be fairly close to the norm. But what if he wished 17? Would this fact make him ab-norm-al, or away from the norm? How far away is "away"?

Standard Deviation

Psychologists have a method of measuring deviations from the norm that they call the **standard deviation**. If you are interested in learning more about this matter, you might wish to look at the Statistical Appendix. However, when all is said and done, the standard deviation is little more than a fairly accurate way of measuring *percentages*.

Psychologists assume that, on any given test (or on the measurement of any given behavior), whatever *two-thirds of the people do* is probably pretty normal. On an intelligence test, for example, the norm (or mean) is arbitrarily set at a score of 100. On many such tests, about two-thirds of the people get scores between 84 and 116. As you can see from Figure 23.3, this fact means that about one-third of the people scored within 16 points *below* the mean, and about one-third of the people scored within 16 points *above* the mean. By definition, then, the *standard deviation* for such a test would be 16 points. If you score within one standard deviation of the norm, your performance is almost always considered "within the normal range."

If you got an IQ of 132 on the test, you would be 2 standard deviations above the mean, and you would be well above average. If you got a score of 148 on the test, you would be 3 standard deviations above the norm. This exceptional score would put you in the upper two-tenths of a percent of the test population.

To summarize (so that we can get back to talking about *psychological deviations* from the norm):

1. If your performance on any measure is within 1 standard deviation of the norm, you are like

Mode. From the Latin word *modus*, meaning "to measure." The highest point or most frequent score on a bell-shaped distribution of scores.

Mean. That which is "middling" or intermediate in rank or order. The arithmetical average.

Median (ME-dee-an). From the Latin word *medius*, meaning "middle." The median on a superhighway is the paved or planted strip down the middle dividing the road in half. The median in a distribution is the score that exactly cuts the distribution in half.

Norm. From the Latin word *norma*, meaning "pattern" or "rule." The expected, the average, the usual. That which is a model.

Standard deviation. (dee-vee-A-shun). The standard deviation is a mathematical way of figuring out how much a test score deviates from the mean, median, or mode (usually the mean). The standard deviation thus gives you a precise way of measuring how significantly your own score on a test varies or departs from the norm.

two-thirds of the population and hence quite normal.
2. If your performance on any measure is between 1 and 2 standard deviations from the norm, you have departed somewhat from the average.
3. If your performance on any measure is more than 2 standard deviations from the norm, you are behaving differently than about 98 percent of the population. Thus your performance should be considered *significantly* abnormal. You may score higher then the rest of the people, or lower—but surely you are measurably *different* from the majority of the others.

Question: *How many behaviors can you think of that are* statistically normal *(in that most people engage in them) but that aren't necessarily "good" or "moral"?*

Normal Sexuality and the Standard Deviation

Now we're ready to put the Smiths' problem into context. Dr. Kinsey's surveys of sexual behavior suggest that young married men like John Smith have, on the average, 4 sexual outlets per week (see Fig. 23.4). The range is from 0 to more than 29. The standard deviation is about 2.

These facts mean that if John Smith desires sexual contact with his wife from 2 to 6 times a week, he is probably like two-thirds of all similar men that Kinsey talked to. In short, *within the society* in which the Smiths live, his sexual demands would seem average, or normal. If he expected sex more than 8 times per week, John would be more than 2 standard deviations from the norm (for his culture), and thus his requests would be at least *statistically* abnormal.

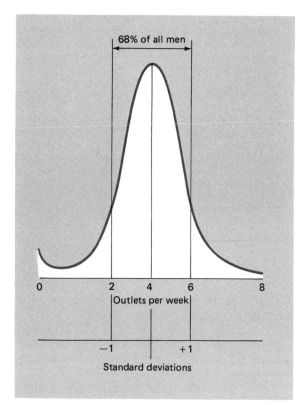

Fig. 23.4. According to Kinsey, two-thirds of all young, white, married, middle-class American males experience 2–6 sexual outlets per week.

Of course, in the long run, the problem that exists between Mary and John Smith is a personal one that cannot be solved by reference to bell-shaped curves. And yet the beauty of Kinsey's work was that he brought sexual behavior out in the open, so that it could be examined statistically as well as personally or theoretically. Lacking this important reference information, the psychologist might well make some very wrong decisions about how to help the Smiths. For we all tend to judge normality *in terms of our own behaviors and expectations*.

For instance, suppose that the counselor was a man who *himself* preferred but one sexual outlet a month—and thought this more than adequate and normal. If John Smith wanted sex four times a week, the counselor might tend to agree with Mary that her husband was a "satyr" who was terribly over-sexed. What kind of therapy might he suggest? On the other hand, if the psychologist was one of those (statistically) rare US men who regularly performed the sex act 20 times a week, he might think that both John and Mary Smith needed to take a few "pep pills" or hormone shots.

Classifying Abnormal Behavior Patterns

As you can gather, it is difficult to define psychological abnormality without a theory of some kind—or some set of data such as Kinsey's—to tell you both what is normal and how any abnormality might have come about.

There is, unfortunately, no one master theory of human behavior that everyone agrees on. Psychologists and psychiatrists have worked out a variety of diagnostic schemes that are supposed to classify people according to their problems. Of these, the best known is surely the *Diagnostic and Statistical Manual of Mental Disorders*, first published by the American Psychiatric Association in 1952. The third edition (DSM-III) appeared in 1980. As we will see, a great many psychologists object to DSM-III. The major complaint raised is that the *Manual* is too *medical* in its approach to what are really *psychological* problems. We will discuss this and other objections to the *Manual* a bit later. First, though, it will pay us to take a look at DSM-III before we go any further in our study of abnormal behavior patterns, sexual or otherwise.

DSM-III

DSM-III was designed to give specific diagnoses for *every* patient who might be referred to a psychiatrist (or possibly a psychologist)—no matter what the patient's problems might be. After interviewing the patient—and perhaps giving the individual various tests—the therapist rates the patient on each of five different **axes** or categories:

Axis 1. Clinical Syndromes and Other Conditions

Axis 2. Personality Disorders; Specific Developmental Disorders

Axis 3. Physical Disorders and Conditions

Axis 4. Severity of Psychosocial Stressors

Axis 5. Highest Level of Adaptive Functioning (during) Past Year

DSM-III stems from what is called the **medical model** of "mental illness." That is, the authors of DSM-III believe that all abnormal thoughts and behaviors are *symptoms* of some psychological "disease." Like most psychiatrists, the people who created DSM-III hold that "insanity" is caused by some "mental germ" that infects your mind much as chicken pox is caused by a virus that infects your body. Thus DSM-III implicitly views all *psychological* difficulties as *medical problems*. You should keep this strong "medical bias" in mind as we discuss the five major axes on DSM-III.

Axis 1

Included on Axis 1 are most of the psychological disorders that the American Psychiatric Association officially recognizes as being "mental illnesses." Generally speaking, Axis 1 is made up of all those severe psychological or behavioral problems that would send you to see a therapist in the first place.

Included in the Axis 1 category are the *psychoses*, all cases of addiction and drug abuse, and most of what DSM-III calls "neurotic disorders." A given patient may have more than one major form of "mental illness," just as a person may also have mumps and measles simultaneously. Also included on Axis 1 are *psychological reactions* to such physical problems as epilepsy and brain damage.

Axis 2

Technically speaking, Axis 2 is limited to what are called the *personality disorders*. In fact, Axis 2 is designed to let the therapist describe the patient's psychological traits or "enduring behavior patterns" rather than any problems that have occurred recently. For example, a severely withdrawn patient would be diagnosed as "schizophrenic" (Axis 1), but a mildly withdrawn or introverted patient *who had been that way for many years* would be diagnosed as having a "schizoid personality disorder" that would appear as an Axis 2 problem.

Many patients will have disorders listed on both Axis 1 and Axis 2. However, since almost all types of "mental illness" are included on Axis 1, many patients will receive no "rating" at all on Axis 2 (or at least none really worth bothering about). A *very* few might have Axis 2 disorders without suffering from any disorder listed on Axis 1.

Axis 3

Axis 3 is a reminder that patients who seek psychological assistance may have physical ailments (such as cancer) that may be related to their mental disorders (such as depression). Included on Axis 3 are all the *physical symptoms* of any type of disease, damage to the brain or any other part of the body, and disabilities caused by accidents or drugs. The *psychological reactions* to these biological problems, however, are generally considered to be mental disorders that would be listed under Axis 1.

Axes (AX-ease). The plural of "axis." An axis is a line about which something rotates. In the DSM-III, the five axes are really "categories" or types of information that the psychiatrist should use in making a diagnosis about what could be troubling a given patient. Whether it is the patient or the psychiatrist who "rotates" around these five axes is an open question.

Medical model. The belief—in psychiatry and psychology—that mental disorders are caused by some "underlying" or "deep-seated" psychological problem, just as influenza is caused by an infectious virus. In fact, what we call the "medical model" should really be termed "the infectious disease model," since there are many other "models" in the field of medicine.

Jargon (JAR-gohn). The "special terms" or "shop talk" of a given profession. As we noted earlier, the word *jargon* comes (appropriately enough) from a French word meaning "the twittering of birds."

Axis 4

Axis 4 is a "social stress scale" that lists such traumatic social stresses as the death of a loved one, changing (or losing) your job, and getting married (or divorced). Again, the patient's *psychological reaction* to these social traumas will probably be a mental disorder listed under Axis 1. Generally speaking, only those stressful events that occurred in the past 12 months are given serious consideration.

Axis 5

Axis 5 is a scale running from "superior" to "grossly impaired" that describes your highest level of psychological adjustment for the past year.

Problems with DSM-III

Table 23.1 gives a *brief* outline of the diagnostic categories included on Axes 1 and 2. However, before you read the material in Table 23.1, there are several things you should understand.

First, DSM-III is filled with psychiatric **jargon**. We will describe many of the disorders later in this chapter, but a complete definition of the terms used in the table would take up several hundred pages.

Second, as we will see in a moment, there is considerable argument both about the *validity* and the *reliability* of the diagnostic categories used in DSM-III. The mere fact that we apply a certain "label" to a person doesn't mean that the label actually fits—or even that a given type of "mental disorder" exists anywhere but in the minds of many present-day psychiatrists.

Third, as we have already noted, DMS-III is based on the "medical model" of "mental illness." There are many other models we could use instead.

Table 23.1. A Brief Outline of the Diagnostic Categories Included on Axis 1 and Axis 2 of DSM-III

Axis 1: Severe Mental Disorders (Including Psychoses and Neurotic Disorders)

Disorders Usually First Evident in Infancy, Childhood, or Adolescence
Mental Retardation
Attention Deficit Disorders
  Hyperactivity
Conduct Disorders
  Undersocialized, Aggressive
  Undersocialized, Nonaggressive
  Socialized, Aggressive,
  Socialized, Nonaggressive
Anxiety Disorders of Childhood or Adolescence
  Separation Anxiety Disorder
  Avoidant Disorder
  Overanxious Disorder
Other Disorders of Childhood or Adolescence
  Reactive Attachment Disorder
  Schizoid Disorder
  Elective Mutism
  Oppositional Disorder
  Identity Disorder
Eating Disorders
  Anorexia Nervosa
  Bulimia
  Pica
  Rumination Disorder
  Atypical Eating Disorder
Stereotyped Movement Disorders
  Transient Tic Disorder
  Chronic Motor Tic Disorder
  Tourette's Disorder
Other Disorders with Physical Manifestations
  Stuttering
  Functional Enuresis
  Functional Encopresis
  Sleepwalking Disorder
  Sleep Terror Disorder
Pervasive Developmental Disorders
  Infantile Autism
Organic Mental Disorders
Dementias Arising in the Senium and Presenium
  Primary Degenerative Dementia
  Multi-infarct Dementia
Substance-Induced
  Alcohol
    Intoxication
    Withdrawal Delirium
    Hallucinosis
    Amnestic Disorder
  Barbiturates
  Opioid
  Cocaine
  Amphetamine
  Phencyclidine (PCP)
  Hallucinogen
  Cannabis
  Tobacco

Caffeine
Substance Use Disorders
(Substance Abuse)
Schizophrenic Disorders
Schizophrenia,
  Disorganized
  Catatonic
  Paranoid
  Undifferentiated
  Residual
Paranoid Disorders
Paranoia
Shared Paranoid Disorder
Acute Paranoid Disorder
Atypical Paranoid Disorder
Psychotic Disorders Not Elsewhere Classified
Schizophreniform Disorder
Brief Reactive Psychosis
Schizoaffective Disorder
Neurotic Disorders
(Included in Categories Below)
Affective Disorders
Bipolar Disorder
  Mixed
  Manic
  Depressed
Major Depression
Other Specific Affective Disorders
  Cyclothymic Disorder
  Dysthymic Disorder (or Depressive Neurosis)
Anxiety Disorders
Phobic Disorders (or Phobic Neuroses)
  Agoraphobia
  Social Phobia
  Simple Phobia
Panic Disorder (or Anxiety Neuroses)
Obsessive Compulsive Disorder (or Obsessive Compulsive (Neurosis)
Post-traumatic Stress Disorder
Somatoform Disorders
Somatization Disorder
Conversion Disorder (or Hysterical Neurosis, Conversion Type)
Psychogenic Pain Disorder
Hypochondriasis (or Hypo-chondriacal Neurosis)
Dissociative Disorders (or Hysterical Neuroses)
Psychogenic Amnesia
Psychogenic Fugue
Multiple Personality
Depersonalization Disorder (or Depersonalization Neurosis)
Psychosexual Disorders
Gender Identity Disorders

Transsexualism
Paraphilias
  Fetishism
  Transvestism
  Zoophilia
  Pedophilia
  Exhibitionism
  Voyeurism
  Sexual Masochism
  Sexual Sadism
Psychosexual Dysfunctions
  Inhibited Sexual Desire
  Inhibited Sexual Excitement
  Inhibited Female Orgasm
  Inhibited Male Orgasm
  Premature Ejaculation
  Functional Dyspareunia
  Functional Vaginismus
Other Psychosexual Disorders
  Ego-dystonic Homosexuality
Factitious Disorders
Factitious Illness with Psychological Symptoms
Chronic Factitious Illness with Physical Symptoms
Disorders of Impulse Control Not Elsewhere Classified
Pathological Gambling
Kleptomania
Pyromania
Intermittent Explosive Disorder
Isolated Explosive Disorder
Adjustment Disorders
With Depressed Mood
With Anxious Mood
With Disturbance of Conduct
With Work (or Academic) Inhibition
With Withdrawal
Psychological Factors Affecting Physical Condition
Conditions Not Attributable to a Mental Disorder That Are a Focus of Attention or Treatment
Malingering
Borderline Intellectual Functioning
Adult Antisocial Behavior
Childhood or Adolescent Antisocial Problem
Academic Problem
Occupational Problem
Uncomplicated Bereavement
Noncompliance with Medical Treatment
Phase of Life Problem or Other Life Circumstance Problem
Marital Problem
Parent-Child Problem
Other Interpersonal Problem

Axis 2: Personality Disorders

Paranoid	Schizotypal	Narcissistic
Borderline	Dependent	Passive-Aggressive
Schizoid	Histrionic	Antisocial
Avoidant	Compulsive	Atypical, Mixed, or Other

Fourth, the theoretical approach underlying DSM-III would please *none* of the personality theorists discussed in Chapter 22 (Freud, Jung, Adler, Erikson, Rogers, Maslow, Skinner, and Bandura). Nor would DSM-III fit very well within a holistic approach such as General Systems Theory.

Why Use DSM-III?

Given the problems associated with DSM-III, why should we pay any attention to it? For two reasons. First, while *far from perfect*, DSM-III offers what is surely the most reliable and valid set of diagnostic categories presently available. Second, as we stated earlier, as psychiatry goes, so goes the entire field of mental health in the US today. Because DSM-III has the approval of the American Psychiatric Association, its viewpoint will prevail—at least until something better comes along.

That being the case, we will follow the general diagnostic scheme used in DSM-III in describing the various types of abnormal thoughts and behaviors that people sometimes experience.

Mental Disorders

DSM-III marks a radical shift in the psychiatric approach to classifying all disorders. DSM-II—published in 1968—was based in part on psychoanalytic theory. Freud believed that almost all types of mental illness were due either to biological or to psychological causes. Some disorders were very severe and were called the *psychoses*. Other forms were not as severe, and were called the *neuroses*.

According to Freud—and DSM-II—the psychoses are characterized by a loss of contact with reality, a disorganized personality, and by extreme deviation from normal patterns of acting, thinking, and feeling. Some of these severe disorders had clear-cut biological causes and were referred to as **organic psychoses**. Other severe disorders had emotional causes and were referred to as **functional psychoses**. But the authors of DSM-II held that the neuroses *always* had emotional rather than organic causes.

DSM-III reflects a strong movement within the field of psychiatry away from Freudian theorizing. Instead of employing such diagnostic categories as "psychosis" and "neurosis," DSM-III uses the more neutral term "disorder." As we discuss the various *disorders*, however, we will also give their older names.

Disorders Evidenced during Infancy, Childhood, Adolescence

Axis 1 of DSM-III begins by listing a variety of mental disorders that "usually first manifest

Organic psychoses (sigh-KOH-sees). Severe mental disorders that supposedly have a clear-cut physiological basis, such as brain damage, stroke, old age, drug abuse, and so forth. In fact, since people react quite differently to brain damage, strokes, old age, and drugs, there is no psychosis that is *entirely* "organic."

Functional psychoses. Severe mental disorders that have no measurable physiological cause. That is, mental disorders that appear to stem from malfunctions of the mind, not the body. In fact, since the body always reacts physiologically to psychological stress, there is no psychosis that is *entirely* "functional."

Dementias (dee-MENT-chee-ahs). From the Latin word meaning "mad," or "insane." A dementia is a severe mental disorder.

Senium (SEE-nee-um). From the Latin word meaning "old." Senium means "senile period," or "old age."

Alzheimer's disease (ALTS-high-mer). A degenerative disease of the nervous system that leads to early senility.

themselves in infancy, childhood, or adolescence." These problems include mental retardation (which we covered in Chapter 20), hyperactivity (Chapter 13), "conduct disorders," including aggression (Chapter 4), separation anxiety in infants (Chapter 19), sleep disorders (Chapter 3), eating disorders (Chapter 11), and infantile autism (Chapter 9).

As you can see, we have discussed most of these developmental problems elsewhere. Some of them have clear-cut biological causes; others don't. We will talk about some of these difficulties again in the next chapter.

Organic Mental Disorders

At the other end of the age scale from the childhood disorders are those problems associated with growing old. DSM-III refers to these as "**dementias** arising in the **senium** and presenium."

Senile Dementia (Senile Psychosis)

Many physical problems associated with old age can cause you to lapse into a child-like state commonly called a *senile dementia*, or *senile psychosis*. You may suffer from a series of slight strokes, or from **Alzheimer's disease**, or even from "hardening of the arteries." In 1974 this type of mental illness accounted for almost 5 percent of the admissions to public mental hospitals. As our life spans increase, however, this figure will surely rise. The average age of admission for patients diagnosed as senile is 75 for both men and women, although the problem may occur as early as age 60 or so.

The symptoms that lead us to call someone "senile" usually develop slowly, but the condition can be hastened by physical illness or psychological stress. The first changes that you might notice in a pre-senile person are usually those of a nar-

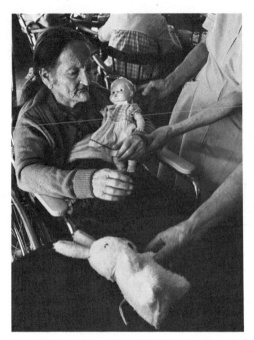

Bernice Neugarten

A patient suffering from Alzheimer's disease becomes senile and may revert to childish behavior patterns. **(left)**

About 6 million US citizens are alcoholics. **(middle)**

rowing of the person's interests, a decrease in alertness, a dislike for change. If Mary Smith were becoming senile, she might seem forgetful, easily irritated, interested primarily in her own thoughts and bodily functions. She might also become more and more hostile and unsympathetic toward others. Eventually she might forget who she is, lose all her memory of recent events, or even refuse to recognize John Smith and their children.

One of the best forms of therapy to *prevent* (or at least retard) the onset of the senile condition seems to be that of giving a sense of meaningfulness to older people's lives, often by helping them maintain family and friendship ties and by making sure older individuals know they are loved and wanted. Robert J. Havighurst and his colleagues at the University of Chicago found—in a series of experiments performed in the 1960's—that older people who remained actively engaged in life were generally happier and healthier than those people who withdrew from society. And, as Bernice L. Neugarten pointed out in 1973, it remains true that people who are well-adjusted and productive during their middle years tend to be those who do best as senior citizens. Dr. Neugarten concludes that, "Within broad limits, given no major biological accidents or major social upheavals, patterns of aging are predictable from knowing the individuals in middle age." In

brief, the seeds of a senile psychosis are typically planted long before the person's fiftieth birthday.

Substance-Induced Organic Mental Disorders

Drug abuse can lead not only to behavioral changes, but organic mental disorders as well. But, as the *Manual* notes, "In most cases, the diagnosis of these Organic Mental Disorders will be made in individuals who also have a Substance Use Disorder."

Substance Use Disorders

Addiction to, or overdose from, many types of drugs can lead to abnormal behavior and thought patterns. A person suffering from such abnormalities is said to have a *drug-induced psychosis*, or a "substance use disorder." We discussed many of the causes for drug-related problems in Chapter 3, and most of the types of drugs that people "abuse" are listed in Table 23.1. By far the most commonly abused substance, however, is alcohol.

Alcoholism

Alcoholism is—at least in the US—a psychological problem associated with aging. In a study reported in 1978, Yale psychologist Jeffrey Blum noted that 35 percent of patients aged 55–64 admitted to VA hospitals were diagnosed as being alcoholics. In marked contrast, only some 5 percent of the patients aged 17–34 were classified as alcoholics.

As we noted in Chapter 3, alcohol selectively destroys brain tissue in the *dominant hemisphere*. Most of the symptoms associated with alcoholism, therefore, are associated with changes in language behaviors, verbal memory, and in logical planning and self-control. The acute alcoholic may show almost all of the symptoms associated with senile psychosis—particularly hallucinations, a denial that any problem exists, memory loss, and a general state of confusion.

Only some 10 percent of chronic alcoholics develop what is called an *alcohol psychosis* and thus require hospitalization. (As we will see in the next chapter, medical treatment for alcoholism is usually far less effective than is psychological or behavioral therapy.)

Schizophrenic Disorders

Psychologists have, in the past, differentiated between the *organic psychoses*, which we have already discussed, and the *functional psychoses*, which are a severe form of psychological disturbances that have no obvious physiological basis. About 40 percent of the first admissions to public mental hospitals are for patients with functional psychoses. Another 25 percent of first admissions are for patients with organic psychoses.

Public health officials estimate that, during any given year, more than one million Americans can be considered psychotic. About two-thirds of these people are hospitalized, more than 98 percent in public institutions. Perhaps 50 percent of the hospital beds in the US are occupied by mental patients, the vast majority being people suffering from psychotic problems. Fortunately, many of these individuals recover completely after treatment and never need hospitalization again.

By far the most common type of functional psychosis is *schizophrenia*. The term comes from the Latin words that mean "splitting of the mind." The use of this term is unfortunate, for the "multiple" or "split personality" we will discuss later as a type of dissociative disorder has nothing to do with schizophrenia.

General mental disorganization is usually the major hallmark of schizophrenia. The authors of DSM-III state that, "Invariably there are characteristic disturbances in several of the following areas: content and form of thought, perception, [emotion], sense of self, volition, relationship to the external world, and psychomotor behavior." Thus if you badly distorted reality, or if you withdrew into a psychological shell and wouldn't come out, you would probably be diagnosed as suffering from schizophrenia.

An older name for schizophrenia is *de-mentia praecox*, from the Latin words meaning "youthful insanity." And schizophrenia *is* primarily a disorder of the young. Jeffery Blum's study of patients at VA hospitals shows that 45.7 percent of patients aged 17–24 were diagnosed as being schizophrenic, while but 8.9 percent of patients over 65 were so diagnosed. About 27 percent of all the patients in Blum's study were classified as suffering from schizophrenia. Furthermore, this disorder is becoming increasingly more common. In 1954, only 22.2 percent of the VA patients were classed as schizophrenic, while in 1974, the figure had risen to almost 31 percent. Schizophrenia affects men and women in equal numbers but single males are particularly susceptible.

There is considerable argument in psychological circles as to whether schizophrenia really exists as a "single" mental illness, or whether we simply call people "schizophrenics" because we don't know what else to call them. The fact that so many people are diagnosed as schizophrenic suggests that this category may be too loose and too large to be meaningfully applied to the complex living systems we call human beings.

DSM-III lists four main types of schizophrenia: disorganized; catatonic; paranoid; and undifferentiated. A fifth category, called *residual*, is reserved for patients who have made some sort of recovery or who are not presently showing all the symptoms of the disorder. However, most schizophrenic patients are not expected to recover fully, and they cannot be considered "cured" until they have been free of all symptoms for a period of "many years."

Disorganized Type

DSM-III lists three main symptoms for the disorganized type of schizophrenia: (1) frequent incoherence; (2) absence of systematized delusions; and (3) blunted, inappropriate, or silly affect. One of the major problems a patient suffering from this

Dementia praecox (dee-MENT'-chee-ah PREE-cox). The original name for schizophrenia. Means "insanity of the young."

Catatonic schizophrenia (kat-tah-TAHN-ick). There are two main types of catatonic schizophrenia. The first (called "catatonic stupor") often comes on rapidly. The patient becomes mute, stares blankly at the floor, and may assume a fixed, stereotyped posture which the patient may maintain for days or weeks. The second (called "catatonic excitement") is characterized by frenzied motor activity. The patient may talk incoherently at the top of the voice, rush frantically back and forth, tear off clothing, and without warning may attack someone or break up furniture. The two states may alternate—that is, a patient may be "stuporous" for a while, then lapse into excitement, then become calm and "freeze" into a strange posture for several days.

Affect. The conscious, subjective aspect of an emotion.

Each year millions of Americans suffer from mild to severe bouts of depression, the worst of which may require medical or psychological treatment of some kind.

type of disorder has is in "talking and thinking logically." The individual may have delusions or hallucinations, but these are not *organized* into any systematic scheme or pattern. And the patient expresses emotions ("affect") in an unusual manner—or not at all.

Catatonic Type
The essential feature of this disorder is what DSM-III calls "psychomotor disturbances." That is to say, the patient may "posture" by assuming a "pose" and holding it rigidly for hours. Or the patient may show excited motor activity, apparently purposeless and not influenced by external stimuli. Or the individual may refuse to talk or fail to respond to environmental stimuli. Some patients alternate between "stupor" and "excitement." This type of disorder was very common several decades ago, but now is rare in Europe and North America.

Paranoid Type
Paranoid schizophrenia primarily involves such symptoms as "delusions of grandeur," and feelings of persecution. Any hallucinations the patient has will almost always involve grandiose schemes and persecutions. In addition, the patient may suffer from intense jealousies. Patients diagnosed as paranoid schizophrenics often show little impairment in their daily functioning—particularly if they do not pay much attention to their delusions. This type of schizophrenia usually occurs later in life than the other types.

Undifferentiated Type
This category is a sort of "grab bag" diagnosis used when the patient is schizophrenic but does

not fit clearly into one of the other three categories—or fits into more than one of them.

Patients who recover from schizophrenia are said to be **in remission**. According to DSM-III, they must be free of all symptoms for a period of several years before they can be considered "cured."

Question: What might Harlow's studies of "motherless" monkeys tell us about the causes of catatonic behavior?

Paranoid Disorders
Some patients have well-organized delusions, severe types of jealousy, and feelings of being persecuted—but show no other evidence of mental illness (such as distorted thought patterns or inappropriate emotions). These patients are often diagnosed as suffering from **paranoia**. But, as the authors of DSM-III note, "the boundaries of this group of disorders and their differentiation from other disorders, particularly severe Paranoid Personality Disorder and Schizophrenia, Paranoid Type, are unclear." The authors of DSM-III also state that deafness, moving to a new country, and other stresses may predispose a patient to the development of a paranoid disorder. The delusions caused by drug abuse are also considered to be a form of paranoid psychosis.

Other Psychotic Disorders
DSM-III lists several minor disorders here that resemble other psychoses but are of very brief duration. Since there is little agreement among psychiatrists on these disorders, we will not discuss them further.

Affective Disorders
People whom we call "schizophrenic" sometimes seem to be stuck in the middle of the "mood scale," being neither very far "up" or "down" no matter what the situation. People suffering from what we call the *affective disorders* (or affective psychoses) often seem stuck at one end of the emotionality scale or the other, although sometimes they "flip-flop" from one extreme to the other.

Bipolar Disorder
If you met a woman on the ward of a mental hospital who was giggling and smiling, racing about, and acting rather as if she had taken too many "pep pills," she would be suffering from what DSM-III calls a "manic episode" in a *bipolar disorder*. In the past, her problem would have been labeled a *manic psychosis*. However, the authors of DSM-III assume that all patients who experi-

ence "manic episodes" will eventually suffer from a major depressive episode. Therefore, DSM-III uses the term "bipolar disorder" to describe anyone who shows manic behavior.

A person afflicted with this disorder is often excessively happy and optimistic even in the face of life's greatest tragedies. During the worst part of an attack of mania, the patient may become so active and agitated that he or she must be forcibly restrained.

Major Depression

If you met a patient overwhelmed by the sadness and futility of life, someone sunk into a deep pit of despair, you would have met someone suffering from a *major depression*. These patients respond as if they had taken an overdose of "downers," and often sink into a state of complete passivity. They may refuse to move from their beds, and sometimes must be force-fed to be kept alive.

There is a curious but not well understood relationship between manic and depressive episodes. Some patients swing wildly from one emotional extreme to the other, while some patients show only the depressive reaction. According to the authors of DSM-III, if the patient shows *both* schizophrenic thought patterns *and* severe mania or depression, the patient probably should be diagnosed as having at least both types of disorder simultaneously.

Question: What might Harlow's research on "depressed monkeys" tell us about the causes of some types of human depressions?

Neurotic Disorders

In a preliminary draft of DSM-III circulated in the late 1970's, the term "neurosis" was discarded completely. Probably no other aspect of the preliminary draft caused so much criticism. In the final version, the authors of DSM-III have again listed the neuroses—but in parentheses after their "new names." On page 9 of the *Manual*, the authors write that, "When Freud first used the term 'psychoneurosis,' he was referring to only four subtypes: anxiety neurosis, anxiety hysteria (phobia), obsessive compulsive neurosis, and hysteria." Over the years, however, the term was broadened to include many disorders that didn't fit Freud's original four categories. And thus, according to the authors of DSM-III, "There [now] is no consensus in our field as to how to define 'neurosis.'"

In fact, most of what DSM-III calls "Anxiety Disorders," "Somatoform Disorders," "Dissociative Disorders," and "Factitious Disorders" are what once were called *neuroses*. The same might

be said for some sexual disorders, "disorders of impulse control," and most of the other disorders that fill out Axis 1 and all of Axis 2 of DSM-III. We will list some of the more common types of neuroses below, following the DSM-III classifications. However, when you hear someone speak of "a neurosis," you should remember that this very broad classification of problems typically means that the person is suffering from some (usually) fairly mild but relatively permanent emotional disturbance.

Anxiety Disorders

Generally speaking, *anxiety* is the hallmark of these disorders. The authors of DSM-III estimate that from 2 to 4 percent of the general population has at some time had a disorder that would be classified as an anxiety disorder.

Phobic Disorders (Phobic Neurosis)

As we mentioned in Chapter 16, phobias are abnormal or unusual fears that have no real basis in fact. If John Smith is unconsciously afraid of sexual activity, he may transfer this unacceptable anxiety to a fear of small or tight places. If the Smiths' bedroom is cramped for space, John may avoid the anxiety associated with entering his wife by refusing to enter the bedroom.

Panic Disorder (Anxiety Neurosis)

Fear begets fear, and panic leads to more panic. If John Smith is unconsciously worried about his masculinity, he may suffer from such acute anxiety that he is unable to perform sexually. The more he tries to satisfy his wife, the more anxiety he experiences, and the worse he performs. Eventually he may break out in a cold sweat if Mary so much as puts her arm around him in the kitchen, fearing that this show of affection is the prelude to another bedroom disaster.

Obsessive Compulsive Disorder (Obsessive Compulsive Neurosis)

Suppose that Mary Smith had, during her childhood attempts to resolve her Electra complex, picked up the attitude that sexual desires are evil

Multiple personality, though a relatively rare mental disorder in real life, often appears in novels and movies, such as "The Three Faces of Eve."

and ought to be resisted even in marriage. And so she attempts to repress her natural instincts and urges, much to John Smith's dismay. But her sexual impulses become so strong that the only way she can keep them safely repressed is to think continually about something utterly irrational—and keep thinking about it again and again and again.

Or perhaps she performs compulsive, repetitive actions—over and over and over. Usually the obsessive thoughts or compulsive actions are symbolically related to her problem. Her mind may be filled with images of germs—she may see them everywhere. Or she may wash her hands (or the bedroom floor) dozens of times each day, all in an attempt to prevent or to get rid of the "dirty sexual thoughts" that occasionally flood her mind.

Obsessions typically deal with thoughts. *Compulsions* typically have to do with behaviors. In either case, the patient is diagnosed as suffering from an "obsessive compulsive disorder."

Somatoform Disorders

Freud called somatoform disorders *hysteria* (see Chapter 17). The essential features are recurrent and multiple complaints about "illnesses" or "body dysfunctions" that apparently are not due to any physical disorder. The patient may experience pain that has no relation to medical problems. Or the individual may so fear having a particular disease that the patient goes to one doctor after another in an attempt to get someone to confirm the patient's fears. This latter type of disorder is called **hypochondriacal neurosis**.

Conversion Disorder (Hysterical Neurosis, Conversion Type)

If Mary Smith suffered from this disorder, she would tend to *convert* hidden or unacceptable wishes or impulses into organic symptoms—presumably in an attempt to divert her feelings of anxiety and perhaps to arouse sympathy and attract attention. If she insisted that her sex organs had no "feelings" at all, that they were "anesthetized," she might be converting her fears about sexuality into a bodily symptom.

Dissociative Disorders

These problems are also closely related to hysteria. The essential feature of most of these disorders is a sudden change in memory, consciousness, identity, or motor behavior.

Psychogenic Amnesia

A type of memory loss brought on by stress or psychological trauma, and not due to any organic problem. As we noted in Chapter 16, the person tends to forget "what" but not "how."

Psychogenic Fugue

If John Smith became badly traumatized by his relationship with Mary, he might assume a totally new identity. Usually this new personality would be more out-going and uninhibited than his previous personality had been. If he later returns to his old identity, he probably won't remember what he did while in the **fugue state**.

Multiple Personality

If Mary Smith's desire for sex bothered her, she might repress all thoughts of sex. But these repressed sexual urges might be so strong that they split off into a separate sub-personality in order to find expression. Mary Smith might refer to this part of herself as "Miss Black," who periodically (usually in bed) seized possession of her body and "did wicked things" with John. In this form of "multiple personality," the dominant personality often forgets the behaviors that the minor personality engages in.

Depersonalization Disorder

If John Smith suffered from this disorder, he might occasionally feel that he had "lost touch with reality." He might believe that he was "living a waking dream," and that his thoughts and movements were under someone else's control. He might even perceive the people around him as being "robots," or even see them as being "dead."

"...AND FLAIR SOAP HAS A SPECIAL OFFER FOR ALL YOU OBSESSIVE-COMPULSIVES WHO WASH YOUR HANDS BETWEEN 30 AND 50 TIMES A DAY..."

Hypochondriacal neurosis (high-poh-kon-DRY-ick-cal). From the Latin word meaning "under the breastbone," which was assumed in olden days to be the "seat" of this disorder. A hypochondriac (high-poh-KON-dree-ack) is someone with a morbid concern about his/her health, or someone with delusions that she/he is sick.

Fugue state (FEWG). Our word "fugitive" comes from the same Latin source. A fugue state is one in which a patient "flees" from his/her old personality, often by getting on a bus or plane and moving to a new place.

Paraphilias (pair-ah-FILL-ee-ahs). From Greek words meaning "love of things above and beyond the normal." These sexual disorders involve a need for abnormal or unusual objects or stimulation in order to achieve climax.

Transvestism (trans-VEST-ism). From the Greek words *trans*, meaning "across," and *vestire*, meaning "to dress." A transvestite is a female who "cross-dresses," that is, who wears masculine clothes, or a male who wears dresses and feminine underwear.

Ego-dystonic homosexuality (EE-go diss-TON-ick). A type of homosexuality in which the person's ego becomes threatened or "torn apart" by the person's sexual thoughts or behaviors. A homosexual who is greatly disturbed by her or his own sexuality.

Psychosexual Disorders

There are four major types of psychosexual disorders.

1. *Gender identity disorders* have to do with a desire to be or dress like the opposite sex (see Chapter 12).
2. The **paraphilias** involve the need for unusual or bizarre imagery or acts in order to achieve sexual excitement. For instance, John Smith might be more excited by the sight of Mary's clothing than by Mary herself, which DSM-III describes as a "clothing fetish." But if John preferred to *wear* women's clothes, this would be a paraphilia called **transvestism**.
3. *Psychosexual dysfunctions* have to do with inhibited desire or performance, or with reaching orgasm too rapidly or too slowly.
4. The last category of psychosexual disorder is **ego-dystonic homosexuality**.

Homosexuality

The authors of DSM-II (1968) considered *any* form of homosexuality to be a "mental disorder" that typically needed treatment. However, in the 1970's, both the American Psychiatric Association and the American Psychological Association voted to remove most forms of homosexual behavior from the official list of "mental illnesses." Indeed, the majority view now is that homosexuality is an "alternative life style," and not a "condition that requires punishment or therapy."

In their 1981 book *Sexual Preference*, Alan Bell, Martin Weinberg, and Sue Hammersmith (all of the Kinsey Institute) report a lengthy study of almost 1,000 homosexuals living in San Francisco.

"In the mid-1970's, both the American Psychiatric Association and the American Psychological Association removed most forms of homosexuality from the official list of "mental disorders." **(left)**

"Transvestism" means "crossdressing," or wearing clothes typically worn only by the opposite sex. **(right)**

Bell and his colleagues also interviewed almost 500 heterosexuals—similar in most respects to the homosexuals—to serve as a "comparison group." This study is remarkable more for what it *disproves* about homosexuality than what it *proves*.

As we noted earlier, Freud assumed that all individuals went through a "natural homosexual period" while trying to solve their Oedipus or Electra complexes during the latency period of the phallic stage of development. He said that most people resolved their complexes by adopting a heterosexual viewpoint during the genital stage (in adolescence). They did this by taking on the values of the opposite-sex parent.

But this natural developmental process could be disrupted, Freud said, if the child's mother was domineering and the father weak or detached. In the case of males, this type of mother might unconsciously "seduce" her sons. And since the father served as a poor model, the boys might take on the mother's values instead of the father's. Thus the boys would fail to resolve their Oedipus complexes in a normal fashion, and

would remain "fixated" at the phallic/homosexual stage. Or they might temporarily "try" heterosexuality, but finding it traumatic, "regress" back to the phallic stage.

Freud presumed that female homosexuality was caused by a similar family pattern. A dominant but hostile mother might overwhelm the girl's feelings for her weak and passive father. Thus the girl would end up rejecting men and would relate to other women instead.

Freud saw homosexuality as "abnormal" (unusual) but not as being **pathological** because it was *learned through experience*, and thus not due to some deep-seated psychological flaw. But, as Bell and his colleagues have shown, the "dominant mother/weak father" family pattern occurs almost as frequently among heterosexuals as homosexuals. In fact, most boys who develop an intense attachment to their mothers early in life turn out to be "straight" in later years. And most girls with weak or detached fathers also become heterosexual rather than **lesbians**. Thus Freud's view of the *genesis* of homosexuality turns out to be a myth.

Bell and his associates also suggest that sexual preference is determined long before the individual becomes sexually active. Thus homosexuality doesn't seem to be *learned*, as many people once feared was the case. A great many heterosexuals Bell and his group interviewed had homosexual encounters at an early age, but became "straight" anyhow. And most of the "gay" individuals interviewed had a number of heterosexual encounters during childhood and adolescence. They didn't find these experiences particularly traumatic. They just found them less rewarding than did the people who became heterosexual during adolescence.

Indeed, the major developmental difference between "straights" and "gays" was that both male and female homosexuals experienced *gender nonconformity* while young. That is, the boys tended not to like sports and other "masculine" activities all that much, while the girls tended to prefer "non-feminine" activities. And they tended to be "nonconformist" in their preferences regardless of which parent was dominant, and whether or not either parent tried to interest them in "traditional" masculine or feminine activities.

According to Bell, Weinberg, and Hammersmith, their evidence indicates that homosexuality is caused by some (as yet unknown) biological cause, not by early experiences, sexual traumas, or "regression to or fixation at the phallic stage of development," as Freud assumed was the case.

Most studies of homosexuality now indicate that "gays" are, generally speaking, as mentally healthy as "straights." In fact, as Bell and his colleagues note, the major problems homosexuals experience stem from society's rejection of what is to them as natural a sexual preference as heterosexuality is to the majority of people.

In his 1980 book *Homosexual Behavior: A Modern Reappraisal*, psychiatrist Judd Marmor writes, "Only when we totally free ourselves from the tendency to put psychiatric labels on homosexuals that singularly differentiate them from heterosexuals with [similar] problems will psychiatrists finally become free from the age-old prejudice in this area."

Ego-Dystonic Homosexuality
The only "mental disorder" that DSM-III recognizes as being associated with homosexuality is that which is *ego-dystonic*. By this term, the authors of the *Manual* refer to someone who experiences great guilt about her or his homosexuality. But the "guilt and anxiety" are what need treating, not the homosexuality itself.

Are Perversions Perverse?
Many forms of unusual or **perverse** sexual behaviors are deviations from the law more than they are from the psychological norm. From 10 to 25 percent of the prisoners in most state penal institutions are sexual offenders. Most are men. Women, when they are arrested for sex offenses,

Pathological (path-oh-LODGE-eye-cal). From the Greek word meaning "study of the emotions." Something is pathological if it is diseased or structurally abnormal in some way.

Lesbians. The celebrated Greek woman poet Sappho (SAF-foh) came from the island of Lesbos. Much of Sappho's poetry sang the praises of other women, a fact that led many scholars to conclude she was a homosexual. Our word for female homosexual comes from the island where Sappho was born.

Perverse (purr-VERSE). From the Latin words meaning "to turn the wrong way." A pervert is someone who gains her or his pleasures in an unusual way—that is, from sexual behavior not approved by society.

are usually charged with prostitution or crimes against children.

In one study of sex criminals in the state of Michigan, 60 percent of all offenses were directed against children. Young unmarried males were the most frequent offenders, but most of them had been sexually delinquent during adolescence. More than 40 percent of those arrested for sex crimes were voyeurs or exhibitionists, who usually were put on probation or given suspended sentences. Fewer than 10 percent had been arrested more than once, and most of these arrests were for very minor offenses.

Only about 5 percent of sexual offenders in the Michigan study inflicted any kind of physical harm on other people. Most of these 5 percent were judged to be abnormal or psychotic in *all* their behaviors, not just in the sexual realm. Very few sexual offenders progressed from minor to major crimes, since they usually persisted in the same type of sexual gratification. And most offenders were not over-sexed but rather the opposite—they were chiefly under-sexed, misinformed, narrow-minded people.

If we assume that sexually deviant behavior is that which is 2 standard deviations from the norm, then what Alfred Kinsey and his associates wrote in 1949 seems particularly appropriate:

> In spite of the many centuries in which our culture has attempted to suppress all but one type of sexual activity, a not inconsiderable portion of all the sexual acts in which the human animal engages still fall into the category which the culture rates as "perverse." The specific data show that two thirds to three quarters of the males in our American culture, and some lesser number of females, engage in at least some "perverse" sexual behavior at some time between adolescence and old age. One half to two thirds of the males engage in such behavior with appreciable frequency during some period of their lives and a fair number engage in such behavior throughout their lives.

Many psychiatrists believe that compulsive gambling is a mental disorder.

Factitious Disorders

The term "factitious" means not real, genuine, or natural. Factitious disorders are, as DSM-III notes, characterized by physical or psychological symptoms that are produced by the individual and are under voluntary control. This tendency to "invent" illness is apparently more common among males than among females. Persons with this sort of problem may often spend all of their lives trying to get admitted to hospitals—perhaps in an attempt to escape from various problems, perhaps because the individual failed in an attempt to become a nurse or doctor. These disorders are not particularly common, and seem to be rather difficult to treat when they do occur.

Disorders of Impulse Control

These disorders include pathological gambling, **kleptomania, pyromania**, and the sorts of "explosive emotional outbursts" we will discuss in the next chapter (see "running amok"). These disorders are more common among males than females.

Adjustment Disorders

According to DSM-III, the essential feature of these disorders is the inability to cope with psychological or social stress (see Chapter 13). Depression; anxiety, and "acting out" are the main symptoms. DSM-III has, in fact, little else to say about this class of disorders.

Conditions Not Mental Disorders but Requiring Treatment

DSM-III lists a number of conditions that may cause a patient to seek treatment but which aren't really "mental disorders" and thus which require a special diagnostic code. Most of these conditions are fairly minor problems that may require little more than "talking things over with an expert." Interpersonal difficulties, mild cases of antisocial behavior, simple grief, and various occupational problems make up the bulk of those on this list.

Personality Disorders

The authors of DSM-III state that, "Personality *traits* are enduring patterns of perceiving, relating to, and thinking about the environment and oneself, and are exhibited in a wide range of important social and personal contexts. It is only when *personality traits* are inflexible and maladaptive and cause either signficant impairment in social or occupational functioning or subjective distress that they constitute *Personality Disorders*."

The personality disorders are coded on Axis 2 of DSM-III, not on Axis 1. Although many of these problems are similar in type to the mental disorders described on Axis 1, they are thought to be "traits," not "mental illnesses." Thus, according to the authors of DSM-III, "The diagnosis of a Personality Disorder should be made only when the characteristic features are typical of the individual's long-term functioning and are not limited to discrete episodes of illness."

The major type of personality disorder not described elsewhere is that of the "antisocial personality."

Antisocial Personality Disorder

Whatever their causes or cures, most mental disorders typically give the most pain and unhappiness to the individual concerned. Someone with an *antisocial personality disorder*, however, is likely to cause more problems for others than for herself or himself. Most criminals fall into this category, as do "manipulators," "con artists," and many types of political rebels.

In previous diagnostic schemes, the terms "psychopath" or "sociopath" were often used to describe individuals with an antisocial personality disorder. Most of these people lack a superego or "conscience," and experience little or no guilt or anxiety about breaking social laws. They often appear to be greedy, impulsive, egocentric men and women who cannot comprehend the social consequences of their actions. Their relationships with others are typically one way: They "get" and the others are expected to "give."

Many people with antisocial personalities are quite intelligent. A few become business and political leaders (such as Adolph Hitler) who are known for their ruthlessness and toughness. Some drift into military organizations, where they may rise rapidly to positions of considerable power. *Most* antisocial people, though, move from one scrape with the law to another and spend much of their time in jails or hospitals. Since they often feel little or no remorse about hurting or killing others, they sometimes become "leaders" in prison societies.

Although a few people with this disorder may suffer from some genetic fault, the main causes for this disorder appear to be poor parental guidance. The majority of antisocial people behave toward others as their parents behaved toward them.

DSM-III: An Evaluation

There are many problems with DSM-III. To begin with, by rejecting Freudian theory, the *Manual* has become much more **eclectic** in its approach than were previous versions. Thus the categories listed above are little more than a hodge-podge of "labels" to be pinned on individuals who don't behave as most of us presumably do. Next, there is the difficulty associated with getting the right label on the right person—that is to say, can we be sure the *Manual* is reliable when used in real-life situations? Last, but not least, we must somehow make sure that the diagnostic categories used are "valid" enough to tell us how to *help* the people we have labeled as being "mentally disordered."

Writing in the October 1981 issue of the American Psychological Association *Monitor*, Robert Spitzer discusses many of the criticisms people have made of DSM-III. Spitzer is a psychiatrist—a medical doctor—who chaired the group that developed DSM-III. Thus some of his arguments are doubtless biased in favor both of psychiatry (as opposed to psychology) and of the use of the *Manual*. However, he does make some good points.

A "Psychiatric Takeover"?

To begin with, Spitzer notes that many psychologists fear DSM-III is yet another attempt by medical doctors to "take complete charge" of the behavioral sciences. Spitzer disagrees. He states that psychologists as well as psychiatrists helped prepare the *Manual*. And more psychologists have bought copies of DSM-III than anyone else, including psychiatrists. Also, most recent textbooks on abnormal psychology have adopted the DSM-III classification scheme.

By implication, then, it would seem that psychology has been more "accepting" of the *Manual* than has psychiatry. Whether this proves to be the case in the long run, though, remains to be seen.

Kleptomania (KLEPP-toh-main-ee-ah). An irresistible urge to steal, usually without any need to do so.

Pyromania (PIE-roh-main-ee-ah). An irresistible urge to set things on fire, often for the perverse sexual excitement associated with "burning."

Eclectic (ek-KLECK-tick). From the Greek word meaning "to gather." To be eclectic is to "gather" or select the best aspects of several different theories or methods.

The "Medical Model"

Spitzer notes that one major objection to the *Manual* is that it "adheres to the medical model." Spitzer denies this is the case. He points out that nowhere in the book do the authors state that "mental disorders are medical disorders." Nor does the *Manual* "assume an underlying biological dysfunction or abnormality for all the disorders."

These points are technically true. However, preliminary drafts of DSM-III *did* state that medical doctors should be the primary care-givers for *all* types of behavioral problems. If psychologists (and many psychiatrists) had not complained loudly about this fact, the final draft would surely have reflected even more of a medical bias than it presently does.

Second, DSM-III still *implies* that most disorders are sets of symptomatic behaviors with an "underlying cause." It matters little, apparently, that the experimental data on this matter simply don't support Spitzer's view.

So, despite Spitzer's comments, it seems clear that the published version of DSM-III *does* adhere to the "medical model," although less so than did the preliminary drafts.

"Labels" versus "People"

The "labels" we stick on individuals who suffer from psychological problems often tell more about our own theories of "mental illness" than about the disorders themselves. Once we label a person a "paranoid," we run the real danger of forcing our perceptions of the person to fit the label. We may unwittingly focus our attention on the few inappropriate things the patient does and ignore all the *healthful* thoughts and behaviors the patient shows.

This problem becomes particularly acute when we realize that DSM-III makes no attempt to describe normal or healthy behavior. Indeed, the *Manual* defines "mental health" almost entirely as the *absence* of any symptoms of "mental illness." And since *almost everyone* has one or more "symptoms," presumably *almost everyone* is to some extent mentally disordered.

David L. Rosenhan

There is a more subtle difficulty here, as well. Once we label someone, we tend to prescribe treatment for the *label*, not for the *person* as he or she exists in real life. As we will see in the next chapter, the vast majority of individuals with psychological problems show improvement *whether or not they are given therapy*. We should not let ourselves get caught in the "correlation fallacy" we described in Chapter 17. Just because we diagnose and treat someone for a particular disorder—and the person subsequently gets better—does not *prove* that the label we used was accurate.

Spitzer disagrees that the *Manual* merely "labels" patients. He states that, "DSM-III classifies and describes disorders (behavior syndromes or patterns), not people. In fact, DSM-III never refers to 'schizophrenics' or 'depressives,' but always to individuals . . . that 'have schizophrenia' or 'depression.'"

Again, Spitzer is technically correct. However, there are two points we should make. First, by saying that a person "*has* schizoprenia," much as one would say that a person "*has* measles," DSM-III implicitly follows the "medical model" described above. A more accurate approach would be to say that a person "displays thought and behavior patterns" of a given type—without assuming that the problem must be totally *inside the individual*.

Second, the vast majority of people who use DSM-III have always referred to patients as "schizophrenics" and "depressives," and there is nothing in DSM-III explicitly warning against this type of *labeling*.

Is DSM-III Valid?

As you discovered in the last chapter, a *valid* psychological instrument is one that "measures what it says it measures." Thus, to prove that DSM-III is a valid diagnostic tool, we would need to have evidence that the categories it uses exist in "real life," and not just in the minds of the *Manual's* authors.

Robert Spitzer states that validity studies on DSM-III are "under way," and he is quite optimistic about their outcome. Other scientists are not so confident. They note that there are but two ways of testing the *Manual's* validity. One way would be to show that most experts using DSM-III agreed that its categories were accurate descriptions of real-life "disorders." A second way would be to show that therapists who used DSM-III had a higher "cure rate" with disturbed patients than did therapists using some other diagnostic scheme. In fact, the experimental data suggest that DSM-III fails both tests.

In a 1978 paper, psychologist Jeffrey Blum notes that the tendency in psychiatry today is to *diagnose what you think you can cure*. In 1954, some 25 percent of the patients admitted to VA mental hospitals were diagnosed as suffering from a neurosis. Today the figure is less than 5 percent. Why the change? Because, Blum says, psychiatrists today prefer medication to "talk therapy," and the neuroses simply can't be cured by pills. In 1954, only 10 percent of the mental patients received medication. Today more than 60 percent of them are given pills—often as the *primary form of treatment*. Only psychiatrists can prescribe medication for a patient, but most scientific experiments show that psychologists are as good at "talk therapy" as are psychiatrists. Therefore, Blum says, DSM-III attempts to turn all behavioral problems into medical problems so that psychiatrists can attempt to "cure" the disorder with a pill. Blum concludes that DSM-III is an invalid instrument.

In truth, the authors of DSM-III admit that their diagnostic categories are not as valid as they might be. On page 8 of the *Manual*, the authors state, "It should be understood, however, that for most of the categories the diagnostic criteria are based on clinical judgment, and have not yet been fully validated by data about such important correlates as clinical course, outcome, family history, and treatment response." We will have more to say on this point at the end of the chapter.

Perhaps, however, we shouldn't worry too much about the *Manual's* validity. For one of the statistical facts of life is that *no test can be valid if it is not reliable*. And, as we are about to see, many scientists have serious concern about the reliability of DSM-III.

Is DSM-III Reliable?

In the June/July 1981 issue of the *Monitor*, Stanford psychologist David L. Rosenhan claims that,

"No proper study of DSM-III's reliability or validity has been published." Spitzer disputes this claim. He notes that DSM-III was field-tested by more than 800 psychiatrists and psychologists prior to its publication. According to Spitzer, "The published results indicate far better reliability than has previously been reported for official classifications of mental disorders."

But is the "far better reliability" Spitzer reports actually good enough? Many psychologists doubt that it is. There is considerable evidence that psychiatrists who use the *Manual* often disagree on what diagnosis to make about a particular patient. Worse yet, psychiatrists often cannot tell (in a reliable fashion) who is a "geniune" mental patient and who is "just faking it."

Rosenhan's "Pseudo-Patients"

In 1973, David L. Rosenhan shocked the psychological world with a report of research he had undertaken on the reliability of psychiatric diagnoses. Rosenhan asked several "normal" people to try to get into mental hospitals by pretending to be mentally ill. These **pseudo-patients**, as Rosenhan called them, asked for voluntary admission to several state and private mental hospitals. The pseudo-patients all stated that they "heard voices," and thus needed help. Other than on this one point, these quite normal people told the admitting psychiatrists the *absolute truth* about their lives and feelings.

To Rosenhan's surprise, *all* of the pseudo-patients were admitted without question. They were all classed as being psychotic, and about 95 percent of the time they were diagnosed as being "schizophrenic."

Once the pseudo-patients were admitted, it was up to each of them to get *out* of the mental hospital as best they could. They were told to ask to see the admitting psychiatrist the next day, to say that the "voices" had gone away, and that they wished to be released. But getting out proved to be much more difficult than getting in. No matter how "normal" the pseudo-patients acted, they found it hard to convince the hospital staff that there was now nothing wrong with them. On the average, it took the pseudo-patients more than two weeks to get out. And, on their release, all of their records were marked, "psychosis *in remission*," meaning that only the symptoms were gone. The "disease" presumably was still present, but hidden. One man was detained (against his will) for almost two months. He finally escaped because, as he put it, the hospital was driving him crazy.

When Rosenhan's data were announced, they caused a furor. Many psychiatrists attacked

him violently for daring to say that they couldn't tell normal people from people who were mentally ill. Rosenhan then agreed to a further study. He promised to send an unspecified number of pseudo-patients to a number of hospitals in the near future. The admitting psychiatrists at these hospitals were asked to "guess" whether each patient they admitted during this time period was a pseudo-patient or not. In fact, Rosenhan sent out no more pseudo-patients. He merely checked all the psychiatric admissions at the end of the time period. To his surprise, he found that some 25 percent of the *actual* patients admitted were thought to be "pseudo-patients" by the psychiatrists.

Rosenhan concludes that psychiatric judgments of what is normal and what isn't—and what is "mental illness" and what is "mentally healthy"—are much less reliable than we had previously suspected.

Other Studies of Diagnostic Reliability

Writing in the September 1981 issue of *Omni*, psychologist Walli Leff notes that there have been many other studies demonstrating that psychiatric diagnoses tend to be highly unreliable. In 1949, Philip Ash arranged to have psychiatrists interview incoming patients jointly at a clinic, then diagnose them independently. The psychiatrists were in total agreement on specific diagnoses less than 10 percent of the time. They were in total *disagreement* about one-third of the time.

In the 1970's, Leff and two colleagues asked staff psychiatrists and clinical psychologists at a VA hospital to indicate how much they agreed with a number of case-history diagnoses. Leff and his associates found very little agreement among the "experts."

Psychologists Maurice Temerlin and William Trousdale had psychiatrists and psychologists listen to a tape-recorded "clinical interview" with what was supposed to be a "disturbed person." In fact, the individual was an actor who was just pretending to have psychological problems. But 60 percent of the psychiatrists diagnosed the actor as being "psychotic." Only about 30 percent of the psychologists did so, and nearly 16 percent of them said the person was normal. But not one psychiatrist diagnosed the actor as being normal.

Psychiatrist Hugh Drummond has made an extensive study of the reliability of DSM-I, II, and III. Walli Leff quotes Drummond as saying, "Each year psychiatrists are more arbitrary in their diagnoses, more smug. They just decide that somebody is psychotic, assume that there's a biochemical cause for it, and treat it with a drug. Psychiatry doesn't work any more; it may do more harm than good. I think we're a bankrupt institution."

Drummond may overstate the case. For, as Robert Spitzer notes, DSM-III does seem to have higher reliability than DSM-I and DSM-II did. However, the bulk of the scientific evidence suggests that the reliability of DSM-III *still isn't high enough* to allow us to help people as much as we should. We will have more to say about this point in the next chapter.

A Holistic Approach to Abnormal Psychology

From a General Systems viewpoint, all behavior is multi-determined—which is to say that everything you do has not one cause but many. Human problems, like human successes, are almost always due to *interactions* of biological, psychological, and sociological forces. Thus any diagnostic scheme that does not view people *holistically* is bound to be both unreliable and invalid.

We can demonstrate this point by returning once more to John and Mary Smith. The authors of the DSM-III consider female frigidity as being primarily the *woman's* problem—a mental disorder (or personality trait) that resides in the woman's mind. But all personality traits (and mental disorders) have a biological background,

and they are always expressed in social, interpersonal situations. In a small percentage of cases, female frigidity may be related to physical causes. But biological difficulties don't really *cause* frigidity. Rather, frigidity is the woman's *response* to her physical condition. And this response is chiefly determined by her own unique developmental history and the social environment she presently lives in. Male impotence—which is defined by DSM-III as being the *man's* problem—can be seen in much the same light.

Frigidity, impotence, and other sexual difficulties are seldom the exclusive problem of just the male *or* the female. A man may have symptoms of impotency at the time of his marriage, but it is his wife's (often unconscious) responses to his condition that help keep him that way. A woman may dislike sex when she marries, but if her attitude does not change after the wedding, it is surely as much her husband's responsibility as it is hers. As Masters and Johnson noted long ago, it typically is useless to treat one of the marriage partners and not the other. For, generally speaking, when a person develops abnormal behavior patterns, everyone the person has close contact with must be considered part of the cause.

In the long run, a theory of mental illness—or a set of diagnostic categories—stands or falls on its ability to help people get better. Thus we cannot make a final evaluation of DSM-III, or any other similar scheme, until we discover what kind of "cure rate" it gives us. As we will see in the next chapter, the holistic approach to treating mental illness apparently yields a higher percentage of cures than does the "medical model" on which DSM-III is based. And perhaps that is the strongest evidence we can offer in favor of viewing human beings as highly complex living systems.

Summary

1. The words **normal** and **abnormal** have no meaning except when they are defined within a given context. What is normal in one social situation may be quite abnormal in another.
2. Personality theorists usually assume that abnormal thoughts and behaviors are **exaggerations** of the mental and behavioral traits that we all have. Thus most **mental disorders** can be viewed as "deviations from a norm."
3. Generally speaking, if the deviation from the norm is slight, the person is said to suffer from a **neurosis**. If the deviation is large, the person is said to suffer from a **psychosis**, and

probably will require hospitalization or extensive treatment.
4. Psychologists often use the terms **mean**, **median**, and **mode** to describe the center of a **normal distribution** of test scores or behavioral measures. This distribution is often a **bell-shaped curve**. An abnormal behavior or score is one that departs two or more **standard deviations** from the norm.
5. Psychiatrists and psychologists use many different **diagnostic systems** to describe and interpret thoughts or actions that are presumed to be abnormal. One such system is described in the **Diagnostic and Statistical**

Manual of Mental Disorders, the third edition of which was published in 1980.

6. **DSM-III** represents a significant change from earlier diagnostic schemes in that it departs significantly from **Freudian theory**. It makes little use of either "neurosis" or "psychosis," but uses the term **mental disorder** instead.

7. A psychiatrist using DSM-III would probably rate a patient on five different diagnostic **axes**:

   a. Axis 1 covers the **clinical psychiatric syndrome(s)** or major mental disorders the patient suffered from.

   b. Axis 2 lists the **personality disorders** or **personality traits** the patient showed.

   c. Axis 3 covers any **physical problems** the patient had, such as brain damage or disease.

   d. Axis 4 describes any **social stressors** the patient had experienced in the past year.

   e. Axis 5 evaluates the patient's highest level of **adaptive functioning** during the past year.

8. There are many problems with using DSM-III, including the fact that it is based on the **medical model** of "mental illness." However, it represents "the shape of the future" in both psychology and psychiatry.

9. Prior to DSM-III, most severe abnormalities thought to stem from physiological causes were called **organic psychoses**, while problems not due to organic causes were called **functional psychoses**. DSM-III uses the term "mental disorders" to cover both types of abnormalities.

10. **Disorders evidenced during infancy, childhood, and adolescence** include such problems as **mental retardation**, **separation anxiety**, and **infantile autism**.

11. **Organic mental disorders** include **senile dementia** or **senile psychosis**, and **substance-induced organic mental disorders**.

12. **Substance use disorders** include **alcoholism** and various other types of **drug abuse**.

13. **Schizophrenic disorders** are of four types: **Disorganized, catatonic, paranoid**, and **undifferentiated**. The hallmark of schizophrenia is usually **general mental disorganization**.

14. **Paranoid disorders** are characterized by such symptoms as **well-organized delusions**, severe types of **jealousy**, and feelings of being **persecuted**.

15. **Affective disorders** involve such severe emotional problems as **mania** and **depression**.

16. For the most part, DSM-III gives new names to what previously were called the **neurotic disorders**, presumably because the term **neurosis** had become so broadly defined as to lose most of its original meaning.

17. **Anxiety disorders** include **phobias, panic disorder**, and **obsessive compulsive disorder**.

18. **Somatoform disorders** (which Freud called **hysteria**) typically involve complaints about **body dysfunctions** that apparently are not due to any physical cause. Included in this category are such problems as the **hypochondriacal neurosis** and the **conversion disorders**.

19. **Dissociative disorders** are closely related to hysteria and involve sudden changes in **memory, consciousness, identity** or **motor behavior**. Included in this category are **psychogenic amnesia, psychogenic fugue, multiple personality**, and **depersonalization**.

20. **Psychosexual disorders** include **gender identity disorders, paraphilias, psychosexual dysfunctions**, and **ego-dystonic homosexuality**. Homosexuality itself is no longer considered a "mental disorder" except when it causes the individual great pain or anxiety.

21. Recent evidence suggests that **homosexual orientation** occurs early in life, usually before the individual is sexually active. Thus homosexuality is probably determined by the genes, rather than being learned or caused by a **domineering mother** and **weak or withdrawn father**. When young, homosexuals differ from heterosexuals primarily in terms of **gender nonconformity**.

22. **Factitious disorders** are characterized by **physical or psychological symptoms produced by the individual**.

23. **Disorders of impulse control** include **pathological gambling, kleptomania, pyromania**, and **explosive emotional outbursts**.

24. **Adjustment disorders** involve the inability to cope with psychological or social **stress**.

25. DSM-III also lists a number of conditions that may cause a patient to seek treatment but which aren't real "mental disorders." These problems typically involve **interpersonal difficulties, simple grief**, and various **occupational problems**.

26. Axis 2 of DSM-III lists **personality disorders**, which are really long-lasting **personality traits**.

27. Among the many objections raised against DSM-III is that it is too **eclectic**, that it repre-

sents an attempt by psychiatrists to "take over" the field of mental health, that it is based on the **medical model**, and that it encourages us to **label** people rather than understand them.

28. Many psychologists believe that DSM-III is not as **valid** or **reliable** as it should be. Several studies show that psychiatrists cannot differentiate between real patients and **pseudo-patients**, and there is little agreement among experts who attempt to **diagnose** any given individual.

29. The best possible **diagnostic scheme** would be a **holistic approach** that took into account the biological, intra-psychic, and social factors that influence the disturbed individual's level of functioning.

(Continued from page 534.)

Steve May looked at the hamburger and burst into tears. "It's the most beautiful thing I've ever seen," he said.

Dr. Mary Ellen Mann nodded her head sympathetically. "Would you like a milk shake to go with it?"

"I'm not sure I could stand that much pleasure all at once," Steve replied in a serious tone of voice. Then he smiled. "But let's order one and see."

Dr. Mann motioned to the waitress and gave her the order. She watched with amusement as Steve demolished the hamburger and sucked up the milk shake in one long gulp. Then the young man sat back in his chair, a contented smile on his face, and uttered a very loud belch. The people at the next table glared at him. "Sorry," Steve said loudly enough for them to hear. "I forgot where I was."

"It's not where you are, but where you've been the past two weeks that I'm interested in," Dr. Mann said. "You said you'd tell me all about your stay at the hospital if I would buy you dinner. I have given you the food of your choice, although I cannot imagine why you chose to celebrate your freedom at Hamburger Heaven. So, for starters, why a hamburger instead of a steak?"

"You miss the things you can't have," Steve explained. "Sometimes the food was okay, but mostly it was terrible. The food at that place is as crazy as the inmates sometimes act." He groaned. "You have no idea what obscenities can be inflicted on innocent objects such as hamburgers and green peas."

"Oh, yes I have," Dr. Mann replied. "I eat at the Faculty Club all the time. But start at the beginning. I want to know what happened, from the moment you walked through the hospital door until the moment you exited in the garbage truck."

Steve stirred his coffee slowly, considering what to say. "Well, I got in, as you no doubt know. The admitting psychiatrist never batted an eye when I told him I heard voices. He just nodded his head and then asked me what the voices said. When I said, 'dull,' and 'thud,' he nodded more vigorously and asked if the voices were male or female. I said I couldn't tell. That seemed to impress him mightily. Then he muttered the words, 'existential crisis.'"

Dr. Mann smiled. "Just as we suspected he'd do, eh? 'Existential crisis'—a type of psychosis that is described in many books, but that nobody's ever seen in real life."

"And then he asked me about my relationship with my mother, and did I have arguments with my father," Steve continued.

"The Oedipus complex, of course."

Steve smiled. "Of course. Seems I've never worked it out. He thought it significant also that I lose my temper a couple of times a year."

"Poor impulse control," Dr. Mann said. "You tend to belch in public places, and terrible things like that."

"I guess you do get back to the elementals in the mental hospital. Nobody thought twice about belching, or even crapping on the floor. They didn't even make you clean it up afterward."

Mary Ellen Mann nodded. "If the people around us didn't complain, we'd all act a lot crazier than we presently do. But to return to the subject, the psychiatrist never guessed you were a 'pseudo-patient,' like the ones in Professor Rosenhan's study?"

"No, he just asked questions for a while, then wrote down on the admission form that I was a certified nut."

"Which you probably are for letting me talk you into the whole affair," Dr. Mann said with a sigh. "I'm really sorry if you suffered very much, Steve."

"Oh, it wasn't all that bad. I did feel terrified at first, but I got over it after a while."

"Terrified of what?" Dr. Mann asked gently.

Steve grinned. "First I was worried that the 'crazies' might attack me. But of course they didn't. In fact, getting to know them was the best part of the whole experience. But after I realized I was physically safe, I got to worrying about not having any control over what was happening to me. I didn't have any money or power or status, so I tried to act sane and sensible and be nice to people. And I smiled a lot."

"Did it work?"

"Not a bit," Steve replied. "One nurse finally told me that smiling was a symptom of my underlying problems. So I stopped. Maybe she was right. Anybody who'd smile in there has to be out of touch with reality."

Dr. Mann frowned. "But they did treat you decently, didn't they?"

"The patients did. The staff treated me more like I was retarded, or some species of vegetable. There was one rather good-looking young nurse's aide I tried to get to know, but she wasn't about to get serious with a 'mental patient,' if you know what I mean. The nurses were much better, but I didn't see much of them. That's one of the things that frightened me."

"Why?" the woman asked.

Steve laughed. "You can't get out of that place unless the nurses and the social workers *see* you and realize that you're 'doing better,' as they put it. And most of them aren't around too much."

"Where are they?" Dr. Mann asked.

"In their offices, filling out papers, I guess." Steve May shook his head. "You can't convince people you're sane if they aren't around to be convinced."

Mary Ellen Mann sighed. "Rosenhan says that if we just valued the patients as people, if we treated them as human assets rather than as liabilities, we might learn a lot from them and simultaneously help most of them get better."

"Some of them don't want to get better," Steve said quietly. "They're afraid they can't cope 'outside,' and it's easier to stay where someone will take care of them. I tried to help a couple of them, as best I could."

"Like how?" Dr. Mann asked.

"Well," said Steve, "There was Crampy Joe. Nice guy, really, but he walked around all stooped over like he had cramps. I started giving him a cigarette every time he walked upright."

Dr. Mann laughed. "Behavior modification to the rescue, eh? Did it work?"

Steve nodded. "It worked until the nurses made me stop. They said it was against the rules for one patient to perform therapy on another."

"A sobering thought, that," Mary Ellen Mann said. "And they never caught on to your game, did they?"

"Oh, many of the patients did," Steve said. "But the staff members never guessed. That's what terrified me most, I guess. The crazy people thought I was sane, but the sane people insisted I was crazy. After a while, I didn't know which group to believe. And that *really* worried me."

"And that's when you decided to get the hell out of there, eh?"

Steve grinned. "You bet. I tried to see the psychiatrist for two weeks, but I couldn't get an appointment. They just increased the number of pills they gave me. And I just kept on flushing them down the toilet, when nobody was watching."

"You aren't as crazy as you look," the professor said.

"No, but I did get to worrying about it." He smiled shyly at the woman. "For a day or two, I even thought you had cooked the whole deal up, because you thought I was nuts and it was the only way you could think of to get me into the looney bin. That's when I knew it was time to leave."

Dr. Mann laughed. "But why make your grand exit in a garbage truck?"

"Only way out. I noticed that the garbage truck always arrived right at lunchtime. So today I waited until they weren't looking and hid under the garbage. Once the truck was outside the gates, I dropped off, cleaned myself up as best I could, and hitch-hiked home. Then I took a very long shower, and called you."

Mary Ellen Mann gave a deep sigh. "Well, I do appreciate what you did, and we'll talk more about it later on. Do you have any final words of wisdom for tonight, though?"

Steve nodded. "Yes, I do. I realize that we can't improve the hospital system until we know it from the inside out, as well as from the outside in. And so you've got to have volunteers like me go in and look for you. But I have a favor to ask. If you talk anybody else into volunteering, tell them one thing for me, will you?"

"What?" she asked.

He smiled. "Tell 'em they're nuts."

Recommended Readings

Bell, Alan P., Martin S. Weinberg, and Sue Kiefer Hammersmith. *Sexual Preference* (Bloomington: Indiana University Press, 1981).

Blum, Jeffery D. "On Changes in Psychiatric Diagnosis over Time," *American Psychologist*, Vol. 33, No. 11 (November 1978), pp. 1017–1031.

Halleck, Seymour L. *The Treatment of Emotional Disorders* (New York: Aronson, 1978).

Kazdin, Alan E. *Research Design in Clinical Psychology* (New York: Harper & Row, 1980).

Task Force on Nomenclature and Statistics, American Psychiatric Association. *Diagnostic and Statistical Manual of Mental Disorders*, 3rd ed. (Washington, D.C.: American Psychiatric Association, 1980).

Woody, R.H., ed. *Encyclopedia of Clinical Assessment*, Vols. 1 and 2 (San Francisco: Jossey-Bass, 1980).

Psychotherapy

Did You Know That . . .

The term "to beat the devil" out of someone refers to a primitive form of psychotherapy?

Many Cree Eskimos believe that they can be "possessed" by a witch or *witigo* who will make them cannibalize their relatives and friends?

A male Chinese may sometimes suffer from a dismal fear that his penis is about to be drawn up into his stomach and disappear?

Psychiatrists, psychoanalysts, and psychologists often disagree on how to define a "cure" of mental illness?

A large number of mental patients will recover spontaneously even if not given treatment?

Prior to the 1600's, mental patients were seldom put in asylums or hospitals?

One form of psychotherapy grew out of the theater?

Encounter groups offer people good opportunities to explore and express themselves, but are not very effective as psychotherapy?

Behavior therapists sometimes pay mental patients for getting well?

"The Odds in Favor"

Mark Evans looked at the little old lady standing by the slot machine. She wore cheap gloves to keep her hands clean, and dirty tennis shoes to keep her feet comfortable. As Mark watched her, she grubbed about in her huge purse, then produced a dollar bill and handed it to a scantily clad young woman who made change for the machines in the casino. The attractive attendant smiled as she handed the older woman a roll of 20 nickels. "Good luck," she said.

"Good juju," the little old lady said in response. Then she tottered along a row of slot machines until she found one to her liking. Mark Evans moved over to watch her as she dumped her purse beside the one-armed bandit, then ever so carefully unrolled the nickels. She counted them one by one. Exactly 20. Examining one of the coins closely, she decided it would do. She spat on it, then rubbed the nickel gently between her gloved fingers to remove the tarnish.

"You'll rub all the luck off it, honey," said a large, red-headed woman who was dropping dimes into the next machine.

"Luck?" cackled the little old woman, taking a grimy cloth bag from her purse and shaking it at the slot machine. "Luck is just a matter of chance, and I don't leave anything to chance. I put a hex on the machines, and they always pay off. I brought my juju bag with me today, so I can't lose. My juju is strong today. I feel its strength in my bones. You just wait and see."

The old lady dropped the coin in the machine and pulled the handle. The three reels spun wildly, then clicked to a stop, one by one. A plum, an orange, and a lemon. She shook her head, and deposited another nickel. Again the reels whirred into action and jerked to a stop—two lemons and a bell.

"Your juju is all lemons today, dearie," the red-headed woman said.

The little old lady gestured wildly at the machine with the bag. "Juju!" she cried. "Give me a jackpot."

The reels produced a cherry and two bells, and the machine grudgingly coughed up two nickels as a reward.

"See! That's a good start. It's going to be a good day. I feel it in my bones!"

Mark Evans shook his head in amazement, then checked his watch. Time to meet his relative-in-law, Lou Hudson, from Chattanooga, Tennessee. Lou, who had married Mark's cousin Betty, was in Las Vegas for a convention of life insurance agents. Betty had called Mark a few days ago, asking Mark to take time out from his graduate studies at the University of Nevada to "show Lou the sights." That was the trouble with studying psychology in Las Vegas—sooner or later everbody you knew showed up and expected you to entertain them.

Lou Hudson turned out to be a thin young man with blond hair and blue but bloodshot eyes. "Stayed up half the night playing blackjack," Lou said, after the introductions were completed. "You wouldn't believe my luck. I was 200 bucks ahead, and I just knew I had a streak going. But then the cards turned against me. I barely broke even."

Mark Evans smiled. He had heard the phrase "broke even" enough to know that it usually meant losing a lot.

"Hey, man, this Las Vegas place is too much!" Lou gestured at the activity in the casino. "Hotels with gambling halls instead of lobbies, people running around 24 hours a day, throwing their money away like there wasn't any tomorrow! Bands playing, and free drinks, and nobody to tell you when to get up or when to go to bed. Why, it's a gambler's paradise!"

"You're here for a convention?" Mark asked, a touch of sarcasm in his voice.

"Yeah. I suppose I really ought to get around to some of the meetings pretty soon now," Lou said with a frown. "But I've been having so much fun, there just hasn't been time." His face brightened suddenly. "Hey, man, they've got every kind of game here you can imagine, haven't they? I mean, I like to gamble a little, just now and then you know. Poker, blackjack, the horses—strictly for small stakes. But they got things here I've only read about, like roulette. You ever play roulette?"

Mark Evans shook his head. "No percentage in it. The odds against winning are too great."

"Whatta ya mean, too great?" Lou demanded almost hostilely, leading Mark toward one of the roulette tables nearby. "See—36 numbers, half of them red, half black. You put a dollar chip on any one of them, and they spin the ball around the wheel. If the little ball drops into your number, the house pays you back 35 to 1. That's pretty good odds, isn't it?"

Mark groaned. "Lou, you forget the two green zeros at the top of the board. There are really 38 numbers, not 36. If you put a dollar down on all the numbers, it would cost you $38 a game. And you'd win back only $35, no matter what number came up. You'd lose $3 each time the wheel spun, because the odds are against you."

"Yeah, but if you pick a lucky number, and put a dollar on it 10 times in a row, and it hits twice, then you've won $70 and it only cost you $10. You can quit a big winner," Lou said.

"*If* you quit, which most gamblers don't. If you keep betting, it doesn't matter whether you play all 38 numbers once, or one number 38 times—you're going to spend $38 to win $35. Because your number is going to win just once in 38 times—on the average."

Lou was plainly annoyed. "You don't understand, man. Look at that fat man over there with the big diamond ring on his pinkie. He's got a stack of chips in front of him that would choke a giraffe. He's bound to be making money on the roulette wheel."

"The only way to make money in Las Vegas is to open your own casino, Lou. That man may be winning now, but if he plays long enough, he'll lose. Because the odds are against him."

Lou shook his head. "You may be right in theory, Mark, but look at that man's stack of chips. Maybe he's got a secret system or something. Maybe he knows what number's going to come up next."

Mark was beginning to understand why the casinos made so much money. "Lou, old man, if that wheel is honest—and out here, they almost always are—there's no way in hell that you or anybody else can make money at roulette if you play long enough."

"Well, how the hell *can* you win at this game, anyway?"

Mark thought a moment. "The only way I know of is to sit for hours and keep a record of each number that comes up. Sometimes the wheel does get out of balance. It gets biased toward one number, let's say 25. Out of 38,000 spins, 25 ought to come up 1,000 times. But if it comes up 2,000 times, or even 3,000, then you know something's abnormal about the wheel."

"You're saying I ought to just sit and take records first instead of just going with my hunches?"

"Absolutely," Mark replied, happy that Lou seemed to be getting the message. "You may not know *why* 25 is better than the other numbers, but the graph tells you it's a winner. So you go with the odds."

"Sounds like a lot of work to me," Lou said, taking a free drink from a cocktail waitress as she passed by. His hands trembled slightly as he sipped the drink. "Oh, I know. You've studied statistics and all that. But Mark, you've neglected the most important thing—the human factor. Man, when I get hot, I get really hot. I mean, I win big. It's like I've got some power over the cards, or the horses, or maybe even the roulette wheel. That kind of power is a helluva lot more important than sitting and watching a wheel turn round 38,000 times."

Mark sighed. "Lou, if you gamble to have fun, then you can just charge your losses off as entertainment expenses. But if you gamble for money—if you absolutely have to win—then you hunt for situations in which the odds are in your favor."

It was obvious that Mark's answer didn't satisfy Lou Hudson. His bloodshot eyes opened wide. "But man, I'm a special case! I get these streaks when I'm hot as hell. How do you explain the power I have over the cards when I've got a streak going?"

"Lou," Mark said gently, "How much money do you have?"

"Me? Well, to tell the truth, I'm pretty near broke right now."

"And you've been gambling all your life. If you have all that power, how come you aren't a big winner?"

Lou took a big gulp of his drink. "Well, I've been down on my luck lately. But just wait until tomorrow. I'm gonna bounce right back with a big killing. I got that special feeling, you see . . ."

Mark sighed heavily. "Lou, friend, listen. How does the insurance company you work for manage to make money?"

Lou frowned. "Why, they sell policies, of course. You wouldn't happen to need some life insurance, would you?"

"No, but pretend I did," Mark replied. "Suppose I bought a million dollar policy from you."

"Nice commission on a policy that big," Lou said dreamily.

Mark nodded. "Yes, but how can the company make any money when I might die an hour after I bought the policy?"

"It's simple," Lou said. "The company knows how many people your age are likely to die in any one year, and they charge enough to cover their expected losses and to make a little dough on the side too."

"They go with the percentages, you mean."

"Sure," Lou replied. "They don't know who's gonna live, or who's gonna die. And I reckon they don't really care. They just go with the odds. I tell you no lie, Mark, those people are pretty hard-nosed when it comes to money." Lou stopped for a moment. Then his head drooped a little, and he continued in a voice grown suddenly hoarse. "Speaking of money, Mark, you wouldn't happen to have a little extra cash on you, would you? Just a temporary loan, you know. Until my luck turns good again."

Mark shook his head. "Sorry, man. The way tuition's shot up recently, students just barely get by these days. But what's the matter? Aren't you selling very many policies?"

Lou's bloodshot eyes filled with tears. "Oh, I sell a few. But the money always seems to go out faster than it comes in. Betty's pretty disturbed about it, I suspect. She says that I'm a compulsive gambler. And she ought to know, her being a psychiatric social worker. You're a psychologist, Mark. Do you think I've gone looney or something?"

Mark sighed, "I'm just a grad student, Lou, and there's lots of things I don't know yet. What do you think?"

"I think I've got a problem, Mark. I mean, I *hurt*. Deep down inside. I hurt real bad." Lou grabbed Mark by the arm. "Man, you gotta help me. What can I do to get rid of the pain? What can I do?"

(Continued on page 584)

Turning Knowledge into Power

There's an old saying that "knowledge is power." Sometimes you study the world to figure out what makes things go. But as soon as you discover some significant relationships about the things you've been studying, you're likely to want to put your knowledge to use to make things go *better*.

At other times, when you're faced with a practical problem, you may try out something new. If it works to your satisfaction, you may sit down and attempt to figure out *why* the new technique succeeded—so that you can use it again, perhaps more effectively. In either case, you're trying to convert knowledge into power.

In the last chapter, we dealt with *knowledge*. For diagnostic schemes are really attempts to discover what abnormal behaviors people engage in, and to determine *why* people act, think, and feel in unusual ways. In this chapter we ask a *power* question—"How do you change or 'cure' abnormal behavior once it occurs?" Generally speaking, the more restricted your viewpoint is about what causes these abnormalities to occur, the more limited your power to change them becomes.

In many primitive parts of the world, for instance, people still believe in the "devil theory" of mental illness. Crazy people are thought to be *possessed* (or at least affected) by devils—outside

spirits that take over a person's mental functioning for one reason or another. Let's look at some examples of the "devil theory" in action before we discuss more modern approaches to the problem of curing mental illness.

Primitive Approaches to Mental Illness

The Cree Eskimos and Ojibwa Indians of Canada occasionally suffer from a psychosis known as **witigo**, or devil-caused cannibalism. The first symptoms usually are a loss of appetite, vomiting, and diarrhea—as well as the person's morbid fear that she or he has been possessed by a *witigo* or witch, who lives on human flesh. The affected individual becomes withdrawn, brooding, and cannot eat or sleep. The person's family—fearing for their very lives—immediately calls in a "witch doctor" to cast out the witigo by saying magic words or casting spells. If a witch doctor can't be found in time, however, the psychotic individual may be overwhelmed by the witigo's powers and kill and eat one or more of the members of the family.

In Malaysia, in Southeast Asia, young males occasionally suffer from a different type of possession by devils, called **running amok**. At first the man becomes more withdrawn, depressed, and brooding than usual. Then he will suddenly leap to his feet with a blood-curdling scream, pull out a dagger, and begin stabbing anyone or anything in his path.

Therapy for "running amok" usually consists of killing the amoker before he can kill you, or keeping everyone out of the amoker's way until he kills himself. The few men who survive the psychotic "seizure" usually say that the world suddenly turned black and they had to slash their way out of the darkness with a knife.

In Spain and Morroco, the name given to this form of "mental disorder" is called *juramentado*, the Spanish word for "cursed person." In the United States, we sometimes call it *homicidal mania*. DSM-III calls it "an explosive disorder of impulse control."

Question: Why would the therapy you suggested for "running amok" vary according to the label you put on the problem?

Koro

Many Chinese believe that mental and physical disorders result from an imbalance of Yang and Yin, the masculine and feminine "powers" that control the entire spiritual universe. Chinese males occasionally suffer from an odd phobia called **koro**—a dismal fear that their penis is

"I FIND THAT AS LONG AS YOU AVOID EYE CONTACT, YOU HARDLY REALIZE THERE IS A CROWD."

Witigo (WITT-tee-go). A Cree Eskimo word meaning an "ice witch" who eats human flesh. Also means the condition of being possessed by such a witch. The Ojibwa (oh-JIB-wah) Indian word for the same condition is *windigo* (win-dee-go).

Running amok (ah-MOCK). The Malaysian word *amok* means "furious attack." To run amok is to undergo a murderous frenzy and attack people at random. Similar to the Scandinavian term "going berserk" (burr-SERK) and the Spanish term *juramentado* (hoor-ah-men-TAH-do).

Koro (KOH-roh). A phobia occurring in the East Indies and southern China. The disorder consists of a sudden fear that the penis will disappear into the abdomen and lead to death.

---

about to be sucked up into their stomachs and disappear, causing death and other disappointments. To prevent this disaster, the man will hold on to his penis for dear life—and when he tires, will ask for help from friends and relatives. The man's wife may "cure" the attack if she practices oral sex on him immediately, but this treatment is not always successful.

Koro is thought to be caused by a sudden upsurge in the strength of the man's Yin, or femininity. Thus, it can be cured by giving the patient "masculine" medicine containing a strong Yang factor—such as powdered rhinoceros horn. If this therapy fails, the man may use a special clasp that holds his penis out from his body mechanically.

On the Pacific island of Borneo, a similar disease affects women—who fear that their breasts and genitalia are being pulled up into their bodies. Therapy in Borneo often consists of asking a witch doctor to remove the curse—presumably laid on the woman by a "witch" jealous of the woman's physical beauty.

Question: Under what diagnostic category would a psychiatrist using the DSM-III put koro?

Four Issues Concerning Psychotherapy

Even in the United States—where most of us no longer believe in witches, demons, and evil spirits—our therapies almost always stem from our theories of what causes human behavior. If we see an organic psychosis as being due *primarily* to physical causes, we tend to treat the patient with physical measures, such as drugs, electric shock, and surgery. If we see a neurosis as being due *primarily* to a conflict between ego and superego, we use psychoanalysis to help bring some rational resolution to the conflict. If we assume that deviant behavior is *primarily* the consequence of inappropriate rewards and punishments, we might prescribe behavior therapy or

563

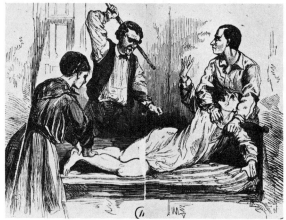

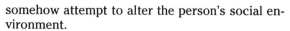

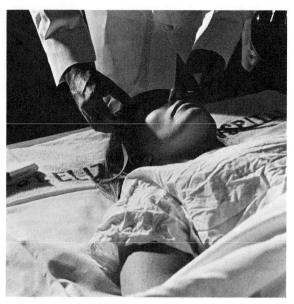

Research suggests that, in primitive cultures, "witch-doctors" and "native practitioners" have as high a cure rate with mental illness as do trained psychiatrists. **(top left)**

A century or so ago, many doctors believed mental patients were "possessed by devils." Treatment often consisted of "beating the devil out of the person." **(bottom left)**

Although Electro-convulsive Shock Therapy continues to be used, particularly with severely depressed patients, recent research casts doubt on how effective it is in the long run. **(right)**

somehow attempt to alter the person's social environment.

In this chapter we will discuss all these special forms of treatment, and the theories that gave rise to them. But before we can evaluate the various forms of therapy, we will have to raise several pertinent (and very hard-nosed) issues:

1. How successful is the therapy? That is, what is its "cure rate"? Would the patient have recovered anyhow, even if we hadn't done anything? Would a "witch doctor," or someone using a different form of treatment, have done as well? In short, does the therapy make a *significant difference* in helping the patient? Is it a *valid* form of treatment?

2. Assuming that the therapy does make a significant difference, how *reliable* it is? Does it work all the time, or just occasionally? Is it effective with all sorts of patients, or does it succeed better with some than with others?

3. What are the *side effects*? What else happens to the patient when we apply the treatment? Is the "cure" sometimes worse than the disease?

4. And, cutting across all these issues is the basic question: "What do we mean by *cure*?" How shall we define improvement and, just as important, how shall we measure it?

We will have much more to say about these issues as we discuss the three main types of psychotherapy. We will also find it all too customary for therapists of opposing views to call each other "witch doctors," and to accuse each other of using "black magic" rather than "scientific magic."

Biological Therapies

Two centuries ago, when the "demon theory" was the accepted explanation of most forms of psychosis, the therapy of choice was *punishment*. The belief was that if you would just whip a patient vigorously enough, you could "beat the devil" out of the person. The fact that many patients did improve after whippings was evidence enough to support the validity of the theory. It was not until *scientific investigations* suggested that the "cure rate" for unbeaten patients was higher than for those who were beaten that we finally hung up the whip in our **lunatic asylums**. Whether our present forms of psychotherapy are all that much more effective than "beating the devil" out of lunatics, however, is a point much debated today in psychology and psychiatry.

As we suggested in the last chapter, the organic psychoses do seem directly related to damage to the central nervous system or to genetic causes. Perhaps for that reason, many of the therapies used to treat organic psychoses are explicitly *biological*—the three main types being artificially induced seizures, psycho-surgery, and drugs. (As we will see, these types of treatment are also occasionally used with patients who have functional psychoses.)

Convulsive Therapy

In 1935 a Hungarian psychiatrist named Ladislaus J. Meduna noted an odd fact—very few of the schizophrenic patients he worked with also suffered from epilepsy. Without considering alternative hypotheses too seriously, Meduna concluded that seizures might somehow *prevent* schizophrenia. If he could induce epileptic-type seizures in his schizophrenic patients, he reasoned, he might be able to cure them of their problems.

As a test, Meduna injected schizophrenic patients with drugs that caused seizures. Many patients did show some improvement, but an alarming number of them were severely injured or died from the treatment. Others showed intense apprehension about the unpleasantness of the experience. Meduna's treatment was abandoned as "barbaric," but the idea lived on.

Question: If therapy is extremely painful—be it whippings or convulsions—might some patients "get well" in order to avoid further treatment?

Electro-Convulsive Therapy

In 1938 two Italian psychiatrists—Ugo Cerletti and L. Bini—began using electrical current rather than drugs to induce seizures. If you were to be given electro-convulsive therapy (or ECT, as it is often called), the psychiatrist would probably apply it in the following way. First you would be given: (1) a muscle relaxant; (2) a drug to prevent you from choking; and (3) a fast-acting anesthetic to put you to sleep. Then you'd be strapped to a padded bed in order to reduce the possibility of your breaking an arm or leg during the seizure.

When you were unconscious, the psychiatrist would apply electrodes to your head, and pass a brief but fairly strong electrical current di-

Lunatic asylums (LOON-uh-tick as-SIGH-lums). In Europe during the Middle Ages, there was a common belief that insanity was caused by some influence the moon had on human behavior. *Luna* is the Latin word for "moon," thus mental illness came to be called "lunacy," and mentally ill individuals were called "lunatics."

rectly through your brain. Your muscles would become rigid for about 10 seconds, then you would go into convulsions much as an epileptic might. The convulsions would last for a minute or two, but you would remain unconscious for up to 30 minutes and would be drowsy or confused for many hours thereafter. Because seizures induce *retrograde amnesia* (see Chapter 16), you probably would not remember the shock or the events immediately preceding it. Typically, you would be given ECT three times a week for a period of a few weeks—or until you showed some recovery.

There is considerable argument about the effectiveness of ECT. Many psychiatrists believe that ECT can be of help with severely depressed patients, and at times with schizophrenic patients. But the data aren't all that clear. In his 1979 book, *Electroshock: Its Brain-Disabling Effects*, Maryland psychiatrist Peter Roger Breggin takes quite a different view. He admits that some patients do show improvement after ECT. However, he states that the effects of ECT on the brain are "severe," "catastrophic," and "devastating."

Breggin notes that ECT is more widely used in private than in public hospitals. The most likely people to receive shock treatment are women, foreign-born, and lower-class patients. Breggin claims that the retrograde amnesia many of these individuals suffer is often very extensive. He says that many patients suffer shame, anguish, and increased dependence on others as a result of the treatment.

Breggin believes that most of the "perceived benefits" of ECT are due to the *placebo effect*. He cites extensively from the scientific literature to prove his point, and notes that the "cure rate" among psychiatrists who refuse to administer ECT is as high or higher than that among psychiatrists who use shock extensively. Breggin urges that ECT be "prohibited by law."

Most of the literature on ECT tends to support Breggin's view. The studies that apparently show ECT of value have, without exception, failed to employ an adequate "no shock" control group. The studies with adequate controls have, again almost without exception, shown that electroshock therapy failed to produce any lasting benefits that couldn't be obtained in other ways.

As Breggin notes, when used extensively ECT can not only damage the brain but the heart

Werner Mendel

Although many mental patients are given medication for their problems, there is growing evidence that pills alone seldom cure a person's psychological problems. **(left)**

and lungs as well. And it is of little or no value at all except in cases of deep depression. Indeed, Meduna's original observations about schizophrenia and epilepsy were based on a mistaken idea. He apparently did not realize that all patients with epilepsy *and* schizophrenia were put in a different ward than the one he was working on.

Question: *Some patients request ECT, particularly after they have been performing badly for a period of time. How might Freud's notions about the causes of* masochism *explain the patients' request for ECT?*

Psycho-surgery

As you will remember from reading the early chapters of this book, emotional responses are controlled by certain parts of the brain called the *limbic system* (see Chapter 4). Portions of the thalamus and the frontal lobes are also involved in emotional reactions. In 1935, John F. Fulton and C.E. Jacobsen demonstrated that surgery on the prefrontal lobes had a *calming effect* on two chimpanzees they were working with. After learning of this research, a Portuguese psychiatrist named Egas Moniz decided that cutting the prefrontal lobes—an operation called a **lobotomy**—might help aggressive or hyper-emotional patients. In 1936 Moniz and his associates reported that lobotomy did seem to be effective with some of these patients.

Lobotomies were introduced to the US in 1942 by Walter Freeman and his colleagues, and Moniz and Freeman later received the Nobel Prize for their work. Other psychiatrists soon reported that cutting the *connections* between the lower brain centers and the prefrontal lobes seemed to

work just as well as *removing* the prefrontal lobes.

The question is, of course, "Work as well as what?" Many lobotomy patients do show an improvement after the operation, but many do not. And the fatality rate from the operation may run as high as 4 percent. Well-controlled comparisons of patients given lobotomies and those given other forms of treatment suggest that the operation is neither as effective nor as reliable as Moniz and Freeman had hoped. (We might note that the "fatality rate" must include Moniz himself, who was shot and killed by one of his lobotomy patients.)

Question: *Why might many physicians be more interested in performing* operations *on patients with mental disorders than in giving the patients long-term* psychotherapy?

Drug Therapy

There are a number of **psycho-active drugs**—that is, chemicals that have a psychological effect. We discussed many of them in Chapter 3. Among the most widely used psycho-active compounds are the major and minor tranquilizers and the antidepressants.

Major Tranquilizers

For many centuries medical practitioners in India have given tense or manic patients a drug made from the snake root plant because it seemed to calm them down. We now call this drug **reserpine**. In 1953 the Indian physician R.A. Hakim reported that reserpine seemed to be effective with some schizophrenic patients. When Nathan S. Kline tried reserpine here in 1954, he stated that it brought about marked improvement in 86 percent of the schizophrenic patients he tried it with.

At about the same time, a French surgeon named Henri Laborit suggested that giving a powerful drug called **chlorpromazine** to schizophrenic patients might make them more manageable. The drug not only calmed these patients down, but seemed to relieve some of their symptomatic behaviors as well.

Reserpine and chlorpromazine were the first of the many tranquilizers now widely used with mental patients. One interesting point about these drugs is that patients often dislike and seldom "abuse" these chemicals. However, since the major tranquilizers make "disturbed" patients easier to handle in hospitals, these drugs are now frequently prescribed by psychiatrists.

Beginning in the mid-1970's, a drug called *lithium carbonate* has been used with varying degrees of success with patients displaying bipolar affective disorders (manic-depressive psychoses). Lithium carbonate can have a calming effect during manic episodes, but has little or no effect on depressive behaviors. However, not all patients are helped by the drug, and it has dangerous (even deadly) side-effects.

Minor Tranquilizers
Drugs such as Valium and Librium are called "minor" tranquilizers because they have less dramatic effects on behavior and mental functioning than do the major tranquilizers. However, Valium and Librium are among the most abused drugs in the US today, in part because many patients seem to enjoy their effects. These drugs are obviously highly addictive, and recent studies suggest they may cause birth defects if taken during pregnancy.

Anti-depressants
As we noted in Chapter 3, these drugs are also called "psychic energizers." Except for the very addictive amphetamines, the anti-depressants are seldom abused and have little effect on people not suffering from depressions. However, all these drugs have dangerous side-effects, particularly when mixed with alcohol.

Drugs Alone Don't "Cure"
Scarcely a month goes by that the popular press doesn't serve up a juicy story about some new drug that seems to offer "miracle cures" for many types of psychological problems. Most of the reports need to be taken with a grain of salt, however.

First, as Nathan S. Kline and Jules Angst note in their 1979 book *Psychiatric Syndromes and*

Lobotomy (loh-BOTT-toe-mee). A surgical technique involving cutting the nerve pathways that run to any one of the four cerebral lobes. Usually means "prefrontal lobotomy," or cutting the connections between the thalamus (THALL-uh-muss) and the prefrontal lobes.

Psycho-active drugs (SIGH-koh). Any chemical compound which affects emotional, cognitive, or behavioral processes, or which relieves symptoms of "mental disorder."

Reserpine (ree-SIR-peen). From the word "serpent." So named because this tranquilizer was first discovered in the snake root plant in India.

Chlorpromazine (klor-PRO-muh-zeen). A tranquilizing drug whose usefulness with psychotic patients was first discovered in France.

Drug Treatment, chemicals *by themselves* seldom solve mental, social, or behavioral problems. Even if the drug "cures" some underlying biological dysfunction, the patient will usually still need psychological and social help in adjusting to life. Thus chemotherapy is *at best* no more than the first step in treating "mental disorders." Second, not all of the drug research has been as well planned and nicely controlled as we might wish. Perhaps a case history will demonstrate these points.

Mendel's Research
Werner Mendel is Professor of Psychiatry at the USC School of Medicine. He was also, for many years, the clinical director of the only public facility for treating acutely disturbed psychotic patients in Los Angeles County.

Like all psychiatrists, Mendel is a medical doctor. After receiving his MD degree at Stanford, he served a year as a psychiatric resident at St. Elizabeth's Hospital in Washington, D.C. Thereafter, Mendel spent several years as a resident at the Menninger Foundation in Topeka, Kansas— one of the best psychiatric training facilities in the world. Once his training at Menninger's was complete, Mendel was qualified to call himself a psychiatrist.

Next, he moved to Los Angeles and studied for several years at the Southern California Psychoanalytic Institute and completed his training as a psychoanalyst. He is an instructor at the Institute. After moving to Los Angeles, Mendel continued a series of experiments on the treatment of mental illness he had begun as a resident in Washington, D.C.

St. Elizabeth's Hospital was the largest of all the US government facilities dealing with psychiatric patients. When Mendel arrived at St. E's, he was put in charge of a ward of Spanish-speaking patients, most of whom came from Puerto Rico or the Virgin Islands. All of these patients were diagnosed as being hostile, aggressive individuals. And many were considered so dangerous to themselves and others that they were confined to "padded cells" or were kept in straight-jackets. Mendel states that he usually took two large attendants along with him whenever he visited the wards. And because the patients spoke little or no English, and Mendel spoke no Spanish, there was little he could do in the way of treatment.

Double-Blind Method

Fortunately, it was just at this time that news of the apparent effectiveness of reserpine spread to the US. The authorities at St. E's decided to test the drug. To make the test scientifically valid, they used the *double-blind method*. That is, they selected certain wards whose patients would be given reserpine. But they needed some *comparison groups* to make sure that the changes they noted in the patients given reserpine (the "experimental groups") were due to the drug and not just to the fact that the patients had been given pills. So the researchers selected an equal number of wards whose patients were given "sugar pills" rather than reserpine. The pills looked the same no matter what was in them. The experiment was "double-blind" because neither the patients nor the doctors in charge of the wards knew which drug the patients on any particular ward were actually receiving.

The experiment ran for several months, during which any improvement in the patients was recorded as carefully as possible. Mendel's ward of Spanish-speaking patients was one of those chosen for the experiment.

Mendel reports that, almost as soon as the study began, he was sure that his patients were receiving the reserpine—for they all calmed down dramatically. Within a short period of time they were so tranquil that many of them could be released from restraint. Mendel was convinced that a psychiatric revolution had begun.

Then the experiment ended and the results were announced. To Mendel's amazement, he learned that his ward had been one of the "controls." All of his patients had received *placebos* instead of reserpine. Yet they had shown marked improvement! It occurred to Mendel that, when the experiment began, he unconsciously changed his attitude toward the patients. Convinced that they were becoming more peaceful, he then treated them as if they were improving. And they did improve—not because of the drug but because of the way in which he responded to them.

The St. Elizabeth's experiment points up one dramatic difficulty in evaluating any psychiatric research: The good results than an experimenter obtains may be due to *chance factors*, or to things that the scientist *failed to control*. Drugs are always given in a social setting. The patient's attitude—and the scientist's—may be more influential than the chemical effects on the patient's body. Or if a surgeon communicates to the patient the belief that psycho-surgery will surely solve the person's problems, the patient may very well get better after the operation—for all the "wrong" reasons.

Intra-Psychic Therapy

Most personality theorists believe that abnormal thoughts and behaviors are mere symptoms of an underlying dysfunction in an individual's basic personality. To "cure" the symptom without handling the underlying problem would, therefore, be as senseless as giving aspirin to a yellow-fever patient. The drug might decrease the fever symptom, it is true. But aspirin won't kill the virus that is really responsible for the disease. Removing the fever with aspirin might delude patients into thinking they had been "cured" when, in fact, the patients might still be carrying the virus. A "deeper" form of therapy is necessary to kill the virus.

Intra-psychic therapy almost always focuses on making "deep changes" in the structure or the functioning of the individual's core personality—the belief being that the symptomatic behaviors will disappear naturally as the cure progresses. As we noted in Chapter 23, this approach to treatment is based on what is called the *medical model of mental illness*.

If you ever have need for intra-psychic therapy, you would seem to have your choice between two major types: (1) those methods that are primarily designed to help you understand your present self by uncovering what has gone wrong in your past; and (2) those techniques that focus on future goals in order to help you change your present mode of existence. (As we will see, the difference between the two types may be more a matter of emphasis than anything else. Highly successful therapists appear to treat their patients in similar ways despite the fact that their theories may be quite different.)

Psychoanalysts usually follow the first method. That is, they concentrate on discovering traumas that occurred during psychosexual development in order to help patients set their "mental houses" in order. Psychoanalytic theory suggests that, if you complete your analysis and become a *fully-functioning individual*, you should be able to handle future problems with little difficulty.

The humanistic psychologists, on the other hand, mostly follow the second method. They hope to make you aware both of your present condition and of your ultimate goals, so that you can shorten the distance between the two and hence move toward self-actualization.

Psychoanalytic Therapy

There is no single accepted and approved method of psychoanalytic treatment—it varies widely according to the patient's needs and the analyst's skills and beliefs. Freud compared analysis to a chess game in which only the opening moves could be standardized. Thereafter, endless variations may develop.

In general, however, the technique is designed to bring about a basic reconstruction of the patient's personality. The analyst achieves this end in two ways. First, by encouraging the patient to build up an emotional relationship, or **transference**, with the analyst. And second, by getting the patient to freely associate about past thoughts and experiences. By interpreting these *free associations*, the analyst can often discover both the content and the dynamics of the patient's unconscious mental processes.

But the task is not an easy one. Psychoanalysis typically takes from two to five years to complete, and the 50-minute-long therapy sessions are usually held three to five times a week. Costs

"MY ASTROLOGER SAYS ONE THING, MY GURU SAYS ANOTHER, MY PSYCHIATRIST SAYS SOMETHING ELSE — I DON'T KNOW WHO TO TURN TO ANYMORE."

Transference (trans-FURR-ents). In psychoanalysis, the patient is subtly encouraged to transfer to the analyst the emotions and attitudes the patient has concerning the "power figures" in the patient's life—chiefly her or his father and mother. That is, the patient is asked to act toward the analyst as the patient does toward the mother and father. Some of the transferred emotions may be warm and loving. Others may be cold, hateful, or angry. In either case, displacing the feelings onto the analyst may help release pent-up libidinal energy. At the end of treatment, the analyst must carefully remove the transference relationship so that the patient stands on his or her own.

for a complete analysis typically run from 10,000 to 30,000 dollars (or more). The most successful patients seem to be between 15 and 50 years of age. They must be bright, verbal, self-motivated, and willing to cooperate with the therapist. Although psychoanalysis is occasionally used with individuals classed as "psychotic," the usual patient is a mildly disturbed or "neurotic" individual.

Most psychoanalysts are males. Although Freud insisted that the medical degree was not necessary for the practice of psychoanalysis, more than 90 percent of the analysts practicing in the US today are physicians who have gone through psychiatric internships and residencies before becoming candidates at a psychoanalytic institute. During the several years of training required for graduation, the candidate undergoes a "training analysis" to make himself or herself aware of personal problems that might prejudice analytic interpretation of a patient's problems. As Freud noted in 1910, "Every analyst's achievement is limited by what his own complexes and resistances permit."

Transference

If you decided to undergo psychoanalysis, you would probably be treated by a male, since less than 10 percent of the analysts are women. You would most likely find your doctor in a private office completely cut off from the outside world. He might well ask you to lie down on his couch and then sit out of sight, just beyond your head, where he could take notes and observe your facial and bodily reactions.

Your analyst would ask you to free associate—that is, to say anything and everything that came to mind. But he would try to direct your attention to your inward world of feeling, emotion, and fantasy. In a variety of subtle ways, he would encourage you to "transfer" to him many of your intense emotional feelings. In a sense, he would become a "father figure" on whom you could rely and trust.

There are currently more than 200 types of "talk therapy," in which patients **(such as this woman)** discuss their problems with a therapist. There is considerable debate over the effectiveness of this type of treatment.

Free Association

Free association is the basic game plan of most forms of psychoanalysis. Freud believed that everything you do and say and think has a *cause*. Thus even trivial and apparently meaningless statements may mask deep-seated emotional conflicts. The more you cut yourself off from conscious control—the more you let your unconscious mind come through to consciousness—the more easily you can bring the buried problems to the surface. If you cannot "free associate" very well, it may be that some part of your mind is blocking the expression of certain traumatic experiences. By noting the things you *avoid talking about*, the analyst can often get a feeling for what your problems are.

Interpretation

During the course of the treatment, your analyst would interpret your thoughts, feelings, and actions in terms of psychoanalytic theory. If inner blocks kept you from expressing important (repressed) material, the analyst might ask you to recall your dreams and talk about them.

Freud believed that many psychic conflicts express themselves in fantasy, particularly when the patient's defenses are down (as during dreaming). He felt it was not so much the actual content of the dream that was important. Rather, it was

what the dream *symbolized* that must be discovered. For Freud, dream analysis was a "royal road" to the patient's unconscious and to the real significance of the patient's childhood experiences.

Psychoanalysis: An Evaluation

Psychoanalysis takes so long—and there are so few analysts available—that only a tiny fraction of the people who need help ever undergo this process. Most patients settle for briefer, less intensive (and less expensive) types of treatment.

Psychoanalytic theory has influenced almost all other forms of intra-psychic therapy. Any form of treatment that concentrates on explaining the present in terms of past experience and unconscious motivations owes a large debt to Sigmund Freud.

Humanistic Therapy

Freud grew up in Austria, a land of kings and emperors who possessed "divine rights" that their subjects dared not question. Austrian fathers typically claimed the same privileges—when the man of the family spoke, the children listened and obeyed. Perhaps it is understandable, then, that in psychoanalysis the fatherly analyst often sets the goals of therapy and urges the patient onward.

Modern humanistic psychologists reject the "divine right" of the therapist to determine what is mentally healthy for the patient. In humanistic therapy, the patient rather than the therapist is king. Humanistic psychologists—such as Carl Rogers and Abraham Maslow—emphasize the conscious determinants of behavior. All human beings are presumed to have a positive drive toward good mental health. As Adolph Di Loreto puts it in the April 1981 issue of *Contemporary Psychology*, Freud's patients may be depicted as fighting for their life, while Rogers' and Maslow's clients are better characterized as fighting for a better life.

The humanistic therapist does not look too deeply into your unconscious nor too far back into your past. For the present and future are considered much more important than events long since forgotten. Therapy, then, should consist primarily of making you aware of your present state of functioning. Therapy should also focus on how you see yourself now, how others perceive you, and what "ideal state" you would like to reach. Once you understand all these things clearly, the therapist need only provide you with objective feedback about whatever progress you are making toward becoming your "self ideal."

Client-Centered Therapy

In Carl Rogers' **client-centered therapy**, the client determines the goals of treatment and the speed at which these goals will be met. Like most humanistic psychologists, Rogers is loath to impose his own standards or values on his clients. Instead, Rogers tries to provide a "psychological mirror" in which the clients can see themselves. He believes the clients will use this reflected information to achieve whatever changes in themselves are necessary to meet their own standards.

If you went to see a "client-centered" therapist, you would most likely find a clinical psychologist who had taken a Ph.D. rather than a medical degree. You would sit in a chair rather than lie on a couch, and you would decide more-or-less what the two of you would do together. The therapist would try to be warm, human, concerned, and supportive. But in theory, at least, the Rogerian therapist would seldom give advice or offer suggestions about what you ought to do or be.

Reflecting

As you talked about your problems, the therapist would frequently restate what you had said—*reflecting back* your own thoughts in slightly different form. In this way the therapist would provide you with an objective "mirror" of yourself and your own mental functioning.

By giving you **unconditional positive regard**—that is, by accepting you and the things you did, rather than criticizing or making value judgments about your emotions and perceptions—the therapist would hope to build a relationship of trust and affection with you. Only

Client-centered therapy. Carl Rogers believes that psychoanalysis is "therapist-centered," in that the analyst typically chooses the goals of treatment. In **client-centered therapy**, the client determines both the goals and the pace at which they are achieved.

Unconditional positive regard. Rogers' technique of accepting whatever the patient says or does as being "normal" for the person at that point in time. Client-centered therapists are taught never to criticize or punish their patients. Instead, the therapists "give acceptance" in a positive fashion for whatever the client is or wants to become.

under such non-punitive conditions, Rogers believes, could you build sufficient courage to see yourself as you really are. This same supportive atmosphere helps you determine what your goals really are—and helps you decide what *you* want to become, not what you think the world wants you to become. But once you can see yourself objectively, and know where you want to go, your own internal motivation will push you toward a better state of mental health and acceptance of yourself.

Is Rogers a Rogerian?

Most of the people practicing intra-psychic therapy in the US today are neither "pure" Freudians nor "pure" humanistic psychologists. Rather, therapists tend to be *eclectic*—they make use of whatever psychological techniques seem to work best for them and their clients. And they may do so almost without realizing what they are doing. Carl Rogers is no exception. For example, in 1966 C. Truax studied movies of Carl Rogers as he performed therapy. Far from providing his patients with "unconditional positive regard," Truax says, Rogers was unconsciously "shaping" his patients by rewarding "healthy self-statements" with head nods and smiles. Rogers also tended to ignore any "unhealthy statements" the patient made. We will have more to say about unconscious "shaping" later in this chapter. For the moment, we need only note that even Carl Rogers is perhaps a bit more eclectic than he sometimes appears to be.

Transactional Analysis and Gestalt Therapy

Both Gestalt therapy and Transactional Analysis were developed by former psychoanalysts with strong humanistic leanings. Since boths types of treatment are somewhat more likely to be used with groups than with individuals, we will postpone discussing them until later in this chapter.

The Effects of Intra-Psychic Therapy

Many factors make it difficult to evaluate the effectiveness of psychotherapy scientifically. Science deals with objective events, things that can

H. J. Eysenck

R. Bruce Sloane

readily be measured. But, by its very nature, intra-psychic therapy concerns itself with personality changes that can seldom be viewed in detail under a microscope. The success rates of various forms of treatment, then, must always be considered in terms of *what changes therapists hope to achieve*.

"Art Form" versus "Applied Science"

Some psychiatrists see therapy as an "art form," thus something that cannot be measured objectively. One such person is Jerome Frank, a professor at the Johns Hopkins School of Medicine. Writing in a recent issue of the *American Journal of Orthopsychiatry*, Frank states that "Psychotherapy is not primarily an applied science. In some ways it more resembles a religion . . . in others, the art of rhetoric or persuasion."

Frank goes on to compare therapy to music. "To try to determine by scientific analysis how much better or worse, let us say, Gestalt therapy is than Transactional Analysis is in many ways equivalent to attempting to determine by the same means the relative merits of the music of Cole Porter and Richard Rodgers. To ask the question is to reveal its absurdity."

Jerome Frank believes that the effectiveness of therapy depends more on the therapist than the technique. Unfortunately, Frank does not give any standards by which to judge who is a "good" therapist, and who isn't.

Although Frank's viewpoint has its merits, other pschiatrists are willing to use less subjective measures of improvement—such as modifi-

cations in the patient's overt behavior and the gradual disappearance of neurotic or psychotic symptoms. At least these changes can be observed and agreed upon by people other than the therapist.

Writing in the February 1981 *American Psychologist*, Sol L. Garfield reviews 40 years of research on the effectiveness of psychotherapy. One of the most widely publicized studies on *psychoanalytic* treatment was performed at the Menninger Foundation and was published in 1972. The Menninger experiment involved 21 patients given psychoanalysis and 21 given analytically oriented "insight" therapy. Both sets of patients were followed for many years. In discussing the Menninger study, Garfield states that, "My understanding or interpetation of this material is that 6 patients were judged to be worse at the end of therapy, 11 were unchanged, 7 showed slight improvement, and 18 (or 43 percent) showed moderate or marked improvement. If one takes my interpretation as provisionally valid, the results cannot be viewed as a very convincing demonstration of the efficacy of psychotherapy—particularly when the therapy is so expensive and time-consuming."

In psychoanalysis, the therapist usually decides whether or not a "cure" has taken place. But in the *humanistic* therapies the patient usually determines whether the therapy was successful or not. Rogers does have objective tests that measure changes in the client's *perceptions* of his or her progress, and the tests do seem to be reliable. But the validity of using the client's subjective impressions as an index of improvement remains in some doubt. The claimed "cure rate" for humanistic therapy is usually in the neighborhood of 75 percent or so.

Eysenck's 1952 Report
In recent years, the behavioral psychologists and social learning theorists have leveled strong criticisms against the "unscientific ways" in which the effectiveness of psychotherapy is usually determined. Immediately after World War II, H.J. Eysenck investigated several thousand cases of mentally disturbed servicemen and women in British hospitals. Eysenck reported in 1952 that the overall improvement rate among those patients given psychoanalytic treatment as about 44 percent. The improvement rate for patients given any other form of psychotherapy (eclectic treatment) was about 64 percent. Several hundred other patients received no psychotherapy at all. Their physical ailments were treated as necessary, but they were given no psychological therapy. The improvement rate among these *untreated* patients was about 72 percent. These data led some scientists to compare psychoanalysis with "witch doctoring," and to suggest psychoanalysis might actually *retard* the patient's progress.

As you might imagine, the psychoanalysts did not take such comments lightly. They pointed out that Eysenck's criteria for improvement were considerably different from their own, since Eysenck focused on easy-to-measure behavior changes. Eysenck ignored all of the basic alterations in the patient's personality that are the stated goal of most psychoanalytic treatment. The analysts also raised the important issue of patient selection. Some patients are better-suited for analysis than others, and the usual feeling is that hospitalized psychotics make the worst clients of all.

Spontaneous Recovery
Eysenck's criticisms deserve more careful consideration than we have space for here, as do the replies of the people he has criticized. We should note, however, that people made **spontaneous recoveries** from their psychological problems long before we had any real form of therapy to offer them. In several recent studies, the spontaneous "cure rate" has turned out to be 40 to 50 percent. Although the term "cured" is admittedly hard to define, it does seem as if the effectiveness of *any form of psychotherapy* must be measured against whatever figures we have on spontaneous recovery.

In his review of 40 years of research on psychotherapy, Sol L. Garfield notes one rather uni-

---

Spontaneous recoveries. Any "cures" or improvements due to natural circumstances, and hence not due to therapeutic intervention. Research suggests that up to 50 percent of people who experience mental problems will recover "spontaneously" in a year or so even if not given treatment.

---

form trend—the more objectively the improvement is measured, the less effective the standard forms of intra-psychic therapy appear to be.

Question: Why would it be more difficult to prove that therapy "works" using objective criteria than if you merely measured the subjective opinions of the clients and therapists?

Sloane's Temple Study
One of the best studies on the effectiveness of therapy was performed by psychiatrist R. Bruce Sloane and his associates at the Temple University School of Medicine in Philadelphia. These researchers selected 94 patients suffering from moderately severe neuroses and personality disorders who had come to an out-patient clinic for help. Roughly one-third of the patients were treated with a brief form of psychoanalytic "insight" therapy. These patients, then, received intra-psychic *psychotherapy*. Another third received *behavior modification therapy*, a type of treatment we have discussed extensively in Chapters 11, 15, and 16. The rest were told that they would have to wait at least four months for help—and hence became an untreated *control group.*

Sloane or another psychiatrist interviewed each patient before treatment and gave an initial impression of how disturbed the patient was and what symptoms the person showed. The assessing psychiatrists did not perform therapy themselves—they merely *evaluated* the patients before (and after) treatment.

After the intake interview, the patient was randomly assigned to one of the three groups mentioned above. The patient was also given several personality tests, including the MMPI (see Chapter 22). At the same time, a research assistant interviewed a close friend or relative of the patient to get this person's evaluation of what might be troubling the patient.

Patients in the treated groups were given an average of one hour of therapy a week for four months. Patients in the untreated control group were called every few weeks to find out how they were doing—and were encouraged to "hang tight" until a therapist could see them. These calls, of course, were themselves a type of treatment. At the end of four months, all the untreated patients who still wished help were put into "insight" therapy.

After four months, all the patients were again interviewed by the assessing psychiatrist, who did not know (and was told not to ask) what kind of therapy (if any) the patients had been given. Each patient retook the personality tests, and the research assistant once more talked with the close friend or relative to determine what progress this person thought the patient had made. Psychiatric assessments of the patients were also made one year and two years after the experiment began.

Sloane and his associates measured as many different aspects of the therapeutic situation as they could. Some of the tests they employed were *objective*. That is, they were aimed at determining success in symptom removal, bettering job performance, improving relationships with others, and so forth. Other measures were *subjective*. For instance, the patients were asked how well they liked the therapists, and the therapists gave subjective ratings of the patients. The patients were also asked about their own inner feelings as to how much they thought they had improved, and what anxiety they were experiencing. Both the assessing psychiatrist and the patient's friend or relative were asked what changes they saw in the patient's emotions and behaviors. In addition to these rather specific measures, the assessing psychiatrist, the patient, the friend or relative, and the patient's therapist (in two of the groups) also made what Sloane calls "global evaluations" of the amount of improvement shown by the patient.

Results

The results of the Sloane study are both complex and fascinating:

1. Some 80 percent of the patients given *either* behavior therapy or "insight" psychotherapy showed significant *symptom removal*, but so did 48 percent of the patients in the no-therapy control group. Thus either type of therapy is better than nothing, but spontaneous recovery did occur in about half the untreated patients.
2. Both the treated groups showed a significant reduction in *anxiety*, but the no-therapy patients also improved so much that Sloane and his colleagues concluded that the differences among the groups were not really significant.
3. The behavior therapy patients showed significantly greater improvement in their *work situations* than did the "insight" or no-therapy patients. The latter two groups of patients performed about the same.

4. As far as *social adjustment* was concerned, the behavior therapy and the no-treatment patients showed significant improvement. Those individuals given "insight" therapy did not do as well.
5. The psychoanalytically oriented therapists gave their patients significantly lower ratings of *sexual adjustment* than did anyone else. The behavior therapists gave their patients significantly higher ratings on the sexual adjustment scale than did anyone else. The patients gave themselves significantly higher ratings than did the insight therapists. Generally speaking, in most of the subjective ratings, the patients (no matter who treated them) and the behavior therapists were much more optimistic about recovery than were any of the other raters.
6. The *global evaluations* of patient improvement made by the assessing psychiatrists yielded the most marked differences among raters. As judged by the psychiatrists (all of whom had psychoanalytic training), 93 percent of the behavior therapy patients showed improvement, while only 77 percent of the "insight therapy" and 77 percent of the no-therapy patients showed improvement. As judged by the patients themselves, 74 percent of those in the behavior therapy group, 81 percent of those given psychotherapy, and but 44 percent of those in the no-therapy group felt they had improved. It would seem that those patients *denied* therapy believed they couldn't possibly have gotten much better without treatment despite the objective evidence to the contrary seen by the assessing psychiatrists.

We might note that the patients in the two treatment groups probably had quite different perceptions of what improvement ought to be. The goal of psychotherapy is often that of giving the person better *understanding* of her or his mental processes. Behavior therapy is a broader-scale type of treatment, in which self-help and self-improvement in many areas are emphasized. It is possible that the "insight" patients did notice a marked improvement in their mental processes and, believing this to be the major goal of therapy, rated themselves highly. The assessing psychiatrists, knowing that things like good job performance and healthy social relations are also necessary to mental health, downgraded the "insight" patients because they had shown little improvement in these areas (while the behavior therapy patients had).
7. Additional findings by Sloane and his group were equally interesting. One of the major ob-

jections raised against behavior therapy is that it merely removes symptoms without curing the underlying cause of the disorder. Hence other symptoms might crop up to replace those the therapy had banished. However, Sloane and his associates found no evidence for *symptom substitution* in any of the patients in any group. To the contrary, it seemed that when a patient's primary symptoms showed improvement, the patient often spontaneously reported improvement of other minor difficulties as well.

Another objection brought against behavioral treatment is that it is a "cold and mechanistic way of pushing people around." In fact, the patients in behavioral treatment rated their therapists as being significantly "warmer, more involved, more genuine, and as having greater and more accurate **empathy**" than the insight patients rated their therapists as being.

8. Sloane and his colleagues found that their psychoanalytically oriented therapists did better with well-educated, middle- or upper-class, verbally fluent patients than with relatively uneducated or verbally passive patients. The behavior therapists did about as well with one type of person as with any other. Perhaps for this reason, none of the patients given behavior therapy got worse, while one or two people in the other two groups showed a *marked deterioration* over the four-month period.

Sloane's Conclusions

R. Bruce Sloane and his colleagues conclude that:

> behavior therapy is at least as effective as, and possibly more so than, psychotherapy with the sort of moderately severe neuroses and personality disorders that are typical of clinical populations. This [finding] should help to dispel the impression that behavior therapy is useful only with phobias and [simple] problems. In fact, only the behavior therapy group in this study had improved significantly on both the work and the social measures of general adjustment at four months. Behavior therapy is clearly a *generally* useful treatment.

Question: *Research such as Sloane's is sometimes criticized as being unethical because individuals in the control group are* denied therapy *for a period of time. Given the findings, what do you think?*

"Sick Talk" and "Well Talk"

One of the most puzzling aspects of the Sloane study is that the psychotherapists saw *less* improvement in their patients than did the patients

---

Empathy (EM-path-thee). From the Greek words meaning "to suffer with." Literally, the ability to understand fully another person's thoughts and feelings.

---

themselves, or the outside assessors. The behavior therapists were just the opposite. An explanation for this finding may come from research by a psychologist named Joel Greenspoon.

In the late 1950's, Greenspoon demonstrated how important the attitude of the therapist is in affecting the behavior of most clients. Greenspoon noticed that when a patient begins talking about sexual abnormalities, or about bizarre thought patterns, the therapist may unconsciously encourage the patient to continue talking. The therapist may lean forward, look very interested, and say to the patient, "Yes, yes, tell me more about that." But when the patient is speaking normally, or discussing solutions rather than problems, the therapist may believe that the patient is making little or no progress. So the therapist may lean back and look disinterested. In Greenspoon's terms, there is always the danger that the therapist may unwittingly *reward* the patient for "sick talk" and *punish* the patient for "well talk."

In more humanistic terms, getting the client to concentrate on achieving mental *health* may be more important than getting the client to understand the causes of his or her mental *illness*. It is possible that the insight therapists in the Sloane study *perceived* their patients as being a "collection of problems" rather than as a "collection of healthy possibilities."

Question: *Given Greenspoon's findings, are you surprised that Rogers may have "unconsciously shaped" his patients toward better health?*

Social/Behavioral Therapy

Up until fairly recently, most of our laws, customs, and philosophies have been based on the assumption that psychological problems existed *within* an individual. When factors *outside* the individual contributed to "mental disorders," these factors were presumed to be primarily supernatural—gods, witches, and evil spirits. Most forms of biological and intra-psychic therapy can be seen as attempts to treat the patient by working from the inside out.

Within the last century rather a different point of view has emerged—a belief that "mental illness" is as much a disruption of relationships *between people* as it is a disruption of *one person's inner psycho-dynamics*. Abnormal behavior

Religious groups often rely heavily on inspirational therapy.

is almost always expressed in social situations. And unless "crazy people" disturb or upset others, they are seldom sent to mental hospitals or to see a therapist. Treatment must not merely alter the functioning of the patient's body or brain—or change the patient's personality—it must also help the patient get along better with others. Indeed, in many instances, the group of people around the patient may actually be contributing to the "craziness" without realizing it. In such cases the best form of therapy may be removing the person from that environment—or somehow getting other people to behave differently toward the patient. This type of treatment obviously works from the outside in.

The three major types of social/behavioral treatment are: (1) group therapy, in which the patient learns better ways of responding to a group of people who often have similar problems; (2) behavioral therapy, including cognitive behavior modification, which we have discussed in earlier chapters; and (3) **milieu therapy**, in which

the patient's social environment or milieu becomes the focus for treatment.

Group Therapy

The history of group therapy probably stretches back to the dawn of recorded time. In a sense the early Greek dramas offered a type of psychological release not much different from the psychodrama we will discuss in a moment. Bull sessions, prayer meetings, revivals—all these are the ancestral forms of today's encounter groups.

Group therapy did not gain any scientific notice, however, until 1905, when a Boston physician named J.H. Pratt made a fortunate mistake. Pratt found that patients suffering from tuberculosis were often discouraged and depressed. He first believed their despondency was due to ignorance on their part—they simply didn't know enough about the disease they suffered from. So he brought them together in groups to give them lectures about "healthy living." The lectures soon turned into very intense discussions among the patients about their problems. Pratt discovered that his patients gained much more strength from learning they were not alone in their suffering than they did from his lectures.

By 1910 group treatment was used by many European psychiatrists who gave "collective counseling" to people with similar psychological problems. Psychiatrist J.L. Moreno tried this method in Vienna with displaced persons, children, and prostitutes. In 1914 Alfred Adler suggested that group techniques might be a more effective way of helping large numbers of patients than the usual one patient–one therapist encounters.

According to R.M. Goldenson, European psychoanalysts were for the most part hostile to group psychotherapy, but this form of treatment soon gained a firm foothold in the United States. Some of the major varieties are psychoanalytic group therapy, directed group therapy, inspirational group therapy, play group therapy, activity group therapy, family group therapy, encounter groups, and psychodrama.

Group Therapy Techniques

As you might guess, these various forms of group treatment differ considerably among themselves. But, as J.D. Frank puts it, they all seem to be based on the belief "that intimate sharing of feelings, ideas, [and] experiences in an atmosphere of mutual respect and understanding enhances self-respect, deepens self-understanding, and helps the person live with others."

Some types of groups are directed by a leader and have a rather formal treatment plan. One purpose these groups often have is that of helping people break through their psychological resistances. The group leader may give lectures or pass out written material that forms the basis of group discussion. This "structured" technique is used particularly with psychotic or withdrawn patients who would not, perhaps, be able to function effectively in a less-structured social environment.

Other groups are more inspirational in character. They are typically led by someone with a strong personality who uses a variety of techniques (including strong criticism, or calling on higher spiritual powers) to inspire change in group members. Some groups concentrate mostly on encouraging the patients to form new behavior patterns and attitudes. Other groups concentrate on breaking down emotional resistances in their members. The 10,000 or more chapters of Alcoholics Anonymous, the Christian Science Church, EST, the Seventh Step Foundation for ex-convicts, and even Weight Watchers, Inc., are examples of groups that rely heavily on inspirational or highly emotional devices.

Milieu therapy (mill-YOU). The French word for "social environment" is *milieu*. Milieu therapy involves changing the patient's environment in order to induce changes in the patient's mind and behavior.

Psychodrama (SIGH-koh-DRAH-mah). A theatrical therapy developed by J.L. Moreno (mor-REE-noh). Some part of the patient's life is usually acted out on a stage, often by professional actors. The patient may play one of the roles, or may simply observe.

Transactional analysis (trans-ACT-shun-al). Psychiatrist Eric Berne believed that people "play games" with each other without realizing what they are doing. Borrowing from Freud, Berne stated that there are three basic "ego states," the Child, the Parent, and the Adult. These three "ego states" correspond (roughly speaking) to Freud's notions of the id, super-ego, and ego. Part of transactional analysis involves determining what "ego state" you and the people around you are in at any given moment.

Stereotyped (STAIR-ee-oh-typed). A routine or unconscious way of acting or feeling.

Psychodrama

Moreno, who first used group therapy with socially displaced persons around 1910, later developed a type of treatment he called **psychodrama**. The therapist usually serves as "director" for the psychodrama, which often takes place on a real stage. The patient stars as "heroine" or "hero" in a "play" that centers around some problem in the patient's life. Trained actor-therapists assist in the production. At times, a whole family or group may act out their difficulties. Moreno often invites audiences to watch the proceedings, for he believes that people in the audience can benefit from seeing problems similar to their own presented on stage.

Transactional Analysis

A very different form of role-playing is found in **transactional analysis**, or TA. US psychiatrist Eric Berne developed a personality theory that was, in part, an extension of Freudian psychoanalysis. He used the term "game" to refer to the **stereotyped** and often misleading interpersonal "transactions" that people frequently adopt in dealing with others. According to Berne, a game is a "recurring series of transactions, often repetitive and superficially rational, with a concealed motivation." He believed that each game is but a tiny part of a "script" that a person uses in "performing" various roles in his or her life. Briefly put, the goal of TA is that of consciously changing your behavior so that you no longer engage in unconscious role-playing.

William and Martha Holloway describe TA as a therapy in which people learn they are responsible for their own feelings, but not for the feelings of others. They describe TA as "being for people who want to change and not those who want to be coddled." The Holloways further state that,

"Change in TA groups is . . . contractual and decisional . . . The duration and extent of the change process for any given individual is entirely dependent upon the goals which that person sets."

In previous chapters, we noted that infants require sensory stimulation in order to survive. The Holloways call this physical stimulation "giving strokes." Positive strokes result in "good feelings," while negative strokes result in "unpleasant feelings." As adults we often seek verbal or psychological "strokes" rather than physical ones. If we can't get positive "strokes," then negative ones are better than nothing. Much of the role playing we engage in, therefore, is unconsciously aimed at "getting strokes."

According to Eric Berne, we have three "ego states," the Adult, the Parent, and the Child. Roughly speaking, Berne has borrowed many of his ideas about the Adult, Parent, and Child ego states from Freud's descriptions of ego, superego, and id.

The parent ego state is a set of "memorized instructions" we learned when young by observing how our parents acted toward us. When playing the role of a "nurturing parent," we use terms such as "I love you," or "You're beautiful." When in a "critical parent" ego state, we use words such as "always, never, must, should, ought to."

The child ego state is one primarily made up of feelings. The "natural child" ego state allows us to express our feelings as they actually are. In the "adapted child" ego state, we react as our parents told us we ought to when we were young.

The Holloways describe the adult ego state as being "like a computer." That is, "The Adult is the part of us that takes in and evaluates information, both from inside us and from the world around us. The Adult also estimates the probabilities and makes decisions." When in this ego state, we tend to "operate with little feeling," and our "Adult decisions are usually well-informed."

When two people speak, the Holloways say, the problem with communications is that one person may be speaking as Adult, while the other may be in the Child or Parent ego state. The Holloways call this "crossed transactions." Thus one goal of TA is to let you identify your states— and those of others—in order to understand how people communicate. Then you must learn to take responsibility for what you do, accept yourself ("I'm OK"), make a contract with yourself to live more successfully in the future, and realize that other people have the potential to do the same ("You're OK").

Gestalt Psychotherapy
Gestalt therapy has its roots in classical Gestalt psychology (see Chapter 9), psychoanalysis, and the analysis of non-verbal behavior. The main object of this type of treatment often seems to be that of *growth through exploration*. The explorations are sometimes emotional, sometimes perceptual, sometimes behavioral. The group leader (or individual therapist) helps clients experiment with new ways of acting and of viewing themselves, their problems, and the world outside them.

Gestalt therapy was begun by Fritz Perls. More than anything else, this type of treatment emphasizes that people should "take responsibility for themselves," and should "focus attention primarily on the here and now." In his 1978 book *Creative Process in Gestalt Therapy*, Joseph Zinker defines Gestalt therapy as an ongoing creative adjustment to the potential in the therapeutic situation.

Encounter Groups
Encounter groups vary so widely among themselves that no simple description of them is possible. In general, an encounter group is made up of people who have had little previous contact with one another. The group may meet one or more times a week for several weeks. Or the members may live together in close, intense contact for a day, a weekend, or even longer. The participants are usually encouraged to bring their feelings out into the open and to learn more honest ways of communicating with each other. Often the focus is on some aspect of non-verbal experience— perhaps on developing better sensory awareness of bodily reactions, perhaps on learning how facial expressions communicate deep-seated emotions. As a means of helping group members strip away their defenses, a few encounter groups meet in the nude.

Evaluating Group Therapy
Perhaps the best evaluation of the effectiveness of different types of group therapy comes from a series of studies performed by psychologists Morton A. Lieberman, Matthew B. Miles, and psychiatrist Irvin D. Yalom. This research on group therapy began at Stanford in 1968 and is still going on. Over the years, Lieberman, Miles, and Yalom have studied just about every type of group treatment offered to the public. Typically, they investigate the group leader's perceptions of what went on, ask the participants to evaluate the experience both immediately after treatment and at some later time, and also ask close friends or relatives of the participants to rate the participants' progress.

In a recent book, Lieberman, Miles, and Yalom report that their studies offer little scientific evidence that group therapy is of much *therapeutic* value. Indeed, it may often do real harm. They state that about 8 percent of the participants are "casualties"—that is, people who show evidence of serious psychological damage that can be attributed to the group experience. Overall, however, about a third of the group members get better, about a third get worse, and the rest seem unchanged immediately after the experience. There are few differences among the various types of group therapy (Gestalt, psychodrama, and so forth) as far as their effectiveness was concerned. Immediately after therapy has ended, almost 65 percent of the participants state that the experience was a positive one. However, six months later, less than a third of them are still enthusiastic about having undergone treatment.

Benefits of Group Therapy

Lieberman, Miles, and Yalom conclude from their work so far that none of the groups they studied were particularly effective as *change agents*. However, the groups can excel at creating *instant, brief, and intense interpersonal experiences*. Lieberman, Miles, and Yalom state that this chance to learn something about yourself from the open reactions of others is real, important, and not often available in our society. But they believe that such experiences are not the crucial ones that alter people permanently for the better.

Environmental Therapy

One of the more interesting discoveries of the past century has been the slow realization of how sensitive we all are to our environments. The **ecologists** have demonstrated rather vividly the disasters that may occur when we pollute the physical world around us. But polluted psychological environments can kill or corrupt your spirit as readily as dirty air and water can kill or corrupt your body. The job of the environmental psychotherapist is similar to that of the ecologist—to identify sources of pollution and remove them. If the therapist cannot easily find ways of removing the "psycho-pollution" from your world, or of helping you live more happily despite the pollution, then more radical treatment is usually needed. Typically this treatment takes the form of moving you to different surroundings—such as a mental hospital.

Mental Hospitals: Past and Present

Yale psychologist Jeffrey Blum points out that mental hospitals first came into existence in 1657, when the General Hospital of Paris was founded. Prior to this time, "mentally ill" people had been free to roam the countryside at will. It was about

---

Gestalt therapy (guess-SHTALT). The German word *Gestalt* means "good form." According to the Gestalt psychologists, we tend to perceive the world in "wholes," which are the "best possible forms." Gestalt therapy often consists of helping you "become a *whole* person again."

Ecologists (ee-KOLL-oh-jists). Ecologists are scientists who study the pattern of relationships between organisms and their environments.

Pauper's prisons (PAW-per). To be a "pauper" is to be poor. Until 100 years ago or so, people who couldn't pay their debts were imprisoned until they obtained enough money to pay their creditors. Since obtaining money in prison was even more difficult than it was outside of prison, most paupers stayed in prison for a very long time indeed.

Protestant ethic. Protestants tend to believe that entrance into heaven is brought about by what you do, not merely what you feel. Thus, anyone believing in the Protestant ethic is likely to assume that people ought to earn their bread and board, or participate actively (and intelligently) in their own salvation. A century ago in the US, anyone who refused to work was deemed either lazy or crazy. Lazy people were put in prison, but could get out by hard work. Crazy people were put in lunatic asylums from which there was little or no hope of escape.

1650, too, when western society first began building large numbers of jails for criminals and **pauper's prisons** for people who couldn't pay their debts. But, as Blum notes, mental patients were at the bottom of society's list. Indeed, in 1657 it was considered *inhumane* to lock up axe murderers, armed robbers, and rapists in a mental hospital because the patients might threaten the physical safety of the *criminals*.

In his monumental work on the history of mental hospitals in the US, David Rothman states that in the 1800's, we built asylums as a way of trying to impress the **Protestant Ethic** on social outcasts who did not work at a steady job, support themselves, and pay taxes. The mental hospital in the mid-1800's was not a place to cure *mental* illness, then, but a place where lazy or disturbed people could learn the benefits of leading a disciplined, scheduled, hard-working life.

Far from being *asylums* where people could flee when the storms of life became too threatening, early mental hospitals were little more than human garbage dumps, crammed with life's failures and misfits. As *ecological systems*, these institutions were often more abnormal and destructive to human egos than was the outside world the patients had sought relief from. Little wonder, therefore, that the "cure rate" in US mental hospitals remained very low from the 1700's until the mid-1900's.

Milieu Therapy

Social/behavioral therapists tend to see mental illness as being *caused* by unhealthy living con-

Eric Berne   Karen Horney

ditions—not by character defects or mental weakness. It was the failure of society to teach people healthy behaviors—not the failure of people to learn—that caused insanity. The best form of treatment, therefore, would be putting the patient in a new milieu—each aspect of which would be carefully designed to help the patient *learn better habits of adjustment*.

The term "therapeutic community" was coined by British psychiatrist Maxwell Jones in 1953 to refer to this type of *milieu therapy*.

Writing in the *American Handbook of Psychiatry*, Dr. Louis Linn points out that our concept of therapy began to change drastically around 1950:

> In former days there was a tendency to regard treatment in the mental hospital as that which takes place during the fraction of a second when the current flows from an electro-shock apparatus, or during the longer intervals involved in other therapies ... In the therapeutic community the whole of the time which the patient spends in the hospital is thought of as treatment time, and everything that happens to the patient is part of the treatment program.

In a sense the therapeutic community is rather like a non-stop, 24-hour-a-day encounter group. However, its primary function is *not* usually that of removing symptoms or merely changing behaviors. Rather, its aim is said to be that of drawing the patient into normal relationships that will give the person confidence, self-esteem, and social competence.

The difficulty in evaluating milieu therapy is the same as with other forms of group therapy—terms like "confidence" and "self-esteem" refer to intra-psychic traits and hence are hard to define or measure objectively. Therapeutic communities certainly are far more humane forms of treatment than the old-style mental hospitals. But as we will

see momentarily, there are serious questions as to whether milieu therapy is as effective in curing people as its proponents claim.

Token Economies

Rather a different type of environmental treatment is favored by behavior therapists, whose aim is that of changing habit patterns rather than altering inner psychological states.

Patients in mental hospitals often develop what is called an **institutional neurosis**. That is, the patients lose interest in the world and the people around them, develop hallucinations and fantasies, and become quarrelsome, resentful, and hostile. Institutional neurosis appears to be caused at least in part by the fact that, in most hospitals, patients often are "given" everything they might need by the "authority figures" in charge. Under these conditions, many of the patients develop a rather child-like dependency on the staff.

Behavioral psychologists believe the best cure for institutional neurosis is making the patients take as much responsibility for their own improvement as possible. To help achieve this goal, the behaviorists have developed what they call the *token economy*. In the money economy that operates in the world outside the hospital, you typically must work to live. The better you work, generally speaking, the more money you make. If you perform poorly or refuse to work, you may very well starve. In contrast, mental hospitals typically operate on a "free economy." That is, the patients are given whatever they need merely by asking for it. In fact, the *worse* they behave, the *more* attention and help they usually receive.

In a token economy, therapy usually consists of having the staff reinforce "socially approved" or "healthy" behaviors and ignore inappropriate or "insane" behaviors. Each patient is encouraged to decide what rewards she or he wants to work for. The patient is then given the tokens as visible evidence that he or she is making progress toward these chosen goals.

In his 1977 book on token economies, Alan E. Kazdin points out that this form of treatment has been quite successful with many different types of mental patients. It works well in helping people with chronic schizophrenia learn to take better care of themselves, get along better with others, and gain the self-control neccesary to reduce some of their bizarre behaviors. It also functions well with mentally retarded individuals who need to acquire job skills and learn to communicate more efficiently with others. But the token economy is often most effective with troubled children, perhaps because it gives them socially approved ways of getting what they want from the adults around them (including their own parents). Kazdin notes that almost all scientific comparisons of the token economy with "traditional" ward treatment in hospitals show the behavioral approach to be superior.

Perhaps the best study comparing the token economy to other forms of treatment was reported by Gordon Paul and Robert Lentz in 1977. Paul and Lentz contrasted the improvement rates in three groups of hospitalized patients—those given traditional "milieu" therapy, those put on a token economy, and those left on the usual ward without any special form of treatment. The patients in the token economy showed far greater improvement than did the patients in either of the other two groups.

The criticism most often raised against the token economy is that it is mechanistic and dehumanizing because it focuses on observable behaviors—on symptoms—rather than dealing with underlying, dynamic psychological problems. The behavioral changes that the token economies do bring about, however, seem to be very reliable (repeatable).

Therapy and the Whole Individual

Psychotherapy is perhaps the most challenging and interesting part of psychology for most of us. It combines the pleasures of intellectual analysis with the warm emotions of "doing good" for individuals who might need our help. These statements, however, are as true of witch doctoring as they are of any other type of psychotherapy. And, whether we like it or not, most "mentally disturbed" individuals get well whether or not they receive treatment. As the noted psychoanalyst Karen Horney said in her book *Our Inner Conflicts*, "Fortunately, analysis is not the only way to resolve inner conflicts. Life itself still remains a very effective therapist." How then can we make sure that our therapy does, in fact, speed up (or add something extra to) what seems to be our inborn way of healing ourselves?

To answer this question, we might turn to Adolf Meyer, who is often called the "dean of US psychiatry."

Meyer's Holistic Approach

Adolf Meyer believed in the *holistic* approach to treating people, and recognized that there were multiple causes for even the simplest of behaviors. Rather than passing verdicts on patients by labeling them as "schizophrenics" or "neurotics,"

Institutional neurosis. Hospital patients are often subtly encouraged to remain "sick" in order to stay in the hospital. The "sicker" the patient becomes, the more dependent the patient is on the hospital, and the more the institution justifies its own existence. When patients develop an abnormally strong dependency on a hospital or its staff, the patients are said to suffer from an institutional neurosis.

Meyer preferred to discover both what was wrong and what was right with the patients at all levels of analysis—the biological, the psychological, and the sociological.

Meyer also attempted to determine those *normal* aspects of behavior that the patient might still have available—and then build on these psychological assets to bring about change. Meyer believed that the patient should set both the goals and the pace of therapy, and that the therapist should work as hard at changing the patient's home (or hospital) environment as in changing the patient's psyche or behaviors. Meyer called his approach "critical common sense."

There are thousands of different kinds of psychotherapy. The surprising thing is that almost all of them "work" with certain kinds of patients and with certain types of problems—and fail with others. If we apply Adolf Meyer's "critical common sense" to an analysis of the strengths and weaknesses of all the various types of therapy, we might discover that most successful forms of treatment have several things in common:

1. Psychological change almost always occurs in a supportive, warm, rewarding environment. People usually "open up" and talk about things—and try new approaches to life—when they trust, admire, or want to please the therapist. Encounter groups whose members focus on expressing hostility toward each other often do incredible damage—unless such expression is embedded in a background of affection so strong that the members can tolerate occasional (but hopefully brief) punishment from each other. Criticism seldom changes thoughts or behaviors, and it often kills all chance of improvement. But sincere expressions of warmth and tolerance for "abnormalities" can provide the atmosphere in which change can occur.

2. Most successful forms of treatment can be seen as feedback mechanisms. That is, they provide you with information about your past, put you in touch with the functioning of your body, and make you aware of how your behav-

ior actually affects other people. Feedback also helps you realize the distance between your desired goals and your present achievements, and offers information on how the social environment influences your own thoughts, feelings, and behaviors. Ideally, a complete form of therapy would do all these things—and also help you learn how to seek out and make even better use of feedback in the future.

3. Magic can "cure" mental illness overnight; all other forms of psychotherapy take a little longer. If you believe that madness is a matter of possession by devils—or that it's due to a "poor attitude" on the part of the patient—then you might expect that beatings or sermons could cure the illness quickly. But if you believe that it takes many years of punishing or stressful experiences—and perhaps a particular genetic predisposition—for a full-blown psychosis to develop, then you might also expect the road to recovery to be a fairly lengthy one.

4. The attitudes of both the patient and the therapist are of critical importance. A Cree Eskimo woman suffering from *witigo* "knows" that she needs a witch doctor. Will giving this woman a tranquilizer help her much? On the other hand, patients often see their therapists as being models of mentally healthy or socially approved behaviors. Effective therapists (witch doctors, psychoanalysts, humanists, or behaviorists) usually practice what they preach.

5. The best forms of therapy seem to build on strengths rather than merely attacking weaknesses. By helping the patient work toward positive improvement—toward problem solving, good social behaviors, and self-actualization—the therapist motivates the patient to continue to grow and change. Therapies that focus entirely on uncovering or discussing psychological problems may merely confirm the patient's attitude that sickness is inevitable.

The Future of Psychotherapy

It is likely that, in the coming years, we will take Adolf Meyer's ideas more seriously than we have in the past, and that we will treat the whole patient as a unique individual rather than treating just one aspect of the person's difficulties. Already in some hospitals there is a *team of therapists* available to work with each patient. One member of the team looks at the person's physical or biological problems. Another deals with the person's intra-psychic dynamics. A third helps the patient change behavior patterns. A fourth team member is an expert in altering social environments. The patient can then get as much—or as little—of each type of therapy as his or her own particular case demands.

Ideally, the goals of therapy should be spelled out in a written contract agreed to by the patient and all members of the therapeutic team, and the patient's progress should be recorded regularly on a graph of some kind so that all team members are aware of the patient's achievements. As this "team-contracting approach" increases in popularity, our success rate in curing mental illness is likely to show a significant increase.

All forms of therapy achieve some success. In 1975 the Research Task Force of the National Institute of Mental Health released a report covering 25 years of research on therapy and mental illness. According to the NIMH report, most types of psychotherapy yield a 70 percent "cure rate." The major exceptions are behavior therapy and drug therapy, both of which (when effectively utilized) have produced cure rates well above 80 percent. But, as the NIMH report suggests, perhaps the single most important thing we have learned about mental health in the past 25 years is that neither problems nor cures occur in a vacuum. No matter how well a patient may respond in a hospital setting—and no matter what insights a client achieves in a therapist's office—the ultimate test of therapy comes when the person returns to her or his usual environment. If the patient can function successfully and happily in the real world, we can then conclude that a "cure" had indeed taken place.

It is thus to the complexities of the social environment that we now must turn our attention.

Summary

1. The types of therapy that we prescribe for mentally ill persons usually stem from our **theoretical explanation** of what causes the persons' problems.

2. In primitive times (and societies), insanity was said to be caused by **possession**. That is, a **devil** of some kind was thought to take over the sick person's mind.

3. Eskimos and Cree Indians believe they can be

possessed by a witch or **witigo** who craves human flesh. In Malaysia, young males occasionally suffer from explosive manic episodes called **running amok**.

4. Primitive forms of **psychotherapy** typically involve the use of magic to "cast out the witch," or painful whips to **beat the devil** out of the patient.

5. As our scientific explanations of the causes of human behavior have changed, so have our types of treatment. In evaluating any form of therapy, we must ask ourselves several questions:

   a. How successful or **valid** is the treatment?
   b. How **reliable** is the therapy?
   c. Are there unfortunate **side effects**?
   d. How shall we define "success" or **cure rate**?

6. Biological treatment typically involves the use of **electro-convulsive shock, psycho-surgery**, and **chemotherapy** or drugs.

7. **ECT** is most often used for **depression**, while **lobotomies** are used with aggressive or highly emotional patients. Both types of treatment have bad side-effects and have not been proven scientifically to be of great worth.

8. The **major** and **minor tranquilizers** and **antidepressants** have limited uses, but many can be **abused** and all may have dangerous side-effects.

9. There are many forms of intra-psychic treatment, including **psychoanalysis, humanistic therapy**, and **eclectic therapy**.

10. In psychoanalysis, the client is encouraged to undergo a **transference relationship** in which the analyst becomes a kind of "father figure." The therapist often **interprets** the client's **free associations**, feelings, and dreams in psychoanalytic terms in order to determine the client's unconscious **psycho-dynamics** and motivations.

11. In humanistic therapy, the client sets his or her own **therapeutic goals** and determines the **pace** at which treatment proceeds.

12. In **Rogerian** or **client-centered therapy**, the therapist gives the client **unconditional positive regard** while **reflecting back** the client's thoughts or feelings.

13. All therapy must be judged in relationship to the rate of **spontaneous recovery** patients show without treatment. In most recent studies, this rate has been between 40 and 50 percent.

14. Some psychiatrists consider therapy to be an **art form** which cannot be judged using the **scientific method**. Other therapists admit that the effects of treatment must be measured **objectively**.

15. In the **Menninger** study of psychoanalytic treatment, the "cure rate" was about 43 percent. However, many patients showed little improvement or were even worse at the end of treatment.

16. The cure rate for humanistic therapy, for eclectic psychotherapy, and for most types of **insight therapy** is about 70 percent.

17. The **Sloane study** suggests that "insight" therapy is better at changing a patient's **self-awareness** than at removing symptoms or changing behaviors. **Behavior therapy** is at least as effective with most patients as is psychotherapy, and is better at helping people improve **job performance** and **social adjustment**.

18. Research by Greenspoon shows that therapists may **unconsciously shape** patient responses by rewarding them for **sick talk** or **well talk**.

19. Environmental therapies include many types of **group therapy**, as well as attempts to change the patient by altering the patient's **milieu** and **social behaviors**.

20. One of the problems with group therapies—such as **nondirective group therapy, psychodrama, transactional analysis, Gestalt therapy**, and **encounter groups**—is that some 8 percent of the clients end up as **psychological casualties** who are worse after treatment than before.

21. Group therapies seem better as ways of encouraging people to explore and express themselves than as **change agents**.

22. **Milieu therapy** involves changing the patient's environment so that the person may grow in psychologically healthy ways.

23. **Behavioral psychologists** often use the **token economy** to help patients overcome **institutional neuroses**. Patients are **rewarded** for achievements with tokens, while inappropriate behaviors are ignored. Research suggests that the token economy is the most effective type of environmental therapy for many behavioral problems.

24. Most effective therapy takes place in a **warm, supporting environment** in which patients are given appropriate **feedback**. The **attitudes** of both patient and therapist are important, as is **building on strengths** rather than merely correcting weaknesses.

25. It is likely that, in the future, a **team approach** to treatment will prove to be highly effective, particularly if **patient-therapist contracts** are employed.

(Continued from page 562)

"I *hurt*, Mark," Lou Hudson repeated, ignoring all of the boisterous activity in the gambling casino as he poured out his heart to Mark Evans. "I've lost almost everything we own. The house, the car, everything—gambled it all away. I've borrowed from everybody in the family and lost it all on the horses. I'm even going to lose Betty and the kids if I can't shape up somehow. But I get those urges, you understand, those times when I just know that I've got a winning streak going, and I have to play my hunches. I've got to get help of some kind, Mark, but what should I do?"

"What does Betty think you should do?"

"She wants me to join the Chattanooga chapter of Gamblers Anonymous. They're a bunch of people just like me that get together regularly to talk over their problems and help each other out. Betty says they've helped lots of folks."

"So, why don't you join and see what they can do for you?"

"Cause it would make your uncle angry at me. I mean your Uncle John, the psychoanalyst. He says I have an unconscious desire to punish myself by losing all the time. He thinks I ought to lie on a couch for a few years and find out what's wrong deep down inside me. He says that group therapy just doesn't get at the roots of the problem."

Mark smiled at the thought of Lou lying on a couch. "Well, why don't you try psychoanalysis, then?"

"Because of your Cousin Sophie," Lou said.

"The Rogerian?"

"Yeah. She thinks I need nondirective therapy to help me achieve self-actualization. Sophie's a wonderful woman, Mark, and she's awful easy to talk to. Every time I say something to her, she just says it back to me in different words. Trouble is, she isn't talking to your Uncle John, and I owe her almost as much money as I owe him."

Mark decided that he needed a drink too, and hoisted a glass off the tray of a passing cocktail waitress. "So, why don't you go in for a little self-actualization?"

Lou groaned. "Your Aunt Beverly would never approve."

"You mean the behavior therapist?"

Lou nodded. "Yeah." He swallowed half his drink in a single gulp. "Man, you've got more different kinds of shrinks in your family than I ever heard of!"

"Psychology runs in my family the way that insanity runs in others. But what does Aunt Beverly, the behaviorist, think?"

"She tells me that all the other forms of therapy are unscientific. According to her, I'd do better to find a witch doctor than to go to your Uncle John for psychoanalysis. She wants to set up a behavioral program that will reward me for not gambling. And I hate to tell you how much I owe that woman, Mark."

"The cure rates for some kinds of behavioral therapy are very impressive, Lou. So why don't you try it?"

Lou shook his head in dismay. "Because it would make everybody else in the family mad as hell at me, including my wife Betty. I wouldn't mind going to any of them if I was sure they could help me. But how can you be sure you're going to be cured, Mark?"

"You can't be, Lou. Any more than you could be sure that if you sold me a life insurance policy, I wouldn't die the next day. All you can do is play the odds."

"What do you mean?"

"Ask each of the shrinks in the family to tell you what the cure rate is for compulsive gambling with their type of therapy. Take a good, close look at what they consider successful treatment to be, and how they measure success, and what the cost to you is going to be. Then pick the one that gives you the best odds for your time and money."

Lou Hudson blinked his bloodshot eyes as he pondered the matter. "That's being pretty hard-nosed about a very human predicament, isn't it?"

"Being hard-nosed about human predicaments is what keeps insurance companies and gambling casinos in business, Lou. You can't be sure that the therapy with the best overall cure rate is going to work for you and your own unique set of problems, but the fact that the odds are in your favor gives you a bit of a head start."

"Yeah," said Lou reluctantly. "I see what you mean."

"But what do *you* want to do, Lou? That's the most important factor of all."

"I kind of like the advice your Cousin Oscar gave me, and I owe him more than anybody."

Mark laughed. "Ah, yes, Cousin Oscar. What does the black sheep of the family recommend?"

Lou grinned. "Well, he knows of this woman who's a fortune teller. She lives in the same trailer park that Oscar lives in. He says that if I slip her a few bucks, she might look into her magic crystal ball and give me a tip on the races. Oscar says she's almost always right. If I could just win a few big ones, Mark, I could pay back my debts, stop gambling, and then I wouldn't need any therapy at all. What do you think of that?"

Mark shook his head. "No dice. If she's so good with crystal balls, how come she lives in a trailer instead of a mansion?"

Lou frowned. "Yeah, I see what you mean. Bad odds, eh? But what can I do? No matter whose therapy I pick, I'm going to make everybody else in the family madder than a wet hen."

Mark scratched his nose. "I have an idea. Lou, *you* haven't got a problem. The *family* has a problem. So we ought to come up with a family group solution."

"What do you mean? Me get a divorce from Betty?"

"No, Lou, nothing that drastic. But I suspect everyone in the family would rather give you free therapy than continue to lend you money."

Lou Hudson rubbed his eyes with the back of his hands. "Maybe you've got something there, Mark. I'd better go call Betty on the phone and see what she thinks."

As the two men walked toward the door of the casino, the little old lady in tennis shoes stopped them. She held up a coin. "My juju's deserted me today, boys, but I feel a change coming over me. This is my very last nickel, and I've got to get a winner. Where do you think I ought to put it?"

"Back in your purse," Mark said.

"Naw, Mark, you don't understand us gamblers." Lou closed his eyes and turned around three times. Then he pointed to a small slot machine far down the row. "Try that one, lady. I gotta hunch."

The little old woman trotted obediently down the row of one-armed bandits and paused to look the machine over carefully. Then she spat on the coin gently, rubbed it lovingly between her gloved hands, dropped the nickel in the slot, and pulled the handle. The reels spun wildly. The first one stopped on a bar. The second one did likewise. When the third reel clicked into place, it too sported a bar.

Suddenly the machine exploded. A bell rang loudly, and lights flashed off like skyrockets.

"Jackpot!" the woman screamed. "I did it, I did it! I've got my juju back! The magic power is with me again!"

A small crowd of people gathered around to watch the slot machine pay off.

Lou Hudson looked at the woman and smiled wanly. "She probably spent $50 in nickels just to win one $10 jackpot. And now she'll put all those nickels right back in the machine, won't she?"

Mark nodded in agreement. "If she's a compulsive gambler, she will."

"You think I can stop that kind of nonsense, Mark?"

"If you really want to, and you get good help," Mark said, "The odds are definitely in your favor."

The slight young man with bloodshot eyes grinned in response. "I'll bet on that!"

Recommended Readings

Breggin, Peter Roger. *Electroshock: Its Brain-Disabling Effects* (New York: Springer, 1979).

Feder, Bud, and Ruth Ronall, eds. *Beyond the Hot Seat: Gestalt Approaches to Group* (New York: Brunner/Mazel, 1980).

Fisher, Seymour, and Roger P. Greenberg, eds. *The Scientific Evaluation of Freud's Theories and Therapy: A Book of Readings* (New York: Basic Books, 1978).

Garfield, Sol L., and Allen E. Bergin, eds. *Handbook of Psychotherapy and Behavior Change: An Empirical Analysis*, 2nd ed. (New York: Wiley, 1978).

Kazdin, Alan E., and G. Terence Wilson. *Evaluation of Behavior Therapy: Issues, Evidence, and Research Strategies* (Cambridge, Mass.: Ballinger, 1978).

Kline, N.S., and Jules Angst. *Psychiatric Syndromes and Drug Treatment* (New York: Aronson, 1979).

Rothman, D.J. *The Discovery of Asylums: Social Order and Disorder in the New Republic* (Boston: Little, Brown, 1971).

Yalom, I.D. *The Theory and Practice of Group Psychotherapy* (New York: Basic Books, 1970).

7

Social Psychology

Person Perception, Attribution, and Social Roles

25

Did You Know That . . .

You tend to perceive your actions as being responses to your environment, but tend to attribute the actions of others to personality traits or flaws of character?

When you meet someone, you tend to judge them more by their looks and "body language" than by what they say or are like "deep down inside"?

You have a "psychological bubble" around you that you defend whenever anyone intrudes on this "personal space"?

The fact that boys engage in team sports more than girls do may help explain why men are often more successful in business organizations than are women?

There seem to be two types of group leaders—the "task specialist," who gets the job done, and the "social-emotional specialist," who facilitates group behaviors?

Successful business managers seem to be motivated by self-actualization and use participatory management techniques, while unsuccessful managers are motivated by security needs and supervise in an authoritarian way?

Guards who behave cruelly toward prisoners are often just normal people who are responding to what they perceive to be "society's rules"?

"The Best of Intentions"

Day 1. I was walking home from the meeting when I saw the police car sitting in front of our apartment house. They had come for Charlie, of course. Charlie is my best friend and bosom buddy.

Charlie and I have been rooming together for two years now ever since we came to college here two years ago. He is a top-notch person, and since we are both pre-legal, we have decided to open up an office together when we get out of Law School. Charlie is a super jock, the sort of guy you'd really want on your team. He is also a born leader, always coming up with great ideas about things to do and giving me advice on what to wear and how to act. Which I guess I sometimes need. I suppose that when we do open that office, his name will be first on the door.

It was Charlie who read the ad in the student newspaper. The one offering to hire us at $25 a day to take part in this two-week-long "prison" experiment that Dr. Wakeman is running. That struck us as a great way to earn some big bucks over the summer vacation. So we showed up, got interviewed, took all those psychological tests, and signed away our rights. I was sort of skeptical about that, you know. Agreeing to give up our basic rights to privacy, and all those good things. But, as

Charlie pointed out, it was only for two weeks. And besides, they promised that they wouldn't use physical punishment of any kind on us. So when Charlie volunteered, I felt sort of obligated to go along with him. And now I am going to make almost 300 bucks, and help science besides.

Funny that they should have selected me to be a guard, and Charlie to play the prisoner's role. Well, maybe the tests showed he was more impulsive or something like that.

I arrived at the apartment house just as the cops were dragging Charlie out the door. He sure did look surprised! We learned at the Guard's meeting this afternoon that the local police were cooperating with Dr. Wakeman. They had agreed to pull the prisoners in unexpectedly, charge them with suspicion of armed robbery, search them, fingerprint them, and take "mug shots" of their faces. Then the cops put blindfolds on the prisoners and we picked them up and drove them over to school where the "mock prison" is. Which we did, all in the spirit of good, clean fun, you understand. Tried to get them in the mood, so to speak.

They needed some mood-setting because the prison is pretty "mock," I tell you no lie. Just some rooms in the basement of the Psych Building, with bars painted on the doors and the tiny windows. Dr. Wakeman said he is repeating a study performed by some professor at Stanford named Philip Zimbardo, who found that isolating people from society was dehumanizing. Well, okay, what's new? But these prisoners are hardly going to be "isolated from society." There will be us guards, three to a shift, and Dr. Wakeman and his students who will be the Prison Staff and actually live there. Plus the guys—the prisoners, I mean—will be allowed visitors twice a week. So I do not think this study is going to work very well.

But maybe it will be fun anyhow, plus the money.

Dr. Wakeman has asked us to keep diaries which he will collect, and we are to write down everything we think and do, even if it seems critical of him and the staff. I don't like criticism or hassling people anyhow, so he shouldn't worry.

Charlie put on a big smile and tried to look very nonchalant when the policemen escorted him out of the apartment. Several of the neighbors were standing outside, watching. I will have to explain to them later what it is all about. I admire Charlie for taking it so calmly. Of course, I did not let on I knew him, since that is one of the Rules.

At the meeting today we decided on the Rules and Regulations for the Uni-Prison. Mostly, they are just common sense things to keep an institution running properly. There is to be no physical abuse, although we can lock a prisoner up in the isolation room if he breaks the Rules. Which, given the sensible nature of the Regulations, a prisoner would be stupid to do anyhow. Charlie being anything but stupid, I figure he will do OK as a prisoner. Unless his Irish impulses get out of hand, or something.

I am not so sure about me in the role of a guard. Sorry. We are to refer to ourselves as Correctional Officers. Anyhow, I put on my uniform at the apartment after the Police Officers took Charlie away. The dumb-looking khaki pants and shirt are a size too big and I feel uncomfortable in them. But I have a whistle and a billy-club, just to make me look "official." And they gave me a neat pair of mirrored sun glasses. Before I left, I stood in front of the mirror for a few minutes. Funny thing. I look pretty tough in that outfit, maybe because you can't see that my eyes are laughing. Mostly at myself.

Then I went over to the Uni-Prison and checked in. They started bringing the "Numbers" in about half an hour later. I call them "Numbers," because that is how I am to address them. Good old Charlie is now #853, which is written on both sides of the nightshirt he wears. He was one of the first Numbers brought in. We stripped him down, then sprayed him with a "de-louser" which, it turned out, was only deodorant. Well, they are going to need that deodorant because they are not going to get a shower while they are in prison. That is one of the Regulations.

Charlie got a little bit teed-off when we put the steel chain around his ankle and then required him to stand naked in the exercise yard for 20 minutes before we gave him his nightshirt. Well, it was necessary to remind him that he is a Prisoner even when he's bare-assed. Of course, underneath, I felt just as foolish as he did, but I don't think he or the other guys noticed. A Correctional Officer should not be embarrassed since he is just doing the job for which he is being paid.

When we checked the guys in—the Numbers—we gave them a nylon stocking to put on over their heads. Makes them harder to tell apart, but they are just Numbers, after all. They have got nothing on under the nightshirts, and that does lead to some comical situations. Charlie complained right off that he wasn't a woman and didn't like wearing a skirt, but I told him to shut up because that is one of the Rules.

Warden Wakeman then assembled the Staff and the Numbers and gave them an Official Welcome. He did a pretty good job of role-playing, I do say that. His talk was really pretty patriotic.

"Listen," he said to the Numbers, "You have shown that you are unable to function outside in the real world. You lack the responsibility of good citizens of this great country. We of this prison, your correctional staff, are going to help you learn what your responsibilities as citizens of this country are. Here are the Rules. We expect you to know them and to be able to recite them by number. If you follow the Rules, repent for your misdeeds, and show a proper attitude, you and I will get along just fine.

"Rule #1: Prisoners must remain silent during rest periods, after lights are out, during meals, and whenever they are outside the prison yard.

"Rule #2: Prisoners must eat at mealtimes and only at mealtimes.

"Rule #3: Prisoners must not move, tamper with, deface, or damage walls, ceilings, windows, doors, or other prison property.

"Rule #4: Prisoners must address each other only by their numbers.

"Rule #5: Prisoners must address the guards as 'Mr. Correctional Officer.'

"Rule #6: Prisoners must obey all lawful commands and orders issued to them by Correctional Officers.

"Rule #7: Failure to obey any of the above rules may result in punishment."

Now, that's what I call *sensible* rules for a place like this!

Well, after the Warden had welcomed them, we put the Numbers away in their cells for Rest Period, and then I was off for the evening. I went back to the apartment, which I admit was sort of empty, what with old #853 being in Prison. Of course, he got himself into this, so I guess it serves him right. But I do not know yet whether I am going to enjoy this experience at all.

Day 2. This morning when I got to work the guys on the night shift told me that they didn't have much trouble handling things. Some of the Numbers broke the Rule about not conversing after Lights Out, but the guys said they stopped that nonsense in a hurry. Charlie likes to talk a lot so I was not surprised to learn that my old buddy #853 got himself shouted at a few times. Sort of wish I'd been around to hear what they said to him.

We got the Numbers through the morning ritual pretty well. Part of their job is to sweep up the place. Naturally #853 complained about having to clean the toilets. Back at the apartment, that's usually my chore. Old #853 got a taste of what's good for him, for a change. I would have given him a chit to see the movie that night if he had done a good job, but he bitched too much, and that's against Regulations. Then at lunch he acted up something awful. Broke the Rules all over the place. Lunch was sausage and potatoes, and being his roommate, I am well aware that he does not like sausage very much at all. So #853 refuses to eat them, although that's illegal, because Rule #2 says that Numbers *must eat* at mealtimes, which means that they must eat *everything* we give them, right?

So I said, "Listen you dumb twerp. Just because you are bigger than me doesn't mean that you are going to get away with breaking the Rules. You don't scare me, 853. You eat that damn sausage or I'll stick it in your ear and let you digest it that way." Of course I didn't say "ear," but you know what I mean.

Well, that must have teed him off, or something, because he started arguing

Person Perception, Attribution, and Social Roles

with me and abusing me, which is definitely against the Rules. So the other guys and I just grabbed #853 by his nightshirt and led him away to solitary confinement. Which is really just a closet he's got to stand in, but it is just what he deserved.

Even then he didn't calm down much, and I had to go down two or three times to shut him up. He got a little nasty the last time, so I shook the billy-club at him, just to let him know who was boss. I wouldn't ever use it, of course, because that's against the Regulations. But it was a little frightening to have this guy I thought I knew threaten me with verbal abuse and physical gestures. Finally, I couldn't take it any more, so I went and got the other guys and we got a couple of sausages and took them down to the "hole" and stuck them in #853's hands.

"Listen you," I told him in no uncertain tone of voice. "You are going to hold on to those sausages until you see fit to obey the Rules and Regulations and eat them. Beggars can't be choosers, and you will stay in this 'hole' until you choose to obey the lawful orders of your Correctional Officers."

To tell the truth, even with the other guys around to protect me, I was a little worried because 853 has got one helluva temper, him being Irish and red-headed and all that. Of course, I couldn't *see* the color of his hair because of the nylon stocking pulled over his head, and maybe that made the difference. Anyhow, 853 shook the sausages at me and stepped forward, like he might be going to hit me with them. So in self-defense I held up my billy-club. Funny thing. He stopped and stared at me, and then he sort of trembled or shivered, like he had a chill. Then he burst out crying, and turned around and hid his face in a corner. I just let the old sissy cry, since he brought it all on himself.

Jeez, I hate sissies. So before I left for the day, I deliberately got in a loud conversation outside the "hole" with one of the Correctional Officers. I had a date that night, and so did the other CO, and we spent a lot of time describing just what we were going to do with the ladies that evening. I figured that would teach 853 a lesson, because he certainly did like his nocturnal activities before he got sent to Prison.

Day 3. The first thing that the guys told me when I came on duty was that 853 still refused to eat the sausages, so they were starving him until he gave in. He had missed supper and breakfast both, which is only proper, under the Rules. I saw right away that we had trouble on our hands, because he was setting the other Numbers a very bad example. What would happen if everybody behaved that way? So I called his two cellmates into the yard, and then I handcuffed 853, sausages and all, and brought him out too.

"Listen you Numbers. This stupid jackass is disobeying the Regulations, and we cannot let him get away with gross violations of the Rules he is guilty of. Therefore, we are going to take away your eating privileges until your cellmate here gives in and eats the sausages we have provided to keep him alive."

Well, naturally, the other two Numbers were not very happy. But we told them to shut up and to get back on the Routine. Which, I am happy to say, they did without too much complaint. Except for 853, the Numbers are mostly a bunch of sheep. Then as I am taking 853 back to the "hole," Warden Wakeman came up and asked me to remove the handcuffs. I am not sure why he did this, since I was just trying to keep 853 from escaping. Which is what I am paid to do.

At lunchtime, when we wouldn't let them eat, the other two Numbers stood in front of the "hole" and tried to talk some sense into 853. Which, I am sad to say, they failed to do, so they went hungry. I would feel sorry for 853, except that he is obviously just being stubborn to show off, and now he is hurting others besides himself. Which is a downright crime, if you ask me.

Naturally, this whole nasty business upset the Routine so much that nobody knew which way was up. Finally, things got so bad that I suggested we ought to take away the eating privileges of all the Numbers until 853 showed he was sorry for his misdeeds and corrected his bad attitude and behaved like any decent human would. The other CO's agreed with me, but they were a little worried about keeping discipline if all the Numbers went hungry.

When we told the Numbers of our decision, they got pretty surly. In fact, one of them started wise-mouthing a bit and showing off, but I tapped him lightly with my billy-club, and he got back into line.

Day 4. I was barely asleep when the CO's on the evening shift phoned. They said the Numbers had gone crazy and were rioting! The Evening Shift got the Numbers cornered by spraying them with a fire extinguisher, but they needed reinforcements.

As I rushed over to help, I really got angry thinking what a sissy jerk 853 turned out to be. Embarrassing us all with that stupid, childish behavior. Why didn't he just give in and obey the Rules, like everybody else?

Well, when I got there, I guess I taught him a lesson, didn't I?

(Continued on page 613.)

Social Psychology

What is *social psychology* all about? What is unique about it? That is, how does it differ from all the other areas of psychology that we have already discussed? According to Theodore Newcomb, the major difference is that social psychology pays attention chiefly to *relations between people*, while most of the rest of the field focuses on *the individual*.

Newcomb believes that there are several major questions that social psychologists typically try to answer. Four of the most important questions are as follows:

1. In describing social relationships, should we look primarily at *attitudes*, or at *behaviors*?
2. Are social behaviors and attitudes primarily *learned*, or are they mostly *determined by the genes*?
3. How shall we describe the *structures and functions* of groups and organizations?
4. How *consistent* are groups and organizations over periods of time?

Some of these questions may sound a bit familiar. But let's look at them briefly from a new perspective before we begin discussing social psychology itself.

Attitudes or Behaviors?

Traditionally, social psychologists have focused more on measuring and describing *attitudes* than on *behaviors*. Since attitudes are "internal processes," this argument boils down to the mind/body problem revisited.

The traditional way of defining an attitude is as follows: It is a consistent way of thinking about, feeling toward, or responding to some environmental stimulus or input. Thus attitudes are composed of cognitive, emotional, and behavioral components. Some social psychologists emphasize the cognitive and emotional aspects of attitudes, and thus come down on the "mind" side of the question. Other social psychologists prefer to deal with measurable behaviors. The social learning theorists—as we saw in Chapter 21—believe that attitudes are "cognitive structures" that allow you to process environmental inputs in consistent ways. Thus in many (but not all) situations, attitudes actually control behaviors. But the social learning theorists also believe that you "create new cognitive structures" as you acquire new behavioral habits. So to explain social relationships completely, you *must* deal both with attitudes and behaviors. As we will see, in recent years the social learning viewpoint has gained considerable strength within the field of social psychology.

Learned or Innate?

The nature-nurture controversy has gained prominence recently in social psychology thanks to a 1975 book by Edward Wilson called *Sociobiology: The New Synthesis*. In this book, Wilson argues that, like all other humans, you are *primarily a biological machine*. And as a "machine," your chief function is that of "surviving." But it's not your *own* survival that motivates you. Instead, it is the survival of your *genes* that stimulates you to act as you do.

According to Wilson, most of your social behaviors are "hard wired" into your brain, which is another way of saying they are determined by your genes. But your genes, Wilson says, are "selfish." Therefore, *most of your social behaviors* are also innately "selfish." Put more clearly, you are genetically programmed to behave in ways that give your own genetic material an "edge" in the race for survival.

But your relatives *share your genes*. Thus you instinctively love and protect members of your family because anything that helps your relatives survive also helps your genes survive. Even when you give assistance to complete strangers, you do so because of an innate response called **reciprocal altruism**. That is, you help others in the selfish hope that they will help you in return and thus increase the chances that your genes will prevail.

In his 1978 book, *The Sociobiology Debate*, Arthur L. Caplan calls sociobiology, "The latest and most strident of a series of efforts in the biological sciences to direct scientific and humanistic attention toward the question of what is, fundamentally, the nature of human nature." As such, Caplan says, sociobiology is more a political point of view than a scientific theory. Caplan notes that almost all of the data that led Wilson to create sociobiology come from studies of insects, birds, and mammals. Wilson notes that most animals behave in selfish ways, and that these behaviors do tend to increase the survival of a given species. But the problem is that Wilson *applies these animal data to humans*. However, Caplan says, studies of human behavior do not support Wilson's theoretical position.

What sorts of conclusions does Wilson reach about human nature? First, that since present patterns of behavior led to our survival, these behaviors *must be* "normal and healthy." Women shouldn't fight for "equality" since male dominance has high survival value. It is only "natural" for men to wish to copulate with as many women as possible because this behavior pattern allows them to "pass on their genes as frequently as possible." And women are "naturally submissive" to men because this is women's instinctual way of getting men to protect the women's children (i.e., genes). Wilson also sees racial prejudice, nationalistic wars, and class struggles as understandable attempts by "people with similar genes" to increase the chances that their group's genes will survive.

Wilson admits that some human behaviors are learned, but sees most social activities as being "unchangeable" since they are part of our animal heritage. However, as we will see, there is considerable evidence that the vast majority of our social behaviors are learned, not innate. Little wonder, then, that after looking closely at all the data, Caplan concludes that the theory of sociobiology is riddled with errors and false assumptions. Furthermore, "There is good reason to fear that the development of sociobiological theories in the present social context will have [disastrous] social consequences."

Question: *What similarities do you see between Wilson's attempts to prove that males have an "innate need to dominate females," and Arthur Jensen's attempts to prove that whites are "innately superior" to blacks?*

Group Structures and Functions

As we noted in Chapter 5, single organisms (such as yourself) and groups are similar in many ways. Groups and organizations have inputs, internal processes, and outputs just as you do. But groups and organizations also have *emergent properties* that make them different from individuals, just as you have properties that your organs and cells don't possess.

One of the major questions that social psychologists have debated for years, however, is how similar the structures and functions of social organizations are to those of individual humans. Do social systems grow and develop in predictable ways? That is, do they pass through the same sorts of developmental stages that Piaget and Freud discussed? Can societies grow "senile"? Can groups experience "social disorders" like the "mental disorders" that some individuals suffer from?

Put another way, what *model* shall we use to describe how social systems operate? We will talk more about these matters in the next chapter.

Group and Organizational Consistency

If social systems are similar to individual humans, then some aspects of social groupings should remain fairly constant over time, while other aspects should change. But are these consistencies due to the fact that the *individuals* who make up the system continue to behave the same over long periods? Or is there something within the structure of social systems themselves that *creates* constant behavior patterns in those individuals within the system?

As you might guess, there are many conflicting answers to these questions. We will talk about these issues more fully in Chapter 26. But we might note here that some social psychologists tend to focus on how social inputs affect individual attitudes and behaviors. Other social psychologists prefer to look at social systems themselves, rather than at the individuals who are "sub-systems" within the groups, organizations, and societies.

We will begin our survey of social psychology by looking at how you *perceive* others—and how and why they perceive you as they do. We will show that your perceptions are often explain-

Person Perception, Attribution, and Social Roles

able in terms of the traits that you attribute to others, and the social roles that people play. In Chapter 26 we will discuss the structure and function of social systems, as well as the ways in which those systems induce you to *conform to their norms*. Finally, in Chapter 27, we will show how social *communications* can promote both attitude change and behavioral consistency.

Person Perception

What is "person perception"? In the May 1981 issue of *Contemporary Psychology*, Edith Greene and Elizabeth Loftus note that the meaning of this term has changed in recent years. They state that, "Traditionally, it has been thought to be the study of how people perceive their human environment. It concerns our ability to know another individual's intentions, attitudes, emotions, ideas, and possible behavior. It is how we know that one person is friendly, another a cheat, and a third is depressingly angry." According to Greene and Loftus, we must now add the term "person memory" to the older definition. Because, as they note, perceptions are primarily *learned*. Thus the way you perceive someone will depend to a great extent on what kinds of "codes" you use to file your memories of people in long-term storage.

But your perceptions are also affected by your needs and motives. Thus the area of *person*

"REMEMBER WHEN YOU WENT BACK TO WORK, AND I DECIDED TO STAY HOME AND TAKE CARE OF THE HOUSE, HOW WE THOUGHT IT WOULDN'T WORK OUT?"

Reciprocal altruism (ree-SIP-pro-kal AL-true-ism). The belief that you help other people so they will help you and thus enable your genes to survive. The evidence that this behavior is innate comes from a limited number of studies of animal behavior.

perception covers not only social perceptions, but social memories and needs as well. Let's attempt to illustrate these points by trying to figure out what factors influence your own perceptions of others.

First Impressions

Suppose some good friends of yours have talked you into taking a blind date to a party. They paint a glowing picture of your date as a kind of superperson in order to get you to agree to the date. When the fatal moment comes, and you first meet the person, what sorts of things do you look for immediately? What clues do you seek as a guide to whether you will like the individual?

Obviously, your answers to these questions may be somewhat different from other people's answers. But the social psychologists who study person perception have come up with some generalities that might interest you.

If you have read Chapter 9, you will remember the primary rule of perception: *You see what you expect to see*. Before you meet your date, your friends will have *biased* your perceptions by their descriptions of the individual. If they have told you the person is warm, affectionate, responsive, and outgoing, you will probably *look for* these attributes in your date as soon as the two of you meet. Certainly your *attitude* toward the person will be different than if you have been told your date is rather intellectual, cold, withdrawn, quiet, and self-possessed.

The question then becomes, how do attitudes affect perceptions?

Attitudes

As we noted earlier, an *attitude* is a consistent way of thinking about, feeling toward, or responding to some aspect of your environment (or toward yourself). Thus an attitude is actually a sort of "cognitive structure" that allows you to process and respond to present inputs in an efficient manner. But an attitude is also a "mental program" for *coding* experiences in order to store them in Long-term Memory. Thus your attitudes affect not only your present perceptions and responses, but how you will remember in the future what you saw and did in the present. We can prove that point by looking at how you form "first impressions" of the people you meet.

Reputations

When your friends describe your blind date to you, they are telling you something about that person's *reputation*—that is, the way that most people presumably perceive your date, or the attitude that most people have toward the person.

Social psychologist Harold Kelley tested the importance of "reputations" in a study performed at MIT in the late 1940's. Kelley told a large class of undergraduates that they would have a visiting lecturer for the day, and that the students would be asked to evaluate this man at the end of the class. Kelley then passed out a brief biographical note about the teacher, presumably to help the students with their evaluation. Although the students did not realize it, the description that half the class received referred to the lecturer as being "rather a warm individual," while the description given the rest of the class called the man "rather a cold intellectual."

After the class had been presented with and read the printed comments, the man arrived and led the class in a 20-minute discussion. Kelley watched the students and recorded how often each of them asked a question or made a comment. Afterward, the students were asked to rate the man on a set of attitude scales and to write a brief description of him.

Although everyone in the class had witnessed *exactly* the same performance at *exactly* the same time, the manner in which each student responded was measurably affected by the descriptions each had read. Those students who had been told the instructor was warm tended to rate him as much more informal, sociable, popular, good-natured, humorous, and humane than the students who had been told the same man was cold.

More than this, the subjects *reacted* to the man quite differently. The students who were told he was warm spoke to him in class much more frequently than did the students who were told he was cold.

Judging from Harold Kelley's research, once you believe you won't like a person, you tend to avoid further contact with him or her. Theodore Newcomb has called this avoidance response **autistic hostility**, and suggests that it may apply to interactions among groups as well as among individuals.

Question: How might Kelley's research help explain the difficulty that Rosenhan's "pseudo-patients" had in convincing mental hospital staffs that they (the "pseudo-patients") were really normal or sane?

Stereotypes

When you don't know a given person's "reputation," your initial impressions are likely to be affected by the **stereotypes**, or biased perceptions, that you have about certain types or groups of people. If you assume that all blacks are lazy, dull, ignorant, but musical, you will tend to "see" these attributes even in an energetic, bright black doctor who perhaps couldn't carry a tune in handbag. If your attitude toward Jews is that they are intelligent, emotional, and penny-pinching, you may respond to each Jew as if she or he had to fit your stereotype.

Any time that you react to an individual *primarily* in terms of that person's membership in some group—or in terms of that person's physical characteristics, race, or religion—you are guilty of *stereotyping*. That is, you have let the reputation of the group influence your perception of the individual who belongs to that group.

Put in more cognitive terms, when you "stereotype" people, you are using what Piaget called the process of "assimilation" (see Chapter 20). That is, you are forcing your perception of the individual to fit your *schema* for remembering or classifying that type of person. When you change your perception to fit the facts, you are "accommodating" to the real world by altering your schema.

Question: How would you explain Newcomb's concept of "autistic hostility" in terms of Piaget's "process of assimilation"?

Primacy Effect

The principle of autistic hostility suggests that getting off on the right foot with a new acquaintance may be very important. For, according to Newcomb, you may have just one chance to get the person to like you. Back in the 1940's psychologist Solomon Asch gave a group of subjects a list of adjectives describing someone they might meet. Half the subjects were told the person was "intelligent, industrious, impulsive, critical, stubborn, and envious." The other half of the subjects were given the same list, but in opposite order: "Envious, stubborn, critical, impulsive, industrious, intelligent." The subjects were then asked to write a brief paragraph evaluating what they thought the person might be like. The responses made by two of Asch's subjects are good examples of what psychologists call the **primacy effect**.

A subject told the person was "intelligent . . . envious" wrote that: "The person is intelligent and fortunately he puts his intelligence to work. That he is stubborn and impulsive may be due to the fact that he knows what he is saying and what he means and will not therefore give in easily to someone else's idea of what he disagrees with."

A subject told the person was "envious . . . intelligent" wrote that: "This person's good qualities such as industry and intelligence are bound to be restricted by jealousy and stubbornness. The person is emotional. He is unsuccessful because he is weak and allows his bad points to cover up his good ones."

You can perceive any person you meet in dozens of different ways. Presumably, the first information you get about a person pulls one particular "memory schema" to the fore. The primacy effect says that you are very likely to "assimilate" any other data about the person into whatever schema you first use to perceive that individual.

Recency Effect

Psychologists often speak of a **recency effect**, which can either counteract or reinforce the primacy effect. If you have recently used a given schema to categorize people—and have found it useful—you are very likely to apply it to the next person you meet. Thus, if one of Asch's students had already encountered a lot of "envious" people that week, the student might well have perceived almost anyone that way despite the fact that "intelligent" was first on the descriptive list the student received.

Two Channels of Communication

The way you perceive someone you have just met is obviously affected by such *internal processes* as attitudes, reputations, stereotypes, the primacy effect, and the recency effect. But your perceptions are also influenced by *present stimulus inputs*. Suppose you want to influence someone else's perception of you. How do you communicate with that person to give him or her a good first impression of yourself? Actually, you have but two main channels of communication—what you do with your body, and what you say with your tongue.

The way you look and dress and move— these are part of your **body language**. What you say, the opinions you express, and the verbal responses you make—these are part of your verbal language. Surprisingly enough, when it comes to first impressions, people are often more influenced by your looks and physical movements than they are by what you actually say.

Autistic hostility (aw-TISS-tic). Autism (see Chapter 8) is the act of withdrawing into oneself, of shutting off external stimulation. Autistic hostility is the act of cutting off or denying favorable inputs about people or things we don't like. "My mind is made up—don't confuse me with facts."

Stereotypes. A stereotype is a fixed or unconscious attitude or perception—a way of responding to some person or object solely in terms of the person's (or object's) class membership. The failure to treat people as individuals, each different from the other, is the act of stereotyping.

Primacy effect (PRY-muh-see). *Primus* is the Latin word for "first." Whenever you remember your first impressions of a stimulus (or person) better than your second or third, you are demonstrating the power of the primacy effect.

Recency effect. The tendency to be more influenced by your last or most recent impressions than by your initial impression.

Body language. The "messages" about yourself that you communicate by how you dress, and by your expressive movements. As opposed to "verbal language," which is what you say out loud. First impressions (and person perception) are often more strongly influenced by body language than by spoken language.

Physical Appearance

According to Ellen Berscheid, the less chance you have to know the people around you well, the more likely you are to judge people in terms of their appearance. "My guess is that anything that increases the number of brief encounters with other people increases the importance of physical attractiveness," Berscheid said in an *Omni* article in November 1981. "People don't have a record of behavior to judge by, and they have to go on superficial characteristics."

Berscheid's own research at the University of Minnesota supports her statements. In one recent study performed with colleagues at the University of Wisconsin, Berscheid found that "most people consider attractive people to be more sensitive, stronger, more modest, more sociable, more outgoing, kinder, more interesting, and sexually warmer and more responsive than their unattractive peers." Berscheid says most people believe that good-looking individuals "have prestigious jobs and happy marriages and . . . enjoy life to the fullest." But this perception of good-looking people is based almost entirely on their looks, not on any real facts about what they are really like.

Karen Dion, of the University of Toronto, has performed research that tends to support Berscheid's views. Dion asked subjects to make judgments about second-grade children who had committed minor misbehaviors. She reports her subjects usually judged the misbehavior as being "much more serious" if the child was unattractive. Furthermore, Dion says, her subjects believed the unattractive children were more likely

Research suggests that most social interactions are strongly influenced by "body language" and by eye contact.

to have a "chronic predisposition to commit bad acts" than were handsome children.

Further evidence comes from research by Elaine Hatfield and her associates at Walster. Hatfield *et al.* tried to match subjects for dates using all kinds of personal data about the people involved. They found that personal attractiveness was the *only factor* that systematically predicted how well the individuals liked their dates. Furthermore, Hatfield reports, the more the couple dated, the more important that physical beauty became in determining whether the two people liked each other.

Beauty may be "in the eye of the beholder," but it obviously does shape our perceptions of others to a greater extent than many of us would like to believe is the case.

Question: *Why do you think beautiful children score higher on individually administered intelligence tests than when they take a written test administered to a whole group of children?*

Non-Verbal Communication

You can't do all that much about changing your looks. But you can alter your physical movements—that is, the way that you present yourself to others. Whether you know it or not, you have a characteristic way of dressing, of combing your hair, of moving your arms and legs, of looking toward or away from people as you speak or listen, of smiling, of frowning, and of giving feedback. This "body language" may not really be a

good indicator of what you are like deep down inside. However, experiments suggest that many people you meet will judge your *intentions toward them* primarily by the way in which you communicate non-verbally.

But what makes up your own unique brand of body language? What can a stranger tell about you just by watching you behave? To begin with, and perhaps most important, is the simple fact that you are either male or female. Every culture has different *social expectations* about the ways that women and men should look and behave. Since these expectations vary from culture to culture, they are obviously learned. In the US we presume that males are bigger, stronger, cruder in their language and movements, and more violent and domineering than women. Men are expected to be interested in such things as automobiles, sports, business and finance, science and technology. Women are expected to prefer the arts, children, home life, cooking, and social relations. Thus you surely have stereotyped beliefs about the psychological differences between men and women that color the first impressions of everyone you meet.

Next most important is probably your age. In our society, young people are expected to be energetic, enthusiastic, idealistic, liberal, but perhaps inexperienced. Older people are expected to be more sedate, conservative, settled, experienced, and perhaps more willing to compromise to get some of the things they want from life. It doesn't matter that these cultural expectations are not entirely accurate. What does matter is that most of us *expect* older people to behave differently than young people.

People, therefore, stereotype you according to your sex, size, age, skin color, dress, and physical beauty. And because of these stereotypes, they expect you to behave in certain ways. Generally speaking, if your behavior *confirms* these expectations, most people will gain a good "first impression" of you. However, if your actions *disconfirm* people's expectations, you are not likely to win very many popularity contests.

Behavioral Congruence

In a 1980 book entitled *Person Memory*, edited by Reid Hastie, Donald Carlston, and several other social psychologists, there are several chapters on how your perception of others changes over time. One important process which influences *perceptual change* is what Hastie calls **behavioral congruence**. If the way people act later on tends to confirm your initial perception of them, then their behaviors are "congruent" with your first impression. If their later actions disconfirm your first impression, you experience *discongruence*. You can reduce this discongruence either by changing your perception of the person, or by disregarding or "explaining away" their later behaviors. The evidence presented by Hastie *et al.* suggests that most people tend to maintain their perceptions by "rationalizing" any data that don't confirm their original impressions.

Oddly enough, Hastie's research shows that most people remember *incongruent* behaviors better than *congruent* ones. Hastie believes that congruent behaviors are readily coded and filed away in Long-term Memory. But when someone acts in an unexpected way, you must try to "explain the behavior" before you can tuck it away in long-term storage. You remember incongruent actions more readily because it takes more time to process them, Hastie says.

Question: *What similarities do you see between "behavioral discongruence" and Piaget's concept of "cognitive disequilibrium"?*

Personal Space

How close people stand to you when they first meet you can often influence your impression of them. California psychologist Robert Sommer has for many years studied what he calls *personal space*. Sommer believes that you carry an "invisible bubble" around your body that encloses what you consider to be your own, personal psychological space. He notes that in a number of studies, subjects have shown a dramatic increase in nervousness when an experimenter moved to within a foot or so of them. Most of the subjects "defended their territories" by either moving away from the intruder, or by becoming increasingly hostile. Put another way, people who invade your personal space tend to give you a bad impression of them.

Sommer states that the size of your own personal space bubble is influenced by such factors as your personality, status, and your culture. For middle-class Americans, this private area extends outward about 2 feet from any part of the body. For Arabs, the space is usually much smaller. For Scandinavians, the bubble is typically larger. People with great status often command a larger personal space than do individuals with little or no status.

People from different cultures often give us the wrong first impression because they either invade our spaces without meaning to, or they stand so far away from us that we perceive them as being distant and aloof. Sommer says we may also perceive someone who stands far apart as pretending to have more status than we believe is the case.

Behavioral congruence (kon-GRUE-ence). Congruent behaviors are those that fit your expectations or match a stereotype. When behaviors and expectations don't match, you are motivated to resolve the discrepancy. Usually you explain or "rationalize" the behaviors and maintain your prior expectations.

Question: *When you change roles—as from Correctional Officer to prisoner—why does the size of your personal space often change?*

Body Posture

Even when you stand at just the right distance from people, the way that you *hold your body* influences the impressions that you give people. In our culture, most people assume that if you lean toward them, you like them (and perhaps are inviting intimacy). But if you lean away from them, they may assume that you dislike or are rejecting them.

In a study on body posture, psychologist Albert Mehrabian asked men and women to act out the ways in which they would sit when speaking to someone they liked or disliked. Mehrabian reports that both men and women leaned *forward* to express liking, but that men (more than women) leaned back or became more tense when addressing someone they disliked.

Once you have established a "proper distance" to stand from an individual, any further movement you make may signal a change in your feelings. Psychologist Don Byrne and his associates set up an an experiment in which couples were selected by a computer for blind dates. After the young man and woman had gotten to know each other briefly, they were called into Byrne's office and stood before his desk for further instructions. The subjects were then separated and asked to fill out a questionnaire indicating how much they liked their dates. Byrne and his colleagues report that couples who liked each other moved closer together in front of the desk than did couples who didn't care much for each other.

Question: *Why might strangers in a crowded elevator stare straight ahead and avoid conversation?*

Eye Contact

Movements of your face and eyes are often as critical to the first impression you give as are how close you stand and whether you lean toward or away from someone. Smiles invite approaches; frowns demand distance. The eye contact you make with people often controls both the flow of conversation and their initial opinion of your honesty and aggressiveness.

Harold Kelley   Robert Sommer

The "rules of eye contact" vary considerably from one society to another, and thus seem to be primarily learned behaviors. If you happen to be a middle-class adult, you probably look *at* people when they are talking or lecturing. For staring directly at a speaker is the way you have learned to encourage that person to continue conversing—particularly if you nod or smile in apparent agreement. When you look *away* from whoever is talking, however, you signal that you are bored or that you want to take over the talking role yourself. Any speaker who is sensitive to your social cue of glancing away will rapidly change the subject or throw the conversational ball in your direction. Most studies show that one person stops talking and another starts speaking primarily when the two people are in direct eye contact.

When you are telling a story or making a point, chances are that you will glance away from your audience, particularly if you are trying to think through a point while talking. While you speak, you may glance back at your audience from time to time to make sure they are still with you (that is, still looking at you), then look away again as you continue talking.

People brought up in lower-class environments have eye signals that are the direct opposite of those found in middle-class US society. Individuals reared in lower-class homes tend to stare directly at people when talking, but avert their eyes when listening to show respect (particularly if listening to someone of higher status).

You learn these "rules of eye contact" so early in life that you may not have been aware of how strongly they influence your perceptions and behaviors. Unless you understand how these rules affect your first impressions, however, you are likely to misinterpret the eye signals that someone from another culture or class gives to you.

Question: If a man stared at you intensely while talking to you, what motives would you attribute to him? If he averted his eyes while listening to you, would you think he was showing disinterest or respect?

The Attribution Process

Why do you "stereotype" people? According to Fritz Heider, you do so to avoid stress. Heider notes that most of us become alarmed (stressed) whenever we cannot guess fairly accurately what will happen to us next. By using what Heider calls the **attribution process**, we attribute to others motives that make their actions understandable (predictable) to us.

As Heider pointed out in 1958, when you perceive a woman's actions as being an expression of her character, you are actually *attributing* certain personality traits to the woman. Most of these *attributed traits* are in fact stereotypes and, in fact, she may not possess these traits at all. But once you stereotype her, you immediately have a ready-made attitude or perception to fit her. Thus you can not only predict her actions, but you can readily respond to her as well.

Edward E. Jones noted in 1976 that we use the attribution process to explain our own faults as well. But we attribute them to the environment, not to our own personality. We see ourselves as merely reacting to whatever situation we find ourselves in. However, when we observe inconsistent behaviors in *others*, we tend to ignore the social background. Instead, we attribute their actions to some inner need, motive, or flaw of character. That is, we perceive ourselves as being *forced* to act in inappropriate ways from time to time. But when others misbehave, we perceive them as *wanting* to behave that way.

Question: It seems a fact that we are often frightened by people whose behavior is highly unpredictable. How could Heider's theory of the attribution process explain why deviant individuals often end up in prisons and mental hospitals?

Kelley's Theory of Personal Relationships

The person who has advanced attribution theory the most in recent years is Harold H. Kelley, who is now at UCLA. His thinking about the attribution process is shown most clearly in his 1981 book, *Personal Relationships: Their Structures and Processes*.

Kelley is interested more in long-term relationships between people than in "first impressions." He believes that three concepts are crucial to understanding enduring **dyads**, or two-person relationships. These three concepts are *interdependence*, *responsiveness*, and *attribution*.

Interdependence

By "interdependence," Kelley refers to the notion that the *outcomes* of a relationship depend in large part on both the individual and the joint actions that people in a dyad undertake. For instance, suppose you are married. Both the benefits and the costs of the marriage—to you and to your spouse—will depend not only on what each of you does individually, but also on the joint actions the two of you perform. Therefore, to get the most out of your marriage, you must not only pay attention to what you do, but you must be able to *anticipate* what your spouse will do as well. Much of your own behavior, then, is dependent on your predictions of how your spouse will behave in certain situations.

If your predictions about your spouse are accurate, you can often use this knowledge to maximize your own personal gains. But if you do, your spouse may suffer. Thus the relationship may break apart unless you are responsive to your spouse's needs as well as to your own.

Responsiveness

By "responsiveness," Kelley means that you take your spouse's needs into account when making decisions about your own behavior. If your partner does the same, Kelley says, both you and your spouse will probably assume this means you have a loving, interdependent relationship. That is, you will *attribute the trait of lovingness* to each other.

To Kelley, the essence of a good personal relationship is the fact that the partners care about one another. And this caring is most readily visible in situations where one partner gives up benefits or endures costs out of consideration for the other.

Question: What similarities do you see between Kelley's notion of "responsiveness" and the sociobiological concept of "reciprocal altruism"?

Attribution

Even loving couples occasionally have problems. Kelley has shown that marriage partners are inclined to explain problems in their relationship in terms of *attributed traits* rather than in terms of *specific behaviors*. Thus a wife who is upset with her husband typically won't speak of the actions that bother her—he leaves his dirty underwear on the floor for her to pick up, doesn't listen to

her, or won't help her with the housework. Rather, she will describe the problem in terms of his personality and his presumed attitude toward her—he is sloppy, lazy, and doesn't love her. This attribution of the causes of his misbehaviors constitutes what Kelley refers to as a *sanction*. That is, the wife calls attention to what the husband is doing wrong and *challenges* him to prove that her attribution of the causes is incorrect.

The husband, on the other hand, will attribute his faults to environmental stress, such as problems he is experiencing at work. He perceives himself as still being deeply in love with her, and believes she ought to forgive him for his minor misbehaviors because his *intentions* are good. When his wife fails to forgive him, he attributes her anger to such traits as "moodiness" and "bad temper."

If the husband changes his behaviors, the wife may not be satisfied if she thinks he is merely trying to appease her. Because she *attributes* his actions to "underlying traits and attitudes," she wants an *attitudinal change* from him rather than a mere shift in the way he acts. The problem is, Kelly notes, the husband is in something of a bind. Since his wife can never see his attitudes or intentions directly, the only thing he can do is to change his behaviors toward her. But she is always free to *interpret* these behavioral changes any way she wishes, and he cannot prove her wrong.

Kelley believes that in successful relationships, the partners tend to *minimize* the attribution process. That is, the partners pay more attention to specific behaviors than to "underlying traits." But if either party begins to believe strongly that her or his attributions are valid, and won't take behavioral change as evidence of attitudinal change, then the relationship is probably in deep trouble.

Question: How does the attribution process help explain the popularity of the "trait approach" to describing human personality?

Social Roles

As Shakespeare put it: "All the world's a stage, and all the men and women merely players. They have their exits and their entrances; and one man in his

According to Judith Bardwick, at age seven, boys typically engage in team sports, while girls form dyadic relationships.

Judith Bardwick

time plays many parts." The lasting impressions that we make depend to a great extent on the *consistency* of the parts that we play in the theater of life. But the traits we attribute to people are often merely parts of the *roles* that they play in life. So perhaps it is time we looked seriously at role-playing.

A *social role* is a more-or-less stereotyped set of responses that you make to related or similar situations. Some roles (such as being male or female) are a basic part of your **repertory** all through your life. Other roles (such as being a cheerleader or class president) are "bit parts" or "walk-ons" that you often discard as you mature. And, like a part in a play, a social role is made up of a characteristic set of body movements and verbal statements.

Question: *What kinds of behaviors and attitudes would you express if you took on the role*

of a policeman? How would you behave if playing the role of a convict?

Male and Female Roles

While basic roles (like traits) surely have a biological component, for the most part we must learn the parts we play in the theater of life. Judith Bardwick states that in middle-class US society, a fundamental shift between male and female roles occurs when a child reaches six or seven years of age. At this time, a girl often builds up an intense dyadic relationship with another girl. This strong friendship is characterized by *complete acceptance*—each girl perceives the other as being "the best in all possible ways." Neither member of the dyad will usually tolerate criticism about the other from any outside source (such as parents).

Sometimes a third girl will become friends with both members of the dyad, thus turning the pair-relationship into a **triad**. But triads are typically less stable than dyads, so the new girl may "capture" one of the others and form a dyad that excludes a member of the original pair.

While young girls tend to form *pair-bonds*, young boys mostly form *teams*, particularly when engaging in social activities such as sports. Bardwick notes that team members "rank" each other according to ability. If you are "choosing up sides" for a game of football, you may select Joe first because he's a good runner, but may choose Bill last because he's too thin and tall. If the game is basketball, you may pick Bill first because of his height, while selecting Joe last since he's poor at hitting the basket. According to Bardwick, boys select their friends in terms of an overall "balance" of pluses and minuses. Boys are also less upset by justifiable criticism since they realize that, while they cannot be "best" in all activities, they still can be a valued and warmly accepted member of "the team."

Heterosexual Relationships

Bardwick believes these early experiences set the basis for later development in male and female *roles* in our society, particularly in heterosexual relationships. Males often select women as they would a teammate—that is, they choose as a wife someone who ranks high on a number of dimensions, including physical beauty. But they don't expect "perfection." Women, on the other hand, may demand *complete acceptance* from men because they are trying to regain the intense emotionality of that childhood dyadic relationship. However, the woman may also have conscious or unconscious fears of rejection, particularly if she was cut out of a triad when young.

The problem in adult male-female relations may come, Bardwick says, when neither party in a marriage understands the needs of the other. The man may believe that the act of choosing a woman "for his team" should be enough to convince her of his affection, while the woman may

Repertory (REP-per-torr-ee). A complete set of social roles. The "parts" that you are able to play in life.

Triad (TRY-ad). From the Latin word meaning "three." The dyad becomes triadic (try-ADD-ic) when a third individual is included. A husband and wife make up a marital dyad. A wife, husband, and one child make up a family triad.

assume that the man surely must perceive her as being "the best person in all possible ways" since he married her. If her husband casually remarks that another woman is pretty, the wife may interpret the remark to mean that he no longer sees her as perfect, therefore he no longer loves her.

Job Performance

The differences in early *socialization* for boys and girls may also affect later performance on the job. Middle-class men may do better than women in organizations because men are accustomed to the mix of criticism and praise that are a part of most team operations. The woman working for a large corporation may attempt to survive by trying to form a "pair-bond," particularly with her manager. If this person criticizes the woman in any way, she may *attribute* the criticism to an attitude of complete rejection.

Bardwick believes that about 70 percent of young boys and girls in our culture go through the socialization process she has described. Males who do *not* acquire the "team mentality" when young often have problems getting along in work (and other) organizations, while young women who are socialized into forming teams rather than pair-bonds tend to rise rapidly through corporate structures.

Leadership Roles

Some roles have innate components, such as "male" and "female." Other roles seem to be entirely learned, such as that of "leader" or "manager." Social psychologists have studied the *leadership role* for many years. Although there still is not too much agreement on why some people become leaders and others don't, some aspects of the leader's role are fairly well defined (at least for our culture).

Two Types of Specialists

Many years ago, Harvard sociologist Robert Bales and his colleagues performed a classic set of experiments on leadership. Their subjects were groups of male college students brought together in a laboratory and given certain intellectual problems to solve. Bales *et al.* measured the men's verbal behaviors as objectively as they

"NOT BAD, FOR A WOMAN."

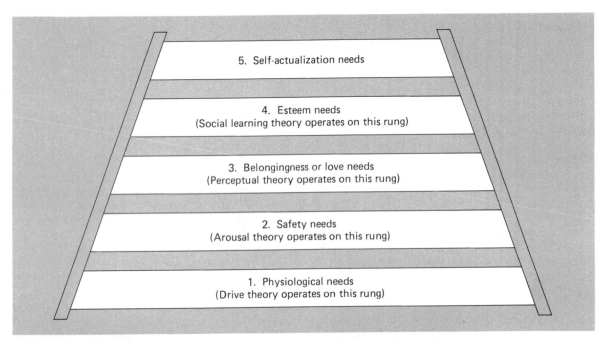

5. Self-actualization needs

4. Esteem needs
(Social learning theory operates on this rung)

3. Belongingness or love needs
(Perceptual theory operates on this rung)

2. Safety needs
(Arousal theory operates on this rung)

1. Physiological needs
(Drive theory operates on this rung)

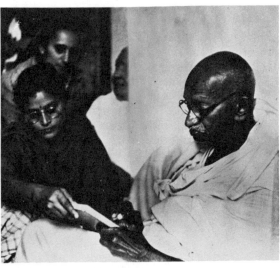

Robert Bales

Fig. 25.1. Maslow's hierarchy of needs.
Mahatma Gandhi, Hindu nationalist teacher, surrounded by young followers. **(left)**

could. And at the end of each problem-solving session, the experimenters asked the subjects to rate each member of the group in a number of ways, including how much the man liked the others and which men seemed to be leaders or have the best ideas.

Bales and his associates found that two types of people got high scores on the leadership rating scales: The "idea man" (or *task specialist*) and the "social facilitator" (or *social-emotional specialist*).

During group sessions, the task specialist gave opinions and made suggestions more often than anyone else. He kept reminding the group of its goals and brought them back to the task at hand whenever they strayed from problem-solving. These behaviors apparently caused other group members to rate the man as a good leader or idea-generator.

The social-emotional specialist, on the other hand, was much more likely to *ask* for suggestions than to give them. He was particularly sensitive to the needs of others. He made extensive use of praise and other forms of feedback, and he smoothed over arguments in order to create what Bales calls *group solidarity*.

According to Bales, the "task specialist" directed the cognitive or intellectual resources of the group, and was respected for his knowledge and expertise. The "social facilitator" directed the emotional resources of the group, and was warmly liked for his ability to keep the group functioning as a **cohesive** unit.

Question: *What similarities do you see between the two types of "specialists" in the Bales study and the functions associated with the two hemispheres of the brain?*

Successful Managers

Harvard psychologist Zick Rubin believes that it is a rare person who is a "natural-born" expert at controlling both the cognitive and emotional processes of groups of people. According to Rubin, such greatness is found only in a very few leaders—Gandhi of India, Mao of China, Winston Churchill of Great Britain, and Franklin Roosevelt of the United States.

A study reported in 1979 by Texas psychologist Jay Hall, however, suggests that leadership skills are more a matter of training than of innate ability. In the course of his survey, Hall measured the attitudes and behaviors of more than 17,000 managers in 50 different US business and government organizations.

Hall began by scoring his subjects on the Rhodes *Managerial Achievement Quotient*, which measures how rapidly and how far a man has risen "through the ranks" in the organizational structure. According to Hall, only some 10 percent of the men had "high MAQ scores," which is to say that only 10 percent of the men had received frequent and rapid promotions. About 50 percent of the men received "average MAQ scores," while some 40 percent of the men had progressed so slowly that they received "low MAQ scores."

Next, Hall gave his subjects the *Work Motivation Inventory*, a test based on Maslow's *hierarchy of needs* that we discussed in Chapter 11. Hall found clear-cut differences among the three groups of managers in terms of what seemed to motivate them. The "successful" managers were most interested in *self-actualization*—that is, in becoming better both as supervisors and as concerned human beings. The "average" managers were motivated by *ego and status needs*. The men with "low MAQ scores" were partially motivated by status needs, but more by *security needs* (such as not being fired). Obviously, from the point of view of Maslow's hierarchy, the most successful managers had risen to the top of the motivational ladder, while the least successful men were stuck on the bottom rungs (see Fig. 25.1).

Cohesive (ko-HE-sive). From Latin and Old English words meaning "to stick, to adhere." Cohesive forces are those that hold things together, like glue. A cohesive unit is one in which the members or parts function efficiently together, usually to achieve some common goal.

Participatory Management

Some organizational leaders *tell* people what to do. Other managers encourage their subordinates to *participate* in the decision-making process. According to Jay Hall, the greatest difference between successful and unsuccessful managers lies in how frequently the men make use of *participatory management*. The "unsuccessful" managers did not encourage much participation at all from their subordinates. The men with "average MAQ scores" asked (and took) the advice of the workers relatively infrequently. The "successful" managers, however, almost always sought the opinions and consent of the people who worked for them.

Jay Hall believes that a manager's *goals* in large part determine how successful the manager will be. Hall reports that men with "high MAQ scores" show both a strong interest in achieving organizational goals *and* in helping their subordinates satisfy their personal needs. Managers with "average MAQ scores," on the other hand, feel a strong urge to "get the task done," but they show considerably less concern about what happens to their employees in the process. The unsuccessful managers appear to be protecting themselves. They seem to have little commitment either to the goals of the organization or to satisfying the needs of those individuals whom they supervise.

Women Managers

Jay Hall's first study dealt exclusively with male managers. In a second study—published in 1980 with Susan M. Donnell—Hall gave similar measures to women managers and to their subordinates. Out of the dozens of measures they took, Donnell and Hall found only two real differences between male and female executives. First, women seem to be more "achievement-oriented" than are their male counterparts. And second, women managers seem to be less open and candid in relating to their colleagues than are males. Donnell and Hall conclude that, "Women, in general, do not differ from men, in general, in the ways in which they administer the management process."

According to Jay Hall, there is a certain irony in these results. For one of the main problems that women managers have is that males

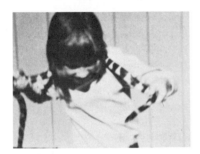

Harry C. Triandis   Albert Bandura

By imitating "models" who handled reptiles confidently, Bandura's clients learned to overcome their fear of snakes.

Question: *What similarities do you see between Jay Hall's findings and Werner Mendel's discovery that his patients at St. Elizabeth's suddenly showed improvement when he started to perceive them differently?*

Role Change

Illinois psychologist Harry C. Triandis believes that your actions are determined primarily by two things: habits, and behavioral intentions. *Habits* are those stereotyped ways you have of responding to specific situations. Your *behavioral intentions* are, more-or-less, whatever set of goals you are trying to reach at any given moment. These momentary goals are affected by many things—the roles you have learned, your emotional reactions, and your cognitive expectancies. Thus, according to Triandis, you can predict an individu-

perceive the women as being skilled at handling social-emotive resources, but as being poor at task achievement. In fact, the truth is just the opposite—males are less oriented toward achievement than are women managers, and males may be more skilled at interpersonal relations than the present crop of female managers are. Yet, as long as males dominate the work scene, it is their *perceptions* of women that make the difference, not the actual behaviors of the women themselves.

al's behavior much better if you know a person's intentions than if you merely know the individual's habits.

Exchange Theory

Triandis views the process of human interaction from the perspective of *exchange theory*. That is, he believes that social relations are governed by "exchanges of resources." You want things from me, and I want things from you. If you know my intentions, you can guess at what I want—and what I am willing to pay for satisfying this goal. But the intentions you *attribute* to me are strongly influenced by your social expectations.

In his 1977 book *Interpersonal Behavior*, Triandis reports a series of studies he has made of what happens when two people from different cultures meet and interact. He finds that most subjects assume that someone from a different country *must* have the same intentions as they do. Thus most Greeks will explain the behavior of Americans in terms of Greek tradition and culture, while Americans find it difficult to believe that Greeks aren't motivated by precisely the same intentions as we have.

Triandis believes that the first thing you have to do when you learn a new role is to discover what behavioral intentions are associated with that role. Thus when you meet someone new, learning what the person's role-expectations are will tell you a great deal about that person's intentions—and how to change or satisfy them.

Observational Learning and Modeling

Roles (and intentions) are learned, but *how* are they learned, and how do you go about *changing* them? Social learning theorist Albert Bandura believes that two of the primary mechanisms of social learning are *observing* and *modeling*. Whenever you see someone act a certain way, you may observe them to see if that action is rewarded or punished. Then you try to imitate those behaviors that you see reinforced, while avoiding those behaviors that lead to punishment. Bandura calls this *observational learning*.

Bandura states that, to some extent, psychotherapy is a matter of choosing a more adaptive role and then learning how to play it well. The technique he finds particularly useful is called *modeling*, in which the therapist demonstrates the new behavior pattern in a step-by-step fashion. The client watches not only the actions the model performs, but is encouraged to note the consequences of the model's behaviors.

In one of Bandura's best-known experiments he used both modeling and observational learn-

ing to help people lose their "snake phobias." At the start of treatment, the clients watched through a glass partition while the therapist played with a snake to show that it wasn't dangerous. The therapist tried to model all of the snake-handling behaviors he wished the subjects to learn. Then in a step-by-step fashion, the clients were encouraged to approach, touch, and finally hold the reptiles. At the end of treatment, *all* the clients could sit peacefully in a chair while a snake crawled all over their bodies.

Clients treated with other forms of therapy were not nearly as successful in shedding their snake phobias.

Question: *Suppose you wanted to learn the role of a policeman. Would you be more likely to model your actions after someone in real life, or after a "cop" you saw on television? Which model would more likely be violent?*

Zimbardo's "Jail"

In the summer of 1971, Stanford psychologist Philip Zimbardo and his students studied the "roles" that people play in prison situations. Zimbardo and his group took over a basement corridor in the psychology building at Stanford and converted it into cells, an exercise yard, observation rooms, and a closet that served as the "hole" for solitary confinement. They turned nearby rooms into space for the guards, the "warden" (Dr. Zimbardo) and his students, and for the videotape equipment.

Next, Zimbardo put an ad in two local papers offering to hire students to play the roles of prisoners and guards for a two-week period. Zimbardo interviewed all the volunteers, screened them for physical and mental health problems, and then selected the 21 men who seemed most healthy, mature, and "normal." On a random basis, 11 of them were chosen to be "guards," while the other 10 were to be "prisoners."

The subjects were told the details of the study and all voluntarily agreed to "play the game" for a period of up to two weeks. They were paid $15 a day for participating, and knew that if selected as a prisoner they would lose all rights to privacy during the 14-day period the experiment was to run. The guards worked 8-hour shifts, but (unlike the prisoners) were allowed to leave when their shifts were over.

The guards were given special uniforms designed to look "official." They were issued police night-sticks, whistles, and reflecting sunglasses (to prevent eye contact with the prisoners). The prisoners were required to wear muslin smocks with no underclothes, a light chain and lock

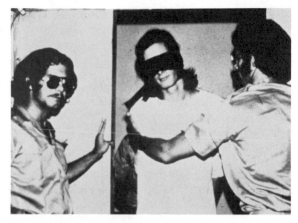

Philip Zimbardo and his students at Stanford University studied the dehumanizing effects of a mock prison environment.

Philip Zimbardo

around one ankle, rubber sandals, and a cap made from a nylon stocking. Each prisoner was given a toothbrush, towels, soap, and bed linen. No personal belongings were allowed in the cells.

Persons and "Non-persons"

Zimbardo and the guards developed a set of "rules" the prisoners were expected to memorize and follow while in jail. One of the most important rules was that the prisoners were to be addressed only by the "numbers" painted on their muslin smocks. The prisoners were expected to "work" in order to earn their $15 daily payment. Twice a week, the prisoners were allowed visitors. The guards could also give them a variety of "rewards" for good behavior, including the right to exercise in the "yard" and to attend movies.

The first clue as to how the study would turn out came during the "count" of the prisoners the guards took three times daily. The first day or so, the "count" took 10 minutes or less. But by the second day, the guards starting using "count time" to harrass the prisoners, so the time increased. By the fifth day, some of the "counts"

lasted for several hours as the guards berated the prisoners for minor infractions of the "rules."

Zimbardo designed his experiment in an attempt to study some of the conditions that lead to *depersonalization*. He found out in a hurry that one primary factor was the behavior of the guards. True, the prisoners had given up their identities and had become "numbers." But they were still human beings, despite the smocks they wore and the chains around their ankles. However, the guards rapidly began treating the prisoners as "non-persons" who weren't really humans at all.

As far as "depersonalization" went, however, the *reactions* of the prisoners were probably just as important as the *actions* of the guards. Instead of protesting their treatment, the prisoners began to act in depressed, institutionalized, dependent ways—exactly the role-behaviors shown by real-life prisoners and mental patients. And, as you might imagine, the more the prisoners acted like "non-persons," the more they were mistreated by the guards.

By the end of the sixth day, the situation had nearly gotten out of hand. The guards began modifying or changing the prison "rules" and routines to make them increasingly more punitive, and even some of Zimbardo's students got so caught up in the spirit of things that they neglected to give the prisoners some of the privileges they had earned.

At this point, wisely, Zimbardo called a halt to the proceedings.

The Results

Afterward, Zimbardo and his students interviewed all of the subjects and analyzed the videotapes they had made during the six days. Perhaps their most important finding is an obvious one—the subjects simply "became" the roles that they played. *All* of the 11 guards behaved in abusive, dehumanizing ways toward the prisoners. Some of them did so only occasionally. But more than a third of the guards were so consistently hostile and degrading that Zimbardo refers to their behavior as *sadistic*.

The prisoners, on the other hand, showed a reaction which (in Chapter 13) we called *learned helplessness*. Day by day, the prisoners did less and less, initiated fewer conversations, became more surly and depressed. Five of the prisoners were unable to cope with their own reactions and asked to leave. But the other five seemed to accept their fates and (in a few cases) didn't even bother to "request parole" when given a chance to do so.

The second important finding Zimbardo made is obvious but, to most people, simply unbelievable. There was absolutely *no prior evidence* that the subjects would react as they did. Before their random selection as guard or prisoner, the two groups did not differ from each other in any way that Zimbardo could discover. All 21 were healthy, normal, mature young men—and not one of them predicted he would act as he did. Furthermore, there is no reason to believe that the study would have turned out any different had the roles of the two groups been reversed.

One of the tests Zimbardo used is the F-Scale, which measures **authoritarianism**. Surprisingly enough, the guards didn't differ from the prisoners on this scale, nor were the "sadistic" guards more authoritarian (as measured by the test) than were the more "humanitarian" guards. However, the prisoners who refused to leave were, generally speaking, the ones who scored as being the *most authoritarian*. Zimbardo believes that these men were psychologically better-prepared to cope with the highly structured and punitive environment of the prison.

The third finding is perhaps less surprising. At no time did any guard ever *reward* a prisoner for anything. The only "correctional" techniques the guards ever employed were criticism, punishment, and harrassment.

Question: Given the data, can you really be sure that you wouldn't have played the guard or prisoner role exactly as Zimbardo's subjects did?

Public Reaction
The results of his experiment distressed Zimbardo so much that he made them available to the

news media almost immediately. Public reaction was swift, and primarily punitive. Many critics found it inconceivable that a "noted Stanford professor" would undertake such a dehumanizing study. Most of these same critics also suggested that Zimbardo must have picked a very abnormal bunch of young men for his subjects, because ordinary citizens surely wouldn't behave in that fashion.

In fact, there is no better illustration of the *attribution process* at work than Zimbardo's study. At first the prisoners blamed their behaviors on the situation they were in. But eventually they became depressed and attributed their failure to cope to their own "innate trait of spinelessness." The guards justified their harrassment in terms of "being paid to do the job," as well as the "criminal instincts" they perceived in the prisoners. The critics attributed both the brutality of the guards and the "helpless" behaviors of the prisoners to innate character flaws in *those* specific men. No one caught up in the experiment—including, at times, Zimbardo and his students—perceived that the *environment* was almost entirely responsible for the behaviors of both guards and prisoners. No one saw that the men were just "playing roles."

Other Similar Studies
Perhaps we shouldn't be too surprised at either Zimbardo's results or the public reaction, for social scientists have reported similar findings many times before. And each time both the majority of psychologists and the majority of the public has found it difficult to believe that human behavior is as strongly influenced by environmental factors as it obviously is.

After World War II, there were hundreds of studies made of the guards and prisoners who had been in Nazi concentration camps. Almost all the results suggested that the guards (on the average) were little different from either the prisoners or from the average European. Zimbardo notes that even some of the worst "Nazi butchers" appeared to be perfectly normal—outside of their actions at the concentration camps.

After the Korean conflict, the US Army did extensive research on the 4,000 American soldiers who returned from Chinese prisoner-of-war camps. Although 85 percent of these men "coop-

Authoritarianism. An authoritarian is someone who believes that discipline and punishment make the world a better place. Someone who believes in "following the rules" set down by higher authority. Generally speaking, most authoritarian individuals also have an external locus of control. See Chapter 13.

erated" with the Communists—even to the extent of "squealing" on their comrades—their personality test scores and prior behavior patterns were no different from those of any other group of army men. Despite this evidence, the official Army explanation of the men's behavior blamed both the men's "psychological weaknesses" and the power of Communist "brainwashing" techniques for the prisoners' behaviors.

Immediately after the My Lai incident during the Viet Nam war, the Army put the soldiers involved through a psychological wringer. In terms both of their personalities and their prior experiences, the soldiers were exactly the same as most other healthy, normal American men of their age and background. The official explanation minimized the Army's role in the affair and attributed the cause of the massacre to the men's failure to "follow the rules."

Social Roles versus "Attributed Motives"

Social roles are patterns of attitudes, emotions, perceptions, and behaviors that are "the norm" for a particular group, organization, or culture. They seem to be learned early in life, primarily through observation and imitation. Although some aspects may be innately determined, roles are primarily determined by the social situation.

Most of the things you do, think, and feel are strongly influenced by the conditions you grew up in and by your present social milieu. But present-day society still *attributes* the causes of human behavior to such internal processes as "personality" and "character." So if you find yourself attributing motives and intentions to other people, perhaps that is merely a role you have been taught to play.

Summary

1. Four important questions that **social psychologists** attempt to answer are these:
   a. Is social psychology the study of **attitudes** or **behaviors**?
   b. Are attitudes and behaviors **learned** or **innate**?
   c. What are the **structures** and **functions** of groups and organizations?
   d. How **consistent** are social systems over time?
2. According to **social learning theory**, attitudes are often formed by observing the behaviors of others. These attitudes then determine future behaviors. Thus social psychology deals with both attitudes and actions.
3. **Sociobiologists** such as Edward Wilson believe most social behaviors are **innate responses** determined by the genes to enhance the genes' chances of surviving. You help others because you hope they will help you, a survival technique called **reciprocal altruism**.
4. Sociobiology stems from studies of **animal behavior**, does not seem applicable to humans, and may be more a **political viewpoint** than a scientific theory.
5. Some social psychologists study **social systems**. Others study the effects of those systems on **individual behavior**. One such effect is that of **person perception**, or how you come to perceive, remember, and respond to people as you do.
6. **First impressions** of people are determined by such factors as **prior attitudes**, **reputa-

tions**, **stereotypes**, the **primacy** and **recency effects**, and by **autistic hostility**, or the tendency to repress favorable data about people or things you dislike.
7. An **attitude** is defined as a consistent way of thinking about, feeling toward, or responding to some aspect of your environment (or toward yourself).
8. First impressions of someone are also influenced by **present stimulus inputs**, including the person's **physical appearance** and **body language**.
9. We tend to attribute **good traits** to good-looking people and **bad traits** to less attractive individuals.
10. Most people tend to think that your body language signals your **intentions**, or your **underlying traits and motives**.
11. If your actions are **incongruent** with people's expectations of you, they tend to "explain away" these behavioral inconsistencies but **remember** them more clearly than actions that confirm expectations.
12. Each of us seems to have a **personal space** around us that we defend as our **psychological territory**. The size of our territory is determined by the culture we grew up in and by our **status** in that culture. We tend to **approach** (or lean toward) people we like, and **retreat** (or lean away from) people we don't like.
13. Each culture has its own rules for **eye contact** that determine the ways in which people converse with each other—and sometimes make

it hard for people from different cultures to communicate with one another.

14. In order to predict and influence the actions of others, we use the **attribution process**. That is, we attribute motives and intentions to them that make their behaviors understandable to us. However, we often see our own actions as responses to the **social environment**.

15. Harold Kelley believes that long-term relationships are determined by **interdependence**, **responsiveness**, and **attributions**.

16. Relationships are interdependent because the **costs and benefits** are a joint function of the behavior of both partners. If the partners are responsive to each other's **needs**, the partners will attribute to each other the trait of **lovingness**.

17. Marriage partners are inclined to explain problems in terms of **attributed traits** rather than **observed behaviors**. To resolve the problems, both partners may desire **attitudinal change** rather than mere **behavioral change**.

18. Both our genes and our early experiences affect our **social roles**.

19. Girls in middle-class US society tend to form **dyadic relationships** about age 7. These relationships are often characterized by each girl's **complete acceptance** of the other. A search for this same acceptance may color the girl's later heterosexual and job experiences.

20. At about age 7, many US boys form **teams** in which each boy evaluates and ranks the skills of the other group members. The adult male role then includes such characteristics as **achievement** and **performance evaluation** rather than dyadic acceptance.

21. Research on problem-solving in small groups suggests that there are two types of **leadership roles**, the **task specialist** and the **social-emotional specialist**.

22. Studies of 17,000 US managers suggest that successful supervisors are motivated by the need for **self-actualization**, while less successful managers are motivated by **security** and **status needs**.

23. Successful managers tend to use **participatory management** techniques, while average or below-average supervisors tend to manage in an **authoritarian** way.

24. Women managers tend to be slightly more **task-oriented** than men, who seem to be somewhat better at **social relations**. Overall, though, there is little difference between men and women managers.

25. Triandis views the process of human interaction as little more than an **exchange of resources**. In order to get what we want from others, we must guess their **behavioral intentions**.

26. Bandura believes roles are learned primarily through **observation** and **imitation**. By using **modeling therapy**, Bandura has been able to cure people of such "psychological problems" as snake **phobias**.

27. Zimbardo's **jail study** suggests that abnormal behaviors such as **authoritarianism, social aggression** and **depersonalization** may be nothing more than **role behaviors** determined primarily by the **social milieu** in which they occur.

28. Critics of Zimbardo's research prefer to **attribute** his results to **innate traits**, but the critics themselves may be just playing a **learned social role**.

(Continued from page 595.)
Day 5. I don't understand why Warden Wakeman stopped the experiment. We had the riot under control, and we hadn't violated the Regulations. I mean, it isn't really physical punishment if you just *poke* the Numbers a little. That sort of stuff goes on in jails all the time, doesn't it? And how else were we going to get 853 to obey the Rules?

I looked at some of the videotapes that Dr. Wakeman took, particularly the last one showing how we settled 853's hash. And I had to grin. I don't think I will ever forget the sight of him standing there, with that sausage sticking out of his mouth.

I watched that final tape twice, and even if I do say it myself, I think I came out of the whole thing looking pretty darn good. Like, when I got there, all of the Numbers were backed into a corner of the yard, and the CO's on the evening shift were pointing the nozzle of a fire extinguisher at them. Old 853 was shaking one of those stupid sausages at the CO's, and they were shaking their billy-clubs back at him. But nobody was getting anywhere. And I saw what I had to do, right off.

I told the CO with the nozzle to keep me covered, and motioned to the other two CO's to come with me. Then we marched right up to 853.

"Grab his arms, men," I said, and they did. He seemed shocked and started to struggle, but the CO's straightened him out right away. Then I grabbed the sausage and stuck it right in 853's face. "Listen, twerp," I said, "We are going to finish this business *right now*. Then you are going to *apologize*, and we are going to get back on the Routine, just like the Rules say."

853 gave me some smart-ass reply, so I jabbed his nose with the sausage and said, "I will give you 5 seconds to start eating, or I am going to cram this thing down your throat, and it will serve you right if you choke."

He gave me this peculiar look, like he didn't recognize who I was because of my mirror sunglasses, or something. Then I started to count, "One . . . Two . . . Three . . . Four . . . Five!"

Well, at that moment 853 opened up his mouth to say something, and I jammed the sausage right between his teeth. "Bite," I said, in a firm tone of voice. But all that animal did was grin at me defiantly. So, I jabbed him in the stomach with my billy-club. A firm little poke, but sudden like, if you know what I mean. Well, his teeth chomped shut automatically, and there was the first bite of the sausage in his mouth.

"Now chew," I said. And to help things along, I jabbed him another good one. I guess the sausage must have had a lot of pepper in it, because his eyes started to water. He stared at me sort of funny, and then his eyes watered some more.

And then, ever so slowly, #853 started to chew.

And everybody breathed a sigh of relief. The Rules were Obeyed.

For some reason, that's when Dr. Wakeman came out and stopped the game. I mean, why then? We had it all under control, and could have gone right back to the Routine. That way, we'd have earned the full 300 bucks.

Well, even if Charlie did cost me the money, he taught me something important. I was looking at the tape, see, and I had this sudden insight. Old friend Charlie was *enjoying* himself, getting all that attention for flouting the Rules that way. The way I see it, Charlie has got some basic flaw in his moral character. He's just a little *bent*, if you know what I mean. Fortunately, I discovered the truth in time, before asking him to take on the role of my legal partner.

Not that I don't still like the kid, sort of. I'm not even mad that he won't converse with me, because I figure he's depressed about how he behaved. He did say we ought to go talk to Dr. Wakeman and apologize for what happened, but I don't see much sense in that. He can go if he wants to, but I have nothing to apologize for.

I was just doing my job.

Recommended Readings

Bardwick, Judith. *In Transition: How Feminism, Sexual Liberation, and the Search for Self-fulfillment Have Altered America* (New York: Holt, Rinehart and Winston, 1979).

Burgess, R.L., and T.L. Huston, eds. *Social Exchange in Developing Relationships* (New York: Academic Press, 1979).

Caplan, Arthur L., ed. *The Sociobiology Debate: Readings on Ethical and Scientific Issues* (New York: Harper & Row, 1978).

Kelley, Harold H. *Personal Relationships: Their Structures and Processes* (Hillsdale, N.J.: Erlbaum, 1979).

Sommer, Robert. *Personal Space: The Behavioral Basis of Design* (Englewood Cliffs, N.J.: Prentice-Hall, 1969).

Triandis, H.C., and W.W. Lambert, eds. *Handbook of Cross-Cultural Psychology*, Vol. 1 (Boston: Allyn & Bacon, 1980).

West, S.G., and R.A. Wicklund. *A Primer of Social Psychological Theories* (Monterey, Calif.: Brooks/Cole, 1980).

Zimbardo, Philip H. "On Transforming Experimental Research into Advocacy for Social Change," in M. Deutsch and H. Hornstein, eds., *Applying Social Psychology* (Hillsdale, N.J.: Erlbaum, 1975).

Social Groups 26

Did You Know That . . .

A group is defined as a set of persons considered as a single entity or system?

Social psychologists are sometimes more interested in how you relate to other members of a group than in what you are like as an individual?

One of the major characteristics of a group is the shared acceptance of group rules and norms by all the members?

If everybody else in your group says that a red rose looks blue to them, you may actually perceive the rose as being bluish?

Many people who claim they are not influenced by group pressures are actually "negative conformers"?

Two-thirds of the subjects tested in an obedience study were willing to shock a person to (seeming) death if ordered to do so by the experimenter?

You may be more likely to aid a wounded stranger if you are alone than if other people are present?

When you do something that conflicts with your moral code, you may be more likely to change your perception of yourself than to change your behavior?

Hostile groups may become friendly if rewarded for cooperating with each other?

"Two (Or More) To Tango"

"Tell me, Mr. Kraus, what area of psychology are you most interested in?"

Norman Kraus squirmed around in the hard, wooden chair. It pained him that his adviser, Professor Ronald Ward, kept such uncomfortable chairs in his office. Professor Ward's seat, of course, was a soft armchair covered with English leather.

"Well, sir, I'm most turned on by social psychology, I guess."

"Good, good. Bloody important field," the Professor said. "Many excellent experiments that you could replicate as your training research."

Norm Kraus squinted at his adviser. Ward spoke with a slight Oxford accent that oddly annoyed Norm. He assumed the man took this means of reminding everyone that he had spent several years in England. Then it dawned on Norm what Ward had said.

"Replicate?"

"Yes, of course. We expect our first-year graduate students to replicate, or to repeat as exactly as possible, some piece of published research. Learn by doing what's already been well done, that's our motto."

"If you don't mind, sir, I'd really rather do something new, something no one's tried before."

Professor Ward nodded sagely. "Yes, I'm sure you would. And did you have something particular in mind?"

Norman Kraus stopped to consider. "No, but I thought we could figure something out."

The Professor's lips pursed into a bitter-lemon smile. "There, you see what I mean. Our attitude is that students should learn to walk before they attempt to run. Try something we know will work first, before they exercise their presumed creativity." Ward coughed discreetly, then continued, "Now, what part of social psychology would you like to work on?"

Norm's anger might have boiled over had he not suddenly recalled his father's advice: "If you want to get along with people, you have to go along with people." Much as Norm hated compromising his own standards, he recognized that his father's comments certainly applied to the present situation. But a devilish urge still prompted him to say, "I'd like to find out why people knuckle under to other people."

Professor Ward glanced at the young man sharply, then frowned. "I presume you are referring to the conformity experiments. The early studies by Muzafer Sherif and Solomon Asch opened the field up, of course, but I've always liked the work that Bob Blake and his group did at Texas back in the '50's. Particularly their use of tape recorders to create synthetic social environments. Have you read Blake's experiments?"

The wooden seat was getting more uncomfortable by the moment. "No, sir."

Ward leaned back in his leather armchair, lit his pipe, and continued. "Asch had students guess the length of lines—a very easy task if no one were around to influence their decisions. But when the students had to judge immediately after several other subjects had spoken, matters got sticky. The other subjects were 'stooges,' paid by Asch to lie about which line was longest. If the stooges gave patently stupid judgments, the students often 'knuckled under' and gave incorrect reports themselves. The presence of the group of stooges was apparently so intimidating that many of Asch's subjects conformed to the false group standard."

"And what did Blake do?" Norm asked, in a slightly desperate tone of voice. This stuff sounded even duller than the flatworm research that another professor had tried to talk him into doing.

Ward tapped his pipe on an ashtray and continued. "Blake and one of his graduate students proved that the stooges didn't have to be physically present. Just hearing a tape recording of the stooges' voices was enough to pressure the subject into conforming. They reported this research at the 1953 meeting of the American Psychological Association in Cleveland, as I recall."

Inwardly, Norm Kraus groaned. Professor Ward's memory for trivial detail was legendary. He should have been a cop instead of a professor, Norm told himself. But aloud he said, "Gee, that's interesting. Do you remember exactly what they did?"

Professor Ward smiled, delighted at the chance to show off. "They used the auto-kinetic effect, as did Sherif. You may recall that if you look at a stationary pinpoint of light in a dark room, the light seems to dance around like a firefly. Because the apparent movement is created by the person's own eyes, everybody sees a rather different dance. Given a 10-second exposure to the light, some people will say that it moved a few millimeters, some will say it danced several meters, while others may insist that it hardly moved at all."

Fireflies? Norm thought. In an experiment on *social* psychology? Maybe he had better go back to the worms after all.

The psychologist plowed right on, as if not noticing Norm's dismay. "Because the auto-kinetic effect is so subjective, it's rather easy to pressure people into conforming to group standards. But that's not what the experiment looked like to the subjects, who were undergraduate males at Texas. They were told it was a study on visual perception. The US Air Force, so they were informed, wanted to find out how people judged the movement of tiny lights on the horizon. So the psychologists had devised a complicated and very expensive piece of apparatus that simulated the movement of airplanes in a night-time sky."

"What was the apparatus like?" Norm asked, beginning to be interested in spite of himself.

Ward snorted with amusement. "An empty tin can with a hole punched in one end. There was a flashlight bulb inside the can that could be turned on and off from the next room. Blake and his student hired four stooges to sit in the dark room and give false reports on how far the light moved. The real subjects were called into the room one at a time and sat directly in the middle of the stooges. During each trial, the light went on for 10 seconds, after which each person was asked to report how far it seemed to move. The four stooges always gave their reports first, before the real subject did."

Norm looked puzzled. "Didn't the real subject know the others were stooges?"

"Certainly not. They looked and acted just like real subjects would have acted—they asked questions and complained about the stupidity of the study. Of course, they asked exactly the same questions with each real subject. Anyhow, the stooges gave ridiculous reports. For example, on the first trial the four stooges reported that the light moved 1.6 centimeters, 1.7 centimeters, 1.9 centimeters, and 2.1 centimeters. Who can make measurements like that in the dark?"

"But it worked?" Norm asked.

Professor Ward lit his pipe again. "Only too well. About two-thirds of the subjects were greatly influenced by what the stooges said."

"And that was news?"

"No, but the second part of the study was. In this part, the subjects sat in the room alone and merely heard the tape-recorded voices of the stooges. Naturally, the subject didn't know a recording was being used. He had met the stooges in person before the start of the experiment and was told they were sitting in different rooms. The stooges asked the same questions and made the same comments on tape as they had in the real-life condition. And, as you might assume, the stooges gave the same ridiculous reports on how far the light moved."

Norm wiggled around on the hard chair. "So, what happened?"

Professor Ward smiled benevolently. "The subjects were just as influenced by the synthetic social background recorded on tape as they were when the stooges were physically present. We seem to conform to imaginary groups as much as to real ones." Ward paused to grind at his pipe with a metal tool. "Yes, I think you ought to replicate that experiment as your training research."

Norm could feel the crunch coming. "But couldn't I jazz it up a bit, just to make it more exciting?"

The Professor looked at the young man sternly. "You will learn a great deal more if you first do it exactly the way the Texas group did. Of course, if you have a streak of serendipity in your personality, you might turn up something unexpected anyhow. But be so kind as to try it our way first."

"But Professor Ward, I don't think . . ."

"Mr. Kraus," the Professor barked in a tone of absolute authority, "Our departmental rule is clear. We will expect you to replicate the Blake work *exactly*, as your training research. Report back to me after you've set things up and have run a few pilot subjects. Do you understand?"

Through gritted teeth, Norm Kraus muttered, "Yes, sir."

(Continued on page 634)

What Is a Group?

In the last chapter, we looked at how your social environment affects you, as an individual. In this chapter, we will discuss *groups* of people—how groups are formed, what keeps them together, and what the structures and functions of groups are. But the first question we must ask is, what *is* a group, and why would you want to belong to one?

Social Groups

Whenever you set up a continuing relationship of some kind with one or more other people, you have in fact either started a new **social group** or joined one already in existence. In the strictest of terms, a group is a *system*—that is, *a set of persons considered as a single entity*.

Actually, this definition is so narrow that it is of little practical use. For it implies that groups exist "in the mind of the beholder" rather than in real life. More broadly speaking, a group is a system of two or more individuals who are psychologically related, or who are in some way *dependent* on one another.

You belong to dozens, if not hundreds, of groups. Some are *formal membership groups*. For instance, you apply for membership in most colleges, churches, synagogues, and tennis clubs. But you are born into *family groups* and *ethnic groups*. Some groups, such as "all the people attending a party," are fairly temporary or very informal systems. Other groups—such as friends and lovers—are informally structured but may exist for months or years.

The most important groups in your life are typically those that (1) last a long time, and (2) are made up of people with whom you have frequent, face-to-face encounters. For obvious reasons, these are called **interaction groups**.

Interaction Groups

Whenever you set up a new friendship, you have begun an interaction group—that is, you have given up some part of your own personal independence to create a *state of interdependence* between you and the other person. Whenever you join or create a group, you lose the privilege of "just being yourself" and of ignoring the other group members. But you may gain many things that compensate for this loss.

Some of the rewards for group membership are social. For example, you now have someone to talk to, someone to be with, and to share things with. Other rewards are more practical or task-oriented. For instance, pushing a car out of the mud, rearing a family, playing tennis, and having sex are activities that typically are more reinforcing if two or more individuals participate.

Most interaction groups, then, are made up of people who have affection and respect for each other, who have similar attitudes toward a number of things, or who have a common set of goals and interests.

Question: As we saw in Chapter 5, the behavior of groups can be described in General Systems Theory terms. How would the process of "feed-forward" operate in groups? What kind of feedback do groups typically give their members?

Group Structure and Function

As Theodore Newcomb notes, groups typically form when two or more people sense that the pleasure of each other's company would be more *rewarding* than remaining socially isolated. Most such groups are informal—that is, they do not have a stated set of rules governing the behavior of their members (as does a formal group). But informal groups have their rules too, most of which are based on *cultural expectations* of how people should behave when they are together informally. If you are too noisy at a party, if you spill drinks on people, or assault the host or hostess, you might well be asked to leave.

As Newcomb points out, one of the major characteristics of any group is the *shared acceptance of group rules by all the members*. This acceptance may be conscious or unconscious, but it is almost always present in one form or another.

Part of the fun of forming a friendship group (becoming friends or lovers) seems to be "psyching out the situation." That is, the early pleasures of *dyadic relationships* often come from determining what *rules of the game* the two of you believe ought to be followed. If the person is very much like you, perhaps little or no discussion of the rules may be necessary. If the person is very different from you, the dyad may not last for long (although it can be an exciting relationship at the very beginning). In most cases, however, where the members of a dyad are neither too similar nor too different, each person will compromise a little. For no group can maintain itself unless there is some minimal agreement or **consensus** as to what its members can and can't do.

Question: As we saw in Chapter 25, Judith Bardwick suggests that women often expect quite different emotional responses from men than men expect from women. How then can heterosexual dyads be maintained over long periods of time?

Group Norms

Newcomb notes that the ability to predict the behavior of people and objects in our world appears to be innately rewarding. One of the most reinforcing aspects of belonging to a group is that each member can to some extent predict what the other members are likely to think and do in most situations. Perhaps that is why group rules are almost always stated in terms of behavioral or attitudinal *norms*. That is, the rules specify what the average or normal behavior of each member should be, or what role(s) each member should play.

Newcomb states that no group member will fit all the norms *exactly*, just as no one is *exactly* average in all aspects of intelligence or sexual behavior. Most groups tolerate some deviation from the norm, so long as the member is not perceived by the group as playing "too abnormal" a role—that is, as being more than about 2 standard deviations from the perceived group midpoint. The more similar the group's members are to each other, and the more emphasis the group places on "following the rules," the less deviation the group will usually tolerate. Perhaps we can demonstrate this point with an example.

Suppose we measure the attitudes toward premarital sex of two different groups—a class of

Social group. A set of persons considered as a single unit. Two or more individuals who are psychologically related to one another. In certain rare instances, such as a child playing with an imaginary companion, or when one person hears tape-recorded voices of others, one or more members of the group may not be real (living) people, or may not be physically present.

Interaction groups. Sets of individuals, psychologically related to each other, who have frequent face-to-face contacts, and who share certain attitudes.

Consensus (con-SENSE-sus). From the Latin word meaning "to feel together, to agree." A consensus is a harmony of viewpoints, opinions, or feelings. One common language mistake we often make is saying "consensus of opinion," for the word "consensus" all by itself means "agreement of opinion." Our word "consent" comes from the same Latin source.

Homogeneous (ho-moh-GEE-nee-us). From the Greek words meaning "same kind." The more alike members of a group are, the more homogeneous the group is. In more technical terms, the smaller the standard deviation of a distribution of test scores, the more homogeneous the scores are.

students taking introductory psychology, and a group of young adults at a campus church or religious center. We will ask the members of both groups to record their agreement or disagreement with the following statement by placing a check mark on the nine-point attitude scale shown in Figure 26.1.

After both groups respond, we measure the position that each person has marked on the nine-point scale. We can then use the number closest to each check mark as a *scale score* that fairly accurately represents each member's attitude toward the statement on premarital sex. And, since we have a number, or score, for each person, we can add these numbers up and calculate the mean or *average attitude* for both groups. This average would, presumably, be the group norm. We can also calculate the *range* and the *standard deviation* of scores for both groups.

For the sake of this discussion, let us assume that the mean or norm for both groups happened to be a scale score of 4: "Agree somewhat." This result might suggest to you that the church group and the psychology class were very similar, since the norm seems to be the same in both groups. But ask yourself this question: If your own position was a 6 ("Disagree somewhat"), would either group perceive you as being "too abnormal" to belong to that group?

The answer is—it depends on what each group's standard deviation is. Church groups, in general, are more **homogeneous** in their attitudes toward sexual behavior than are the more random collections of students who make up classroom groupings.

The distribution of scores for the church group might look like those shown in Figure 26.2.

"ANALYZE YOUR HOSTILITY. EXAMINE YOUR AGGRESSION. WEIGH YOUR ANGER. IF THAT DOESN'T HELP, THEN THREATEN TO LICK ANY MAN IN THE HOUSE."

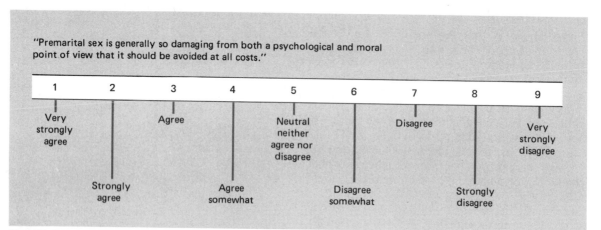

"Premarital sex is generally so damaging from both a psychological and moral point of view that it should be avoided at all costs."

| 1 | 2 | 3 | 4 | 5 | 6 | 7 | 8 | 9 |

Very strongly agree

Strongly agree

Agree

Agree somewhat

Neutral neither agree nor disagree

Disagree somewhat

Disagree

Strongly disagree

Very strongly disagree

Fig. 26.1

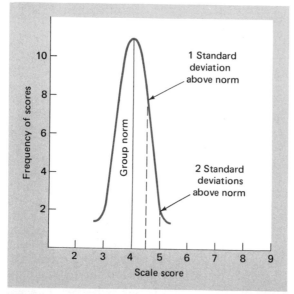

Fig. 26.2

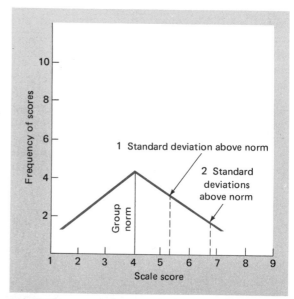

Fig. 26.3

A bar mitzvah is a formal induction into a religious group.

However, the distribution of scores for the classroom group might look like those shown in Figure 26.3.

As you can see, your score of 6 would be more than 2 standard deviations from the church group norm, but well within the "normal" range for the psychology class. Presumably, the church group would consider your attitude too deviant, while the classroom group probably would not.

Generally speaking, the more homogeneous the group, the smaller its standard deviation will be on most scales. And the more **heterogeneous** the group, the larger its standard deviation will be on most measures.

Question: What do you think would happen to the standard deviation of the church group's scores if you attacked the group for being narrow-minded on the subject of premarital sex?

Group Cohesion

According to Theodore Newcomb, *cohesiveness* is the psychological glue that keeps group members sticking together. The more cohesive a group, the longer it will typically last and the more resistant it will be to external pressures.

In ordinary situations, cohesion is often a function of the homogeneity of the group—the more homogeneous the attitudes or behaviors of the members, the more cohesive the structure of the group will be. However, even such heterogeneous groups as introductory psychology classes can be made momentarily cohesive if the group is threatened by some outside force.

People riding together in an elevator are not usually considered a group, for they have no real psychological interdependencies, and their attitudes are likely to be very dissimilar on most subjects. However, if the electric power fails and the people are trapped together in the elevator for several hours, this very heterogeneous bunch of people may quickly form into a group. They will give each other psychological support and comfort, and work together on the goal of escaping.

As soon as the people are released from the stalled elevator, however, the common threat to their survival is removed. At this point, the heterogeneity of the members' attitudes and behaviors will probably overcome the temporary cohesion and the group will disband (although individual members of the group may be similar enough to strike up friendships as a result of the experience).

Question: Why do groups that were close-knit in high school tend to become less cohesive if some of the members go on to college, while others don't?

Heterogeneous (HETT-turr-oh-GEE-nee-us). From the Greek words meaning "different kinds." The more dissimilar the members of a group are, the more heterogeneous the group is, and hence the less cohesive the group is.

Group Commitment

The individual organs in your body cannot wander off to join some other person as they please, but the members of a group system are often free to abandon the group whenever they wish. A group can survive only if it can hold its members together. One of the functions of any group, then, seems to be that of inducing the highest possible *commitment* among its members. For the more committed to the group's norms and goals the members become, the more cohesive the group typically will be and the more homogeneous its attitudes.

In an interesting study of nineteenth-century communes, psychologist R.M. Kanter found that these groups often demanded considerable sacrifice from their members. Some communes required their members to sign over all money and worldly goods to the group and thereafter to work on commune property "for free." Other communes prohibited their members from wearing jewelry or expensive clothes, from smoking tobacco, eating meat, or having sex. Kanter reports that communes demanding such sacrifices tended to last longer than communes that did not.

A similar finding comes from an experiment by social psychologists Elliot Aronson and Judson Mills. They offered college women a chance to participate in a discussion group—if they were willing to pay a price. Half of the women were required to suffer a very painful initiation in order to "buy" entrance to their discussion group. The other half of the women were put through a much milder form of initiation. Those who suffered less liked their discussion group significantly less than did the women who had committed themselves to paying the much higher psychological price.

Question: Which country club would seem more desirable to you, one that charged a $1,000 membership fee or one that charged but $100?

Group Pressures To Conform

Most of us believe that our attitudes toward such things as sexual behavior, politics, economics, and religion are primarily the result of our own soul-searching and logical deduction. In truth, as Harold Kelley points out, we use the groups we

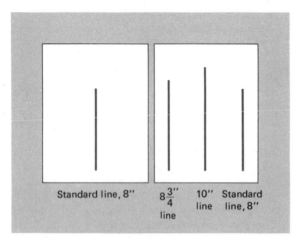

Fig. 26.4. The lines used in Solomon Asch's experiment.

belong to as reference points, or guides, for much of what we think and do.

According to Kelley, these **reference groups** influence your behavior in at least two ways. First, by providing comparison points which you use in evaluating yourself and others. Second, by setting standards or norms and enforcing them by rewarding you when you conform and by punishing you when you do not conform to these standards. As Kelley has shown, members who express opinions, attitudes, or judgments too far from the reference group norm are typically pressured by other members to fall back into line.

Question: Your most important reference group is usually your family. How did your mother, father, and siblings enforce *group norms when you were growing up?*

The Sherif Experiment

The study of how groups induce their members to conform to group norms is one of the most fascinating areas of social psychology—and probably one of the most relevant. Scientific experiments on this topic date back to 1935, when social psychologist Muzafer Sherif first demonstrated the effects of group pressures on visual perception. Sherif asked students to observe a pinpoint of light in a dark room and tell him how much the light moved.

When the students made their judgments sitting alone in the room, each went his or her own way. But when the students were tested in groups, the first members to give their judgments created a perceptual "group norm" that the others had trouble resisting.

Attitudes expressed verbally in groups almost always tend to be more homogeneous than those the group members express if questioned in private.

Question: Can you explain the phrase "divide and conquer" in terms of destroying group cohesion and reducing group pressures toward conformity?

The Asch Experiment

Several years after Sherif reported his findings, social psychologist Solomon Asch carried the matter a step farther. Asch first tested the perceptual abilities of a group of students who served as "control subjects" for the latter part of his experiment. Asch showed these controls a white card that had a black line 8 inches long drawn on it, as shown in Figure 26.4. He referred to this as the "standard line" and asked the controls to remember it well.

Then Asch removed the first card and showed the subjects a second card that had three "comparison lines" drawn on it. The first of these lines was 8.75 inches long, the second was 10 inches, while the third was the same 8-inch length as the standard. Asch then asked the control subjects to report *privately* which comparison line matched the standard. To no one's surprise, the controls picked the correct answer some 99 percent of the time.

With his "experimental subjects," Asch played a much more subtle game. He asked these volunteers to appear at his laboratory at a certain time. But when each young man arrived, he found several other students waiting to participate in the experiment. What the experimental subject did not realize was that the others were stooges, who were paid by Asch to give occasional false judgments. After the stooges and the experimental subject had chatted for a few moments, Asch ushered them into his laboratory and gave them several opportunities to judge line lengths for him. The judgments were given *out loud*, so that everyone could hear, and the stooges were always called on to report *first*—before the experimental subject did.

During the first two trials, the stooges picked the *correct* comparison line—as did the experimental subject. But on the third trial, each of the stooges calmly announced that the 10-inch line matched the 8-inch line! These false judgments created an *incorrect group perceptual norm*, and apparently put the experimental subjects under tremendous pressure to conform. In this first study, the experimental subjects "yielded" to group pressures about one-third of the time by reporting that the two lines matched. In later studies, when the judgments were more difficult to make, the experimental subjects yielded to the group of stooges about two-thirds of the time.

Size of the Group
In another experiment Asch varied the number of stooges who reported before the experimental subject did. While the presence of one, two, or three stooges did induce some conformity, the maximum pressure to yield apparently was reached when there were four stooges giving false reports. Having 14 or even 40 stooges doesn't increase conformity much more than having four. However, if even one stooge out of 40 gives the "correct" answer, the homogeneity of the group is broken, the group pressures are lifted, and the experimental subject typically gives the correct answer also.

Reasons for Conforming
The importance of the Asch study lies not merely in its dramatic demonstration that people tend to conform to temporary reference groups, but in the *reasons* they gave for doing so.

If you were to ask the subjects who "conformed" why they judged the 8-inch line as being as long as the 10-inch line, about half of them would look at you sheepishly and confess that they couldn't stand the pressure. They might say that they figured something was wrong, or that they thought the stooges "saw through a trick" that they hadn't recognized, or that they simply didn't want to "rock the boat" by giving a judgment that went against the group norm.

The other half of the "conformers" are far more interesting, however. For they typically insist that they *actually saw* the two lines as being identical. That is, they were not conscious of "yielding" at all.

Group norms not only influence your attitudes toward complex social issues, but your perceptions of even the simplest objects as well.

What Makes People Conform?

Shortly after Asch reported his initial results, a number of psychologists began to study how groups induce conformity in their members. Perhaps the most detailed of these studies was a series of experiments by Robert R. Blake, Harry Helson, and their colleagues at the University of Texas.

In one of the first of these, which I performed under Professor Blake's direction, we demonstrated that the "stooges" did not have to be physically present in order to pressure the

---

Reference groups. Those groups that set social norms you are expected to live up to. Reference groups typically give you feed-forward by stating the goals you and other group members should attain, as well as giving you rewarding or punishing feedback as you move toward or away from the goals.

Adaptation-level Theory. A theory proposed by Harry Helson that accounts for judgments, perceptions, and attitudes in terms of three factors—the physical and social dimensions of the stimulus input, the background in which the stimulus appears, and the personality structure (traits, attitudes, past experiences) of the perceiver. Often called A-L Theory.

---

experimental subject into conforming. If the subjects merely heard tape-recorded voices of the "stooges," the subjects still conformed about two-thirds of the time.

In further studies, Blake and his students showed that subjects would volunteer for difficult tasks, donate large or small sums of money to a fake charity, violate social rules ("Don't Walk on the Grass!"), and change their reported attitudes toward war and violence in order to conform to the behavior of various groups of stooges.

Adaptation-level Theory
Robert Blake is a social psychologist with a long-standing interest in group behavior. Harry Helson, however, was an experimental psychologist who spent many years studying visual perception in individuals, not groups. Some of Helson's best-known research had to do with the effects of the *background* on the perception of a visual stimulus—for example, the fact that a white rose appears reddish when seen on a background of blue-green velvet (see Chapter 9).

Originally, Helson had little interest in social psychology. However, he soon perceived that the stooges in Blake's studies were really a "social background" that affected perceptual judgments much as the blue-green velvet "colored" the perception of the white rose. Thus conformity behavior could be explained by reference to **Adaptation-level Theory**, which Helson had devised to account for the way that humans perceive the world. The discovery that their interests were similar led Blake and Helson to form a research group—and to jointly direct a series of experiments that helped clarify the conditions that induce people to conform to group norms.

According to Adaptation-level Theory, all behavior (including conforming) is influenced by three factors:

1. *Stimulus factors*. These influences include the task or problem set before the subject—what the subject looks at or is told to do.

Isolated individuals who happen to be together in an elevator. **(left)**

The Shakers lived in communes in the last century. **(top right)**

The farm, a modern commune in Tennessee. **(bottom right)**

2. *Background factors*. These influences include the social situation or context in which the stimulus is presented.
3. *Personality factors*. These influences include such matters as innate response tendencies, traits, and past experience.

According to Adaptation-level Theory, if you want to understand why people do or do not yield to group pressures, you must look at all three factors in detail.

Stimulus or Task Variables

The physical properties of the stimulus you must judge in a conformity experiment have a lot to do with whether or not you will yield to group pressures. In general, the *vaguer* the stimulus, the more likely it is that you will conform. It is a rela-

tively simple task to get you to change your opinions about the beauty of a work of art or the melodiousness of a piece of music. However, it is much more difficult to get you to say that a 10-inch line is shorter than an 8-inch line.

Attitudes about almost anything are easier to shift than are *judgments of concrete facts*, as Richard Crutchfield reported several years ago. However, strong *personal preferences* for things like food are harder to influence than are guesses about such vague facts as the distance from New York to London.

The more *difficult the stimulus task* appears to be, and the more *confusing the instructions* about the task, the more likely it is that the group will be able to influence your behavior. For this reason, perhaps, group pressures are most effective if you must judge the stimulus from *memory*.

Situational or Background Variables

If the group is to have an influence on you, then you must know what the group's opinion or norm actually is. One of the most important situational factors, therefore, is how much information you have about what the group is like, and what the other group members believe. In general, the more *knowledge* you have concerning the group, the more strongly you will feel pressured to yield.

Group pressures to conform develop when stimulus and background factors are in conflict—that is, when your perception of the stimulus *differs significantly* from that offered by some reference group you belong to. Up to a point, the larger the difference between your judgment and that of the group, the more likely it is you will be influenced by group standards. However, if the matter is carried to ridiculous extremes, the pressure on you may lift. It is all very well to ask you to report that an 8-inch line is the same length as one 10 inches long. It is something else to expect you to report than an 8-inch line is identical to one several feet in length.

The way that you perceive the other group members is also critical. The more *prestige* or status or competence members of the group seem to have, or the more *trustworthy* they appear to be, the more powerful agents they become in pressuring you to conform. You are more likely to conform to friends than to strangers, and more likely to yield to strangers who say they like you than to strangers who don't.

The more *out in the open* you are forced to be in making your judgments, the more likely it is that you will yield to group pressures. If you must state your name, or respond so that the rest of the group can hear, then you are more likely to submit to group pressures—at least in public. But if you get the impression that the group may be on the verge of rejecting you, then you may conform in public but not when you're given a chance to make your judgments in private.

If you are told that the whole group must come to a *unanimous decision* on the matter at hand, you will be strongly pressured to yield. Also, the greater the *reward* for yielding, or the more importance the judgment is supposed to have, the more likely it is that you will be swayed by incorrect or inappropriate group norms.

Question: Why is it particularly important that juries, who often decide matters of life and death, should always take secret ballots?

Personality Factors and Past Experience

Some people seem to conform much of the time, some practically never. Most of us, however, yield in some situations and not in others. The *personality traits* of the individual who readily yields to group pressures have often been measured—but not all of these studies have come up with the same results. There are at least three reasons why this conflict might be expected.

First, as we noted in previous chapters, most of our personality tests are not as valid and reliable as we would like them to be.

Second, with the notable exception of the investigations by Blake and Helson, many of these studies of the "conformist personality" have never been replicated. As a general rule, you probably should not trust any scientific finding until it has been successfully repeated several times.

Third, there is no reason why we should expect that all people who conform to group norms should have the same sort of personality. In fact, judging from Zimbardo's research on prisoners and guards (see Chapter 25), we might assume that we would *all* yield if the situational factors were strong enough.

But there are literally dozens of studies in which personality traits have been correlated with yielding or conforming. Looking at the broad picture, we find that yielders are reported to have had harsh parents who gave their children very little "independence training." Yielders are also reported to be "followers" rather than "leaders," but are rather rigid and *authoritarian* in the way they respond to rules. Men who yield more than average are reported to score as being more "feminine" than average on masculinity tests.

There is some evidence that women are more responsive to group pressures than are men, but this difference may reflect cultural values more than basic personality traits. Blake and Helson report that men tend to conform more in areas of traditional interest—such as politics and economics—while women are more likely to yield to group pressures in matters of art and social affairs.

Past experience also has its effects on conformity. If you are an expert on the task at hand, or if the experimenter somehow makes you *think* you are an expert, you are less likely to yield. If you are rewarded for going against the group, then you will yield less than if you are punished for refusing to conform.

There is little or no evidence that conformity is an innate or inherited trait. Rather, it seems to be a behavior that you learn—primarily because your reference groups *reward* you when you conform and *punish* you when you deviate. There is also evidence that even high yielders can be trained to resist group pressures.

Question: Would you expect "internalizers" or "externalizers" to be more likely to conform to group pressures?

Solomon Asch

Robert Blake

Harry Helson

Stanley Milgram

Negative Conformity

In our society, we all make use of reference groups, and we all conform (one way or another) to group norms at one time or another. Indeed, as we will see, one of the *chief functions* of a group is to induce "normative behavior" in its members. And yet we often talk as if we placed a high premium on being independent of the people around us. People brag (and even write songs about) "doing things *my* way." But are we really as non-conformist as we often think we are?

In one study, Blake and Helson discovered a very amusing thing about many people who consider themselves to be "independent thinkers." In fact, they yield to group pressures just as much as do the rest of us, but they yield *negatively*. Let us return to our attitude scale on premarital sex to see what these *negative conformers* are like (see Fig. 26.1).

"Premarital sex is generally so damaging from both a psychological and moral point of view that it should be avoided at all costs." Suppose we ask a young man to respond to this statement while he is *alone*, and he marks #8, "Strongly disagree." Later, we present him with a similar statement that he must respond to *publicly*, after four stooges have given their opinions out loud. The stooges have been paid to say that they too "Strongly disagree" with the statement. What would you think of this young man if he now switches and gives his score as #2, "Strongly agree"? Is this man really acting *independently* of the stooge group? If you wanted to trick him into doing something, couldn't you figure out a way to do so?

Question: How might you use the information on stimulus, background, and personality factors to minimize the effects of group pressures on your own behavior?

Despite protests from the "learner" **(seated in chair),** many subjects in Milgram's "obedience" experiments did obey command's to deliver what they thought were highly painful shocks to the "learner."

Obedience

One interesting sidelight to the conformity studies is this—in most of the experiments, the subject was never told that he or she *had to yield* to the group norm. Indeed, many of the subjects were quite unaware that they had given in to group pressures and *denied* that they had done so. So let us next ask a very important question: What might the results have been had the subjects been *ordered* to yield by the experimenter?

The Milgram Experiments

The answer to this question apparently comes from a fascinating set of experiments performed by psychologist Stanley Milgram in the 1960's at Yale. His subjects were men who ranged in age from young to old, and who came from many different walks of life. These men were paid to participate in what they thought was a study on the effects of punishment on learning.

"Teachers" and "Learners"

In the first experiment, each man arrived at Milgram's laboratory to find another subject (a stooge) also present. The stooge was supposed to be the "learner" who would have to memorize a list of word pairs. The experimental subject was supposed to be the "teacher" who would punish the stooge if he made any mistakes. The stooge was sent into another room and was strapped into a chair so that he couldn't escape when the punishment became severe. The stooge was then out of sight for the rest of the experiment.

Sitting in front of the experimental subject was a very impressive piece of electrical equipment that was supposed to be a powerful shock generator. In fact, the machine was a fake. *No shock was ever delivered during the experiment.* This "fake" generator had 30 switches on it to control the (apparent) strength of the electrical current. Labels on these switches ranged from "Slight Shock" (15 volts) to "Danger: Severe Shock" (450 volts). The first time the stooge made a mistake, the subject was to give him 15 volts of shock. For each subsequent mistake, the subject was to increase the shock intensity by flipping on the next highest switch. The apparatus was so ingeniously designed that none of the subjects guessed that the stooges actually weren't receiving shocks from the machine.

At the beginning of the session, things were easy for the experimental subject. The stooge got most of the word pairs correct, and the "shocks" delivered were presumably very mild. As time wore on, however, the stooge made more "mistakes" and the "shocks" became more and more severe. When the shock level reached what seemed to be a fairly high point, the stooge suddenly pounded on the wall in protest. Then the stooge *stopped responding entirely*, as if he had fainted or had suffered an attack of some kind.

At this point Milgram told the "teacher" to continue anyway—no matter how dangerously high the shock might get. If at any time the subject wanted to stop, Milgram told him in a very stern voice, "Whether the learner likes it or not, you *must go on* until he has learned all the word pairs correctly. So please go on."

What would you do in this situation? Would you refuse to continue, or would you "obey" Milgram and go on shocking the stooge right up to what you believed were the limits of the electrical generator?

And how do you think most other people would react if they faced this challenge?

Some "Shocking" Facts

After he had completed his first study, Milgram asked a great many college students this question. If you are like them, you will insist that you—and most other people—would refuse to continue the experiment when a dangerously high shock level was reached (and particularly when the stooge apparently had fainted or died in the other room). But, in fact, your guess (at least about other people) would be wrong. For out of the first 40 subjects Milgram tried, *almost 65 percent* continued to obey Milgram's orders right up to the bitter end. Most of these subjects were extremely distressed about doing so. They complained, they showed tension, and they told Milgram again and again that they wanted to stop. But some 65 percent were *completely obedient* in spite of their inner conflict.

Question: *What similarities do you see between the people who "obeyed" Milgram and the young men in Zimbardo's experiment who became "brutal" in their behaviors toward men who were playing the role of prisoners?*

Factors Inducing Obedience

In Adaptation-level Theory terms, Milgram's verbal orders to the subjects were "stimulus factors," while the behavior of the stooge can be considered part of the "background or situational factors." By manipulating each of these factors in subsequent experiments, Milgram was able to determine a variety of ways in which obedience can be increased or decreased.

As you might expect, the weaker the stimulus, the fewer the number of people who obeyed. When Milgram stood right over the experimental subjects, breathing down their necks and ordering them on, about 65 percent followed through to the end. But when Milgram was out of the room and gave his orders by telephone, only some 22 percent of the subjects were completely obedient.

In the first experiment, the subjects could not see or hear the stooge in the other room. In subsequent studies, Milgram altered this "background factor." If the stooge began moaning, or complaining about his heart, fewer subjects obeyed orders. Having the stooge physically present in the same room so that the subject could see the supposed pain from each shock reduced obedience even more. And if the subject had to grab hold of the stooge's hand and force it down on a metal "shock plate" before each punishment, very few of the subjects followed Milgram's instructions to the end. As you might guess, the subjects were more likely to deliver severe punishment if they couldn't see the *consequences* of their actions.

Group Pressures and Obedience

In a later experiment, Milgram added the group-pressures technique to his own method of studying obedience. In this experiment, Milgram used three stooges with each experimental subject. One of the stooges, as usual, was the "learner" seated in the next room. The other two were supposed to be "teachers" working in a team with the subject.

The experiment proceeded as before, except that one of the stooge-teachers backed out as soon as the "shock" reached a medium-low intensity. Saying that he refused to continue, this stooge simply took a seat as far from the shock machine as he could. When the "shock" reached a medium-high level, the other stooge-teacher also refused to go on. The subject then was faced with *conflicting social norms*. Milgram kept pressuring him to continue, while the "group" of stooge-teachers was exerting pressure to stop. Under these conditions, the "social background" factors won out over the "stimulus" of Milgram's orders. More than 90 percent of the subjects refused to complete the experiment.

We are taught to obey, just as we are trained to conform. If you consider the great rewards and massive punishments that groups can administer to their members, perhaps it is not so surprising that many of us obey and conform rather readily.

Question: What would have happened in Zimbardo's prison study had the "warden" ordered the guards to punish the prisoners severely for infractions of "the rules"?

Attribution Theory and Obedience

Before we go any farther with our discussion of obedience, let's ask a question. Suppose, in one of his studies, Milgram had allowed the "teacher" to *set the shock level himself*. That is, rather than insisting that the "teacher" blindly increase the amount of shock given the "learner" after each trial, Milgram had told the "teacher" to decide how much punishment would be "appropriate." The "teacher" could increase the shock to the maximum level, keep it in the "mildly painful" range, or decrease the shock to almost zero.

Under these circumstances, how much shock do *you* think the "average teacher" would eventually administer? And what percentage of the "teachers" do you think would give the maximum amount of electricity? Why not write your predictions down on a sheet of paper, and then see what actually happened.

In fact, Milgram actually performed this experiment and reported the results in 1974. He began by giving all the teachers themselves a mildly painful shock of 45 volts, so they would "understand how shock felt." Thereafter, the "teachers" were allowed to administer (false) shock to the "learner" that could vary from 15 up to 450 volts. Milgram found that almost all of the "teachers" maintained the shock in the "mildly painful" range (45 to 60 volts). Only one "teacher" out of 40 administered the maximum shock of 450 volts. That finding itself is very interesting. However, an extension of this research by Martin Safer of Catholic University of America yielded even more intriguing results.

Safer began by showing a film of Milgram's research to 132 students in an introductory psychology class. He then asked the students to *predict* what the "teachers" would do if allowed to set their own shock levels. Safer found that the students systematically *overestimated* the amount of shock they thought the "teachers" would administer. They guessed that about 12 percent of the "teachers" would give 450 volts, and that the average "teacher" would end up giving about 175 volts!

Safer believes that his students *attributed evilness to the "teachers."* That is, the students apparently assumed that most people have a "cruel streak" in them, and that they will express this trait if given a chance. Safer points out the paradox of his findings. First, before learning about Milgram's research, most students presume that *almost nobody* would shock an innocent "learner." When they learn what actually happened in Milgram's laboratory, however, the students attribute the results to some character flaw inside the "teachers." For the students failed to perceive that the "teachers'" actions were due to the *social environment*, not some personality trait. Thus, when asked how the "teachers" would react when allowed to set their own shock levels, the students predicted on the basis of *attributed traits*, not on the basis of the actual situation the "teachers" were in (and responding to).

Martin Safer concludes that few people "appear to have insight into the crucial situational factors affecting behavior in the obedience . . . experiments."

Question: What level of shock did you think the "teachers" would use? What have you learned about your own perceptions from these studies?

The Ethics of Deception

The Milgram studies, the Zimbardo prison research, and many other experiments raise a number of complex but important questions about the *ethics* of using humans as subjects in scientific experiments. One of these questions involves the morality of *deceiving* the subjects as to the real purpose of the study, even if the experimenter believes such deception is necessary because people seldom act naturally when they know they're being observed.

Milgram's Critics

When Milgram's research was published, a storm of protest was raised by sincerely concerned individuals who urged that studies such as Milgram's be banned or prohibited. This same barrage of criticism, as we noted in the last chapter, occurred when Zimbardo released the results of his prison experiment. In consequence, a number of codes of ethics were proposed, but workable guidelines for experimentation on humans are not easy to agree upon. For, given a little time and motivation, we could all think of certain types of studies in which deception might be morally justified, and other experiments in which misleading the subjects would be both a legal and an ethical outrage.

When Is Deception Ethical?

Obviously we should always consider the *actual results* of experiments before drawing hasty conclusions about what is ethical and what isn't. Viewed in this perspective, Milgram comes off fairly well, for he did discover some fascinating facts, and there is no evidence that any of his subjects suffered ill effects. In truth, Milgram seems to have employed little more deception in his work than is used regularly on TV programs such as "Candid Camera." Yet the nagging question— "When is it ethical to use deception?"—remains for the most part unanswered.

Some of the emotional reaction to Milgram's experiments probably stemmed from the rather unflattering picture his results gave us of ourselves. Had most of Milgram's subjects *refused* to obey blindly, perhaps he would not have been so vigorously attacked. Milgram's research—as well as Zimbardo's, and the early research on conformity—suggests that we all have "psychological blind spots" about the true *causes* of human behavior. Since many of us find it difficult to perceive how influential the social environment is, we apparently prefer to attack people like Milgram instead of "changing our minds" about what inputs actually influence our actions.

However, despite the emotionality of some of Milgram's critics, the issue of experimenter responsibility remains a crucial one, and the American Psychological Association has recently taken a stand against the unwarranted use of deception in similar research.

Apathetic (app-pah-THET-tick). From a Greek word meaning "without sympathy, lacking passion or interest, being indifferent to the fate of others."

We will have more to say about these complex ethical issues in the next chapter.

Question: *Under what circumstances do you personally think that deceiving subjects in a scientific experiment might be ethically warranted or justified?*

Bystander Apathy

Milgram created problems for his subjects because he told them what to do. In real-life conflicts, there often isn't anyone around to give you directions, and you must act (or fail to act) on your own. If there are other people around you when a crisis occurs, however, you may look at them as "models" of what you ought to do. And you may assume that *they are as responsible as you are* for taking action (or not doing anything) in an emergency. Thus if your "models" fail to react, you may feel strong group pressures to follow their lead. Keep that thought in mind as we describe a particularly gruesome murder.

What would you do if, late some dark night, you heard screams outside your place? Would you rush out at once, or would you first go to the window to see what was happening? If you saw a man with a knife attacking one of your neighbors, how would you react? Might you call the police, or go to the neighbor's aid? Or would you remain **apathetic** and unresponsive? And if you failed to assist the neighbor in any way, how would you respond if someone later on asked why you didn't help?

Before you answer, consider the following facts. Early one morning in 1964, a young New York woman named Kitty Genovese was returning home from work. As she neared her front door, a man jumped out of the shadows and attacked her. She screamed and attempted to defend herself. Because she screamed loudly, 38 of her neighbors came to their windows. And because she fought valiantly, it took the man almost 30 minutes to kill Kitty Genovese. During this period of time, not one of those 38 neighbors came to her aid—and not one of them even bothered to call the police.

The Darley-Latané Studies

Kitty Genovese's death so distressed scientists John M. Darley and Bibb Latané that they began a study of why people refuse to help others in similar situations.

John Darley   Bibb Latané

In one experiment, Darley and Latané staged a disaster of sorts for their subjects. They paid people 2 dollars to fill out a survey form which was given to them by an attractive young woman. While the people were in an office filling out the forms, the woman went into the next room. Shortly thereafter, the subjects heard a loud crash from the next room, and the woman began moaning loudly that she had fallen and was badly hurt and needed help.

Now, how many of the subjects do you think came to her rescue?

The answer is—it depends. Some of the subjects were exposed to this little drama when they were all by themselves in the testing room. About 70 percent of the "alone" subjects offered help. Another 40 subjects faced this apparent emergency in pairs. Only 8 of these 40 people responded by going to the woman's aid. The other 32 subjects simply sat there listening to the moans and groans.

Were the subjects who failed to rush to the woman's assistance merely apathetic and uncaring? In this case, yes. Many of the "apathetic bystanders" informed the experimenters that they hadn't really thought the woman was seriously hurt and were afraid of embarrassing her if they intervened. But we should note that the subject's *perception* of the emergency was strongly influenced by whether or not there was someone else present in the testing room.

In another experiment, subjects heard a young man (presumably in the next room) discuss the fact that he frequently had seizures similar to grand mal epilepsy. Shortly thereafter, the stooge began crying for help, saying that he was about to have an attack and would die if no one came to help him. About 85 percent of the subjects who were "alone" rushed to the stooge's assistance. However, only 62 percent of the sub-

jects who were in pairs offered aid, while but 31 percent of those in 5-person groups overcame their apathy.

Latané's Theory of Social Impact

In an article in the April 1981 issue of the *American Psychologist*, Bibb Latané proposed a "theory of social impact." Latané states, "As social animals, we are drawn by the attractiveness of others and aroused by their mere presence . . . We are influenced by the actions of others, stimulated by their activity and embarrassed by their attention . . . I call all these effects, and others like them, 'social impact.'"

Latané goes on to say that the impact of your social environment can be determined by three factors: The *strength*, *immediacy*, and the *number* of people around you. The more people involved in a given situation, the more *diluted* you will perceive your own responsibility as being. Thus, Latané says, each person who witnessed Kitty Genovese's murder felt but 1/38th of the responsibility for helping the woman or reporting the crime. Thus, while the murder itself had a strong and immediate impact on the neighbors, the *number of people* was so great that it diluted each person's sense of responsibility to the point where no one took action.

Question: Consider those 38 neighbors as an Asch-type "conformity group." Why would each person be under strong pressures not to intervene if none of the other 37 did?

Subways Are for Slipping

Darley and Latané note that most of Kitty Genovese's neighbors said after the murder that they didn't *perceive* anything really terrible as taking place. This inaccurate perception then excused the neighbors' failure to take action—at least in their own minds.

More recent research by I.M. Piliavin, J. Rodin, and J. Piliavin tends to confirm the accuracy of this explanation. In the late 1960's, Piliavin and his group turned the New York subway system into an experimental laboratory. Four people involved in the study would board one car of a subway train through different doors. Once the train was underway, one of the male experimenters would stumble down the aisle, slip, and collapse on the floor, face up. Two of the experimenters recorded how long it took the "innocent bystanders" in the subway car to come to the stooge's aid. If no one helped out, one of the other experimenters would then assist the stooge.

From a humanistic point of view, the results of the Piliavin research are fairly encouraging.

When the "victim" was carrying a white cane, and acting as if he were blind, people came to his aid in 95 percent of the tests. Even when the stooge reeked of whiskey and pretended to be drunk, he received assistance in about half the tests.

Question: People tend to conform to groups less in situations in which they think they are experts. What would happen to "bystander apathy" if we began teaching children how to handle social emergencies as part of their normal training in school?

Cognitive Dissonance

Not all the conflicts we face involve a choice between satisfying group expectancies or satisfying our consciences by living up to a moral code. Sometimes the problem has to do with trying to explain to ourselves why we picked a biological reinforcer rather than an intra-psychic one. For instance, most of us are taught that sexual intercourse is immoral except when engaged in by a married couple. Yet, if Kinsey's data are true, many of us violate this ethical standard at some time during our lives. Afterward, rather than admitting that our ids got the better of our super-egos, we may *rationalize* our actions in a variety of ways: "I did it only because I loved him (her)," "She (he) needed me," or "I was forced into doing it."

Doomsday Prophecies

Over the years, Leon Festinger has conducted a series of intriguing studies on how human beings react to situations involving social conflicts. In one of his first studies, Festinger worked with H.W. Riecken and Stanley Schachter. These social scientists made an extensive study of a "doomsday group" whose leader had predicted that the world would end on a certain day. As the fatal day approached, the members of the group became more and more excited and tried to convince others to repent and join their group in order to "save their souls." When "doomsday" arrived, the members of the group gathered together to await final judgment and to pray for deliverance. To their amazement, the day passed, and so did several other days, and the world continued to speed on its merry way.

And how did the leader of the "doomsday group" react to the failure of her predictions? Apparently, by finding a "rational excuse" for what actually happened. Several days after the date the world was supposed to end, she told the members of her clan that "God had spoken to her, and had spared the world in answer to the group's prayers." The group members then reacted with great joy. Rather than rejecting the leader, they

> **Cognitive dissonance** (KOG-nih-tiv DISS-oh-nance). The feeling you get when your behaviors differ markedly from your intra-psychic values. According to Leon Festinger, you are strongly motivated to reduce this dissonance. You do so either by changing your values or by changing your behaviors. For the most part, people experiencing cognitive dissonance tend to change their attitudes or explanations—and then keep right on behaving as they always had.

accepted her more warmly and believed even more firmly in her prophecies.

Changing Perceptions To Reduce Conflict

The "failed prophecy" study led Festinger to hypothesize that people tend to reduce mental conflict by changing their *perceptions* of what really happened to them. In perhaps the best known of his experiments—reported in 1959 by Festinger and J.M. Carlsmith—college students were asked to do about 30 minutes of very tedious and boring work. The subjects performed these repetitive and uninteresting tasks while alone in a laboratory room.

After the students had completed the chores, Festinger and Carlsmith offered some of them a dollar as a reward to tell the next subject what an exciting and thrilling task it had been. Other subjects were paid 20 dollars for doing exactly the same thing. Afterward—no matter how good a "selling job" the person had done—each subject was asked to give her or his actual opinion of how pleasurable the work was.

Festinger and Carlsmith report that the students paid one dollar thought the chores were really pretty interesting and enjoyable. However, the subjects paid 20 dollars rated the tasks as dull, as did a group of subjects who were not asked to "sell" the experiment to another student.

Why did the subjects paid but one dollar rate the work as being much more pleasant than one might have expected? Festinger believes that they had a difficult job rationalizing their own actions. For they had *lied* to the other subject about how interesting the task was supposed to be. The subjects paid 20 dollars for lying apparently were willing to face the fact that they had "fudged" a bit for that much money. The students paid but a single dollar couldn't admit to themselves that they'd "sell out" for so little money. Thus they changed their *perception* of the enjoyability of the task "after the fact."

Dissonance Theory

In the early 1960's, Festinger suggested that in conflict situations we experience **cognitive dissonance**. That is, whenever we do something we

Leon Festinger   Muzafer Sherif

think we shouldn't, we face the problem of explaining our actions to ourselves and to others. Festinger stated that we are usually highly motivated to reduce cognitive dissonance when it occurs, and that we do so chiefly by changing our *beliefs or attitudes* to make them accord with our *actual behaviors*—and then we go right on behaving the way we always had.

Perhaps you will have noticed a certain similarity between the group pressures experiments, the obedience studies, the research on bystander apathy, and the cognitive dissonance experiments. In all these cases, the actual conflict arose when people failed to recognize that we are all immensely sensitive to group pressures, and that it is a *natural function of a group* to exert these pressures.

Given the fact that so few of us ever perceive what strong control our environments exercise over us, perhaps it is not surprising that we must invent all kinds of "rational explanations" that over-emphasize the importance of intra-psychic processes in determining how individuals think and behave. These "inventions" include most of our theories about "traits," "attitudes," "personality factors," and "mental illness."

Question: What similarities do you see between Festinger's theory of cognitive dissonance and Piaget's description of how "disequilibrium" drives us to change our perceptions of the world?

Inter-Group Conflict

For the most part, the studies on conformity, obedience, and cognitive dissonance have dealt with individual subjects put under strong psychological pressure to avoid conflict with other members of a group, or with their own value systems. From the standpoint of General Systems Theory, however, we can consider the group itself as a kind of "super-organism" that should be subject to social pressures to conform to the standards set by other groups or organizations. Groups should also show many of the same sorts of *internal processes* (structures and functions) as do individuals. Not unexpectedly, most of the factors that influence individual conformity and internal conflict have their direct parallels when we study the behavior of groups as groups.

Sherif's "Camp" Experiments

Muzafer Sherif was one of the first social psychologists to undertake scientific experiments on conflict between groups. Several years ago, Sherif and his colleagues helped run a camp for 11- and 12-year old boys. These youngsters were all from settled, well-adjusted, white, middle-class, Protestant homes. The boys were carefully selected to be happy, healthy individuals who had no difficulty getting along with the others. None of the boys knew each other before being admitted to the camp—nor did any of them realize that they were to be subjects in Sherif's experiments.

Eagles and Rattlers

The camp itself had two rather separate housing units. The boys living in one unit were called the "Eagles," while the other group's name was the "Rattlers." Because Sherif had purposely selected boys who were very similar in attitudes and behaviors, he predicted that the boys in each unit would form into a group very readily.

On the first day of camp, since there were no pre-existing friendships among the boys, group commitment and cohesion in both units was very low. Then Sherif gave both the Eagles and the Rattlers various real-life problems that could be solved only if the boys *in each separate unit* worked together effectively. As each unit overcame the difficulties Sherif put to it, the boys came to *like* the other boys in the same unit more and more. Both Eagles and Rattlers became a "natural group," and commitment to each of the groups (and to its emerging norms) increased significantly.

Competition versus Cooperation

After the Eagles and the Rattlers had shown considerable cohesion, Sherif introduced a series of contests designed to make the two groups hostile toward one another. As the groups competed for prizes, conflict developed, since one group could win only at the expense of the other. Very soon the Eagles were making nasty comments about the Rattlers, and vice-versa. Most of this hostility consisted of one group's *attributing* selfish or hostile motives to the other group. Name-calling, fights, and raids on the cabins belonging to the other group became commonplace. At the same time, Sherif reports, there was a marked *increase* in cooperativeness and cohesiveness within each of the groups.

Reducing Inter-Group Hostilities

Once the groups were at each other's throats, Sherif tried to bring them back together again. In his first experiment, Sherif attempted to unite the two groups by giving them a common enemy—a group of threatening outsiders. This technique worked fairly well, in that it brought the Eagles and the Rattlers closer together. But they still held *hatred* for their common enemy.

The next year Sherif repeated the group-conflict experiment with a different set of boys. Once inter-group hatred had reached its peak, Sherif brought the two units into very pleasant, non-competitive contact with each other. They sat together in the same dining hall while eating excellent food, and they watched movies together. However, this approach didn't succeed, for the groups merely used these occasions for fighting and shouting at each other.

Sherif then confronted the hostile groups with problem situations that could be solved only if the two units *cooperated* with each other. First, a water shortage "suddenly developed," and all the boys had to ration themselves. Next, Sherif offered to show the whole camp an exciting movie—but to see it, both units had to pool their resources. And one time when all the boys were particularly hungry, the transportation for their food "broke down." It could be fixed only if both groups worked together quickly and effectively.

Sherif reports that his technique worked beautifully. The two groups did indeed cooperate—reluctantly at first, but more and more willingly as their initial efforts were reinforced.

Before the crises occurred, almost none of the boys had friendships outside their units. Afterward, some 30 percent of the friendships were inter-group rather than in-group. During the hostile period, about one-third of the members of each group rated the members of the other group as being "stinkers," "smart-alecks," or "sneaky." Afterward, less than 5 percent of the boys gave the members of the other group such highly unfavorable ratings.

Conflicting Attitudes

When you feel conflict *within yourself*, as Festinger has shown, it is often because you hold two dissonant attitudes at the same time. In Chapter 25, in describing Harold Kelley's research on married couples, we noted that *dyadic conflicts* arise when the two partners attribute incorrect attitudes to each other. And when hostility arises *between two groups*, as Sherif has demonstrated, it is often their norms or group attitudes that are in conflict. Turning enemies into friends thus is sometimes a matter of changing their attitudes and actions toward one another.

In the next chapter we will take a careful look at how attitudes are formed, how consistent they are, how they are changed, and how attitudes relate to behaviors.

Question: Suppose you wished to help a group of whites get along better with a group of blacks. What would you try to do, and what changes would you hope to make in the attitudes and attributions of both groups in order to promote cooperation?

Summary

1. A **group** is a set of persons considered as a **social system**—a collection of two or more individuals who are psychologically related to or dependent upon one another.
2. There are many types of groups, including **formal membership groups, family groups, and ethnic groups**.
3. **Interaction groups** are made up of individuals who have frequent face-to-face encounters and who share **common attitudes**.
4. One of the major characteristics of any group is the **shared acceptance of group rules (goals)** by all the members.
5. The more similar the members, the more **cohesive** the group and the more **homogeneous** it becomes.
6. The more cohesive a group, the more **commitment** the members are likely to have toward the group and its goals.
7. Our **reference groups** are those we look to as social **models** or **norms**.
8. Reference groups give us **feedback** on our behavior by rewarding movements toward and punishing movements away from the **group norm**.
9. Whenever we make a judgment or give an opinion that is different from one shared by other group members, we typically find our-

selves under strong psychological **pressure to conform** more closely to the group standard or norm.

10. **Group pressures** become most effective when at least four group members have announced their judgments or opinions without being openly contradicted. If even one group member disagrees openly, **group cohesion** may be destroyed.

11. Some group members know when they are conforming (but do so anyway), but others **yield to pressures** because these pressures affect their **perceptions** of what has taken place. Conformity occurs even when the other members of the group are not **physically present**, if the subject hears their voices on tape.

12. Conformity behavior can be explained in terms of Helson's **Adaptation-level Theory**. A-L Theory states that judgments, perceptions, and attitudes are influenced by three factors—the stimulus, the background in which the stimulus appears, and the personality and past experience of the individual under pressure.

    a. **Stimulus factors** include the vagueness of the stimulus, the difficulty of the stimulus task, and the instructions given. **Attitudes** are easier to influence in conformity situations than are judgments of concrete facts.

    b. **Background factors** include the size of the group, how the group members feel about each other, how expert they are in the task at hand, the openness with which judgments must be made, and whether the group decision must be unanimous.

    c. Although there does not seem to be a "conformist personality," **yielders** in conformity experiments are frequently reported to be more **authoritarian** than are people who tend to resist group pressures. Conformity increases when it is **rewarded**.

13. Some people are **negative conformers** who tend to move away from the group norm no matter what they perceive it as being.

14. Milgram's research suggests that, when given orders from a higher authority, most of us tend to show **obedience** even if we sometimes end up hurting ourselves or others. We are particularly likely to obey orders if the people around us are doing so.

15. Most people tend to **underestimate** the amount that subjects will actually "obey" in Milgram's studies. Once exposed to his research, however, they tend to **overestimate** obedience because they assume it is due to **personality traits** rather than to **social influence**.

16. Latané's **theory of social impact** states that the impact of the social environment is determined by the **strength, immediacy**, and the **number** of people around you. **Bystander apathy** occurs in part because groups tend to **dilute** feelings of responsibility.

17. **Cognitive dissonance** develops when you hold two conflicting attitudes. According to Festinger, all people act to **reduce dissonance**, usually by changing the way they **perceive** the situation rather than by changing their actual behaviors.

19. **Social conflicts** can occur between groups that must compete for limited resources. These group conflicts are in many ways similar to conflicts between two people, or to dissonant attitudes within a single individual.

20. Sherif has shown **inter-group conflicts** can be reduced if the groups are either **threatened** by an outside danger or **rewarded** for working toward a common goal.

(Continued from page 617)

"All right, Mr. Kraus, please calm down and tell me what happened."

Norm Kraus leaned forward excitedly, hardly noticing the hardness of the chair in Professor Ward's office. "Well, the Blake experiment worked just like it was supposed to. I put a flashlight bulb inside an empty cocoa box to make the auto-kinetic light, and I got some friends to act as stooges. We made tape recordings of their voices, but I wanted to start with the situation where the subject was sitting right in the middle of my four friends."

Taking a quick breath, the young man hurried on before Ward could interrupt him.

"I got an undergraduate named Dan Gorenflo to volunteer for the experiment. I introduced Dan to the stooges, and then we all went into the lab. The cocoa box was hidden behind a black curtain that I didn't open until the lights were off when nobody could see what it was. Then I gave Dan and my friends the song and dance about airplanes moving on the horizon, turned off the overhead light, and left them to adapt to the dark."

"Sounds fine so far," Ward said.

Norm Kraus smiled. "The lab next door was my control room, where I ran the experiment. I could open the curtains, turn the flashlight off and on, and talk to the subjects over a loudspeaker. I put a mike right in front of Dan so I could hear his voice. And, of course, I could also hear the stooges and make sure they said what they were supposed to say."

Professor Ward nodded in an absent-minded fashion. "Yes, yes, just like Blake and his student did it. But how did your stooges know what to say?"

"I gave them their responses written out on a card."

Ward's eyebrows rose a millimeter or so. "And they read these numbers in the dark?"

Norm smiled broadly. "I wrote the numbers in dark-glow paint. The stooges could just make out the numbers if they squinted at them."

"Didn't this Dan Gorenflo fellow get suspicious?"

"No, sir. You see, I gave him a card with a scale marked across it in centimeters, also in dark-glow paint. It looked just like the cards the stooges had. I told them to look at their cards frequently to make sure they could judge how far 1 centimeter was."

Professor Ward coughed politely. "Not half bad. But how did it go?"

Norm beamed. "Beautifully, at least at first. I was sitting in the control room recording Dan's reactions. The first trial, he seemed to ignore the group. But on the next 14 trials, he hit the midpoint of their judgments right on the nose. I couldn't believe it! I was so excited at the end of the test that I rushed over to the next room to congratulate everybody and turn on the lights. And that's when it happened."

"Dare I ask what?"

"Well, Dan came bolting out of the lab and went rushing down the hall toward the toilet. I had to chase after him to catch up. He was shouting at me over his shoulder, 'Don't believe a word I said. You can't use my results.'"

"Did he tell you why?"

Norm nodded. "Yes, sir, he did. He said, 'You put me in a bad seat. I couldn't see the damned light at all. I just said whatever the other subjects said. You shouldn't do things like that, it curdles the stomach.'" Norm frowned rather theatrically. "And then Dan rushed into the john and was sick all over the place."

Ward picked up his pipe and stuffed it with tobacco. After a moment, he asked, "Why do you think Dan responded that way? Were the group pressures to conform that strong?"

Norm tried to hide the smirk that kept creeping over his face. "Serendipity, sir. After I left your office the last time, I looked the word up."

"Oh, yes, the Persian fairy tale about the three princes of Serendip, or Ceylon, as many people call it today. They were always going out on expeditions to search for something like iron and discovering a mountain of gold instead. Serendipity is the gift for finding very valuable things you weren't really looking for. Invaluable in scientific research, serendipity is." The Professor smiled rather warmly. "And you think you have the gift?"

Norm attempted a modest grin. "Well, I did luck onto something strictly by accident. It isn't every day you can upset a subject that much without laying hands on him."

"All right, Mr. Kraus, tell me exactly what happened."

Norm Kraus leaned back in the hard chair and relaxed. "Well, at first I couldn't figure it out, and neither could the stooges. But then I checked out each piece of equipment, just to make sure. Guess what I found?"

"I'm veritably breathless with anticipation," Ward said, smiling with encouragement.

"The flashlight bulb had burned out! As far as I can tell, the light went on during the first trial, but then it got shorted or something. I kept saying the light would go on . . . NOW. And the stooges kept giving their reports. But for the last 14 trials, the light simply didn't appear."

"Why didn't your friends, the stooges, notice it?"

"They were too busy trying to read the night-glow numbers on their little cards. Besides, it didn't matter to them if they couldn't see the light at all. Their job was just to read off their reports."

Professor Ward poked at the tobacco in his pipe with a match. "But why did the poor young man get sick?"

"How would you like it if you were sitting smack in the middle of four people who all acted as if they could see something that you saw once, but couldn't see thereafter? Dan told me later that he looked and looked, but the light just wasn't there. He thought he was going crazy. But he didn't want to upset the experiment, so he just sat there and gave the same reports the stooges were giving. He couldn't disobey orders by leaving, and he couldn't violate the group standard by saying he didn't see what everybody else was seeing. The stress was so great that his stomach curled up into a tight little ball. He said he'd never felt so much pressure in his life."

A stern tone crept back into Professor Ward's voice. "I hope you explained things to him and tried to make amends."

"Oh, yes sir. I took him over to the clinic and had the doctors examine him. They gave him a tranquilizer and two aspirins and told him to call them in the morning if he didn't feel better. While we were walking back to Dan's place from the clinic, I told him about what we had done, and why. Now he wants to be a stooge if we continue the experiment."

"If?"

Norm sighed dramatically. "Well, sir, it does seem we've discovered an interesting way to measure psychosomatic responses to social stress. I was talking to some of the doctors at the clinic about it. They thought we might do some joint research. You know, trying to figure out how group pressures toward conformity can lead to ulcers and hypertension and things like that. I realize that's not a replication of the Blake experiment, and I wouldn't want to break the rule . . ."

Professor Ward interrupted. "Mr. Kraus, we have two departmental rules about graduate students. The first is that they should begin by repeating a piece of published research. The second rule is that, if the student finds something exciting on his or her own while performing the replication, we expect them to follow it up. You wouldn't want to violate our departmental standards, now would you?"

Norm Kraus smiled slyly. "Oh, no sir."

"Good work, Norm. I'm pleased with your progress. Let me know if I can help, and keep me posted on how you come along. And by the way, why don't you call me Ron instead of Professor Ward?"

Norm could hardly believe his ears. "Yes sir, Profes . . . I mean, bloody good of you, Ron!"

Recommended Readings

Barnes, J.A. *Who Should Know What?: Social Science, Privacy and Ethics* (Cambridge, England: Cambridge University Press, 1979).

Berkowitz, Leonard, ed. *Advances in Experimental Social Psychology*, Vol. 12 (New York: Academic Press, 1979).

Festinger, Leon, ed. *Retrospections on Social Psychology* (New York: Oxford Press, 1980).

Hare, A. P., ed. *Handbook of Small Group Research*, 2nd ed. (New York: Free Press, 1976).

Helson, H. *Adaptation-level Theory* (New York: Harper & Row, 1964).

Latané, Bibb. "The psychology of social impact," *American Psychologist*, Vol. 36, No. 4 (1981), pp. 343–355.

Lindzey, Gardner, and Elliot Aronson, eds., *The Handbook of Social Psychology*, 2nd ed. (Reading, Mass.: Addison-Wesley, 1969).

Safer, Martin A. "Attributing Evil to the Subject, Not the Situation," *Personality and Social Psychology Bulletin*, Vol. 6, No. 2 (1980), pp. 205–209.

Persuasion, Communication, and Attitude Change

27

Did You Know That . . .

You are probably exposed to 1,500 different ads each day of your life?

Although you may reject propaganda if it comes from what you consider to be a biased source, later on you may forget the source and be influenced by the message?

Many student activists of the 1960's have found ways to maintain their "radical attitudes" despite pressures to change?

People involved in presenting propaganda are often more affected by it than is the intended audience?

Propaganda messages that arouse a high degree of fear are usually not as effective as low-fear appeals that tell you how to cope with the threatening situation?

Some youthful offenders who were exposed to a "scared straight" program actually became *worse* than did similar offenders not treated with scare tactics?

You cannot make valid ethical judgments about persuasive attempts unless you understand how strongly influenced you are by the attitudes and behaviors of the people around you?

"The Mind Benders"

Once upon a time, not so long ago, there was a shining kingdom-by-the-sea called Nacirema. The capital of Nacirema was Imperial City. At its very center, right on Empire Avenue, a concrete castle stretched up to scrape the sky. On the 100th floor of this castle there lived an Iron Duke, one of the Great Wizards of all Nacirema. The Duke's brand of magic was so strong that, for a great many years, he had influenced the minds of almost everyone in the country. But now, after years of mystical success, the Iron Duke feared that his occult powers might be slipping.

"Peasants" said the Duke loudly, glaring out of his 100th floor window at the people marching meekly below. "The peasants be damned!"

Humbly born to poor but proud parents named Mr. and Mrs. Steele, the Iron Duke had risen from obscurity to the Royal life through sheer guts and hard work—although neither the guts nor the labors were entirely his own. After obtaining a degree in Applied Arts (Basketweaving) from Imperial City College, the Duke had immediately take a position with the Royal Advertising Agency. By means of judicious apple-polishing—and a few lies and magical spells—he had climbed up the corporate ladder until he was just two rungs from the top: Vice-wizard in Charge of Practically Everything.

"Giants," said the Duke with a curse in his voice. "Double-damn the giants."

In Nacirema at this time there existed many giants—huge corporations that wanted to sell their products, but lacked the mystical power to do so effectively. So the giant corporations hired expert wizards such as those at the Royal Agency to create their advertising for them. Each giant was called a Sponsor, and the Agency kept track of each Sponsor's business in a separate financial account. Every account had its own wizardly Royal Executive who saw to it that things went right. It was the Executive's job to cast spells on the peasants to coax them into buying the giants' products, and to stroke the giants when they became unhappy. And as everyone on Empire Avenue knew, the Royal Surgeon had long ago determined that stroking giants can be hazardous to your wealth.

"And triple-damn the widget!" roared the Duke, still standing morosely at his window.

The Duke was, in fact, a glorified Account Executive. His Sponsor was a giant called General Widgets, Inc. In order to keep his job, the Duke had to perform many boring and trivial tasks, such as spending millions of dollars, traveling all over the world, attending parties with other members of the Imperial Court, and drinking three martinis for lunch each and every day. When the Duke had time, he tried as well to work a little magic on the giant's behalf.

As successful as the Duke had been, however, gold and power had not brought him security. He still quivered and quaked whenever His Highness, the Chairman of the Royal Agency Board, or His Grace, the Presiding Wizard, called the Duke on the magic carpet. He quivered and quaked even more when the giant called him on the telephone—as the giant had just done—complaining bitterly that widget sales were busting instead of booming. The giant blamed the Duke for the drop in widget sales, and threatened to hire some other agency. The Duke knew that if this evil event occurred, His Highess, the Chairman, would lose his royal temper—and the Duke would lose his Royal head.

As the Duke stood looking out of the castle window at the traffic moving along Empire Avenue far below, cold fear gripped his cast-iron guts. Was he losing his magic touch? Could he think of a new spell to cast on the peasants that would motivate them to buy all those unwanted widgets the Sponsor had sitting in the warehouse? What had the Future in store for him?

At this point in time, Fate intervened: There came a gentle knocking at the castle gate.

"Prithee, enter!" roared the Duke.

A young girl with a crown of golden hair burst happily into the Iron Duke's office. Trailing right behind her was an equally happy and longhaired young man.

"Father!" the girl cried, kneeling quickly before the Duke and then embracing him warmly.

"Princess!" responded the Duke gruffly. "I thought thee still at Lady Bennington's School for Gentlewomen. What brings thee to town?"

"Father, I wish to present Rodney, my Prince Charming."

"Hail to thee, Rodney, and welcome to our humble abode," cried the Duke, extending one of his huge hands.

"Pleased to meet you, Mr. Steele," said Rodney, shaking hands perhaps a bit too eagerly, his flowing locks bobbing as he did so.

"Just call me Duke," the older man said, shaking his head in dismay at the length of Rodney's hair.

"Yes, Sir, Mr. Duke," Rodney responded.

"Rodney has come to ask you for my hand in marriage, Father. You see, Rodney is my soul-mate."

"Rodney is what?" demanded the Duke in an appalled tone of voice.

"He's a Taurus. And I'm a Libra. That makes us soul-mates," the Princess said, a gentle smile on her radiant face.

"I had thought thee a Virgo," murmured the Duke.

"Ah, well," the lass said defiantly, "now I am Liberated."

"Harrumph," said the Duke ominously, casting steely eyes at his daughter's escort. "But what does thy Prince Charming do for a living?"

"Rodney's a genius," the girl said earnestly.

"Gadzooks!" groaned the Duke loudly. "Then he wants a job."

The young princess caressed her father. "Well, you're always saying that everyone who serves you is either a fool or a knave."

The Duke took a monogrammed handkerchief out of his pocket, mopped his noble brow, and then turned back to the window. "I regret that I cannot add your princeling to my retinue. I fear I have giant problems."

"You mean, the *Sponsor*?" the Princess whispered, a trace of terror in her voice.

The Duke nodded sagely. "General Widgets. They have doubled their budget for advertising, but sales are lower than a dragon's belly. We've tried every trick known to man, and a few known only to women, but the damned peasants just won't buy. If the Olde Iron Duke doesn't come up with some new magical incantations right away, his name is mudde."

"Yes, Sir, Mr. Mudde," responded Rodney.

"But what's wrong, Father? Why aren't your advertisements working? It's the same old widget it's always been."

"I know not," replied the Duke. "Perhaps thy genius soul-mate can enlighten us."

Rodney cleared his throat. "Widgets stink," he said quietly.

"What!" roared the Duke.

"Widgets stink. They're too big, too expensive, too clumsy, and Sir Ralph Nadir says they're unsafe."

"Nonsense!" cried the Duke haughtily. "You just don't understand, my boy. The product doesn't matter. It's the magic in the advertisement that counts. Royal prides itself on being able to bend the peasant minds whatever way the Sponsors wish it bent."

"How do you work that kind of miracle?" Rodney asked innocently.

"Follow along, my boy, and I'll show thee how magic is made."

The Duke led Rodney and the Princess down a long golden-carpeted corridor into a huge, well-lighted room. A bank of computers lined one wall. The machines clicked and chirped softly as large numbers of Elves scurried about, feeding incantations into the devices.

"This be our Market Research Department," the Duke said. "We gather every known fact on the Nacirema peasants and insert the gatherings into our Merlin computer. We know where the peasants live, how much gold they earn, what visual entertainments they watch, and whether they've ever bought a widget. Isn't that marvelous?"

Rodney didn't seem overly impressed. "What use do you make of all this information?"

The Duke frowned. "Forsooth, I never bothered to ask. Anyway, it really doesn't matter. It's the Creative Department that actually conjures up the magic. I'll show thee what I mean."

The Duke pressed a button on the wall to summon an elevator. "We lock the creative types in the dungeon, to keep them out of mischief." He ushered Rodney and the Princess into the Royal Lift.

Moments later the doors opened out on a dark basement cavern. Several yards away was a roaring wood fire. Huddled around the blaze was a mixed bag of tiny Gnomes and Witches dressed in oddly colored clothes. One of the Witches was stirring a bubbling pot that hung above the fire. The Gnomes passed a large, smoking object among themselves.

"What's that peculiar smell?" asked Rodney, a sly grin on his face.

"Incense," coughed the Duke discreetly. "They use it in casting their occult spells."

The smallest of the Gnomes rushed up to them and bowed several times. "Most noble liege lord, what brings thee to our nether regions? What action, fair or foul, has caused thee to descend to our dank depths? In short, what's cooking, Wiz?"

"Thy flesh and mine, I greatly fear," the Duke said grumpily. "The Sponsor hath just called. That last magic potion you created turned sour, and widget sales are faltering like a knight in a daze. If we cannot discover some spectacular new means of ensnaring the peasants' desires, thy whole crew will be back to reading palms by next week."

The tiny Gnome scratched tenderly under his arm, a sad look on his wizened face. Then he suddenly brightened. "I've got it, your Wizardship! The Double Whammy, the Evil Eye, and the Final Curse! We'll mix them all together in our little pot and boil up the most magical brew the world has ever smelt! We'll push more widgets through the market place in a week than the Sponsor can make in a month. Leave it to us, Wiz!"

"If you don't succeed, I'll personally turn thee back into a pumpkin," said the Duke.

The Gnome bobbed his head respectfully, retreating back toward the fire. One of the Witches came up and whispered in his ear. "Oh, your Wizardship," the Head Gnome called after the departing trio. "We need a new lid for our pot, and sundry things like that . . ."

"That's what we give thee an expense account for," replied the Duke, ringing for the Royal Lift.

Once back in the 100th floor office, the Duke poured himself a glass of Sir Johnny Walker's Black Magic, and took his glass to the window. "That be it. You've seen almost the entire Royal operation. But wherewith have we failed?"

"You've shown us *everything*?" asked Rodney.

"Methinks so," replied the Duke.

"Then I have the solution to your problem," said Rodney proudly.

"Oh, Father, I told you he was a genius!" cried the Princess pridefully.

"Young man, although I find it difficult to believe, perhaps I have underestimated thee," said the Duke craftily. "If you can help me keep the widget account, I will not only give thee a job, but the Princess' hand in wedlock as well."

"What kind of a job will you give Rodney?" interjected the Princess practically.

"Well," responded the Duke, "the Head Gnome needs a new assistant. And there are always availabilities as a Merlin-tender."

"I'm more the Wizard Executive type myself," mused Rodney hopefully.

"Let us haggle over unseemly trifles later on," said the Duke brusquely. "Tell me thy bright idea first."

Rodney looked the Duke squarely in the eye and spoke quietly for two minutes.

As Rodney talked, a look of great astonishment blossomed on the Duke's visage. When the young man had finished, the Iron Duke turned pale as a goblin's bedsheet.

"Thou canst not mean it?" cried the Duke.

"Ah, but I do," responded Rodney sincerely.

The Iron Duke collapsed in a dead faint.

(Continued on page 655.)

Ads and Attitudes

What brand of toothpaste do you use? No matter what your answer, there's a much more interesting question to ask: How did you happen to pick that particular brand? Was it the flavor that attracted you to it, or the approval of a dentists' organization, or the low price? Or did you "choose" it because it's the same brand that the rest of your family uses?

Whatever reason you give, chances are that you probably won't list *advertising* as the factor behind your choice. And yet, if you think about it, how would you have known about this brand if it had never been advertised? Furthermore, if you were subjected to "blind" tests (where you couldn't tell which brand you were trying), are you absolutely confident you could pick your favorite toothpaste or brand of beer, soup, or cigarette from others on the market?

Most of us like to think our decisions to buy a particular product, to vote for a certain politician, or our opinions about war and sex and minority groups are *rational* decisions. However, while we do sometimes think through such matters logically, our viewpoints are often created *unconsciously*, without our being aware of how various forces in our social environments shape our thoughts and preferences. One such force is advertising.

You probably encounter about 1,500 ads each day of your life. Some of these advertisements appear on radio and televison. Others show up in books, magazines, and newspapers. And still others flash out from billboards and signs, from bumper stickers on cars, and from the shelves of supermarkets. Americans spend more money each year on advertising than they do on education, or on pollution control, mental health, poverty relief, or scientific research. If the advertisers didn't believe that they could influence your attitudes toward their products (whether or not you were aware of their efforts), would they spend so much?

"IT WON'T BOTHER US IF WE'RE NOT ALLOWED TO AIM OUR ADS AT THE KIDS. THE ADULTS ARE EASIER TO FOOL ANYWAY."

Public relations. Most large firms and government agencies have employees whose jobs are to see that the firm or agency receives favorable attention in the news media. These employees are typically called "public relations specialists," because their task is making sure that "the public" knows about—and likes—the firm or agency. In fact, these PR specialists are often little more than "flacks," despite their fancier title. E.L. Bernays, who invented the term "public relations" back in the 1920's (and who was a nephew of Sigmund Freud), once described PR as being "the engineering of consent." It was the public whose attitudes were to be "engineered" by PR specialists, and not vice-versa.

Public Relations

Nor are advertisers the only ones who wish to bend your opinions to their purposes. Almost every press release put out by the government, or by individual politicians, is aimed at getting you to think favorably of the person or agency involved. News stories about movie stars, rock musicians, professional athletes, and university professors are almost always "handouts" from publicity agents. In fact, up to *90 percent* of what passes for "news" on television and in the newspapers actually comes from **public relations** specialists and not from a reporter who has "dug up the facts" on her or his own time.

Whenever a teacher criticizes or praises a certain theory, whenever a religious leader preaches, whenever a parent "lectures" or a friend offers advice—aren't these people trying to affect your attitudes? And whenever you "dress up to make a good impression," or compliment someone in authority, aren't you "advertising" too?

In the past several chapters we have talked at length about how attitudes (or personality traits or types of behavior) are created. In this chapter, let us look at why attitudes are important, why some of them remain fairly stable throughout our lives, and why other attitudes appear to be so changeable. We will then discuss the relationship between attitudes and behaviors, and the ethics involved in trying to persuade people to change.

Question: *How has the author of this book attempted to influence your attitudes toward psychology?*

Attitude Stability

In an earlier chapter we defined an attitude as a relatively enduring way of thinking, feeling, and behaving toward an object, person, group, or idea. And, as we noted, attitudes almost always involve some bias or pre-judging on your part. When you *label* someone as "stingy" or "psychotic," you both state an attitude and reveal the way in which

You are probably exposed to more than 1500 advertisements a day.

Theodore Newcomb

you perceive the person. In a sense, then, attitudes are *perceptions* (cognitive schemas) that involve emotional feelings, and that pre-dispose you to act in a certain way.

You could not do without attitudes, for many reasons. To begin with, the attitude (or schema) that you have of someone or of some object allows you to predict the future behavior of that person or thing. If you made no pre-judgments about things, you would have difficulties walking across a street or carrying on even the simplest of social conversations. For example, when you say that you "hate pollution" to a man wearing an ecology button on his shirt, you not only can predict the man's response but also influence his attitude toward (or perception of) you.

Attitudes and Memories

A second important aspect of attitudes has to do with memory. As you learned in earlier chapters, you seem to file your experiences in Long-term Memory according to certain *categories*. That is, you attach "cognitive labels" to the important features of the experience, and then file the memory according to these "labels." When you try to remember something that happened in the past, you search your memory files using this same set of cognitions. Another word for "labels," of course, is *attitudes*.

Psychologists believe that the more you know about a person, thing, or idea, the more *stable* your attitude will usually be. Likewise, the

more strongly you feel about something, the more difficult it will probably be to get you to change the "memory labels" attached to that thing. Furthermore, the better your attitude allows you to predict future events or inputs, and the more you are rewarded for holding a certain percept, the less susceptible that percept or attitude is to being changed.

Since the attitudes of individuals are affected by the groups to which they belong, *attitude consistency* is also a property of social groups and organizations. Generally speaking, the more important a given attitude is to the continued functioning of a group, the less likely it is that group members will give up or change this attitude.

Question: *Studies show that most college students have attitudes very similar to those held by their parents. Can you think of at least five reasons why this might be the case?*

Newcomb's Study of Bennington Women

As Theodore Newcomb notes, liberal arts colleges are populated by professors who often have very liberal political opinions. When a student from a politically conservative family arrives on such a campus, the student often comes under fairly intense social pressure to change his or her attitudes. If you were such a student, do you think you would change, or would you retain, your old attitudes despite the pressure?

Bennington College

Newcomb answered this question many years ago. At the time he began his research, he was teaching at Bennington, a women's college in Vermont noted for its fine programs in the liberal arts. Because the student body was limited to about 600, Newcomb was able to work with the entire college population in his study of political attitudes.

Most of the women attending Bennington in the mid-1930's came from wealthy and rather conservative homes. The faculty members, however, were quite liberal in their views. Indeed, they felt duty-bound to familiarize the students with the social and political implications of a Depression-torn America and a war-threatened world. Therefore, the faculty encouraged the students to become politically active and socially concerned.

The college itself, nestled between the Taconic and the Green mountains of Vermont, was physically isolated from much of the rest of the world. The nearest town, a village of less than 15,000 people, offered few excitements. The students visited the town infrequently, and went home for the weekend less than once a month. Hence, the students made up what advertising executives call "a captive audience."

Student Reference Groups

In the first part of his research, Newcomb found that the more prestige or *status* a woman had among her fellow students, the more likely it was that she was also very liberal in her views. Conservative students typically were looked down upon; liberal students were very much looked up to. Seniors were significantly less conservative than were freshmen.

Under these conditions, the entire college population acted rather like a **reference group** that rewarded liberal attitudes and punished political conservatism. Those women who identified with the college community tended to become much more liberal during their four years at Bennington. By their own admission, many of them were quite conscious of how they had changed. As one woman put it, "What I most wanted here was intellectual approval of teachers and the more advanced students. Then I found you can't be reactionary and be intellectually respectable."

Those women who resisted the liberal college tradition tended to identify more with their parents than with their classmates. As one woman said, "I'd like to think like the college leaders, but I'm not bold enough and I don't know enough. So the college trend means little to me. I guess my family influence has been strong enough to counterbalance the college influence." Newcomb notes, incidentally, that this woman was given to severe emotional upsets and told the college staff that she felt "alone and helpless except when with her parents."

Reference group. That group of people whom you look to for your social feed-forward (models, "rules and regulations") or against whose behaviors you measure or judge your own actions.

Question: How many Bennington women would have become politically liberal had they lived at home and commuted to their classes? What if they had taken most of their courses by television and seldom met their teachers or other students?

25 Years Later

To find out how their attitudes would change over time, Newcomb followed 150 of the most liberal of these women for the next 25 years of their lives. Although he had originally suspected they might revert to a more conservative position, this turned out not to be the case with many of them. In fact, during the entire 25 years, most of the women remained liberal in their outlooks *despite family pressures*. But why?

Newcomb reports that most of these women *deliberately* set out to remain liberal in spite of their social backgrounds. They tended to select liberal (or non-conservative) husbands who would reinforce their political views. They found little pockets of liberalism in their environments and tried to stay entirely within these pockets. And they kept in close touch with their Bennington classmates who were also liberal (and tended to ignore those who weren't).

Newcomb believes that if maintaining a given attitude is important enough to you, you will consciously or unconsciously select environments that will continue to support that attitude. You may also shut out incoming sensory messages that might tend to disrupt the attitudes you already hold (a form of *autistic hostility*).

1960's Student Activists

The November 1980 issue of *Psychology Today* reports a study by Alberta J. Nassi that confirms Newcomb's findings. Nassi looked at how many of the "student activists" at Berkeley had fared 15 years after they had been arrested in the 1964 sit-in. Nassi reports that these individuals "do not appear to have grown out of the political philosophy that galvanized their activist youth." That is, they still hold relatively radical or liberal attitudes toward most things. Nassi notes that they have maintained these attitudes much as the Bennington women did—by seeking environments that would protect them from change. Most of them had found jobs in "social service" and "creative" occupations, and tended to socialize with people who held similar views.

Studies of people who belonged to the "Free Speech" movement in 1964 showed that they have maintained their radical beliefs by seeking out environments that shelter them from conflicting viewpoints.

The one change Nassi does report is that the former activists were now "strikingly uninvolved in political activities." In this respect they differ little from their non-activist former classmates who, Nassi says, also tend to shun the political scene.

The studies by Newcomb and Nassi are among a very few aimed at measuring *stability* of attitudes. Attitude *change* is much easier to investigate, in no small part because the subjects need not be studied over such a long time span. Indeed, it seems that most of what we know about attitude stability comes from experiments designed to change people's opinions. So now let us look at the factors that bring about shifts in attitudes. Perhaps this information will be useful not only if you wish to change someone's mind—but also if you wish to protect yourself against the influence of the millions of people who would like to persuade you to be different than you presently are.

Question: Ethnic and religious minority groups often tend to "flock together" even when they are economically free to do otherwise. How might this tendency be related to a desire to maintain attitude stability within the group?

Persuasion and Attitude Change

Suppose you are in the market for a new automobile. You shop around, looking at Fords, Plymouths, Chevrolets, Eagles, and a number of other cars. As you can now see, you come to this situation with a number of biases, or attitudes, about cars in general and these automobiles in particular. If your prior attitude toward Fords is highly favorable, how might a Chevy sales person try to change your viewpoint?

In 1940, Solomon Asch pointed out that there are two basic ways to induce attitude change toward an object like an automobile. The first way is to change the *object* or product itself, so that your own perception of the car simply isn't **consonant** with the facts any more. The second way is to leave the car "as is" but somehow get you to change your perception of its good and bad points. In either case, the sales person must somehow get certain types of information across to you. For without new *sensory inputs* of some kind, your attitudes will presumably remain very stable. Thus the most important aspect of **persuasion** is the *flow of communication* from the outside world into your nervous system.

Asch remarks that, in most real-life situations, attitude change usually comes about because of some change in the *object* of the attitude.

When psychologists study attitude change scientifically, however, they don't always have the power to make changes in the objects of your attitudes. If you wished to examine the biases that people have toward Escorts, for instance, could you readily get the Ford Motor Company to build a totally new product just to satisfy the rigid requirements of your experiment? The most scientists can usually do, therefore, is to try to get subjects to view reasonably familiar objects (or people or ideas) in a new light. To do so, the psychologist often attempts to control some aspect of the *communication process*.

Question: What sorts of television commentators are you most likely to watch or to place faith in?

The Communication Process

Psychologists tend to look at persuasive communication as having four main factors—the communicator, the message, the audience, and the feedback loop that exists between the audience and the communicator.

The *communicator* is the person (or group) trying to induce the attitude change. As we will see, the way that the audience *perceives* the communicator often affects the readiness with which the audience will change.

The *message* is the information that the communicator transmits to the audience. The type of language or pictures used, and the channel through which the communicator chooses to transmit the message, can be of critical importance.

The *audience* is the person or group whose attitude is to be changed. Obviously a clever communicator will wish to know as much as possible about the personalities and attitudinal characteristics of the audience in order to make the message as persuasive as possible.

Until fairly recently, the *audience-communicator feedback loop* was perhaps the least-studied aspect of the communication process. Yet it is of crucial importance (see Fig. 27.1). Unless the communicator knows what type of response the audience *actually* makes to the message, the communicator is very likely to misjudge the success of the persuasive project.

Let us see, then, what kinds of experimental evidence social scientists have provided so that we can understand the effects of each of these four influences on persuasion.

Question: Why do you think the audience-communicator feedback loop was so little studied until recently?

"AT LEAST WITH WASHINGTON AS PRESIDENT, WE WON'T HAVE A CREDIBILITY GAP TO WORRY ABOUT."

Consonant (KON-so-nant). From the Latin words *con*, meaning "with," and *sonare*, meaning "to sound." Consonant thus means "to sound at the same time," or "to agree." The consonants are those letters of the alphabet that are "sounded with" the vowels (a, e, i, o, u, and y).

Persuasion (purr-SWAY-zhun). From the Latin words meaning "to urge" or "to advise." To persuade is to induce someone to adopt a certain attitude or behavior by argument or pleading, or to win someone over to your way of thinking.

Credibility (kred-ih-BILL-it-tee). From the Latin words meaning "worthy of lending money to." Literally, the power or ability to inspire belief.

The Communicator

If your best friend told you that a given product was incredibly good, would you be more likely to believe this communication than if you heard a TV announcer say the same thing on a television ad? Chances are you'd put more **credibility** in your friend's endorsement than in the TV announcer's. And credibility seems to be one of the most influential traits a communicator can possess.

The first reliable experiments on communicator credibility came from a group of Yale psychologists almost 30 years ago. This group of scientists, led by Carl I. Hovland and Irving L. Janis, were pioneers in the study of the communication process. Some of their early findings have stood the test of time. However, as we will see, many of their conclusions are of limited value because they were *laboratory* studies. And the real world is—for better or worse—much more complicated than scientific laboratories are. Suppose we first look at what Hovland, Janis, and their colleagues found. We will discuss the limitations of their findings a little later.

High Credibility Sources

In one of the first of the Yale studies, Hovland and Walter Weiss tested the influence of "trustworthiness" (credibility) on attitude change. They began by making a list of "communicators" they figured were very trustworthy, and another list of communicators they figured few people would trust. The "high credibility sources" included the *New England Journal of Biology and Medicine*, a Nobel-Prize-winning physicist, and *Fortune* magazine. The "low credibility sources" included a noted gossip columnist, the Russian newspaper *Pravda*, and a well-known US publication that specialized in scandals and sex-oriented stories. When Hovland and Weiss asked students to judge the credibility of these sources, about 90 percent of the subjects rated the first group as being very trustworthy and rated the second group as being exceptionally untrustworthy.

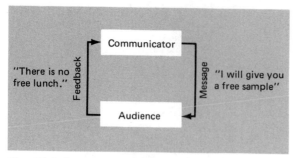

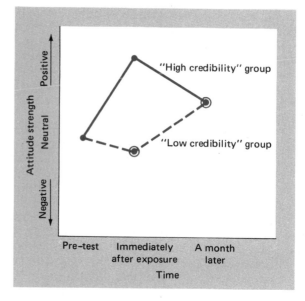

Fig. 27.1. Successful communication depends on feedback from the audience to the communicator. **(left)**

Fig. 27.2. The "sleeper effect." Effects of exposure to propaganda on "effectiveness of atomic submarines." **(right)**

Next, Hovland and Weiss tested the "attitude toward the effectiveness of atomic submarines" in two similar groups of students. They found that most of the students were rather neutral about this highly complex topic. If we were plotting their attitudes on a graph, we would say the students were right in the middle—at the "neutral" point on the graph shown in Figure 27.2.

Hovland and Weiss then wrote a "message" in which they argued that atomic submarines would indeed be a very important weapon in any future war. They showed this message to the two groups of students. The first group was told that the message came from one of the high credibility sources (such as *Fortune*). The second group was told that the message came from one of the low credibility sources. Immediately after exposing the students to the message, Hovland and Weiss retested their subjects' attitudes.

As you might surmise, the subjects in the "high credibility" group tended to accept the arguments and their attitudes became significantly more positive. The students in the "low credibility" group tended to reject the arguments as being "biased and untrustworthy." If anything, their attitudes became slightly more negative.

Apparently you tend to move *toward* the position of someone you trust, and *away* from the position of someone you distrust—even if this movement involves giving up your original attitude.

Question: *How does this study compare with the experiment on "negative conformity" mentioned in the last chapter?*

The "Sleeper Effect"

Had Hovland and Weiss stopped their work at this point, we might well have misunderstood the real importance of communicator credibility. However, they continued by retesting all their subjects a month later. To their surprise, they found significant attitude changes in both groups over this period of time. The attitudes of the "high credibility" subjects became significantly *less* positive, while the attitudes of the "low credibility" subjects became significantly *more* positive. As Fig. 27.2 suggests, the students had apparently forgotten the *source* of their information on submarines, but remembered the *arguments* rather well. Hovland and Weiss call this the **sleeper effect**.

The sleeper effect suggests that the credibility of a source has an immediate and often strong effect on whether you accept or reject incoming information. However, once the message has gotten through to you, chances are that you will soon forget the source and recall only the information itself.

Question: *There is an exception to the sleeper effect. What do you think would have happened had Hovland and Weiss reminded their subjects of the message source before testing their attitudes a month later?*

Credibility and "First Impressions"

A number of further experiments by Hovland, Janis, and their associates demonstrate that the factors which influence credibility are much the same as those which influence first impressions (see Chapter 25). People whom you like, or who are like you, or who seem to be acting naturally rather than "playing roles," are people whom you typically trust. Persons with high social status—such as doctors, scientists, and church leaders—

are somehow more believable than are people with low social status. In the long run, then, it is your *perception* of the communicator—and what motives you *attribute* to this person—that determines how much you will be influenced.

Question: *If you were trying to sell a cold remedy on television, what kinds of TV actors would you choose, and how would you have them dress?*

The Message

In 1956, University of Michigan professor Sam Eldersveld decided to run for mayor in Ann Arbor as a "class project" to help his political science students learn about politics in the "real world." Eldersveld planned and carried out his campaign with the assistance of his students. The students not only performed several interesting experiments during the heat of the contest, but they also managed to get their professor elected (he became a very effective mayor).

In one of the Ann Arbor studies, potential voters were approached in one of three ways. Either the voter received four mail appeals to vote, or the voter was contacted in person, or both. A fourth group of voters served as an "untreated control group." A much higher percentage of the voters contacted in person actually voted than did voters who received just mailings (or no messages at all). The combination of mail appeals and personal contact was no more effective than was just asking the voter in person.

In another study, Eldersveld compared the *content* of the appeals. Some voters were given highly emotional arguments—either by mail or by personal contact. Others were given very rational reasons for voting. As it turned out, the *content* of the message seemingly didn't much matter. But again, personal contact was much more effective in "bringing out the vote" than were mail appeals—no matter what the content of the appeals happened to be.

Question: *How could you be sure that the voters sent messages by mail actually read them?*

Fear-Arousing Messages

Many of us seem to believe that people would behave in more socially acceptable ways if someone in authority just threatened them enough. In recent years, for instance, nation-wide campaigns against venereal disease, the use of hard drugs, cigarette smoking, and the dangers of not wearing seat belts have employed the "hellfire and damnation" approach. That is, the main thrust of the propaganda has been to describe in exquisite detail the terrible consequences of various types of misbehavior.

Sleeper effect. As Hovland and Weiss showed, people tend to remember the facts of an argument rather well but often forget the source of those facts. The credibility you place in a source may cause you to accept or reject a message as soon as you see or hear it. However, the facts are somehow "sleeping" in your Long-term Memory and will emerge on their own long after you have forgotten who told you those facts.

But are such threats really as effective as we sometimes think them to be? The experimental evidence suggests that the actual effects of "the punitive approach" are more subtle and complex than we might previously have guessed.

In 1953, Irving Janis and Seymour Feshback investigated the effects of fear-arousing communications on high school students. These scientists picked "dental hygiene" as their topic. They wrote three different 15-minute lectures on tooth decay. The first was a "high fear" lecture that contained 71 references to pain, cancer, paralysis, blindness, mouth infections, inflamed gums, ugly or discolored teeth, and dental drills. The second or "moderate fear" lecture was somewhat less threatening. But the third or "minimal fear" lecture was quite different. It made no mention at all of pain and disease, but instead suggested ways of avoiding cavities and decayed teeth through proper dental hygiene.

Janis and Feshback presented each of the three appeals to a different group of 50 high school students (a fourth group of students heard no lecture at all and thus served as a control group). Janis and Feshback found that *immediately afterward*, the subjects exposed to the "high fear" lecture were highly impressed with what they heard. A week later, however, only 28 percent of them had brushed their teeth more often, and 20 percent of them were actually doing worse. In marked contrast, the "low fear" students were not particularly impressed with the lecture—but a week later 50 percent of them were "brushing better" and only 14 percent were doing a worse job.

The high fear appeal apparently evoked strong emotional responses in the students, many of whom thought that being frightened was somehow "good for them." When it came to actually *changing behaviors*, though, the high-fear message simply didn't work as well as did the minimal-fear message. In fact, for reasons we will make clear in a moment, the high-fear propaganda seems to have had exactly the opposite long-term effect than one might have predicted.

Example of a "high-fear" campaign to change attitudes. (How effective was it?) **(top)**

Although the prisoners who participated in the Scared Straight program enjoyed their attempts to "straighten out" juvenile offenders, there are conflicting reports on how effective the program actually was. **(left)**

Counter-Propaganda

Propagandists often point out that it is not enough to change the attitudes an audience has—you must also make sure that the audience resists any further attempts that might push them back toward their original beliefs. Effective propaganda, then, is that which not only causes attitude shifts but also protects against *counter-propaganda*.

A week after the high school students in the Janis-Feshbach experiment had listened to the dental hygiene lectures, the experimenters exposed the students to information that contra-

dicted what they had originally been told. The students were then asked whether they believed this counter-propaganda or not.

Twice as many subjects in the high-fear group were affected by the counter-persuasion as were subjects in the minimal-fear group. Janis and Feshbach conclude that "under conditions where people will be exposed to competing communications dealing with the same issues, the use of a strong fear appeal will tend to be less effective than a minimal appeal in producing stable and persistent attitude changes."

Question: Given the data on the subject, why do you think so many people in the US still believe that "high-fear" propaganda works?

Fear and Failure

Why don't fear and threats work the way many people think they should? The answer seems to be twofold. To begin with, as Janis and Feshbach report, there seems to be a tendency for people to repress frightening information. Second, and perhaps more important, our emotions can *arouse* us, but they don't always *direct* us in our thoughts and behaviors. Janis and Feshbach believe that fear-inducing communications focus your attention on *problems* and not on *solutions*. You become excited by the terrifying message, but you don't know what you must do to avoid or prevent the disaster the message warns you of. In fact, the fearful message may do little more than convince you that disaster is inevitable, and so you give up and do nothing at all.

Scared Straight

In the spring of 1979, a film called "Scared Straight" was shown on many US television stations. The movie shows how inmates at a prison in New Jersey use "scare tactics" to frighten troubled young people into avoiding further scrapes with the law. The youths spend several hours in the prison, mostly listening to the convicts describe the effects of homosexual rape, fights, and prison brutality. The film is highly dramatic, and implies strongly that the "Scared Straight" program has been a great success. The film won an Academy Award in 1979, and after it was broadcast, many state legislatures debated whether or not to make such treatment compulsory for all juvenile offenders.

Unfortunately, the actual data did not support the effectiveness either of the first version of the program or of the film's fear-arousing message. In the August 1979 issue of *Psychology Today*, Rutgers professor James O. Finckenauer reports on a detailed study he made of the juvenile offenders involved in these jail visitations. Finckenauer discovered that only some 60 percent of the juveniles in the program avoided further arrest. By contrast, some 90 percent of highly similar offenders in Finckenauer's control group "went straight" *without being scared*. Worse than this, of 19 youngsters who had no criminal record before they visited the New Jersey prison, 6 later broke the law.

Because of Finckenauer's research, the "Scared Straight" program was drastically changed. The fear-arousing messages were toned down, and most of the youngsters were also given "one-on-one" counseling and were encouraged to write or call the prisoners for help. The prisoners then could monitor and encourage any progress the youngsters made. In a 1980 study, Sidney Langer reports that 47 percent of the "Scared Straight" youngsters showed improved behaviors, as against only 25 percent of a similar group not in the program.

There is, however, a basic flaw in Langer's reseach. His experimental subjects were both

Deterrent (dee-TURR-ent). From a Latin word meaning "to frighten, or to discourage from acting." Punishment is usually thought to be a highly effective deterrent that keeps "sane" people from committing crimes. In fact, many studies suggest that fear of punishment seldom keeps people from doing things that they really want to do, or that they find particularly rewarding. If punishment really deterred criminals, those countries with the most punitive laws would be those with the lowest crime rates, which doesn't happen to be the case. Closer to home, punitive laws have obviously not stopped people in the US from smoking marijuana, or from exceeding the 55 mile per hour speed limit.

"scared" and given individual counseling. His control subjects *got neither type of treatment*. But he credits the "scare tactics" for the success, not the counseling. As we will see, the "scares" may actually have been less effective than just giving the youngsters guidance and skill training.

Question: *Why do you think the prisoners doing the "scaring" were so convinced that the program was a great success? How would their attitudes compare with the leaders of therapy groups (discussed in Chapter 24) who incorrectly believed that* all *members of their groups showed improvement?*

Nothing Succeeds Like Success

According to *attribution theory*, you see your own actions as being a response to environmental circumstances, but you see the actions of others as being determined primarily by their personality or character traits. Thus you may believe that "punishment works" because others need a fear-evoking **deterrent** to keep their anti-social impulses under control. But the data show that many criminals—particularly youthful offenders—simply don't have the social skills to succeed in a complex environment. What would happen if juvenile delinquents were given skill-training rather than being threatened?

In 1979, Carolyn Mills and Tim Walter gave an answer to this question. They reported achieving a marked reduction in anti-social behaviors among a group of youthful offenders who were given special training in how to get and hold a job. Mills and Walter began with a group of 76 young people aged 14–17 who had been arrested 4 times or more prior to the start of the experiment. Mills and Walter randomly selected 23 of the young people to be a "no-treatment control group." The other 53 were put into a behavioral training program.

In the first part of their program, Mills and Walter recruited a number of local business people who were willing to offer employment to youths who were "on probation." These business

Carolyn Mills   Tim Walter

Almost 95 percent of the US population knew about President John F. Kennedy's death within 90 minutes after the first news bulletin, but the vast majority learned about the assassination from friends and relatives rather than from the news media.

people signed contracts agreeing, among other things, to give the subjects' day-by-day feedback on their performance and to meet with the experimenters weekly to discuss the youths' progress.

Next, Mills and Walter asked the youths to make a list of the behaviors they thought would be expected of them while working. If the subjects could not guess, they were given a list of job-appropriate activities produced by the employers. The youths then "role-played" the behaviors they thought would help them get and hold the job. They were rewarded for learning these skills and, once they were on the job, they got written feedback *daily* by the employer.

When the subjects had been successful "on the job" for a period of several weeks, Mills and Walter began to fade out their assistance. The experimenters also began trying to help the youths gain skills in handling personal and school-related problems (rather than focusing primarily on job-related tasks). All in all, the subjects were followed for a period of 18 months or more.

Mills and Walter report that more than 90 percent of the experimental subjects had no further arrests, while but 30 percent of the control subjects stayed out of trouble. Some 85 percent of the experimental subjects stayed in school, but only 14 percent of the control subjects did.

Mills and Walter note two further points of interest. At the beginning of their intervention program, their subjects got considerable verbal harrassment from their peers for "giving in to the system." However, as the subjects began earning good paychecks, many of these peers voluntarily requested placement in the training program. Second, while the training program was fairly costly, the "re-arrest" rate among the trainees was so small that the juvenile court sponsoring the program ended up saving many thousands of dollars.

Thus changing people's attitudes may be important—but teaching people the skills that will allow them to *maintain healthy attitudes* may be the best form of propaganda presently available to us.

Question: *Does criticism or punishment for inappropriate behaviors* by itself *tell you what to do in order to succeed?*

The Audience

In terms of Helson's Adaptation-level Theory, the "message" is a *stimulus* factor, while the social context in which the message appears is a *background* factor. The character traits and past experiences of the audience are, as you might expect, *personality* factors that affect how the audience will perceive and respond to the message.

Obviously, the most persuasive messages are those created with all three factors in mind. A good communicator thus attempts to discover as much as possible about the audience, and then *shapes* the message to suit both the occasion and the people receiving it.

The Cincinnati Study

Knowing something about your audience doesn't always guarantee that you will be able to get your message through to them, however. Several years ago, Shirley Star and Helen Hughes helped lead a monumental advertising campaign designed to inform the citizens of Cincinnati of the great value of the United Nations. Star and Hughes began by taking surveys to determine what people thought about the UN. The groups who knew the least about the UN (and who liked it the least) included the relatively uneducated, the elderly, and the poor.

Once Star and Hughes knew the characteristics of their target audience, they carried on a six-month campaign aimed at changing their attitudes. Unfortunately, the messages apparently reached or persuaded few of the target population. Instead, the propaganda was effective primarily with young people, and the better-educated and relatively well-to-do segment of the general public. These were, of course, the very people who were already favorably disposed toward the world organization.

In marked contrast to these results, studies by several investigators show that more than two-thirds of the American public learned about the assassination of President John F. Kennedy within 30 minutes after the news first broke. And more than 95 percent of the population knew about Kennedy's death within 90 minutes after the first radio bulletin hit the airwaves. The vast majority of the public, however, first learned about the assassination from *friends and relatives*, not from the news media.

Obviously mass communications *are* successful from time to time—but primarily when the "message" meets some need the audience has, or when the information imparted is so important or stimulating that people *talk to each other* about what has been printed or broadcast.

Question: How might you explain the response of the "target audience" in the Star and Hughes study in terms of autistic hostility?

Audience Responses

Why did the Cincinnati campaign fail? There probably are many different reasons. To begin with, we have no guarantee that Star and Hughes knew what kinds of messages would be most likely to reach their target audience (the poor, the uneducated, the elderly). Nor can we be sure that those involved in creating the propaganda knew what sorts of appeals would convince the targets to change their attitudes.

A more glaring mistake, however, was that Star and Hughes did nothing to establish feedback loops to monitor continuously the effects of their propaganda campaign. The Cincinnati communicators talked—the audience was merely supposed to listen and to respond appropriately. We will have more to say about this point momentarily.

The one "success story" in the Cincinnati study was that people who *actually engaged* in the propaganda campaign showed significant attitude change in the desired direction. As they worked on the project, this group of people apparently became more and more committed to

making the study a success. Since the group was favorable toward the UN, anyone who joined the group was under strong pressure to conform to the group norm. These individuals also had the greatest exposure to the persuasive messages.

Question: How successful would the Mills and Walter study of juvenile offenders have been had the experimenters not monitored continuously the youths' actual "on the job" behaviors?

The Yale Studies: An Evaluation

As Richard Petty, Thomas Ostrom, and Timothy Brock point out in their 1981 book *Cognitive Responses in Persuasion*, the Yale studies dominated research in the field of social psychology in the 1950's. However, during the 1960's, many experimenters had difficulties in replicating some of the work by Hovland and his associates. There seem to be three reasons for these difficulties.

First, Hovland and Janis assumed that what they found in the laboratory would readily translate to real-life situations. But that turned out not to be the case, for the Yale group had almost completely ignored the *social context* in which messages are presented. Thus the model of human behavior that the Yale group used was far too simple to be applicable in most situations outside the laboratory.

Second, Hovland assumed that the "audience" was a passive receptacle into which the communicator poured a message. Indeed, Hovland once defined his research as the study of "Who says what, how, and to whom." Thus the Yale group almost completely ignored the *response* of the audience to the inputs that it received. And as research in the 1960's soon showed, the audience was anything but passive. They most frequently were actively engaged in "processing" messages from communicators. And the audience frequently would argue with the communicators, reject what was said to them, or refuse to listen further to a given message or communicator. By the 1970's, most scientists studying the persuasive process had begun to focus as much on active audience responses as on "communicator, message, and (passive) audience."

Third, the Yale group had assumed that *attitudes control behavior*. But by 1965, psychologists had discovered an unexpected difference between what people *said* their attitudes were, and what the people actually *did* in real-life settings. Few people who conform see themselves as being conformist. And few authoritarian people are likely to call themselves by that name on a pen-and-paper test. Furthermore, many people apparently have very inconsistent or conflicting attitudes. As Peter Drucker put it in the July 6, 1981 issue of the *Wall Street Journal*, "In a good many social matters, attitudes are secondary and attitude surveys are a snare and delusion. What matters is what people do, not what they will say they will do."

One great benefit of the Yale research, then, was that it led social psychologists to pay more attention to the differences between attitudes and behaviors.

Attitudes versus Behaviors

According to most social psychologists, whenever you state an attitude, you are making a prediction about your future thoughts, feelings, and behaviors. But what are we to think if your attitudinal statement doesn't predict what you actually do at some future time?

Chinese and Blacks Keep Out!

The research study that first opened up this problem was reported many years ago by R.T. La Piere. Just after World War II, La Piere spent considerable time driving through the US with a Chinese couple as his companions. Despite the very strong "anti-Chinese" prejudice to be found among many Americans at that time, La Piere and his friends were refused service only once during 10,000 miles of travel.

Later, when they were safely home, La Piere sent questionnaires to all the hotels and cafes where they had stopped. One item on the questionnaire asked, "Will you accept members of the Chinese race as guests in your establishment?" More than 90 percent of the places responded with a very firm "no," and yet all but one of these hundreds of establishments actually had accepted the Chinese couple without question or comment. Obviously there was a very marked difference between "attitude" and "behavior" on the part of these establishments.

In a similar study reported in 1952, B. Kutner, Carol Wilkins, and Penny Yarrow had three young women visit various restaurants in a fashionable suburban community in the northeastern part of the US. Two of the women were white; the third was black. The two white women always arrived at the restaurant first, asked for a table for three, and were seated. Shortly thereafter, the black woman entered, informed the head waiter or hostess that she was with friends who were already seated, found the table, sat down with the two white women, and was served without question.

Two weeks after each visit, Kutner, Wilkins, and Yarrow wrote a letter to each restaurant asking if they would serve blacks. Not one replied. The experimenters then called the manager of each establishment on the phone. The managers uniformly responded in a very cool and distant manner, suggesting that they held a highly prejudiced attitude toward serving blacks. Yet, as in the La Piere study, this attitude was simply not translated into action when the restaurant personnel were faced with seating a black person.

Since 1965, there have been dozens of other experiments, all of which suggest that attitudes (as measured by questionnaires) are very poor indicators of what people actually do, think, and feel in many real-life situations. Furthermore, there is often little relationship between attitude *change* and a subsequent change in the way a person *behaves*. Just as important, as we noted in the previous chapters, people often change their behaviors without changing the attitudes related to the behaviors.

Question: How would you explain La Piere's results in terms of Adaptation-level Theory?

Attitudes toward Attitudes

In their classic book *Opinions and Personality*, M. Brewster Smith, Jerome Bruner, and Robert W. White ask a most important question: "Of what possible use to you are your opinions?" The answer to that question is not an easy one to find. Smith, Bruner, and White believe that attitudes or opinions *serve needs*. That is, whenever you express an attitude, you are really describing some need or goal that you are "driven" to fulfill. When you state your attitudes to the people around you, therefore, you are presumably hunting for others with similar needs who might assist you in achieving mutual goals. Like most social psychologists, Smith, Bruner, and White believe that attitudes are *internal processes* that somehow guide or direct your behaviors.

A radically different approach to the subject, however, was stated in the late 1960's by Daryl Bem. According to Bem, attitudes are simply *verbal statements* about your own behaviors. Bem believes that most of what you do is under the control of external stimulus inputs, most of which you simply aren't consciously aware of. Bem points out that La Piere really measured two quite different responses that occurred in two very different environments. La Piere's questionnaire, for example, seemed designed to elicit negative responses from the hotel and innkeepers to whom it was sent. But when La Piere presented himself and a well-dressed Chinese couple at the desk of the hotel, the stimulus situation was so different that the behavioral response of the innkeeper was bound to be different as well.

Bem believes that there really are no such things as "attitudes," unless you wish to consider them as verbal explanations of why you do what you do. Attitudinal statements then don't predict well at all—they merely give a *rationalization* of what you've already done. We might summarize Bem's position as follows: "How do I know my attitude until I see what I've done?"

Reciprocal Determinism

Are your thoughts and actions regulated primarily by internal processes such as attitudes? Or by environmental inputs that directly influence your visible behaviors? Do you "change your mind," and let your actions follow suit? Or do you first change the way you act, and then alter your attitudes to fit your behaviors?

According to Albert Bandura, you do both at the same time. Writing in the April 1978 issue of *American Psychologist*, Bandura states that, "Explanations of human behavior have generally favored unidirectional causal models emphasizing either environmental or internal determinants of behavior. In social learning theory, causal processes are conceptualized in terms of **reciprocal determinism**." Bandura goes on to say that, from his point of view, psychological functioning involves a *continuous* interaction between behavioral, cognitive, and environmental influences.

Bandura believes that you first build up "behavioral standards" by observing others and by noticing the consequences of their actions. You may then test these standards yourself, to determine if you will be rewarded or punished for thinking and acting in a given way. Once your standards are set, though, you tend to *evaluate* future social inputs in terms of (1) the situational context in which the input appears; (2) your own internal standards; and (3) the possible consequences of acting or thinking in a given way. But these three factors are *reciprocal influences* on each other. Other people influence your internal standards, true. But, as Newcomb has shown, you tend to avoid people who don't share your standards and seek out those who do. And, as we noted in Chapter 11, when you're trying to lose weight, you use your internal standards to help you stay away from pastry shops because you know you will respond to the sight of cookies by purchasing and eating some.

The notion of "self-regulating systems" lies at the heart of Bandura's position. He sees you not as the "passive audience" for persuasive messages from your environment as Hovland does. Nor does he view your mind as a "behavior-producing machine," as do trait theorists. Neither does he assume that all of your responses are

Reciprocal determinism (ree-SIP-pro-cal dee-TURR-min-ism). Bandura's belief that psychological functions are a joint function of behavioral, cognitive, and environmental influences. According to Bandura, you build up schemas (behavioral standards, or perceptions) that allow you to evaluate both social inputs and your own reactions to those inputs. Your evaluations affect both your attitudes and your behaviors. And because you monitor the consequences of having a given attitude or acting a certain way, your attitudes and behaviors can affect your future evaluations. Thus each part of the process—behavior, attitudes and cognitions, and environmental inputs—affects every other part in a reciprocal manner.

learned reactions triggered off by external inputs, as does Bem. Instead, Bandura believes that there is a reciprocal *interplay* between your social inputs, your perceptions, and your responses. You continually evaluate the consequences of perceiving a given stimulus in a particular way. And you change both your behaviors and your attitudes in order to achieve your own particular goals.

The Ethics of Attitude Change

Whatever solution you take to the attitude/behavior (mind/body) problem, there is a deeper issue involved. We *do* know ways of inducing attitude change, and we *do* have methods for creating new behaviors. Given this knowledge, we must then face the following issue: *Who has the right to use these powerful techniques?*

Is it right to talk someone into buying an expensive new car? Is it ethical to convince people that the United Nations is worthy of support? Is it a morally responsible act to persuade a mentally disordered person to seek professional help? Is it ethical to teach children religion or economic theories? Shouldn't all individuals be free to make up their own minds without interference from persuasive sources?

The ethical questions involved in persuasion and attitude formation are numerous and complex. And the questions become even more difficult to answer in cases of *unintentional* persuasion, such as the influence parents have on their children or the subtle and indirect propaganda found in many textbooks, movies, newspapers, and television programs.

Psychology, as an objective science, is not in a position to answer ethical questions. Psychology can, however, attempt to provide some of the information and facts that you will need in order to make your own ethical decisions. One important point that psychology makes about attitude formation is this one: *No one is free of the influence of others or free of the responsibility of influencing others*. Every member of society is involved in attitude formation, both as communicator and as audience. Whenever two or more people get together, the outputs (messages) of one individual become the inputs of others. And this exchange of outputs can result in behavior or attitude change.

If everything you do in the presence of someone else affects that person, then the only way you can hope to judge the ethical value of your actions is to have an *objective* understanding of how your behavior influences others. And since you acquired many of your own attitudes from others, you will also need as much *scientific* information as possible about how you were "shaped" to be what you presently are. For only when you know the full facts of how people communicate with and influence each other can you hope to make good ethical decisions about human attitudes and actions.

As Carl Rogers noted long ago, people need people, and no one ever achieved self-actualization without considerable assistance from hundreds of other individuals. The debt you owe these people, in return, is to help them achieve their own unique goals.

And perhaps that is what ethics is all about, at some deep psychological level—helping others so that they in turn can help you. Therefore, the more that you learn about human behavior (and attitudes), the more likely it will be that you can achieve your own form of self-actualization, and the more likely it will be that you can be of *optimal* assistance in helping others.

Summary

1. **Social psychologists** have long sought answers to the following questions:
   a. Where do our **attitudes** come from?
   b. What personal and environmental factors promote **attitude stability**?
   c. What factors promote **attitude change**?
2. Although some of our opinions, feelings, and preferences are the product of **rational decision making**, many of our attitudes are unconsciously influenced by attempts of other people to **persuade** us to think and act as they do (or as they would like us to think and act).
3. Attitudes are important because they allow you to **predict** future events. They also aid you in **remembering** past experiences.
4. In general, the more you know about something, the more **stable** your attitude toward that thing will usually be.
5. The stronger you **feel** about something, the more difficult it probably will be to get you to change your perception of or attitude toward that thing.
6. The more you are **reinforced** for holding a certain **percept**, the less susceptible that percept or attitude is to being changed.
7. In Newcomb's study of Bennington women, he found that students felt **group pressures to conform** to the liberal environment at the college. The most liberal of the students tended to create post-college environments that would help them **maintain** their liberal attitudes.
8. The Bennington students often showed **autistic hostility** to non-liberal attitudes and opinions.
9. **Student activists** from the 1960's have tended to maintain their "radical" attitudes over the years much as have the Bennington women.
10. The **communication process** is influenced by at least four different factors: the **communicator**, the **message**, the **audience**, and the **feedback** (if any) from the audience to the communicator.
11. Studies suggest that one of the most important aspects of the communication process is the **credibility** the audience places in the communicator.
12. Immediately after hearing a message, we tend to accept the word of **high credibility sources**, but reject the word of **low credibility sources**. Several weeks later, we tend to be more influenced by the actual content of the message than by its source—a phenomenon called the **sleeper effect**.
13. Many studies suggest that **person-to-person communication** is by far more effective than **mass communication** involving the news media.
14. When we receive **fear-arousing messages**, our first impression may be that the stimulus is a very persuasive one. However, studies show that fear usually achieves little more than **repression** and does not protect the audience from **counter-propaganda**.
15. Youthful offenders exposed to the first **scared straight** program actually had a higher rate of subsequent arrests than did a control group not exposed to the fear-arousing experiences. The success rate increased when **individual counseling** was added to the "scare tactics."

16. Youthful offenders given **job-skill training** and **positive feedback** about their attitudes and behaviors showed a much lower rate of subsequent arrests than did control-group subjects.

17. The more that a **propagandist** constructs the message to fit the prior beliefs and attitudes of the audience, and the more the communicator pays attention to **audience feedback**, the more successful the persuasive attempt will usually be.

18. People involved in presenting **propaganda** are usually more affected by it than is the intended audience.

19. The Yale researchers had problems because (1) they ignored the **social context** in which persuasion occurs; (2) they assumed the audience was **passive** and thus ignored **feed-back**; and (3) they presumed that **attitudes always determine behavior**.

20. Some studies suggest that attitudes are poor predictors of what people actually do.

21. Bandura believes that psychological functions are determined by **reciprocal determinism**—that is, a continuous interaction between behavioral, cognitive, and environmental influences. Thus you change both your attitudes and behaviors **simultaneously** in order to achieve your goals.

22. The **ethical questions** raised by research on attitudes are highly complex and not easily answered. However, we probably should evaluate ourselves objectively in terms of what we really do, rather than evaluate ourselves subjectively in terms of our intentions and attitudes.

(Continued from page 640.)

It took several minutes for the Princess to revive the Iron Duke from his faint. While the young girl was alternately wiping her father's brow and slapping him on the cheeks, Rodney poured himself a glass of Black Magic.

"Thou canst not be serious," the Duke said, when he had finally recovered sufficiently to make it to his huge leather chair.

"Dead serious," said Rodney.

"But to give forth the whole, unadulterated, 100 percent *truth* about our Royal products! Why the whole fabric of society would be torn to shreds. Such folly would lead to the complete collapse of the Nacirema economy."

"Nonsense," said Rodney. "Things would change a little, but perhaps for the better."

"Well, it would surely mean the undoing of General Widget, which is just as bad," replied the Duke, thinking of his own position.

"I doubt even that," said the younger man. "The trouble with a widget is not that it's so terrible but that it just isn't as good as it could be. As long as the Sponsor can sell the present model, why should he change? It's cheaper to use your agency's 'word magic' to cover up the problems than to put out a noticeably better product. If you had to tell the truth about the widget, the Sponsor would no longer have that choice."

The Duke poured himself a large tumbler of the amber liquid. "Thy suggestion would never work," he said finally. "The peasants would never stand for it. They love their illusions, and we but keep them happy. Peasants have no love for the truth."

"Then why have they stopped buying widgets?" Rodney asked smugly. "It seems to me that you and the Sponsors are the ones who don't want the truth. Give the peasants a better product, and maybe they'll start buying widgets again."

"Ah," said the Duke softly, "there's the rub. What meanest thou by better?"

Rodney moved to the window and stared at the traffic 100 floors below. "I must admit that I don't really know."

"And this princeling calls himself a genius!" the Duke said to the princess.

"But I know how to find out," Rodney continued.

"Like how?" asked the Duke, his voice ringing with sarcasm.

"Ask the peasants what they want. Tell the Sponsor your findings. And then do your level best to see that the Sponsor tries to meet the peasants' needs. Then you don't have to be afraid of the truth."

The Duke laughed hollowly. "Thou kiddest."

"No, I kid thee not. Business, politics, education—they've all become like Empire Avenue down below—a one-way street. The Sponsor builds widgets and tells you to sell them. You use glowing descriptions to trick peasants into buying widgets whether they need them or not. But how do you know what they really want or need?"

"We spend millions of dollars each year peering into the peasant mentality," the Duke said gruffly.

"So you can persuade them better, not so they can persuade you to give them a better product. You've cut off all feedback from your customers. No wonder widgets are selling poorly."

"But I tell thee Wizards like me know what the peasants really want!" the Duke roared.

Rodney turned away from the window. "Papa knows best—is that what you mean?"

The Duke nodded slowly.

"Mr. Steele, have you ever gone out and bought a widget?"

"Heaven forfend!"

"When was the last time you really talked to someone who has?"

The Duke looked puzzled. "Princess," he said slowly, "I don't suppose . . ."

"I wouldn't be caught dead with one, Father."

The Duke picked up his phone and buzzed his secretary. She didn't have a widget either. And neither did the Director of Marketing, the Chief of Production, nor the Head Gnome.

"See what I mean, Sir? A one-way street. Everybody talks, and nobody listens. What you need is a Vice-wizard in Charge of Feedback."

The Iron Duke grumbled to himself for a moment, then managed a half-hearted smile. "Methinks the matter needs serious contemplation. Get thee hence, you two. The Iron Duke has a giant to kill."

After the young couple had gone, the Duke hunched over in his huge chair, considering what Rodney had said. After a while, the big man wearily picked up the telephone and dialed a number.

"Hello, Mama? This is Sonny. How are things? Yes, I know I haven't talked to you in quite a while. Oh, has it been that long? Well, you know how busy I've been. What? Yes, the Princess is doing just fine. She's got a new boy friend, a prince of a fellow. There may be wedding bells any day now. Oh, certainly, I do want you to meet him. He's got long hair and some strange ideas, but he'll learn, he'll learn. Incidentally, we may be hiring him here at the firm."

The Duke listened for a moment, nodding in silent response to what he had heard. Then he took a deep breath. "Oh, say, Mama. What's your attitude toward widgets?"

Recommended Readings

Bandura, Albert. "The self system in reciprocal determinism," *American Psychologist*, Vol. 33, No. 4 (1978), pp. 344–358.

Hovland, Carl I., Irving L. Janis, and Harold H. Kelley. *Communication and Persuasion* (New Haven, Conn.: Yale University Press, 1953).

Moscovici, Serge. *Social Influence and Social Change* (London: Academic Press, 1976).

Newcomb, Theodore M., Ralph H. Turner, and Philip E. Converse. *Social Psychology* (New York: Holt, Rinehart and Winston, 1965).

Petty, Richard E., Thomas M. Ostrom, and Timothy C. Brock, eds. *Cognitive Responses in Persuasion* (Hillsdale, N.J.: Erlbaum, 1981).

Stumphauzer, J.S., ed. *Progress in Behavior Therapy with Delinquents* (Springfield, Ill.: Charles C Thomas, 1979).

Zimbardo, P.G., Ebbe B. Ebbesen, and Christina Maslach. *Influencing Attitudes and Changing Behavior: An Introduction to Method, Theory, and Applications of Social Control and Personal Power*, 2nd ed. (Reading, Mass.: Addison-Wesley, 1977).

A Conclusion 28

"What's in It for Me?"

Like most scientists, I believe in the future. I suppose I always have. I am much more interested in new things than in old, and I am more intrigued by what a person might become than in what a person has already been. Indeed, about the only time I think about yesterday is when I need information that might let me better understand what tomorrow could be like.

Humans seem to be the only animals that can look far into the future and plan accordingly. This ability to change some parts of the present world *deliberately* in order to shape the world of tomorrow is, in my opinion, one of the essential characteristics of being human.

Science is (among other things) the fine art of predicting the future in objective terms. It is therefore one of the most human of occupations. It took human beings a long time to learn how to make their predictions accurate, however, for at least two reasons:

First, being emotional or subjective seems easier for most of us than being rational or objective. Perhaps this fact is not too surprising. As we noted in Chapter 4, when we discussed Paul MacLean's "Theory of the Triune Brain," the brains of lower animals are dominated by emotional centers. The "thinking" or "processing" centers in the cortex reach their fullest development in humans. But these are *additions to* (rather than subtractions from) the basic blueprint of the highly reactive animal brain. The sheer size of the human cortex gives us the potentiality of bringing the lower centers—and hence our passions and desires—under *voluntary control*. But we need training and experience in order to learn how to be rational. However, we need precious little training to be emotional.

Language is one of the keys to rational thought, and hence to emotional control. As we noted in Chapter 5, in order to think logically, you have to be able to translate parts of the world into verbal symbols, so that you can manipulate the world *symbolically* in your mind. But speech alone is not enough. As human society developed, we had a long heritage of animal emotionality to overcome. Thus we had to develop such symbolic languages as mathematics in order to help us gain control of our passions.

If this line of thought seems odd to you, ask yourself this question: How many "dirty" numbers can you think of? One or two, perhaps. But how many hundreds of "dirty," emotion-laden words can you think of? A computer (which has no emotions) can translate numbers directly. But how can a computer "process" (i.e., understand) any of the hundreds of put-down terms we use to refer to ethnic groups, minority groups, or sexual functions? It is only when we get the emotionality out of our language that we can think objectively, and hence make rational projections about the future.

Second, even when early men and women attempted to view the world in objective terms, they often lacked sufficient data to make good predictions. It probably wasn't until around the year 1600 A.D. that we had gathered enough hard, unemotional facts about the world—and had the proper mathematical tools—for science to prove a worthwhile occupation.

The Industrial Revolution

Perhaps because it is easier for most of us to look at *things* objectively than for us to be objective about ourselves, the physical (or "thing") sci-

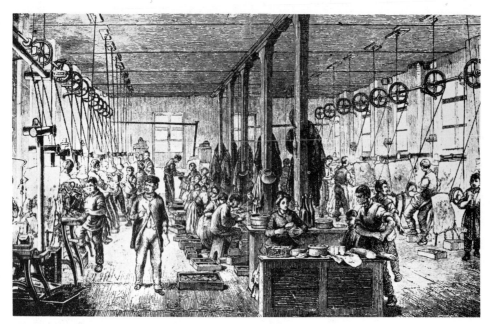

The Industrial Revolution gave us control over the physical environment, but gave us little knowledge about how to help people survive in that environment.

ences were the first to develop. Modern physics and astronomy date from the 1600's. Chemistry came a little later. These scientific disciplines soon matured enough to let us understand and predict the behavior of a few objects under certain specified conditions—for that kind of prediction is science's job. But once we could *guess* how physical things would behave, we could also hunt for ways to *control* the future behavior of these objects. This ability to control "things" marked the rise of physical technology.

The first major applications of physical technology in Europe began in the mid-1700's, and led to what we call the "Industrial Revolution." Before this time, almost everyone in Europe lived on farms or in relatively small towns, and almost every "thing" was handmade. Life changed little from one generation to another. A man typically became what his father had been, and a woman married the sort of man her mother had married. As greater and greater application of the physical sciences gave humans the ability to shape their physical environments, however, the tempo of cultural change speeded up noticeably.

The Medical Revolution

By the 1800's, we had learned enough to begin viewing our bodily reactions in an objective manner. Biology became a true science, and medical

technology became a reality. As the "Medical Revolution" gathered steam in the early 1900's, we discovered ways to predict and control some of our biological reactions. Because of this applied knowledge, we are now bigger, stronger, healthier, and we live longer than at any previous time in human history.

The Psychological Revolution

During the last part of the 1800's and the first part of the 1900's, we took the next step up the ladder—we discovered ways to look at our minds and behaviors objectively. Psychology and the social sciences came into being. We are just now starting to build a technology based on our new-found objective knowledge of ourselves. We call this technology *applied psychology*—that is, the application of psychological facts and theories to help us solve real-life problems. In short, we are now in the midst of what might be called the "Psychological Revolution." The cultural changes this third revolution has brought about are, in their way, as "mind-blowing" as those caused by the Industrial and Medical Revolutions.

What will scientific psychology be like in the future? That question is difficult to answer, since it depends in part on the often unpredictable outcomes of all the thousands of experiments that psychologists are conducting right at this moment.

The future of applied psychology is somewhat easier to predict, however, since tomorrow's technology will lean heavily on today's scientific knowledge. In these final pages, let me share with you my guesses about the changing world of human behavior, and what these changes might mean to you. Other psychologists will surely see things differently, and predictions are often little more than wild speculation.

Still, it might pay us to try to answer three interesting questions:

1. What will the world be like in the year 2000?
2. What kinds of job opportunities might be open to you then?
3. What types of psychological services will probably be available to you by the end of this century?

In defense of my answers to these questions about the year 2000, let me remind you of one fact. At least half of the *types* of jobs available to college graduates today simply didn't exist as "job classifications" 25 years ago.

The Future of Biological Psychology

There seems little doubt that we will shortly gain a great deal more control over our heredity (and hence our instinctual behaviors) than we would have dreamed possible a few years back. In 1973 scientists at the University of Wisconsin announced that they had synthesized a gene in a

"GILMORE SPEAKING. ANATOMY ISN'T DESTINY."

test tube. That is, they had taken ordinary chemical molecules and combined them to "build" a very simple gene. By the late 1970's, other scientists had shown that "artificial genes" could function *normally* in very simple organisms. And, by 1982, dozens of corporations had been formed in the US alone to exploit the possibilities of "genetic engineering." Thus it seems clear that in the very near future we will indeed be able to change a person's heredity (genes) both before and after that person is born (see Chapter 18).

Once the biologists give us greater control over our inheritance, psychologists will be able to determine with much greater precision what the genetic contribution to behavior really is. We should also be able to learn much more about how to overcome genetic handicaps that people already have. By the year 2000, many psychologists should be employed as "genetic counselors," giving advice to prospective parents both before and after they get married. Other psychologists will be able to offer physically handicapped people much better training than now exists. These psychologists may also offer surgeons advice on what kinds of drugs and operations might be helpful to maximize the *psychological* potential of brain-damaged individuals.

The Two Hemispheres

There is no part of physiological psychology presently more exciting than the study of the functions of the two hemispheres. As we noted earlier, there is now considerable evidence that such "mental illnesses" as schizophrenia and autism are related to a *functional imbalance* between the two halves of the brain. Fifty years ago, autism was thought to be a type of schizophrenia. But in the last two or three years, brain scan research has clearly shown this isn't the case. Autistic children process information primarily with their right hemispheres, while patients diagnosed as schizophrenic process inputs primarily with their left hemispheres. I would guess that our whole approach to treating these two "mental disorders" will change markedly in the next decade. Instead of locking schizophrenic patients up in asylums, or just using chemotherapy, we surely will begin training them to process information with *both hemispheres*. Already, as we noted in Chapter 8, several of us at Michigan are doing precisely this sort of thing with autistic children.

We are also likely to be able to help normal children who have language problems by measuring how they input information to their two hemispheres. In the June 29, 1979 issue of *Science*, Joseph Cioffi and Gillray L. Kandel report that young boys tend to process information in quite a differ-

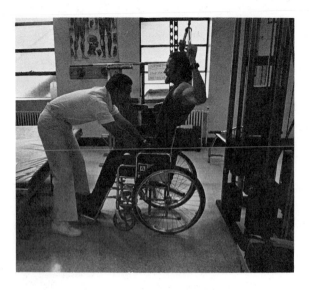

Charles Seigerman

In the future, psychologists may well be intimately involved in helping medical patients maintain painful or stressful types of therapy, such as that involved in strengthening weakened or damaged muscles. **(left)**

ent manner than do young girls. When Cioffi and Kandel gave "word-shapes" to more than 100 young subjects, the girls tended to respond to the "word value" of the stimulus, while boys tended to respond to the "shape" of the input. Boys also tend to have more language development problems than do girls, while girls typically have more difficulty learning spatial concepts and the correct use of mathematical symbolism than do boys.

Psychologist Leona Tyler states that the *main psychological difference* between men and women lies in this area—men do better at perceptual problems than do women, and women do better at language problems than do men. This difference is found at all ages and in all cultures. Although we often think of women as being more emotional, soft-minded, and submissive than men—and men as being more dominant, tough-minded, and logical—Tyler notes that these are *cultural expectations* rather than empirical facts. Indeed, as we noted in Chapter 25, Jay Hall has shown that male managers are better at "social relations," while female managers seem more "task-oriented." And throughout the ages, males have always been better at right-hemisphere tasks (such as art, musical composition, and abstract mathematics) than women have. And women have often excelled in linear logic and language skills.

Male hormones, it would seem, tend to bias the brain toward processing information with the right hemisphere, while female hormones tend to bias the brain toward processing information with the left hemisphere.

Now that we know what the *major* psychological difference between the two sexes may

really be, perhaps we can help parents and teachers overcome a variety of hormone-induced problems. By giving boys special training to improve their "left hemisphere" skills, and by giving girls training to improve the functioning of their "right hemispheres," we can surely come closer to achieving a psychological *equality of the sexes* than if we focus on changing such character traits as "dominance" and "emotionality."

Behavioral Medicine

There are very few psychologists working in hospitals today. By the year 2000, however, hospitals may employ more behavioral technologists than they do physicians and surgeons. This surprising situation will be a direct consequence of the three revolutions we mentioned earlier. For, thanks to our increased knowledge of the physical and biological sciences, the major health hazards are no longer diseases that have a purely physiological cause—such as pneumonia, influenza, and tuberculosis. Medical technology has "cured" us of these maladies, for the most part. But medical technology is presently ill-equipped to help us with health problems that have an intra-psychic or behavioral component, for few physicians are trained in psychological technology.

In the summer of 1975, the US Department of Health, Education, and Welfare released its *Forward Plan for Health*, a long-range blueprint of US needs in the health sciences. According to this report, the major killers today are heart disease, cancer, stroke, and—in younger people— automobile accidents, murder, and suicide. As stated in the *Forward Plan for Health*, "A distinctive feature of these conditions is that most of them are caused by factors [that is, the environment and individual behavior] that are not susceptible to direct medical solution."

Writing in the *Forward Plan for Health*, physician John H. Knowles states that, "The people have been led to believe that national health insurance, more doctors, and greater use of high-cost, hospital-based technology will improve health. Unfortunately, none of them will. . . . The next major advances in the health of the American people will come from the assumption of individual responsibility for one's own health and a necessary change in life style for the majority of Americans."

In brief, our biological systems *interact* with our intra-psychic and our social/behavioral systems. And the next breakthroughs in medicine will come from the wise and human use of a psycho-technology that helps *coordinate* the inputs and outputs of all three systems.

Already many of my students are working with doctors and patients at several medical facilities in the Ann Arbor area. The students have been particularly successful with "problem patients" whose thoughts and behaviors interfere with improvement in their physical health. Helping patients stay on diets, give up smoking, and stay on medical treatment plans are three of the areas that the student-therapists have done well in. And sometimes the students can achieve near-miracles with patients the medical profession has "abandoned."

The Case of "Ennis"

In the late 1970's, four of my undergraduates—directed by Charles Seigerman, then an undergraduate himself—began helping the nursing staff at the local VA hospital. One of the patients the students worked with was a young man whom we will call Ennis, who had suffered severe brain damage in an automobile accident when he was 19.

The accident left Ennis paralyzed and unable to walk. He spoke but two phrases, "God," and "God damn." He had no voluntary control over his bowels and bladder, he had to be spoon-fed, and he threw amazing temper tantrums whenever anyone tried to wash him or get him into a bathtub. Ennis had little in the way of effective social behavior. He avoided eye contact with people who tried to talk to him, and he did not respond to the requests the nurses and doctors made of him. He had been shuffled from one hospital to another because he was a "problem patient" and was diagnosed as being "uncurable."

The students found Ennis lying on the floor of the neurology ward. The nurses would pull him out of bed each morning, clean him up as best

they could, feed him, and then stretch him out on the floor to keep him from getting bed sores. At night, the nurses would put Ennis back to bed. They had little other contact with him because Ennis would scream "God damn" and resist any attempts they made to help him get better.

Self-Care Behaviors

Seigerman and the other four undergraduates began by trying to teach Ennis how to feed himself, since (they thought) the nurses might be willing to spend more time with Ennis if he could manage some self-care behaviors. A member of the hospital staff recorded their efforts on videotape. In the first taped episode, Ennis looks like a wild man. He screams at the students as they put a spoon into his hands, dip it in food, and forcibly move it toward his mouth. He thrashes about, avoiding eye contact, apparently paying little attention to the constant flow of praise and encouragement that the students gave him. But he did eat—once the food was shoveled into his mouth.

By the end of the first week, Ennis had developed into quite a different person. He was still clumsy, but now he looked at the students directly, he responded to their requests, and he obviously enjoyed the positive reinforcement and his newly acquired ability to move his hands and arms voluntarily. By the end of two weeks, he was able to eat almost entirely on his own. After a month of training, Ennis could pick up a cup and drink without spilling the liquid all over him. He now had become skilled enough at feeding himself so that he no longer required much assistance at mealtimes.

The rapid progress that Ennis made impressed the nursing staff quite favorably, so they recommended he be given physical therapy to help him recover his ability to walk. The physical therapists worked closely with the students, and by the end of a month or so of daily sessions, Ennis was able to walk on a level surface without assistance (although he still needed help going up and down stairs).

Next the students built a "potty-trainer" for Ennis that rang a bell whenever he used it properly. The nurses would immediately praise him for showing voluntary control over his bowels and bladder whenever he "rang the bell." It took about a week or so of constant reinforcement for Ennis to complete his "toilet training."

Bathtubs and Applesauce

The most difficult problem of all was Ennis's fear of bathing. The physicians had assumed that this inappropriate behavior was due to his brain injury, but the students discovered the real cause.

661

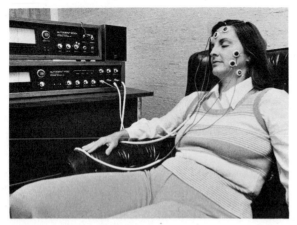

Patients who use biofeedback to consciously lower skin temperature often find it helps relieve headaches.

At another hospital, whenever Ennis would throw a temper tantrum, the attendants would punish him by dragging him into the shower room and sticking his head into a tub of water. The students attempted to *de-sensitize* this conditioned fear of water using the "modeling" techniques developed by Albert Bandura at Stanford (see Chapter 25).

Charles Seigerman put on a hospital gown similar to the one Ennis wore. Seigerman then sat down next to Ennis and began talking with him. A nurse approached them and offered Seigerman some applesauce (Ennis's favorite food) if Charles would let her wash his arms. Seigerman agreed, the nurse washed, and gave Charles his reward. She then turned to Ennis and asked if he would like to earn some applesauce too. Ennis replied by sticking out his arms to be washed—a behavior he had not shown previously.

Day by day, the therapy was expanded so that, within a couple of weeks, Ennis was allowing the nurse to wash his entire body (for the applesauce reward). Then the wash-sessions were slowly moved closer and closer to the shower room. Again, within a week or so, Ennis had been "shaped" into the bathroom with little or no difficulty.

However, a near-disaster occurred at this point. Two of the hospital attendants became angry at Ennis one day. To punish his "misbehavior," the attendants took him into the washroom, stuffed him in a shower stall, and turned on the cold water. Ennis naturally regained his fear of bathing after this episode—but the students "reshaped" him within a few days. The final videotape shows Ennis calmly sitting in a tub of water, playing with a rubber duck, happily muttering "damn" over and over again.

Regression and Relearning

The Ennis story has a sad (but realistic) ending. Shortly after the students had desensitized his fear of bathing, the medical staff at the local hospital decided that Ennis was so dramatically improved that he should be returned to his "home" hospital. The students wrote up a full report of what they had done and asked that the staff at the other hospital be made aware of how effective their work had been. But, as we later learned, the staff either didn't read the report, or didn't believe it. Whatever the case, Ennis soon regressed to many of his old ways of acting. The hospital authorities became so discouraged that they gave up and "parked" him in a nursing home several hundred miles from here.

In the summer of 1979, Charles Seigerman happened upon Ennis at the nursing home. Ennis was no longer able to feed himself, and many of his social skills seemed to have vanished. But the important thing to note is this: When Seigerman spent a few minutes retraining Ennis, the man rapidly *regained his ability* to use a fork and spoon, and to hold a cup in his hands. Seigerman estimates that, given two weeks of intensive therapy, Ennis would be right back at the high level of performance he had shown just prior to his leaving the Ann Arbor hospital. The real problem that Ennis has, then, is not that he is brain-damaged, but that the staff at the nursing home simply didn't give him the *environmental support* he needed in order to function at his best.

Biological Feedback

Quite often physicians use drugs to try to influence biological processes that might better be brought under the patient's voluntary control. There are already promising hints that some milder forms of epilepsy may be helped by conditioning procedures. If the epileptic patient can be hooked to an EEG machine, the patient can sometimes see a visual representation of the chemical storm building up in her or his own brain. By training the person to detect the subtle biological "cues" and intra-psychic "feelings" that accompany the onset of an epileptic seizure, the psychologist may be able to teach the patient to relax or otherwise change thought patterns so that the seizure is prevented.

In similar fashion, patients recovering from heart attacks may use machines that record their heart beats, much as the EEG records brain waves. By seeing this graphic representation of the heart's outputs, the patient may discover how to condition the heart to respond in healthier ways. High-blood pressure, digestive upsets, urine production, and internal bleeding may also turn out to be controllable through conditioning. It is even possible that we may learn how to influence the production of human sperm and eggs through conditioning techniques. Rather than giving a woman "the pill" to prevent her from becoming pregnant, we may be able to train her to become fertile only when she consciously wishes to do so.

Applied Psychology Involving Drugs

We already know that chemicals such as caffeine speed up learning, and that "downers" typically retard it. By the year 2000, psychologists may use a wide variety of drugs that will help people achieve goals not presently within their reach. Chemicals to slow down or help reverse the process of senility are a possibility, as are drugs that will help prevent some types of mental illness. It is highly probable that all such compounds will be used *in conjunction with* psychological and social/behavioral treatment, but there is no reason not to use drugs if they can be helpful.

As we learn more about "consciousness," we will surely discover more effective means of inducing whatever "altered states of consciousness" anyone might desire to experience. Both drugs and biofeedback techniques seem likely candidates in this type of research.

Applied Psychology Involving Sensory Processing

Computers are crude models of our brains. As we gain more insight into how your cortex "inputs" sensory inputs and processes them, we should be able to build dramatically better yet simpler computers than we presently have. It is already theoretically possible to use, for example, the brain of an ant or a worm as a "biological computer." The problem at the moment is in controlling the sensory inputs and the motor outputs. Biological computers should be able to handle complex decision-making much better than present-generation electrical or mechanical computers—and brains are likely to be smaller and easier to handle than machines. Thus it is possible that some "computer technologists" in the year 2000 will be, animal trainers rather than machine-tenders.

And, as we learn more about how your receptors actually sense the world, and how your motor centers control your muscles, we might be able to build "electronic eyes and ears" that would be connected directly to the brains of blind and deaf patients. Perhaps, too, we can build artificial arms and legs that will be directly connected to the motor-output centers of the brain, so that the mechanical "limbs" will respond to a person's thoughts almost exactly the way that flesh and blood would respond.

Biological engineering will be a part of our future whether we like it or not. But it seems reasonably certain that it will always be used *along with* improved ways of "engineering" our thoughts and behaviors. So let us look next at what applied intra-psychic psychology may be like in 2000 A.D.

Applied Intra-Psychic Psychology

Technology implies measurement. The more accurately you can describe or measure anything, the better chance you have of being able to exercise some kind of control over it. As you may have gathered from the earlier chapters in this book, one of the major problems with the intra-psychic or subjective approach to human existence is that internal events are most difficult to describe in quantitative or measurable terms. For this reason alone, we can probably expect greater immediate technological development in biological and behavioral psychology than in the intra-psychic area.

There are a number of highly promising developments, however, that we should take note of. Personality theory in the past has been based on the assumption that your character was fairly well fixed by the end of the first few years of your life. Freud, for instance, thought that only superficial or "surface" changes occurred in people once they had passed the years of early adolescence. Personality tests were usually designed to measure the intellectual and emotional traits a person already possessed, not the traits that the person might acquire with training and encouragement. The intelligence test, for example, tells you something about what you are, but not very much about what you could become.

Tests do have their uses, though. In the spring of 1982, the National Academy of Sciences released a report on testing. The NAS states that, *under the right conditions*, aptitude and performance tests can indeed predict future performance. However, these tests are useful indicators of future performance *only* when the subjects aren't given the sort of "special training" that many of them need in order to maximize their potentials.

The humanistic psychologists emphasize growth and perpetual change. One of the greatest challenges of the coming 20 years will be to develop new types of intra-psychic tests that will tell us more about the *potentialities* of people than present tests do. We will have to find new types of traits to measure (as best we can) that emphasize the process-of-becoming rather than "fixed" or supposedly unchangeable traits such as "intelli-

There is no reason why people should be locked into the same profession all their lives.

gence" or "mental disorders." The humanistic psychologists are also likely to discover more about human (and humane) goals and values in the coming years than we presently know. In many ways, the humanists are in a unique position—that of functioning as a conscience or "superego" that can help keep the more applied technologies oriented toward *ethical* solutions of human problems.

Psychotherapy

Psychotherapy is one of the most important and exciting areas in psychology because it involves *people helping people*. And the belief that you have assisted some other individual to overcome his/her problems is incredibly *reinforcing*. Little wonder, then, that when therapists have a choice, most of them pick clients who are most likely to improve. According to a recent study by Georgianna Shick and Anthony DeVino of Fordham, most therapists prefer to treat YAVIS—young, attractive, verbal, intelligent, and successful people. And, as Shick and DeVino point out, YAVIS are the most likely individuals to cure themselves *without* therapy. Therefore they're the easiest patients for therapists to achieve positive results with.

As we noted in Chapter 24, there is considerable debate right now as to whether "talk therapy" does most people any good. The National Institute of Mental Health has begun an extensive, long-term study of the effectiveness of psychotherapy. The results of this research probably won't be released until late 1983 or early 1984. However, Morris Parloff, a chief of research at

NIMH, has analyzed 475 studies already in print. He concludes that there is some evidence that psychotherapy does help a small number of people. But he also discovered the following rather interesting facts:

1. There are now more than 250 types of "talk therapy," and they all yield about the same "cure rate."
2. The amount of experience a therapist has apparently has little effect on the cure rate. Indeed, there is some evidence that beginners (including relatively untrained undergraduates) do slightly better than do psychiatrists with many years of experience.
3. The "cure rate" is much the same whether treatment is brief or lasts for many years.
4. Both patients and therapists tend to *overestimate* the benefits of treatment.
5. Even when treatment does seem to work, the effects apparently don't last. Parloff notes that two years after therapy ends, about half the benefits of treatment have disappeared.
6. About 10 percent of the patients in treatment end up in worse shape than before they started therapy.

As Philip Hilts notes in the November 1980 *OMNI*, Parloff's findings tend to support one amusing study done recently in India. Half the patients at a mental health clinic were randomly selected to be treated by trained psychiatrists, while the other half were entrusted to native faith healers and "witch doctors." At the end of five years, the "cure rate" for both groups was about the same. In fact, the only measurable difference between the two groups was that the "witch doctors" released their patients a bit sooner than did the psychiatrists.

"Psychic Explorations" versus Psychotherapy

According to Philip Hilts, there is a growing realization among psychotherapists that "talk treatment" is really a form of *psychological exploration* rather than a type of *treatment*. In a society as mobile as ours, it is not always easy to find someone to talk your troubles over with. More than this, not even your friends can always guide you through a full-fledged "investigation into the self." And yet, that is just what most forms of psychotherapy turn out to be.

We might suspect, therefore, that in the future people will seek out a therapist when they have minor problems and anxieties, or when they want to find out more about their own intra-psychic functioning. For more severe problems, however, a *combination* of therapies is more likely to yield good results. This combination will surely include biological therapy, behavioral therapy, and family and work counseling as well as the more traditional types of psychotherapy.

Applied Developmental Psychology

One of the fastest growing fields within the behavioral sciences is that of *developmental psychology*. Although this term once meant much the same thing as *child psychology*, we now realize that people continue to change throughout their lives. In the future, developmental specialists will work with people of all ages, helping them solve whatever "growth" difficulties arise at any time in a person's life.

Life-Long Learning

As our health gets better and our lives get longer, we will realize that there is no reason why we should commit ourselves to one occupation, or to one style of life, and stick with it forever. Indeed, studies of "job burn-out" and "career plateauing" suggest many people may *benefit* from changing occupations in mid-life. By the year 2000, therefore, some psychologists may specialize in helping middle-aged individuals acquire new job skills.

For that matter, we now realize that education should not stop when some college places a degree in a person's hands. Rather, learning should continue up to the moment of the person's death. So even those middle-aged individuals who are content with their jobs may well decide to take additional college courses just to "freshen up their minds."

Later Life

Some of our greatest untapped resources are the skills and abilities of our senior citizens. As we learn how to maintain psychological youthfulness even when our bodies have started to creak and groan a bit, we will need specialists to help older people continue to be useful and contributing members of society.

Death is as much a part of the business of living as is life itself, yet we often avoid the topic, and it has seldom been studied scientifically. Developmental psychologists will probably be called upon as much to help people prepare psychologically for facing death as for facing life.

Applied Behavioral Psychology

The engineering profession really got its start with the beginning of the Industrial Revolution. Part of an engineer's job is to take known scientific data and use them to transform the physical environment. But in doing so, engineers often discover new scientific principles on their own. And, in putting well-known scientific theories to practical tests, the engineers may uncover flaws in the theory that laboratory scientists were unaware of.

One of the most important new professions is that of behavioral engineering—women and men who use psychological data to help create new and more satisfying social and work environments. My private opinion is that, by the year 2000, half the psychologists in the US will be employed in jobs demanding behavioral engineering skills. Let us look at some of the things they might be doing.

Community Mental Health

As long as we believed that "mental illness" was primarily the fault (or responsibility) of the individual, we could ignore the effects of the social environment on human behavior. But we now know that—just as dirt and germs breed physical illness—bad cultural conditions can breed crime, violence, "mental disorders," and personal misery.

At present we have sanitary engineers who inspect restaurants and grocery stores to make sure that food is clean and healthy. Perhaps by the next century we will have behavioral engineers who will inspect businesses, schools, and industries to make certain that employers show as much concern for the mental health and happiness of their employees, students, and customers as they do for cleaning up dirt and preventing physical disease.

"Parenting" Skills

Already we have a great many community mental health centers scattered across the US and Canada. We will need many more of them, and they will surely take on a variety of new tasks. The data suggest, for instance, that many parents who mistreat their children were mistreated by their own parents. If we are to stop this destructive behavior toward innocent children, we will have to find effective ways of teaching some parents to manage their children without resorting to violent physical punishment. Since most high schools and colleges fail to give training in "parenting skills," probably the community mental health centers will have to fill in the educational gap.

What we call "mental illness" tends to run in families partly because of genetic factors, in part because certain types of parental responses induce "insane" behavior in children. To break this self-perpetuating pattern of mental illness, we will need more effective forms of family counseling.

**Child abuse
hurts everybody**

National Committee for Prevention of Child Abuse. A Public Service of Outdoor Advertising and The Advertising Council.

Write: Box 2866, Chicago Ill. 60690

In the future, psychologists may help discover better ways of helping parents solve the problems associated with child abuse.

We will also have to make some rather difficult moral decisions concerning society's right to intervene in unhealthy family situations when the parents may resent or fight against outside intervention.

Sheltered Environments

Mental hospitals as we presently know them may well vanish during the first part of the next century. These "asylums" will be replaced by clinics, re-education centers, halfway houses, group homes, and other forms of "sheltered environments" where people with mental problems may go for relatively short periods of time. Behavioral engineers—working in teams with psychiatrists, psychologists, and social workers—will help these disturbed people find solutions to their problems. The patients will then be eased back into society bit by bit, rather than being discharged abruptly with little in the way of aftercare. Behavioral psychologists will also be involved in helping to change the social environment (such as a family situation) into which the patient will return.

The importance of the "step-by-step" method of bringing mental patients back into society is emphasized in recent work by Wayne State psychologist Jacobo A. Varela and his students. Varela noted that many ex-mental patients were housed in cheap hotels where violence was rampant. Terrified by their new environment, the patients often remained locked in their rooms and thus were even more cut off from other people than when they had been hospitalized. Varela and his students slipped notes under the doors of the patients' rooms inviting them to join "rap" groups in the hotel that would discuss problems they all had in common. Varela states that 19 out of 20 ex-patients responded enthusiastically and "came out from behind their locked doors." Unfortunately, this type of carefully engineered "aftercare" is seldom offered by the present mental-health establishment.

The sprawling concrete prisons we presently send criminals to will also slowly fade from the scene. As we gain greater control over the social environment, fewer people will "want" to become law-breakers. Rehabilitation and re-education are much more effective ways of dealing with criminals than are merely punishing them and locking them away behind bars. Thus prisons too should develop into "schools for social and personal learning" and be staffed as much by psychologists as by wardens and guards. And prisoners—like ex-mental patients—should be given extensive assistance after leaving jail in order to help them learn the skills necessary for day-to-day survival.

Industrial Psychology

Psychologists have long been employed by business firms and governmental agencies in many capacities. One of the chief functions of these industrial psychologists has been that of personnel selection. A great many intelligence and aptitude tests have been developed that, under the right conditions, allow psychologists to evaluate the knowledge and skills of potential employees. Psychologists also have tried to develop "job descriptions" that would state what abilities were needed to handle a particular position. It was then up to the psychologist to match the person to the job. As we learn more about how to help people grow and develop, however, industrial psychologists will probably spend more time *training* personnel than *selecting* them.

Improving Job Performance

A worker's performance is not dependent entirely on her or his own talents. It also depends on the type of encouragement and feedback the worker's supervisor gives, and on how rewarding and satisfying the job happens to be. In his 1978 book *How To Improve Human Performance*, Thomas K. Connellan points out that gaining some control over their own destinies—that is, being able to participate in decision-making—is a major reinforcer for most workers. And, as we noted in Chapter 25, most successful supervisors do in fact use "participatory management" as one of their main managerial tools.

Giving employees appropriate feedback on job performance is a large part of "participatory management." Indeed, the so-called *quality control circles* used by many Japanese companies are little more than feedback devices in which both workers and managers can let each other know "how things are going" and suggest ways of improving matters.

The Hawthorne Effect

For almost half a century, industrial psychologists have spoken of the "Hawthorne Effect," meaning that one must be careful in real-life experiments because subjects will often produce the results they think the experimenters want. The effect gets its name from a series of studies performed at the Hawthorne (Chicago) plant where the Western Electric Company manufactures equipment for the Bell Telephone System. This research, done between 1927 and 1932, was designed to discover how much productivity and morale might be improved when the experimenters made various changes in the work environment.

According to the initial reports the experimenters issued, productivity increased *no matter what the experimenters did*. The usual interpretation of these data has been that the subjects knew they were being measured—and hence worked harder—whether the experimenters made conditions better or worse. Very recently, though, psychologist H.M. Parsons has gone back and re-examined all of the original data in this study. Parsons was able to show that productivity increased *only* in those situations in which the workers could have gotten some feedback as to how well they were performing. Parsons believes the so-

called "Hawthorne Effect" is just another example that productivity tends to increase *primarily* when employees are given appropriate feedback about their performance.

Management "by Exception"

Generally speaking, most US managers and supervisors "manage by exception," which is to say that they tend to ignore appropriate work behaviors and focus on punishing inappropriate or off-target behaviors. But, as Thomas Connellan points out, "management by exception" actually tends to punish productive responses and reinforce (with attention) unproductive and disruptive responses.

As an example of how behavioral engineers might help managers overcome this tendency to "manage by exception," suppose we look briefly at industrial absenteeism. Connellan notes that employees who stay away from their jobs cost the US more than $40 billion a year. In some companies, 10 percent of the employees are likely to be absent on a given day. For many years the "cure" for absenteeism has been punishing those workers who had no excuse for their failure to show up at work. Most managers *attributed* the cause of "playing hookey" from work to some innate character flaw in the employees' personalities.

In fact, as recent studies show, high absence rates are primarily an index of poor employee morale and of job dissatisfaction. In general, the more a worker dislikes the supervisor and/or the work group, the more likely it is that the worker will have a high absentee rate. When jobs are extremely scarce, threatening to fire an employee may have some effect on absenteeism. When jobs are more plentiful, a rather different solution seems to be called for. Many corporations have found that offering workers "time off" for good attendance often cuts the absentee rate in half.

However, as E.E. Lawler and J.R. Hackman showed in 1969, by far the best way to reduce absenteeism is to ask employees what incentives or job changes they want, and then to reward the workers with what they asked for when they do show up for work. (Some employees may prefer other rewards than "time off.")

Industrial corporations often count their buildings, machines, and profits as "corporate assets." As psychologist Rensis Likert points out, however, the finest resources available to any company are the skills and talents of its employees. Two of the major jobs for future industrial psychologists will be to: (1) help executives measure these human assets; and (2) treasure these assets by developing work environments that are maximally satisfying to all employees.

Thomas K. Connellan

Large corporations often call in psychological consultants for assistance much as individuals seek help from psychotherapists.

Organizational Development

In the January 1982 issue of *Contemporary Psychology*, Clayton Alderfer defines organizational development as "a professional field that attempts to improve human organizations by using the theory and methods of behavioral science." The problem with this field is that we know much more about people working in organizations than we do about organizations themselves. The reason for this lack of knowledge is not hard to discover. There probably have been a thousand times as many studies of individuals as of groups, and a thousand times as many studies of groups as of organizations. Indeed, as a recent book on *organizational development* shows, even when psychologists do study large social systems, they tend to focus on the effects these systems have on the individual, not the structures and functions of the system itself.

A Theory of Behavior in Organizations, published in 1980 by James Naylor, Robert Pritchard, and Daniel Ilgen, is essentially an application of social learning theory to the study of organizational development. Thus Naylor and his colleagues assume that productivity is a function of the *collective perceptions* of the individuals within the organization. If employees perceive a given act as likely to yield a reward, they will perform that act. Thus managers shouldn't just offer reinforcers for good behavior, Naylor *et al.* say, but they should also attempt to alter the "attitudes and perceptions" employees have about work-related actions. As an application of cognitive behavioral psychology to the workplace, the book is excellent. As a description of how organizations

function, the book has certain obvious weaknesses.

Systems Theory for Organizational Development, a 1980 book edited by Thomas Cummings, is quite a different kettle of fish. Most of the authors of the various chapters attempt to apply an information-processing model or General Systems Theory to the study of large organizations. Will McWhinney's chapter on "how to design an organization" is a particularly apt description of how to use systems technology in creating and maintaining new social systems.

In the future, I suspect, psychologists will probably adopt the strategies found in both these new books. That is, they will utilize *change strategies for individuals* (as Naylor *et al.* suggest), and they will apply various psychological theories to the *study and understanding* of social systems (as described in the Cummings book).

Psychology in Your Future

Fifty years ago most Americans were employed in producing "things"—farm products and manufactured goods. Today more than half of all Americans are employed in service occupations—that is, in processing information, helping other people, or taking care of people's possessions. As we learn more effective ways of assisting one another, the need for psychological services will grow tremendously. The behavioral sciences have rapidly become one of the most popular undergraduate majors in US colleges and universities. My own estimate is that by the year 2000 at least

10 percent of the US work force will be able to lay claim to the title "psychologist" or "behavioral engineer."

Whether you choose to become a psychologist yourself is, quite naturally, a decision that only you can make. But perhaps reading *Understanding Human Behavior* will have given you some notion of what the future possibilities in psychology will be. And no matter who or what you choose to become, your life will surely be affected by what I call the "Psychological Revolution."

At its best, psychology can offer you the tools to shape your body, your mind, and your social environment somewhat closer to your heart's desire. We do not as yet know what the real limits of human potential are—we know only that people are capable of greater growth and development than we dreamed possible a mere 50 years ago. It is up to you to use the tools available to you, and to plot your own course into the future.

Let me close by thanking you for making me your guide through some of the frontiers of psychology, and by wishing you the happiest of life's journeys.

Statistical Appendix

The Red Lady

I was sitting in the student union not long ago, talking with a friend of mine named Gersh, when two young women came over to our table and challenged us to a game of bridge. The two women—Joan and Carol were their names—turned out to be undergraduates. They also turned out to be card sharks, and they beat the socks off Gersh and me. Joan was particularly clever at figuring out how the cards were distributed among the four bridge hands—and hence good at figuring out how to play her own cards to win the most tricks.

One hand I will never forget, not merely because Joan played it so well, but because of what she said afterward. Joan had bid four spades, and making the contract depended on figuring out who had the Queen of Diamonds—Gersh or me. Joan thought about it for a while, then smiled sweetly at Gersh. "I think you've got the Red Lady," she said, and promptly captured Gersh's Queen of Diamonds with her King.

Gersh, who hates to lose, muttered something about "dumb luck."

"No luck to it, really," Joan replied. "I knew you had 5 diamonds, Gersh, while Doc here had only 2. One of you had the Queen, but I didn't know which. But since you had 5 of the 7 missing diamonds, Gersh, the odds were 5 to 2 that you had the Little Old Lady. Simple enough, when you stop to think about it."

While Gersh was dealing the next hand with noisy frustration, Joan turned to me. "I know you're a professor, but I don't know what you teach."

"Psychology," I said, picking up my cards for the next hand. The cards were rotten, as usual.

"Oh, you're a psych teacher! That's great," Joan said with a smile. "I really wanted to study psych, but they told me I had to take statistics. I hate math. I'm just no good at figuring out all those complicated equations. So I majored in history instead."

Statistics—A Way of Thinking

I shook my head in amazement at what Joan said. I don't know how many times students have told me much the same thing—they're rotten at mathematics, or they just can't figure out what statistics is all about. But these same students manage to play bridge superbly, or figure out the stock market, or they can tell you the batting averages of every major league baseball player, or how many miles or kilometers per gallon their car gets on unleaded gasoline.

Statistics is not just a weird bunch of mathematics—it's a way of thinking. If you can think well enough to figure out how to play cards, or who is likely to win the next election, or what "grading on the curve" is all about, then you're probably already pretty good at statistics. In fact, you surely use statistics unconsciously or intuitively every minute of your life. If you didn't, you'd be dead or in some institution by now.

Sure, a few of the equations that statisticians throw around get pretty fancy. But don't let that fact discourage you. I've been a psych prof for more than 20 years, I minored in mathematics, but even I don't understand all the equations I see in the statistical and psychological journals. But those "fancy formulas" are usually of interest only to specialists. Forget about them—unless you happen to be a nut about mathematics.

The truth is that you *already know* most of the principles involved in basic statistics—if, like Joan, you're willing to stop and think about them. Yet many psych students reject statistics with the same sort of emotionality that they show when somebody offers them fried worms and rattle-snake steak for dinner. Well, worms are rich in protein, and rattlesnake meat is delicious—and safe to eat—if you don't have to catch the snake first. But you may have to overcome some pretty strong emotional prejudices before you're willing to dig in and see what snake meat (or stat) is all about.

Odds and Ends

I've been a gambler all my life, and I really enjoy trying to "psych people out" at the bridge or poker table. So maybe I didn't get conditioned to fear numbers and "odds" the way a lot of people do. But whether you realize it or not, you're a gambler too. And you (like Joan) are pretty good at figuring out all kinds of odds and *probabilities*. Every time you cross the street, you gamble that the odds are "safely" in your favor. Each time you drive your car through a green light without slowing down, you gamble that some "odd" driver won't run the red light and hit you broadside. Every time you study for a true-false exam, you're gambling that you can learn enough to do better than somebody who refuses to study and who just picks the answers randomly. And whenever you go out with somebody on a date, you're gambling that you can predict that person's future behavior (on the date) from observing the things that the person has done in the past.

So you're a gambler, too, even if you don't think of yourself as being one. But if you're going to gamble, wouldn't it be helpful to know something about odds and probabilities? Because if you know what the odds are, you can often do a much better job of achieving whatever ends or goals you have in mind.

One way or another, almost everything in statistics is based on *probability theory*. And, as luck would have it, probability theory got its start some 300 years ago when some French gamblers got worried about what the pay-offs should be in a dice game. So the gamblers—who were no dummies—hired two brilliant French mathematicians to figure out the probabilities for them. From the work of these two French geniuses came the theory that allows the casinos in Las Vegas and Atlantic City to earn hundreds of millions of dollars every year, that lets the insurance companies earn even more by betting on how long people will live—and that lets psychologists and psychiatrists employ the mental tests that label some people as being "normal" and other people as being "abnormal."

The Odds in Favor

If you want to see why Joan was so good at playing bridge, get a deck of cards and pull out the 2, 3, 4, 5, 6, 7, and Queen of Diamonds. Turn them face down on a table and shuffle them around so you won't know which card is which. Now try to pick out the Queen just by looking at the back of the cards.

If the deck is "honest" (unmarked), what are the odds that you will pick the Red Lady instead of the 2, 3, 4, 5, 6, or 7? As you can see, the odds are exactly 1 in 7. If you want to be fancy about all this, you can write an equation (which is what Joan did in her mind) as follows:

The probability (p) of picking the Queen (Q) is 1 out of 7, therefore

$$pQ = 1/7$$

Next, shuffle the cards again, place them face down on the table, and then randomly select 2 of the cards and put them on one side of the table, and the remaining 5 on the other side of the table. Now, what are the odds that the Queen is in the stack of 5 cards (Gersh's bridge hand), and what are the odds that the Queen is in the stack of 2 cards (my bridge hand)?

Well, you already know that the probability that any 1 card will be the Queen is 1/7. I have 2

" I THINK YOU SHOULD BE MORE EXPLICIT HERE IN STEP TWO."

Learning how to use statistical reasoning is no more difficult than learning how to play bridge.

cards, therefore, I have two chances at getting the Queen, and the equation reads:

$$p\text{Q (Me)} = 1/7 + 1/7 = 2/7$$

Gersh had 5 cards, so his probability equation is:

$$p\text{Q (Gersh)} = 1/7 + 1/7 + 1/7 + 1/7 + 1/7 = 5/7$$

So if you dealt out the 7 cards randomly 70 times, Gersh would have the Queen about 50 times, and I would have the Queen about 20 times. No wonder Joan wins at bridge! When she assumed that Gersh had the Queen, she didn't have a sure thing—but the odds were surely in her favor.

Outcomes and Incomes

Now let's look at something familiar to everyone, the true-false examination. Suppose that you go to a history class one day, knowing there will be a test, but the teacher throws you a curve. For the exam you get is written in Chinese, or Greek, or some other language you simply can't read a word of. The test has 20 questions, and it's obviously of the true-false variety. But since you can't read it, all you can do is guess. What exam score do you think you'd most likely get—0, 10, or 20?

Maybe you'd deserve a 0, since you couldn't read the exam. But I'm sure you realize intuitively that you'd most likely get a score of about 10. Why?

Well, what are the *odds* of your guessing any single question right, if it's a true-false exam?

If you said, "Fifty percent chance of being right," you're thinking clearly. (See what I mean about statistics being a way of thinking?)

The probability (p) of your getting the first question right (R_1) is 50 percent, or 1/2. So we write an equation that says:

$$p\text{R}_1 = 1/2$$

The probability of your getting the first question wrong (W_1) is also 50 percent, or 1/2. So we write another equation:

$$p\text{W}_1 = 1/2$$

Furthermore, we can now say that, on the first or any other equation, the

$$p\text{R} + p\text{W} = 1/2 + 1/2 = 1$$

Which is a fancy way of saying that whenever you guess the answer on a true-false exam, you have to be either right or wrong—because those are the only two *outcomes* possible.

Now, suppose we look at the first two questions on the test. What is the probability that you will get *both* of them right, if you are just guessing at the answers?

Well, what outcomes are possible? You could miss both questions (W_1W_2), or you could get them both right (R_1R_2), or you could get the first answer right and the second answer wrong (R_1W_2), or you could get the first one wrong and the second right (W_1R_2).

$$p\text{R}_1\text{R}_2 = 1/4$$
$$p\text{W}_1\text{W}_2 = 1/4$$
$$p\text{R}_1\text{W}_2 = 1/4$$
$$p\text{W}_1\text{R}_2 = 1/4$$
and
$$p\text{R}_1\text{R}_2 + p\text{W}_1\text{W}_2 + p\text{R}_1\text{W}_2 + p\text{W}_1\text{R}_2 = 1/4 + 1/4 + 1/4 + 1/4 = 1$$

Thus, there are 4 different outcomes, and since you would be guessing at the right answer on both questions, these 4 outcomes are *equally likely to occur*. Only 1 of the 4 outcomes (R_1R_2) is the one we're interested in, so the odds of your getting both questions right is 1/4.

In a sense, getting both questions right is like selecting the Queen of Diamonds when it is 1 of 4 cards face down on the table in front of you. In both cases, you have 4 equally likely outcomes, so your chances of getting the Queen (or being right on both answers) is 1 out of 4, or 1/4.

As you can see, if you're taking an exam, playing bridge, or trying to add to your income by buying a lottery ticket, it will surely pay you to consider all the possible outcomes.

Actually, we can figure the odds of your answering the first 2 questions correctly in a much simpler way. We simply multiply the odds of your getting the first question right (pR_1) by the odds of your getting the second question right (pR_2):

$$pR_1R_2 = pR_1 \times pR_2 = 1/2 \times 1/2 = 1/4 = 25\%$$

Maybe you can see, too, that the odds of your getting both answers *wrong* would be exactly the same:

$$pW_1W_2 = pW_1 \times pW_2 = 1/2 \times 1/2 = 1/4 = 25\%$$

If the exam had just three questions to it, the odds of your getting all the answers right by chance alone (that is, by guessing) would be:

$$pR_1R_2R_3 = pR_1 \times pR_2 \times pR_3 =$$
$$1/2 \times 1/2 \times 1/2 = 1/8 = 12.5\%$$

To put the matter another way, on a 3-question exam, there are 8 different outcomes:

$$R_1R_2R_3$$
$$R_1R_2W_3$$
$$R_1W_2R_3$$
$$R_1W_2W_3$$
$$W_1R_2R_3$$
$$W_1R_2W_3$$
$$W_1W_2R_3$$
$$W_1W_2W_3$$

Since only 1 of these 8 possible outcomes is the one you want ($R_1R_2R_3$), the odds in your favor are only 1 in 8.

If the test had 4 true-false questions, there would be 16 different outcomes—twice as many as if the test had but three questions. These outcomes would range from $R_1R_2R_3R_4$, $R_1R_2R_3W_4$ . . . . all the way to $W_1W_2W_3R_4$ and $W_1W_2W_3W_4$. If there are 16 different outcomes, only one of which is "all answers right" or $R_1R_2R_3R_4$, what would be the odds of your guessing all the answers right on a 4-question true-false test?

(If you said, "1 in 16," congratulations!)

Now, let's take a giant leap.

If the exam had 10 questions, the odds of your getting all 10 answers right by guessing would be:

$$pR_1R_2R_3R_4R_5R_6R_7R_8R_9R_{10} = 1/2 \times 1/2 \times 1/2 \times 1/2$$
$$\times 1/2 \times 1/2 \times 1/2 \times 1/2 \times 1/2 \times 1/2 = 1/1024$$

So if you took the exam 1024 times and guessed randomly at the answers each time, just *once* in 1024 times would you expect to get a score of 0, and just *once* in 1024 times would you expect to get a score of 10.

Now, at last, we can answer the question we asked you a few paragraphs back: If you took a 20-question exam on which you had to guess at each answer, what exam score do you think you'd most likely get—0, 10, or 20?

Well, what are the odds that you'd get a score of flat 0? In fact, the odds are astronomically against you, just as they are astronomically against your getting a score of 20 right. In either case, the probability would be:

$$pW_{1-20} = pR_{1-20} = 1/2 \times 1/2 \times 1/2 \ldots$$
$$(20 \text{ times!}) = 1,048,576 \text{ to } 1!$$

So the odds are more than a million to one that you won't get all the answers right or all the answers wrong on a 20 question true-false exam just by guessing. Which might give you good reason to study for the next exam you have to take!

Normal Curves

Next, let's throw in some pictures just to liven things up a bit. Statisticians have a way of plotting or graphing probabilities that may make more sense to you than equations do.

Let's make a diagram of the *distribution* of outcomes when you take a 10-question true-false exam (see Fig. A.1):

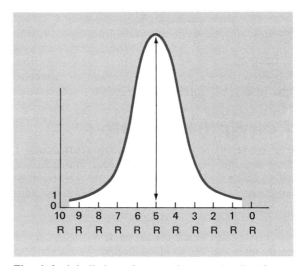

Fig. A.1. A bell-shaped curve showing the distribution of "right answers" expected by chance alone when taking a 10-item true-false exam.

Table A.1 Table of Grade Point Averages

Course	Hours Credit	Grade	Hour × Grade
History	3	A	3 × 4 = 12
Psychology	4	A	4 × 4 = 16
Mathematics	4	C	4 × 2 = 8
Spanish	4	B	4 × 3 = 12
TOTALS	15		48

GPA = 48/15 = 3.2

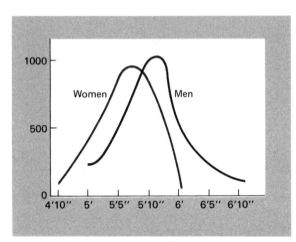

Fig. A.2. A bell-shaped curve showing the distribution of heights of a thousand men and a thousand women selected at random.

As we mentioned earlier, the number of possible outcomes in a 10-question exam is 1024. So the odds of getting all 10 questions right by just guessing ("by chance alone") would be 1 in 1024. Not very good odds. But the probability of your getting 4, 5, or 6 questions right would be well above 60 percent! That makes sense, because just looking at the curve you can see that better than 60 percent of the possible outcomes are bunched up right in the middle of the curve.

Descriptive Statistics

The curve we've just drawn is the world-famous, ever-popular "bell-shaped curve." In fact, the curve describes a *random distribution of scores* or outcomes. That is, the curve describes the outcomes you'd expect when students are forced to guess—more-or-less at random—which answers on a true-false exam are correct. Naturally, if the exam were written in clear English, and if the students knew most of the material they were being examined on, the curve or *distribution of scores* would look quite different.

There are many sorts of "outcomes" that fit the bell-shaped curve rather nicely. For example, if you randomly selected 1,000 adult US males and measured their heights, the results you'd get would come very close to matching the bell-shaped curve shown in Fig. A.2. Which is to say that there would be a few very short men, a few very tall men, but most would have heights around 5'10" (178 centimeters). The same bell-shaped curve would fit the distribution of heights of 1,000 adult women selected at random—except that the "middle" or peak of the bell-shaped curve would be about 5'5" (166 centimeters).

Measures of Central Tendency

As we noted in Chapter 22, intelligence tests are constructed so that the scores for any age group will approximate a bell-shaped curve. In this case, the peak or "middle" of the distribution of IQ's will be almost precisely at 100. A very few individuals would have IQ's below 50, a very few would have scores above 150. But some two-thirds of the scores would fall between 84 and 116 (see diagram page 536).

Why this bulge in the middle as far as IQ's are concerned? Well, think back for a moment to the true-false test we were discussing earlier that had 10 questions on it. There are 1024 possible outcomes. If you wanted to get all 10 questions right, there was only one way you could answer the 10 questions—all had to be correct. But there were 256 ways in which you could answer the questions to get a score of 5—right in the middle.

There is only one way you can earn a top score on an intelligence test—you've got to answer all the questions rapidly and precisely the way the people who constructed the test say is "right." But there are thousands of different ways you can answer the questions on the usual test to get a "middle score," namely an IQ between 84 and 116.

In a similar vein, there are precious few ways in which you can earn a million dollars, but there are dozens and dozens of ways in which you can earn between $10,000 and $15,000 a year. So if we selected 1,000 adult US citizens at random, asked them what their incomes were, and then "took an average," what kind of curve (distribution of incomes) do you think we'd get?

Whenever we measure people psychologically, biologically, socially, intellectually, or economically, we often generate a distribution of outcomes that looks very much like a bell-shaped curve. Each person in the world is unique, it's true. But it is equally true that, on any given *single* measuring scale (height, weight, grade-point average, income), most people's scores will be somewhere in the *middle* of the range of possible outcomes.

Psychologists have a variety of tools for measuring the "middle" of any curve or distribution of outcomes. These techniques are often called *measures of central tendency*, which is a fancy way of saying that these techniques allow us to measure the center or midpoint of any distribution of scores or outcomes.

Mean, Median, Mode

1. *The Mean*. The *mean* is simply the statistical "average" of all the scores or outcomes involved. When you figure your grade-point average (GPA) for any semester, you usually multiply your grade in each course by the number of credit hours, add up the totals, and divide by the number of hours credit you are taking. Your GPA is actually the *mean* or mathematical average of all your grades (see Table A.1).
2. *The Median*. Since the mean is a mathematical average, it sometimes gives very funny results. For example, according to recent government figures, the "average" US family was made up of about 4.47 people. Have you ever known a family that had 4.47 people in it? For another example, if you got two A's and two C's one semester, your average or "mean" grade would be a B. Yet you didn't get a B in any of the courses you took.

There are times when it makes more sense to figure the exact *midpoint score* or outcome, rather than figuring out the *average* score. At such times, psychologists often use the *median*, which is the score that's in the precise middle of the distribution—just as the "median" of an expressway is the area right down the middle of the highway.

The median is often used as a "measure of central tendency" when a distribution has one or two extreme scores in it. For instance, if 9 people earn $1 a year, and a tenth earns $100,000, what is the *mean* income of these 10 people?

About $10,001 a year, which is a misleading statistic, to say the least. However, the *median* income is $1, which describes the actual income of the *majority* of the group somewhat better than does the mean of $10,001.

3. *The Mode*. The word *mode* is defined in the dictionary as "the prevailing fashion or most popular custom or style." When we are talking about distributions of scores or outcomes, *mode* means the most popular score. That is, the mode is the highest point (or points) on the curve. If the distribution has two points that are equally high, then there are two scores that are *modal*, and we can call the curve *bi-modal* (having two modes).

Skewedness

If the distribution of scores is more-or-less bell-shaped, then the mean, median, and mode usually come out to be the same. But not all curves do us the favor of being so regular in shape. For example, suppose you were interested in whether a particular teacher—Dr. Johnson—started and ended her classes on time. To find out, you take a very accurate watch with you all semester long and make a scientific study of Dr. Johnson's behavior.

During the term, let's say, there are supposed to be 50 lectures by Dr. Johnson. So the number of possible start-time scores or outcomes will be 50. For the most part, Dr. Johnson begins on time, but occasionally she starts a minute or two early, and sometimes she's a minute or two late. Now and again, she is fairly tardy in getting to class, and once she didn't show up at all. But she *never* begins a class more than two minutes early. If you put all of her starting times on a graph, it would look something like the curve on the left side of Figure A.3. If you plotted all her closing time scores on a similar graph, it would look like the curve on the right in Figure A.3.

The term we use to describe these curves is *skewedness*, which means they are "slanted" or "pushed out of shape." In the starting-time example, the curve slants out far to the right-hand side, so we say that the curve is "skewed to the right." The other curve has a tail that slants out to the left, so the curve is "skewed to the left." As is the case in many distributions where the scores are measures of reaction times or beginning times, the mean, median, and mode are fairly different.

Range and Variation

There are two more important concepts we have to get out of the way before we can finish our discussion of *descriptive statistics*—which is to say, statistics that measure or describe some-

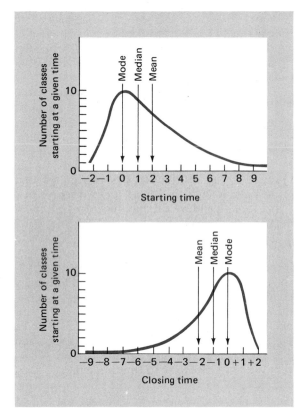

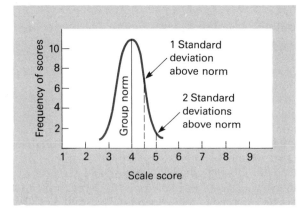

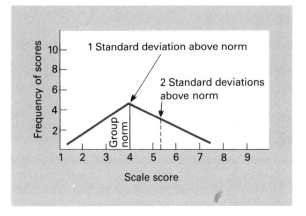

Fig. A.3. A plot of Dr. Johnson's "beginning times" and "closing times." **(left)**

Fig. A.4. A distribution of attitude scores for a homogeneous group. **(top right)**

Fig. A.5. A distribution of attitude scores for a heterogeneous group. **(bottom right)**

thing. The first concept is the *range* of possible scores or outcomes; the second is the *variability* of the scores. The first concept is easy to understand, but the second will take some careful thought on your part.

What is the *range* of possible scores on a 10-item "fill in the blanks" test? From 0 to 10, of course. And since you can't guess as easily on this type of test as on a true-false examination, you can't really tell ahead of time what the class average is likely to be. The range on a 100-item test would be from 0 to 100—and again, you have no way of knowing before you take the test what the "mean" or average score is likely to be.

Let's suppose that you took a 10-item "fill in the blanks" exam and got a score of 8 right, which also turned out to be the mean or average score for the whole class. Then you took a 100-item "fill in the blanks" test and again you got a score of 8, which again turned out to be the class average. What does knowing the *range* of possible scores

tell you about the level of difficulty of the two tests? Wouldn't you say that the 100-item test was considerably more difficult, even though the class average was the same on both tests?

Now, let's add one more dimension. Suppose that on the 10-item examination, *everybody in class* got a score of 8! There would be no *variation* at all in these scores, since none of the scores *deviated* (were different from) the mean. But suppose on the 100-item "fill in the blanks" exam, about 95 percent of the class got scores of flat zero, you got an 8, and a few "aces" got scores above 85. Your score of 8 would still be the *mean* (but not the median or mode). But the *deviation* of the rest of the scores would be tremendous. Even though you scored right at the mean on both tests, the fact that you were better than 95 percent of the class on the 100-item test might well be very pleasing to you.

The variation or variability of test scores is simply a measure of *how spread out across the range* the scores actually are. Thus the variability of a distribution of scores is a very important item to know if you're going to evaluate how you perform in relation to anybody else who's taken the test.

The Standard Deviation

If you know the range of scores, plus the mean, median, and mode, you can usually get a fairly good notion of what shape the curve might take. Why? Because these two bits of information tell you something about how the scores are *distributed*. If the mean, median, and mode are almost the same, and they fall right at the center of the range, then the distribution curve must be "vaguely" bell-shaped, or regular in shape.

But why do we say "vaguely" bell-shaped? In Chapter 26, we discussed the distribution of scores on an attitude questionnaire in two different groups. In the homogeneous group, as Fig. A.4 shows, the range of scores was very small. But in the heterogeneous group, as Fig. A.5 shows, the range was much larger. The means for the two distributions were the same, and if the groups had been large enough, we might even have found that the ranges of the two distributions were the same. However, in the homogeneous group, the scores were all bunched up close to the mean, while in the heterogeneous group, the scores were broadly *dispersed*, or spread out.

In Chapter 23, we found that we needed a concept we called the *standard deviation* to describe the *dispersion of scores* across the range (or around the mean). The larger the standard deviation, the more widely the scores vary around the mean (and the more heterogeneous the group probably is). The smaller the standard deviation, the more bunched up the scores are around the mean (and the more homogeneous the group probably is).

We can now define the *standard deviation* as a statistical term meaning the variability of scores in a distribution.

There are a variety of mathematical formulas for figuring out such statistics as the standard deviation. Once upon a time, students were required to memorize these formulas and grind out statistical analyses using nothing more than their brains (and perhaps their fingers and toes to count on). Nowadays, however, even cheap pocket calculators will figure out the standard deviation of a distribution of scores almost instantaneously (if you input the right data in the first place). If you wish to learn one of the formulas for calculating the standard deviation—or if you are required to do so—you will find them in many places, including the *Student Manual* that accompanies this book.

However, as we said earlier, statistics is more a way of thinking than it is a bunch of fancy formulas. *Descriptive statistics* are short-hand ways of describing large bunches of data. They are "thought tools" that let you think about the world in convenient symbols.

Let's now see how you can use "descriptive" statistics to help you *make inferences* or draw conclusions about the data you're mulling over in your mind.

Inferential Statistics

Whenever you test a hunch or a scientific hypothesis, you often are hunting for *reliable* differences between two groups of subjects or between two sets of data. Again, there are *many* different formulas for figuring out how reliable (or important) the group differences really are. But one of the simplest—and most often used—is the standard deviation. By convention, scientists accept differences as being "real" if the means of the two groups depart by 2 or more standard deviations from each other.

We pick the figure 2 standard deviations for a very understandable reason. If on a bell-shaped curve we measure out from the mean a distance of 2 standard deviations, we will take into account about 95 percent of all the IQ scores described by the curve. Any score falling outside of this distance will be there *by chance alone* less than 5 percent of the time. So the odds of your getting an IQ of 132 are but 5 in 100, or 1 in 20. Since these odds are pretty impressive, we can assume that your score didn't occur "by chance alone," and thus the score suggests you are "brighter than average."

To summarize, the greater the standard deviation, the greater the odds are that the score didn't occur "by chance alone."

Differences between Groups

Now, suppose we compare the IQ's of two people, Bill and Mary. Bill has an IQ score of 84, which is exactly 1 standard deviation from the mean of 100. He might have "below average" intelligence, true. But he's so close to the mean that we might as well call him "average" since he might have been overly tired when he took the test. (In fact, even if his *true* IQ was 100, Bill would get a *measured* score of between 84 and 100 about one-third of the time that he took the test. Can you guess why this would be the case?)

Mary has an IQ score of 116, which is exactly 1 standard deviation above the mean. But again, her score isn't all that different from the mean, so we could (technically speaking) say that she too has "average intelligence." (She too would be expected to get a *measured* score between 100 and 116 one-third of the time if her *true* IQ was

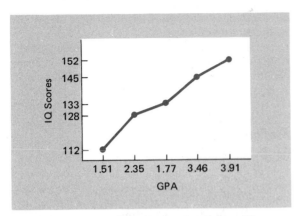

Fig. A.6. A scatter diagram showing the positive correlation between IQ's and grade point averages.

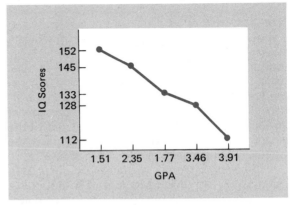

Fig. A.7. A scatter diagram showing a negative correlation between IQ's and grade point averages.

100. And, like Bill, she would also get a *measured* score between 84 and 100 a third of the time.)

Since both Bill and Mary have IQ's that "vary" from the mean by 1 standard deviation, their scores of 84 and 116 don't differ reliably from each other, right?

Wrong! (As if you didn't know that intuitively anyhow.)

Bill's score differs from Mary's by *2* standard deviations, thus the odds are at least 20 to 1 that Mary's *true* IQ score is significantly higher than Bill's. (And wouldn't you have been willing to make a small wager that was the case the moment you knew what their IQ scores were?)

Significant Differences

Whenever you hear scientists say that their "findings are significant at the 5 percent level," you can translate this to mean that their groups differed by about 2 standard deviations. In general, if the odds are not at least 20 to 1 in support of the hunch you're trying to prove, you probably shouldn't use the word "significant" in describing your results.

There are many different tests or formulas that you could use for calculating whether the results of an experiment were significant or not. Among the best-known of such statistical devices are the *t-test* and the *critical ratio*. Should you ever need to employ one of these tests, you'd do well to read about them in a statistics text.

Correlation Coefficients

In several chapters of this book, we have mentioned the term *correlation* to suggest that two events or traits were somehow connected or associated with each other. The mathematics underlying correlations are not too difficult to understand. However, the correlation concept itself has a "problem" buried deep within it that makes it one of the most misunderstood and misused ideas in all of human experience. We'll come back to this problem in just a moment. First, let's look at how one figures out if two sets of scores are correlated.

As we noted in Chapter 22, there is a strong relationship between IQ's and grades in school, and for a very good reason. Intelligence tests are usually devised so that they will predict academic success, and the items on most such tests are juggled around until the final score does in fact yield the expected predictions. Thus if we give intelligence tests to all incoming freshmen, and we know their grades at the end of their first collegiate year, we should expect to find the sort of relationship between these measures shown in Table A.2.

Table A.2
Relationship between IQ Score and GPA

	Entrance Test IQ Score	Grade Point Average (GPA)
Ann	152	3.91
Bill	145	3.46
Carol	133	2.77
Dick	128	2.35
Elmer	112	1.51
Σ (Sum of)	670	14.00
Mean	134	2.80
SD	15.54	0.94

Just looking at the rank orderings of these scores, you can tell that a strong correlation exists between the two distributions. As Fig. A.6 shows, if we plotted the data on what is called a *scatter diagram*, we'd get pretty much a straight line. (A scatter diagram shows how the scores for each subject are *scattered*, or distributed, across the graph or diagram.)

If we reversed the scores, so that Ann got an IQ score of 152 but a GPA of 1.51, Bill got an IQ score of 145 and a GPA of 2.35, and so forth, we'd get a scatter diagram that looked like the one in Fig. A.7.

Generally speaking, the closer the scatter diagram comes to being a straight line tilted to the right or left as these are, the higher the correlation between the two variables (scores).

There are several formulas for figuring out the *mathematical* correlation between two sets of scores that we needn't go into here. All of these formulas yield what is called a *correlation coefficient*, which is merely a "coefficient" or number between $+1$ and -1.

A correlation coefficient of $+1$ indicates that the two sets of scores are *perfectly correlated in a positive way*. Which is to say, the person who got the highest score on one test got the highest on the second test, the person who got the second highest score on one test got the second highest score on the other test, and so forth.

A correlation coefficient of -1 indicates the two sets of scores are *perfectly correlated in a negative way*. Which is to say that the person who got the *highest* score on the first test got the *lowest* score on the second, the person who got the second *highest* score on the first test got the second *lowest* score on the other test, and so forth.

A correlation coefficient of $+.75$ suggests there is a strong (but not perfect) association between the two sets of scores. A coefficient of $-.75$ would indicate the same strength of association, but in a negative direction.

A correlation coefficient of 0 (or close to it) tells you that there is little or no significant relationship between the two sets of scores.

Uses and Abuses of Correlation Coefficients

The ability to make quick correlations is just about the most useful trait that your mind has available to it. Whether you realize it or not, your brain is so built that it automatically makes connections between incoming stimuli. Think back to the discussion of Pavlovian conditioning you read about in Chapter 14. When you ring a bell, and then give food to a dog, the animal's brain soon comes to associate the sound of the bell with the appearance of the food. When the dog eventually salivates to the sound of the bell *before* food arrives, its nervous system has calculated a crude sort of "correlation coefficient" between the onset of the bell and the presentation of the food. Since (in the experiment) the two events *always* occur together, the correlation coefficient of the two events would be close to $+1$. Thus the dog can anticipate (predict) the stimulus input "food" as soon as the stimulus input "bell" has occurred.

If dogs could talk, how might they explain their conditioned responses? Don't you imagine that Pavlov's beasts might explain matters in *causal* terms? That is, might not a well-conditioned canine remark that the bell has "magic powers" that cause the food to appear?

As peculiar as this notion may sound to you, evidence in its favor comes from some real-life experiments. In several studies, bell-food conditioned animals have later been trained to turn on the bell themselves by pressing a bar in their cages. What do you think the animals do when they become hungry?

As we mentioned earlier, the concept of correlation has a problem buried in it. The problem is this: We too often assume that if event A is correlated with event B, then A must somehow *cause* the appearance of B. This "causal assumption" gets us into a lot of trouble. For example, does the sound of the bell really *cause* the food to appear? Do high IQ's really *cause* students to get good grades? As you can see, the answer in both cases must be a resounding *no*.

Scores on an intelligence test don't cause much of anything (except, perhaps, favorable reactions from college admissions committees). The underlying trait of intelligence presumably causes both the high IQ and the good grades. Thus *intelligence* is responsible for the correlation between the two events, just as Pavlov's desires were responsible for the correlation between the bell and the food.

There are times when highly significant correlations may seriously mislead us. As we have mentioned several times, there is a high correlation between going to a psychotherapist and "getting better." But as many studies have shown, you are just about as likely to show improvement if you *don't* seek help as if you do. But the fact that you (1) went to a therapist and (2) solved some of your problems may incorrectly convince both you and your therapist that it was the *treatment* that primarily caused your improvement.

At their very best, correlations can help us predict future stimulus inputs and give us clues as to what the underlying causal connections among these inputs might be. However, in daily life, we too often misuse correlations. If you want to make your psychology teacher very happy indeed, say "Correlations don't determine causes" over and over again—until you're conditioned to believe it!

Experimental Design

Why statistics? Or, to phrase the question more precisely, is there any correlation between knowing something about stat and knowing something about yourself and the people around you?

As it happens, the difference between knowing stat and not knowing it is highly significant. All of your future life you will be performing "little experiments" in which you try to psych out the people around you. It's likely (at the 5 percent level) that you will probe your environment better if you know how to interpret the results of your informal experimentation. If you are introspective, an understanding of correlations and conditioning could help tell you some very important facts about how you have acquired many of your values and attitudes. And, if nothing else, understanding what a bell-shaped curve is all about could save you a lot of money should you ever happen to visit Las Vegas.

The second reason for imposing statistics on you, willy-nilly, is that you may wish to take further courses in psychology. If you do, you may be encouraged (or even required) to perform one or more controlled experiments, either in a laboratory or in a real-life setting. Therefore, you might as well learn the first law of statistics right now:

Your statistical inferences are never better than your experimental design will allow.

The topic of how to design a good experiment has filled many a thick textbook, and there's little sense in subjecting you to more grief than we've done already. What we can say is this—the secret of good experimentation lies in *controlling variables*. If you want to pick a random sample of people for a political poll, make sure your sample is *really random*. Just asking a few friends what they think won't do, because your method of choice highly biased—and hence not random at all.

Several times in this book we've mentioned the concept of a "control group" that some scientist(s) used in an experiment. There probably is no more powerful way of making sure your results are reliable than by incorporating as many groups as possible in your study—one group to *control* for each factor (variable) that might influence the results of your study.

But, most important of all, if you must run a scientific study, think it through carefully *before you start*. Then you can design your study intelligently so that the data you gather will be easy to analyze, and so your expected results will be as truthful and as reliable as you can make them. Scientists are probably about as honest and as open in their work as any professional group can be. And yet all of us might unconsciously bias our results if we feel passionately about the subject we're studying. So we should use control group after control group—just to make sure that we screen out our unconscious biases before they can affect our results. Anything that you love, or that is important enough to you, is worth working hard for—and worth being entirely honest about.

Animals show a lot of intelligent behaviors. They "sing," and monkeys even draw pictures of a sort. But only human beings run experiments, control for bias, select their subjects randomly, and perform statistical analyses. Being a scientist is thus one of the most *humane* occupations you can have, because we all need reliable and valid data about how things are now so we can make things (including ourselves) better in the future.

As it happens, I love science. To me, it is a "fun game," a way of wisdom, and a means of achieving self-actualization. My parting hope is that you will someday come to appreciate this art form as much as I do. And if the scientific love bug does bite you, perhaps then and only then will you come to enjoy statistics and experimental design as much as most scientists do.

I wish you the best of luck!

(Meanwhile, Gersh and I are reading several books on probability theory as applied to bridge. Joan and Carol, you'd better watch out!)

For permission to use copyrighted materials the authors are indebted to the following:

Chapter 1: p. 4, Jeff Albertson/Stock, Boston/p. 8, Erika Stone/Peter Arnold, Inc.; p. 16, Erika Stone/Peter Arnold, Inc.; p. 18, Dan McCoy/Rainbow.

Part I: Fernand Rausser/Black Star.

Chapter 2: p. 30, photo courtesy of the American Museum of Natural History; p. 34, photo courtesy of the Brookhaven National Laboratory; p. 44, © Marjorie Pickens 1974.

Chapter 3: p. 60, photo courtesy of the News & Publications Service/Stanford University; p. 68, photo courtesy of the Museum of the American Indian, Heye Foundation; p. 70, Kenneth Karp; p. 74, Wide World Photos; p. 76, Phyllis Graber Jensen/Stock, Boston.

Chapter 4: p. 86, (left to right) Bettmann Archive, National Library of Medicine, Culver Pictures; p. 96 (top right) Jill Freedman/Archive Pictures; (top left) Chris Steele-Perkins/Magnum Photos; (bottom right) George Roos/Peter Arnold, Inc.; p. 98, German Information Center.

Chapter 5: p. 116, (top left) American Cancer Society; (top right) American Lung Association; (bottom left) Robert Flamholtz; (bottom right) Erika Stone/Peter Arnold, Inc.; p. 124, (left to right) Eugene Kowaluk, Culver Pictures, Bettmann Archive, Christopher S. Johnson/Stock, Boston; p. 128, Samuel Teicher; p. 130, (left) Joan Liftin/Archive Pictures, (right) Sybil Shelton/Peter Arnold, Inc.

Part II: The Lighthouse

Chapter 6: p. 146, (top) Dan Brinzac/Peter Arnold, Inc., (bottom left) Museum of Modern Art/Film Stills Archive, (bottom right) Wide World Photos; p. 154 (top left) Ginger Chih/Peter Arnold, Inc., (top right) Anestis Diakopoulos/Stock, Boston, (bottom left) Bruno Barbey/Magnum Photos.

Chapter 7: p. 160, photos by Kenneth Karp; p. 166, (left) Samuel Teicher, (right) James R. Holland/Stock, Boston; p. 170, (left) Ellis Herwig/Stock, Boston, (right) Ira Kirschenbaum/Stock, Boston; p. 174, (top left and top right) Michael Weisbrot, (bottom left) Jane Hamilton-Merritt; p. 178, University of Texas News & Information Service.

Chapter 8: p. 186, (left) Thomas Ives, (right) University of California, Los Angeles; p. 190 (top) © Jerry Howard 1981/Stock, Boston; p. 194, Birth Defects Foundation/March of Dimes; p. 196, (left) Nancy Ellison/Sygma; p. 200, (left) Liane Enkelis/Black Star, (middle) University of Denver, Department of Psychology, (right) Samuel Teicher; p. 202, Phonic Ear International.

Chapter 9: p. 210 (bottom left) Michael Weisbrot; (middle right) photo courtesy of the Port Authority of New York and New Jersey, (bottom right) photo courtesy of NASA; p. 212, David Linton; p. 214, (right) Neil Selkirk/courtesy of The Lighthouse; p. 220, (bottom right) Bettmann Archive; p. 226, (left middle) William Vandivert; p. 226 (top) photos by Kenneth Karp.

Chapter 10: p. 238, (bottom left) Lam Mediflex Photo Lab, (top right) Harvey Stein/Black Star; p. 244, photos by Kenneth Karp; p. 246, Mimi Forsyth/Monkmeyer Press Photo Service.

Part III: © Gerry Granham (Rapho/Photo Researchers).

Chapter 11: p. 258, Brandeis University, Public Affairs Office; p. 260, (top right) © Raymond Depardon/Magnum Photos, (top left) Mimi Forsyth/Monkmeyer Press Photo Service, (bottom left) Nancy Hays/Monkmeyer Press Photo Service, (bottom middle) Phyllis Graber Jensen/Stock, Boston, (bottom right) Abigail Heyman/Archive Pictures; p. 266, University of Miami; p. 268 (right) Dr. Neal E. Miller, Rockefeller University; p. 270, (top right) photo courtesy of the University of Pennsylvania News Bureau, (top left) Bettmann Archive, (bottom left) University of Pennsylvania, (bottom right) Columbia University Office of Public Information; p. 274, (top left) © Andy Levin 1979/Black Star, (top right) Samuel Teicher, (bottom left) © 1979 Josephus Daniels/Photo Researchers, (bottom right) Teri Leigh Stratford/Monkmeyer Press Photo Service.

Chapter 12: p. 286, (left) photograph by Dellenback/Kinsey Institute for Sex Research, Inc., (right) Bob Levin/Black Star; p. 288, University of Wisconsin, Madison; p. 290, (top) Owen Franken/Stock, Boston, (bottom) Photo courtesy of the American Museum of Natural History; p. 292, courtesy of Peter M. Milner; p. 294, © Erika Stone 1982/Peter Arnold, Inc.

Chapter 13: p. 304, © Karsh, Ottowa/Wide World Photos; p. 308, (right) L. Fabian Bachrach; p. 310, (top) Nicholas Sapieha/Stock, Boston, (bottom left) Cornell Capa/Magnum Photos, (bottom right) Marc Riboud/Magnum Photos; p. 314, (top left) photo courtesy of United Airlines, (top right) © Jerry Berndt/Stock, Boston, (bottom right) Abigail Heyman/Archive Pictures.

Part IV: Sybil Shelton/Peter Arnold, Inc.

Chapter 14: p. 330, (middle) Hanna W. Schreiber/Photo Researchers, (bottom) Culver Pictures; p. 334, (left) Anna Kaufmann Moon/Stock, Boston, (right) © Bruce Roberts 1977/Photo Researchers; p. 336, © 1979 Arthur Sirdofsky; p. 338, (top right) Public Relations Department, Temple University, (bottom left) Museum of Modern Art/Film Stills Archive, (bottom right) The New York Times.

Chapter 15: p. 350, (left) photo courtesy of Teachers College, Columbia University; p. 352, photo courtesy of Routledge & Kegan Paul, Ltd., from *The Mentality of Apes* by Wolfgang Köhler; p. 360, (top left) E.F. Bernstein/Peter Arnold, Inc.; (right) Cary Wolinsky/Stock, Boston; (bottom left) Jane Hamilton-Merritt.

Chapter 16: p. 372, (top) Hugh Rogers/Monkmeyer Press Photo Service; (bottom) photo courtesy of the National Library of Medicine; p. 374, photos courtesy of Elizabeth Loftus, University of Washington; p. 378, (left) photo courtesy of Data General Corporation; (right) Jane Hamilton-Merritt; p. 380, (left) photo courtesy of the University of Chicago; (right) Robert Burroughs/Black Star; p. 382, (middle) photo courtesy of the American Museum of Natural History.

Chapter 17: p. 392, photo courtesy of the National Library of Medicine; p. 394, (top) photo courtesy of the National Library of Medicine; (bottom) Mimi Forsyth/Monkmeyer Press Photo Service; p. 396, (left) Yale University Archives, Yale University Library; (right) photo courtesy of Cushing Hospital, Framingham, Massachusetts; p. 398, (left) Fabian Bachrach; (right) photo reproduced by permission of Harcourt Brace Jovanovich, Inc., from "Divided Brain & Consciousness," produced by Lee R. Bobker, copyright © 1977 by Harcourt Brace Jovanovich; p. 402, (bottom) photo courtesy of McGill University.

Part V: Erika Stone/Peter Arnold, Inc.

Chapter 18: p. 414, © Rene Burri/Magnum Photos; p. 416, (top right) photo courtesy of the American Museum of Natural History; (middle left) photo courtesy of the March of Dimes, Birth Defects Foundation; p. 418, © Rick Winsor 1981/Woodfin Camp & Assoc.; p. 420, Erika Stone/Peter Arnold, Inc.; p. 422, (top left) Suzanne Szasz; (bottom left) Erika Stone/Peter Arnold, Inc.; (top right) David Burnett/Contact; p. 426, (top) photos courtesy of Andrew N. Meltzoff, University of Washington; (left) Nina Leen, LIFE Magazine, © Time Inc.

Chapter 19: p. 436, photos by Harry F. Harlow, University of Wisconsin Primate Laboratory; p. 438, courtesy of John Bowlby; p. 440, (top) © Richard Kalvar/Magnum Photos; p. 444, (top left) Erika Stone/Photo Researchers; (top right and bottom left) Erika Stone/Peter Arnold, Inc.; p. 446, (left) photo by Harry F. Harlow, University of Wisconsin Primate Laboratory; (right) © Michal Heron 1982/Woodfin Camp & Assoc.; (bottom left) photo courtesy of the University of Virginia.

Chapter 20: p. 454, Yves de Braine/Black Star; p. 460, (top left) © Frostie/Woodfin Camp & Assoc.; (top right) © Christopher Morrow/Stock, Boston; (bottom left) Burt Glinn/Magnum Photos; (bottom right) Frank Siteman/Stock, Boston; p. 462, (left to right) courtesy of Charles Ferguson; courtesy of The New School; Erika Stone/Peter Arnold, Inc.; p. 464, (top left) Jean-Claude Lejeune/Stock, Boston; (top right) Erika Stone/Peter Arnold, Inc.; (bottom left) Paul Conklin/Monkmeyer Press Photo Service; (bottom right) courtesy of Otto Weininger.

Part VI: D. Goldberg/Sygma

Chapter 21: p. 482, Pictorial Parade; p. 486, photos by Erika Stone/Peter Arnold, Inc.; p. 490, (left to right) photo courtesy of the National Library of Medicine; Bettmann Archive; United Press International; p. 494, (top left) Doug Wilson/Black Star; (top right) Fred Kaplan/Black Star; (bottom left) Michael Weisbrot; (bottom right) © Ian Berry/Magnum Photos; p. 498, photo courtesy of the Center for Studies of the Person, La Jolla, California.

Chapter 22: p. 510, (left) Library of Congress; (right) photo courtesy of the National Library of Medicine; p. 512, (left to right) photo courtesy of the Harvard University News Office; courtesy of the University of Illinois; Bettmann Archive; courtesy of the Stanford University News & Publications Service; p. 516, (top left) George Roos/Peter Arnold, Inc.; p. 518, (left) photo courtesy of Yale University; p. 520, (left) Erika Stone/Peter Arnold, Inc.; p. 524, (left) Sybil Shelton/Peter Arnold, Inc.; (right) George Roos/Peter Arnold, Inc.

Chapter 23: p. 532, (left to right) Susan Meiselas/Magnum Photos; J. Brian King; Donald Rocker, courtesy of the Department of Behavioral Sciences, University of Chicago; p. 544, Kenneth Karp; p. 546, Twentieth Century Fox; p. 548, (left) Kenneth Karp; (right) Ken Robert Buck/Stock, Boston; p. 550, © Bob Adelman/Magnum Photos.

Chapter 24: p. 564, (top and bottom left) The Bettmann Archive; (right) photo courtesy of the National Institute of Mental Health; p. 566, (left) Kenneth Karp; (right) photo courtesy of the University of Southern California; p. 570, Freda Leinwand/Monkmeyer Press Photo Service; p. 572, photo courtesy of the University of Southern California, Department of Psychiatry; p. 576, The Bettmann Archive; p. 580, (left) Fred Kaplan/Black Star; (right) The Bettmann Archive.

Part VII: Rosemary Ranck/Black Star

Chapter 25: p. 600, Frank Siteman/Stock, Boston; p. 602, (left) photo by Carol Tyler, courtesy of Robert Sommer; (right) University of California, Los Angeles; p. 604, (top left) Erika Stone/Peter Arnold, Inc.; (top right) Bob Fitch/Black Star; p. 606, (bottom left) The Bettmann Archive; (bottom right) courtesy of the Harvard University News Office; p. 608, (top) courtesy of Alfred Bandura; (bottom left) courtesy of the University of Illinois; (bottom right) photo courtesy of the Stanford University News & Publications Service; p. 610, (top) photos courtesy of Philip Zimbardo; (bottom) photo courtesy of the Stanford University News & Publications Service.

Chapter 26: p. 620, Maury Englander; p. 624, (left) Featherkill Studios; (top right) The Bettmann Archive; (bottom right) The Farm, Summertown, Tennessee; p. 626, (top, left to right) photo courtesy of the Rutgers News Service; photo courtesy of Scientific Methods; photo courtesy of Harry Helson; photo courtesy of Stanley Milgram; (bottom) copyright 1965 by Stanley Milgram. From the film *Obedience,* distributed by the New York University Film Library; p. 630, (right) photo courtesy of Wooten-Moulton Studio; p. 632, (right) photo courtesy of The Pennsylvania State University, Department of Public Information and Relations.

Chapter 27: p. 642, (left) Jeff Albertson/Stock, Boston; p. 644, (top) United Press International; p. 648, (bottom) photo courtesy of Golden West Television from "Scared Straight"; p. 650, (right) Wide World Photos.

Chapter 28: p. 658, The Bettmann Archive; p. 660, (left) © Kathleen Foster 1982/Black Star; (right) photo courtesy of Charles Seigerman; p. 662, Peter Southwick/Stock, Boston; p. 664, Samuel Teicher; p. 666, photo courtesy of The Advertising Council; p. 668, (left) photo courtesy of Thomas K. Connellan; (right) Peter Menzel/Stock, Boston.

Appendix: p. 672, Kenneth Karp.

Name Index

Maccoby, Eleanor Emmons, 450
MacLean, Paul D., 100–101, 102, 107, 657
Maddi, Salvatore R., 514
Maddox, Victor, 73
Magee, Kenneth, 401
Magellan, Ferdinand, 114
Magoun, H. W., 186–189, 284
Maher, Brendan, 127
Mao Tse-tung, 607
Mark, Vernon, 103, 107
Marlatt, G. A., 75
Marmor, Judd, 549
Marolla, Francis A., 519
Maslach, Christina, 656
Maslow, Abraham H., 258, 259–262, 272, 279, 492, 497, 498, 499, 501, 503, 541, 570, 571, 606, 607
Massie, Henry, 438–439
Masters, William, 285–286, 295, 298, 554
Mayer, J., 266
McBurney, Donald H., 156
McCaleb, M. L., 269, 270
McCleary, Robert, 241
McClelland, David C., 526
McClintock, Martha, 152
McConnell, James V., 1–20, 200–201, 204, 249, 381–383, 623, 657–669, 670–680
McDermott, William, 75–76
McEwen, Bruce S., 298
McGinnies, Elliott, 240
McNeal, E. B., 249
McWhinney, Will, 668
Mead, Margaret, 444
Meadow, Kathryn P., 181
Meduna, Ladislaus J., 565, 566
Mehrabian, Albert, 601
Meltzoff, Andrew, 427
Melzack, Ronald, 401, 403
Mendel, Werner, 566, 567–568, 608
Merskey, Harold, 405
Mesmer, Anton, 387, 392, 393–395, 403
Mesulam, Marek-Marsel, 45
Meyer, Adolf, 581, 582
Meyer, Knarig Katchadurian, 421
Michael, Richard, 152
Miles, Matthew B., 578–579
Milgram, Stanley, 626–629, 634
Millar, Susanna, 461, 468, 473
Miller, James G., 132, 243–245
Mills, Carolyn, 649–650, 651
Mills, Judson, 621
Milner, Peter, 292–293, 294
Moniz, Egas, 566
Monnet, Mary, 242
Moreno, J. L., 577
Morris, Naomi M., 152, 153
Morrison, Adrian, 58
Morton, Adam, 132
Moscovici, Serge, 656
Murray, Henry A., 525
Mussen, P. H., 431
Myers, R. D., 269, 270
Myers, R. E., 40, 41, 43, 47

Nassi, Alberta J., 643–644
Naylor, James, 668
Neugarten, Bernice L., 542

Newcomb, Theodore, 595, 598, 618–619, 621, 642–643, 644, 653, 654, 656
Newton, Isaac, 145
Norman, Donald A., 386

Olds, James, 292–293, 294
Olson, Mary, 204
Orne, Martin, 397, 398, 399
Ostrom, Thomas M., 651, 656

Panksepp, Jaak, 76
Parke, Ross D., 444
Parloff, Morris, 664
Parsons, H. M., 667
Paul, Gordon, 581
Pavlov, Ivan, 325, 329–335, 337, 339, 340, 341, 344, 345, 352, 353, 359, 360, 362, 363, 381–382, 392, 679
Peckham, Robert, 523
Peele, Stanton, 313, 315
Petty, Richard E., 651, 656
Piaget, Jean, 451, 453–462, 464, 467, 468, 469, 470, 471, 473, 482, 490, 500, 501, 596, 598, 601, 632
Piliavin, I. M., 630
Piliavin, J., 630
Plato, 468, 511
Pleck, Joseph, 445
Plutchik, Robert, 320
Pomeroy, Wardell B., 298
Poon, Leonard W., 496, 506
Pratt, J. H., 576
Premack, David, 467
Prescott, James W., 438, 439, 448
Pribram, Karl, 103, 132, 307–308, 317
Price, Kenneth P., 364
Pritchard, Robert, 668

Rabbitt, Patrick, 496
Rader, Nancy, 214
Randi, James, 245, 249
Randle-Short, J., 197
Rayner, Rosalie, 335, 336, 341
Reiser, Martin, 397
Reschly, D. J., 523
Restak, Richard M., 426–427, 435
Richter, Curt, 309–311, 313, 317
Riecken, H. W., 631
Rimland, Bernard, 200
Ritvo, Bernard, 197
Rodin, J., 630
Rogers, Carl, 480, 497, 498–499, 501, 503, 527, 534, 541, 570, 571, 572, 575, 654
Rohsenow, D. J., 75
Roosevelt, Eleanor, 499
Roosevelt, Franklin D., 607
Rorschach, Hermann, 507, 515
Rosenhan, David L., 552–553, 598
Ross, Elliott, 45
Rothman, David J., 579, 586
Rotter, Julian, 308, 309, 317, 320, 392, 396
Rowell, T. E., 466
Rubin, Zick, 607
Rumbaugh, Duane, 466–467
Russell, Michael, 152

Sacher-Masoch, Leopold V., 333
Safer, Martin A., 628, 636
Sagan, Carl, 246
Sanders, Louis, 435
Sappho, 549
Savage-Rumbaugh, Sue, 466–467
Sawin, Douglas, 444, 450
Scarr, Sandra, 518
Schachter, Stanley, 272, 277, 631
Schafer, Roy, 506
Schechter, Marshall, 201
Schmidt, Frank, 523–524
Schmidt, Helmut, 245
Schuldberg, David, 527
Scott, J. P., 97
Scott, T. H., 192
Seidler, Maren, 495
Seigerman, Charles, 660, 661, 662
Seitz, Victoria, 522–523, 530
Seligman, Martin, 320
Selye, Hans, 305, 315, 316, 320
Shakespeare, William, 571, 603
Shelby, Jessie, 383
Sheldon, W. H., 507, 511–512, 528
Sherif, Muzafer, 616, 622, 632–633, 634
Shick, Georgianna, 664
Shor, R. E., 405
Shorkey, Clayton, 337–338
Shulman, Bernard H., 506
Siebert, Al, 20
Simon, Herbert A., 132
Simon, Theophile, 515, 516, 517, 521, 528
Singer, Barry, 245–246
Singer, Jerome E., 320
Skeels, H. M., 518
Skinner, B. F., 125–126, 345, 353, 354–362, 363, 364, 499–501, 503, 541
Sloane, R. Bruce, 572, 573–575, 583
Smith, Donald E. P., 200–201, 204
Smith, M. Brewster, 652
Smith, T. G., Jr., 80
Smith, W. L., 405
Snellen, Herman, 173
Snyder, Solomon H., 70, 74
Solomon, Philip, 204
Sommer, Robert, 231, 601, 602, 614
Sorenson, James, 427–428
Spanier, G. B., 450
Spearman, Charles, 517, 528
Spencer, Herbert, 468, 471
Sperry, R. W., 40–41, 43, 45, 46, 47, 50, 126
Spitz, Rene A., 439–440
Spitzer, Robert, 551–552, 553, 554
Springer, S. P., 50
Squire, Larry, 376
Star, Shirley, 650–651
Steinfeld, Jesse, 94
Stellar, Eliot, 269–270
Sterman, M. B., 50
Stern, Daniel, 435, 441
Strickland, Stephen, 107
Stuart, Richard B., 272–273, 277, 279
Stumphauzer, J. S., 656
Stunkard, A. J., 271, 272
Sudia, Cecilia, 445
Suedfeld, Peter, 195, 196, 201, 204
Suomi, S. J., 439, 450

Subject Index